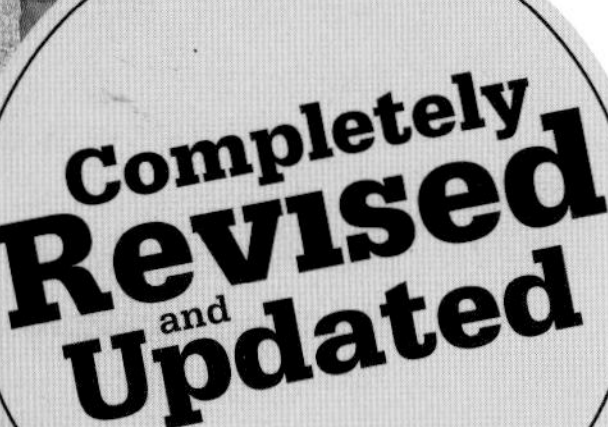

Complete Do-It-Yourself Manual

With the Editors at The Family Handyman

Reader's Digest

The Reader's Digest Association, Inc.
Pleasantville, NY • Montreal

For Reader's Digest

U.S. Project Editor:
Kim Casey

Copy Editor:
Barbara Booth

Canadian Project Editor:
Pamela Johnson

Canadian Technical Consultant:
Jon Eakes

Senior Designer:
George McKeon

Consulting Designer:
Andrèe Payette

Executive Editor, Trade Publishing:
Dolores York

Director of Production:
Michael Braunschweiger

Associate Publisher, Trade Publishing:
Christopher T. Reggio

President & Publisher, Trade Publishing:
Harold Clarke

For The Family Handyman

Senior Project Editor:
Spike Carlsen

Assistant Project Editor:
Mary Flanagan

Senior Graphic Designer:
Patrick Hunter

Production Coordinator:
Lori Callister

Archive Management:
Roxie Filipkowski, Alice Garrett, Shannon Hooge, Lisa Pahl Knecht

Editor-in-Chief:
Ken Collier

Editor:
Duane Johnson

Publisher:
Jim Schiekofer

Vice President, General Manager, North American Publishing Group:
Bonnie Bachar

The entire staff of *The Family Handyman* and *American Woodworker* magazines (see p. 528)

Contributors

Senior Writers:
Bill LaHay, Mike Satterwhite

Contributing Writers:
Andy Rae, John Williamson

Graphic Designers:
Rick Dupre, Evangeline Ekberg, David Farr, Barbara Pederson, Gregg Weigand

Copy Editors:
Jean Cook, Dinah Swain Schuster

Photographers:
Mike Habermann, Patrick Hunter, Mike Krivit, Phil Leisenheimer, Shawn Nielsen, Bill Zuehlke

Illustrators:
Ron Chamberlain, John Keely, Don Mannes, Doug Oudekerk, Frank Rohrbach, Eugene Thompson

Indexer:
Harriet Hodges

Administrative Assistants:
Ronelle Ewing, Shelly Jacobsen, Peggy McDermott

Consultants

Electrical:
Al Hildenbrand, John Williamson

Plumbing:
Charlie Avoles, Les Zell

Painting and Wallcovering:
Butch Zang

Tile:
Dean Sorem

Landscaping:
Jeff Timm

Woodworking:
Bruce Kieffer, Bruce Wiebe

Heating and Cooling:
Robin Huber, Dan Holohan

Structural Engineering:
Dave Macdonald

Kitchen and Bath Design:
Mary Jane Pappas

Interior Design:
Katherine Hillbrand, Susan Moore

Library of Congress Cataloging in Publication Data
Complete do-it-yourself manual / the editors of The family handyman magazine.—
Rev. and updated p. cm.
Rev. ed. of: Reader's digest complete do-it-yourself manual. 1973.
ISBN 0-7621-0579-8
1. Dwellings—Maintenance and repair—Amateurs' manuals. I. Reader's Digest complete do-it-yourself manual.

TH4817.3.C626 2005
64'.7—dc22 2004050945

Address any comments about *Complete Do-It-Yourself Manual* to:
The Reader's Digest Association, Inc.
Adult Trade Publishing
Reader's Digest Road
Pleasantville, NY 10570-7000

For more Reader's Digest products and subscription information, visit our websites:
www.rd.com (in the United States)
www.rd.ca (in Canada)
www.familyhandyman.com

Printed in China
9 10 8

A Note to Our Readers

All do-it-yourself activities involve a degree of risk. Skills, materials, tools and site conditions vary widely. Although the editors have made every effort to ensure accuracy, the reader remains responsible for the selection and use of tools, materials and methods. Always obey local codes and laws, follow manufacturer's operating instructions, and observe safety precautions.

About This Book

In 1973 Reader's Digest published a uniquely shaped book based on a uniquely shaped proposition. The book's shape was long and rectangular, so it stood out on bookshelves, making it easy to locate, grab and use. The book's unique proposition was, given enough information and encouragement, home improvement projects and repairs could be tackled successfully by the average homeowner.

The book was titled, aptly enough, *Reader's Digest Complete Do-It-Yourself Manual*, and over the course of the next 30 years it sold over eight million copies. Other home improvement books have come and gone, but none has succeeded in covering the subject matter as extensively and authoritatively.

This version of the book took a classic and made it even better. The editors of *The Family Handyman* magazine—a Reader's Digest publication and the largest home improvement magazine in the world—completely revised and updated the old book. This edition combines the best elements of the original *Do-It-Yourself Manual, The Family Handyman's* rich informational and photographic archives, new illustrations and photography and the wisdom and experience of the best experts in the field today. The book continues to be comprehensive, with added information on buying materials, safety and ways to save time and money. We've added chapters on two topics that hit home with nearly every homeowner: landscaping and storage. And we've "brought the book up to code" so you know what you're reading is the most current information around.

So even if you own the *Complete Do-It-Yourself Manual* and the *NEW Complete Do-It-Yourself Manual,* you'll find tons of fresh new information on projects and repairs in this version. We think it's still the best resource around. We think you will, too.

Circa 1973

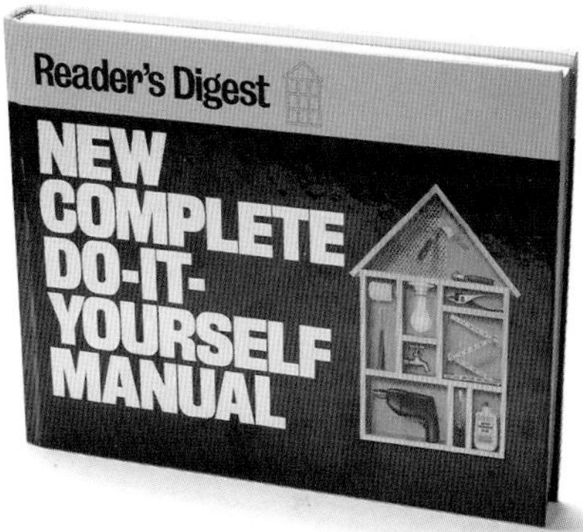

Circa 1991

About Your Safety

Nearly every home improvement activity involves some form of risk. You can greatly reduce your chances of injury by using the right tools and protective gear, taking the proper safety precautions and following manufacturer instructions for the products and tools you use.

As much as we encourage "doing it yourself," if you don't feel comfortable tackling all or part of a project—don't. Hire a pro. Throughout the book we've highlighted areas where we feel you should exercise extra vigilance. But always use the best piece of safety equipment you own—common sense.

About Metric Conversions

This book was researched and written with both Canadian and U. S. markets in mind. Since both countries—at varying rates of speed and with varying degrees of success—are converting to the metric system, we've included both metric and standard (also referred to as "imperial," "English," and "U.S.") systems for most measurements and weights. In areas where products, materials and practices are entrenched in "nonmetric" terminology, only "standard" terminology and measurements were used. When in doubt about converting from metric to standard and vice versa, consult the information in the back of this book.

Contents

Contents

Your Home

The Do-It-Yourself Attitude

Electrical Codes and Permits 128
Hazardous Materials 480

There are two approaches to home improvement: DIY and PAP. If you're of the DIY (do-it-yourself) persuasion, you roll up your sleeves and tackle the job yourself. You know you can save money, control the schedule, learn new skills and add your own personal touches. But you may be more of a PAP (point-and-pay) person. You call the electrician or plumber, point out the problem, then pay a pro to do the work.

The truth is, most homeowners alternate between these two approaches—and that's just fine. Some feel comfortable with a router but run at the sight of a dripping faucet. Others may feel confident installing a new light fixture but cringe at the thought of hanging a new exterior door.

Regardless of your approach, knowing more about the steps, tools, materials and pitfalls will help your projects go more smoothly. And know-how is what this book is all about.

10 Guidelines for Successful Home Improvement

1. **Be realistic.** Most manuals, TV shows and books present projects and repairs in a perfect-world scenario. But we live in an imperfect world where bolts stick and floors aren't level. Things may very well take longer, cost more and use more materials than you expect.
2. **Be safe.** Wear hearing, eye and breathing protection to save yourself from injury and years of misery.
3. **Invest in the best tools you can afford** to buy (or rent). You'll work faster, safer and with more enjoyment.
4. **Know when to stop.** Figure out the logical stopping points and then stop. Most accidents happen when people get tired.
5. **Measure twice, cut once.** You'll save tons of time and material.
6. **Be prepared.** There's no such thing as one trip to the hardware store. Buy extra and return what you don't use. Before you take it apart, take a picture of it.
7. **Remember the big picture.** What you do at point A may affect point B. For example, if you insulate your attic, make certain you don't block the roof vents.
8. **It's OK to ask directions.** Really.
9. **Think like a drop of water.** Water in the wrong place—whether from a broken pipe, condensation or rain—causes more problems than anything else.
10. **Finish the job.** If you don't install that last piece of molding while your tools are out, the project may go on forever.

Planning

Most projects and repairs are done twice: first in your head or on paper, next with a wrench or saw in your hand. Don't shortchange the first part of the process. Whether it's ordering the right amount of lumber for your deck or plotting out your bathroom remodeling project so your family isn't without water for three days, planning can make or break a home improvement project. This first step takes a little extra time up front, but in the end you'll experience fewer hassles and more peace of mind.

The best time to gather information, determine a game plan, arrange for outside help and round up your tools and materials is before the dust flies. Think ahead.

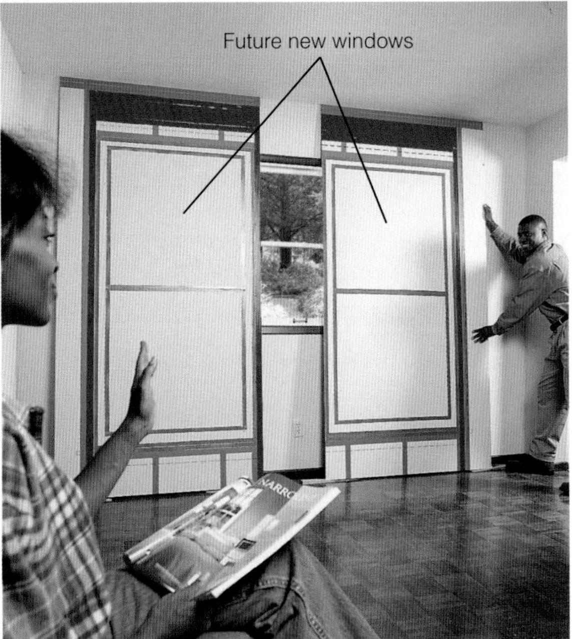

Project planning. It doesn't matter whether you plan your project using graph paper, computer software or life-size models, as shown here–just make sure you plan.

Permits, Inspections and Contractors

Permits

Many home-improvement projects require you, or your contractor, to obtain a permit. Obtaining permits can be a hassle, but getting caught doing work without one, or using substandard building practices, can be much worse.

Frequently required permits

Permit requirements vary greatly from one community to the next. Some common projects requiring permits include:

■ Projects involving structural alterations to your house, such as adding a larger window or removing a wall.
■ Installing a deck, fence, outbuilding or pool.
■ Finishing a basement or attic space.
■ Adding an electrical branch circuit, outlet or fixture.
■ Installing or replacing a water heater, furnace, air conditioner or fireplace.

Depending on the project, you may or may not be required to submit a blueprint or plan.

Inspections

Some small projects may require a single inspection, while larger ones may require a dozen or more. Make certain you know when and where inspections are required. Also remember you may not be able to move to the next step of your project until the inspection has been completed. Plan and schedule ahead.

Frequently required inspections

■ Footing inspections (after the footings are formed, but before the concrete is poured).
■ Framing inspections (after the framing materials and sheathing are in place).
■ Rough plumbing/gas line inspection (while pipes are exposed).
■ Final plumbing inspection (supply and drain-waste-vent pipes are pressure tested for leaks).
■ Insulation inspection (sometimes after the vapor barrier is installed).
■ Drywall inspection (often after drywall has been fastened, but before taping begins).
■ Rough-in electrical inspection (rough wiring completed in electrical boxes but devices such as switches, outlets and light fixtures not installed).
■ Final electrical inspection (all switches, outlets and lights in place and wiring at circuit panel complete).
■ Final inspection (final check to make sure all codes have been followed).

Working with Contractors

Though stories of unscrupulous contractors abound, most in the business are honest, hardworking folks. Most live and die by their reputations. Those who take the money and run or do substandard work don't stay in business long.

Yet, there are things you should check out.

Questions to ask, things to check

1. **Legal matters.** Do they have the proper licenses and insurance to work in your community? Ask to see the actual documents.
2. **Contract.** The more specific, the better. Specify the exact materials to be used, right down to the manufacturer, when necessary.
3. **References.** Will they provide names and contact information for their most recent clients? If the references are old or few-and-far-between, ask why. How long have they been in business? Check with the Better Business Bureau to see if any complaints have been filed.
4. **Down payment and money matters.** Determine at what points in the project payments will be made. One-third down for materials is common.
5. **Work schedule.** What date will the project start and what is a realistic date of completion?
6. **Changes.** Commonly, a change order spelling out the design and financial implications is drawn up and signed by the homeowner and contractor when there is a change in the initial contract.
7. **On the job.** Determine whom you'll speak with regarding the day-to-day operations. Who handles questions? How early in the day would work start and how long would it go on in the evening? What about a bathroom, smoking and eating? Who cleans up and when?

Utility Shut-Offs

Emergency Plumbing Shutoffs 88
Circuit Breakers and Fuses 127
Fire Safety 481

You may not pay much attention to the service pipes and wires that enter your home, but at times, during remodeling or an emergency, you may need to shut off the electricity, gas or water. Locate the main shut-off valves and switches, then tag them for future reference.

Electrical

The primary switch is usually in the main electrical panel that contains the breakers or fuses. This panel is usually on an inside wall behind the outside electrical meter, or in the basement below. Snap the circuit breaker switch, normally at the top, labeled "Service disconnect" or "Main" to OFF to cut electrical power to the entire house.

Older homes with fuses usually have a plastic block labeled "Main," which you pull out to cut power. Never reach into this open space with fingers or tools; it contains powerful "live" terminals.

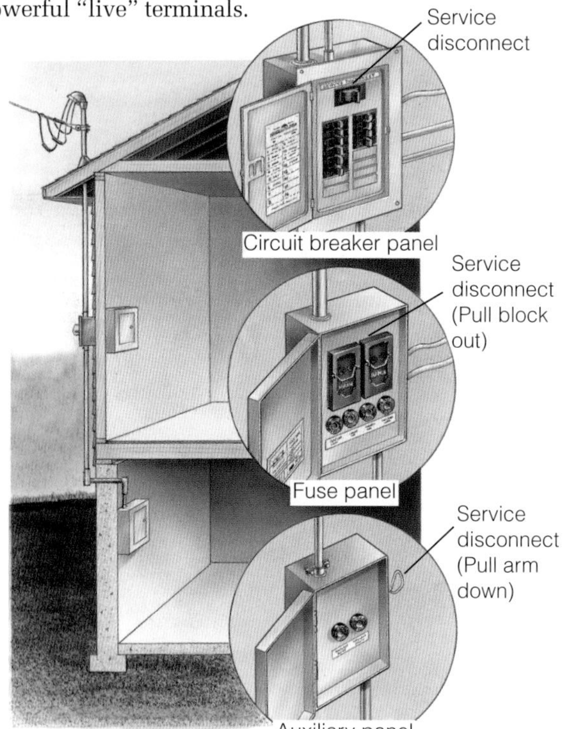

Water

Water enters your home through a 3/4- to 1-1/2-in.-diameter pipe connected to a water main that usually runs under the street. This pipe, normally plastic or steel, is buried below frost level to avoid freezing. The easiest way to locate the water shut-off valve is to locate the meter. In mild climates the meter will probably be in a box located close to the street. In colder regions the meter is inside the house. In either case, you'll find the shut-off valve on the water main side of the meter. There's often one on the house side as well.

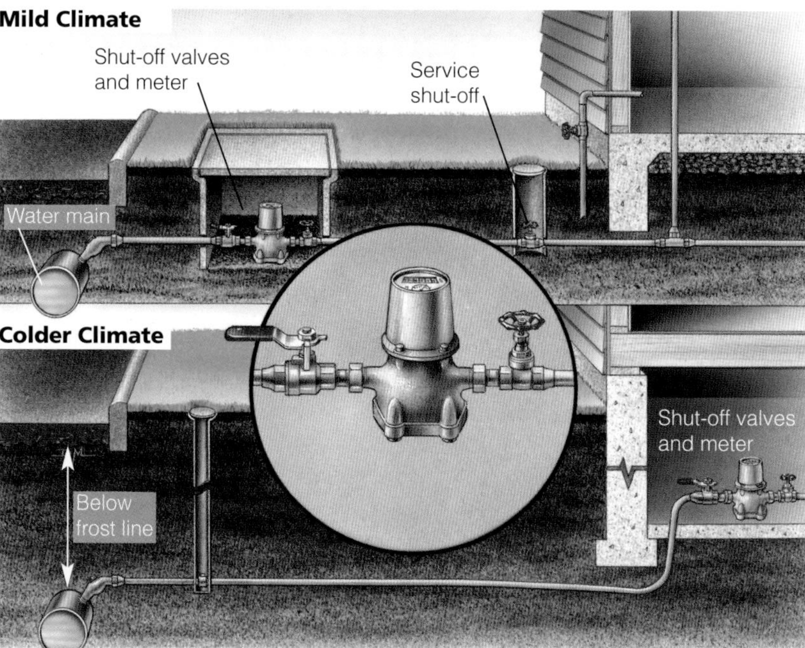

Gas

The main gas line generally runs 18 in. (45 cm) underground and surfaces next to the house in a steel sleeve by the meter. Just before the meter there is a rectangular shut-off knob that must be turned with a wrench to stop the gas flow. In some cases, the meter and shut-off valve are inside the house. Most utility companies prefer only their employees, professional contractors and fire personnel use this "street-side" valve. They prefer homeowners use the shut-off valve located after the meter.

Caution: If you smell gas, get everyone out of your home and call the gas utility from a neighbor's house or a cell phone outside. Don't switch any lights or appliances on or off because the smallest spark can trigger an explosion.

Detectors and Alarms

Smoke Detectors

The majority of smoke alarms that fail to sound in a fire either have dead batteries or are missing them entirely. Perform the basic maintenance shown here and replace any smoke detector more than 10 years old. When you install smoke detectors, follow these guidelines:

- Place smoke detectors at least 12 in. (30 cm) away from corners and on surfaces that have fairly stable temperatures, like high on an inside wall or against the center of an insulated ceiling.
- Don't place smoke alarms in kitchens, bathrooms, furnace rooms or workshops where fumes, dust and smoke can trigger false alarms and contaminate the alarm's detectors.
- To prevent air movement from delaying the alarm, position alarms away from windows and at least 3 ft. (1 m) away from furnace ducts.
- Position alarms within 15 ft. (5 m) of bedrooms (some codes require one in each bedroom) so they can be heard through closed doors.
- Don't place alarms on tall walls, over stairways or other areas where it is inconvenient or dangerous to test them.

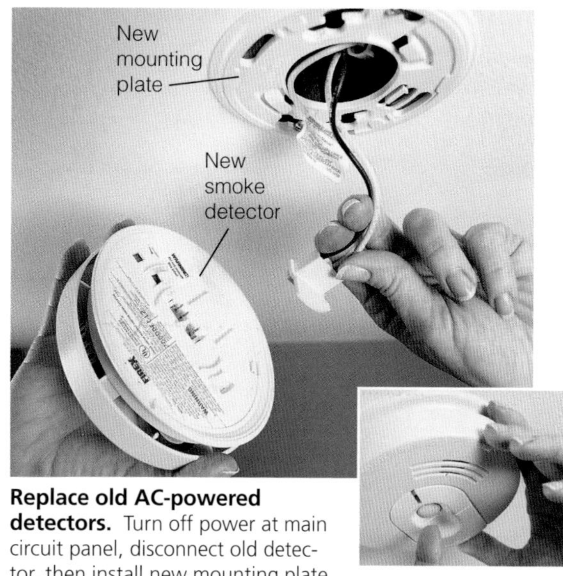

Replace old AC-powered detectors. Turn off power at main circuit panel, disconnect old detector, then install new mounting plate and detector. Replace interconnected alarms at the same time with compatible units from the same manufacturer. Turn on power and test. **Tip:** Jot the installation date on the mounting plate so you'll know when to replace the detector.

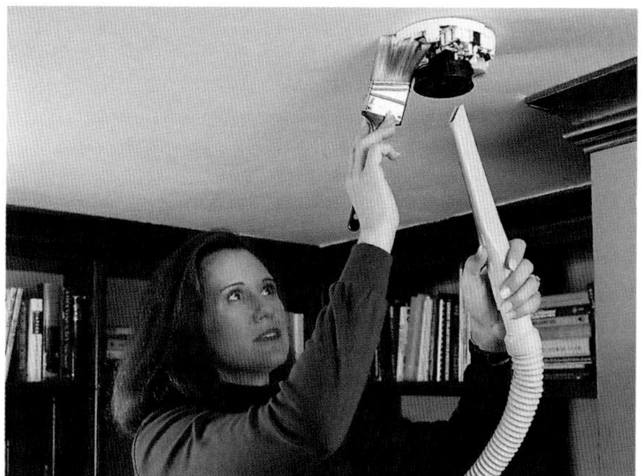

Clean detectors and test batteries. Vacuum the interior of detectors once a year, test detectors monthly with test button and install new batteries every six months.

Smoke test. Test your smoke alarms once a year by blowing out a match and letting the smoke roll over the alarm—or use that cigar you've been saving. Incense works, too.

CO Alarms

Carbon monoxide (CO) is an invisible, odorless gas produced by fireplaces, furnaces, stoves, water heaters and other appliances and heaters. When blocked chimney flues, poor natural drafting and leaks allow CO to spill into your home, it can be absorbed in the blood stream and result in serious illness or death. Accidental CO poisoning accounts for several hundred deaths in the United States and Canada every year. Most could be prevented with a warning from an inexpensive CO alarm.

Install a CO alarm near the sleeping rooms on each level of your home on ceilings or walls away from drafts and solvents. Read directions for specific details.

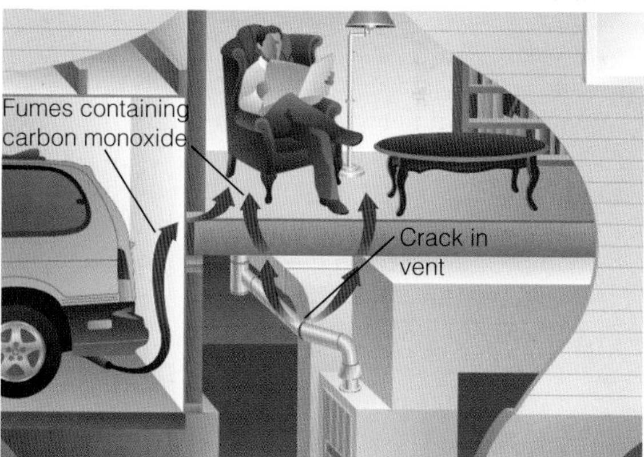

Sources. Carbon monoxide is produced by gas-, oil- and wood-burning devices. Auto exhaust and poorly vented furnaces are the most common dangerous sources in a home.

Alarms. Test CO alarms monthly. Those with a digital display will also show the peak CO level in your home when you push the peak level button.

Home Security

Home Security Systems **158**
More Secure Windows **372**
Installing Deadbolts **376**
Door Reinforcement and Security **378**

Basic home security consists of two things: keeping your home from looking like an easy target, and making a forced-entry troublesome for those trying to break in. Here are a few tips:

10 Common Home Security Mistakes

1. Unlocked windows and doors are the means of entrance in almost half of all burglaries. And most occur between 8 A.M. and 5 P.M. Lock up the house, even if you'll be out only a short period of time.
2. Weak strike plates allow your door to be opened with a few kicks. Install strike plates with screws long enough to penetrate into the wall framing.
3. Door chains can be yanked out with one good shove or kick.
4. Unchanged garage door openers allow crooks with a handful of common transmitters to click away until they find a garage door that responds.
5. Complete darkness is an invitation to break-ins. Install a motion-detector light.
6. Wimpy windows can often be jimmied open. Use sturdy locks.
7. Vulnerable sliding glass doors can be lifted out of their tracks. Use the precautions shown at right for making them more secure.
8. Hidden windows and doors are another invitation for crime. Keep bushes and trees trimmed back for increased safety.
9. Flimsy exterior doors are highly vulnerable. Replace hollow-core doors with those of steel, fiberglass or solid wood.
10. Burglar bait includes leaving empty boxes outside that advertise big purchases of computers, TVs and stereos. Ladders and other break-in tools left outside may also attract thieves.

Simple Security Measures

Some of the most effective security measures are free or inexpensive; they just take a little time. Here are a few small projects that offer big-time security:

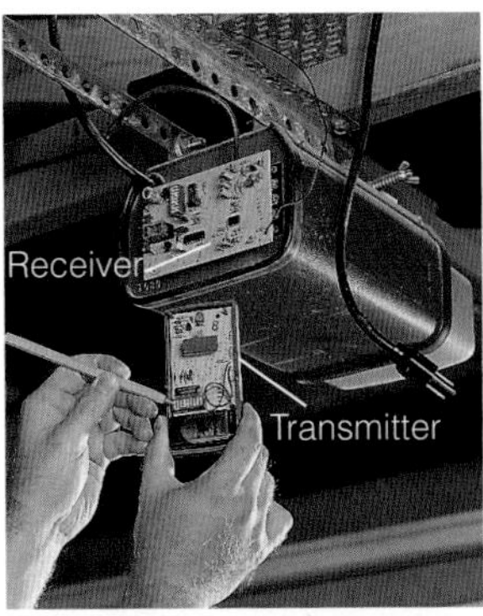

Garage door openers. Randomly reset the tiny switches in the transmitter, then set the switches on the receiver to match.

Top door track. Drive a couple of screws into the top track leaving the heads protruding so the door can't be lifted and removed from the outside.

Bottom track. Supplement your existing lock by laying a cut-to-fit dowel in the lower door track.

Motion Detectors

There's no need to arrive home in the dark or be kept in the dark about noises in the night. Outdoor lights that are activated by motion detectors can solve many safety and security problems. These electronic eyes can be adjusted to detect movement 70 ft. (20 m) or more away, in an area of up to 240 degrees. A timer can be set to determine how long the light stays on.

Installation can be as simple as shutting off power, removing the old fixture, then connecting the new wires and fixture. Follow the manufacturer's instructions and bear in mind:

- Heat from the bulb can confuse the detector; keep the bulb and detector as far apart as possible.
- Moisture can damage the detector and light sockets. Locate the fixture under an eave or buy one that has special bulb seals then angle the bulbs downward.
- Adjust the field of view angle to avoid nuisance trips from traffic, animals, wind-blown shrubs and other moving objects.
- Most fixtures allow you to double-flip the switch to keep the light on as long as you want, then double-flip again to return to motion-sensor mode.

Flood

Decorative

Remote

Universal Design

The concepts of universal design and accessible housing are based on the notion that people have a wide range of abilities and needs and that houses should be designed accordingly.

These design considerations range anywhere from installing lever-type handles and rocker light switches to aid those with limited hand strength to installing lifts for those who have trouble navigating stairs.

The three sections on this page are focused primarily on wheelchair accessibility for kitchens, bathrooms and entryways, and are guidelines only. For more complete information, contact the resources listed on p. 516.

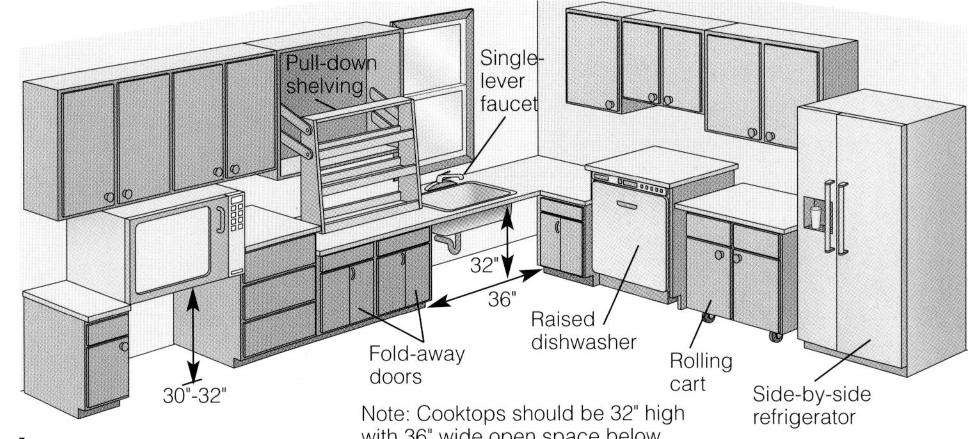

Bathrooms

Bathrooms, with their slippery surfaces and hard fixtures, can pose a danger to anyone. Consider these measures for better accessibility:

- Widen doorways to 32 in. (81 cm) or more. Consider replacing swinging doors with pocket doors.
- Try to provide a clear space of 5 ft. (152 cm) in diameter to provide room for wheelchair maneuverability.
- Install grab bars on walls around the toilets and bathtub for fall prevention and support.
- Install a toilet with adjustable-height or power-lift features. Wall-mounted toilets allow installation at a more convenient height.
- Provide roll-under space, 29 in. (74 cm) high and at least 32 in. (81 cm) wide, for accommodating wheelchairs in sink areas. Install pipe insulation to prevent accidental burns from hot pipes.

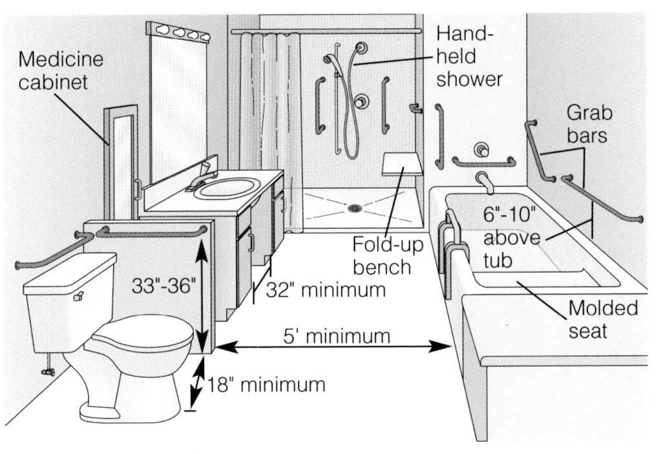

Kitchens

There are many products and design ideas that can make kitchens more accommodating to wheelchairs. Consider the following measures:

- Try to provide a clear space, at least 5 ft. (152 cm) in diameter, for wheelchair maneuverability. When possible, allow 48 in. (122 cm) for pathways and clear space in front of appliances and work areas.
- Elevate the dishwasher 6 in. (15 cm) or install a drawer-style model for better access.
- Install full-extension drawer slides to minimize reaching.
- Install ovens, microwaves and sinks at a height of 30 to 32 in. (76 to 81 cm).
- Install one or more sections of countertop at 32 in. (81 cm). Keep the space below open or install foldaway doors to provide roll-under access.
- Modify upper cabinets with pull-down shelf units and base cabinets with glide-out and swing-up shelves.
- Install single-lever faucets and provide roll-under access in sink areas.

Entrances, Doorways and Ramps

Entrances can be made safer and more convenient by installing better lighting and lever-type handles on doors. Other measures for wheelchair accessibility include:

- Make walkways at least 3 ft. (91 cm) wide; 4 ft. (122 cm) is better yet.
- Keep thresholds to a maximum of 1/4 in. (6 mm) in height. If that's not possible, provide threshold ramps.
- Install a "package shelf" at a convenient height.
- Install a ramp or electric lift for accessibility. Ramp slope should not exceed 1:12. In other words, the ramp should rise no more than 1 in. for every 12 in. of length.

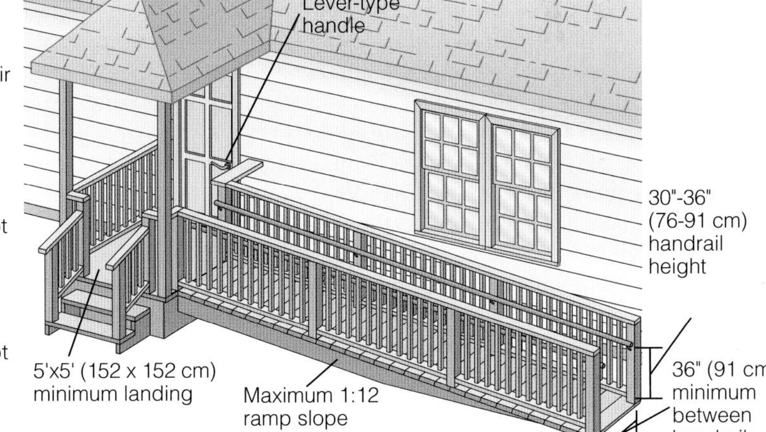

House Structure

Notching and Boring Rules 119
Enlarging a Door Opening 381
Lumber 427
Plywood 431

Bearing vs. Nonbearing Walls

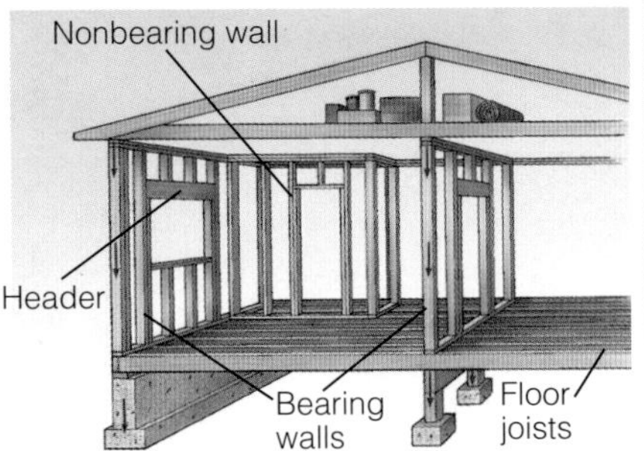

There are two kinds of walls in your house—bearing and nonbearing. Bearing walls are exterior and interior walls that transfer the weight of the roof, floors and walls above them down to the foundation. Since these walls carry a lot of weight, studs removed during remodeling must be replaced by a header that transfers the weight over to the sides of the opening, then down to the foundation. Bearing walls usually (but not always) run perpendicular to the floor and ceiling joists. And exterior walls are usually bearing walls if the rafters overlap them. If you check your basement for posts, walls and beams, the interior walls located above them are usually bearing walls. But there are exceptions. Joists and roof members can change directions.

Nonbearing walls need to support themselves, but not much weight from above. Interior nonbearing walls simply divide up space. Nonbearing exterior walls usually run parallel to the roof trusses and floor joists above. But if you create an opening in a nonbearing wall, it's still a good idea to install a substantial header, so the opening doesn't sag under its own weight. When in doubt, consult an inspector.

Wall Bracing

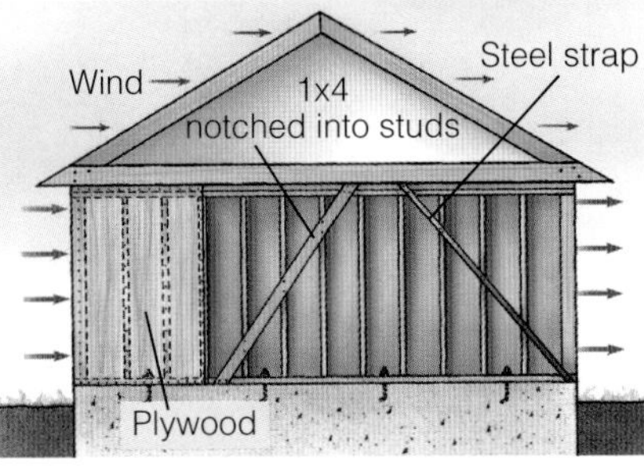

If you've ever carried a sheet of plywood in a strong breeze, you know how strong a force the wind can be. Your house needs to stand up to these same winds, year after year. And occasionally it needs to stand up against the violent forces of a thunderstorm, hurricane or tornado. To withstand all this, your home contains several types of bracing.

Wall bracing, which prevents your walls from going out of plumb, can be in the form of plywood or other sheathing nailed to the studs or in the form of steel or wood cross-bracing notched into, or secured to, the studs. Chances are, if you crawl around in your attic, you'll find other types of diagonal bracing nailed to the trusses or cross ties that also help keep your walls straight and strong.

In areas with a threat of earthquakes, many other forms of bracing are required. Suffice it to say, you should not remove braces or parts of braces in the course of remodeling. When in doubt, consult a building inspector.

Typical Exterior Wall

The 2x4 or 2x6 studs and plates that create the framework for an exterior wall do triple duty: They support the roof and floors above; create a cavity for pipes, wires, ductwork and insulation; and provide a flat, uniform surface for applying plywood, drywall and other materials.

On the exterior, most walls are covered with plywood, rigid foam or some other sheathing. Over that, felt paper or, more recently, house wrap or wind infiltration barrier, is often installed. The final layer can be wood, vinyl or steel siding, stucco or brick.

On the interior side, most walls contain insulation and a vapor barrier along with drywall or plaster.

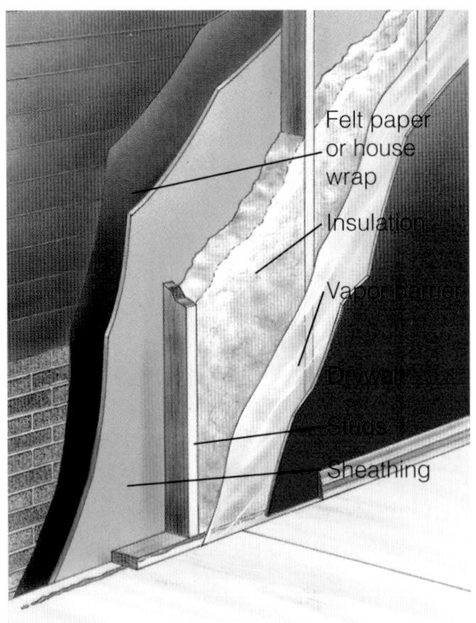

Typical Interior Wall

Before you pick up a sledgehammer and bash out that wall, think about what's inside. Any given wall can contain electrical wires, phone lines, cable TV lines, gas pipes, hot and cold water lines, drain and vent pipes, heat ducts, cold air return ducts, radiator piping and more. These "surprises" may need to be rerouted and can turn a small project into a big one or, worse yet, a doable project into an impossible one.

As you plan, pay visits to the basement and attic to find out what pipes, wires and ducts enter or leave the wall. Walls around kitchens and bathrooms usually contain the most stuff, while exterior walls, especially in cold climates, usually contain only wires.

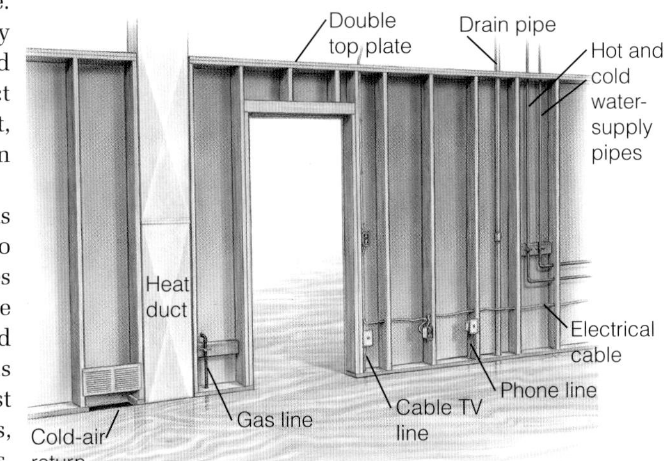

Basic Structure

Our homes rarely let us down because, even as they evolved architecturally, wood frame houses maintained basic design principles that make them sturdy.

Below is a an example. The weight from the roof compresses the rafters and tenses the ceiling joists. These forces transfer the weight to the load-bearing walls. Weight compresses the wood along the top of the floor joists. It also tenses the wood along the bottom, which allows the floor joists to transfer weight to the bearing walls. The foundation transfers weight to the ground.

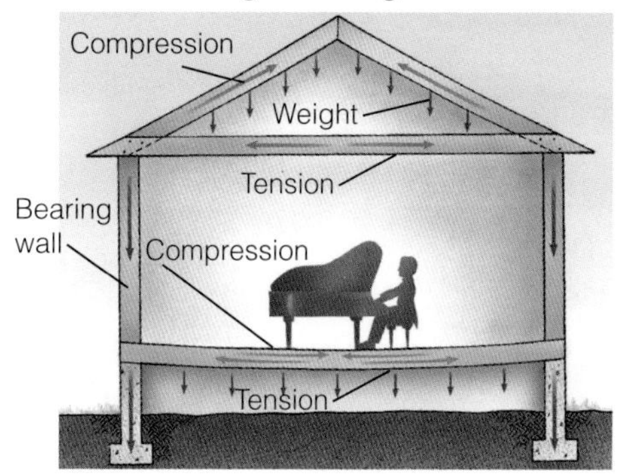

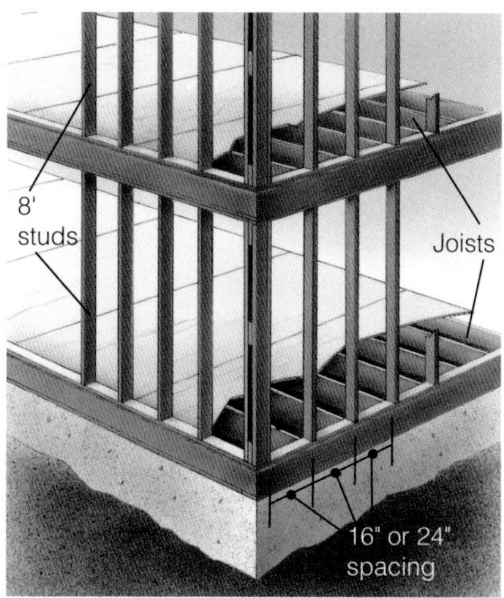

Platform framing is the standard residential construction method used today. It allows builders and do-it-yourselfers to use shorter and lighter framing members than houses of the past. Studs, joists and rafters are typically spaced at 16- or 24-in. intervals to create strength and make optimum use of standard materials such as 2x4 studs, 4x8 sheets of plywood and 4x12 sheets of drywall.

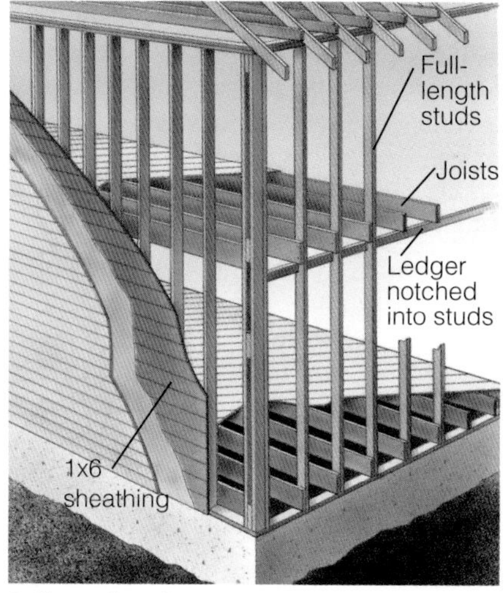

Balloon framing, employed primarily from 1850 through the early 1900s, made use of studs that extend from foundation to roof. Intermediate floors are supported by ledger boards notched into the studs. Walls were usually sheathed with 1-in.-thick boards to stiffen the structure, then finished with wood lap siding, stucco or brick.

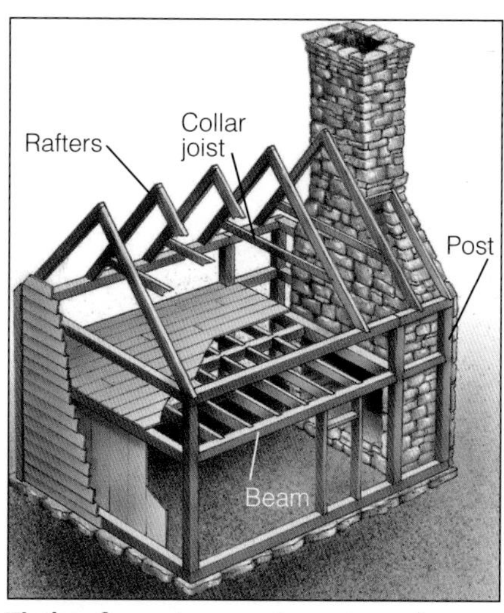

Timber frame houses rely on strong, large-dimension posts and beams to support the roof, walls and floors. Originally the spaces between beams and posts were filled with mudded and plastered sticks or whatever materials were available. Eventually wood sheathing and siding were used to make the structures more weather-tight.

Beams

Beams are used to support weight in areas that aren't supported by walls. You'll see them running down the centers of basements and across large openings. Consult a structural engineer before adding, moving or modifying any beam.

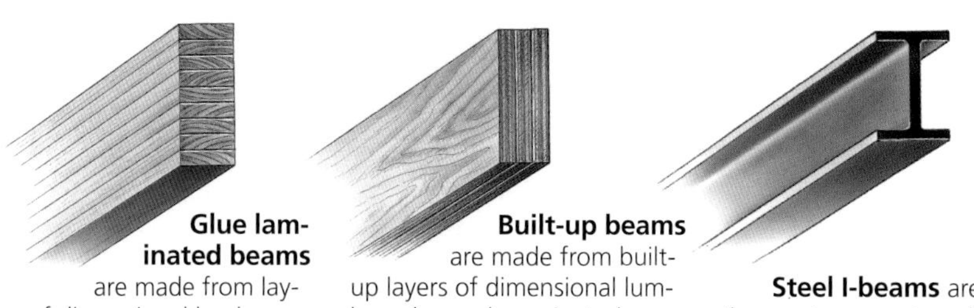

Glue laminated beams are made from layers of dimensional lumber, stacked and glued.

Built-up beams are made from built-up layers of dimensional lumber, plywood or oriented strand boardlike materials.

Steel I-beams are the most compact, making them ideal for long spans.

Joists

Joist size is determined by the distance they span, how closely spaced they are and the weight they carry. Wood truss joists and I-beam joists can be manufactured in a variety of depths, thicknesses and lengths to accommodate these variables.

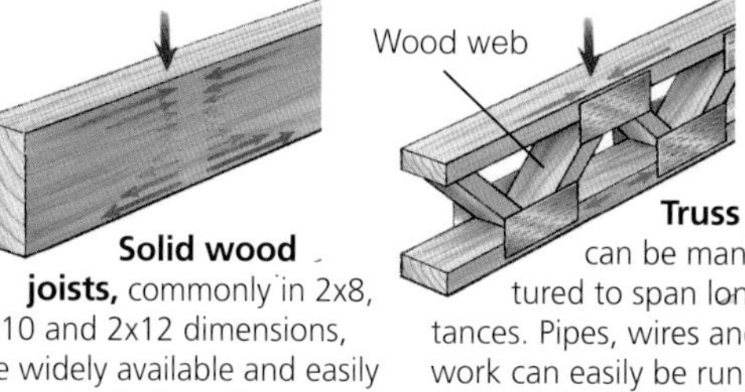

Solid wood joists, commonly in 2x8, 2x10 and 2x12 dimensions, are widely available and easily cut and nailed on site.

Truss joists can be manufactured to span long distances. Pipes, wires and ductwork can easily be run through the web openings.

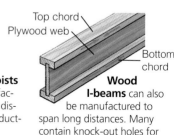

Wood I-beams can also be manufactured to span long distances. Many contain knock-out holes for running wires and small pipes.

Roof Styles

Ladder and Scaffold Safety **311**
Roof Safety **312**
Understanding Ice Dams **330**

A roof has to endure summer temperatures hot enough to grill a burger (really!) as well as resist bitter cold, shoulder tons of snow and shrug off hurricane-force winds. All that while still looking good and remaining darn near maintenance-free. There's not just one perfect roof that does all this, but several. Here are three common styles, each with its own pros and cons.

A gable roof is the easiest and least expensive to build. Most of the weight rests on the two outside walls that the roof overlaps. Dormers, intersecting roof lines and trim provide unique character. Steeper roofs contain more attic space, which can be converted into living space. Gable roofs are easy to vent, meaning they're relatively easy to keep cool in the summer and less prone to ice dams forming in the winter.

A hip roof looks like a gable roof with the ends clipped off at an angle, which makes the roof less prominent. A hip roof is more expensive and more complicated to build than a gable roof, and the extra angles reduce headroom and amount of usable space. Since rafters lap over all the outside walls, the weight is more evenly distributed.

A mansard roof has two pitches, a shallow top and a steep side. The roof overlaps and bears on all the side walls. These roofs can provide a great deal of living space. The roof is very prominent and can make a house look boxy unless carefully designed.

Gable Roof

Hip Roof

Mansard Roof

Trusses vs. Rafters

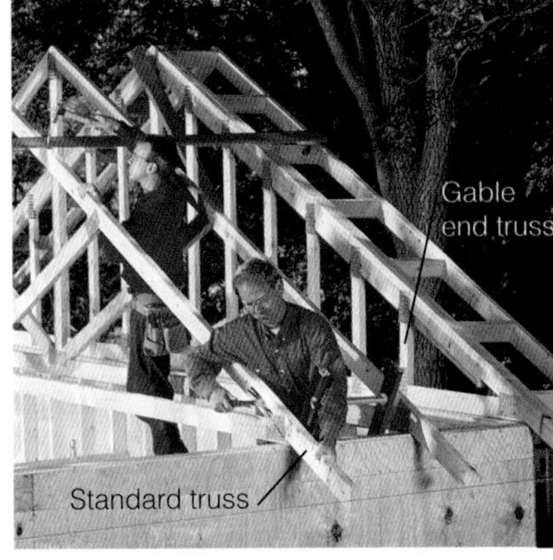

There are two ways to create a roof structure: by installing trusses or by installing individual rafters.

Factory-built trusses (left), triangles of 2x4s and 2x6s reinforced with metal plates and a web of more 2x4s and 2x6s, can be installed easily, even by novices. Computerized systems can make all the calculations to allow even complex roof designs to be manufactured and installed using trusses. Energy-efficient trusses are also available. On the downside, all of those interior 2x4s and 2x6s make the attic space largely unusable. Special trusses that carve out living and storage space can be ordered, but they're expensive. Never cut into, or modify, a truss.

Hand-framed roofs (right) consist of rafters that are individually cut and installed. Since the rafters are usually made from dimensional lumber, such as 2x10s that can span greater distances, there are fewer internal supports to interfere with the space below. Deeper rafters also provide a handy space for insulation. The result is a roof with more usable space, but also one that's harder and more expensive to build.

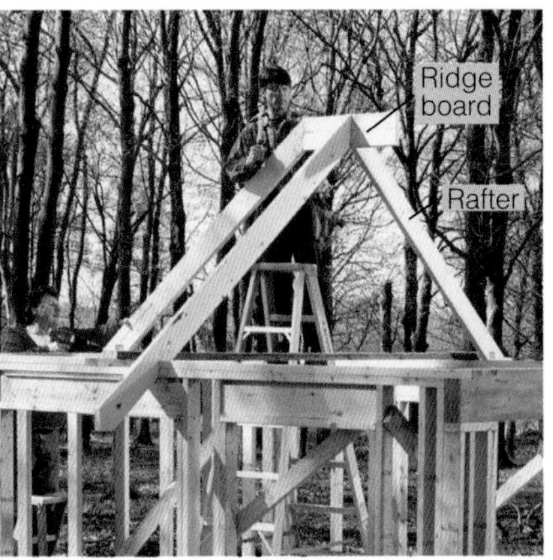

Hand Tools

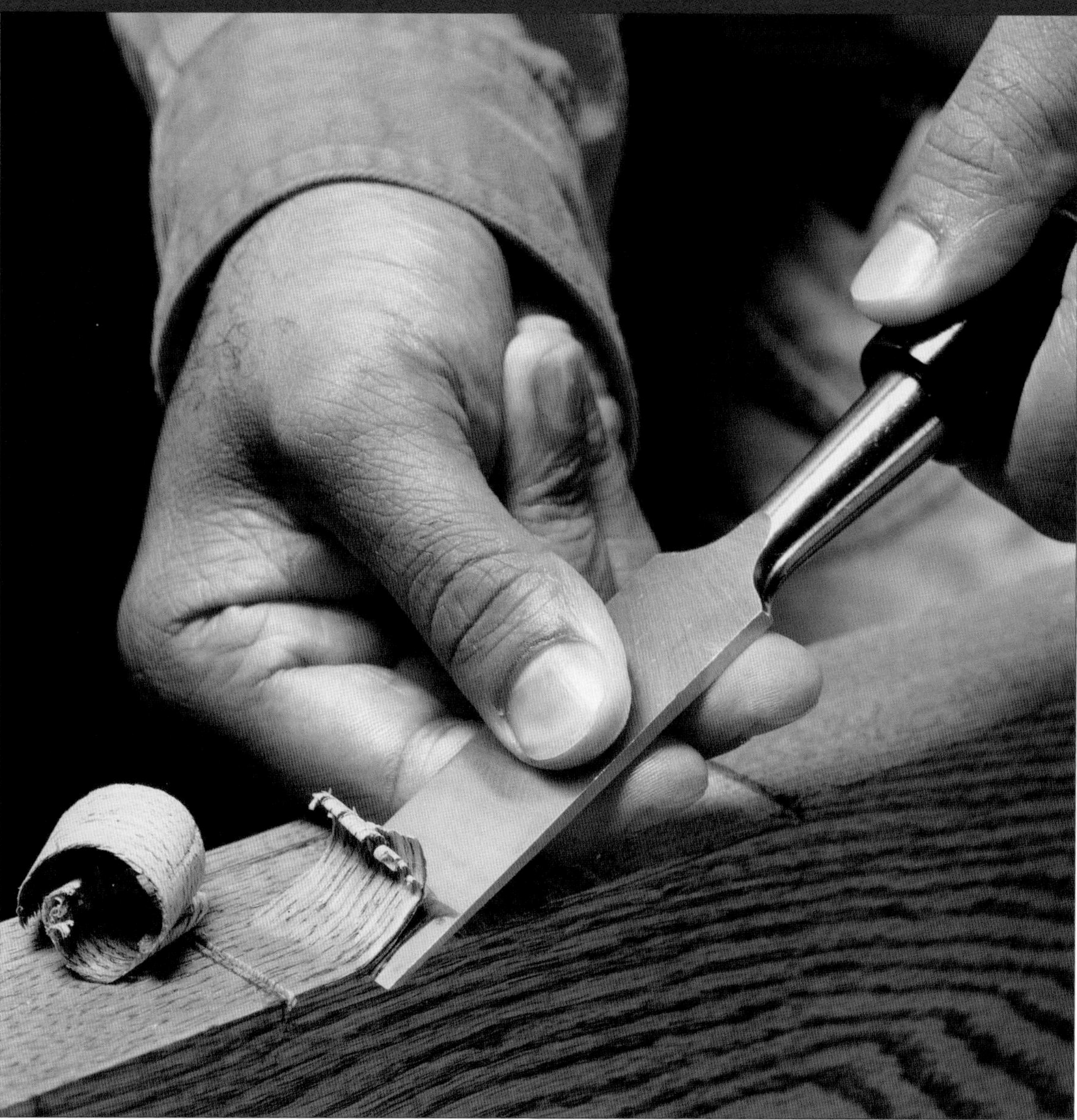

Basic Tools

Dust Collection 73
Adding Branch Circuits 138
Garage Wiring 140
Fluorescent Lights 152

Safety and Safety Equipment

Whatever tools you might assemble for a project, the list should start with items that help keep you safe and healthy. Item one? Your brain. Trust its intuition when a task seems inherently dangerous or too difficult to tackle alone. Don't work in adverse conditions that can make a routine job dangerous, and never work with tools if your judgment or motor skills are impaired by medication, alcohol or other substances.

Equally important, don't think only in terms of acute injuries or accidents. Cumulative health risks often pose greater hazards to your sight, hearing and respiratory functions, so take preventive measures to protect yourself.

Hearing protection. Irreversible hearing loss from exposure to loud noise is deceptively gradual, often going undetected until it's too late. You can prevent this by taking simple precautions in the form of disposable foam earplugs, reusable rubber earplugs (tethered pairs stay intact longer) or earmuffs.

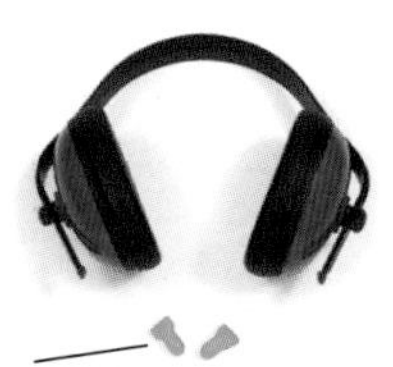
Foam earplugs

Eye protection. A ricocheting nail or a splash of harsh solvent can permanently damage an eye before you have time to react. Safety glasses or goggles help protect you from these and other needless injuries. The best have impact-resistant polycarbonate lenses and wraparound side shields to prevent indirect impact.

Respiratory protection. Fine sawdust, drywall dust, insulation fibers and vapors from solvents or adhesives all pose respiratory risks. To avoid breathing these and other airborne contaminants, wear a dust mask or a respirator, depending on the task at hand. Moldable form-fitting masks are better than the single-layer disposables. Use a respirator with cartridge filters for fumes.

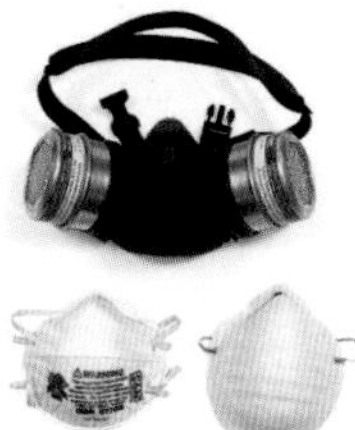

The Indispensable Dozen

True do-it-yourselfers know you can never have too many tools, but if you were stranded on the proverbial desert island (with an electrical outlet and a house that needs remodeling!) and had to pick your best 12, here's a mix that would be tough to beat. Opinions vary, but these tools rank as must-have items in even the most modest toolbox, and they'll allow you to tackle a wide array of projects. If we had to add a 13th, it would surely be the basic pliers.

16-oz. hammer
25' tape measure
Pry bar
Non-contact voltage tester
Multi-head screwdriver
Chalk box
Angle square
Cordless drill
24" level
Utility knife
Adjustable wrench
Circular saw

16-oz. hammer. Nimble enough to drive a small finish nail and stout enough for a 16-penny sinker, these midsize hammers have a curved claw for nail pulling or rip/straight claw for prying.
Pry bar. Great for dismantling framing, pulling nails, removing trim and moldings, and for demolition work.
Multi-head screwdriver. This self-contained kit typically features #1 and #2 Phillips tips, plus small and midsize standard slotted or square-drive tips.
Non-contact voltage tester. Guesswork is not recommended when working on electrical repairs or improvements. A non-contact voltage tester detects live current in a wire or cable.
25-ft. tape measure. A 25-ft. tape measure is light and compact for small-scale work and still stretches enough to handle bigger chores, such as framing.
Cordless drill. A middleweight 12-volt model will handle most drilling and screwdriving tasks. Get a kit with two battery packs and a one-hour charger; add a good set of drill and driver bits.
Angle square. Use this versatile tool for layout or cutline marking, to check corners for square or to find and mark angles from zero to 90°. It's great for rafter layout.
Circular saw. Get a model with 7-1/4-in. blade diameter with a ball-bearing motor rated at 12 amps minimum. Substituting specialty blades allows you to cut plastics, metals and concrete.
Adjustable wrench. A 10-in. (25-cm) model is a good all-around size; buy a smaller one as a spare and because you often use them in pairs.
24-in. level. This midsize level is compact enough for aligning pictures, yet big enough to plumb a fence post or level a deck beam.
Utility knife. Use to cut vinyl flooring, roofing shingles, builder's felt and other building materials.
Chalk line. Use a chalk line to snap straight guidelines for cutting plywood, installing shingles or establishing tile layout on a floor. Locking versions double as plumb bobs.

Organizing a Workshop

An improvised work area on the back porch might suffice for the occasional screen-door repair or for assembling a piece of store-bought garden furniture, but to tackle more complex projects or actually make anything, you need a real workshop. For most homeowners, the garage presents the best site for setting up a shop, but that big boxy space is just the beginning. Aside from such essentials as shelter, adequate light and ventilation, you need organized storage, a stable workbench and accessories, such as a heater or air cleaner to make the shop safe and comfortable. To keep the space available for parking cars, try to concentrate all the shop storage around the garage's perimeter. Large items, such as workbenches and machines, should be mounted on casters for mobility, so you can roll them aside when they're not needed. Walls and even the ceiling are prime candidates for mounting shelves, cabinets, racks and other storage accessories. After you set up these basics, tailor the details to the kind of work you do most.

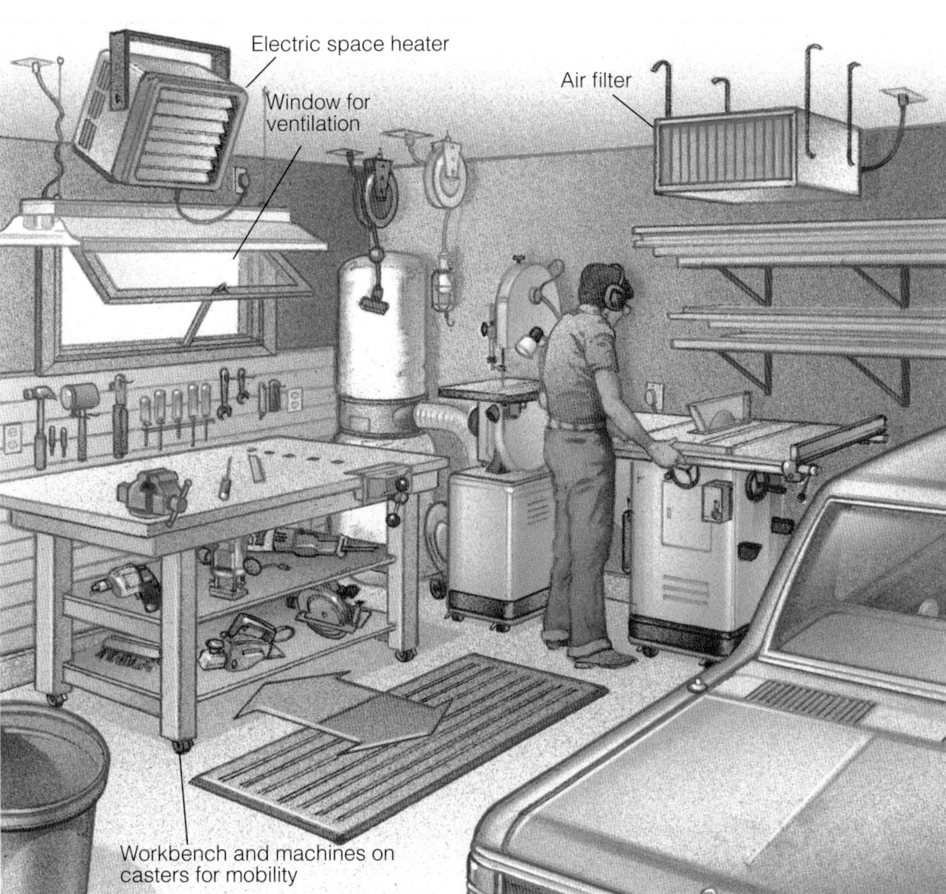

An efficient workshop. Compact but well-organized, this shop area can expand by rolling the machines and workbench into the center of the garage. An awning window provides natural light and ventilation, supplemented by a ceiling-mounted light fixture and air cleaner. Also overhead are an electric space heater and two reel-type extension cords, one with a built-in service lamp. Slat-wall sheeting provides hand-tool storage; portable power tools have a home on platform shelves built into the workbench.

In colder climates, insulate walls and ceiling, warm up wood for one to two days before gluing, and store paints, glues and liquids in an area not subject to freezing.

Light and Electricity

Most garages sport only an overhead outlet for an electric door opener plus one or two wall receptacles, all for 110-volt current. Plan to upgrade your home's electrical panel with several dedicated shop circuits—two 20-amp single-pole (110-volt) breakers and two 20-amp double-pole (220-volt) breakers make a good combination—to handle the requirements for running common power tools, stationary machines, a dust collector and a space heater. In most locales, you'll need a permit and inspection.

Some of your added electrical capacity will go toward lighting, which should be a mix of general ambient and specific task lighting. Ceiling-mounted fluorescent fixtures are inexpensive and efficient; combine them with spot-type fixtures to create a good mix.

Electrical upgrades. Work efficiency and safety concerns should be equal priorities in a home workshop. For best results, mix lighting types and route wiring to locate receptacles at convenient locations throughout the shop. Target a worst-case scenario of combined electrical demands—a table saw, dust collector and space heater, for example—to calculate how much of an upgrade your system will need. If it's substantial, consider adding a separate electrical subpanel in the garage.

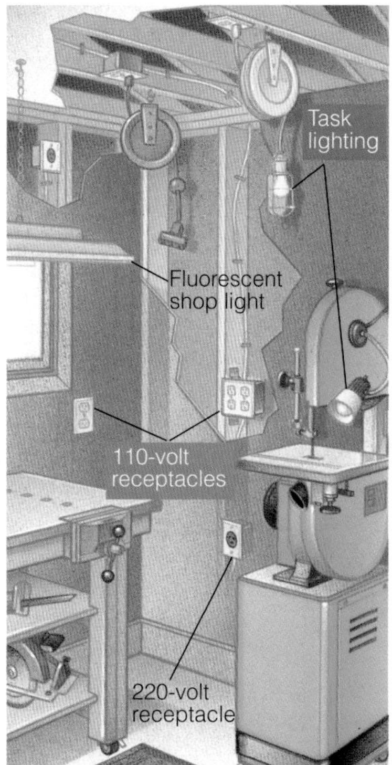

Workbenches

Vises 33
Garage Storage 492
Workshop Storage 512

Simple

Workbenches don't have to be complicated or expensive. Space-saving wall-mount versions have been around for decades, used by apartment dwellers or homeowners who didn't have the space or need for a large fixed bench. The foldaway version shown here cleverly employs a pre-hung solid-core door fitted with reinforced jamb corners and a wood flange for fastening to the wall studs. The flange also provides a mounting base for a pegboard panel to store and organize tools; the storage bay is deep enough to hold most hand tools. To support the bench when it's in the open position, a pair of 3/4-in. pipe legs thread into flanges attached to the door face.

If even this seems too ambitious, plenty of workbench kits are available at home centers and tool outlets. Most are freestanding benches, without the wall-mount option, but they offer a large, flat work surface and usually some storage features.

Customized

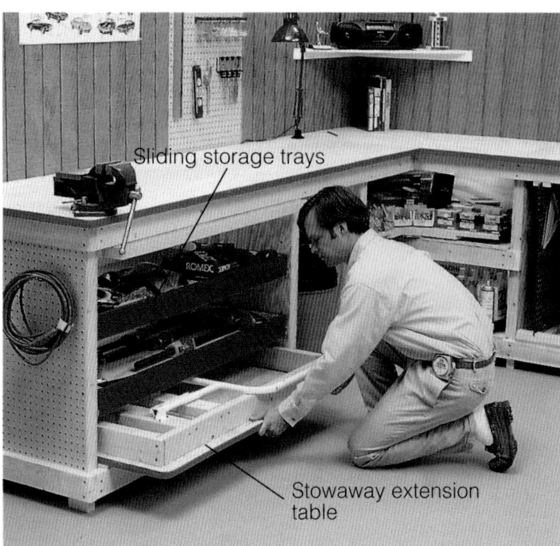

Tailoring a workbench to your shop space and your specialized uses can help you complete projects more successfully. The bench's shape, dimensions, storage, clamping features and materials should all reflect an intended specific purpose but offer versatility for other tasks. Whether you restore vintage jukeboxes, make wood jigsaw puzzles or tinker with small-engine repairs, imagine a typical project scenario and design from there. Designate separate storage features for the tools of your craft and the hardware and materials you use regularly. Use modular construction so you can change storage options without rebuilding the entire bench.

This L-shape corner bench features sliding tool-storage trays mounted on ball-bearing drawer guides; roll them out and quickly scan the contents to find what you need. Below the drawers is a stowaway table extension to provide an additional work surface as needed. The bench's other end stores fasteners, hardware and other materials, all organized for ready access.

Woodworking

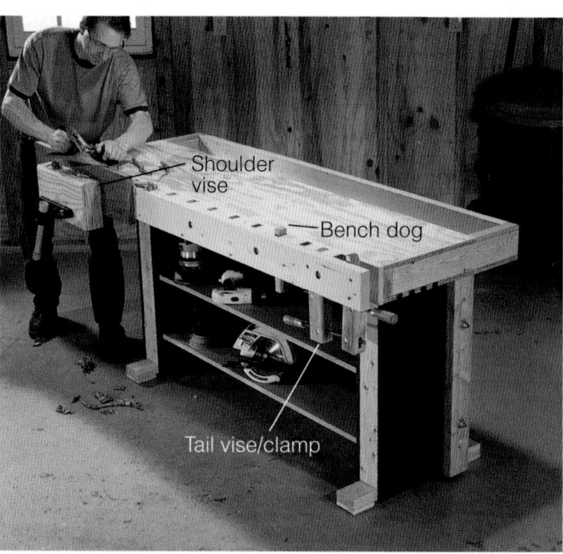

When home-shop woodworkers get serious about their craft, their all-purpose workbench suddenly seems less purposeful. Unlike the generic table-style work surface, a traditional joiner's bench is an exercise in heft and clamping capacity. Hand-planing a hardwood plank or cutting precise joinery demands a weighty, unshakable workbench that won't deflect or shimmy across the floor. Heavy bases and thick hardwood tops provide the mass; built-in vises secure the material.

The shoulder vise (shown in use, above) excels at gripping stock for edge planing or cutting joinery. At the other end of the bench is a tail vise, capable of clamping stock edge-to-edge so it can lie flat and unobstructed on the benchtop. The bench featured above substitutes a traditional joiner's clamp (called a hand screw) to accomplish the same thing; holes in the work surface accept adjustable bench dogs, which are retractable stops used to grip and hold material at its edge or end. Base cabinets or shelves provide storage for tools (or for sandbags if you want even more weight).

Sawhorses

Adjustable Sawhorses

These versatile sawhorses offer a feature most don't—adjustable height settings. You can vary the setting according to your own height or preferences, the type of project or a table saw's height to provide outfeed support of long boards. Although it looks more complicated than a standard sawhorse, it's an assembly of two fairly simple structures: a splayed-leg base with a wide footing for support, and a movable center frame that incorporates the work rail. It's made from standard nominal 1x4 and 2x4 lumber, so no special milling is required.

The unusual feature is a pair of adjustable slides, which are vertical frame members with 1/2-in. (13-mm) holes drilled at a 2 in. (5 cm) center-to-center spacing along the length of their faces. Two hardwood dowels, tethered to the frame rails with chains, function as locking pins to secure the height setting you want.

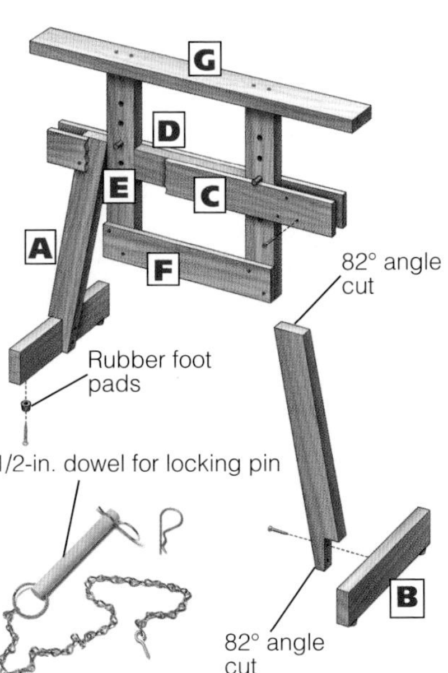

Cutting List

Key	Pcs.	Size & Description
A	2	1-1/2" x 3-1/2" x 25" legs
B	2	1-1/2" x 3-1/2" x 18" feet
C	2	3/4" x 3-1/2" x 36" upper rails
D	1	1-1/2" x 3-1/2" x 13" spacer block
E	2	1-1/2" x 3-1/2" x 21"adjustable slides
F	1	3/4" x 3-1/2" x 20" slide brace
G	1	3/4" x 3-1/2" x 40" work rail

Square-cut Sawhorses

The only materials required to build this sturdy sawhorse are a pair of 12-ft.-long 2x4s and a handful of 3-in. drywall or all-purpose screws. Cut one of the 2x4s into three equal lengths for the I-beam rail assembly; use screws to secure upper and lower flanges to the center rail, as shown. (If during use you'll be cutting through workpieces and into the upper flange, drill counterbores so the screw heads nest about 1/2 in. (13 mm) below the surface.) For the legs, cut the remaining 2x4 into four equal lengths, up to 36 in. (90 cm) long.

The upper ends can be cut square, but if you want to bevel the lower ends, as shown here, clamp the legs in place for a test fit. Place a 1x4 gauge block on the ground, scribe a pencil line on the leg to indicate the bevel angle and cut accordingly.

To attach the legs, nest them against the sides of the I-beam as shown above; then drive screws to fasten them to the center rail and lower flange.

Hammers

Hammers look simple, but they are the result of complex metallurgy and engineering to ensure they perform well over a lifetime of use. Although most are versatile enough to handle a variety of situations, each is in fact designed to excel at a few specific tasks.

The head's size, shape and weight determine its best uses, so don't expect a common 16-oz. household hammer to work as effectively as something much larger or more specialized.

Good balance and a comfortable handle help prevent unnecessary fatigue; if a tool doesn't feel right in the store, odds are it won't improve when you're swinging it on your project site.

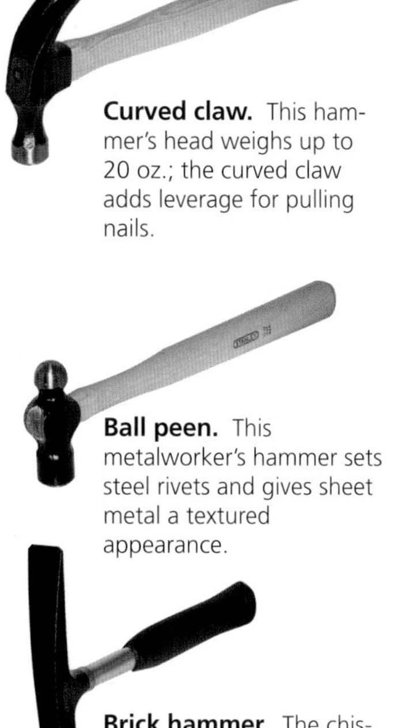

Curved claw. This hammer's head weighs up to 20 oz.; the curved claw adds leverage for pulling nails.

Ball peen. This metalworker's hammer sets steel rivets and gives sheet metal a textured appearance.

Brick hammer. The chiseled end can trim bricks, chip mortar or score a break line on stone or brick.

Straight claw. The head weighs up to 28 oz.; the straight claw excels at prying boards apart.

Tack hammer. The narrow magnetic head holds small nails and gets into tight spaces.

Sledgehammer. With a 2-lb. or larger head, this heavyweight offers brute force for driving stakes.

Shop Smart: Hammer Handles

In the days when Henry Ford offered the Model A in any color, as long as it was black, hammer handles offered a similarly singular option: wood. The toughness, durability and relatively low cost of straight-grained ash or hickory handles still merit their use, but today the playing field is much bigger.

Solid-steel hammers cured the broken-handle problem by forging the head and stem of the hammer from a single piece of steel and fitting it with a rubber cushion grip. But some stress and vibration still are transmitted to the user's arm and hand. Fiberglass and graphite handles, also fitted with cushion grips, are better at dissipating the impact shock before it reaches your arm, and the latest generation of hammers combine these proven materials with polycarbonate, vinyl or other composites for a mix of comfort and durability. Most also feature molded head-to-handle connections to enhance their shock-absorbing properties.

Replacing a Wood Handle

A broken wood handle is no reason to discard a perfectly good hammer. Whether the head has worked irreparably loose over time or is dangling dangerously from a splintered shaft, your local hardware store or home center is likely to have a replacement handle kit for a hammer of almost any size or age.

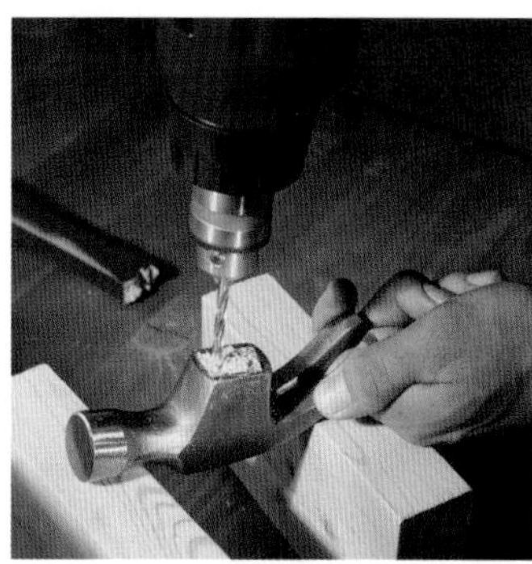

1 Start by drilling multiple holes in the handle remnant. Then use a nail set or punch to clear the debris from the eye of the head.

2 Fit the head on the new handle. Seat it firmly by rapping the handle end on a solid surface. Trim part of handle protruding past head.

3 With the head firmly seated, drive a tapered wood shim into the precut kerf in the handle.

4 Check the head for a tight fit; then drive a metal wedge at an angle to the wood shim.

Using a Hammer

Simple as they are, hammers still warrant some basic safety guidelines. First, always wear eye protection to avoid injuries from ricocheting nails, debris or a shattered hammer head. This latter danger is a relatively rare occurrence, but the hardening treatment that makes nail hammers so durable also makes them brittle. Never strike one hardened hammer face to another or use a hardened nail hammer to strike other hardened tools, such as cold chisels or punches. Also, don't strike anything with the side, or cheek, of the hammer. When nailing, always use at least one set stroke to ensure the nail tip is firmly embedded in the material before taking a full swing. Always keep your attention focused on the nail or other target, not on the hammer.

Swing. Adjust your swing and pivot point to the size of nail you're driving. Swing from the wrist for smaller nails, elbow for midsize nails and shoulder for large nails. Release the nail after the set stroke; then swing in a smooth arc.

High places. Reaching above your head to drive nails sometimes requires a one-hand trick. Wedge the nail between the hammer claws to hold it, seat it with a light set stroke, then resume normal grip on the hammer to drive the nail home.

Leverage. To increase the tool's leverage for pulling nails, insert a scrap block under the hammer's head. This not only reduces the effort required but helps prevent breakage of wood handles.

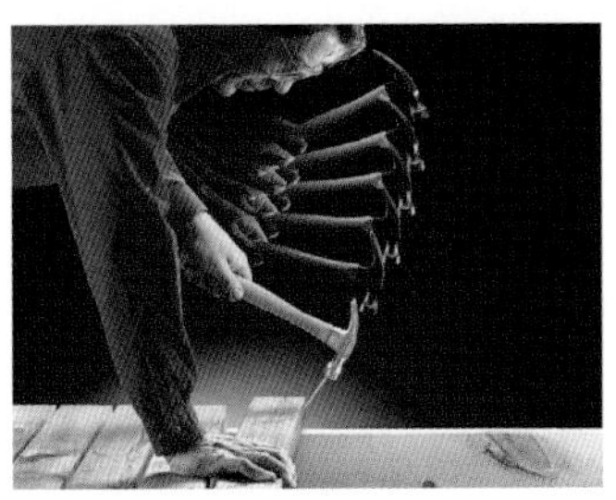

Toenailing. When face nailing isn't possible because of space constraints or you want to conceal the nail head in the edge of a board, driving nails at an angle—a technique called toenailing—offers a simple solution.

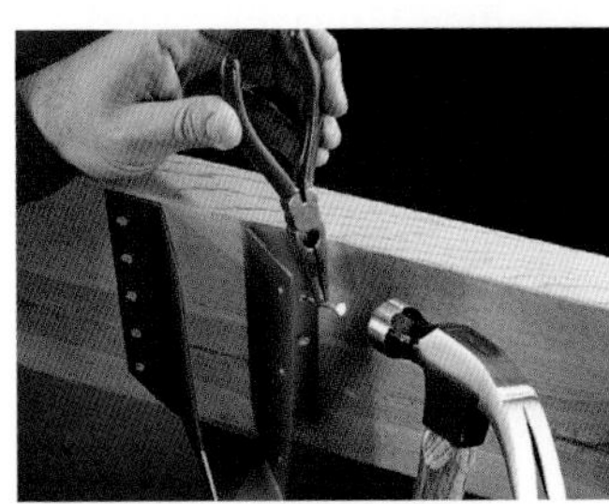

Awkward spaces. For tight spaces where you can't fit your fingers at all or without exposing them to hammer blows, use a pair of needle-nose pliers to hold the nail until you set it.

Sidewinder. To remove nails in tight spaces or with broken heads, wedge the nail shank in the hammer claws and "walk" it out by turning the hammer on its side in one direction and then the other.

Replacing a Fiberglass Handle

When it's time to replace a broken or damaged wood handle, fiberglass tool handles offer a more durable option and cost only slightly more than a wood replacement kit. Especially common for sledgehammers and other large tools, these fiberglass repair kits substitute epoxy for the wedges that secure wood handles.

1 After cutting off the wood handle, place the hammer head onto an open bench vise and drill multiple holes in the remaining plug.

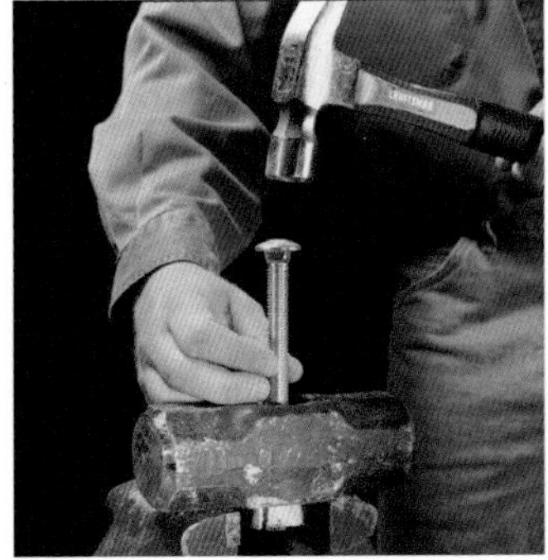

2 Knock the plug from the head using a hammer and the largest bolt you have available. Hard blows will loosen the plug until it releases.

3 After wire brushing the hole sides, fit the new fiberglass handle into the sledge head and seal the connection with caulking cord.

4 Mix the supplied epoxy packet as per the instructions and pour it into the tool eye, around the handle. Let it cure one week before using.

Saws

It's no secret that stationary and portable power saws have displaced manual cutting tools for many tasks, but handsaws still have a vital role in every kind of woodworking, from rough carpentry to building fine furniture. Featuring a thin flat blade with one or two serrated edges, handsaws offer cordless convenience and can make deep or close-quarters cuts that are off-limits to many power saws. Handsaws are usually defined by the number of teeth per inch (tpi) or "points," and by the particular grind and set (offset angle) of the teeth, which determines what kind of cutting they do best. Some can be resharpened and reset; others feature replaceable blades.

Handsaws

The traditional Western-style handsaw for general carpentry features a long blade with a hardwood handle, and excels at cross-cutting. The teeth are offset alternately to create a cutting gap (called a kerf) slightly wider than the blade thickness. Recently, shorter saws have become more popular, and a chisel grind on the teeth cuts on both the pull and push strokes.

Position. For accurate, safe cutting, place the workpiece on steady supports at about knee height. Cut with the blade and your arm square to the board.

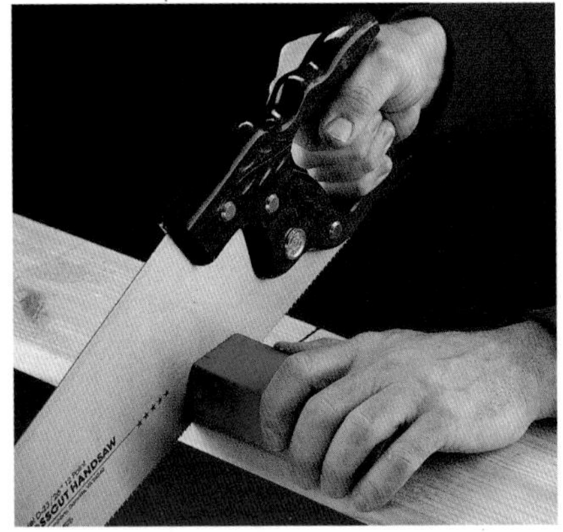

Start cut. Start a cut by pulling the saw backward at a low angle for a few strokes. Use a guide block to protect fingers and ensure a square cut.

Finish cut. Use a steeper angle (about 45°) as you progress through the cut. For a stopped cut like the one shown, the saw should finish at a 90° angle.

Pull Saws

Pull saws, such as the Japanese-style dozuki (above), differ from traditional Western saws in two ways: They typically have in-line rather than transverse handles, and the teeth cut on the pull stroke, allowing for thinner blades, smaller kerfs and, proponents say, better control in the cut. A dozuki saw has a steel reinforcing channel along its back, ensuring a straight blade for cutting precise joinery.

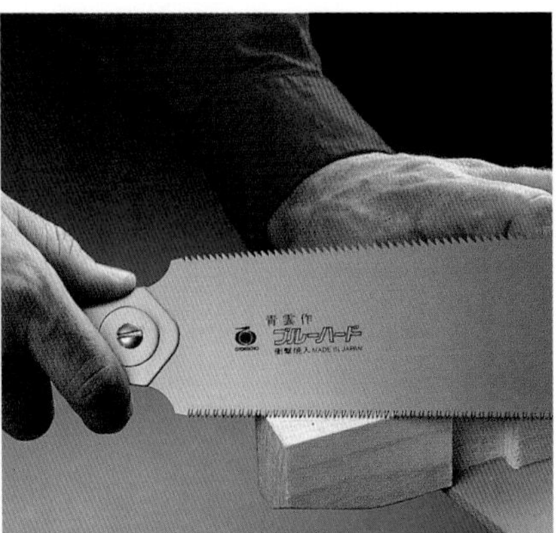

Using a pull saw. Use light touch when starting cut, letting blade score the wood first. Double-edge varieties have one side for cross-cutting, the other for ripping boards to width.

Coping Saws

Featuring a very narrow, flat blade tensioned in a steel bow frame, a coping saw excels at cutting intricate curves. These saws are commonly used to cut contours on the ends of wood molding. Smaller versions, called fret-saws, are used in making jewelry and musical instruments.

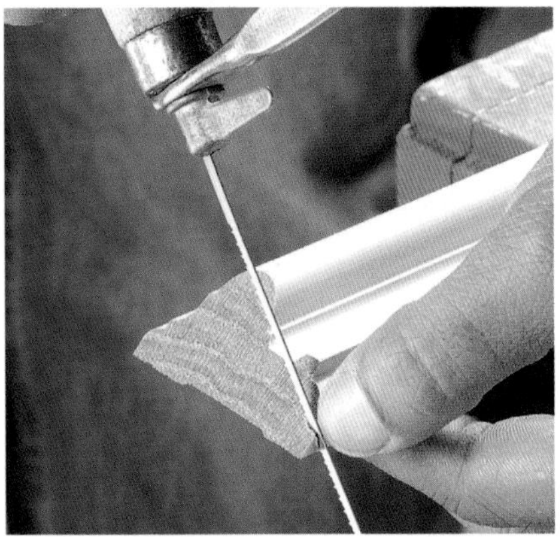

Using a coping saw. To cope the end of a molding, first cut an inside miter on the piece. Then follow the contour line of the molding face with the coping saw.

Miter Saws

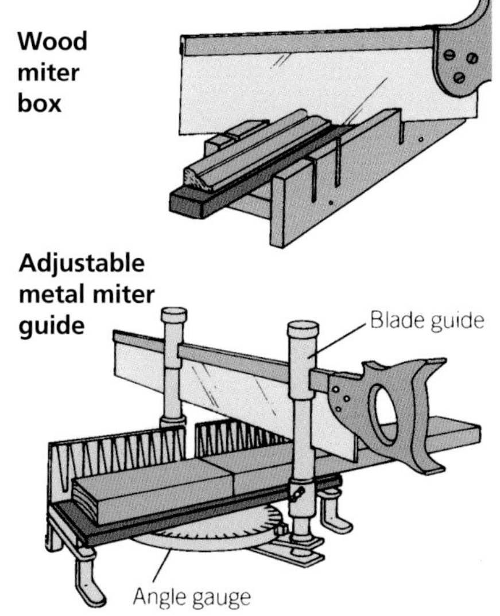

Miter saws are actually two tools—a saw that does the actual cutting and a guide to create a precise, controlled cut. Metal versions feature an adjustable-angle base; wood versions are simple boxes with precut kerfs at 90° and 45°.

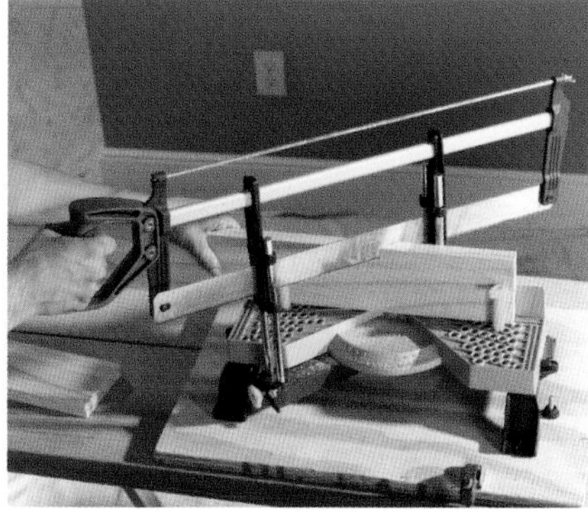

Newer metal miter saws feature lightweight tension-type blades and telescoping post guides that control the saw's movement.

Hacksaws

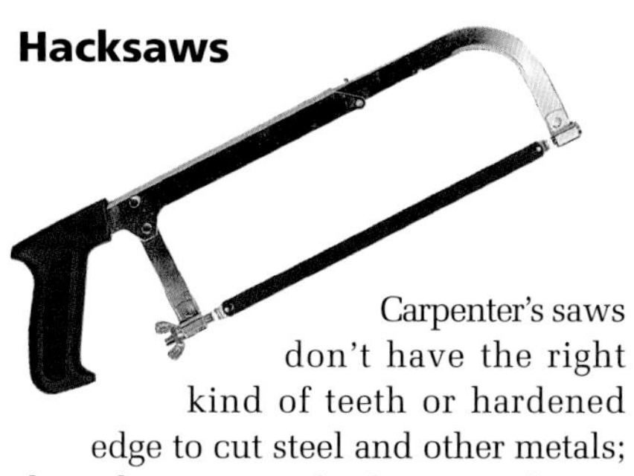

Carpenter's saws don't have the right kind of teeth or hardened edge to cut steel and other metals; that job requires a hacksaw. Hacksaws use a narrow replaceable blade tensioned in a bow frame, and the teeth are much smaller and shorter than those found on woodworking saws. Blades are typically classified by the number of teeth per inch—fine (32 tpi), medium (24 tpi) and coarse (18 tpi). Coarser blades cut faster and more aggressively but leave a rougher edge. A properly tensioned blade is critical for making a clean, accurate cut; with too little tension, the blade will flex and drift rather than cut straight.

Hacksaws are great for plumbing and electrical work, but never work on pipe or conduit without shutting the water or electricity off.

Keyhole Saws

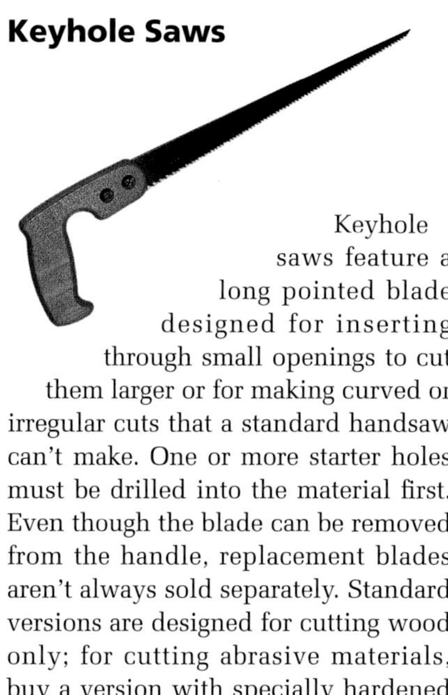

Keyhole saws feature a long pointed blade designed for inserting through small openings to cut them larger or for making curved or irregular cuts that a standard handsaw can't make. One or more starter holes must be drilled into the material first. Even though the blade can be removed from the handle, replacement blades aren't always sold separately. Standard versions are designed for cutting wood only; for cutting abrasive materials, buy a version with specially hardened teeth for that application.

Keyhole saws work more effectively if you predrill holes and use the saw just to cut through the remaining waste portion.

Making the Cut

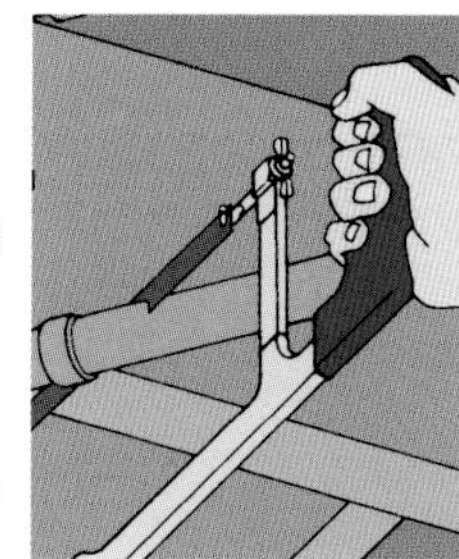

1 When required, a hacksaw blade can be installed upside down with the cutting edge toward the frame.

2 To use a coping saw for a closed cutout, drill a starter hole and feed the blade through it. Then reattach the blade to the frame.

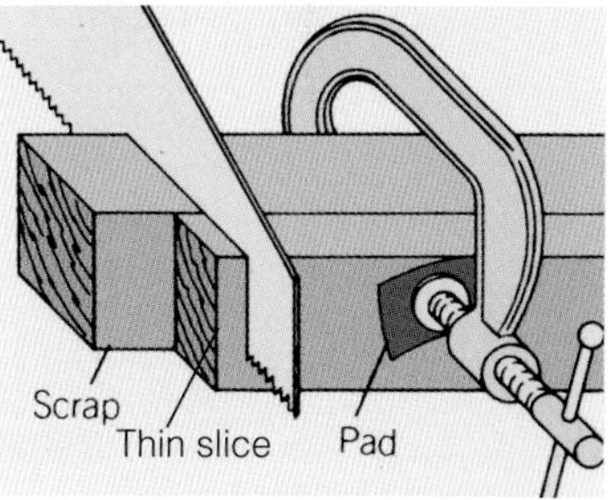

3 To prevent tear out and splintering a workpiece or to cut a thin slice, clamp a sacrificial wood block to the board, then saw through both pieces.

Staple Guns

Nails, bolts and screws might be the fasteners you typically associate with home improvements and repairs. For some projects, though, those items are outnumbered by a much smaller piece of hardware—the staple. Used to fasten fabric, felt roofing underlayment, screen mesh, insulation, carpet padding and dozens of other materials, staples for home use vary in length from 1/4 in. to 9/16 in. long, typically in 1/16-in. increments. The guns that drive them are medium-duty tools, beefier than a household stapler but less powerful than an industrial pneumatic tool.

You'll find three basic types of staplers designed for building or project applications: a standard manual gun, a manual hammer tacker and an electric staple gun. If you tackle a variety of home improvement projects, the two manual versions are affordable enough to warrant owning one of each. An electric gun is slightly more expensive but requires only a light trigger pull to operate; for frequent use, it might be worth the investment.

Standard

A standard staple gun features a spring-action drive that activates when you grip the tool body and press the lever handle down firmly with your palm. Precise placement of the staple is this gun's strong suit, so it's great for tasks where careful work is more important than speed.

Hammer Tacker

Use a hammer tacker for covering large areas quickly. Installing carpet padding or securing roofing felt are two prime uses. As the name implies, you swing it like a hammer. On impact, the tool's momentum compresses the head and drives the staple. It's fast, but not designed for precision work.

Electric

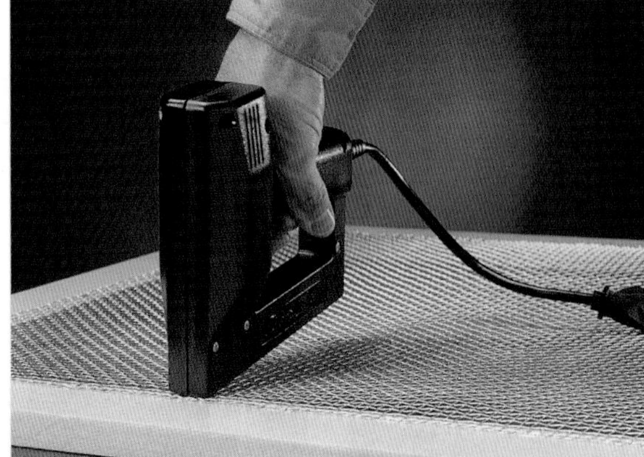

Electric staple guns take the fatigue out of firing repeatedly and make it possible to drive staples into and through tougher materials. Unlike the blunt force of a standard staple gun or a hammer tacker, the electric gun's direct impact is to the staple only, not the workpiece, so delicate materials fare better.

Utility Knives

Many flexible materials have to be cut before or after installation. For such trimming, there's no better tool than a utility knife. This inexpensive cutting tool can feature a retractable or fixed blade. Each blade typically has two cutting ends, which you can rotate before swapping the blade for a new one. Some have multi-section blades that snap off on scored lines to give you a fresh edge. The interchangeable blades provide versatility. Standard blades cut screen cloth, roofing felt, the paper face on wallboard and dozens of other materials. Linoleum blades specialize in cutting resilient sheet flooring; laminate-scoring blades etch a razor-thin line in plastic laminates to snap a clean break. Hook blades slice through shingles and other material in one pass without cutting the surface below.

Newer generation blades include more durable "tri-metal" blades and special serrated blades designed for cutting drywall. Newer-generation handle designs feature quick-change features and ergonomic contours and cushioned grips for comfort.

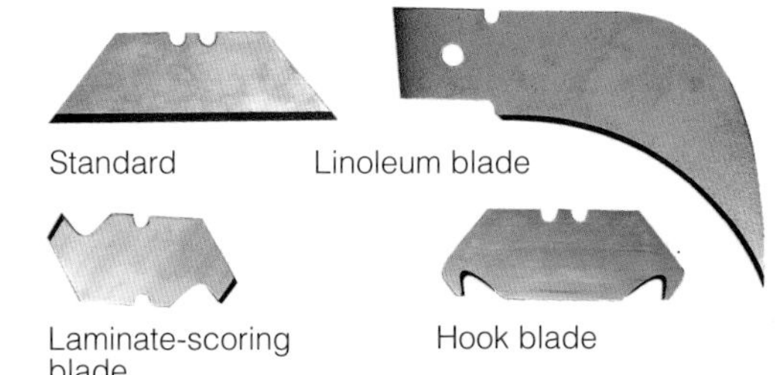

Utility knives outperform almost any other tool, manual or powered, for precise trimming of flexible materials. A sharp blade is less likely to stray from where you direct it, so change blades as often as required.

Screwdrivers

Few tools are this basic and essential. Screwdrivers have a centuries-old history, but modern versions have evolved from the simple flat-blade type to include other drive tips. The Phillips drive offers a greater grip area for the fastener head and the convenience of a tip that screws can cling to. Square-drive, or Robertson, tips provide an even better grip with less chance of slipping or stripping.

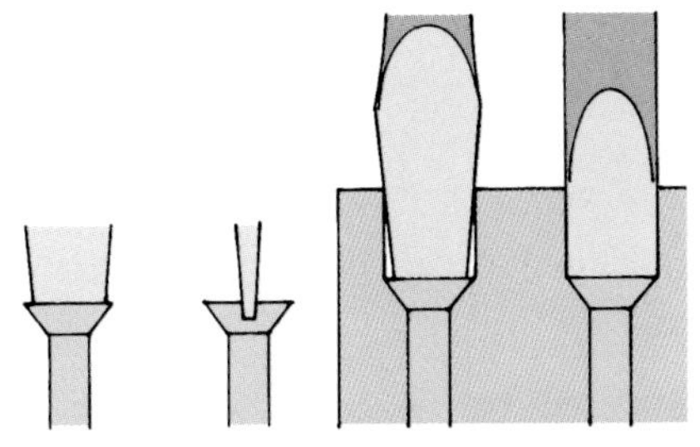

Basic Types

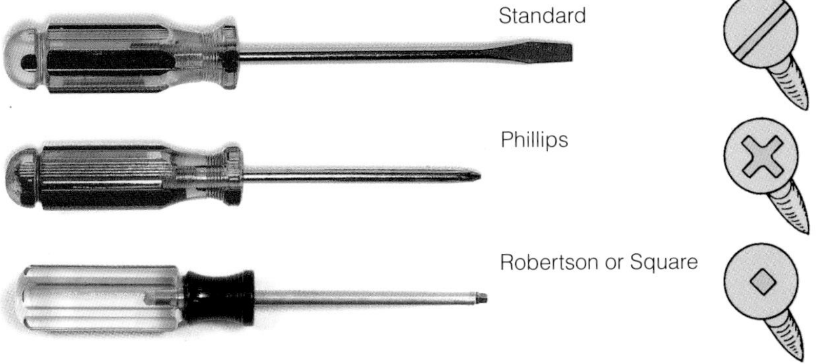

Specialty Screwdrivers

Stubby. Working in confined spaces—a car engine is among the worst—often doesn't allow room for a full-size screwdriver with a normal handle and blade length. "Stubby" short-handled versions pack the function into a compact size.

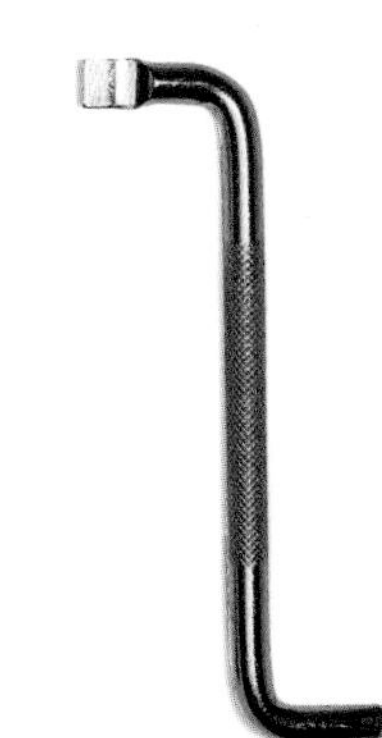

Offset. For clearances so tight even a stubby won't fit, an offset screwdriver features a bent double-ended blade and no handle. Available in standard and Phillips versions, you can also find these with ratcheting heads to work a little faster.

Renewing the Tip

When screwdrivers lose their edge and start slipping, they can easily be renewed. Square-drive tips can be restored by simply filing back the blunt end.

Phillips. Start by filing the nose or point of the tip down slightly to flatten it. Then use the edge of the file (inset photo) to shape and sharpen the grooves.

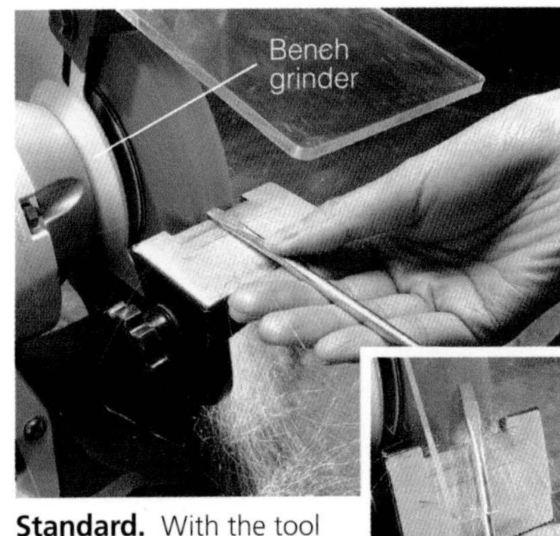

Standard. With the tool rest set square to the wheel edge, grind off the worn or damaged portion. Change to a steep angle (see inset photo) to taper the new tip.

Handy Hints: Work Smarter

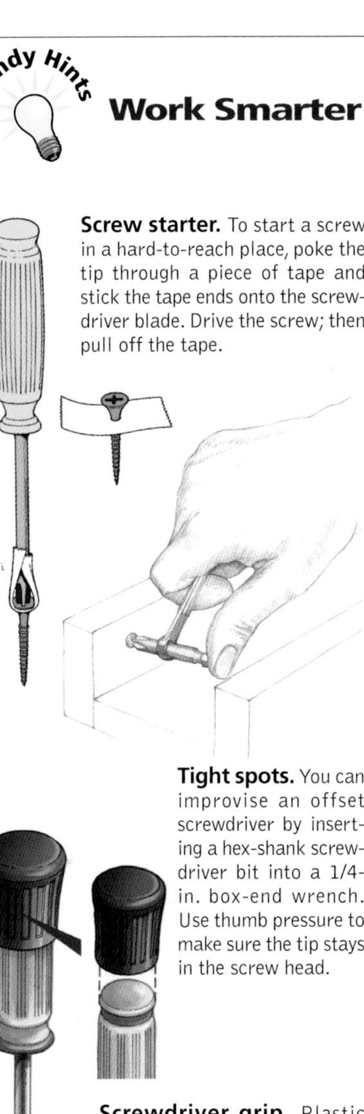

Screw starter. To start a screw in a hard-to-reach place, poke the tip through a piece of tape and stick the tape ends onto the screwdriver blade. Drive the screw; then pull off the tape.

Tight spots. You can improvise an offset screwdriver by inserting a hex-shank screwdriver bit into a 1/4-in. box-end wrench. Use thumb pressure to make sure the tip stays in the screw head.

Screwdriver grip. Plastic screwdriver handles are tough on your palms. Improve your grip and comfort level by pressing a rubber chair leg tip onto the handle.

Wrenches

Virtually every household has items that require wrenches for assembly, adjustment or repair. There are other variations, but the nuts, bolts and screws that require wrenches typically feature a hexagonal (six-sided) shape (square heads were common in older hardware but are seldom used today). Whatever the wrench type, it works by gripping two or more sides of the nut or bolt head so it can be rotated. Some versions are adjustable, but others are fixed sizes that must be matched precisely to the fastener size.

In fixed-size wrenches, two standards are common. Imperial sizes, common in the United States and the United Kingdom, are labeled in fractions of an inch (7/16 in., for example). Metric sizes are labeled with a single number that indicates millimeters (12 mm, for example).

Socket Wrenches

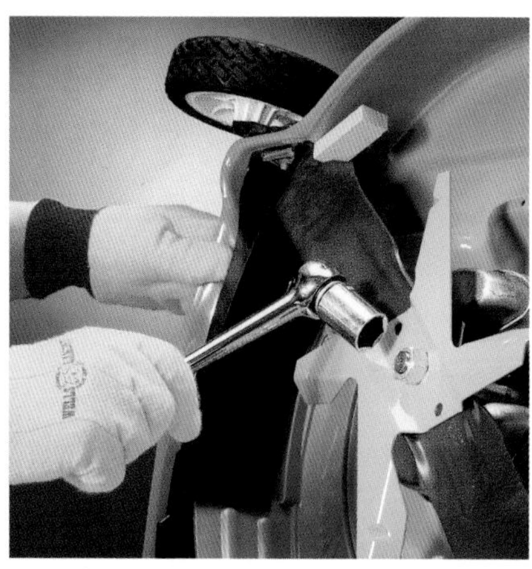

Socket wrenches are hollow cylindrical wrenches with flat or angled edges machined on their inside faces. They nest snugly over the bolt head like a cup. The socket's other end is machined to accept a square driver, typically on a ratcheting handle that can be set to engage the driver in only one direction, to tighten or loosen. A 3/8-in.-drive socket set is the most common for household use, but 1/4- and 1/2-in. sizes are also widely used. (Industrial-duty sockets often feature even larger drives.) Most socket wrenches are fixed-size models purchased in sets, although adjustable versions with movable jaws are available.

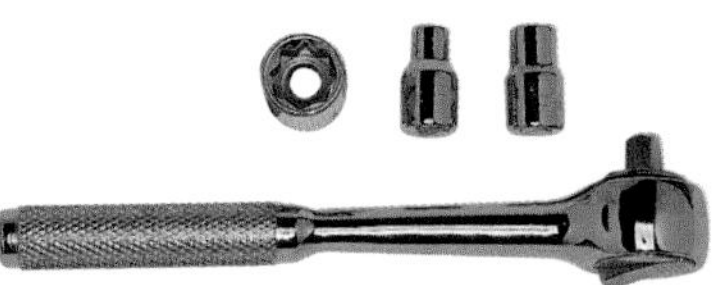

Ratchet handle and socket. Ratchet handles, which work with interchangeable sockets, are much faster than fixed-handle wrenches.

Box-end ratchet. Box-end ratchets fit where there isn't clearance for a standard ratchet handle and socket.

6-Point vs. 12-Point

If you're shopping for socket sets, you might notice that some have a different internal shape. Mechanics like 12-point sockets because they fit onto bolt heads faster, but they grip only at the corners and can sometimes strip a nut. They'll also grip square-head nuts. A 6-point socket provides a bearing surface on the flats, creating a stronger grip.

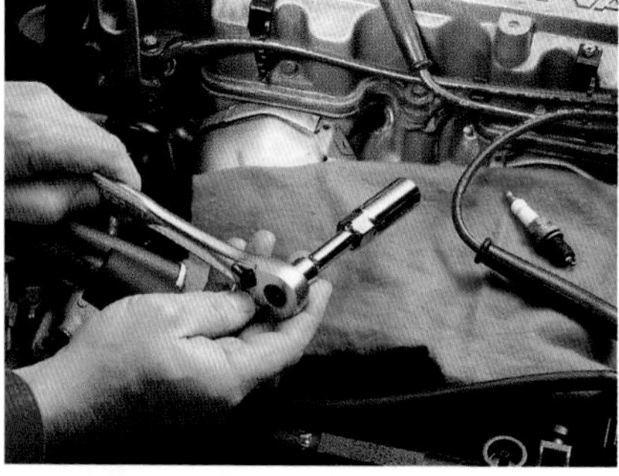

Extensions. Hard-to-reach areas can be made more accessible by fitting a drive extension between the ratchet handle and the socket.

Cheater bar. For dealing with stubborn nuts or bolts, extending the ratchet handle length with a pipe will increase the tool's leverage.

Adapters. Driver adapters let you fit a socket onto an electric drill, offering better power and speed for driving lag screws or tightening bolts.

Nut Drivers

Nut drivers work on hex-head bolts and nuts, but they're fitted with an in-line handle like a screwdriver—hence the name. Nut drivers are convenient for getting into tight spaces where a wrench won't fit. They're available in fractional inch and metric, but in a limited range of smaller sizes.

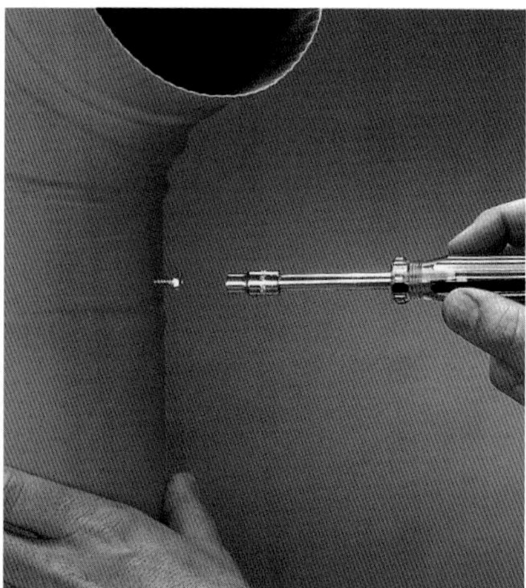

Spinner handles. A spinner handle is a variation on the nut driver. It features a square-drive tip (usually 1/4 in.) designed to accept interchangeable sockets like a ratchet handle.

Fixed

With fixed-size wrenches, you have to buy multiples to handle different fastener sizes, but the crisp, exact fit is worth the expense. They're faster to use and maintain a solid grip.

A stubby wrench has the same "business ends" as a standard wrench, but the shorter handle allows you to get into cramped spaces.

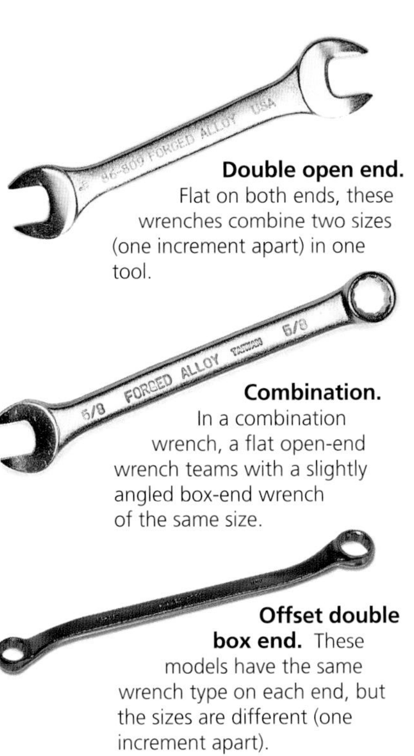

Double open end. Flat on both ends, these wrenches combine two sizes (one increment apart) in one tool.

Combination. In a combination wrench, a flat open-end wrench teams with a slightly angled box-end wrench of the same size.

Offset double box end. These models have the same wrench type on each end, but the sizes are different (one increment apart).

Wrenches

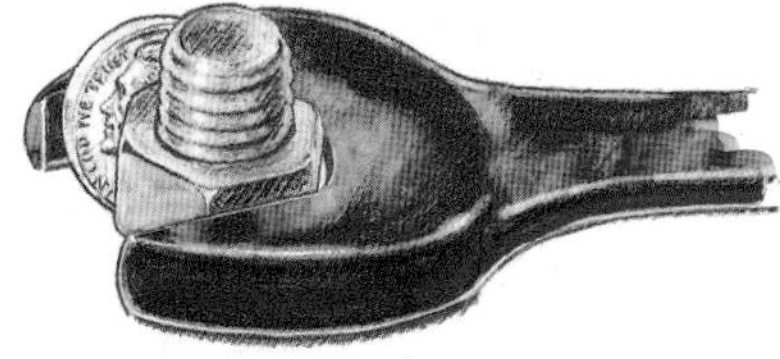

Improvised size. If you don't have an adjustable wrench or the exact fixed size you need, try inserting a coin as a shim between the jaw and the nut.

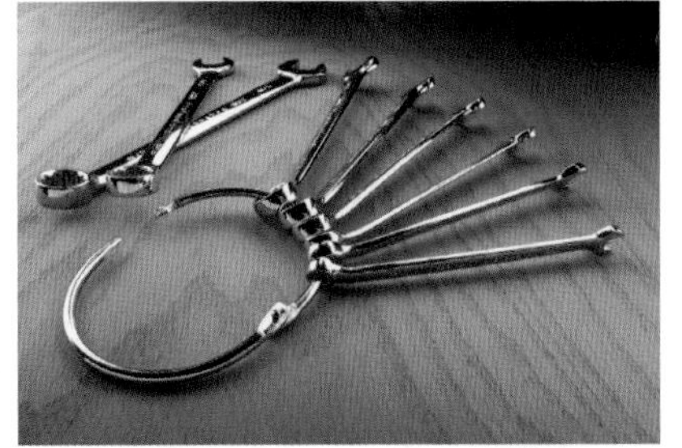

Stay organized. To avoid searching your toolbox for one elusive wrench, thread the whole set onto a loose-leaf binder ring and store them together. Open the ring to free the size you need.

Adjustable

Like any general-purpose tool, an adjustable wrench offers versatility in exchange for a slight loss in precision. It's difficult to get the snug fit that a fixed wrench provides, and the movable jaw tends to creep slightly during use. But a single adjustable wrench can sometimes substitute for an entire set of open- or box-end wrenches. Because their jaw size is not fixed, adjustable wrenches are designated by their handle length; the maximum jaw opening is usually stamped on the handle. Plan to buy at least one small and one large size. Using an oversize wrench on a small fastener is awkward, and you often use wrenches in pairs anyway, so it pays to have two.

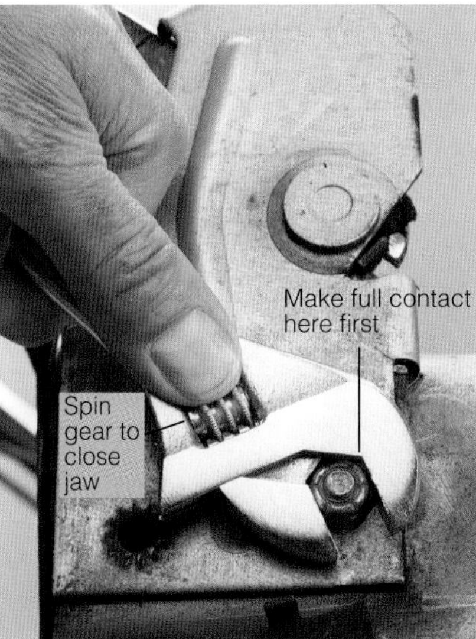

To ensure a tight fit with an adjustable wrench, place it firmly against the nut before threading the jaw closed. For best results, turn the wrench handle toward the lower jaw, never away from it.

Pipe wrench
A pipe wrench has a coarse thumb-wheel adjustment and jaws lined with angled teeth. The jaws grip when rotated in one direction and release in the other.

Monkey wrench
Designed to handle flat-sided fasteners, such as square-head bolts and pipe plugs, the monkey wrench is one of the oldest styles of adjustable wrench.

Adjustable wrench
A mechanic's-style wrench has slightly angled jaws oriented toward the tool's end. The adjustment mechanism is fairly fine.

Multi-wrench
The pivoting ends on this wrench self-adjust to fit nuts and bolts of different sizes and can adapt to irregular shapes, if necessary.

Pliers

Gripping Pliers

Where fingers can't fit or offer a sufficiently tight grip, these tools are indispensable. Most have wire cutters built into the jaws.

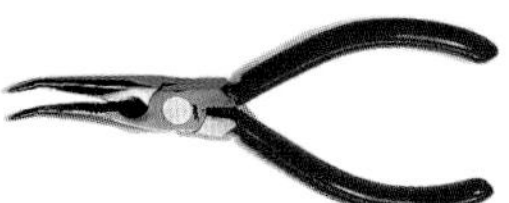

Bent-nose pliers. Almost as precise as tweezers but much stronger, these pliers reach into tight or awkward spaces.

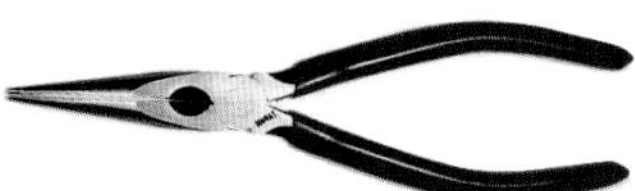

Long-nose pliers. With a long reach, these pliers are great for narrow spaces and for electrical work. They can form tight wire loops to connect terminals.

Lineman's pliers. Designed for heavy-duty electrical work, these pliers can cut through thick cable. They have flat, serrated jaws for a strong grip.

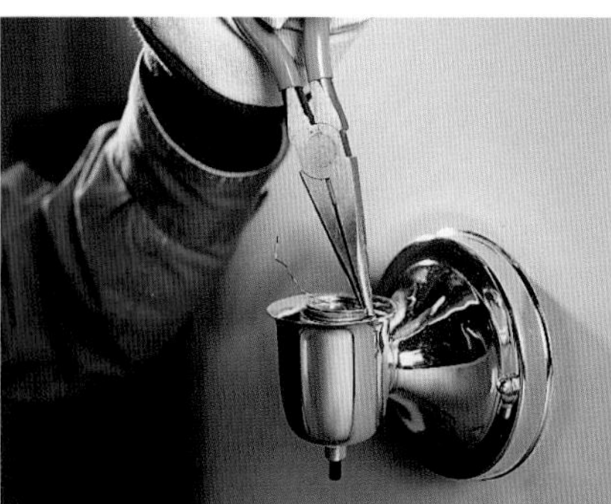

Freeing the base of a broken light bulb is an easy task for the narrow tip of a long-nose pliers. (First, confirm that the power is off!)

Adjustable Pliers

Because one size really can't fit all, these pliers feature movable pivots that allow them to expand or reduce the jaw opening range as required.

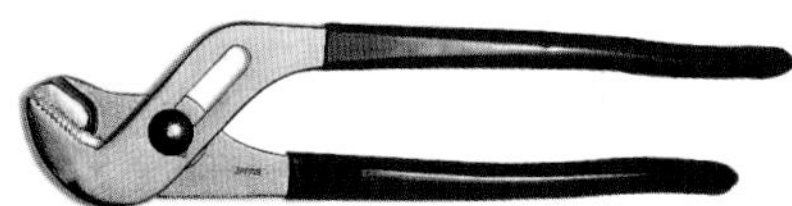

Groove-joint pliers. These tools feature multiple curved grooves on the inside face of one part and a matching tongue machined on the other. By repositioning the pivot post along the slot, you can adjust the jaws' working range to create the size you need.

Slip-joint pliers. Similar in concept to groove-joint pliers, slip-joint pliers offer just two pivot positions and a narrower range of jaw sizes. The jaws feature flat and curved portions, both serrated, for gripping a variety of objects.

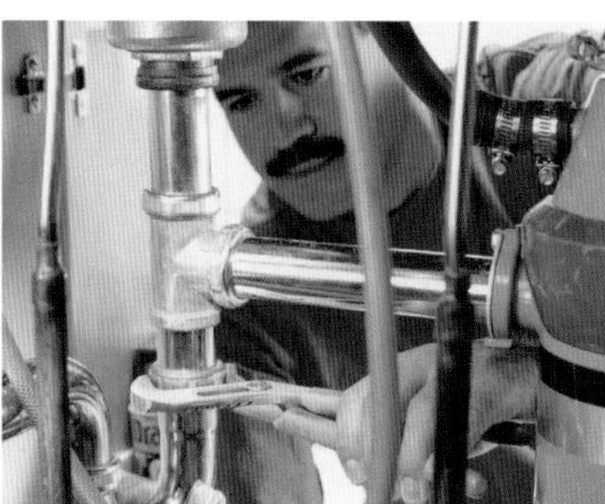

Plumbing repairs, especially involving the large pipe sizes used in drains, are an ideal application for groove-joint pliers.

Cutting Pliers

Like their name implies, these tools are designed to cut—specifically wire, small nails and other small metal parts.

Diagonal-cutting pliers. With a spear-shape nose and an offset side-cutting jaw, these pliers can get into tight spaces to snip wires or nails.

End-cutting pliers. With sharp chisel-edge jaws and a rounded head, end-cutting pliers can snip nails virtually flush with a surface.

Salvaging wood molding requires pulling finish nails through the wood, a task made easy by the tenacious grip of an end-cutting pliers.

Locking Pliers

When hand strength isn't enough to keep standard pliers gripping an item, locking pliers provide crushing jaw pressure that won't let up.

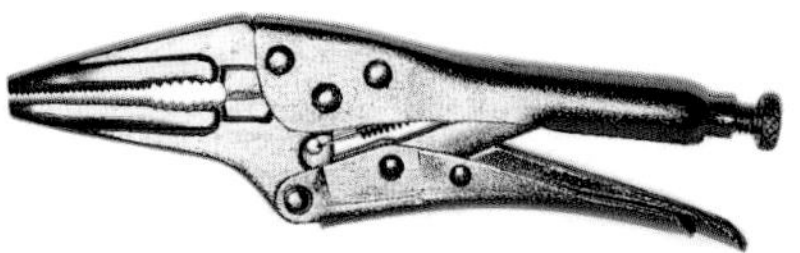

Long-nose pliers. Like other long-nose pliers, these locking models are designed for hard-to-reach places. Turning the knurled end knob adjusts the clamping pressure at the jaws' tips.

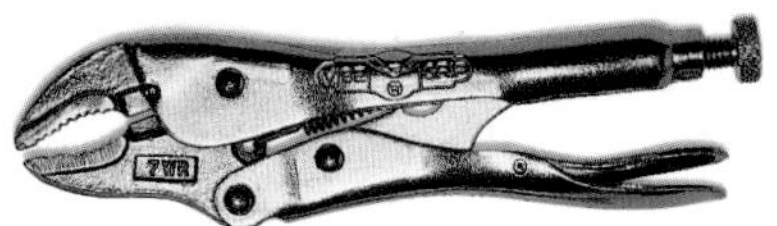

Curved-jaw pliers. To get a secure grip on pipes and other round or irregularly shaped items, use a locking curved-jaw pliers. Pressure is released by the small lever inside the handle.

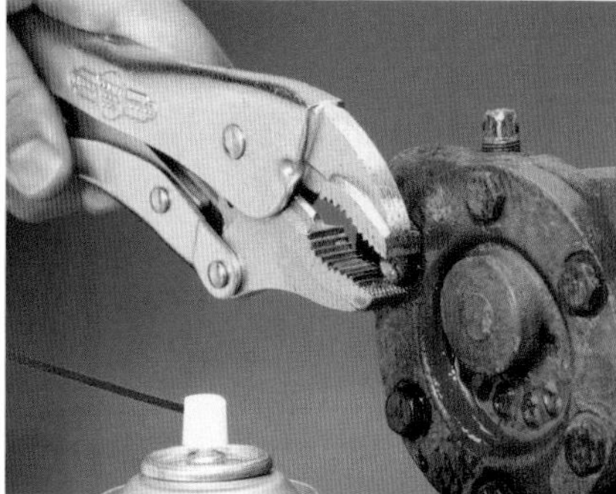

Rusted bolts or nuts may be too corroded to turn with an ordinary wrench. Locking pliers have serrated jaws that dig in better.

Vises

Metal-Jaw Vise

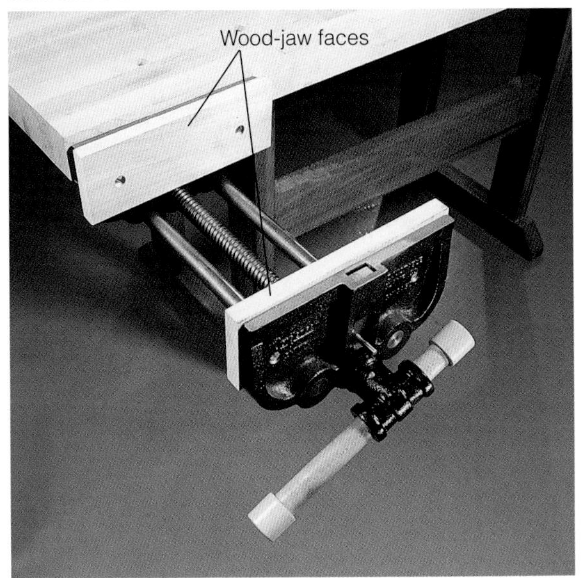

For quick, efficient clamping of workpieces, most woodworkers give top honors to metal-jaw vises. A metal-jaw vise offers a complete package, with cast-iron jaws and a base fitted to guide rails and the center screw. The only thing you'll want to add is a pair of wood-jaw faces. The metal jaws are often taller than the workbench thickness; for a flush mount, simply secure a wood block on the underside of the benchtop and then install the vise. The simplest way to mount the vise is butted against the bench's edge, which leaves the fixed jaw slightly proud, as shown in the example. Some users prefer the jaw face flush with the benchtop edge, so they notch the bench to create an inset fit.

For light-duty use, jaw width can be in the 6- to 7-in. (15- to 20-cm) range, although serious woodworkers usually opt for a larger vise. User-friendly features include a quick-release screw for fast adjustment, "toe-in" jaw alignment for a better grip and a vise dog, which is a retractable stop that's used for clamping a workpiece at its edge or end.

Wood-Jaw Vise

A more traditional style for a cabinetmaker's bench, the wood-jaw vise typically comes with only mounting hardware, guide rods and a vise screw. Some versions use the bench edge as a fixed jaw and require a thick wood block for the movable jaw. Others require that you make two wood jaws. A few versions have quick-release screws, but most do not, and you often have to make your own handle out of steel pipe or a wood dowel.

On the plus side, a wood-jaw vise is less likely to nick plane irons and chisels if they stray from the workpiece. Their feel isn't quite as crisp as that of metal-jaw vises, however, and you don't get the toe-in feature that makes metal-jaw vises grip so well. Still, most provide plenty of clamping power.

The hardware for wood vises varies according to where it will be mounted. The proportions and mounting details for a shoulder vise mounted to the front edge of a bench differ from those for mounting a tail vise on the end of the bench.

Machinist Vise

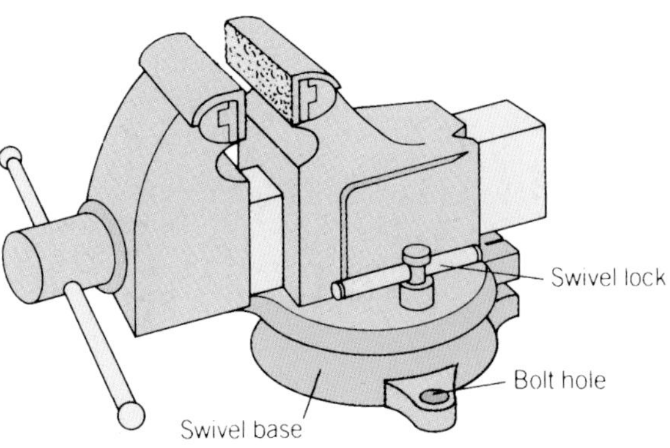

For general shop work that involves metalworking or small parts, a machinist vise is a great accessory to your workbench. This type surface-mounts to the bench and features much smaller jaws, which are serrated to grip hard or smooth metals. Most also feature a notched area below the jaws, ideal for gripping pipe. A swivel base lets you rotate the work for easier access.

Handy Hints

Make it Portable

If your machinist vise sees only occasional use and you don't want it occupying permanent space on your workbench, simply bolt it to a thick plywood base and use clamps to secure it to the bench when in use.

Clamps

Edge Gluing 442
Regluing Chairs 462

For tools that have just one basic purpose—to create and hold pressure in a concentrated spot—clamps come in a remarkably wide range of sizes and shapes. Even limiting the category to home-workshop uses doesn't pare it down much. It's true that all clamps perform basically the same function, but their size, the amount of pressure they generate, their speed and range of adjustment and the particular ways they hold items together can vary greatly. Furniture and other woodworking projects often require clamps—lots of them—but even simple tasks, like sharpening a lawn mower blade or repairing a damaged door, require more holding power than hands can provide.

Sometimes, clamps coax stubborn parts into position or just keep an assembly together while fasteners can be driven or adhesive cures. Whether the task is a moment's holding power or an overnight glue up, clamps provide the muscle.

C-clamps

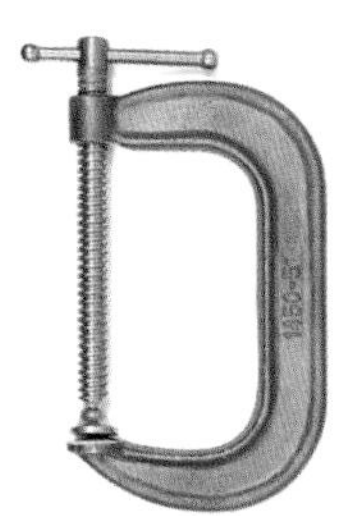

Named for their body or frame shape, C-clamps are among the oldest and simplest clamp designs. Relatively compact, they can fit into tight spaces. Sizes from 1- to 8-in. (2.5- to 20-cm) length are common for general shop use. Typically, the threaded spindle features a small sliding handle on the outboard end and a ball-and-socket shoe that swivels and pivots to accommodate slightly irregular angles. These are not fast-adjusting clamps and their overall capacity depends on throat depth and spindle length, so sizes tend to be modest.

Pipe and Bar Clamp

For longer reaches, pipe or bar clamps work best. Pipe clamps feature interchangeable fittings that thread onto standard plumbing pipe. Bar clamps have permanent bars of rectangular steel or aluminum. One jaw operates via a threaded spindle at the clamp head, the other slides along the pipe or bar.

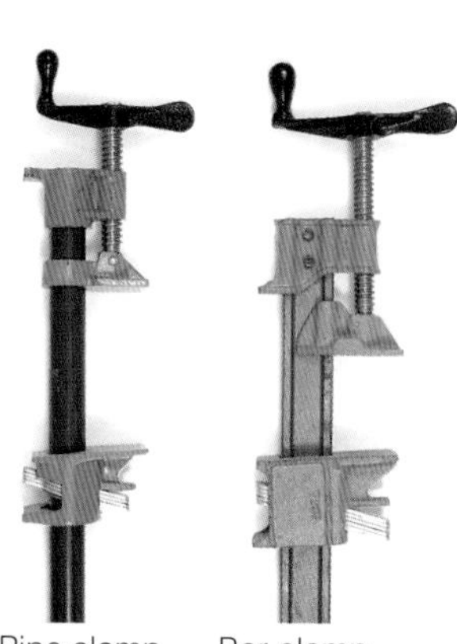

Pipe clamp Bar clamp

Hand Screws

Used mostly for making furniture, hand screws are a traditional joiner's clamp. The large hardwood jaws help prevent dents in the workpiece. "Floating" spindles let you adjust the clamping angle and the jaw offset if the shape of the assembly requires it. Opening capacities are fairly limited, with spindle lengths from a few inches (centimeters) to about 1 ft. (30 cm) for larger sizes.

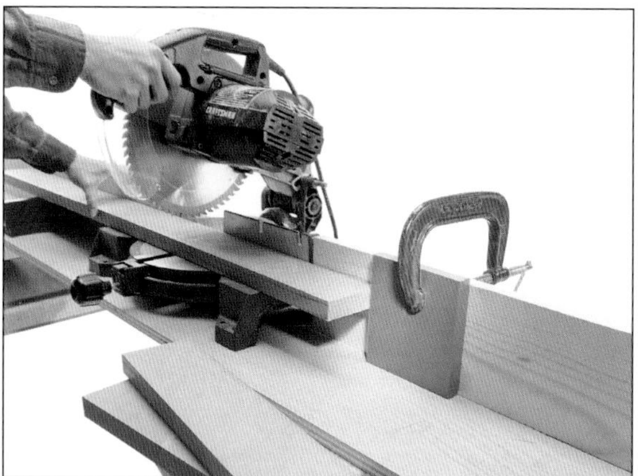

C-clamps, with their compact size and strong holding power, excel at improvised shop setups, like this simple miter-saw cutoff stop. The jaws typically dent the surface, so for finished pieces, use scrap blocks to absorb the pressure.

Gluing up wide wood panels is a typical job for pipe clamps. Alternate the clamps along both sides to equalize clamping pressure, and use spacer blocks to keep panel flat.

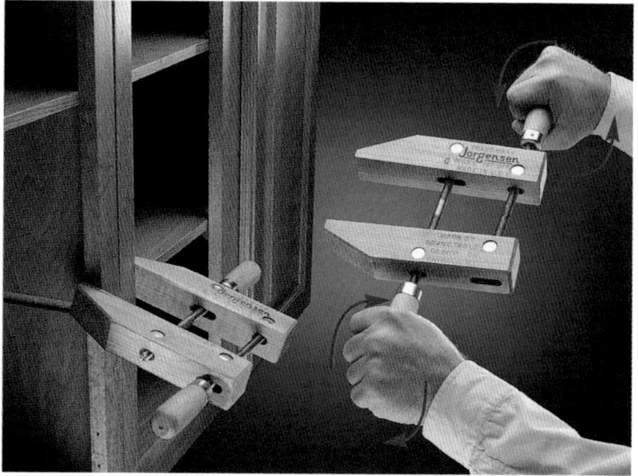

Hand screws are kinder to wood surfaces than metal clamps. To close or open the clamp quickly, grasp both handles as shown and rotate the jaws end for end, like peddling a bicycle.

Squeeze Clamps

Traditional clamps have always required one hand to hold the clamp and one to tighten it, leaving no hands to steady or align the items you're clamping. Some newer designs feature trigger grips that let you hold and tighten the clamp single-handedly, freeing your other set of digits.

On-site carpentry presents no end of opportunities for squeeze clamps. Here, a straightedge is secured in place to guide a saw cut.

Lighter loads, like this copper pipe being soldered in place, can be supported by the clamp bar if the jaws have a firm hold on a solid base—in this case, a pair of floor joists.

Spring Clamps

Spring clamps are compact, fast and easy on wood surfaces. They are the original one-handed clamp. They're inexpensive and convenient but tend to creep when you first set them.

Specialty Clamps

Sometimes an item's shape, size or placement relative to another part defies the limits of a standard clamp. For those situations, an entire class of specialty clamps exists. Some are too exotic or expensive for the typical home workshop, but several types prove useful on a regular basis.

Band clamp. No chair restorer worthy of the title could live without band clamps. Consisting of a sturdy web strap as long as 25 ft. (7.6 m) and a ratcheting or tightening mechanism, band clamps are ideal for cinching around large or irregularly shaped objects.

Edging clamp. Fitting decorative trim or molding to the edge of a plywood or wood composite panel is a common technique in cabinetmaking. If you don't want to use finish nails or screws to hold the trim, these three-way edging clamps apply pressure directly where you need it.

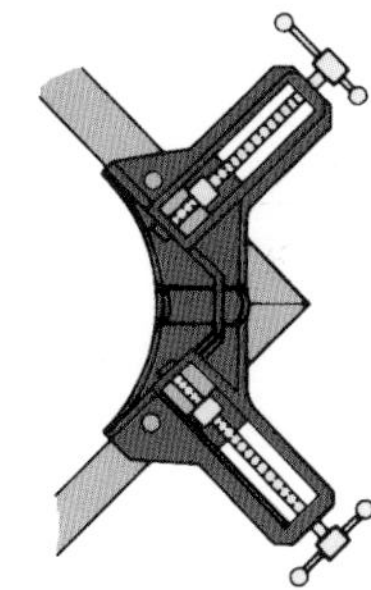

Miter or corner clamps. Precise 90° alignment of corners is much easier to achieve with a miter, or corner, clamp. Sometimes called a framer's clamp because of its usefulness in assembling art frames, this type also helps ensure square drawer and box assemblies.

In a Squeeze

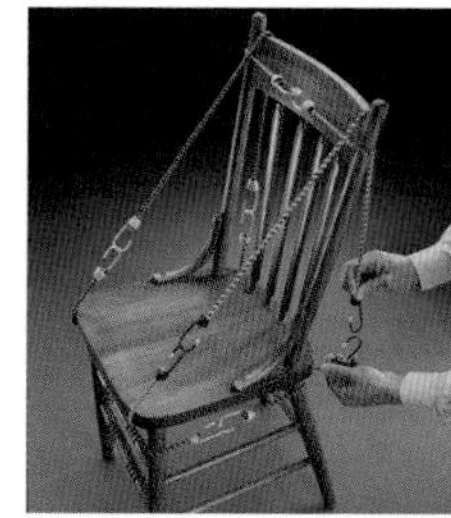

Bungee cords. For light to moderate pressure on large or irregular-shape assemblies, try stretching bungee cords to hold everything together. Check the parts' alignment as you work.

Quick vise. Don't have a bench vise handy? A pair of handscrew clamps can substitute. Secure the workpiece in one hand screw, and then use the other to secure everything to a stable work surface.

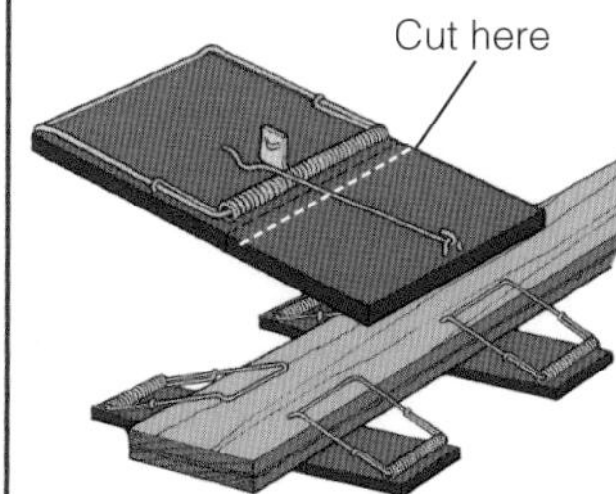

Mousetrap clamp. Small assemblies can be clamped with light pressure, the perfect application for a spring-type mousetrap.

Clamp storage. Small clamps tend to be indistinguishable and hard to find when they're heaped together on a shelf. To avoid the pileup, mount an ordinary towel bar to the wall and hang the clamps there.

Wood Chisels

Sharpening 46
Hanging a Door 383

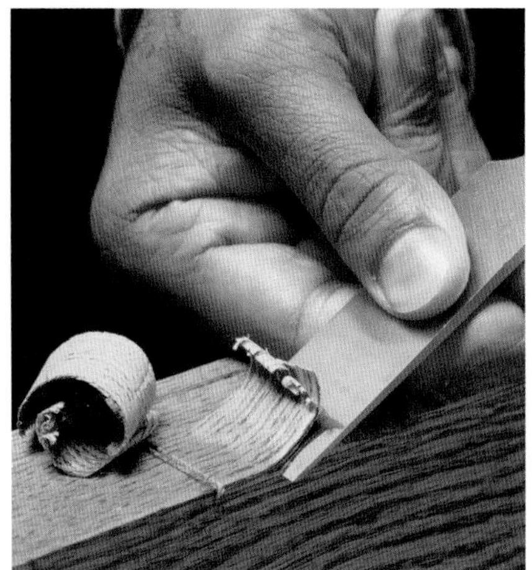

Made of hardened tool steel and shaped with a cutting bevel at the tip, a sharp chisel will sever wood fibers cleanly to cut shallow notches or deep mortises into a wood surface. For general use, start with a small set of three sizes, such as 1/2, 3/4 and 1 in. (12, 19 and 25 mm). Choose some with plastic handles that have a steel striking cap at the end. Keep them sharp by periodically honing them on an oilstone or waterstone; regrind the bevel only when necessary, and with care.

Keep Control

Like any cutting tool, chisels should be handled with respect. Work with the blade traveling away from your body and let the edge take small bites. If brute force is required, whether from the palm of your hand or a mallet, you're cutting too deeply or working with a dull edge. The likely result is an abrupt breakaway from the workpiece—and a serious wound.

The Basics

Even a sharp chisel will sometimes wander with the wood grain rather than cut a straight line. For accurate mortises and other cuts, always outline the cutting area by scoring the wood with a knife or the chisel itself. As a general rule, cut first across the grain, then follow with a cut along the grain. Repeat this sequence as you cut deeper; this reduces splitting.

Grain direction. To prevent the edge from burrowing too deep, make paring cuts with the direction of the grain, not against it.

Chopping cut. Make small chopping cuts to sever the fibers across the grain. Follow with paring cuts to remove the waste chips and then repeat the process.

Demolition chisel. To keep your better chisels in good shape, designate an older chisel for tasks that don't require a perfect edge.

Cutting a Hinge Mortise

Before electric router use became widespread, cutting a hinge mortise by hand was something every carpenter learned to do. The shallow depth of a hinge mortise involves less work than a furniture joint, but it does require precise control. The trick is to take small controlled bites and follow a sequence that helps ensure a uniform mortise depth.

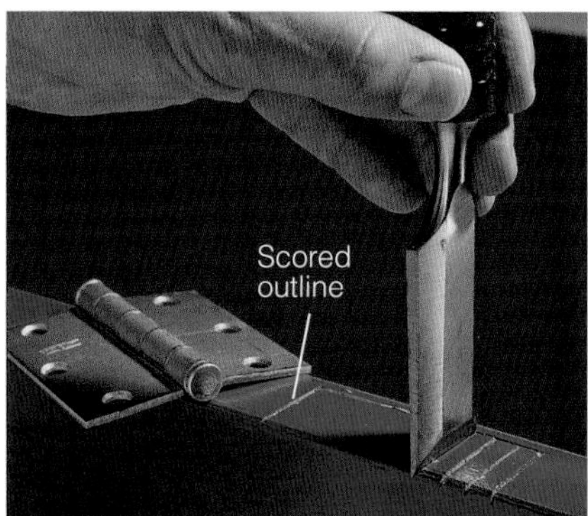

1 After scoring the hinge outline with a chisel or a utility knife, use a 1-in. (25-mm) chisel to make a series of vertical plunge cuts.

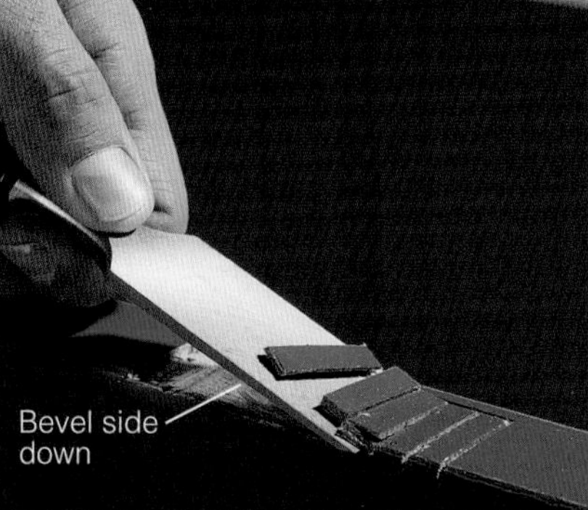

2 With the bevel side down to control the cutting depth, remove the small wood segments created by the plunge cuts.

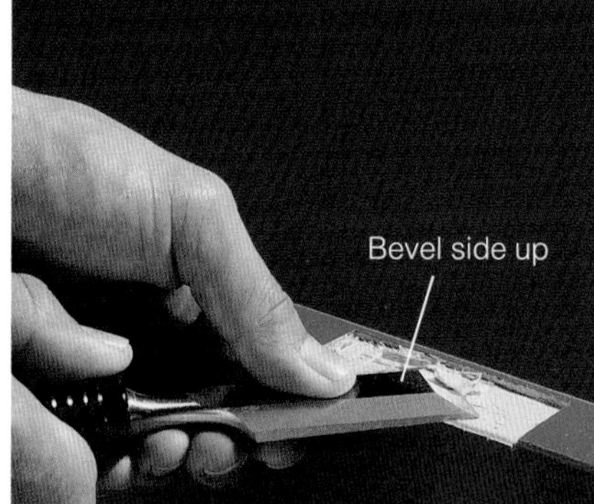

3 Turn the chisel bevel side up and use a circular or angled (skewed) motion to pare the mortise bed smooth and flat.

Demolition Tools

Demolition is the "paying your dues" phase of any major remodeling project. Before you get to the fun parts—installing new windows or cabinetry, picking out paint colors and flooring—you have to tear out old materials and clean up the mess. The process isn't typically as painstaking or precise as building or installing new elements, but it does require planning and careful work. Haphazard demolition can undermine the structural integrity of a house, particularly if you don't identify critical load-bearing supports correctly. Just as important, you have to stay safety-minded so the chaos and debris around you doesn't result in an injury. As with all tasks, having the right tools is essential.

Cat's Paw

When embedded nails in framing can't be cut away, you have to dig them out one at a time. Use a hammer to drive the curved "claws" of a cat's paw under the nail head; then pry out the nail.

Sledgehammer

With head weights ranging from 8 to 20 lbs. (3.5 to 9 kg), full-size sledgehammers can break up concrete slabs and footings. For most interior work, though, try a smaller version; a heavyweight like this is overkill.

Flat Bar

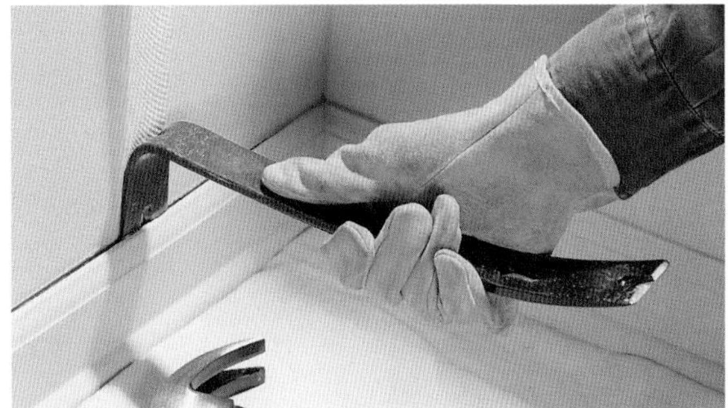

A versatile demolition tool, the flat bar can be used to remove molding, pry apart framing lumber and pull nails.

Cold Chisel

Use a smaller mallet and a cold chisel to create controlled breaks where the brute force of a sledgehammer would be too much.

Containing Dust

If it isn't contained at the source, fine gypsum and plaster dust from demolition work will quickly migrate throughout an entire house. To keep the dust under control, cover floors and seal off ventilation registers and ducts with plastic sheeting. Set an exhaust fan in an open window to pull the dust outside.

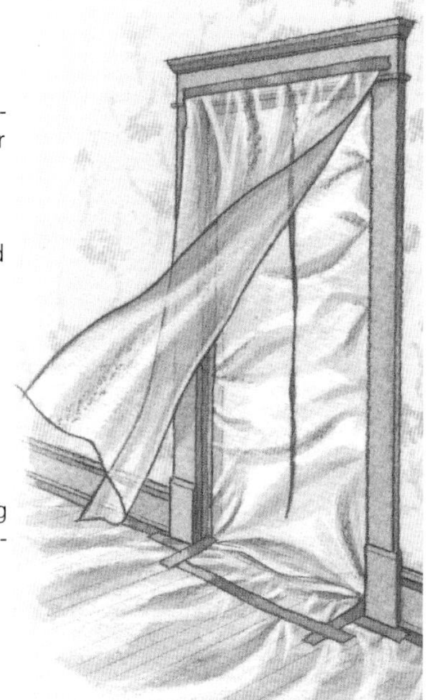

Doorway dust curtain. To keep access doorways from becoming escape routes for airborne dust, use clear plastic sheeting to create a two-layer dust curtain. Tape the first layer around the entire doorway and cut a center slit that stops about 6 in. (15 cm) short of the top and bottom ends. Then tape a second cover sheet along the top of the doorway; it will hang closed but allow passage when necessary.

Don't Wreck Your Health

As crude and simple as demolition techniques are, the work can still be dangerous. Take basic precautions by shutting off potential hazards, such as electrical circuits or water and gas lines, and never cut blindly into a wall without knowing what's inside. Keep the area well lit and ventilated, and always wear eye protection, gloves and a dust mask.

Planes

Sharpening 46

Use a dull, poorly adjusted bench plane and you'll wonder why anyone would bother with such an ineffective tool. Try a well-tuned version with a sharp iron in it, and you'll know why no woodworker would live without one. Before the advent of power machinery, hand planes were used to surface rough-sawn lumber until it was smooth and flat, to straighten crooked board edges, to cut furniture joints and to put decorative edge profiles on moldings.

Today's jointers, thickness planers, routers and other power tools can perform most of these tasks more quickly and with less effort from you, but for the trimming and detail work that's part of almost any woodworking project, a few good hand planes more than earn their keep in your workshop.

Planes are precision tools, but their anatomy is fairly simple. The cutting blade, called the iron, resembles a wide flat chisel blade without the handle. It's held firmly at an angle in the body of the tool, which can be wood or even plastic but typically is made of cast iron. The body's flat underside, called the sole, has a throat opening through which the iron protrudes to make precisely controlled cuts in the wood, typically just a thin shaving. Bench planes come in numbered sizes that vary in length from about 6 in. (15 cm) to more than 2 ft. (61 cm); a block plane and a midsize smooth or jack plane make a versatile pair.

Types

Standard block plane. Designed for one-handed use, a block plane works well for such light tasks as beveling a sharp corner or trimming a cabinet door's edge. The iron is set at a relatively low angle (20° to 25°) with the bevel up.

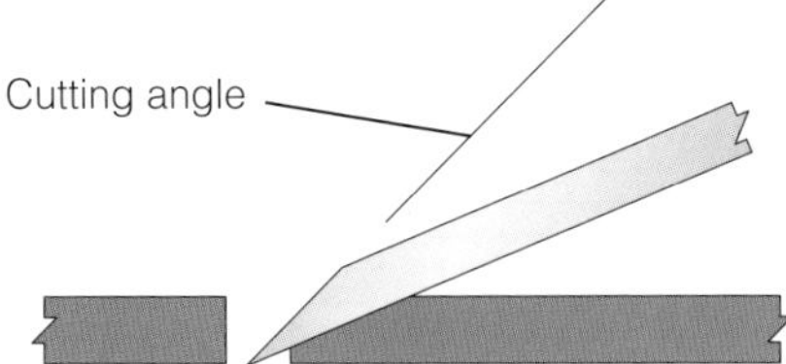

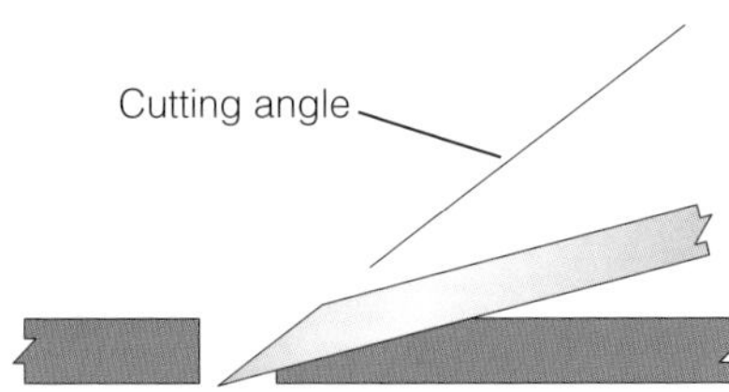

Low-angle block plane. Similar in size and shape to a standard block plane, the low-angle version has the iron bedded at about 12°. This produces a shearing cut that can cleanly trim end grain.

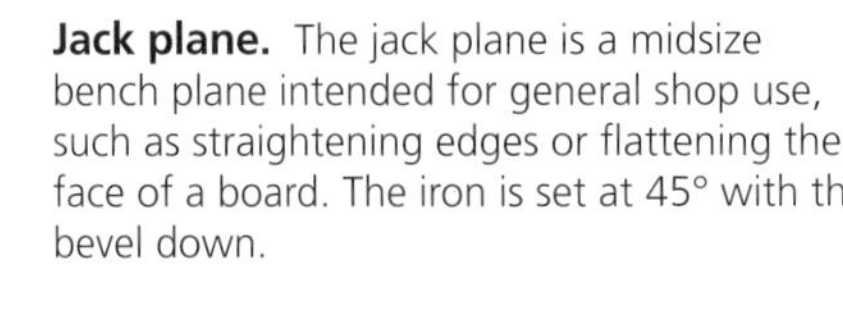

Jack plane. The jack plane is a midsize bench plane intended for general shop use, such as straightening edges or flattening the face of a board. The iron is set at 45° with the bevel down.

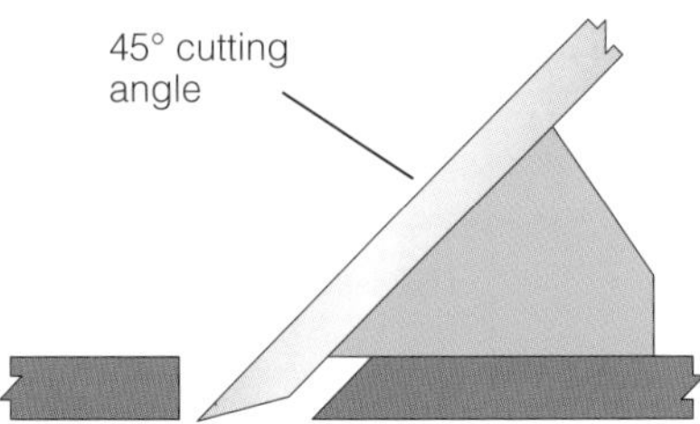

Adjustments

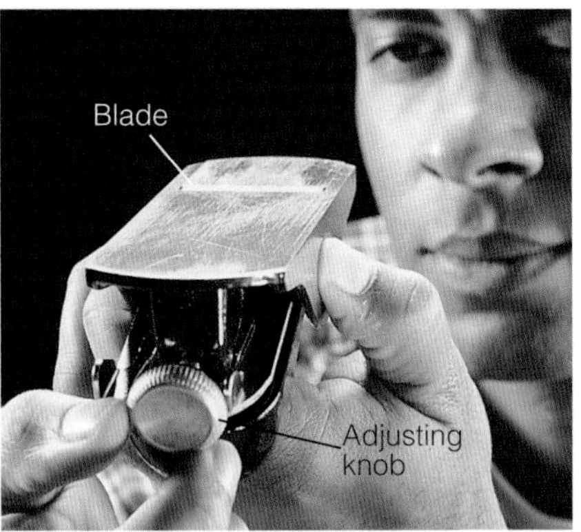

Even with a razor-sharp iron, a plane will perform well only if properly adjusted. This means having the iron set to the right depth of cut and parallel to the opening in the sole. If the sole seems warped or uneven, flatten it by backing off the iron and stroking the plane against wet/dry sandpaper taped to a thick piece of glass. Then turn the plane upside down, sight the sole and turn the adjustment knob until the iron just emerges through the throat.

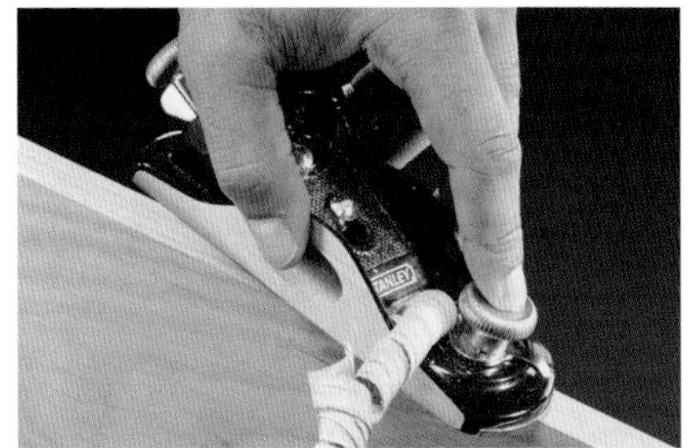

The right cut. Different woods and circumstances call for slight variations, but normally a sharp, well-tuned plane produces a thin, uniform shaving that curls up as it exits the throat.

Using a Block Plane

Grain direction. The cardinal rule for any hand plane, especially for a low-angle style, such as a block plane, is to work with the direction of the grain. With the plane body skewed at a slight angle to produce a shearing cut, the iron will sever the wood fibers cleanly and leave a smooth surface. Pushing against the grain will cause the iron to snag the fibers and break them off, leaving a rough surface condition called tear out.

Back bevel. You can tighten up the fit of a mitered end cut by using a block plane to relieve the cut angle slightly. Plane from the short side toward the long side of the miter to avoid cutting against the grain. Applying slightly more pressure along the back side of the miter will allow the face of the joint to close tighter.

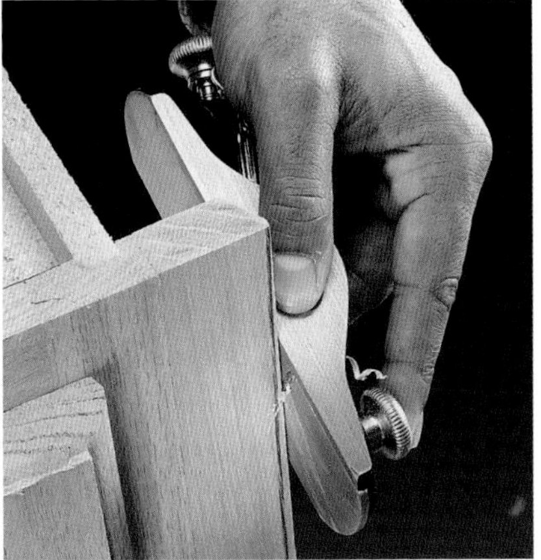

Angle plane. The length of a plane's sole is designed to straighten board edges, but you can work around that trait when necessary. Holding the plane at a sharp angle to the board effectively shortens the body and lets it follow or create curved contours. Here, the plane is skewed to trim the edge of a cabinet face frame that's been scribed to fit an irregular wall.

Ease edges. Jointers and table saws might leave board edges crisp looking and sharp, but a chamfered or rounded edge is much easier to the touch. Create a rounded edge easily with a block plane by making a few passes at a 45° angle to the edge for a chamfer, following up with several passes at 22.5° on either side of that bevel.

Other Planes

Although bench planes rank first in utility for general woodworking, specialty versions apply similar cutting principles in different packages. Some have shorter bodies and irons, some are designed to cut joinery or curved profiles rather than plane a smooth surface and some are all cutting blade and no body. Many were developed for now-obsolete tasks or have been supplanted by power tools, but each still fills its own niche.

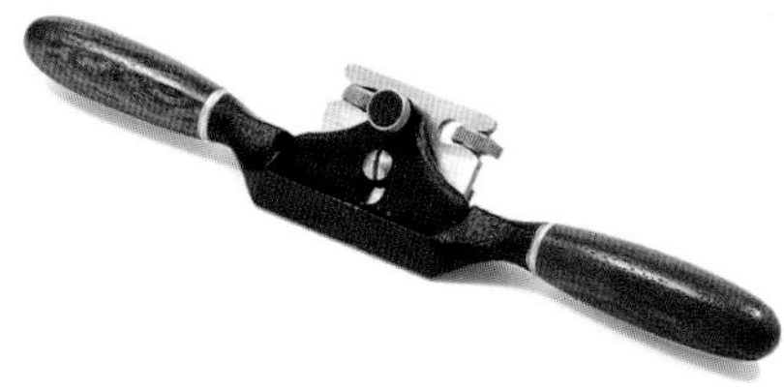

Spokeshave. As the name implies, this twin-handled tool was developed to shape wood spokes for wagon and carriage wheels. The short sole—offered in straight, convex and concave versions—and wing-shape handles allow the user to follow and shape abrupt contours.

Rabbet plane. Several variations exist on this theme—some more versatile than others—but all of them will cut an L-shaped ledge, called a rabbet, on the end or edge of a board. Some will also cut grooves in the face of a board.

Scrapers. Scrapers—used solo or with a body to grip—feature a thin, flat blade that's burnished on the edge to produce a small cutting burr or hook. They can produce a finer surface than most sandpapers can match and are great for smoothing wood with difficult or unruly surface grain.

Files and Rasps

Sharpening 46
Cutting Drywall 212

Files are used primarily to sharpen or remove burrs from metal edges, but they also work on wood and plastics. They are classified by shape, cut (the arrangement of the teeth), length and sometimes coarseness. The most common shapes are flat, square, triangular, round and half-round, with either blunt or tapered ends. A file's teeth are actually ridges cut into the faces and edges. A single-cut file has parallel diagonal ridges; a double-cut file has two sets of diagonal ridges that crisscross each other. Typically, both faces of the file feature the same cut; most files also have teeth cut on both their edges. For general shop use, files from 6 to 12 in. (15 to 30 cm) in length are common. The cut pattern grows proportionately larger with the length, so longer files typically have coarser teeth.

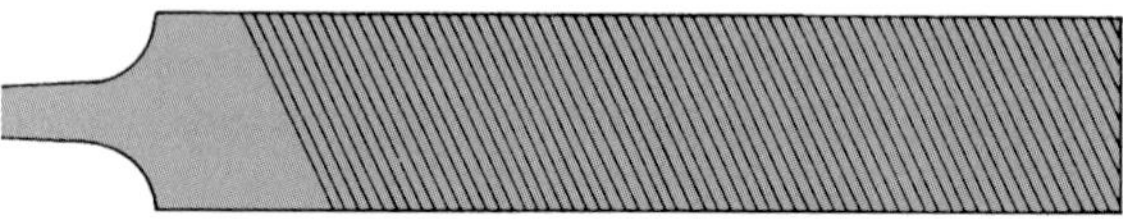

Single-cut file. A single-cut file produces a smooth surface and works well for sharpening steel edge tools.

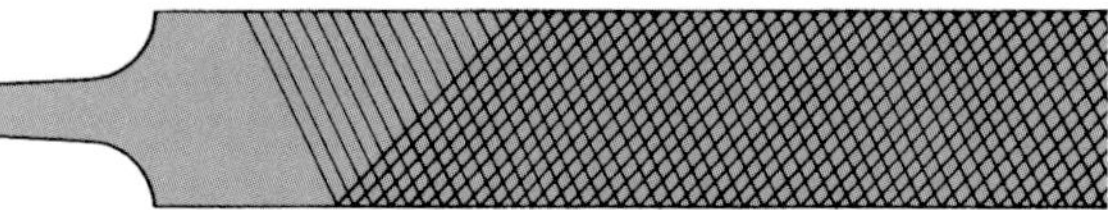

Double-cut file. A double-cut file removes material more quickly and leaves a slightly rougher surface than a single-cut file.

Four-in-hand file. This is a combination tool—half double-cut file and half rasp. Typically, one side is flat and the other convex.

Rasps

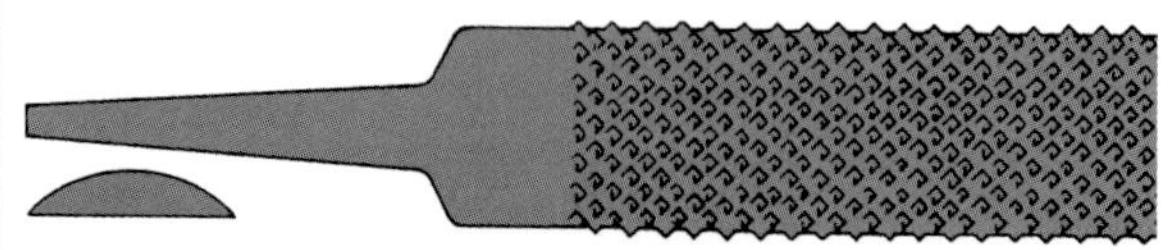

Similar to files in size, shape and purpose, rasps have individually cut teeth that are much coarser than a file's ridges. They cut aggressively, remove material quickly and are used to shape wood, rigid foam, plastic and some nonferrous metals. Like files, they cut on the push stroke and feature two working faces. But on a rasp, one face typically is flat and the other a half-round profile. Because of the coarse surface they produce, rasps are used for rough shaping; for a smoother finish, switch to files, sandpaper or fine carving rasps called rifflers.

Sharpening. Files are indispensable for sharpening garden shears, mower blades, axes and other large edge tools. Use a double-cut file to dress the edge quickly, but finish with a single-cut file for sharpness.

Shaping. The four-in-one is a great tool for general shop use since it is able to do coarse shaping of wood quickly and then follow up with a smoothing cut from the file end.

Cleaning. To clean a file, rap it on a hardwood block to dislodge loose debris. Follow up if necessary with a short-bristle wire brush called a file card.

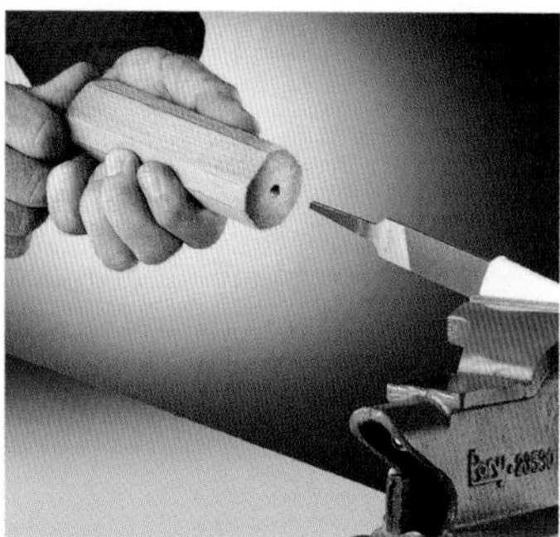

Handles. Files have sharp tangs that can easily puncture a palm. Make a simple handle by shaping a scrap wood block and drilling a hole in the end. Heat the tang; then press the handle on firmly.

Rasp Planes

Shorthand for "surface-forming tool," Stanley Tools' Surform, or rasp plane, is a type of rasp that features rows of sharp open teeth punched into a thin steel "blade." Unlike a conventional rasp, a Surform requires a body to support the cutting blade; small versions resemble block planes, but larger versions may have handles. Not only do the open teeth cut quickly, but they resist clogging; each "bite" of new material forces the previous one through the tooth gullet. This self-cleaning feature is especially welcome on wallboard, dense foams and other soft materials that tend to clog rasps.

Measuring Tapes

There's hardly a home improvement or repair project that doesn't require you to measure something. Years ago that meant brandishing a yardstick, a story pole or a folding carpenter's rule—all useful tools but hardly convenient. Today, retractable measuring tapes put far more capacity into a pocket-size package. Choices range from 3-ft. (1-m) key-chain versions to reel-mounted 100-ft. (30-m) tapes. Stay in the neighborhood of 16- to 25-ft. (5- to 7.5-m) tapes to get the most versatility in a compact package. For features, look for a positive blade lock, a belt clip and an ergonomic case.

Basics

Inside-outside. The loose fit of the hook at the blade end is designed to compensate for the tip thickness, whether you're taking an inside measurement, with the tip butted or pushed, or an outside measurement, with the tip hooked or pulled.

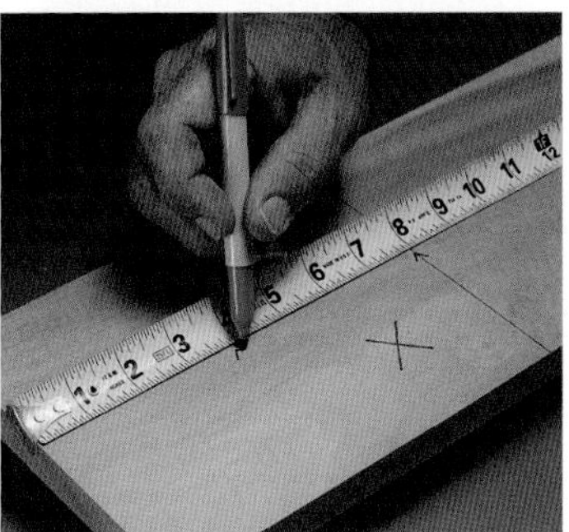

Marking. Mark accurately by tilting one edge of the blade flat against the workpiece. Indicate the exact measurement by marking it with the point of a V. An X designates the waste side of a line or sometimes where another piece will intersect.

Burn an inch (or a centimeter). If there's no reliable spot to hook the blade tip, shift the blade slightly to align the 1-in. (1-cm) mark with the starting point. Then compensate for the 1-in. (1-cm) offset when you mark.

Special Situations

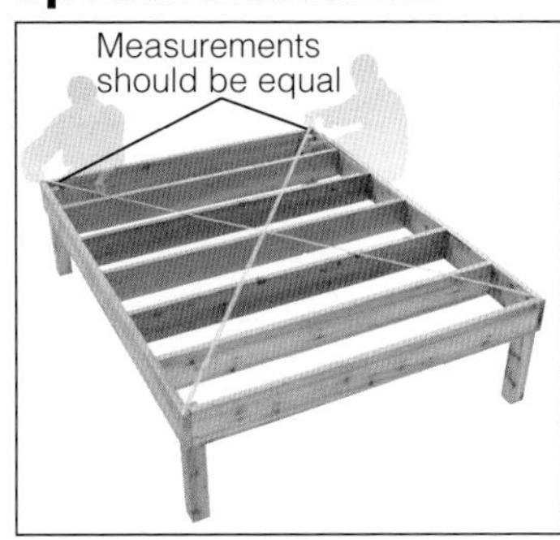

Diagonals. To see whether a square or rectangle is square, in other words, has four 90° corners, measure both diagonals. Adjust the corners until the measurements are equal.

Squaring. To check for squareness in a single corner, measure and mark 3 ft. (90 cm) on one side and 4 ft. (120 cm) on the other side. The distance between the marks will be 5 ft. (150 cm) if the corner is square.

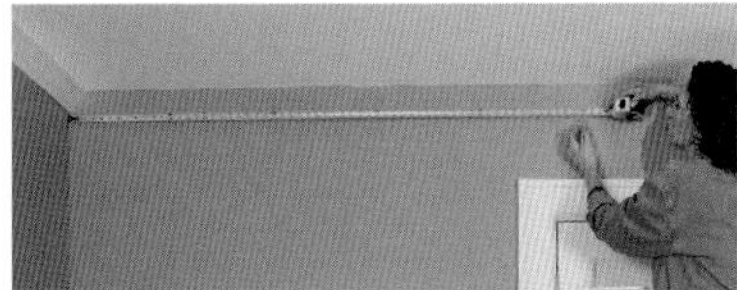

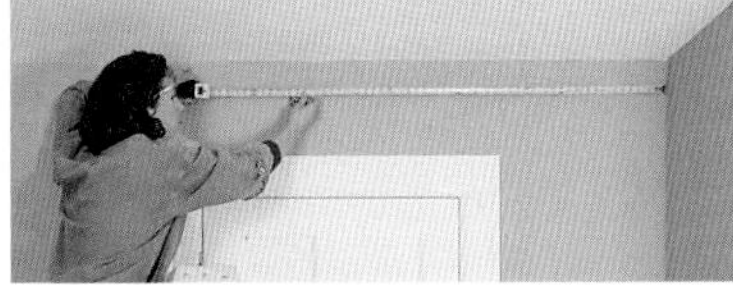

Long walls. Taking accurate inside measurements on a wall is difficult when you're working solo. Butt the tape into the corners and take two readings, noting where they intersect. Then add the total.

Measuring Tricks

Dollar bill. Some common items, like a dollar bill, have consistent dimensions (in this case, 6-1/8 in./about 15.5 cm) you can use when a measuring tape isn't available. Note the number of full lengths. Then fold the bill to mark the last partial segment.

Masking tape reminder. Rather than struggle to remember multiple measurements, use masking tape as an impromptu note pad for jotting the numbers down.

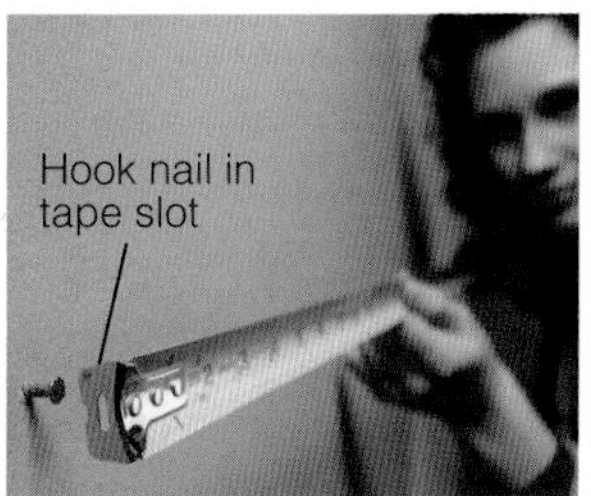

Use a nail. When you need a field reference point to measure from and don't have anyone to hold the tape, drive a nail partway into the surface and hook the tape's slotted tip over the nail head.

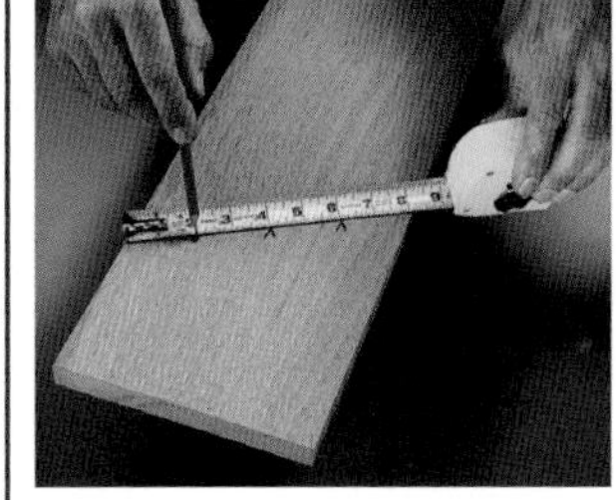

Dividing. Need to divide a distance into equal segments? Angle the blade until it reads a false distance that's easily divisible by the number of segments you need; then mark the increments.

Marking and Scribing

Jigsaws 54
Belt Sanders 68
Creating Curves 443

Chalk Boxes

Familiar to any carpenter, a chalk box (sometimes called a chalk line) shares the simplicity common to most good tools. Inside the pear-shape case is a chamber that holds powdered chalk and a reel of string. As the string is pulled from the case, chalk clings to it until the line is stretched taut, then snapped on a surface, leaving a straight line.

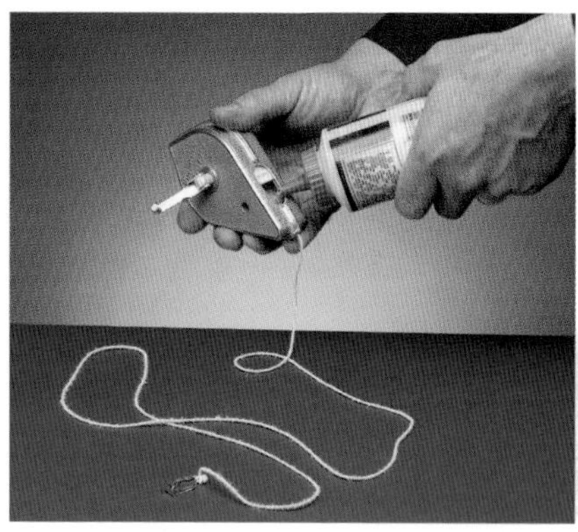

Load the box. A sliding cover or screw-on cap provides access for filling the box with chalk. Leave a few feet of string out, so when you reel it in, the chalk powder will be distributed throughout the box.

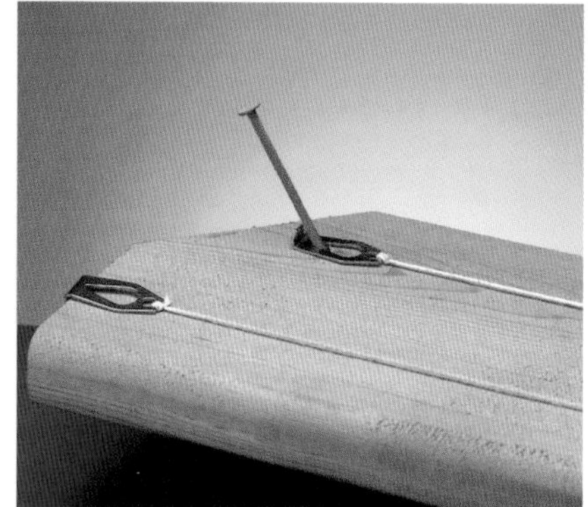

Secure the end. The metal end tab can be hooked on an edge or secured with a nail or screw. Note the different colored chalks: White, blue and red are most common, and high-visibility fluorescents help in low-light situations.

Long distance. Marking consistency can waver on long runs. To avoid problems, stretch the line tight, press down at the center point and snap the two segments separately.

Straight cut. Deck builders save time and get clean results by letting decking boards run long during installation. Then they snap a chalk line and cut off the ends in one pass.

Scribing

Anyone who has remodeled a house knows square corners, plumb walls and flat surfaces are abstract notions that rarely exist in real life. Scribing is a technique for transferring the irregular contours of a surface onto a straight workpiece so it can be trimmed to fit exactly. Cabinet installation is a common application, but the technique can work anytime you need to create a custom fit.

Fitting cabinets. For small gaps along cabinet edges, position and level the cabinet, then slide a pencil along the wall, so the point transfers any irregularities onto the face frame. If you don't have much material to remove, a belt sander can offer gradual, controlled stock removal right up to the scribe line.

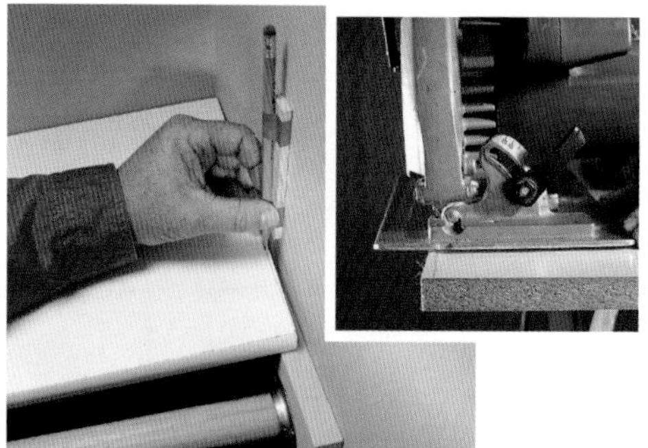

Fitting shelves. Built-up drywall compound or other irregularities can leave most inside corners out of square, requiring custom-cut shelves. With a spacer as thick as the largest gap taped to a pencil, scribe the end of the shelf. Then trim to the line using a circular saw.

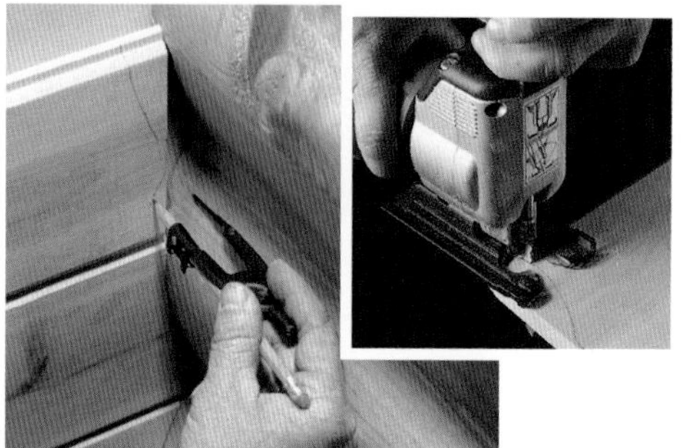

Irregular shapes. The minimum scribing offset always equals the largest gap in the surfaces, so highly irregular shapes, such as these log walls, require a compass or similar tool to transfer the contours. When there's this much material to remove from your workpiece, cut close to the line with a jigsaw, test the fit and use sandpaper to fine-tune the final shape.

Angles and Curves

Framing Square

Also called a rafter square because of the rafter calculation tables embossed in its surface, this tool is useful for layout marking and for checking 90° corners. It consists of a 2- x 24-in. (5- x 61-cm) metal body, or blade, and a shorter, narrower perpendicular tongue. The clamp-on gauges shown are an accessory for marking consistent, accurate stair layouts.

Combination Square

An essential general-purpose layout tool, the combination square can check 45° and 90° angles, function as a depth or marking gauge and, thanks to a bubble vial built into the body, take plumb and level readings. The most common version sports a sliding, locking blade, etched with double scales on each side.

Sliding T-bevel

For situations that involve irregular angles, a sliding T-bevel lets you take the angle reading directly from one surface or corner and mark it on the workpiece. There is no scale on the blade to tell you the angle size, but with the direct transfer, there's no loss of accuracy and less potential for error.

Circles and Curves

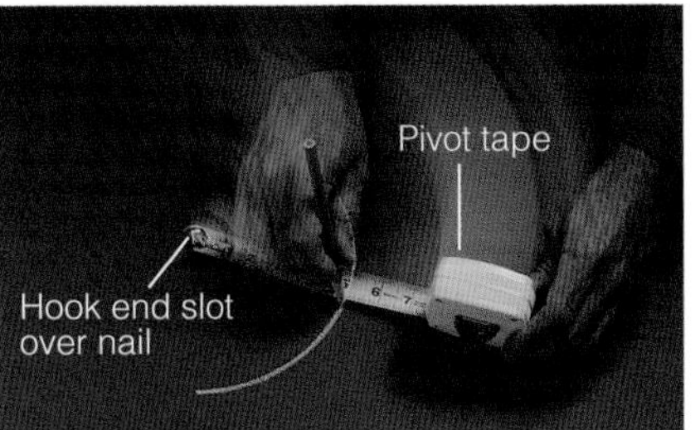

A tape measure becomes an improvised compass (see above) when you hook the tip on a nail and pivot the blade in a circle. To lay out a large sweeping arc (at left), tension a string on a thin slat of wood to create a bow.

Angle Squares

Prized by framing carpenters for their compact size and near indestructibility, angle squares make quick work of layout marking. Offered in pouch-size and larger versions and made of thick plastic or aluminum, they have angle scales etched into both faces for marking rafter end cuts. They're plenty accurate, but not intended for precision work. Some versions, called protractor squares, feature a pivoting fence to lock variable angle settings at other than 90°.

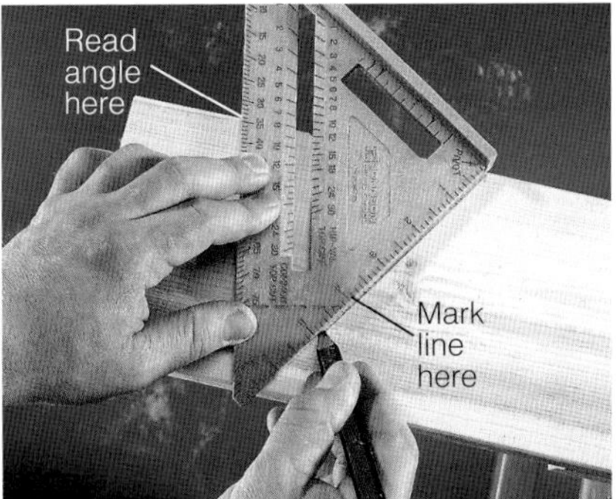

Marking angles. One side of an angle square features a double-lipped edge. By using the square corner as a pivot point, you can read the desired angle on the long edge, then mark the board.

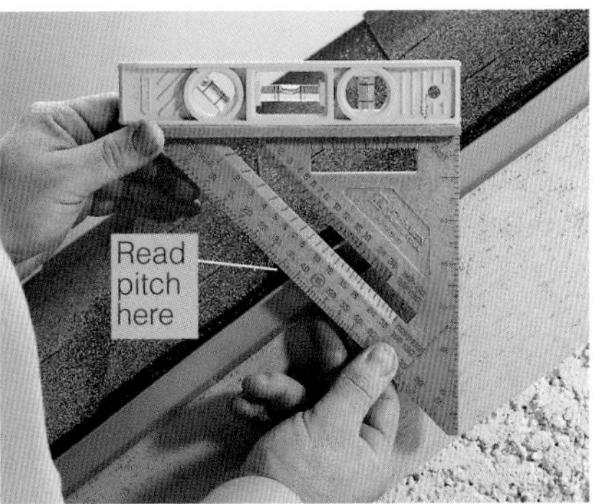

Finding roof slope. With the help of a torpedo level, an angle square can indicate a roof slope. With the pivot point on the roof edge, adjust to get a level reading. Then check the angle scale.

Cutting guide. With the lipped edge of the square pressed tight against the board's edge, you can get accurate, square cuts by guiding the saw base along the body.

Level and Plumb

With the exception of mud huts and a certain Italian cathedral tower, buildings and other large structures rely on accurate engineering and layout to remain standing upright over time. No matter what the final size and shape is, that effort starts with a level foundation. Keeping other major elements level and plumb as you work is just as critical. During a project's excavation and early rough stages, it's tempting to settle for close enough and figure you'll take care of the adjustments when you install the molding. This is a fool's bargain that will make most of the project's later work much more difficult.

It's important to remember that level footings, square corners or plumb walls aren't more technically difficult to build than shoddy work is; they just require a little more patience and a few more adjustments until you get them right. Even on projects that you deliberately want to miss the mark, such as a deck or patio slab that slopes away from the house for drainage, you still need accurate readings. Modern professional tools include high-tech laser transits and levels with digital readouts; but for the projects most homeowners will tackle, the tools are much simpler, more affordable and proven by decades, if not centuries, of use.

Leveling a Level

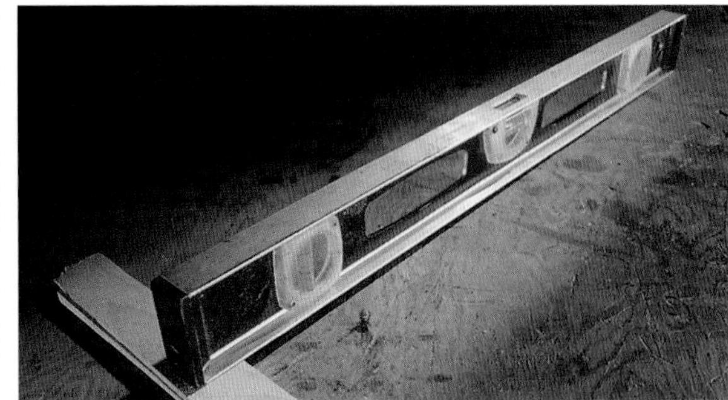

Levels with adjustable vials may need to be periodically recalibrated. Adjust one end until you get a dead-level reading. Rotate the level end for end. If the bubble stays centered, the vial setting is still good.

Long-distance leveling. To extend the reach of a short level, place it on the edge of a straight board. If necessary, be sure to compensate for the board width when marking. Here, that simply means marking at the bottom edge to match the height of the other end.

Line levels. Longer readings over uneven ground can be handled with taut string and a pocket-size line level. This is especially effective for taking coarse readings before or during excavation, but might require adjustments with more precise tools later.

Finding the slope. For an accurate way to determine exact slope, use a long straight board as a base for a level. Shim underneath the level until you get a level vial reading. Here, the shim thickness indicates how much the end of the door threshold will have to be raised.

Torpedo levels. Named for their streamlined shape, torpedo levels are favored by plumbers for getting into tight spaces and checking drain pipes for proper slope. Most have a magnetic strip on one edge so they'll stay put on metal pipes.

Which Level Is Right?

Sometimes a general-purpose tool is versatile enough to handle all your projects. A traditional 24-in. (61-cm) wood carpenter's level would probably qualify, especially if you limit your do-it-yourself efforts to simple projects. If working on a larger scale suits you, a laser level offers the accuracy of a pinpoint beam projected for long distances. A digital-readout level indicates the angle of incline, useful for more complex structures. If you're going to lay brick or block walls and want something simple that can get wet and take a beating, get a cast-aluminum version. Whichever you choose, set aside a few bucks for a torpedo level, too; they're inexpensive and really handy around the house.

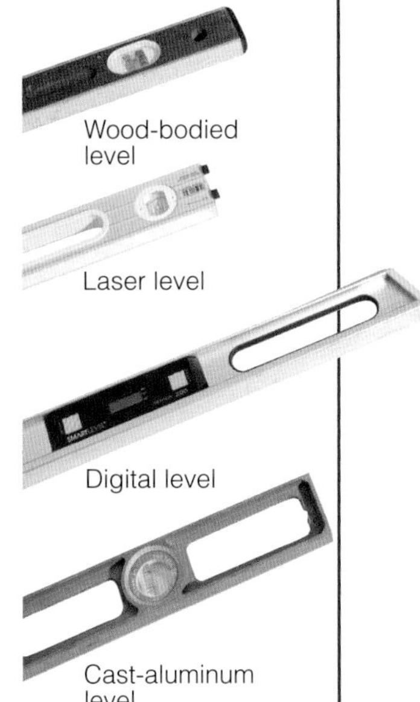

Transits

Transits are used mostly for foundation layout and other large-scale projects. Perched on a tripod, the transit body consists of an adjustable base and a rotating optical scope. A bubble vial lets you know when the scope is level. Then a helper can mark the level reference lines directly onto a surface or use a gauge rod.

Water Levels

Simple, accurate and affordable, water levels consist of a length of clear, flexible tubing (or two short segments that attach to a garden hose). The water inside seeks its own level, reading the same height at both ends.

Plumb

Establishing plumb simply means verifying that an edge or surface has a true vertical orientation, perpendicular to a level line. You can do this with a level, which typically has at least one vial positioned to read plumb, or with a plumb bob, a precisely machined weight suspended by a string.

Checking a door opening. Door jambs have to be plumb and parallel to ensure a door aligns and opens properly. For a more accurate reading, extend the level's range using a long, straight board. Never assume either door jamb is plumb without checking it.

Laser Levels

Laser levels represent the newest technology in leveling tools and, predictably, they cost more than conventional levels. The simplest version resembles a standard level but has an internal laser diode that projects a beam that can be read at distances of 25 to about 100 ft. (8 to 30 m), depending on the model. You'll also find self-leveling tripod-mount versions with multiple beams or a rotating head, some capable of providing accurate readings at distances as far as 200 ft. (60 m). The multiple-beam units feature perpendicular beams that make corner alignments easier and more accurate. Rotating beams spin continuously to cast a level line around a room or an excavation site. Consider renting rather than buying these tools.

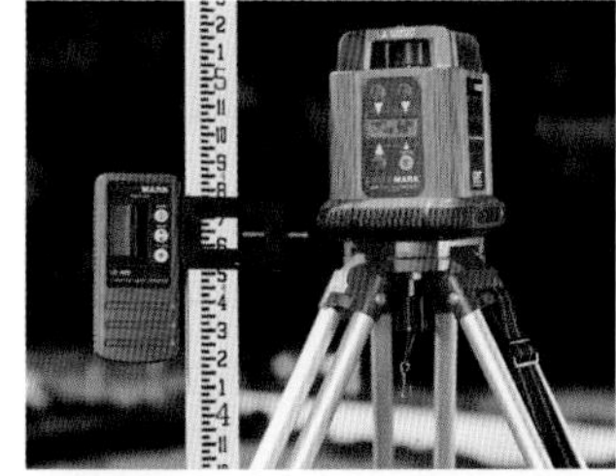

Rotating laser. Rotating lasers perch on a tripod and spin around to cast a beam. Most have an electronic sensor on the elevation rod, useful for bright daylight conditions. The sensor produces an audible signal when the beam hits the sensor.

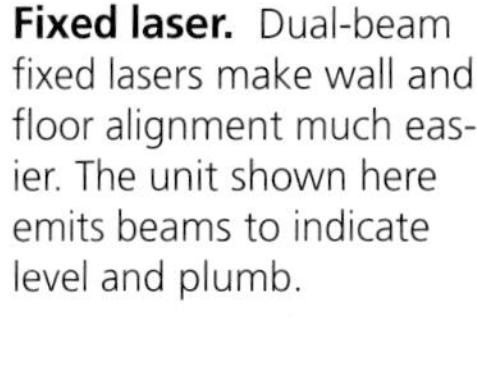

Fixed laser. Dual-beam fixed lasers make wall and floor alignment much easier. The unit shown here emits beams to indicate level and plumb.

Chalk-line plumb bob. Most chalk lines are designed with locking reels so they can double as plumb bobs. Give the chalk line a minute for gravity to stop the pendulum swing before you take your reading.

Sharpening

Planes 38
Drill Bits 52
Bench Grinders 71

Sharpening techniques are often among the last workshop skills people learn, yet among the most used and appreciated once they're mastered. Buyers often assume chisels, knives, plane irons and scissors are sharp when they come out of their packages, but those edges are typically far from precise. Mass-production manufacturing doesn't allow for the sometimes painstaking process of producing a fine cutting edge. Fortunately, honing edge tools involves simple skills and mostly inexpensive accessories. A bench grinder removes material quickly and can ruin a blade's ability to maintain a sharp edge, so limit it to occasional use. A couple of oil- or water-lubricated whetstones, or even fine sandpaper on a piece of glass, can quickly restore a tired or poorly prepared tool edge.

Watch Your Fingers!

Sharpening safety is mostly common sense: Don't use dull chisels and other tools, as they require more force and are more likely to jump erratically out of a cut. Watch your fingers as you sharpen and (although it's tempting) never run your finger lengthwise along a cutting edge to assess its sharpness. Instead, make a test cut.

Chisels

With their many uses, chisels need sharpening regularly. If the edge is maintained periodically by honing, regrinding the bevel should be an infrequent chore. When it is necessary, remove material slowly to avoid ruining the temper.

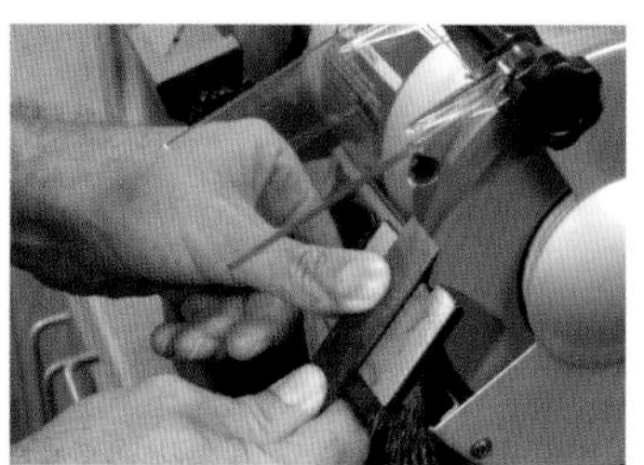

1 Adjust the tool rest of a bench grinder to the required angle (typically 25° to 30°). Slide the chisel side to side as you work. Quench the tool in water periodically.

2 Use a whetstone to flatten the back of the chisel, a technique called "lapping." This is essential for a precise cutting edge.

3 Turn the chisel over and use a circular motion on the stone to hone just the bevel. Keep the surface lubricated to float metal particles away.

Knives and Scissors

Knives and scissors might come from the store in better shape than a chisel or plane iron would, but they'll eventually need resharpening. For a very dull or beat-up edge, start with a coarse whetstone and work to a finer grade.

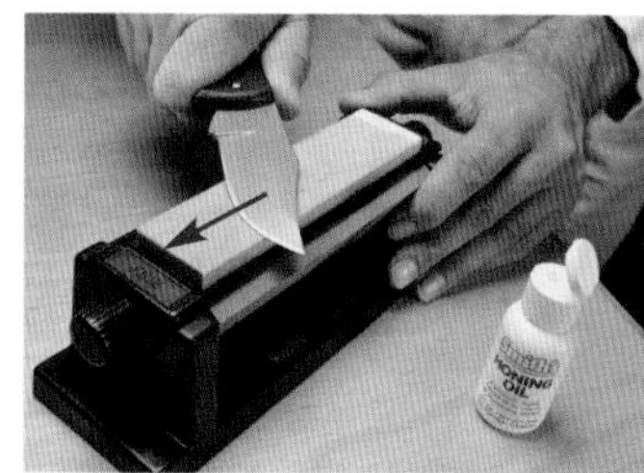

1 Adjust your grip until the knife edge's angle seems aligned to the stone. Then lock your wrist and push forward with a firm stroke.

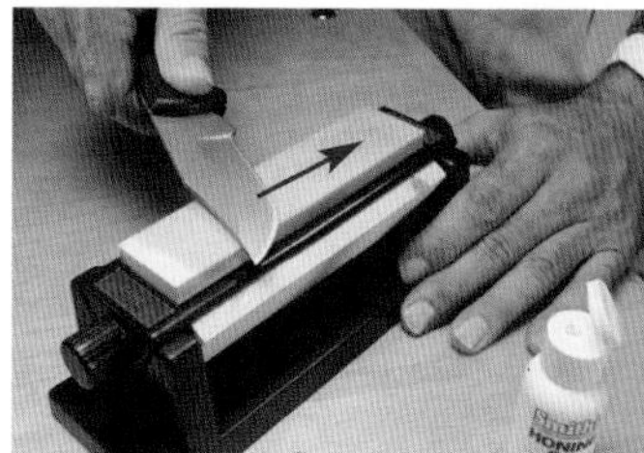

2 For the return stroke, reverse the knife blade and apply light pressure as before. Keep lubricant on the stone throughout.

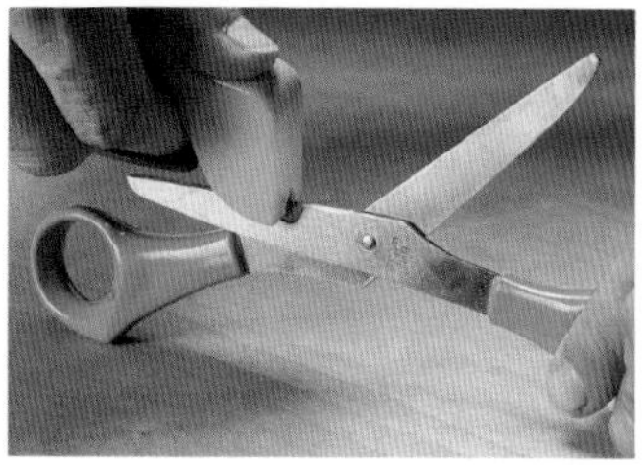

Scissors. Specialized sharpeners for scissors have a V-shape stone that simultaneously hones and straightens the edge. The offset handle keeps knuckles at a safe distance.

Block Plane

The small size and low cutting angle of a block plane demand a sharp blade. End-grain trimming, especially, requires a fine edge. Plan on a two-step process to flatten, or lap, the back of the iron and hone the bevel.

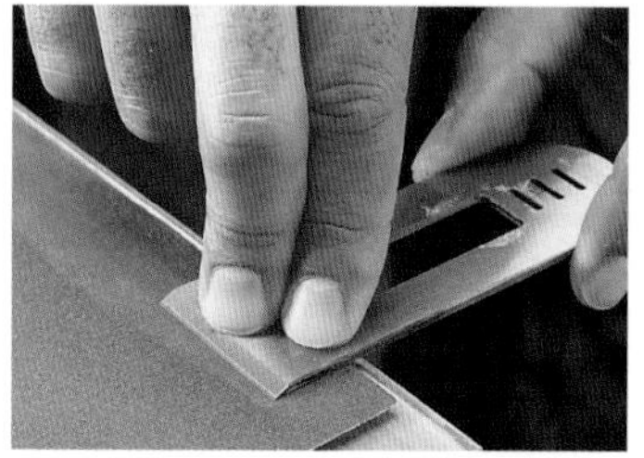

1 Starting with 220-grit silicon-carbide sandpaper applied to a thick piece of plate glass, lap the back face of the plane iron to ensure a flat surface.

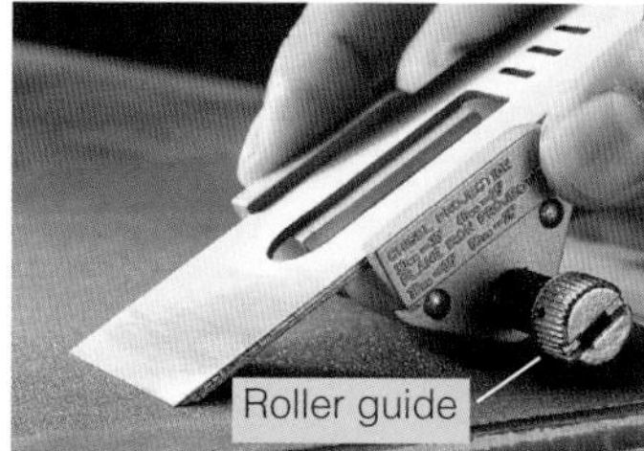

2 Use a roller guide to set the correct bevel angle. Sharpen the bevel on successively finer grits of silicon-carbide sandpaper, working up to 600 grit.

Double bevel. Some users hone a double bevel on a plane iron to strengthen the edge or change the cutting angle.

Lawn Mower Blade

A dull blade makes your mower's engine work harder and tears the grass rather than cutting it cleanly, leaving it ragged looking and susceptible to disease. To keep the blade cutting like new, pop it off the mower shaft and follow this simple regimen:

1 Use a bench grinder to clean up the cutting-edge portion and remove any large nicks. Grind off only what's necessary to get a clean edge.

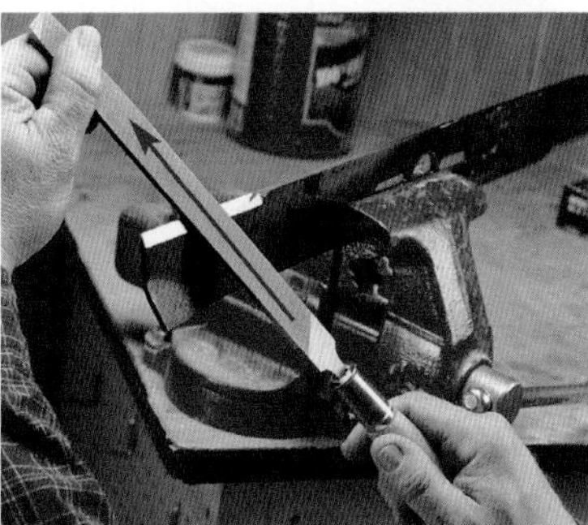

2 File the ground edge with a 10-in. (25-cm) single-cut mill file. Keep the angle consistent and use long, broad strokes away from you.

3 Balance the blade with a special plastic balancer available at hardware stores. Mark the heavy end and grind away material from the very end of the blade.

Garden Tools

Dirt is abrasive and unfriendly to tool edges, so it's not surprising that garden tools take a beating with regular use. Most don't require precision sharpening the way a wood chisel or knife does, so files and coarse whetstones will suffice.

File an axe. Clamp the axe head firmly in a machinist's vise. Use a double-cut file to shape the edge and remove any large nicks. Stroke from the back of the head toward the edge.

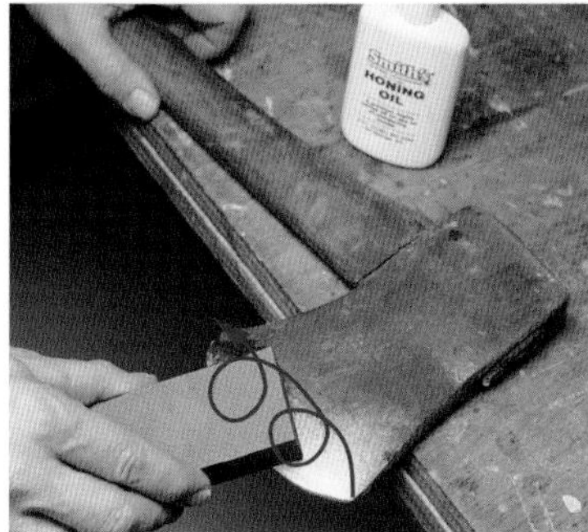

Fine-tune an axe. After the edge has been restored and reshaped, fine-tune the edge with a coarse oilstone to hone it sharp. Use a circular motion and plenty of sharpening oil.

Sharpen a shovel. Even shovels and spades need reasonably sharp edges to cut through clay or packed soil and to sever small roots. File on the top face, stroking toward the tip.

Drill Bits

Whether boring in wood or metal, a dull drill bit will overheat and also cause tear out at the edge of the hole. Some specialty bits have to be sent out for professional sharpening, but simpler cutting profiles can be done at home.

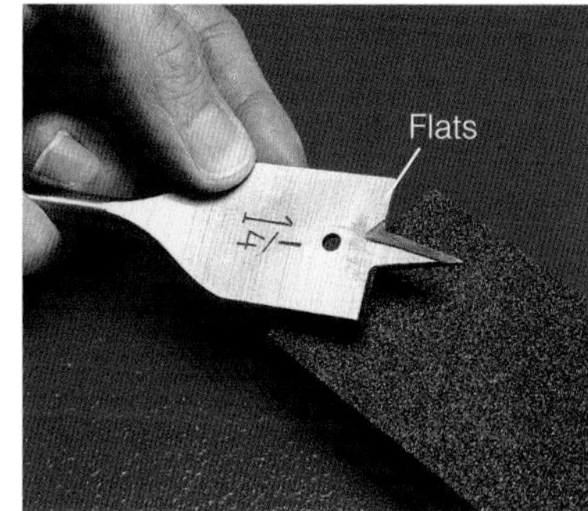

Spade bits. Use a file to reestablish all four cutting edges of a spade bit: the point and the flats on both sides. Remove the burrs by stroking the bit on a whetstone.

Twist bits. A simple angle jig can hold a twist bit at a precise angle for sharpening with a fine-grit wheel and bench grinder. Rotate the bit in the V-shape groove to sharpen the entire tip.

Twist-bit sharpening machines. Specialized sharpening machines offer precision control for renewing a drill bit with a two-step factory-style grind.

Sanding

Repairing Wood with Epoxy 366
Sanding 452
Wood Preparations 453

Hand-sanding is a simple but important skill. The rules are few, but when you ignore them, everyone can see the glaring error. Stains and finishes look blotchy or scratched and an exceptional wood figure takes on a muddied look. Stick with the basics shown at right for best results.

Standard papers. The two most common abrasives intended for dry use (without water or solvents) are: garnet, a reddish orange natural stone, and aluminum oxide, a manufactured compound. Garnet cuts and wears more quickly; aluminum oxide holds up better in power sanders. Common grits range from very coarse, about 36 grit, to very fine, about 320 grit.

Wet-dry papers. Capable of sanding wood, metals and some plastics, wet-dry sandpapers typically feature a black silicon-carbide abrasive. The binder and paper are designed for use with water and ordinary solvents, so these abrasives can be used for wet-sanding finishes. Grits run as fine as 600 for general shop use.

The Basics

Sand with the grain. Working across wood grain leaves deep scratches, so always sand in the direction of the grain. Where two pieces intersect in a frame, as shown, sand the crosspiece first.

Use a sanding block. The contours of your palm or fingers will exert spot pressure on sandpaper, which can result in an uneven surface. Use a sanding block to ensure flatness.

Use progressively finer papers. Making big jumps between grits is a slow and unreliable way to remove scratches from the previous grits. For best results, work in a reasonably close sequence, especially on finishes.

Special Situations

Sanding sponge. Unlike the hit-and-miss pressure of loose sandpaper in your hand, sanding sponges conform to slightly irregular shapes, ensuring uniform abrasion on an entire surface.

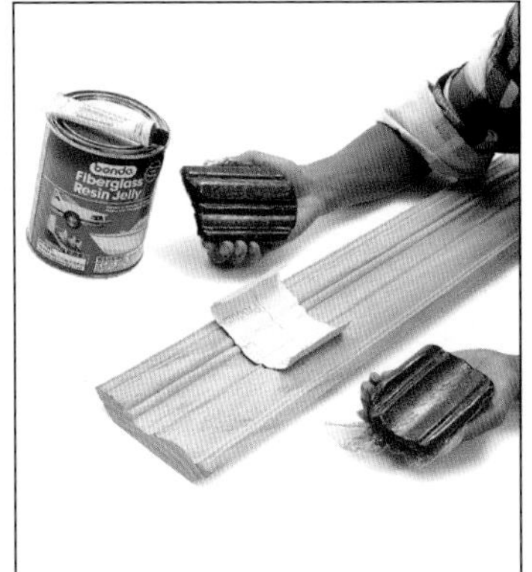

Custom sanding blocks. Automotive filler compounds can be used to create custom sanding blocks for complex shapes. Press the compound onto plastic wrap on the molding or object and let it harden.

Sanding pads. Abrasive pads work well to sand burrs and dust out of layers of finish. They conform to irregular shapes and don't leave residue, the way steel wool does.

Power Tools

Drills / Techniques

Clamps 34
Installing a Deadbolt 376
Drilling Metal 470

A portable electric drill is probably the power tool most homeowners buy first, for good reason. No other tool lets you tackle as many repairs or do-it-yourself projects simply by installing different low-cost accessories. Aside from drilling holes in wood, metal, masonry or plastics, a drill can spin a sanding disc or wire brush, stir paint, churn a drain-cleaning auger or drive screws for hours at a pace you could never match with a manual screwdriver.

Its anatomy is simple. The motor, drive gears and trigger switch are contained in a plastic housing or handle. On the business end is the chuck, a geared sleeve with adjustable metal jaws that close to grip the shank of a drill bit or other accessory. Drills are classified by the maximum capacity of their chucks (typically 3/8 in. for standard-duty drills, 1/2 in. for heavy-duty versions), but the motor amperage (power rating), bearing type and speed range can vary among drills of the same size.

The Basics

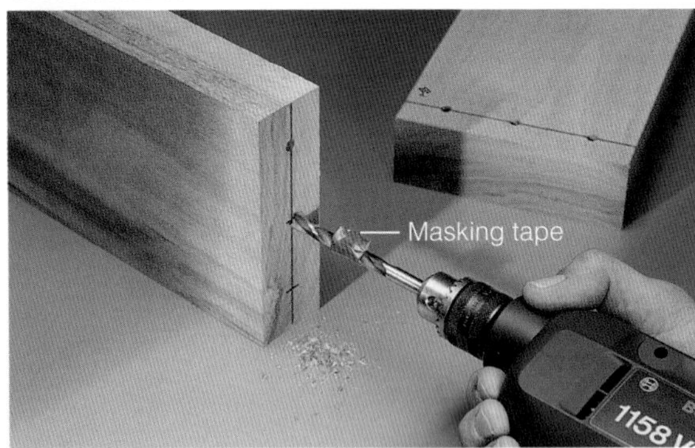

Depth guide. Many projects require a stopped hole. You can buy metal depth-stop collars for this purpose, but a piece of tape on the bit can substitute in a pinch. Check the tape's position periodically to make sure it hasn't shifted.

Backer board. Even if a drill bit cuts cleanly entering a workpiece, it often splinters the exit side as it pushes through, resulting in a ragged hole edge. Called blowout, this defect can be prevented by using a scrap piece as a backer board.

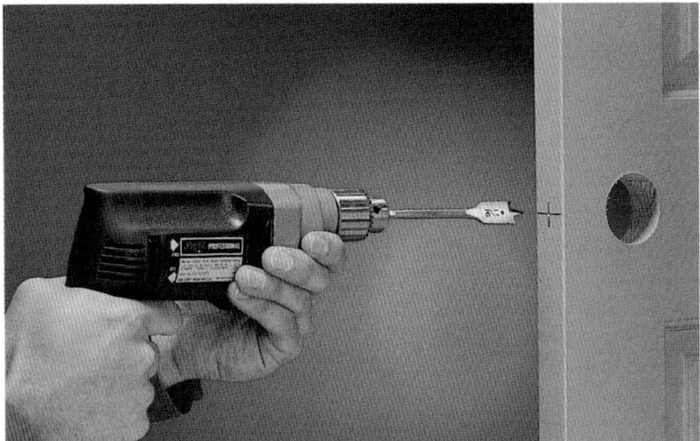

Center mark. Most drilling situations, such as boring for a lockset latch on this door edge, require precise placement of the hole. Mark and punch a center point to start the bit accurately.

Clamp it. The drill's rotary action can cause a workpiece to spin, especially with larger bits if the bit edge grabs the piece faster than it can drill through it. For the sake of both safety and accuracy, use clamps to secure the work.

Features

Chuck. Keyless chucks, like the one shown, feature a rubberized grip sleeve, allowing hand pressure to open or close the jaws. On traditional drills, the chuck has a toothed ring that requires a special key for opening and closing.

Clutch. For driving screws, it often helps to control the drill's power so the screw doesn't break off or strip the hole. Most cordless drills feature an adjustable clutch that disengages the drive gear when a certain level of resistance is met.

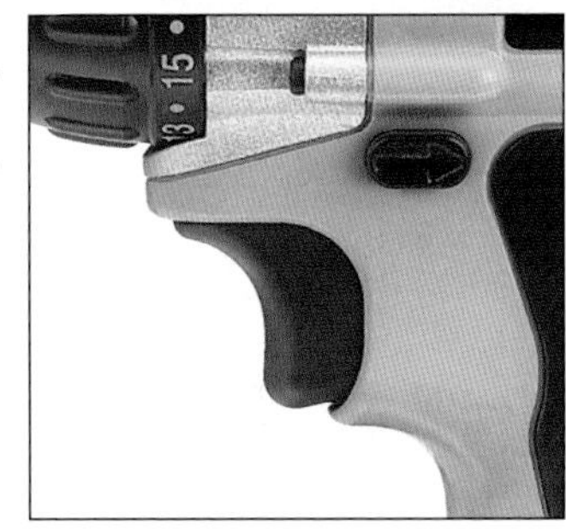

Variable speed and reverse. Dubbed VSR for short, this feature comes standard on any good, all-purpose drill. A typical speed range is 0 to 1,200 revolutions per minute (rpm); slower speeds provide greater control. The reversing feature lets you back screws out or free stuck bits.

Drills / Special Materials

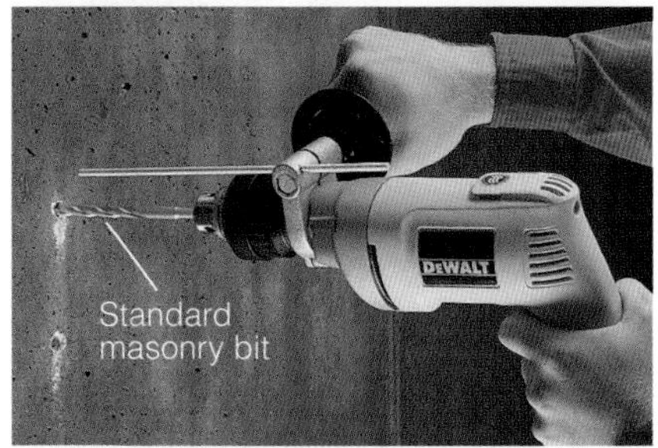

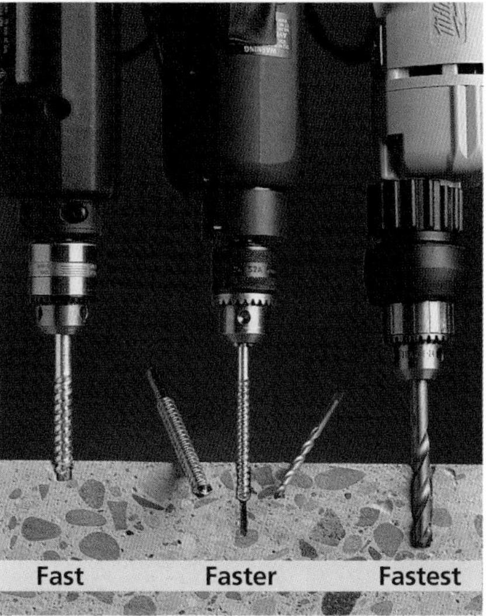

Concrete

Drilling holes in concrete, brick, plaster or stucco requires special carbide-tipped bits that can withstand these abrasive materials. Concrete is typically harder and thicker than the others, and it contains large rocks, called aggregate, that can stop a drill bit in its tracks.

Two things will improve your odds. First, a hammer drill (photo, top left) combines the rotary motion of a standard drill with a hammering action, so it pounds away at stubborn rocks until they break apart. This type of hammering can destroy common masonry bits, however, so special hardened percussion bits are usually paired with this type of drill. If the concrete is still uncured or "green," or you are drilling in a softer masonry material, a standard drill and masonry bit (photo, middle left) will often suffice.

Drills, bits and speed. You can take three basic approaches when drilling concrete: patience, brute force or strategy. This sample drilling test demonstrates the difference.

On the left is the patient approach: a masonry bit chucked into a standard drill. It makes for slow going, but you don't have to spend money on specialized tools.

On the right is the brute-force option: an industrial-duty hammer drill fitted with a percussion bit. You'll work faster, but both the drill and the special bits cost more.

In the center is the strategic approach. A standard drill is fitted first with a small masonry bit. After drilling that hole, you switch to an intermediate-size bit, and then repeat with the large bit. This approach is reasonably quick, easier on your drill motor and requires only inexpensive masonry bits.

Metal

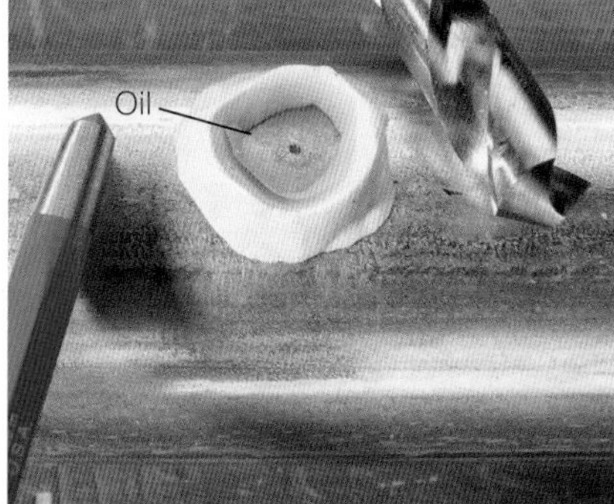

Lubrication reduces the friction and heat that can prematurely dull a drill bit or ruin the temper of its cutting edge. Here, a steel pipe was dimpled with a center punch; then glazing putty was used to create a small oil reservoir.

Ceramic Tile

Ceramic tile, another tough material, should be immersed in water for cooling and lubrication. Large holes require carbide-grit hole saws, like the one shown. **Caution: Use a cordless drill to avoid a dangerous electrical shock.**

Glass and Mirrors

Drill bits tend to skate on this smooth, brittle surface. Use a spear-point carbide bit, and start in a piece of dense cardboard taped to the glass. After you dimple the glass, remove the cardboard to finish drilling.

Thick Wood

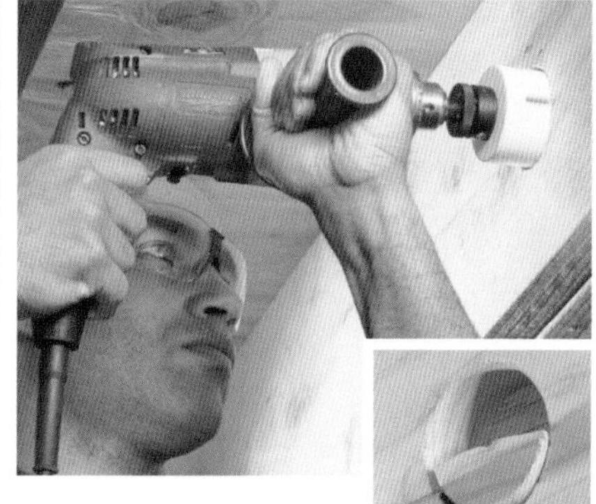

If you don't have large specialty bits, drilling deep holes may require a few steps. A hole saw will cut the outline of the plug, which can be removed with a chisel. Then the hole can be deepened by drilling and chiseling again.

Drills / Bits

Installing a Deadbolt **376**
Mortise-and-Tenon Joints **436**

Large Holes

Even ordinary do-it-yourself projects can exceed the limits of some tools. That 10-piece twist drill set you have might be fine for hanging pictures or installing cabinet hardware, but how about routing drain pipe through a stud or drilling for a lockset in a new door? That's when you need large specialty bits, such as a Forstner or a multi-spur bit; hole saws also fit these applications and can cut metal and plastics.

1 To install a new lockset, use the lock template to mark the center of the lock body; then drill a small hole through the door. For best results, mark both sides and drill from each, meeting in the center.

2 Use a hole saw (2-1/8 in. is the standard size for locksets) with a pilot bit to continue. Drive the saw slowly until the cutting rim starts to touch evenly on the door's surface.

3 Increase the drill speed and apply moderate pressure to keep the saw cutting. Back out periodically to clear the sawdust and give the cutting teeth a chance to cool.

4 After cutting halfway into the first face of the door, switch to the other side and finish drilling from there. The plug will break free and come out with the hole saw.

Specialty Bits

The renowned versatility of the portable drill doesn't come from the drill itself but from the dozens of accessories you can use with it. Some allow you to drill deep or curved holes, some create customized pockets where fastener heads can nest while others let you drive specialized fasteners. You could fill an entire toolbox if you had them all, but here are four of the most popular ones.

Magnetic bit holder. These simple tools feature a hex shank that fits into the chuck and a magnetized hex pocket that accepts driver bits. Steel screws stay put without help.

Rotary rasp. For efficient but controlled removal of wood along curved contours, a rotary rasp lets you rough out the shape quickly. Files or sandpaper finish the job.

Self-centering bit. The spring-loaded nosepiece on this bit centers itself in hinge and other hardware holes, then retracts as you plunge the drill bit in for the pilot hole.

Hex driver bit. Many sheet-metal screws—especially appliance fasteners—feature hexagonal heads. Hex driver bits come in several sizes for these screws.

Drill Presses

To use a portable drill, you bring the tool to the workpiece. For some projects, like furniture or toys, it's faster or more accurate to bring the workpiece to the tool. For these situations, a drill press offers a lot of advantages.

A drill press is a stationary machine, typically either a full-height floor model or a shorter bench-top version. Power comes from an induction motor mounted to the rear of the head; this type of motor is designed to run quietly and continuously, unlike the noisier universal motors found on portable power tools.

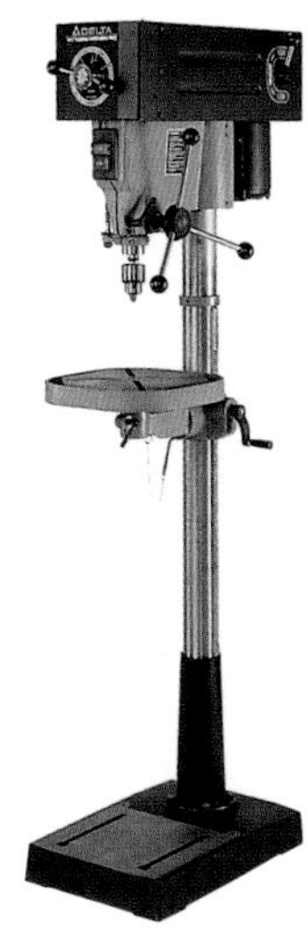

Floor

Drill presses are classified by their throat size, which is the distance from the support column to the drill center; you double this dimension to get the model rating. Drill presses feature adjustable tables that raise, lower, and sometimes tilt to support a workpiece. Some versions also have a rack-and-pinion system that adjusts the table position via a hand crank. Typical chuck capacity is 1/2 in., though industrial versions are larger.

Aside from convenience, drill presses provide greater accuracy because the standard table position ensures a 90° drilling angle. They also offer greater safety with large-diameter bits and much faster operation for repetitive drilling. You can set a depth stop to limit the drill's travel and use jigs to position workpieces accurately.

Benchtop

Jigs and Accessories

Fence. A fence helps position stock for consistent, accurate drilling. When fitted with adjustable stops, a fence can index both the edge and the ends of the workpiece so you won't have to mark each hole location—a time-saving feature for creating identical pieces.

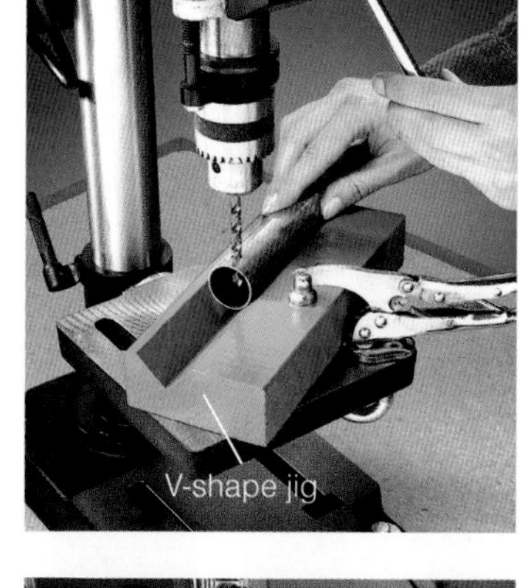

Dowel and pipe jigs. Pipe and other round stock tends to roll or shift when the drill bit first contacts the curved surface. Centering and clamping a simple V-shape jig to the table provides a stable base that helps restrain the workpiece to keep the bit drilling on center.

Flat-bottom holes. The accurate 90° table alignment and the adjustable depth stop make it easier to drill flat-bottom holes with large Forstner or multispur bits. When using these large-diameter bits, always clamp the workpiece firmly to the table to prevent it from spinning.

Mortising attachment. Though not as efficient or heavy-duty as a dedicated hollow-chisel mortiser, a drill press fitted with a mortising bit and attachment can cut square mortises in wood. The drill bit turns inside a square four-edged chisel, which is forced into the cut by spindle pressure.

Controls

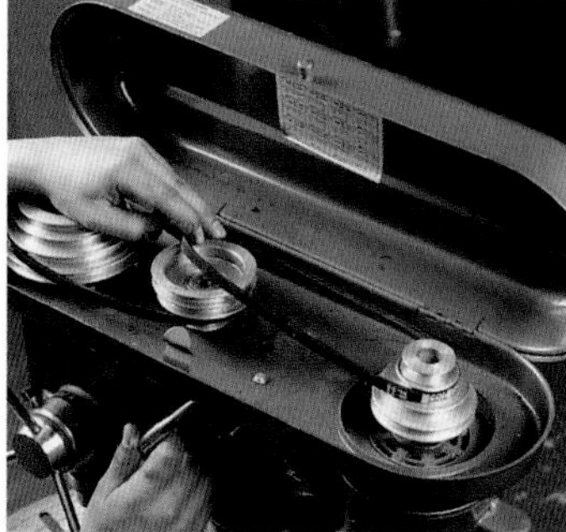

Speed. Unlike a variable-speed portable drill, most drill presses have a single-speed motor. At the drill head, the machine will feature either a step-pulley-and-belt drive or a variable-speed dial to adjust the rpm. The slowest speeds (about 300 to 400 rpm) are safest for large bits.

Height. Many older drill presses require you to adjust the table height by loosening the clamp on the column and moving the table manually. Newer versions typically feature a rack-and-pinion system that you adjust using a hand crank.

Jigsaws

Baseboard Moldings 230
Crown Moldings 232
Interior Trim 388
Creating Curves 443
Cutting Metal 469
Laminate Countertops 476

Jigsaws rank among the most versatile, user-friendly power tools you can own. This tool, which cuts by the up-and-down reciprocating stroke action of a thin steel blade, can rip and crosscut wood, but it's especially useful for cutting curves. Many saws have an orbital action feature that speeds the cutting rate. A variety of blades lets you choose the tooth size and type for different situations and materials, such as rough cuts in framing lumber, notches in ceramic tile or intricate shapes in metal.

Though the slight blade drift that's normal with jigsaws doesn't always yield the crisp, square edges a circular saw blade would provide, a jigsaw will deliver accurate cuts without the risk of dangerous kickback or other surprises to intimidate the user. For stopped cuts or controlled contours, the jigsaw excels.

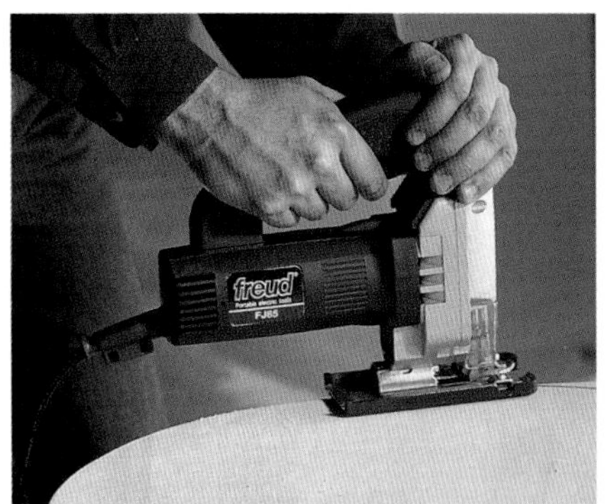

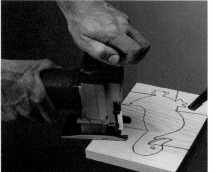

Curves. No other portable power saw offers the same control in cutting curves. The top-handle version shown is the most popular type, but many manufacturers offer barrel-grip models and even in-line jigsaws.

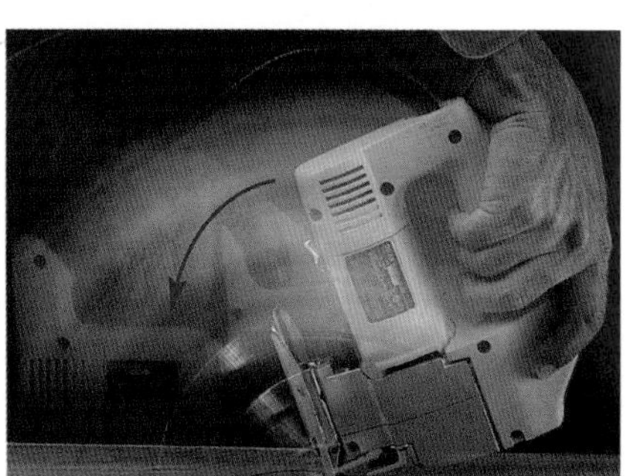

Relief cuts. For tight curves, make a series of relief cuts in the workpiece's waste portions. Cut from the board edges to the outline so scrap sections will fall away as the pattern is cut. This helps prevent blade binding.

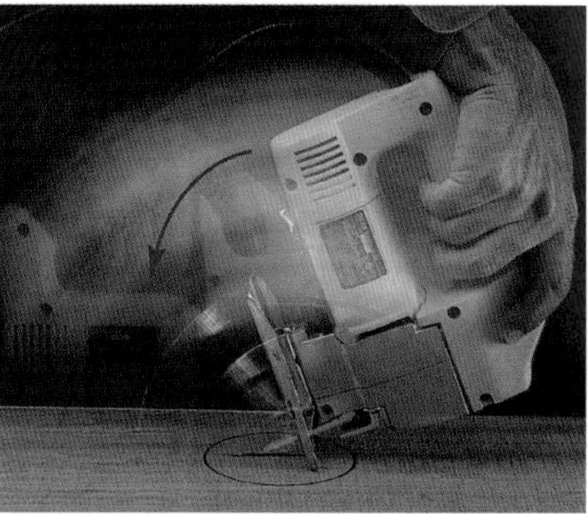

Plunge cuts. If you can't drill a pilot hole for the blade, you can often make a plunge cut in thin materials by resting the tool on the front edge of its baseplate, or shoe, then slowly and carefully tilt the saw back as the blade cuts its way into the surface.

Coping. Narrow, fine-tooth blades can cut tight contours for coped molding joints. Clamp the stock to a bench or sawhorse and make relief cuts in the miter face, if necessary.

Bevel cuts. Most jigsaws feature a tilting base that lets you adjust the bevel angle all the way to 45°. Clamp an edge guide in place and block the workpiece up off the bench to allow clearance underneath for the blade.

Finish cuts. Where perpendicular cuts meet, as on this staircase stringer, a circular saw can't make a stopped cut at the corner. For these situations, finish the cut with a jigsaw to avoid overcutting the material.

Special Blades and Uses

Jigsaws are ideal for woodworking projects but, with special blades installed, they can easily cut other materials as well.

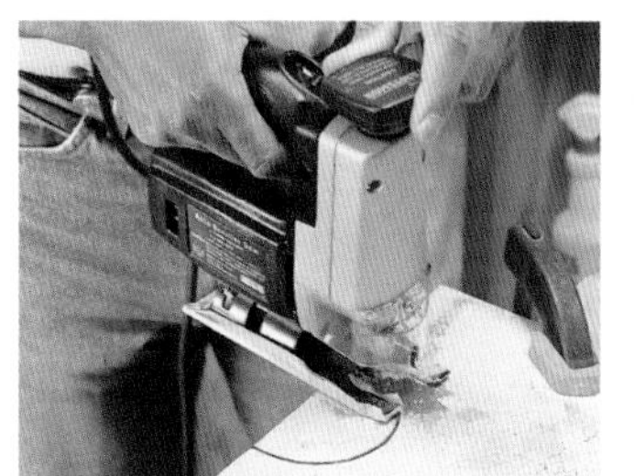

Tile. Blades edged with carbide grit are used to cut this hard, abrasive material. Cut slowly to avoid blade breakage and overheating.

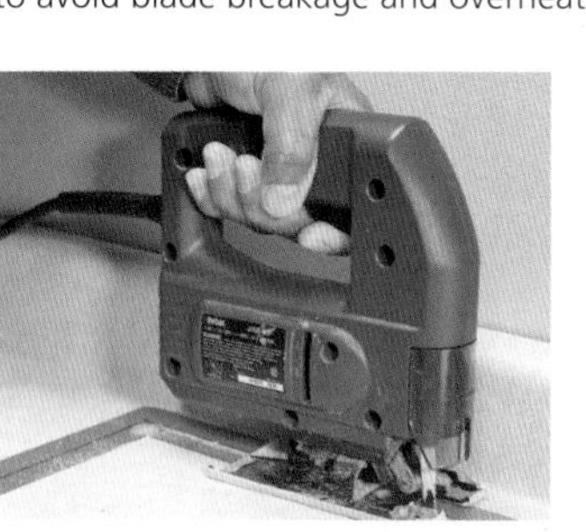

Laminate. Laminate blades have teeth that cut on the down stroke. This orientation helps prevent chipping of brittle plastic surfaces.

Metal. Metal-cutting jigsaw blades resemble hacksaw blades, with fine teeth and a slightly wavy edge that helps prevent binding.

Miter Saws

With an adjustable-angle turntable base and a saw head that pivots down or slides forward to make the cut, miter saws specialize in precise cuts for molding, picture frames, other trim stock, framing lumber, decking and even fence posts.

The locking turntable offers precise repeatability for angled cuts from square (90°) to a steep miter (at least 45°, sometimes as much as 60°).

Most saws have positive stops, called detents, at 0°, 15°, 22.5°, 30° (or 31.6° for crown molding) and 45°. Most models also have a locking override feature to bypass the detents and cut at intermediate angles. Blade diameters of 10 or 12 in. offer the most versatility and capacity at a reasonable cost.

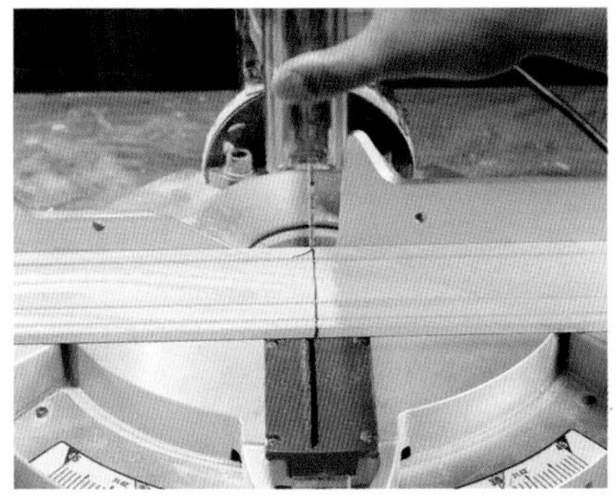

Align the cut. Lift the blade guard and sight down the edge of your blade to align the cut—allowing for the blade thickness—on the waste side of the line.
Caution: Your fingers should be off the trigger switch as you do this.

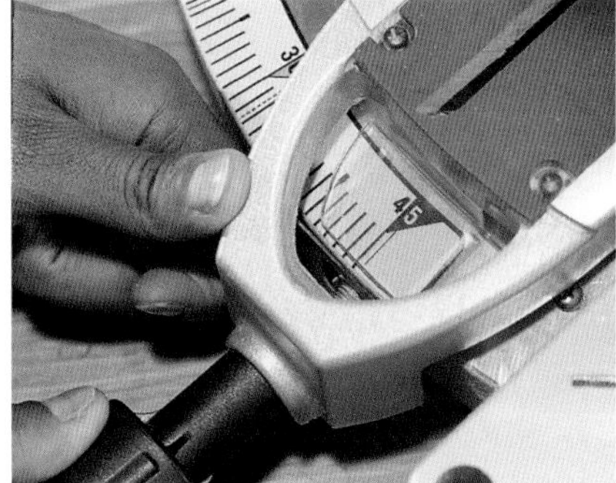

Fine-tune. Angle settings required for trim carpentry often vary from a perfect 45° or 90°. If the detent stop isn't at the exact angle you need, loosen the locking knob and shift the turntable slightly. Then lock the knob to hold the setting.

Increase cutting depth. To cheat the cutting limitations of a miter saw, set a flat spacer board on the turntable. This raises the workpiece toward the center portion of the blade, closer to its full cutting diameter.

Support. Portability requirements keep miter saw bases compact, so long stock tends to dangle loosely and then drop harshly when the cut is made, compromising accuracy. For support, fashion a simple T-block to match the base height and support the stock end.

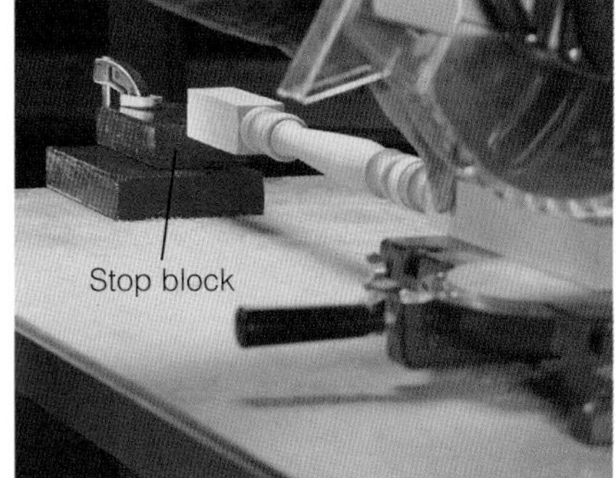

Repetitive cuts. Even with its narrow base, a miter saw can handle precise repetitive cuts on longer stock. Set up the saw on a flat, stable surface and clamp a stop block firmly in place to establish a consistent cutting length.

Small pieces. Small cutoffs tend to slip past the saw fence and will often get launched through the air like a missile. Prevent this by using a sacrificial backer board behind the workpiece. Properly supported, the cutoff will typically drop harmlessly.

Making the Cut

Blade sizes—from 8 in. to 15 in. dia.—are only one factor to consider. Miter saws also come in three styles:

Standard miter saw. The least expensive type, these pivot-style saws have a nontilting head to cut simple miters up to 45°.

Compound miter saw. These pivot-style saws have a tilting head for angled or bevel cuts. With the turntable also adjusted to an angle, they will cut compound miters.

Sliding miter saw. The sliding-carriage feature on these tilting-head miter saws allows them to cut wider stock than a standard saw.

Circular Saws

Cutting Dadoes 434

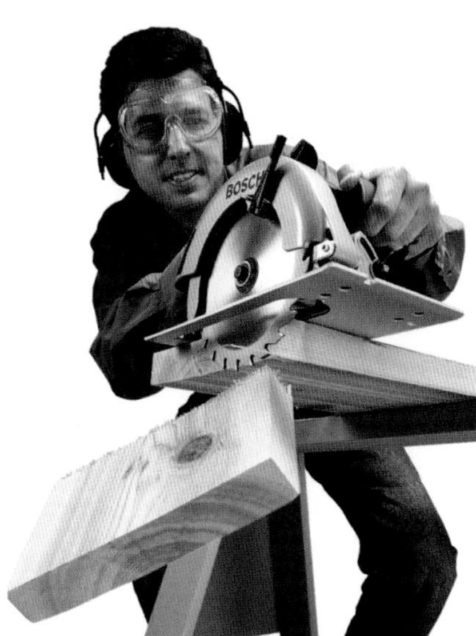

For the better part of a century, the portable circular saw has been the primary job-site tool for most carpenters. Properly adjusted and fitted with the right blade, this is a compact, lightweight machine that can do anything from rough framing work to cutting up plywood sheets. When fitted with specialized blades, a circular saw can cut materials ranging from sheet metal to concrete. For most do-it-yourself use, though, woodworking is its number-one role.

Start shopping for a circular saw and you'll quickly find common standards amidst a few significant design differences. Most models for the North American market have a round 5/8-in. arbor shaft that accepts a 7-1/4-in.-dia. blade, and will run on standard household current.

Pricier models have quality differences you don't necessarily see—better bearings, heavier motor windings and a heavy-duty trigger switch—and benchmark features, including a 15-amp motor rating, precision-machined aluminum baseplate, smooth blade-depth adjustment, and a magnesium housing for light weight. The most common configuration, sometimes called a sidewinder, fits the motor on one side of the tool and mounts the blade directly to an in-line arbor on the other side. (The blade can be on the left or right side.)

On commercial job sites, you're more likely to see worm-drive circular saws. These long-bodied tools feature oil-bath gears, transverse arbors and heavy-duty motors to give them plenty of cutting power. Most worm-drive circular saws have rear-mounted handles for better ergonomics. The increased cost and added weight—typically about 40-percent higher than a sidewinder in each cost and weight category—make this type primarily a professional's tool. Whatever the type you choose, always wear hearing and eye protection when using the saw.

Caution: Always unplug saw when making adjustments.

Basics

Set depth. The saw's base, or shoe, has a front mount that pivots to adjust the blade's cutting depth. For most situations, set the blade depth so the teeth fully clear the underside of the workpiece. Unplug saw before making adjustments.

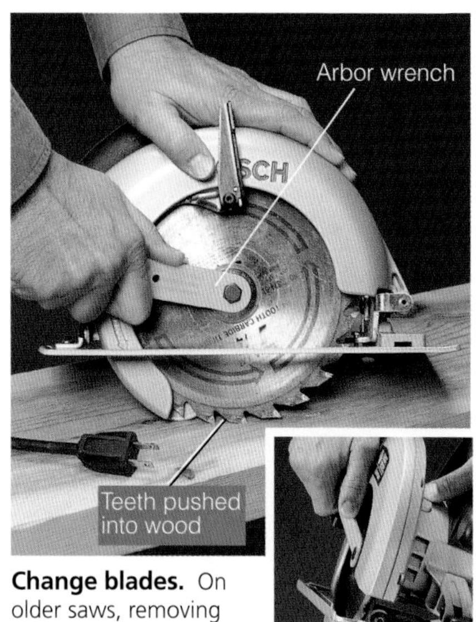

Change blades. On older saws, removing the arbor nut requires pushing the blade into a soft board to prevent rotation. On newer versions (see inset photo), you press an arbor lock button.

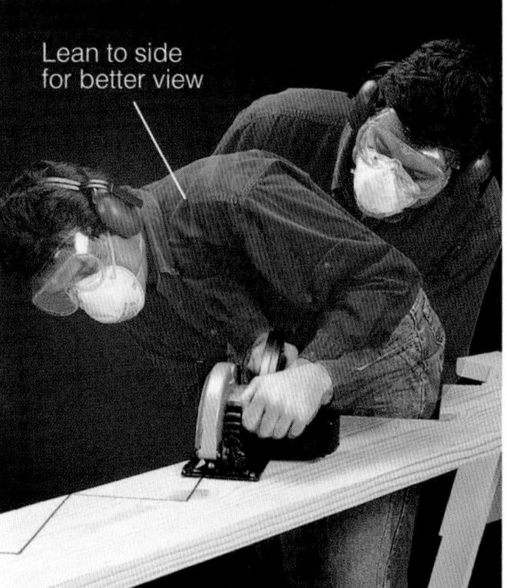

Straight cut. When cutting freehand along a layout line, try sighting the cut from the side of the blade, not from behind. You'll be able to make slight corrections as you proceed, resulting in a straighter cut.

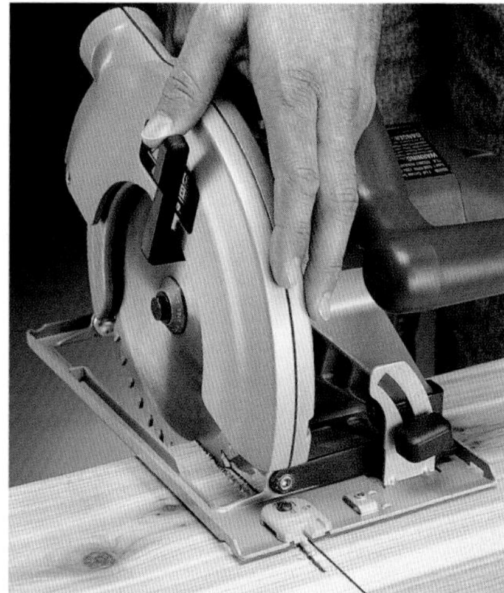

Mistakes. If your cut goes off the line, stop the saw, lift the saw out of the cut and start over. You can't twist a circular saw back into line the way you can a jigsaw.

Crisp Cuts

Just because you're working with portable tools doesn't mean you can't get top-notch results. Using the correct blade, keeping it sharp and oriented correctly toward your material, and using guides or accessories when appropriate can mean the difference between craftsmanship and chaos. If a procedure seems unsafe, find an alternate tool or technique.

Guided. For precise straight or square cuts, use edge guides rather than relying on freehand skill.

Good-side down. To avoid a splintered edge on finish surfaces, place the material good-side down; any tear-out will occur on the side facing you.

Plunge cuts. Tilt the saw onto its nose, then retract the blade guard and lower the spinning blade slowly as you push the saw forward. **Caution: Saw can kick back toward you.**

Dadoes

Wide grooves, called dadoes, or notches can be cut efficiently with multiple passes of a single blade. Set the

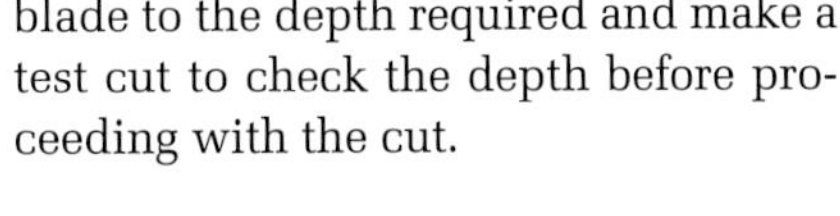

blade to the depth required and make a test cut to check the depth before proceeding with the cut.

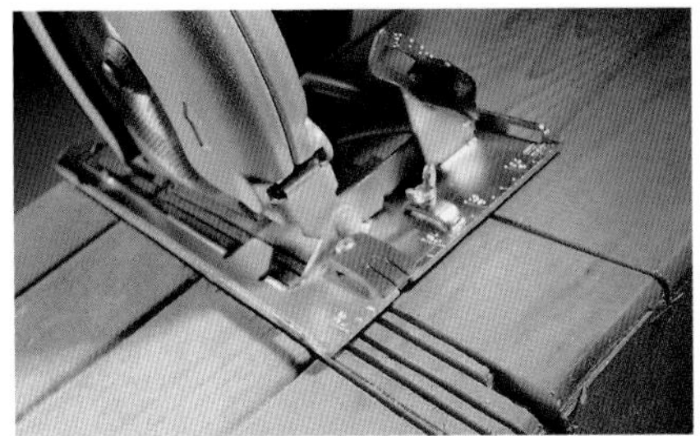

1 After making the two guided outermost cuts to define the dado width, make closely spaced freehand cuts inside the area.

2 Use a sharp wood chisel to break the waste material out of the dado and then to pare the bottom surface flat.

Shop Smart

Selecting the Right Blade

Get all the power and fancy accessories you want, but the wrong blade for the job will negate those features by overburdening the saw's motor, leaving a poorly cut edge or even ruining both the blade and material. Whatever you're cutting, there's a blade designed with just that application in mind, so resist the temptation to make do with the blade that happens to be mounted on the saw. Blade changes take only a few minutes.

Basic Blades

Finish blade. Blades with more teeth leave a smoother finish cut on plywood, paneling and other sheet goods.

Framing blade. With fewer, more sharply angled teeth, a framing blade leaves a rougher edge but cuts quickly.

Combination blade. Designed for general-purpose use, combination blades offer a compromise for making rip and cross-grain cuts.

Specialized Blades

Diamond blade. Studded on its edge with small diamond spurs, this blade will cut concrete, stone and ceramic tiles.

Abrasive blade. Abrasive blades—in versions for masonry or metal—cut by grinding away the material.

Remodeling blade. This carbide-tipped blade is for demolition work and cutting nail-embedded wood.

Circular Saws / Jigs

Straight-cut Jigs

Guided by a straightedge, a circular saw can make cuts nearly as precisely as most tablesaws, but it can't do it as expeditiously. There's a whole routine involved: You have to mark the cutline, allow for the saw-base edge's offset from the blade, position the straightedge accurately and clamp it down. Even then, it often takes a couple of test cuts before you have the guide precisely where you need it. This simple shop jig fixes that problem by letting you align the jig right on the cutline, with no need to calculate an offset dimension.

1 Start with a 3-in. (8-cm)-wide piece of 3/4-in. plywood with one factory edge. Fasten it to a 12-in. (30-cm)-wide plywood base as shown. The narrow offset on the outboard edge provides a clamping ledge.

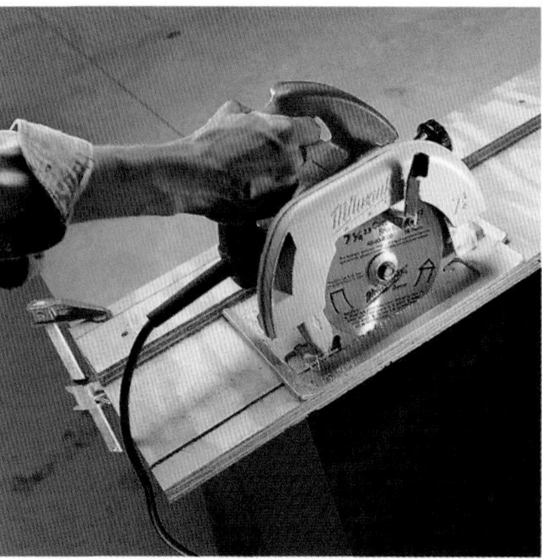

2 Clamp the jig to a stable surface; then trim the excess material from the base's wide part. Allow enough overhang so that you cut only the jig base and not the support surface underneath.

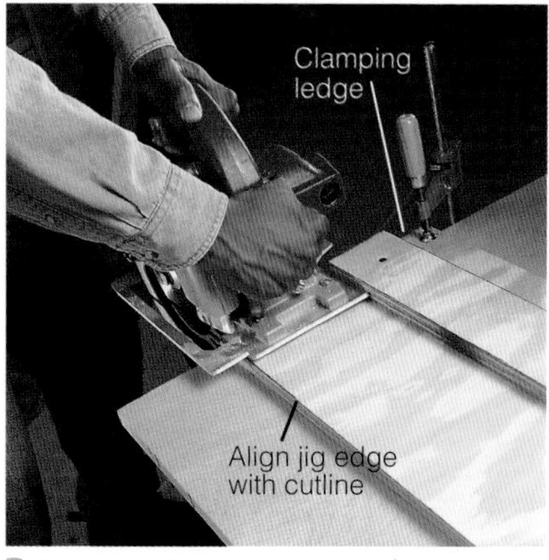

3 To use the jig, align the cut edge of the base with the layout marks on your workpiece. Adjust the cutting depth so the blade makes it completely through. **Note:** The clamping ledge provides clearance for the saw motor.

Crosscut Jigs

This jig also controls the saw's position and cutting path but is suited best for square-cutting the ends of boards. The base is made of two layers of 3/4-in. plywood, glued and screwed together and then cut to finish size (12 in. / 30 cm or wider). Next, fasten a pair of sides (1x4 poplar is a good choice here) to the long edges of the plywood base. Cut another pair of hardwood strips for the runners, and rout or cut a rabbeted or grooved ledge along one edge. Fasten the first runner to the jig, perpendicular to the sides, as shown. Then set your saw base in the rabbet to align and attach the second runner.

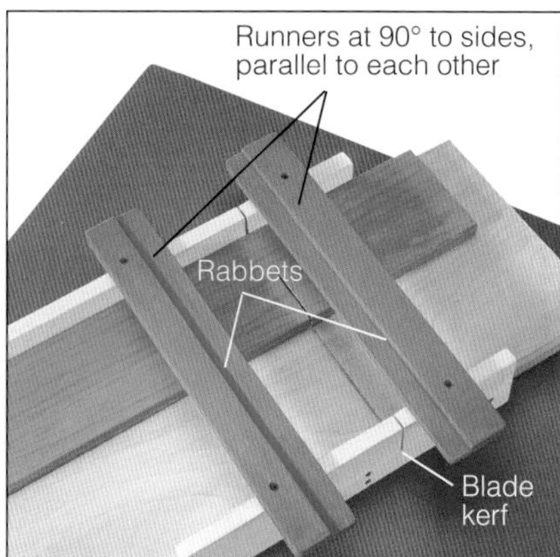

1 Careful assembly is critical to building an accurate crosscut jig. Make sure the sides are parallel and at the same height, and that the runners are exactly perpendicular to the sides and parallel to each other with rabbeted edges to the inside.

2 To use the jig, adjust the blade depth for a shallow cut in the plywood base. Then align the workpiece against the back side.

Quick Rip

You can get surprisingly accurate results with narrow cuts by using your hand as a guide. Mark the cutline, pinch the saw base with your fingers and let your forefinger glide along the board's edge. Use extreme caution.

Reciprocating Saws

Most power tools help you build things. Think of a reciprocating saw as a tool designed to help you unbuild things. Named for its blade's back-and-forth cutting action, a reciprocating saw excels at demolition work. It accepts blades from 2-1/2 to 12 in. long with varying tooth configurations to cut wood, plaster, metal, nails and other materials. The longer blade sizes allow you to cut deep into walls, sometimes through them, at a much faster rate and with better access than using other tools.

"Recip" saws, once used primarily by remodeling contractors and tradespeople, are now a worthwhile investment for homeowners involved in large-scale projects. Base models have 10- to 12-amp motors and straight-line cutting action. Better versions feature 15-amp motors, variable-speed control and orbital-cutting action. If purchasing a reciprocating saw doesn't make sense, don't worry; they're widely available at rental centers.

Caution: Always brace yourself well when using this saw; if the blade tip hits a solid surface, it can push the saw and you backward with a violent jolt.

Demolition. The in-line model shown here can sometimes get in tighter spaces than most rear-handle reciprocating saws—a useful feature when cutting away framing.
Caution: Use care around wiring!

Rough cuts. Reciprocating saws are ideal for jobs where speed is more important than beauty. Here, the blade self-guides along the window framing to cut the plywood flush.

Plunge cuts. For plunge cuts, start the blade at a very low angle and at a relatively slow speed. As it enters the material, increase the cutting speed and tilt the saw blade down until the pivoting shoe rests flat.

Metal. Cutting away steel pipe or conduit with a reciprocating saw is quicker than trying to dismantle old fittings.
Caution: Always shut off the water or electrical circuit beforehand.

Nails. Nail-embedded wood is an unavoidable hazard of remodeling. The hardened teeth and rapid cutting action of the saw's thin blade make it well-suited for this task.

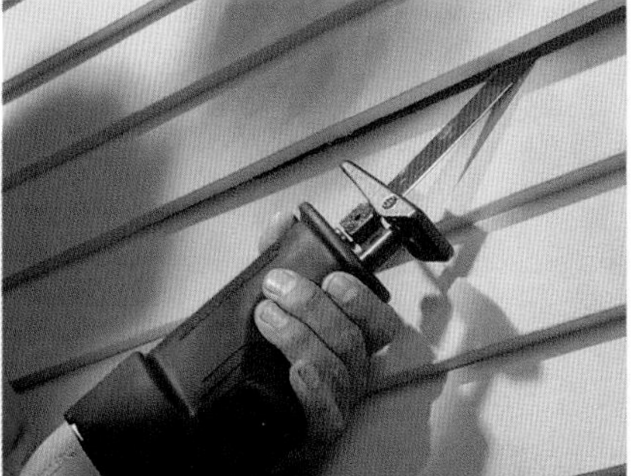

Reverse blade. For cuts where clearance is especially tight, such as replacing damaged siding, reverse the blade to get the body of the saw closer to the surface.

Convenient Options

Variable-speed and orbital action are two features that offer better control and more efficient cutting. For that reason, you'll find them on most professional-quality reciprocating saws, but convenience features are now showing up just as often on consumer models. Battery power and tool-free blade changes rank at the top. An adjustable, articulating head comes in handy in awkward situations, too.

Cordless. Used on the roof, around the backyard and other places where running extension cords can be a hassle, reciprocating saws are ideal candidates for cordless design. Most are 18- or 24-volt models.

Wrenchless. Early generations of reciprocating saws had you fumbling with a hex key wrench to change the blades. Now most models have spring-loaded blade clamps that require no tools.

The Cordless Revolution

Early-generation cordless drills showed plenty of potential, but the everyday reality of the 1970s often meant a bulky battery pack and not much power to show for it. Today's technology seems like a quantum leap from those early days, and the variety in cordless tools has grown from a handful of drills to an arsenal of powerful portable tools. Hammer drills, jigsaws, circular and reciprocating saws, even routers and sliding miter saws come in cordless versions.

Some light-duty drills come in the under-10-volt category. For most household projects, a 12-volt model is a good choice. Professional-duty tools typically feature 18- and 24-volt battery packs and motors. Whenever possible, get a kit with two batteries and a 1-hour charger.

Longer battery life. Almost anyone who has owned a cordless tool and used it regularly knows about the fade that afflicts aging batteries. They don't seem to have the punch they did when they were new, and a full charge doesn't last as long as it used to. Conventional wisdom used to hold that recharging a battery before it was fully spent would eventually handicap its ability to hold a charge, making it develop a memory or pattern that required frequent fill-ups. While that problem affected some earlier batteries, it's not a factor for today's cordless tools.

The biggest culprit in lost battery life is actually heat, which destroys the electron-storing chemicals inside the battery. Some of this is unavoidable, because heat is a by-product of charging and discharging the battery. Also, high-voltage batteries are more susceptible because they contain more individual cells. To improve your odds, occasionally leave the battery pack in the charger for a few hours to equalize the charges, and use corded tools when working in temperature extremes—hot or cold—that stress or degrade batteries.

Understanding Voltage and Amps

Start shopping for a cordless tool and you'll quickly encounter the jargon of volts and amps, but not much explanation for what they mean. In simple terms, battery voltage is somewhat like a horsepower rating. It indicates the force, or torque, the tool's battery can generate. If you do the math, you'll discover that the voltage ratings are always multiples of 1.2, because that's the voltage of the individual battery cells used in the packs.

1.2-volt cells

An amp-hour rating indicates the battery's stamina or endurance. The higher the rating, the longer the run time. Better-grade batteries are rated at 2 amp hours or higher.

Replacement Batteries

Even under the best circumstances, cordless-tool batteries eventually need replacing. When that day arrives, don't discard your old battery. Most contain cadmium, a heavy metal that is environmentally harmful. Ask at local tool retailers whether they accept batteries for recycling or offer rebuild services. If they offer the latter, they'll be able to replace the individual cells with new ones and you can reuse the old battery case. Otherwise, buy a new battery and ask about a more environmentally friendly nickel-metal-hydride (cadmium-free) version.

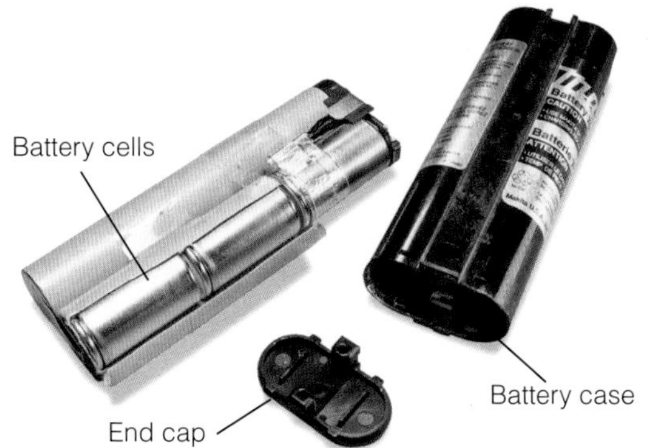

Bandsaws

Bandsaws derive their name from the type of blade they drive—a thin steel band with cutting teeth along one edge. The blade, which is tensioned between an upper idler wheel and a lower drive wheel, passes through guides and a table where the workpiece is cut. Bandsaws are quieter and safer to use than many saws; with their downward cutting force, there's no kickback.

These machines are classified by their throat sizes—the distance from the frame to the blade—which is roughly equivalent to the wheel diameter. Home-shop versions are typically 10- to 14-in. models. The flexible thin blade allows a bandsaw to make curved cuts that aren't possible with a tablesaw, circular saw or radial-arm saw. Bandsaws will make straight cuts, but at a slow pace and can be used for cutting joinery.

Relief cuts. To keep the blade from binding in tight curves, make a series of relief cuts beforehand. Cut from the board edges to the outline so the scrap sections will fall away as the pattern is cut.

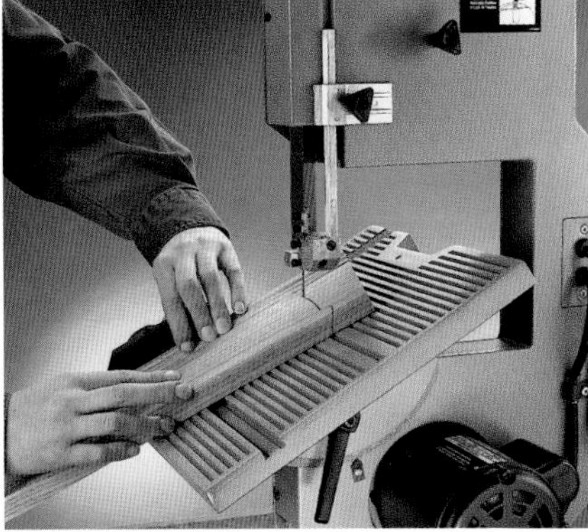

Angle cuts. Normally set for a square or perpendicular cut, a bandsaw table can tilt as much as 45° to make an angled cut. You can cut freehand or use a fence or miter gauge as a guide.

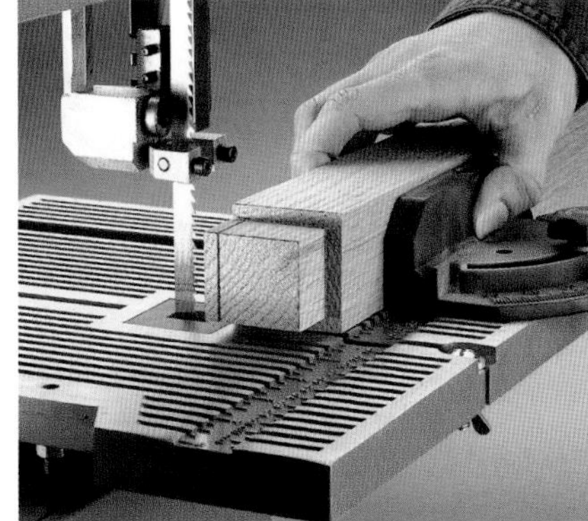

Miter gauge. Although it's usually safe to make freehand cuts on a bandsaw, using a miter gauge offers more precision for joinery. Many bandsaws also come with a fence for making rip cuts.

Resawing

Besides cutting curves, bandsaws excel at other tasks, and resawing is one of them. With this technique, the blade enters the board's edge rather than its face, allowing you to make the board thinner or to cut multiple layers or veneers from a single board. The upper blade guides can be adjusted to create clearance for wide boards. Most home-shop bandsaws can resaw stock up to 4 in. (10 cm) and sometimes 6 in. (15 cm) wide; professional-duty models typically have the extra horsepower required to cut materials at least 12 in. (30 cm) wide.

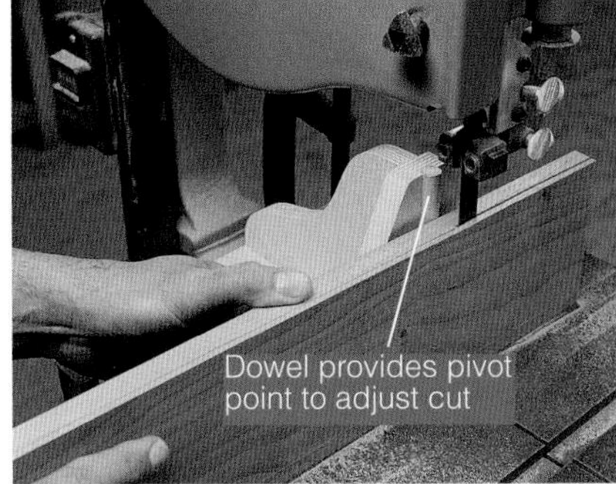

Resaw jig. Accurate resawing requires precise alignment of the board's vertical face but a flexible feed angle to compensate for normal blade drift. This shop-built jig allows both.

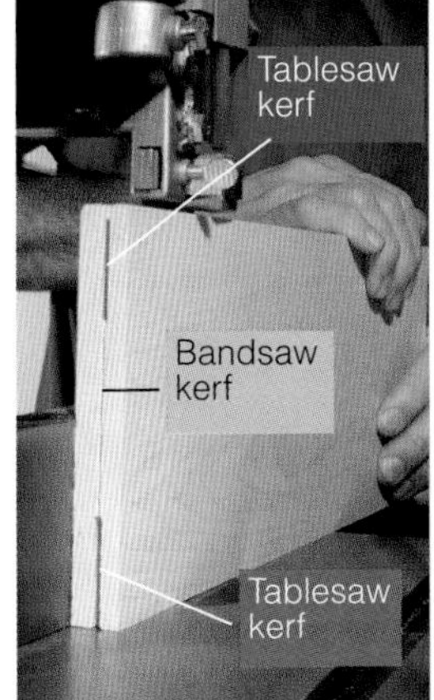

Combination cut. If wide resawing cuts tax your bandsaw's motor, use a tablesaw to make partial cuts in both edges first. This requires more machining, or surface planing, afterward, resulting in slightly more material being lost to the blade kerf.

Scrollsaws

A scrollsaw is a tool specializing in one task—cutting intricate designs and curves. The blades are very narrow, about 1/16 in. (1.5 mm), so they can make sharp turns without binding. The saw's wide throat allows the workpiece to be constantly repositioned as needed. Although used primarily for woodworking, scrollsaws can also cut leather, plastics and nonferrous metals.

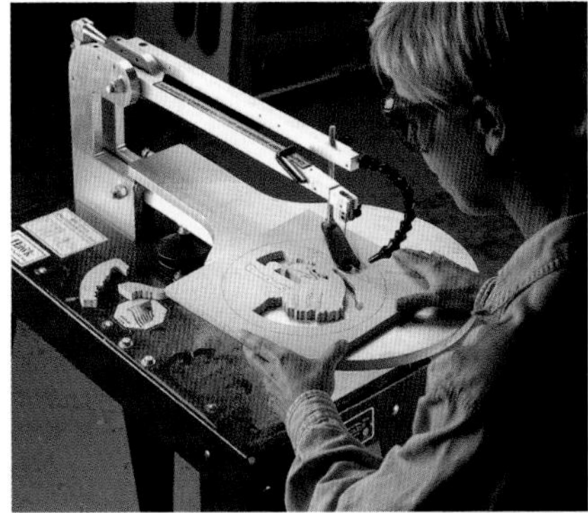

Scrollsaws' detail-cutting capabilities make them ideal for fretwork, veneer marquetry and puzzle making. Better-quality models have quick-change blade systems and anti-vibration features to ensure smooth cutting.

Threading. To make enclosed cutouts, you have to disconnect the upper end of the blade, feed it through a starter hole in the workpiece and then reattach it to the upper blade clamp.

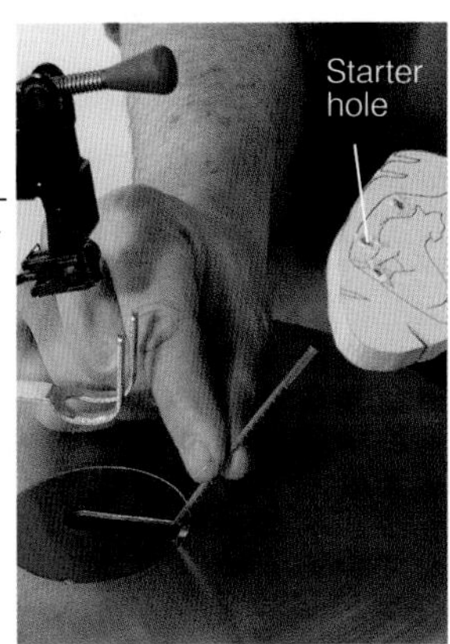

Tablesaws

Framing Square 43
Rabbets 435
Tablesaw Miter Jig 444

As the name suggests, these machines feature a flat table with a perpendicular blade that adjusts for height and angle. Portable bench-top versions, made of aluminum and lightweight plastic composites, usually have a direct-drive motor and arbor assembly mounted to the underside of the table. Larger stationary models sport cast-iron tables and are usually belt-driven, with the motor suspended behind or inside the saw base. Classified by blade diameter, sizes can vary from a 4-in. modelmaker's saw to a 16-in. industrial heavyweight, but 10-in. saws are the most popular for home use.

Tablesaws are versatile, but their most basic function is to make cuts with the lumber's grain, called rip cuts. An adjustable guide, called a rip fence, lets you find and lock a setting quickly, then slide the board alongside to make the cut. Aside from ripping, though, these indispensable tools can crosscut lumber, cut plywood and other sheet goods down into manageable parts, machine precise joinery in furniture parts and even make decorative moldings.

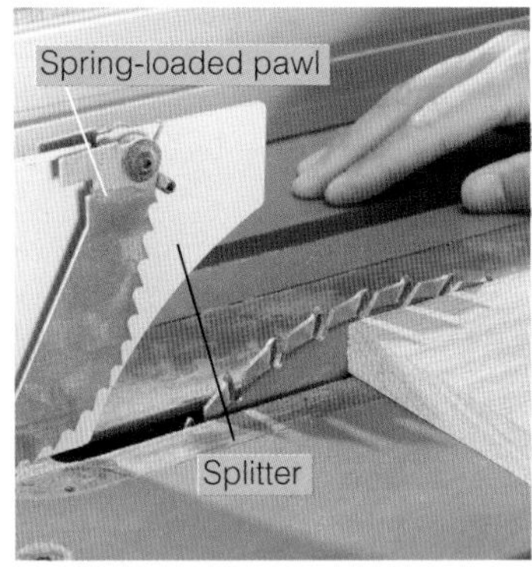

Blade height. To avoid unnecessary exposure to the blade, adjust the cutting height so the tooth gullets just clear the top of the workpiece. This helps the blade run more coolly and clears sawdust from the cut. At left are a splitter and a spring-loaded pawl, which help prevent kickback.

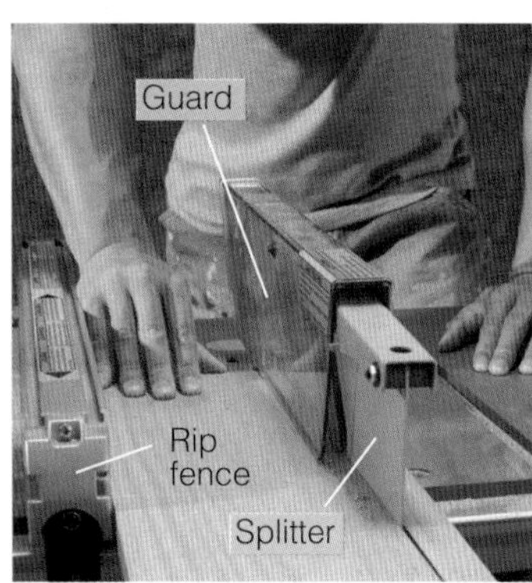

Basic rip. Safe technique for ripping involves using a blade guard, observing a minimum width of 6 in. (15 cm) for hand-feeding, using your thumb to push forward on the end of the board and keeping your little finger in contact with the rip fence.

Narrow rip. To rip narrow boards safely, start with the basic ripping technique, but as your pushing approaches the saw table, switch to a push shoe to feed the board past the blade. Stand to the side of the cutting line to avoid injury from unexpected kickback.

Adjusting Tablesaws

All of the precision inherent in a tablesaw is just wasted potential if the machine isn't set up properly. Most factory settings are reasonably accurate and can be tuned with help from the owner's manual. The crucial adjustment is having the blade parallel to the miter-gauge slots in the table. For the settings that you change on a regular basis, however, you should make periodic checks, adjusting as needed.

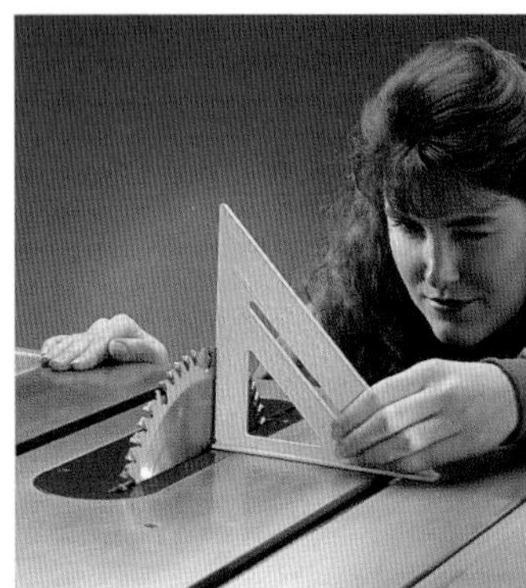

Blade angle. The angle scale relies on an accurate original setting of the blade in its normal position—perpendicular to the top. Check this with a square and adjust the stop or pointer, if necessary. Make a test cut and check it with a square to ensure your adjustment is accurate.

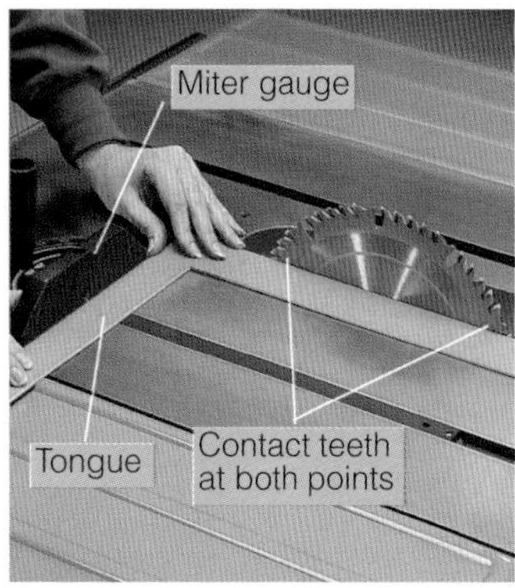

Miter gauge. To tune the miter gauge, rest the body of a framing square against the blade so teeth contact the edge in two places. Then nest the square's tongue against the miter-gauge face. The cursor arrow on the gauge should point to zero; adjust if it doesn't.

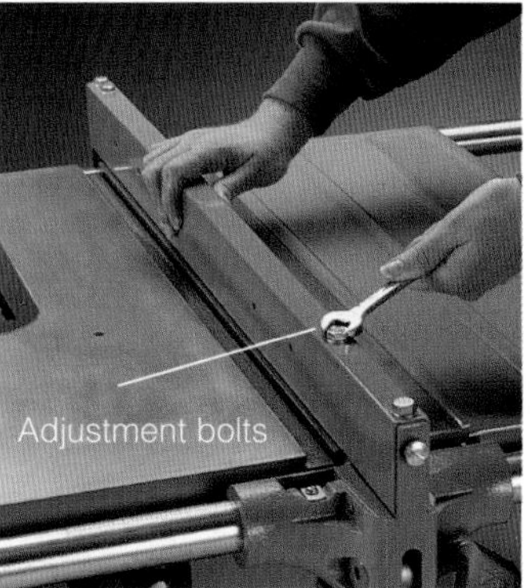

Rip fence. The rip fence must have an accurate width readout on the guide scale and be parallel to the blade. Adjustment mechanisms vary depending on the manufacturer, but if tuning is required, align the fence parallel to the miter-gauge slot in the table.

Blade guard. To align the guard and splitter, place a framing square or a straightedge alongside the blade. If they are not exactly in line, make minor adjustments by bending the splitter with a hand-screw clamp. For larger adjustments, shim the guard mount with washers.

Cutting Thin Strips

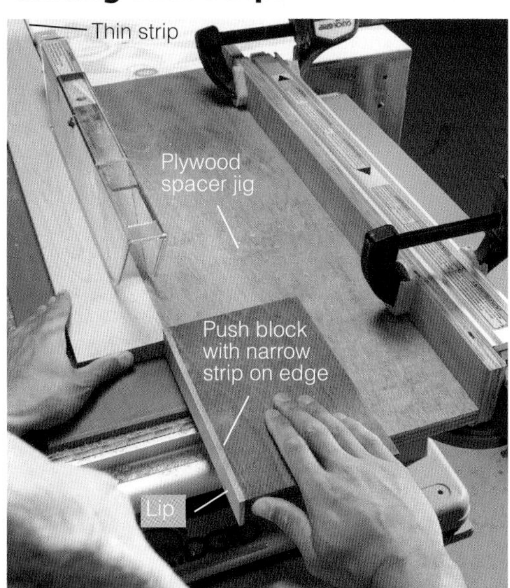

When ripping thin pieces, the guard and rip fence compete for the same turf leaving little space for a push stick. Make room by clamping a 10-in.-wide (25-cm-wide) plywood spacing jig to the fence. Add the jig's and strip's widths to determine the fence setting. Then make a push block with an L-shaped lip to feed the stock safely.

Ripping Crooked Boards

If you don't have a jointer, you can use the tablesaw to straighten board edges. Use screws (positioned to avoid the blade) to fasten the board to a straight piece of plywood; it functions like a sled to guide the cut. With the first edge straight, remove the board from the jig, flip it over and align it directly against the fence for the second cut.

Cutting Dadoes and Rabbets

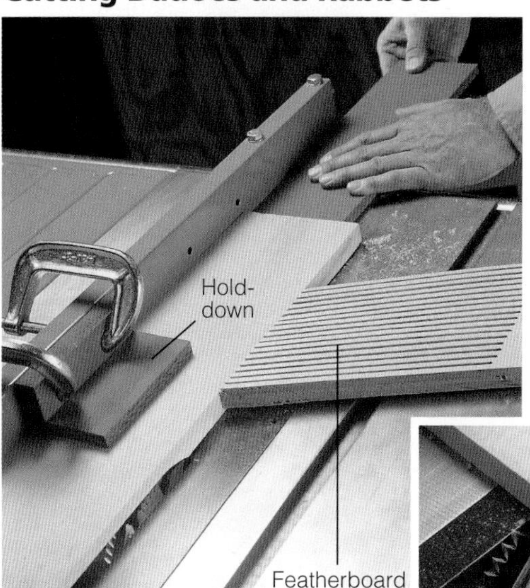

Special dado blade sets cut grooves, (called dadoes), and grooved edges (called rabbets), in one pass. To ensure uniform depth and width, use a hold-down and a featherboard to keep the workpiece tight against the table and fence.

Making Repetitive Cuts

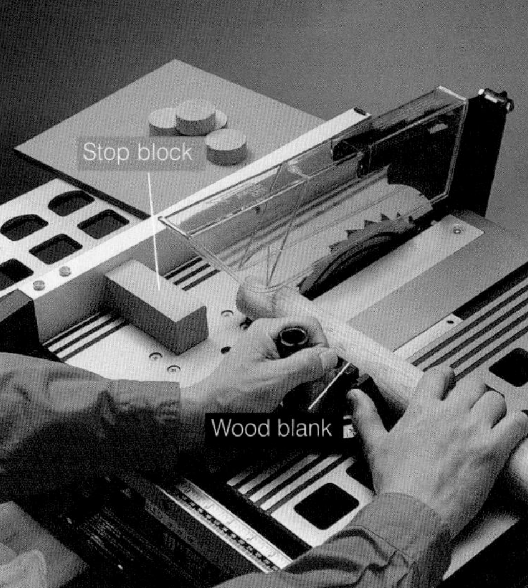

Making batches of identical small parts, such as blocks or round plugs, is difficult when the sections are too small to fit securely in a jig. The technique shown here remedies that with a stop block screwed to the rip fence. Nest a long wood blank against the miter gauge and butt the end against the stop block; push forward and the part will be cut safely and accurately.

Safety First

Push Sticks and Shoes

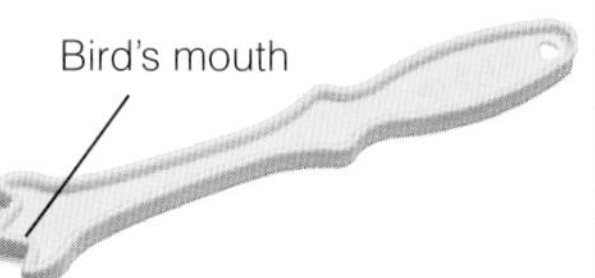

In woodworking, the expression "rule of thumb" ought to refer to safety rules that help you keep your thumbs, and your other digits as well. First on that list would be to never use a technique that puts your hands near a spinning saw blade. A simple way to observe this rule is to use push shoes or sticks to feed workpieces. Both accomplish the same goal, but push shoes are larger and have a saw-type handle. Manufactured versions are plastic and have some handy features that let you check angles or find the center point of a dowel. A heel on the lower edge catches the workpiece to push it forward while the forward part keeps the wood pressed firmly against the table. Push sticks are long, narrow tools that have a contoured handle on one end and a single or double bird's-mouth jaw on the other. You can make either tool out of scrap plywood—a good idea as they often get damaged in use.

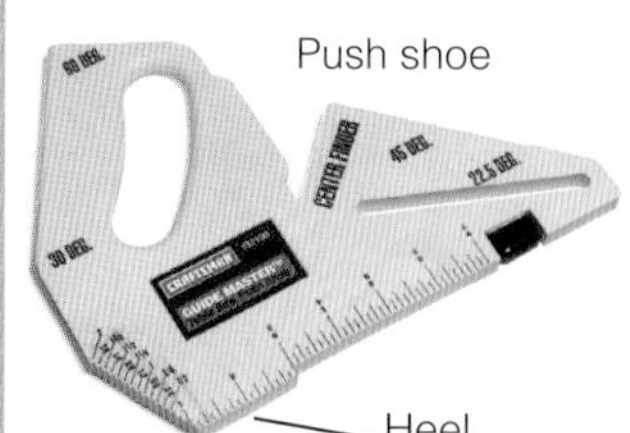

Radial-Arm Saws

A few decades ago, you could drop in on any home-building site or do-it-yourself workshop and find a radial-arm saw getting plenty of use. Designed primarily for crosscutting wood, but capable of making rip, miter, bevel and dado cuts, these machines pack a lot of function into a relatively small package.

The saw's versatility stems from the quick-change configuration of the radial-arm design, which supports a sliding saw carriage (motor, blade and guards). But suspending the heavy motor assembly on a long adjustable arm often creates deflection during heavy cuts. This compromise has prompted some to label the radial-arm saw a "jack-of-all-trades, master of none." That might be a harsh assessment, but specialized tools, such as tablesaws and sliding compound miter saws do perform some tasks more precisely.

Except when it's used for ripping, the cutting action of a radial-arm saw differs from that of other circular saws. Instead of rotating against the feed direction, the blade spins forward as the motor carriage moves forward. Care is required to prevent the blade from binding or from unexpectedly climbing out of the cut.

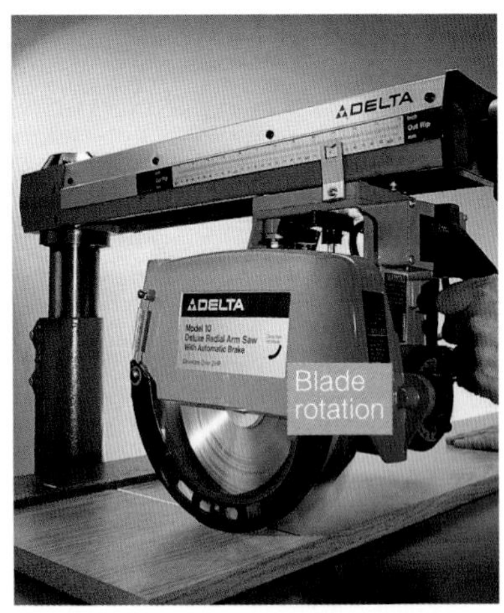

Crosscutting. With the saw carriage back against the post, place the stock flat on the table and firmly against the rear fence. Then slowly bring the blade forward. The cutting action may require you to find a balance between pulling and pushing on the handle.

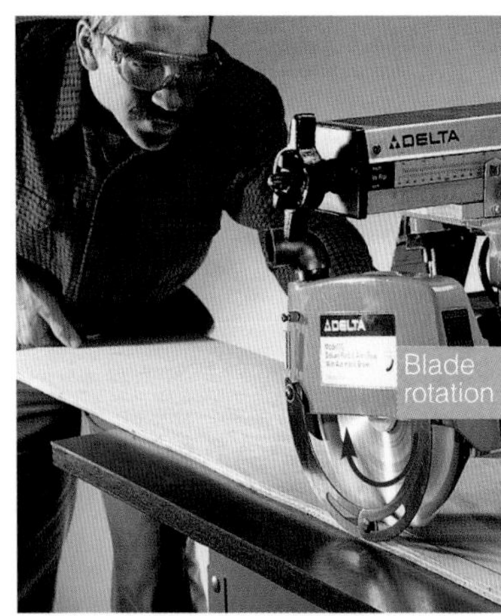

Ripping. The motor housing can be rotated and locked at 90° for making rip cuts. Use the safety devices for control and feed the workpiece the way you would on a tablesaw—opposite the blade rotation so you're pushing material against the teeth.

Miters. Since the saw carriage can travel the full length of the arm, you can miter wide boards you couldn't cut with most miter saws. Here, the arm is angled slightly and the blade is tilted for a bevel cut, producing a compound miter/bevel.

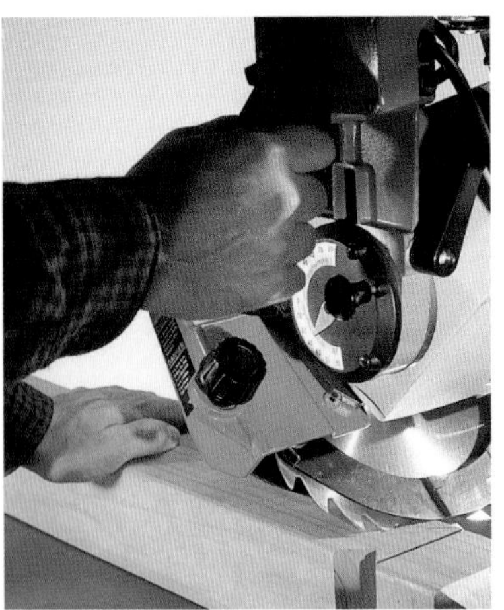

Bevels. Keeping the arm set at 90° and tilting the blade produces a bevel cut. By elevating the blade, as shown here, you can cut decorative details and bevels rather than cut all the way through the workpiece.

Dadoes. The arbor and blade housing allow installation of a dado blade, so you can cut dadoes, grooves and rabbets more efficiently.

Caution: The lower guard is shown lifted for photographic clarity; always cut with guard in normal position.

A Kinder, Safer Blade

Most circular saw blades have teeth set at a positive rake—that is, angled toward the direction of rotation. This is fine for most tools, but on radial-arm saws it aggravates the tendency of the blade to climb the cut faster than it can sever the wood fibers. To avoid this, install a zero or negative-rake blade (right) for a less aggressive scraping cut.

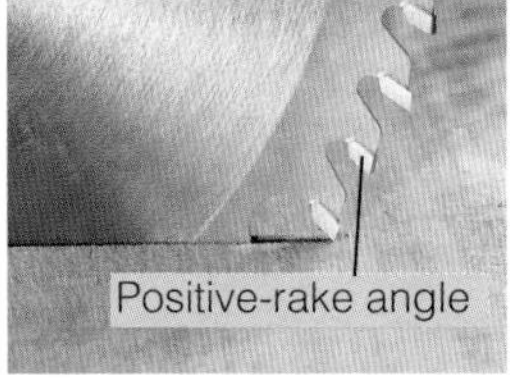

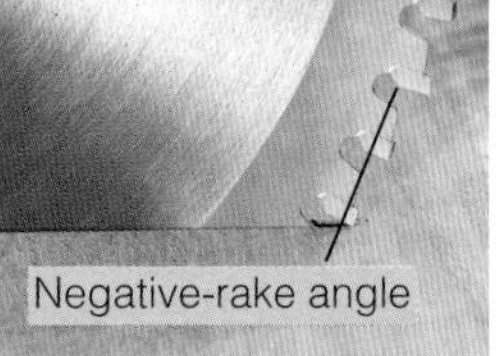

Wood Lathes

The wood lathe is an exception to just about every rule of woodworking equipment. Most machines noisily spin a cutter at high speed, most of them trying to make or keep a workpiece straight and square. A lathe quietly spins the workpiece itself against the cutting tool and produces cylindrical objects. The anatomy is simple—a narrow body, called a bed, supports a motor-driven headstock at one end and a sliding tailstock at the other. Lathes can make such parts as chair or stair rail spindles, called "between centers turning," or bowls and other objects when secured to just the headstock, often referred to as outboard turning.

Lathes are classified by their maximum turning diameter, called the swing, and by the maximum distance between the headstock and tailstock centers.

Mounting a Blank

Aspiring woodturners should always get hands-on instruction, but the basics of mounting a workpiece are easy to grasp. First, mark the center point on each end of the blank. Press one end onto the spurs of the drive center, slide the tailstock against the other end and tighten and lock the tailstock.

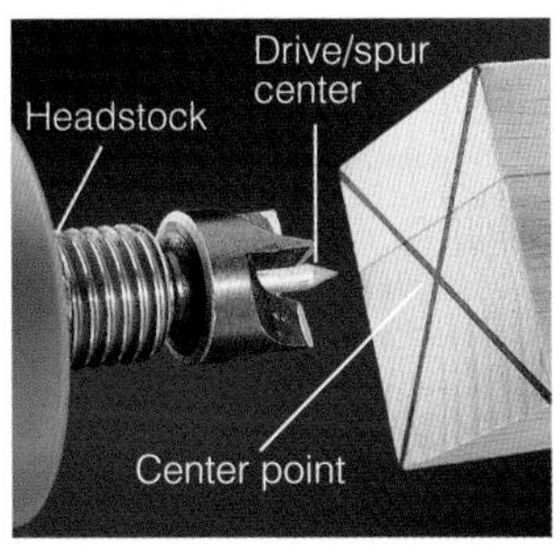

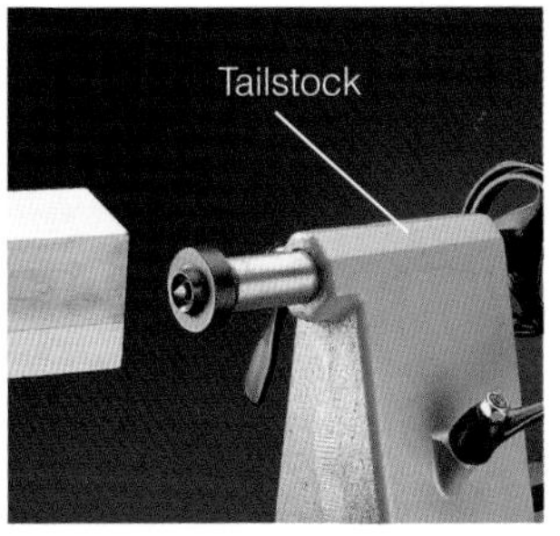

Turning Tools

Different turning tools produce different textures and details. Better-grade tools feature blades made of high-speed steel so they can withstand friction and heat without losing their ability to hold an edge.

Parting tool. This narrow double-bevel tool cuts directly into the wood, creating a narrow groove. It cuts very quickly, so use light pressure.

Skew. This chisel has a slightly angled double-bevel edge that makes fine cuts to smooth a roughed-out blank or to shape a bead.

Roughing gouge. With a heavy body and a thick curved edge, this gouge removes wood rapidly to get the rough blank close to its finished size or shape.

Small gouge. This is a narrower, more delicate gouge typically used for making inside curves and for bowl turning.

Basic Steps

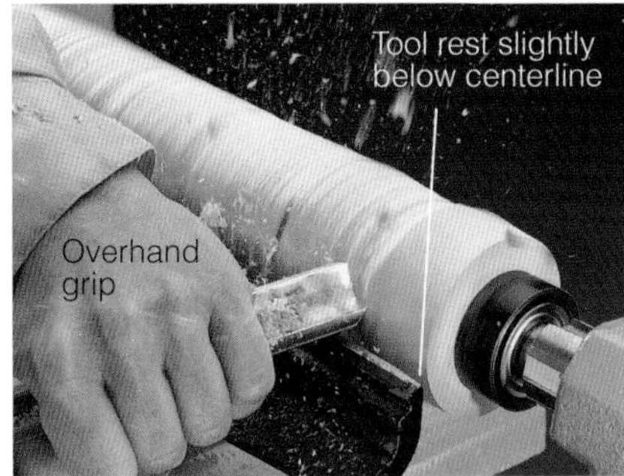

Rough rounding. You can precut square corners or knock them off with a roughing gouge. Hold gouge firmly and glide it along tool rest, shaving the blank as you go.

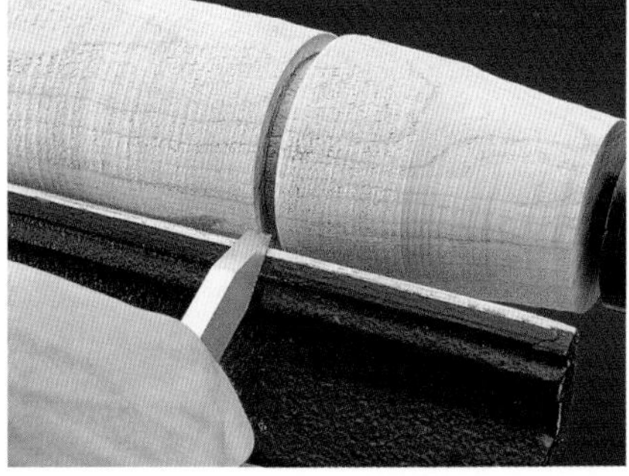

Parting. Use the parting tool to cut into the blank to specific diameters, creating a built-in index you can follow as you remove surrounding material.

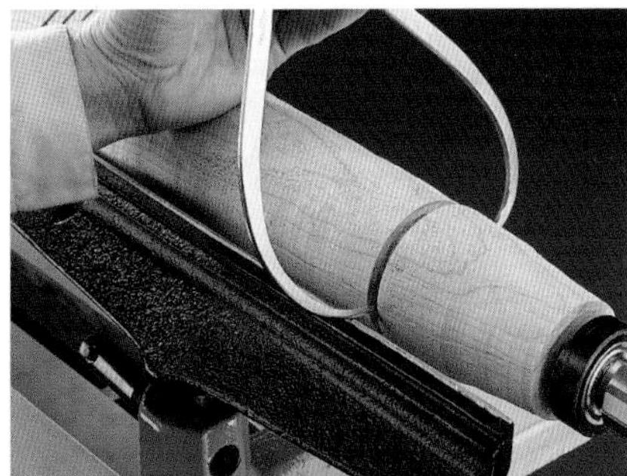

Measuring. Set a caliper from a full-scale drawing or a prototype piece and use it to check diameters along the blank as you work.

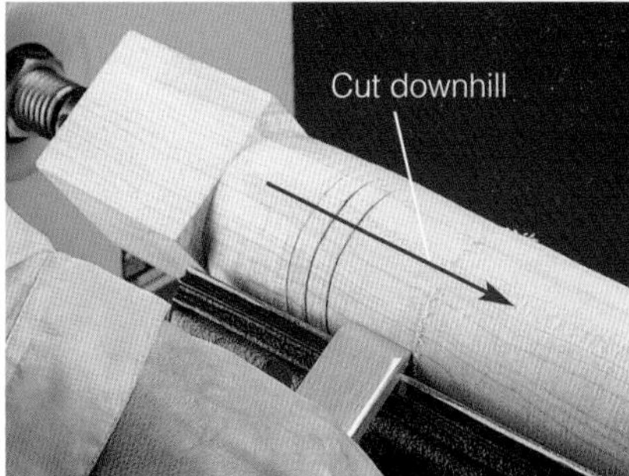

Shaping. Skew chisels can make scraping cuts to smooth and shape the blank. For tapered shapes, work downhill with the grain, from fat end to thin.

Routers

Dadoes 434
Rabbets 435
Router Jigs 445

No portable tool offers more versatility for detail work and for applying finishing touches than a router. These simple tools—basically just a height-adjustable motor, a base with handles and a collet to hold the bit—can cut all kinds of joinery, including dadoes and dovetails, and they can mill decorative details on the face or edge of a board. Routers can also cut complex shapes repeatedly and precisely with help from a pattern template.

Actually, the bits or cutters provide the versatility; the router itself simply spins them at 20,000 or more rpm and lets you control the depth and direction of cut. Start with a lightweight, easy-to-control router that accommodates 1/4-in. shank bits, then move up to a larger model.

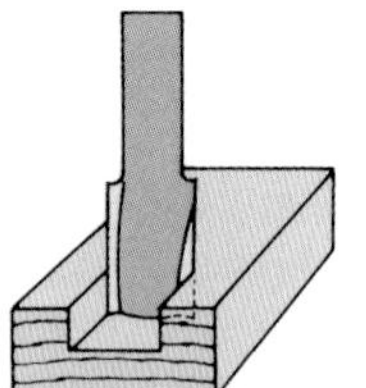

Straight. These bits cut flat grooves, dadoes, rabbets and other joinery details.

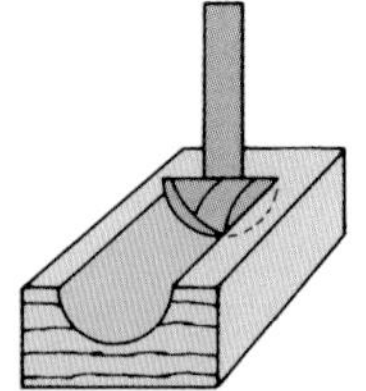

Grooving. Grooving bits cut flutes and other decorative shapes into the face of a board.

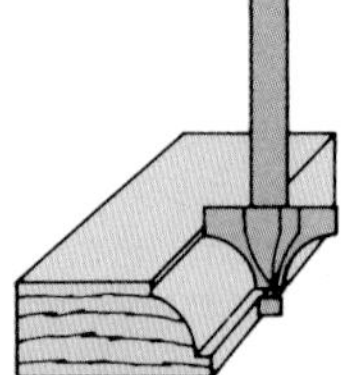

Edging. Edging bits are for machining a rounded, beveled or decorative profile on a board's edge.

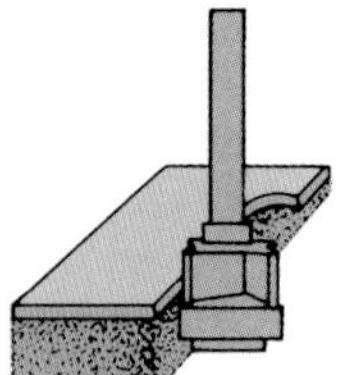

Trimming. Use these on trimming surfaces or edges flush with a substrate or template.

Basics

Direction of cut. Like most rotary-type cutting tools, routers are designed to cut against the direction of feed. That is, the bit should rotate against the workpiece edge in a direction opposite the movement of the router itself. For an edge facing you, this means moving the tool from left to right. For routing around the entire outside edge of a workpiece, the router should travel counterclockwise. For routing inside edges, as on the frame shown here, move the tool in a clockwise direction.

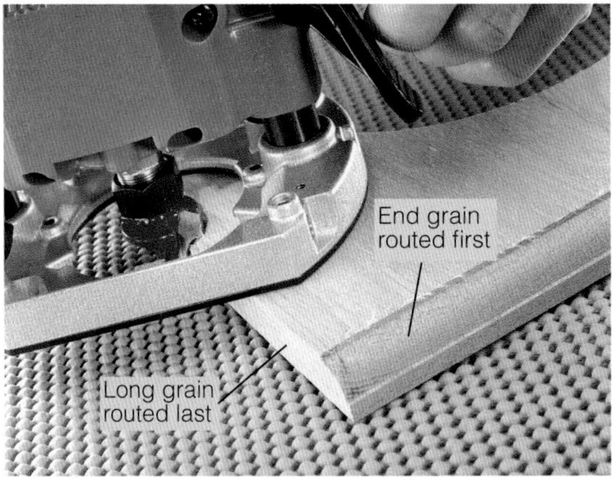

End grain. When edge-routing the perimeter of a piece of solid wood, two edges will feature long grain and two will have end grain. The bit is most likely to splinter the wood at the corner where end grain transitions to long grain. To prevent this, rout end-grain edges first; minor tear-out at corners will be removed as you rout the long-grain edges.

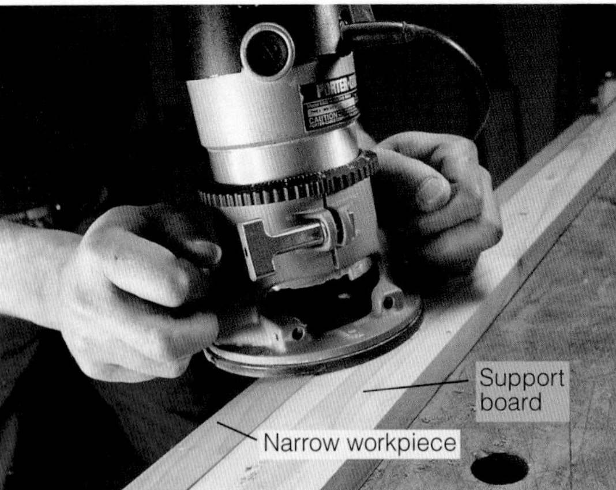

Narrow stock. Stable support of the router base is essential for accurate cuts. This isn't a problem when you're routing the face or edge of a wide board, but with narrow workpieces the small area of contact can easily allow the base to tilt or wobble, perhaps ruining the cut. You can improve your odds by fastening a scrap board of the same thickness behind the workpiece, as shown here. For improved safety and accuracy, fasten stop blocks at the ends to keep the workpiece from shifting.

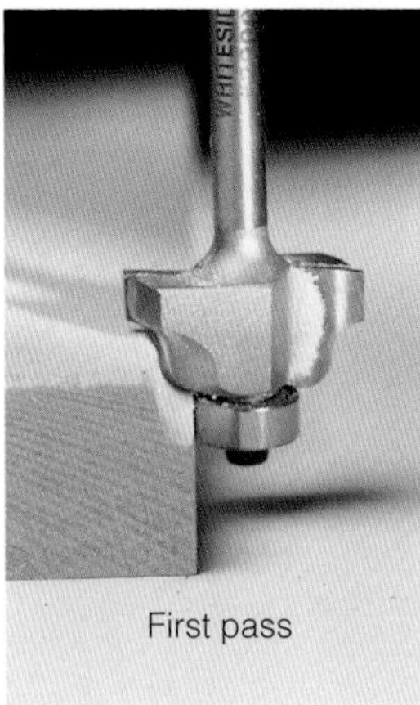

Deep cuts. Whether due to an underpowered router, a hard workpiece or a large-diameter cutter, some routing situations call for making cuts in stages. Because any taper in a router bit typically goes from narrow at the tip to wider near the shank (dovetail bits are a notable exception), you can work your way down, using a shallow cut to make the first pass or two, then resetting the cutting depth to make a final pass. Not only is this easier on your router motor, but it tends to leave a smoother finish on the cut.

Making Moldings

With the wide variety of edge-forming bits available, you can use a router to make your own moldings. Most shaping bits have a guide bearing that rides along the edge of the workpiece creating a consistent profile.

1 Start by clamping a wide workpiece to your workbench and routing the profile along one edge. It's likely the finished molding will be narrower, but leaving the board wide for now helps support the router base.

2 After you rout the edge profile, use the tablesaw and a push stick to rip the narrow molding from the board. Repeat the process to make as many moldings as the board can safely yield.

Cutting Dadoes

For dadoes and other cuts that require a router guide, the setup often takes longer than the actual routing. This simple T-shaped jig guarantees a 90° angle and lets you quickly align its precut dado with layout marks on the workpiece.

1 Glue and screw the crossbar perpendicular to the body of the jig, make a test cut at the correct routing depth, then align the jig's dado with the marks on your workpiece and clamp it in place.

2 Start the cut at the top of the jig, at the crossbar, and proceed into the workpiece. Keep firm, uniform pressure against the guide edge so the router doesn't stray.

Router Tables

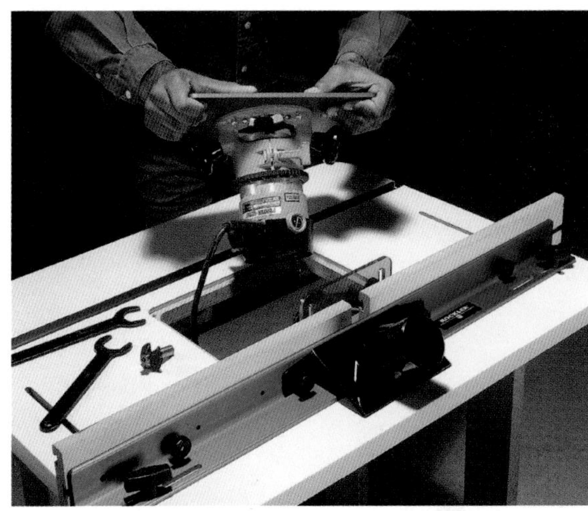

By suspending a router upside down from a tabletop, you create a mini-shaper that can add efficiency and precision to your projects and can let you work with larger cutters that you can't use freehand. A simple homemade version can be nothing more than a piece of plywood with a hole in it, but fancier varieties, either store-bought or built in your shop, feature insert plates, adjustable fences and dust collection.

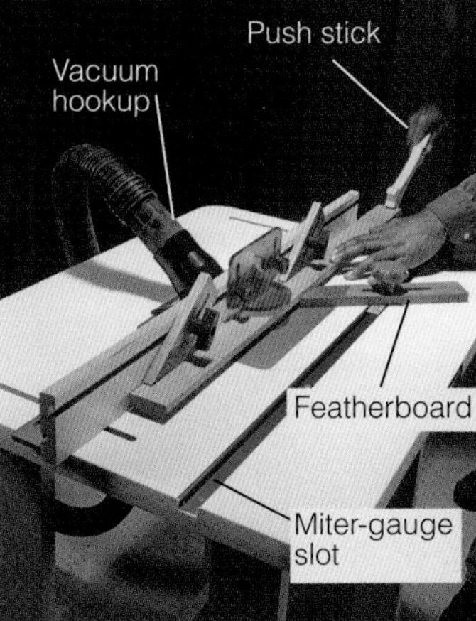

Router tables are ideal for machining narrow stock or other material that would be difficult or time-consuming to rout freehand. An array of basic safety devices—cutter guard, hold-downs and featherboards—keep your hands safe and the material tracking straight. This version also features a miter-gauge slot and a vacuum hookup.

Shop Smart

Plunge or Fixed Base?

Apart from horsepower ratings, the most significant difference you'll find in router designs is the type of base that holds the motor. The traditional fixed-base router (far right in photo) offers adjustment of the cutting depth, but once you have the desired setting, you keep the motor position locked during use. A plunge router (left in photo) supports the motor on a pair of spring-loaded steel rods that allow you to start the motor, then lower, or plunge, the bit straight down to a preset depth. This feature is useful for routing furniture mortises and other joinery details, but isn't used much for general routing work. Some manufacturers offer router kits that contain a motor and one of each base.

Sanders

Scribing 42
Sanding 48
Hang a Door Slab 383

Belt Sanders

A belt sander is the fastest portable sander around. It's ideal for removing stock quickly, flattening large panels and leveling glue joints. However, the aggressive action requires care to avoid gouging the workpiece or sanding through veneer. They create a lot of dust, and most newer versions have dust collection bags or ports that you can hook up to a shop vacuum. A variable-speed unit with a 3 x 21-in. belt size is a good choice for a home workshop.

Reshaping cabinet frames to fit tightly against irregular walls is a perfect application for a belt sander. After scribing the line onto the frame, turn the cabinet on its back and shape the edge with the sander.

Finishing Sanders

Finishing sanders use either a circular or straight-line pad motion to sand surfaces. They provide slower, more controllable stock removal than a belt sander, with far less cross-grain scratching. This is especially important for sanding veneered surfaces or hardwood plywood, and also helps prepare surfaces for finishing. Various models accept a quarter-sheet or a half-sheet of sandpaper.

Detail Sanders

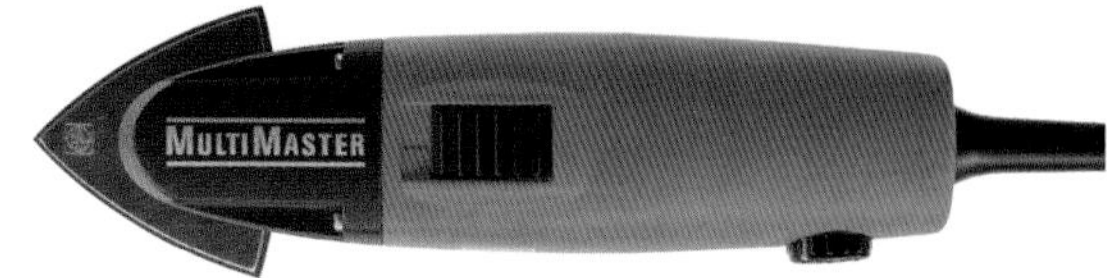

When you're building a woodworking project and can sand parts before assembly, standard finishing sanders work fine, but refinishing an existing piece of furniture often means getting into corners and other tight spaces. For those situations, a detail sander can access areas no other sander can reach and provide faster results than hand sanding. Most detail sanders have a triangular-shaped head that accepts interchangeable precut sandpaper. Some manufacturers offer accessories that let you adapt the sander for scraping or cutting tasks. A few versions feature assorted contoured pads for sanding moldings and curved edges.

Random-orbit Sanders

The random-orbit sander is the closest thing to a do-it-all sanding tool. This versatile machine combines a spinning disc with an orbital action, allowing it to remove material quickly with coarse abrasive discs but provide a smooth, swirl-free finish with fine abrasives. Other welcome features include quick-change sanding discs (with either hook-and-loop fastening or a pressure-sensitive adhesive backing) and dust pickup directly through ports in the sanding pad. Two-handed versions tend to have larger 6-in.-dia. sanding pads and more powerful motors; a palm-grip style (shown above) features a 5-in.-dia. pad and is designed for one-handed use.

Random-orbit sanders excel at eliminating cross-grain scratches, an essential feature when you're working with assembled cabinets or furniture. Glue joints on cabinet face frames can be leveled quickly without leaving unsightly marks.

Stationary Sanders

As versatile as portable sanders are, they aren't very user-friendly or efficient for sanding very large or small parts or for precisely shaping workpieces. In those situations, it's easier to bring the part to the tool than vice versa, which means using a stationary sanding machine designed for home shop use.

Belt-disc Sanders

These machines combine a large belt sander with a large disc sander, both driven simultaneously by the same motor. Each has a cast-iron table to support the workpiece, and the belt sander adjusts from a vertical to horizontal orientation to suit the work you're doing. Use with a shop vacuum or dust collector; you'll need it.

Spindle Sanders

Curved contours are often cut with a bandsaw or a jigsaw, both of which leave workpiece edges a little rough. Getting good results by hand sanding is difficult and time consuming, but a spindle sander offers good sanding control and much faster cleanup. To reduce visible scratches, the spindle oscillates up and down while rotating.

Drum Sanders

Gluing up wide panels of solid boards typically creates a slightly uneven surface with prominent glue joints and maybe even a slight cup or wave. A drum sander features a power-feed conveyor that guides the panel under a metal drum lined with a wide abrasive strip, rendering it smooth and flat. Dust collection is a must with these sanders.

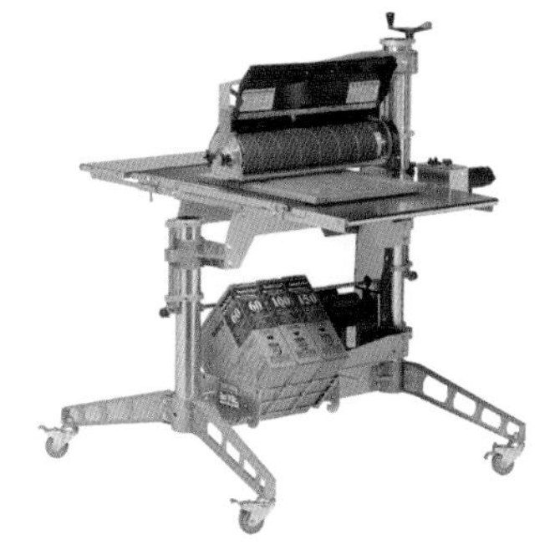

Power Hand Planers

As the name implies, power hand planers do what hand planes do, but with the help of a motor and high-speed rotating cutterhead. Using either straight jointer-type knives or a spiral cutter, a power planer can take off as much as 1/8 in. (3 mm) of material in a single pass. These tools are indispensable for trimming large doors.

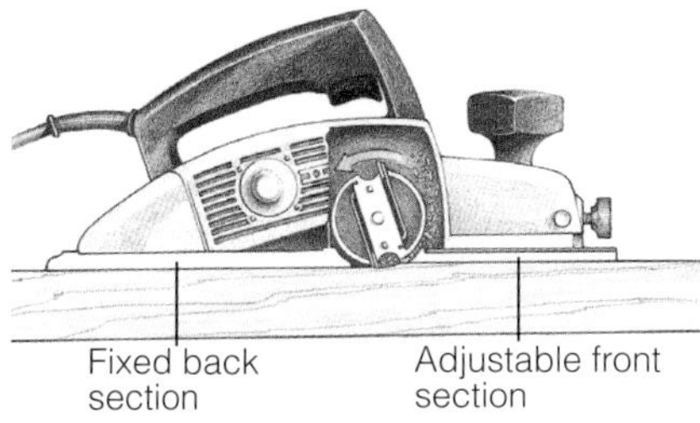

How they work. Like a hand plane, a power planer rides on a shoe or sole plate, but in this case, the shoe is split into a fixed rear section and a movable front section. An adjustment knob changes the front shoe's elevation, creating an offset from the rear shoe (and the cutterhead) to control the depth of cut.

Scribing. Though it can't follow the curved contours possible with a belt sander, a power planer will quickly trim excess material from a cabinet frame so it fits properly against a wall.

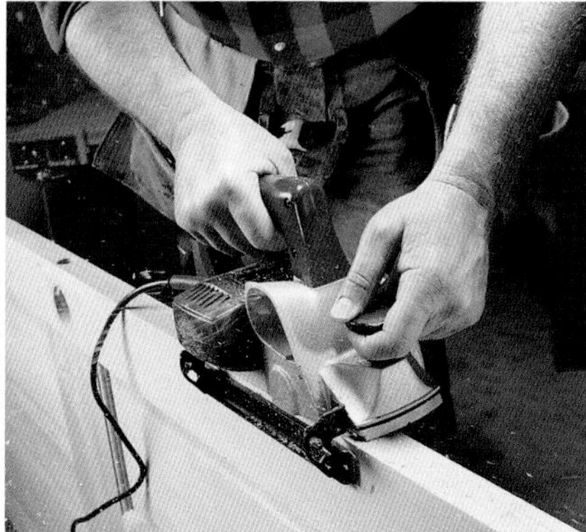

Beveling. An adjustable fence lets you tilt the plane for cutting beveled edges. This is commonly done on entry doors to provide the necessary clearance for the door to close against the jamb.

Leveling. A power planer can quickly and accurately trim unevenly aligned joists to create a flat base for installing ceiling or flooring materials.

Caution: Use ear, eye and respiratory protection.

Rotary Tools

Wood Chisels 36
Sharpening 46
Removing Stubborn Bolts 80

As a rule, power tools have three virtues—muscle, precision and speed. Most rotary tools can lay claim to only the last, but speed is enough to make these compact tools compensate for their shortcomings. Shaped like a fat-handled screwdriver with a collet at one end, rotary tools are like routers in that they get their versatility mostly from the cutters and bits they spin. Some actually have attachable bases that let them function like a router, but for most tasks they are used freehand or in a base that holds them with the business end up. The collet accepts rotary files, grinding wheels, sanding drums, cutoff wheels and other accessories. Their small scale lets them get in places that are off-limits to most power tools. Some drive flex-shaft accessories that can get into even tighter spaces.

Rotary tools do come in variable-speed versions, but most of their work gets done at very high speeds—around 30,000 rpm is typical. It's the high-speed rotation, not horsepower, that gets the job done, so don't force the tool with heavy pressure.

Grind. Grinding wheels and stones remove metal quickly in situations where a hand file might fit but its progress would be slow. Here the opening in a strike plate is enlarged so the latch will align properly.

Engrave. Marking items for identification is easily done with an engraving bit. Different engraving tips are available for different materials, such as metal, plastic and wood.

Cut. A stripped bolt head, its corners rounded off, can be salvaged by cutting a slot for a screwdriver. If necessary, the wheel could cut all the way through the bolt.

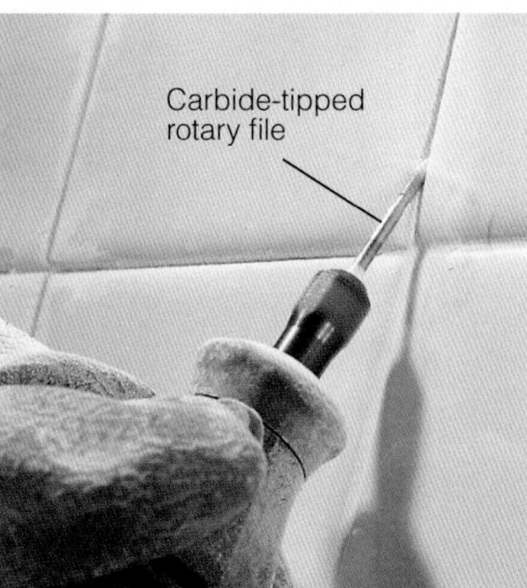

Remove. Removing old tile grout is a tedious chore done by hand, but a rotary tool with a carbide-tipped file does it quickly. Keep the bit at a low angle to the surface and work downward.

Spiral Saws

The spiral saw is a close cousin to the rotary tool. The collet size and high-speed rotation are similar, but spiral saws tend to have larger motors and a built-in base. They're designed to be used more like a router—with the base pressed or supported against a flat work surface. With fewer bit types available, this tool isn't designed to have the versatility of a rotary tool. In fact, they are often called cutout tools because of the task they excel most at—making cutouts in drywall, cement backer board, tile and other materials used to cover walls and ceilings.

Drywall. Cutouts for electrical boxes don't have to be marked precisely. Just use an X to designate the box location, set the drywall loosely in place and drive a few screws to hold it. Find the outer box edge and rout counterclockwise around it.

Paneling. For freehand cutting in paneling, mark the outline of the cutout and make a plunge cut to start. Then follow the outline, making a full stop at each turn to keep the corners crisp.

Bench Grinders

Spend a few years tackling home-improvement projects and your assortment of chisels, planes and other cutting tools is likely to include a few battered edges. Those that are just slightly dull can be sharpened with a few strokes on a whetstone, but if any are severely worn, you'll want to renew them with a bench grinder. Bench grinders are compact, affordable and nearly indispensable when it comes to keeping a sharp edge on tools. They'll sharpen chisels, plane irons, scissors—just about any hand tool that cuts—plus mower blades, drill bits and other accessories.

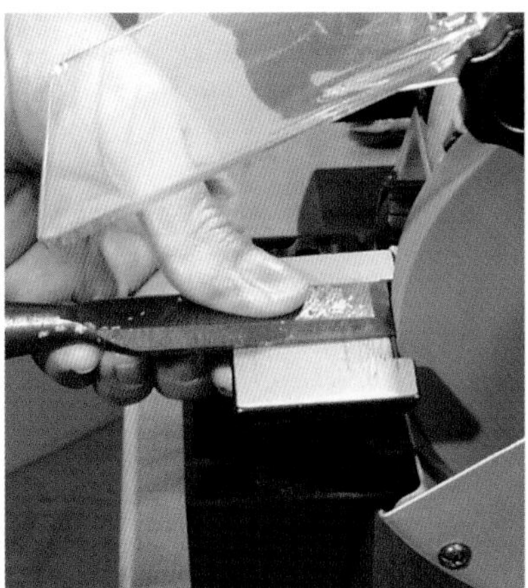

Tool rest position. Begin by setting the tool rest close to the grinding wheel and as squarely as possible to the wheel edge. Apply light pressure to grind off nicks and leave a square, blunt edge on the tool.

Quenching. Dunk the blade in water every two passes to prevent heat buildup near the edge. A straw- or bluish-colored area on the bevel means you've overheated the chisel and ruined its ability to hold an edge.

Most bench grinders work at speeds exceeding 3,000 rpm, faster than the ideal speed for regrinding tools. At that high speed, the biggest risk is overheating the tool edge to the point that it loses its ability to hold a sharp edge. Unless it's heat-treated again (not a task for beginners), the tool's steel will soften and never hold its edge as well again. But if you exercise care, you can learn to use the grinder quickly and efficiently without damaging any tools. Practice on expendable tools until you get the hang of it.

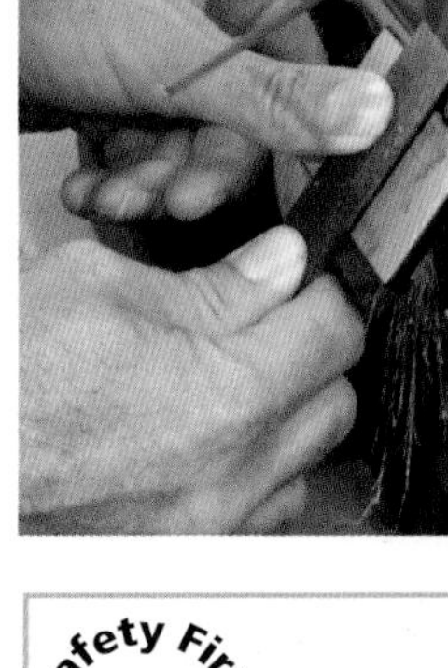

Tool rest angle. Reset the tool rest to match the tool's bevel angle (typically 25° to 30° for chisels) and make light passes, moving the tool from side to side. Check often to ensure a square edge.

Grinder Reminders

They may not have sharp teeth, but bench grinders should be used with respect. Here are a few rules to observe:

- Always wear safety glasses. There will be sparks (hot fragments of metal) flying, and the wheel itself can shatter and disintegrate.
- Don't wear loose clothing, unrestrained long hair, gloves or anything else that might catch on the wheel.
- To reduce risk of wheel failure, never install a grinding wheel that isn't rated for the speed of your grinder or has been dropped.
- Inspect the wheels before each use and stand to the side when starting the machine.
- Never grind on the side of the wheel, only the edge.
- Unplug the tool when it's not in use.

Grinding Wheels

Chances are any bench grinder you buy will come equipped with gray aluminum-oxide grinding wheels, probably medium and coarse. A coarse wheel (about 36 grit) will grind very aggressively but also will run slightly cooler. A medium- or fine-grit wheel will remove material more slowly and leave a smoother surface on the tool, but will run slightly hotter. Fine-grit wheels clog with metal particles sooner, a condition known as glazing, that increases the risk of burning tool edges. A 100-grit wheel is a good compromise for sharpening woodworking tools; you'll get a reasonably fine surface but a lower risk of edge-burning than a finer wheel would produce.

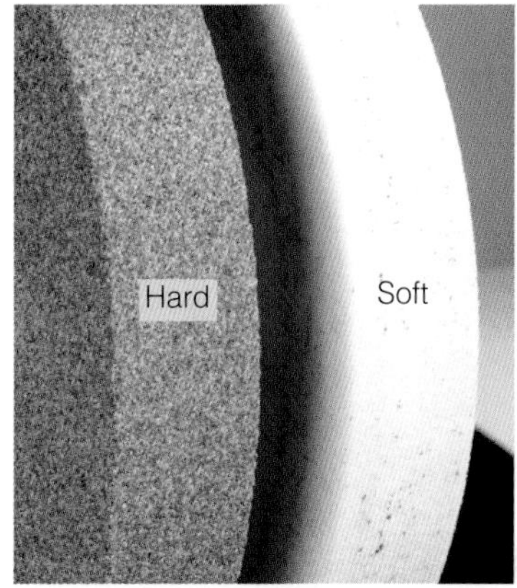

Types. Apart from the hard (gray) variety of aluminum-oxide grinding wheels, a softer grade (white, or vitrified) offers an advantage for tool sharpening. These wheels have an edge that breaks away faster, exposing fresh cutting grains, and they run cooler.

Dressing. While grinding wheels are reshaping other materials, they are being deformed themselves and becoming loaded with metal particles. A wheel dresser has a hardened steel head that cleans and reshapes the wheel edge so it can perform at its best.

Jointers

For most woodworking projects, accurate work starts with having lumber that's flat, straight and milled exactly to the correct size. Of course, wood rarely comes from the lumberyard in such pristine shape. Those crooked edges and warped boards have to be remilled to straighten them, and a jointer is the first tool in that process.

The jointer bed is actually two separate tables supported on a common base, with the cutterhead nesting between them. Except for periodic adjustments when new knives are installed, the outfeed table stays at a fixed height, flush with the top of the cutterhead, while the infeed table travels up and down to change the depth of cut. The tables remain parallel but offset in height. As the board travels past the cutterhead, its newly milled edge is supported by the outfeed table.

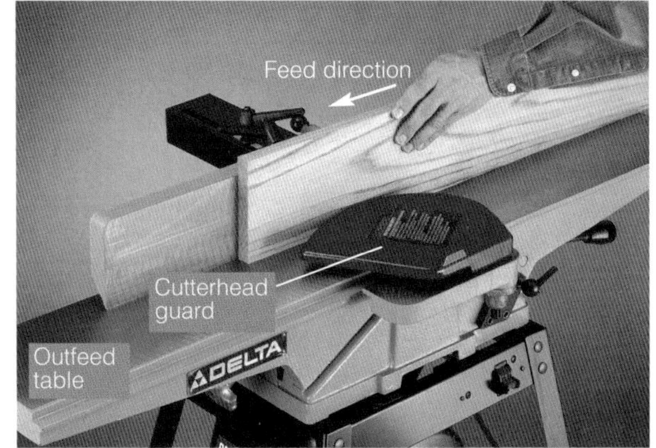

The basics. Precision from the jointer depends on having accurate settings and applying firm pressure to keep the workpiece pressed against the tables and the fence. As the board passes over the cutterhead, gradually shift the pressure to the outfeed table to ensure a consistent cut. The machine shown here has a 6-in.-wide (15-cm-wide) cutterhead, a good size for most home workshops.

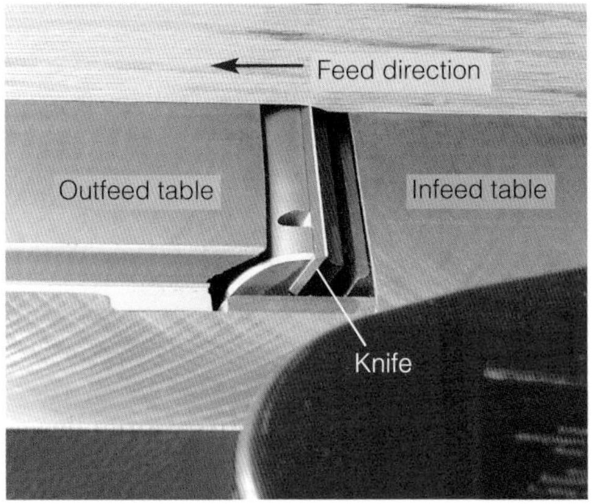

Set infeed table. Set the infeed table height according to the material and conditions. Edge-jointing, shown here, allows deeper cuts because the material is relatively narrow, but stay within a range of 1/32 to 1/16 in. (0.75 to 1.5 mm) for best results. Heavier cuts tend to produce more tear-out and a rougher surface. When jointing the wide face of a board, you may have to make shallower cuts (1/32 in./0.75 mm or less) to avoid overloading the motor. Whenever possible, try to feed the board with the edge's grain direction pointing back toward the infeed table.

Thickness Planers

The thickness planer is partner to the jointer in producing flat, uniform boards for your projects, but it works a little differently. The table is much shorter and sits underneath the cutterhead, so material is removed from the top surface of the board. When a board is fed into the machine, feed rollers propel it slowly forward and under the cutterhead. In the process, the board is milled smooth and thinner, with the faces exactly parallel.

Until a few decades ago, thickness planers were expensive, heavy industrial machines that seldom found their way into a home workshop. Since then, smaller versions and even portable models have become widely available and affordable. Most portable units feature cutterhead widths of about 12 in. (30 cm) and can accept material up to 6 in. thick (15 cm). They also have fixed cutterheads and height-adjustable tables.

The basics. Thickness planers are noisy and produce a lot of chips, but they are simple to use. Typically, a hand crank adjusts the thickness by moving the cutterhead assembly on portable models or the table on larger stationary planers. When the scale indicates the correct setting, you feed the board into the machine's power rollers, which are concealed alongside the cutterhead.

Snipe. Snipe is a dip or shallow trough that gets cut across the ends of a board as it travels through a thickness planer. On portable models, snipe is caused by a slight tilt in the cutterhead when only one of the feed rollers is contacting the workpiece, which is why it occurs only at the board's ends. Some snipe is unavoidable, but you can reduce it by feeding boards through the planer in a continuous "train," with the ends butted together. This helps keep the cutterhead assembly stable and level.

Dust Collection

It's not uncommon for some woodworkers to buy a dozen tools that generate dust before they ever think about buying one to collect it, but those who make dust management a priority will find their shops cleaner and themselves breathing easier.

For reasons involving workers' health, fire safety and insurance coverage, dust management has long been an essential part of nearly every commercial woodworking facility. Home-shop woodworkers often employ makeshift or even no solutions, even though they face the same risks as their professional counterparts. Accumulated dust and shavings not only constitute a fire hazard, but create slippery floors that make workshop falls and other accidents more likely. Worse still, the fine dust that lingers airborne in a shop has been reliably identified as a factor in nasal cancer. Even without those severe health risks, however, wood dust is a nuisance that can meander into a ventilation system and settle throughout an entire home.

It doesn't take a complicated or expensive system to manage woodshop dust, but it does require a diversified strategy. That's because there isn't just one kind of wood dust. Planers and jointers create mostly large shavings that quickly pile up if they aren't collected. Tablesaws and routers generate a mix of small shavings and coarse dust, while sanders can send up plumes of fine dust that will stay airborne for hours, or until you breathe them in. Plan your dust control around the amount and type of woodworking you do.

Shop Vacuums

Shop vacuums provide an affordable and reasonably effective means of capturing limited amounts of wood dust. They can be moved around the shop to where you're working, but the loud operating noise can be bothersome.

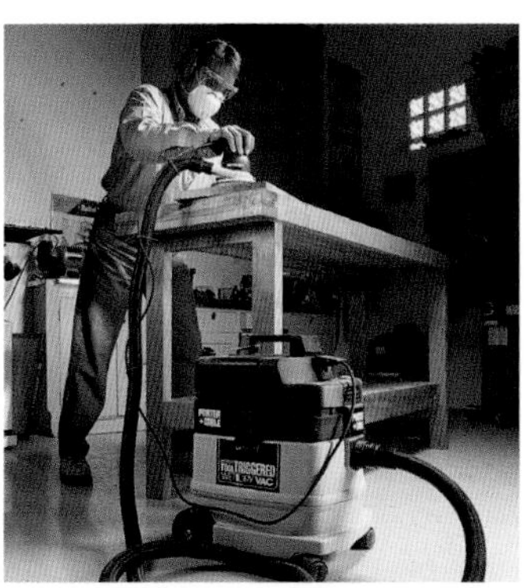

Direct connect. Many portable power tools now come with built-in dust collection ports. Pair one up with a tool-activated shop vacuum and the dust collection starts automatically when you turn on the tool. This is an ideal setup for belt and finishing sanders.

Open port. A quick-adapt feature lets a shop vacuum cover an entire shop. Here a common plastic reducer plumbing coupling is fitted with a magnet and connected to a vacuum hose. It will mount instantly to any machine with a steel or cast-iron table.

Air Scrubbers

Air scrubbers target the fine dust that tends to stay afloat. Flow is rated in cubic feet per minute (cfm). The blower should be able to recirculate the air in the shop at least every 10 minutes.

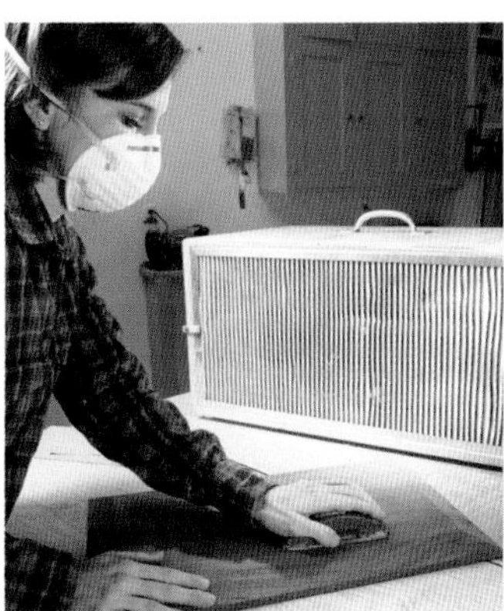

Bench-top scrubbers. For projects that involve working in one spot for an extended period, bench-top air cleaners filter dust from the air before it circulates into the shop. If the dust generation is not localized, use ceiling-mounted air cleaners instead.

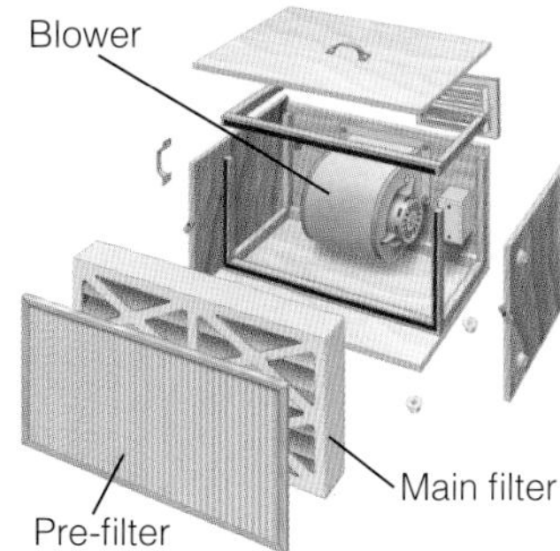

How they're made. Whether manufactured or shop-built, air scrubbers typically feature an airtight housing that encloses a blower fan and motor. On the intake face, an inexpensive pre-filter and a finer main filter scrub the incoming air, which is then exhausted through the blower.

Ducted Systems

Also called source capture systems because they are ducted directly to machines, these large built-in vacuum systems use a network of branch ducts to convey dust-laden air to a central fan and filter.

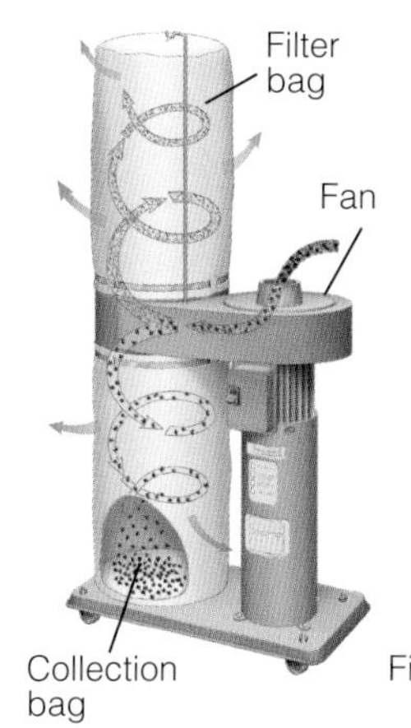

Single-stage collectors. This is the simplest form of ducted dust collector. It can be hooked temporarily to just one machine at a time or permanently to a fixed central duct that branches off to several machines, each controlled by a separate blast gate. The airstream and its entire contents travel through the impeller fan and into a collection bag, where the heavier particles drop to the bottom.

Cyclonic collectors. Also called a two-stage system, a cyclonic collector pulls the contaminated airstream into a conical drum, where it slows to allow large particles to drop into a bin. The air flow then continues through the fan and a filter.

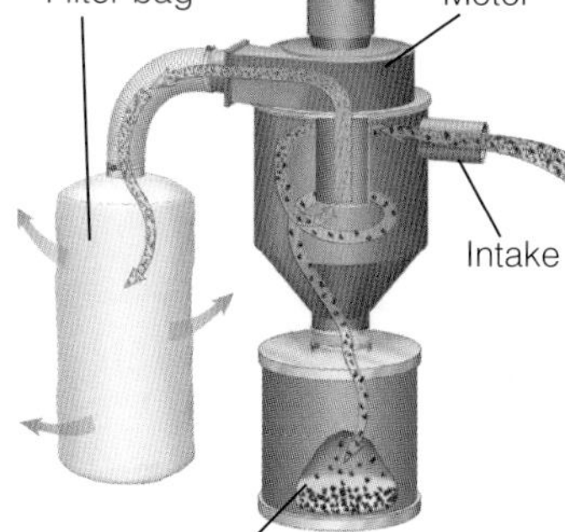

Air Compressors and Tools

AIr Nailers 389

If all they did was blow dust off of a project before you applied the finish, air compressors would still be worth the cost. Fortunately, these machines offer far more versatility than that. They drive pneumatic staplers and nailers of every variety, spray finishes, power vacuum veneering systems and even drive tools, such as drills, sanders and impact wrenches.

Although pump types vary, the basic anatomy and function of an air compressor is fairly consistent from model to model. A power source—either an electric motor or a gasoline engine—drives a pump that compresses air into a holding tank. The maximum pressure for standard units is about 125 pounds per square inch (psi). Most compressors have a pressure-activated switch that turns the motor on as soon as the pressure drops to a prescribed level. The pump will run until the upper threshold is reached again, then automatically shut off or divert the air out through a relief valve. Electric-powered air compressors are more convenient for shop and home use. Tank sizes may range from portable 2-gal. (7.5 l) units to 60-gal. (225 l) floor models.

Compressors

Unless you spray a lot of finishes or have multiple air tools running simultaneously, you can probably get by with a portable compressor. The unit should be light enough to hand-carry or be fitted with wheels.

Oil-less. A relatively recent development, oil-less compressors have pumps that feature low-friction coating on the moving parts. They are subject to faster wear than oil-lubricated pumps, but for home workshop use, that only means a simple rebuild must be done every few years.

Oil lubricated. Oil lubrication lets these pumps last longer between rebuilds, but they do require oil changes and other regular maintenance. If you want to spray finishes, install an in-line filter to prevent oil contamination.

Nailers

Pneumatic fastening tools only recently became a staple (no pun intended) in the home workshop, but the speed and holding power they provide quickly makes them indispensable to an avid do-it-yourselfer. Always use great caution.

Brad and finish. These nailers shoot fine nails up to 2-1/2 in. long, making them ideal for installing door and window trim or for assembling woodworking projects. They're often sold in kits with small compressors.

Roofing. The repetitive nature of fastening roof shingles makes that task an ideal application for a pneumatic nailer. The nails are collated in coils to fit in a compact magazine. Roofing staplers are also available.

Framing. Worth renting if you've got a garage or addition project to frame, these large nailers have the power to drive nails up to 3-1/2 in. long. The nails are typically collated in strips.

The Right Size

Though labels on most air compressors clearly state the horsepower rating and tank size, a better indicator of a compressor's capacity is its air delivery rate, expressed both in standard cubic feet per minute (scfm) and pressure (psi). Your requirements will vary with the uses you plan for the tool. For example, a small brad nailer's intermittent bursts typically aren't as taxing as the nonstop pressure you would need to run a spray gun or a sander. To be on the safe side, check the air requirements on the tools you'll use most before you buy a compressor.

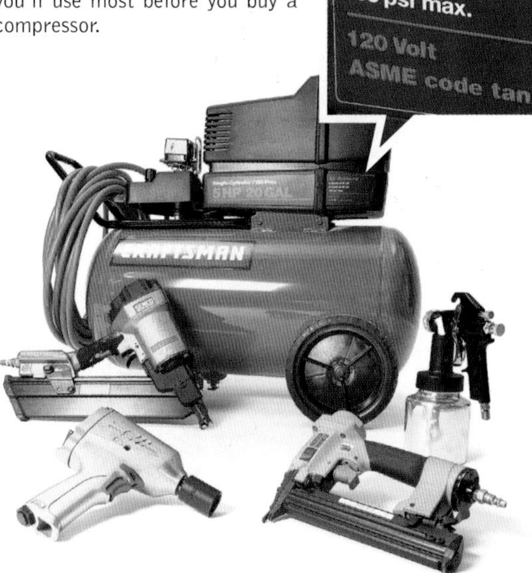

Fasteners & Adhesives

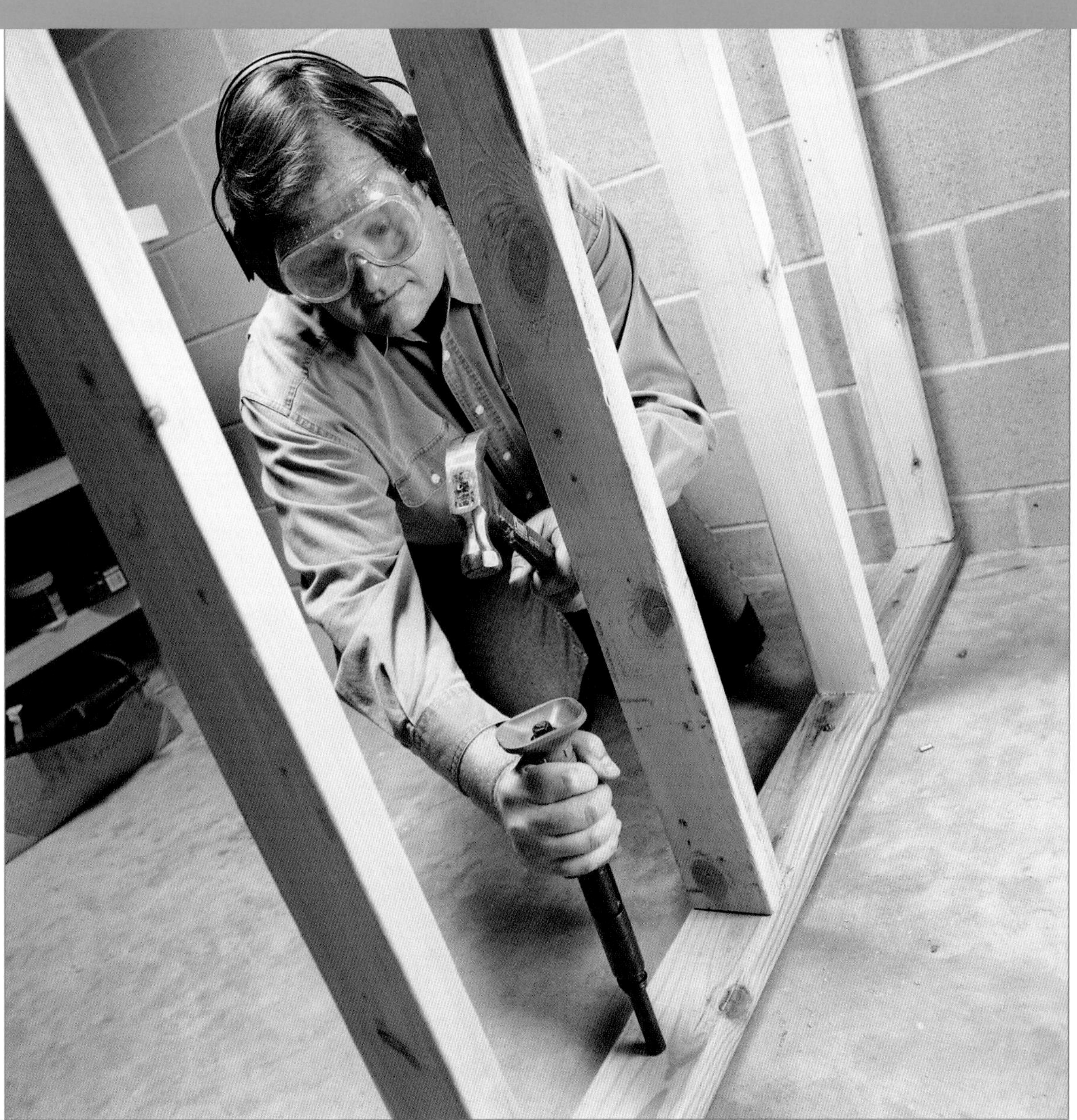

Nails

Hammers **24**
Deck Building **354**

The most widely used nail types are common and sinker nails, for their holding power, and finish nails, for their ability to hide. Most other nails are either variants of these or special-purpose fasteners with enhanced holding or penetrating power.

The length of most nail types can be designated by penny size—a term abbreviated with a small letter "d." Most nails come in a wide range of lengths and their shaft diameters increase with length. Common nails are available in lengths from 1 in. or 2d, to 6 in. or 60d (see illustration, lower right). The nail's diameter increases four times over that range.

Many special-purpose nail types, such as roofing nails or drywall nails, have only one diameter and vary only in length. Small wire brads and wire nails are sized in inches and by wire-gauge number. The higher the gauge number, the thinner the nail.

The approximate number of common nails in a 1-lb. (.45-kg) box is given along the bottom of the illustration below left. A box of finish nails of equivalent size will yield about 75 percent more nails.

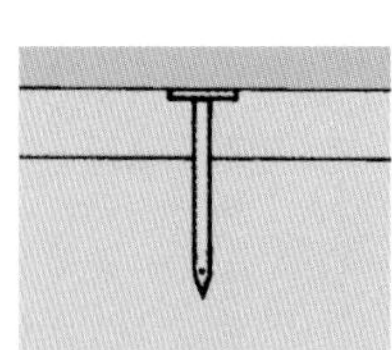

Thin to thick. Nail a thinner piece to a thicker one using a nail with a length three times the thickness of the thinner piece.

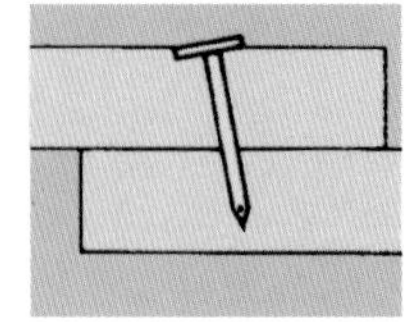

Equal thickness. If board thicknesses are the same, use a nail equal to the combined board thickness. Angle the nail to avoid piercing the other side.

Nail Types

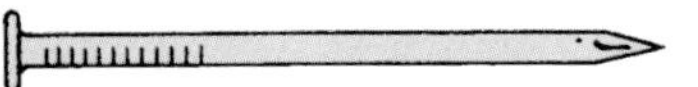

Common nail. For use in heavy construction and rough framing. Large head won't pull through.

Box nail. Lighter gauge version of the common nail. Used for general-purpose framing. May be galvanized.

Sinker. Coated to ease penetration and increase holding power. Used commonly for rough framing. Textured head reduces hammer slippage.

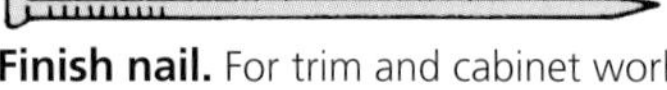

Finish nail. For trim and cabinet work where nailheads must be sunk and filled.

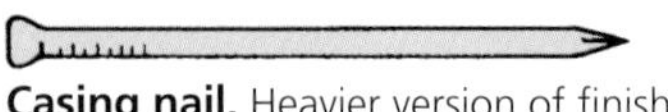

Casing nail. Heavier version of finish nail, with more holding power. Usually galvanized and used for door and exterior window trim.

Wire brad. For small, easily split moldings. Measured by gauge size and length.

Drywall nail. Tightly secures drywall panels with broad head and ringed or barbed shank. May be resin coated.

Ring-shank or annular-ring nail. Used for sheathing. Sharp-edged ridges on shank lock into wood, increasing holding power.

Spiral nail. Turns like a screw when driven. Harder to drive but has tremendous holding power.

Metal roofing nail. For corrugated metal and plastic roofing. Plastic or rubber washer under head seals hole.

Roofing nail. Extra-large head holds asphalt shingles and metal lathe in place. Galvanized.

Masonry nail. Made of hardened steel. Used for fastening to concrete and concrete block.

Double-headed or duplex nail. For temporary work, such as concrete forms. Upper head projects for easy removal.

Cut nail. A flat nail with blunt tip used for blind-nailing flooring and fastening to concrete.

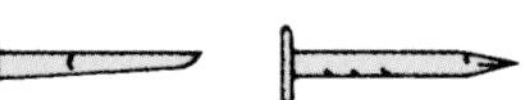

Tacks. Made in cut or round form. Used to fasten carpet or fabric to wood or similar light fastening jobs.

Staples. Made in many forms for varied uses, including carpet and wire fencing installation. Those with insulated shoulders are used for low-voltage wires.

Corrugated fastener. For securing light-duty miter and butt joints, such as on screens or picture frames. Driven across joint.

Pointed fastener. For strengthening joints—sharp prongs spread apart in wood to provide gripping strength.

Penny Nail Gauge

Penny or "d" are terms derived from the ancient coin called the denarious and are now used to indicate nail length.

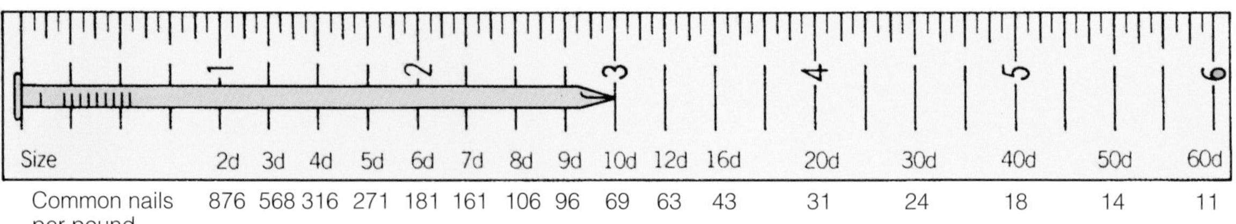

Size	2d	3d	4d	5d	6d	7d	8d	9d	10d	12d	16d	20d	30d	40d	50d	60d
Common nails per pound	876	568	316	271	181	161	106	96	69	63	43	31	24	18	14	11

Metal Hangers

Nail Composition

Using a nail made from the right material is just as important as using a nail that's the correct size.

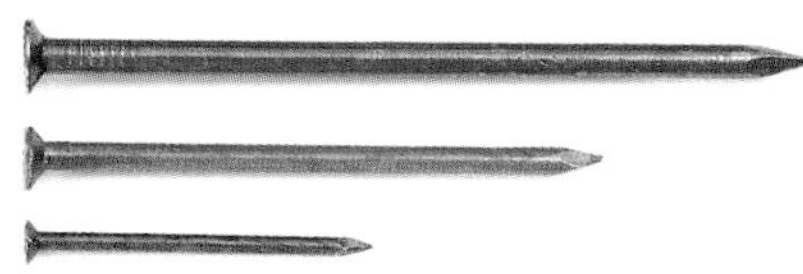

Steel. Use steel nails for framing and interior work where corrosion will not be a factor.

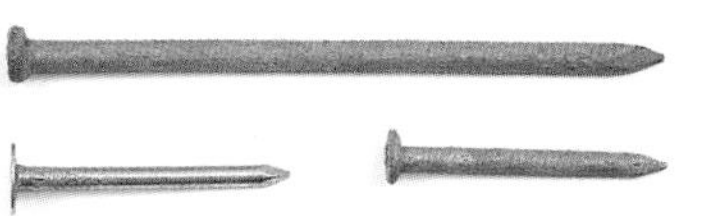

Galvanized. For exterior work and use in damp interior areas. Electroplated versions are smoother and less corrosion-resistant than chunkier hot-dipped versions.

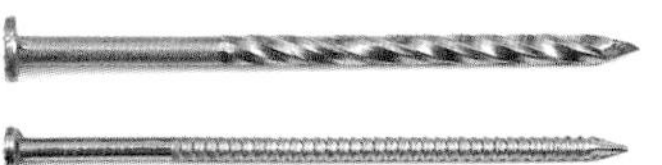

Stainless steel. Resists corrosion and staining of surrounding wood surfaces. Commonly used with cedar, redwood and treated wood.

Holding Power

Nail shanks with indented rings, spirals and grooves give wood fiber a better grip and are less likely to loosen. Hot-dipped galvanized and cement-coated nails also have extra holding power.

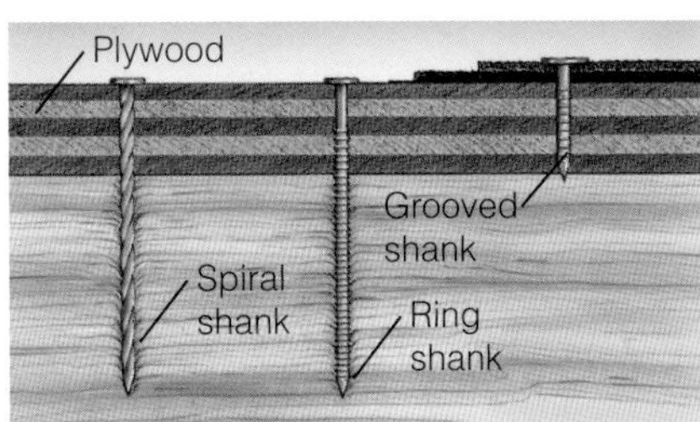

Handy Hints

Neater Nailing

Clinched. For extra holding power, drive extra-long nails through the wood, bend the nail tip with the hammer claw, then pound the nail over so it bites into the wood again, forming a J-shape.

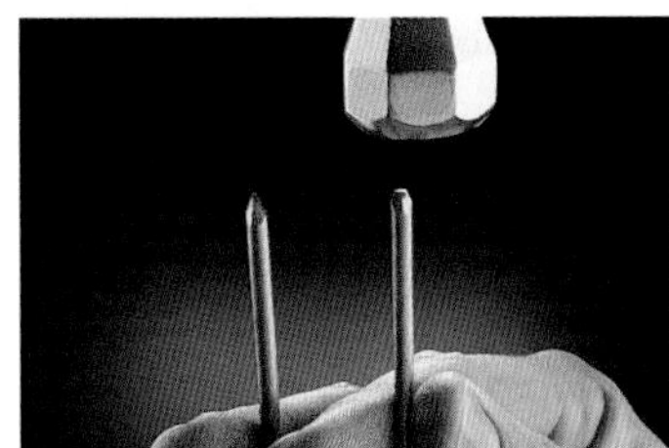

Blunted. Blunt nail tips crush their way through wood fibers, helping to avoid splitting lumber near the ends of boards. Tap the sharp point with a hammer to blunt the nail.

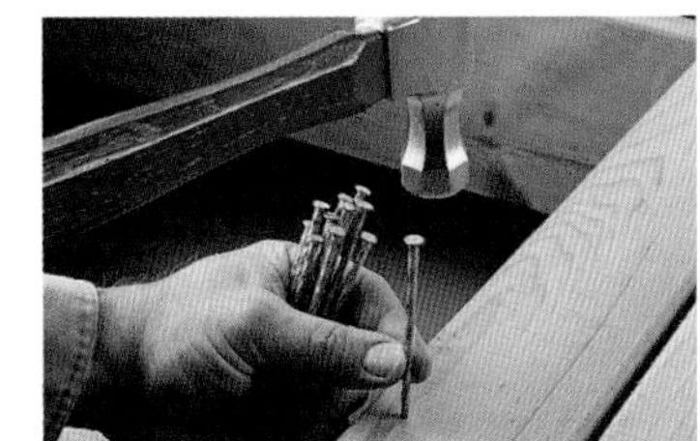

Driven. Arrange a fistful of nails, heads up, then use your pointer finger and thumb to roll them out and into position for nailing to increase your NPM (nails per minute).

Metal hangers are designed to solidly anchor framing members throughout your home, but are most commonly used to anchor joists in floors and decks. Properly installed, they make a joint far stronger than nails would alone.

Joist hangers come in many sizes to support different dimensional sizes of lumber and manufactured joists. Most hangers have a galvanized coating and will work indoors and out. Specialized hangers are available for unusual situations, such as building in a corrosive salt-air environment or joists that run at an angle.

When selecting and installing metal hangers, follow these rules:

- Install the largest hanger that fits Never use a 2x6 hanger on a 2x10 joist.
- Fill all holes in each hanger with the proper size joist-hanger nail.
- Don't reuse or modify joist hangers.

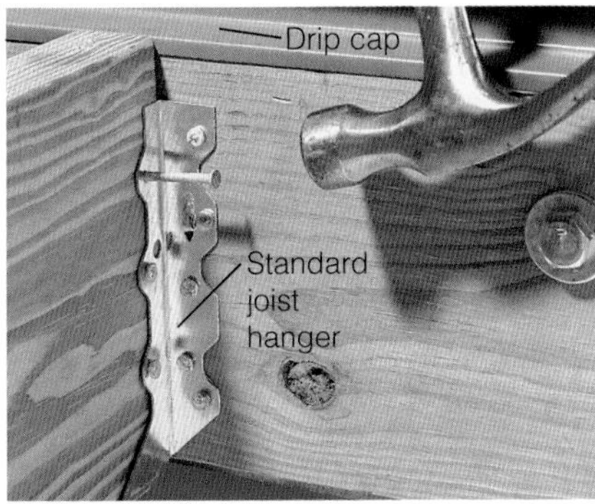

Standard. Secure standard joist hangers using 1-1/2-in.-galvanized joist-hanger nails. To protect fingers, hold nails with needle-nose pliers while starting them.

Double shear. For double-shear joist hangers, toenail 3-in. nails at a 45° angle through the hanger and joist, and into ledger board.

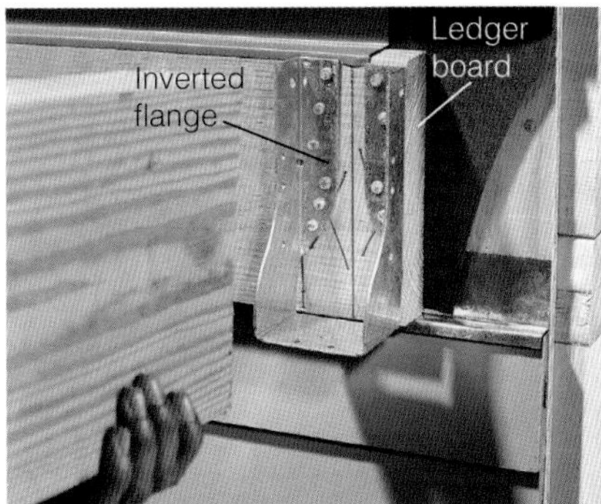

Inverted flanges. Use double or single versions to install joists at the end of the ledger board. Predrill holes to avoid splitting.

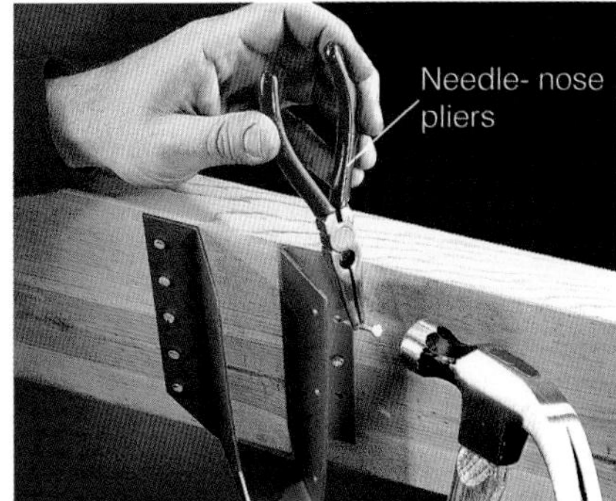

Angled. Specialized hangers, such as angled hangers, expand your options when designing the frame for your deck or floor.

Screws

Screwdrivers 29
Drills 50

Use screws when you need strong holding power and want to be able to take a joint apart without damaging it. Wood screws, which come in many sizes and head types, are traditional for joining wood. But many special-purpose screws (such as sheet-metal, drywall or deck screws) can also create sturdy wood joints. Screws with sharp points and threads are designed to be self-tapping—they pull themselves into the material—and seldom need a pilot hole when driven into softwood or sheet metal with a power drill or screw gun.

The square-drive (Robertson), Phillips, and star-drive screwheads are designed to help prevent bit slippage. Hex heads allow you to use nut drivers or sockets to drive small or large screws. One-way screw heads, once driven in, are not easily removed.

When purchasing screws, specify the length in inches and the diameter by a gauge number. Gauge numbers range from 2 (the smallest) to 16 (the largest). The exception is lag screws that are sold by diameter from 1/4 in. to 5/8 in.

Use an awl or nail to make a pilot hole for smaller screws. For larger screws, drill a pilot hole with a bit the same diameter as the threaded part of the shaft, minus the threads. Two-thirds of a screw's length, or at least 1 in. (2.5 cm), should go into the second piece of wood. To lubricate screws for easier driving, coat the threads with soap or any kind of wax.

Drive Heads

Slotted

Phillips

Square-drive (Robertson)

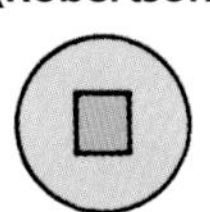

Star-drive

One-way

Hex-head

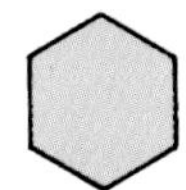

Screw Types

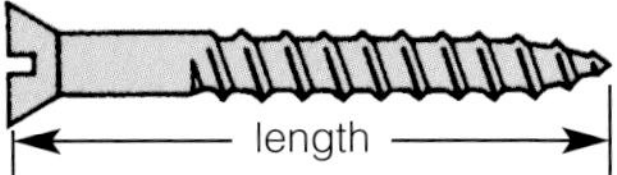

Flathead screw. A general-purpose wood screw driven flush with surface or countersunk below. Designated length refers to entire screw.

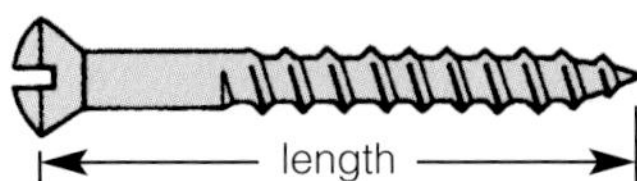

Oval-head screw. A protruding head offers a decorative appearance. Upper part of head is not counted in designated length.

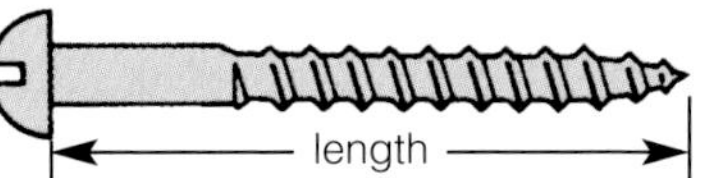

Roundhead screw. Used for fastening a thin board or metal to thicker wood. Head is excluded in designated length.

Particleboard screw. Has wide, deep threads for extra holding power. A sharp point cuts through tough particleboard.

Drywall or all-purpose screw. Thin, sharp and hardened. A bugle-shaped head dents drywall surface and deep threads cut into studs.

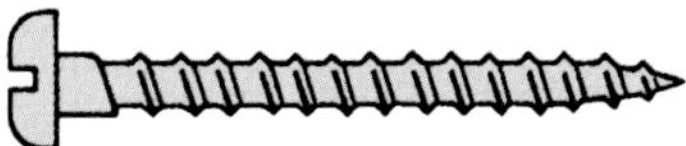

Sheet-metal screw. Threaded along its entire length. May also have hex-shaped head. Self-tapping.

Lag bolt (or screw). A heavy-duty wood screw sold by diameter and length. Commonly used to attach a deck ledger board to the house frame.

Dowel screw. Joins leg to tabletop. Screw into top of leg using locking pliers, then screw leg into top.

Hanger bolt. One end has wood-screw threads and other end has machine-screw threads that will accept a nut.

Hooks and Washers

Screw hook

Screw eye

L-hook

Flush for flathead screw

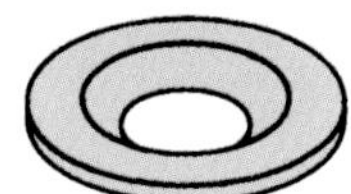

Countersunk for oval-head screw

Flat for roundhead screw

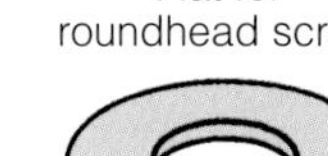

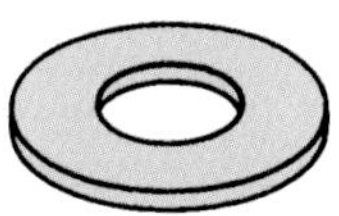

Screw Sizes

Gauge number	2	3	4	5	6	7	8	9	10	11	12	14	16
Actual size of screw													

Countersinking Screws

Flathead screws are designed to be driven so the screwhead is flush with, or recessed below, the surface of the material. Some screws, like cement-board screws, have ridges underneath the head to help make them self-countersinking. Drywall screws have a gradual, bugle-shaped slope underneath the head that helps dimple, rather than tear, the drywall facing as it drives deeper. Wood screws, however, need the help of countersink bits (below).

Each screw type is designed for a specific purpose and is not necessarily interchangeable. Drywall screws are made of hardened, brittle steel, and the shaft will often snap during installation. Wood screws are thicker, more snap-resistant and designed for woodworking projects; drywall screws are not.

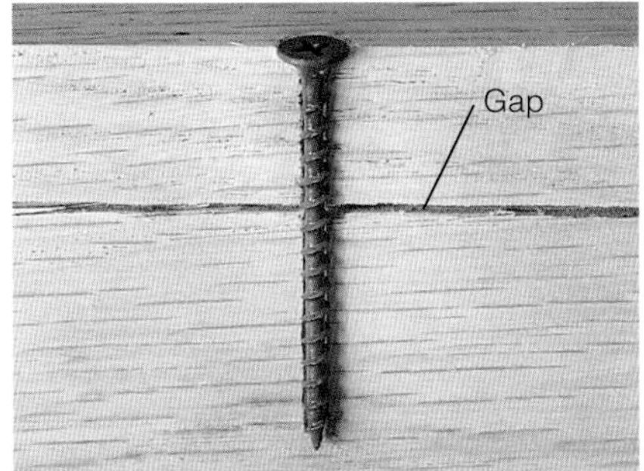

Boards held apart. When a fully threaded screw is used, the top threads can anchor into the top board and keep the boards apart rather than pull them together.

Boards held together. Wood screws have a smooth shank section that slides through the top layer of wood so the screwhead and the threads pull the two boards together.

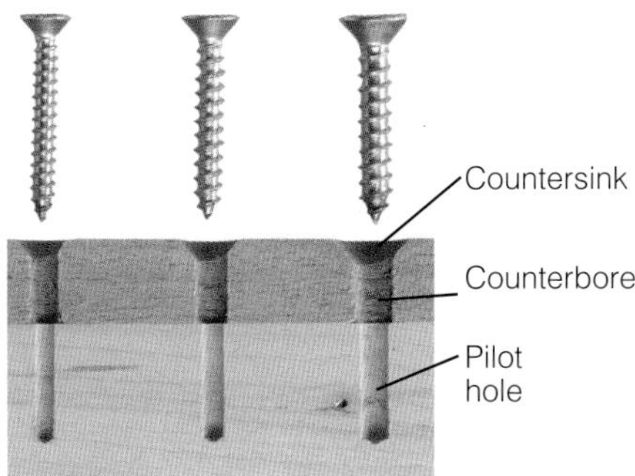

Hole sizes. A properly drilled hole for a wood screw has three elements: a pilot hole for the threads, a wider hole through the top board, and a countersink hole for the head.

Countersink bits perform all three predrilling chores for wood screws at once. The primary bit is tapered like a screw shank. A set of three will handle most common screw sizes.

Extracting Stubborn Screws

The best way to remove screws with stripped or broken-off heads is to use a screw extractor. To center the drill bit in the jagged face, start with a very small bit, then drill another hole large enough to hold the extractor. Extractors come in sizes small enough to remove even very small screws.

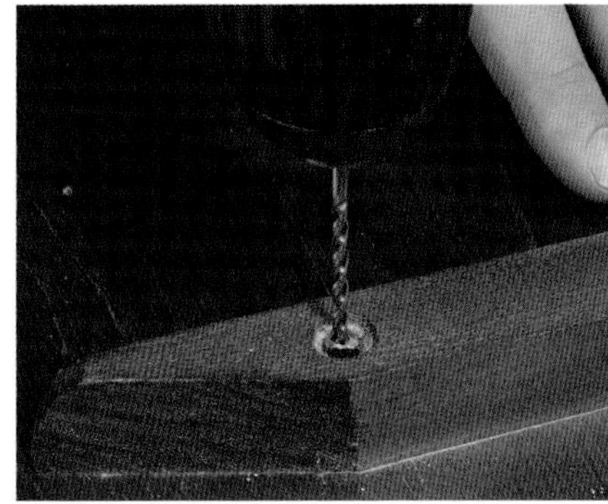

1 Drill a hole in the screw shank 1/8 to 1/4 in. (3-6 mm) deep. Oil the drill bit to improve cutting ability and preserve bit.

2 Remove broken screw by inserting extractor and turning counterclockwise. Extractor will lock into hole and twist out screw.

Screwy Ideas

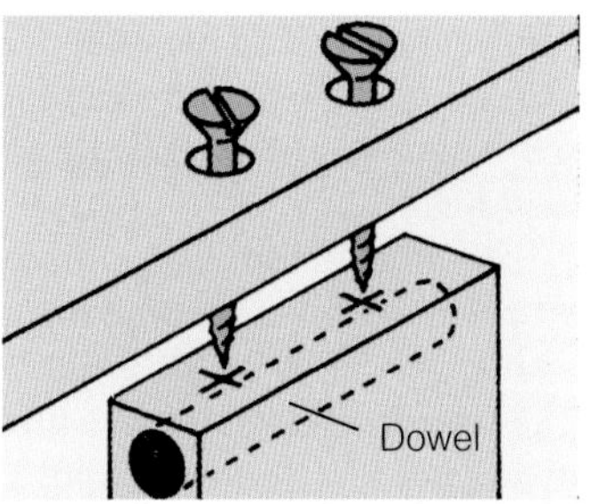

To strengthen a weak end-grain joint, drill a hole and insert a hardwood dowel. The same trick can be used when screwing into the edge of plywood.

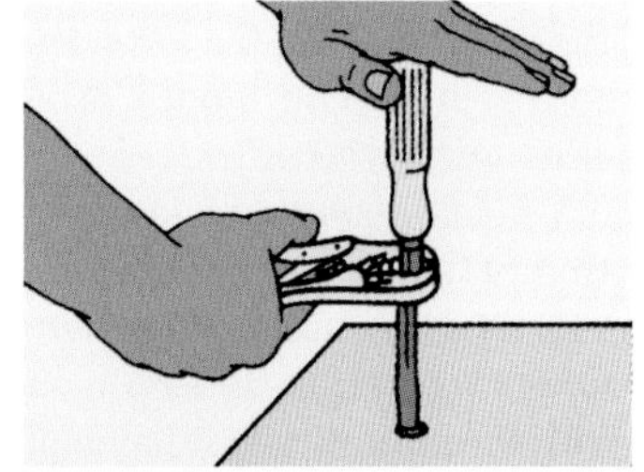

Loosen stubborn screws by inserting a square-shanked screwdriver, clamping a locking pliers onto the shank and pushing down hard while turning the screwdriver.

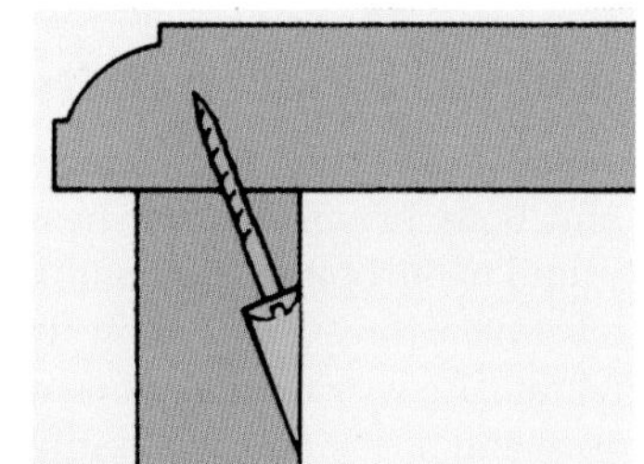

Use the pocket screw method when attaching a tabletop. First drill a long, angled hole for the screwhead, then drill a pilot hole in the pocket at the same angle.

Nuts and Bolts

Nuts and bolts act like very powerful mini-clamps that can be easily removed and offer more adjustability options than screws or adhesives. Select machine bolts or stove bolts (or machine screws) for metal and other thin materials. Select carriage bolts for woodworking applications where you don't want a sharp, exposed head.

Specify a bolt's size by its diameter, thread pitch, and length. For instance, for a bolt sized 1/4 in.-20 x 1-1/2 in.: 1/4 in. is the diameter, 20 is the number of threads per inch, and 1-1/2 in. is the length. Metric bolts are becoming increasingly common. Diameter and thread pitch combinations commonly range from 1/8 in.-40 to 1/2 in.-13. As a rule, the larger the bolt, the fewer threads per inch it has. The length of a bolt excludes any protruding part of the head. A machine screw is a stove bolt less than 1/2 in. in diameter and its diameter is given as a gauge number.

Always tighten or loosen a nut or bolt with the appropriate wrench or tool to avoid damage.

Bolt Types

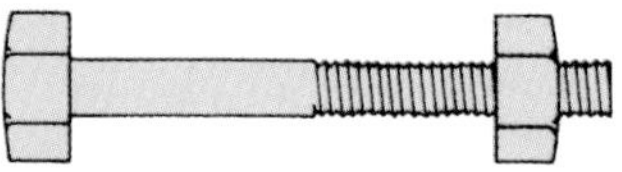

Machine bolts. Come with hex heads or square heads and accept hex or square nuts.

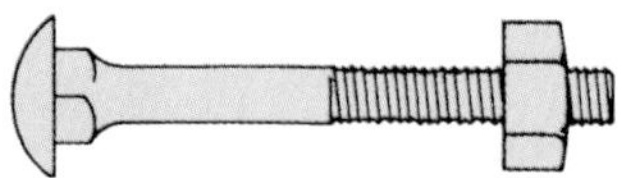

Carriage bolts. Have an unslotted oval head. Square shoulders sink into wood to prevent turning.

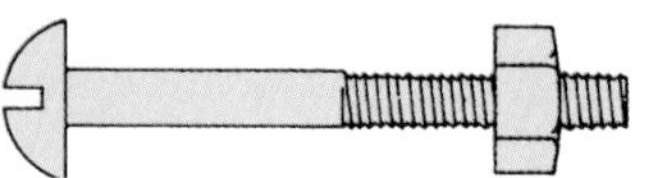

Stove bolts. General utility bolts with slotted heads.

Flat Oval Round

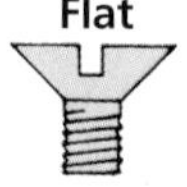

Stove-bolt heads. Can be flat to sink flush, oval for easy removal, or round to accept a washer.

Nut Types

Common nuts. Include locknuts designed to lock themselves in place. Cap nuts are decorative and protective. Wing nuts are hand tightened. Castle nuts let a secured part move (a cotter pin holds nut in place).

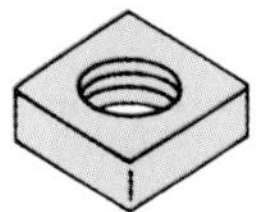

Square nut

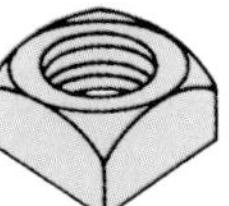

Hex nut

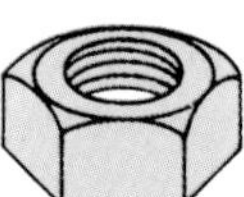

Jam nut

Locknut

Castle nut

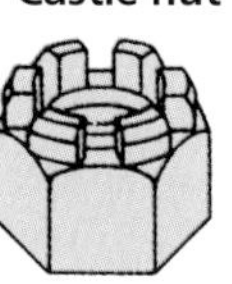

Cap nut

Wing nut

Washer Types

Common washers. Include a flat washer, which goes under a bolt head or nut to spread the load and protect the surface. Split-ring and toothed lock washers prevent a nut from working loose.

Flat washer

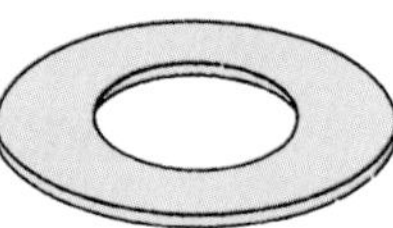

Split-ring lock washer

Toothed lock washer

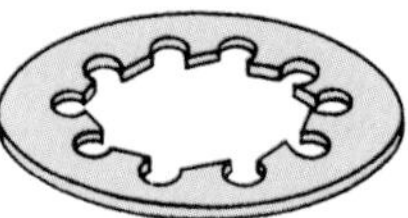

Removing Stubborn Bolts

Heat, oil and tapping will loosen most nuts and bolts in metal. After heating, tap the end of the bolt with a hammer to help release the threads and allow the oil to penetrate. Be very careful when combining oil and heat since penetrating oil is flammable.

1 Apply only enough heat to expand the entire bolt—about a minute or so.

2 When bolt cools enough to touch, squirt penetrating oil on and around it.

Nut splitter. If heat fails, a nut splitter will crack a nut without damaging bolt threads.

Hollow-wall Fasteners

Wall studs are rarely conveniently located for wall-mounted accessories. To hang a towel rack, mirror or small shelf on any hollow wall or door, use one of these hollow-wall fasteners. Just be aware of the advantages and limitations of the fastener you choose.

Most wall surfaces are 1/2-in. drywall. If you have an older home with plaster and lath, the walls will be thicker. Knowing the wall thickness is critical when selecting most hollow-wall fasteners; they just won't work in a wall that's thicker or thinner than what they're made for. The package, or the fastener itself, will tell you the required thickness.

Beyond accounting for wall thickness, there are some other basic rules to follow for hollow-wall fasteners. First, use the correct sized mounting screw. Too heavy a screw will break the fastener loose before it's secured. Second, drill the hole size specified on the package. Third, don't overtighten the mounting screw or the housing could break loose. Finally, don't expect too much from a fastener. Some items, such as cabinets, stair rails and heavy shelves must be mounted to wall studs for safety reasons.

All weight ratings below are based on vertical weight in 1/2-in. drywall.

Toggle Bolts

These bolts are heavy-duty anchors with spring-loaded wings that work in drywall, plaster or hollow-core doors. Fold wings together and measure across fold to determine hole size. Once installed, you can't remove screw without losing the wings.

1 With wings folded together, expose enough screw shank for wings to pop open behind wall surface.

2 As wings begin to tighten, adjust position of object being attached. Supports up to 30 lbs. (13 kg).

Expanding Plastic Anchors

These anchors hold by expanding within the drywall hole and use legs that spread out behind drywall. They require drilling a hole of precise diameter. Overtightening can ruin anchor's effectiveness.

Expanding legs. Medium-duty anchor secured by spreading legs. Designed to hold 20 lbs. (9 kg).

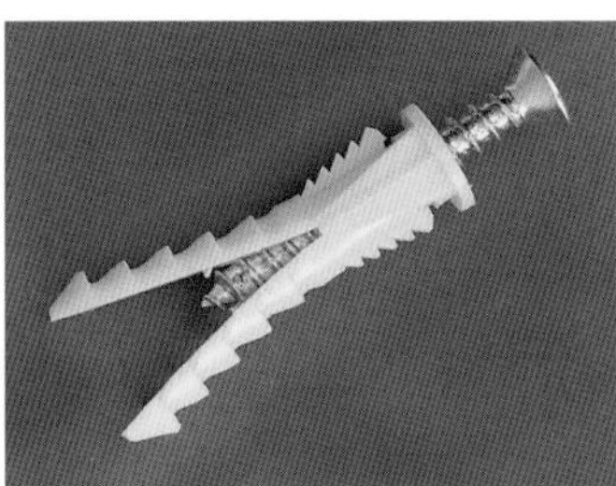

Expanding throat. Light-duty anchor secured by wedging action. Holds 15 lbs. (7 kg).

Hollow-wall Anchors

These anchors' housings mushroom as screw is tightened to form securing arms. The short-shank version is designed for anchoring the thin skins of hollow-core doors.

1 Drill hole, insert anchor making sure face points bite into surface to prevent spinning.

2 Remove screw, position object to be hung, and then reinstall screw. Supports about 25 lbs. (11 kg).

Plastic Toggles

Inexpensive, quick and easy to use, toggles provide a sturdy bite. Toggles have wings that you squeeze together to insert into a hole. If wings haven't opened after installation, poke them with a nail through the toggle hole. Supports about 25 lbs. (11 kg).

1 Drill hole to size specified and drive anchor into hole until face ring is flush with surface.

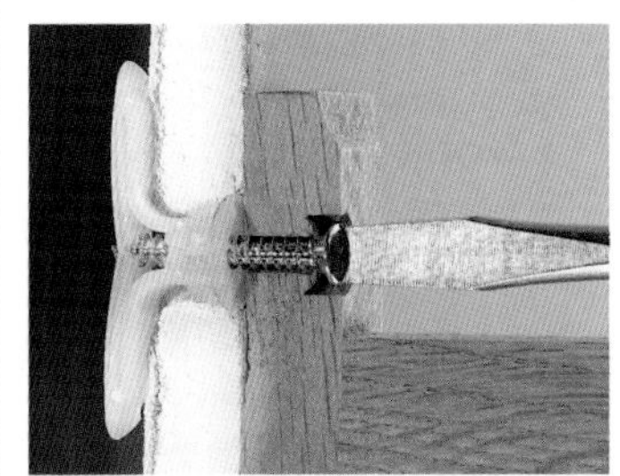

2 Before driving screw, be sure wings have popped fully open by trying to pull out toggle.

Screw-in Anchors

These anchors are intended exclusively for drywall. With a sharpened end, they drill their own mounting hole as you drive them with a large Phillips screwdriver. Coarse threads anchor the housing to the drywall.

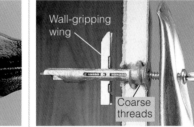

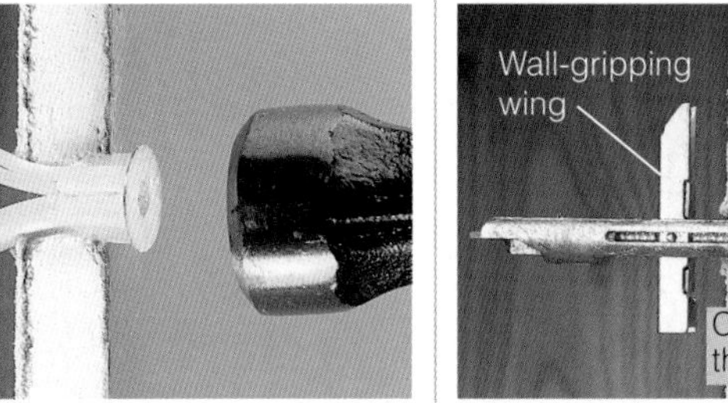

Wall-gripping wing. These anchors support 35 lbs. (15 kg). As you turn mounting screw, the wing pulls tight against back of drywall.

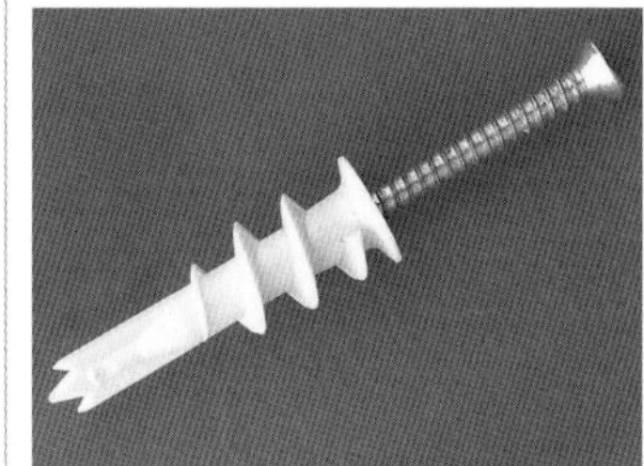

Light weight. In some versions, only threads hold anchor in drywall. These support about 20 lbs. (9 kg).

Concrete and Masonry Fasteners

Safety Equipment 20
Drilling Concrete 51

Concrete continues to harden for decades after it's poured. Consequently, it provides a reliable foundation for a solidly mounted anchor. On the downside, it can create a great deal of frustration in making the hole for the anchor. The key to emphasizing the positives and dealing with the negatives is using the right tools and the best anchors for the project.

Most fasteners, including some masonry nails, require a pilot hole into which you slip the fastener or anchor. The fastest way to drill a hole in concrete, concrete block, mortar or brick is to use a hammer drill. If you don't have a hammer drill, borrow, rent or buy one. Most hammer drills have a switch or collar so you can change from percussion drilling to regular drilling.

Masonry nails work best to attach furring strips, window frames, and other wood pieces to masonry block or concrete. Plugs and anchors provide more security when hanging hooks, shelves, and other heavy fixtures on masonry and concrete walls. Most work by expanding against the sides of a hole when you insert a screw, bolt or plug. In some cases, you can use a plastic toggle or anchor if you're concerned about cracking brick.

Hammer drills. When you need to make many holes in hard, cured concrete, a hammer drill and percussion bit can make the daunting task doable.

Plastic Anchors

Plastic anchors are an excellent light-duty fastener for shelf brackets, towel bars, rake and shovel brackets, and hardware weighing less than 50 lbs. (23 kg). They require a pilot hole at least as deep as the screw will penetrate. Each package will give the hole size and the screw size that work best.

To use them, drill a pilot hole to the proper depth with a hammer drill and masonry bit. Tap the anchor into the hole with a hammer. If the concrete is soft or crumbly, the anchor may break free as you turn the screw. If this happens, try a bigger screw or wedge in a sliver of plastic from another anchor alongside the first.

Soft Metal Anchors

Soft metal shield anchors work especially well in softer materials like brick and mortar that can't take the stress from heavy-duty anchors.

To use these anchors, drill the correct sized pilot hole (consult package instructions) with a masonry bit. To drill into softer brick and mortar, you may not need a hammer drill. The hole must be deep enough for the shield and the length of the bolt or screw that will protrude through it.

Soft metal anchors can strip out when overtightened. If the shield becomes loose, cut strips of wire solder and push them in along the outside of the shield.

Nails

Masonry nails are made of steel, hardened to withstand being driven into concrete and masonry. These nails snap easily and can chip a cast-iron hammer, so always wear goggles and use a hardened-steel hammer. Use them in conjunction with construction adhesive for best results.

Hammer-set Anchors

Installed by drilling holes and pounding them in place, these anchors work best to secure furring strips, light straps and brackets to sound concrete, concrete block, mortar and brick.

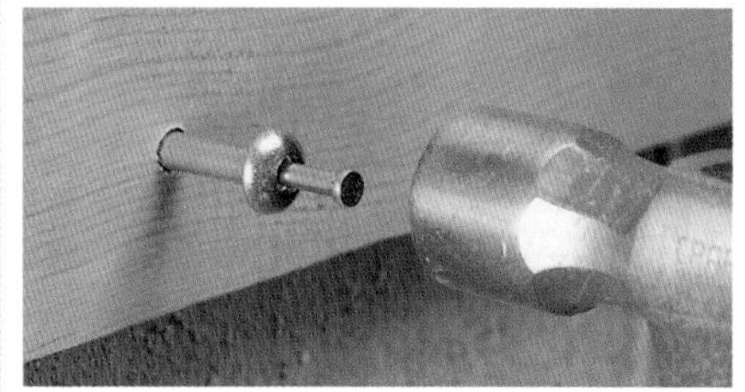

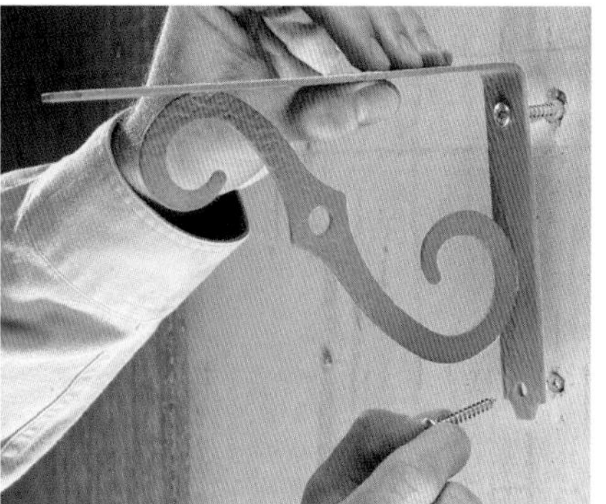

Plastic anchors are ideal for fastening many types of light-duty brackets to concrete, concrete block, mortar, brick or stone.

Soft metal shield anchors are perfect for securing downspout straps to brick and mortar.

Concrete Screws

Concrete screws offer a fast, relatively inexpensive method to attach furring strips, window and door frames, conduit clamps and electrical boxes to concrete and concrete block. The big advantage is that you hold the wood or object in place, drill right into the concrete, and drive the screw home. This saves the hassle of marking holes and trying to realign the work piece.

To use concrete screws, drill a pilot hole with the appropriate masonry bit and a hammer drill. Larger packages of concrete screws usually include a free bit. Drive the screw with a power screwdriver. Use 3/16-in.-dia. screws for light-duty tasks and 1/4-in.-dia. screws for heavier jobs.

Concrete screws are ideal for attaching conduit and electrical boxes to concrete block. Available in hex-head and flathead types.

Sleeve Anchors

Sleeve anchors are available in several sizes and will hold up to 200 lbs. (90 kg), making them the best choice for heavy-duty applications. The sleeves pinch the sides of the predrilled hole as the tapered plug on the bottom is pulled into the sleeve when you tighten the bolt. They can be used in concrete, concrete block, or mortar and brick.

To use sleeve anchors, first drill the correct sized pilot hole through the wood or metal and into the concrete. Slip the sleeve into the hole and hold the object you're fastening firmly to the surface because the anchor will only draw it slightly tighter as you tighten the screw or bolt.

Heavy-duty sleeve anchors are ideal for attaching a deck ledger board to concrete or concrete block.

Powder-Actuated Tools

Powder-actuated tools (also called PATs or stud guns) offer the quickest, most efficient and cost-effective way to fire multiple fasteners into concrete slabs and concrete-block walls. PATs use gunpowder cartridges to drive hardened-steel nails through wood and into concrete. When it comes to finishing a basement, these heavy-duty tools quickly pay for themselves by saving hours of drilling and pounding. However, the fasteners won't work well in very hard concrete or stone, so it's usually best to test-fire a few fasteners into your concrete to see if you'll get reliable results.

Always follow the recommended spacings for placing drive pins and for working near the edges of concrete slabs.

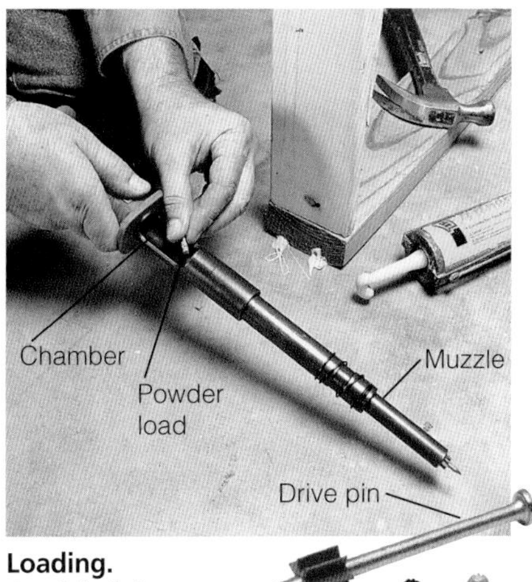

Loading. Carefully follow manufacturer's instructions. For safety, insert the fastener (drive pin) into the muzzle first. Next, place a powder load into the chamber.

Gun-Control Laws

Keep powder-actuated tools and unspent powder loads locked up and away from kids. Injuries and deaths have occurred when ricocheting projectiles have struck bystanders or when common nails were used in stud guns. When the tool is dropped, check for damage to the barrel and other moving parts and don't use it until it's repaired. Always wear safety goggles and hearing protection.

Improve the fastener holding power by using construction adhesive on sill plates and behind furring strips. Avoid overdriving power fasteners by selecting the right size powder load. Overdriving will damage the gun and weaken the bond.

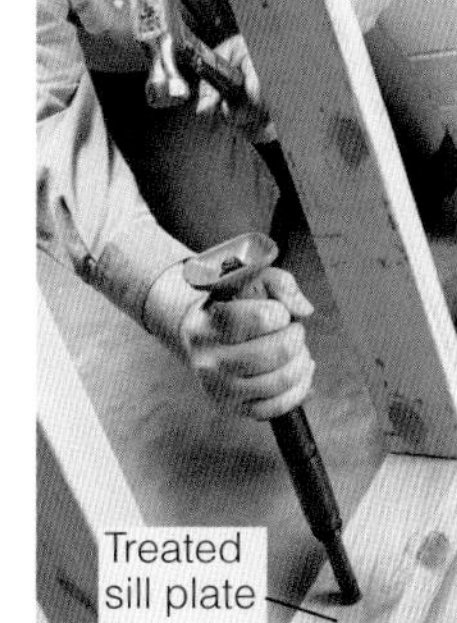

Floors. Quickly fasten sill plates to concrete slabs using a PAT. Firmly hold the tool at 90° angle, push down and hold to cock it, and then strike the firing mechanism with a strong hammer blow.

Walls. Attach furring strips to walls using 1-1/2-in. drive pins or drive pins equipped with washers if the wood splits.

General Purpose Adhesives

When the right adhesive is used in the appropriate application on properly prepared surfaces, the adhesive can form a strong, permanent bond that's often stronger than the material itself.

Most adhesives require clamping until they set. Setting time refers to the interval before the glue hardens. Curing time is the period it takes the bond to reach maximum strength. In most cases, an object shouldn't be used until the adhesive has cured. For glass, china, and other items that are difficult to clamp, fast-setting glues are ideal.

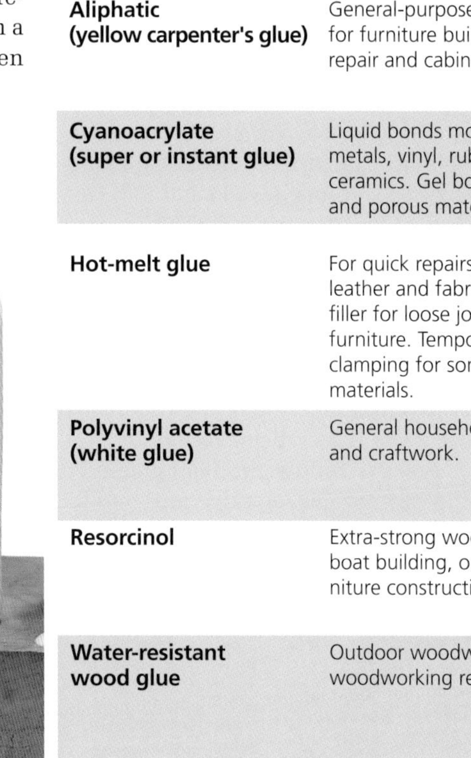

Adhesive	Typical Uses	Application	Characteristics	Solvent
Aliphatic (yellow carpenter's glue)	General-purpose adhesive for furniture building and repair and cabinet work.	Apply from squeeze bottle; clamp for at least 45 minutes.	Sets within 1 hr.; cures overnight. Water soluble, not for outdoor use. Rigid, dries clear, easy sanding.	Warm water
Cyanoacrylate (super or instant glue)	Liquid bonds most plastics, metals, vinyl, rubber and ceramics. Gel bonds wood and porous material.	Apply in drops from tube. Short working time. **Caution:** Avoid contact with skin.	Sets in seconds or minutes depending on product. Cures rapidly. Water-resistant and gap-filling.	Acetone (nail polish remover)
Hot-melt glue	For quick repairs on leather and fabrics. Gap filler for loose joints on furniture. Temporary quick clamping for some sheet materials.	Melt glue with hot-glue gun. **Caution:** Avoid contact with skin.	Very fast setting to slower setting formulas available. Not ideal for permanent bonds or repairs.	Acetone (nail polish remover)
Polyvinyl acetate (white glue)	General household repairs and craftwork.	Use applicator for small jobs; apply with brush for large jobs. Sets in about 8 hrs. at room temperature.	Cures in 24 hrs. Water soluble, dries clear, poor sanding.	Soap, warm water
Resorcinol	Extra-strong wood repairs, boat building, outdoor furniture construction.	Two parts: liquid and powder.	Sets and cures slowly (up to 10 hrs. at room temperature). Waterproof, rigid, dries dark red.	Cool water before hardening
Water-resistant wood glue	Outdoor woodwork and woodworking repairs.	Apply from squeeze bottle; clamp for recommended time.	Some have fast-tack qualities. Some of the no-drip/no-run formulas have better gap-filling qualities.	Warm water before hardening

Storing Glue

Always follow manufacturer's instructions for storing adhesives. Many are sensitive to freezing or will quickly dry out if not properly capped or stored. If you use an after-market applicator bottle, don't store the glue in it. Dried glue can quickly foul many of these applicator tips.

Many adhesives contain toxic, flammable solvents or resins that release noxious fumes. Always use these adhesives in a well-ventilated area and store away from fire sources.

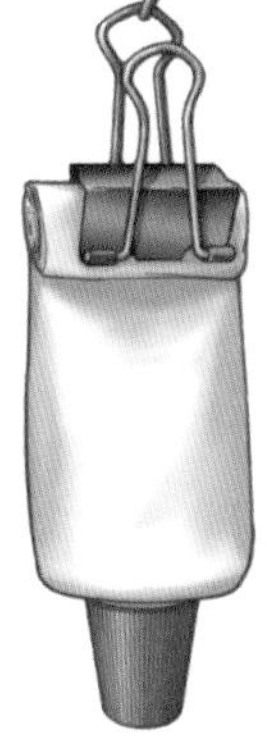

Hang it. Use binder clips to keep the empty portion of tube glues and caulks rolled up. These same "handles" can be used to hang the tubes for neat, easy-to-see storage.

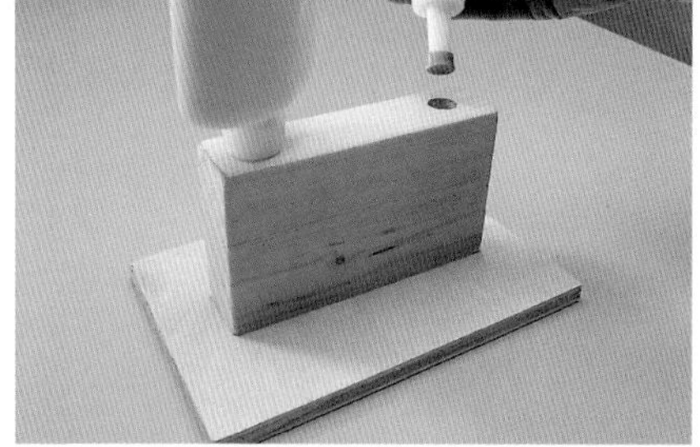

Ready to go. If you hate waiting for glue to come out, make this handy glue holster by drilling holes in a piece of 2x4. Make sure to put the cap on before inserting the bottle.

Cap it. Glue bottle caps have a tendency to disappear. If this happens, a rubber pencil eraser makes a nice substitute that's airtight and readily available.

Specialty Adhesives

Specific materials often require special adhesives. In fact, manufacturers often specify the adhesive to use with their product in order for the warranty to be valid. Beyond manufacturer recommendations, choose an adhesive based on its characteristics. Water- or latex-based adhesives have the convenience of water cleanup and low odor, whereas others require noxious, flammable solvents for cleanup and good ventilation for application. Other characteristics to consider are gap-filling capability, flexibility, spreadability, ease of use, and ease of sanding. The most important characteristic, of course, is that it works.

Adhesive	Typical Uses	Application	Characteristics	Solvent
Bolt-locking compound (anaerobic resin)	For locking threads of bolts, screws and setscrews.	Squeeze from tube or bottle.	Hardens in absence of air between closely fitted metal parts.	Soap and warm water before hardening
Contact cement	For bonding laminated plastic to countertops. Also for tasks where clamping is difficult.	Coat both mating surfaces and let dry until tacky to touch, then join parts.	Remains flexible. Parts cannot be moved once brought together. May be water-based or solvent-based.	Acetone (nail polish remover)
Epoxy	For wood, metal, china, glass and most other materials. Especially good for rebuilding moldings and bonding dissimilar materials.	A two-part formula, usually mixed in equal amounts. May be in liquid or putty form.	Sets at room temperature in 5 min. to overnight depending on product. Waterproof; excellent gap-filling and sanding. Ventilate working area well.	Acetone (nail polish remover)
Hide glue	Repairing furniture assembled with hide glue. As a base for creating a crackle-paint finish.	May be ready to apply or in flake form that's mixed with warm water.	Water soluble. Incompatible with aliphatic and polyvinyl acetate glues.	Warm water
Latex-based mastics	For applying ceramic wall tile or other uses as recommended by manufacturer.	Apply with recommended notched trowel.	No-slip formulas available for installing wall tile.	Warm water beore curing
Polyurethane	Multi-purpose applications. Especially good for wood-to to-wood bonding.	Most formulas require dampening mating surfaces with water before application.	Water resistant. Foams and expands as it sets. Good gap-filling and sandability. Limited shelf life.	Mineral spirits when wet, scrape after drying
Solvent-based mastics	For ceiling, wall and floor tiles, engineered wood floors, cork and other uses as recommended by manufacturer.	Apply with recommended notched trowel.	Tends to be messy. Generally offers stronger bond than latex formulas.	Mineral spirits or follow manufacturer's recommendations

Sticky Situations

Sometimes the best adhesive for a task isn't really an adhesive per se. Expanding polyurethane foam, often used around doors and windows, has tremendous bonding strength. Pure silicone is one of the best building adhesives around. It adheres tenaciously to most surfaces, has excellent gap-filling qualities, doesn't shrink and remains flexible. Contractors use it to install slab granite countertops and other materials such as solid-surface or cultured-marble shower surrounds.

Mini trowel. When face-gluing boards, use a credit card snipped along its wide edge with pinking shears. The serrated edge spreads the glue like a notched trowel.

Dispensing. If you hold onto a glue bottle and swing it around a couple of times with the cap on, the centrifugal force concentrates the glue at the top of the bottle for easy dispensing.

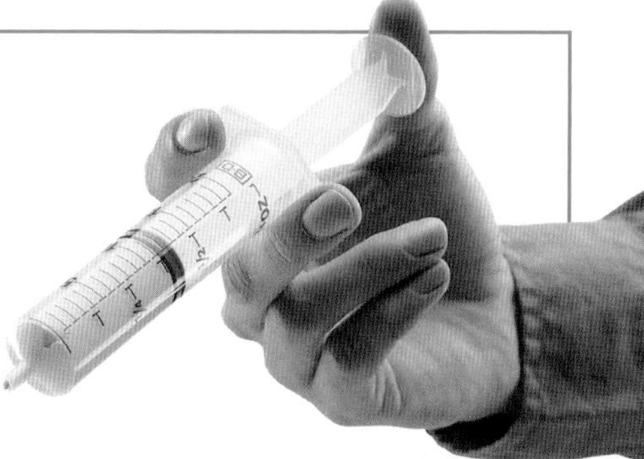

Applying. Ordinary caulk guns are too big for working in tight spots such as behind a sink. For these places, try a 20 cc plastic syringe (without a needle) as a mini caulk gun.

Tapes

Masking Tape 282

While tape doesn't usually have the holding power or permanence of glue or other adhesive, it does many jobs that a liquid can't.

Electrical tape can insulate an outlet or switch from the sides of a metal electrical box and different colors can designate the purpose of a particular wire. Metal foil tape, the true duct tape, conveniently and effectively seals leaks in duct runs. Masking tape can be used as a temporary clamp for parts that are too awkward to clamp with other methods. Double-sided carpet tape can be used to hold a part in place while you drill pilot holes and drive the first screw.

Tape	Description	Typical Uses
Anti-slip or Anti-skid	Heavy weatherproof plastic with rough-textured surface and strong adhesive.	For sure footing in tubs and showers, on steps, in entrances and on ladders.
Carpet	Plastic or cloth with moderately strong adhesive on two sides. Also made in waterproof form for outdoor use.	Securing carpets and rugs to floor. Apply tape to floor, then peel off backing and press carpet against top side.
Duct	Strong, plastic-coated cloth with moderately strong adhesive. Resistant to moisture, heat and cold.	A versatile tape with many uses indoors and out. Often used for temporary repairs and seals.Contrary to its name, it should not be used on heat ducts.
Electrical	Flame-retardant, stretchable vinyl with moderately strong adhesive. Comes in a variety of colors.	Helps insulate electrical connections, switches and outlets against shorts and shocks. Can be used to mark wire's function.
Foam mounting	Flexible foam core with strong adhesive on both sides of core.	Mounting lightweight items on rough-textured surfaces, such as brick or concrete. Apply like carpet tape.
Masking	Paper tape with minimal tacking adhesive. Residue becomes difficult to remove if left on for a long period.	A wide variety of temporary uses such as defining paint lines or holding glued parts together.
Mesh fiberglass	Strong, thin fiberglass mesh with slightly tacky surface.	For repairs and joints on drywall and cement board. Used in conjunction with joint compound or adhesive.
Metal foil	Heavyweight aluminum foil with strong adhesive.	Sealing duct seams and joints. Temporarily repairing aluminum siding and gutters.
Weather-sealing	Heavyweight weatherproof tape with strong, permanent adhesive.	Sealing gaps around protruding pipes, cables, windows and refrigeration lines.

Tape Tricks

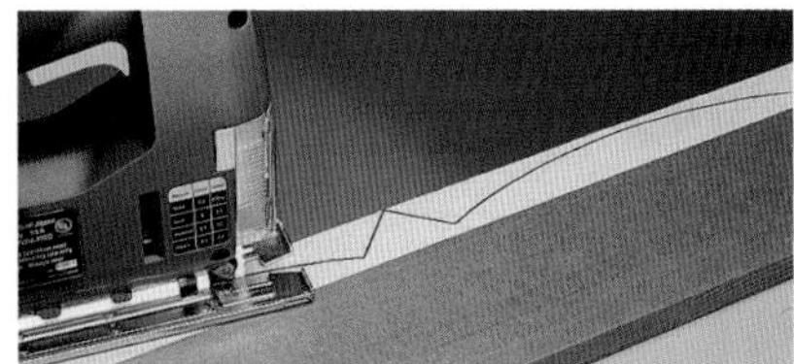

Marking. Make cutting lines easy to see and follow on dark surfaces by marking on masking tape applied to the surface.

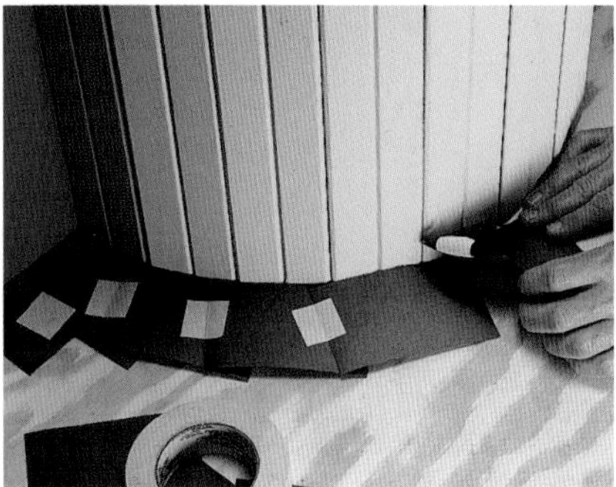

Patterns. Create patterns from cardboard and masking tape. The pattern can be transferred to vinyl or other flooring materials for cutting.

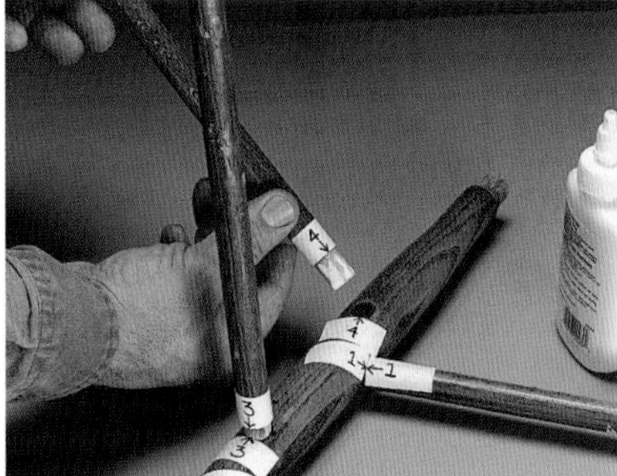

Labeling. Masking tape labels can help you remember the exact position and order of parts when disassembling and regluing furniture.

Holding. Use masking tape to hold onto and position screws located in awkward or hard-to-reach places.

Plumbing

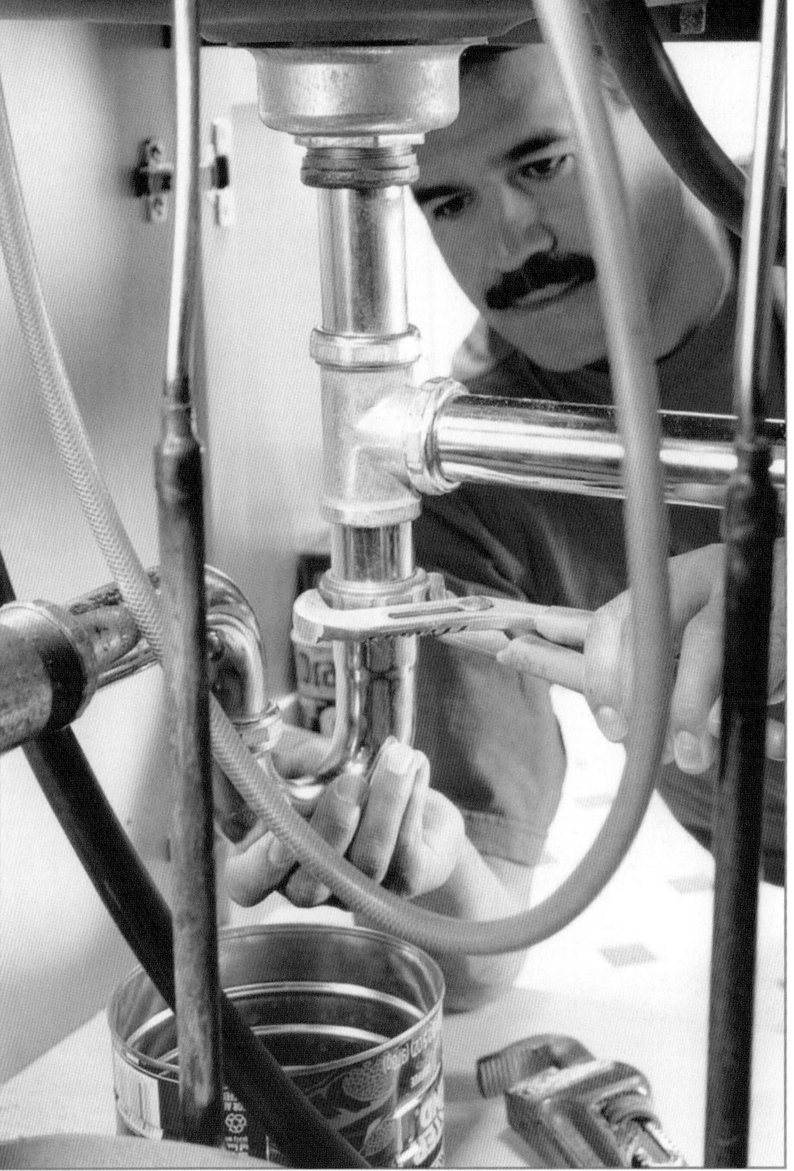

Basic Systems

Unclogging Main Drains 95
Installing Shutoff Valves 100
Replacing a Faucet 101
Pipes and Pipe Fittings 107

We tend to take our plumbing for granted—until something clogs or starts leaking on a Saturday afternoon. That's when a little plumbing know-how pays off, both in dollars saved and convenience gained.

Your home's plumbing consists of two basic systems: a water-supply system and a drain/waste-vent (DWV) system. In the water-supply system, the water usually enters the house through a main service pipe and meter, unless you have a private well. Pressure, supplied by gravity from a local water tower or from a well pump, pushes the water through the system. Parallel supply lines carry hot and cold water to fixtures and appliances.

The DWV system is a separate set of nonpressurized pipes that carry water, waste and gases out of the house. Because the force of gravity carries off the waste, the horizontal drain pipes slope. Each main horizontal section of drain should contain cleanout plugs for removing blockages. At each fixture, the drainpipe contains a U-shaped trap, also called a P-trap, that traps water in its curve to create a seal that prevents sewer gas from escaping into the house. A toilet has a built-in P-trap.

The vent system, connected to the drainage system, allows sewer gases to escape, improves drainage, keeps P-trap seals in place and prevents water from backing up between fixtures.

Water-Supply System

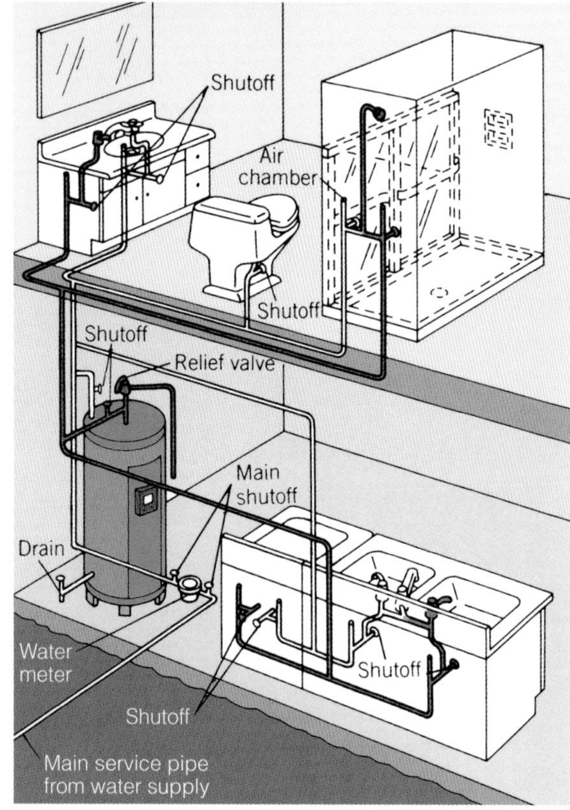

Drain/Waste-Vent System

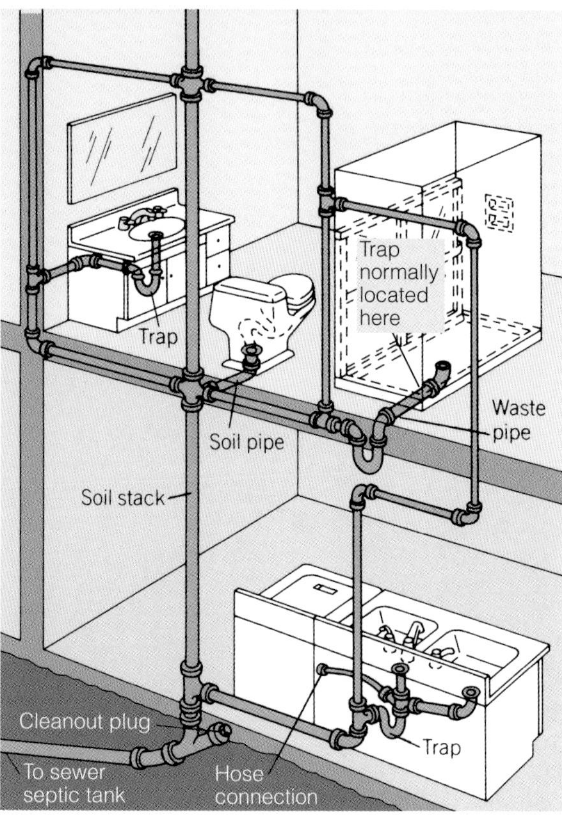

Emergency Shutoff Valves

Shutoff valves allow you to control water flow to all or parts of the water-supply system to reduce damage from a supply leak or to make repairs or replace fixtures. The main shutoff, whether indoors or outdoors, is generally near where the service line enters the house, usually next to the meter. On a private system, it will be near where the line leaves the pressure tank. You'll also find shutoff valves at the water heater, boiler, individual fixtures and outdoor water lines.

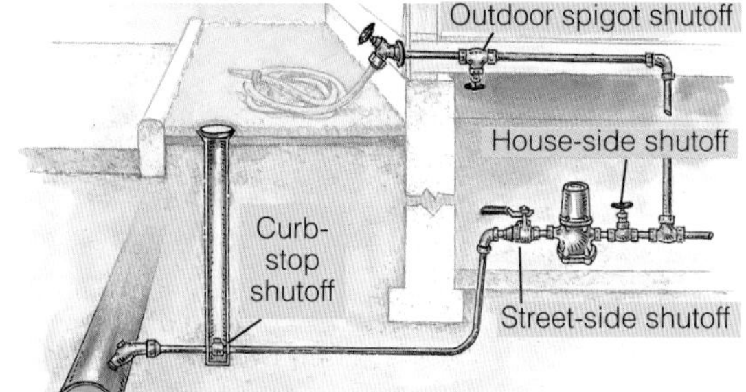

Main shutoff. This valve controls the flow of all water entering the water-supply system.

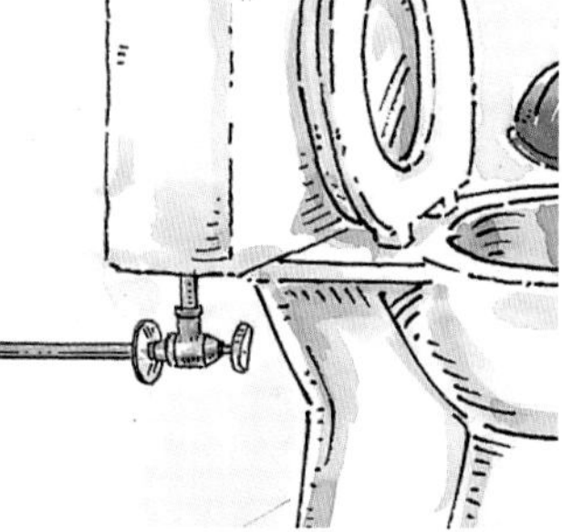

Toilet shutoff. This valve is usually on the cold-water supply located underneath the tank.

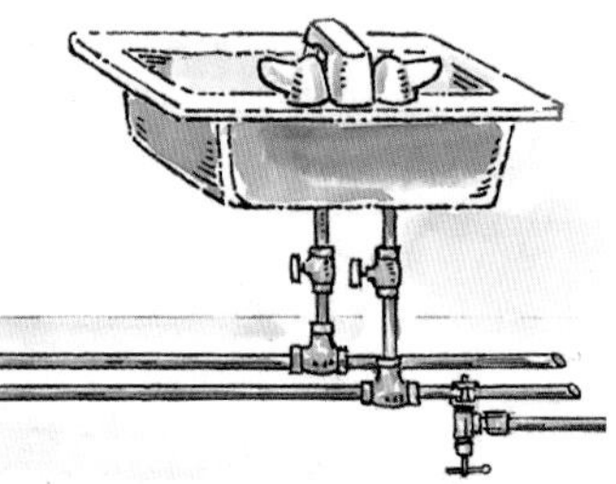

Faucet shutoff. Separate valves control the hot and cold water.

Water Supply

Most large cities rely on water from lakes or rivers for their water needs. Because water drawn from lakes and rivers doesn't benefit from the natural filtering that groundwater undergoes, larger communities usually pump water to a central treatment facility where it is treated before being stored in water towers. Small to midsize communities often rely on water—naturally filtered—pumped from stable underground aquifers. Often only minimal treatment is required to purify the water.

Water towers or elevated tanks serve two functions. They provide storage, so if a power failure shuts down the pump or the well becomes contaminated, the reserve water continues to meet immediate needs. Towers and tanks also provide pressure, so gravity can feed water to all of the surrounding homes and businesses.

Water from private wells is naturally filtered but should be tested once a year for coliform bacteria, nitrates and other impurities. In-home filters can often improve water purity, flavor and clarity.

Avoiding Lead Contamination

Your home's plumbing system may contain lead from several sources. Municipal water mains laid before 1960 may have lead-sealed joints. Supply pipes installed before 1930 may contain lead. Until about 1986, the solder used to join copper pipe and fittings contained lead. And many faucets with brass fittings and spouts still contain small amounts of lead. Here are some simple steps to avoid waterborne lead exposure:

- When remodeling, replace old pipes or fittings while they're accessible.
- Use lead-free solder or solderless pipe like PEX.
- After working on supply pipes, remove faucet aerators and let water run for five minutes to remove dislodged pieces of lead or solder.
- Don't drink, cook or make baby formula with water from the hot-water faucet if you suspect lead in the system; hot water dissolves lead more readily than cold.
- Flush water for one minute if it has been sitting in pipes for more than six hours.
- Have your water tested by a qualified lab.

Large-City Water-Treatment System

A surface water-treatment system has several steps. First, chemicals are mixed with the raw water. These chemicals cause suspended particles to clump together, or coagulate, and form larger particles, called floc. During sedimentation, floc, silt and other particles sink to the bottom of the tank where the particles are removed. Next, the water is filtered through gravel, sand and anthracite coal to mimic nature's purification process. In the final steps, the water is disinfected to kill disease-causing organisms and bacteria, it is softened by removing calcium and magnesium, and fluoride is added to reduce tooth decay.

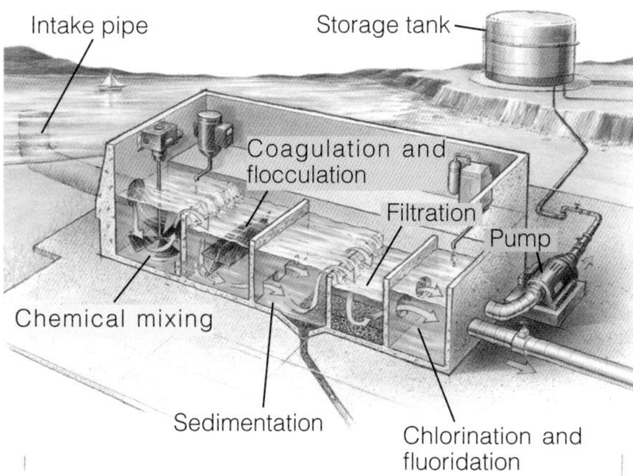

Small-Town Water System

Smaller municipal systems usually consist of a deep well—often in excess of 700 ft. (210 m) deep—a pump to move the water, a chlorinator for disinfecting the water, a fluoride dispenser and a water tower that provides both storage and pressure.

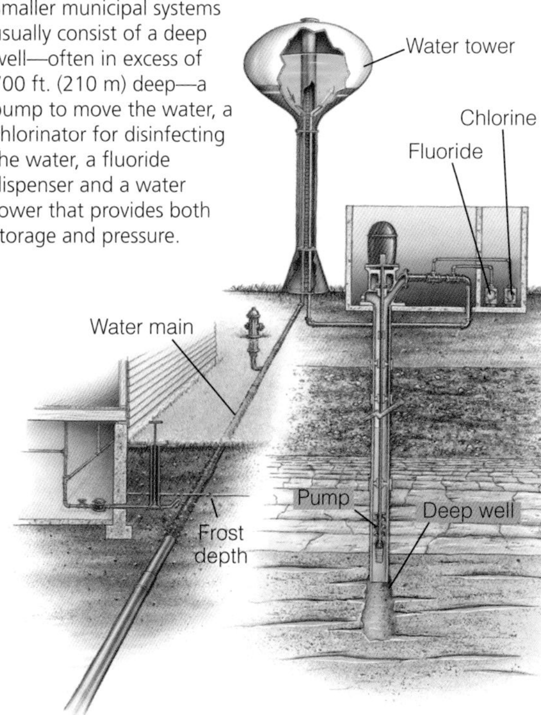

Private-Well System

In a private well, a pressure sensor and gauge, usually located inside the house, send messages to a pump submerged in the well to push more water up into the pressure tank as needed. Since the water is drawn from a deep source, it's filtered as it works its way down and is less susceptible to surface pollution. However, as the water percolates down, it dissolves calcium, magnesium and other minerals. This "hard" water can create rocklike deposits in pipes, water heaters and plumbing fixtures, reducing both the efficiency and life span of a plumbing system and fixtures. Consequently, many homes with private wells need water softeners to filter out the minerals.

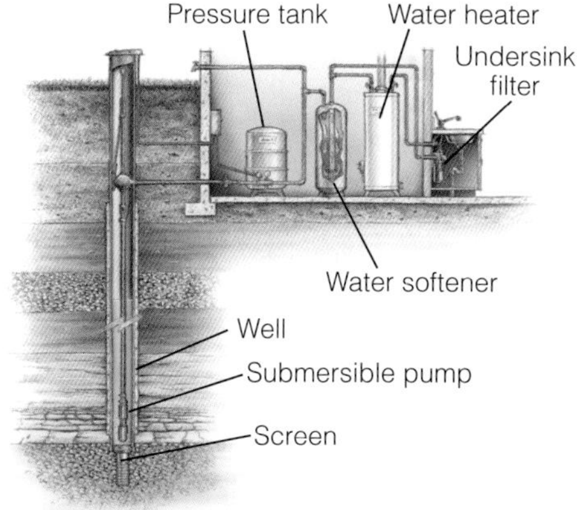

Pressure Tanks

In older pressure tanks found in homes with wells, the incoming water pushes air into the upper third of the tank, where it forms a springlike cushion. When the air pressure reaches a preset level, a pressure switch is triggered, shutting off the pump. As water is drawn from the tank and the pressure diminishes to a preset level, the switch turns on the pump again.

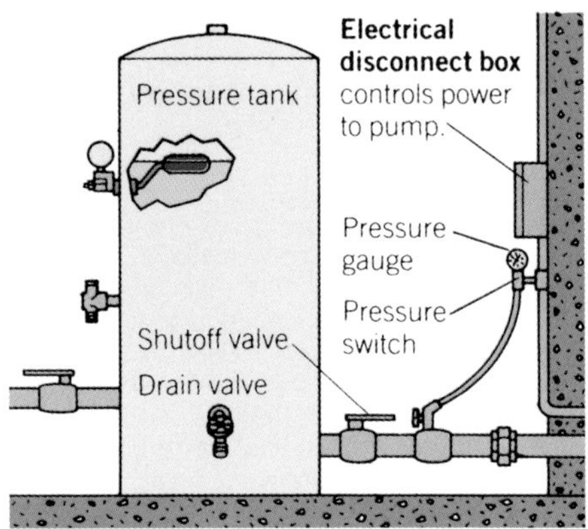

If a tank, like the one shown, loses too much air pressure, it becomes waterlogged, causing the pump to switch on and off frequently. To solve the problem, shut off power to the pump and use the drain valve to drain the tank. Then, open a faucet to drain any remaining water. With the tank empty, shut off the faucet, close the drain valve and turn the pump back on. Newer versions with diaphragms or floats to separate air and water are less likely to have this problem.

If periodic blasts of violent air come from the faucets, the pressure tank may be air-bound. Troubleshoot the problem by draining the tank and replacing the air-volume control if there is one. If you have an air-bound air-cell pressure tank, which has no air-volume control, call a well contractor, because you probably have a leak somewhere between the well and the house.

Safety First

Keeping Water Systems Safe

A cross-connection occurs when water that should go into a pool, DWV system or other location gets into the supply system, where it pollutes the drinking water. This happens when a vacuum is created from a heavy draw elsewhere in the house and another part of the water supply, such as the nose of a faucet or a water hose sitting in dirty water, siphons water into the supply system. To solve this, replace old faucets that have spouts below the spill line and install anti-siphon valves, or vacuum breakers, on outdoor faucets.

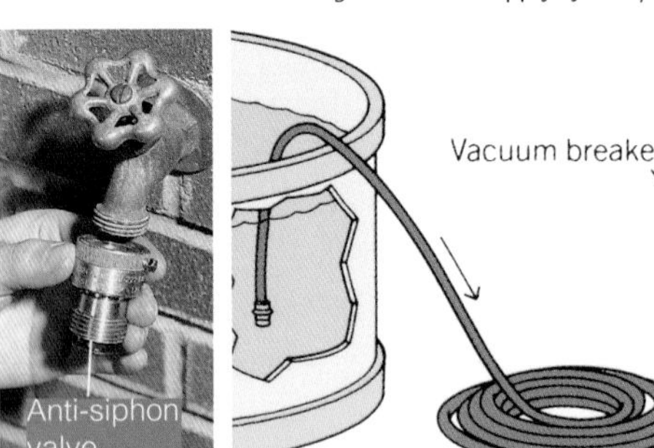

Wastewater-Treatment Systems

Wastewater treatment simulates nature's purification process, but at a much accelerated pace. Although water released from a treatment facility isn't pure, it is likely to match or exceed the purity of the body of water where it is released. The treatment has five basic steps, though processes may be combined and vary greatly from plant to plant.

1. In **preliminary treatment**, the wastewater flows through bar screens to remove trash and debris, then slowly moves through a grit tank, where sand and heavy particles settle and are removed.
2. During **primary treatment**, water moves into sedimentation tanks, where it's undisturbed for a few hours. Solids that sink are scraped from the bottom of the tank and removed. Grease and oils that float to the top are removed with large rotating skimmers.
3. **Secondary treatment** begins when the water enters a chain of aeration tanks, where bacteria feed on incoming waste solids and organic matter, forming a heavy sludge. The water then moves on to a clarifying tank where the sludge settles out.
4. In some plants, the final step is **disinfection**, where harmful bacteria and other microorganisms are killed through chlorination or use of intense ultraviolet lights.
5. Before the treated water, or effluent, is released into the main body of water, it may undergo **advanced treatment** to remove phosphorus and nitrogen, ingredients that stimulate algae growth and eventually deplete the oxygen levels of lakes and rivers.

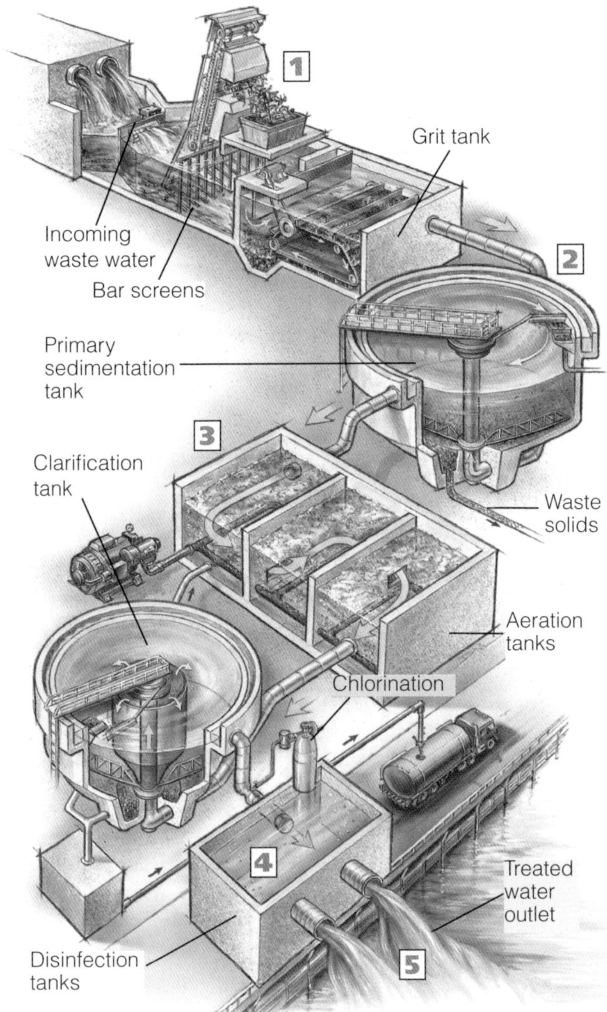

Septic Systems

In a typical private septic system, waste is piped out of the house into a watertight holding tank, or septic tank, where bacteria breaks down the waste into solids, called sludge; liquid, called effluent; and scum. The sludge settles to the bottom of the tank, the scum rises to the top and the effluent flows into a distribution box, which channels it through perforated pipes to different parts of a drainage field of loose gravel.

The proportions of sludge, effluent and scum must be carefully balanced for the tank to function properly. If particles of sediment get into the effluent and clog the drainage field, a health hazard results. Pumping removes the sludge and part of the scum to restore the proper balance. Consult your city or local septic-tank service about how often you should have your tank inspected and cleaned. To help with cleaning and inspection, locate and mark the caps and outlet covers of your system. If you don't know where they are, refer to the septic system's original design plan or check with your local building department.

Practicing water conservation is essential for you to have a long-lasting septic system. Large volumes of water, especially when delivered to the system over short periods, flush suspended, untreated particles into the drain field and clog it. Bathrooms account for 60 percent of the water used in a typical home, so it's the first place to start saving. Replace old toilets with new ones that use less water. Install water-saving showerheads and take shorter showers. Repair dripping faucets and shut off the tap when shaving or brushing your teeth. Water-saving clothes washers and dishwashers can further save hundreds of gallons or liters per month.

Caution: Keep a tight lid on your septic tank. Most tank lids can be secured to deter curious children from dangerous exploration.

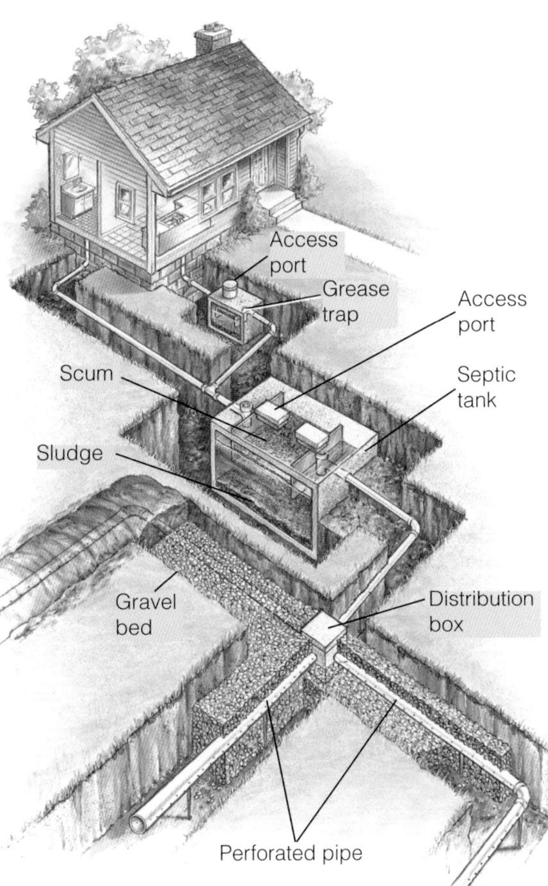

Septic systems are designed to separate liquids from solids, allowing the liquids to drain into the soil, where the earth's natural filtering process treats the wastewater as it percolates through the gravel and soil. From the house, wastewater enters the septic tank, where solids drop to the bottom to create sludge, and grease and oils rise to the top to create scum. The wastewater between the two layers flows to a distribution box, which sends it out to a series of absorption, or leach, trenches. The wastewater is absorbed by the surrounding gravel and soil. The sludge on the tank bottom decomposes with the help of bacteria. Excess grease or other contaminants can destroy the bacterial action and, if allowed to flow into the leach field, can coat and clog the rock and soil and prevent absorption. A grease trap and careful maintenance can prevent this problem.

Maintaining a Septic System

Most septic systems are designed to last 20 or more years; however, if you carefully maintain your system following these rules, it can last indefinitely.

- Have the tank cleaned every two or three years.
- Stagger baths and wash loads to avoid overloading the system.
- Don't pour paints, chemicals, drain cleaners or oils into drains or toilets.
- Never dispose of grease, fat, coffee grounds, paper towels or facial tissues in sinks or toilets.
- Be sparing in use of any cleaning product not labeled septic-safe, especially those with bleach or antibacterial agents.
- Use a garbage disposer sparingly or not at all.
- Direct runoff from gutters or drainage spouts away from the drainage field.
- Don't park or drive over drainage fields.
- Call for service if smelly water rises from the drainage field or if water backs up out of drains.
- Don't use commercial tank treatments—they can liquefy sludge, allowing it to flow into drainage fields and clog leach lines.

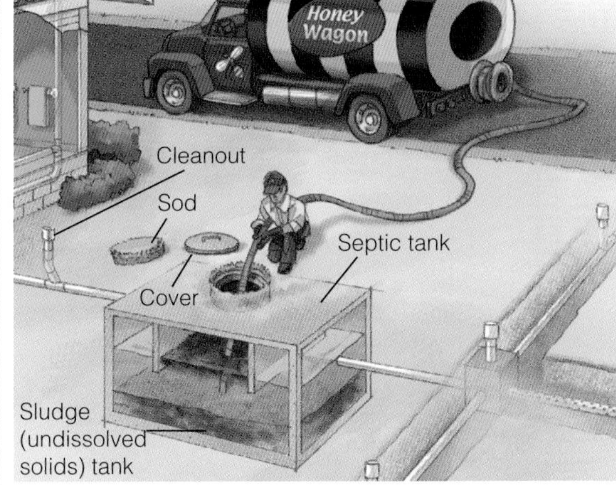

Septic tanks should be inspected and pumped out every two or three years, depending on the size of the system and the number of people using it.

Plumbing Tools

Unclogging Drains 93
Pipes and Pipe Fittings 107

Drain-Cleaning Tools

Generally, it's far better to clear drains using mechanical methods than to use chemical drain cleaners. Chemical cleaners can harm some drain pipes and be very damaging to septic systems. Further, splashing drain cleaners can harm humans, pets and surrounding surfaces.

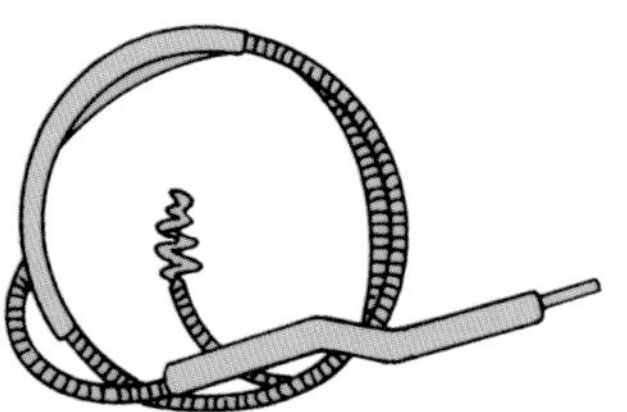

Trap-and-drain auger. Used to clear stubborn, distant clogs. Also called a snake, it's a long, flexible springlike metal tube with a spiral hook at one end and a locking handle at the other. The design helps push and break up the clog. Manual and drill-powered augers are available in varying lengths and thicknesses. Power augers are available for clearing main drains.

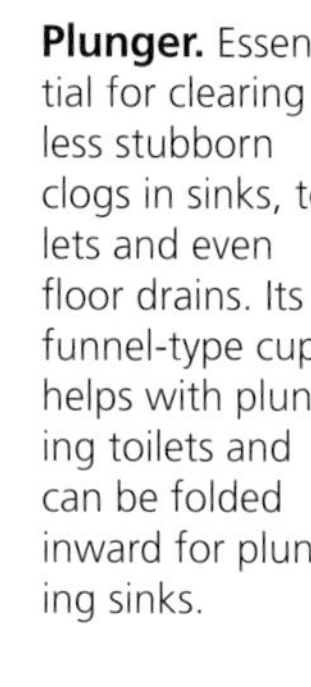

Plunger. Essential for clearing less stubborn clogs in sinks, toilets and even floor drains. Its funnel-type cup helps with plunging toilets and can be folded inward for plunging sinks.

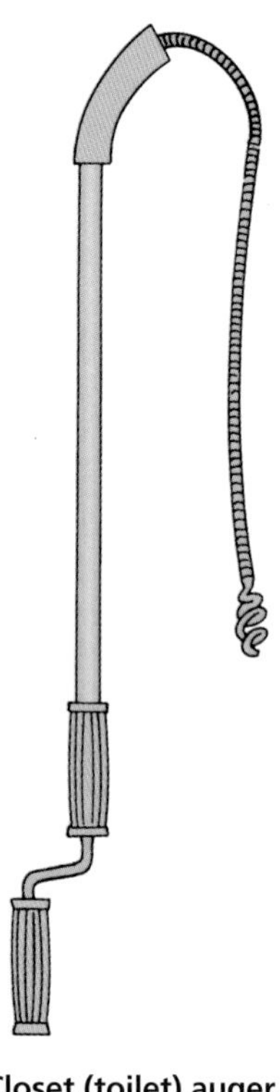

Closet (toilet) auger. A shorter auger with a crank handle specifically designed for clearing stubborn toilet clogs.

Specialty Wrenches

In addition to conventional tools, several specialized wrenches quickly pay for themselves when you're doing plumbing work. These days, many plumbing fixtures, especially faucets, include specialty tools such as deep sockets and hexagonal Allen wrenches in the packaging; hold on to them for later use.

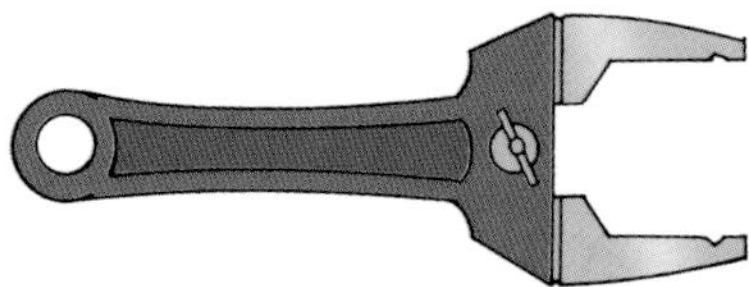

Spud wrench. Used for turning large, flat-sided nuts, such as locknuts on a sink drain. Get one that's adjustable.

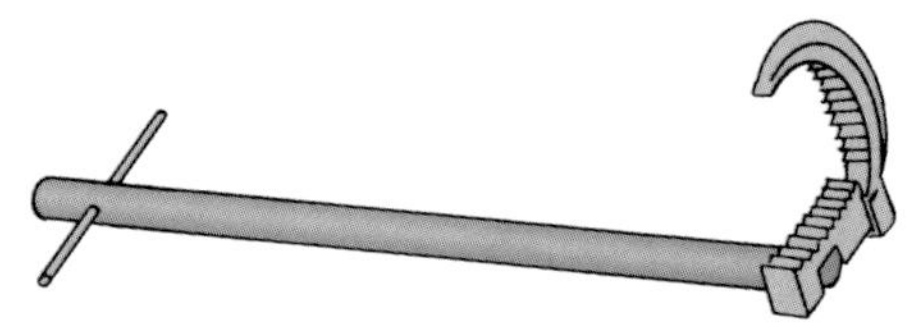

Basin wrench. Used to tighten hard-to-reach nuts on the underside of a faucet behind the sink bowl. Has spring-loaded jaws at a right angle to its long handle.

Chain wrench. Used for large-diameter and hard-to-reach pipes. The chain loops around a pipe to hold it.

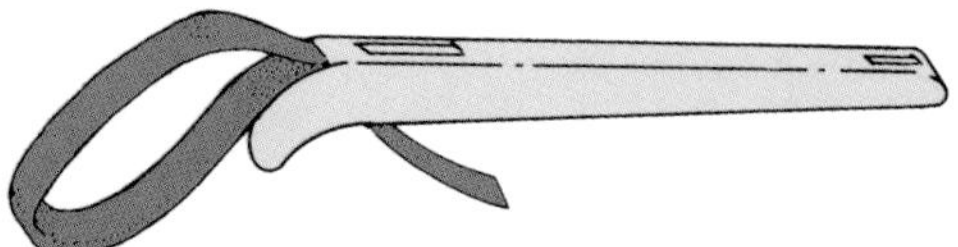

Strap wrench. Functions in a manner similar to a chain wrench except a strap replaces the chain to protect pipes with polished surfaces.

Tools for Working with Pipe

With a few relatively inexpensive cutting and shaping tools, you can work efficiently with almost any type of pipe, except galvanized and black pipe, which most hardware stores will cut to length and thread at little or no extra cost.

Pipe cutter. Primarily for cutting copper pipe, but can be used for plastic pipe. Guide wheels and cutter wheel work together to make a clean, round cut. Smaller, tight-area cutters are ideal for remodeling work.

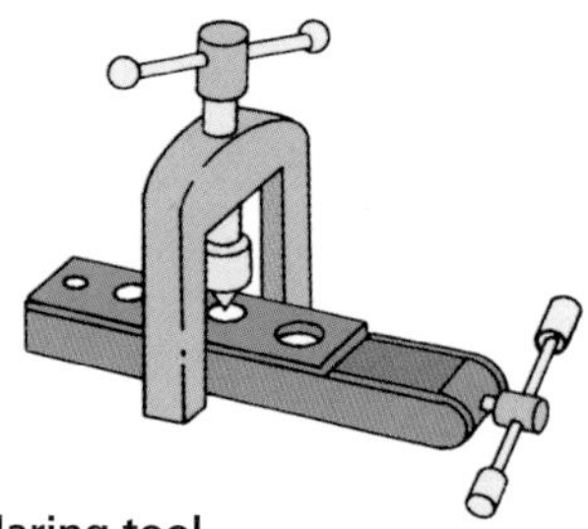

Flaring tool. Used to widen ends of flexible metal pipe before joining with a flare fitting. Flaring tool shown works for multiple sizes of pipe, but specifically sized flaring tools are also available.

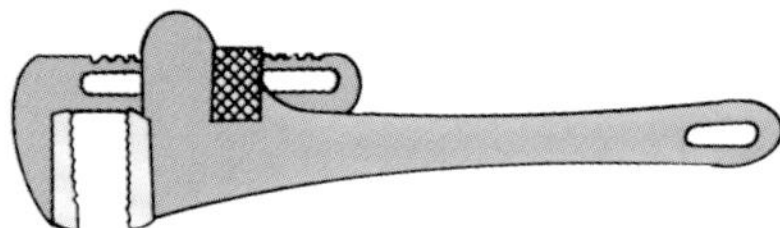

Pipe wrench. An adjustable wrench with serrated jaws. Keep two on hand—one large wrench for holding the fitting and a medium-size one for turning the pipe.

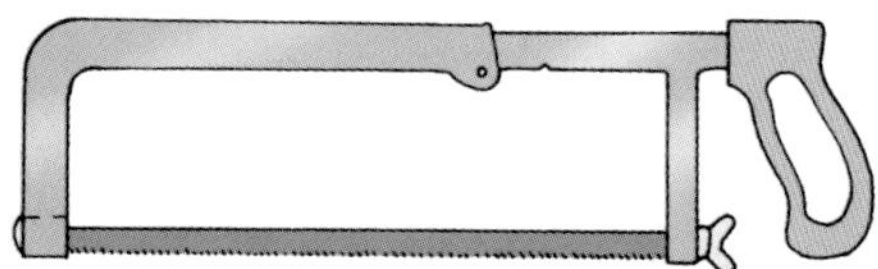

Hacksaw. Cuts most pipe, but ends tend to be rough and uneven. Works best with small pipe.

Unclogging Fixtures / Sinks and Tubs

Clogged or slow-draining sinks and tubs are more than a nuisance; they can put your entire bathroom or kitchen out of action and disrupt your family's busy schedule. But as frustrating as they make life, most drain clogs can be quickly cleared, even by a novice, in 10 to 15 minutes.

The first step in clearing a clog is locating it. This task often takes some trial and error, but here are some clues. If only one fixture is clogged, the problem is either in the stopper mechanism, the P-trap or the drain leading away from the fixture. If a group of fixtures is affected, look for the clog downstream from where their drains join.

In bathrooms, by far the most common source of clogs is a wad of hair and soap scum wrapped around the stopper mechanism or, in a shower, lying just underneath the drain cover. Always check for this problem before resorting to taking drains apart for snaking. In kitchens, the most common causes are excess grease poured down the drain and overused garbage disposers—problems most easily solved by developing better waste-disposal habits.

Grease-free Drains

Keep kitchen drains grease-free by pouring in a few spoonfuls of baking soda every few weeks. Then fill the sink with hot water, remove the plug and let it drain freely to flush debris. The best way to prevent clogs is to limit the amount of grease and other solids going down the drain in the first place.

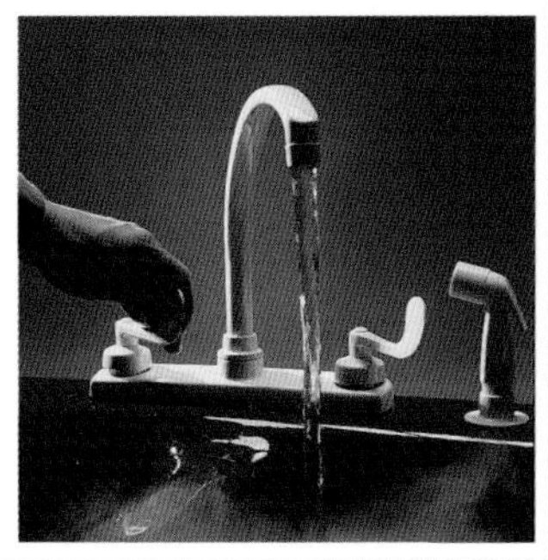

Unclogging Sink Drains

Plunge the sink drain. Fill the sink with 2 in. (5 cm) of water. Completely cover the drain hole with the plunger bell. Cover overflow hole with a wet sponge to maintain pressure. Make the first plunge slowly to expel air from bell; then plunge in and out vigorously 15 to 20 times. Add water as needed to keep the bell covered and air out.

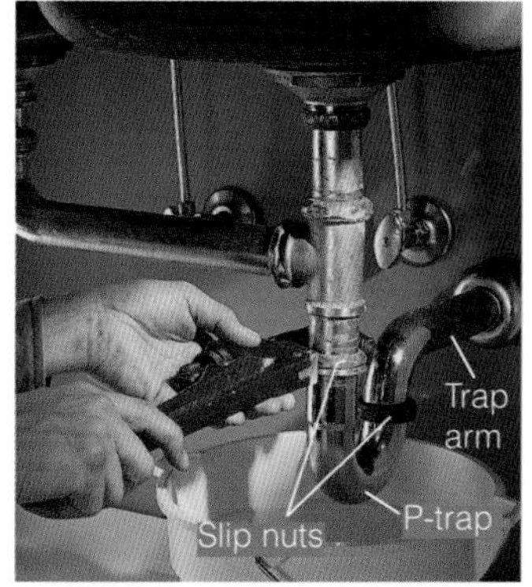

Clear the P-trap. Place a bucket under the trap, loosen slip nuts using pipe wrench if necessary, remove the trap and clear the debris. Reassemble the trap.

Clear stoppers of hair and debris. For sinks with stoppers locked in place by a pivot rod, first remove all standing water from the sink. Unscrew the retaining nut on the back of the sink drain and remove the pivot rod from the stopper. Remove stopper and clear away clog. Reinstall stopper assembly and test drain to make sure retaining nut doesn't leak.

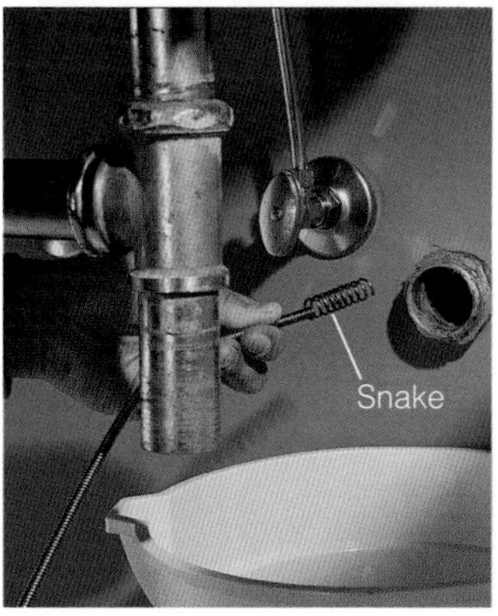

Snake the drain. Remove trap arm, slide spiral end of snake into drain and feed it all the way to the clog if possible. Don't mistake an elbow in the drain pipe for the clog. Lock snake's offset handle in place and crank snake clockwise while pushing it forward. Slide handle back and relock as necessary. Spiral end helps work snake around bends and break up clogs.

Unclogging Bathtub Drains

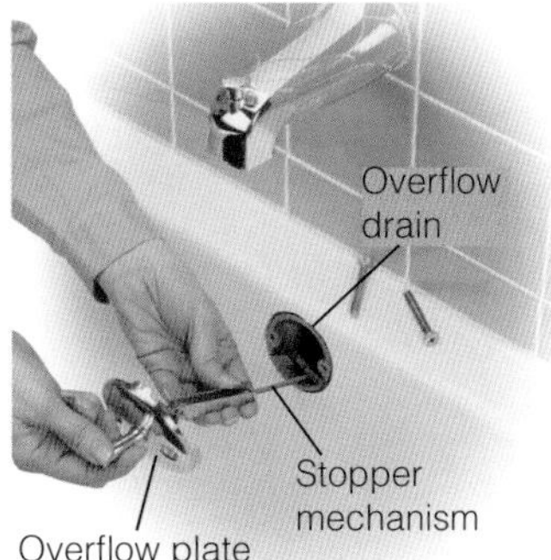

1 Unscrew overflow plate and remove it and the stopper mechanism from the bathtub drain. Some tub stoppers have two main parts—a spring or weight in the vertical overflow drain and an arm attached to the stopper plug in the horizontal tub drain. Clean stopper parts, cover overflow hole and plunge drain. Reassemble stopper.

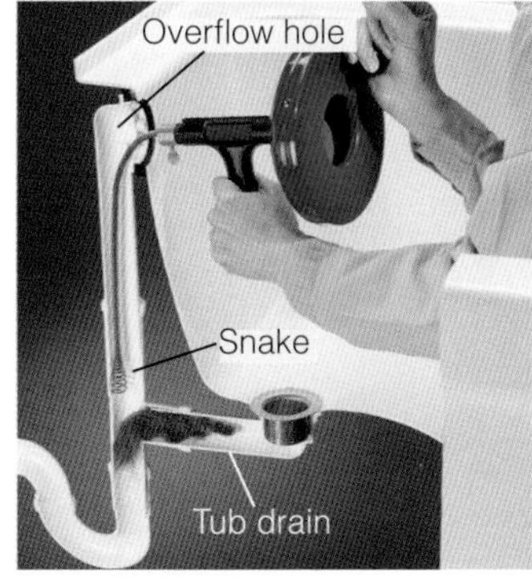

2 If clog remains, run the snake down the overflow hole to clear obstructions. If still unsuccessful, replace overflow plate and stopper mechanism, and remove P-trap through access hole or from below. Then run snake down the drain as you would a sink drain.

Unclogging Fixtures / Toilets

For about 90 percent of toilet clogs, you need only one special tool—a plunger with a flange-type cup. Toilet clogs are relatively easy to clear because after the clog passes the wax ring, the drain pipe becomes significantly larger, allowing the clog to float away.

Understanding how toilets work will help you diagnose your toilet troubles. Toilets require two things to flush well—a smooth, unobstructed drain and good siphoning action. As the flapper valve lifts, water flows into the rim chamber. Some of the water will exit through the rinse holes to clean the bowl and create the swirling action at the bottom; the rest passes through the siphon-jet chamber, where it picks up speed as it exits the siphon-jet hole. Together, these two water sources create the force necessary to carry waste over the back part of the drain and leave behind a clean bowl. When any part of the water path is limited, troubles begin.

Anatomy of a Flush

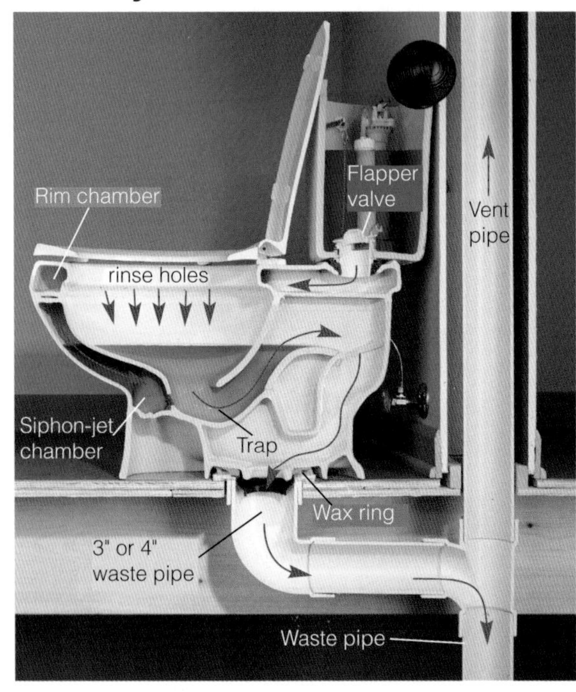

Clearing a Clog

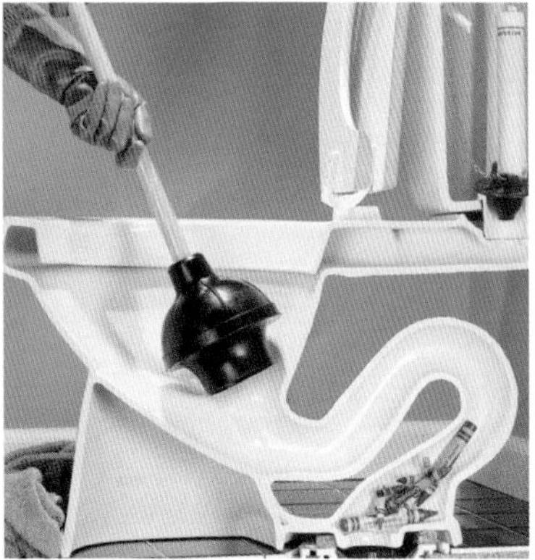

1 Don't flush the toilet if you suspect a clog. Make a first plunge gently to expel air from the plunger bell; then plunge vigorously in and out. Keep the plunger covered with water. If the plunger fails to clear a clog, use a closet auger, as shown in Step 3.

2 Test the drain by letting in small amounts of water—don't use the flush handle. Instead, remove the tank lid and manually open and close the flapper to see whether water goes down easily. If it's still plugged, you'll have to push the flapper down to restore seal quickly.

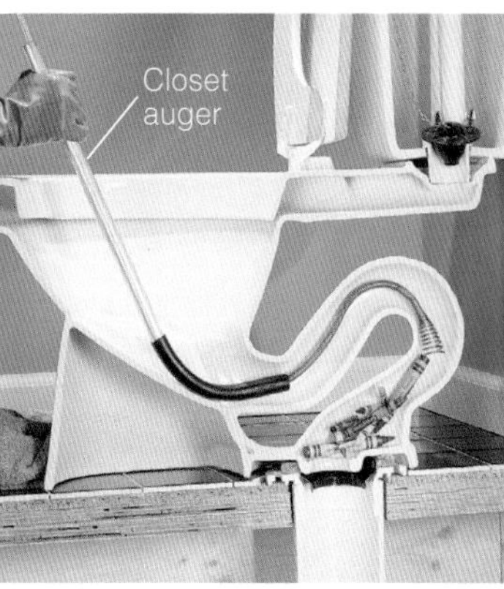

3 For stubborn clogs, spin a closet auger or regular snake through the drain. The hooked spring end should break through the clog or grab the obstruction (such as a rag) so you can pull it out. Once a clog passes the wax ring into the wider drain, it should move easily.

Fixing a Slow-Flushing Toilet

A toilet needs siphoning action to pull waste out of the bowl. If you have problems, first check the water level in the tank. If it's low, there might not be enough water released to put the siphoning action in motion. If your water is hard, calcium deposits can clog the rinse and siphon jet holes. To clear the calcium, use the following approach.

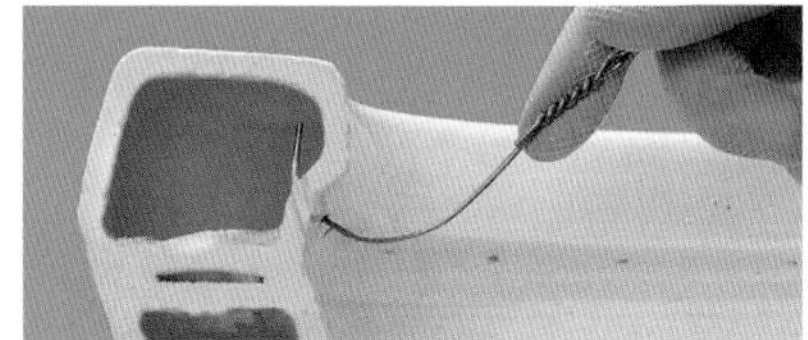

1 Use coat hanger to ream out rinse and siphon holes. Be careful not to damage glazed surfaces.

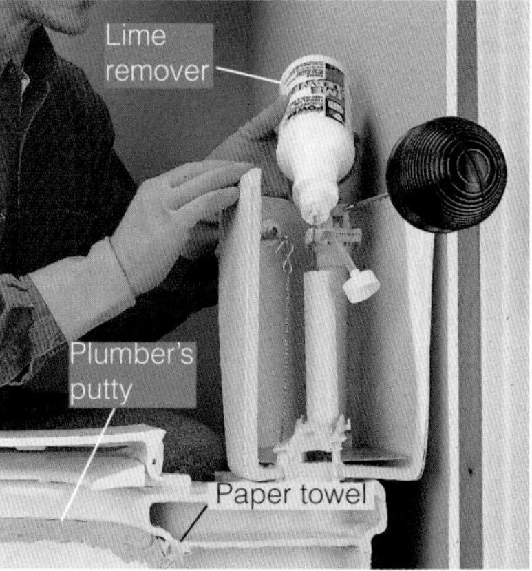

2 Dissolve remaining deposits by plugging siphon holes with wet paper towels and plumber's putty after draining water from tank. Pour lime remover down the overflow pipe or valve seat and let it sit in the rim for 24 hours. Flush toilet several times before using.

The Buzz on Low Flush

Many first-generation low-flush toilets (1.6 gal. / 6 l) worked poorly because of a number of design flaws. Bowls were the wrong shape and traps weren't engineered for the lower flow. These problems led to toilets that, because of multiple flushes, often used more water than the ones they replaced. Today, most new low-flush toilets work well, but for a better one, look for a fully glazed trap, 2 in. (5 cm) or greater in diameter. Some models even use compressed air to assist the flush, but these tend to be a bit noisy and expensive.

Unclogging Fixtures / Main Drains

If a group of fixtures, or a floor drain, is backed up, you have a clog in one of the main drain lines. These clogs often require that you remove cleanout plugs and open the drain using heavy-duty power-driven augers. Frequently these clogs form when tree roots penetrate the main drain or when certain foreign objects are sent down the drain.

To clear the drain, you can call a professional or rent a drain-cleaning machine. Be careful removing the cleanout plug—it may release a flood of backed up wastewater, so be prepared with buckets and rags.

Caution: Never attempt to remove a cleanout plug from, or run a cable into, a drain that contains chemical drain cleaner.

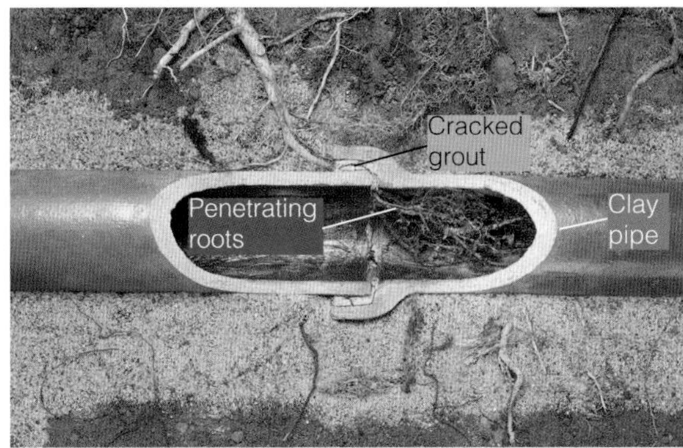

Tree roots work their way through cracks or joints in older sewer lines made of clay tile, cast iron or other piping. Newer sewer lines, made of plastic, don't suffer from this problem. When a drain becomes rootbound, it needs to be reamed out using a root saw, but the problem will soon recur unless one of the following extra measures is taken:

- Dig up the old line and replace it with plastic.
- To slow root growth, treat the drain with poison formulated to kill nearby roots.
- Seal the line by having the existing pipe lined with an internal plastic fabric and epoxy.

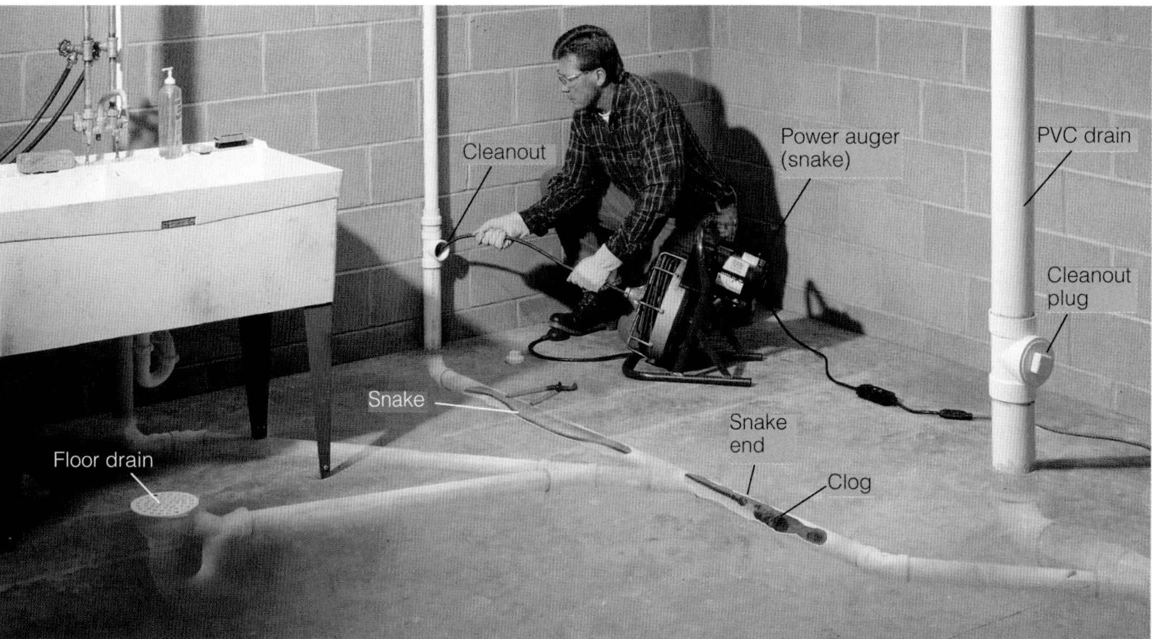

1 Remove the cleanout plug from the floor drain or cleanout. Feed cable into the drain with the motor off until you can't push any farther. Start and stop the motor using the foot switch as you feed cable. Proceed slowly. Do not allow tension to build up if the cable head stops and the cage continues to rotate. To chew through the clog, tighten the cable-lock bolt and loosen and feed cable as needed.

2 If necessary, attack the clog through the main drain cleanout. Correctly installed systems will ensure the snake follows the correct path. Stubborn or stripped cleanout plugs can be replaced with special friction-fit plugs.

Toilet Tank Problems

Plumbing Tools 92
Replacing a Toilet 120

When you flush a toilet, a carefully balanced series of events takes place in the tank. As you push the flush handle, the tank-stopper ball is lifted from its valve seat, allowing water to flow from the tank into the bowl. When the tank is nearly empty, the tank ball falls back into the valve seat, cutting off the flow.

As the tank's water level falls, so does the float, opening up the supply, or ballcock, valve just as the tank ball seals the tank. The tank then refills through the tank fill tube, and the bowl and trap refill from the bowl fill tube directing water down the overflow tube. As the float rises, it shuts off the ballcock valve and the toilet is ready for action once again. When any part of this balancing act is out of whack, you'll need to make one of the repairs shown in the chart below.

If your toilet tank or bowl develops a leak, check all pipes and connections. If a pipe or tube is corroded or the tank or bowl is cracked, replace it. If the leak appears near a joint, clean away any corrosion, replace any gaskets or washers and tighten the connection. Be careful when tightening bolts and nuts mounted to porcelain—the porcelain may crack and ruin the toilet.

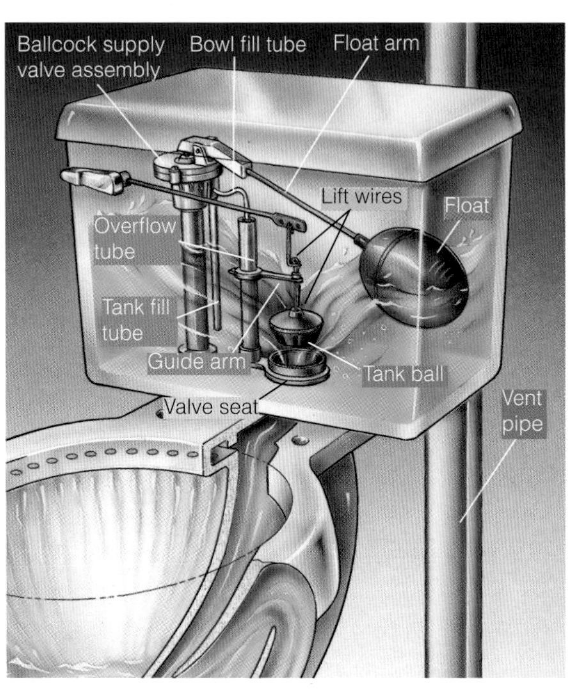

Problem	Solution
Water runs continuously.	Adjust lift wires or chain to align tank ball. Clean valve seat.
Water spills into overflow tube.	Bend the float arm down.
Water runs after flushing.	Bend the float arm. Clean the valve seat. If the float is waterlogged, replace it. Replace tank ball or flapper.
Whistling sounds occur.	Put new washers in the ballcock-valve plunger. Replace ballcock assembly.
Splashing sounds are heard.	Reposition the refill tube to eject directly into overflow tube. Put new washers in the ballcock-valve assembly.
Tank flushes partially.	Shorten the lift wires or chain to make the tank ball rise higher. Bend the float arm upward to raise the water level.
Tank sweats.	Insulate the tank by lining it with sheets of polystyrene or foam rubber. Have plumber install tempering valve to warm the water in the tank.
Tank leaks.	Tighten connections to the water-supply line. Check gaskets and washers around discharge pipe and mounting bolts to the bowl.
Toilet leaks at base.	Tighten bolts at base of bowl. Disconnect the toilet from the floor and replace the wax seal under the bowl.

Quick Fixes

Most toilet tank problems are simple to repair with minor adjustments or cleaning. Here are some common adjustments for standard (not low-flush) toilets:

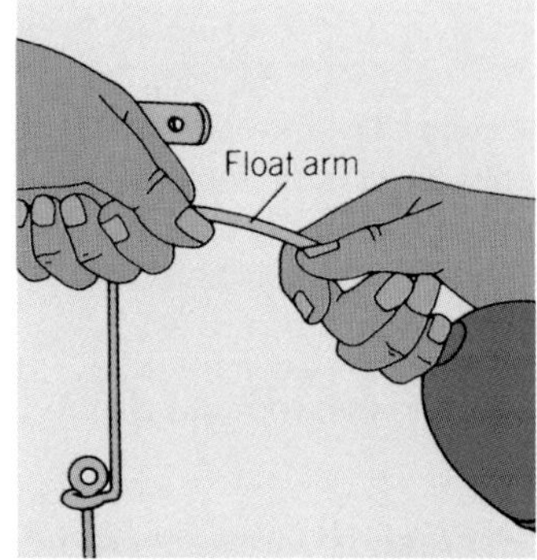

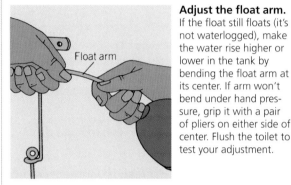

Adjust the float arm. If the float still floats (it's not waterlogged), make the water rise higher or lower in the tank by bending the float arm at its center. If arm won't bend under hand pressure, grip it with a pair of pliers on either side of center. Flush the toilet to test your adjustment.

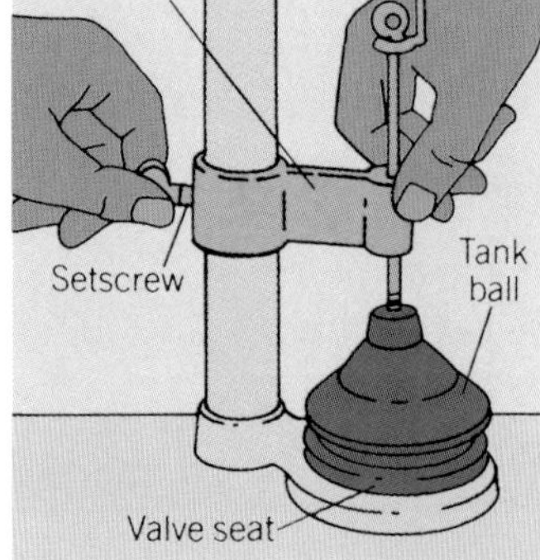

Check the tank ball alignment. Shut off the water supply to the tank and look inside it as you flush to watch the tank ball drop. If it doesn't fall straight into the valve seat, loosen the setscrew on the guide arm, and reposition the arm so the tank ball is directly above the valve seat. Tighten setscrew, refill the tank and flush to test.

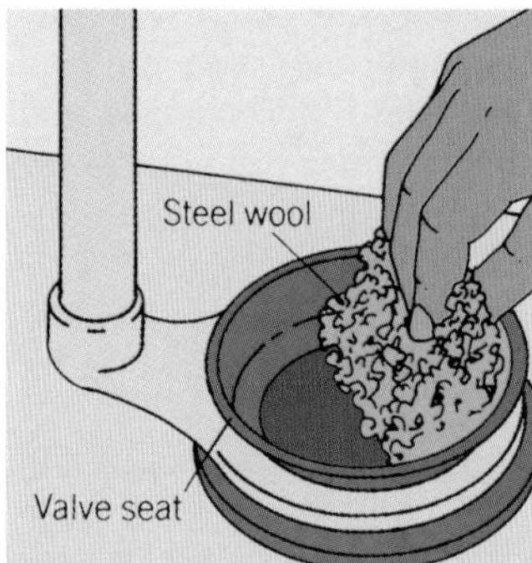

Clean the valve seat. When the tank ball seats properly and water still escapes, mineral deposit buildup on the tank ball and valve seat may create a poor seal. Completely empty the tank, remove the tank ball and clean the ball with warm water and detergent. Gently scour the rim of the valve seat using fine steel wool.

Overhauling a Toilet Tank

It's often easier to replace the entire working mechanism inside the toilet tank rather than to replace it piecemeal. A universal replacement kit and a few tools will soon silence the annoying watery sounds keeping you awake at night. First, shut off the water supply at the shutoff underneath the toilet or at the home's main shutoff. Be prepared to replace the toilet shutoff—corrosion or disuse frequently causes it to seize or not close completely.

With the water off, flush the toilet to drain the tank. Sponge up the remaining water in the tank. Be sure the tank is completely empty before you remove any parts.

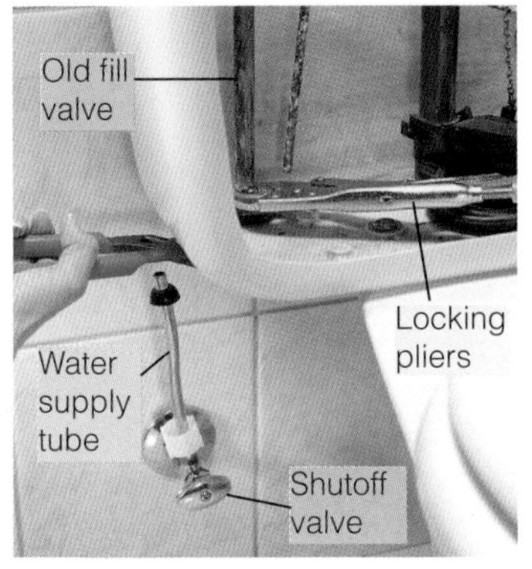

1 Disconnect the water supply tube located under the tank's bottom left side. Inside the tank, attach locking pliers to base of old fill valve to keep it from spinning. With adjustable pliers, remove locknut on outside of tank.

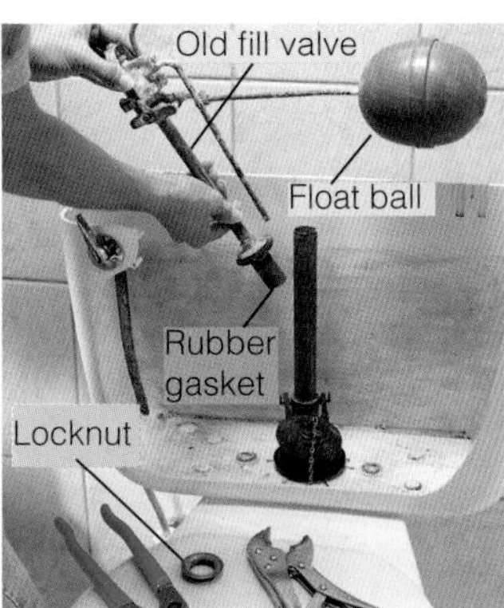

2 Remove old fill valve by lifting it out of the tank. Float ball and refill tube are attached and will come out with it. Clean area around the hole where the fill valve mounts to the tank.

3 Adjust the length of new fill valve by twisting fill valve base stem until the critical water mark (see Step 4) is 1 in. (2.5 cm) above top of overflow tube. Install rubber gasket and test-fit height by setting valve in place. Orient fill valve so bowl refill tube points toward overflow tube. Secure fill valve with locknut.

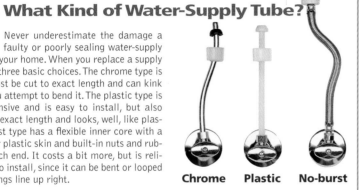

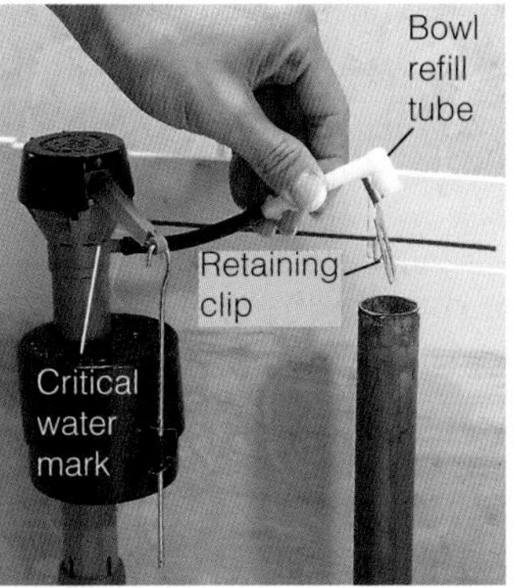

4 Trim bowl refill tube to length to avoid kinking and install it. Push refill tube over stem on valve and clip it to rim of overflow tube so water will be directed straight into overflow. Install and tighten water supply tube and turn on water to test toilet.

5 Clean out new valve to remove any dislodged mineral deposits. To do this, turn off water, take off cap, and then open water shutoff valve slowly to let water bubble out.

Shop Smart

What Kind of Water-Supply Tube?

Never underestimate the damage a faulty or poorly sealing water-supply tube can do to your home. When you replace a supply tube, you have three basic choices. The chrome type is reliable but must be cut to exact length and can kink easily when you attempt to bend it. The plastic type is the least expensive and is easy to install, but also must be cut to exact length and looks, well, like plastic. The no-burst type has a flexible inner core with a woven metal or plastic skin and built-in nuts and rubber seals at each end. It costs a bit more, but is reliable and easy to install, since it can be bent or looped by hand, so things line up right.

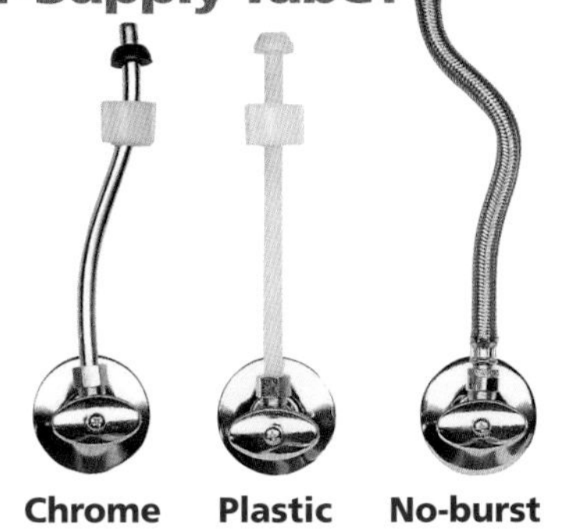

Wax Rings

When water leaks out from under a toilet, the wax ring must be replaced immediately to avoid water damage. Shut off and drain the water, and loosen one end of the supply tube. Remove the two flange nuts holding the toilet in place—be prepared to use a hacksaw to cut them if they're frozen in place. Plug the drain temporarily with a rag, then scrape the old wax from the toilet base and flange. Install a new wax ring with a rubber or plastic collar. Remove the rag and lower the toilet straight onto the bolts. Sit on the toilet to compress the wax; it will reseal the connection between flange and toilet bowl. Reinstall the nuts, washers and supply tube.

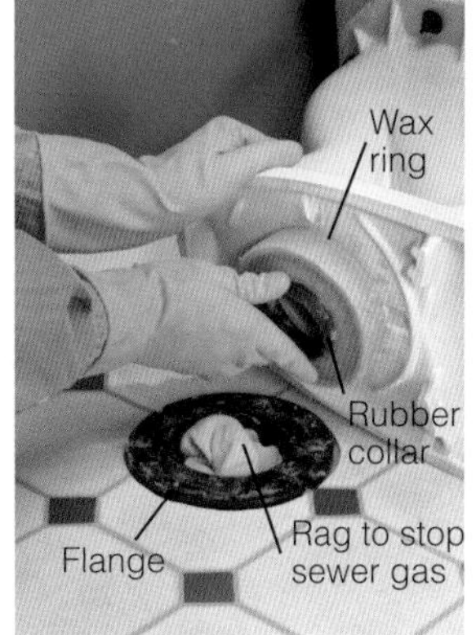

Faucet Repair / Washer Type

A leaky faucet has a torturous way of wearing on nerves and water resources. Even a slow drip can waste hundreds of gallons or liters per month. Luckily, most dripping washer-type faucets can be cured in 30 minutes for less than a dollar.

To repair a washer-type faucet, you'll need to replace the washer on the bottom of the valve stem and sometimes replace the valve seat as well. Replace washers for both the hot and cold water while you're at it, not just the one that's leaking. Before you begin, turn off the water-supply valves and close the sink stopper so small parts won't disappear down the drain.

Most faucet handles are secured by a screw, which is sometimes covered by a snap-on cap or button. You may need to tap, wiggle or pry the handle a bit to remove it. The washer on the end of the valve stem may be flat or beveled. The new washer should be the same profile and fit snugly inside the circular lip without having to be forced.

With your finger, feel down inside the area where the stem assembly enters the faucet to determine whether the valve seat is rough or grooved. If it is, replace it with a new valve seat that exactly matches the old in diameter, height and threads.

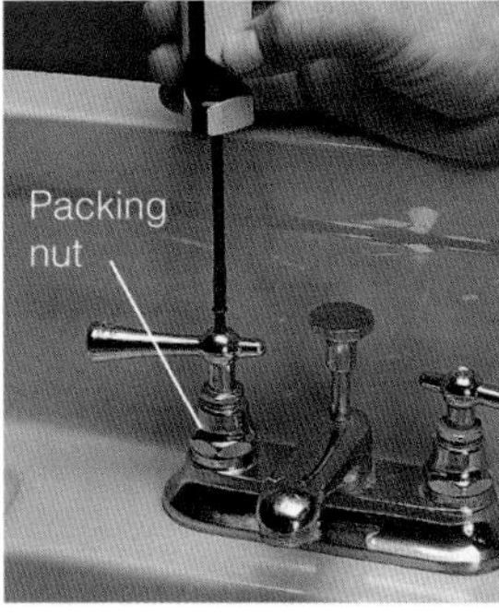

1 Remove screw holding handle, then loosen and remove packing nut. Remove stem assembly.

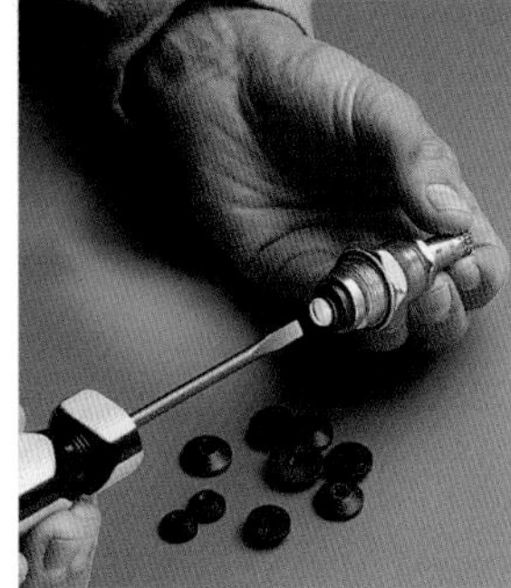

2 Remove worn washer and replace it with correct type: flat or beveled. New washer should fit snugly without being forced.

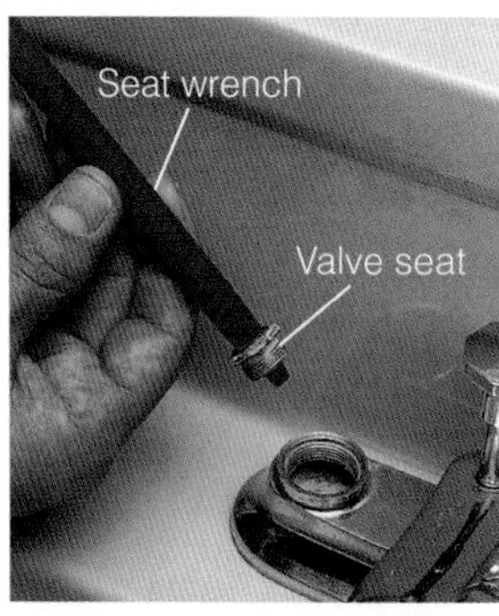

3 Use seat wrench to remove worn valve seat. New seat must match old one exactly in diameter, height and number of threads.

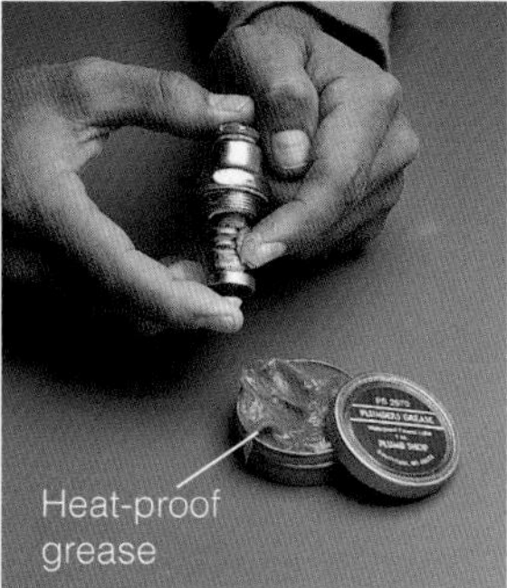

4 Lubricate working parts of stem assembly with heat-proof faucet grease. Reassemble faucet.

Repairing an Outdoor Faucet

Most outdoor faucets, including the freeze-proof one shown, have a washer at the end of the valve stem. Freeze-proof faucets are particularly prone to worn washers because, when the faucet is turned off, it continues to drain for a few seconds; consequently, people tend to turn the faucet tighter, damaging the rubber washer. Before beginning your repair, turn off the faucet's water supply.

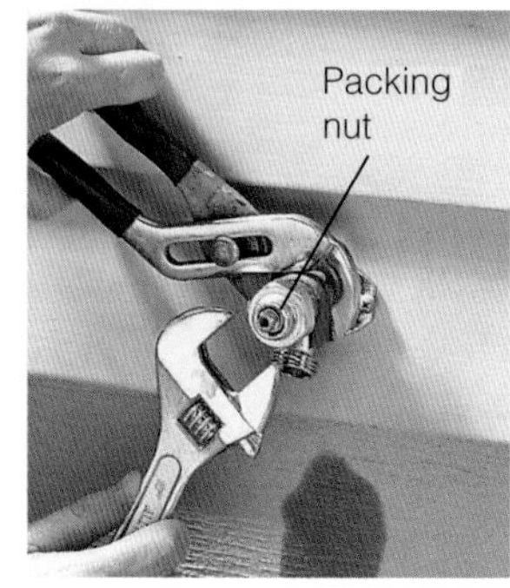

1 Unscrew handle and remove packing nut. Hold faucet steady while loosening the nut to avoid twisting the interior pipe. Even hard copper pipe can be twisted.

2 Pull stem out of faucet. For removal, some stems have to be turned so a key lines up with a slot; reattach handle to turn and pull stem.

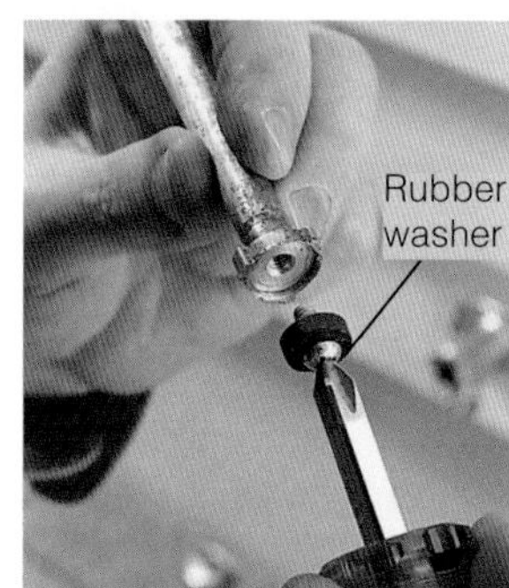

3 Remove and replace rubber washer on the stem end. If there are rubber O-rings on stem, replace these as well.

Installing a Frost-proof Faucet

Frost-proof faucets work by shutting off water flow inside a heated space, away from freezing temperatures. New frost-proof faucets frequently have a built-in anti-siphon device to prevent cross-connections (p. 90). Install the faucet at a slight downward pitch to allow the stem housing to drain.

Faucet Repair / Cartridge and Ball

Usually the hardest part to repairing a faucet is finding the right replacement parts. Hardware and plumbing supply stores normally carry parts for common models, but if you have a faucet from a small manufacturer, you may have to special-order replacement parts. (Sometimes it's easier to simply replace the whole darn faucet.) Most repair kits include thorough instructions and some of the specialized tools you'll need.

Examine the faucet closely to determine where the leak is coming from. Leaks around the base of a spout require a different repair than a drip from the end of a spout. After you turn off the water supply, open the valve in the center position to relieve water pressure.

Pay close attention to the order and orientation of the parts as you remove them. A digital camera is handy for recording each step in case you forget later. Set the parts aside in the order you removed them. When all the parts are out, inspect the interior of the valve for bits of deteriorated gaskets or mineral deposits. To clean these surfaces, use a cloth or fine-abrasive nylon pad.

Slow water flow can be caused by plugged holes in the faucet body. Use a small screwdriver to clean them out. Before you replace worn parts and reassemble the faucet, hold a rag over the faucet and open the water shutoff valve slightly to flush out loosened debris, catching it in the rag. Here are other tips to remember when you repair a faucet of any type:

- Always take old faucet parts with you to the store to get an exact match.
- Plug or cover drains and strainer baskets to avoid losing small parts.
- Line sink with a towel to prevent dropped tools from damaging it.
- Slow flow is frequently caused by a plugged aerator. Simply remove it, clean it and return it to its place. If it still works poorly, replace it.
- Always pay attention to alignment of parts as you reassemble the faucet.
- Many faucet manufacturers offer a lifetime guarantee. Take them up on it if yours drips or malfunctions.

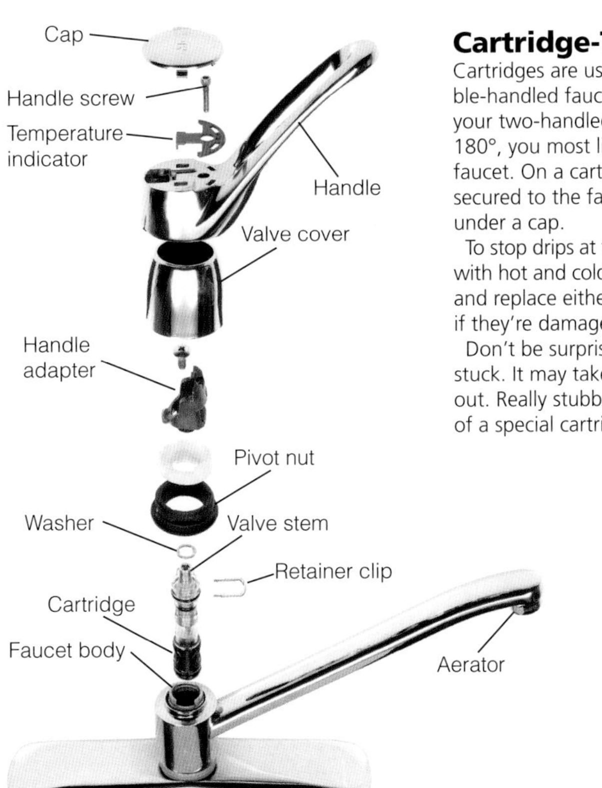

Cartridge-Type Faucet

Cartridges are used in both single- and double-handled faucets. If the levers or knobs on your two-handled faucet turn only 90° to 180°, you most likely have a cartridge-type faucet. On a cartridge faucet, the handle is secured to the faucet by a screw that's hidden under a cap.

To stop drips at the spout or correct problems with hot and cold mixing, remove the cartridge and replace either the O-rings on the cartridge if they're damaged or the entire cartridge.

Don't be surprised if the cartridge seems stuck. It may take considerable force to pull it out. Really stubborn cartridges require the use of a special cartridge-pulling tool.

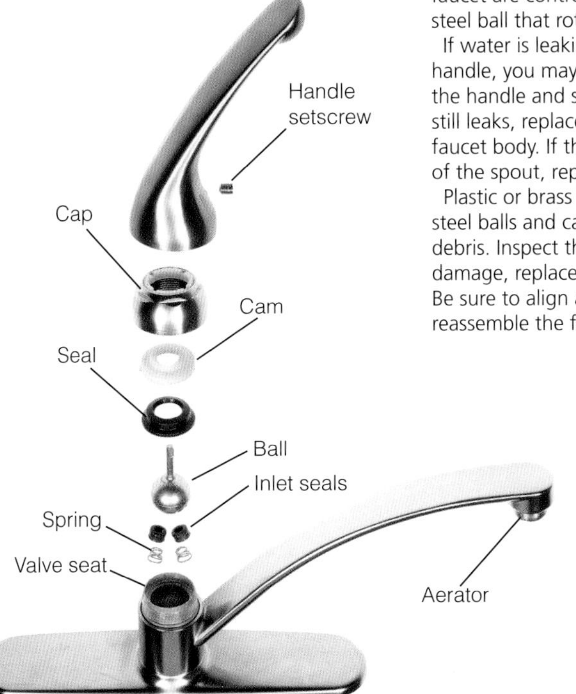

Ball-Type Faucet

Water flow and temperature in a rotary-ball faucet are controlled by a hollow plastic or steel ball that rotates in a socket.

If water is leaking around the base of the handle, you may be able to fix it by removing the handle and simply tightening the cap. If it still leaks, replace the O-rings around the faucet body. If the faucet drips from the end of the spout, replace the seats and springs.

Plastic or brass balls are softer than stainless steel balls and can become scratched by debris. Inspect the ball and, if you see damage, replace it with a stainless steel one. Be sure to align all the parts properly as you reassemble the faucet.

Faucet Repair / Ceramic Disc

Plumbing Tools 92
Pipes and Pipe Fittings 107

Ceramic-disc faucets are like cartridge faucets except discs inside the cartridge control the water flow. This type of valve is sturdy and reliable and rarely needs fixing. In fact, many manufacturers offer a lifetime warranty on the cartridge. Leaks can result from faulty rubber seals or a cracked disc inside the cartridge. Since replacement cartridges are expensive, start by replacing the seals and reassembling the faucet. If it still leaks, replace the cartridge.

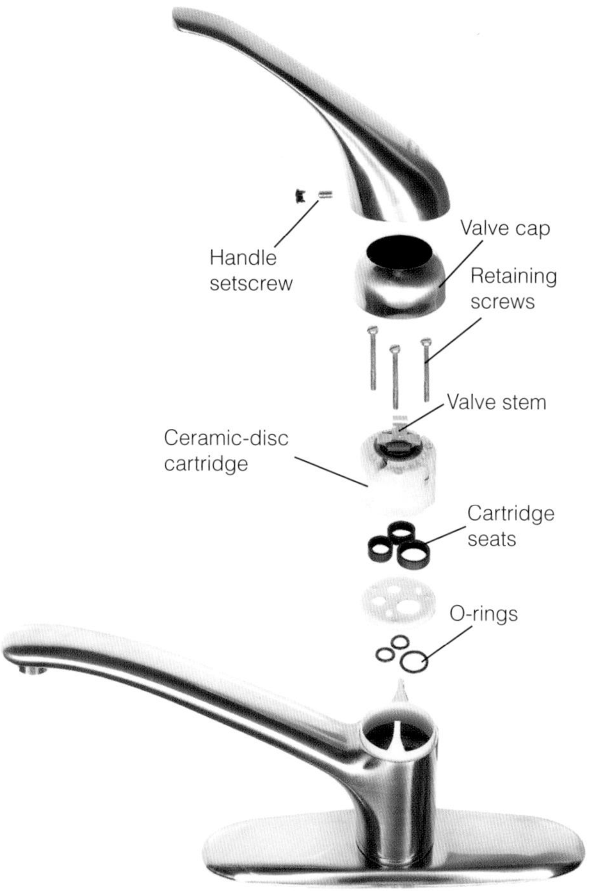

Repairing an Aerator

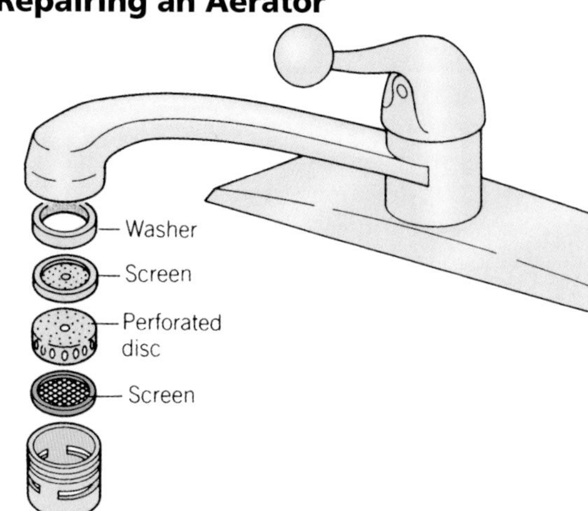

Slow water flow. Unscrew aerator, remove debris, soak parts in vinegar and clean. Flush debris out of faucet and reinstall aerator.

Repairing a Spray Attachment

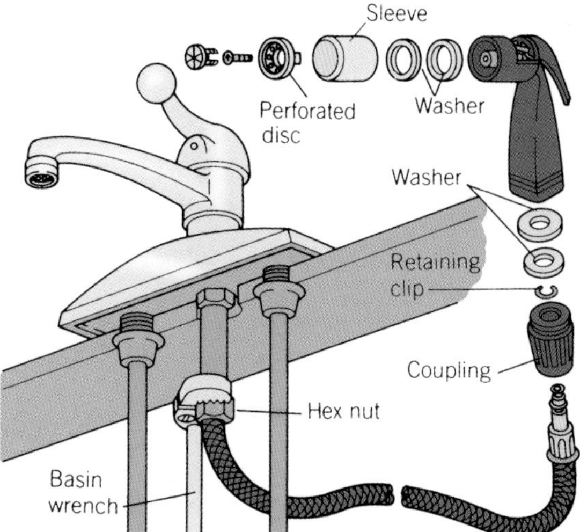

Faulty sprayer. Clean sprayer head and replace sprayer hose, if necessary. If problems persist, remove faucet and clean the sprayer diverter in faucet body.

Installing Shutoff Valves

Shutoff valves on every water-supply line simplify repairs and allow you to quickly deal with emergency faucet and toilet leaks. For long-term reliability, use ball-type valves (p. 114) and determine whether you need a straight or angled valve.

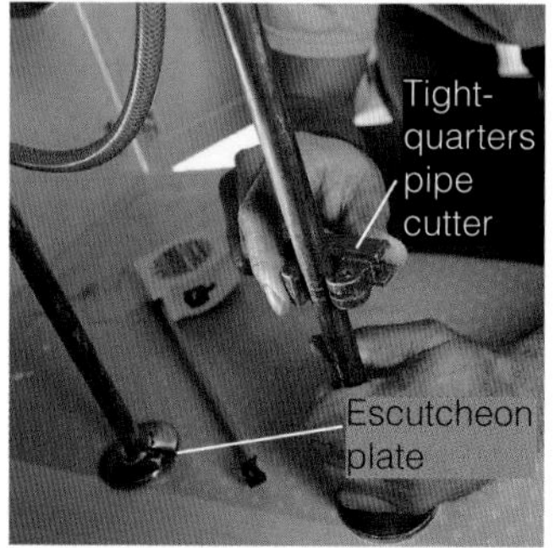

1 Shut off main water valve. Cut pipe at a point that leaves room to work. Pipe may come up from floor or out of wall. Disconnect old faucet supply lines. Remove burrs from inside and outside of pipe. Install escutcheon plate. Shutoffs are available for compression, solder or threaded fittings.

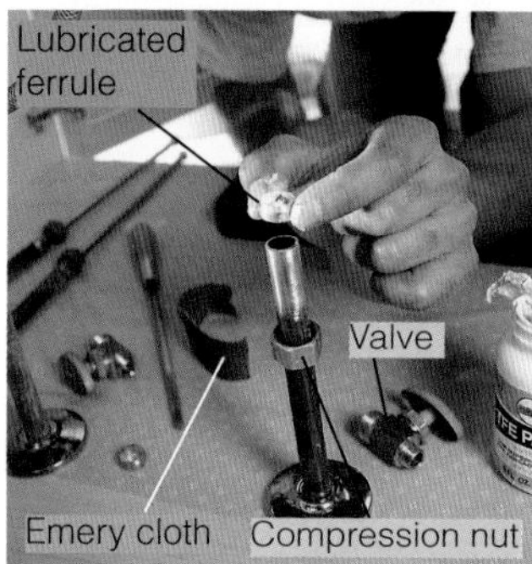

2 Clean copper pipe with emery cloth or steel brush. For compression fittings, slip compression nut over pipe, lubricate ferrule with Teflon pipe compound and slip ferrule over pipe. For sweat joints, open valve to avoid heat buildup while soldering the joint.

3 Attach supply lines to faucet first. Slide shutoff valve onto pipe. Coat threads with pipe compound. Use two wrenches to tighten compression fittings to hold the valve steady with its handle facing out. Check valve packing nut to make sure it's tight.

Faucet Repair / Replacement

Often the hardest part of replacing a faucet is removing the old one. To get at it, you'll need to clear the cabinet jungle and you may need to remove the drain for access. Plan to replace supply lines. Replace defective valves or add shutoff valves if you don't have them. The basin wrench (Step 3) is a must-have tool for getting the job done right.

New faucets are surprisingly installer-friendly. Manufacturers provide good instructions, custom tools and easy-to-use fittings. If you install a faucet with a pull-out sprayer spout (like the one shown), you'll use only three of the four holes in the sink's rim. Cover the extra hole with a blank plate or use it for a soap or filtered-water dispenser. When selecting a faucet, look for solid-brass bodies with durable plating and washerless controls for longevity.

1 Disconnect drain lines and P-trap if they block your access to the faucet and supply lines. Plug main drain with a rag to block sewer gases. Use a towel on the bottom cabinet edge as a back cushion.

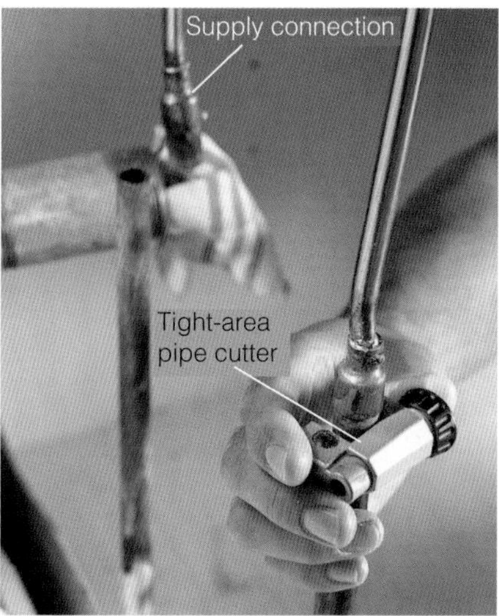

2 Shut off water supply and open faucet. When possible, open a lower faucet to drain the lines. If replacing or installing shutoff valves, turn off water main and cut pipe below old supply connections.

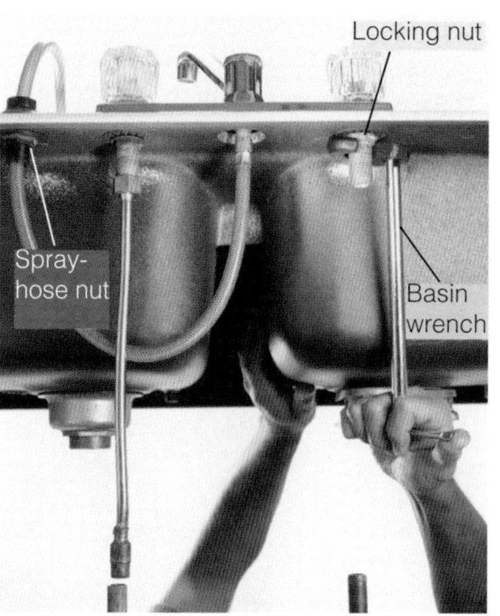

3 Reach behind sink to fit basin wrench around the locking nuts that hold the old faucet. Disconnect spray-nozzle hose and remove sprayer hose and faucet.

4 Follow manufacturer's preassembly instructions and hand-tighten flange nuts. Check alignment of flange, faucet and sink hole from above.

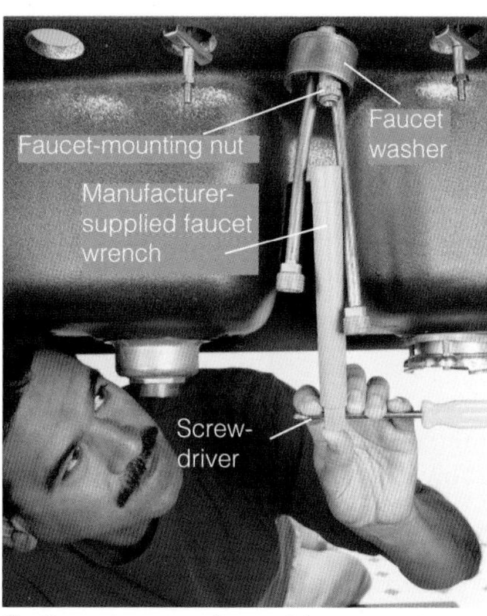

5 Slip on faucet washer and face-mounting nut. Gently spread supply tubes to make room for the tool and test whether sprayer hose fits through the opening. Tighten the nuts.

6 Thread sprayer hose through faucet body and attach it. Attach counterweight and test that hose moves freely. Attach shutoff valves and supply lines.

Handy Hints

Make It Easy

If you're replacing the kitchen sink along with a new faucet, install the faucet and strainer baskets before setting the sink into the countertop. You'll save yourself a lot of reaching, straining and frustration.

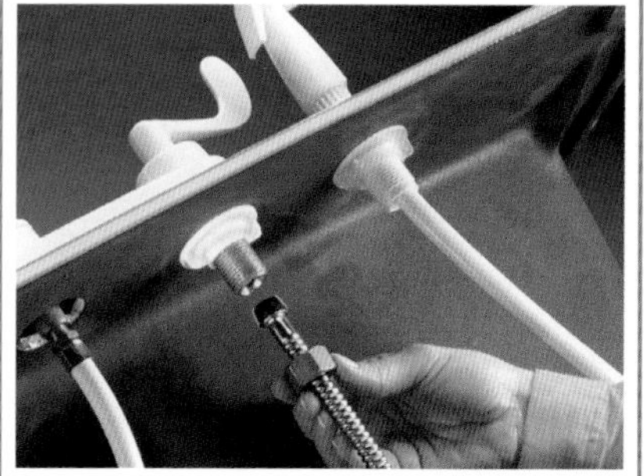

Faucet Repair / Tub Faucets

Plumbing Tools 92
Copper Pipe 112

The operating parts inside a tub faucet are similar to those in a sink faucet, and the repairs are very similar. Some shower valves have a diverter in the valve body that may need repairing or replacing; others will have no diverter or it will be on the tub spout (see below right). Shut off water before making repairs.

Washerless Faucet

Internal parts, including the O-rings, springs or the cartridge may need cleaning or replacing. You may have to remove the handle and escutcheon to access parts.

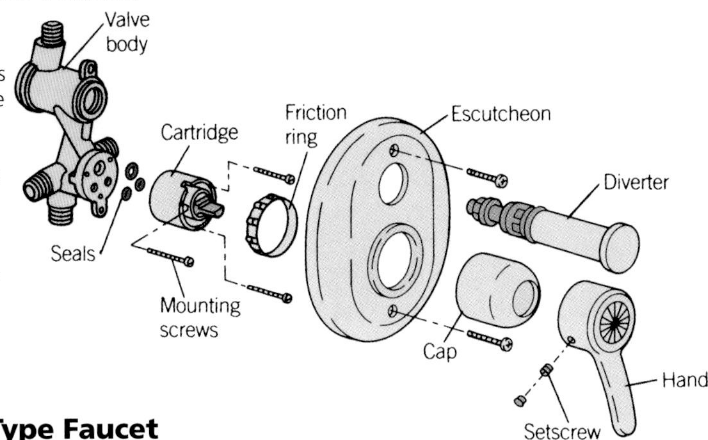

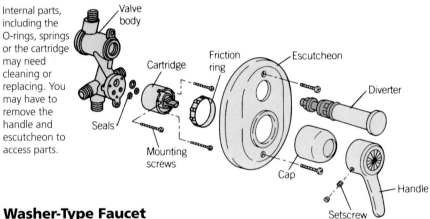

Washer-Type Faucet

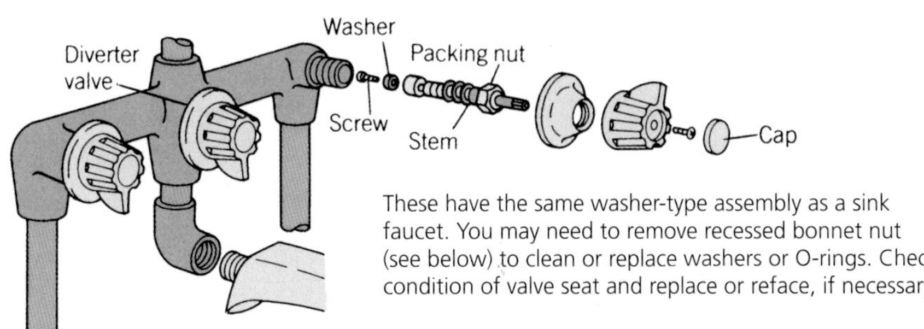

These have the same washer-type assembly as a sink faucet. You may need to remove recessed bonnet nut (see below) to clean or replace washers or O-rings. Check condition of valve seat and replace or reface, if necessary.

Removing a Bonnet Nut

To reach a recessed bonnet nut, you may need to chip away surrounding tile with a hammer and cold chisel or with a rotary tool with a ceramic-tile bit. Remove only enough material so you can slip a deep socket wrench over the nut. Turn the wrench counterclockwise to loosen the nut. Coat parts with heat-proof grease before reinstalling.

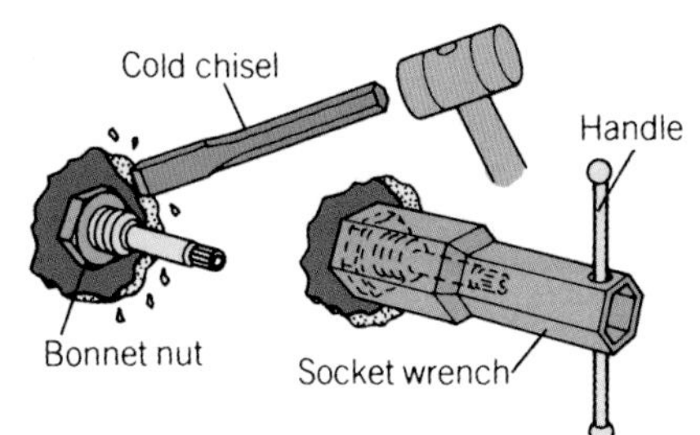

Hand Spray Attachment

When it comes time to wash the kids or the dog, if you like a mobile showerhead or if you shower while sitting, replacing an existing showerhead with a detachable handheld model may be the best—and least expensive—way to handle the job. Some models even offer a vertical support arm that allows you to reposition the showerhead to make it more child friendly.

1 Remove the old showerhead by holding the shower arm with a pipe wrench and protective cloth. Twist off showerhead using pliers or a wrench.

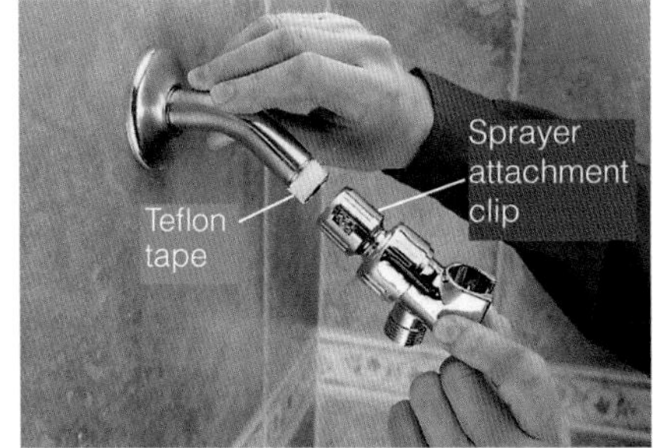

2 Wrap Teflon tape around the shower arm threads in a clockwise direction. Screw on sprayer attachment clip and tighten with pliers and protective cloth.

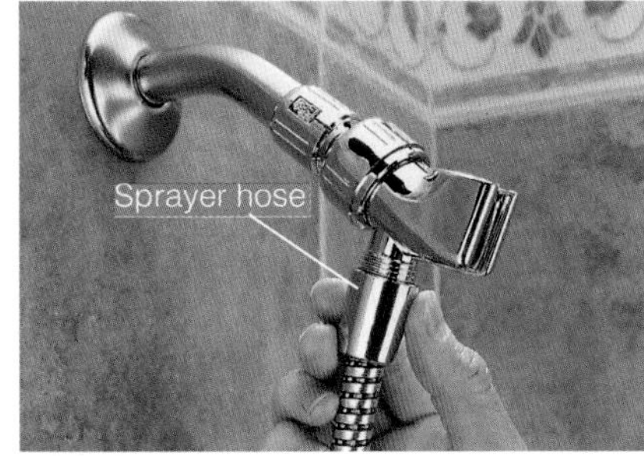

3 Attach sprayer hose to attachment clip and tighten. If necessary, wrap clip threads with Teflon plumbing tape.

Tub Spout Diverter

A tub spout diverter is a simple device that blocks water flow through a tub spout and redirects it through the shower pipe above the actual valve. The most common style uses a plunger rod that pulls up a gate to block the flow. If the diverter is faulty, your best bet is to replace the entire spout. The old spout will most likely be threaded, but some are held in place by a setscrew underneath the spout.

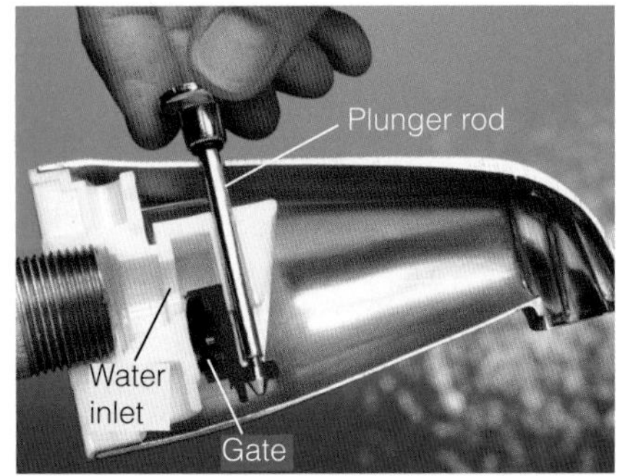

Faucet Repair / Shower Faucets

Antiscald, also called pressure-balance, valves are designed to prevent sudden blasts of hot or cold water coming through the showerhead when another plumbing fixture is turned on or the toilet is flushed. A jolt like this poses a very real hazard, because it can cause you to slip and injure yourself. Burns are another danger, especially for children and older folks who have sensitive skin.

Antiscald valves work by detecting and compensating for changes in pressure in the hot and cold supply lines. Even better, you can set the maximum temperature for an individual valve (see "Adjusting an Antiscald Valve," far right).

Most antiscald valves have a single handle; however, many older homes have two- or three-handled valves. In this situation, you can either look for a two-handled antiscald valve or special order an escutcheon plate that will cover the old handle holes.

To avoid or minimize tile repairs, install the valve from the back side of the tub or shower wall and tie into the existing copper pipe. If you have galvanized pipe, you can transition from galvanized to copper by using a dielectric union to prevent corrosion.

Protect your tub and shower and keep debris out of the drain by taping an old sheet to the tile wall below the work area. When dry-fitting pipes, make sure all the joints seat completely so the measurements will be accurate. Finally, install the shutoff valves right away so you can turn the water back on to the rest of the house.

1 Remove handle and escutcheon plate from valve. Shut off water supply to shower. Measure setback from tile surface to center of pipes in wall. To simplify installation, buy a valve with a similar setback.

2 Cut an access hole behind the valve if you don't already have one. Remove tub spout and shower arm and cut supply pipes where shutoff valves will be located. Remove old faucet valve and all old pipe above shutoff cuts.

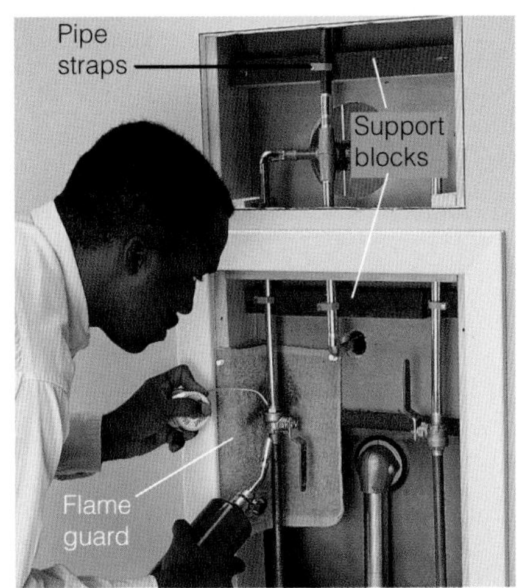

3 Use old valve and pipes as a template for sizing new valve assembly. Solder connections. Use a fireproof cloth to protect flammable materials in the work area. Open the shutoff valves and remove valve cartridge while soldering.

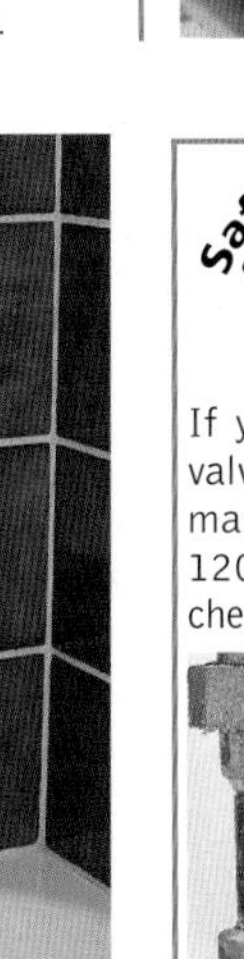

4 Secure valve and pipes with support blocks and pipe straps (see Step 3). Install escutcheon plate, set antiscald limiter and install handle. Install tub spout and shower arm and test the valve and connections.

Adjusting an Antiscald Valve

Antiscald valves usually have a gear-like rotational stop behind the handle that controls the hot water flow by limiting how far the handle can be turned in the "hot" direction. Just remove the handle to gain access.

Safety First

Not So Hot!

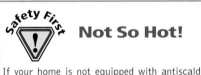

If your home is not equipped with antiscald valves, lower the water heater setting so the maximum hot water temperature is around 120° F (50° C). Use a cooking thermometer to check the temperature.

Sink and Tub Pop-up Stoppers

Plumbing Tools 92
Installing Tubs and Showers 122
Reducing Noise 278

Most bathroom sinks and tubs have a pop-up drain stopper. Although stopper adjustments are simple, it may take several tries to get them just right.

Many stoppers simply rest on a pivot rod (or a rocker arm in tub drains) and can be easily lifted out for cleaning. Others attach to a pivot rod and require that the pivot rod be removed before the stopper can be pulled. Usually, the stopper needs to be pulled to clear a hair clog that's causing slow drainage, but if the stopper is clean, it may need adjusting to raise it higher to open the drain.

To raise or lower a sink stopper, you can adjust the clevis, which is a flat rod with holes, on the lift rod for minor adjustments or move the pivot rod to a different clevis hole for larger adjustments. The point where the pivot rod hooks into the sink drain is a common source of leaks. The plastic pivot ball becomes worn, the seals holding it wear out or the retaining nut cracks. Whenever you remove or replace a retaining nut, wrap the threads with Teflon plumbing tape.

After replacing any or all parts on a drain, always test the drain by filling the basin with water and allowing it to drain. Sometimes, leaks only show up when the drain is subjected to maximum water flow.

For a tub stopper, remove the overflow plate and the striker assembly (see photo, right). The striker assembly has a threaded rod that controls how far the striker spring drops onto the rocker arm.

In sink stoppers, the lift rod controls a three-part linkage consisting of the lift rod, a clevis and a pivot rod that raises and lowers the stopper. If a part of the stopper assembly breaks, it can be hard to find a new part that correctly fits the old assembly. Even minor part differences can cause major problems. As a result, you may need to replace the entire drain and stopper assembly.

Setting Lift Rod

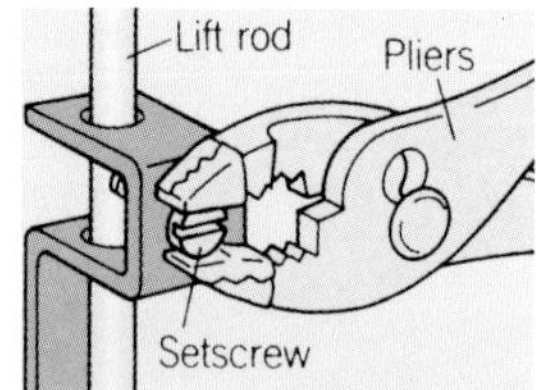

Loosen setscrew, push stopper down, adjust rod and retighten setscrew.

Setting Pivot Rod

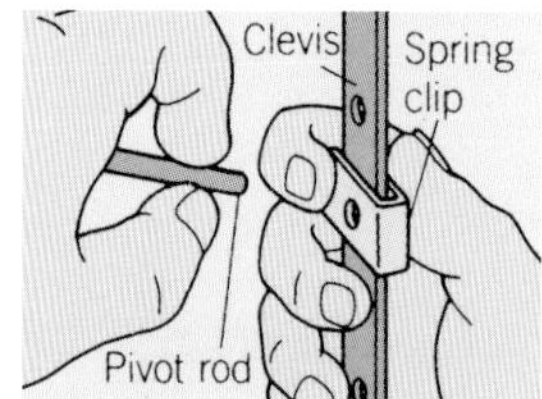

Squeeze spring clip and slide pivot rod out of clevis. Install rod in new hole.

Pivot Ball Leaks

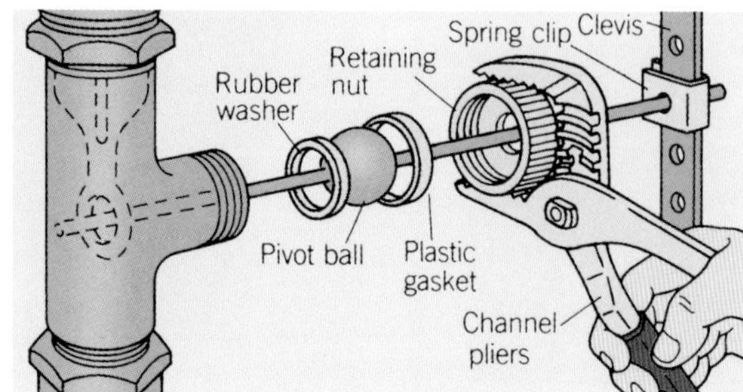

Remove retaining nut and check condition of pivot ball, gasket and retaining nut. If parts are in good condition, wrap threads with Teflon plumbing tape and reinstall. Make sure the concave side of plastic gasket goes over the pivot ball and the gasket is underneath the retaining nut.

New Tub Stopper

Replacement stoppers are now available that allow you to dispense with the troublesome internal mechanisms of the old-style tub stopper. However, it can be difficult to match the threads of the new stopper body to those of the old tub drain.

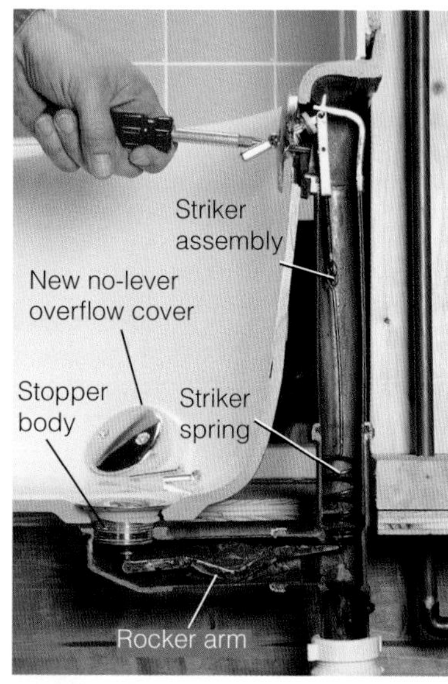

Remove old stopper by unscrewing overflow, pulling out striker assembly and installing no-lever overflow cover. Pull out stopper and rocker arm. Remove old stopper body with pliers wedged into cross arm. Take old stopper body to plumbing store to find compatible replacement. Adapter bushings are available to allow replacement stoppers to fit older drains.

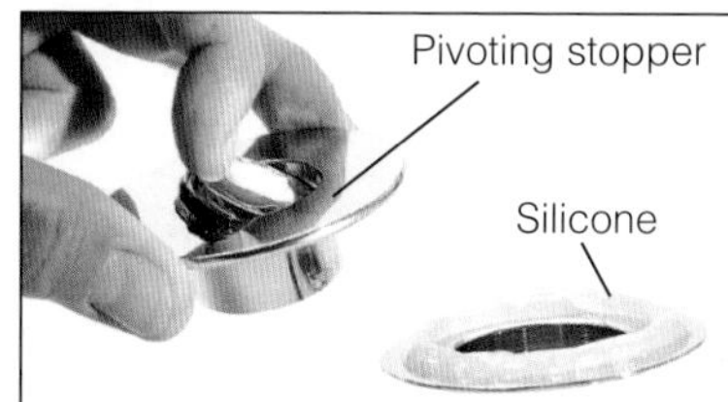

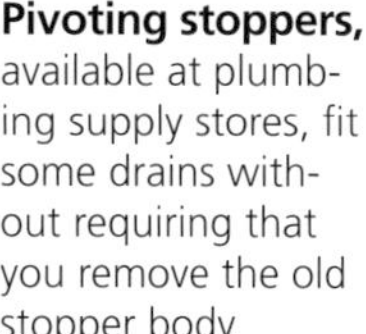

Pivoting stoppers, available at plumbing supply stores, fit some drains without requiring that you remove the old stopper body.

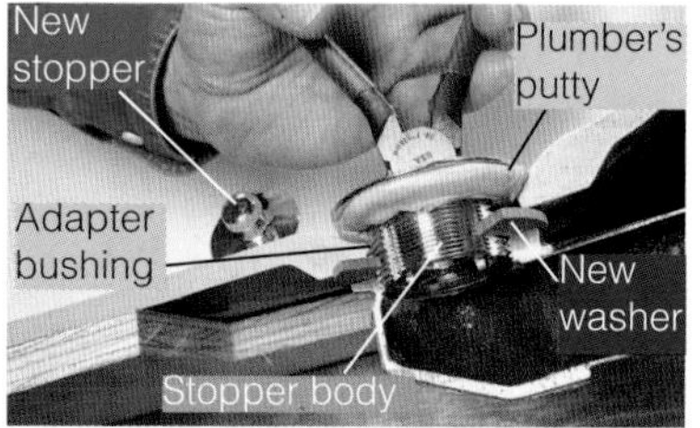

Stopper kits have lift-and-turn or spring-loaded stoppers that replace the lever system. These require replacing the stopper body.

Plumbing Noises

Houses have sounds. Some are normal and you learn to live with them. Others are an indication of a problem that needs correcting. Most plumbing noises fall somewhere in between. Banging pipes, water hammer and whistling sounds can all be corrected. If you have access to your water-supply pipes, the solutions may be fairly simple and affordable. But it can be another story if the pipes are covered by drywall.

Water hammering is caused by the quick shutoff of water-supply lines. The energy of flowing water has to go somewhere, and when a valve is shut off, the pipes can flex and "hammer" against anything close—nearby studs, joists or other water pipes. Solenoid-triggered valves, like those in dishwashers, washing machines and water softeners, shut off almost instantly. This instant shutoff not only causes the most ferocious hammering, but also puts a strain on flexible supply hoses and soldered copper fittings. Hand-controlled faucets usually don't cause as much hammering, because the shutoff is more gradual.

Sometimes the solution is as simple as adding one or two supports to the affected pipe. A piece of felt or rubber between the pipe and support can further deaden the noise. This felt cushion works especially well for pipes that are too tightly anchored. These pipes make clinking or ticking sounds when a fresh flow of hot water causes the pipe to expand.

If adding or cushioning pipe supports doesn't solve the problem, you may need to add water hammer arresters. Arresters have a chamber of air that acts as a cushion for the force of water to push against when the flow is stopped. If your home is already equipped with arresters and you still have water hammering, the arresters may need maintenance or replacing.

Whistling sounds are usually an indication of a shutoff valve that's not fully open or of high water pressure. High water pressure can exacerbate water hammer problems. In some cases, you may need to install a pressure-reducing valve to lower water pressure to the house; however, lowering the pressure may negatively affect upper-floor fixtures.

Water Hammer Arresters

Arresters have an air chamber that cushions against the moving water when the flow is stopped. If your home has arresters and water hammering persists, the arresters may need maintenance or replacing.

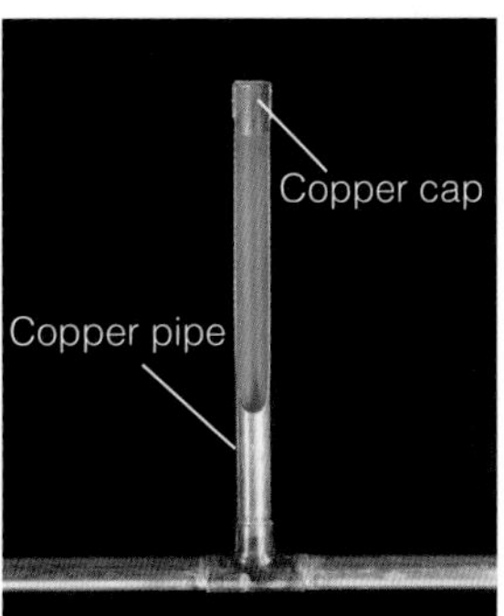

Vertical air chambers are simply a capped length (usually 12 in. / 30 cm) of pipe added to a supply line. These arresters eventually fill with water as the air gets absorbed into the water supply. If this happens, turn off the main water supply and open all the faucets to drain the lines, then close the faucets and turn the water back on.

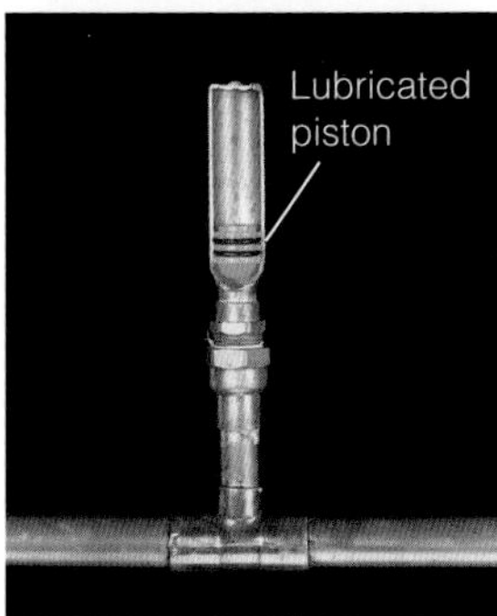

Manufactured arresters offer a more permanent water hammer solution. These arresters use a rubber-gasketed piston to isolate a pocket of air from the water in the pipes. The closer you locate the arrester to the affected valves, the better. The supply pipes for dishwashers and water softeners, which are frequent offenders, are usually accessible to add arresters.

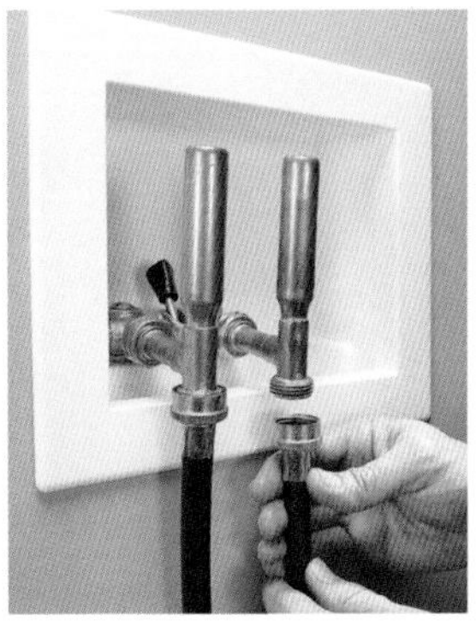

Screw-in arresters offer the perfect solution to water hammer caused by a washing machine. These mount between the faucet and the washing machine supply hoses. Look for arresters at hardware or plumbing supply stores.

Isolating Sound

Pipes can bang, rattle and squeak where they contact wood. An oversized hole with a pipe insert and pipes hung from special J-hooks will isolate vibrations and reduce noise.

Pipe inserts are split and can be installed where pipes pass through a support block and the diameter of the hole around the pipe is large enough to accommodate the insert. Generally, it's best to put these in when you initially install the pipe.

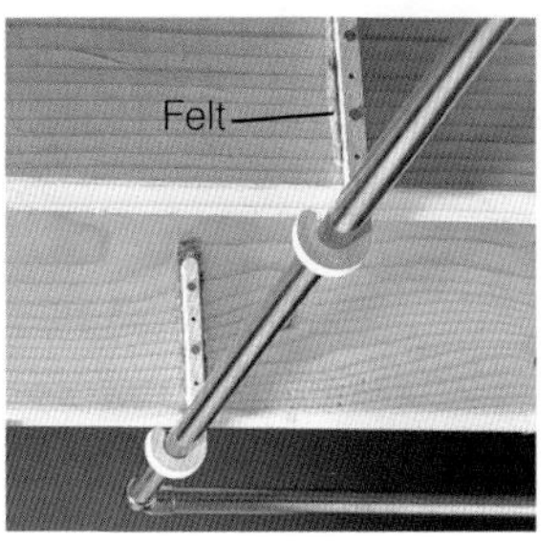

J-hooks can be used during new construction or they can easily be retrofitted to existing pipe. Nails through the side of the J-hook hold it to the supporting joist. Securing felt between the hook and joist helps to further isolate any vibration.

Pressure-Reducing Valves

Install this valve near the water meter. Cut the pipe and add adapters and unions. Screw on the valve and tighten using two wrenches. Set the pressure with the adjusting screw on top of the valve.

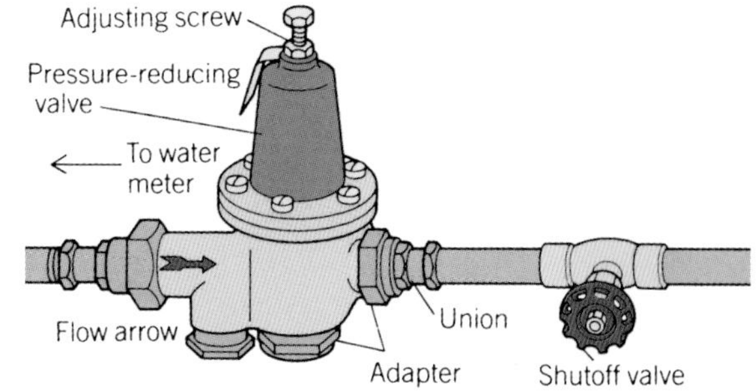

Protecting Pipes

Utility Shutoffs 12
Emergency Shutoff Valves 88
Plastic Pipe Types 108

Thawing frozen pipes is a time-consuming process. Water expands as it freezes, so frozen pipes or joints may burst or leak. For this reason, in cold climates, water-supply pipes are rarely installed in exterior walls or other unheated areas. Thaw pipes, heat or insulate problem spots and make repairs using one of the following methods.

Heat the wall cavity containing pipes by adding return-air grills near area where drain comes out of wall. Slide 1-in. (2.5-cm) piece of rigid foam behind pipes for further protection. If possible, add second grill to cabinet side to let more heat in.

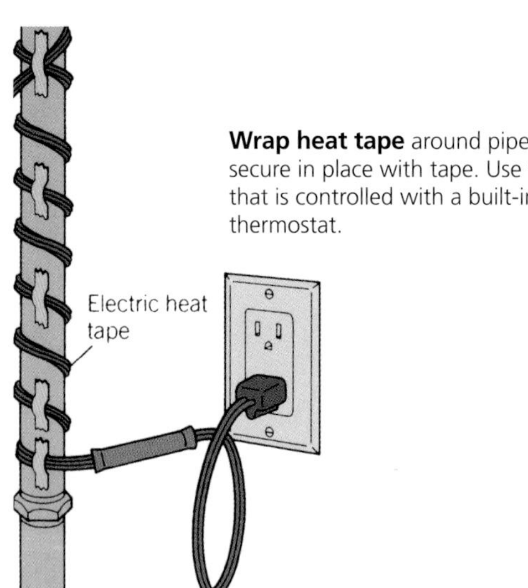

Wrap heat tape around pipes and secure in place with tape. Use tape that is controlled with a built-in thermostat.

Thawing Pipes

Before thawing a frozen pipe, close shutoff valve or main water valve. Open faucet to allow melting ice to run out and let steam pressure escape—this is especially important if you use a propane torch on metal pipes. Work from the faucet toward the frozen area. As ice melts, check for leaks and take note of any you find. For plastic pipe, heat using a hair dryer or heat lamp. Keep the heat source moving; the pipe must remain cool enough to touch.

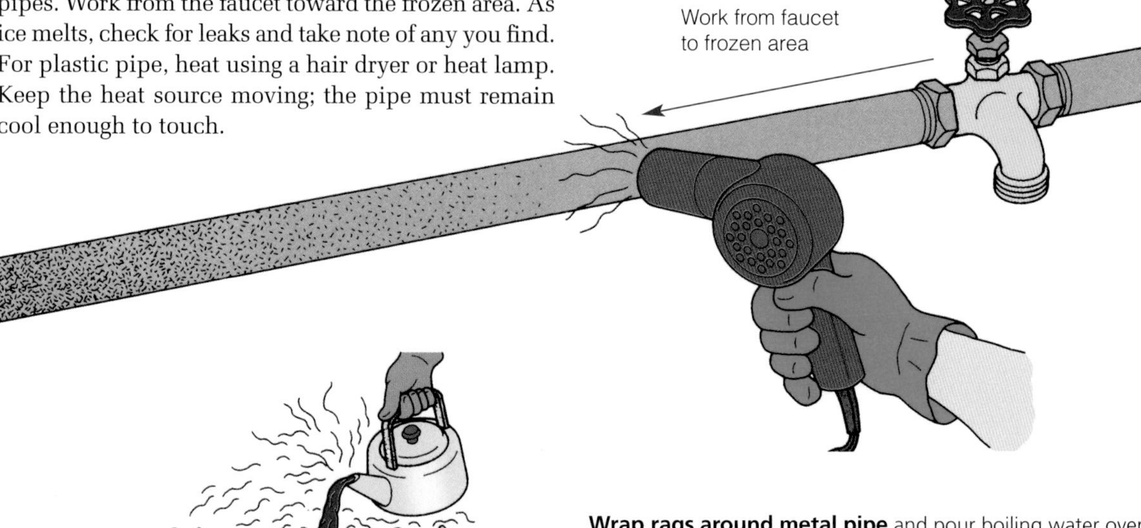

Wrap rags around metal pipe and pour boiling water over the rags. When the rags cool, repeat the process. You can also wrap a grounded, waterproof heating pad around pipe.

Pipe Insulation

Wraparound foam pipe insulation is available in several sizes. It will help maintain the temperature of water in the pipes, but it won't protect pipes in areas prone to long-term freezing. The insulation is split to allow it to slip over the pipe and cuts easily with a serrated knife. The insulation also keeps warm, humid air from condensing on pipes, stopping the pipes from sweating in the summer.

Handy Hints: Quick Fix for Holes

The best way to deal with a hole in plumbing is to replace the section of pipe, but a temporary fix helps you deal with emergency leaks. First, shut off the water supply. Next, slit a section of hose or a rubber coupler, available at hardware stores, and place it over the hole. Finally, secure the rubber patch with hose clamps. Larger holes will require multiple clamps placed side by side.

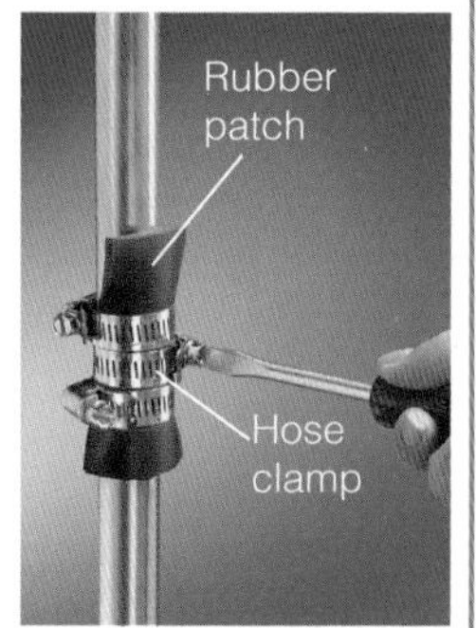

Pipes and Pipe Fittings

The type and size of pipe you can use in your home is regulated by plumbing codes. Before undertaking any plumbing job, check your local codes to determine whether you need a permit and to find out what restrictions exist on pipe types and sizes. Generally, water-supply pipes may be approved plastic, copper, galvanized steel or brass. Drain waste vent (DWV) pipes may be approved cast iron, copper, plastic or steel.

Fittings join sections of pipe. A large variety of fittings exist for connecting pipes of different types or diameters, for making curves with rigid pipe or for joining sections of pipe in straight runs or branches. If you can't find a single fitting to make a particular connection, try a combination of two or more.

Fittings are often available in two styles—standard and flush wall. Standard fittings are used for water-supply pipes. Flush-wall fittings are needed for drainage pipes—they have smooth inside joints that offer no obstruction to the flow of waste.

Rigid pipes are always referred to by their inside diameter (i.d.). However, the nominal size of a pipe sometimes bears little relation to its actual size. A pipe that is labeled 1/4 in. may actually be slightly larger or smaller than that. If you are buying pipe to connect to an existing line, measure the pipe's actual inside and outside diameters and, if possible, take a fitting or a piece of pipe with you to the plumbing supply store.

Always pick up valves or caps for the pipes you're working with so you can seal the system if you can't complete the project.

Copper Pipe Fittings

No-stop coupling. Used to join copper pipe when there's no space to drop pipe into hub. Most useful for repairing damaged copper pipe.

Street elbow. Differs from standard elbow by having one hubless joint to allow tighter turns.

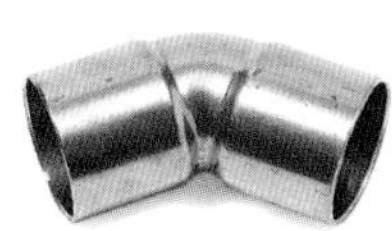

45° elbow. Allows a gradual turn in rigid pipe systems, with 22.5° curves.

Male adapter. Transitions from soldered or cemented joints to threaded joints. Female adapters also available.

Cast drop-ear elbow. Ears allow firm support of pipe, and its female threads accept shower arm or other threaded fittings.

Cast-copper tee. Designed to provide easy installation of washer supply shutoff valves. Has female threads to accept valve.

PVC Pipe Fittings

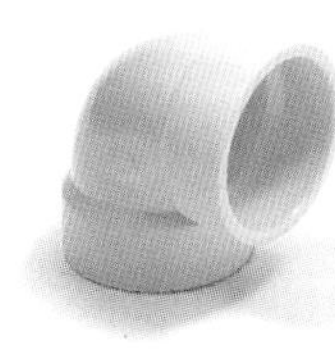

Vent elbow. A tight-turning 90° elbow to be used only with venting system. In drains, it would interfere with using augers (snakes).

Sanitary tee. Used for 90° connection in drain line, usually to join vent, fixture drain and main drain.

Wye. Connects horizontal branch line to horizontal drain line at 45° angle.

Steel Pipe Fittings

Reducer coupling. Joins pipe of different sizes. Available for threaded, soldered, cemented and compression-type joints.

Pipe cap. Used to seal stub-outs or out-of-service pipes. Plugs with male threads also available.

Dielectric and Other Unions

When joining pipes made of different materials, particularly copper and galvanized steel, use dielectric couplings to prevent deterioration. Other types of unions include:

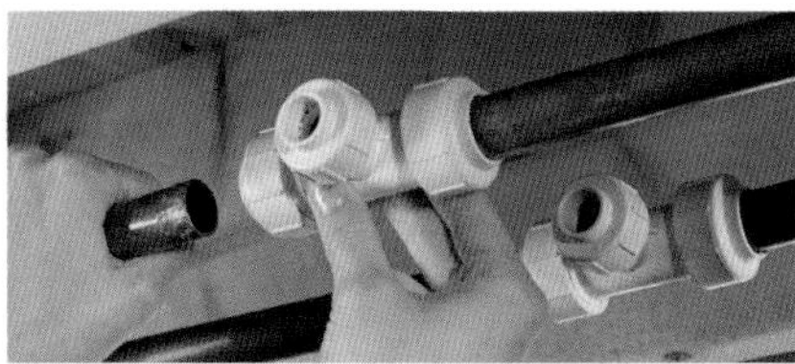

CPVC transition union compensates for thermal expansion between CPVC and copper or steel piping.

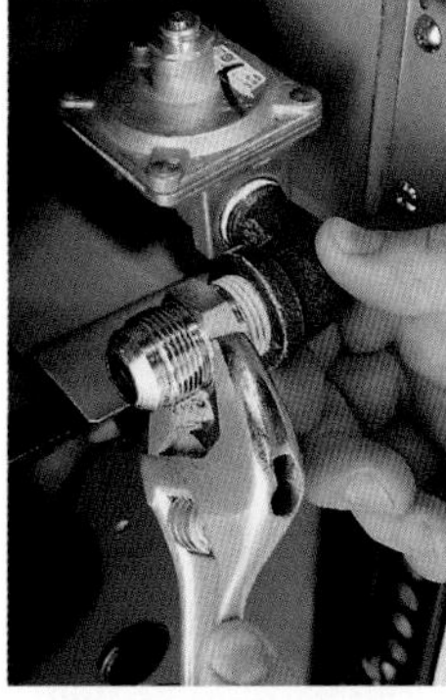

Flare-end connector fittings help make the transition from threaded-steel pipe to flexible, corrugated gas line.

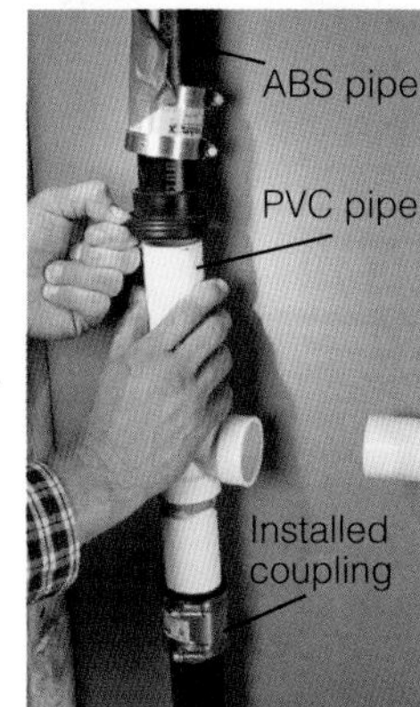

Transition couplings with neoprene rubber sleeves and metal jackets make the transition from ABS pipe to PVC, from plastic to steel, and with other dissimilar materials. Always check label for approved uses.

Pipes and Fittings / Plastic

Plastic pipe is a dream material. It's inexpensive, won't rust or deteriorate, lasts almost indefinitely, and its smooth interior surface allows water and waste to flow unimpeded. It cuts easily and the fittings are precisely molded to reduce the risk of leakage.

Although cutting and joining plastic pipe is relatively easy, planning any plumbing project is not. To plan a plumbing project, you have to figure out pipe sizes, slopes, vent locations and other important factors. Contact local building inspectors for guidance and be aware that local plumbing codes sometimes prohibit the use of plastic pipe in certain situations.

You'll find many types of plastic pipe used in homes: ABS, PVC, CPVC and others. The ABS (black) and PVC (white) pipes are larger, usually between 1-1/2 in. and 4 in. inside diameter, that plumbers use for drains and vents. CPVC, PB and PEX are used for water-supply lines that run to faucets and toilets. If you have trouble identifying any type of plastic pipe or fitting, look for a label printed or stamped somewhere on the plastic.

Use pipe with the pressure rating prescribed by local codes. Most plastic-pipe joints are chemically glued together—a process called solvent welding. The solvent melts the plastic, so when you push the pipe and fitting hub together, the two fuse as the solvent evaporates. Note that dry-fitting (Step 3) won't allow the pipe to go as far into the hub as when you have applied the solvent. Allow for this slight difference when planning.

Plastic Pipe Types

The four types of plastic pipe shown below are commonly used inside homes. Another common type, polyethylene, is a flexible black pipe used for lawn and plant irrigation. Look for the pipe type stamped on the pipe or fittings.

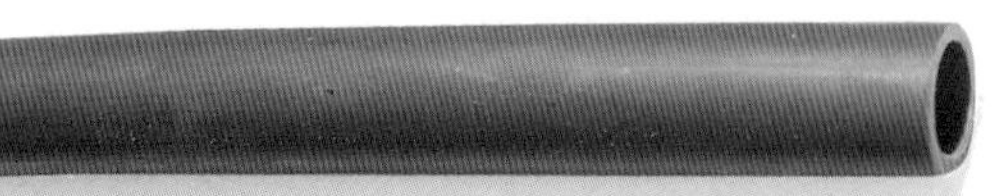

PEX (cross-linked polyethylene). Flexible pipe, commonly used in 1/2- and 3/4-in. sizes, is joined with special compression or crimped fittings. Used for water-supply and in-floor heat lines.

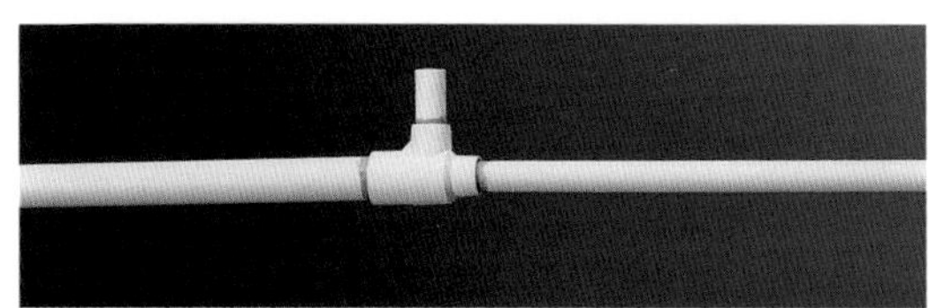

CPVC (chlorinated polyvinyl chloride). Rigid, cream-colored pipe used for hot and cold water lines. Normally used in sizes 1 in. and smaller. Requires primer for solvent-welded joints.

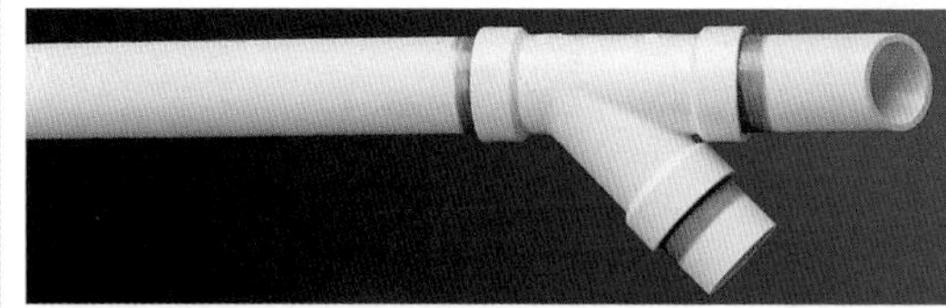

PVC (polyvinyl chloride). Rigid white pipe used for drains, vents and, in certain cases, cold-water lines. Available in 1/2 in. and larger sizes. Requires primer for solvent-welded joints.

ABS (acrylonitrile butadiene styrene). Rigid black pipe used for drains and vents. Available in 1-1/2 in. and larger sizes.

Transition Fittings for Plastic

Plastic pipe can be joined to virtually any other type of pipe as long as both types are code approved for the job. To transition from galvanized or copper pipe to plastic, use special plastic transition fittings that have one threaded side. For transitions to larger galvanized or cast-iron drains or vents, use rubber transition couplings with steel sleeves. Some codes allow rubber couplings without a steel sleeve to be used to join new plastic drain lines to existing plastic systems.

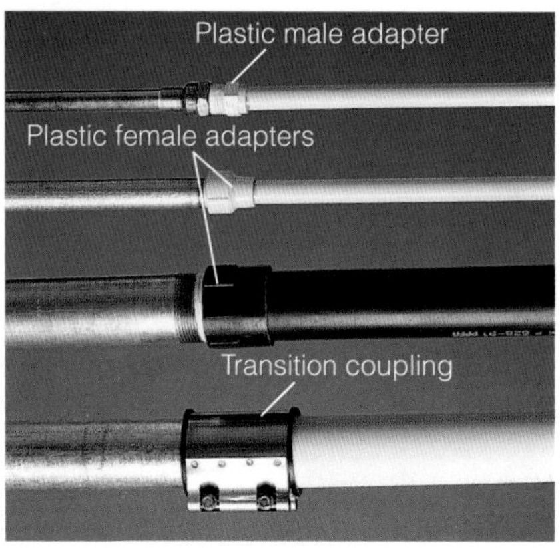

Plastic Pipe Tips

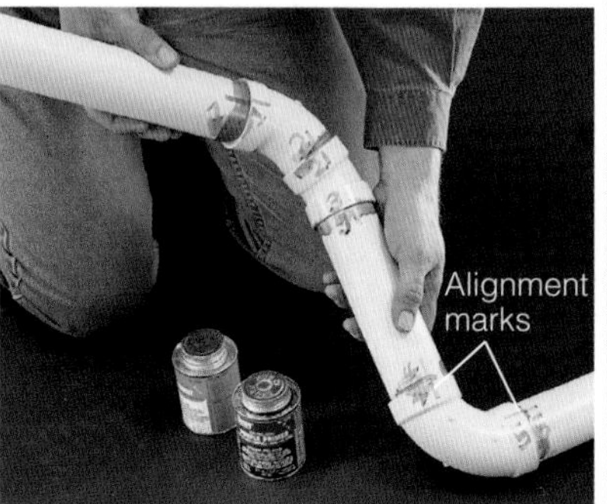

Assembling a run. When assembling plastic pipes, you should cut, mark and dry-fit everything before cementing the components. Without this assembly, you can't properly orient the fittings so the pipes run in the right direction. With the cut, unglued and unprimed pipes assembled, number and make alignment marks on the pieces so you can join them exactly in their original positions. Once the puzzle is solved, glue the run together.

String saw. If you have to cut plastic pipe buried in a wall or some other tight spot, you can do it with a simple string. Mason's line works best.

Pipes and Fittings / PVC

Cutting and Joining PVC

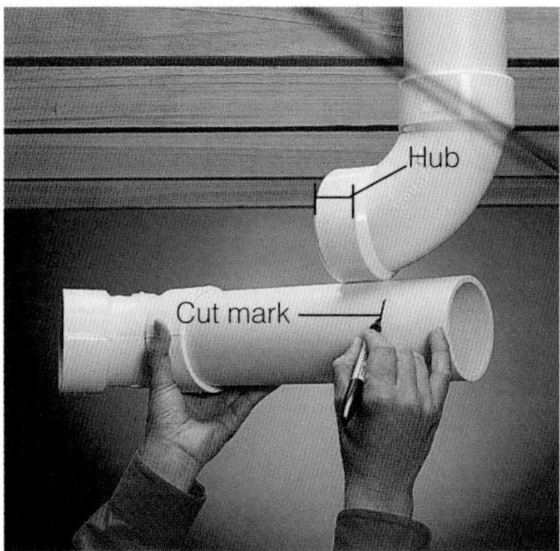

1 Measure correct pipe length or hold section in place and mark it. Be sure to include depth of hub. The goal is that when pipes and fittings are joined, no interior gaps can slow water flow or collect debris.

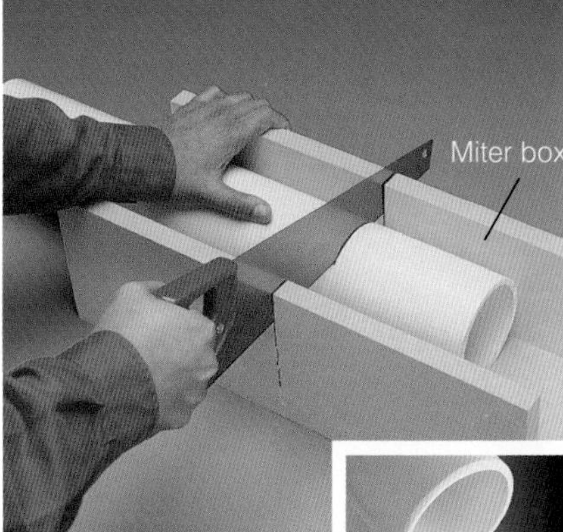

2 Cut off pipe perfectly square using a miter box and stiff fine-tooth handsaw. A power miter saw works even better. Remove burr left by the saw with a file or sandpaper. Bevel edges slightly for a smoother fit.

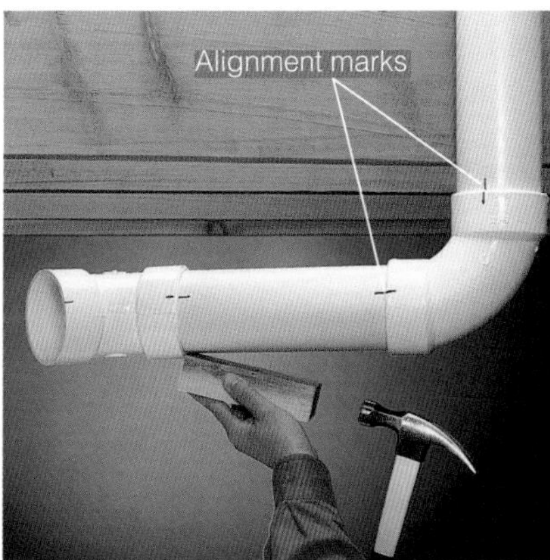

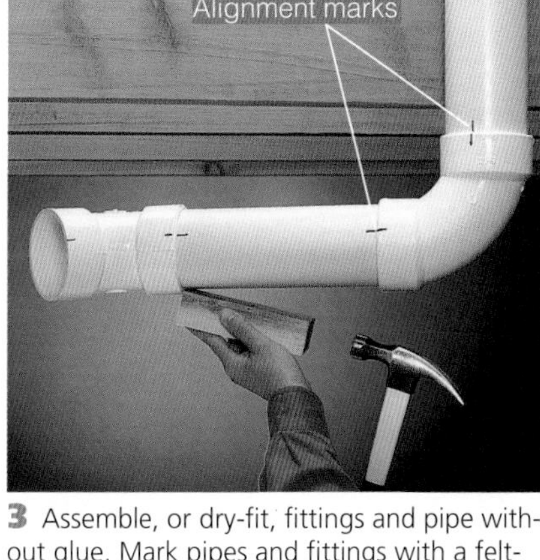

3 Assemble, or dry-fit, fittings and pipe without glue. Mark pipes and fittings with a felt-tip pen to make sure they line up again when you glue them together. If joints stick together when you disassemble the run, tap them with a hammer and wood block. Where possible, dry-fit an entire run.

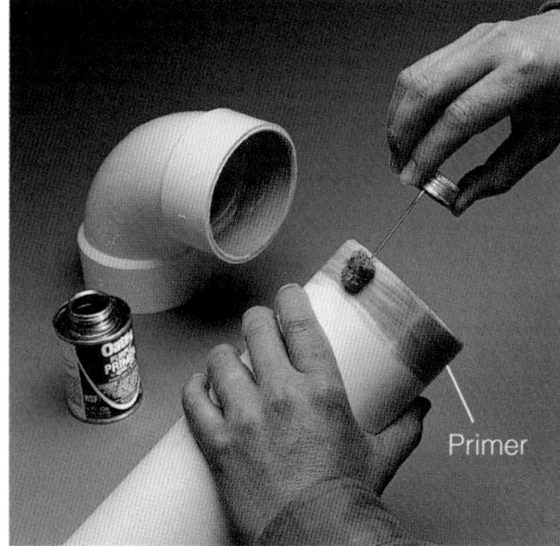

4 Clean joint surfaces with clean cloth. For PVC and CPVC (not ABS) coat surfaces to be joined with a special primer/cleaner. The primer is prone to splashing and dripping, so protect finished surfaces with a drop cloth.

5 Spread solvent liberally inside the hub and on outer pipe surface. Use solvent specifically designed for the pipe you're joining. Solvent gives off fumes and is flammable, so ventilate area and wear a respirator. Push fitting and pipe together quickly, making a quarter turn with either piece to seat the pipe fully.

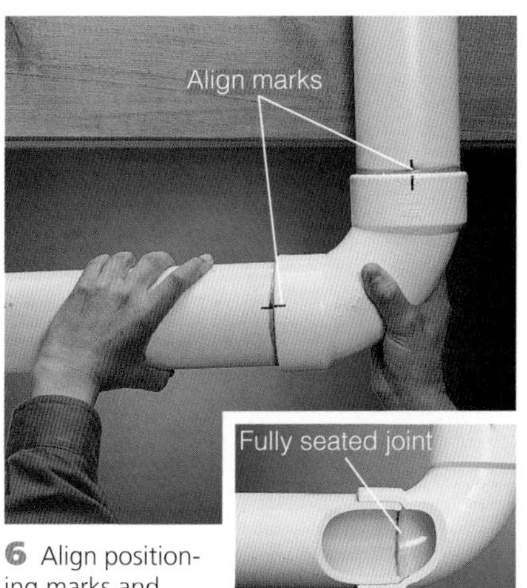

6 Align positioning marks and hold tightly for 15 seconds, because initially the joint may want to spring apart. Finished joint should be completely seated so water flows smoothly without obstruction.

Installing Plastic Pipe

J-hooks. Use plastic hangers called J-hooks to hang pipe from joists every 32 in. (80 cm) to support horizontal runs. You can also use flexible plastic or steel banding. Pay close attention to slope as you install a horizontal run.

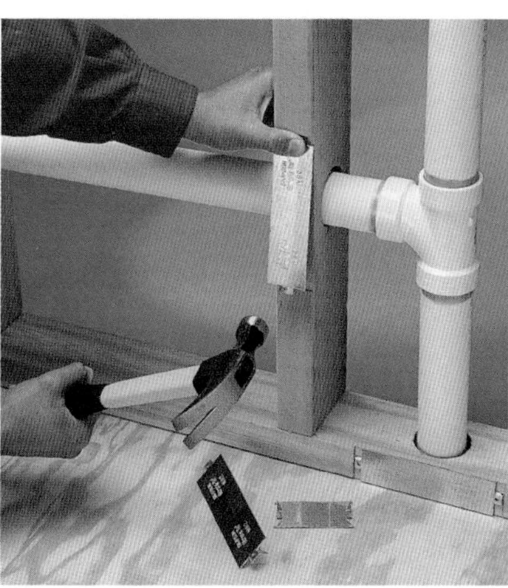

Protective steel plates prevent accidental puncturing of pipe when hanging drywall. Add plates whenever pipe passes within 1-1/4 in. (32 mm) of surface of wood framing. Drill oversize holes in framing so pipes won't squeak when they expand and contract.

Pipes and Fittings / CPVC

Pipes and Pipe Fittings 107
Wet Basement Cures 273

CPVC piping has been successfully used in homes since 1965. In some cases, CPVC is actually better than copper, since some areas of the country have corrosive water that eats away at copper pipes.

This piping system is designed to be user-friendly and versatile. The outside diameter of CPVC tubing is sized the same as copper pipe. This means grip-style mechanical fittings can be used to join copper to CPVC.

Be aware that many copper- or steel-pipe systems are used as grounding for electrical wiring. Adding CPVC may change your grounding system, so consult an electrician about your plans.

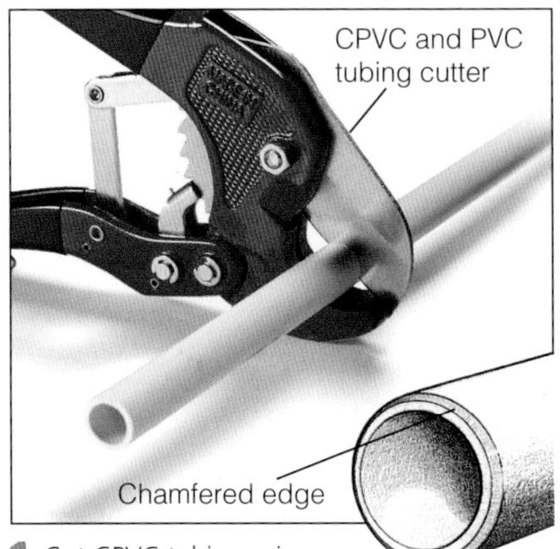

1 Cut CPVC tubing using tubing cutter or handsaw. A cutter makes straight, burr-free cuts ready for cement or mechanical fitting. Chamfer (taper) the edge with a utility knife for a better joint.

2 Add shutoff valves with mechanical fittings to CPVC or copper pipe. Add a drop of liquid soap to pipe's end for lubrication. Loosen nut on fitting about two turns and seat pipe into fitting. Hand-tighten each nut.

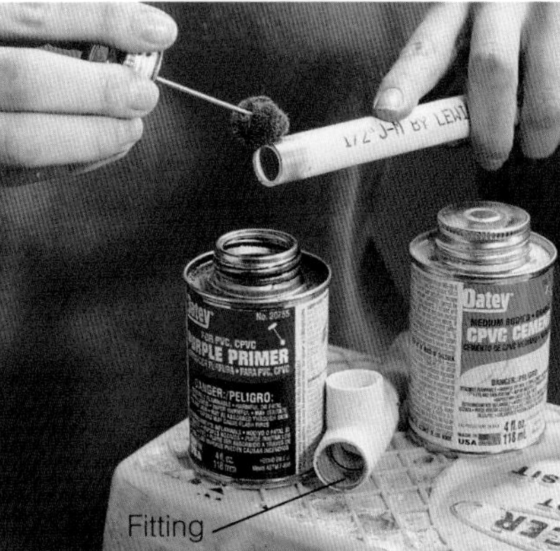

3 Swab primer onto pipe end and inside fitting to clean and etch surface. Primer gives cement a better grip. Ventilate the work area and wear a respirator. Some codes permit use of CPVC cement without primer.

4 Apply CPVC cement to outside of tubing and inside of fitting. Push tubing into fitting with a slight twisting motion and hold for 15 seconds until joint sets. Initially, the pipe may try to pop out of the fitting.

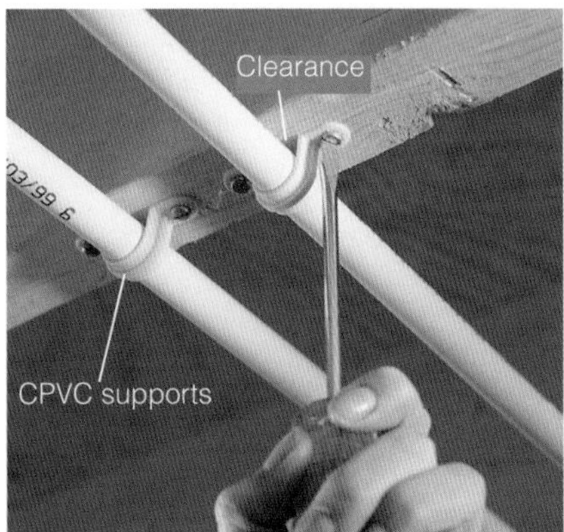

5 Support CPVC lines every 32 to 36 in. (80 to 90 cm) with CPVC supports. Tubing should slide freely within each hanger to allow movement. Leave 1/2 in. (12 mm) clearance to obstructions to allow tubing to expand and contract.

6 Cement stub-out tube to every water supply and cap stub-out. After one hour, turn on water supply to check for leaks.

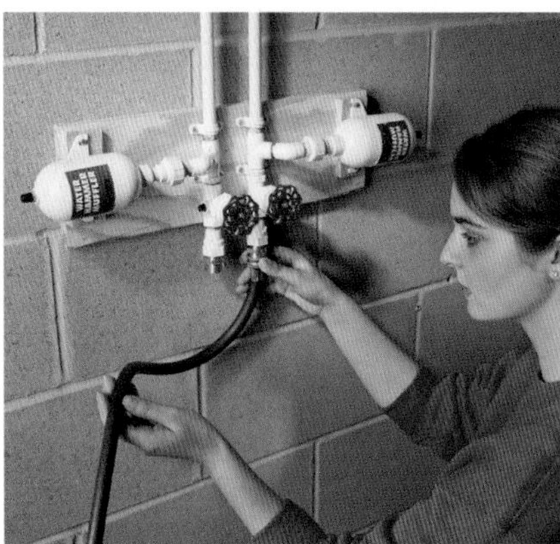

7 Use water hammer arresters to keep pipes from banging. The ones shown are specifically for CPVC systems. Other types of arresters may be used with appropriate fittings and if the water supply doesn't deteriorate copper.

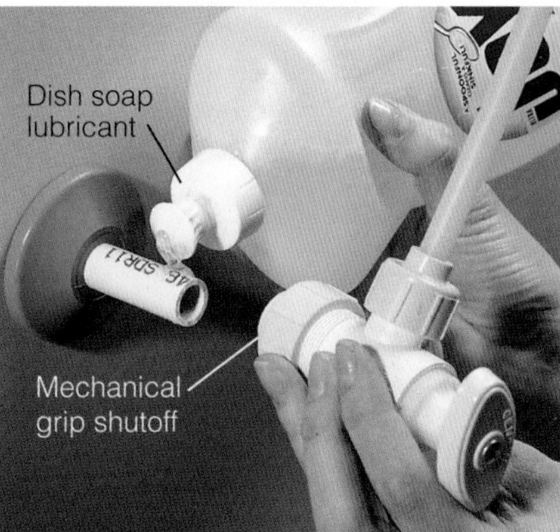

8 To add shutoff valves for fixtures, turn off the water supply, cut stub-outs to desired length and add escutcheon plate. Use mechanical grip or cement-on shutoff valves.

Pipes and Fittings / PEX

PEX (cross-linked polyethylene) plumbing systems are relatively new players in the world of plumbing, but are rapidly gaining acceptance by plumbers, homeowners and building code officials.

These systems consist of flexible tubing that's joined to specially designed fittings by way of compression fittings or a crimping tool. The tubing itself—which can be used for hot and cold water lines as well as in-the-floor radiant heating systems—is flexible, can be installed in long lengths with fewer joints, is freeze-break resistant and is relatively easy to install. Continuous "home run" lengths can be run from a central manifold to individual fixtures to further minimize the number of joints and connections.

It can't be used for outdoor, aboveground applications, its use hasn't been okayed in all jurisdictions and, though it's expected to last as long as copper, some will argue it hasn't withstood the test of time. There are several systems available; the one shown employs clamps and a crimping tool.

Pipe types. Some systems offer the option of red tubing for hot water and blue tubing for cold water.

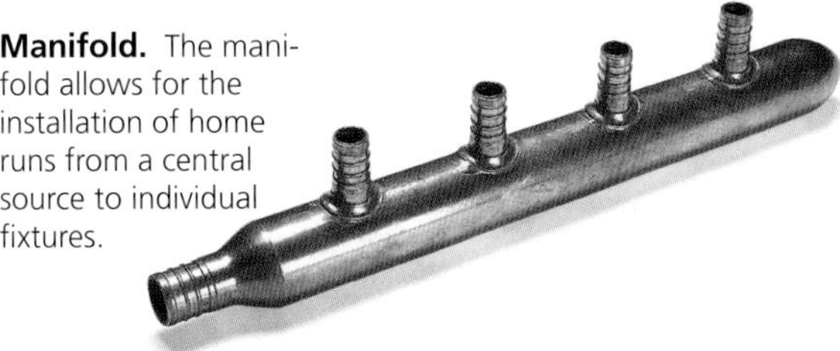

Manifold. The manifold allows for the installation of home runs from a central source to individual fixtures.

Fittings. A wide variety of male and female connectors, shutoff valves and elbows makes it easy to make connections to standard faucets and fixtures.

Elbow bracket. Helps ease the tubing around sharp corners.

Crimping tool. The crimping tool compresses the specially designed ring around the tubing and fittings.

1 Select the correct size clamp and slip it over the tubing.

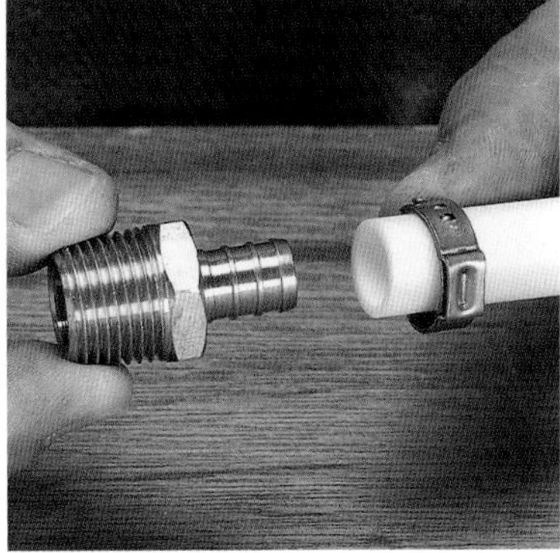

2 Slide the fitting into the tubing until it's fully seated.

3 Secure the clamp with the special crimping tool.

Sump Pumps

If your basement is prone to flooding, you may need to install a sump pit to collect the water and a sump pump to pump it out. Perforated pipes around your foundation perimeter and underneath the basement floor direct water into the pit. When water in the sump pit reaches a certain level, a float-operated switch turns on the pump, which discharges water, bringing the water level back down until the pump switches off.

A check valve between the pump and the discharge pipe keeps the water in the pipe from flowing back into the pit. Do not use the flexible corrugated pipe that comes with many sump pumps for discharging water; instead, use 1-1/2-in. rigid plastic pipe for long-term reliability.

Inspect and test the pump at least four times a year and any time you plan to be away for an extended period. To test it, fill the sump pit with water and make sure the pump operates correctly. If the pump works slowly or makes labored noises, clean the inlet screen underneath the pump.

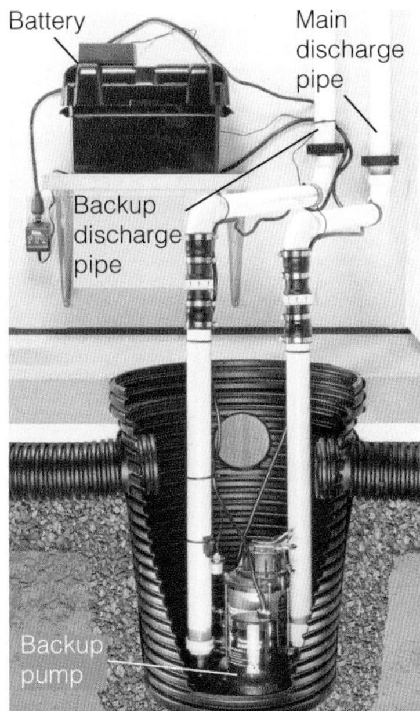

Battery-powered backup sump pumps automatically start pumping if the regular unit loses its power source. Some models can be retrofitted to supplement an existing AC-powered pump, but many new AC-powered pumps have the battery backup pump built into the unit. Most backup sump pumps have an automatic charger and can run 6 to 8 hours on a fully charged battery. A car battery can be substituted in an emergency.

Pipes and Fittings / Rigid-Copper

The recipe for soldering success calls for two parts prep work and one part craftsmanship. If you do the critical preparation steps well—joint cleaning and heating—the solder itself will finish the job.

The basic soldering tool is a propane or MAPP-gas torch, which consists of a regulator and tip that you screw onto a small tank. To operate it, open the fuel valve and light the tip with a handheld striker or built-in igniter. Adjust the flame so the blue cone in the center is about 1-1/4 in. (3 cm) long. The longer the cone, the hotter the flame. The hottest point is at the tip of the cone, so hold the flame so the cone tip just touches the fitting. When the joint is heated properly, molten solder quickly flows into and surrounds the joint, hardening as it cools.

Be sure to drain water lines in the area being soldered and open a faucet at one end of the line so any pressure that builds up in the pipe during soldering can escape.

Safety First: Tame the Flame

To avoid fires, use a special heat-shield cloth when you solder near wood or other combustible materials. Also, shut off your torch whenever you set it down; the propane tank is top-heavy and can fall over and burn something if it's left on. Finally, keep a fire extinguisher nearby.

Cutting Copper Pipe

Copper is soft and relatively easy to cut with a tube cutter. In addition to a larger cutter, a small tight-area cutter will quickly pay for itself in time saved during remodeling work in confined areas.

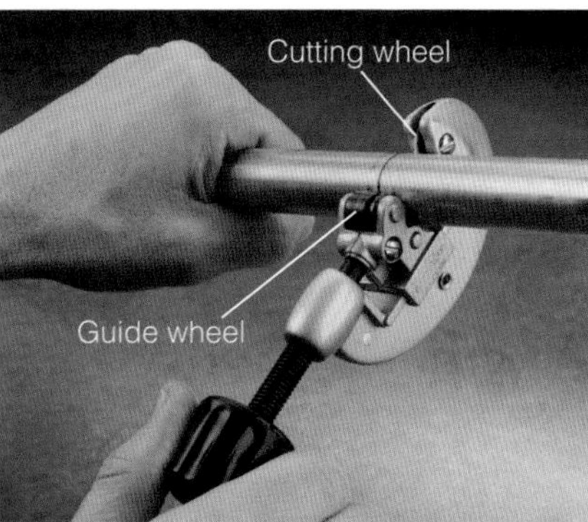

1 Lightly pinch pipe between the cutting wheel and guide wheel. Rotate the cutter, scoring all the way around the pipe. When cutting resistance eases, tighten cutter knob a quarter turn and rotate again. Repeat until the pipe snaps off.

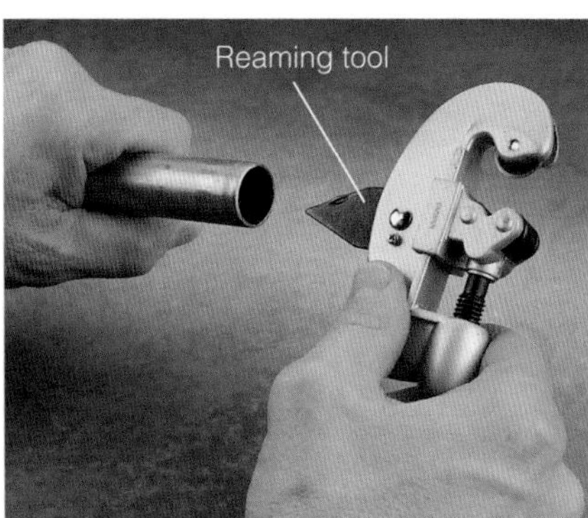

2 Remove inside burr by inserting the reaming attachment squarely and twisting a full revolution.

Cleaning Copper Pipe

Even if you're working with new pipe and fittings, all mating surfaces must be smooth and oil free. Clean outside surfaces with emery cloth and the insides of fittings with wire brushes sized to fit.

1 Clean dirt and corrosion off the outside of a pipe end using emery cloth until the pipe shines evenly. Don't touch the cleaned surface with your bare hands. Skin oils can disrupt solder flow and negatively affect the joint.

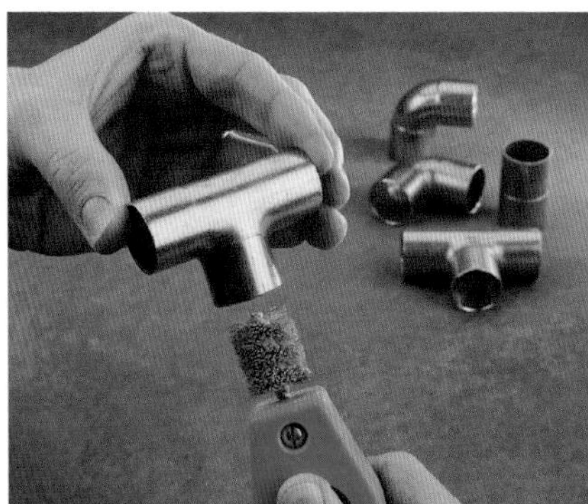

2 Clean inside of fittings with a wire brush sized to fit the pipe diameter. You can also wrap emery cloth around your finger to clean inside.

Soldering a Joint

Flux is an acidic paste that etches the copper and helps carry the solder into the joint. When the temperature of the copper reaches the solder melting point, the solder liquifies and flows into the joint—even if the joint is upside down.

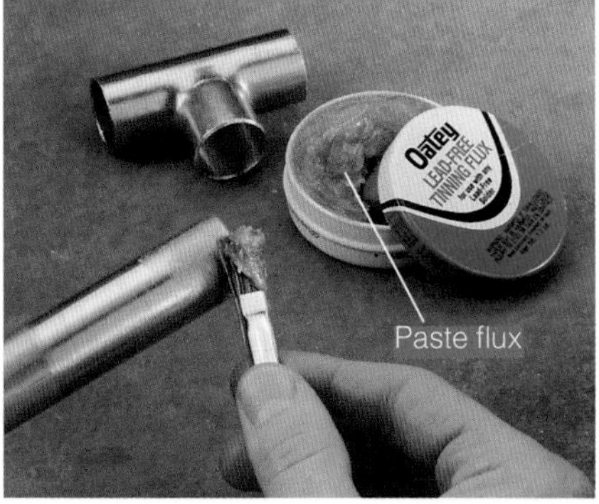

1 Brush an even layer of flux over surfaces to be joined—pipe ends and the inside of fittings. Push the joint together until pipe and fittings seat fully. You can prepare multiple joints at the same time.

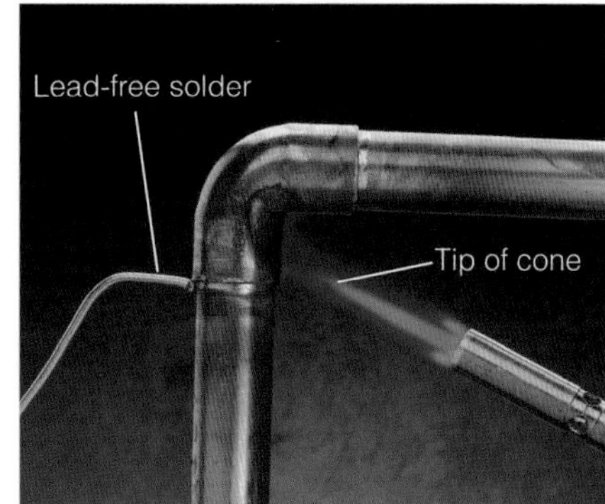

2 Heat joint with a propane or MAPP-gas torch, moving its blue cone back and forth to heat fitting evenly. Hold lead-free solder against the joint on the flame's opposite side until it flows into joint and appears full on all sides.

Flexible-Copper Tubing

Soldering Valves and Adapters

Soldering brass fittings, like shower and shutoff valves, requires more heat than soldering solid-copper fittings, so leave valves open to avoid pressure buildup. If the valve has soft plastic or rubber parts, remove them when possible to avoid damage.

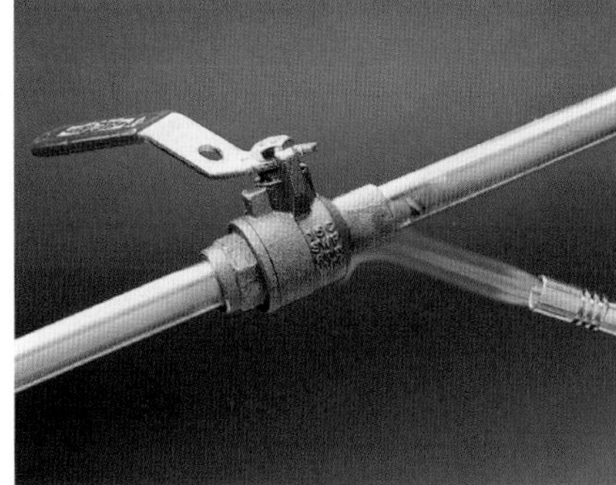

Be patient when soldering brass valves. Use a propane or MAPP-gas torch as for copper fittings and heat the joint from several sides, if possible. Always leave valves open and remove soft parts when soldering.

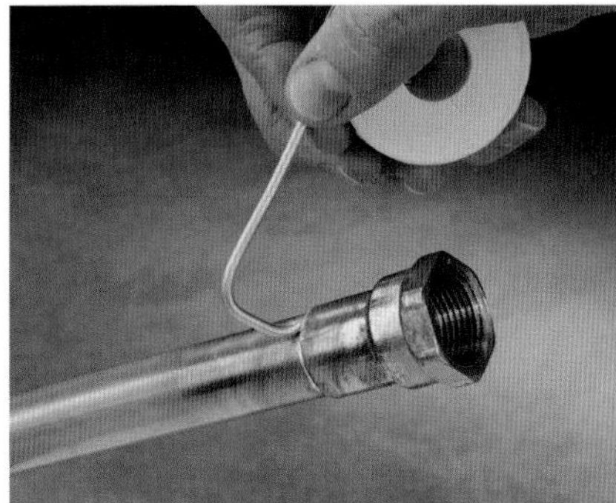

Angle the tube end upward when soldering on threaded adapters to avoid filling threads with excess solder. As a rule of thumb, the amount of solder needed is equal to the pipe's diameter; for example, a 1/2-in. pipe needs 1/2 in. (12 mm) of solder.

Flexible-copper tubing is most frequently used to run gas lines or as water-supply lines for dishwashers and evaporative air coolers. It's particularly useful when access is limited, because it comes in coils up to 100 ft. and requires fewer fittings than rigid pipe. There are two common weights: type "L" is used for household plumbing and type "K" is a heavier tube used for underground and other installations.

Flexible-copper tubing can be joined with flare fittings or compression fittings, or it can be soldered the same as you would rigid-copper pipe. A well-soldered joint is stronger and more durable than a flare-fitted joint, but flare fittings can be taken apart using a wrench. Remember, flare joints can leak unless carefully made. Even a small dent in the tube end can create a problem.

When you buy flexible copper and fittings, pay close attention to the size. Unlike other types of pipe, it's sold in both inside diameter (i.d.) and outside diameter (o.d.) sizes.

Making a Flare Fitting

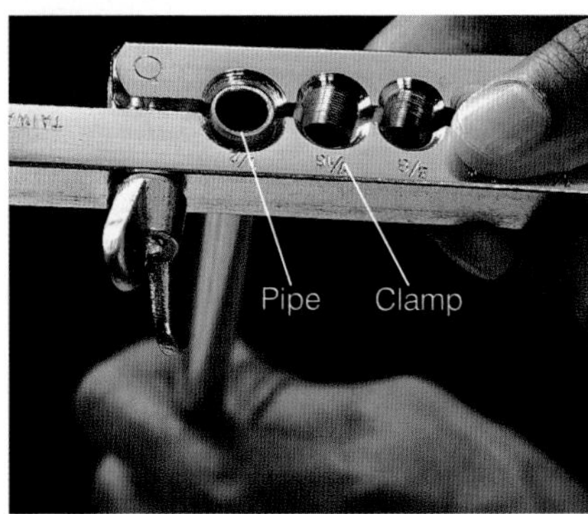

1 Cut copper pipe squarely with a tube cutter and remove burrs from rough inner edge. Slip a flare nut on the pipe and clamp pipe tightly between the flaring tool's two bars so the pipe's rim is even with the bars' top surface.

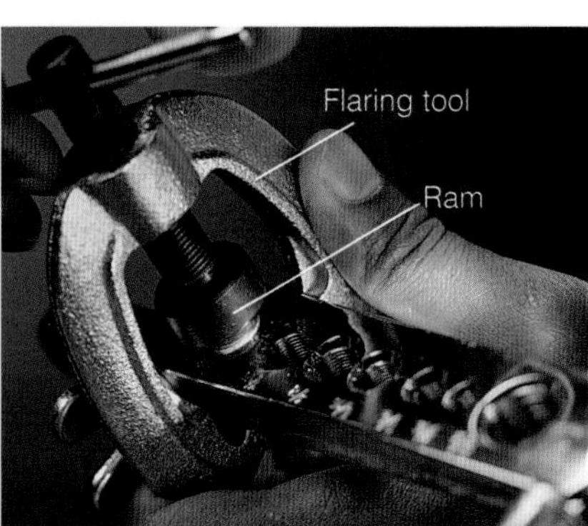

2 Mount shaper to bars and screw down ram to expand copper into cone-shaped mold. Remove pipe and inspect flare for cracks, unevenness or other damage.

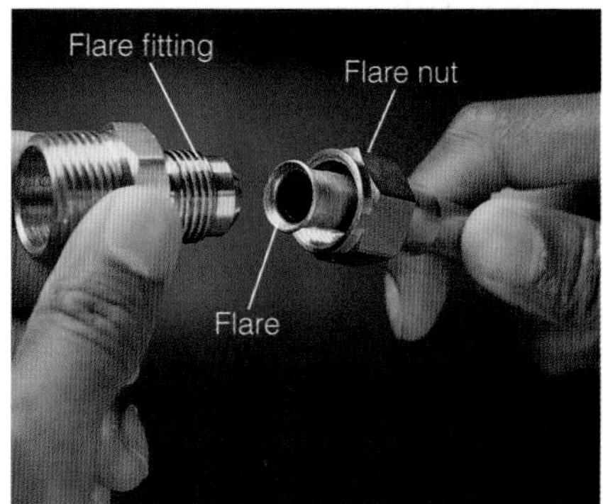

3 Screw a flare nut to the fitting, using two wrenches to tighten the joint—one to hold the fitting, one to tighten the flare nut. If the joint leaks, cut off the flared end and start over.

Bending Tubing

You can make gradual bends in tubing by hand or by molding it around a form. However, do this with caution; the tube can kink suddenly and you'll have to cut and join the pipe to use it. For sharper bends, insert the tubing into the bending spring, shown here, using a clockwise twisting motion, to the point of the intended bend. Slightly over-bend the tube, then ease back to the desired angle or curve and twist off the spring.

If you don't have a bending spring, you can fill the tube with sand while bending; however, this trick only works if the pipe is loose on both ends and you can thoroughly clean it out afterward.

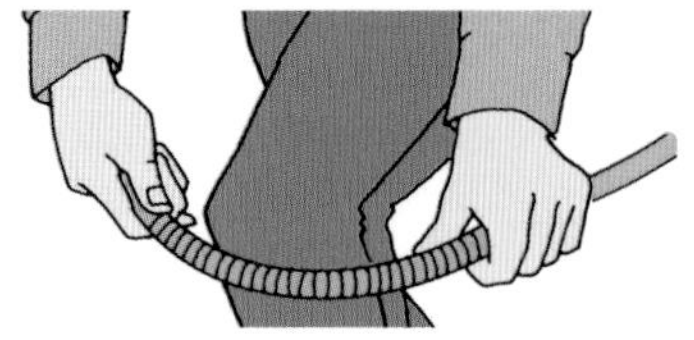

Pipes and Fittings / Steel

Hacksaws 27
Adjustable Wrenches 31
Pipes and Pipe Fittings 107

Threaded pipe, also referred to as steel or iron pipe, carries hot and cold water to sinks, fixtures and radiators. In larger diameters, it serves as drain, waste and vent pipe. Today, copper and plastic have taken over most of threaded pipe's duties, but you may need to repair existing pipe—and it continues to be used for gas piping.

Galvanized pipe is rust resistant and used for water lines. Black pipe is less expensive but susceptible to rust and should be used only for indoor natural gas and propane lines. Usually, you can have pipe cut to exact lengths and threaded at your local hardware store for a small fee. Standard nipples, short pieces of pipe threaded on both ends, are normally kept in stock. Any time you work with threaded pipe, keep these tips in mind:

- Loosen rusted or stubborn joints by applying penetrating oil and using a large pipe wrench or a cheater bar on the wrench handle to gain leverage.
- Don't hammer on pipes. Hammering can loosen mineral deposits, which will clog valves and faucets.
- Check for leaks in gas-line fittings by brushing soapy water around joints, then watching for bubbles.
- Many electrical systems are grounded by the cold-water pipes, so replace any grounding wires you remove.

Tapered threads on threaded pipe provide an ever-tightening seal as a pipe and fitting are screwed together, making threaded pipe joints particularly strong. Female fittings and couplings are likewise tapered.

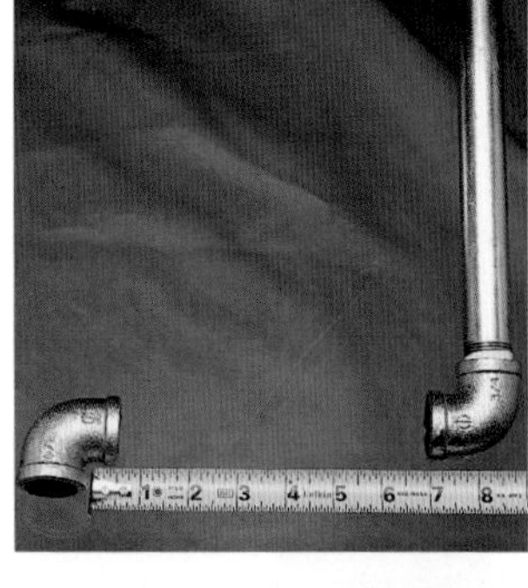

When measuring, account for the distance the pipe and its fittings overlap once joined. Measure distance between fittings and add 1/2 in. (19 mm) per threaded end for 3/4-in. pipe. For 1/2-in. pipe, add 7/16 in. (11 mm) per threaded end.

Wrap Teflon plumbing tape in clockwise direction around threads to lubricate, protect and seal joints. Use at least three clockwise wraps to provide a tight seal.

Loosen and tighten threaded steel pipe and fittings using a pipe wrench. The wrench has sharp teeth that bite into pipe and an upper jaw that pinches pipe as the wrench is turned. Always use two pipe wrenches, one to twist the pipe and one to hold the adjacent fitting.

Shutoff Valves

When you visit a well-stocked plumbing supply store, you'll discover dozens of shutoff valves for virtually every type of pipe, fitting and application. They're commonly made of plastic, solid brass or chrome-plated brass.

The valves can be connected by soldering, with threaded connections or with compression joints. Select a valve based on intended use and space limitations. Those marked WOG can be used for water, oil and gas. The heart of the valve—the internal shutoff mechanism—will be one of only three types: stop, gate or ball. Stop valves are most often used as shutoffs for such fixtures as sinks, toilets and outdoor faucets.

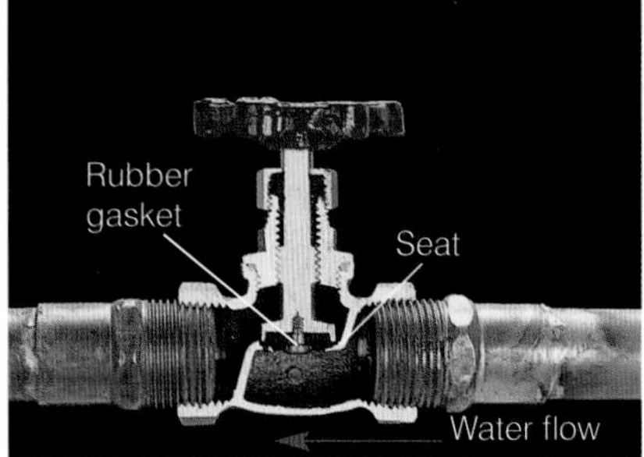

Stop valves are washer-type valves that seal by screwing a rubber gasket against a seat. Flow is inefficient because the fluid takes a circuitous route. The valve must be oriented correctly so flow goes against bottom of rubber gasket. Gaskets sometimes need replacing.

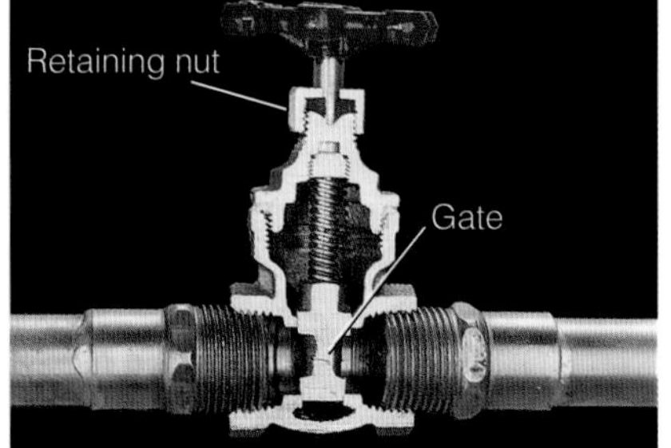

Gate valves have a wedge-shaped brass gate that lowers into a machined slot to close the valve. This valve allows full, unobstructed flow for fluid. It should either be completely open or completely closed; water flowing through a partially open gate valve wears away the metal and causes premature failure.

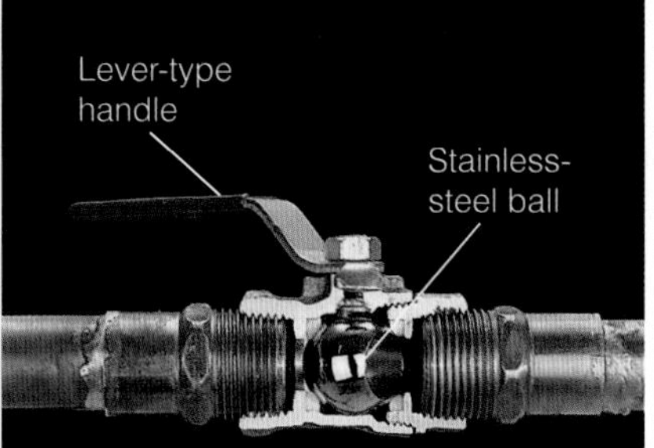

Ball valves employ a stainless-steel ball with a port drilled through it that pivots in plastic bushings. It allows full or partial flow and completely opens and closes with only a quarter turn. In the closed position, the lever is perpendicular to the pipes; when open, it's parallel.

Pipes and Fittings / Cast-Iron

Steel Pipe Repairs and Add-ons

You can't simply unscrew a section of threaded pipe from the middle of your plumbing system to tap into it or make a repair. You need to cut and remove the affected piece of pipe and then use a union (Step 3) and some shorter pieces for reconstructing the section.

1 Turn off water. Cut pipe using a hacksaw. Avoid using a reciprocating saw, because vibration can knock loose mineral deposits that can clog fixtures and faucets.

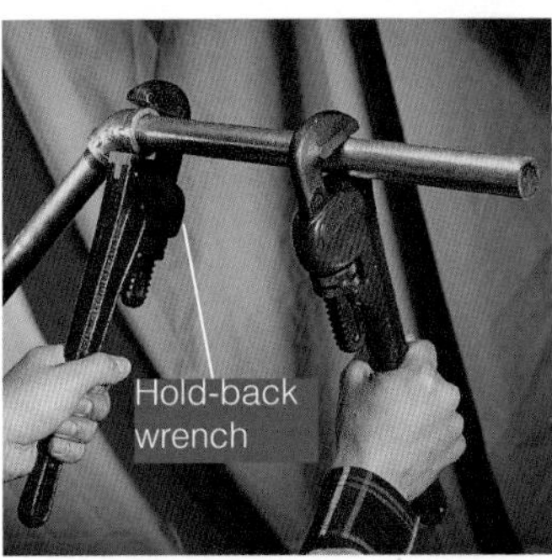

2 Use two pipe wrenches for disassembly. One turns the pipe, while the hold-back wrench prevents damage farther down the line.

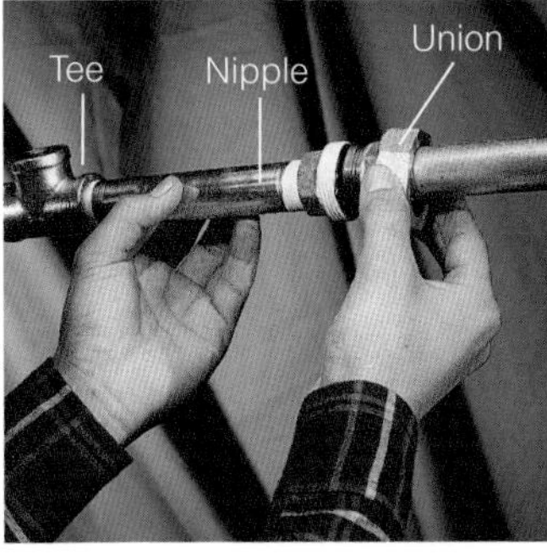

3 Install a union to reconnect pipe sections after adding a tee or making repairs. Unions have three parts—a part with male threads that goes onto the first pipe, a part with only female threads and a tapered-type joint that goes onto the facing pipe, and a tapered nut that pulls the parts and pipe together.

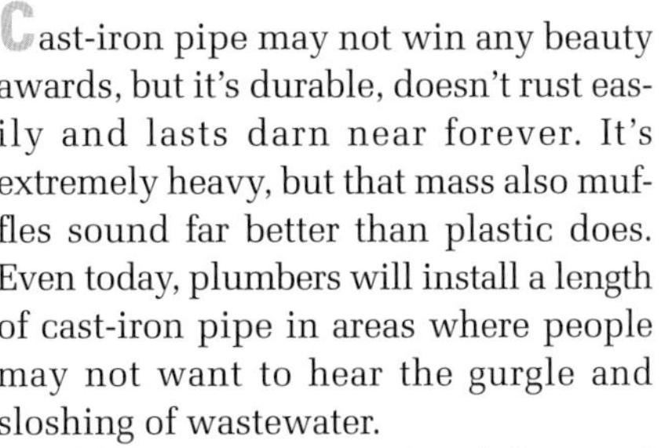

Cast-iron pipe may not win any beauty awards, but it's durable, doesn't rust easily and lasts darn near forever. It's extremely heavy, but that mass also muffles sound far better than plastic does. Even today, plumbers will install a length of cast-iron pipe in areas where people may not want to hear the gurgle and sloshing of wastewater.

Older cast-iron pipe (see left image) was joined by packing hubs with oakum and sealing the joint with molten lead. Newer no-hub cast iron is joined using no-hub couplings (see right image) consisting of neoprene sleeves and stainless-steel band clamps. Special transition couplings can be used to tie newer plastic pipe into existing cast-iron systems.

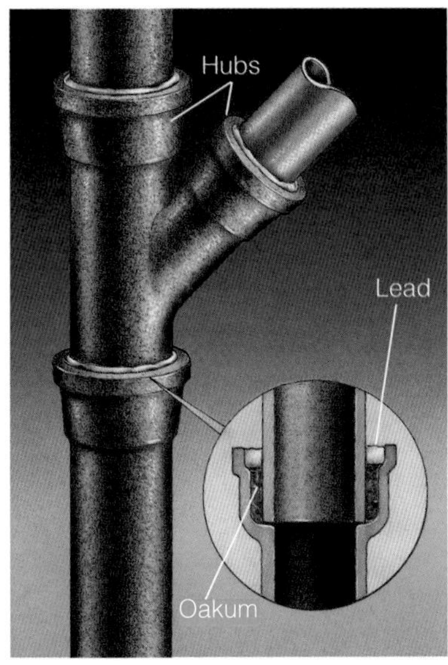

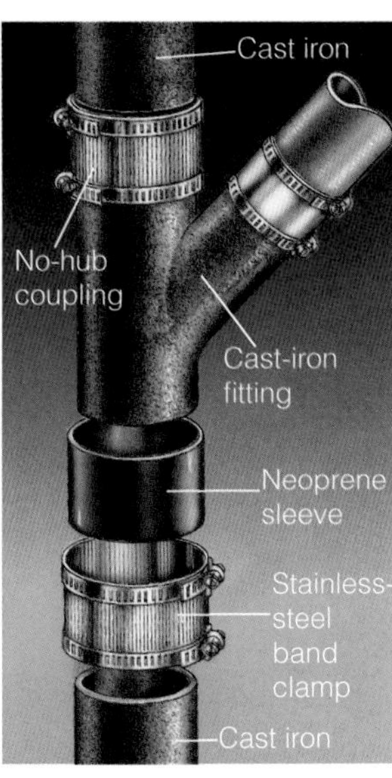

Tying Into an Existing Soil Stack

Cast-iron pipe was once commonly used in household plumbing, particularly for the large main soil stack. Cast iron contains about 4 percent carbon, which makes it so hard you can barely cut it with metal-cutting blades. Snapping it, as shown below, is the best way to remove a section while remodeling. Always make certain the pipe is secured well with riser clamps, as shown, before you cut into it to keep the heavy stack from dropping down.

Snap cast-iron soil stack. Measure new cast-iron tee and mark stack for cutting. Add 1/4 in. (6 mm) to measurement to make sure tee slips in. Wrap cutter chain around the pipe so cutting wheels rest on mark. Lever tool until pipe snaps. Cut at second mark and knock out the section using a hammer and block of wood.

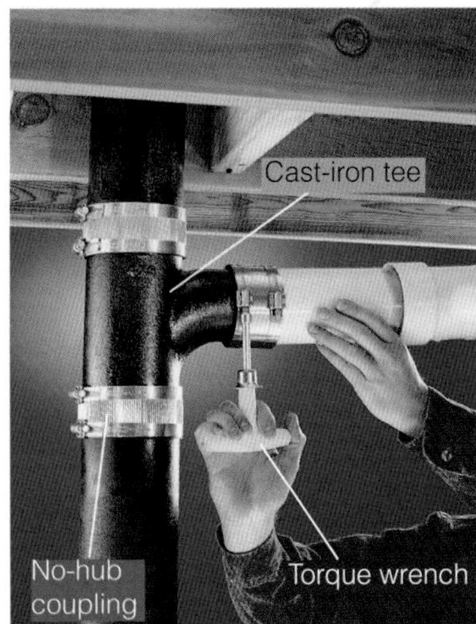

Steel-sleeved rubber couplings. Slip rubber and steel couplings onto cut pipe ends first. Insert cast-iron tee fitting and work couplings over joints. Use torque wrench to tighten band clamps. Rubber gaskets should be crimped firmly, but not so tightly that they bulge out from pressure.

Water Filters, Water Softeners and Water-Saving Devices

Residential water filters are primarily designed to back up your local water treatment facility. They're good for improving water's aesthetics—for reducing unpleasant odors and tastes, discoloration and other annoying qualities. You can also use them to reduce potential health risks, like lead, that your water utility can't always control. However, if you have your own well, don't depend solely on these devices. Follow the water-testing procedures established by your state or province.

Although some filter systems go a long way toward purifying water, don't rely solely on them to solve serious water problems. A water engineer from your local utility can almost always tell you what's in your water and what's causing a problem. If you have health concerns, follow up with a call to your local department of public health.

When you know which contaminants are causing trouble, pick a filtration device that solves that particular problem. A good rule to remember is that water softeners excel at taking care of your plumbing system and fixtures. Filtration systems excel at taking care of your needs for taste and healthy water.

Labels on the packaging advertise what each filter does. Usually they list more contaminants than you need removed. Look for a National Sanitation Foundation (NSF) or other listing mark that indicates the unit has been tested to meet a certain NSF standard.

Water Problems and Their Remedies

Symptom	Cause	Solution
White deposits build up in faucets, showerheads and electric coffee pots. Soaps and detergents don't lather well.	Magnesium and calcium compounds making water hard.	Install ion-exchange water softener on hot-water pipes or whole system. Clean affected fixtures and flush out water heater.
Rust forms around drains in sinks, bathtubs and laundry tubs. Rust-colored slime appears in toilet tank.	Iron compounds or bacterial ion.	Install ion-exchange water softener. Use rust-removing softener salt. If problem persists, install an oxidizing filter or a chlorination feeder and an activated carbon filter.
Water has rotten-egg smell. Washed silverware tarnishes. Water looks black.	Hydrogen sulfide.	Install oxidizing filter. If problem persists, install chlorination feeder system, particle filter and activated carbon filter. Replace badly corroded pipes.
Rust or green stains form around drains. Metal pipes become corroded.	Acidic water (low pH).	Install a neutralizing particle filter. If problem persists, install continuous chemical feeder with alkaline solution. Check pipes for corrosion.
Water has unpleasant taste and slight yellow or brownish color.	Algae or other organic matter suspended in water.	Install a particle filter. For a serious problem, install continuous chemical feeder with chlorine solution and add an activated carbon filter.
Water looks cloudy or dirty.	Suspended particles of silt, mud, sand and organic matter.	Install particle filter first, then use activated carbon filter to remove color caused by organisms.
Illnesses in family, such as diarrhea, dysentery or hepatitis.	Disease-producing bacteria or viruses in water.	Test for coliform bacteria first, which indicates potential contamination from human or animal waste. A water-quality expert can help identify contaminant and recommend treatment.

Types of Water Filters

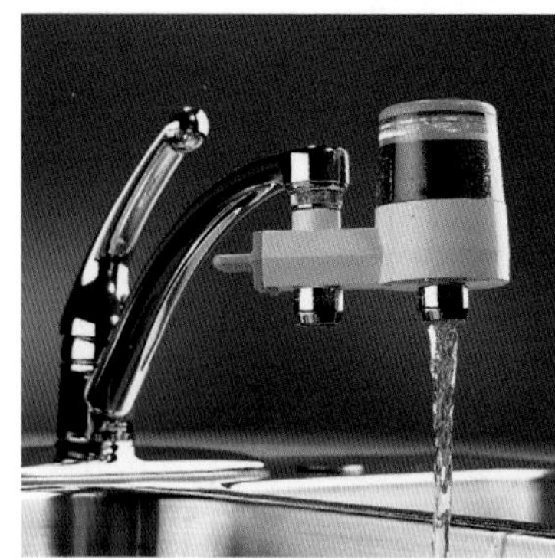

Faucet filters are inexpensive and easy to use and install. They contain filter elements similar to those in more expensive systems. Usually they're low volume, require frequent cartridge changes and are bulky, although some systems are made with the filter built into the faucet.

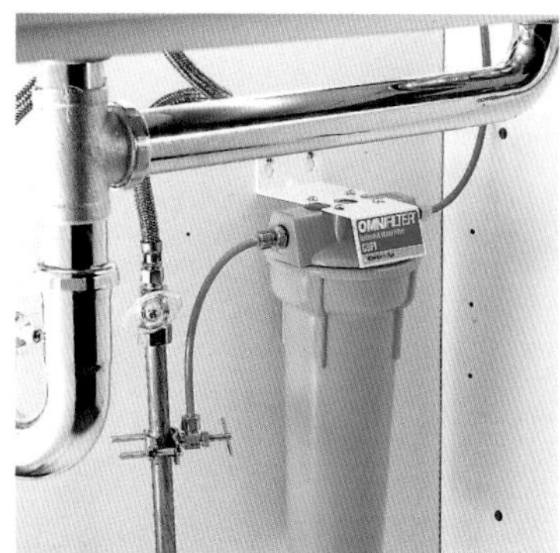

Under-sink filters have lower long-term cost per gallon and more filter types available. They can serve several points of use, including ice makers. Below-sink installation can be somewhat difficult and requires extra hole in sink for mounting special filter faucet.

Reverse-osmosis filter systems filter out virtually all biological contaminants and most other contaminants, including lead. But they are bulky, have a high initial cost, waste 2 to 5 gal. (7.5 to 19 l) of water for every purified gallon and require a drain for wastewater.

Installing a Refrigerator Water Filter

Install a refrigerator water filter to remove bad tastes from drinking water and ice cubes. An in-line filter reduces chlorine, rust, sediment and odors. It splices into the standard copper or plastic refrigerator water-supply line. Locate the filter as close as possible to the shutoff valve. When you've installed the system, quick-connect fittings make it easy to change the filter.

Strap the filter to any nearby support to take the stress off the tubing. Write the installation date on the filter and replace as directed.

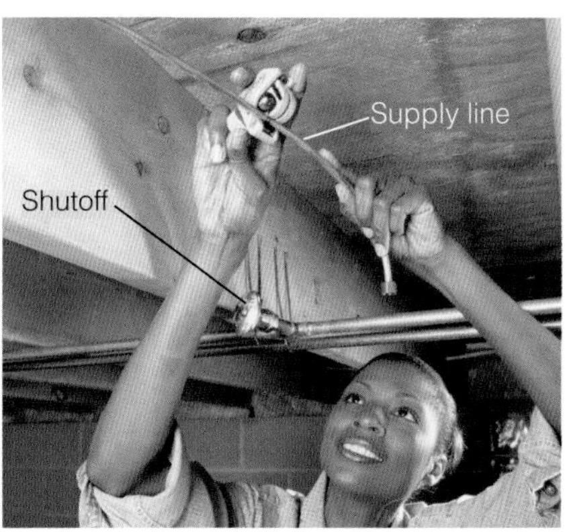

1 Shut off the water supply and mark filter space on supply line. Cut out and remove the section. Tighten the cutter in small increments to avoid pinching the soft copper tube.

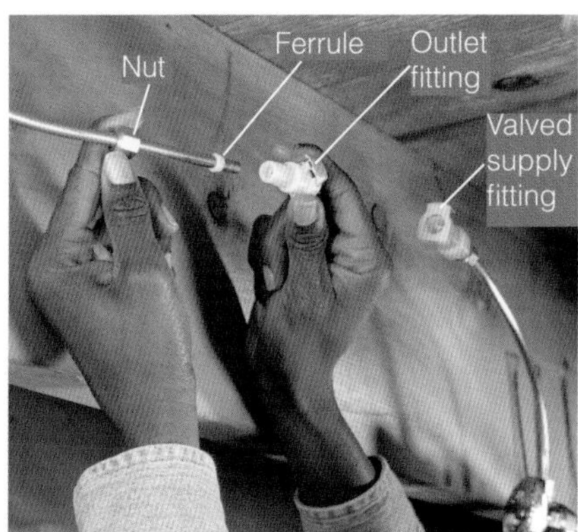

2 Slip nut and ferrule onto tubing. Thread nut onto fitting until it's finger tight and then use wrenches to twist one full turn. Install supply fitting on supply side.

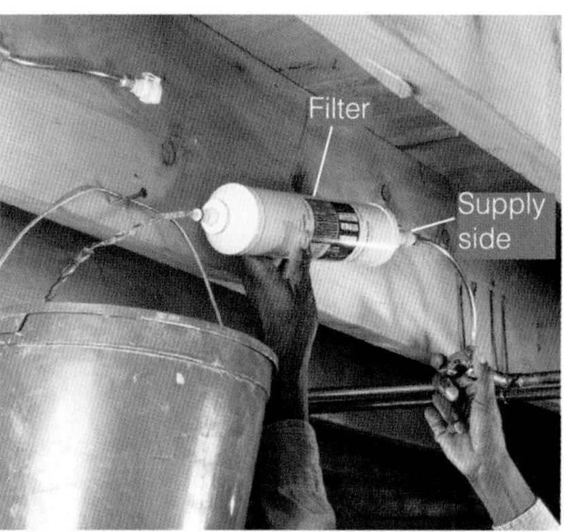

3 Snap filter into supply side. Make sure water-flow indicator points toward the fridge. Flush water through filter for five minutes, and then snap filter into other fitting.

Maintaining Water Softeners

These maintenance steps will help softeners keep running efficiently. Consult your instruction manual or a specialist for more details before performing any tune-up.

1. Clean the brine tank. Sometimes the salt forms a hard, hollow dome in the tank if you add too much salt.
2. Purge an iron-fouled resin bed by running a rust remover through the system. Iron-rich water can eventually foul the resin bed that removes the hard-water particles and replaces them with sodium. Follow the directions for the amount to add to the brine tank; then run your softener through a manual regeneration to purge the wastewater. Also, use rust-remover salt to help prevent future problems.
3. Clean the resin tank injector. The injector screen sometimes gets plugged with sediment caused from dirty salt. To clean it, consult your softener's instruction manual for information.

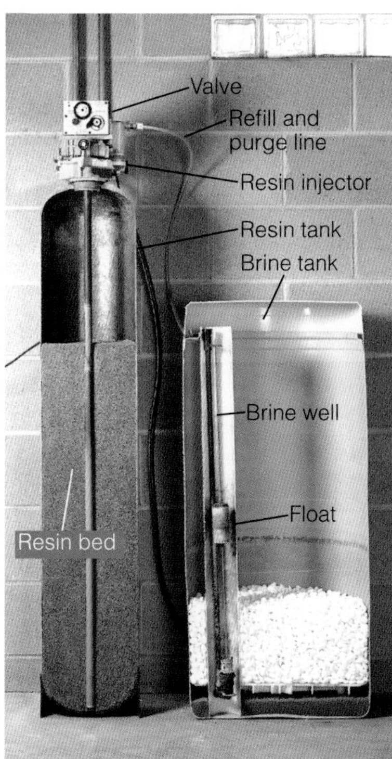

Saving Water

Changing habits can, over the course of a year, save more water than investing in water-saving appliances. Taking shorter showers or shutting off the tap while you brush your teeth can make a big difference. You can also wait until you have a full load before running the dishwasher or washing machine. Plumbing maintenance is another huge water saver—a dripping faucet or running toilet can waste thousands of gallons or liters of water, so make prompt repairs.

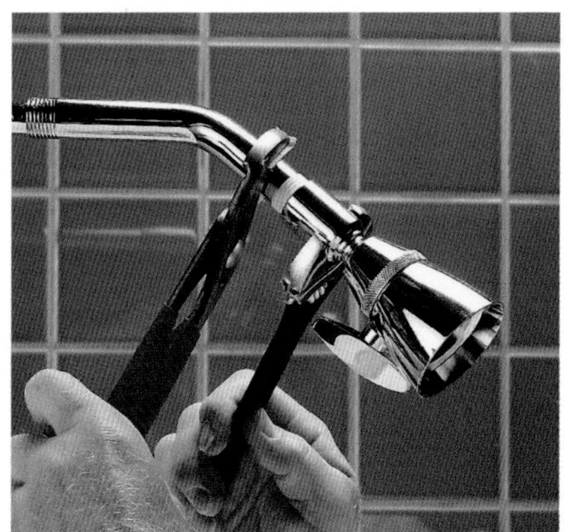

Low-flow showerhead. By converting from a 5-gal.-per-minute (19-l-per-minute) showerhead to a 2.5-gal. (10-l) model, you'll save water and the cost of heating it.

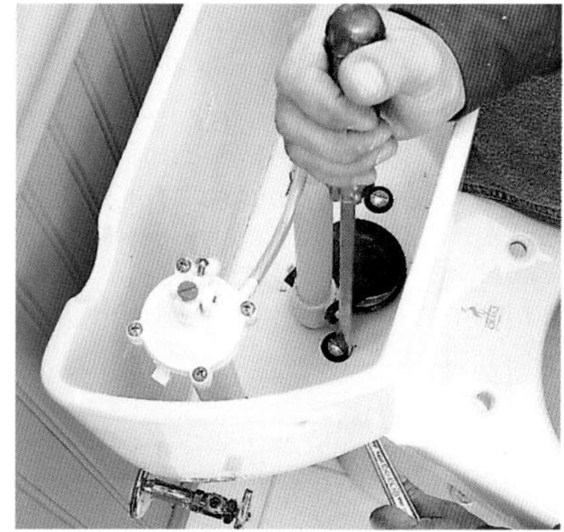

Water-saving toilet. Older toilets use as much as 5 gal. (19 l) of water per flush. New toilets are required to use only 1.6 gal. (6 l) per flush.

Roughing-in a Half Bath

If you have an older home or a growing family, you could probably use another bathroom. A half bath often works well because it's small enough to squeeze into your current floor plan. But even with a half bath, building an entirely new bathroom is a big project, involving carpentry, plumbing, electrical, drywall, tiling and other skills.

Space issues. Closets, pantries and portions of bedrooms are the most likely places to steal space for a half bath. At a minimum, you'll need 30 x 66 in. (76 x 168 cm) of floor area if the fixtures are on opposite walls, or 48 x 54 in (122 x 138 cm) if the fixtures rest against the same wall. You might have to shift a wall or two to get the right dimensions. Some non-bearing or partition walls are simple to shift. Others—if they're load-bearing or contain heat ducts, plumbing pipes and electrical wires—are best left alone.

Location issues. The main waste line is a 3- or 4-in. pipe called a soil stack when run vertically and called a building drain when run horizontally underground. At a minimum, you'll have to attach a 3-in. waste line from your new toilet to this main waste line. In a slab-built home, this main line can be difficult to find, because it runs under concrete.

Framing issues. Keep the subfloor intact and frame the new bath walls with 2x4s. If you have to frame a wall that contains the 3- or 4-in. waste lines, use 2x6s. The open space in your half bath might be too small for a normal inward-swinging door, so you may elect to install an outward-swinging or a pocket door. When you install the wall studs, leave space and access to run plumbing, electrical circuits, heat ducts, exhaust fan and blocking for things like grab bars and wall-mounted sinks.

Plumbing issues. If the toilet drain is over a joist, see if you can shift the toilet; cutting a floor joist can seriously weaken the floor and additional framing will be required. Another problem: Half-inch pipe can serve only two or three fixtures, so you might have to tap into a 3/4-in. supply line for the added fixtures.

Five Steps for a Top-notch Job

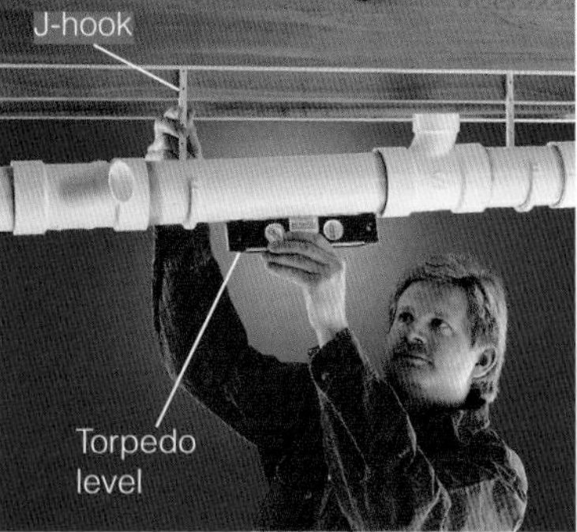

1 Slope all horizontal drain lines a minimum of 1/4 in. per foot (2 cm per meter) and support pipe every 32 in. (80 cm).

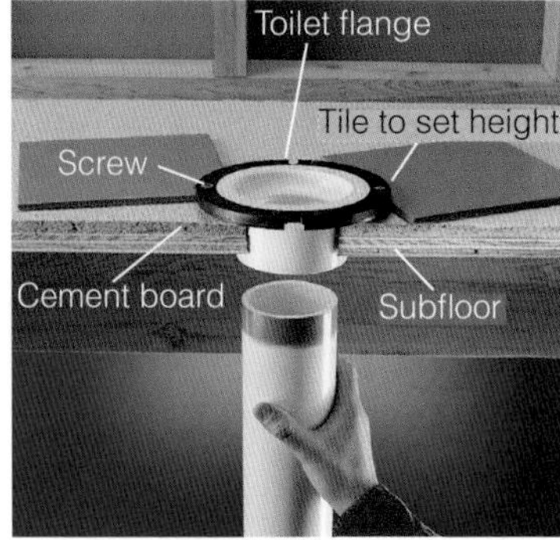

2 Anchor flange with screws at finish floor height to provide a solid point for drain assembly.

3 Tap into existing water lines and install supply lines for new bathroom. Run hot and cold for faucet and cold for toilet.

Half-bath plumbing and electrical rules

Codes vary, so confirm your plans with a local building inspector. Here are some generally accepted rules to follow:

- Position a 2-in. vent to rise vertically from drain within 4 ft. (1.2 m) of toilet flange.
- Position a 1-1/2-in. vent to rise vertically within 42 in. (1 m) of a 1-1/2-in. sink trap.
- Maintain uniform slope on all drain lines (see Step 1, p. 118).
- Run sink and toilet vents vertically to a point 6 in. (15 cm) above overflow level of fixture.
- Slope horizontal vent runs back toward drain.
- Whenever plastic or copper pipe or electrical wire pass within 1-1/4 in. (32 mm) of a framing surface, protect lines with protective steel plates.
- The bathroom should have its own 20-amp circuit.
- Use a GFCI-protected electrical outlet.
- Provide a ventilation fan, vented to the outside, over the toilet.

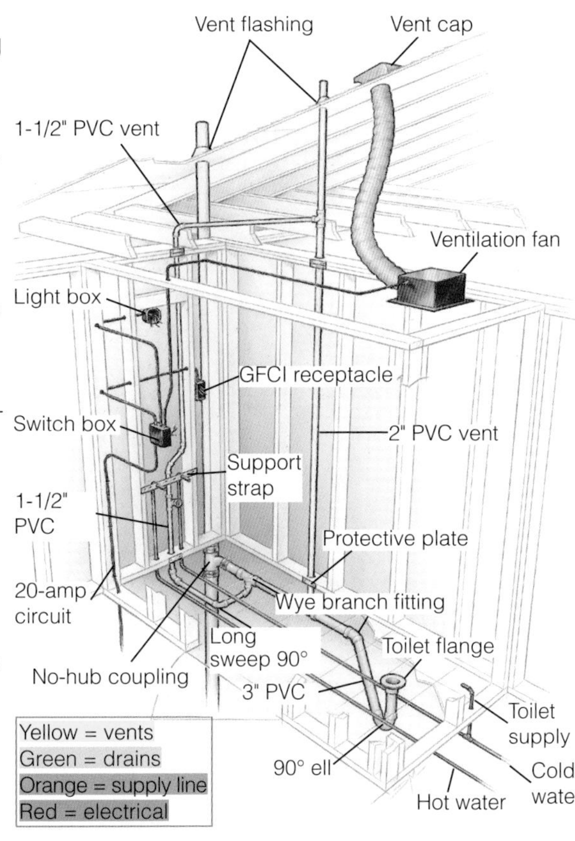

4 Stub out faucet supply lines above drain for pedestal sinks. Support copper pipe with wood blocks or special copper strap.

5 Before connecting to main soil stack, rent pressure gauge to pressure-test DWV system. With the system temporarily plugged, it should hold 5 lbs. (2.27 kg) for 15 minutes.

Notching and Boring Rules

As you remodel, you can't simply cut, notch and bore through structural members and expect your house to remain strong and your floors solid.

If you have solid wood joists, follow these rules to maintain structural integrity:

- Holes must be at least 2 in. (5 cm) from top and bottom edges of joist.
- Maximum hole size is one-third of joist depth.
- Avoid locating holes and notches near loose knots.
- The maximum depth of a notch at the end of a joist can't exceed one-quarter of the joist's depth.
- Maximum notch depth in the outer third of a joist is one-sixth of joist depth.
- Maximum notch length should be no more than one-third of joist depth.
- Do not notch anywhere in the middle third of a joist along its length.

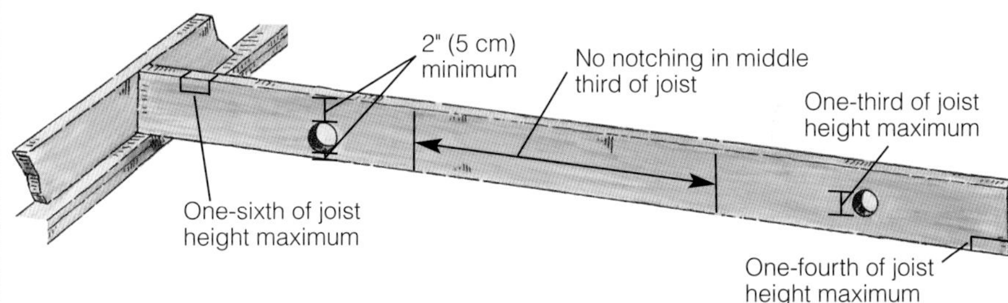

Instant Hot-Water System

If the inconvenience and waste of water, energy and money that occurs while waiting for hot water to reach a fixture bothers you, install a recirculating pump that brings hot water to your fingertips in seconds. The unit shown is compatible with most plumbing codes and requires only basic tools and skills. To work, a pump and controller unit are installed under the sink farthest from your water heater. This way, the system automatically works for any other sink or shower that runs off the main hot-water line.

The pump unit connects the hot-water line to the cold-water line. When activated, the unit pumps the cool water in the hot-water line into the cold-water line and back to the water heater. As soon as the hot water arrives, a temperature sensor shuts off the pump.

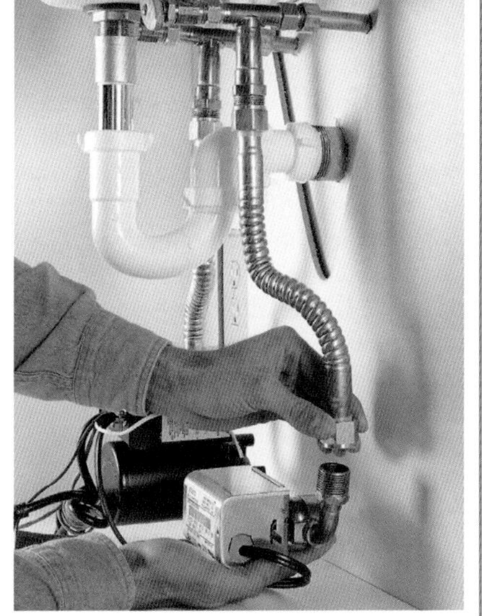

Replacing a Toilet

Demolition Tools 37
Scribing 42
Plumbing Tools 92
Toilet Wax Rings 97
Supply Tubes 97
Shutoff Valves 114
Drywall Repair 217
Installing a Vinyl Floor 248
Ceramic Tile Floor 253

There are many reasons to replace a toilet. An old one might have worn-out internal workings that can't be replaced, or it might be cracked, leaky, noisy, out of style or using too much water. Even if you've never replaced a toilet before, don't be afraid to tackle this job. Few tools are needed and it's a pretty straightforward job, unless you run into stubborn pipes, fittings or bolts.

One complication frequently accompanies a toilet replacement project—the floor. The floor beneath your toilet may be waterlogged or rotted, meaning you may need to replace or patch the finished floor and at least part of the one or two layers of plywood and floorboards below. Even if your floor is sound, there's a chance the new toilet base won't match, or even cover, the profile left by the old toilet base. Again, new flooring or patchwork will be required.

Here are some tips to help the installation go smoothly:

- Before going to work, have the new toilet at hand, as well as a new wax ring, supply line, shutoff valve, if necessary, and two sets of new flange bolts and nuts (you can use the extra flange nuts and washers to firmly hold the bolts while you set the new toilet).
- Don't be tempted to stack wax rings to make up a height difference caused by a higher new floor. Instead, install or stack plastic flange extenders and use a single wax ring with a rubber flange that helps direct waste.
- The simplest way to set the new wax ring is to simply sit on the toilet.

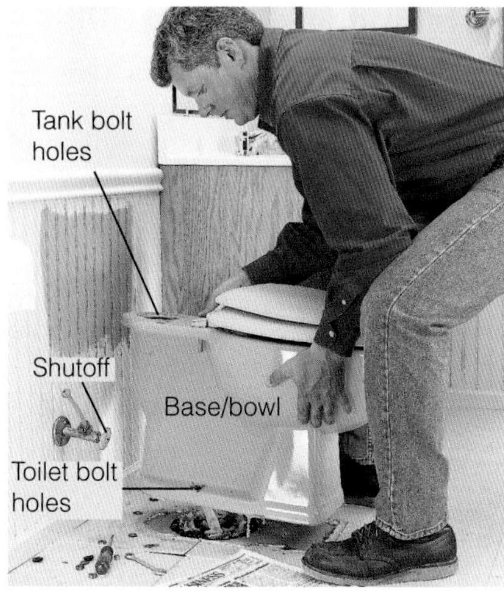

1 Empty the bowl and tank of water. To lighten the load, disconnect the tank from the bowl (usually held by two bolts). Unscrew flange nuts securing toilet to floor. If flange nuts spin, use a hacksaw to cut bolts below the nuts. Lift toilet off bolts and floor.

2 Replace any rotted subfloor. You'll likely have to split new subfloor to go around toilet flange. Support all plywood edges with 2x4s under split and where old and new subfloor meet. Screw down new subfloor. Patch or replace floor covering.

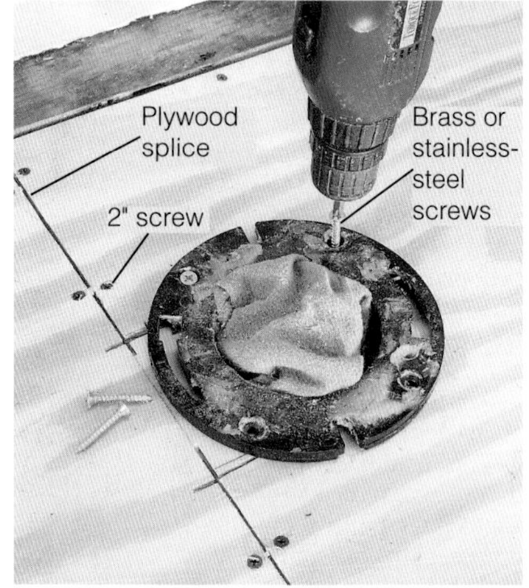

3 Screw toilet flange to subfloor with 2-in. brass or stainless-steel screws. If new flooring will raise finished floor height 1/2 in. (6 mm) or more, add flange extenders before screwing down flange. Install new flooring tight to the existing flange.

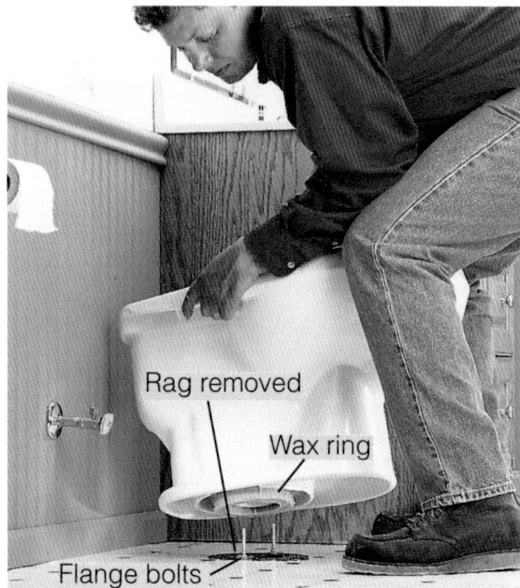

4 Install new flange bolts in flange. Stick new wax ring on bottom of toilet. Set toilet by lining up flange bolts with toilet base holes. Push toilet down or sit on it to set wax ring. Install washers and nuts on flange bolts.

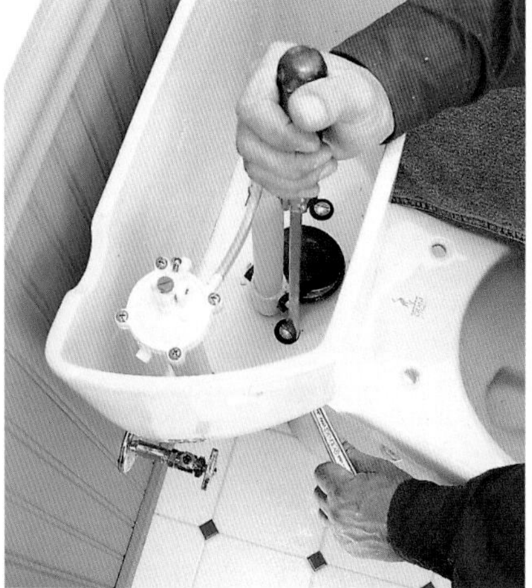

5 Bolt tank onto bowl with new bolts and washers. Tighten cautiously to avoid cracking the porcelain and to keep tank level. Tank installation varies by manufacturer, so follow directions included with your toilet.

6 Install new no-burst supply line and, if necessary, new shutoff valve. Attach supply line to toilet tank. Turn on water and flush a few times. Check for leaks around water supply, tank-to-bowl connection and base.

Installing a Vanity

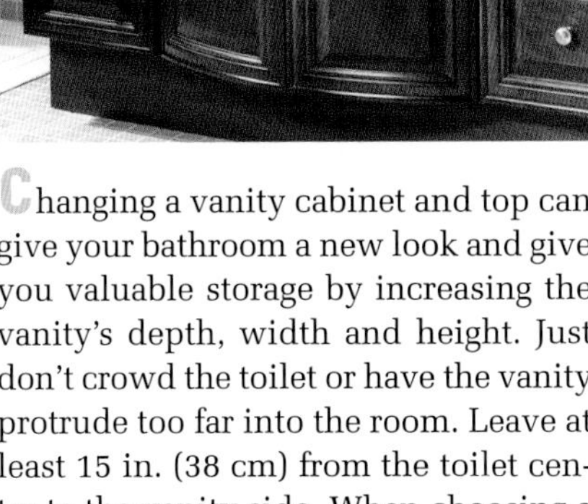

Changing a vanity cabinet and top can give your bathroom a new look and give you valuable storage by increasing the vanity's depth, width and height. Just don't crowd the toilet or have the vanity protrude too far into the room. Leave at least 15 in. (38 cm) from the toilet center to the vanity side. When choosing a taller vanity, be aware of obstructions, such as electrical outlets.

Always check the flooring material to see whether it runs underneath the old vanity. If it doesn't go underneath, get a vanity with a similar footprint or larger. Also, if a vanity side will rest against a wall, make sure drawers will clear any protruding trim. To create clearance, you can add a thin filler strip to that side of the cabinet.

1 Shut off water. Disconnect supply lines and drain. Remove backsplash if it's separate from top. Remove screws or cut through adhesive holding the top. Pull top free from vanity; lift straight out to minimize wall damage.

2 Remove fasteners holding old vanity to wall. Use a cat's paw to remove nails. Scrape away glue or adhesive left on the wall and patch any wall damage. Repaint the room. Locate studs and mark level lines on wall for cabinet-edge locations.

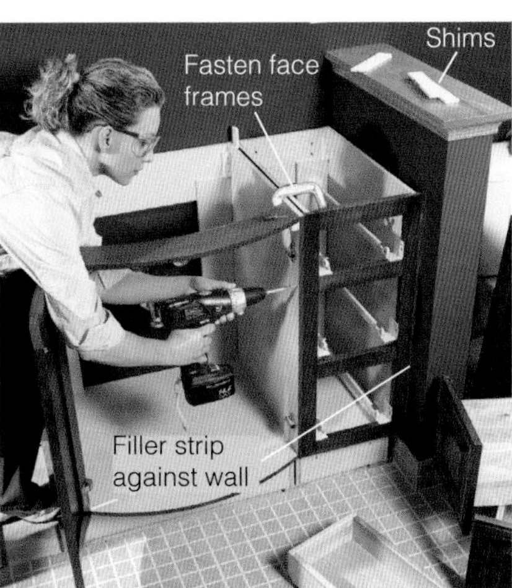

3 Nail filler strips to cabinet sides, if necessary. Assemble cabinets and screw face frames together. Cut holes for plumbing. Level cabinets side to side and back to front using tapered shims and secure cabinets to wall.

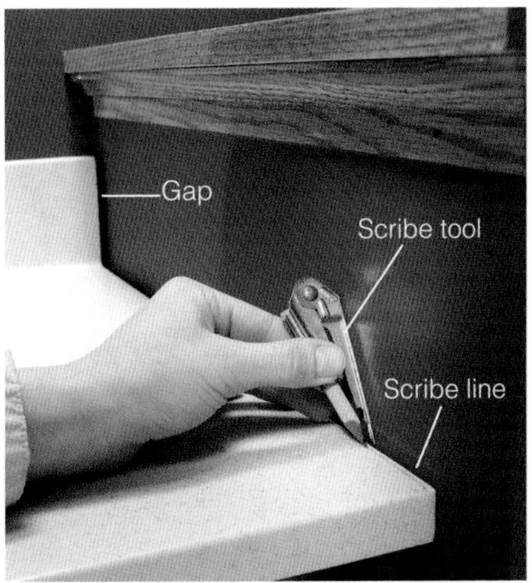

4 Set top onto cabinet to check fit against side wall. For gaps greater than 1/16 in. 2 mm), mark a scribe line. For solid surface and cultured marble, use belt sander to remove material. Side splashes cover some gaps.

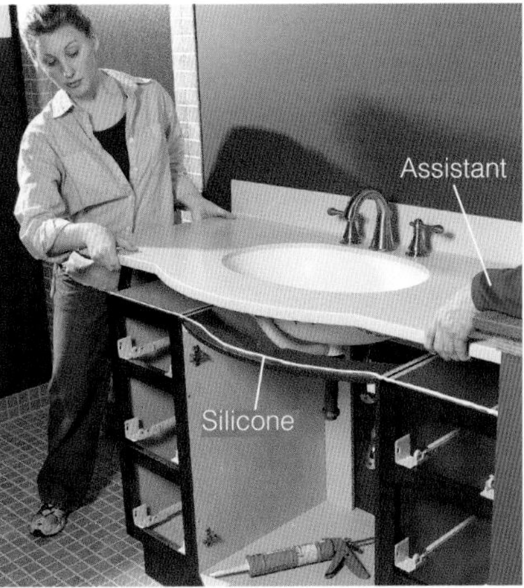

5 Install faucets and drain assembly to molded sink top before installing it. Apply 3/8-in. (5-mm) bead of clear silicone to top cabinet edge. With assistance, drop vanity top straight onto cabinet and silicone bead.

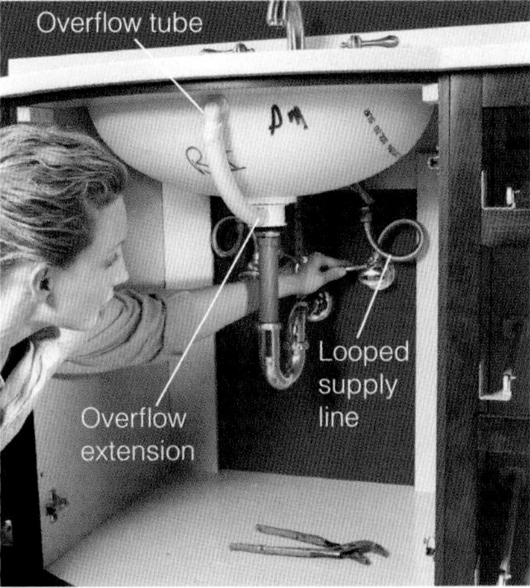

6 Connect faucet supply lines to shutoff valves and reconnect drain. Some molded sinks have built-in overflow tubes. Others have separate overflow tubes that must be attached with an extension between sink and drain.

Installing Tubs and Showers

Demolition Tools 37
Anti Scald Tub Valve 103
Soldering Joints 112
Flexible-copper Pipe 113
Shutoff Valves 114
Connecting Wires 137

In the past, your choices for bathtubs were limited to cast iron or steel and the bowl shapes and colors were fairly limited as well. Today, you still have cast iron and steel, but there's also fiberglass and composite materials available in countless shapes, sizes and colors.

To get the new tub in place, you'll likely need to remove wall tile, drywall or plaster, flooring and usually the sink or toilet. Further, you may need to install a newer antiscald valve to meet current codes. In short, since getting the old tub out and the new tub in involves so much demolition and patchwork, this project makes most sense when done as part of a whole-bathroom remodel.

1 Shut off water. Remove drain and overflow. Cover cast-iron tubs with heavy blanket to control flying shards and break up using a sledgehammer. Wear protective gear. Lightweight tubs can be removed intact.

2 Cut hot- and cold-water supply lines using a tight-area pipe cutter to remove old valve and tub and shower lines. For galvanized pipe, disconnect unions, install transitional fittings and convert to copper or CPVC pipe.

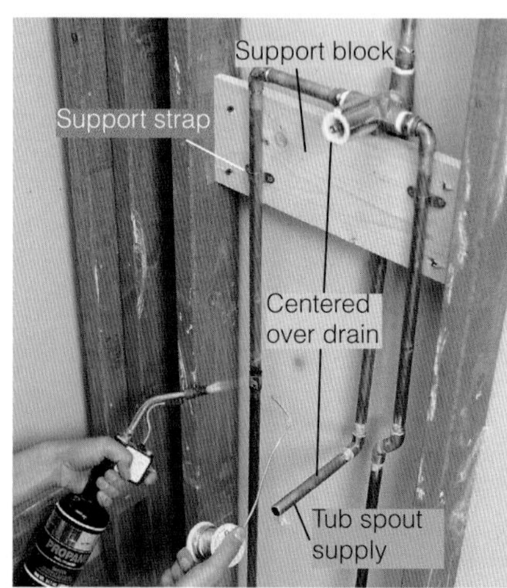

3 Hook up new faucet valve so it's centered over new tub's drain. Use valve's finished-surface-plate template to gauge valve's front-to-back position in wall. Add support block to support valve and establish its position.

4 Install new tub according to manufacturer's instructions. Some tubs require a level ledger board to support back of tub. Others use hanger clips for support. Slide tub into position on 2x4 skids and make sure it doesn't rock.

5 Connect new drain and overflow. For deeper tubs, you'll need a tall, whirlpool-type overflow. Install overflow gasket according to manufacturer's directions. Connect tub drain to main drain with P-trap. Test drain and overflow.

Installing a Shower Base

Several manufacturers offer preformed shower bases that range in size from 32 x 32 in. up to 60 x 32 in., the same footprint as a tub. The rules for installation are basically the same as those for tubs. The primary difference is that the shower drain is generally centered and there's no overflow to worry about. For nonstandard floor spaces—a common problem when you remove a tiled shower base—you may be able to special order a base to fit.

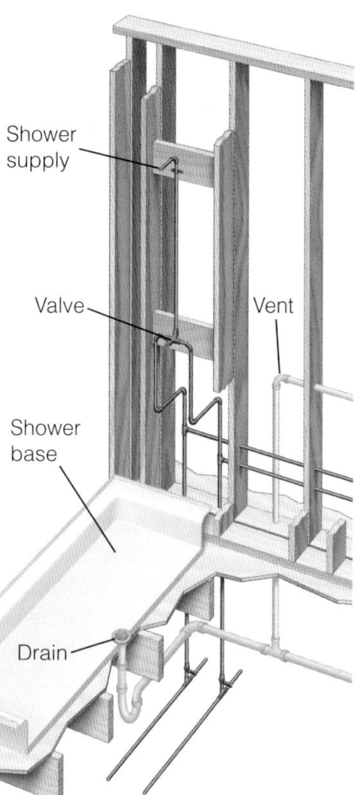

Installing a Dishwasher

If you're simply replacing your old dishwasher with a new one, this project is fairly straightforward. Standard dishwasher sizes make them largely interchangeable. Most manufacturers use a standard mechanical configuration that allows you to reuse the same supply lines. However, some models may require new supply lines fed from a different direction.

To remove the old unit, shut off water and disconnect water-supply line. Next, shut off power and remove electrical connection. Remove the anchor screws from the countertop and lower the unit using the adjustable feet for clearance. Save the 90-degree fitting and the electrical cord if you have a plug-in setup, provided the parts are in good condition. The new unit will usually include a new drain hose. After installation, run dishwasher through a complete cycle and test for leaks.

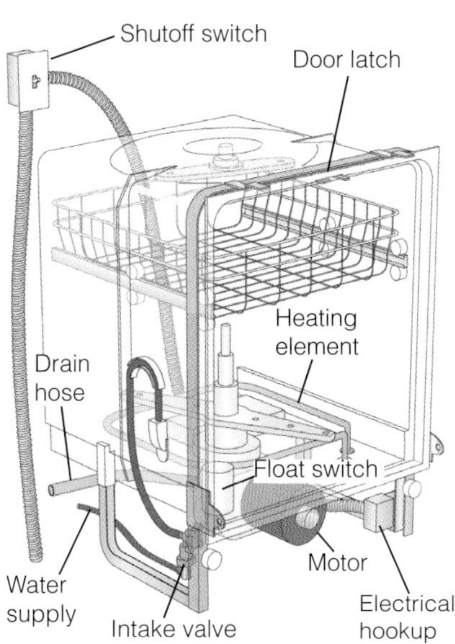

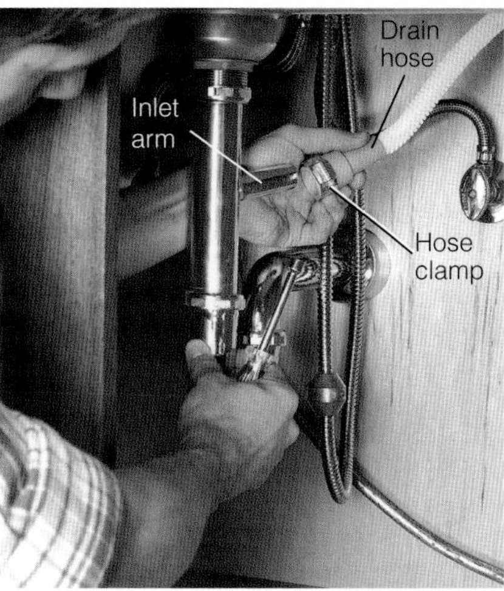

1 Thread new drain hose into cabinet. Loop drain hose up to bottom of countertop or special air-gap fitting, if required by code, and clamp. Pull drain hose down to inlet arm on sink drain or garbage disposer.

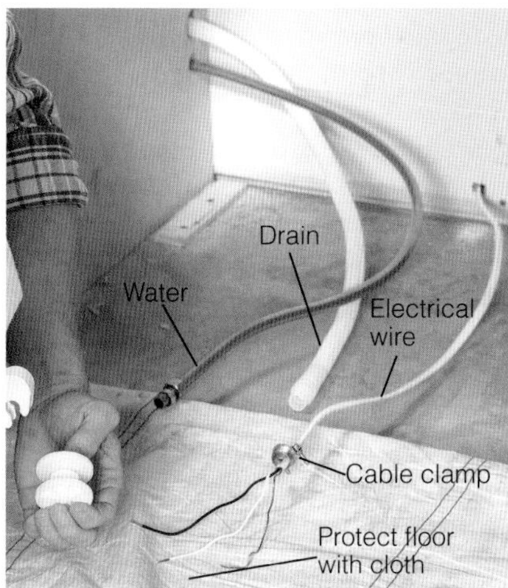

2 Lay out water line, drain hose and electrical wire so they clear obstructions underneath the dishwasher as you slide it back. If required by code, sheath electrical wire in flexible-steel conduit.

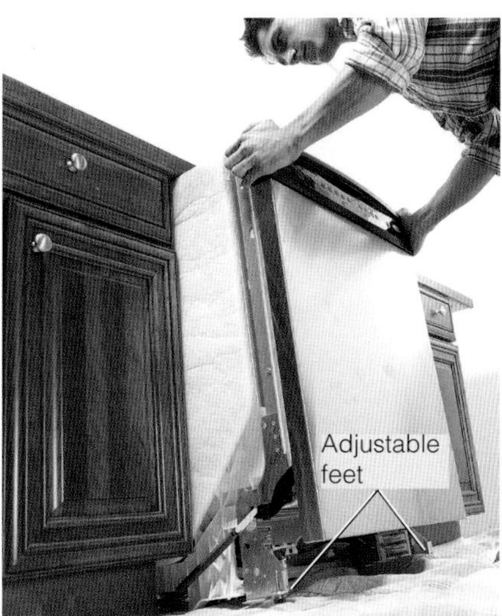

3 Adjust front feet to roughly fit the opening's height. Carefully slide dishwasher into opening. Adjust feet so door is level and gap between cabinets is equal on both sides of the unit.

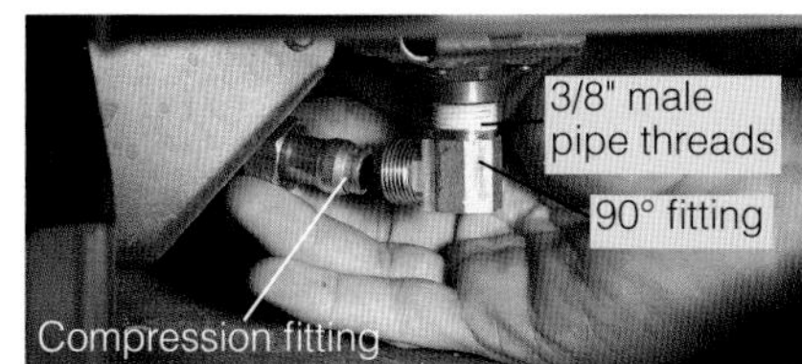

4 Install 90° fitting and align it so water supply slides straight into fitting. Use plumbing tape on threads and tighten fitting.

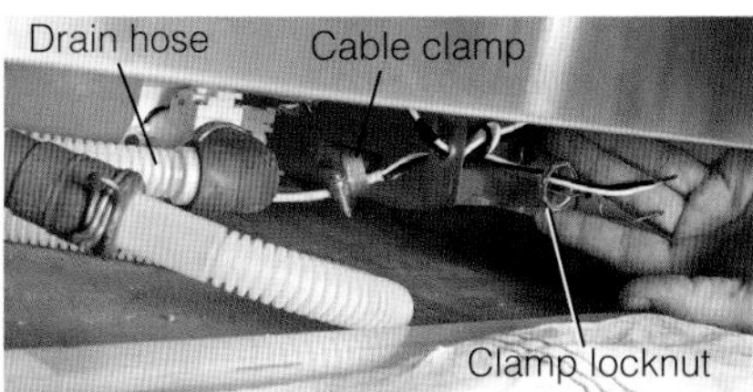

5 Clamp drain hose to dishwasher. Install cable clamp and connect electrical wires. Double-check dishwasher position and screw dishwasher brackets to underside of countertop.

Repairing Door Leaks

A poorly sealing door is the source for most dishwasher door leaks. Look for drips directly under the door when it runs. If a puddle appears after washing, remove the lower front panel and check for drips around the hoses and water connections. Also, check for a stuck float switch causing the tub to overfill.

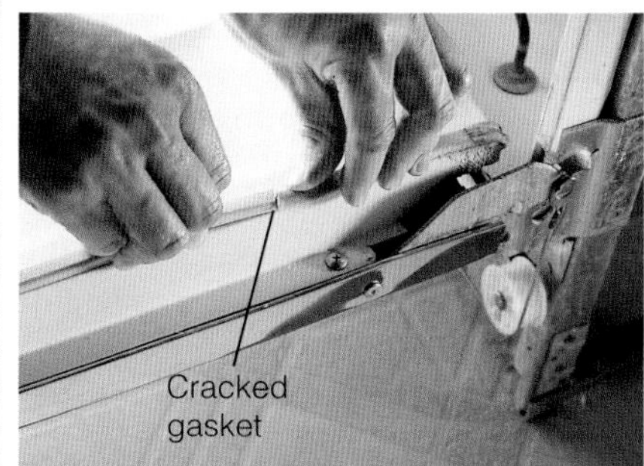

Replace a gasket that's cracked, brittle or worn. Observe how the old one fits when you remove it. Soak the new gasket in hot water to soften it, and use petroleum jelly to lubricate flanges for easier installation.

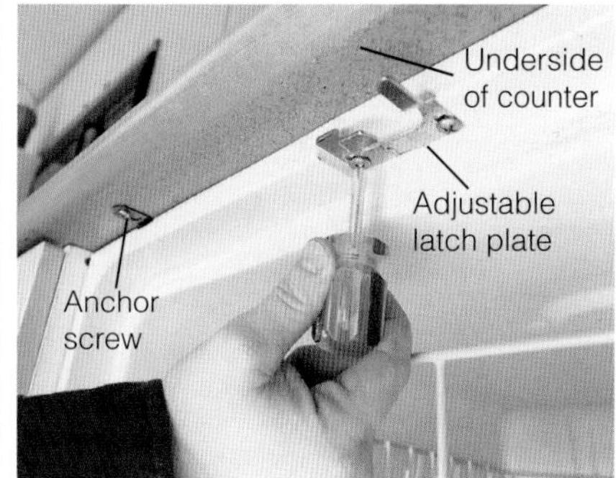

Tighten the latch if you can jiggle the door after it's latched. Loosen screws holding adjustable latch plate and move inward in small increments, testing the door's fit after each adjustment.

Installing a Garbage Disposer

Septic Systems 91
Plumbing Tools 92
Pipes and Pipe Fittings 107
Branch Circuits 128
Connecting Wires 137

A garbage disposer can be a great convenience but shouldn't be used as a trash can. Overloading can lead to frequent drain clogs and, if you have a septic system, can clog and ruin the leach field. Many kitchen drains function perfectly well with no disposer at all. As you install your disposer, keep these factors in mind:

Mounting assembly. Disposers are held in place by a mounting assembly that takes the place of a strainer basket in the sink. This mounting assembly is installed separately from the disposer. Setscrews tighten the assembly by pushing against a setscrew plate, pushing the mounting ring against a split ring to pull the flange tight against the sink.

Drain systems. The disposer discharge opening must be at least 3 in. (8 cm) above the drain stub-out in the wall for proper drainage. A disposer-replacement project is also a good time to replace and simplify the sink drain. A single P-trap system, shown below, works well and often frees up valuable space. Just make sure the tee fitting has an internal baffle to help prevent discharge backup into the other sink bowl.

Electrical requirements. Make sure your disposer is on a dedicated circuit not shared with any other outlets or light fixtures. If the disposer is hardwired rather than plugged in, the electrical cable or wires should be protected by flexible-metal conduit. If the old disposer has a plug-in cord in good shape, save it for use with the new disposer.

What's included. The new disposer will include detailed installation instructions and a new mounting assembly and stopper. Use the new assembly because the old one may not precisely fit the new disposer. Most new disposers will not include an electrical cord or the straight discharge tube shown below.

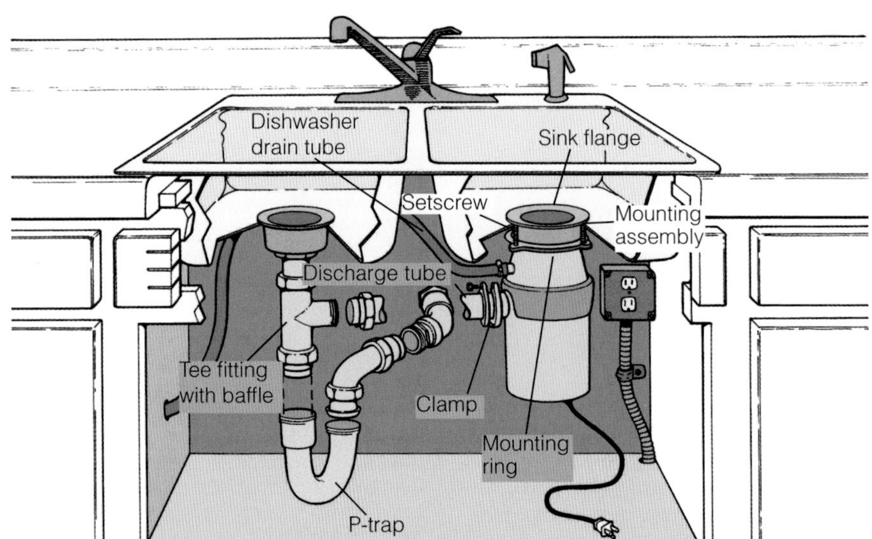

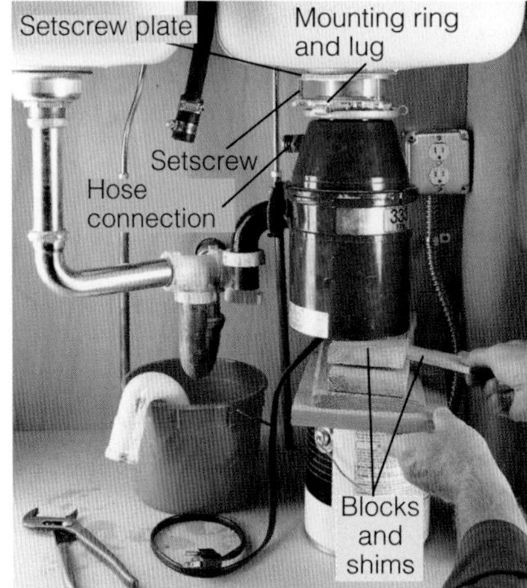

1 Shut off power. Disconnect disposer drain and dishwasher drain hose. Use blocks and shim to slightly wedge up disposer for easier removal. Lightly hammer on mounting ring lug to knock ring loose. Remove disposer.

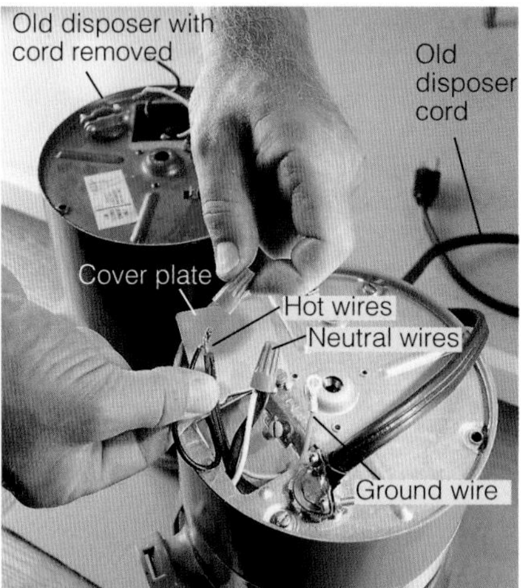

2 Follow manufacturer's wiring instructions to install electrical cord. On a flat, three-wire cord, ground is in the center, positive has smooth sheathing and neutral has raised ridges or indentations on sheathing.

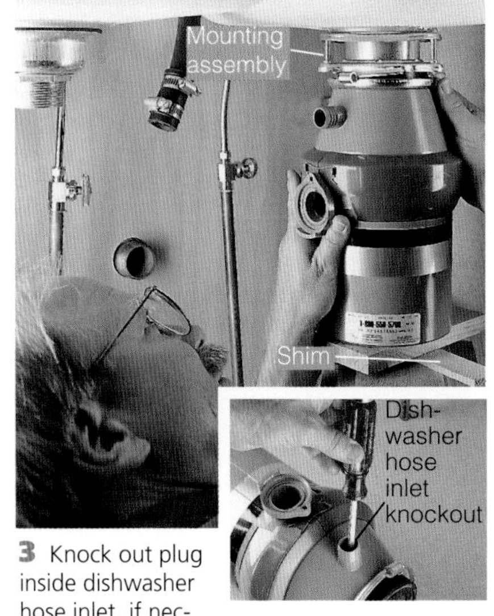

3 Knock out plug inside dishwasher hose inlet, if necessary. Wedge new disposer in place and partially tighten lugs.

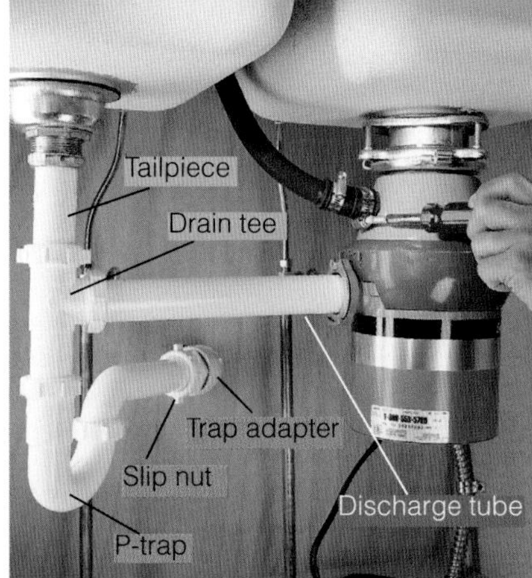

4 Attach tailpiece and drain tee. Slope the discharge tube slightly toward the drain. Mark and cut the discharge tube to length. Slide retaining ring and gasket over discharge and secure to disposer and drain tee. Tighten mounting ring.

Electricity

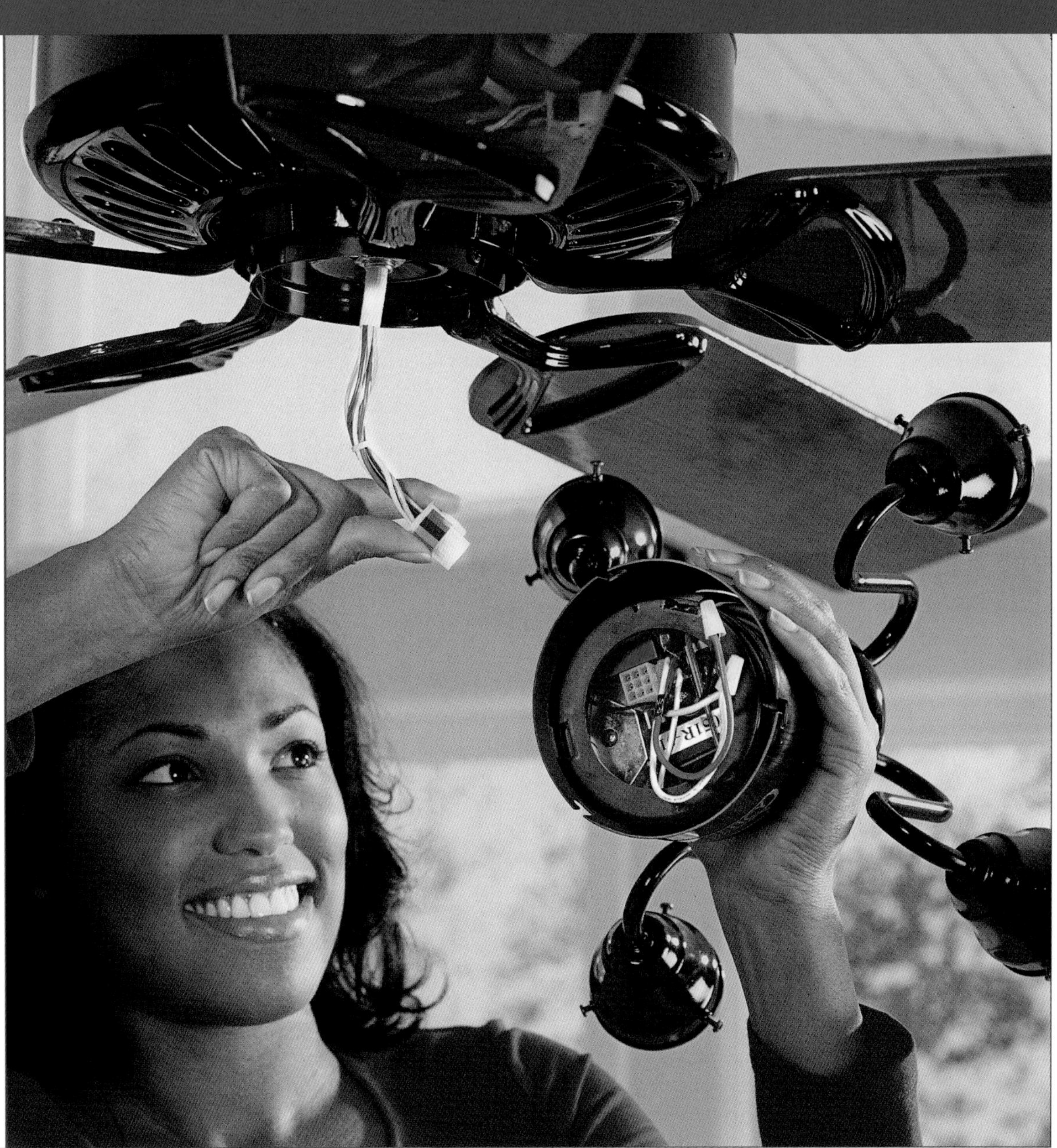

Understanding How It Works

Working with electricity is neither difficult nor dangerous as long as you understand this powerful phenomenon and treat it with respect. Here you'll learn how your system works and how to assess it, upgrade it, add to it and make repairs. You'll also be able to tell whether a wiring job is within your reach or best left to a licensed electrical contractor.

If you're a beginner, read the chapter carefully before attempting any electrical projects. Pay special attention to all safety precautions and learn how to safely use electrical testers and tools.

Just what is electricity? Think of it as a stream of negatively charged particles, called electrons, flowing at 186,000 miles per second (the speed of light) through a conductor, a wire, much the way water flows through a pipe.

The electrical pressure that causes current to flow through a conductor is measured in volts. Light fixtures and small appliances operate on 120 volts, and electric ranges and other heavy-duty appliances require 240 volts.

Resistance to the flow of electrons will vary with different materials. Copper is a good conductor and has low resistance, unlike plastic wire insulation that has very high resistance.

The rate that electric current flows is measured in amperes (amps). One ampere is the amount of current that will flow through one ohm—a measure of resistance—with a pressure of 1 volt.

The amount of power delivered by a current under pressure to a lamp or appliance is measured in watts. Watts, volts and amps are all interrelated. If you know two of the variables, you can figure out the third (see "Amps, Volts and Watts" below right). You can also determine the cost of running appliances and equipment.

Simple circuits. To do work, electricity must flow in a closed loop or circuit from a power source to a load, such as a lightbulb, then back to the source. If the circuit is interrupted by a switch or blown fuse, the current flow stops.

How power reaches your home. The electricity generated by a power plant and delivered to your home by your local utility is called alternating current (AC) because it flows alternately, first in one direction, then in the opposite, completing 60 cycles every second. Batteries produce direct current (DC) that flows through a circuit in only one direction. From the power plant, current travels over high-voltage transmission lines to substations, where transformers reduce the voltage for distribution to local lines. Neighborhood transformers lower the voltage to 120 and 240 volts for household use.

Homes built after the late 1960s will have 100-amp (or larger), 120- and 240-volt, three-wire service. Some homes built in the early 1900s may still have 30-amp, 120-volt, two-wire service. The most common pre-1960s service was three-wire, from 30 to 60 amps.

Electrical service may be supplied through overhead or underground wires. The utility's overhead service drop is connected to the home's service-entrance wires at the weatherproof service head, where they are installed in conduit to the meter enclosure. For underground services, the utility's direct-buried wires run to the home, where they emerge from the ground in a short conduit sleeve and connect inside the electrical meter box.

From the meter enclosure, the service-entrance wires run to the service panel usually inside your home where they terminate at the main service disconnect (see next page). The service disconnect is the first overcurrent protective device in the home; therefore, the length of unfused service-entrance wires inside the home must be kept as short as possible. From the service panel, electricity is distributed by branch circuits.

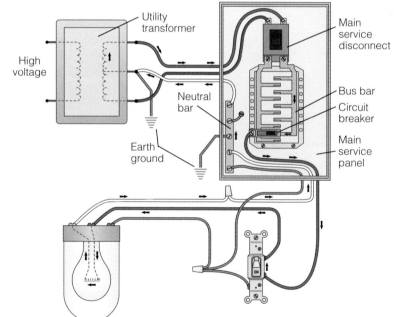

A simple circuit. In a typical lighting circuit, current flows at 120 volts from a common hot bus bar in the main service panel through a hot wire (usually color-coded black) to a lightbulb's wire filament, where it produces heat and light. From the bulb, a neutral wire (usually color-coded white) completes the circuit path back to the panel's neutral bar, which is grounded, connected to the earth. If a circuit malfunctions, a grounding wire (bare copper or color-coded green), running with the hot and neutral wires, provides a safe path to the source for abnormal current flow. The grounding wire enables overcurrent protective devices, like circuit breakers, to work.

Amps, Volts and Watts

Watts = volts x amps
Amps = watts ÷ volts
Volts = watts ÷ amps

Use these formulas to determine unknowns. For example, a 1,200-watt heater will draw 10 amperes at 120 volts.

To determine the cost of running an electrical item, all you need to know is:

- A thousand watts = 1 kilowatt.
- A kilowatt used for 1 hour = 1 kilowatt-hour (kwh), which is the unit utilities use to measure and bill you for electricity.

Circuit Breakers and Fuses

Branch circuits that distribute electricity throughout your house are typically rated from 15 to 50 amps. When a circuit draws too much current, wires can overheat, insulation can degrade and fail and the risk of fire greatly increases. To prevent this, each circuit is protected at the service panel by an overcurrent protective device. Most pre-1965 panels have fuses, and newer panels have circuit breakers. If a circuit draws excess current, the breaker will trip off or the metal strip inside the fuse melts open, stopping current flow.

Circuit failures are often caused by overloads, short circuits and ground faults. **Overloads** are caused when too many lights or appliances are on a circuit. **Short circuits** occur when a hot wire touches the neutral wire or another hot wire. A hot wire that touches a grounded metal box would be a **ground fault**. Before resetting the breaker or replacing the fuse, identify and correct the problem.

A heavily used circuit that fails when you turn on a high-wattage appliance is probably overloaded. The solution is to move portable appliances to a different circuit with unused capacity.

If the circuit still fails, check for a short circuit or ground-fault condition. Unplug lamps and appliances and look for damaged plugs or cords. Look for discoloration and smell for burned odors at receptacles, switches and fixtures. With lamps and appliances still unplugged, reset the breaker or replace the fuse. If the circuit fails again, there may be hidden problems in the house wiring. If the circuit fails only when you turn on a lamp or appliance, the problem may be corrected by repairing the item.

Panels

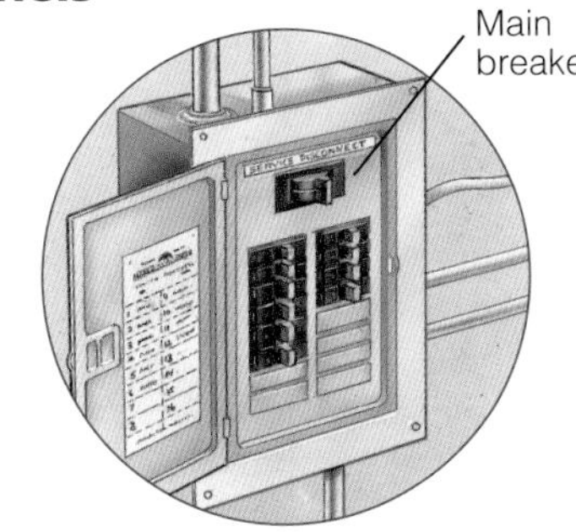

A circuit-breaker panel will usually have a double-pole main breaker and single-pole or double-pole branch breakers.

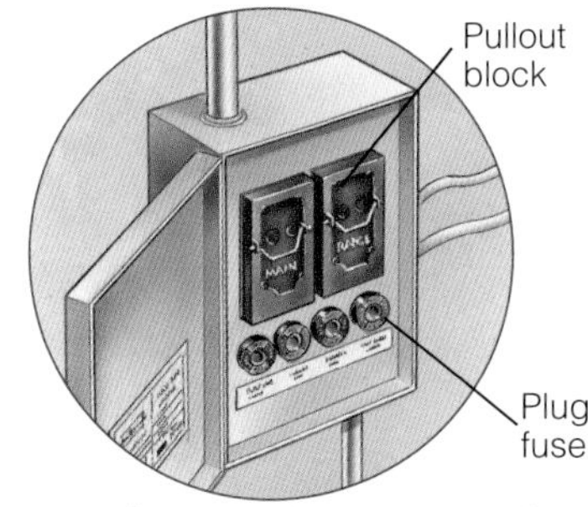

A fuse panel will usually have main pullout blocks with cartridge fuses and plug fuses for the branch circuits.

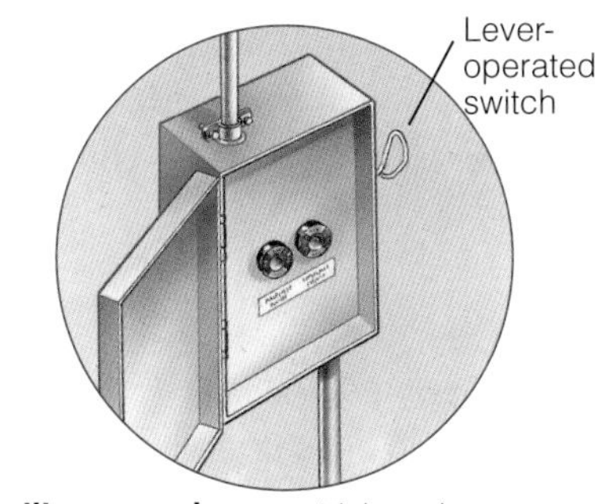

Auxiliary panels vary widely and may include lever-operated main switches with circuit breakers or cartridge or plug fuses.

Circuit Breakers

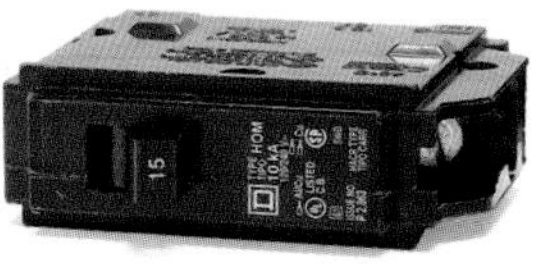

Single-pole breakers protect 120-volt lighting and appliance circuits usually rated at 15 or 20 amps.

Double-pole breakers protect 240-volt circuits rated at 15 to 50 amps, for appliances like clothes dryers and ranges.

Ground-fault circuit-interrupters (GFCI) protect people in damp locations from fatal electrical shocks.

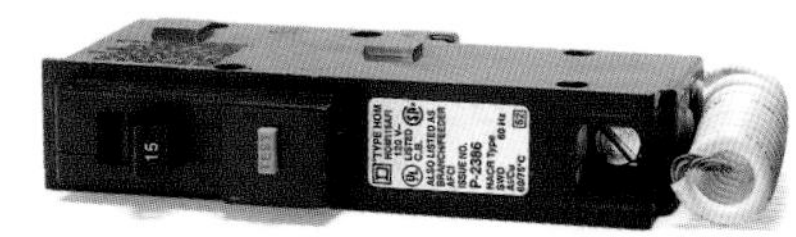

Arc-fault circuit-interrupters (AFCI) de-energize bedroom and other circuits when arcing faults, such as damaged lamp cords, are detected.

Fuses

Standard Edison-base plug fuses (15 to 30 amp) can only be used as replacements in existing installations. Many local requirements mandate upgrading to type S plug fuses.

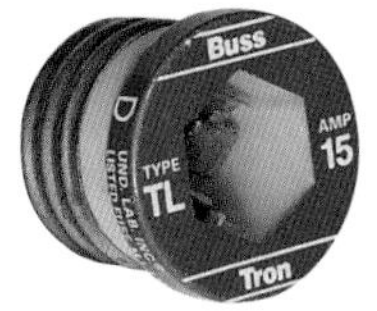

Time-delay plug fuses (15 to 30 amp) will tolerate the quick burst of a high motor-starting current without blowing and needing replacement.

Type S plug fuses and their matching permanent adapters prevent the wrong size fuses from being used.

Screw-in circuit breakers can replace existing standard plug fuses. When a breaker trips, its button can be reset. These can be replaced by type S fuses for safety.

Ferrule-type cartridge fuses, rated up to 60 amps, usually protect large-appliance circuits.

Knife-blade cartridge fuses, rated up to 600 amps, usually protect service or feeder wires.

Distribution

Electrical Testers 132
Wiring Variations 143
Undercabinet Lighting 149

Service Panel

Modern services are rated from 100 to 400 amps. After passing through the electric meter, the three-wire, 120/240-volt service-entrance wires enter the service panel. The two black hot wires (each supplying 120 volts) are attached to the terminals of the service disconnect, which feeds the two hot bus bars. Single-pole breakers plug into one bus bar and supply 120-volt circuits. Double-pole breakers plug into two adjacent bus bars supplying 240-volt circuits. The neutral wire (marked white) attaches to the neutral bar, which is bonded to the metal enclosure and the ground bar with a screw or strap. Grounding wires from ground rods and water pipes and in the branch-circuit cables connect to the ground bar.

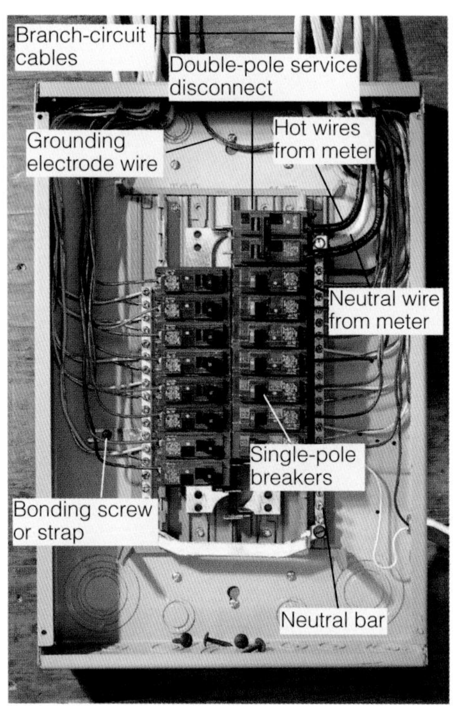

When to Upgrade the Fuse Box

Older 60-amp services are only adequate in smaller homes with no more than one 240-volt appliance, like a water heater or range. Home-loan programs and insurance companies often require existing homes to have a minimum of 100-amp service. Upgrading old fuse boxes enhances your safety, adds convenience and value to your home and allows you to easily add circuits to accommodate modern appliances.

Consult a licensed electrical contractor to evaluate the load supplied by your service to determine if an upgrade is necessary.

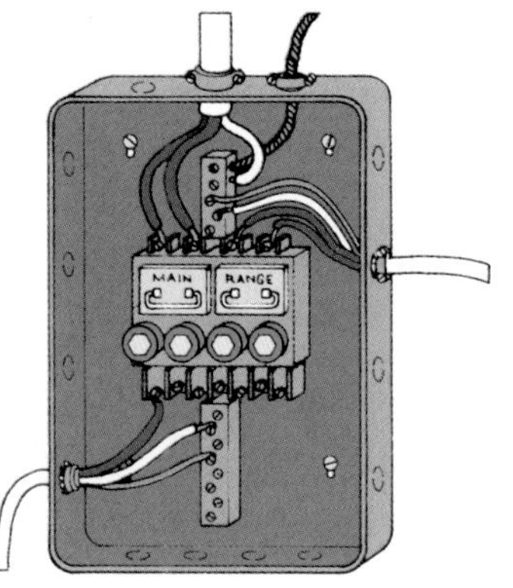

Older-style fuse box

Branch Circuits

Branch circuits carry electricity from the service panel's breakers or fuses to receptacles, light fixtures and appliances. There are three categories of branch circuits. **General-purpose circuits** supply two or more outlets for lighting and appliances, **appliance circuits** supply only appliances, and **individual circuits** supply only one item, such as a water heater. A 120-volt circuit consists of a black hot wire connected to the breaker, a white neutral wire connected to the neutral bar and a bare copper or green insulated equipment grounding wire connected to the ground bar. A 240-volt circuit will have two hot wires and a grounding wire and may include a neutral wire if required by the appliance served. Unlike hot wires that are interrupted by light switches, neutral and grounding wires must never be switched.

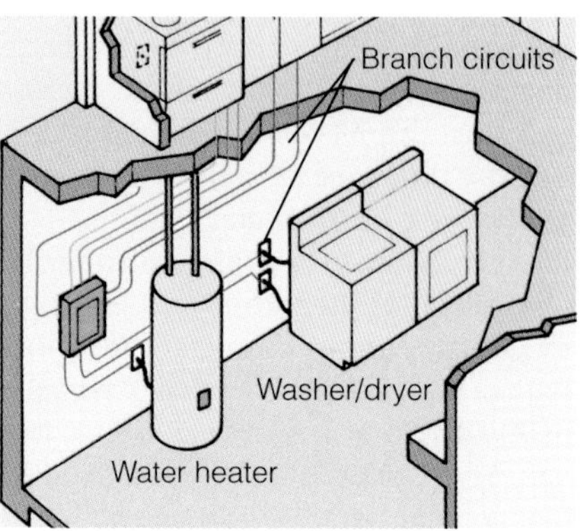

Codes, Permits and Inspections

The National Electrical Code (USA) and the Canadian Electrical Code contains rules necessary for safeguarding people and property from hazards associated with electricity use. Before doing any electrical work, contact your local, county, state or province inspector for up-to-date information.

Except for minor repairs, such as replacing a broken receptacle, you usually need to apply for a permit, submit plans or pass a simple proficiency test to do the work. Wiring usually must be inspected before it is covered or concealed; final inspections ensure the wiring is complete and safe to use. Electricity can be deadly—when in doubt, hire a licensed electrical contractor to handle the tough jobs.

All electrical equipment should be third-party certified. Look for the Underwriters Laboratories (UL), Underwriters Laboratories Canada (ULC) or Canadian Standards Association (CSA) mark or label.

A Few Projects You Need Permits For:

- Wiring new homes
- Upgrading electrical services
- Room and porch additions
- Finishing basements
- Replacing light fixtures and ceiling fans
- Installing or replacing appliances, furnaces and air conditioners
- Installing wiring to detached garages and sheds
- Installing outdoor wiring and wiring for hot tubs and swimming pools

Circuit Mapping and Planning

Mapping an Electrical System

The first step in assessing your electrical system is to determine whether you have two-wire (120-volt) or three-wire (240-volt) service. To do this, check the number of wires entering the service head outside. Also look for the system's service rating in amps, usually stamped on the service disconnect.

Before doing any electrical work, make a map of all existing circuits. Create a panel index card and assign a number to each circuit breaker or fuse in the service panel, noting its ampere rating. Draw a floor plan of your home that includes the attic, basement, garage and exterior wiring. Use a full sheet of graph paper for each floor and label all rooms and spaces. Using the common electrical symbols shown below, record the location of all receptacles, switches, lights and other equipment. Simply turn off a circuit breaker or remove a fuse at the service panel, then walk through the house with a tester or portable light to determine which outlets are dead. Turn that circuit back on and repeat the process for each additional circuit, recording the assigned circuit number next to the symbols on your floor plan.

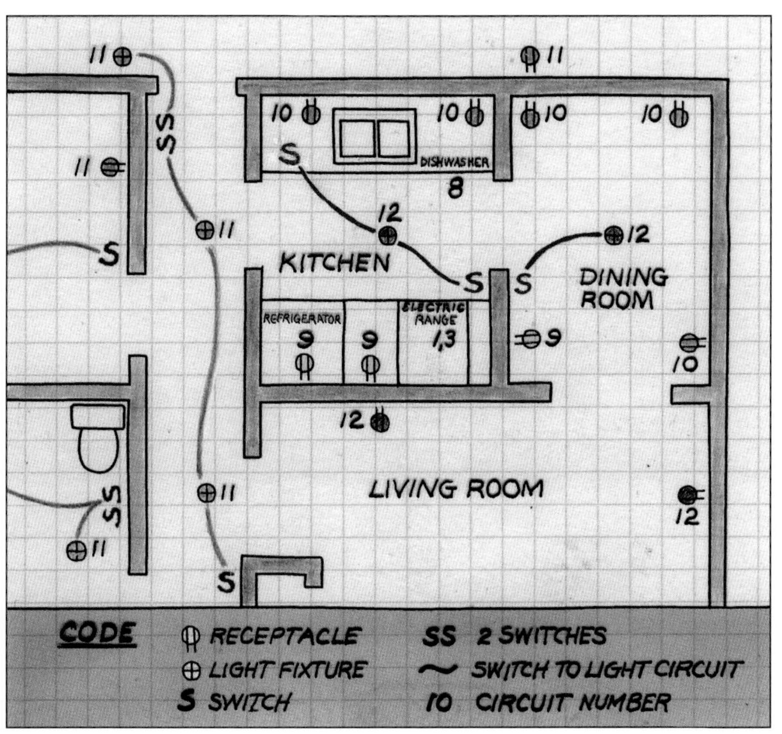

Basic Code Guidelines

Most codes use a minimum load of 3 watts per sq. ft. (33 watts per sq. m) to calculate the general lighting load and the number of general-purpose lighting circuits that supply light fixtures and receptacles. Keep it simple—a rule of thumb is one 15-amp circuit for every 600 sq. ft. (56 sq. m) of floor space, or better yet, only install a combination of 10 lights and outlets on a 15-amp general-purpose circuit.

Code also requires a minimum of two 20-amp circuits for kitchen receptacles, one 20-amp circuit for laundry receptacles, one 20-amp circuit for bathroom receptacles and a dedicated circuit for central heating equipment.

Generally, receptacle outlets in habitable rooms must be installed so no point measured horizontally along the floor line in any wall space (24 in. / 600 mm or greater) is more than 6 ft. (1.8 m) from a receptacle outlet.

Generally, at least one wall switch-controlled lighting outlet must be installed in every habitable room, bath, hallway, stairway, attached garage and the exterior side of entrances. For habitable rooms other than kitchens and bathrooms, a wall switch-controlled receptacle can be used for the lighting outlet.

Note: The above information is based on United States codes; The Canadian Electrical code (CEC) differs in some areas. See Resources, p. 516 for more information.

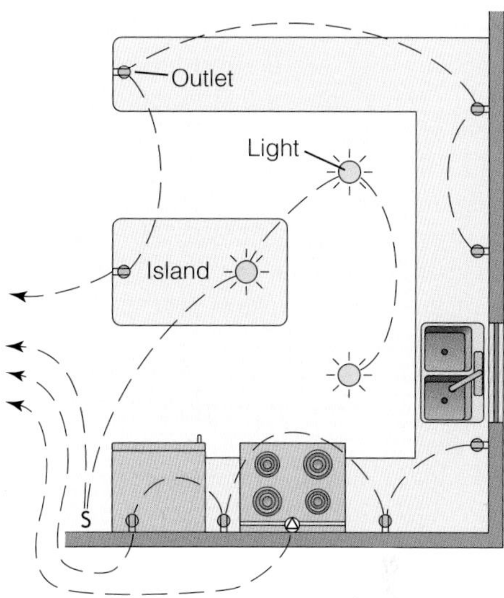

Kitchens. Ground-fault circuit-interrupter (GFCI)-protected outlets should be installed at countertops so no point measured horizontally along the wall line is more than 24 in. (600 mm) from a receptacle outlet. Islands and peninsulas each must have one GFCI outlet.

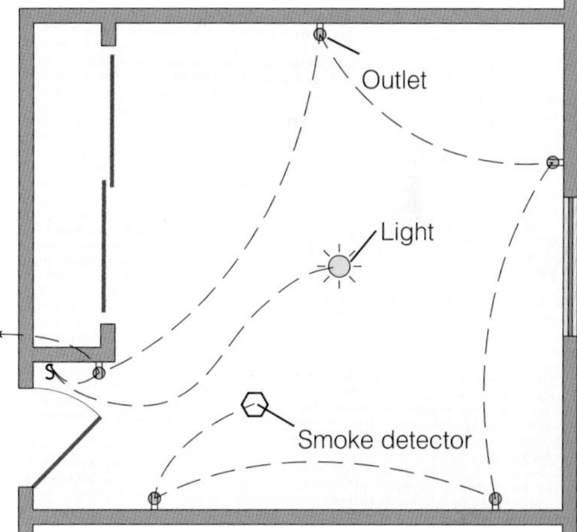

Bedrooms, living rooms. All branch circuits that supply 125-volt, 15- and 20-amp outlets in bedrooms must be AFCI protected. This includes receptacle and lighting outlets and smoke detectors.

Grounding

Amps, Volts and Watts 126
Circuit Mapping 129
Lightning Protection 162
Hazardous Materials 480

Circuit breakers, fuses, ground-fault circuit interrupters (GFCIs), arc-fault circuit interrupters (AFCIs), transient-voltage surge suppressors (TVSSs) and other protective devices are a home's first line of defense against electrical accidents. Equally important is the grounding system, which normally doesn't carry current but must always be on guard to provide a safe path for abnormal current flow and to ensure protective devices' quick operation.

The basics. The principles of grounding are simple but often misunderstood, even by experienced electricians. The term grounded is defined in the code as meaning "connected to earth or to some conducting body that serves in place of earth," such as a grounded metal electrical box. The earth as a whole is a conductor and is assumed to have a voltage potential of zero, but it is made of different types of soil that resist current flow and do not conduct electricity very well.

Electricity always seeks the path of least resistance to return to its source, usually the utility's transformer. Instead of the earth itself, grounding wires are used to ground all metal objects and provide an effective low-resistance, highly conductive path for abnormal current. Grounding all metal objects also ensures they are at the same safe zero-voltage potential as the earth. If a hot wire comes in contact with a grounded metal object, the low-resistance grounding wires carry the maximum current necessary to quickly trip the circuit breaker or protective device. The grounding wires try to keep the metal object close to the earth's zero-voltage potential to reduce the shock hazard.

Electrical systems and equipment are connected to ground rods, underground metal water pipes and other electrodes to limit and stabilize the voltage to ground during normal operation and to prevent excessive voltages from lightning strikes, power surges or accidental contact with high-voltage utility lines.

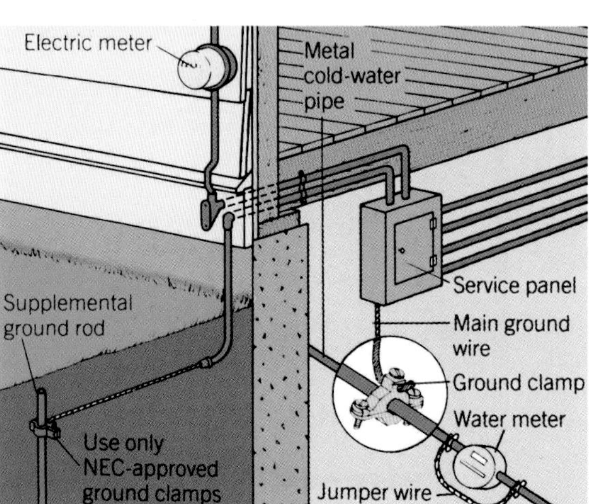

Service equipment is usually grounded to the underground metal water pipe within 5 ft. (1.5 m) of the point of entrance into the building. Because of the growing use of plastic water pipe, the code requires one or more supplemental electrodes, such as a ground rod. Copper-coated ground rods must be at least 8 ft. (2.5 m) in length, 1/2 in. (13 mm) in diameter and driven flush with or below the earth. Interior metal piping systems must be grounded by installing a wire called a bonding jumper around water meters and filters. Use only approved clamps for ground rod and metal pipe connections.

Making Older Receptacles Safer

You can increase the safety of your old two-prong outlets in two ways. Installing GFCI outlets will protect against a deadly shock even if the outlet is not connected to a grounding wire. If you have grounded metal conduit and boxes, new three-prong outlets can be installed.

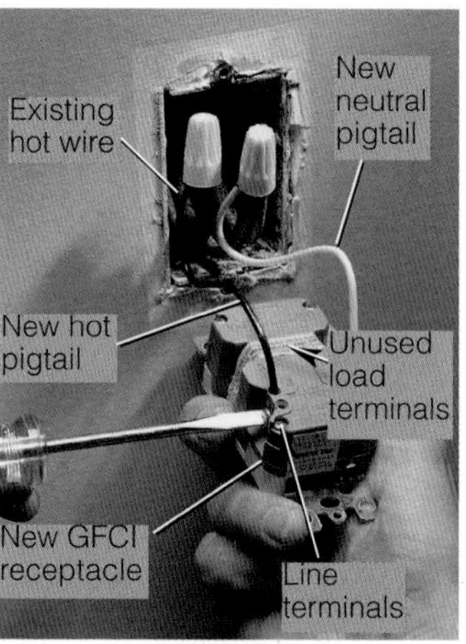

GFCI. Turn off power to the receptacle outlet at the service panel. Check to make sure the power is off. Carefully unscrew the outlet and pull it out of the box. (You may need to install a larger box to safely contain the wires and new GFCI). Disconnect wires from the old outlet and splice them to 6-in. (15-cm) pigtails of white or black wire. Connect the new wires to the GFCI terminals marked "Line," attaching the black wire to the brass screw and the white wire to the silver screw. Fold wires neatly into the box, fasten the GFCI and plate, and attach the stickers that say "No Equipment Ground."

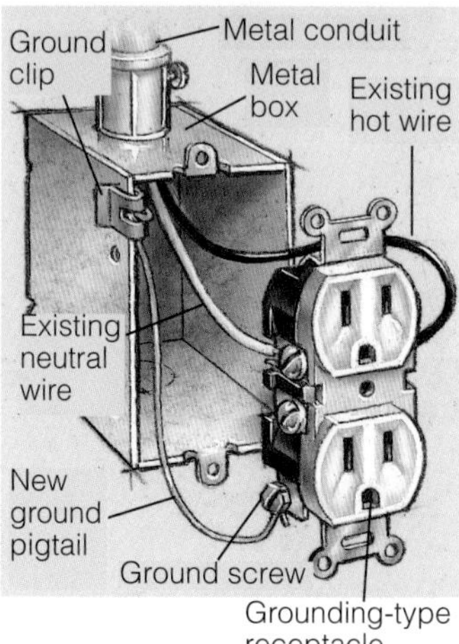

Three-prong. Three-prong grounding-type outlets can be installed only as replacements where a grounding means is available, such as metal conduit, metal armored cable, flexible-metal conduit and their metal boxes. One can also install a ground from elsewhere on the grounding electrode system by using a wire of the same gauge as the branch-circuit conductors. Turn off power to the receptacle outlet at the service panel. Check to make sure the power is off. Carefully unscrew the outlet and pull it out of the box. Connect the black wire to the brass screw and the white wire to the silver screw. Install a bare or green-insulated bonding jumper from the green ground screw on the outlet to the metal box using a green ground clip or green ground screw threaded into the back of the box. Fold wires neatly into box and install the outlet and plate.

Assessing Your Electrical Service

If your home has two-wire (120-volt) electrical service or if you have a 60-amp three-wire service, consult a licensed electrician about converting the two-wire (120-volt) service to three-wire (120/240-volt) service or upgrading to at least 100 amps. While the minimum requirement for new homes is 100 amps, 200 amps is common in larger homes. Some may have 400-amp service. If you have doubts about the grounding system, consult a licensed electrician.

Got aluminum? Millions of homes were wired with inexpensive aluminum (AL) cable because of high copper prices in the late 1960s and early 1970s. Such wiring can be unsafe if it is not properly installed and maintained. Aluminum wires are dull gray, not the dull orange characteristic of copper wires (see p. 480). Cables may be marked AL or Aluminum. To ensure your safety and the value of your home, hire an experienced electrical contractor to work on aluminum wiring systems, which require special techniques and wire connectors.

If your wiring is aluminum, replacement switches and receptacles, rated 20 amps or less, must be marked CO/ALR. Replacement devices rated 30 amps and more must be marked AL-CU. Replacement light fixtures and devices with pigtails, like dimmers, require special wire connectors.

Need more lights and outlets? As long as you don't exceed the capacity of your service panel, you can add new receptacles and fixtures by either extending an existing circuit or installing a new one. Before extending a circuit, check your circuit map (see p. 129) to make sure the additional receptacles or fixtures will not overload the circuit. To install a new circuit, the service panel must have space for a new breaker. To add a new circuit, combine underused circuits, substitute half-size for full-size breakers (if your panel is listed for half size) or connect a subpanel to the main panel. Contact a licensed electrician for this type of work.

Typical Wattage Ratings

The wattage figures listed here are averages. Your appliance wattage ratings may vary significantly. Always check the appliance nameplate ratings for the correct voltage, wattage and amperage. If the rating is given in amps, multiply the amps by the volts to obtain the approximate wattage (use either 120 volts or 240 volts).

Appliance	Watts	Appliance	Watts	Appliance	Watts
Air conditioner, central	5,000	Food processor	200	Refrigerator	600
Air conditioner, room	1,300	Frying pan	1,200	Saw, table	1,200
Blender	300	Freezer	500	Saw, circular	1,200
Broiler, countertop	1,500	Furnace, gas forced-air	800	Stereo	400
Clothes dryer	5,000	Garbage disposer	600	Television	300
Clothes iron	1,200	Hair dryer	900	Toaster	1,500
Coffeemaker	1,000	Heater, portable	1,200	Trash compactor	600
Computer	500	Microwave oven	1,500	Vacuum cleaner	800
Dishwasher	1,200	Range, oven	5,000	Washing machine	1,300
Fan, ceiling	400	Range, cooktop only	4,000	Water heater	5,000

Shop Smart

Surge Protectors

Surge protectors are designed to protect sensitive electronic equipment, such as computers, televisions and stereos, from spikes and surges that occur on power, telephone and coaxial cable lines. The warranties for such equipment are often void if you fail to provide surge protection.

Surges and spikes can be caused by utility switching operations, lightning strikes or motors and appliances in the home. Surge protectors absorb and dissipate excess energy, often sacrificing themselves to protect the equipment. Replace protectors that are worn out.

Surge protectors are required to be plugged into grounded outlets to operate properly and dissipate excess energy. All connected equipment must be plugged directly into the protector. Extension cords, adapters or other electrical connections are not advisable. Whole-house surge protectors are also available.

Surge suppressors carry a rating for a unit of electrical energy called a joule. Higher joule ratings mean surge protection devices will absorb more damaging energy from overvoltage surge conditions.

Multiple strip with phone, fax and coaxial cable protectors

Simple point-of-use surge protector

Point-of-use with telephone protector

Testers and How to Use Them

Wires and Connectors 134
Lamp and Cord Repairs 153
Communication Wiring 160

You can work safer and track down problems faster using electrical testers.

Continuity testers. Electricians and homeowners alike find a good basic diagnostic tool in a continuity tester—a battery-powered device with a lightbulb, probe and alligator clip. The bulb will glow when you have a complete circuit. Check the tester by touching the clip to the probe. Use this tester to detect short circuits, open circuits or other problems in lamp sockets, switches, cords, and to see if a fuse is good. Never use a continuity tester on wires or equipment that are, or may become, energized.

Voltage testers. Equipped with a neon bulb and two probes but no battery, the 90- to 600-volt neon-bulb voltage tester lights up when voltage is present. Always check the tester's bulb in a known live receptacle before each use. Use it to detect voltage between hot and neutral, hot and ground, or two hot wires on 240-volt circuits.

Volt-ohm meters. These battery-powered tools, also called multimeters, test for continuity, AC and DC voltage and DC amps, and measure resistance (ohms). Some testers have digital readouts; others have a needle that sweeps across a dial. Choose one that measures 250 volts AC and has RX1, RX10 and RX100 settings to test resistance. Take time to read the owner's manual to avoid damaging the meter.

Caution: Always use a voltage tester to make sure that any switch, receptacle, circuit or appliance you are going to work on is really dead.

Using a Continuity Tester

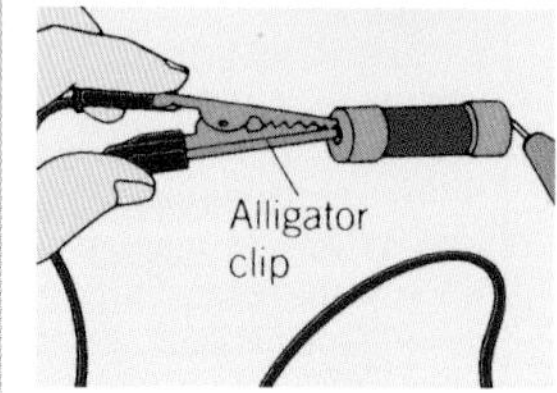

Fuses. Touch ends of fuse with clip and probe. If fuse is good, bulb will light.

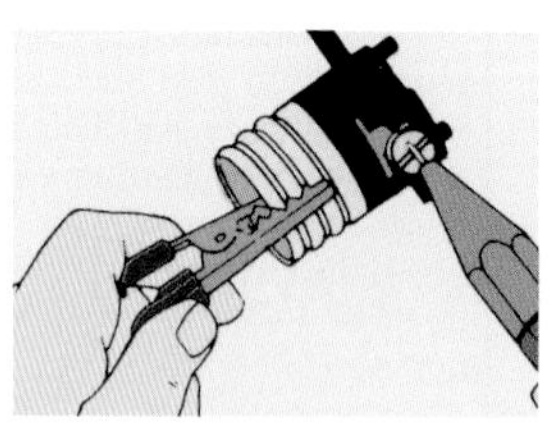

Lamp socket. Test for continuity between socket shell and silver screw, and center terminal and brass screw.

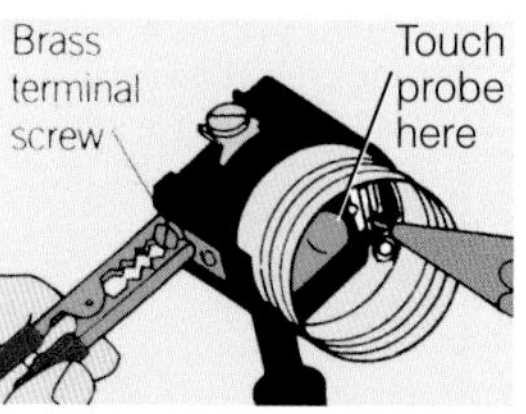

Lamp switch. Testing is similar to lamp socket (above) but switch operation can be checked.

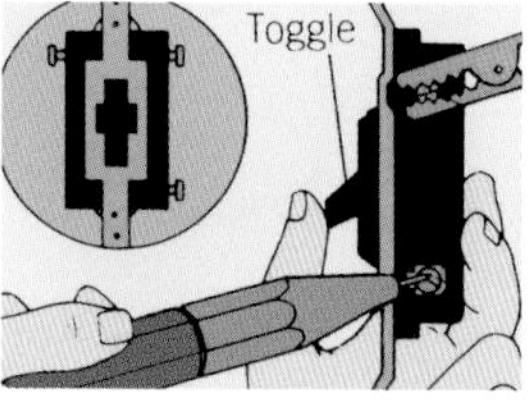

Three-way switch. Operate toggle up and down with clip on common screw and probe on each traveler screw.

Using a Voltage Tester

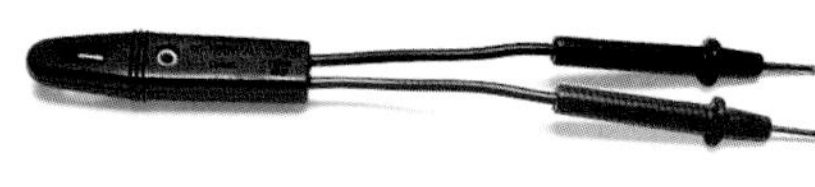

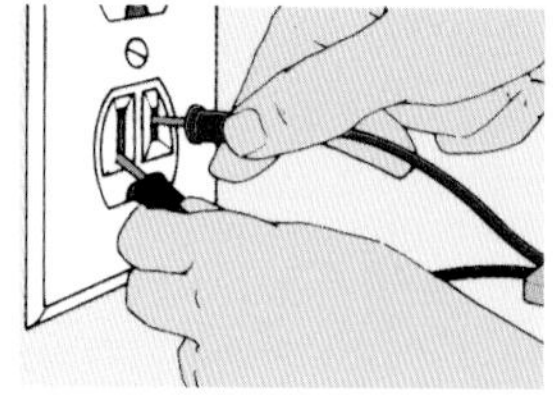

Test for power at receptacles. Check to determine that power to a receptacle is off before working on it. If bulb doesn't light, power is off.

Test for grounding with power on. Place one probe in short (hot) slot and the other probe to grounding slot or plate screw.

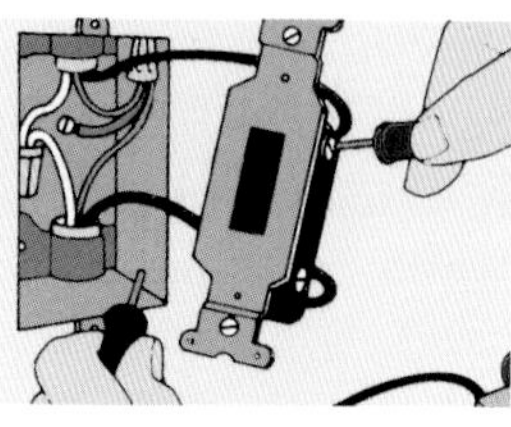

Test for power at switch. Set one probe on metal box and the other probe to each terminal.

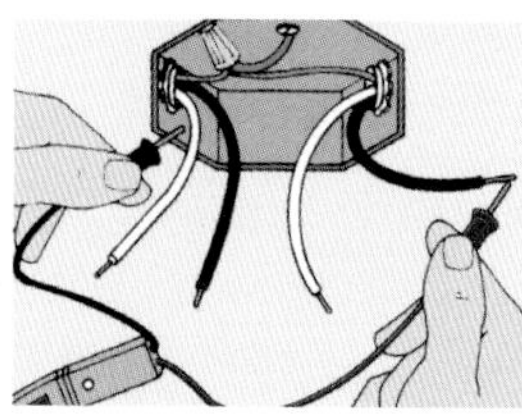

Test hot wire in a metal box. Touch one probe to metal box and the other probe to each wire.

Using a Volt-ohm Meter

Be safe—read the owner's manual carefully to avoid damaging your multimeter. Rotate the switch to select the proper test function, such as volts, amps or ohms, before you start testing. Select a voltage or amperage range that's higher than the top value you anticipate testing.

Use the resistance, or ohms, function to test switches. An "infinity" reading may indicate a defective switch.

Touch probes to heating element leads. Compare the appliance specifications with the resistance readings in ohms on your multimeter.

Wire Strippers

Voltage "Sniffers"

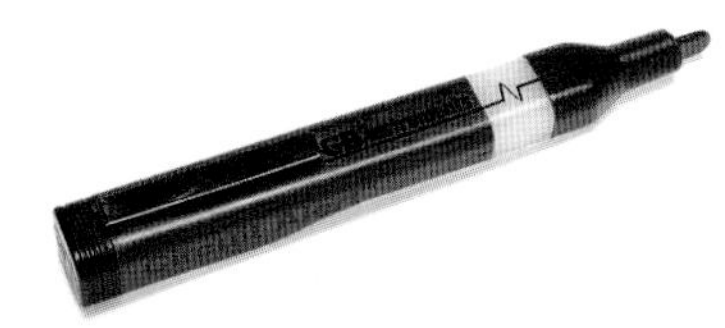

Noncontact voltage testers detect the presence of AC voltage from 50 to 600 volts anywhere along an insulated wire. An audible signal and LED indicator alert the user.

Outlet Analyzers

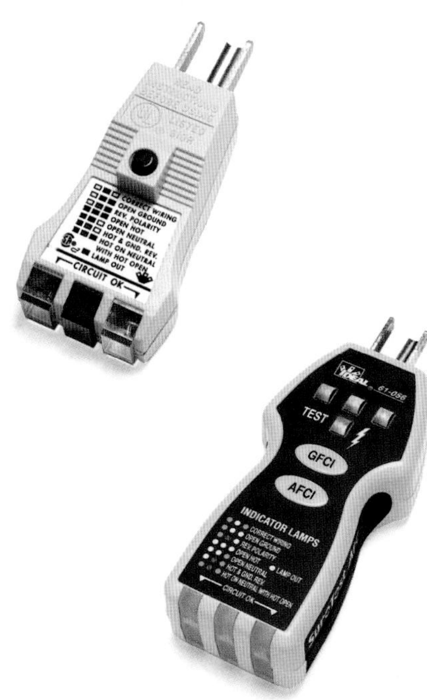

Circuit analyzers are used to make sure receptacles are energized, grounded and polarized. Some also test GFCI receptacles and breakers and AFCI breakers.

Electrical Smarts

To ensure your safety when working with electricity, always take these basic precautions:

- Turn off power to a circuit before working on it. Place a sign at the service panel to warn others. Affix a piece of tape over breaker handle or fuse.
- Wear safety glasses when working around electricity.
- Never stand on a wet or damp floor when working with electricity. If necessary, cover the floor with rubber mats or dry boards.
- After you've turned off a circuit breaker or pulled a fuse, use a voltage tester to check that the power actually is off.
- Before touching any wire, use a voltage tester to make sure it isn't live.
- When working on electrical wiring or appliances, avoid touching grounded metal pipes or fixtures.
- Never replace a fuse with one of higher amperage.
- Check your work with a voltage tester or outlet analyzer to make sure that it's properly wired and grounded.
- Use rubber- or plastic-handled tools.
- Never use aluminum or wet wood ladders near overhead wires.
- Wear heavy rubber gloves if you are working on or in a service box.
- Unplug appliances before working on them.
- To protect small children, install safety covers in unused receptacles.
- When unplugging a lamp or an appliance, pull the plug, not the cord.
- Extension cords are not a substitute for permanent wiring—put them away after each use. Don't run cords under rugs or where they may be stepped on or tripped over.

Nearly every cable or wire has some form of sheathing to protect it and keep it separated from other wires. Specialty tools allow you to strip sheathings quickly and with less chance of damaging the wire inside.

Plastic-Sheathed Cable

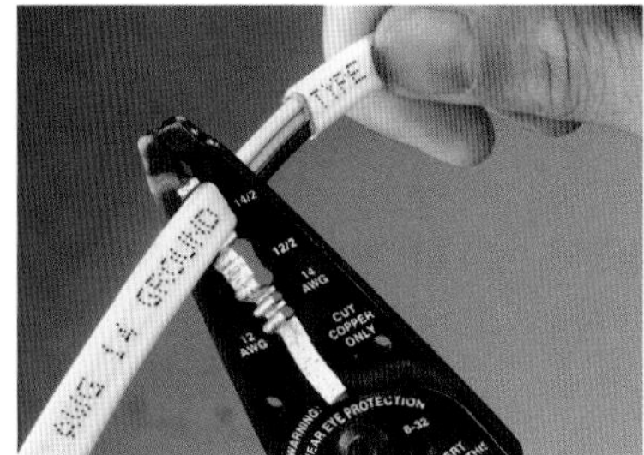

1 Align plastic-sheathed cable with the notch that matches the wire gauge.

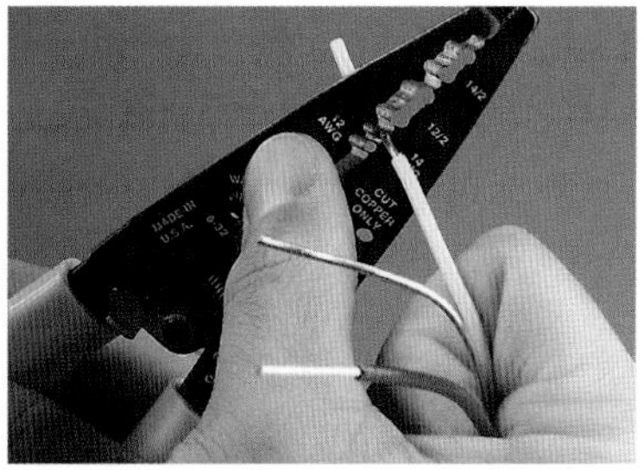

2 Strip individual wires using correct notch. Keep stripper perpendicular to wire.

Coaxial Cable

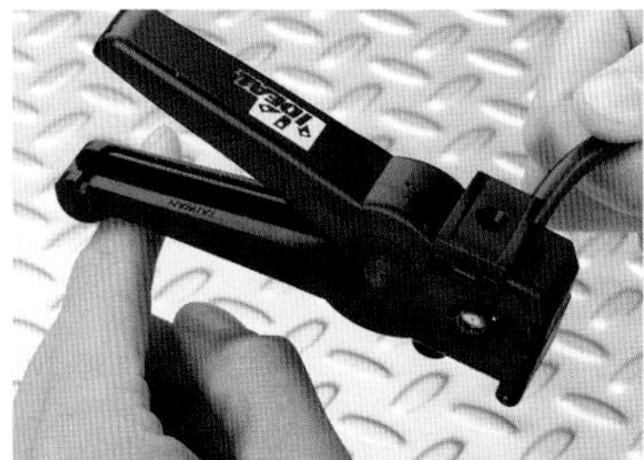

1 Set triple-bladed stripper to match cable size. Rotate cutter five or six times.

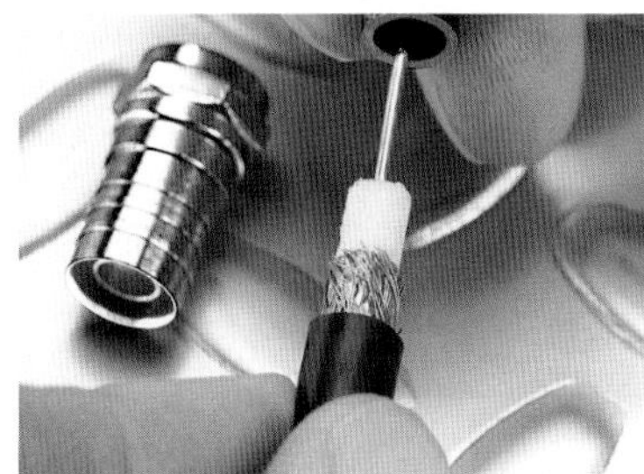

2 Remove inner and outer sheathing. Use fingernail to gently scrape foil from plastic insulation.

Communication Wire

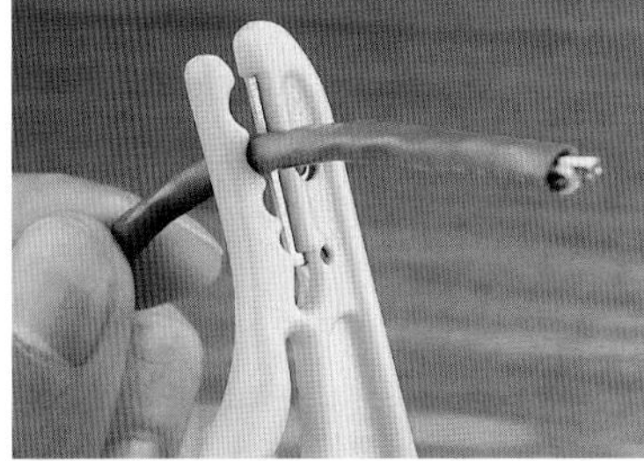

1 Place cable in largest groove and rotate. Move to next smaller notch, if necessary.

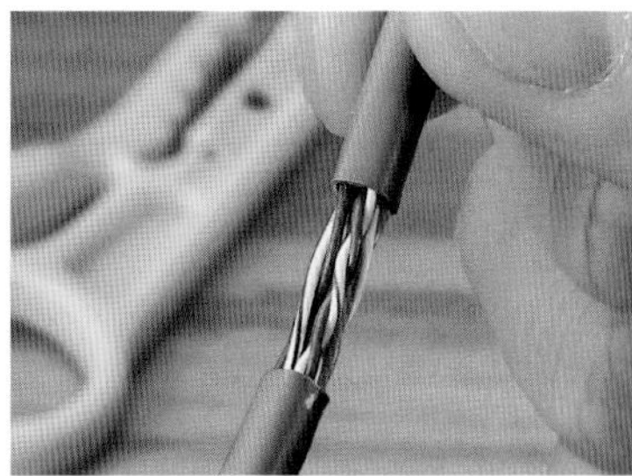

2 Bend cable to break, and remove sheathing. Inspect wires for damage.

Wires and Connectors

How to Read Cable

It's critical to understand the information imprinted along the length of wires or cables. Manufacturers abbreviate the descriptive code names for all of the different types of wires and cables. In this example:

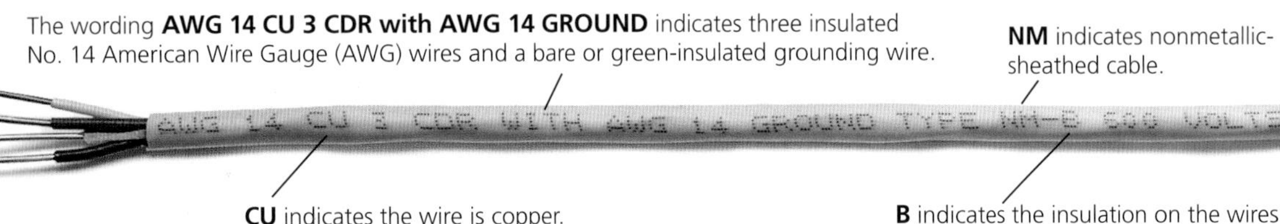

The wording **AWG 14 CU 3 CDR with AWG 14 GROUND** indicates three insulated No. 14 American Wire Gauge (AWG) wires and a bare or green-insulated grounding wire.

NM indicates nonmetallic-sheathed cable.

CU indicates the wire is copper. **AL** indicates aluminum.

B indicates the insulation on the wires in the cable is rated for 90°C.

Wire Gauges, Ampacity, and Use

3/0 Gauge — **200 Amps** Service entrance

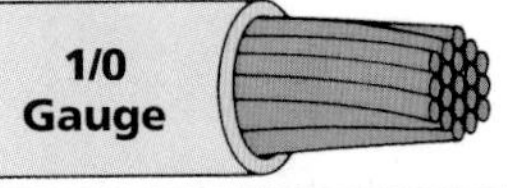
1/0 Gauge — **150 Amps** Service entrance and feeder wire

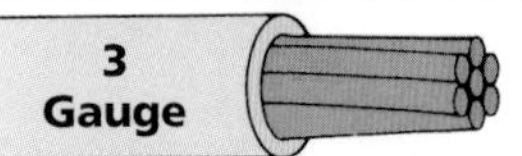
3 Gauge — **100 Amps** Service entrance and feeder wire

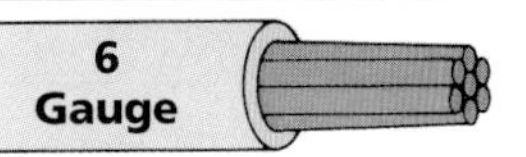
6 Gauge — **55 Amps** Feeder and large appliance wire

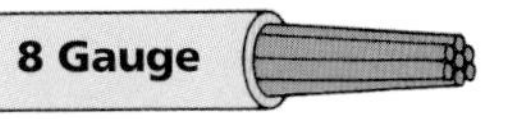
8 Gauge — **40 Amps** Feeder and large appliance wire

10 Gauge — **30 Amps** Dryers, appliances, and air conditioning

12 Gauge — **20 Amps** Appliance, laundry and bathroom circuits

14 Gauge — **15 Amps** General lighting and receptacle circuits

Note: The amperages listed above are based on equipment terminations rated at 75°C. For dwelling-service installations, smaller conductors may be permitted by code.

Types of Cable

2-wire with ground

3-wire with ground

Type NM-B (nonmetallic-sheathed) cable contains two or more insulated wires and a grounding wire with a nonmetallic outer sheath that is flame retardant and moisture resistant. NM-B cable is only permitted in dry locations and can be installed in both exposed and concealed work in one- and two-family dwellings.

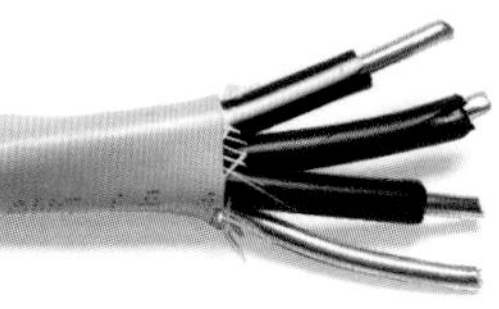

Type SE (service-entrance) cable is often used indoors for feeding subpanels or large appliances. Type USE (underground service entrance) cable is approved for direct burial to detached garages and other structures.

Type UF-B (underground feeder and branch-circuit) cable is approved for direct burial and is used to run power to garages, outdoor lights and well pumps.

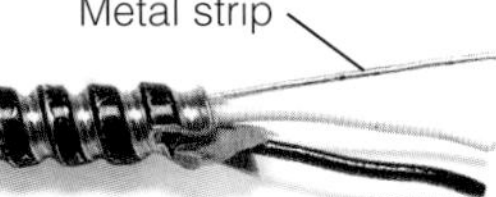

Type AC (armored cable) contains a metal strip to qualify the sheath for grounding purposes. Plastic inserts inside connectors prevent wire abrasion. Use in dry indoor locations only.

Wire Connectors

Always use the right connector for the job. Read the package instructions to determine the size, type (solid or stranded) and number of wires that can be used with each connector, how much insulation to strip from each wire and whether the wires first need to be twisted together.

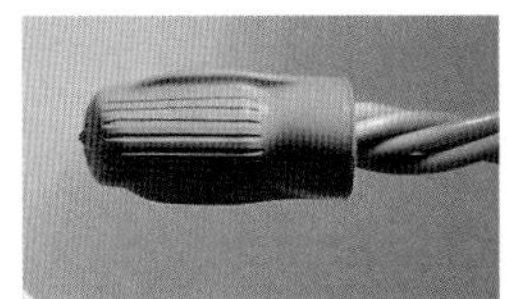

Screw-on connectors. Strip insulation, hold wires parallel to each other with ends lined up and twist connector in clockwise direction. No bare wire should show below connector skirt.

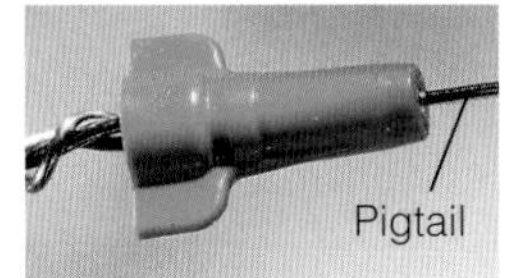

Grounding connectors. Special connectors for splicing only grounding wires allow one longer wire to protrude as a pigtail to connect to receptacles and switches.

Direct-bury connectors. Connectors approved for direct burial are filled with silicone sealant and often used for lampposts, lawn sprinklers or other high-moisture applications.

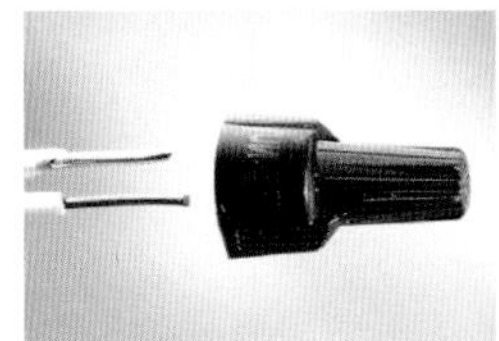

AL/CU connectors. For homes with aluminum wiring, special AL/CU connectors allow aluminum and copper wires to be spliced together. Copper pigtails then connect to standard receptacles and switches.

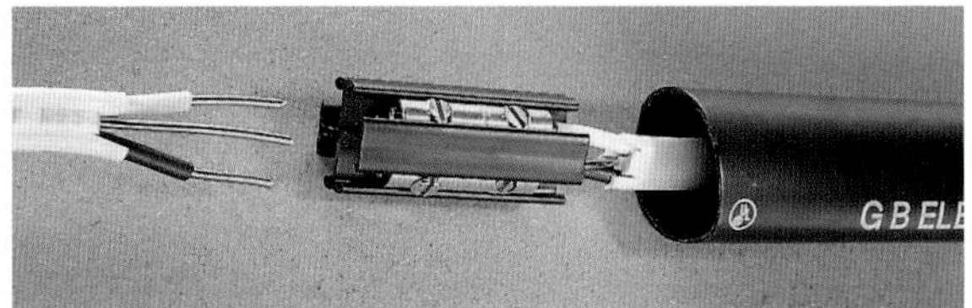

Direct-bury splice kit. Underground splice kits allow simple repair of damaged cables.

Electrical Boxes and Sizing

Wherever electrical wires are spliced together or connected to the terminals of switches, receptacles or fixtures, they must be enclosed in an electrical box. Made of steel, plastic or fiberglass and available in many sizes and styles, boxes isolate energized connections from flammable building materials and safeguard people, as well. Switches and receptacles are generally housed in rectangular or square boxes, lighting fixtures in octagonal or round boxes. Boxes must be securely supported by the building structure, and unused openings must be effectively closed. They must be installed so the wiring in them can be rendered accessible without removing any of the building finish. In completed installations, all boxes must have a blank cover, a fixture or a device and cover plate.

Go Figure Electrical Box Calculator

Boxes must be of sufficient size to provide free space for all enclosed wires. Nonmetallic boxes are marked with their cubic-inch (or cubic-centimeter) capacity. Official volumes for metal boxes are listed in the codes, but you can measure the inside of the metal boxes to approximate the volume.

Here are simplified code rules to help you decide what box size you need:
- Count each hot and neutral wire as one wire each.
- Count all ground wires combined as one wire.
- Count all cable clamps combined as one wire.
- Count all devices that mount in the box each as two wires.
- Multiply the total wire count by either 2.0 cu. in. (14-gauge wire) or 2.25 cu. in. (12-gauge wire) to determine the minimum box volume required.

Metal Remodeling Box

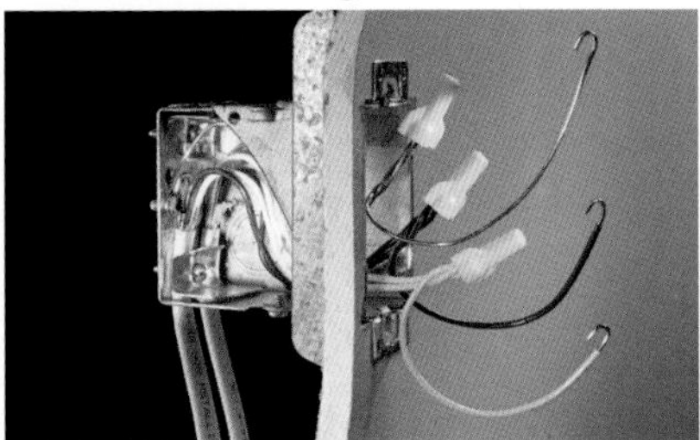

To determine the minimum metal box volume required in this situation, calculate as follows:
- All conductors entering box (hot and neutral): 4
- Ground wires (count 1 for all present): 1
- Cable clamps (count 1 for all present): 1
- Receptacle that fits into box: 2

Since the total is 8 wires and you should allow 2 cu. in. per wire, the minimum box size in this situation is 16 cu. in.

Standard Plastic Box

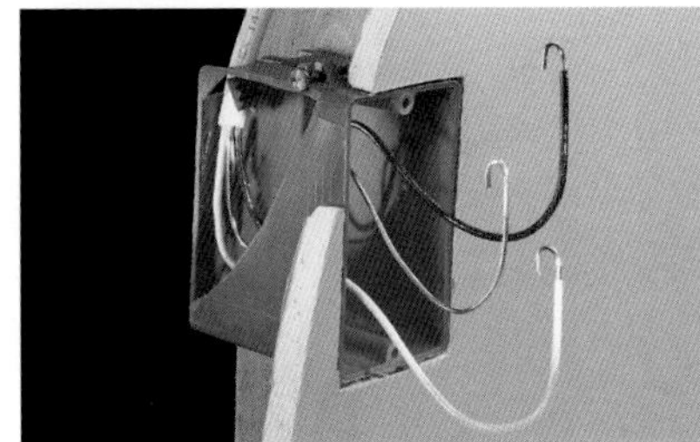

To determine the minimum plastic box volume required in this situation, calculate this way:
- All conductors entering box (hot and neutral): 2
- Ground wires: 1
- Cable clamps: 0
- Switch or receptacle: 2

Since the total is 5 wires and you should allow 2 cu. in. per wire, the minimum box size in this situation is 10 cu. in.

Basic Boxes

New-work nonmetallic boxes are used with type NM cable only and come in a variety of sizes. They require access to the wall cavity to be nailed in place.

New-work metal boxes can be used with all types of wiring. The mud ring gives the outward appearance of one outlet, while providing more volume for wires, connectors and other fittings in the larger box behind it.

Metal and nonmetallic ceiling boxes on bar hangers allow easy positioning between framing members. Check load rating for heavy fixtures.

Remodeling Boxes

Spring brackets on some old-work, or remodeling, boxes secure box to the drywall, plaster or other surface.

Wings and ears on some remodeling boxes are used to secure the box to the wall surface.

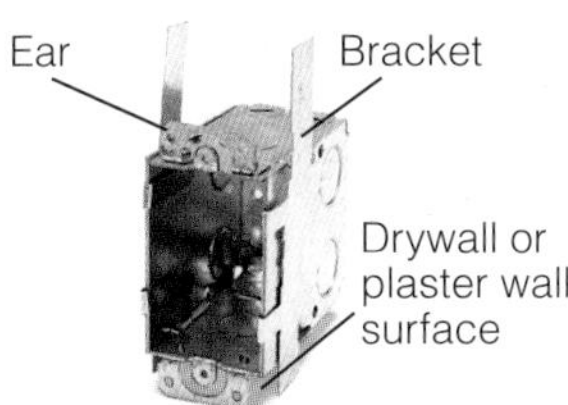

Adjustable ears and separate brackets on some remodeling boxes lock the box to the wall surface.
See p. 138 for installation.

Specialty Boxes

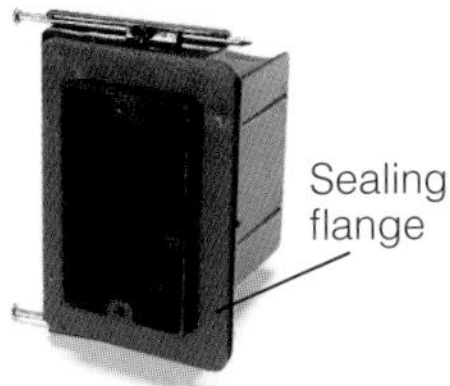

Sealing flanges for attaching vapor barriers meet strict energy code requirements in cold-climate regions.

Floor boxes are common in homes. Adjustable-height floor boxes allow receptacle placements where wall space is limited.

Adjustable boxes can be tweaked after installation to ensure they are flush with wall materials such as paneling and tile.

Switches

Electrical Testers 132
Wiring Variations 143
Outdoor Outlet 154

Since you must never interrupt or switch the neutral wire, a switch is connected in series only with the circuit's hot wire. (Receptacles are connected to both the hot and neutral wires of a circuit.) Connections made using wire-binding screws are more secure than those with push-in connections.

The most common type of wall switch, the single-pole switch, controls a receptacle outlet or fixture from one location. It has two brass-colored terminal screws and its toggle is marked On and Off. Used in pairs to control a fixture from two locations, a three-way switch has two brass-colored traveler terminals for the wires between the two switches and a dark common terminal, which connects the incoming hot wire or the switched wire up to the fixture. The toggle on a three-way switch has no On or Off markings.

Switches in the United States are now required to be grounded and have green grounding screws. Replacement switches must have the same voltage and amperage ratings. Note: Standard dimmer switches should not be used for ceiling-fan control.

Reading a Switch

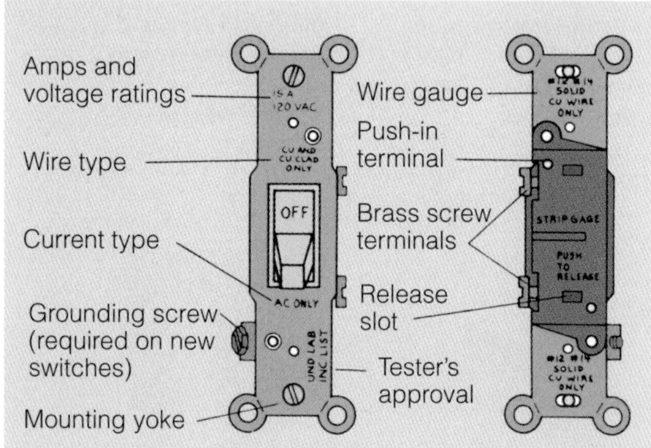

There's a lot of information on the front and back of a typical snap switch. Markings include voltage and amperage ratings, wire material (CU means copper), third-party certification and the size of wires that may be terminated. Electricians normally use screw terminals, not the less reliable push-in terminals.

Replacing a Single-pole Switch

Use a noncontact voltage sniffer to make sure power is off. Remove switch cover plate and switch. Disconnect wires from the old switch and reconnect to new switch. Install a pigtail from grounding screw on switch to grounding wires or metal box. Tighten screw terminals and fold wires and switch into box. Screw switch to box and reinstall cover plate. Restore power and test the switch.

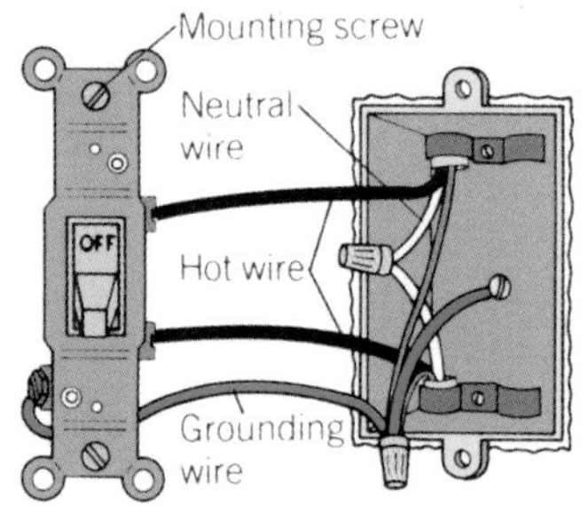

A middle-of-circuit switch has two black wires attached to the brass screws. One black wire is the incoming hot wire. The other black wire is the switch-leg to the light fixture.

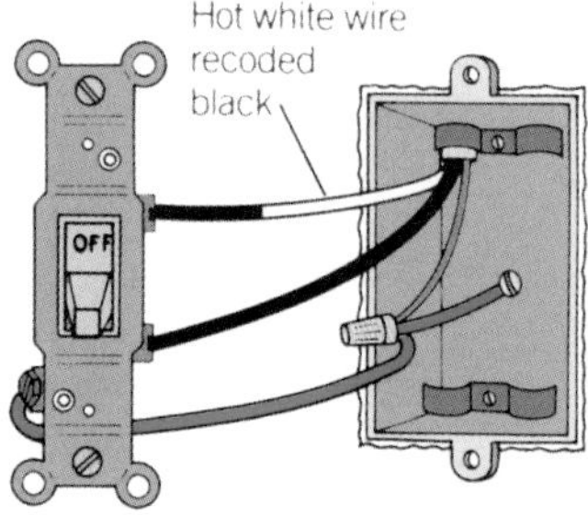

In a switch-loop circuit using two-wire NM cable, the incoming hot wire is white, reidentified with black tape. The other black wire is the switch-leg to the light fixture.

Installing a Dimmer Switch

Dimmer styles include rotary, slider, toggle and digital electronic types for controlling incandescent, low-voltage and fluorescent lighting (fixture modification may be required). Some dimmers replace single-pole switches for controlling lights from one location; other special dimmers replace three-way switches for multiple location control. To avoid electrical accidents and risk of fire, make sure dimmer-switch ratings match the load and type of light and that electrical boxes are big enough to accommodate the larger wires and wire connectors. Dimmers are required by code to be grounded.

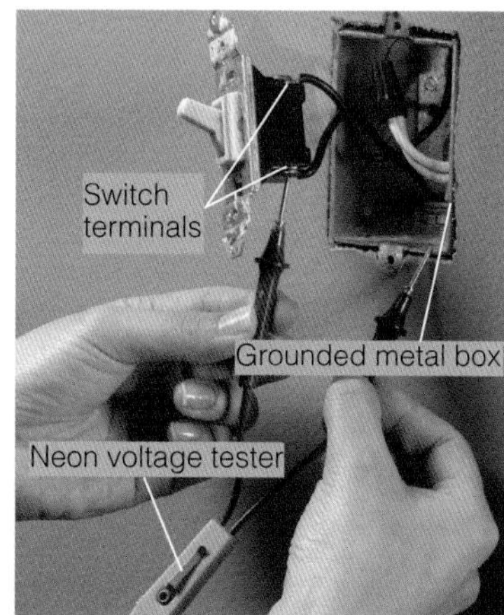

1 Pull switch out and turn power on. Check for voltage between box and each terminal. If tester lights, box is grounded. Turn off power to proceed.

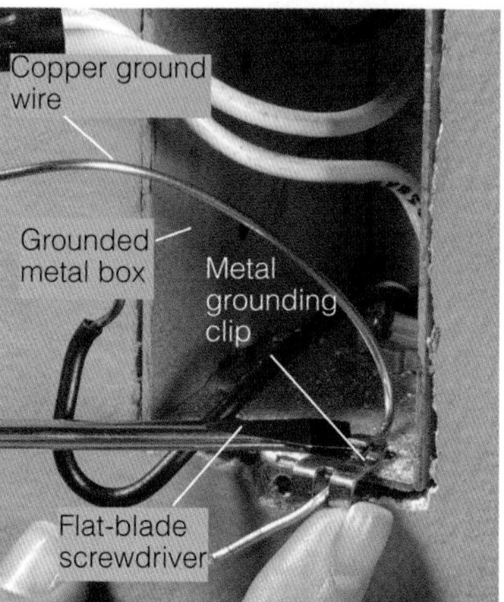

2 Press grounding clip and 6-in. (15-cm) length of bare copper wire onto box's edge using a screwdriver. Notch drywall to provide clearance for clip.

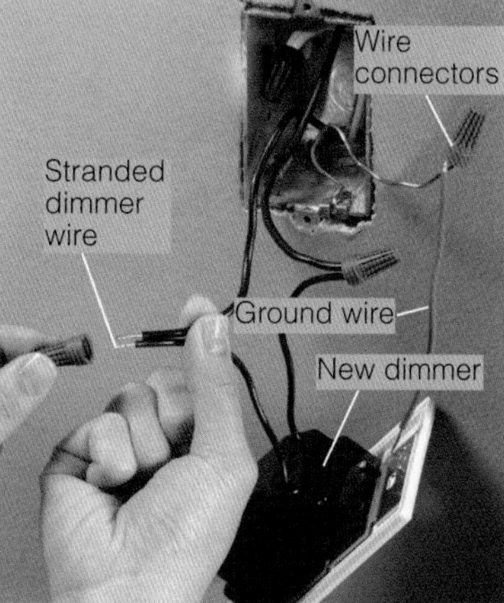

3 Select proper connector based on wire sizes. Hold stranded wire 1/8 in. (3 mm) beyond solid wire and twist wire connector clockwise until it is snug.

Connecting Wires

Making proper wire connections is one of the most important skills to learn to have a safe, trouble-free electrical installation. Loose connections result in open circuits and inoperative equipment, blown fuses or tripped breakers, arcing and sparking, overheating and fires. Connections need to be clean and secure without damaging the wires. The most common connections include pressure terminal connectors on circuit breakers, wire-binding screws on receptacles and switches and pressure cable-connectors, which are twist-on connectors for splicing wires. Always make connections with power off.

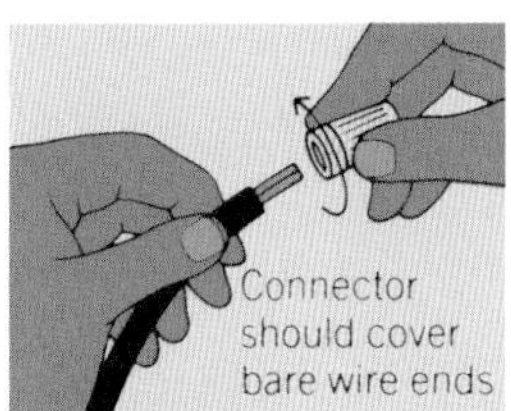

To splice wires, strip 3/4 in. (20 mm) of insulation from wire ends. Hold wires parallel with ends even or twist the wires together with side-cutting pliers. Twist connector clockwise until tight.

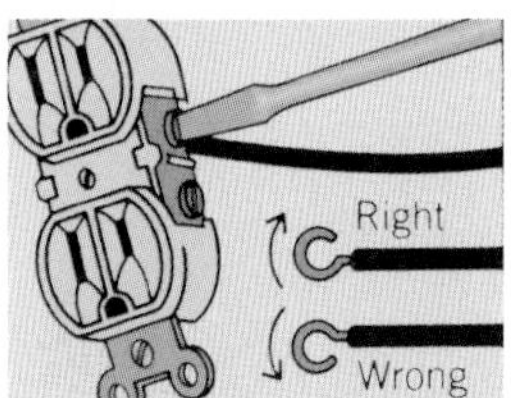

To attach wire to screw terminal, strip 3/4 in. (20 mm) of insulation off wire end. Use needle-nose pliers to bend wire into loop. Hook wire clockwise around screw and tighten.

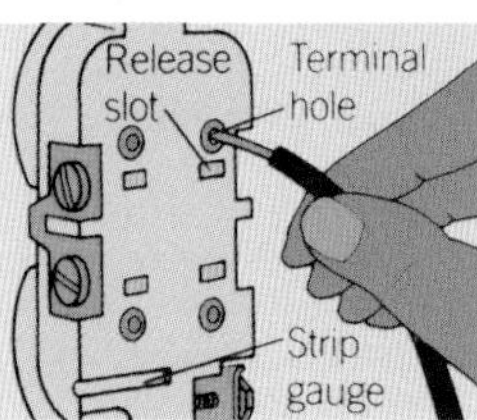

A strip gauge on devices with push-in terminals shows how much insulation to remove. Push-in terminals are restricted to 14-gauge solid copper wires. Some have screws to clamp the wire securely once the wire is inserted. Push a thin screwdriver into the slot to release wire.

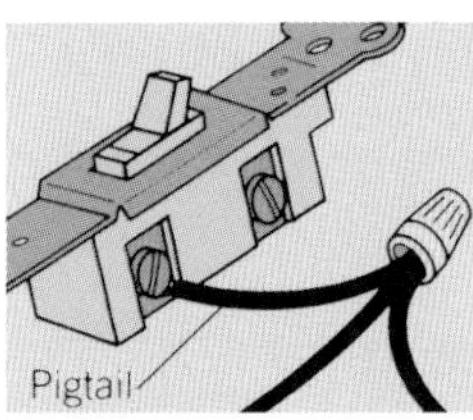

A pigtail is a short wire linking two or more circuit wires to one terminal. Never connect two wires directly to one screw terminal. Attach the end of the pigtail to the screw terminal.

Receptacles

A 120-volt, 15- or 20-amp duplex receptacle consists of two receptacle outlets, each accommodating a standard 120-volt plug. For new installations, three-slot grounding type receptacles are required. Three-slot receptacles should be used to replace old two-slot receptacles if the new receptacle can be properly grounded (see p. 130). Receptacles have screw terminals and/or push-in terminals. A duplex receptacle has silver-colored screws for connecting neutral wires, brass-colored screws for connecting hot wires and a green grounding screw for connecting grounding wire. Break-off tabs between the outlets allow you to split-wire a duplex receptacle to supply each outlet from a different circuit. Another option is to control the lower outlet by a wall switch, with the upper outlet hot all the time. Make sure the ampere and voltage ratings of new replacement receptacles match those of the old receptacles.

120/240-volt, 30-amp grounded receptacle for clothes dryer

Large appliances often require 240- or 120/240-volt receptacles rated 30 amps or more. A receptacle's ampere and voltage ratings determine its slot design, which must match the configuration of the appliance plug.

Replacing a Receptacle

Defective or worn receptacles won't hold a plug properly or may cause circuit failure whenever you plug in an appliance. To replace, turn off power to the circuit and check the receptacle using a tester. Connect wires to new receptacle, restore power and test receptacle.

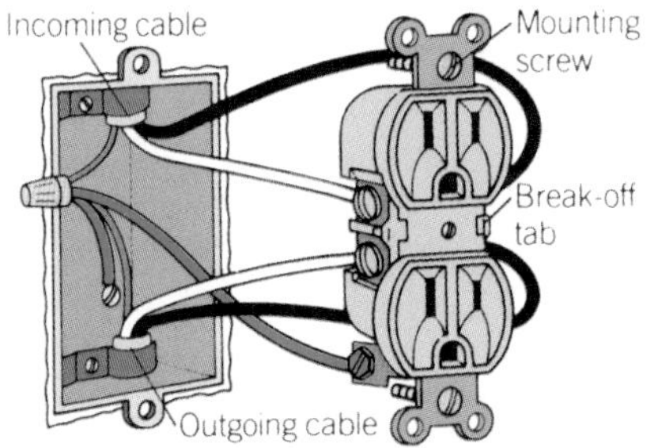

A middle-of-circuit receptacle is connected to incoming and outgoing cables. Pigtailing the hot and neutral wires similar to the ground wire is preferable.

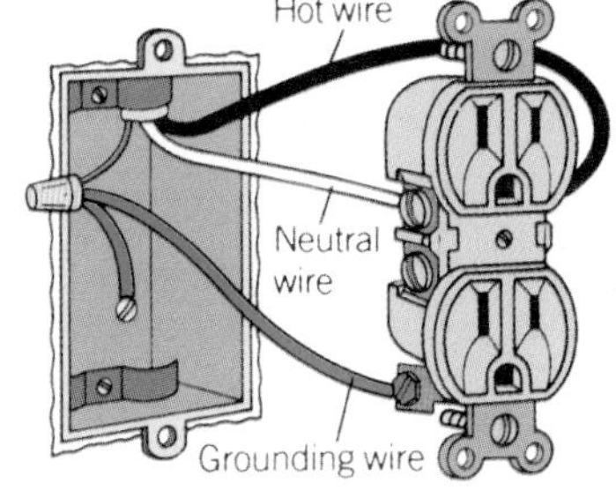

In an end-of-circuit receptacle the grounding wire connection is pigtailed because there is only one ground screw on the receptacle.

Installing a GFCI Receptacle

Ground-fault circuit-interrupters (GFCIs) have saved countless lives. They prevent lethal shocks by stopping current flow within 25 milliseconds if they sense ground-fault current of 5 milliamps. GFCI protection devices include circuit breakers, receptacles and portable devices. GFCI protection is required for receptacles installed outdoors and in bathrooms, garages, accessory buildings, crawl spaces, unfinished basements, kitchens and wet-bar areas (Canadian requirements differ). It's also required for hydromassage bathtubs, spas and swimming pool areas. Read all instructions carefully and test GFCIs monthly (photo, far right).

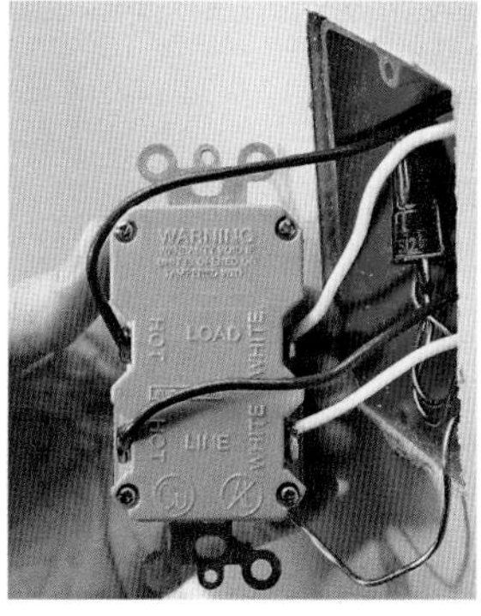

Adding or Extending a Branch Circuit

To install new switches, fixtures and receptacles, first determine the types you want and where you want them. Either run a new circuit from the service panel or extend an underutilized existing circuit. Before adding a new circuit, calculate your power usage to make sure the new circuit won't overload the service panel. Check to see whether the panel has space for a new breaker or fuse.

Extend an existing circuit only if it's grounded and not already operating at or near capacity. If an extension is possible, pick an accessible box to serve as its power source. The simplest source is a junction box in which wires from the new and existing cables are spliced together. The power source must always be hot, so don't use an end-of-circuit switch, a fixture or a switch-controlled receptacle. Junction and device boxes must be replaced with larger ones if the additional wires will exceed the box's volume limitations.

To estimate cable lengths, plan the shortest route from power source to the new outlet(s). Add a foot for each box plus 25 percent for errors. Wire sizes for new wiring must match that of the existing wiring. Check local codes for specific requirements and have your work inspected.

Caution: Cut power to an electrical box before working on it. Use a voltage tester to make sure all wires are dead.

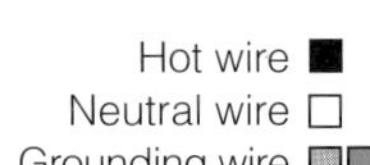

Tapping into an Existing Circuit

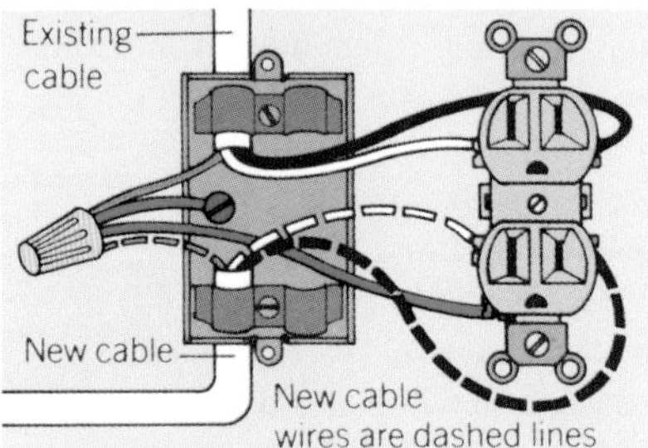

An end-of-circuit receptacle is a good place to start a circuit extension, as long as the receptacle isn't switch-controlled. Connect the new cable's black wire to the receptacle's unused brass screw, its white wire to the unused silver screw. Splice grounding wires in the box.

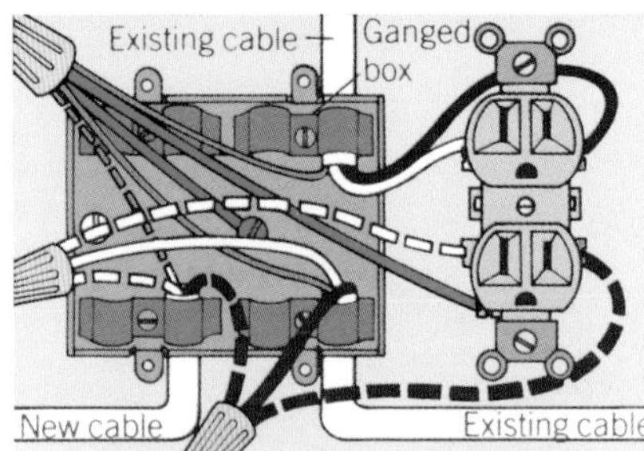

A middle-of-circuit receptacle has wires from two cables connected to it. Adding a third cable may require a bigger box. Use pigtails to attach new and existing black wires to the brass screw, white wires to the silver screw. Splice all grounding wires.

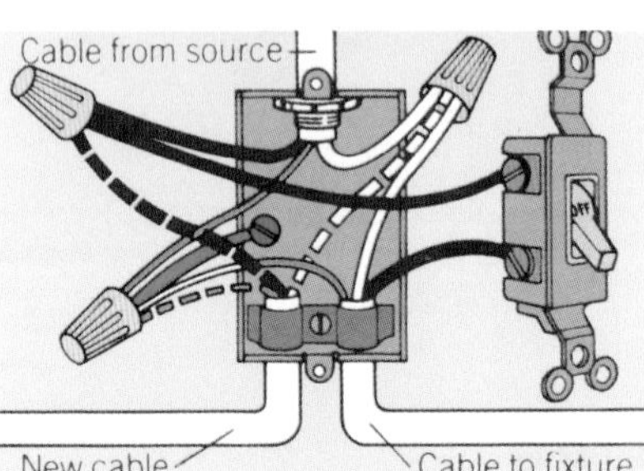

To tie into a switch, carefully identify the incoming hot wire with a voltage tester. Cut power and disconnect the hot wire. Pigtail new and incoming black wires to the switch terminal. Splice new white and grounding wires to existing white and grounding wires.

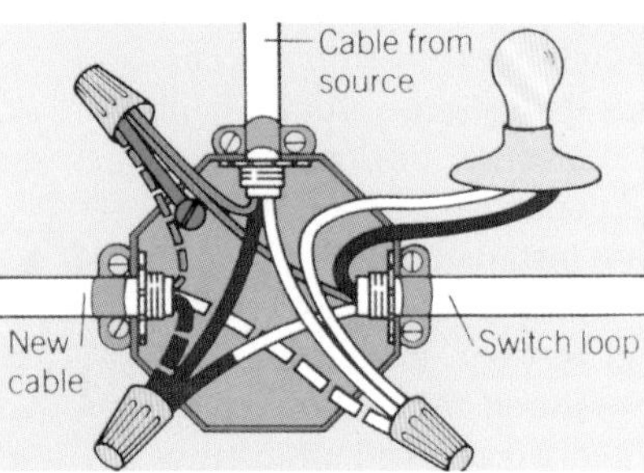

To tap a middle-of-circuit fixture, use tester to find incoming hot wire. Shut off power and splice black wires from new and incoming cables to the switch loop's hot white wire (marked black). Splice white wires from new and incoming cables and fixture.

Mounting Boxes

The type of electrical box and mounting hardware you'll need depends on whether they'll be set in drywall, wood or plaster. You also need to determine the size of the boxes you'll need based on the number of wires and devices in each box (see p. 135). Before routing the cable, cut holes for all the boxes. Securely clamp cable to boxes with separate clamps or the clamps that may be incorporated into the box design. Mount wall boxes at the same height from the floor as existing boxes (usually 4 ft. / 122 cm for switches, 12 to 18 in. / 30 to 45 cm for receptacles).

When you've decided where you want a box, locate studs or joists that might obstruct it. To check for pipes and other obstacles, drill a test hole into the wall. Bend a short length of stiff wire to a 90-degree angle, insert it into the hole and turn it full circle. If you hit anything, repeat the test nearby until you find a clear area.

Mounting Boxes in Existing Wall Surfaces

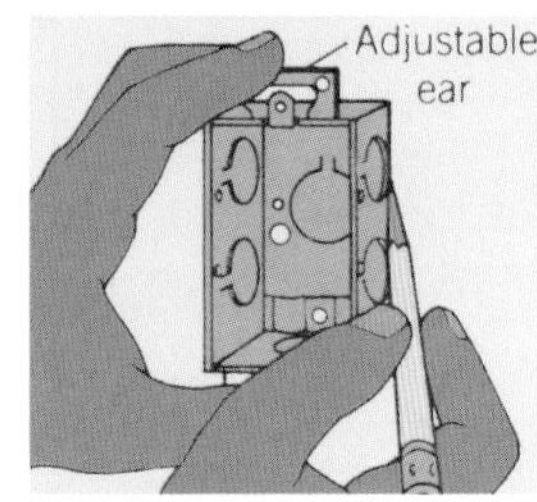

1 Select the proper size and type of remodeling box and make sure the desired location is free of obstructions. Trace a box outline on the wall, omitting adjustable ears. Score the drywall along the outline with a utility knife. Cut inside the score line with a drywall saw.

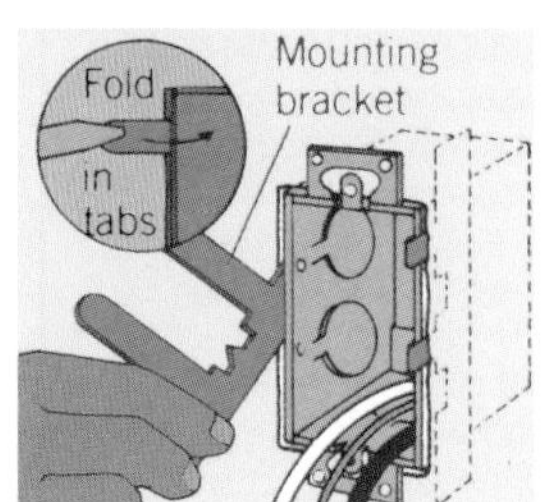

2 Fasten the cable to the box with a cable clamp. Adjust ears so the box front is flush with the wall. Hold the box in the wall and slip brackets between the box sides and wall. With a long-nose pliers, pull each bracket tab forward, folding tightly against the box side to pinch it in place.

Installing a Floor Outlet

Mounting Boxes from an Attic

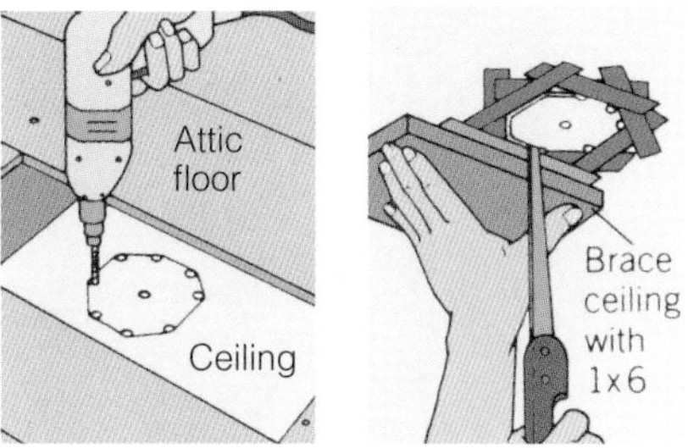

In the attic, remove flooring, center the box on pilot hole, trace its outline and drill a series of holes. From below, cut opening using a keyhole saw. For a plaster ceiling, tape the outline before cutting.

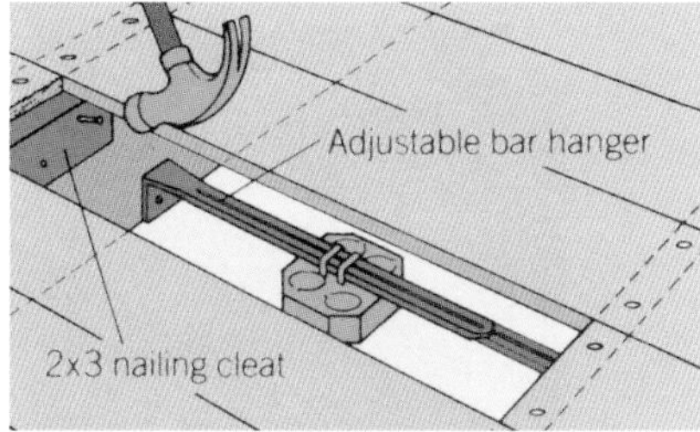

Fit adjustable bar hanger and box between joists so box is directly over hole, its front edge flush with the ceiling. Screw hanger to joists. Nail cleats to joists.

Mounting Boxes from Below

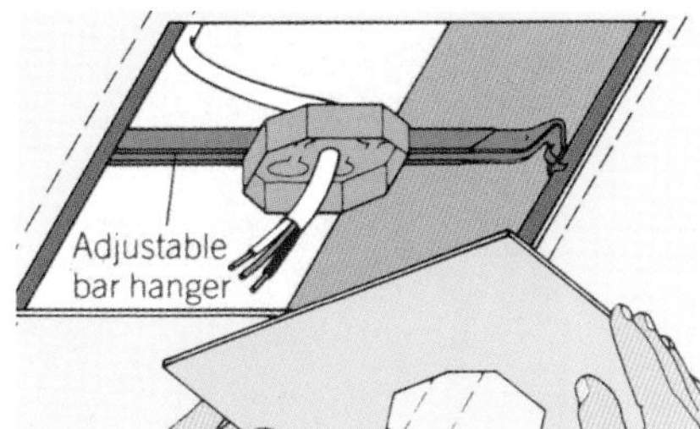

Locate framing members and check for obstructions. Mount box so it's centered on opening. Run cable to box. Screw patch to joists with drywall screws and seal edges with joint compound and tape.

Not all lamps or appliances are destined to be wallflowers, especially when you're furnishing a large space. The solution is a strategically placed floor outlet. Plan the project with wire routing problems in mind. Working over an unfinished basement offers the simplest solution; finished ceilings present greater challenges.

Most local codes require floor outlets to be part of an approved assembly consisting of a special box, gasket seal, special receptacle and strong cover plate with a moisture-proof cover. Locate the floor box where you can tie into a nearby circuit.

1 Position outlet so it falls between joists. Drill through wood floor with long bit or through carpeted floor with straightened clothes hanger wire with angled tip to avoid carpet snags. Locate wire below.

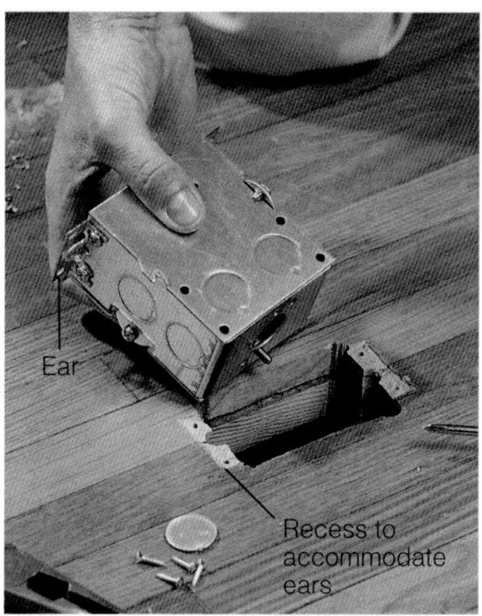

2 Outline box on floor. Cut out hole using a jigsaw or keyhole saw. For carpeted floor, cut away carpet and pad, drill through corners and cut out hole from underneath.

3 Attach cable clamp to cable, then snap clamp into box. Secure cable to joist within 12 in. (30 cm) of box with a cable staple.

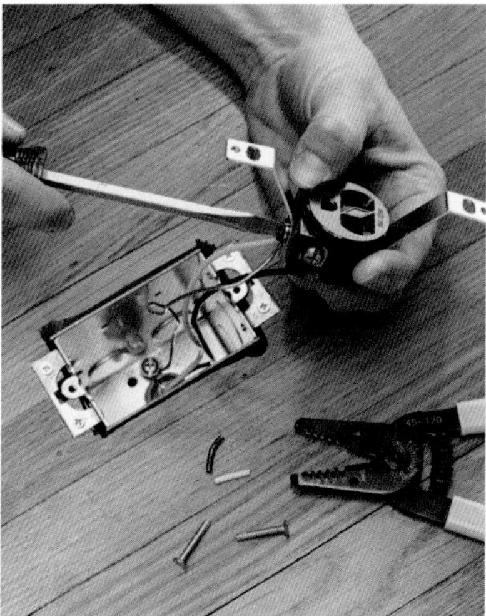

4 Fasten box to floor and attach wires to receptacle. Connect ground wire to ground screw in box, then to receptacle. Position receptacle in box and secure it.

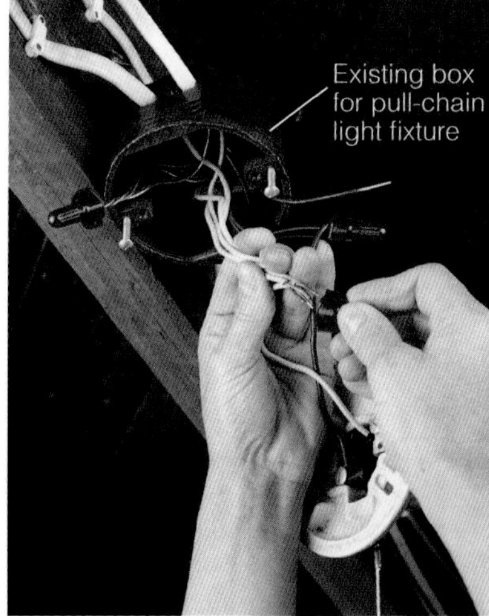

5 With power off, tie new outlet to existing circuit in box with constant (not switch-operated) hot feed. Find incoming hot wire and connect new wires with wire connectors.

Running Cable

Drills 50
Wiring Variations 143

In New Construction

For installing new cable, you'll need a 3/4-in. (20-mm) spade or auger bit, a drill (right-angle drill, if possible), wire stripper and basic hand tools. Select the proper types and sizes of boxes, then lay out and fasten them to framing members at the code-required and desired locations. Fasten boxes so their faces will be flush with the finished wall surface. Lay out, line up and drill holes—holes should be drilled in the center of framing members. Cables must always be at least 1-1/4 in. (32 mm) from both faces of studs to prevent damage from nails and screws. If not, install metal protector plates. Before pulling the wire through the holes, unroll and straighten a long length of it, so it slides through the holes without tangling. Staple cable within 8 in. (20 cm) of boxes and every 4 ft. (1.2 m), when running along joists or studs.

1 Bore 3/4-in. holes through center of framing members about 12 in. (30 cm) above outlet boxes.

2 Pull cable through holes between boxes, leaving 12 in. (30 cm) of excess cable at each box.

3 Fish cable around corners by bending a sharp hook in it. Use your finger as a guide.

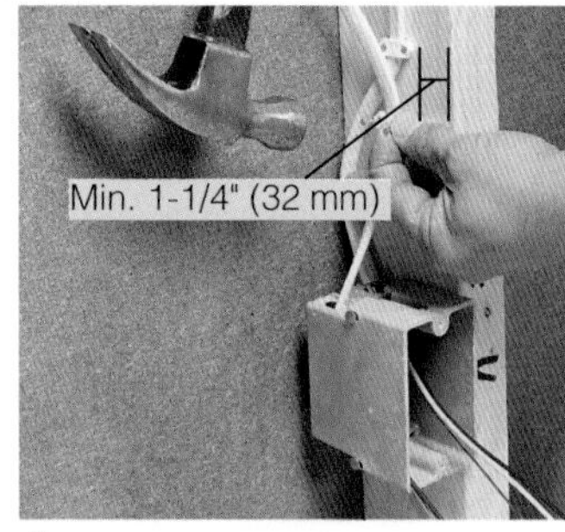

4 Secure cable with a staple 1-1/4 in. (32 mm) from front edge of stud and within 8 in. (20 cm) of box.

In Thin Walls

Protect cable in 1-1/2-in. walls by running it through 1/2-in. thin-wall metal conduit. Fasten 4 x 4 x 1-1/2-in. metal boxes (drill extra hole in wall for ground screw) and attach a length of conduit with a conduit connector. You'll need one conduit for each cable entering the box. Install a conduit connector at the top of the conduit to protect the cable from sharp edges where it exits the conduit. Secure the conduit with a strap within 3 ft. (90 cm) of the box and at a maximum of 10 ft. (3 m) thereafter. Attach the ground wire to the threaded hole in the back of the box with a green ground screw. Install a plaster ring.

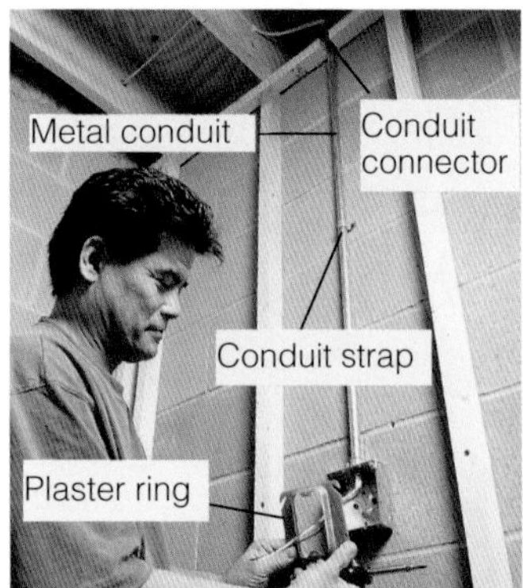

In Unfinished Garages

Special rules apply and extra care is required when installing Type NM cable in unfinished garages, sheds, workshops or other structures with unfinished walls and ceilings. In finished areas, wiring is protected by drywall or wood. The key to safe wiring in unfinished areas is to properly route the cable and use the framing members for protection. Remember these guidelines:

- Don't span stud or joist spaces where cables could be damaged. Run cables so they closely follow framing members. This often means taking a longer route between boxes, but cable is relatively cheap and easy to install.
- Unwind and straighten cable before installing it to avoid potentially damaging twists. Don't bend the cable too sharply around corners—gentle bends look better and won't damage the cable.
- Secure cable within 8 in. (20 cm) of boxes and every 4 ft. (1.2 m). Use lots of staples at bends and where necessary to prevent cables from sagging.
- Use metal boxes and thin-wall metal conduit where cable is installed on masonry walls or already finished walls.

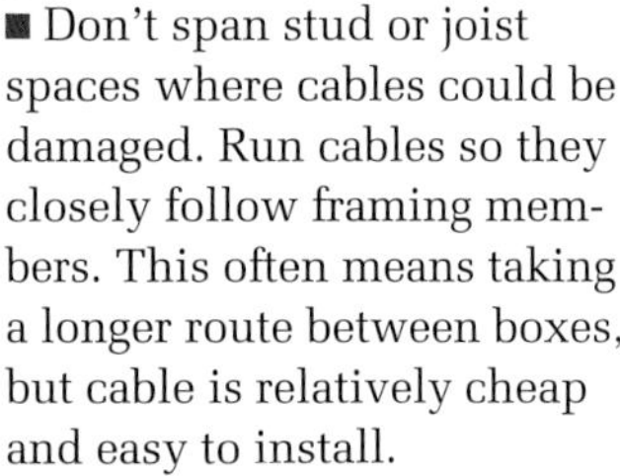

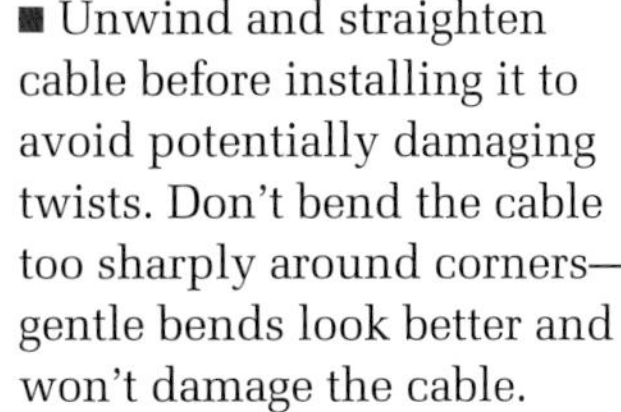

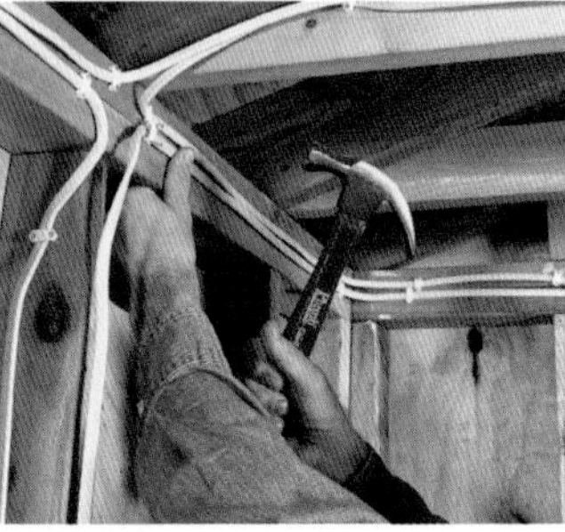

Follow framing members closely, bend cable gently around corners and secure cable often with plastic staples.

Run cables perpendicular to ceiling joists by securing them to the sides of wood braces.

Run cable on face of gable-end framing where it remains visible and not subject to damage.

Fishing Cable

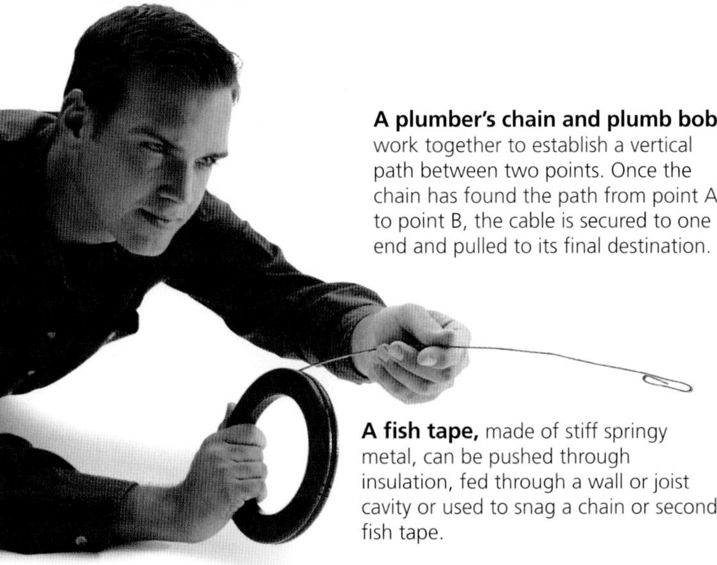

A plumber's chain and plumb bob work together to establish a vertical path between two points. Once the chain has found the path from point A to point B, the cable is secured to one end and pulled to its final destination.

A fish tape, made of stiff springy metal, can be pushed through insulation, fed through a wall or joist cavity or used to snag a chain or second fish tape.

Fishing cable is a task that frequently arises during the course of remodeling or adding on. In some cases you only need to run new wire a few feet, but in other cases you may need to run a new cable from the circuit box in the basement to the new light you're installing in the attic. Regardless of the distance, remember these key points:

- Plan the easiest route, not the most direct route. A winding route that requires an extra 50 ft. of cable is better than a direct route that means more cutting and patching.
- Whenever possible, run cable through unfinished spaces. Crawl spaces, unfinished basements and attics let you run cable with the least hassle.
- Avoid running cable through exterior walls where insulation makes the task more difficult.
- Avoid cutting textured ceilings or walls. Patching and matching those surfaces can be difficult. Instead, cut into areas inside closets, near the floor or in spots hidden by furniture.

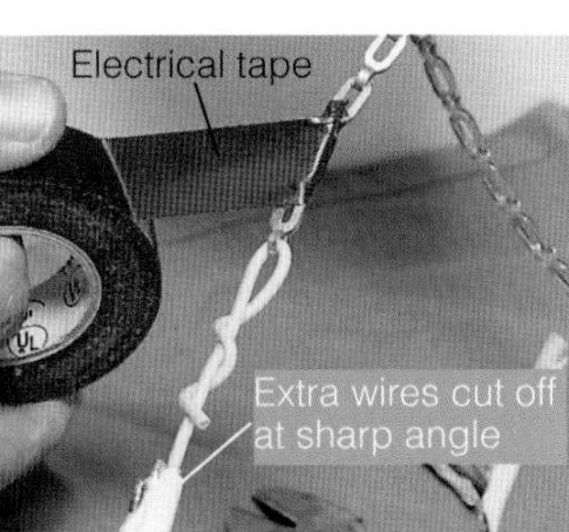

Loop one wire from the cable through chain (cut off extra wires). Tightly wrap entire connection with electrical tape, beginning on the chain and ending on the cable.

Home Run

Fishing cable is the art of running cable from one place to another with minimal cutting into walls and ceilings. The more you cut, the more patching, painting and carpentry you need to do later. The key? Plan the easiest route, not the most direct route. One good option is along the vent stack, as shown above.

Through Offset Walls

To create a path between offset walls, begin by cutting two small access holes and drilling holes at a steep angle through the 2x4 plates. At the lower wall, you'll also have to cut a notch into the plate so the cable can pass down into the wall cavity. Feed a plumber's chain into the joist cavity from above and hook the chain from below using a coat hanger or fish tape. After pulling the cable, install steel protector plates (see below).

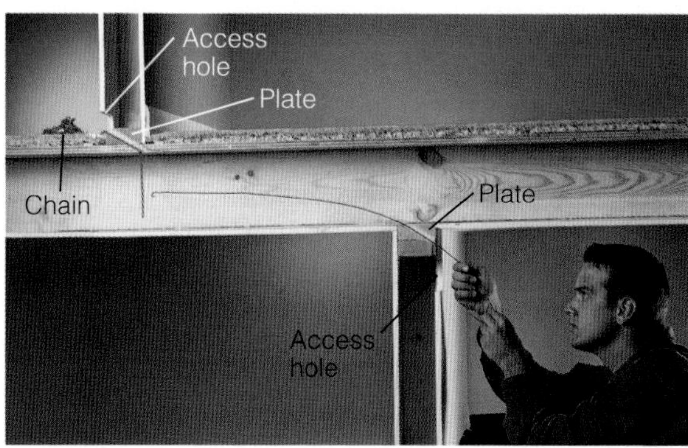

Behind Baseboard

Remove the baseboard and cut access holes at each stud, making sure you don't cut any higher than the height of the baseboard. Using a chisel, cut a notch into the base of each stud just deep enough for a plastic staple. Feed the cable through the notches, staple the cable at each stud and cover the notch with a metal protector plate.

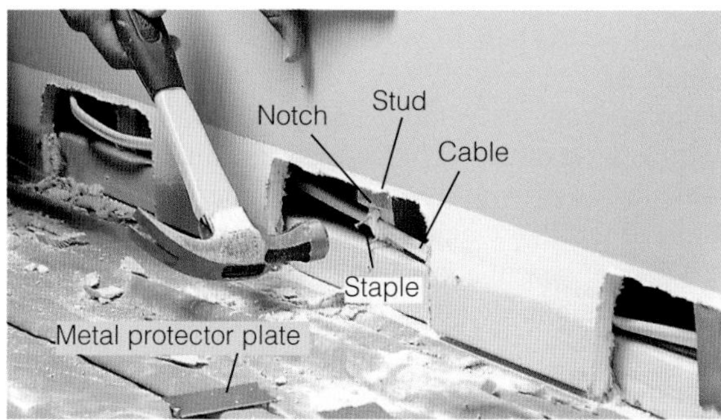

Surface Wiring

Electrical Boxes 135
Connecting Wires 137
Home-Automation Systems 159

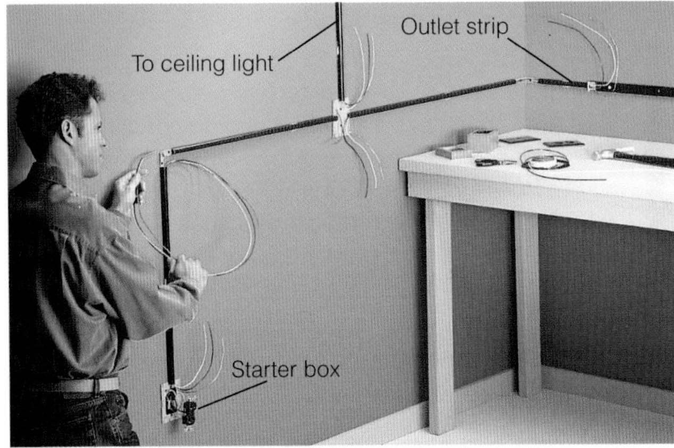

If you can't run cable behind walls and ceilings, an easy alternative is to install surface wiring in which wires travel through metal or plastic channels or raceways attached to walls and ceilings. With a one-piece metal raceway, you still have to fish wires through the raceway. Two-piece metal or plastic raceways have snap-on covers that eliminate the need for fishing wires. Check local codes before starting this project.

Surface wiring systems come with specific manufacturer's instructions that must be followed carefully. Components aren't interchangeable among brands. These are the general steps:

- Select an existing receptacle with excess capacity to power the circuit extension.
- Plan and mark the raceway path and box locations.
- Determine the amount of raceway needed and the number and type of boxes and fittings needed.
- Turn off the power. Remove existing receptacle from its box. Screw the base of outlet extension box to the existing wall box.
- Cut raceways to length using a hacksaw and install bases of all new boxes. Attach one-piece channels with clips or fasten bases of two-piece channels.
- Install wiring in raceway.
- Wire and mount all new devices and fixtures.
- Rewire and mount existing receptacle in outlet extension box.
- Install channel, elbow and connection covers as necessary.

Outlet Starter Box

Select an existing receptacle with excess capacity to power the surface wiring circuit extension. Turn off power to that circuit. Remove existing outlet and install the starter box mounting bracket. Install raceway, bushings, wire and surface-mount starter box. Make final wiring connections, then install outlet and cover plate.

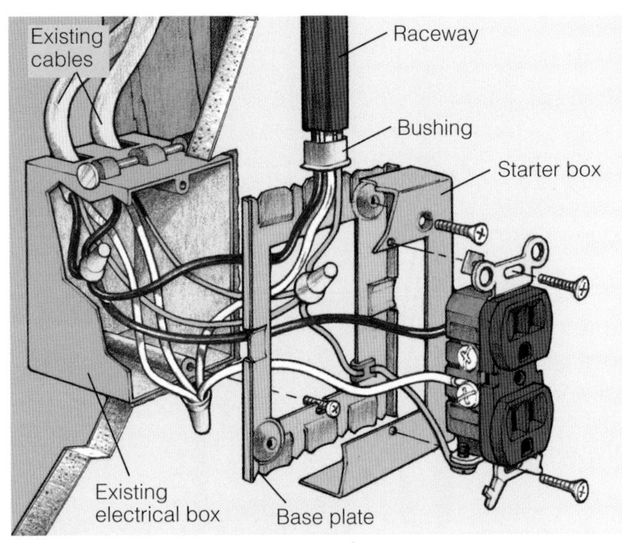

Light Fixture Detail

Install base plate, then run raceway and wiring from switch to fixture. Install fixture box. Make final wiring connections, including connection to grounding screw, then install fixture.

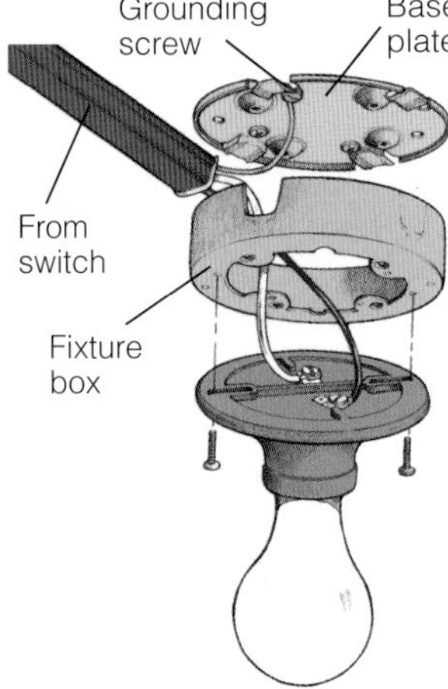

Remote Switching

There are a variety of ways to control or operate lights without adding in-wall or surface wiring. Here are two options:

Wireless electronic devices control lights and appliances for convenience, security, safety or energy savings. Plug a lamp or appliance into a receiver module and then into a receptacle outlet. The battery-operated wall switch module can then be mounted at a convenient location.

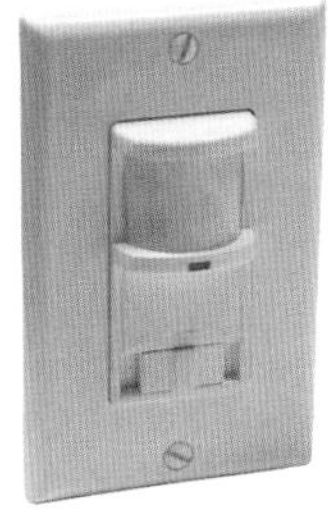

Motion-activated wall switches that use motion-activated passive infrared (PIR) technology provide cost-effective lighting control and help conserve energy. PIR units turn on lights automatically when people enter or leave a space and turn off after a preset time delay.

Wiring Variations

Scores of wiring variations exist for any combination of switches, fixtures and receptacles. These basic diagrams can help you get started. The nonmetallic boxes and fixtures shown are not grounded. Metal boxes and metal fixtures must always be grounded.

White wires in cables are normally used only as the neutral wires. However, in a two-wire switch-loop circuit, the white wire is used as the hot wire to supply power to the switch, so it must be reidentified with tape or similar marking. For example, the black wire in the switch-loop circuit, shown below, is the switched hot wire that completes the circuit to the fixture. This prevents having both a white neutral wire and a white hot wire at the fixture. This rule also applies to three-way and four-way switch circuits.

Caution: Always turn off power and use a voltage tester to make sure the circuit you're working on is off.

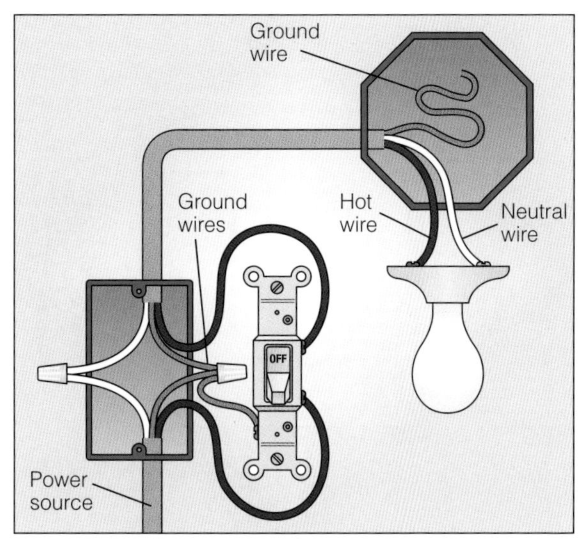

Switch controlling a ceiling fixture. Power from the source feeds the switch box first. The hot wire connects to the switch. The switched hot wire completes the circuit to the fixture.

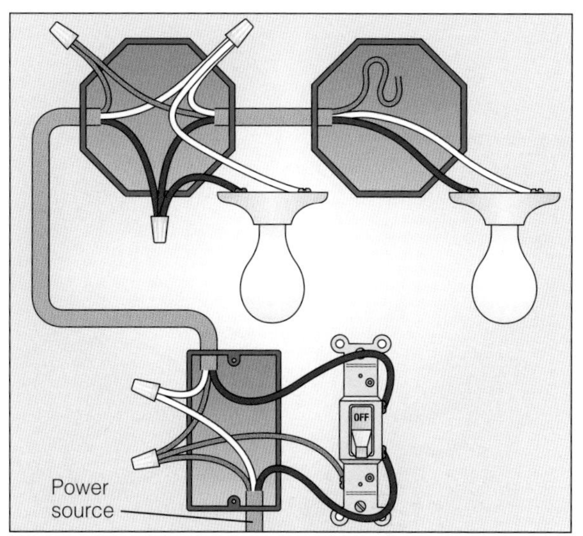

Switch controlling two or more fixtures. Power from the source feeds the switch box first. The switched hot wire, neutral and ground wires continue to two or more fixtures.

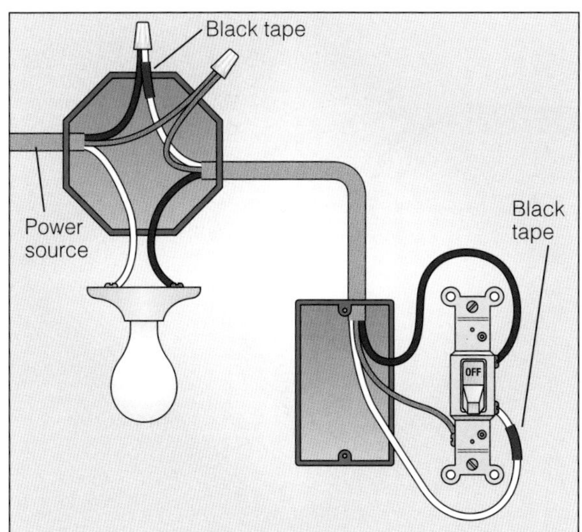

Switch loop. Power from the source enters fixture box first. White hot wire, reidentified with black tape, supplies power to switch. Black switched wire completes the circuit to the fixture.

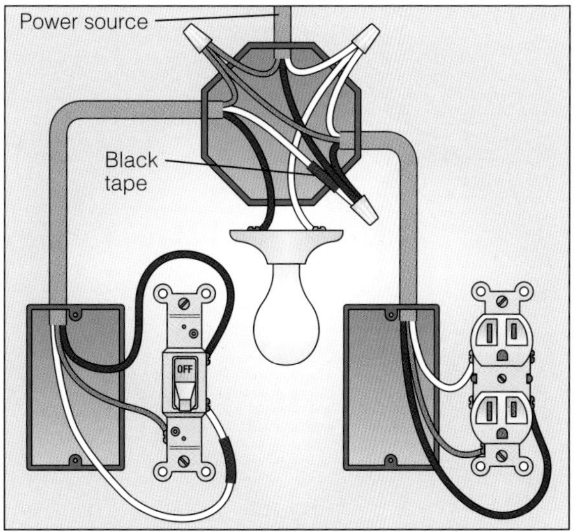

Switch loop with receptacle added after fixture. In this configuration, the switch loop controls the fixture only. The unswitched receptacle is hot all the time.

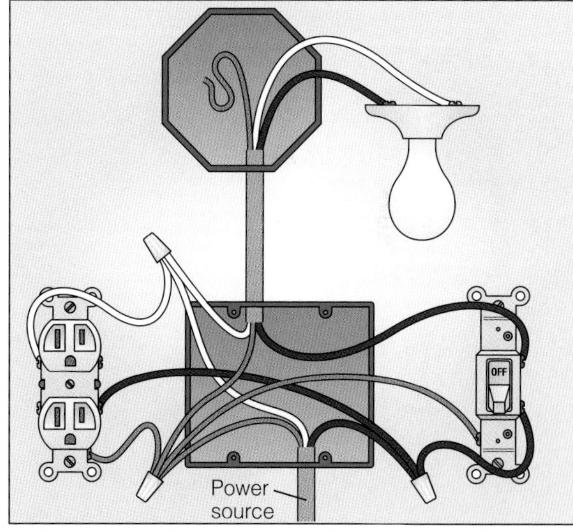

Switch loop with receptacle in the same box. The switch loop controls the fixture only. The unswitched receptacle is hot all the time.

Wiring Variations

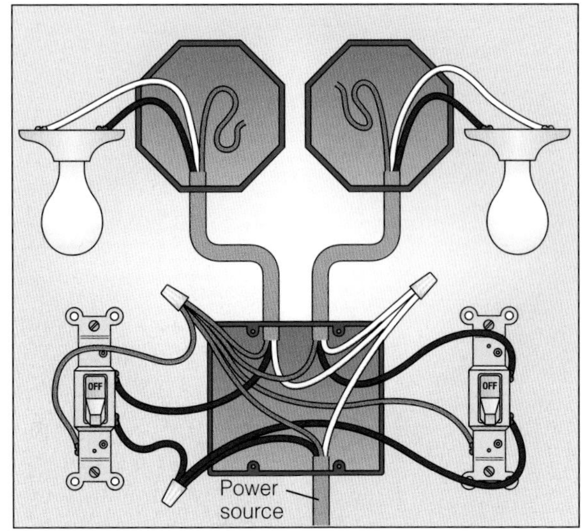

Two fixtures with two switches, power entering switch. The circuit that supplies power to the switch box is used for two switches and two separate switched circuits.

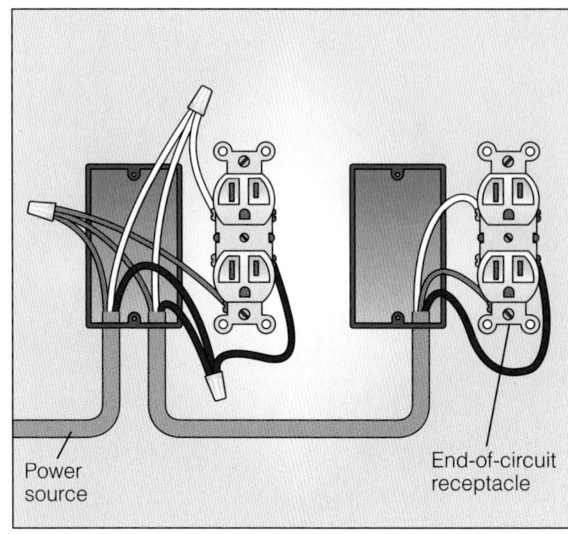

Receptacles wired in tandem. Power passes through one (or more) middle-of-circuit receptacles to end-of-circuit receptacle.

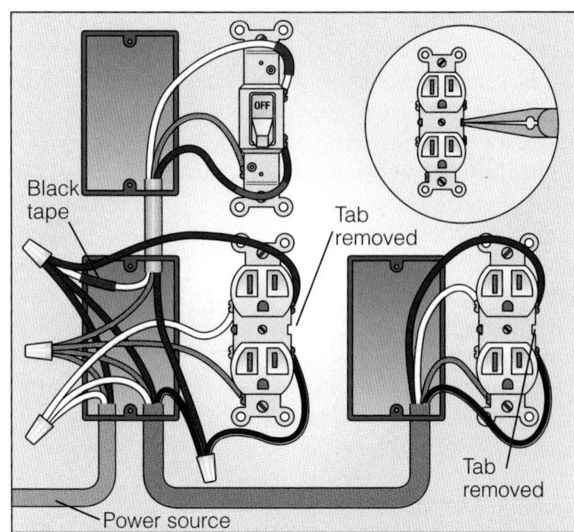

Split receptacles. The top half of split receptacles are always hot. The bottom half are switch-controlled. To split a receptacle, break off the tab between the hot brass terminals.

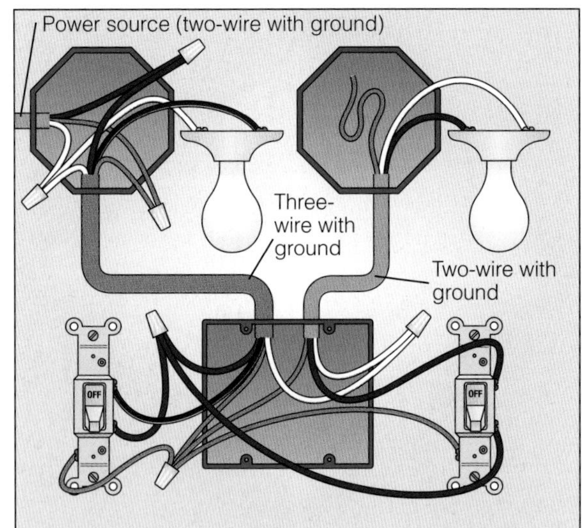

Two fixtures with two switches, power entering one fixture. The black wire supplies power to both switches. The red wire is a switched hot wire back to fixture.

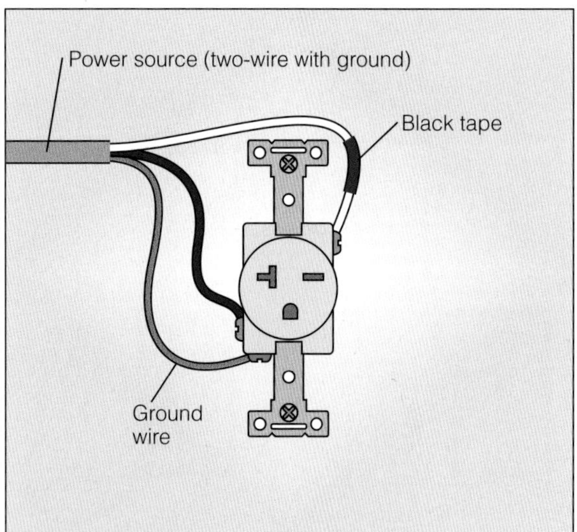

Wiring a 20-amp, 240-volt receptacle. Two-wire with ground cable for 240-volt receptacle for window air conditioner. No neutral wire required. Hot white wire in cable is reidentified with tape at all terminations.

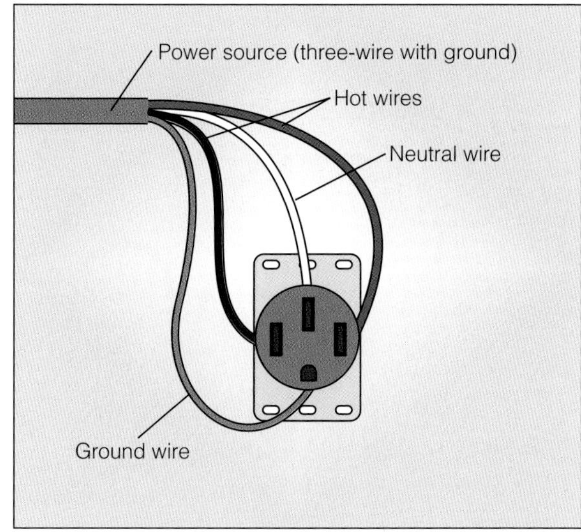

Three-wire with ground cable for power supply to a 50-amp, 125/250-volt receptacle for electric range. Two hot wires, a neutral wire and a grounding wire are required.

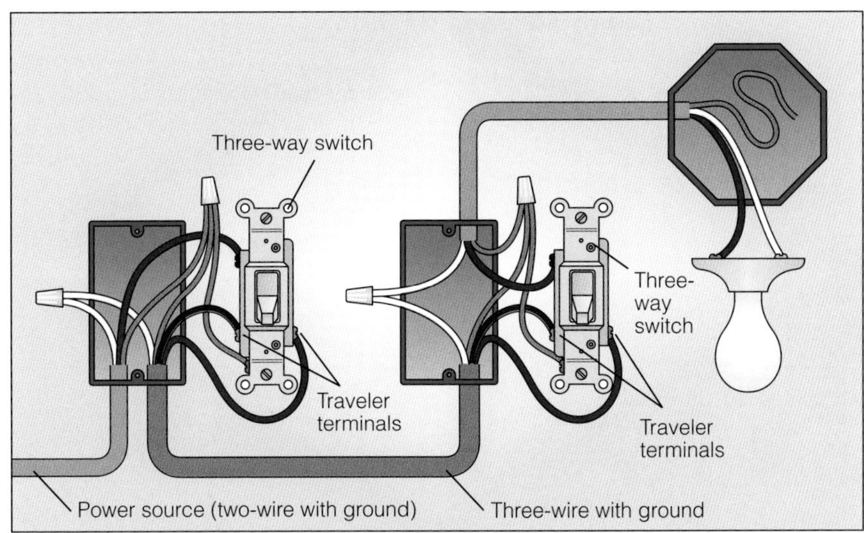

Three-way switches, fixture after switches. The incoming hot wire attaches to the first switch's common dark-colored terminal. The two hot wires of three-wire cable connect to a pair of brass-colored traveler terminals on each switch. The fixture's hot wire connects to the second switch's common terminal.

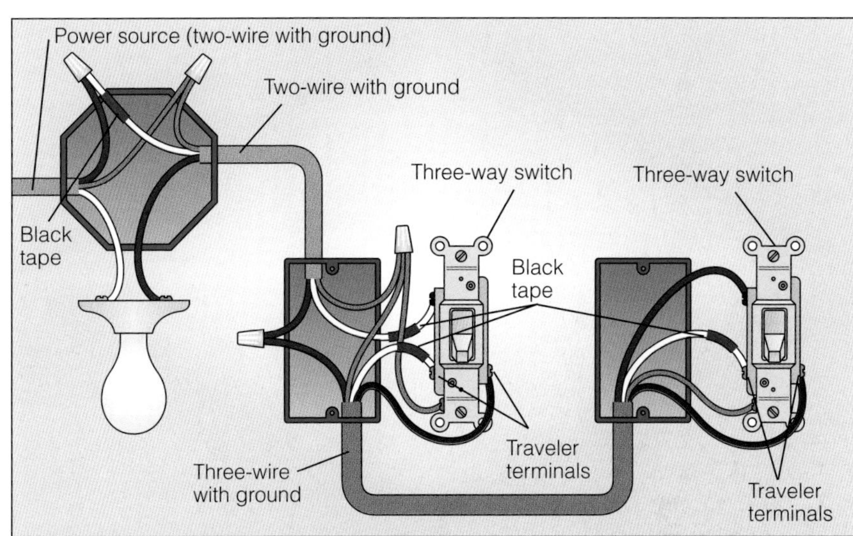

Three-way switches, fixture before switches. Power enters the fixture box. The reidentified white hot wire connects to the first switch's common terminal. Red and reidentified white wires link traveler terminals of both switches. Black wire, which is connected to the second switch's common terminal, leads back to the fixture.

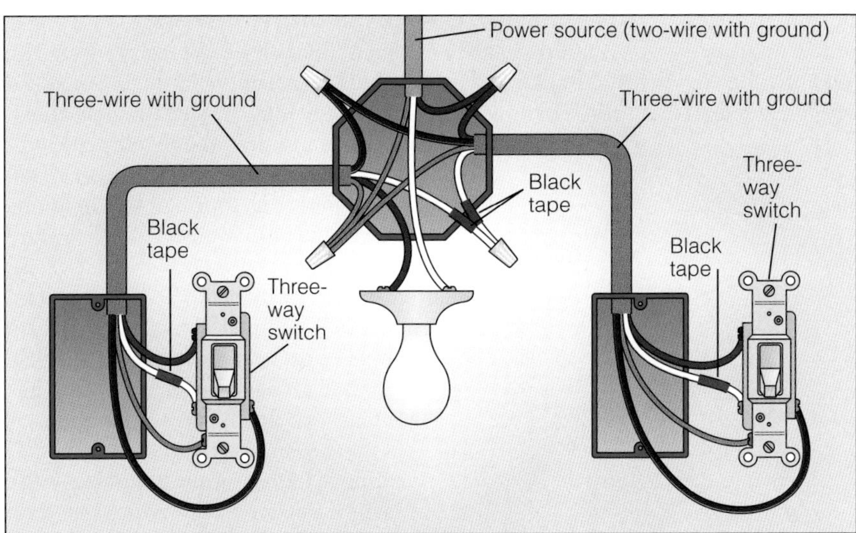

Three-way switches, fixture between switches. Power enters the fixture box. The incoming hot wire is connected to the right switch's common terminal. Two lengths of three-wire with ground cable, joined at the fixture box, link the right and left switches to each other and to the fixture. Reidentify white traveler wires as shown.

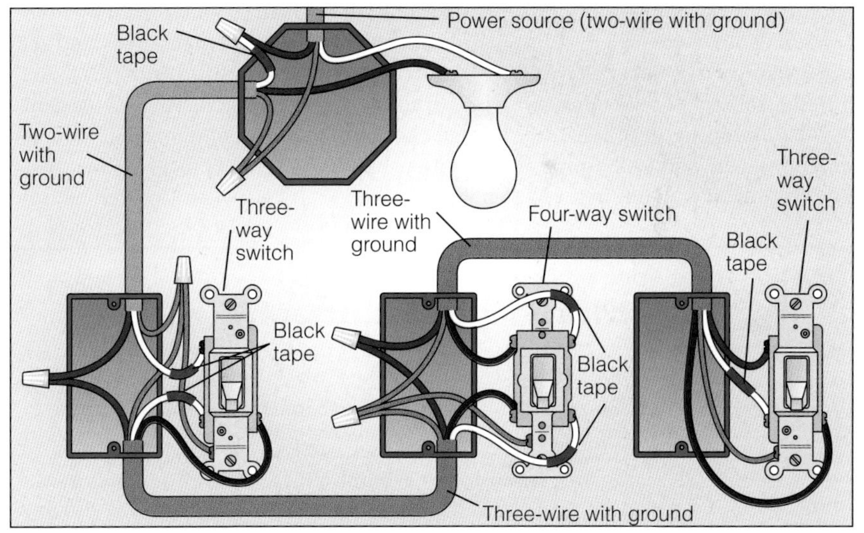

Controlling a light from three places using a four-way switch and two three-way switches. The incoming hot wire is routed through the fixture box to common terminal of the left three-way switch. Three-wire with ground cable connects all three switches. Black wire from the common terminal of the right three-way switch leads back to fixture.

Lighting Basics

Grounding 130
Voltage Tester 132
Safety First 133

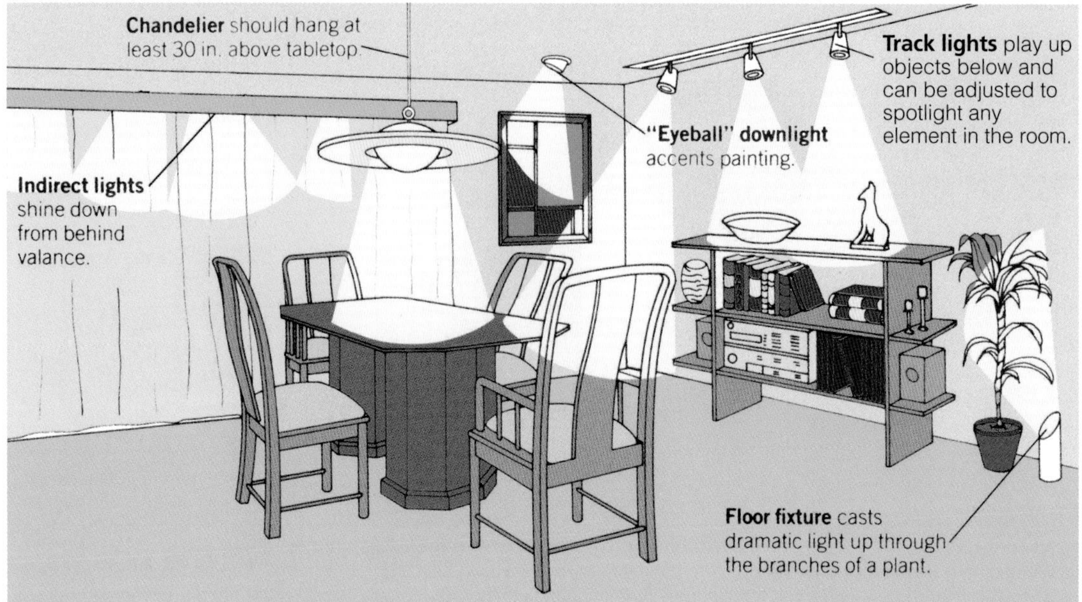
Chandelier should hang at least 30 in. above tabletop.
Track lights play up objects below and can be adjusted to spotlight any element in the room.
"Eyeball" downlight accents painting.
Indirect lights shine down from behind valance.
Floor fixture casts dramatic light up through the branches of a plant.

Beam Spreads of Bulbs

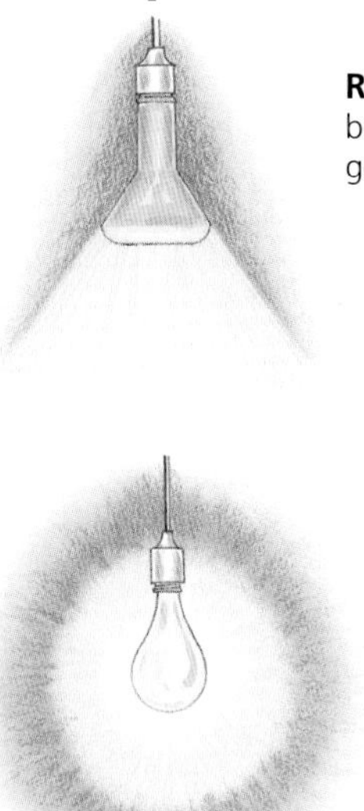

Reflector-type floodlights cast a wide beam of light (about 70° angle), which is good for general lighting.

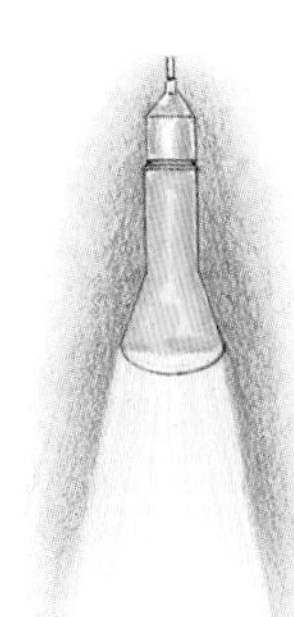

Reflector-type spotlights cast a narrow beam of light (about 20° angle), which is good for task or accent lighting.

Standard incandescent bulbs, unlike reflector-type bulbs, cast light very broadly in all directions.

Good lighting can do wonders. It can accentuate or soften colors, create a festive or soothing mood, call attention to objects you want to show off and provide safe work areas and snug places to read.

Residential lighting falls into three categories: general, accent and task. **General lighting,** usually from ceiling or wall fixtures, radiates light throughout a room, as sunlight does. **Task lighting** focuses on individual areas and may come from portable lamps, undercabinet fixtures, track lights or recessed spotlights. **Accent lighting** is more decorative and may be in the form of halogen lights focused on artwork or spotlights accenting architectural details.

How Distance Affects Light Levels

A bulb's capacity to light a surface is dramatically affected by distance. A standard lightbulb mistakenly placed in a recessed or track fixture will only provide a fraction of the light that a reflector bulb would provide. If 100 percent of the light from a bulb reaches a surface 1 ft. (30 cm) below it, only one-fourth of that light hits the surface if the bulb is raised to 2 ft. (60 cm) above the surface, one-ninth at 3 ft. (90c m) and a mere one-sixteenth at 4 ft. (120 cm) When you need bright task lighting, keep the light close to the work surface, use a bulb that focuses more light and has wattage near the fixture's maximum.

Be sure to use the proper type and rating of bulbs in your fixtures. For fire safety, never exceed ratings listed on a fixture.

Go Figure

How Much Light Is Enough?

Opinions vary on the right amount of light needed for a room; so much depends on personal preference, type of light, color of room and activities performed there. But there are a few rules of thumb:

- **Kitchens, laundry rooms and workshops.** 3 to 5 watts of incandescent light per square foot (32 to 54 watts / sq. meter) of floor.
- **Living rooms, dens and bedrooms.** 1 to 2 watts of incandescent light per sq. ft. (11 to 22 watts / sq. meter.)
- **Bathrooms.** 6 watts per sq. ft. (66 watts / sq. m), with vanities receiving 30 to 40 watts per running foot (30 cm) of vanity top.

Note: When installing fluorescent light, divide the number of watts above by about one-third.

Ceiling Fixtures

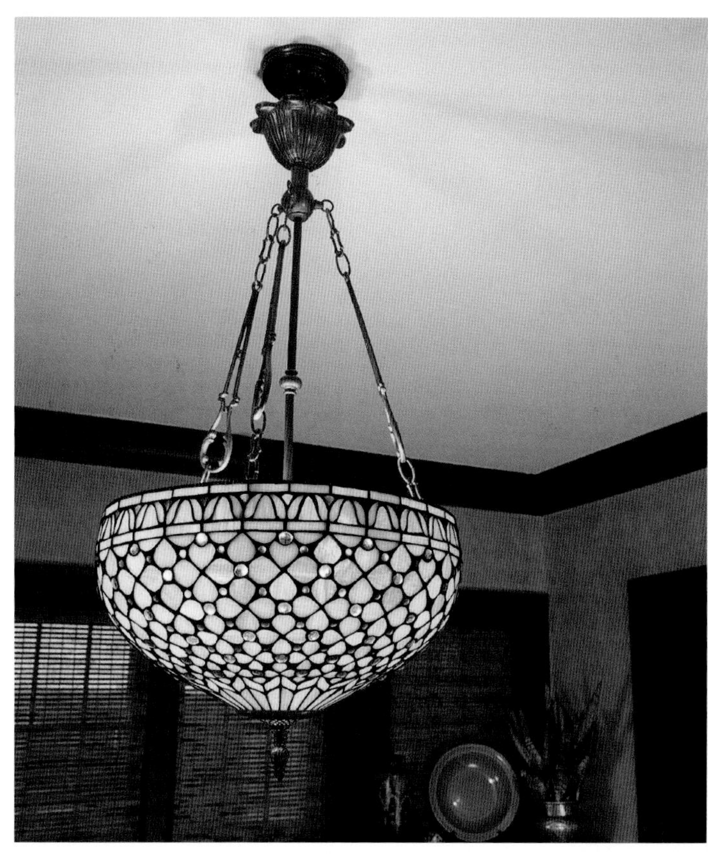

Installing a new light fixture is a great way to transform a drab room into a dazzling one. However, correct wiring and solid installation are critical. This page shows how to hang a fixture safely and securely.

Learn the temperature rating of your existing wires and verify your new light will be compatible. Many lights, especially ceiling-hugging fixtures, require connection to standard 90-degree C-rated wire. Wires installed before 1985 often don't have insulation that can withstand this higher temperature.

Heavy fixtures require strong electrical boxes. Inspect your existing electrical box and make certain it's firmly mounted to solid framing, especially for heavier fixtures. If the new fixture is particularly heavy—more than 25 lbs. (12 kg), consider replacing the old box with a ceiling-fan-rated box.

Key Installation Steps

Avoid trouble by assembling and adjusting the mounting parts before you climb up the ladder. Also, if the new fixture has silver or gold lamp-cord wire, identify the neutral side by feeling for ridges, indentations or square edges; the hot wire will be smooth.

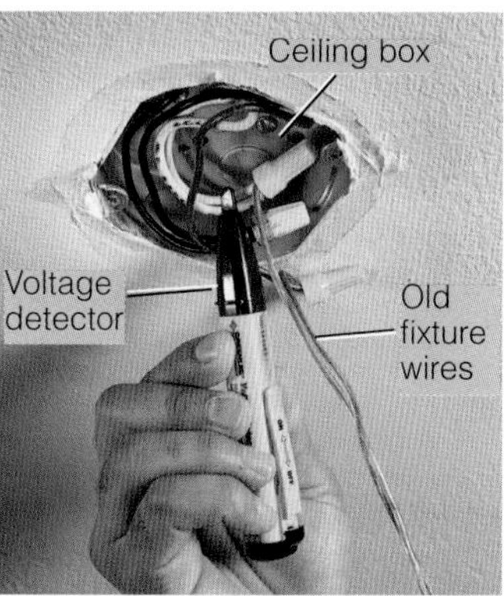

1 Turn off power and test all wires with a voltage detector to make sure the power is off. Disconnect the light fixture wires and remove the old fixture. Inspect and test the box for secure mounting.

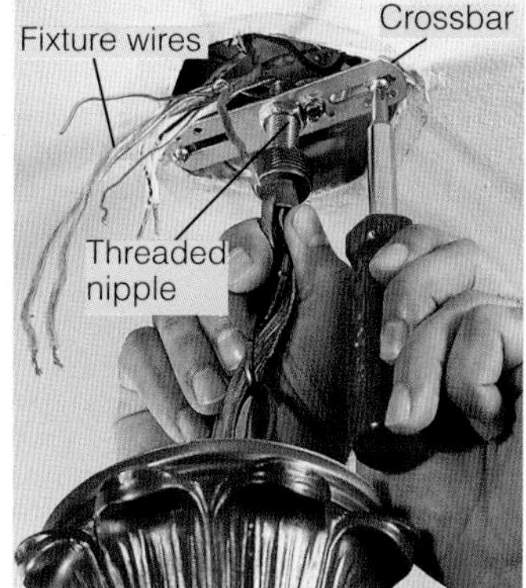

2 Install fixture strap and threaded nipple. Lift fixture into position and thread fixture wires through threaded nipple. Attach fixture firmly to ceiling box.

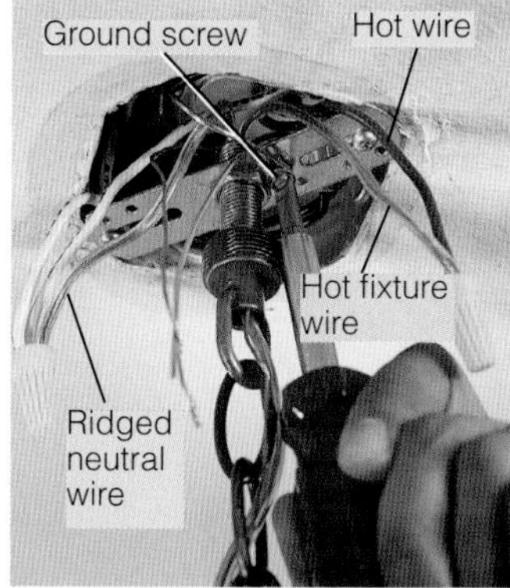

3 Connect the wires after you identify the neutral fixture wire and hot fixture wire. Attach the ground wire around the ground screw and test the fixture before installing canopy.

Mounting Systems

A screw and cap nut assembly holds the fixture to the fixture strap with screws mounted to a two-piece offset fixture strap. Before installation, thread the screws through the offset fixture strap and test-fit the canopy over the screws. The screws should protrude only enough that the cap nuts will hold the fixture firmly against the ceiling.

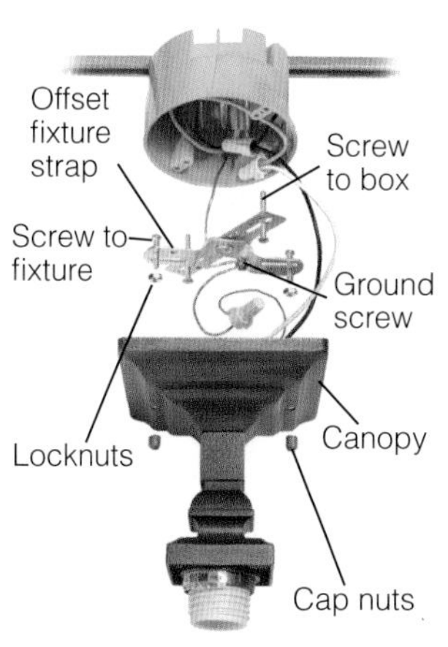

A threaded nipple assembly mounts to the center of a single flat fixture strap. This threaded nipple holds the fixture to the fixture strap and acts as a conduit for the fixture wires into the box.

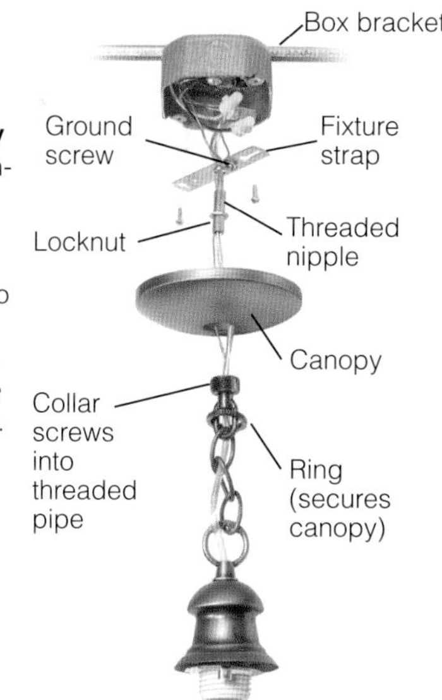

Ceiling Fans

A quiet, elegant ceiling fan can add year-round beauty and comfort to any space. It cools in the summer by pushing air toward the floor, and a reverse feature warms in the winter by pushing warm air off the ceiling, along the walls and back toward the floor.

You can mount ceiling fans to either flat or sloped ceilings. If your room has a flat ceiling, keep in mind that the blades should be no less than 7 ft. (2.15 m) from the floor. To shorten the overall fan depth, ceiling-hugging kits are available for some fans. For a sloped-ceiling installation, consult a fan expert to calculate the downrod length you'll need for the room.

New, properly installed ceiling fans run quietly with minimal wobble; most new fans include a balancing kit to help correct any problems.

Key Installation Steps

Begin by turning off the power and removing the old fixture. Test all the wires and knock the old electrical box free of the framing by using a block of wood against the inside of the box. It's okay to leave the old box in the ceiling cavity.

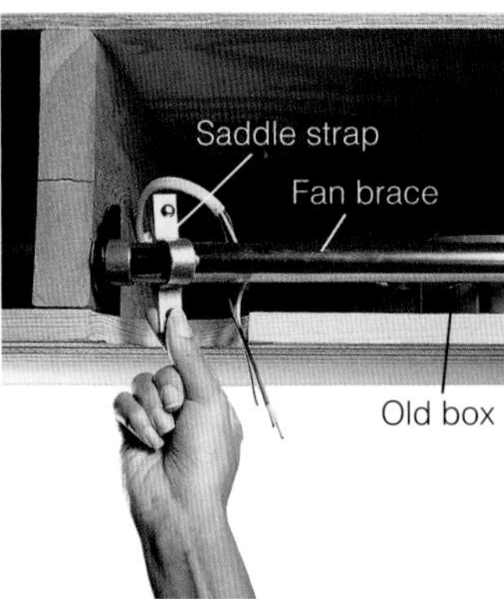

1 Slip a fan brace through the hole, set the appropriate box depth and secure brace against the framework by twisting. Feed existing wire into fan box, secure with cable clamp, then fasten the box to the brace with saddle strap.

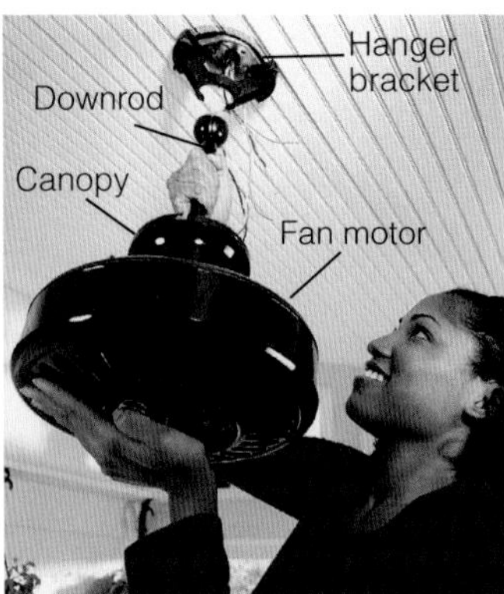

2 Secure hanger bracket to box. Connect down rod and canopy to motor and set motor assembly in bracket. Make wiring connections based on manufacturer's instructions and local codes.

3 Install blades and blade brackets on the fan motor. If necessary, connect the remote-control kit to light-kit housing and attach the light kit to the motor. Turn on power and test the fan.

Fan Supports

Most local codes require ceiling fans to be mounted to a fan-rated brace and box. Buy a fan brace and box when you purchase your fan. If the framing is accessible from the attic, choose a brace that fastens with screws. Otherwise, pick a brace that's designed to slip through the hole left by the removal of the old electrical box. These braces expand to fit between the framing members in your ceiling; you just rotate the shaft to anchor them.

Selecting a Fan—It's a Breeze

With a host of ceiling fan options available, it pays to do your homework before you shop. In general, avoid inexpensive bargain models and begin searching in the moderately priced category. These fans are more efficient at moving air and tend to have quiet, durable motors. Pay attention to blade size, blade pitch and motor quality.

A fan that's mounted close to the ceiling needs a steeper blade pitch and a tough motor to work well. A remote-control option can be added to most fans, if it's not already installed, and light kits are relatively interchangeable. If you're installing the fan in a damp area, select a damp-rated or wet-rated fan. Make certain speed control switches are designed for fans, not lights.

Undercabinet Lighting

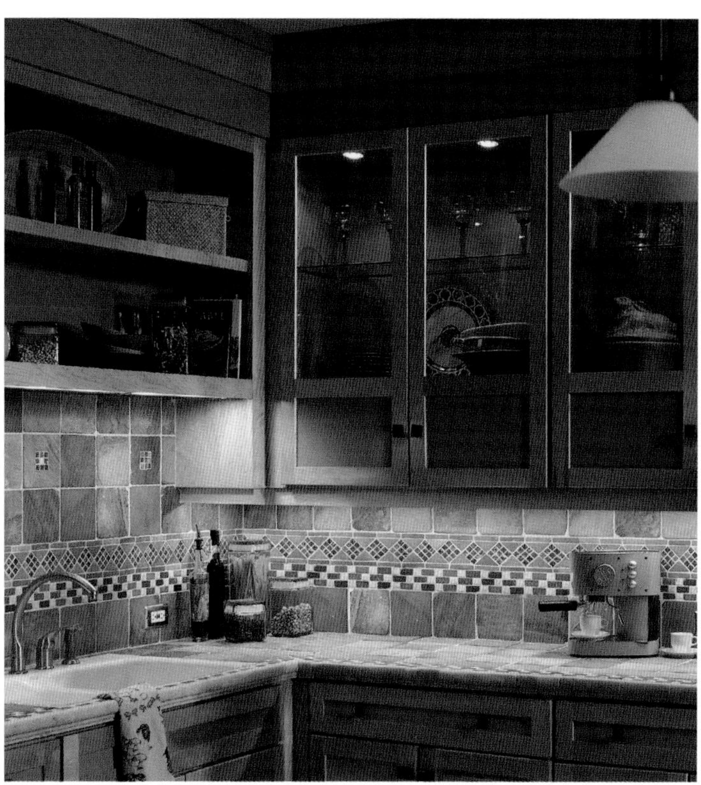

Undercabinet lighting is a weekend project that provides lifelong benefits. It can set the mood for a romantic dinner, provide bright light for slicing and dicing or glow softly for a midnight raid on the refrigerator.

Begin by solving the power source problem. Unfortunately, most electrical boxes in a kitchen area belong to dedicated circuits and most local codes prohibit any connections to these circuits. Look for an outlet serving another space that backs up to the lower cabinets.

Next, plan the wiring route. To simplify the project, you can run the cables through your lower cabinets. Most local codes require plastic-sheathed cable be protected inside metal conduit in lower cabinets and other areas where the cable is subject to damage.

Finally, you may also want to hide the lighting fixtures by adding a small valance to the lower edge of the upper cabinets.

Key Installation Steps

Using a long bit, drill a hole next to an existing power source in an adjacent room, then insert a coat hanger. Locate the hanger inside the cabinet, and use it as a reference point for marking and cutting an access hole for wiring in back of the cabinet.

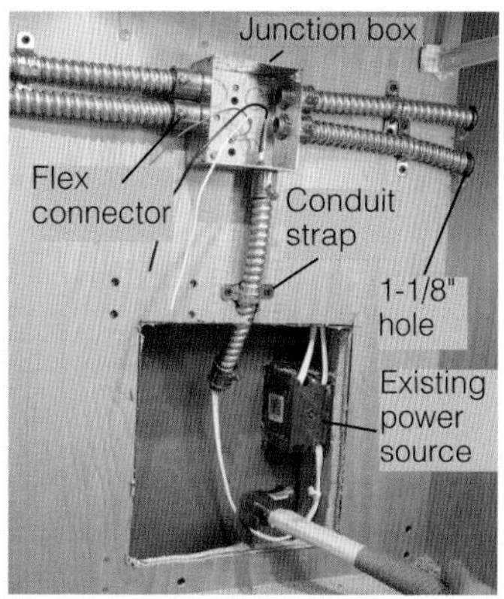

1 Run cable from an existing outlet, through flex conduit, into a new junction box. Install connectors and more flex conduit for undercabinet lights and switches. Strap conduit within 12 in. (30 cm) of junction box.

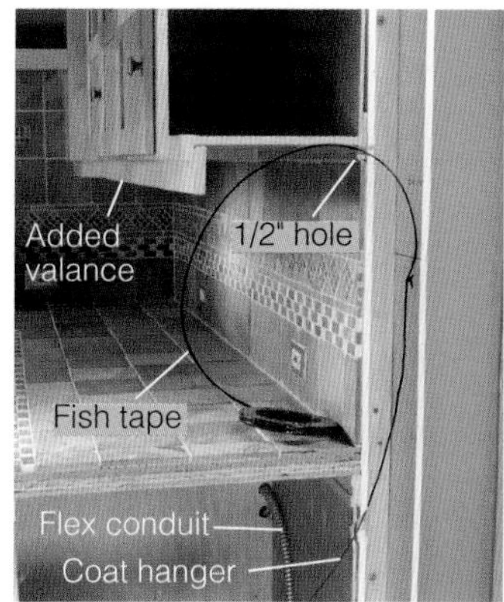

2 Fish cable from the base cabinets to the upper cabinets' lower edge. Run conduit to remodeling box for switch. Wire must run in flex conduit when running through the back of cabinets.

3 Secure the cable to the fixture with a cable clamp, connect wires according to manufacturer's instructions, then screw fixture to cabinet bottom. Test lights.

The Big Picture

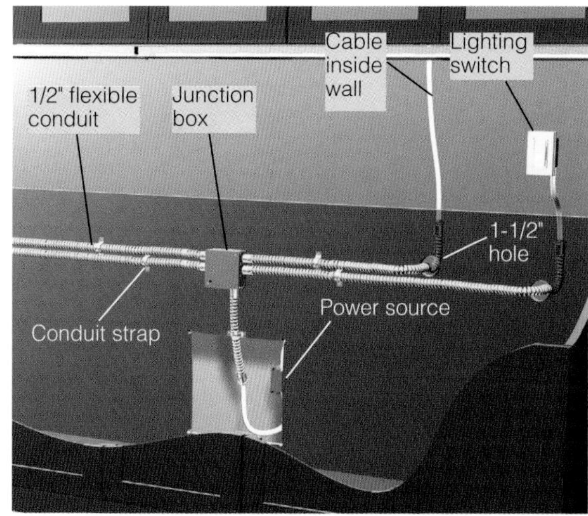

The Right Light

The most common choices for undercabinet lighting are halogen, xenon, fluorescent and thin, tubular rope lighting. Halogen and xenon are generally low-voltage fixtures that use built-in transformers to reduce the 120-volt current to 12 volts. Both halogen and xenon are dimmable using special switches. Install a continuous row of fixtures for the most evenly distributed light.

Track Lighting

Extending a Branch Circuit **128** Voltage Tester **132**
Grounding **130** Fishing Cable **141**
Wattage Ratings **131** Wiring Variations **143** Lighting Basics **146**

If you want to transform the look and feel of a room with minimum effort, installing a track lighting system is a good place to start. Focused halogen bulbs allow you to strategically light a room by placing emphasis on particular objects or spaces. Individual fixtures can be easily moved to accommodate changing needs, and halogen bulbs provide sunlike light.

Plan your project with lighting goals and potential problems in mind. Rigid track systems come in a variety of lengths and are joined with fittings to form L-shapes, U-shapes, V-shapes or crosses. Some systems even use flexible or cable-type tracks.

Pay attention to clearance issues, such as rooms with low ceilings or doors that might interfere with the lights. In general, keep the track at least 2 ft. (60 cm) away from walls or doors.

Key Installation Steps

You can easily install track lighting by removing an old fixture and connecting the new track. The tracks are prewired and a mounting plate or canopy covers the connection. Use drywall anchors and screws for securing the track. Shut off power at panel while working.

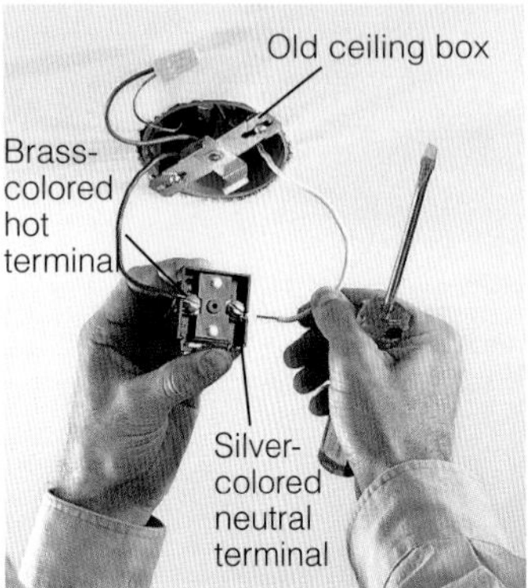

1 Pay close attention to a track fixture's polarity. Hot and neutral wires must go to correct terminals. Keep the hot and neutral wires separate and consistent throughout the track system.

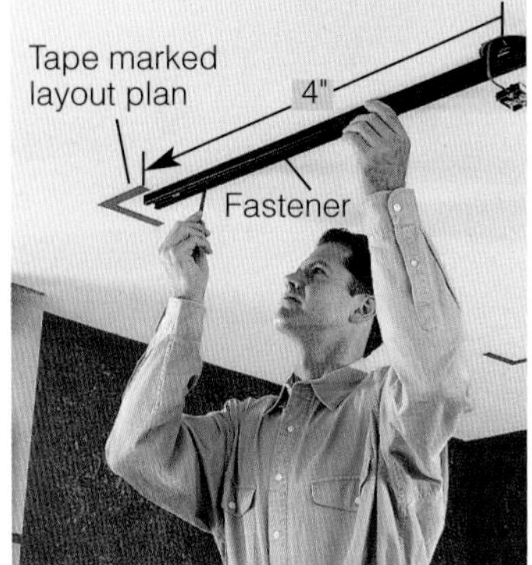

2 Mark the track's layout plan on the ceiling using masking tape. Next, mark locations for fasteners to connect the track to the ceiling. Use at least one fastener for every 4 ft. (1.3 m) of track.

3 Push a fixture into the track; turn and lock it into place. Contact prongs in the fixture base will carry current to the bulb. Adjust bulb direction and fixture location as desired.

High or Low Voltage?

Track-lighting systems can be either low or high voltage. Some systems can accommodate both fixture types by use of lights with individual built-in transformers. A system with all low-voltage fixtures can operate from a single transformer.

Line voltage heads use standard 120-volt current and work well for general lighting because their wider beam provides softer light.

Low-voltage fixtures with built-in transformers provide focused accent lighting in systems that also provide general lighting.

Low-voltage fixtures powered through a single transformer are available. Some have flexible track for more layout options.

Recessed Lighting

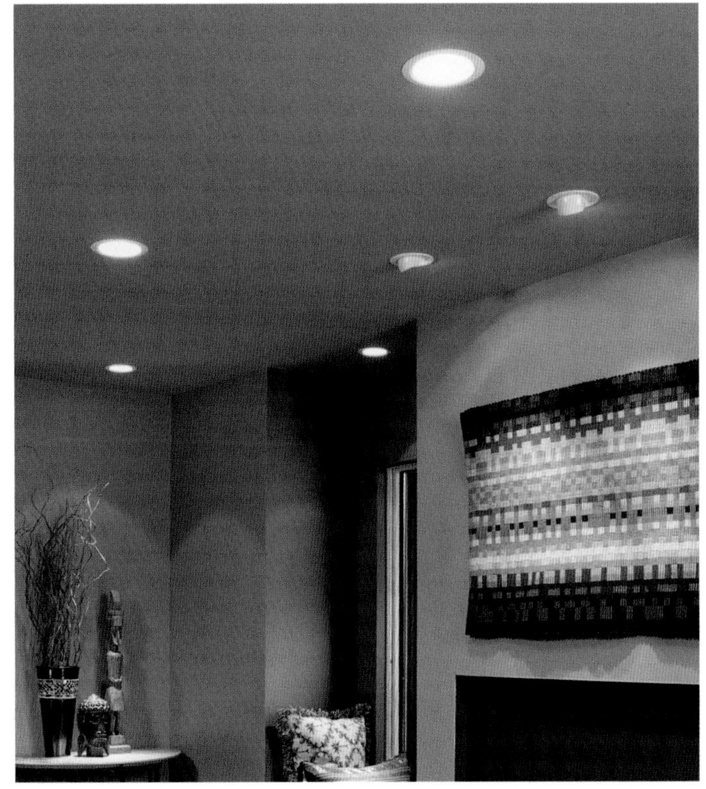

Recessed lights can provide general illumination, focused task lighting or decorative accent lighting. They clean up a ceiling by eliminating fixture clutter and even make a ceiling feel higher. Good planning is the key. Make sure the housings will fit into the ceiling spaces where you plan to install them. If you plan to use an existing ceiling electrical box as a power source and get rid of the fixture, you'll need a blank cover for the box so it can be accessed after the project is finished.

A recessed light assembly consists of the housing, trim and bulb. Labels inside the housing list the compatible trim styles, as well as bulb types and wattages for each. Special remodeling housings, like those shown being installed (above right), allow you to install recessed lights with minimal patching and repairs. See "The Right Type of Light" (right) for information on housings installed in insulated ceilings.

Key Installation Steps

Find a convenient power source for the new lights. Determine the joist locations with a stud sensor. Try to anticipate obstructions, especially water and drain lines, and mark the fixture locations. Before permanently installing the trim kits, plan to paint the entire ceiling.

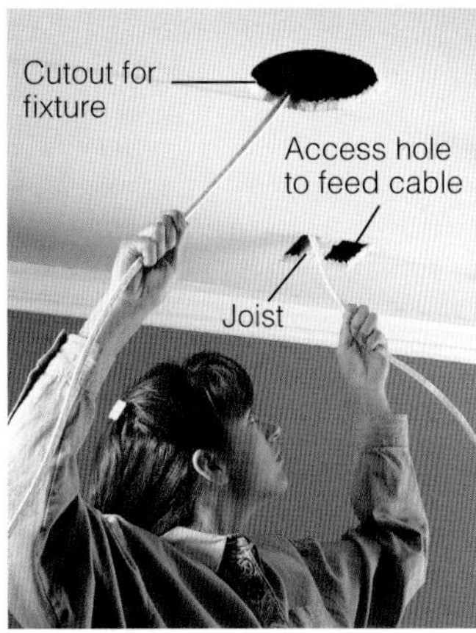

1 Cut housing openings, using caution to avoid plumbing and electrical lines. Run cable from power source to the nearest opening, then continue running cable to remaining openings. Use access holes and cable protector plates where necessary.

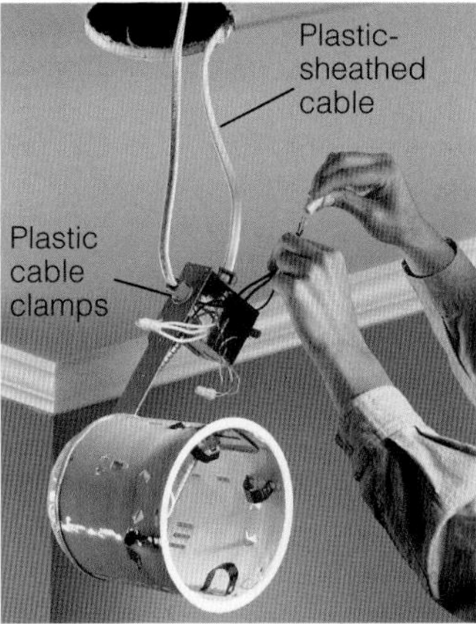

2 Fasten cables to junction boxes with plastic cable clamps. Make connections at the power source and each housing junction box. Secure all connections with wire connectors, and fold the wires into the junction box.

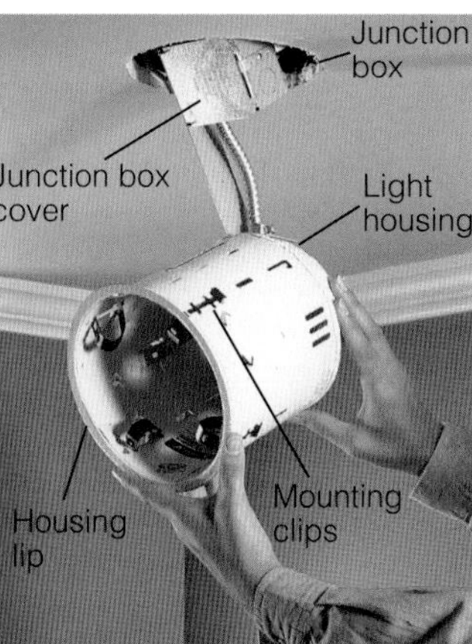

3 Install a junction box cover and slip housing through opening. Mount housing to ceiling or framing using built-in clips. Adjust housing so its lip lies flush against the ceiling surface. Install bulb and attach trim kit.

The Right Type of Light

If you're installing recessed lights in an existing ceiling without attic access, buy remodeling housings that mount to the drywall or other surface rather than the framing. Buy insulation contact (IC)-rated housings if they will be touching insulation. For extra energy efficiency in insulated ceilings, buy IC-rated airtight housings. Select the fixture trim style (right) based on your needs.

Down-light trim pieces cast a cone-shaped beam of light. The area lit will roughly equal its distance from the light.

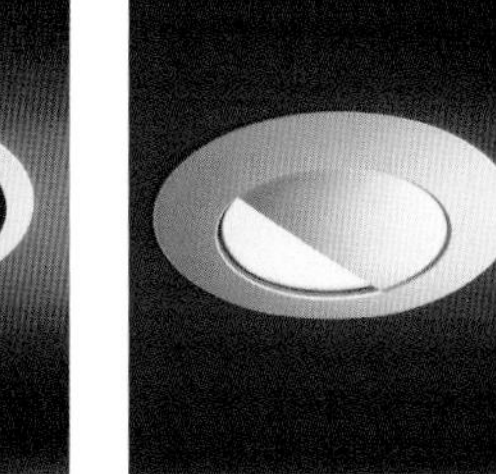

Wall washers cast an arc of light down a wall to accent a painting or fireplace or to softly light a room.

Eyeballs have a protruding, movable port that lets you focus light on a countertop, desk or other workspace.

Fluorescent Lighting

Grounding 130
Voltage Testers 132
Safety First 133
Wiring Variations 143

A fluorescent light fixture is a terrific energy saver, consuming up to 75 percent less electricity than an equivalent incandescent bulb—and the fluorescent bulb lasts up to 10 times longer.

They're worth keeping in good repair. If your fluorescent light flickers or makes an annoying hum, a degrading ballast is the likely culprit. You can easily replace it, as shown (top right). Just make sure the wiring configuration, voltage and current match the old one. Make sure the cost of the ballast does not exceed that of a new fixture—ballasts can be expensive and fixtures are relatively inexpensive.

If your fixture won't light, flickers on and off or won't hold a bulb, you may need to replace a lamp socket. Consider installing full-spectrum bulbs that cast a more natural-looking light.

Replacing a Degrading Ballast

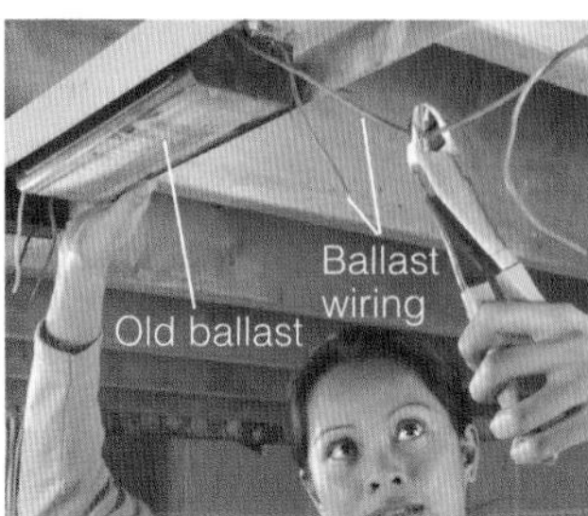

1 Turn off the power. Remove the bulbs and ballast cover. Snip old wiring several inches (centimeters) from the ballast's end.

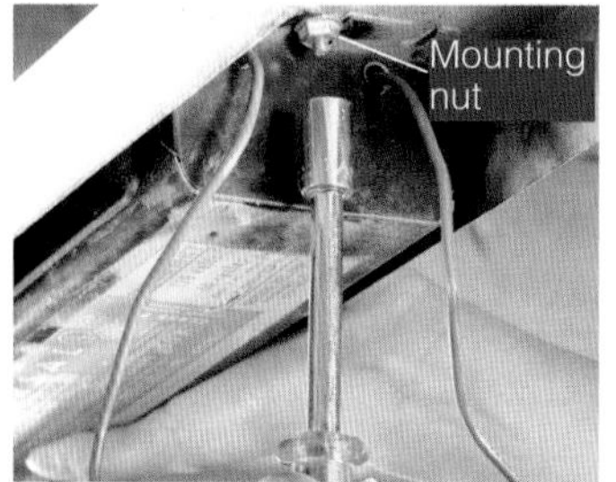

2 Remove the old ballast by loosening mounting nuts. A ballast is heavy, so use caution as it comes loose.

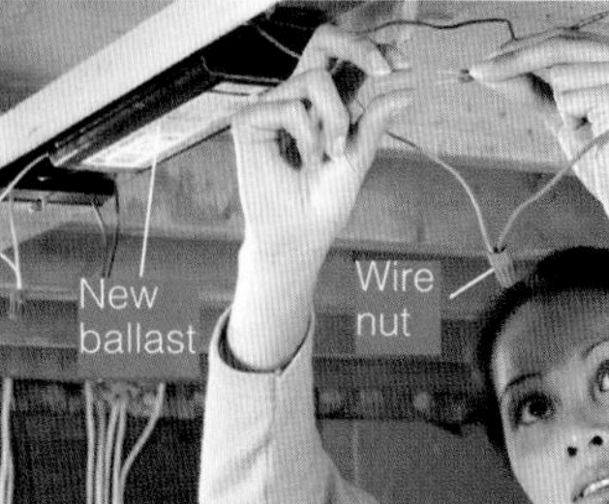

3 Install a new ballast with adequate cold-starting temperature. Connect the wires and reinstall bulbs and cover.

Replacing a Malfunctioning Lamp Socket

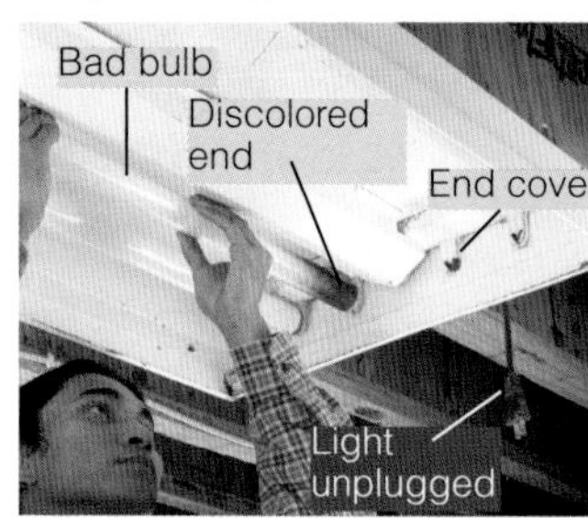

1 Turn off power. Remove bulb by twisting 90° with both hands. Pull one end straight down to free bulb.

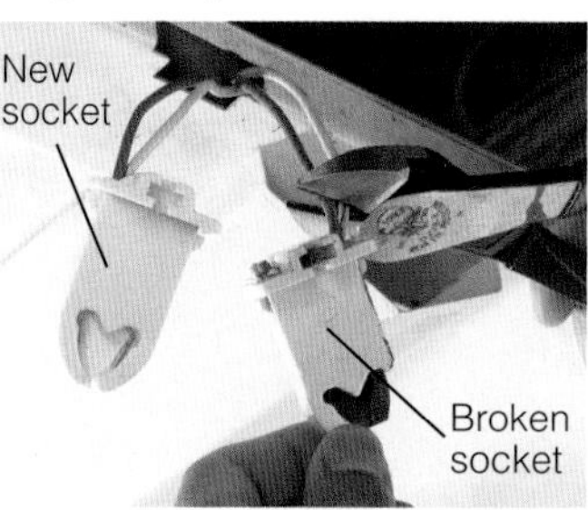

2 Unscrew fixture end cover, then slide out socket to expose wiring. Cut wires close to the socket.

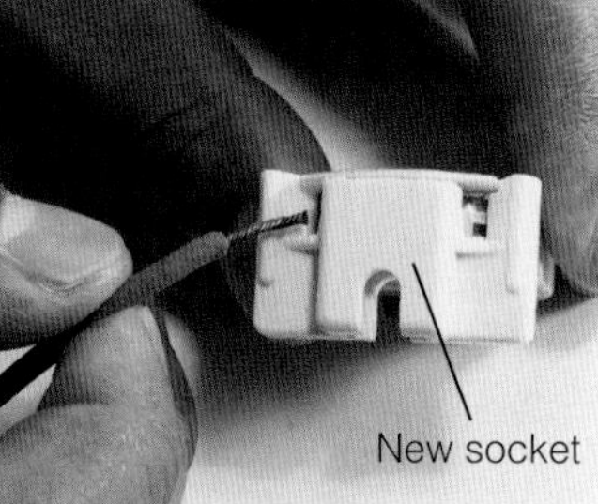

3 Strip 1/2 in. (12 mm) of insulation from wires and push wires into new socket terminal slots.

Shop Smart: Compact Fluorescent Bulbs

It makes good sense to use compact fluorescent lightbulbs (CFLs) to replace hard-to-reach incandescent bulbs or those lights used more than three hours a day. Since CFLs use far fewer watts, buy bulbs based on the lumen output. Also, CFLs tend to dim slightly with age, so buy bulbs with 20 percent greater lumen output than the standard bulb equivalent.

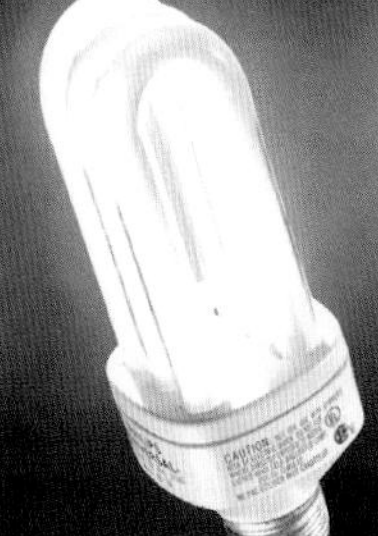

Standard CFLs can be used to replace ordinary bulbs.

Decorative CFLs are available for fixtures with visible bulbs.

Three-way CFLs often use a separate ballast and bulb.

Repairing Lamps and Cords

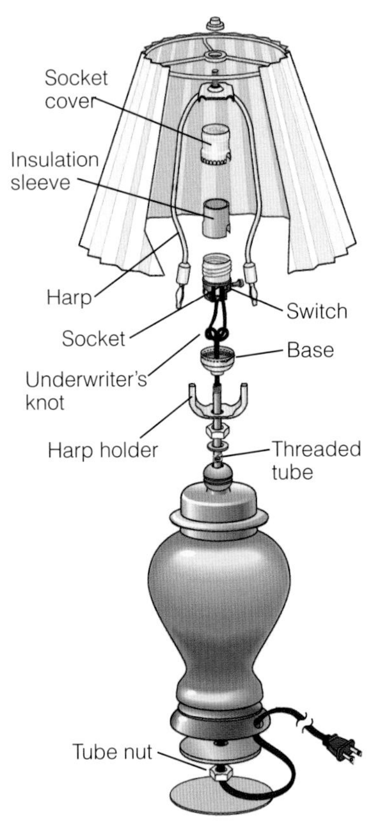

Rewiring a Lamp

When a lamp goes kaput, it's often easier to replace the three working parts—the socket, switch and cord—rather than trying to diagnose and fix the actual problem.

Most sockets, like the one shown, have a switch inside, but stores carry parts for cord-mounted switches as well. You can install a switched cord in a lamp that originally had a socket switch and vice versa.

Caution: The screw shell must be connected to the neutral wire, which is connected to the wide prong on two-wire polarized plugs. This keeps any metal parts of the lamp safe to touch and operate. The insulation for the neutral wire in a two-wire lamp cord will be identified with ribbed lines, a sharp ridge or another marking. If the cord is transparent, the neutral wire is silver.

1 Unplug the lamp. Pry the socket shell out of the base with a small screwdriver. Disconnect socket from cord by loosening screw terminals. Remove the base by turning it counterclockwise. Screw on a new socket base and feed a new cord up through the lamp body.

2 Tie an Underwriter's knot about 1 in. (2.5 cm) from the end of the cord. This strain-relief knot prevents tugs on the cord from pulling the wires loose from the screw terminals, which could create a shock hazard.

3 To make each connection, gently twist wire strands together to form a more solid wire. Then wrap the wire clockwise around the terminal screw. Connect the neutral wire to the silver screw and the hot wire to the brass screw. Reassemble and test lamp.

Wiring Plugs

Replace older plugs with bent, corroded or loose prongs, or plugs missing their insulating faceplates. Also replace damaged plugs when the ground prong is broken or has been cut off. Closely match the replacement plug to the original plug. Older two-prong plugs, though, should always be replaced with polarized two-prong plugs that have one wider prong. Most new plugs preclude the need to use the strain-relief Underwriter's knot.

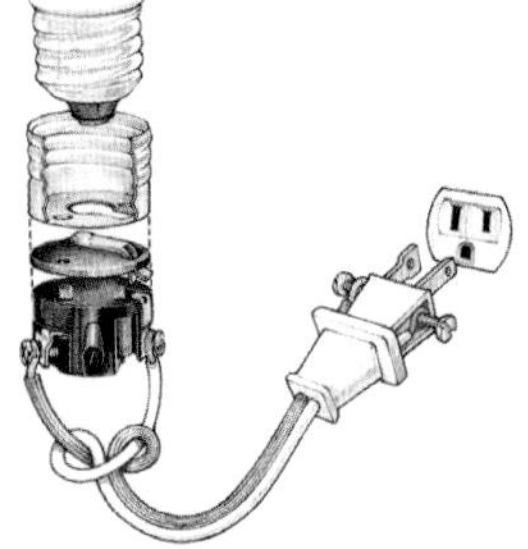

Polarized two-prong plug. The identified neutral cord wire connects to the silver screw in the wide-prong plug and the silver screw on the lamp socket. The wide prong connects to the neutral slot in the receptacle.

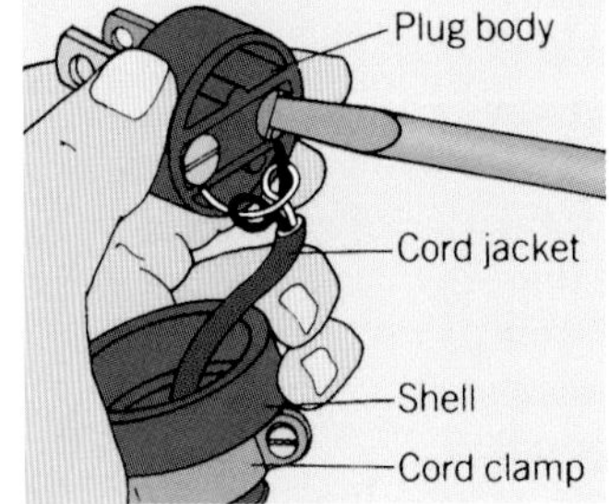

Two-prong plug. Remove cord jacket and strip wire insulation. Connect white wire to silver screw and black wire to brass screw. Assemble the plug body and tighten the cord clamp.

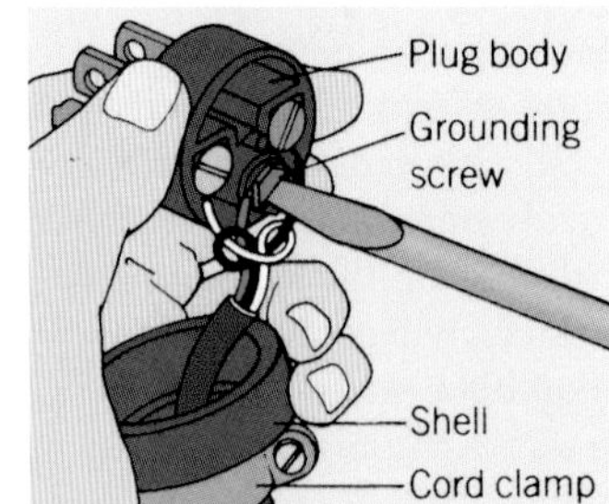

Three-prong plug. Strip wire insulation. Connect white wire to silver screw, black to brass screw and ground wire to green screw. Assemble the plug body and tighten the cord clamp.

Outdoor Wiring

Voltage Testers 132
Wiring Variations 143

By bringing power outdoors, you can extend the usable hours of your backyard or patio, do away with awkward, and sometimes dangerous, extension cords and enhance your home's security. Basic wiring techniques are the same indoors and out, but because receptacles and switches are exposed to the elements, they must be housed in weatherproof boxes. Outdoor light fixtures must be rated for use in wet locations. Outdoor receptacles must also be provided with ground-fault circuit-interrupter (GFCI) protection.

Working underground. When buried underground, outdoor wiring can be either individual Type THWN heat- and moisture-resistant insulated wires installed in metal or plastic conduit or Type UF (underground feeder) cable. The code permits direct burial of UF cable in a trench at least 24 in. (60 cm) deep. Some local codes may require that conduit protect all underground wiring. Above-ground outdoor wiring must be run through conduit for protection from physical damage. PVC plastic conduit is easy to cut and join with PVC cement, but it must be buried at least 18 in. (45 cm) deep. Rigid metal conduit is joined with threaded couplings. It's harder to cut than plastic and bending it takes some effort, but it requires only a 6-in.-deep (15-cm-deep) trench. Thin-wall metal conduit corrodes easily and is not suitable for direct burial.

Planning and permits. Before starting an outdoor wiring project, check building and electrical codes and obtain needed permits. Determine where and how to run power from inside to outside the house. You can tap an existing general-purpose circuit as long as it's not already operating near capacity, or you can run a new circuit from the service panel if you plan extensive outdoor wiring. Next, map out an efficient route for the outdoor circuit. When planning outdoor lighting, be aware of glare and its effects on neighbors and passersby. Use shielded fixtures placed well out of sightlines.

Caution: Before working on a circuit, turn off the power at the service panel and use a voltage tester to make sure the power is off.

Installing an Outdoor Outlet

A convenient way to bring power outside is to run cable between back-to-back boxes on opposite sides of an exterior wall. Locate an existing receptacle on a general-purpose circuit with excess capacity inside an exterior wall, near the desired site of a new outdoor GFCI receptacle. (Do not connect to dedicated kitchen, bathroom or laundry-room circuits.)

To add an outdoor outlet, begin by turning off the power at the service panel. Remove receptacle cover of existing indoor receptacle and use voltage tester to make sure power is off. Disconnect receptacle; remove a knockout from box. Locate studs, then mark new exterior box location; trace box outline on wall. Drill pilot holes through siding; carefully cut outline using a jigsaw with a short blade. Feed cable from indoor box to opening for outdoor box. Run cable through cable connector into new box and secure box to wall. Make connections at indoor receptacle and attach new wires to outdoor GFCI receptacle. Reinstall indoor receptacle. Fasten GFCI receptacle to new box and install an in-use-type weatherproof cover.

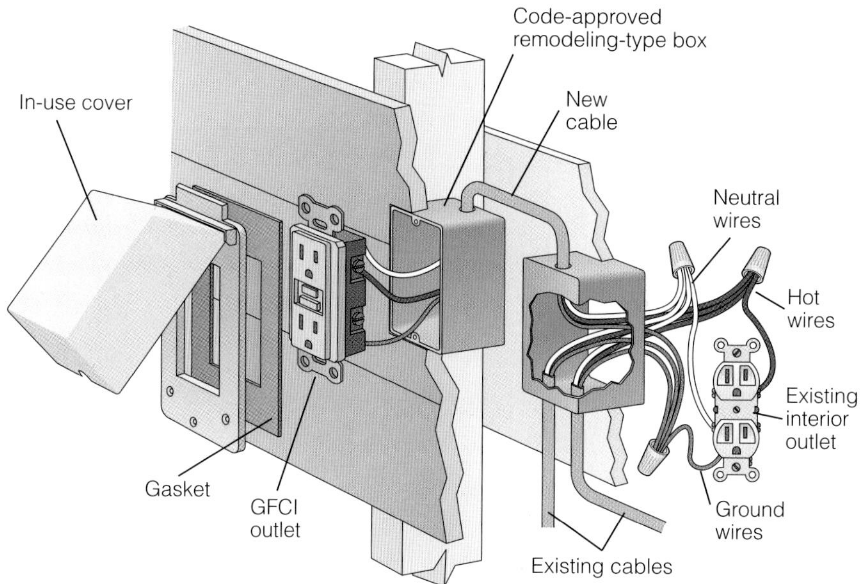

Weatherproof Boxes and Fittings

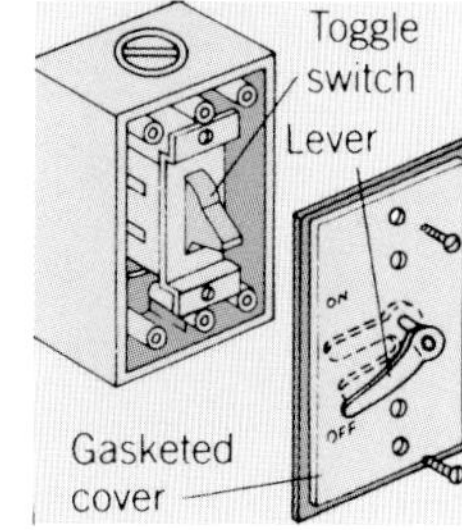

A weatherproof outdoor switch box has an external lever that activates the toggle of a standard snap switch. The cover's gasket seals the box against entry of exterior moisture and water.

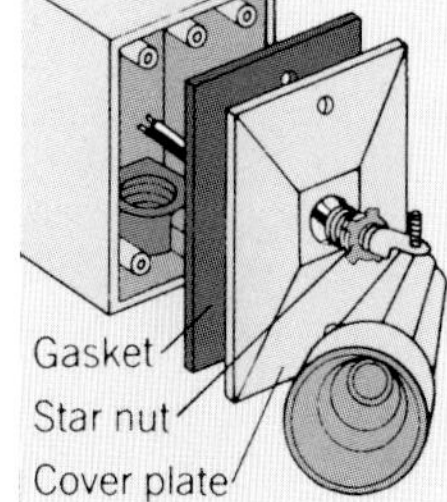

Outdoor lampholders have captive lamp-sealing gaskets and require outdoor-rated bulbs made of shock-resistant glass that won't shatter if they come in contact with water.

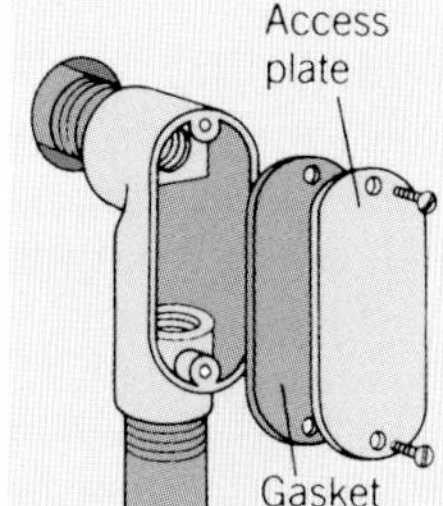

LB fittings with weatherproof gaskets are used with metal or plastic conduit. Removable covers let you pull wire around corners or make a transition through a wall into the ground.

Mounting a Soffit Light

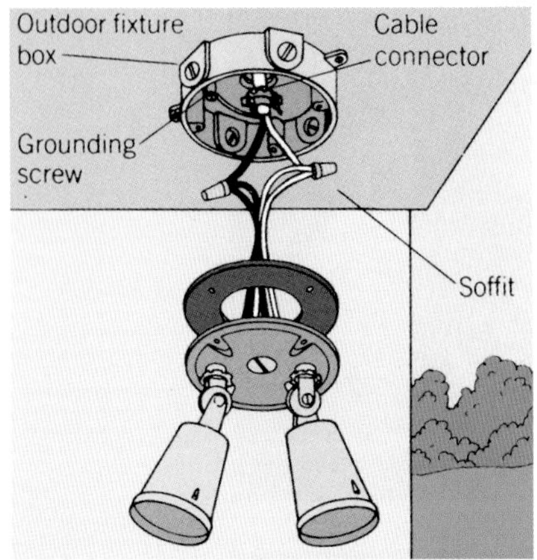

With the power off, run cable from switch-controlled circuit to soffit. Secure cable to outdoor fixture box using cable connector. Secure box to soffit. Connect hot and neutral wires to fixture wires, grounding wire to grounding screw in box. Mount fixture on box.

Tapping an Existing Outdoor Fixture

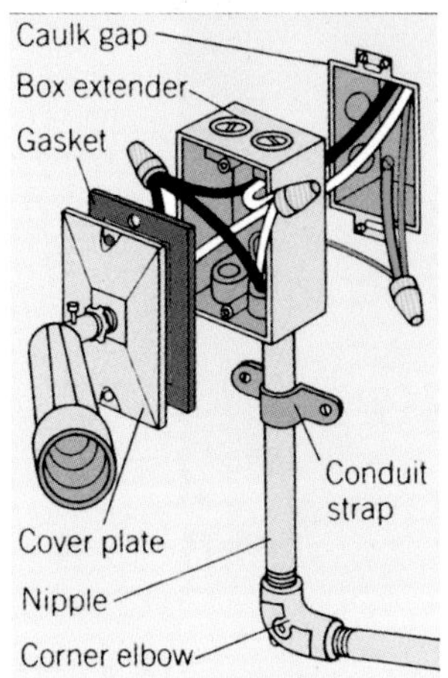

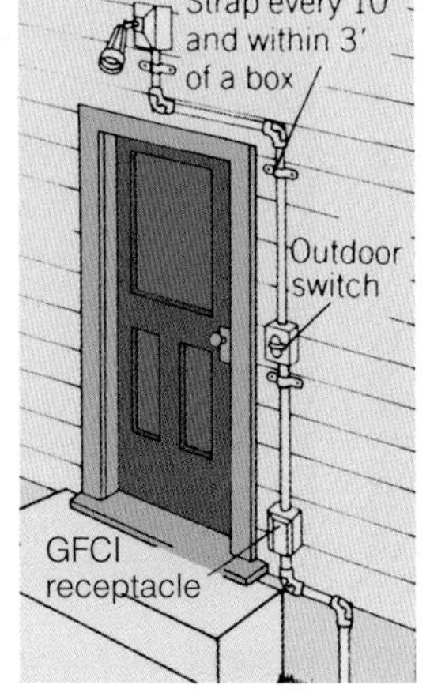

Turn off power to fixture and disconnect it. Attach box extender to fixture box. Effectively seal around extender box to prevent water intrusion. Install metal or plastic conduit from extender box to the other surface-mounted switch boxes, receptacle boxes or underground trench location, as desired. Secure conduit within 3 ft. (1 m) of boxes and every 3 ft. (1 m) thereafter. Install Type THWN insulated above-ground wire or Type UF underground cable, as required. Connect new wiring at extender box and replace fixture.

Handy Hints: Working Down Under

No need to tear up your sidewalk to run cable. Flatten the end of rigid metal conduit, dig a trench on both sides of the walkway and use a sledgehammer to drive conduit horizontally under the walkway. Cut off both ends of the conduit using a hacksaw, file any sharp edges inside the conduit and add connectors to protect the cable. Feed Type UF cable through the conduit.

Running Underground Wiring

PVC conduit is easy to install and can be cut with any good saw. Use PVC cement to glue conduit and fittings together. A variety of boxes, fittings and preformed elbows are available. Type UF cable is another easy alternative. However, PVC conduit offers better protection from physical damage and does not have to be buried as deeply as direct-buried UF cable. Standard Schedule 40 PVC conduit can be used in horizontal trenches, but heavy-wall Schedule 80 PVC conduit is required where you move from underground to above ground or where the conduit is subject to damage, such as an exterior wall. Type THWN moisture-resistant wire is used in the conduit: black or red for hot wires, white for neutral wires and green for grounding wires.

How Deep to Bury Cable

Wiring that emerges from underground must be installed in rigid metal conduit or Schedule 80 PVC conduit for protection from physical damage. This protection for direct-buried nonmetallic (NM) cable must extend from at least 18 in. (45 cm) below grade to the aboveground termination point. The minimum amount of cover (from top surface of finished grade to top surface of any wiring) is as follows:

- Rigid metal conduit: 6 in. (150 mm).
- Residential 120-volt GFCI-protected branch circuits rated 20 amps or less: 12 in. (300 mm).
- Rigid PVC conduit: 18 in. (450 mm).
- Direct-buried cable: 24 in. (600 mm).

Low-voltage Outdoor Lighting

Voltage Testers 132
Connecting Wires 137
Outdoor Outlets 154

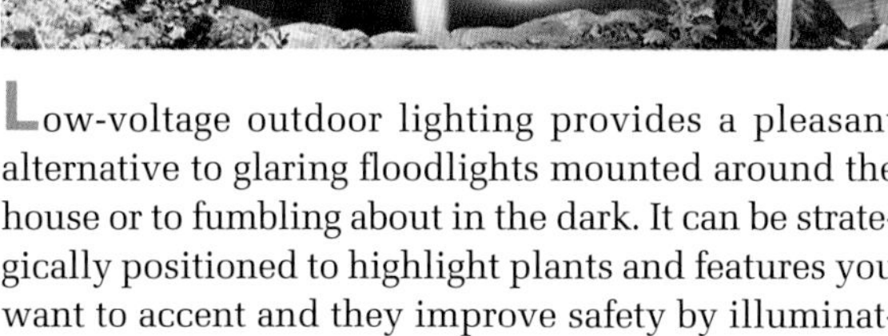

Low-voltage outdoor lighting provides a pleasant alternative to glaring floodlights mounted around the house or to fumbling about in the dark. It can be strategically positioned to highlight plants and features you want to accent and they improve safety by illuminating paths, steps and dark zones.

Durable lighting systems may cost more, but they'll last longer and be more dependable. Low-voltage halogen bulbs provide the best light and last up to 10,000 hours. To anchor the lights, don't use manufacturer-supplied stakes; instead, build the PVC anchors shown in steps 3 and 4.

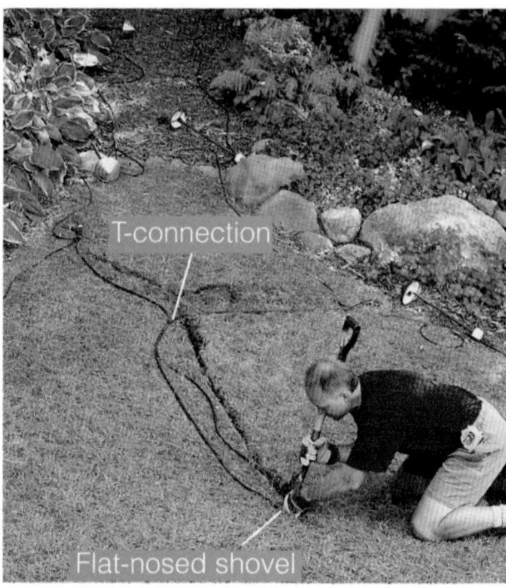

1 Lay out the light fixtures and wire. To avoid a voltage drop, create wire T-connections wherever you'll have more than five fixtures. Bury wires 6 in. (15 cm) deep. Test the lights and system before burying the wire and installing lights.

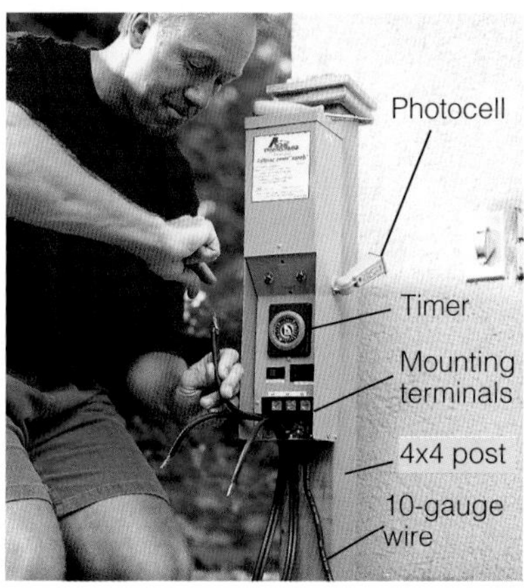

2 Install a transformer near an outdoor GFCI outlet with an in-use cover. Buy an oversized transformer so you can add more lights later. Mount transformer to a post to avoid damaging the house and allow free orientation of photocell. Connect 10-gauge main wires to mounting terminals.

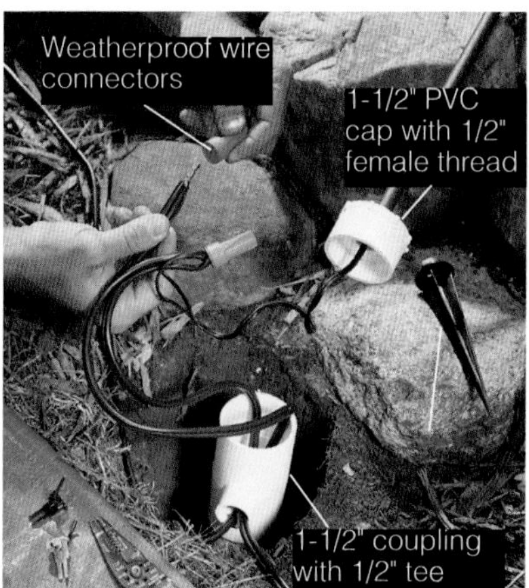

3 Connect wires with connectors approved for direct-burial—they contain sealant to resist corrosion. For taller lights, build the indestructible PVC anchors and junction boxes shown.

4 Level lights and anchor them in place. Bury wire 6-in. deep throughout the installation. To keep ground clean, use a tarp to contain the dirt while you dig.

Types of Lights

Pond lights are watertight with weighted bases. They illuminate pools, fountains and other water features.

Path lights are offset for lighting pathways. Use one 24-in.-tall (60-cm-tall) light with 20-watt bulb for every 10 ft. (3 m) of path.

Cone lights broadcast general light and illuminate walkways and the surrounding plants.

Floodlights work best to emphasize tree trunks, shrubs, statues or a home's architectural features.

Moon lights are mounted 15 to 30 ft. (4.5 to 9 m) high in a tree to simulate moon shadows in the branches.

Doorbells and Chimes

A doorbell or chime system consists of the sounding device, a front-door button, an optional rear-door button and a transformer that reduces 120-volt current to the lower voltage most systems require. Bell wire connects the components. The transformer must be connected to an unswitched branch circuit in a junction box, often in the basement or near the service panel.

Caution: Before installing the transformer, turn off the power to the circuit you're tapping into and use a voltage tester to make sure the power is off.

When estimating cable, measure the distances between components and add another 15 ft. (4.5 m) for connections and route turns. Follow the manufacturer's instructions. Although bell wire can be exposed, fish it behind finished surfaces where possible.

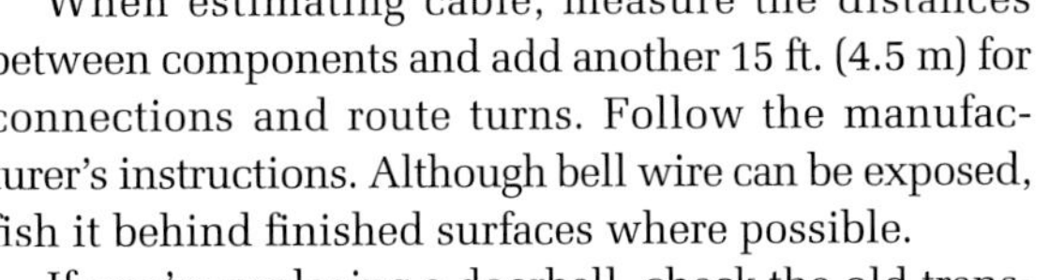

If you're replacing a doorbell, check the old transformer to make sure it has the same voltage rating. Replace the transformer, if necessary. Before repairing a doorbell, check the service panel for a tripped breaker or blown fuse.

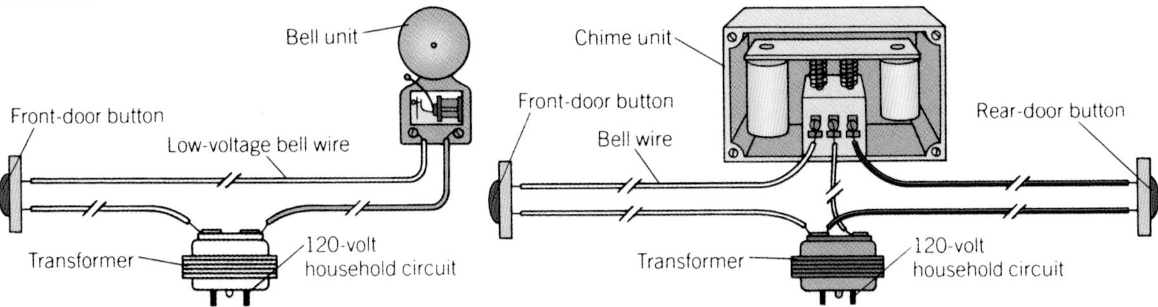

A typical single-button doorbell circuit.

A chime unit wired to both front and back door buttons.

Installing a Doorbell or Chimes

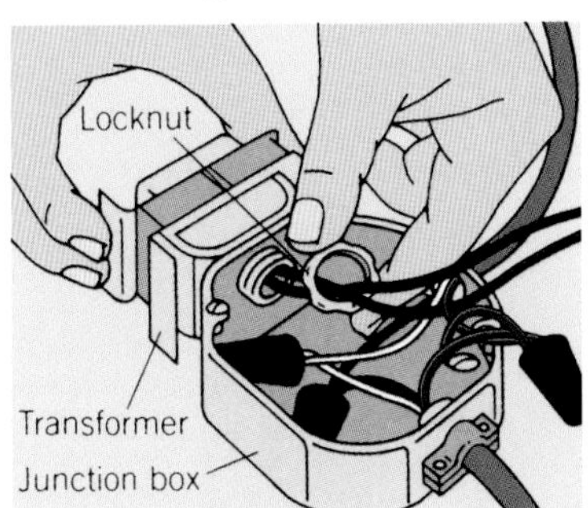

1 With power off, remove a knockout from the junction box; insert transformer wires. Fasten transformer to box with locknut. Use wire connectors to join one transformer wire to a black wire, the other to a white wire.

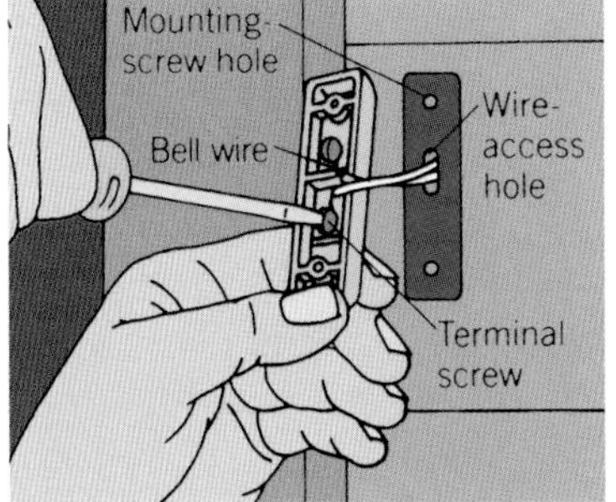

2 Drill holes for door button wires and mounting screws at doorknob height adjacent to the door's edge. After running the bell wiring, connect one wire from the transformer and one from the bell or chime unit to the button's terminal screws.

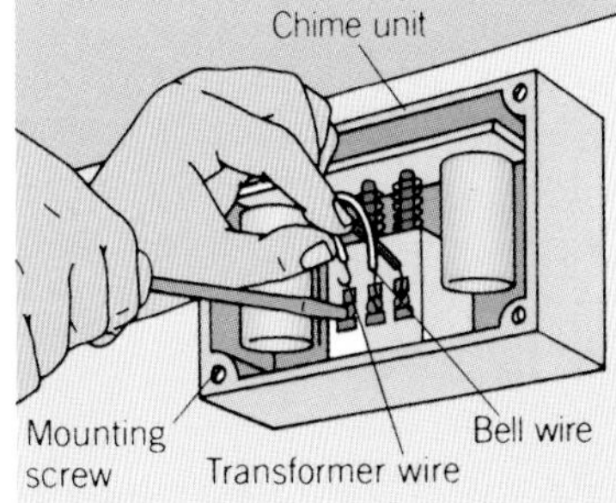

3 Determine chime location on the wall. Drill wire-access and mounting-screw holes for chime. Mount chime unit and connect wires from the transformer and door button(s) to the correct terminals on the chime unit (they're usually marked by the manufacturer).

Troubleshooting and Repairing

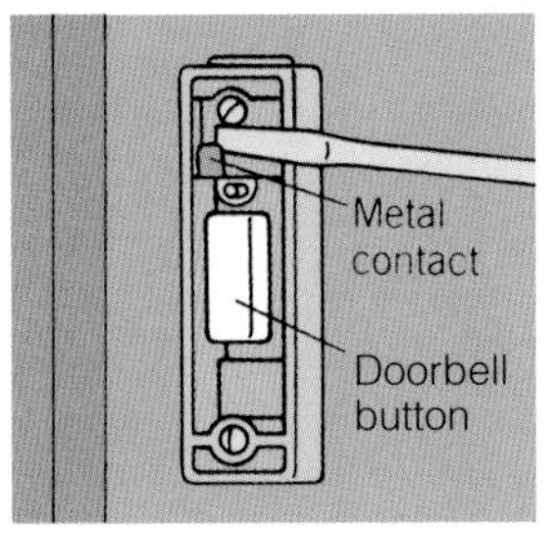

1 If the doorbell won't ring, remove the button cover and clean contacts with sandpaper; pry them up with screwdriver. If this fails, loosen mounting screws and pull out the button. Disconnect wires and touch ends together. If the bell rings, the button is faulty; replace it.

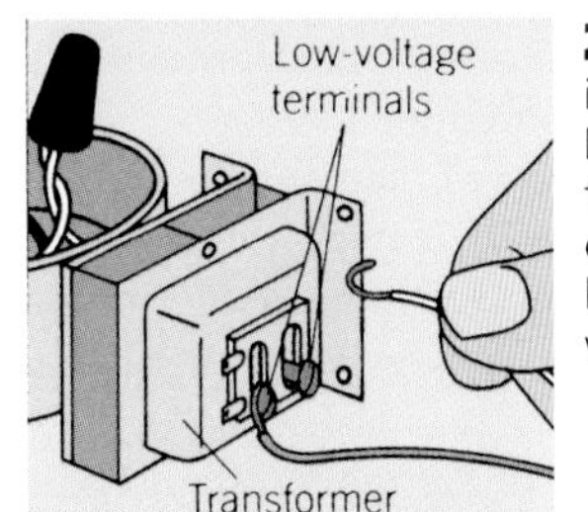

2 Turn off power when working at the transformer. Tighten loose wires at the bell or transformer. Wrap frayed wires with electrician's tape. To repair breaks, strip ends; join with wire connectors.

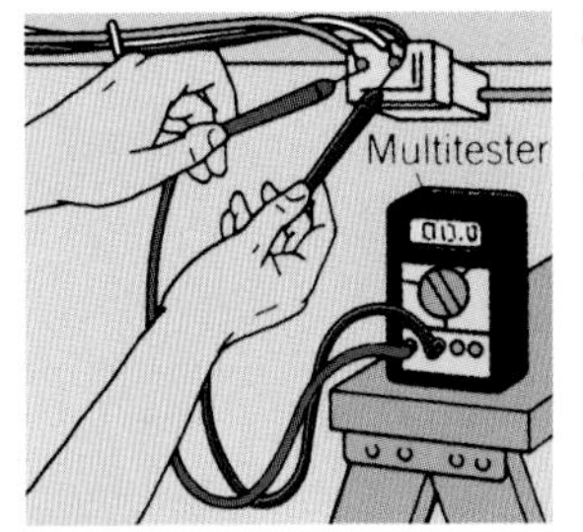

3 Test transformer by restoring power to its circuit. (Remember, incoming wires will be hot!) Set a multimeter to its AC volts scale and turn the dial to the 50-volt range. Touch multimeter probes to the transformer's low-voltage terminals. If the tester registers no voltage, the transformer is defective; replace it.

A Simpler Way

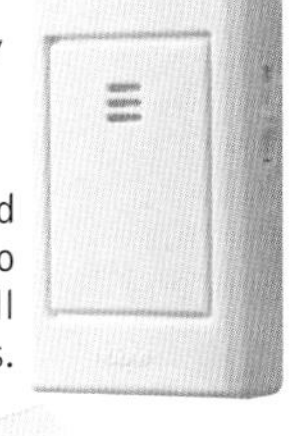

Wireless chimes offer an alternative to wired units. They can be used in new construction or to replace older units where wires inside the wall may be damaged or broken and hard to access.

The battery-powered push-button transmitter sends a radio signal to the battery-powered chime unit. Transmitter buttons cannot be mounted on metal surfaces that will interfere with signal performance.

ELECTRICITY

Home-security Systems

Homeowners have a multitude of security systems and products from which to choose. Some products are simple and only need a screwdriver for installation. Some systems are more complicated and require installing wiring. Always follow the manufacturer's installation instructions.

Security systems can be hardwired or wireless. **Hardwired systems** operate using low-voltage wire and circuits. Typical system components include the master control panel, backup batteries, control keypads, door and window sensors, motion detectors, smoke and heat detectors, a siren, a phone dialer and a key-chain remote control. Sophisticated systems may also include sensors for monitoring water intrusion, freezing temperatures and carbon monoxide.

A wireless system consists of many of the same components as the hardwired systems. However, the wireless system uses radio frequency signals to monitor the components, many of which are separately powered by batteries or plug into a receptacle outlet.

You'll also have a choice of alarms: A silent alarm automatically dials a police station or security company, often for a monthly fee, whereas on-site alarms may take the form of piercing sirens and flashing lights. A system may have both types of alarms.

Typical Home-security System and Components

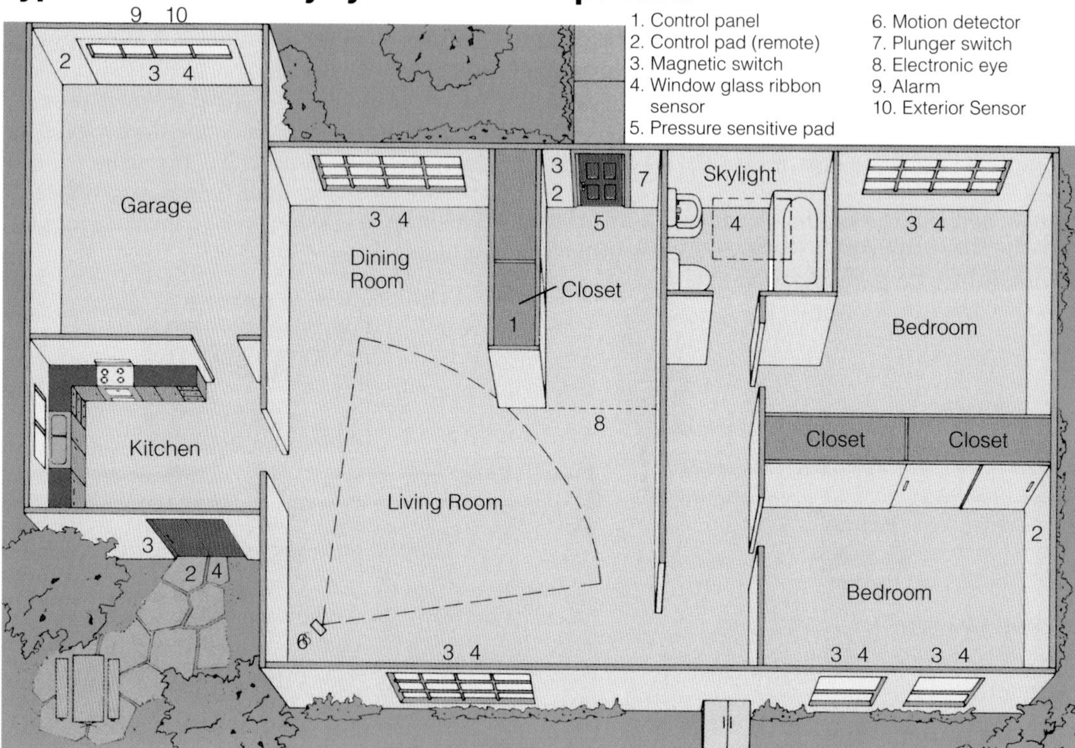

A Hardwired System

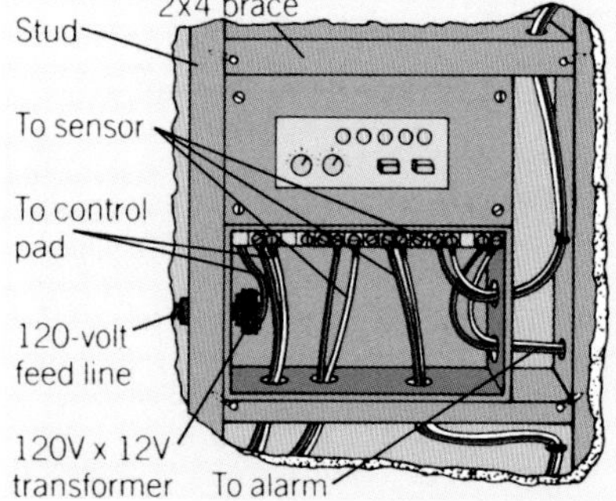

Place control panels in inconspicuous, secure locations. Carefully connect all components according to the manufacturer's instructions.

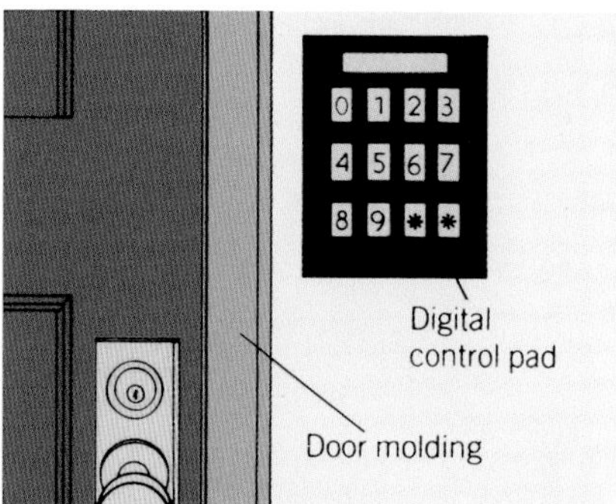

Position control keypads near all entrance doors. Allow a 30-second delay for entering and exiting without tripping the alarm.

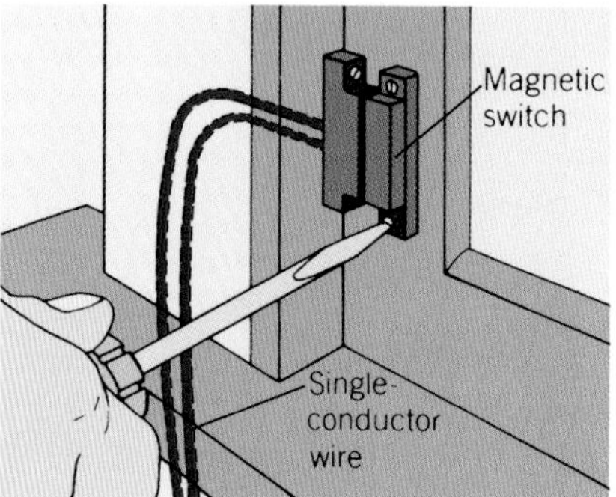

A magnetic switch keeps a monitored alarm circuit closed when a window is closed. When the window is opened, the circuit opens, triggering the alarm.

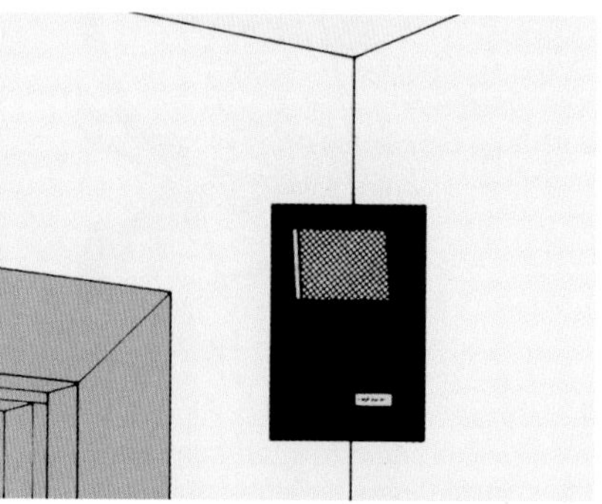

Passive infrared motion detectors protect large interior areas and hallways. An alarm is triggered when the monitored area is entered.

Home-automation Systems

Technology is advancing at the speed of light, and wireless technology is being used to make our homes very "smart." We are constantly striving to enhance the safety, comfort and convenience of our homes and to help save time as we scurry about in our daily activities.

Home-automation systems can integrate personal computers, handheld computers, communication systems, home network systems, audio and video systems, home entertainment systems, lighting controls, security systems, heating and cooling controls, appliance controls, garage-door openers and scores of other features and products that enter the marketplace on a continuous basis.

The X10 system is one communication language that allows compatible products, devices, controllers and components to talk to each other using the existing electrical wiring in a home.

Transmitter devices that are plugged into receptacle outlets or otherwise connected to the home's existing wiring send signals to receivers in other locations in the home that are also connected to the existing wiring. A lighting controller on the nightstand in the bedroom can turn on all the exterior lighting around the home's perimeter in case of emergency, simply by sending signals over the existing 120-volt wiring.

Home-automation Components

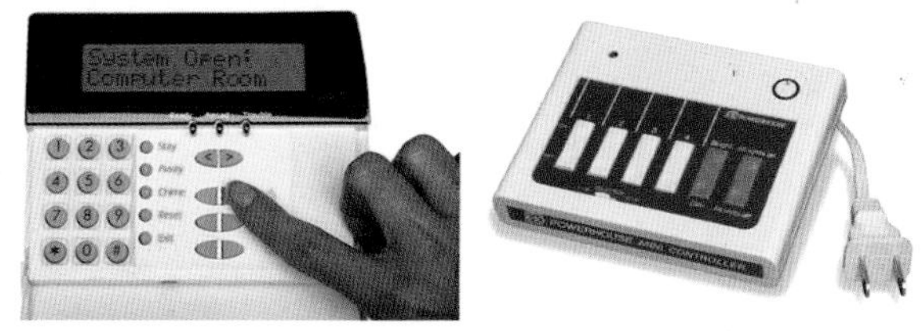

Wall-mounted keypads and remote minicontrollers allow you to control lighting, drapery, thermostats, alarm systems, communications equipment and other automation devices around the home.

Wireless wall switches allow you to operate lamps and other items via special transmitters plugged into receptacle outlets.

Home-automation System Options

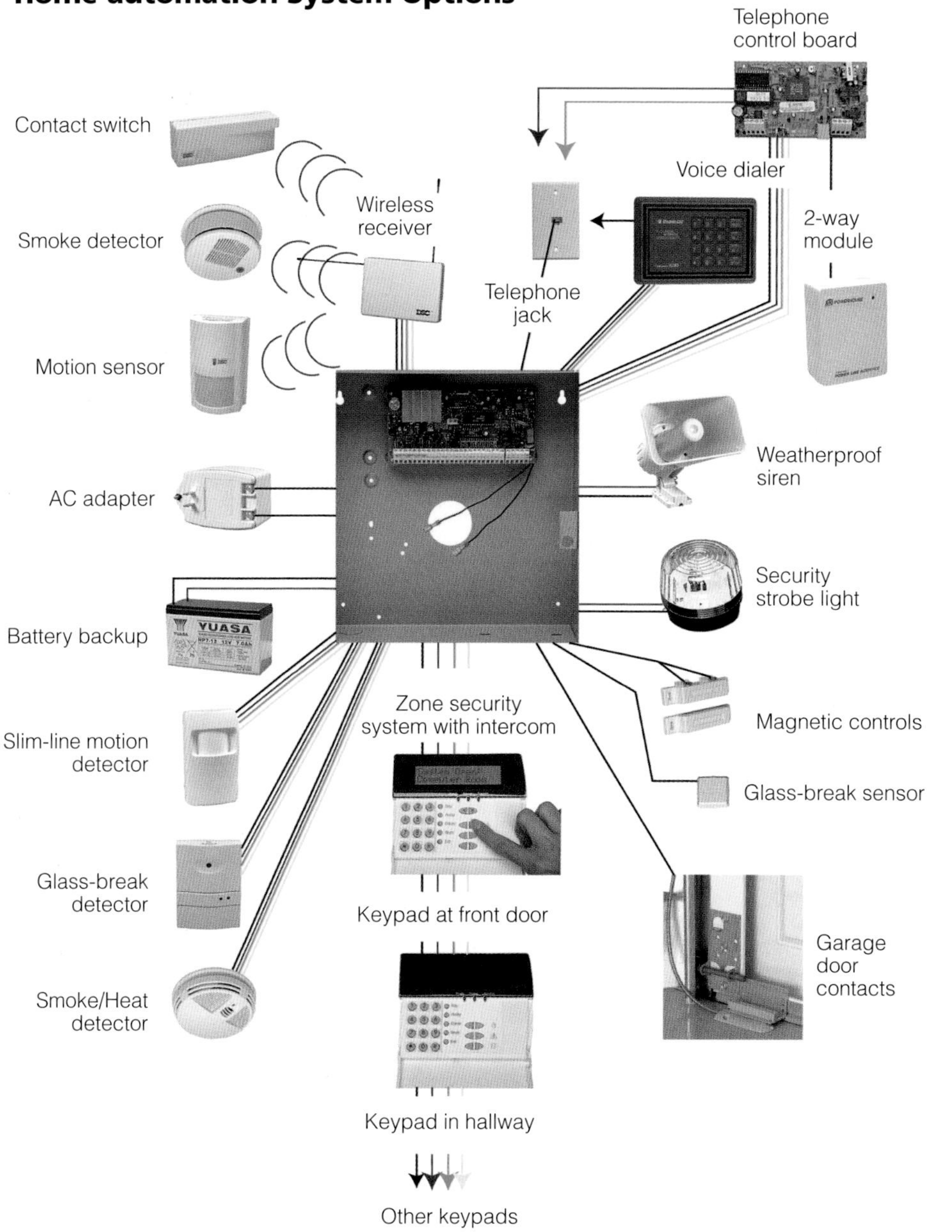

Telephone control board
Contact switch
Smoke detector
Wireless receiver
Voice dialer
Telephone jack
2-way module
Motion sensor
Weatherproof siren
AC adapter
Security strobe light
Battery backup
Zone security system with intercom
Magnetic controls
Slim-line motion detector
Glass-break sensor
Glass-break detector
Keypad at front door
Garage door contacts
Smoke/Heat detector
Keypad in hallway
Other keypads

Communication Wiring

Plastic Pipe **108**
Wire Strippers **133**
Fishing Cable **141**

The older phone wiring and coaxial cables in our homes are rapidly becoming outdated for supplying digital televisions and Internet connections with high-speed, high-performance connectivity.

Home-network-distribution systems can be installed in both new construction and during remodeling projects to help consolidate, simplify and organize all your audio, video, telephone and other systems in one convenient location. These needs can generally be handled by installing only two types of cable—Category 5e UTP (unshielded twisted pair) cable for voice and data, and RG-6 shielded coaxial cable for television or video. As your needs change, a central distribution system allows you to easily reconfigure, enhance or expand a system. Similarly, compatible devices can be connected in the distribution box by using "jumper" cables. The distribution system essentially connects all information outlets in each room directly to a central hub.

Buy high-quality cable and be sure to select a distribution box that will accommodate your expansion needs.

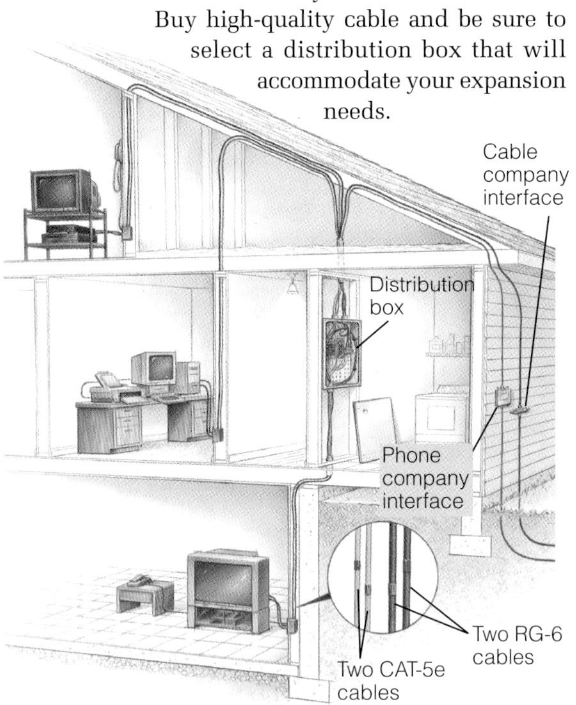

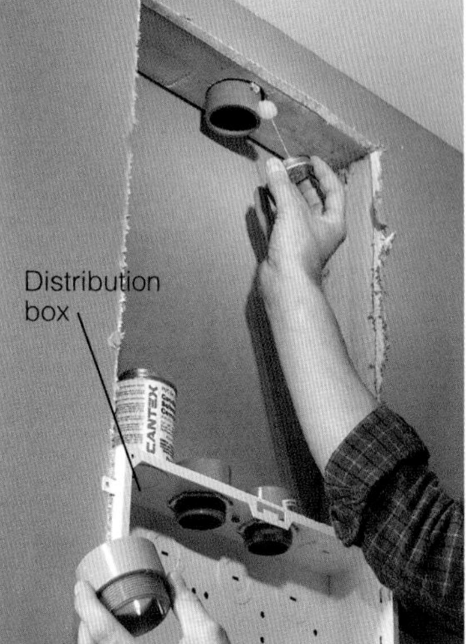

1 Install distribution box. Drill 2-1/2-in. holes in wood framing and install 2-in. PVC conduit sleeves for routing cables to attic and basement.

2 Install low-voltage open-back remodeling boxes at desired locations. Check for hidden obstructions inside walls before cutting holes for boxes.

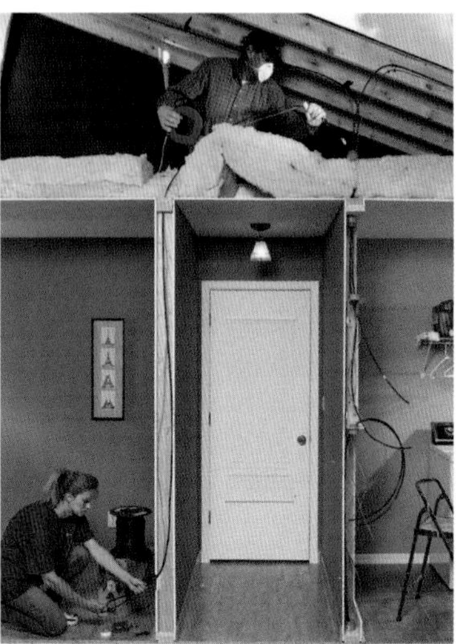

3 Fish cables from distribution box to outlet locations. Clearly identify or label cables on both ends. Leave extra cable length at all boxes.

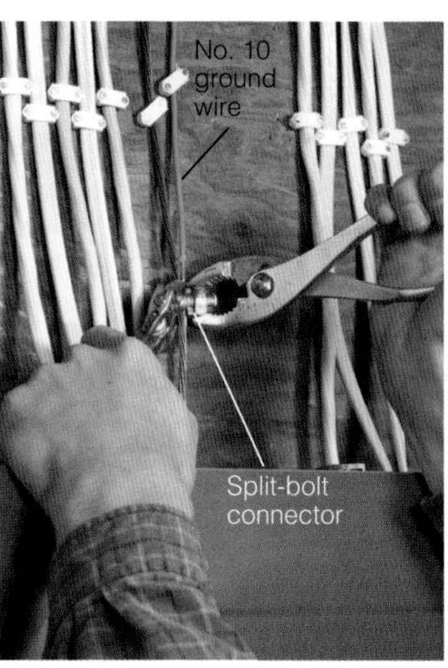

4 Install a ground wire from the distribution box to the main electrical service location in accordance with local code and manufacturer's instructions.

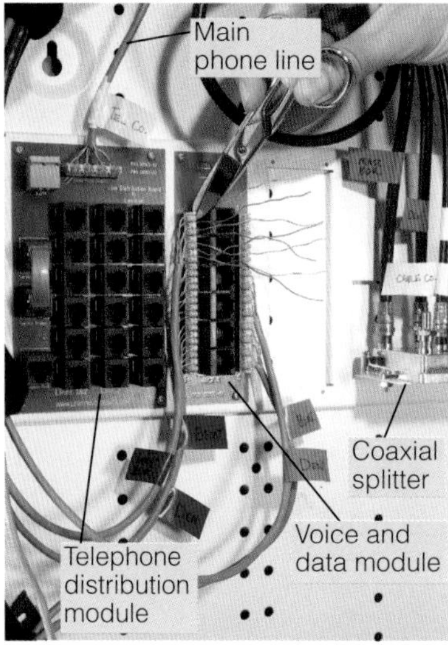

5 Neatly install cables and wires using appropriate connectors or terminals. To ensure good system performance, avoid sharp bends in cables.

Invest in the Future

With communication wiring and other systems in the house, you gain these options and home-theater systems.

- Transmit DVD, satellite or cable signals to multiple televisions.
- Network computers for file sharing and printing.
- Monitor closed-circuit televisions for home security.
- Install high-speed Internet connections in every room.
- Have unlimited telephone and fax capability for home offices.
- Improve whole-house audio and home-theater systems.
- Integrate fire and security systems.
- Monitor cooling and heating.
- Control lights and smart appliances remotely.

Older Phone Systems

Connecting CAT-5e Cable

To connect Category 5e cable, cut into the end of the cable with an electrician's scissors (don't use a knife). Pluck out the internal string and "zip" open a few inches (centimeters) of cable jacket. Carefully remove the jacket. Gently untwist the colored wire pairs and bend them into the terminals on the jack. Use a punch-down tool to terminate the wires. Snip off excess wire length.

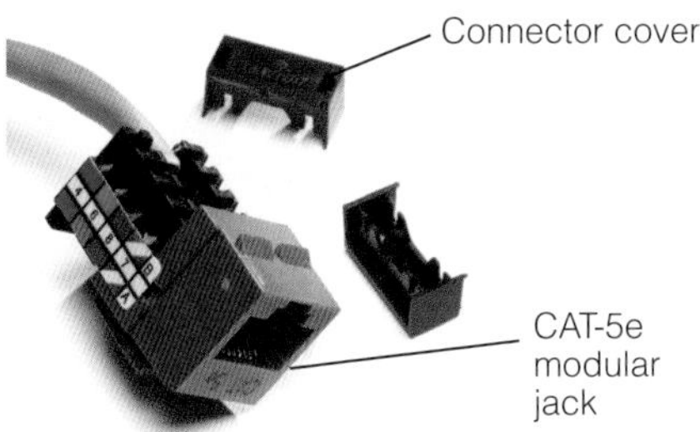

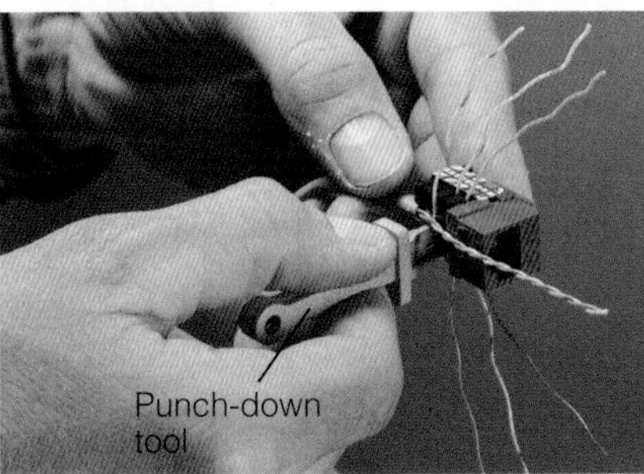

Connecting Coaxial Cable

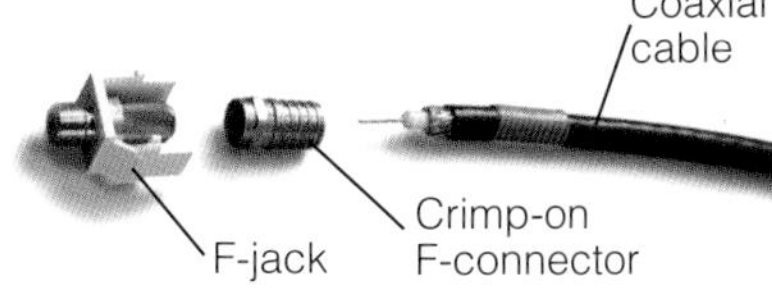

To connect coaxial cable, adjust the stripper, then spin it around the cable with 5/8 in. (16 mm) of cable projecting past the tool. Use your fingernails to expose the inner signal wire, white insulation and metal shielding. Push on the F-connector and crimp with the tool. Leave 1/8 in. (3 mm) of wire past the end of the connector. Screw F-connectors to F-jacks and snap into cover plate.

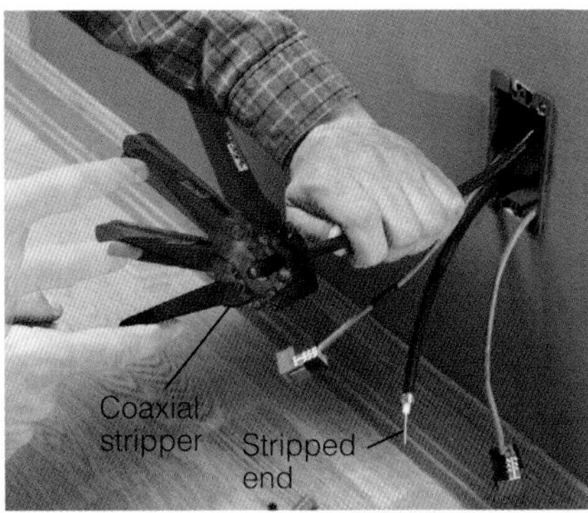

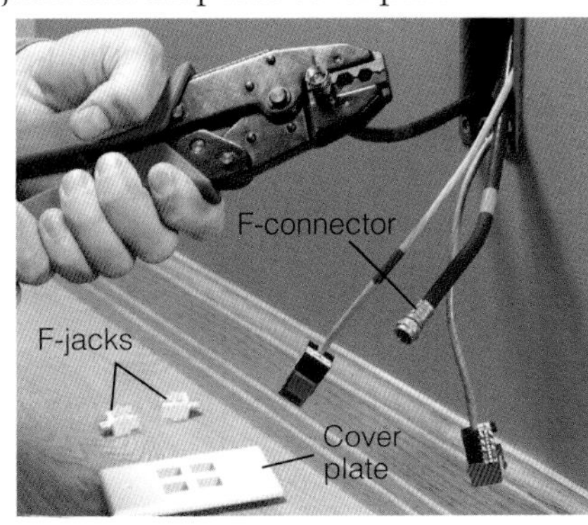

Replacing a Phone Jack

When your phone quits working or static develops on the line, your phone jack may need to be checked and replaced. Be careful and don't let the bare low-voltage phone wires touch each other.

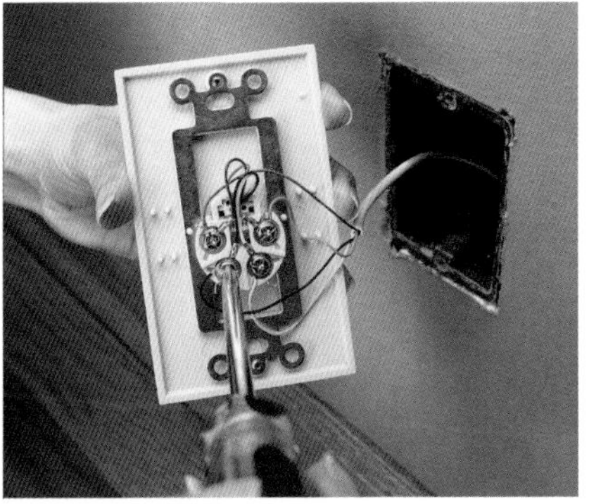

Checking. Remove screws and jack faceplate. Check wires for corrosion or nicks. Note color coding of wires, loosen screw terminals and disconnect old jack. Don't let the existing cable slip back into the wall.

Replacing. Match the color of the old cable wires to the wires on back of the new jack. Pinch each wire against back of new jack with your thumb. With needle-nose pliers, wrap each wire clockwise around the terminal screw.

Connecting New Phone to Old Jack

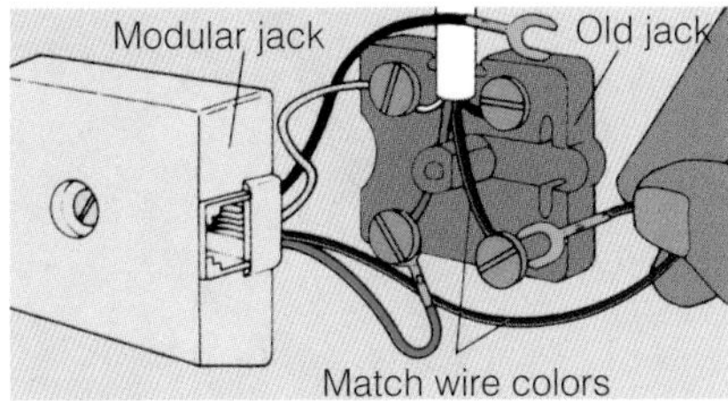

Modular connections make phone installations a snap. If your phone wiring is pre-1974, you can convert it to a modular system.

Adapters are available to convert old jacks to modular ones, switch old phones to fit modular jacks, turn one line into two to five lines and extend the length of a line without splicing it.

To connect a new phone to an old jack, convert the jack. At the terminals, cut the wires to the old phone. Leave house cable wires alone. Attach the modular jack's spade clips or caps to the terminals.

Adding Extensions

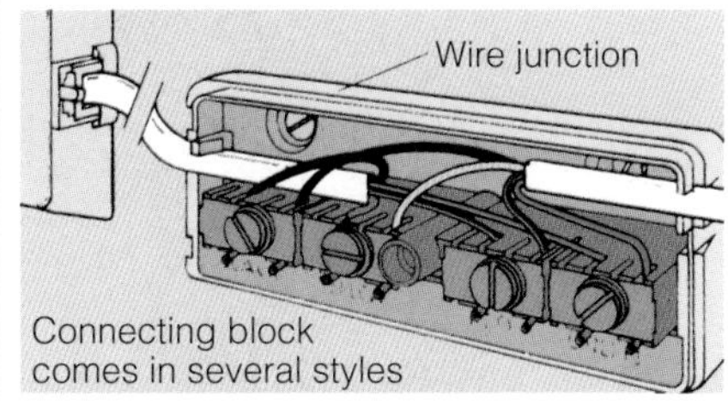

Determine the best route for running cable to the new phone location. Fish wiring behind walls and along floor joists, hide it in surface wiring channels or behind baseboards, staple it to the baseboard with insulated staples or rout a groove on the inside of the baseboard.

To add two or three extensions, install a wire junction box at the connecting block where telephone wiring comes into the house or at a jack for an existing line. To connect wires, follow manufacturer's instructions. To add as many as five extensions, install another wire junction box.

Antennas

You can improve or expand television reception, in some areas, by installing an antenna. Antennas will pick up VHF and UHF telecasts and FM radio transmissions as well.

Antennas are rated by mileage range and gain. Mileage range is the distance from which a signal can be pulled. Gain refers to the antenna's ability to increase the signal's strength.

The antenna you buy will depend on where you live. Different sizes of antennas are available for city, suburban or rural locations. Remote-controlled antenna directional rotors and signal amplifiers can be installed to improve reception. Install antennas and masts at safe distances from power lines. Carefully follow the manufacturer's instructions.

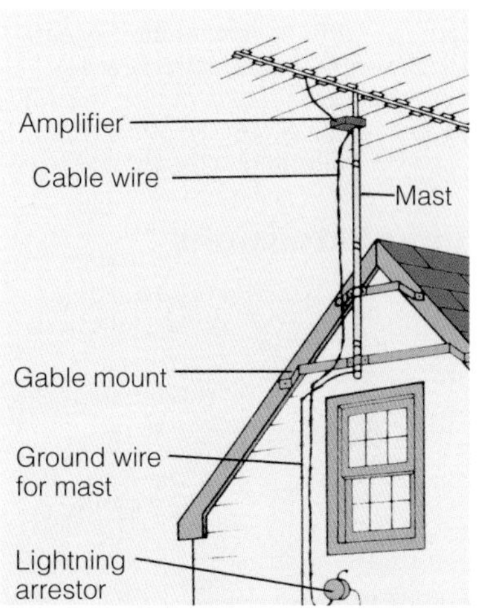

Assemble antenna, mast and lead-in wire before mounting. Run lead-in wire through row of standoffs spaced 1 to 2 ft. (30 to 60 cm) apart. Provide a drip loop in the cable. Install a lightning arrester and No. 10 AWG copper wire to the mast in accordance with the manufacturer's installation instructions.

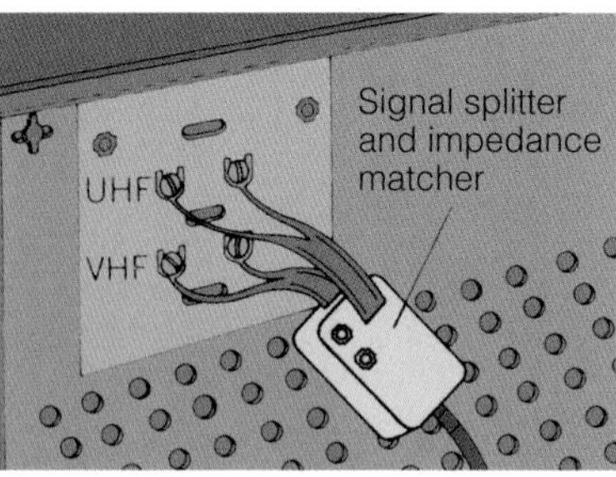

If needed, connect the lead-in wire to a signal splitter, which divides antenna signal into VHF, UHF and FM. Plug unused splitter outlet with terminator to prevent interference.

Dishes

No matter how remote your home, a satellite dish antenna and receiver allow you to watch your favorite programs. Dishes that had been the size of a tractor tire or larger are being replaced with dishes the size of a frying pan. In addition to television programming, satellite dishes can be used for Internet subscriptions.

A satellite dish must be positioned with a clear view of the southern sky, free from any obstructions, such as trees or other buildings. Although a homeowner can set up a system, most are professionally installed and tuned.

Azimuth (compass direction), elevation (angle up) and skew (dish rotation) angles must be properly set to receive clear signals.

Satellite dishes must be grounded according to local code requirements.

Satellite television systems are available for do-it-yourself or professional installation. Typical systems include the satellite dish, one or more receivers, infrared remote-control units and the necessary cabling, accessories and grounding components.

Lightning Protection

Lightning causes billions of dollars in property damage each year. It kills more than 100 people each year in North America alone and injures hundreds of others. Unprotected homes can be damaged by resulting fire, gas explosions or damaging electrical surges. Certified professionals can install lightning protection systems in accordance with national standards published by the National Fire Protection Association (NFPA) and Underwriters Laboratories.

Have your lightning protection systems inspected annually. Check for loose or damaged air terminals and ground rods, and make sure that the conductors are securely clamped and all their connections are tight.

To guard your appliances from lightning strikes, have a surge protector installed at the service panel and use portable surge protectors plugged into your receptacle outlets for protecting sensitive electronic equipment and appliances, such as computers.

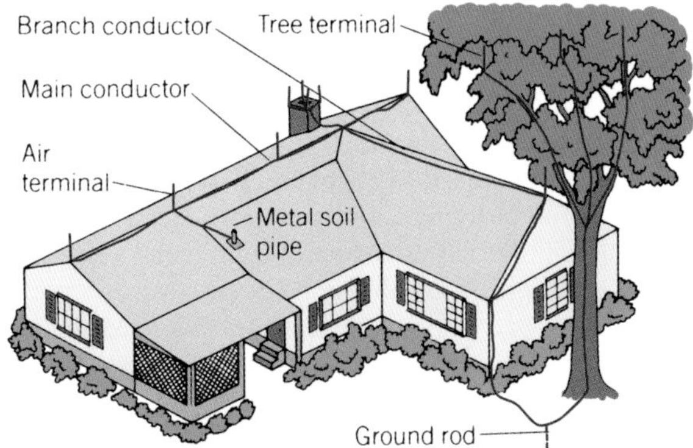

Lightning protection system. Air terminals are small metal rods placed about 20 ft. apart along high points on the roof. Braided copper or aluminum conductors connect the terminals to each other. All metal objects on the house are interconnected, such as vent pipes, gutters and aluminum siding. Air conditioners, plumbing, electrical and telephone systems are also connected to the main conductor or to branch conductors. At least two copper ground rods are driven into the ground at opposite corners of the house. These rods direct the massive electrical charge into the earth and away from the home.

Home Climate

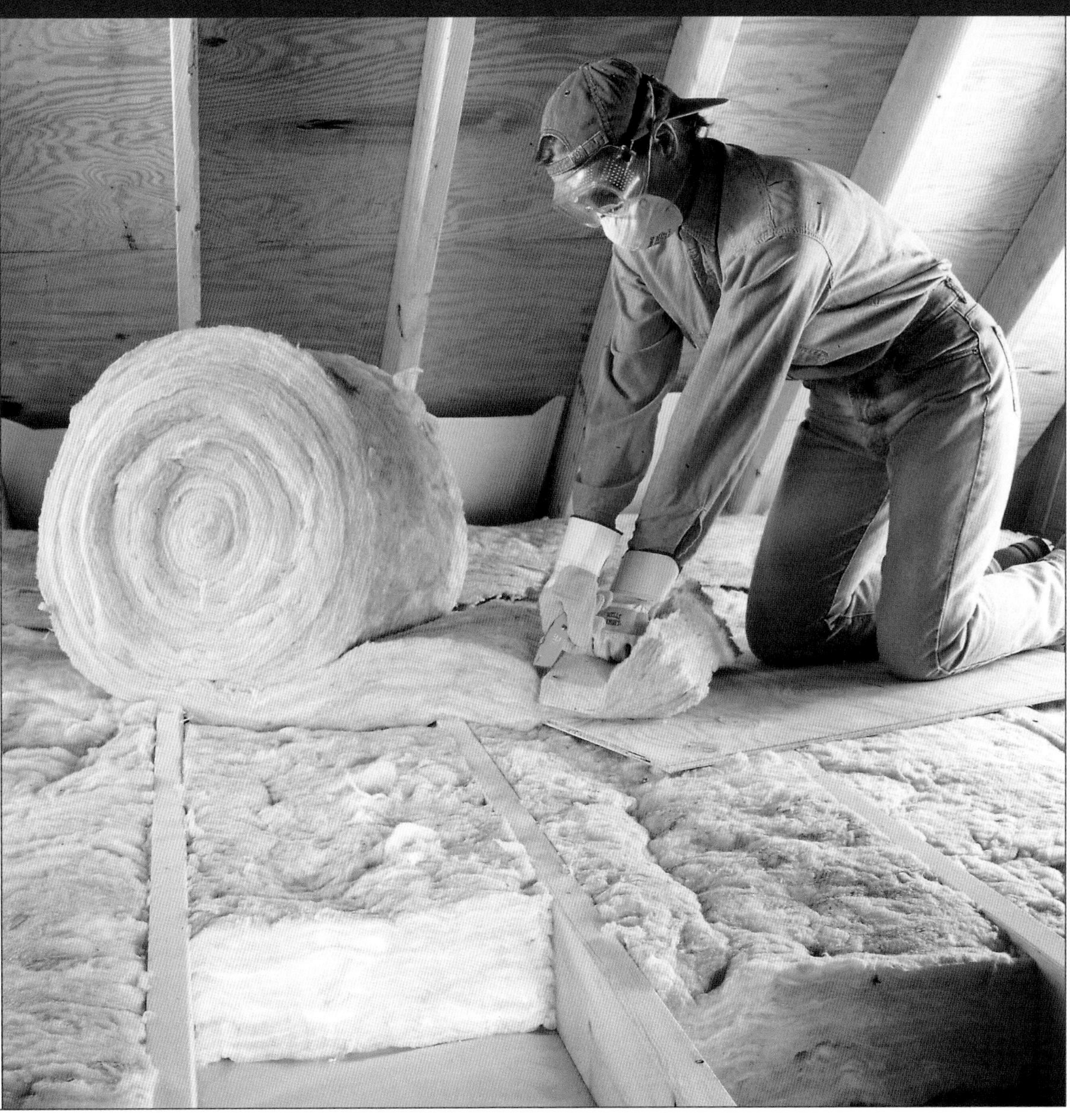

A More Comfortable Home

Attic Insulation and Bypasses **168**
Furnace Tune-up **174**
Replace a Thermostat **184**

Through frigid winter cold and sweltering summer heat, we expect our homes to keep us comfortable within a fairly small temperature range—around 72 degrees F (22 degrees C), give or take a few degrees. You can't change the weather, but there are factors you can control. A well-insulated, leak-free structure is the first goal. Properly sized and well-maintained heating, cooling and ventilation systems are close seconds. Energy-smart personal habits rank right up there, too.

For starters, see if your local utility company offers an energy-audit service to find out exactly where your home is losing heat. Or do your own audit by moving through your home and searching out all drafts, cold (or hot) surfaces, improper humidity and stale air.

When you've located your home's problem areas, get busy. This chapter is full of home-comfort ideas. Many low-cost, energy-saving jobs can be done in a weekend, with tools and skills you have, and provide measurable improvements. If you're remodeling or adding a room, seize the opportunity to make energy-saving improvements.

Common Causes of Cold Rooms

1. Register is closed.
2. Furnace filter is dirty or clogged.
3. Drapes and furniture block heat flow.
4. Ducts are clogged with debris.
5. Ductwork dampers are improperly adjusted.
6. Thermostat is located in a warm area.
7. Duct has too many bends or is undersized.
8. Too few or no cold-air returns exist.
9. Windows are drafty.
10. New addition is designed with too many windows.
11. Attic or walls are poorly insulated.
12. Floor over crawl space is cold.
13. Basement is cold.
14. No air chutes, or poorly installed ones, to vent the roof cavity.
15. Heat loss occurs due to leaks.
16. Floor is uninsulated.

Ways to Warm Up a Cold Room

1. Open heat registers.
2. Change the furnace filter.
3. Rearrange furniture and modify drapes to increase airflow.
4. Remove or vacuum debris as far as you can reach.
5. Adjust dampers for optimum airflow.
6. Close registers in close proximity to thermostat or move thermostat.
7. Install larger or more ducts, when possible.
8. Shorten door slightly or add louvers to increase airflow.
9. Caulk and weather strip; add storm windows.
10. Add supplemental heat, like electric baseboards and gas fireplaces.
11. Increase attic and wall insulation.
12. Insulate crawl space area.
13. Insulate rim joists and basement; add more heat registers.
14. Install attic vent chutes to reduce attic moisture.
15. Seal air leaks to attic.
16. Encourage better air mixing with ceiling fan; add pad and carpet.

Insulation and Air Leaks

What Is R-Value?

The capacity of an insulating material to resist heat flow is called its R-value. The higher the material's R-value, the better it insulates. Recommended R-values differ for various parts of your home and vary by region. Check with your local utility company or insulation manufacturer's literature.

Type	R-Value per Inch	Cost	Pros & Cons
Fiberglass	R-3.0 to R-3.8	Low	**Pros:** Easy-to-install batts press into place; made in standard stud and joist widths; available with Kraft paper facing attached. **Cons:** Can be irritating to installer's skin and lungs; susceptible to air gaps during installation.
Loose fill	R-2.2 to R-4.0	Low	**Pros:** Better coverage in irregular spaces and over trusses; can be poured or blown into walls. **Cons:** Messy to work with; quality can vary; lower R-value; can shift or settle; may need to rent insulation blower.
Extruded foam	R-5.2	High	**Pros:** High compressive strength; great performance underground. **Cons:** Cover with drywall or other fireproof material.
Expanded foam	R-3.8 to R-4.3	Medium	**Pros:** Lowest-cost among foams. **Cons:** Not for underground. Cover with drywall or fireproof material.
Sprayed urethane foam	R-6.0 to R-7.3	High	**Pros:** Makes a tough, seamless thermal and vapor barrier; covers irregular surfaces; adds structural strength **Cons:** Must be professionally applied. Very expensive. Cover with drywall or other fireproof material.

Note: To convert R-value to metric RSI values, divide the R-value by 5.679.

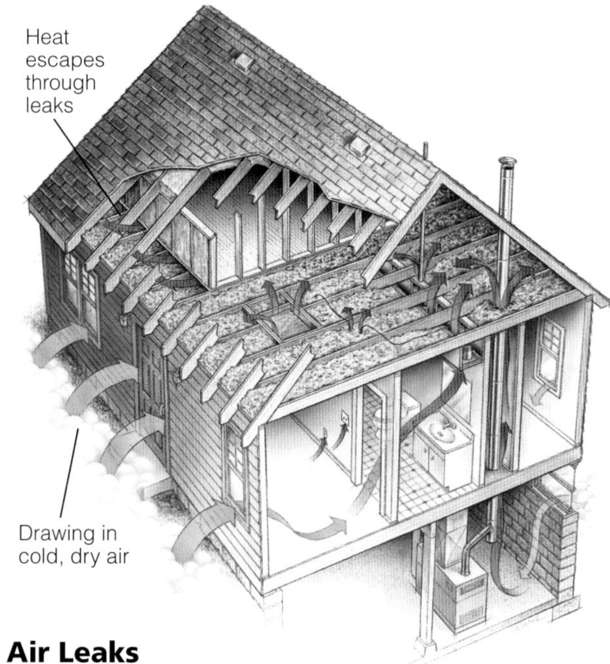

Air Leaks

The typical house has many small air leaks in the ceiling. Their area, when combined, can be equivalent to the size of a small chimney. The drafting this creates pulls heated air out through the attic and sucks cool air in from around windows and doors. This is also a primary cause of ice dams. Plumbing vents, open soffits, recessed lights, spaces between joists and the attic hatch are all areas that can benefit from sealing and insulating.

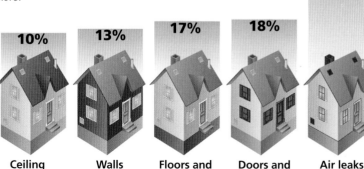

Where Energy Goes

To improve your home's energy efficiency while making the best use of your time and money, take a look at where heat loss typically occurs. Focus first on the simple steps that provide the biggest benefit. Air leaks—especially those in the attic—are responsible for the majority of a home's heat loss, followed by poor-performing windows and doors. Next on the list of energy wasters is heat loss through floors, foundations and basements. Since walls account for only about 13 percent of the heat loss in a house—and retrofitting wall insulation is difficult and expensive—this area may be lower on your priority list. Curbing heat loss through the ceiling is often the easiest approach, because attic insulation is inexpensive and easy to add.

10% Ceiling
13% Walls
17% Floors and basement
18% Doors and windows
35% Air leaks

Insulating Walls

Utility Knives 28
Drilling Large Holes 52

Properly installed wall insulation makes your home more comfortable year-round. In the winter, your home will be warmer with more pleasant humidity levels and, in the summer, your air conditioner will work more efficiently.

The best time to insulate is during construction or remodeling when you have clear access to the wall framing and gaps around windows and doors. Fill the cavities completely and seal all potential leaks. Do it right! Even small gaps can reduce energy efficiency by 25 percent. Note that fiberglass can irritate skin, eyes and lungs. Wear a long-sleeved shirt, long pants, safety goggles and a two-strap dust-particle mask rated for insulation.

Push batts into place and completely fill cavity, leaving no voids or gaps. Batts should be cut slightly longer and wider than the space to ensure a tight fit.

Split batts to fit around both sides of electrical wiring. Pull fiberglass batts apart at the desired thickness, press into place and rejoin.

Cut batts for installation by pressing a straightedge down on the batt at the desired width and use it to guide the utility knife. Remember to cut batts slightly oversize.

Cut batts in place by positioning the top and cutting to length against the bottom plate. Cut slightly long to ensure a tight fit.

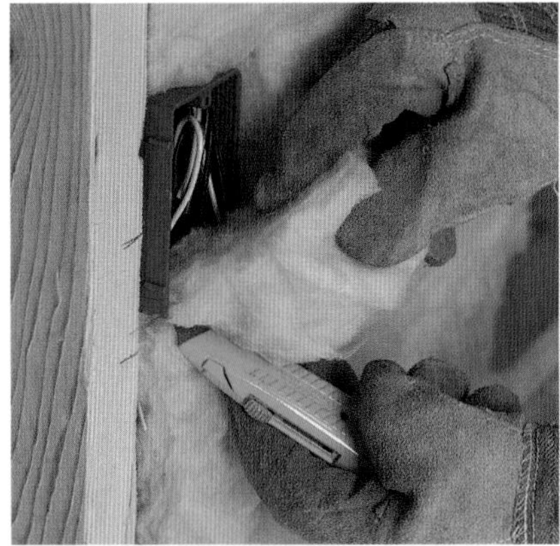

Split and cut to fit tightly behind electrical boxes. Slide the back half behind the box. Then closely cut the front half to fit tightly around the box.

Insulate around windows and doors by snugly tucking fiberglass into the back of the cavity, and then filling the remaining space with low-expansion foam.

Vapor Retarders

Vapor retarders, often referred to as vapor barriers, limit the movement of warm, moist air into the wall cavity, where it can lessen the effectiveness of insulation and can promote mold growth.

Plastic sheeting. Use 6-mil plastic sheeting to cover unfaced fiberglass batts. Overlap and tape seams to reduce air leakage. Fire-retardant and reinforced varieties are available.

Kraft-faced paper. Kraft-faced paper batts allow you to secure batts in individual stud cavities using a staple gun. It must be covered for fire-prevention purposes and isn't as effective or seamless as plastic sheeting.

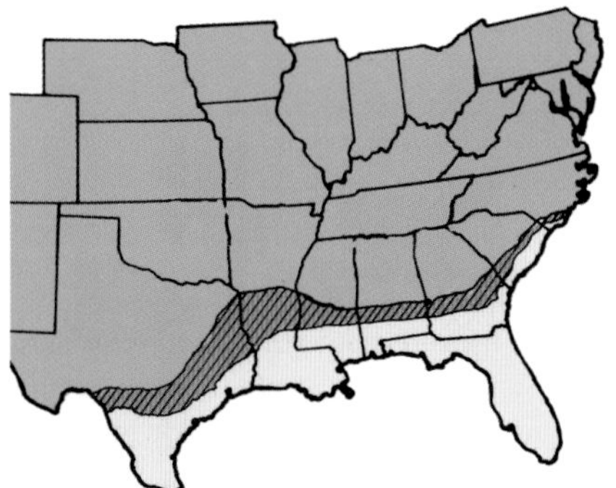

Vapor barrier zones. The green states and all areas north and west are cold climate zones that require an interior vapor barrier. Pink indicates fringe climates, and yellow indicates humid climates where an interior vapor barrier is not needed.

Blown-in Insulation

If your older house lacks wall insulation, you can add it by blowing it in. The basic procedure is to drill holes in walls, blow in insulation and plug the holes. Because of the mess, it's often better to work from outside. Some pros remove a single strip of siding and blow the top half of the stud cavity (it will usually stay put) followed by the bottom half. Others will drill two or more sets of holes. If your home is brick, you'll have to work inside. Stucco is hard to patch, so consider an inside job there, too.

Cellulose paper treated with a fire retardant is a common loose-fill insulation. It's sold at lumberyards and home centers, which will usually rent or lend you a blowing machine. When blown into walls at the proper density, cellulose can reduce air leakage as much as 33 percent. Make sure the product you buy is code-approved.

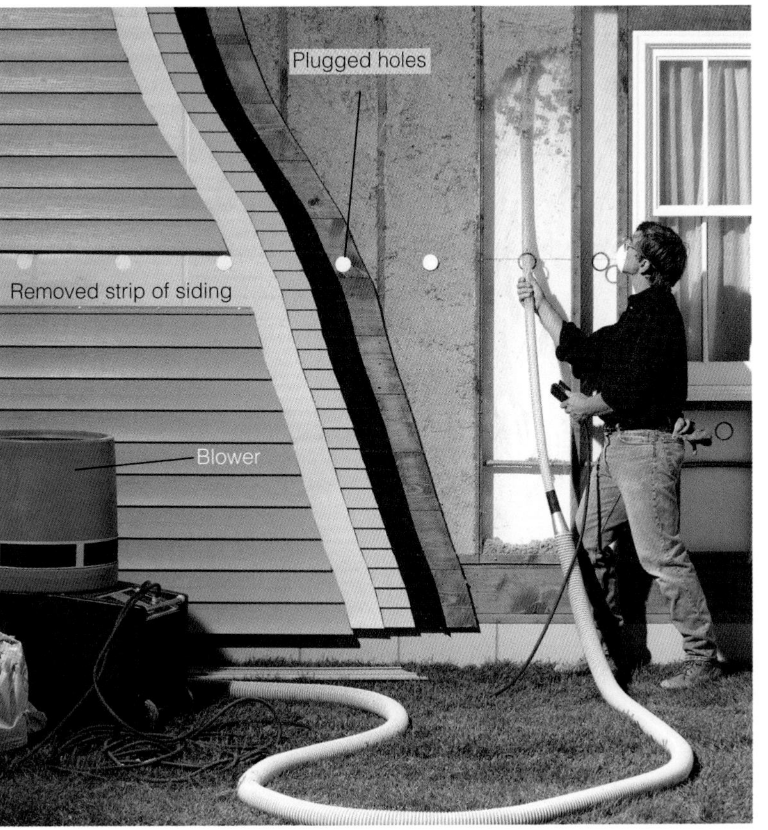

Drill access holes. Using a hole saw, cut holes in each stud cavity. Some pros remove a single strip of siding in the middle of each wall, blow the top half of the cavity first and then blow the bottom half. Others bore holes at the top and midpoints and blow insulation downward.

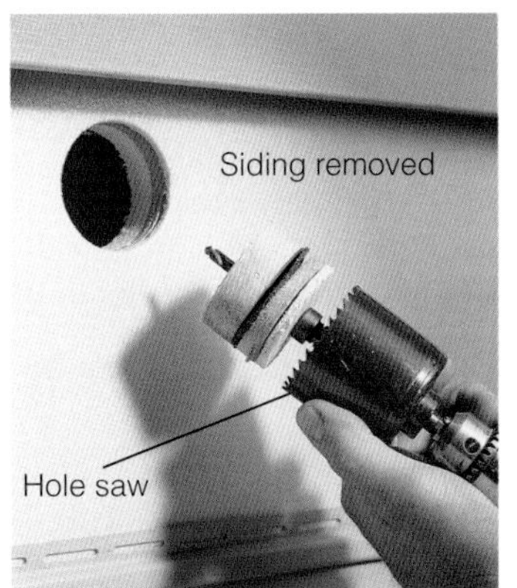

Plug holes. Tapered plugs are available in standard sizes to match your hole saw. If possible, choose cork or plastic plugs; they fit and seal better than wood. Tap in plugs until they're flush with the siding or wall sheathing. Caulk them in place for a tight seal.

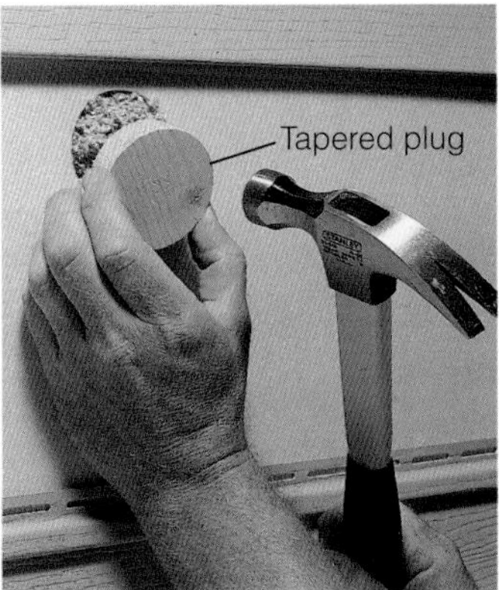

Crawl Spaces

To warm your feet, you can wear thicker socks, but a more permanent solution is to insulate crawl spaces. The standard procedure is to insulate ceilings of unheated crawl spaces and walls of heated crawl spaces. (Check with your building inspector about venting.) If you're using Kraft-faced batts in cold climates, install them with the paper up against the floorboards. Cut each batt oversize for a tight fit; then secure it in place using friction-fit insulation bands or staple wire mesh (chicken wire) or house wrap to the bottom of joists.

To ensure the effectiveness of insulation and prevent mold growth, keep it dry. Ground moisture is the main source of humidity in crawl spaces, so cover dirt floors with 6-mil plastic sheeting. Overlap generously and tape seams; hold edges down with bricks, long boards or other heavy objects.

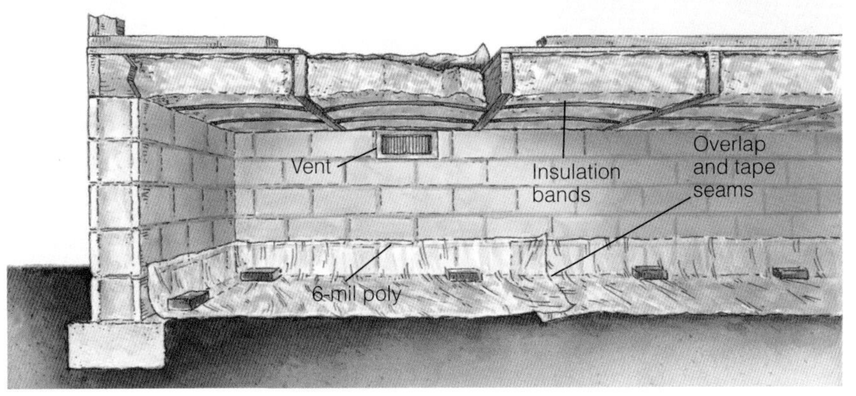

Attic Insulation and Bypasses

Safety Equipment 20
Staple Guns and Utility Knives 28
Adding a Roof Vent 323

It's dusty, dirty work, but sealing and insulating your attic is an extremely effective way to cut your energy bills. The average attic has gaps around pipes, chimneys, walls and light fixtures that waste your energy dollar.

For little money and a day's labor, you can seal these gaps. To find leaks, set a fan in an open window, aiming it to blow inward and sealing it tightly with tape and cardboard. Close all other doors, windows and ducts leading to the outside. Turn the fan on high to pressurize your house. Go into the attic to feel for drafts and look for insulation being blown around.

Vermiculite Insulation Alert

Some attics have vermiculite insulation—a lightweight, pea-size, flaky gray mineral—which may contain asbestos. Don't disturb it unless you've had it tested by an approved lab.

Plugging Large Holes

Put on protective gear and clothing, then seal any large open joist cavities and the areas above stairwells, soffits and dropped ceilings.

1 Cut a square piece of unfaced fiberglass batt, fold it into a plastic garbage bag, punch a few holes on the cold side, and stuff it into the top of each open soffit cavity.

2 Cut a larger rectangle of fiberglass batt, place it into a garbage bag, fold and stuff it into the joist space under kneewalls.

Sealing Flues and Chimneys

Insulate around furnace or water-heater flues to stop air leaks. The pipe gets hot, so install a heat shield to protect the insulation.

1 Cut aluminum flashing to fit around the flue, press it into a bead of latex caulk and staple it down. Overlap all the seams generously.

2 Create a collar to prevent insulation from contacting the flue: Cut slots and bend tabs in. Wrap the collar around the flue and staple it down.

Sealing Small Gaps

Seal openings around plumbing vent pipes and electrical wires with expanding foam. It works well, but it's messy stuff, so wear latex gloves.

1 Stuff strips of fiberglass batts into gaps as backing. Then follow the directions on a can of expanding foam to fill the gap completely.

2 Fill wiring and plumbing holes with expanding foam. Caulk around electrical boxes, fill the holes with caulk and replace insulation.

Weather Stripping Hatches

Seal the attic hatch door by installing foam weather stripping and using hook-and-eye fasteners to hold the door airtight.

Installing Insulation

Fill joist, rafter and stud spaces with fiberglass batts. In cold climates, install overlapping layers.

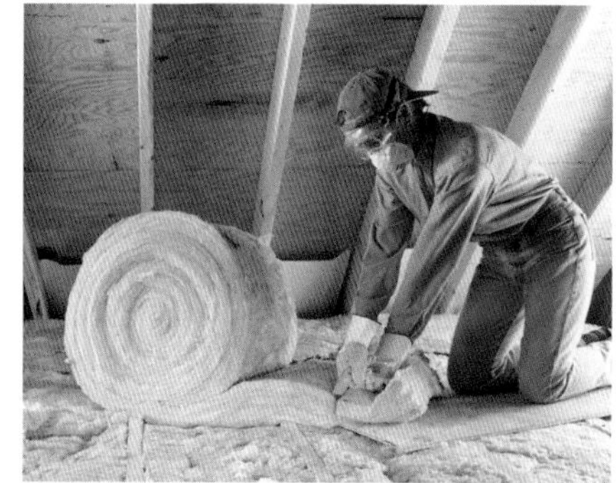

Attic Ventilation

Good ventilation helps dissipate attic moisture and hot air in spring, summer and fall. It curbs mildew growth and structural rot, extends shingle life, prevents ice dams and, in summer, reduces cooling costs. To create airflow, place vents in the soffits or low on the roof to let fresh air in and add vents at or near the ridge to let air escape. Most building codes require 1 sq. ft. (.09 sq. m) of screened venting for each 150 sq. ft. (14 sq. m) of attic, ideally split half and half between lower and upper roof vents.

Use air chutes over exterior walls to keep the airflow pathway open, and in winter, make sure roof vents aren't blocked by snow (use a snow rake, p. 331). In sunny climates, consult your local building inspector about adding a radiant barrier of shiny foil to the rafters' bottom edges to keep the attic cooler.

Soffit Vents

The standard way of providing lower roof ventilation is with soffit vents. Rectangular vents are easy to install anytime; continuous soffit vents are most easily installed during new construction.

Rectangular vents. Drill starter holes, cut an opening between rafters using a jigsaw and attach the vent with self-tapping screws. Angle the louvers toward the house to block snow and debris—and to look better, too.

Continuous vents. These allow an even ventilation along the eaves but are difficult to retrofit in existing soffits. Be sure to leave a strong strip of plywood on both sides, at least the width of your palm.

Roof Vents

Attic heat rises and escapes through roof vents. The best time to add them is during reroofing, but they can be added any time to improve ventilation.

Roof cans. These are best for hip and pyramid roofs with a short ridge line. To install, cut through the shingles and sheathing, slip the tops of the vents under shingles, nail them down in front and seal by cementing shingles over the side flanges.

Ridge vents. These blend into the roof, distribute ventilation evenly along the ridge and are frequently used for vaulted or cathedral ceilings. To install the type shown, cut and remove a strip of shingles and sheathing along the ridge, nail down the vent and cover it with ridge cap shingles.

Gable and Turbine Vents

Gable and turbine vents can be less effective than other methods at consistently moving air. Both depend on wind speed; gable vents are affected by wind direction, too.

Turbine vent. Mount these near the roof's ridge, on the least-visible side. When the wind blows, they spin and the turbine acts as an exhaust fan. They can be very effective but have a limited effect on hot, still days, and unbalanced units can be noisy.

Gable vent. These are inexpensive and they leave the roof uncluttered. However, they are poor performers, as they tend to circulate air only near the gables. They work much better when used to supplement other vents.

Bath and Kitchen Fans

Replacing a Bathroom Fan

If your bathroom fan is noisy, underpowered or broken, you can install a new one yourself. If access isn't a problem, the job can be completed in less than a day and requires only basic carpentry and electrical skills. While you're at it, upgrade to a new-generation fan—they're more powerful, more efficient and virtually silent. This job will reward you every morning with a quieter bathroom and a clear mirror.

You'll need basic hand tools, a power drill and a jigsaw. The basic steps include creating a larger opening, installing or retrofitting ductwork and installing the roof or wall vent.

1 Turn off power at the main panel. In the attic, unscrew the fan housing, detach old cable and disconnect wiring. Remove tape, clamps or screws securing the ductwork.

2 Hold the new fan housing in place. Check to make certain there are no obstacles. Cut or enlarge the opening with a drywall saw. Screw the housing to a joist and caulk seams.

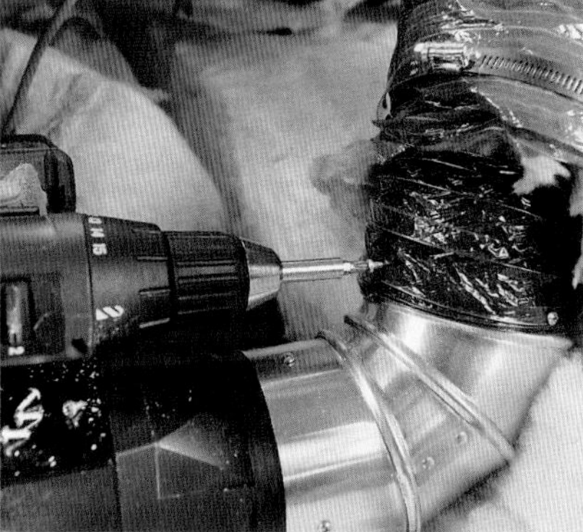

3 Screw an elbow to the fan's exhaust port using self-tapping screws. Attach flexible ductwork to the elbow. Use insulated ductwork to reduce noise and condensation.

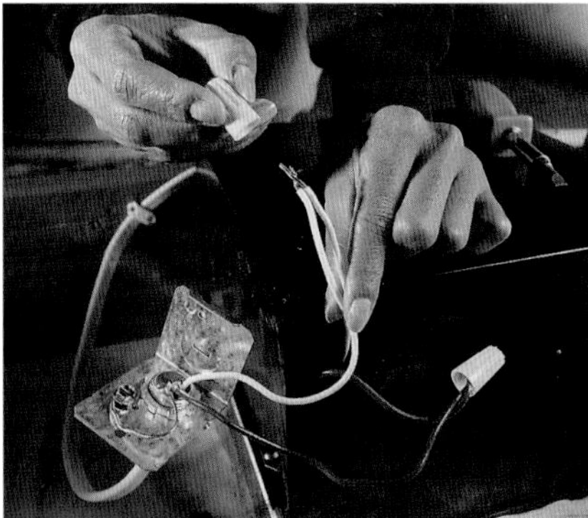

4 Remove the cover plate at the electrical splice box and pull out the wires. Twist the wires together and secure them with connectors according to the manufacturer's directions.

5 Enlarge the existing vent hole if required and pull the duct's end about 3/4 in. (2 cm) above the roof surface. Secure it to roof sheathing with sheet-metal screws and caulk around the gap.

6 Slide the new vent cap under shingles to check the fit. Remove, apply roofing cement to shingles where nailing flanges will rest and nail in place.

Range Vents

Vented kitchen-range hoods exhaust smoke, grease, heat, odors, combustion products and moisture generated by cooking. By installing a combination range hood/microwave oven, you can unclutter your counters and clear the air.

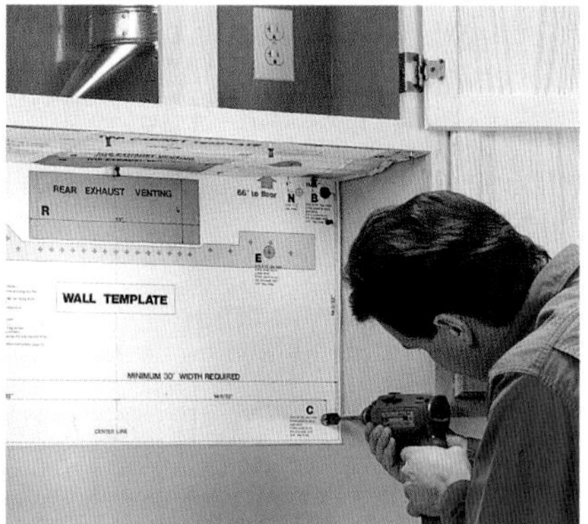

Drill mounting holes by following the directions and template supplied with the new vent. Electrical and duct connections are similar to bathroom fans.

Beware of Backdrafts

Studies show that the combination of a well-sealed, energy-efficient house, a high-volume kitchen exhaust fan and certain combustion appliances can be dangerous. Powerful exhaust fans can move so much air that they can pull dangerous furnace and water heater combustion gases down the chimney and into your living space. Two possible solutions are to provide a dedicated combustion air supply to the furnace room or install sealed combustion equipment that brings in its own combustion air.

Dryer Vents

Replacing a Dryer Vent

A defective dryer vent can allow drafts, bugs and mice into your home. In less than an hour and at a reasonable price, you can replace it with a sturdier unit that is easier to clean, seals out vermin, reduces the risk of fire and saves energy.

1 Remove the old vent by unscrewing the four corners. Pull out the vent far enough to access the hose clamps and loosen them. Vacuum lint from the old duct.

2 Connect your old ducting to a metal duct collar and insert that into the bottom of the new elbow. Caulk the new elbow mounting base and screw it to the house with galvanized screws.

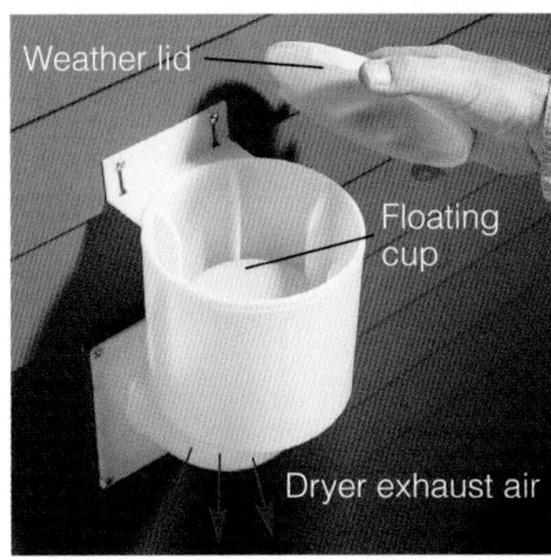

3 Slide the vent body onto the elbow and screw it to the house with galvanized screws. Drop the vent closer, or cup, onto the vent body and add the weather lid. Clean every 90 days.

Heat-recovery Ventilators

Tightly built homes can experience problems with lingering odors, stale air and high humidity, resulting in damaging condensation. Generally, these problems can be solved with ordinary ventilation or by cracking open a window. If you live in a moderately cold climate with high utility rates, and conventional methods don't solve your problem, your home may be a candidate for a heat-recovery ventilator (HRV), also called an air-to-air heat exchanger.

Compared to opening a window, an HRV provides continuously controlled ventilation. Heat from stale exhaust air is used to temper the incoming air so fresh air enters your home closer to room temperature; about 70 percent of the heat is transferred. The air streams don't mingle or contaminate one another, but weave and bypass one another through a series of chambers. Operating costs are about the same as those for a 100-watt lightbulb.

Most HRVs are designed to ventilate the entire home. Typically, four to eight supply-and-return ducts connect to the HRV. The ideal system exhausts air from moisture-laden rooms, such as the kitchen, bathrooms and laundry room, and dumps the fresh air into a closet, hallway or other space where the cooler air and increased movement won't affect comfort. Adding this kind of whole-house ventilator can be expensive and is normally done by a professional.

It is also possible to install a small, plug-in, single-room HRV on an exterior wall or in a window. Some models include multiple filters that clean the air as well. For the most effective air mixing, install a wall-mounted unit high on an outside wall, but avoid mounting it up against the ceiling. Keep it away from thermostats and seating areas, in a spot where some fan noise and cool air movement won't be a bother.

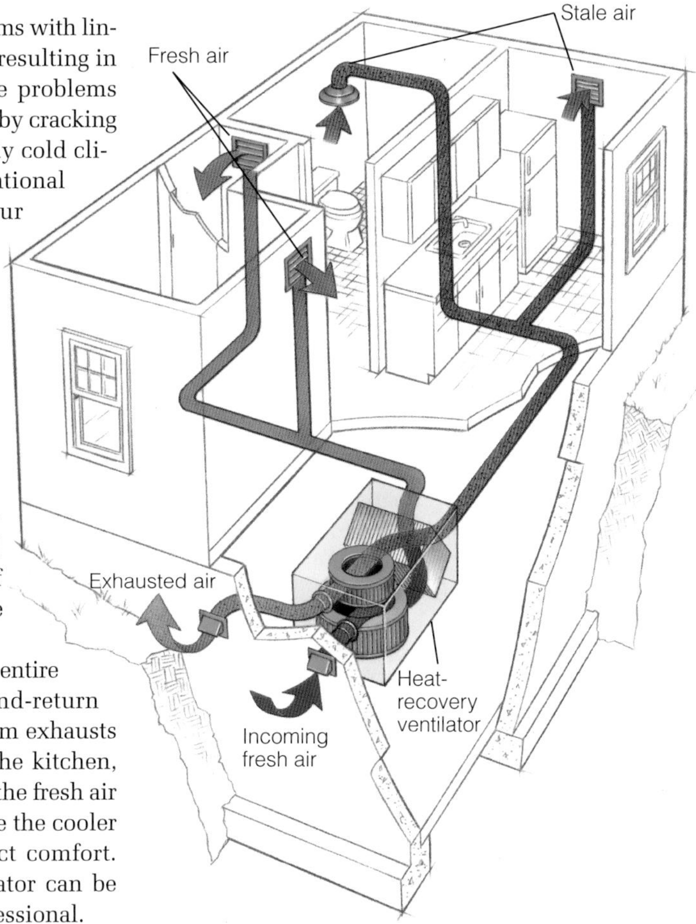

How a heat-recovery ventilator works. In an HRV, one fan exhausts stale, moisture-laden indoor air while another draws in fresh outside air. Both air streams pass each other, separately, through a core of many thin metal or plastic surfaces. As it passes through the core, exhaust air from the house transmits its heat through core walls or fins to the cooler outside air coming in. A heater can be added to a supply duct in some systems to further warm the incoming air during severely cold weather. In summer-operating mode, HRVs work in reverse. A drain carries away any condensate.

Whole-house Heating Systems

Heating systems convert fuel or energy into heat and distribute it throughout the house. Regardless of the type, they all do the same job: keep our homes warm and comfortable. Heating systems differ mainly in the fuels they use and in the ways they generate and distribute the heat.

The most common whole-house systems are warm air and hot water. In both cases, air or a liquid is heated in a furnace or boiler and sent to the various parts of the house through ducts, pipes or tubes. The heated air in a warm-air system is blown into the rooms through ducts and registers. In hot-water systems, water or steam heats radiators, convectors or even the house's floors, ceilings or walls; these in turn give off their heat to the rooms. The furnace of a warm-air system and the boiler in the other systems have a burner that can be fueled by gas, oil, propane, butane, electricity, even wood or coal, depending upon their availability and the local preference. Other systems heat the home entirely by electricity, as in electrical radiant heat and baseboard convectors.

Heat pumps extract heat from outside air and pump it indoors. Solar panels, fireplaces, wood-burning stoves and space heaters are also used. Generally, these heat sources provide auxiliary heat to supplement a whole-house system, although they may be all you need in warmer climates where only occasional heating is required.

One or more thermostats control a whole-house system. The thermostat may also perform other functions, such as controlling the forced-air system blower fans or hot-water system valves.

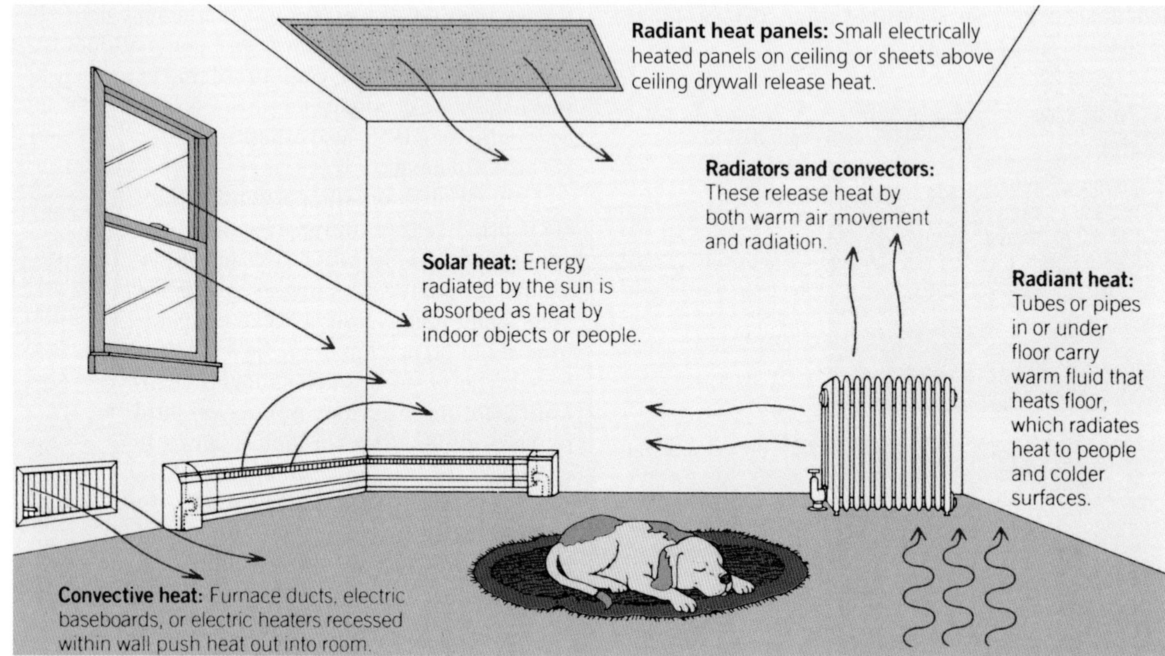

Radiant heat panels: Small electrically heated panels on ceiling or sheets above ceiling drywall release heat.
Radiators and convectors: These release heat by both warm air movement and radiation.
Solar heat: Energy radiated by the sun is absorbed as heat by indoor objects or people.
Radiant heat: Tubes or pipes in or under floor carry warm fluid that heats floor, which radiates heat to people and colder surfaces.
Convective heat: Furnace ducts, electric baseboards, or electric heaters recessed within wall push heat out into room.

Common Heating System

System	Heat Delivered By	Most Common Fuels	Means of Distribution	Pros	Cons
Warm air	Forced convection blower	Natural gas, fuel oil, propane, or electricity	Ductwork from furnace, electric heaters mounted on exterior walls or recessed into interior walls	Can also filter, humidify and air-condition. Rooms heat quickly. Wall heaters are inexpensive.	Large ductwork required. Fans can be noisy, can circulate mold and other allergens. Require regular filter changes.
Hot water	Convection, or convection and radiation	Natural gas, fuel oil, propane, or electricity	Pipes and convectors or radiators	Efficient and quiet. Holds steady temperatures. Boiler can be small.	Slower temperature rise. Radiators or convectors take floor or wall space.
Steam	Convection, or convection and radiation	Natural gas, fuel oil, propane, or electricity	Pipes and radiators	Efficient and hot. Warms rooms quickly. Boilers can be small.	Can be noisy. Radiators can be hot to the touch. Boiler systems are tricky to maintain.
Radiant heat	Radiation, or radiation and convection	Gas, oil, propane, butane for floor systems; electricity for ceiling systems and exposed panels; wood and coal for stoves	Pipes or tubes in or under floors, wiring within plaster or above wallboard, panels mounted on ceilings or walls, firebox and flue pipe for stoves	Quiet, even heating. Embedded systems make floors pleasantly warm. Hydronic systems can use most-efficient energy source or fuel.	Slow to warm up and cool down. Expensive to install initially. Embedded elements or pipes are very difficult to repair.

Forced-Air

Forced-air systems are relatively inexpensive to purchase and easy to maintain, making them one of the most popular types of whole-house heating. Because their design includes air ducts throughout the house, you have the option to add whole-house air-conditioning, humidification and air cleaning to the system.

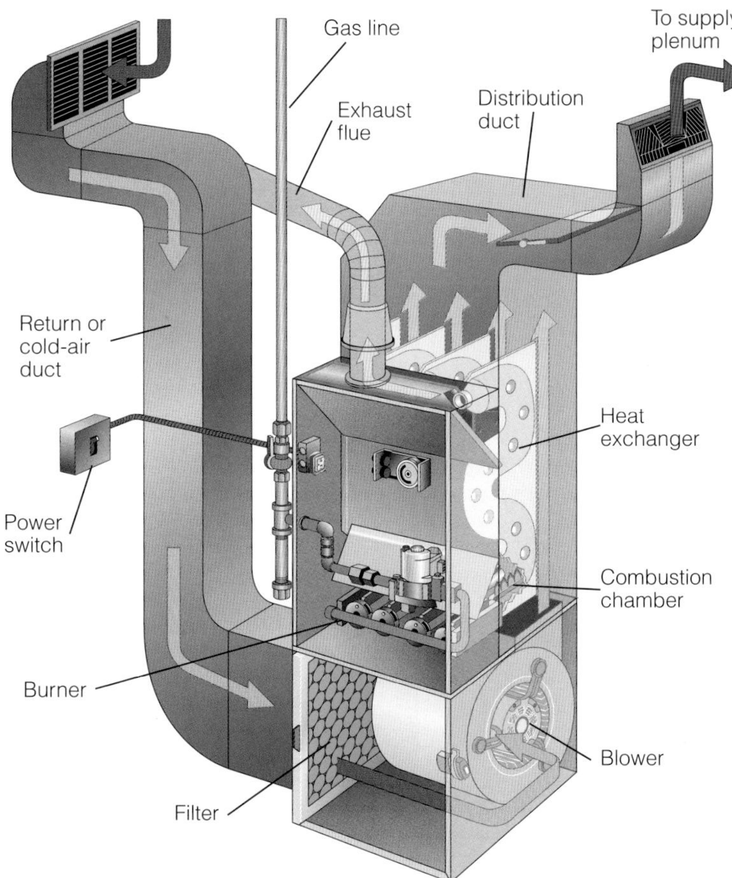

How a furnace works. The thermostat sends a signal to the burner located inside the combustion chamber, which heats the outside of the heat exchanger. When the heat exchanger gets hot, the blower starts and pulls cool air into cold-air registers, through the cold-air return ducts, to the furnace. The return air goes through a filter to keep the blower clean. The air then passes through the inside of the heat exchanger, where it is warmed, safe from the burner combustion gases, which exit through the exhaust flue. Warm air is carried through the supply plenum and distribution ducts to warm-air supply registers in rooms.

A forced-air system contains five main elements: a furnace, a network of distribution ducts, registers on walls or floors, an exhaust flue and a thermostat. A motor-powered blower circulates air through the system. A few old furnaces still use gravity circulation, which relies on the natural convection created by the buoyancy of hot air and the fact that cold air falls. These systems have larger ducts and no blower.

Homes with ductwork can leak noticeably more air and require more heating and cooling energy than homes without ductwork. The reason is that forced air creates pressure differences within the house that can draw in outside air, force air out through cracks in the house or pull outside air in through cracks in the house, all of which waste heat.

To make sure your warm-air system works efficiently, clean or replace the filter regularly and follow the furnace tune-up steps on the following pages. Also, be sure your system has enough return ducts—at least one per level. In addition, seal all seams in ductwork, and insulate ducts in unheated spaces. For improved comfort, adjust dampers and registers to balance heat distribution. Some furnaces and thermostats allow you to run the blower constantly at a low speed. It costs more for the electricity to run the blower, but your house will be more comfortable and evenly heated, and your burner may run less.

High-efficiency Furnaces

Top-of-the-line furnace models can operate at very high levels of efficiency—95 percent or more. Their design features a second heat exchanger to draw usable heat from the exhaust gases. The cooler exhaust gas can then be routed through a small vent, often of PVC pipe, through an outside wall—no conventional chimney is required. They also have a sealed combustion chamber and draw air from the outside, rather than inside. The downside is that the initial cost is greater and extra water-condensate from the exhaust must be piped or pumped to a drain.

Furnace Tune-up

Bending Metal 468
Cutting Metal 469

When it comes to furnaces, an ounce of prevention truly is worth a pound of cure. Simple maintenance will cut heating bills, prolong furnace life and make your home warmer and safer. To help prevent furnace trouble, follow these simple steps that will keep it in top shape. This maintenance operation normally takes an hour or two and costs only a few dollars, which is pretty inexpensive insurance. Put it on your calendar each year, at least a month before the heating season begins.

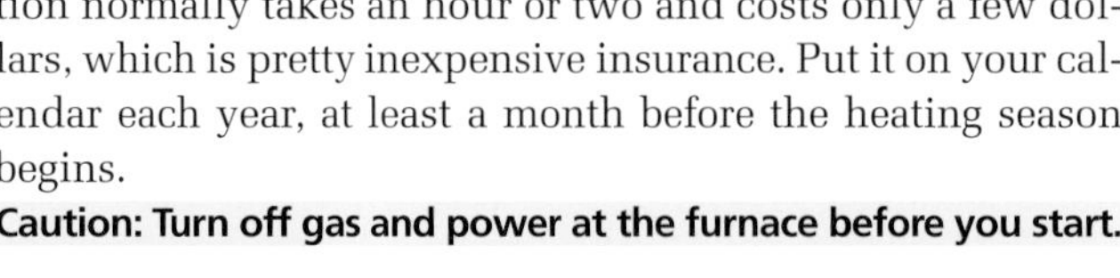

Caution: Turn off gas and power at the furnace before you start.

Safety First: CO Alarms—Get One!

Install an approved carbon-monoxide alarm near sleeping rooms on each floor and test them regularly. They are inexpensive, so don't wait. Carbon monoxide is a colorless, odorless gas sometimes produced by malfunctioning flues and fuel-burning appliances, such as oil-, gas- and wood-burning furnaces, stoves and fireplaces. If carbon monoxide spills into your home in high enough concentrations, it can be fatal. Plug alarms into outlets or directly wire them into the electrical system. Position alarms on walls, away from drafts and solvents.

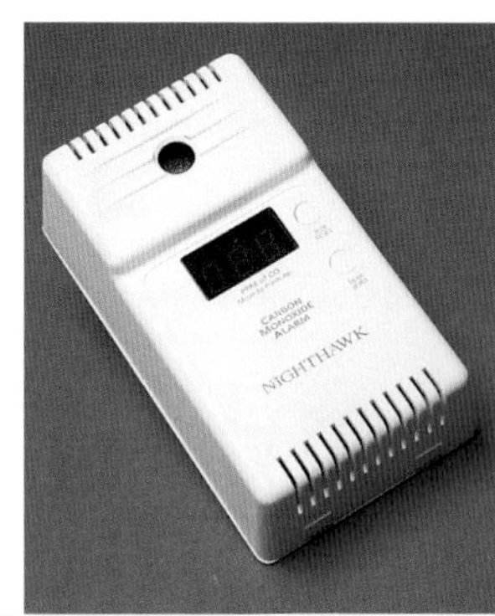

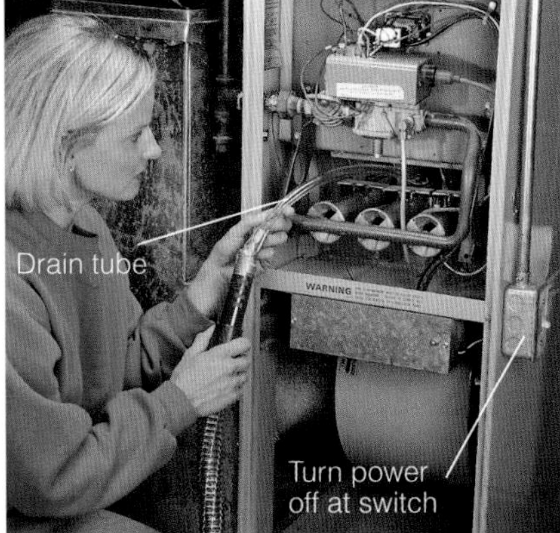

Vacuum burners and furnace base. With electrical power and gas off, vacuum the burners and the furnace base. To reach way in back, tape a drain tube to the vacuum hose.

Clean blower blades. Remove bolts holding the blower in place, lift the blower out and use a vacuum and small brush to clean the blades. Take care not to stress wiring or disturb fan blade counterweights.

Change filter. Change the filter every one to three months. Inexpensive fiberglass filters will protect the blower and blower motor; check the manual before installing more restrictive, higher-efficiency filters.

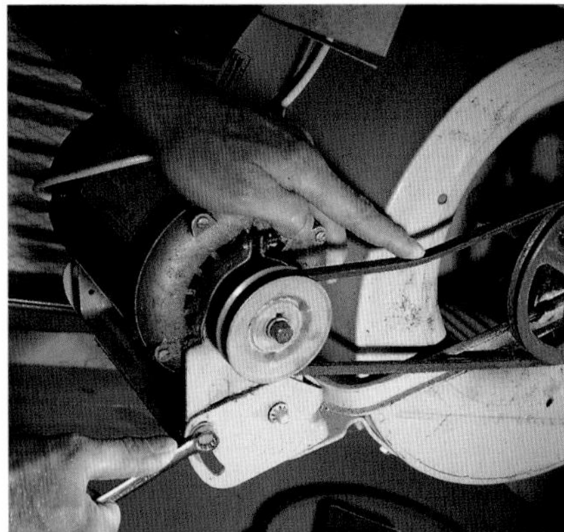

Inspect belt. Belts need periodic adjustment or replacement. Inspect for cracks or frayed areas. Tension a new belt so that it deflects about the thickness of a finger.

Oil bearings. Some older furnaces have two motor and two blower shaft bearings that need oiling every year. Clean around oil caps, remove and apply two to three drops of oil—but no more!

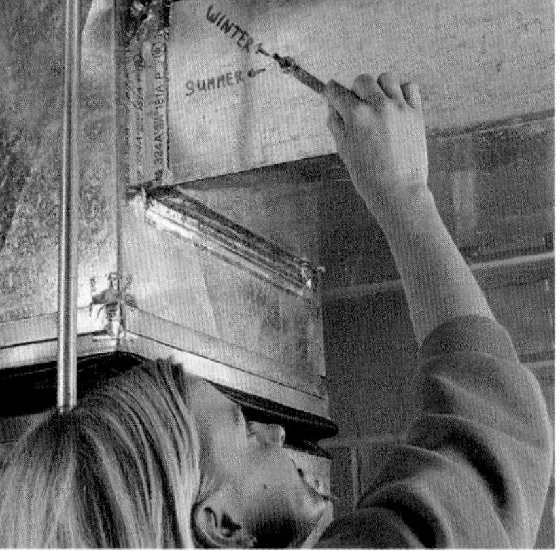

Adjust dampers. If your ducts serve both heating and air-conditioning duties, they may have marked settings for seasonal adjustments. Rotate the damper handles to adjust.

Seal leaky ducts. Special metal tape is available for sealing leaky ducts. High-temperature silicone works, too. Return air ducts are especially important to seal.

Ductwork

Working with Round Ducts

Round ductwork comes in preformed but unconnected sections. You can cut it before snapping the edges together or cut it in the round, as shown below. Gloves are a must when cutting, shaping or installing any ductwork.

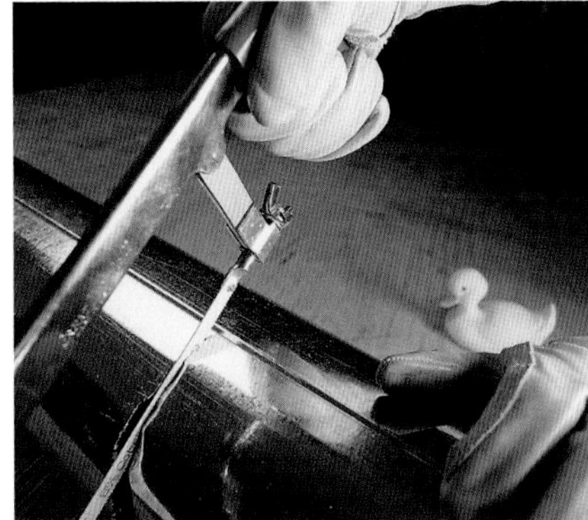

1 Start the cut by making a slit with a screwdriver (see right) then cut the perimeter with aviation snips. Cut through the seam with a hacksaw, as shown here.

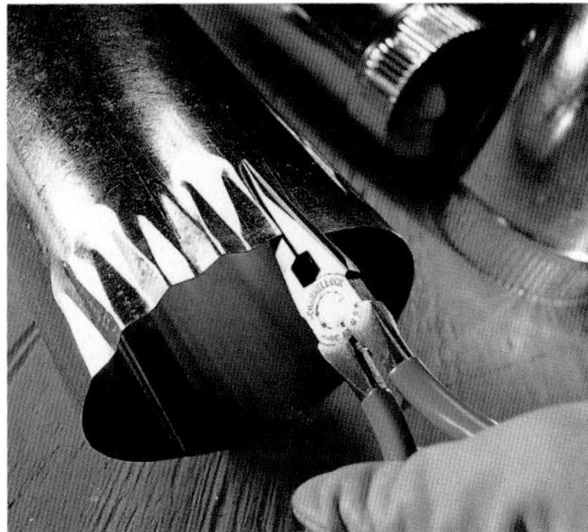

2 You can create a male-end by using a specialized crimping tool or a needle-nose pliers with a series of pinches and light twists.

Adding a Takeoff Collar

Heated air from the main furnace supply duct is usually delivered by way of smaller round ducts. Create the opening in the main distribution duct for the takeoff collar, as shown below.

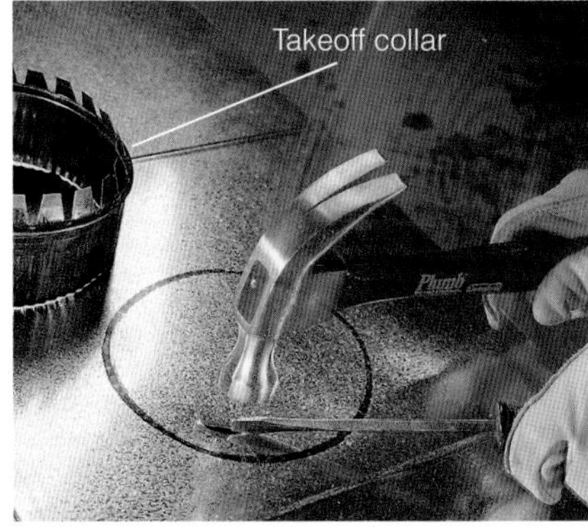

1 Lay out the collar's size and location. Drive a screwdriver blade inside the area to be cut out and twist it to make room for your snips.

2 Use your left- and right-hand aviation snips to cut the hole. Carefully follow the circle so the collar fits snugly.

Duct Accessories

Two specialty items can help solve some tricky forced-air heating problems. A duct booster is an add-on fan that helps deliver extra air to rooms located far from the furnace. Always turn off power before making electrical connections. For difficult-to-reach or unusual connections, use flex duct.

Duct booster. Locate unit as near as possible to the cold room. You can wire it to a manually controlled switch or furnace's blower-fan wiring. Shut off power while working.

Flex duct. For short runs of up to 5 ft. (1.5 m) or to connect ductwork in tight spaces, insulated flex duct is the ticket. You can attach it securely with hose clamps.

Shop Smart: Which Filter?

Walk down the aisles of your local home center or hardware store and you'll find furnace filters ranging in price from under $1 to $40 or more. What's the difference?

The least expensive **woven fiberglass filters** screen out some pollen and mold spores but mostly keep dirt and debris from damaging your blower motor.

Accordion-like **pleated filters** have a larger surface area, meaning they can capture smaller particles for longer periods of time without impeding the airflow of your furnace.

The more expensive, higher efficiency **electrostatic filters** can filter out and magnetically attract contaminants, including bacteria, dander, odors and smoke particles. Consider these if you have household members with allergies or asthma.

Many filters carry a minimum efficiency reporting value (MERV) rating, which basically indicates their effectiveness. The higher the MERV rating, the higher a filter's effectiveness.

Remember, changing filters isn't only a heating-season chore. Many blower motors work at a higher speed in air-conditioning mode than in heating mode, which means you should clean or change your filters more often in the summer. A clogged filter will make both your furnace and air conditioner work harder and less efficiently.

Hot-water Heating

Radiators 178
Gas Burners 182
Oil Burners 183

In a hot-water, or hydronic, heating system, water is heated in a gas, oil or electric boiler and circulated through pipes to radiators or their modern counterpart, convectors, located in the rooms. Radiators and convectors are designed with many fins, folds or tubes that add up to a large surface area, which allows them to give off considerable heat to the room. Various piping arrangements are used, as illustrated below.

A pump called a circulator drives the water through the pipes and convectors whenever the thermostat calls for heat. It's usually positioned near the boiler in the return line; however, it's better positioned on the supply line, pumping away from the expansion tank. This allows for a quieter system and fewer air-binding problems with the radiators and convectors. A flow-control valve keeps the water from flowing when the pump is not operating; this keeps the system from overheating the convectors. Some older systems have no circulator but rely on the principle that water expands and becomes lighter when heated. The lighter hot water rises through the pipes and replaces the cooler, heavier water, which is pulled down through the return pipes by gravity.

Water expands when it is heated. Without room for expansion, pressure could build up rapidly, causing the safety relief valve to open. To prevent pressure buildup, an airtight expansion tank is installed near the boiler. As water in the system heats, it expands safely into the tank. If over time the expansion tank fills, excess water escapes through the safety relief valve on top of the boiler. Older types of tanks must be drained when they get too full of water; newer tanks have an elastic diaphragm separating the air from the water and should be drained only by a boiler specialist or plumber.

Improving efficiency. To reduce heat loss, insulate any pipes that run through crawl spaces or other unheated areas. To help balance heat throughout the house, adjust shutoff valves on individual radiators or convectors (no cost) or install separate thermostatic valves (more expensive).

One-pipe system. In a one-pipe system, the supply pipe carries hot water past the convectors or radiators and back to the boiler. Convectors connect to the supply pipe by short branch pipes. When a convector's heat-control valve opens, a special T-fitting diverts some water from the main line into the branch line. If a convector is shut off, hot water bypasses that branch and proceeds to the next one. The single-pipe system is most often used in small- and medium-size houses.

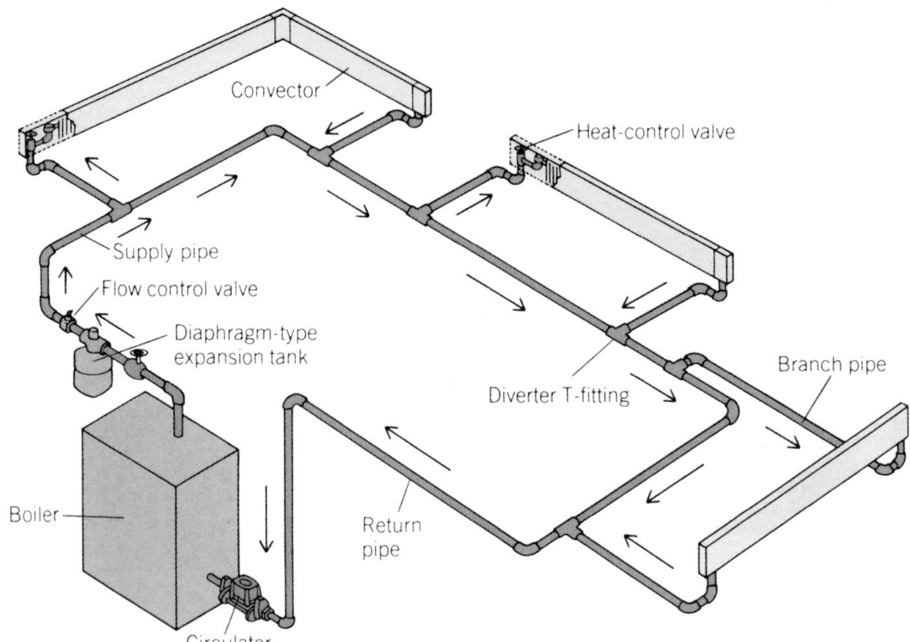

Two-pipe system. Best for large houses, this system uses one pipe to carry hot water to convectors or radiators and another to return water to the boiler. Cooler return water flows through a separate pipe, not through the convectors, so the supply water remains hotter as it travels to the far ends of the system.

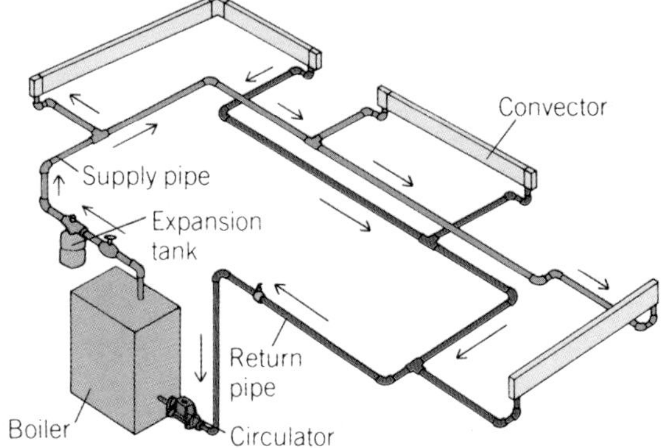

Series-loop system. In this simplest hot-water system, one pipe runs from the boiler through each convector or radiator (in one end, out the other) and back to the boiler in an uninterrupted loop. You cannot turn off one convector in the loop without shutting them all off, but a system may have two or more loops.

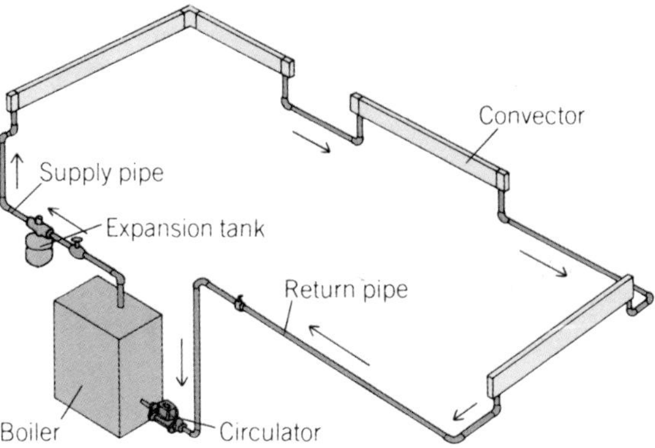

Zoned Heating

To save energy, a hot-water system can be divided into zones. This lets you make occupied rooms warm while keeping others cooler. Typically, a two-zone system combines living areas, kitchen and bathrooms in one zone and bedrooms in another.

Zones are created by running branch lines off a main supply pipe to each desired zone and adding thermostatic zone valves in each branch to turn the hot-water supply on or off. One boiler and one circulator (or two of each in large houses) are used with multiple zone valves. Alternatively, a separate circulator can be used for each zone, eliminating zone valves.

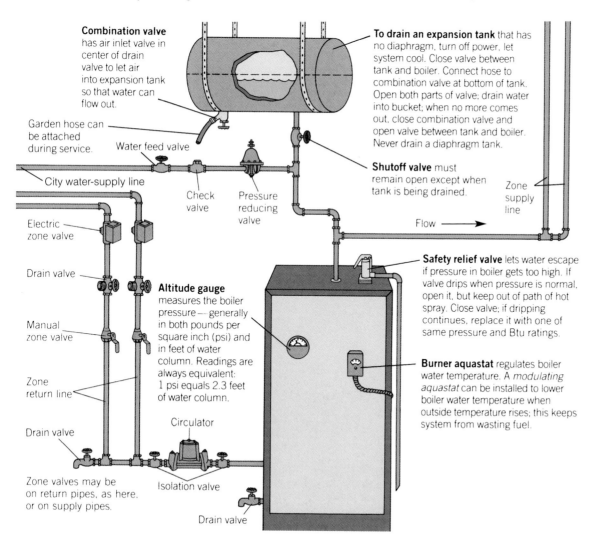

Combination valve has air inlet valve in center of drain valve to let air into expansion tank so that water can flow out.

Garden hose can be attached during service.

Water feed valve

City water-supply line

Check valve

Pressure reducing valve

To drain an expansion tank that has no diaphragm, turn off power, let system cool. Close valve between tank and boiler. Connect hose to combination valve at bottom of tank. Open both parts of valve; drain water into bucket; when no more comes out, close combination valve and open valve between tank and boiler. Never drain a diaphragm tank.

Shutoff valve must remain open except when tank is being drained.

Zone supply line

Flow →

Electric zone valve

Drain valve

Altitude gauge measures the boiler pressure—generally in both pounds per square inch (psi) and in feet of water column. Readings are always equivalent: 1 psi equals 2.3 feet of water column.

Manual zone valve

Zone return line

Drain valve

Circulator

Isolation valve

Zone valves may be on return pipes, as here, or on supply pipes.

Drain valve

Safety relief valve lets water escape if pressure in boiler gets too high. If valve drips when pressure is normal, open it, but keep out of path of hot spray. Close valve; if dripping continues, replace it with one of same pressure and Btu ratings.

Burner aquastat regulates boiler water temperature. A *modulating aquastat* can be installed to lower boiler water temperature when outside temperature rises; this keeps system from wasting fuel.

Venting a System

Trapped air prevents hot-water flow to a radiator or convector. Open an air vent (some require a special key) until water spurts out; catch it in a cup. Be careful, it's hot! Start with the convector at the lowest level if more than one is cool.

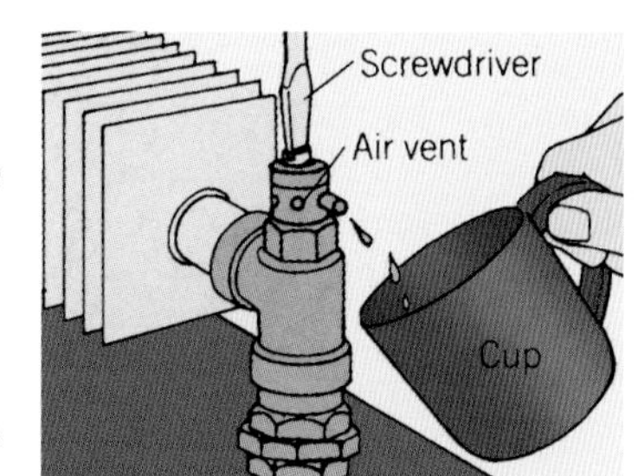

Valves. When venting a convector, open its zone valve, if any, by turning it manually or by setting the thermostat in that zone to well above room temperature. After venting air from the system, check the boiler pressure. Add water, if necessary, to restore pressure to 12 pounds per sq. in. (psi) or recommended pressure. If a water feed line has a manual valve but no automatic fill valve or pressure-reducing valve, close the manual valve when the recommended pressure has been reached.

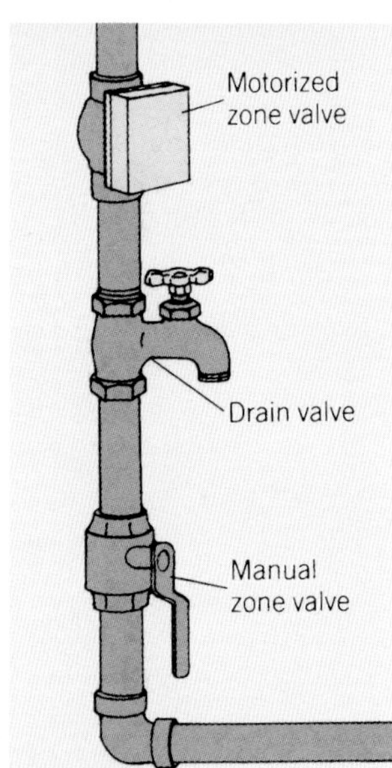

An automatic vent valve slowly releases air from a convector as the system fills with water, ensuring good flow and even heat. The vent should be kept clean. If it drips water, replace it.

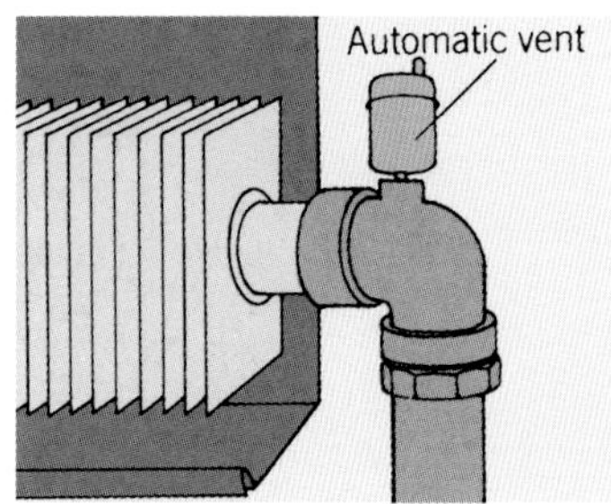

Radiators and Convectors

Dielectric and Other Unions 107

Replacing a Radiator with a Convector

Metal convectors and radiators give up part of their warmth by radiation, but most of the heat comes from convection-air circulating past the hot metal. Generally found only in older systems, radiators are made of cast-iron tubing. Convectors, much lighter in weight, are either grilled cabinets or long, low baseboards. Inside they contain thin-wall copper or steel tubing surrounded by metal fins that increase the surface area. You can replace one or more radiators with convectors, as shown at right, but use dielectric fittings to connect pipes of different metals. Make certain the replacement convector's output rating matches that of the radiator you're removing.

Vent all the convectors or radiators in the system to ensure maximum efficiency. Never place anything on or in front of a convector or radiator; it could obstruct the airflow. If you paint a convector or radiator, use standard paint; metallic paint will substantially reduce the heat transfer. Dust also cuts down on efficiency; vacuum convectors and radiators regularly. Straighten bent convector fins with needle-nose pliers and be sure that the convector covers are not bent or misaligned.

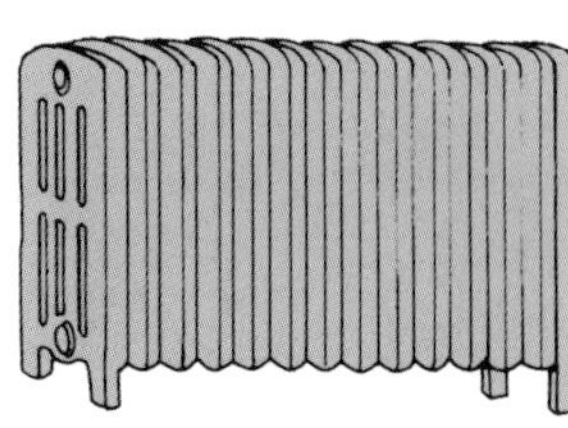
Cast-iron radiator

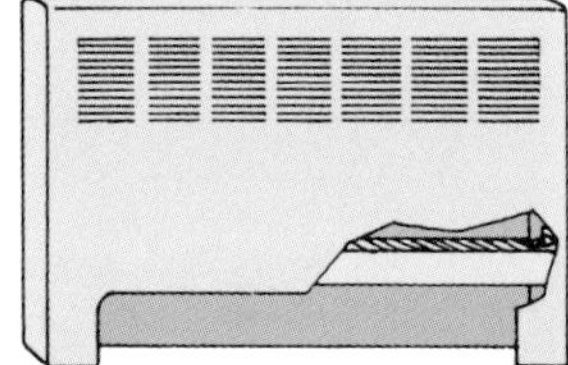
Upright convector

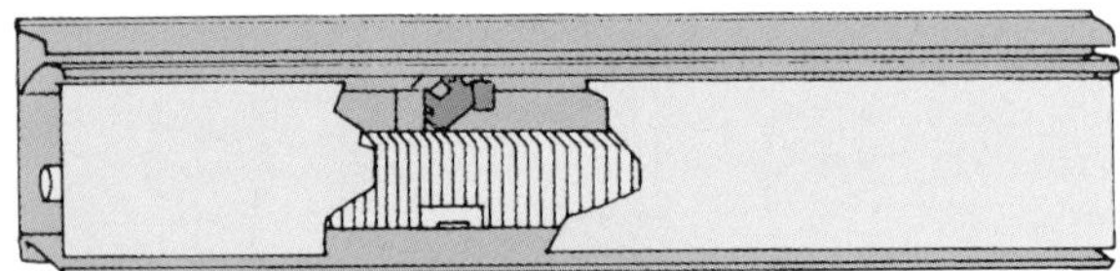
Baseboard convector is low-lying, but still should not be blocked.

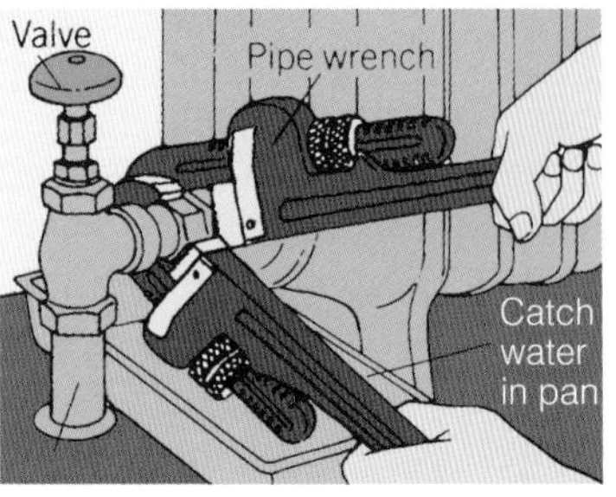

1 Turn off system and let cool. Close feed valve and open radiator valves. Attach hose to boiler drain valve, open radiator vent and drain water. Use pipe wrenches (or propane torch, if soldered) to remove radiator.

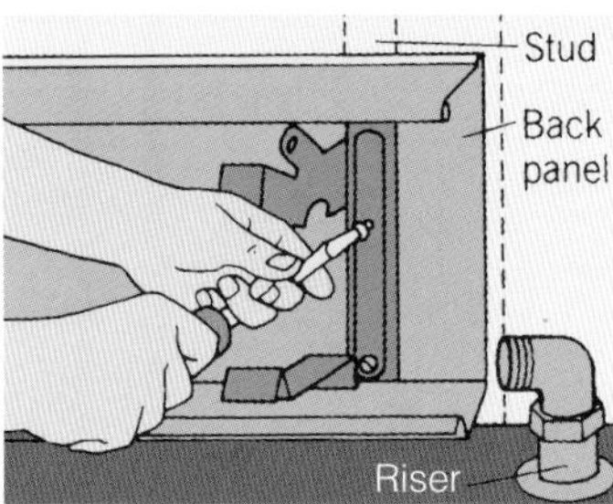

2 Align baseboard convector with riser pipes and align convector's back panel so it can be screwed directly into studs. Mark position for back-panel screw holes, drill pilot holes and screw into place.

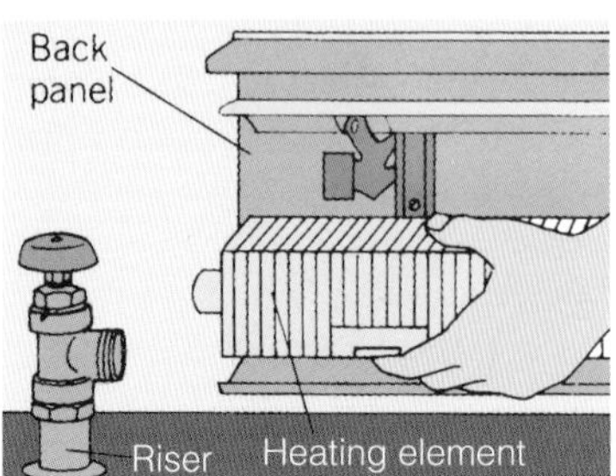

3 Install the finned heating element on back panel. Clean riser threads using a wire brush; wipe with a clean rag and wrap with pipe tape. If riser is too far away, add needed extensions and fittings.

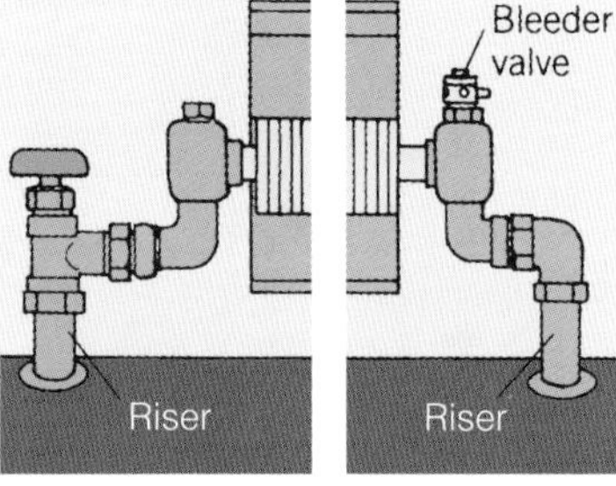

4 Make plumbing connections. Open inlet valve, attach convector cover, turn on water and flush out boiler. Close boiler drain valve; fill boiler. Turn system on and wait a bit; then vent system.

A New Face in Radiators

The two most common complaints about radiators are that they take up too much floor space and that they're less than attractive. Fortunately, there are radiators on the market that address both complaints.

The wall mounted, vertical panel radiators (near right) are available in a wide variety of colors and sizes and are ideal for entryways and other rooms where floor space is limited. The European-style towel radiators (far right) provide both even heat and the luxury of warm, dry towels and bathrobes. These hydronic units can be used to replace fin-tube or cast-iron radiators and are compatible with most closed loop, forced-hot-water heating systems. Electric versions are also available.

Heating an Addition

Most electrical and plumbing systems can accommodate the additional demands of a room addition, especially if that room is something other than a kitchen or bathroom. But heating systems are another matter. In many cases furnaces and boilers are sized to handle the demands of the existing house and not much more.

Even if the heat plant does have the extra capacity to handle an addition, getting the heat there can present more obstacles. Heat ducts are large and best run without a lot of twists and turns, radiator pipes can freeze if run through uninsulated spaces. So looking at alternatives is wise.

If it's a family room, office or bedroom addition, consider installing a gas fireplace. You'll need to install a gas line and chimney, but you'll get ambiance and heat in one shot. If it's a bathroom, laundry room or entryway with a tile floor, consider installing in-the-floor electric resistance heat (p. 188). It requires fishing just a single wire from your circuit box to the new addition.

The following are a few other options and considerations:

Forced-air System

If the furnace and blower have excess capacity and the main trunk line runs near the addition, you can tap into it. However, calculating a furnace's excess capacity and balancing the system are activities best left to a pro. The system must remain balanced so you may also need to install an additional return-air duct.

Distribution duct

Cold-air return duct

Addition

Hot-water System

If you have space for a dedicated water heater (never mix domestic hot water with heating water since this can breed dangerous bacteria) or your boiler has excess capacity, consider adding a hydronic radiant system. Heat is delivered via warm water or fluid pumped through a system of mixing valves, water pipes or tubing embedded in a lightweight concrete or dry-tamped mortar. The system is quiet, there are no heat registers or baseboards to take up space, and heat is delivered to what are usually the coldest body parts—your feet. Check local codes; water heaters are not approved for this use in some areas.

Electric Radiant-heat System

If you can fish wires from your existing circuit box to your new addition—something you'll almost surely be doing anyway—you can consider a wide range of electric-resistant heat options. The radiant heating panels shown here come in standard sizes and mount on any flat surface—so they're easy to add to an existing ceiling or wall without major remodeling. Rigid panels are typically made of fiberglass insulation board with an aluminum frame and a textured surface, and contain a heating element that is charged by either 120 or 240V. Follow manufacturer's recommendations for installing and wiring a thermostat designed for your panels.

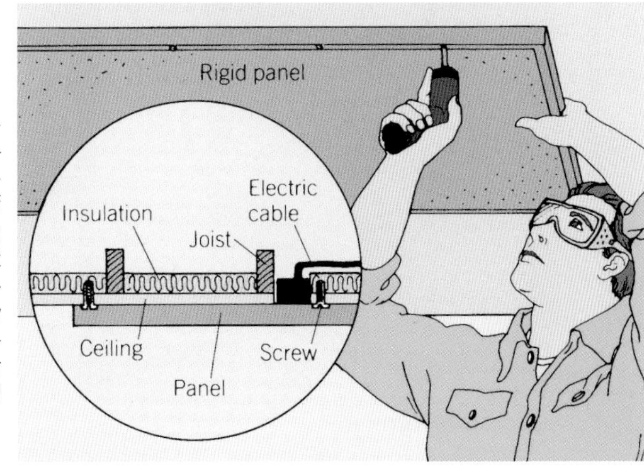

Steam Heating

Radiators 178
Gas Burners 182
Oil Burners 183

How They Work

Steam systems heat water in a boiler until it vaporizes and rises through pipes to radiators and convectors that radiate heat into the room. When the steam hits the cooler radiator surfaces, it condenses and the water runs back to the boiler. As steam rises in the pipes, quick-release air vents let air escape from the main steam lines and individual radiators. As the steam advances, pressure forces the air out of the vents. (Change a vent that spits or drips water, leaks steam or fails to open.)

Steam systems come in two basic types. In a **two-pipe system**, the steam flows through one set of pipes and the condensate, water, returns through another. In a **one-pipe system** (like the one shown below), the steam and water travel through the same pipe in opposite directions.

When water is heated to steam, pressure builds in the boiler. Check the pressure gauge just after the boiler switches off. If it is far above the recommended pressure setting (generally 2 psi or less), have the boiler pressure control replaced immediately. Boilers also have a pressure safety valve that will open before an unsafe pressure level is reached. Test yours regularly. Another safety feature: The low-water cutoff turns off the burner if the water in the boiler falls below a safe level. Release about a quart of water from the low-water cutoff once a week. Do this while the burner is operating to make sure that it shuts off. Be careful, though, the water is very hot.

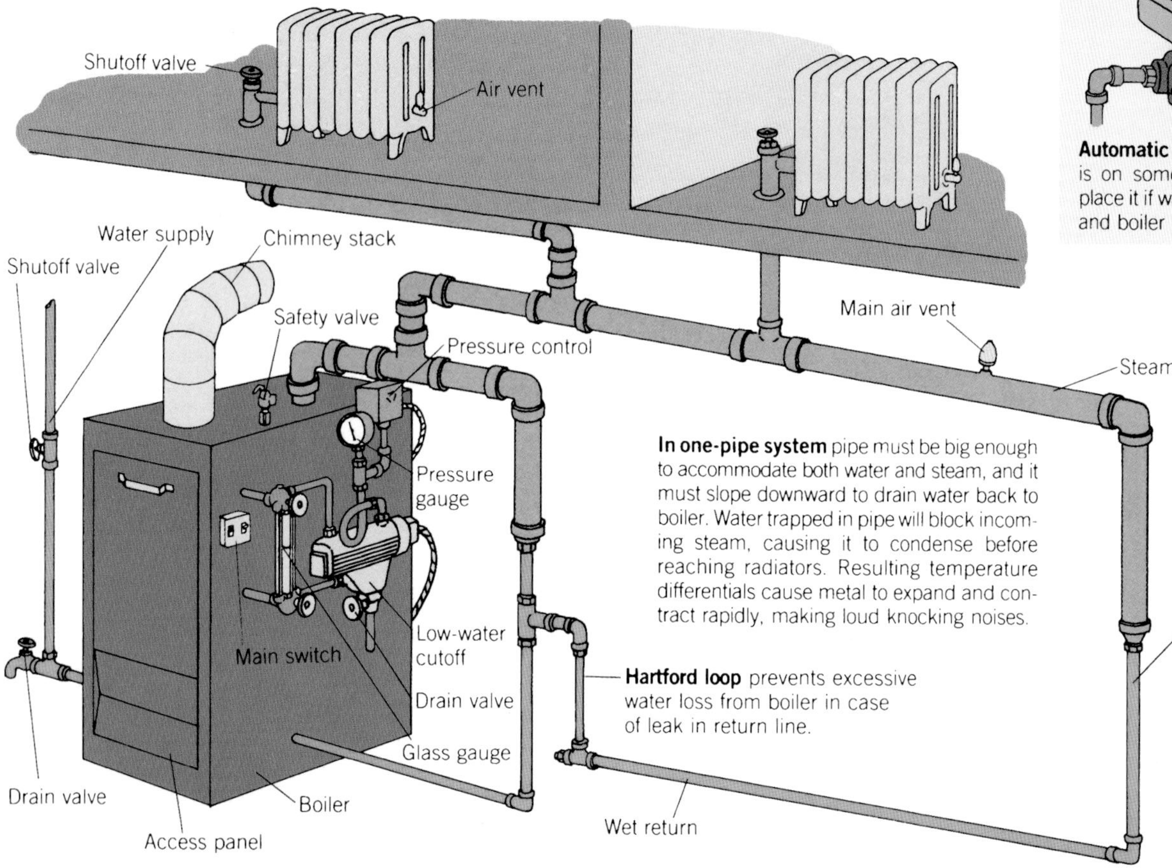

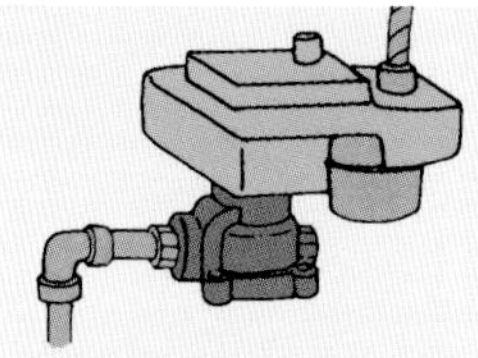

Shutoff valve
Air vent
Water supply
Chimney stack
Shutoff valve
Safety valve
Main air vent
Pressure control
Steam main
Pressure gauge
Low-water cutoff
Main switch
Drain valve
Glass gauge
Reducer
Drain valve
Boiler
Access panel
Wet return

Automatic water feeder is on some boilers; replace it if water level falls and boiler doesn't refill.

In one-pipe system pipe must be big enough to accommodate both water and steam, and it must slope downward to drain water back to boiler. Water trapped in pipe will block incoming steam, causing it to condense before reaching radiators. Resulting temperature differentials cause metal to expand and contract rapidly, making loud knocking noises.

Hartford loop prevents excessive water loss from boiler in case of leak in return line.

Steam Trap

On some two-pipe steam systems, each radiator is fitted with a steam trap (instead of an air vent). The trap holds steam inside the radiator until it gives up all its heat. If return pipes feel very hot or if steam comes out of main air vent in great quantities, one or more traps may be defective; have them checked. If a trap leaks, steam will pass directly into return pipe and be wasted; replace leaky trap.

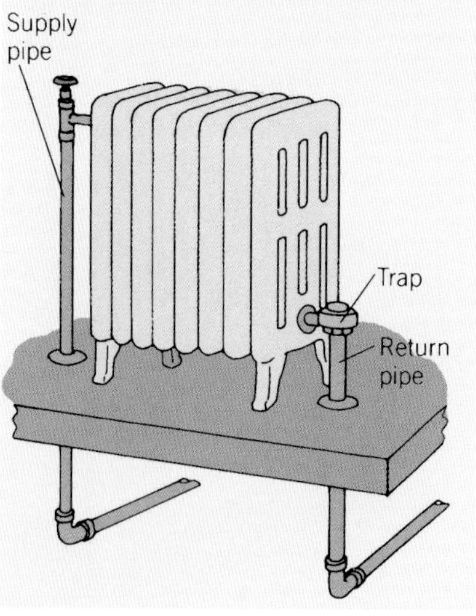

Maintenance

Steam systems operate at high temperature. Regular maintenance improves efficiency and, more importantly, ensures your family's safety. Have the system checked annually by a service person. If the system operates poorly, call a professional. Malfunctions can be difficult to pinpoint without special equipment.

Radiators require a free flow of air to work efficiently. Don't block them with furniture, and cover them only with special vented covers. Vacuum radiators often. Inspect exposed piping runs for breaks or gaps in insulation, but be careful, as some old systems used asbestos. You can perform some simple maintenance steps by following the procedures shown here.

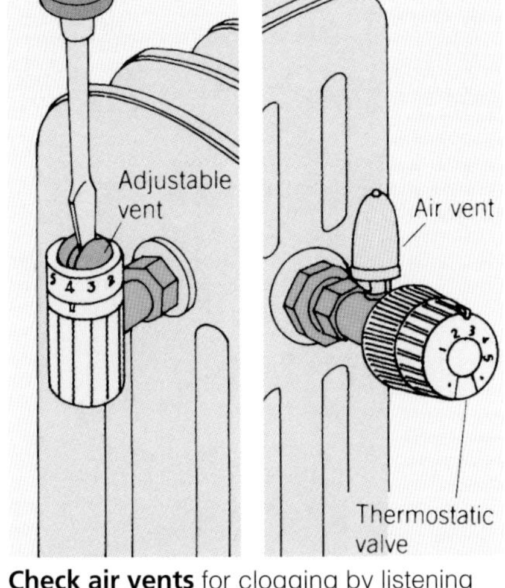

Check air vents for clogging by listening for a hissing sound and checking radiator for heat. If valve is adjustable, open fully when checking. Replace clogged vent with one of the same size. If a room overheats, add a thermostatic valve to radiator.

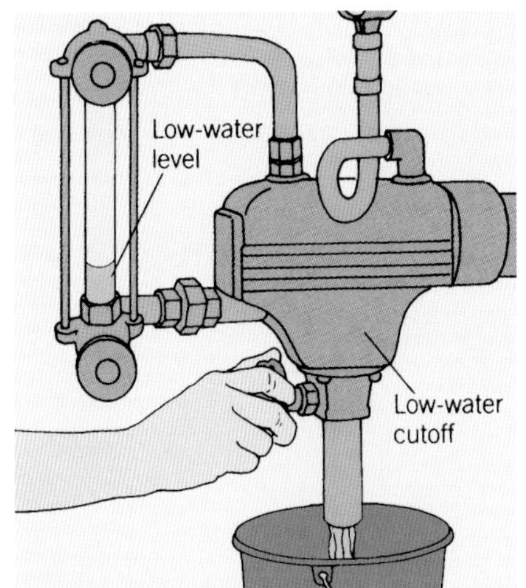

Flush low-water cutoff once a week in heating season to prevent sediment buildup. Turn down the thermostat, put a bucket under the pipe, open the valve and let water run until it's clear. Be careful; water will be hot. Close valve; refill boiler to proper level.

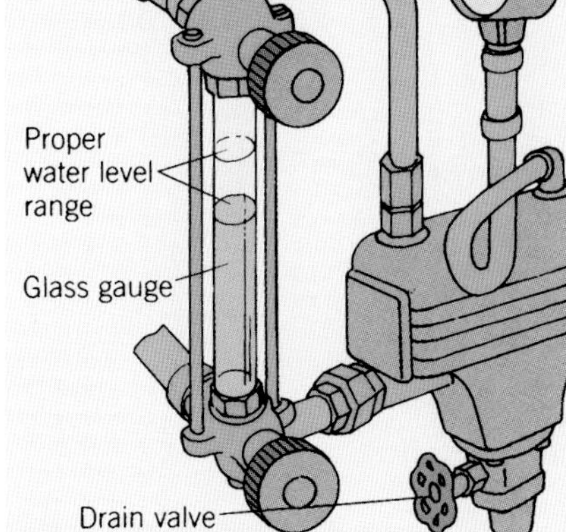

Check water level when boiler is off, every l0 to 14 days in cold weather. If water level is less than halfway up glass gauge, open water-supply valve after the boiler has been shut off for an hour or so, until water reaches the proper level.

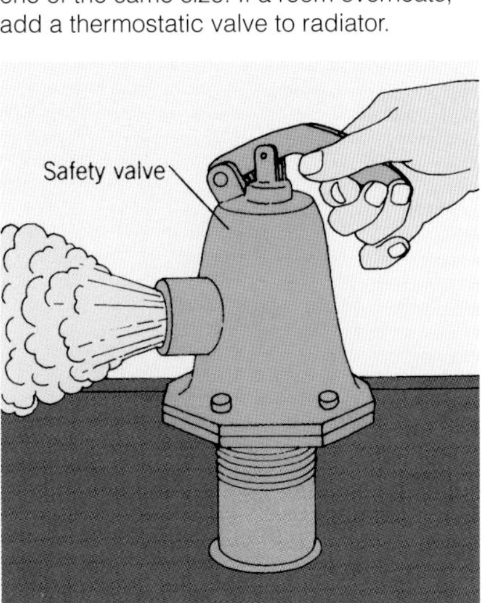

Check safety valve once a year. With boiler running, pull up lever and let small amount of steam escape. Watch that valve reseals and doesn't leak. If it sticks or is clogged, shut off power and have the valve replaced.

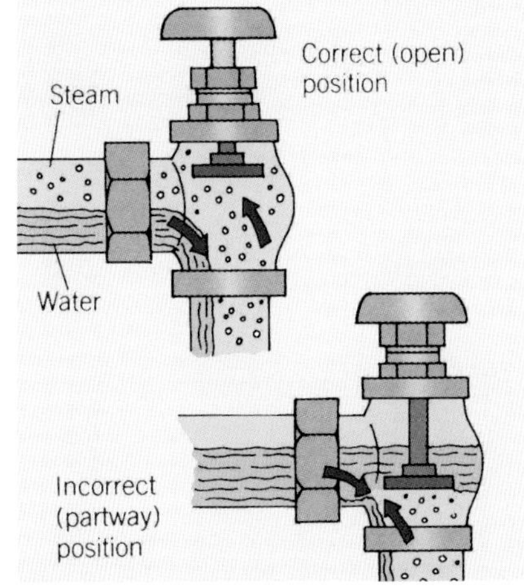

Prevent knocking in a one-pipe system by opening or closing valves fully. Because steam enters and water leaves through same valve, a half-closed valve mixes water and steam, causing knocking at the valve.

Stopping Knocks

In one-pipe radiator, tip end opposite pipe a bit higher to keep water from collecting at bottom and blocking incoming steam. If radiator has height-adjustment bolts in legs, simply loosen them; otherwise slide shims or checkers under legs.

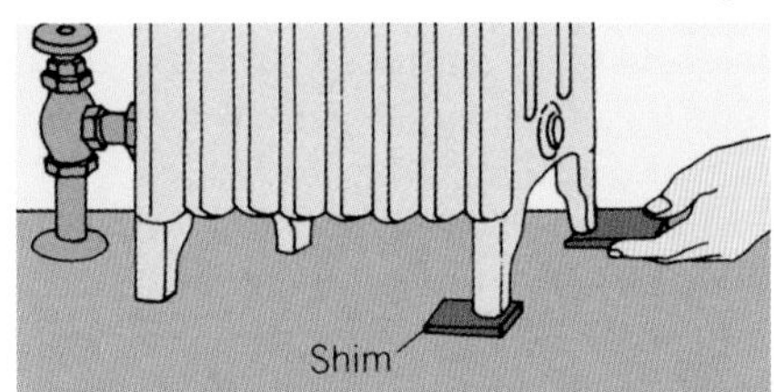

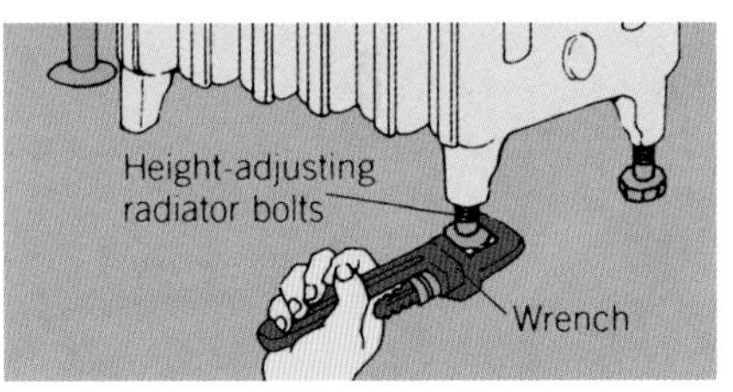

Increasing Efficiency

Increase radiator efficiency by sliding a reflector between it and outside wall to reflect heat back into room and keep it from being lost to outside wall. You can buy insulated reflectors or make them with corrugated cardboard and aluminum foil.

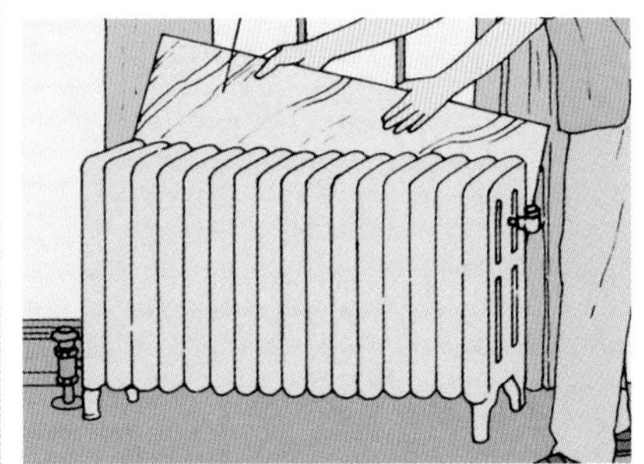

Gas Burners

Hot-water Systems **176**
Steam Systems **180**

A gas burner is designed to efficiently burn propane or natural gas to heat water or air in a boiler or furnace. When the thermostat calls for heat, it signals the burner control to open a valve, sending gas to the burner ports, where it mixes with air and is ignited by the pilot light or electronic ignition. Burning gas heats the heat exchanger containing air or water. Combustion gases escape through a vent pipe. A draft diverter hood on the vent pipe or furnace outlet stops air currents from blowing out the pilot light. A thermocouple stops gas flow if the pilot light goes out.

Energy efficiency. If you significantly improve your home's energy efficiency, you may be able to reduce furnace output. Talk to an expert about reducing the size of the burner's orifice. To allow an efficient flow of gases, keep the burners and air shutters free of dust and dirt. If you want to convert an oil burner to a gas burner, look into a power burner because it uses less gas.

Maintenance. Have a heating contractor or the utility company inspect, test, adjust and clean the burner as needed every year. To clean the burner yourself, turn off its main gas valve and electric power. Slide the burners out; some disassembly, twisting or lifting may be required. If the pilot and thermocouple are attached to a burner, remove them. Clean the burners, air shutters and combustion chamber with a stiff brush, then vacuum. Unplug gas ports carefully with a toothpick.

Caution: Make sure the burner has an adequate air supply; an outside air source is best. Don't relight the pilot light or make any repairs if you smell gas. Close the main valve and call the gas company from a neighbor's house. Don't operate any electrical switches.

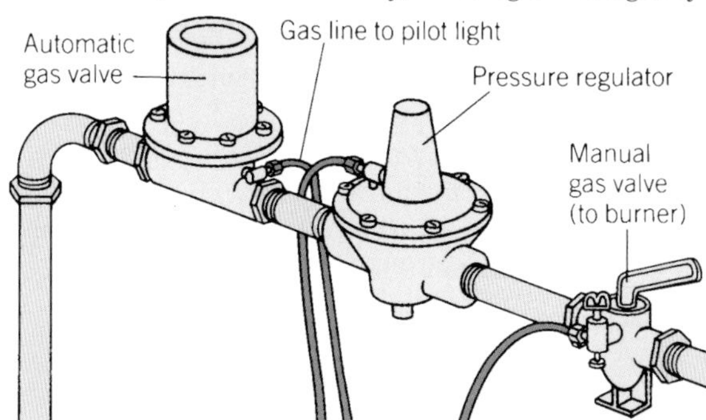

The gas train. An automatic gas valve regulates flow of gas supplied to burner; an automatic pressure regulator controls gas pressure. In newer systems, they are combined in a combination control. A pressure regulator is supplied by the utility company in areas where gas pressure is medium to high. Do not try to adjust the regulator yourself; call the utility for service.

Anatomy of a Gas Burner

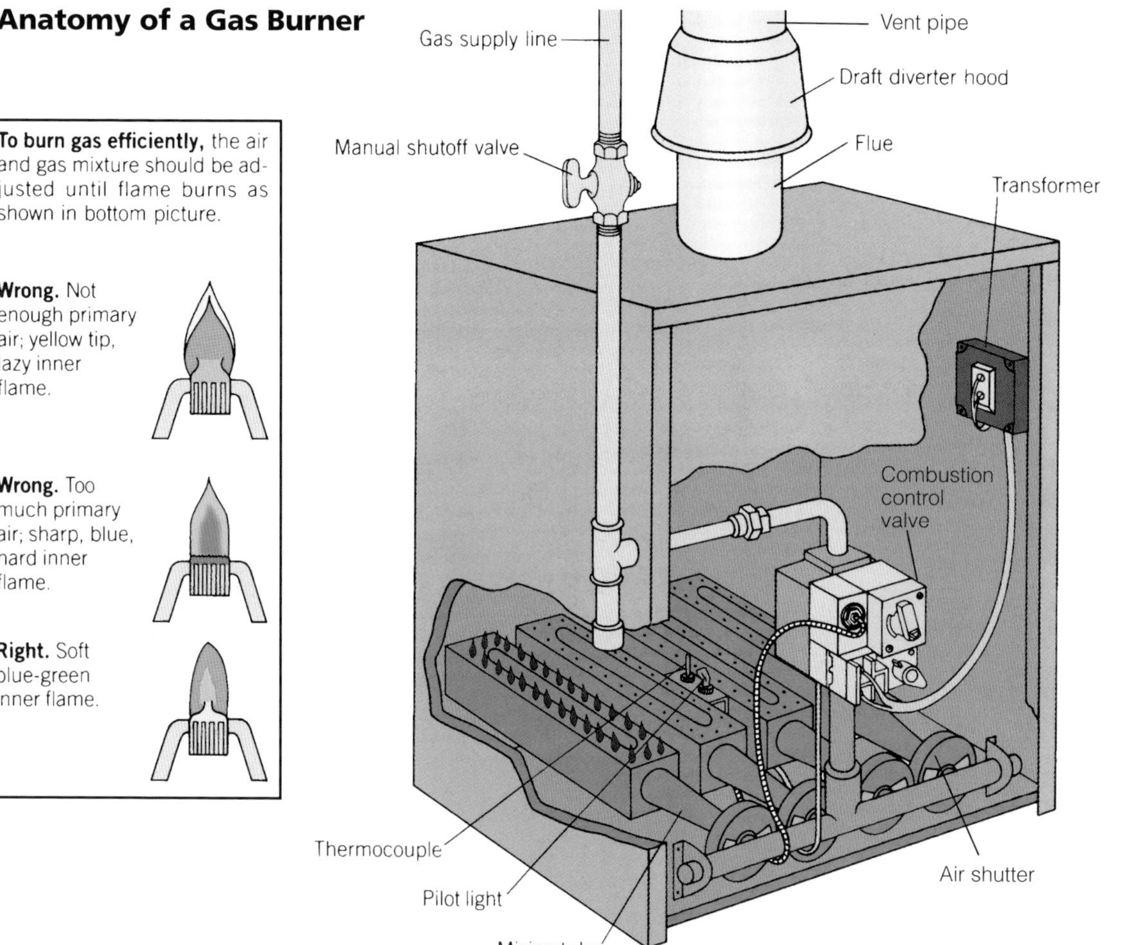

To burn gas efficiently, the air and gas mixture should be adjusted until flame burns as shown in bottom picture.

Wrong. Not enough primary air; yellow tip, lazy inner flame.

Wrong. Too much primary air; sharp, blue, hard inner flame.

Right. Soft blue-green inner flame.

How It Works. When the thermostat calls for heat, it signals the burner control to open a valve, sending gas into the ports in the burners. There the gas mixes with air and is ignited by a pilot light or electronic ignition. Burning gas heats the heat exchanger, the chamber containing air or water. Combustion gases escape through a vent pipe.

Oil Burners

Relighting a pilot. For an older burner, turn the manual gas valve and pilot gas valve to "off." After airing the burner 5 minutes, turn the pilot gas valve to "on." Press in the red button on the switch for one minute while lighting the pilot. If pilot doesn't light, wait five minutes, then repeat steps. If it still doesn't light, replace thermocouple (see below) or call the gas company.

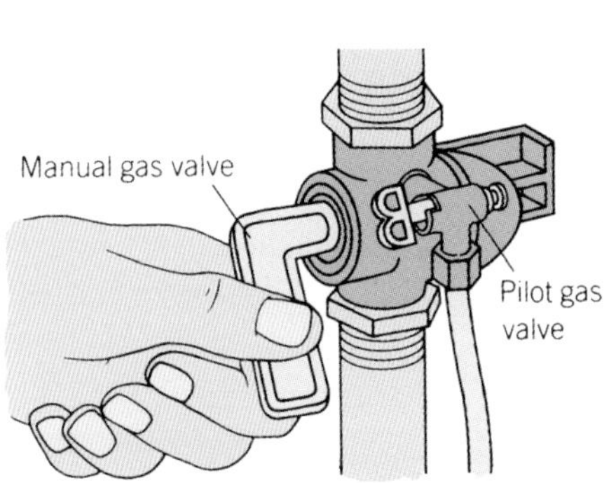

Cleaning the pilot orifice. If the pilot doesn't light, its orifice or air-shutter orifice may be clogged. Turn off the main shutoff valve and electrical switch. Remove the access panel by unscrewing its bracket. Carefully clean orifice with a toothpick. Remove debris from the edges with a cotton swab or paintbrush.

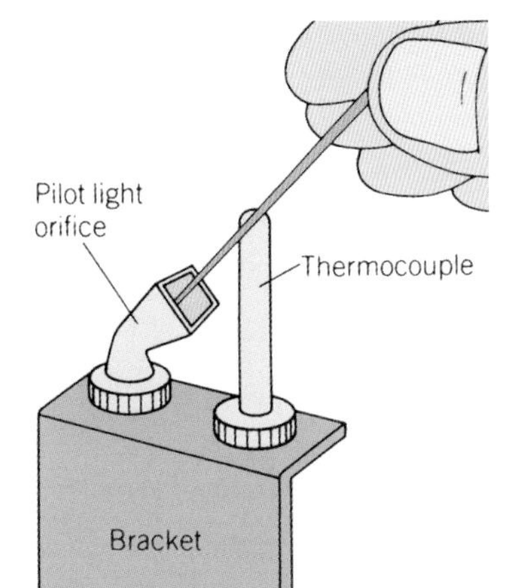

Replacing a Thermocouple

Turn off gas knob (or manual and pilot gas valves) and power to burner. Air 5 to 10 minutes. Unscrew lead from combination control valve; wipe threaded area with clean rag. Unscrew nut holding thermocouple to bracket. Fasten new thermocouple to bracket, lead to control valve.

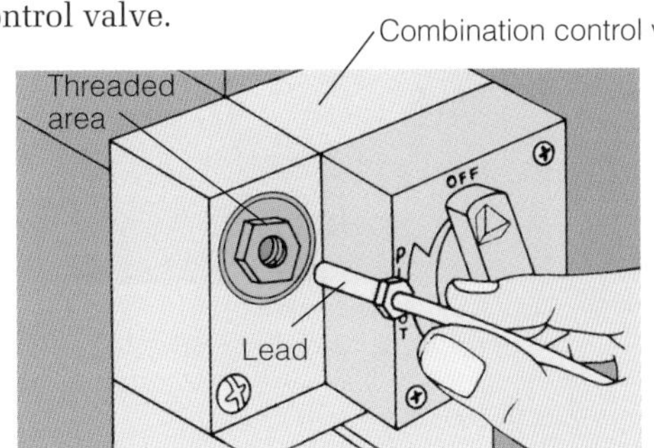

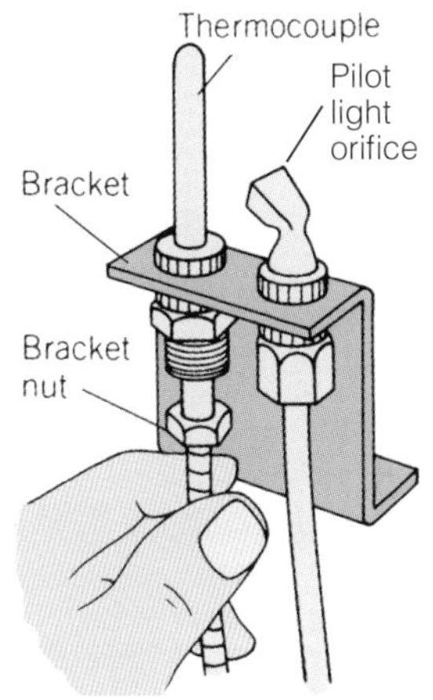

Of the several oil-burner varieties, the gun-type high-pressure oil burner is the most common. The oil burner is usually bolted to the outside of the furnace. In addition to a thermostat, an oil burner has a primary control relay connected to a flame sensor. It shuts off the burner if the oil spray doesn't ignite, preventing dangerous oil buildup.

Maintenance. Before each heating season, have your system checked, cleaned and adjusted by a service person; it's not a do-it-yourself project. Keep the burner area clean. Periodically vacuum with a crevice tool in the openings that admit air to the burner's blower. Do not sweep dirt under the burner.

Increasing efficiency. If there is an observation window, look at the flame; it should be bright yellow and produce no smoke. If it's dark orange or sooty, or if you can see smoke exiting from the chimney outside, have the burner adjusted.

The oil burner is usually bolted to the outside of the furnace or boiler, but sometimes it's inside the jacket. In this case, a removable metal panel provides access to the burner. If you have a service contract, think twice before doing any work on the burner. Most contracts are voided if you work on the burner.

Note: A modern oil burner uses a flame-sighting control (built into the burner itself) instead of a stack switch.

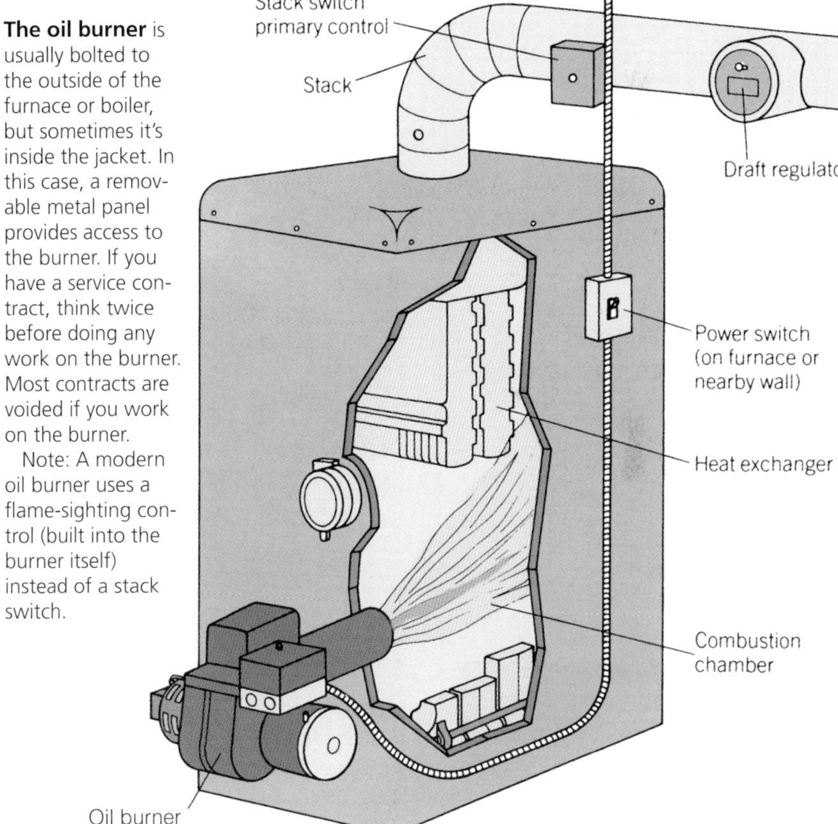

Thermostats

The thermostat is the bridge between a home's climate-control system and the comfort of its occupants. The core component of this mechanical-type, temperature-sensitive switch is a bimetallic coil composed of two thin metal strips. Fluctuations in temperature cause the coil's metal strips to expand or contract, automatically tripping a switch to turn the climate-control system on or off. Most older thermostats control only a furnace or boiler and often have a simple rotary dial or a lever to set the desired temperature threshold. Modern versions perform the same function for an air-conditioning unit as well, and most are programmable so you can preset selected temperatures for certain times of the day or week. Most thermostats work on low-voltage current, usually provided by a transformer on the furnace.

Shop Smart: Setback Thermostats

A setback thermostat lets you set varying temperature controls ahead of time; newer units offer electronic programming. By allowing an empty house to get warmer or cooler than normal and adjusting the temperature only when occupants are due or at home, energy consumption is reduced. Some people even adjust them to save energy while they're sleeping. These thermostats can pay for themselves in short order.

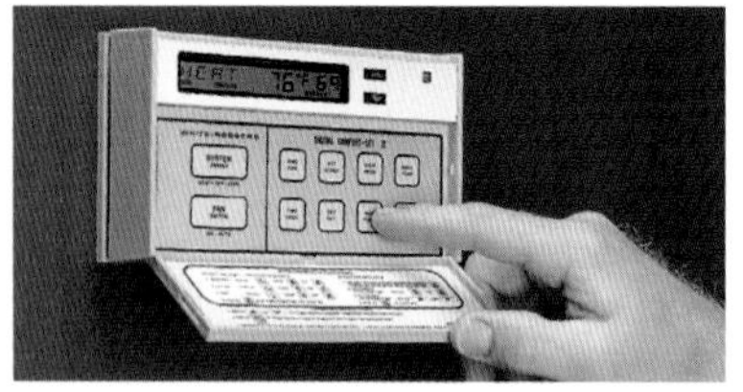

Replacing a Thermostat

If your thermostat doesn't function properly or doesn't offer programmable features, you can replace it with a new one, provided it operates on the same voltage and is compatible with your climate-control system. Most gas or oil forced-air furnaces and air-conditioning units can operate with modern programmable thermostats, but heat pumps, electric baseboard heaters and some other systems require special features. Always shut off the power to the furnace and air-conditioning unit before making repairs such as this, even with low-voltage systems. Be aware that upgrading to a more versatile or full-featured thermostat may also require replacing the wire feed. (You may have to have a professional installer run new cable for you.) Note the model or specifications of any appliance that's thermostatically controlled (furnace, air conditioner or humidifier) and have that information with you when you shop for a new thermostat. Verify that the new unit has the programmable features you want, plus a manual override you can use without altering the program settings.

Location. If the thermostat's current location creates false readings from nearby heat sources, sunlight or drafts, reroute the wire feed to another spot. Choose an inside wall; keep it away from fireplaces, heat-generating appliances or drafty windows, and don't place it above a heat register.

How to do it. Turn off power to the furnace. Disconnect your old thermostat and tie the wire feed into a loop or clip it with a clothespin to keep it from slipping back through the hole in the wall. The wires should be color-coded, but if they're not, use tape tags to mark the letters of the terminals to which they were attached. Affix the new mounting plate to the wall with screws and anchors; then make the wire connections (and set the programming) according to the installation instructions provided with your thermostat. One final note: If your old thermostat contains mercury (look for a small glass tube with a shiny silver ball inside), don't throw it in the trash. Mercury is toxic, so the thermostat should be brought to a recovery facility or a hazardous-waste disposal site.

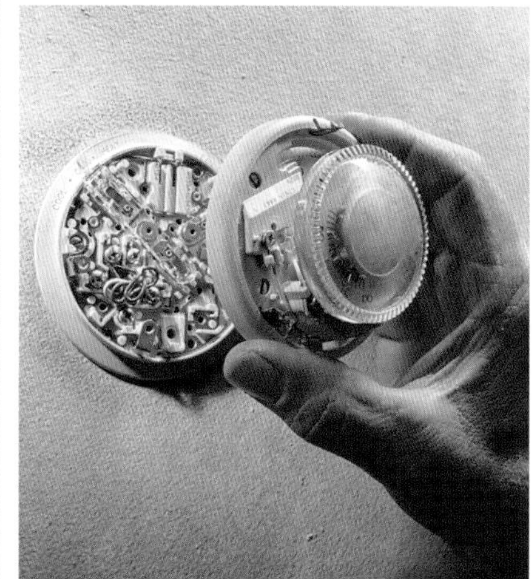

1 Turn off the system power, mark the wires to identify their correct terminal and disconnect the old thermostat. Dispose of the old unit properly.

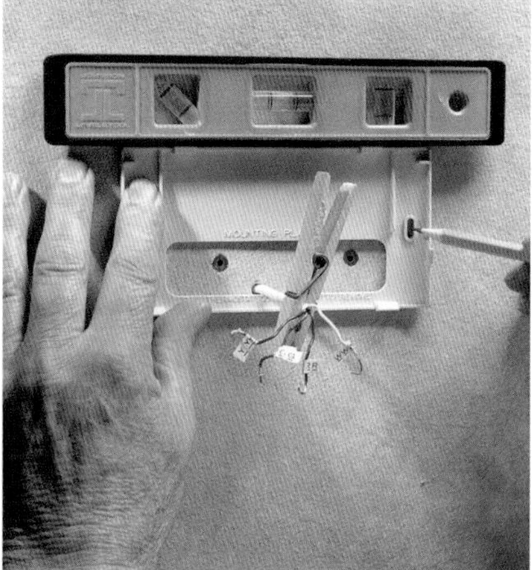

2 Level the new mounting plate on the wall and mark the fastener locations. Use drywall anchors and screws to secure the plate firmly.

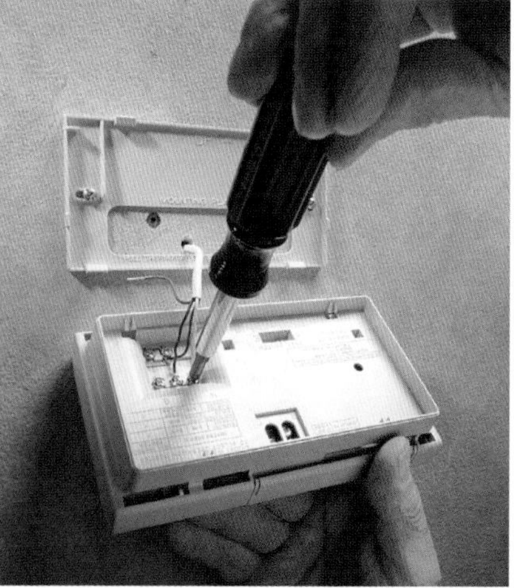

3 Using lettered tape tags to keep track of new hookups, connect the wires to the terminal screws of the new thermostat, then snap onto mounting plate.

Adjusting Thermostats

A thermostat that's not working properly doesn't always need to be replaced. As with almost any mechanical object with moving or adjustable parts, sometimes a tune-up is all that's required.

First, check the thermometer, which has to be calibrated accurately to trigger the system on and off as required. Place another accurate thermometer next to the thermostat and adjust the setting; with some types, you use a screwdriver to turn a shaft in the center of the bimetallic coil, but other versions require a wrench or pliers to turn a nut behind the coil.

The next step is leveling the thermostat itself to ensure that the mercury switch functions accurately.

Finally, set the anticipator. This device controls the on-off cycling by compensating for the heat or cooled air that has yet to make its way through the system. It's like turning off a stove burner and letting the residual heat in the pan finish cooking the food. The net effect is a more consistently modulated temperature range.

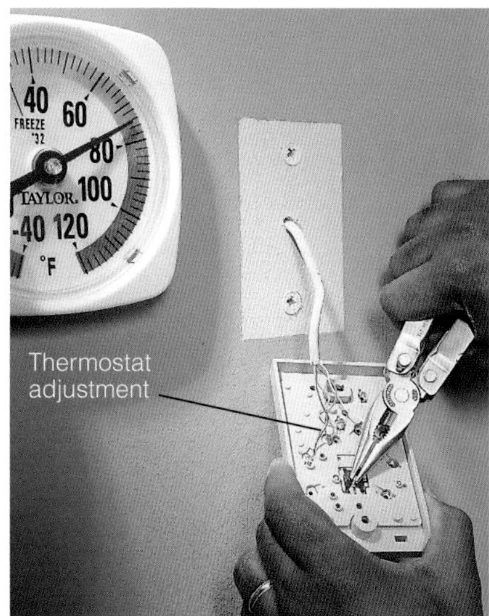

1 Like a bathroom scale that occasionally needs recalibration to true zero to record an accurate weight, the thermometer provides the benchmark readings that control the thermostat's automatic functioning. Follow the instructions in the thermostat manual if it's available; otherwise, look for an adjustment screw or nut behind the bimetallic coil.

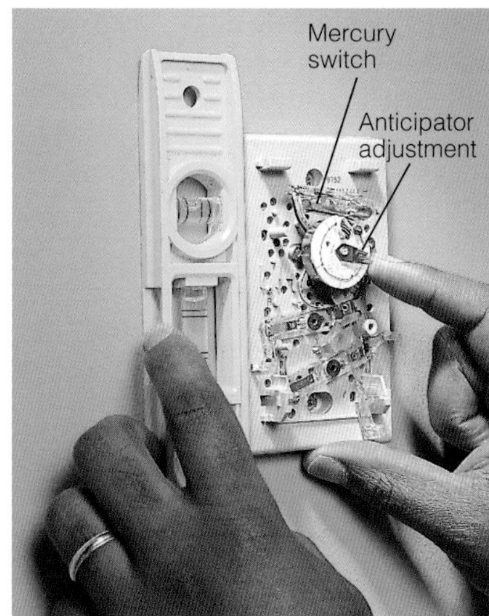

2 The thermostat's switch is often a glass tube containing mercury, which, when tilted by the movement of the bimetallic coil, flows to connect a pair of electrodes. This connection turns the system on. Leveling the thermostat provides the base, or off, position for the switch. The anticipator adjusts via a lever and dial to control on-off cycling intervals.

In-line Thermostats

In-line thermostats are used to control single appliances, typically an electric wall or baseboard heater. Newer electronic thermostats maintain a more even temperature by cycling on and off more frequently and sending only the required amount of power to maintain the desired temperature. Some electric heaters consume a large amount of current and require their own dedicated 240-volt circuit; check with the heater's manufacturer and your local building officials before installing and wiring one of these units.

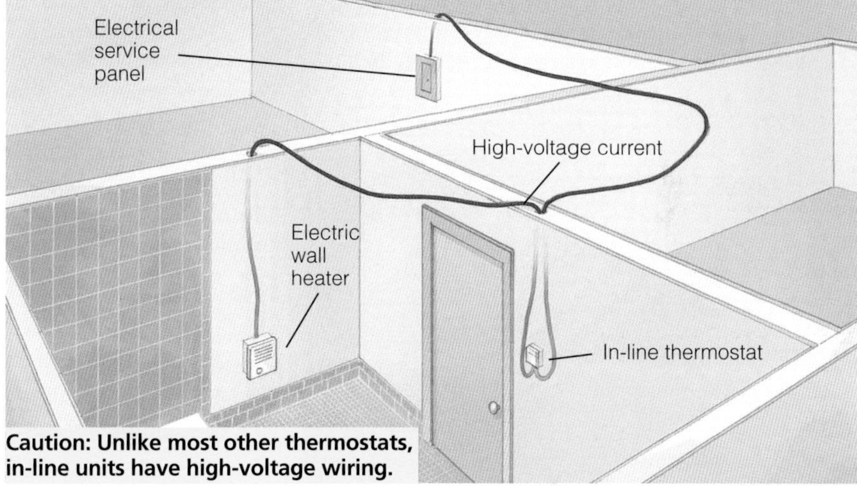

Caution: Unlike most other thermostats, in-line units have high-voltage wiring.

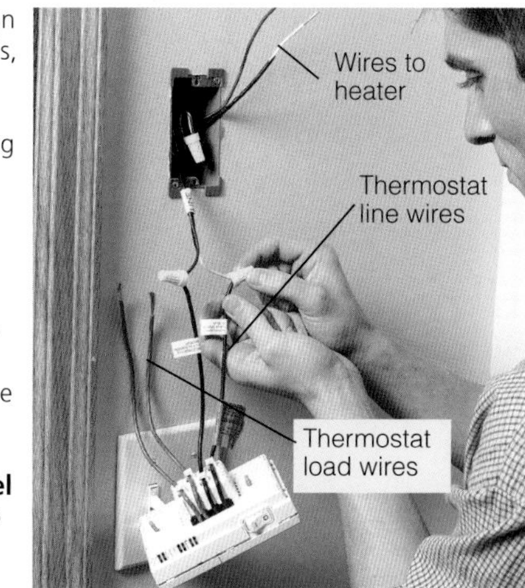

How they work. Although individual units can vary, the basic wiring for an in-line thermostat is, in most cases, similar in principle to that of a wall switch. The thermostat shown here is a 240-volt unit with two wire leads for connecting to the incoming wiring, called the line wires, and two wire leads, called the load wires, that connect to the lines going to the wall heater. Unlike in a standard wall switch, however, the direction of current travel is critical. Whereas a switch merely has to complete the wire loop to get current to flow and turn on a light fixture, for example, an in-line thermostat has to receive incoming current at the correct terminal(s) and send it out through the correct terminal(s). **Always shut off power at the circuit panel before working on or installing an in-line thermostat.**

Electric Heat

Volt-ohm Meter 132

Cove Heaters

Cove heaters offer an effective means of heating individual rooms—especially bathrooms. But to many people, they seem like a counterintuitive solution. We know hot air rises, so why put the heater near the ceiling and expect it to heat the floor? The answer lies in the nature of radiant heat. Convection heaters heat air, which rises when warmed, but radiant heaters heat objects directly, not the space between them. A cove heater transmits its heat energy directly to the floor, so tile and other hard surfaces are ideal recipients, acting as a sort of thermal bank to store and release the heat.

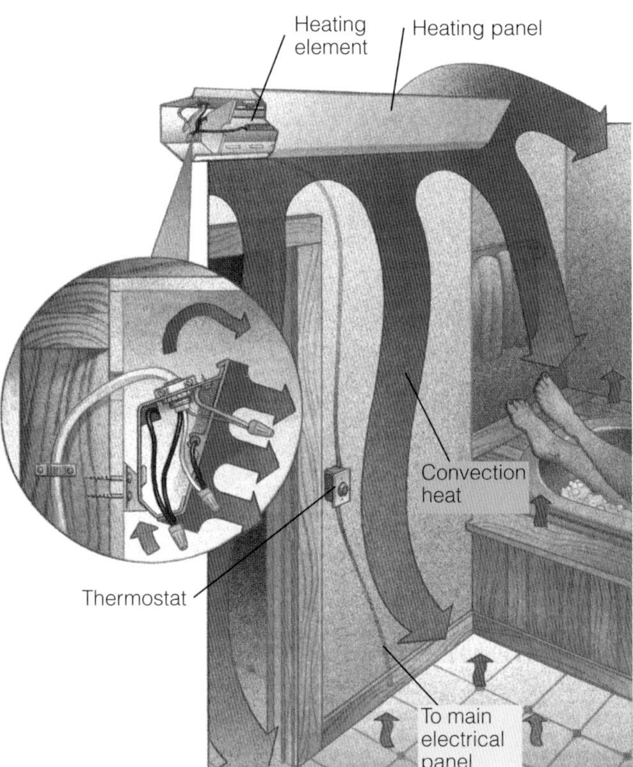

Cove heaters, requiring relatively simple routing of wires in the wall, come in a variety of lengths and can be controlled by a wall-mounted timer or thermostat. Insulated floors are best at holding the heat.

Wall Heaters

Wall heaters can be convection or radiant units and, though most are electric, some models use propane or natural gas. Electric units often require a dedicated electrical circuit, one that has no other load except the heater. Most are intended for heating a single room and will operate on 120-volt current for smaller areas, such as bathrooms, or on 220-volt current. The general guideline for heater capacity is to allow at least 10 watts of heating power for every sq. ft. (110 watts per sq. m) of floor area, unless there's already a primary heat source in the room. If you don't find anything that provides that exact ratio, install one with the next larger size or rating.

Installing a wall heater requires cutting open the wall surface between two studs and running wiring to the opening, typically through the top or bottom plate of the wall. Most wall heaters have a built-in thermostat or timer with adjustment controls right on the front panel, so wiring a separate wall thermostat isn't necessary. You'll also have to add horizontal 2x4 blocking above and below the heater housing. The blocking provides a secure mount and also a backing surface for the drywall around the opening's perimeter.

Bathrooms are an ideal application for wall heaters. Radiant versions heat one or more electric coils and have a reflective back panel to channel the heat energy into the room. Convection units have a fan mounted behind the heating coil and actively circulate heated air. Most units require their own electrical circuit, so plan to run new wiring and add a circuit breaker to your main electrical panel (a substantial job). Avoid installing them in exterior wall cavities.

Baseboard and Kick-Space Heaters

Positioning supplemental heat sources low helps keep feet warm, a benchmark for comfort. Baseboard heaters are long, slender units that provide passive convection heat via an electric-wire element or a coil of copper tubing that circulates hot water. Kick-space heaters are fan-forced convection units that fit inside a cabinet toe-kick.

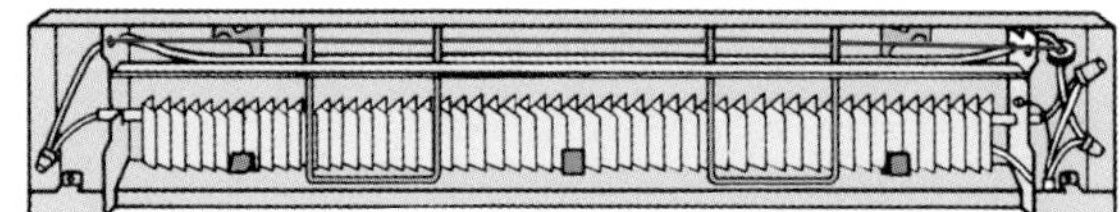

Baseboard. Too slender to accommodate an internal fan, a baseboard heater relies on passive convection to draw cool air from just above the floor. The air rises as it flows past the long core of heating fins and exits through a vent along the top of the heater.

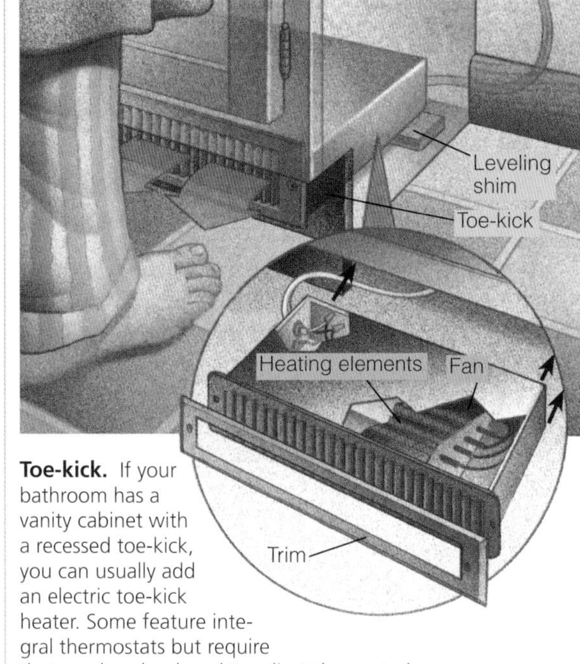

Toe-kick. If your bathroom has a vanity cabinet with a recessed toe-kick, you can usually add an electric toe-kick heater. Some feature integral thermostats but require that you bend or kneel to adjust the controls.

Troubleshooting Electric Heaters

Problem	Possible Cause	Solution
No heat	Thermostat is set too low.	Adjust thermostat until heat goes on.
	Draperies or furnishings block airflow.	Remove the obstruction(s).
	Circuit breaker tripped or fuse is blown.	Switch the breaker to on or replace fuse.
	Circuit breaker trips again; new fuse melts.	Check for short-circuit in wiring.
	Resistance wire in heating element is defective.	Turn off circuit breaker to heater and check wire with continuity tester; replace element with one of same voltage rating.
	Wiring connections inside heater are loose.	Turn off circuit breaker or pull fuse to heater circuit; check and tighten all connections.
	House wiring is defective.	Have an electrician check wiring.
Heater cycles on and off frequently	Draperies, furniture or debris block airflow.	Remove the obstruction(s).
Heater will not shut off	Heat loss from room is greater than heater's capacity.	Close doors and windows. Add weather stripping and/or insulation. Supplement with additional heaters.
Heater emits smoke or odors	Thermostat is defective.	Rotate thermostat knob to lowest setting; if heater continues to run, replace thermostat.
	Dust, dirt or lint have accumulated inside.	Vacuum heater using an extension tool.
Fan doesn't operate on fan-equipped heater	Blades are jammed.	Turn off power to heater; remove cover and inspect. Remove any obstruction(s).
	Wires are not connected to fan motor.	Turn off power to heater; connect fan wires.
	Fan motor is defective.	Use volt-ohm meter to see whether current is reaching motor. If so, replace motor; if not, check wiring, switch and circuit breaker.
Fan rotates but no heat is produced	Resistance wiring in heating element is defective.	Turn off circuit breaker to heater or check wire with a continuity tester. Replace element with one of the same voltage rating.
	Wiring connections inside heater are loose.	Turn off circuit breaker to heater; check and tighten all wire connections.

Caution: Before making any repair, unplug heater or turn off power to heater.

Types of Electric Heaters

Permanent electric convection heaters come in three types; recessed wall-mount or floor-mount units, kick-space units, and baseboard units.

Recessed heaters nest between wall studs or floor joists and feature a fan and either a built-in or in-line thermostat.

Toe-kick space heaters are designed to fit in the space under a kitchen base cabinet or a bath vanity cabinet. These units provide fan-forced heat.

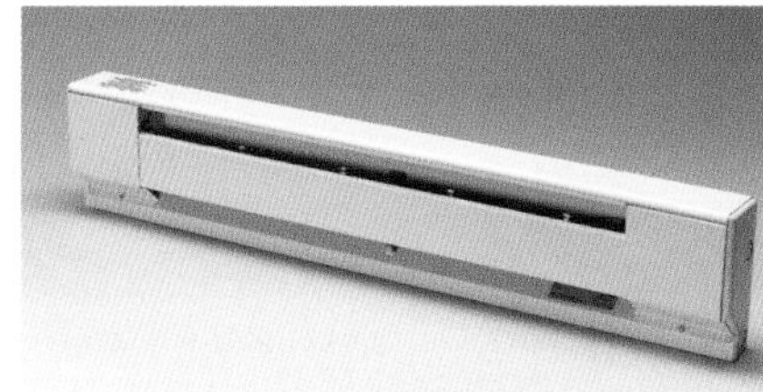

Baseboard heaters rely on natural convection, drawing cool air in through the lower slot. The heated air flows out the top slot.

Sizing an Electric Heater

Electric heaters for single rooms are rated according to their energy consumption, with ratings typically ranging from 750 to 5,000 watts.

The first step in selecting the right size of heater is to determine the floor area; simply multiply the room's length by its width. To determine heater size for a room with normal ceiling height, figure on about 10 watts per sq. ft. (110 watts per sq. m).

Factors, such as climate, location of room, number of exterior walls, and amount of insulation can greatly effect these numbers.

Prevent Fires

Although they are usually of lower wattage than built-in units, portable heaters are responsible for more residential fires. Undersize or damaged extension cords can result in overheated wires and arcing current. For safety, always plug the heater directly into a wall outlet. Always keep heaters away from flammable materials or objects.

Electric Resistance Floor Heat

Circuit Mapping and Planning 129
Electrical Testers 132
Heating an Addition 179
Ceramic Tile and Stone 250
Tiling Floors 253

Tile floors are popular in bathrooms for their practicality and durability, but even in mild climates, they tend to be too cold for bare feet. Imagine the comfort of stepping out of the shower onto a warm floor, and you'll understand why in-floor electric heating systems have become so popular. For small residential spaces, such as bathrooms, simple electric-heating mats borrow the principle of commercial hydronic (water-filled tubing) systems to provide a reliable, affordable heat source.

Embedded in the thin-set mortar used to secure the tile, these mats feature a continuous loop of resistance heating cable amid a thin plastic mesh. There are different systems and types of heating cable available, so shop around. Like other heaters, the system can be controlled by a thermostat, a timer or even an on-off wall switch. Be extra cautious during installation to avoid nicking any wires. Insulate under floor, if possible.

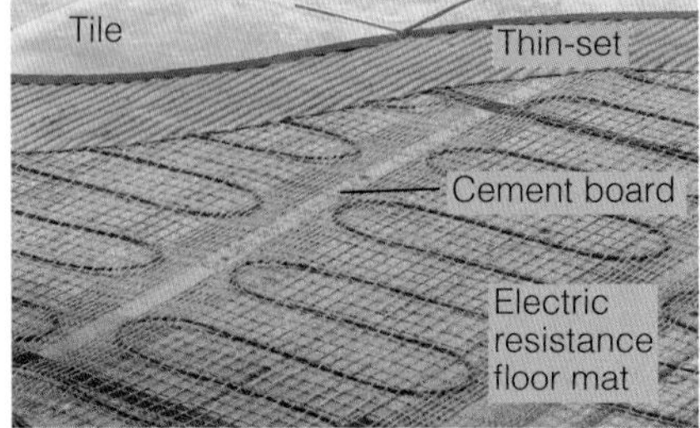

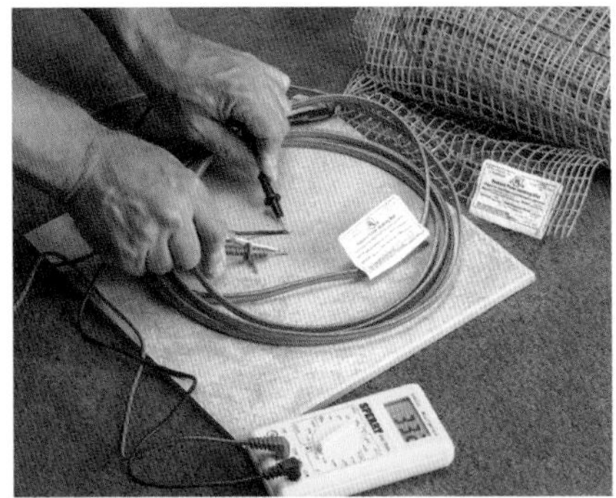

1 Test the heating cable with a volt-ohm meter to make sure the resistance reading is within 10 percent of the rating on the product label. If it's not, check the manufacturer's instructions before you proceed.

2 After laying a cement-board subfloor, test-fit the mat, making sure the heating cable is at least 4 in. (10 cm) away from any walls, fixtures or cabinets. Do not cut the heating cable or allow it to overlap itself.

3 Chisel a shallow trench in the cement board near the wall where the line wiring is, to make room for the mat's thicker wire lead. Also notch the bottom plate for the thermostat cable and power lead.

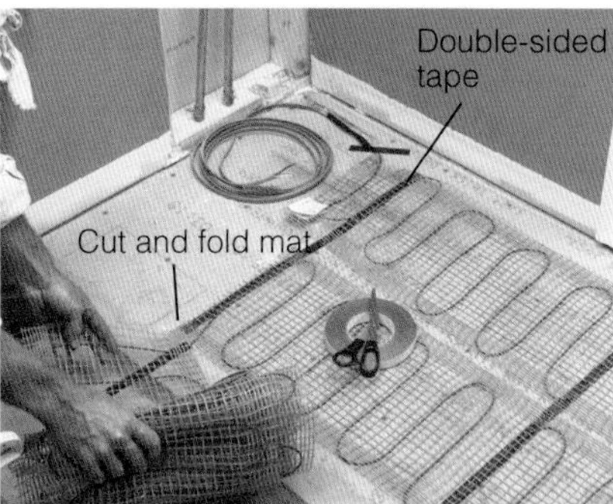

4 Secure the mat to the cement board subfloor with double-sided tape. At the end of each run, cut the mat, not the heating cable itself, so you can fold it over and reverse direction to start the next course.

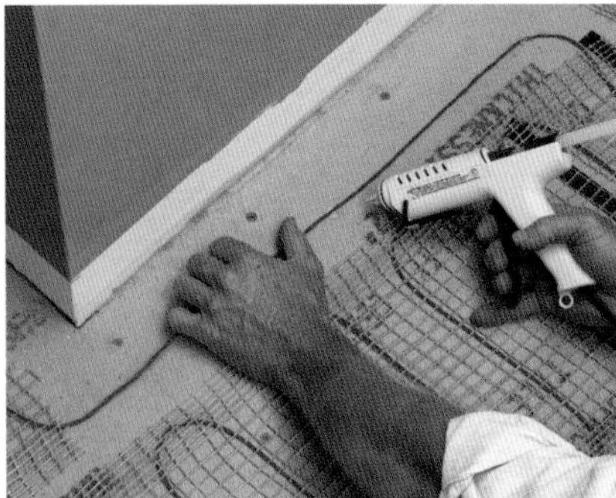

5 For sections where the mat won't fit, such as around a fixture, cut the plastic mesh away and secure the heating cable to the floor with hot-melt glue. Glue down any loose ends or humps in the mat, too.

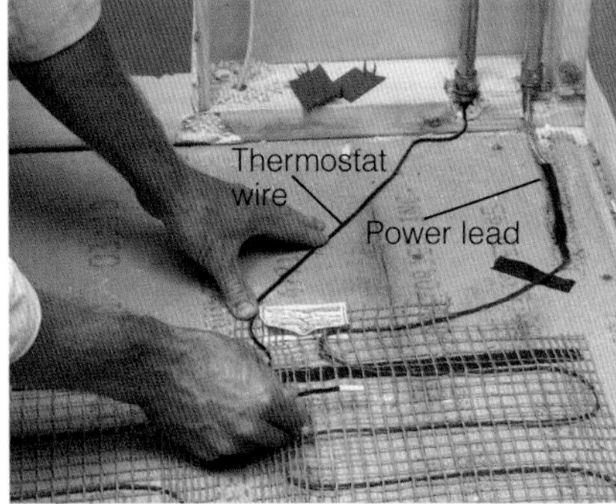

6 Feed the power lead and the thermostat wire through the conduit and to a wall-mounted electrical box. Connect the power lead to the house wiring (it may require a new circuit) and install the thermostat wire and sensor.

7 With the mat secured, use a notched trowel to apply thin-set mortar to cover it and provide a bed for the tile. Take care to avoid nicking or cutting the heating cable with the trowel's sharp edges.

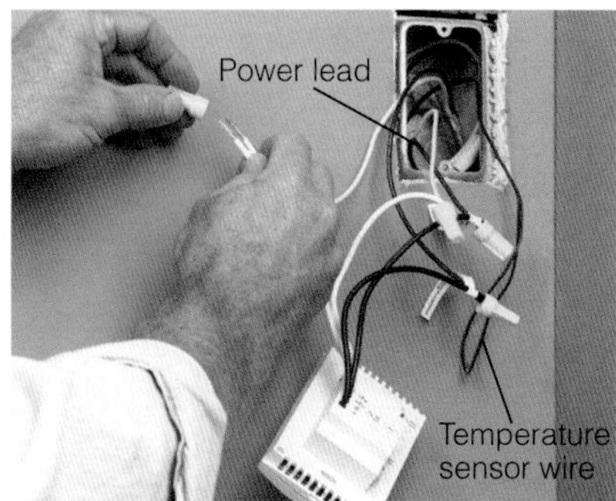

8 After setting the tile and doing another continuity-resistance test, wire the wall thermostat. Shut off power to the thermostat while you're working on it. Let mortar cure one week before turning on the current.

Passive Solar Heating

As reliable as most of them are, the systems commonly used to provide heat to our homes all cost money to operate and come from outside sources. Whether they rely on electricity, natural gas, propane or heating oil, the cost and sometimes availability of their fuel can vary widely with the regional, economic, even political forces that are out of a homeowner's control. Solar energy offers a "free," inexhaustible source of heat energy, but it doesn't provide the same consistency and control that conventional systems provide. Although it is possible to harvest solar energy for storage in battery systems or link a solar collector-converter to a commercial power grid, the simplest gains can be had from passive solar systems, which convert the sun's energy directly into usable interior heat. Even on cold winter days, the sun's energy can be captured to provide heat for a home.

An effective passive solar-heating system relies on two primary conditions, aside from the basic requirement of daylight. First is a clear surface, like glass, that allows the passage of solar energy into the interior space. Second is a storage feature that can absorb that energy so the space doesn't overheat, then release it later when the sun goes down and temperatures drop. A material with this ability to store and release heat energy is said to have thermal mass. Water is a common example, as is almost any masonry material, especially concrete or brick. Other features that help make a sun-warmed space more livable allow you to control the rate of heat gain and release; roof overhangs and venting windows are two common examples.

In North America, passive solar features are normally installed on the south side of a structure. This prevents overheating during the summer months when overhangs block out the high summer sun and captures more energy during winter months, when the earth's orbit causes the sun to appear lower in the sky. Solar features are sometimes costly to retrofit onto an existing home, and the rate of financial return is sometimes slow, but energy savings and a light-filled interior environment are two good reasons to welcome solar energy where possible.

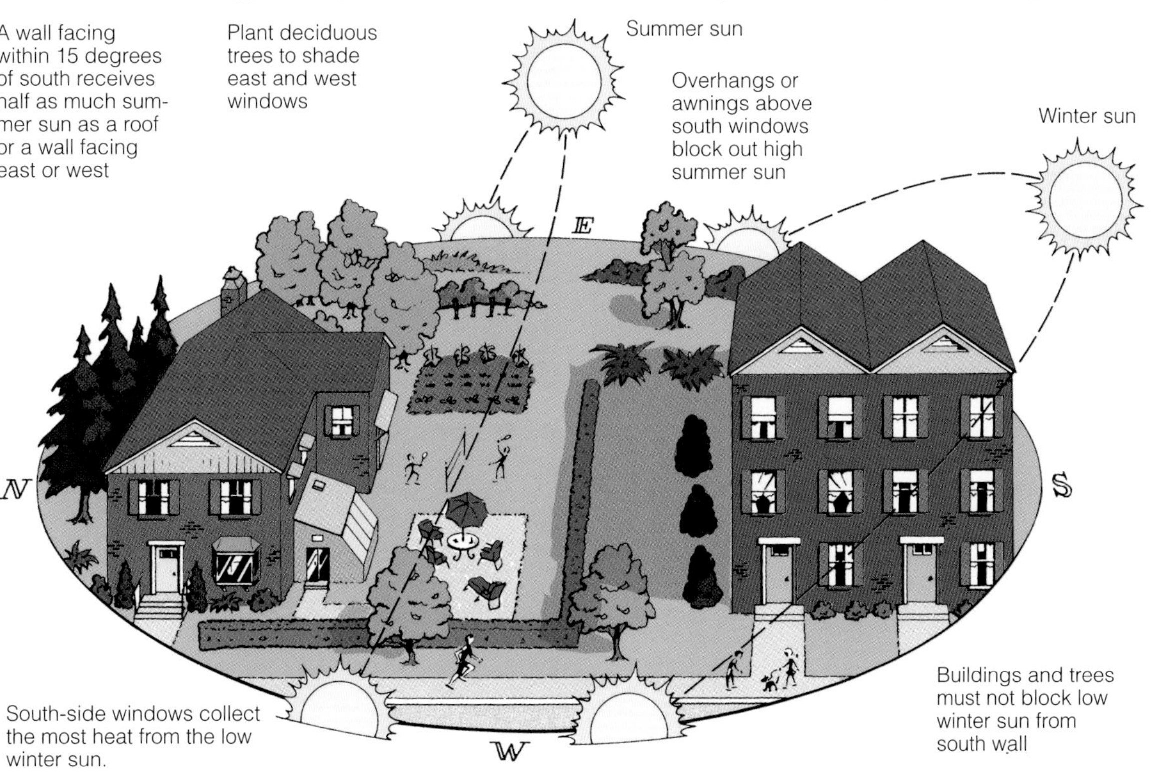
A wall facing within 15 degrees of south receives half as much summer sun as a roof or a wall facing east or west
Plant deciduous trees to shade east and west windows
Summer sun
Overhangs or awnings above south windows block out high summer sun
Winter sun
E
N
S
W
South-side windows collect the most heat from the low winter sun.
Buildings and trees must not block low winter sun from south wall

Shop Smart

Sun-powered Heat, Electricity and Light

Despite decades of interest and product development, solar technology is still largely an emerging industry. Some applications show increasing promise; photovoltaic panels, like the one shown for charging batteries, now feature a flexible thin-film technology and are more efficient at converting sunlight into electricity. Many solar technologies remain supplemental rather than primary energy systems, especially for controlling home climates. Rooftop water-heating systems and south-facing sun spaces still represent the most practical applications of passive solar gain. As these simple technologies improve, they will likely contribute a higher percentage of a home's energy needs. Expect increased performance and decreased costs eventually, as well as a wider range of products and applications.

Tracking down solar products can start with familiar sources, such as your local Yellow Pages or business directory under "Solar Products and Services" or through Internet searches. There already exists a solar-energy trade show, called Solar Power, as well as a trade group, the Solar Energy Industries Association (SEIA), that can direct consumers to solar-powered products for residential use.

Installing a Gas Fireplace

Drywall 211

There's no denying that a fireplace adds character and ambience to a home's interior, but when the traditional coal- or wood-burning fireplace lost its central-heating role to the automatic furnace, many homes went hearthless. Retrofitting a traditional masonry fireplace in most of those homes is an expensive and complicated project, but a modular metal fireplace that burns gas can provide a convincing substitute, without the need for a heavy, expensive masonry chimney. Most units operate with the flick of a wall switch or remote control, and optional blower units expand their heating ranges by actively distributing heated air into the room.

Aside from their simpler, more affordable installation, direct-vent gas fireplaces eliminate the need to haul firewood through the house or clean out ashes, and more flexibility in locating the unit. The insulated metal duct that exhausts hot gases and brings in combustion air can usually be installed through either an exterior wall or the roof.

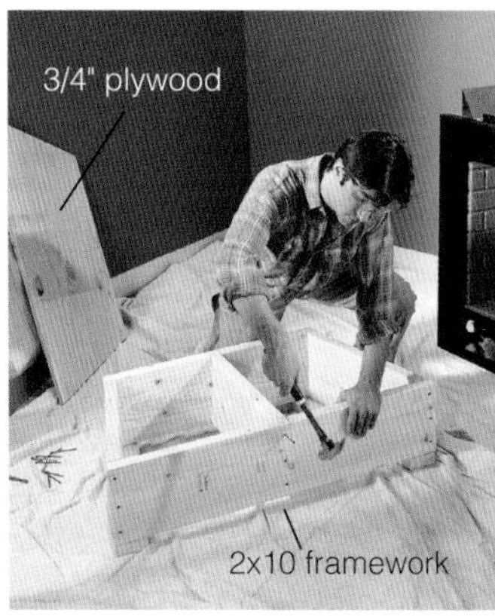

1 After mocking up the fireplace in several locations or test-fitting the unit itself, use framing lumber to construct a base platform the same size as the fireplace module. Fit a 3/4-in. plywood top onto the base and fasten it with screws. Slide it temporarily into position to check the fit against the wall or corner.

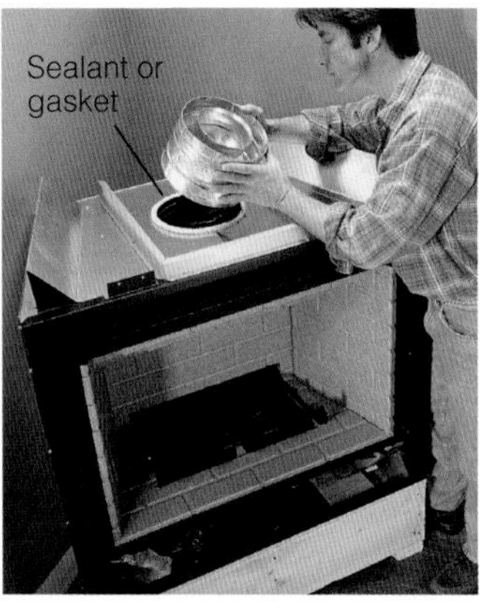

2 With the necessary sealant, which is typically a stove cement, rope gasket or high-temperature silicone caulk, fit the first vent-pipe section in place. Fasten it securely according to the instructions and add the next fitting. In this installation, it's a 90° elbow with a straight pipe extension on the back end.

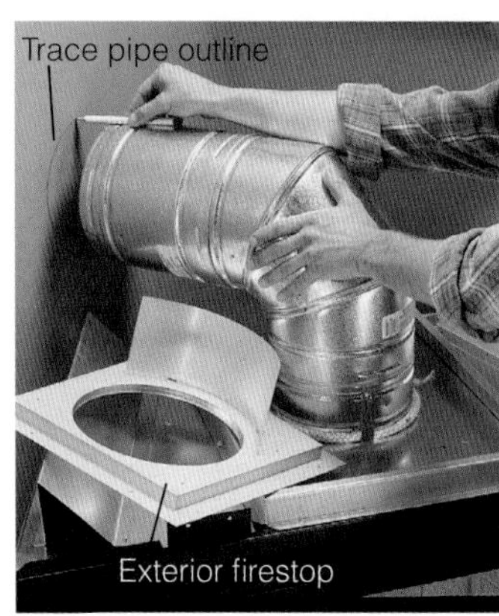

3 Mark an outline of the vent pipe on the wall surface and temporarily move the fireplace out of the way. Cut a 12-in. (30-cm) square opening around the vent-pipe location; add blocking and a header around the opening. If a wall stud obstructs the path, cut a larger opening to alter the framing, as shown in Step 4.

4 Drill holes at the corners of the square vent opening, penetrating the exterior wall sheathing and siding. This transfers the opening to the outer face of the wall so you can cut through the siding and sheathing. Next, fit the outer fire-stop and cap against the siding and trace the outline; cut through only the siding.

5 Replace the wall insulation and patch the interior wall surface—a rough patch is fine if you'll add a fireplace surround and mantle to cover the area. Apply a bead of caulk around the patch and around the perimeter of the vent opening; press the interior fire-stop into the caulk and fasten it to the wall with screws.

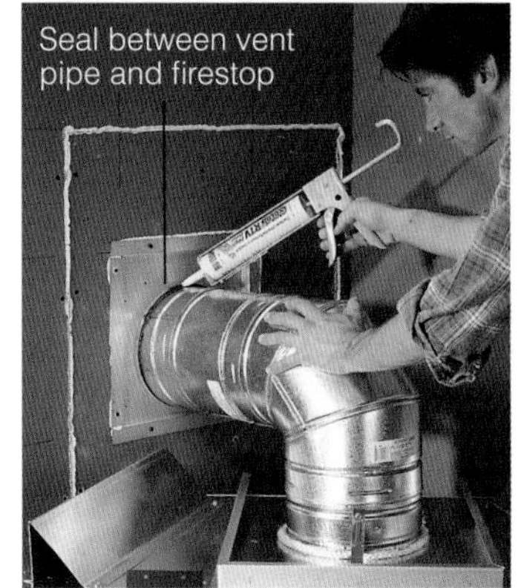

6 Move the fireplace unit into position and insert the interior vent pipe through to connect with the exterior fire-stop. The procedure for making the vent-pipe connection can vary with the manufacturer and model, so follow the instructions provided. Seal around the vent pipe with a bead of high-temperature silicone caulk.

7 Slide the exterior vent fitting (a combination fire-stop and cap) onto the pipe coming through the wall. If necessary, install a metal drip cap under the siding, as shown here, and use screws to fasten the fire-stop flange to the wall. Use caulk to seal the joints between the siding and the metal flange.

8 After installing the required gas and electrical lines (we suggest you hire pros for this), level and fasten the wood platform. Using the illustration at far right as a guide, frame the remaining structure for the fireplace surround. The detailing can vary from the example shown, as long as you provide a nailing base for the drywall.

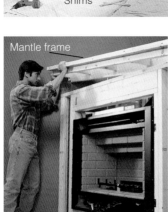

9 The mantle frame is the next assembly required to complete the structural framework for the fireplace surround. Slide it into position atop the main façade frame and fasten it with screws. Follow this step by installing the angled frame pieces at each end; then build and install the hearth extension and upper wall frame.

10 Cut the column parts from 2x10 and 2x2 stock and screw them to the lower wall frame of the surround. Note that the vertical 2x2 cleats taper to a point at their lower end and that the lower 2x10 block is beveled 45° on its upper edge. When complete, fasten drywall over the entire assembly.

11 Cover all the outside corners with metal drywall corner bead. Where two or more corner beads meet, cut angles at the ends to form a point so the flanges don't interfere with each other. Nail the bead tight with drywall nails. For corners greater than 90°, install a special 120° metal bead.

12 At inside corners, embed paper drywall tape in joint compound and apply the compound to all surfaces to cover the joints and corner bead. Let dry; then sand and repeat one or two applications until joints and surfaces are smooth and flat. If desired, apply a troweled or sponged texture, prime and paint.

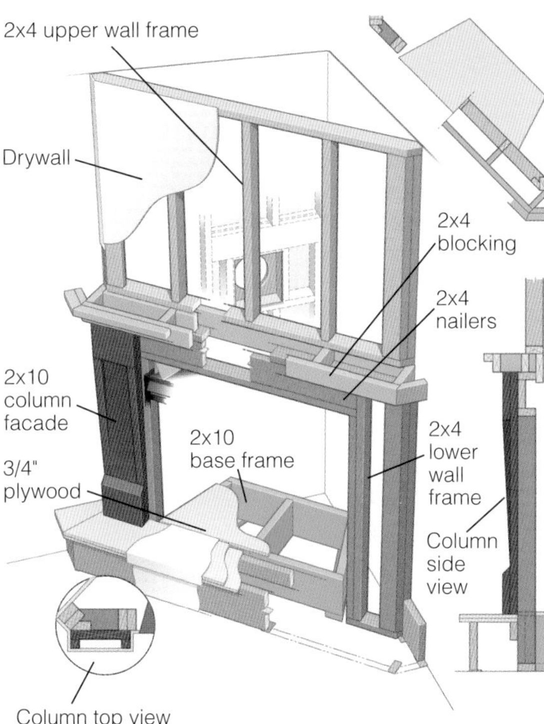

Fireplace surround details. This illustration reveals the basic framing components of the fireplace surround, mantle and hearth. Make certain to follow the manufacturer's guidelines, which specify safe clearances from combustible materials.

No-vent Gas Fireplaces

No-vent, or vent-free, gas fireplaces represent the simplest route to getting a fireplace, but they aren't legal everywhere because of air-quality concerns. Like a gas kitchen range, they burn natural gas or propane and do it so cleanly that the tiny amounts of combustion by-products generated don't require a vent. These units have an oxygen-depletion sensor that automatically shuts the gas off if the oxygen level in the room falls below 18 percent; many also integrate carbon-monoxide detectors. Air circulates around the firebox by natural convection, but the heat output is modest.

Efficient Wood-burning Fireplaces

The Problem

Heat (and money) go up the chimney. Despite its undeniable aesthetic appeal and that toasty feeling on your face, a crackling wood fire in a traditional fireplace is not your friend. It's sending most of its heat straight up the chimney, and its appetite for oxygen can actually displace the warm air in your home with cold, resulting in a net energy loss.

To keep smoke from back-drafting into the house, a fireplace has to draw air from the outside. In most homes, this means cold air will enter through leaky windows and other openings, forcing warm air up the chimney. In a weather-tight home, a window will have to be opened to provide air for combustion.

Solution #1

Add glass door and air-intake vent. If your fireplace sits above grade in an exterior wall, and if local codes allow it, install a box vent, lined with fireproof material, to provide combustion air directly to the fire. This helps prevent warm inside air from being lost up the chimney. Glass fireplace doors radiate the fire's heat but block the loss of interior air.

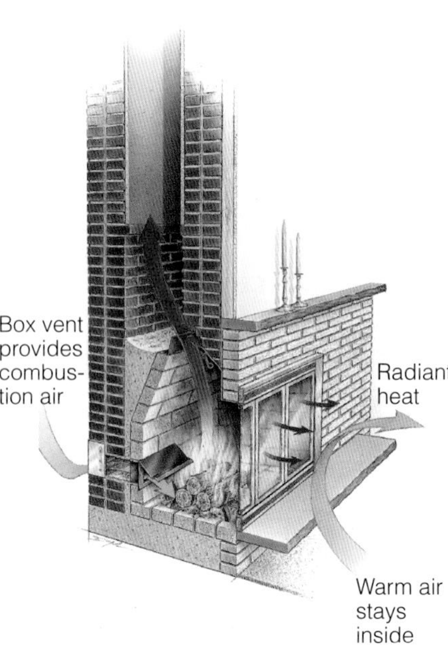

Two modifications can interrupt a fireplace's cycle of inefficiency by stopping the loss of warm inside air. The first step is to provide an alternate source of combustion air by adding a vent that opens directly into, or in front of, the firebox. Second, a set of glass fireplace doors prevents interior air from entering the chimney.

Solution #2

Wood-burning insert. Similar in function to a freestanding wood stove but nested inside the fireplace opening, a wood-burning insert offers much greater efficiency than an open fireplace. The key is a heat-exchange chamber that surrounds the firebox; room air, helped by an electric blower, enters this chamber for heating and recirculation.

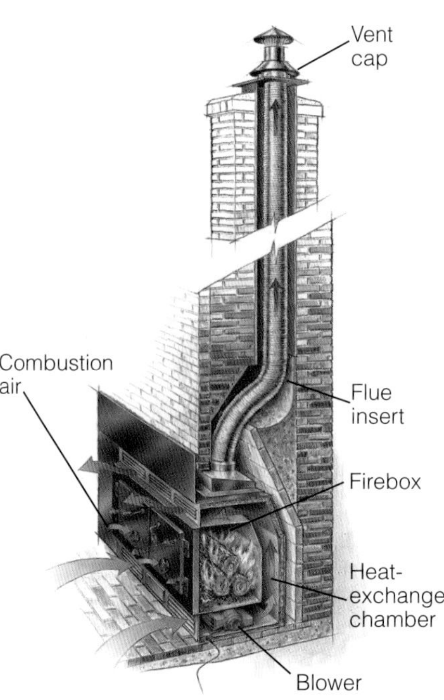

Adjustable vents in the insert doors provide combustion air for the firebox, but air that enters the heat-exchange chamber is heated and returned to the room. The smoke stream exits through a metal flue insert so no cross-contamination occurs with the air circulating through the heat-exchange chamber.

Solution #3

Gas-fired insert. Although it relies on a heat-exchange chamber much the way a wood-burning insert does, a gas-fired fireplace insert has a sealed combustion chamber, so no interior air is used for combustion. Instead, two metal flue inserts are used: one for combustion air intake and one for an exhaust vent. It's convenient and efficient.

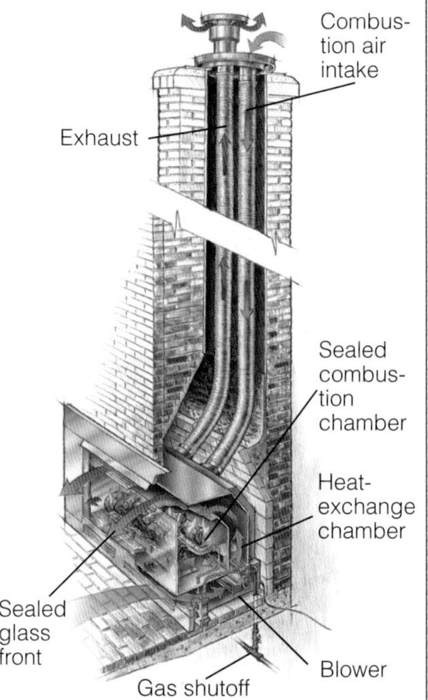

With no wood to haul in and no ashes to clean out, a gas-burning fireplace insert offers convenient use of a converted fireplace. The combustion chamber is sealed off from the home's interior; its heat is captured by air in the surrounding exchange chamber and circulated by an electric blower.

Wood-burning Stoves

A freestanding wood-burning stove can provide much of the ambience of a traditional masonry fireplace and do so with efficiency ratings as high as 75 percent compared with a fireplace's low or even negative efficiencies. Some stoves can burn with their doors open, but all provide the most heat when closed and properly vented. Part of the key to their efficient heat transfer is the amount of exposed surface area; lined with firebrick and built of heavy steel plate or cast iron, a wood stove's firebox radiates heat in all directions, warming surrounding objects and surfaces. For safety, minimum clearances for combustible materials are mandated by codes and manufacturers (see examples at right).

Relative to a fireplace, a woodstove offers much more control over combustion air intake and burn rates, but for peak efficiency and lower emissions, the smoke-exhaust temperature should stay between 300°F and 400°F (150°C and 200°C). For this reason, don't buy more stove capacity than the space requires. It's better to install a smaller stove and burn it hot rather than burn a too-large stove slowly to avoid overheating the room. Also, don't slow-burn a stove to make the fire last through the night; instead, install a masonry surround with enough thermal mass to store and release the heat after the fire burns out.

You'll get the most efficiency by burning seasoned hardwood or manufactured pellets made from compressed sawdust. Never burn unseasoned "green" wood, railroad ties, pressure-treated lumber or plastics in a woodstove.

Cleaner Burning Woodstoves

Only about half the potential energy from a fire comes from the wood; the rest lies in the heated gases we call smoke. Newer woodstoves feature a catalytic combustor, similar to the devices used for reducing emissions in automobile exhaust, that reburns the smoke to extract heat energy and reduce airborne pollutants. Often required by law, many of these stoves produce only 2 to 5 grams of smoke per hour—a 95-percent reduction.

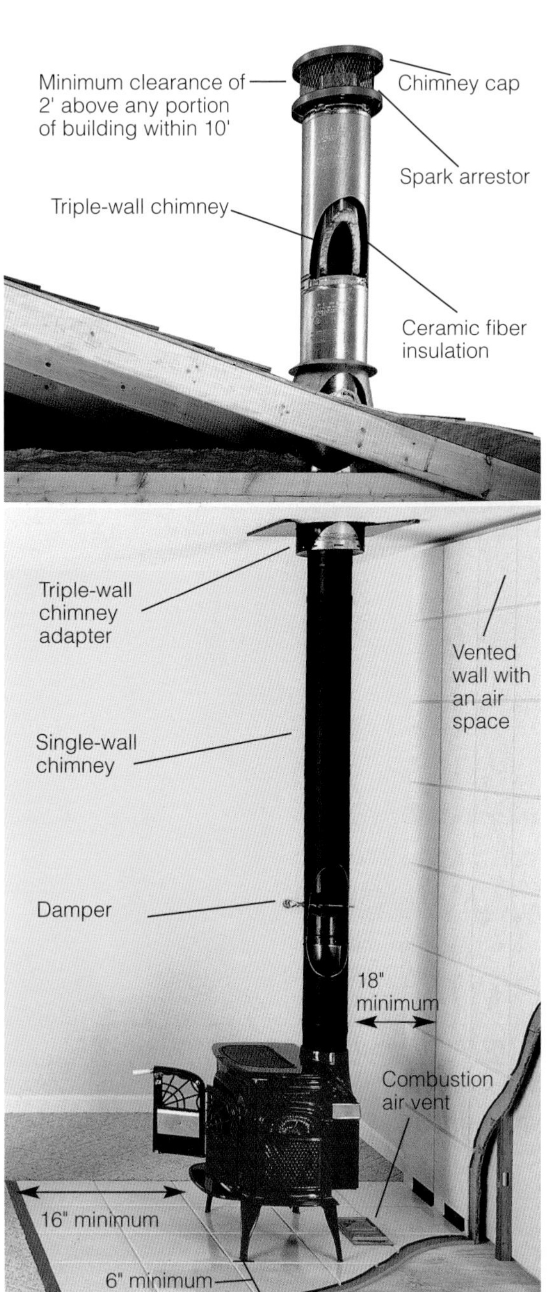

Roof Components

Where the stove chimney exits the roof, an adjustable support bracket positions it to maintain a 2-in. (5-cm) clearance from combustibles. Flashings and caulk keep rainfall at bay.

Ceiling Components

Entering the ceiling, the single-wall stove pipe must be fitted with an adapter to connect to a triple-wall chimney or other approved insulated chimney. Cover plates can include decorative trim or a simple flange to cover the clearance hole in the ceiling.

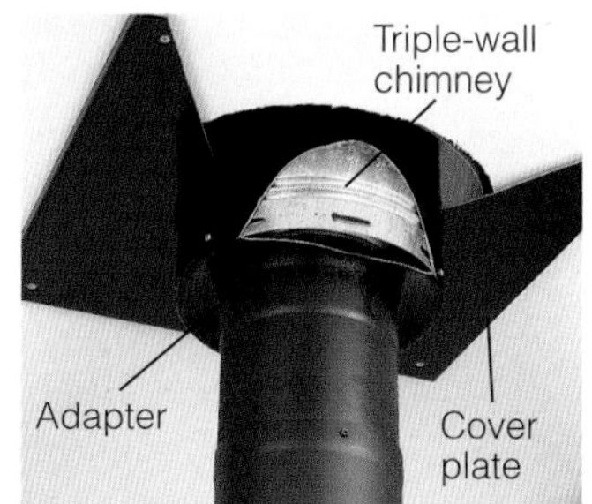

Floor and Wall Components

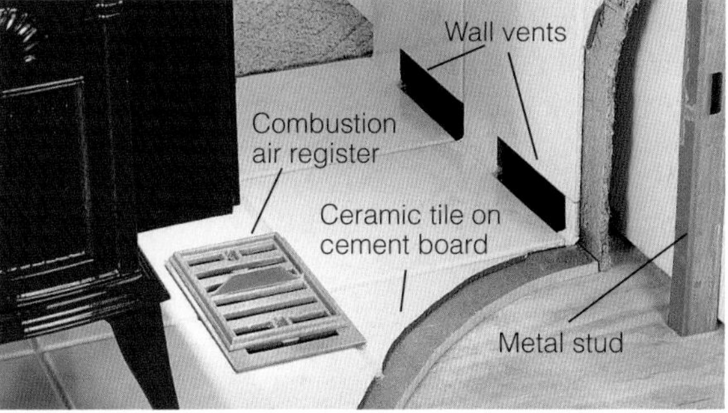

Surfaces below and behind the stove should be noncombustible materials, such as ceramic tile or masonry. A floor register provides outside combustion air. The wall surface features a vented air space for keeping the wall cool.

Heat Pumps

A heat pump is a refrigerant system, much like an air conditioner or refrigerator, that can both heat and cool your home. Most heat pumps are split systems, with an outdoor coil, an indoor coil and a compressor. During the winter, the system extracts low-grade heat from outdoors and transfers it indoors. During the summer, the heat pump is reversed, absorbing unwanted heat from indoors and sending it outdoors. A thermostat, ducts and blowers control and distribute the warm and cool air.

Although it is hard to imagine squeezing any useful heat energy from 30°F (-1°C) wintertime air, a refrigerant at -20°F (-29°C) will be warmed when circulated through the outdoor coil in air that is 50°F (27°C) warmer. During this cycle, the compressor and fans consume energy to deliver the heat. The ratio of the amount of heat delivered to the amount of energy consumed is called the coefficient of performance (COP). Depending on the outdoor temperature, the COP of a good heat pump in the heating season ranges from 1.0 to 3.0—meaning 1 to 3 BTUs of heat delivered per BTU of electricity consumed. Most heat pumps are slightly more efficient during the cooling season.

Other rating systems used for heat pumps are the heating season performance factor (HSPF) and the season energy efficiency ratio (SEER). These ratings use the watt as a unit of measure and are simply 3.4 times the size of the COP because there are 3.4 BTUs per watt.

As outdoor temperatures fall, a heat pump's heating capacity declines, although high-quality units can still extract heat with outdoor temperatures as low as 9°F (-13°C). To compensate, supplementary electric heating elements switch on at the crossover point, which is the point at which an air-source heat pump does not have enough heating capacity to satisfy a home's needs.

Have a heat pump serviced annually by a qualified contractor. In addition, routinely vacuum the indoor coil, change the blower filter and wash the outdoor coil with a hose.

Heating Cycle

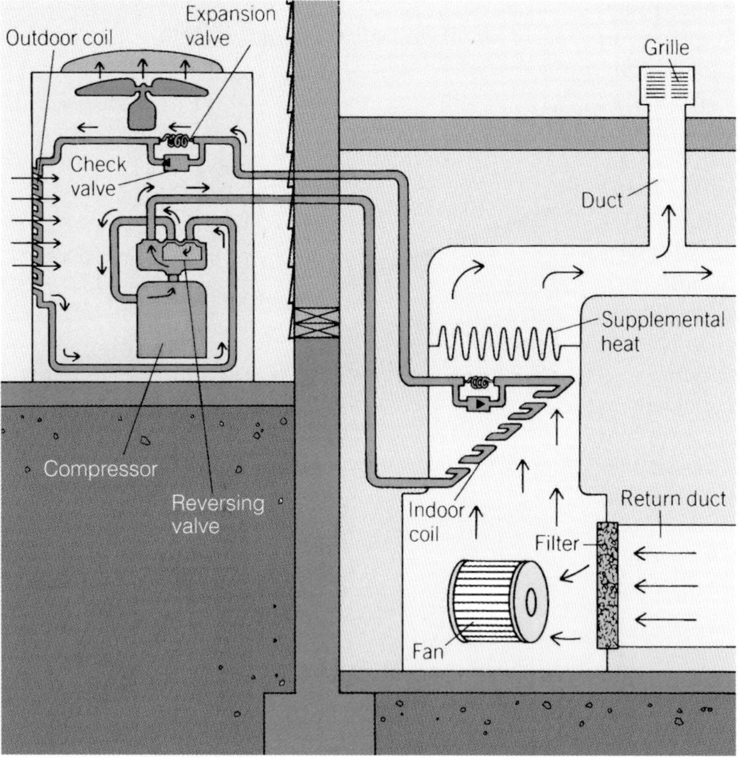

Cooling Cycle

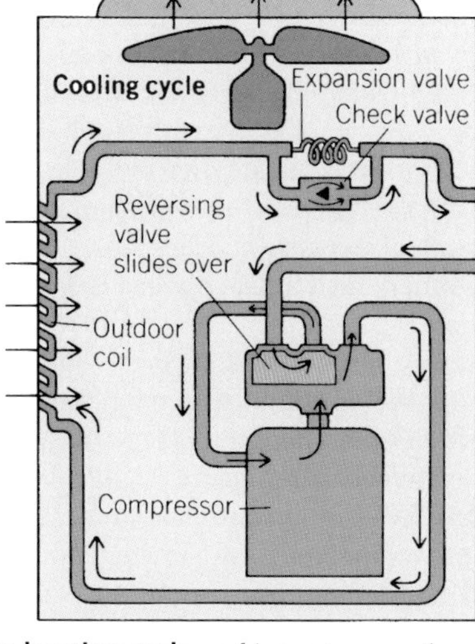

In heating cycle, refrigerant passes through outdoor coil as gas, drawing heat from air. Gas moves to compressor, where high pressure raises its temperature. Compressed gas moves to indoor coil, where it releases heat and condenses into liquid. Expansion valve allows liquid to move from high pressure to low, lowers temperature and vaporizing again. For cooling, a valve reverses the system.

Heat Pump Troubleshooting

Problems	Possible Solutions
Frost on outdoor coil in winter and on indoor coil in summer; irregular defrosting patterns.	Buildup is a normal function of humidity, temperature and coil design. Keep coils and condenser clean. Replace filter because more airflow reduces defrost cycle length. If problem persists, check manual to locate and clean airflow sensing tube.
Refrigerant leaking red dye.	Call for repair. If unattended, a leak can lead to compressor failure.
Odors when heat pump kicks on.	Check that drip pan, which catches condensate from indoor unit, is draining.
Inadequate heat in very cold weather.	Unit may be undersize. Shut off vents in unused rooms. Consider adding duct boosters or auxiliary heaters. Supplementary heating coil may need replacing.
Frequent on-off cycling.	Check thermostat; it could be broken or have an improperly set anticipator.
Cold air from register blowing onto frequently used seating places.	Adjust diffusers to direct air away from seating; seal any ductwork in attic or crawl space; have in-line supplementary heater installed in problem duct.
Frequent compressor burnout.	Mismatched indoor and outdoor units. Have contractor evaluate system as a whole.

Water-Based Heat Pumps

Most heat pumps extract heat from the air, but some use heat from water for heating or cooling. In a water-based system, the pipes may be submerged in a lake or stream. But, since groundwater temperatures vary less than lake and stream water, the most common type uses well water brought to the heat pump and either discharged or reinjected into another well, as shown below.

Though much more expensive to install, heat pumps that rely on ground and water temperatures are vastly more efficient than air systems, because ground and water temperatures don't go to the extremes of air temperatures. Check local building codes about regulations in your area.

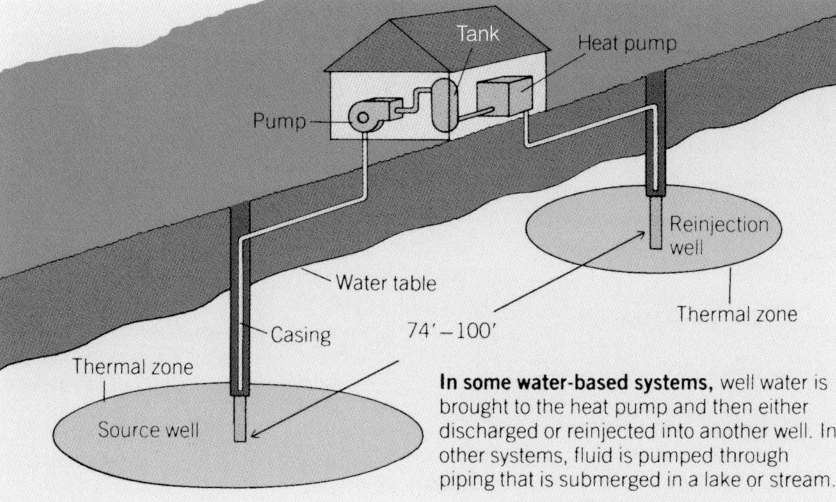

In some water-based systems, well water is brought to the heat pump and then either discharged or reinjected into another well. In other systems, fluid is pumped through piping that is submerged in a lake or stream.

Improve Efficiency

An air screen greatly improves a heat pump's cooling efficiency in the summer, especially in warm, humid climates. It shades the outdoor condensing coil to make it possible for the cooling coil to dissipate heat faster. In the winter, remove the screen to better capture the sun's warming rays.

Ground-Source Heat Pumps

Ground-source heat pumps, also called geothermal systems, tap into the huge storehouse of energy contained in the earth by removing heat stored in the soil and transferring it into your house, making these systems extremely efficient. Whereas the best gas furnaces run at 92-percent efficiency, geothermal units run at a whopping 300-percent efficiency, because they're tapping into and transferring existing heat rather than burning fuel to create it.

Geothermal systems have three main components: the ground loop that gathers heat, the heat pump that condenses the heat and the duct system that distributes the heat. The ground loop can be one of two varieties. Closed-loop systems circulate an antifreeze solution through polyethylene pipe buried at least 6 ft. (2 m) underground, where year-round temperatures hover at around 55°F (13°C). Open-loop systems rely on a supply of water, usually well water, rather than antifreeze. Water is circulated through the heat pump, heat is extracted and the cooled water is discharged, usually to a pond.

The heat is absorbed by a refrigerant, which is compressed and rises in temperature to about 160°F (71°C). Air passing over a heat exchanger is warmed and distributed throughout the home through a network of ducts, similar to a forced-air system.

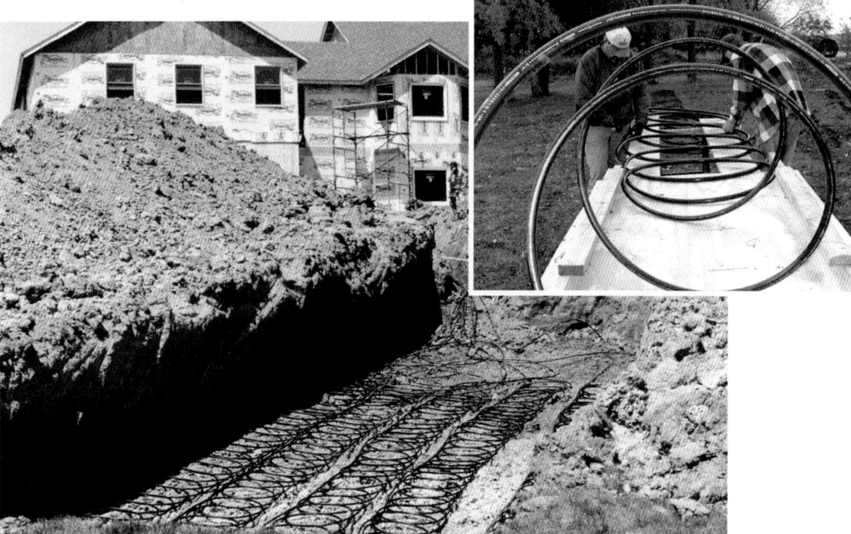

Geothermal pipe can be buried in trenches, circulated beneath ponds or run in a series of deep, vertical well holes. The pipe can be installed in straight, parallel lines or coiled like a Slinky toy. The earth warms the antifreeze mixture or water, the heat is withdrawn by the heat pump and the cycle repeats. The earth around the pipe slowly cools, but never to the point that the system stops working. Summer sun reheats the earth for the next heating season.

Cooling Your Home

Extending a Branch Circuit 138
Compact Fluorescent Bulbs 152
Window Tint Films 368
Window Choices 369

Keeping your home cool during the heat of summer requires a multifaceted approach to maximize comfort and energy savings. About 25 percent of the summer heat that enters a house comes through the windows, another 25 percent seeps through cracks and 20 percent enters through walls and ceilings. Most of the rest is generated inside by cooking, bathing and heat-producing lights and appliances.

For most homes, the first line of defense is air-conditioning, but these systems can be expensive to operate. To reduce energy costs, don't rely on air-conditioning alone to make your home comfortable. Take the steps shown in the checklist at right to help keep the heat out.

Air-conditioners cool, dehumidify and filter the air. They can be bought to condition a single room (p. 198) or the whole house (p. 200). In areas where nights are cool and dry, a whole-house fan (p. 197) can cool a house at a fraction of the cost of air-conditioning.

If you live in a dry climate, consider air conditioning your home with an evaporative cooler. These coolers use the natural process of water evaporation to cool indoor air at a fraction of the cost of refrigerated air. They contain a blower, fibrous pads, a small pump and a water reservoir. When the unit is operating, the pump draws water from the reservoir and distributes it to the pads to keep them saturated. The blower draws outside air through the pads to cool it, forcing the cooled air into the house and the warm, stale air out.

Cooling with shade. Before air-conditioning, shade was the best defense against summertime heat. Today, shade has taken a back seat to the on-demand predictability and convenience of air-conditioning in homes, workplaces and cars. But don't dismiss shading strategies as outdated; they will still provide plenty of comfort and energy savings. Shade can reduce your air-conditioning bill by as much as one-third and will make your yard cooler and more pleasant as well.

The sun's path dictates the best placement for shading devices. The west and south sides of a home are hardest hit by the summer sun. During the heat of the day, the south side takes the brunt of the sun's rays. In the late afternoon and evening, when temperatures are highest, the west side becomes the victim.

Landscape shading blocks the sun before it hits your house, so it's a great house-cooling strategy. For maximum energy savings, place trees and other foliage so the house is shaded in summer but not in winter. Moderate-size trees block late morning and early evening sun. Tall trees placed fairly close to the house cast shade over the roof during midday hours.

Energy-efficient roof design should include overhangs, awnings and porch roofs to shade the south walls and windows during the middle of the day.

No one shading device or landscaping idea is best for every home. But basic shading principles will help you choose what fits your home's style, your local climate and your budget.

Cool-house Checklist

Steps, both simple and complex, can go a long way in lowering your home's cooling costs. Check out these areas; they can go a long way in lowering your home's cooling costs.

- ☐ Attic ventilation moves hot air out. Ridge, gable and soffit vents provide passive movement. Whole-house fans provide mechanical means for removing hot air.
- ☐ Adequate insulation in the attic and exterior walls keeps out heat, as well as cold.
- ☐ Deciduous trees on the south and west sides of a house provide shade in summer but allow passive solar heating in winter.
- ☐ Use ceiling or other fans to provide a chill effect while reducing air-conditioning costs.
- ☐ Replace incandescent light bulbs with compact fluorescent bulbs to cut energy consumption and reduce heat output.
- ☐ Protect sunny windows with drapes, shades, blinds, awnings or heat-reflecting film.
- ☐ Install thermal windows with low-E glass and argon gas.
- ☐ Seal around windows and doors to keep hot air from seeping in.
- ☐ When it's time to replace, consider installing light-colored shingles to reduce attic temperatures.
- ☐ Choose light-colored paint which reflects heat better than dark-colored paint.

Whole-house Fans

Whole-house fans are an economical, energy-efficient alternative to air-conditioning. In some regions, it may be the only cooling mechanism you need; in others, it can shorten the length of time you need to run your air conditioner and save hundreds of dollars annually.

Capacity. Whole-house fans come in different sizes to accommodate different attic construction and house sizes. Increase the convenience by installing a timer or thermostat. Fans are sold according to their cubic feet per minute (CFM) capacity, which indicates how much air they move. Depending on the climate, you need a fan that will change the air in your house every two to three minutes. To determine the CFM requirement, take the total above-ground square footage and multiply it by three for moderate climates or four for warmer climates.

Location. For this type of fan to work effectively, install it in a central location on the upper level of the house; usually the hallway that leads to the bedrooms. Check for obstructions in the attic after you've determined the best location. In cold climates, make certain the units can be tightly sealed and insulated during heating season.

Operation. Use a whole-house fan only when the outside temperature is cooler than the inside temperature. To use it, shut off the air-conditioning and, in the rooms you want cooled, open the windows about 2 to 3 in. (5 to 7.5 cm) and block open the doors.

Caution: Don't use the fan when windows are closed. This will cause interior air to be exhausted without being replaced with fresh outside air. When this happens, backdrafting can occur, which means deadly carbon monoxide fumes given off by water heaters and other gas-burning appliances may be drawn into your home rather than exhausted through their venting systems.

How attic fans cool. Attic fans cool by pulling cooler, outside air in through windows that are open by 2 to 3 in. (5 to 7.5 cm) and drawing the warm air in the house up into the attic. The warm air in the attic then exhausts under pressure through vents in the roof.

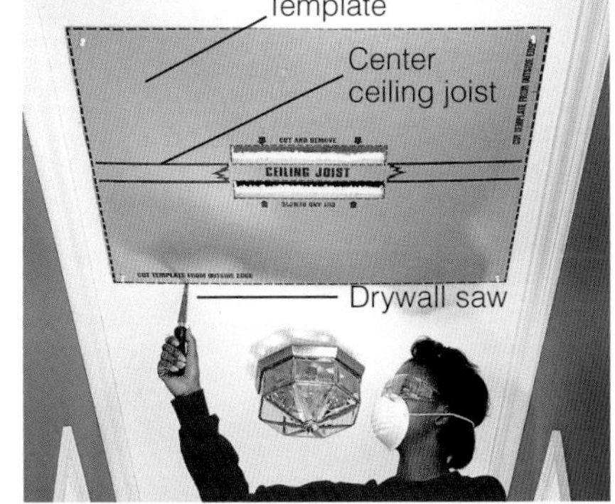

1 Locate center ceiling joist for fan location and cut out a slot on either side. Align and position template on center ceiling joist and, after checking for obstructions, cut completely around outer edge. Remove drywall.

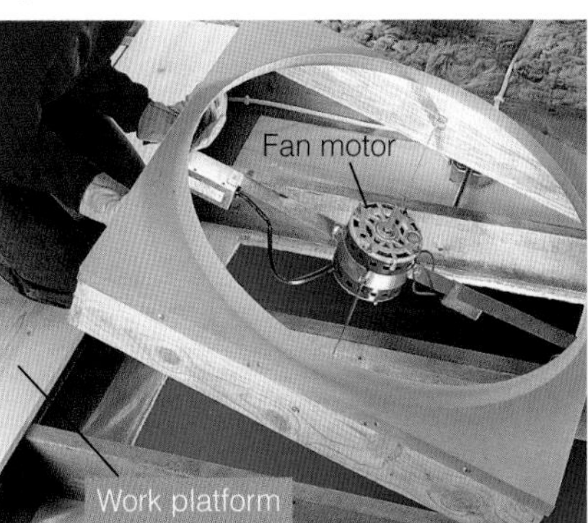

2 Position the fan by placing its motor over the center ceiling joist with fan edges aligned with the drywall cutout. Place plywood or lumber across joists for a comfortable work platform.

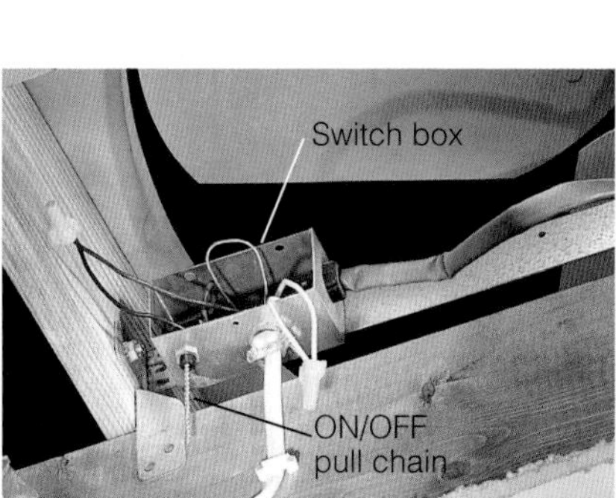

3 Mount the switch box to the ceiling joist. Run cable from a new circuit or nearby power source and make connections. The switch box may contain a pull chain for operation or you can install a wall switch.

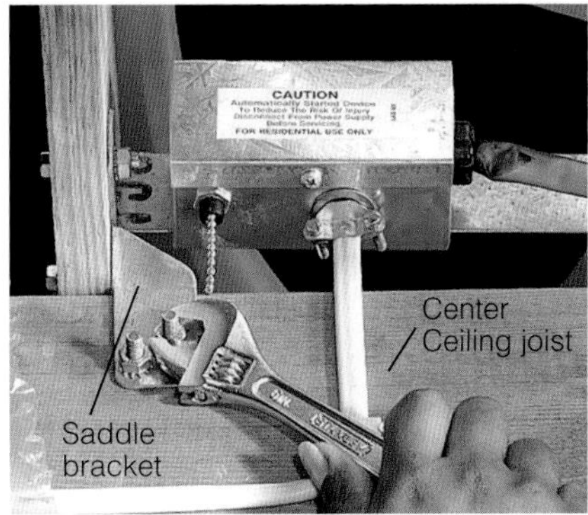

4 Secure saddle brackets to the center ceiling joist with nuts and bolts. Make sure the fan is centered before you drill holes in the joist.

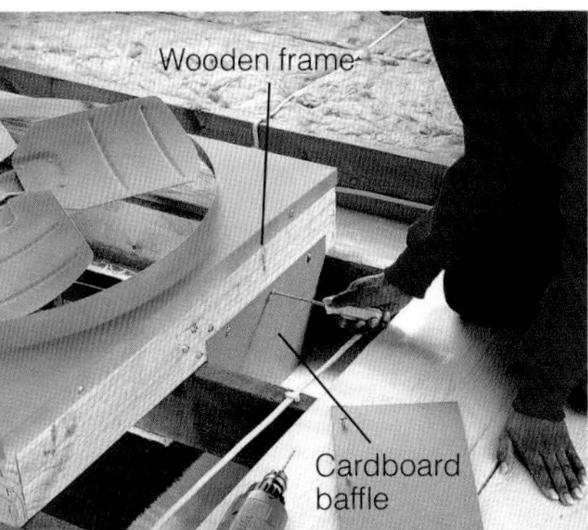

5 Fill the gap between the ceiling and fan frame with cardboard baffles; some manufacturers supply them. Cut baffles to fit between ceiling joists and screw the baffles to the fan frame. Cut insulation to fit up to the baffles.

6 Attach the louver panel to the ceiling with screws into the joist and drywall anchors into the drywall. Louvers are drawn upward when fan is turned on and weighted to shut tightly when the fan is off.

Room Air Conditioners

Drywall Repair 217
Installing Windows 370

The components of a room air conditioner are essentially the same as those of a central air-conditioning unit, except they're contained in a compact box that can be mounted to a window or through a wall. Individual room units are less expensive to install in an existing home than a central system, especially if there is no ductwork. Because room air conditioners can be controlled on a room-by-room basis, they may also be more energy-efficient than a central system.

Room air conditioners are labeled with an energy efficiency ratio (EER). The EER is calculated by dividing the unit's capacity, in BTUs per hour, by the number of watts of electrical energy needed to run it. Efficient room units will have an EER of 9 or higher.

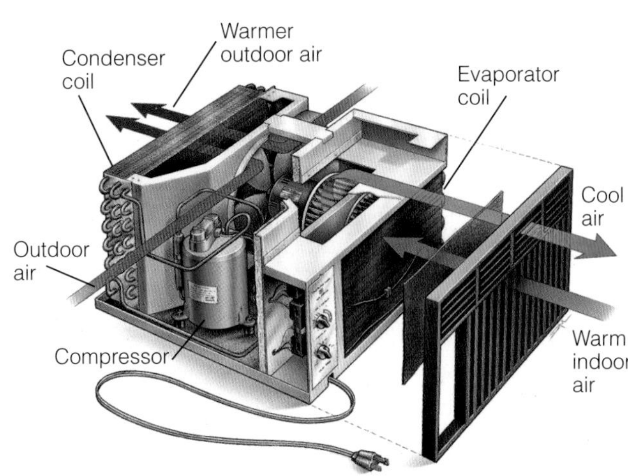

How a room air conditioner works. Every air conditioner contains two coils, which are composed of panels of aluminum fins and loops of copper tubing. A compressor circulates refrigerant through both of the coils. One fan draws room air across the evaporator coil, where the air is cooled and dehumidified. Another fan blows outdoor air over the condenser coil, where the heat absorbed from the indoor air is ejected. A barrier with a door separates indoor air from outdoor air.

Window Installation

Window-mounted air conditioners work best with double-hung windows. Measure the window opening before purchasing a unit. Many units cannot be removed from the casing, as shown below, and must be installed fully assembled.

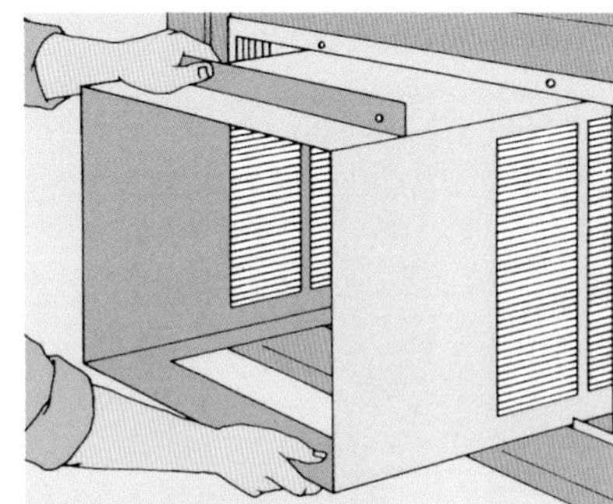

1 Remove air conditioner from its casing. Slide the casing into the window opening and screw it into the sill and sash. The casing must tilt slightly toward the outdoors so condensate will drain away from window.

2 If casing extends more than 12 in. (30 cm) beyond the outside sill, it needs exterior bracing to support it. Fasten bracing to the wall and adjust the pitch with leveling screw.

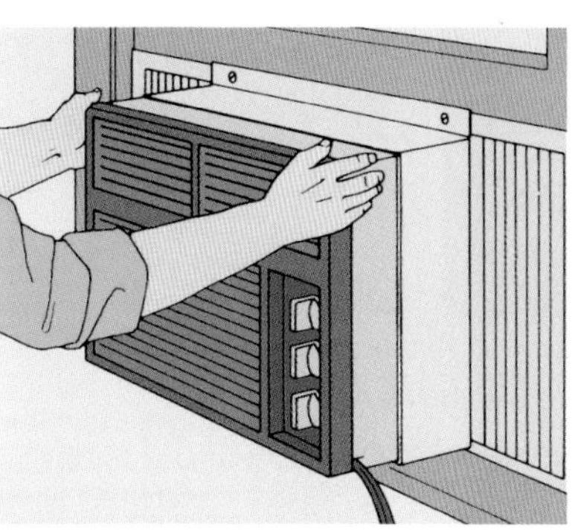

3 Slide the air conditioner into its casing. Most units require two people to install. Seal around the casing and the gap between upper and lower sashes with foam rubber. Install expandable curtain for side gap.

Wall Installation

The advantage of a wall unit is that you can choose an optimum location, preferably on an eastern or northern wall out of the heat of the sun. The disadvantage is it takes significantly more effort to install.

1 Outline the cutout on the exterior wall. Make the cutout 1/4 in. (3 mm) higher and wider than the air-conditioner casing. Nail a straightedge to the wall as a guide and saw through the sheathing and siding. From inside, cut back studs above and below the opening to make room for header, sill and jamb that will create the opening.

2 Frame air-conditioner opening as you would a window. Attach a header and sill to the existing wall frame and add 2x4 side jambs. Inside dimensions of the finished jamb are the same as those of the outside wall cutout. Jamb thickness is equal to stud width plus interior sheathing. Slip the jamb into the rough opening and fasten.

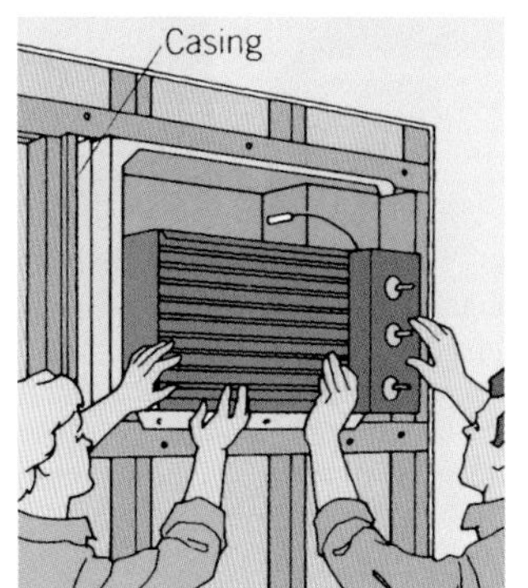

3 Install the unit using the same steps as for window units. Screw the casing into the finished jamb and slide the air conditioner into the casing. Always lift the air conditioner from the base pan on the bottom; never pull or lift from the plastic parts. Take care not to damage fins or electrical wiring. Seal around exterior and interior of the unit. Cover in winter.

Maintenance

The secret to room air-conditioner maintenance is simply good, regular cleaning. When an air conditioner doesn't seem to cool well, most people assume the coolant needs recharging. But most often the culprit is dirt, a problem solved by cleaning the coils.

Room air conditioners, like central air conditioners, have two sets of coils. A coil is an arrangement of fins and tubes for efficient heat transfer. The condenser coil is on the outside and the evaporator coil is on the inside. Keeping these coils clean is 90 percent of the battle in keeping your air conditioner operating efficiently.

The most important maintenance steps are easy, but if this is the first time you've cleaned the unit, allow about half a day to pull things apart and put them back together. To clean it properly, you'll have to remove the unit from its window or wall opening. Air conditioners can be very heavy, so recruit some help before you begin.

Unplug the unit and lift it from the opening. Remove the front cover and lift off the case, following your instruction manual, to expose the compressor, fan motor and evaporator coils. If you have a well-sealed wall unit, you may want to leave the casing in place and slide out the air conditioner to work on it.

Vacuum the fins. Vacuum evaporator fins with a soft brush attachment. The evaporator coil is protected by a filter; replace it or wash and reuse the old one.

Lubricate the motor. Lubricate the motor with five drops of electric-motor oil (oil made specifically for electric motors), if you can find oil ports. Check owner's manual for specific lubrication instructions. Don't apply too much oil—more is not always better.

Straighten bent fins. Straighten bent fins. Fins are delicate and can easily bend when you handle the unit. Straighten bent fins with a special, inexpensive plastic fin comb to improve air circulation. You can use fin combs on outdoor units of central air conditioners, too.

Wash condenser coil. Wash the condenser coil with a spray of water from outside inward. Cover the fan motor with plastic to keep it dry. Rinse and wipe up as much dirt and crud as possible from the bottom pan, making sure drain holes or overflows are open.

Split Air Conditioners

A split air conditioner is similar to a conventional window air conditioner except that its operations are split in half. The unit that contains the noisy compressor is usually on the ground outside the house. Refrigerant lines connect it to an indoor air handler, or condenser, that's typically mounted to a wall or ceiling in the area you wish to cool. A very quiet fan blows room air over the cool coils to distribute the conditioned air.

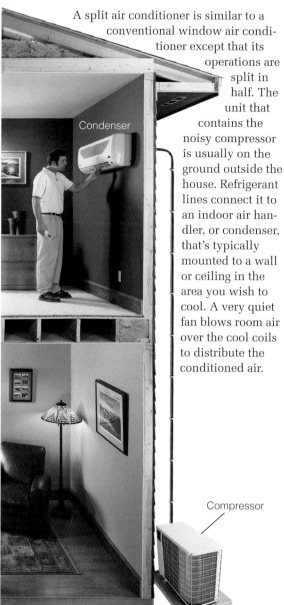

Condenser

Central Air Conditioners

A central air-conditioning system circulates cool air throughout the house with a network of ducts. Typically, these same ducts are used for heat distribution in winter. When the thermostat calls for cooling, the outdoor compressor switches on and circulates refrigerant through both coils. The furnace blower forces indoor air through the evaporator coil, where it is cooled, dehumidified, and then circulated throughout the house. Heat taken from the indoor air stream is transferred to the condenser coil and then to the outdoor air.

When adding a cooling system to a home that already has forced-air heating, central air-conditioning is often less expensive and far more convenient than equipping every room with an individual wall or window unit. However, if your home has no ductwork, you will have to add it. Large ducts can be installed economically in an open basement, crawl space or attic, but when walls and ceilings have to be opened, the cost can become prohibitively expensive. A pressurized or high-velocity system, which distributes air through small, easier-to-install pipes that can be run through standard 2x4 walls rather than ducts, is another option worth considering.

Central air conditioners usually range from 1 to 1-2/3 tons for every 1,000 sq. ft. (93 sq. m) of living area. However, the amount and quality of insulation and the amount and location of window area also effect sizing requirements. Accurate sizing is critical. An oversize unit will cycle excessively, causing inefficient operation, shortened compressor life and inadequate dehumidification. Your best bet is to have a professional size the unit.

Central air conditioners are labeled with a seasonal energy efficiency ratio (SEER) number. The higher the SEER number, the more efficient the unit. Although 10 is suitable for most locations you may want to check whether a unit with a higher rating is worth the added expense: in some areas regulations require more efficient units. Compare the unit's price plus installation costs with the money you can save in energy costs to determine the payback period. Utility companies can help determine an accurate figure and sometimes offer rebate incentives for installing higher-efficiency units.

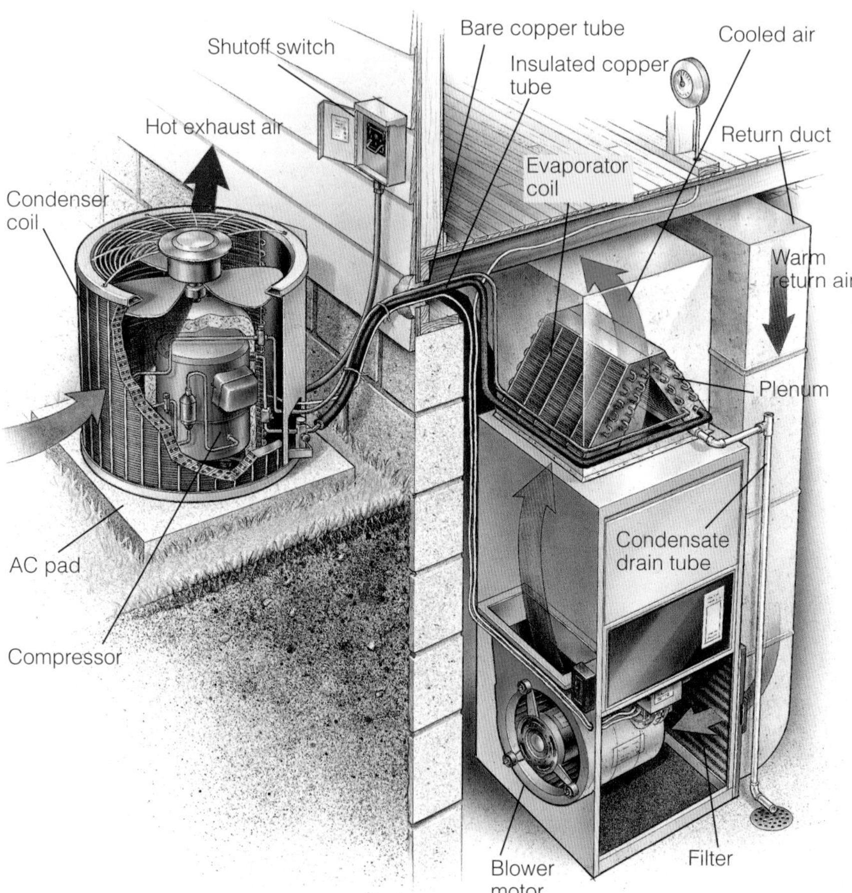

How a central air conditioner works. The two main parts of a central air system are the outdoor compressor with a condenser coil and an indoor evaporator coil that's located in the plenum above the furnace blower. Two copper tubes, one bare and one insulated, connect the two coils and transfer refrigerant between them. If you have a heat pump, both tubes will be insulated.

Refrigerant in the copper tubes absorbs heat at the evaporator coil inside, cools indoor air, and then releases heat at the condenser coil outdoors. To carry away that heat, the fan inside the condenser coil sucks air through the fins.

As a result of this process, the fan pulls dirt and debris with it. Dust, leaves, dead grass and anything else that collects on the fins will block airflow and reduce the unit's efficiency. Grass clippings thrown by a lawn mower, "cotton" from cottonwood trees and dandelions are particularly guilty offenders.

Cutting the Power

Begin the maintenance of your central air-conditioning unit by shutting off the 240-volt power at the shutoff box. It's usually outside within sight of the outdoor unit. Some shutoffs simply pull out; others have a handle to pull down or a fuse to remove. If there isn't an outdoor shutoff, turn off the outdoor unit's power at the circuit breaker on the main electrical panel.

When the power to your compressor is shut off for more than four hours, follow these steps when restoring power. First, move the switch from "cool" to "off" at the thermostat. Second, switch power back on and let the outdoor unit sit for 24 hours to allow the warming element to warm up the compressor's lubricant. Finally, switch the thermostat to cooling mode, then set the temperature to turn on the outdoor unit.

Central Vacuum Systems

Plastic Pipe 108
Circuit Mapping and Planning 129
GFCI Outlets 130

Although often associated with new construction and expensive homes, central vacuum systems can be installed in an existing home. Unfinished basements and attics simplify the task by allowing good access.

Central vacuums are quieter and more efficient than even the best portable machine. The long hose makes stair cleaning easier, and attachments are available for any cleaning task. But the most compelling reason to consider a central vacuum system is indoor air quality.

Research suggests that the dust and dander floating around our homes contributes to any number of health problems, including asthma. The filters in most standard portable vacuums remove only the largest, least dangerous particles, spewing the rest back into the air. A central vacuum, on the other hand, can be exhausted to the outdoors so all the dust it picks up leaves your house.

Choose a motor size to match the cleaning power you want, not the size of your house. Vacuum motor power is expressed as water lift, or suction power, and cubic feet (cubic meters) of airflow per minute.

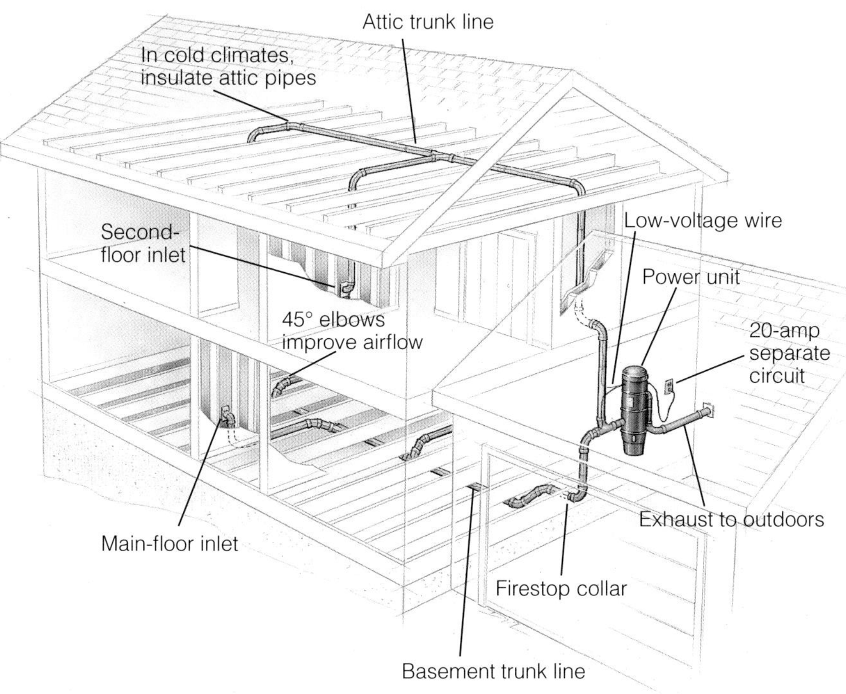

Key Components

When installing a central vacuum system, plan pipe routes to avoid obstacles. First choose a place for the power unit. An attached garage or utility room is the usual location. Check the instructions for power requirements and hire an electrician to add a separate circuit or additional outlet, if necessary.

If you plan to use a power head attachment with rotating roller brushes, make sure there's an electrical outlet within 6 ft. (2 m) of each inlet valve. The inlet valves must be connected to the main trunk line, located in either the attic or basement.

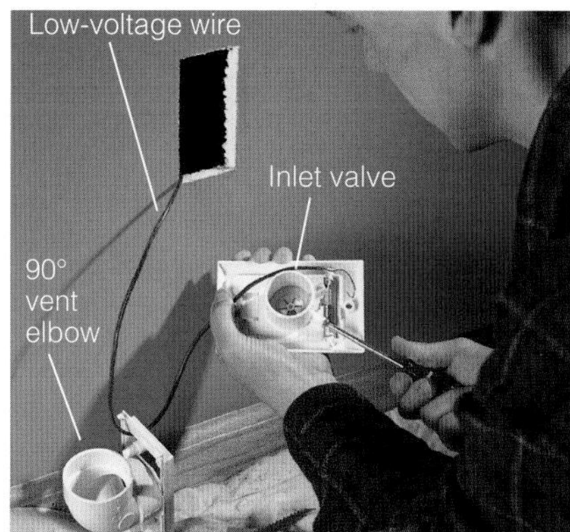

Inlet valve. Inlet valves are located so long flexible hose reaches all areas easily. Plugging the hose into a valve activates the system.

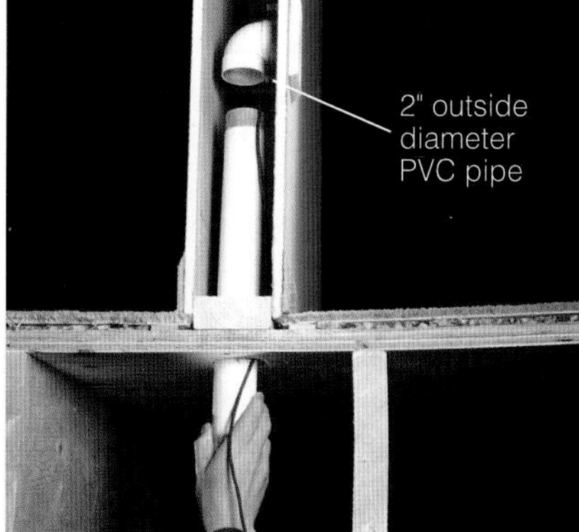

Pipe. A network of 2-in. thin-walled PVC pipe, manufactured for central vacuums, carries debris to a canister in power unit.

Low-voltage wiring. This wiring, installed alongside pipes and attached to inlet valves, switches on the power unit when the hose is plugged in.

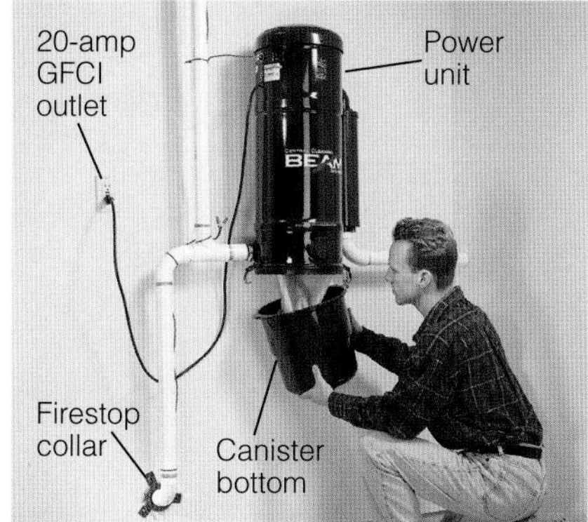

Power unit. The power unit is located in an attached garage or basement to reduce noise level and is plugged into a standard 20-amp ground-fault circuit-interrupter outlet.

Humidifiers

Adding moisture to dry heated air in winter can ease dry throats, reduce static electricity, stabilize wood furniture and floors, and allow you to lower the thermostat a few degrees and still feel warm. Unfortunately, the process can also spew white mineral dust, molds and bacteria into the air if you are not meticulous in following the manufacturer's instructions, although some newer units have a self-cleaning feature.

Three basic types of portable humidifiers exist: evaporative, ultrasonic cool mist and warm mist. Evaporative units blow room air over a rotating belt of dampened sponge. These are particularly prone to mineral, mold and bacteria buildup. Ultrasonic cool-mist units use high-frequency vibration to break water into tiny droplets that are impelled into the air as a mist. These require frequent cleaning and use of distilled water to avoid buildup problems. Warm-mist units first heat a reservoir of water before dispersing it as a warm mist. Heating the water distills out minerals and kills bacteria and molds, reducing some of the humidifier maintenance problems.

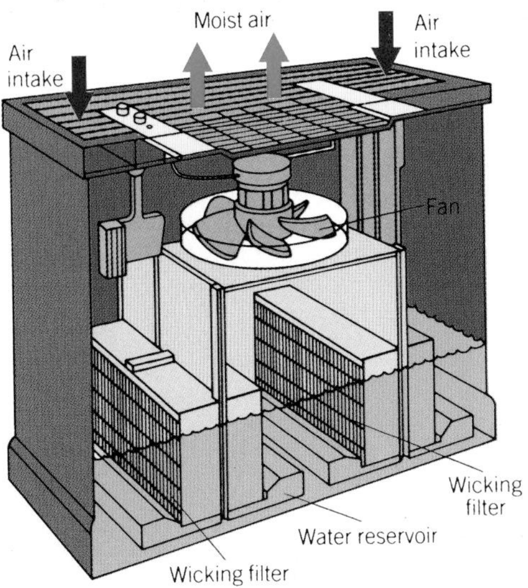

Evaporative humidifiers use filters to trap minerals in water and to act as wicks in drawing water up to the fan, which sends moisture into the air. Replace filters as recommended.

Tuning-up Portable Unit

Periodically, you need to remove the mineral scale that builds up on a warm-mist humidifier's electrical heating element and in the water reservoir pan. The more fouled a heater element becomes with mineral scale, the less efficiently it vaporizes water. Clean off accumulated scale, as shown below, to keep a humidifier running efficiently. Finally, work carefully around the heating element so it doesn't get damaged.

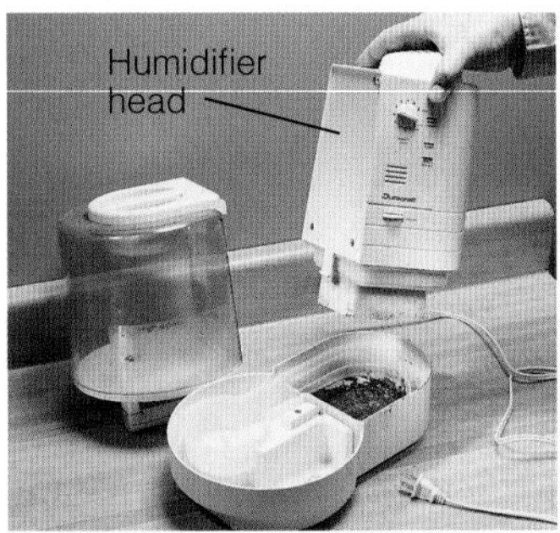

1 Unplug the humidifier, empty the water tank and pull off the humidifier head to reveal the reservoir pan. Empty out the water, loose mineral scale and sludge, give the pan a quick scouring and rinse it well.

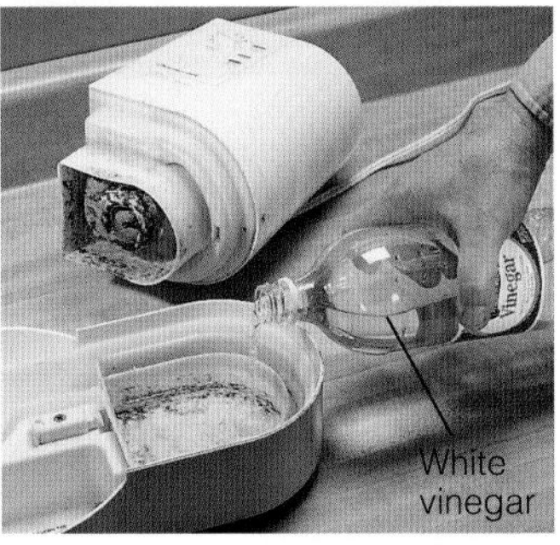

2 Fill the reservoir pan with white vinegar and reinstall the humidifier head. Leave the humidifier unplugged and soak the heater element in vinegar overnight to loosen mineral scale.

3 Scrape mineral scale off the heater element using a utility knife and toothbrush. It's not necessary to scrape it down to bare metal everywhere to accomplish your task

Central Humidifiers

A central, or whole-house, humidifier offers the optimum in convenience, effectiveness and low maintenance if you need to humidify dry, winter air. Installing a central humidifier involves several skills: cutting sheet metal, electrical wiring and plumbing.

This type mounts on the heating ductwork near the blower on both furnaces and heat pumps. If your home has no ductwork or is heated by hot water or electric baseboard heat, you can't use a central humidifier.

Whenever your furnace blower switches on, the low-voltage electrical circuit that operates the humidifier also turns on. The humidifier itself operates when the humidistat, which is a moisture-sensing device mounted in a room, senses the air in your home is too dry. If you have condensation buildup on your windows, turn the humidistat lower. Check your owner's manual for any required seasonal adjustments.

To check the humidifier's operation, open the water-supply valve, make sure it has power and open the damper. Turn the humidistat up to high and adjust the thermostat so the furnace blower switches on. After a few minutes, you should see water coming out of the drain tube. Note: Saddle valves may not be code-compliant in all areas.

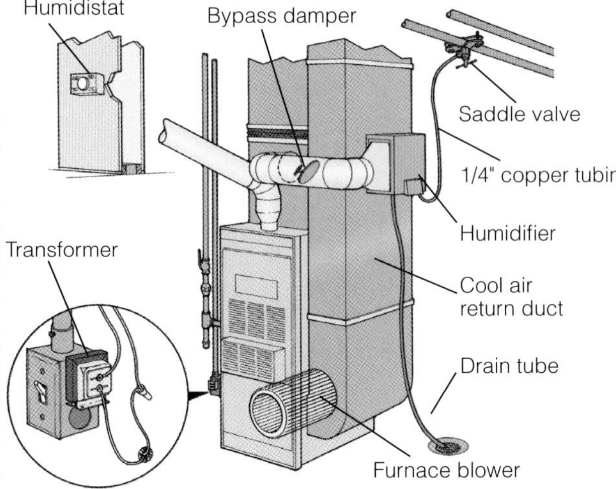

Water Heaters

Shutoff Valves **114**
Electrical Testers **132**

Normally, a water heater is so reliable and maintenance free, you can practically ignore it. On average, it takes about 13 years for one to go bad, but with faithful maintenance, it can last indefinitely.

Rust is the terminal disease for a water heater. Once it eats through the steel tank and causes it to leak, you have to replace the unit. Although the tank's inside surface has a glass coating baked onto it, this coating eventually cracks and rust begins. Failure typically begins around the tank-pipe joints, at the welds or on the bottom where sediment collects.

Heavy sedimentation from the minerals in the water, especially hard water, causes sediment to pile up on the bottom and trap heat from a gas burner, raising the temperature on the bottom higher than normal and stressing the steel tank and glass coating. On gas units, you can detect this problem by a rumbling or popping sound that occurs soon after the burner comes on.

The best defense against sediment buildup is to annually drain the tank through the drain valve and flush it according to the directions in your owner's manual. Unfortunately, many manufacturers use cheap drain valves, so plan to replace it with a more reliable ball-type valve during the first cleaning.

Besides the glass coating, your water heater's other defense against rust is a special rod called a sacrificial anode (see illustrations) made of magnesium or sometimes aluminum. The anode helps stop the chemical reaction that causes the steel tank to rust. In the process, the anode itself corrodes, or sacrifices, itself. Anodes typically last five years or longer, and some heaters have two to prolong the water heater's life. Replacing them generally requires a professional.

How they work. In most water heaters, cold water enters the bottom of the storage tank through a dip tube, where the water is heated to about 120°F to 140°F (50°C to 60°C) until there's a demand for it. Hot water then exits the tank at the top, pushed out by the pressure of incoming cold water. On the cold side inlet, the valve is open so there's always water pressure in the tank. Since hot water is more buoyant than cold, it rises to the top and remains somewhat separate until the cold is heated. A thermostat near the bottom senses when cold water arrives and automatically switches on the heating device.

Gas heaters must be vented through a flue or a power vent. The base of this vent's draft hood is an excellent place to check for back-drafting problems. Because gas heaters heat water more quickly than electric models, they tend to be smaller. The most common problem with a gas heater is a failed thermocouple (see next page).

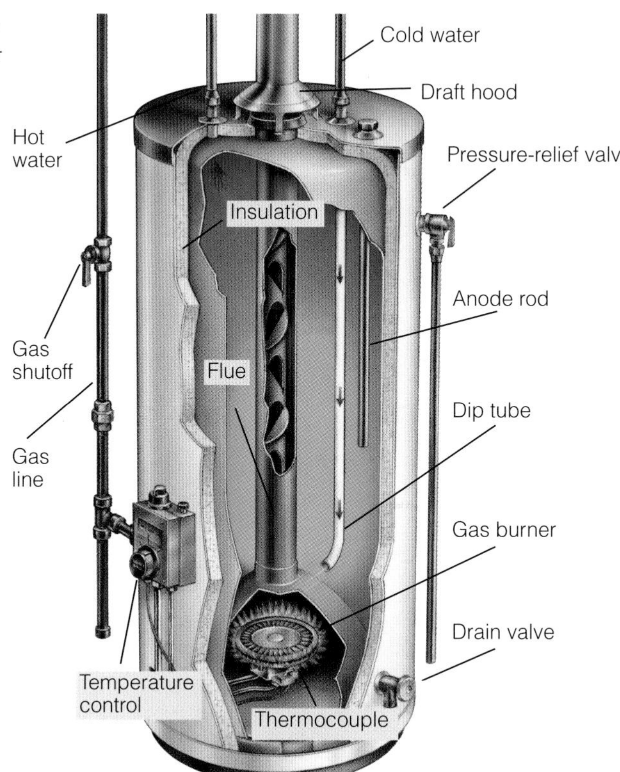

Electric heaters use one, or more often two, heating elements. If an electric heater has two elements, the upper element acts as a supplemental heater that only operates during heavy demand; consequently, it rarely fails. Electric heaters take longer to heat the water, tend to be larger and cost more to operate. However, not requiring a venting system makes them significantly easier to install.

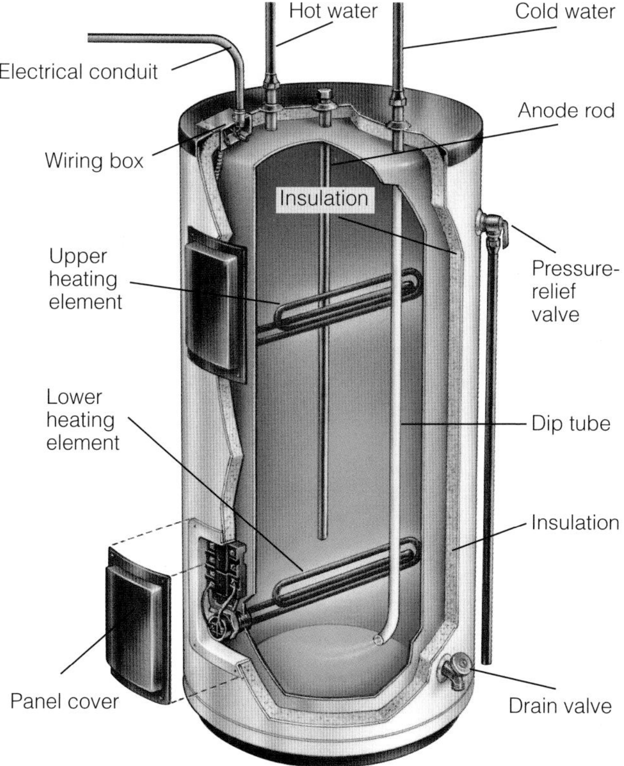

Electronic Air Cleaners

As houses have become better sealed for energy efficiency, concern about indoor air quality has grown. Common indoor pollutants—dust, pollen, bacteria, viruses, spores, animal dander and tobacco smoke—not only effect people but can clog and interfere with electronic equipment and heating and cooling systems.

Good housekeeping, including frequent vacuuming with a high-quality, high-filtration vacuum is the first requirement. Removing dust-trapping furnishings, such as deep-pile carpeting and heavy, dust-trapping draperies, may help those with severe reactions. If you're still suffering or you want to reduce such airborne contaminants as smoke and pollen, try an electronic air cleaner. These appliances offer relief by a process called electronic precipitation (see below).

Installed in the return-air duct of a heating and air-conditioning system, an air cleaner will extend the life of that equipment and other electronic equipment in your home. For houses with other kinds of heating or cooling systems, there are a variety of room-size models.

To maintain the cleaner's prefilter and plate, clean them monthly by scrubbing them or running them through a dishwasher. Also, electronic air cleaners produce ozone, a respiratory irritant also produced by hair dryers and power tools. High airflow dilutes the ozone and good maintenance minimizes it.

Some indoor pollutants are still best removed by ventilation. To clear out smoke, unpleasant odors or noxious gases, open a window or turn on exhaust fans.

Air Cleaner Anatomy

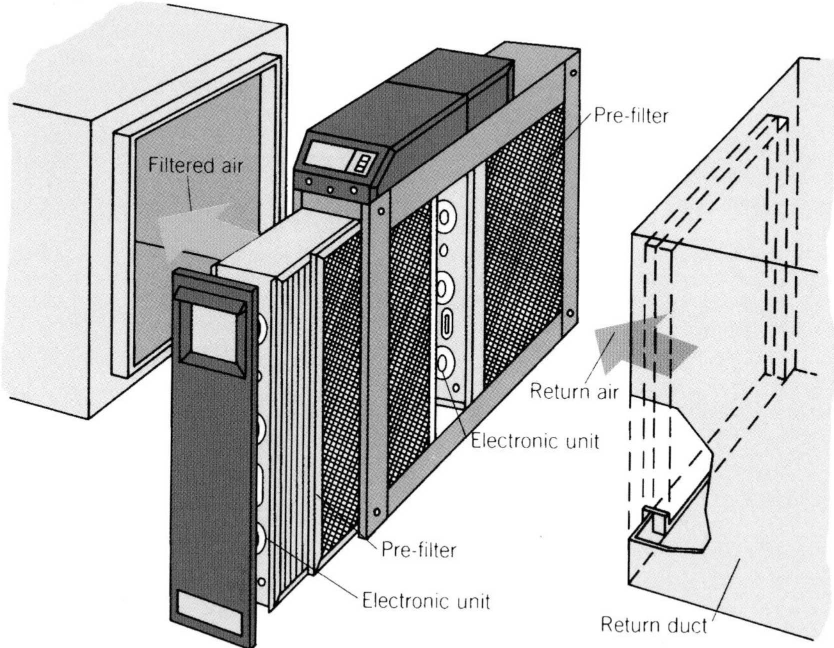

An electronic air cleaner cleans by a process called electronic precipitation in which a prefilter first screens out large particles. Next, in the electronic unit, small particles are electrically charged and collected on a plate that acts like a magnet. This plate and prefilter must be cleaned monthly.

Location. Units can be mounted vertically or horizontally in a return air duct with up or down airflow.

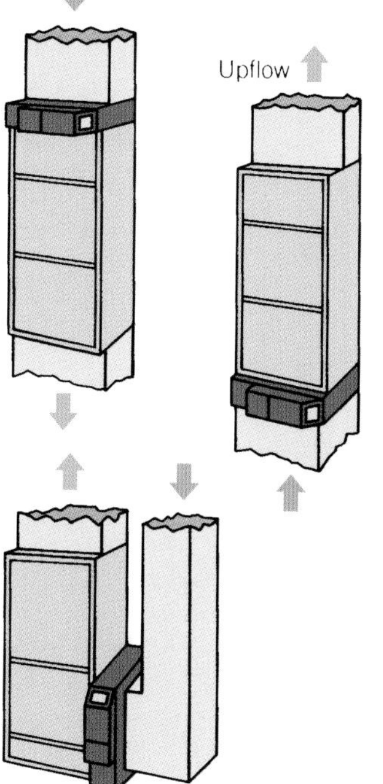

A Breath of Fresh Air

When it comes to filtering the air in your home, the best performance for the money comes from electronic air cleaners, like the one shown below. The installed price of a central electronic air cleaner can be high, but operating costs are very low. Furthermore, since these cleaners replace the filter in your heating and air system, manufacturers claim that you can cut air-conditioning costs by up to 10 percent, because an air cleaner keeps the evaporator coil clean. The most convenient electronic cleaners have easy-to-remove collectors that are simple to clean; a necessary step for good performance.

Electrostatic filters and pleated filters (see "Which Filter?," p. 175) are inexpensive, easy to install and usually just replace your existing furnace filter. Neither type requires an electrical hookup; however, their performance is only marginally better than that of ordinary filters.

High-efficiency particulate air (HEPA) cleaners are the most effective and expensive approach. They have a huge surface area and hundreds of small folds packed into a small space and they remove even the smallest particles, like viruses. However, the installed cost of a whole-house HEPA-cleaner system can easily exceed $1,000 and the operating costs can be significant. If a central air cleaner isn't feasible, the best portable models are nearly as effective, at least for a single room. Buy one with a cubic feet per minute (CFM) rating that will give you four changes of air per hour in the room where the unit is located.

Water Heater Repair

Replacing a Thermocouple

Inside the burner compartment of your gas water heater, right in front of the pilot light, is a small metal cylinder called a thermocouple (unless you have a unit with electronic ignition). The thermocouple is a safety device that senses when the pilot light is burning. If the pilot light goes out, the thermocouple signals the gas valve to remain closed until the pilot light is relit. If your burner is shut off and the pilot light refuses to stay lit, a worn-out thermocouple is the likely culprit. Remove the old thermocouple, measure it and buy the same size replacement at a hardware store. Also, take the opportunity to clean the burner while it's out. Before beginning, turn off the gas to the water heater and turn the temperature control valve to OFF.

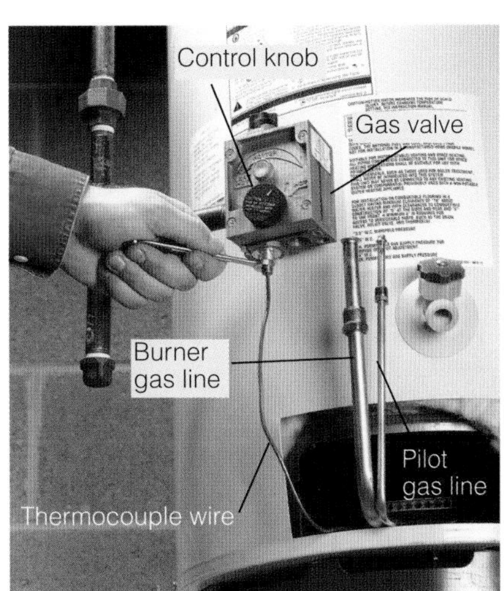

1 Remove the burner by disconnecting the burner gas line, pilot gas line and thermocouple. Pull lines out of the gas valve and remove the burner.

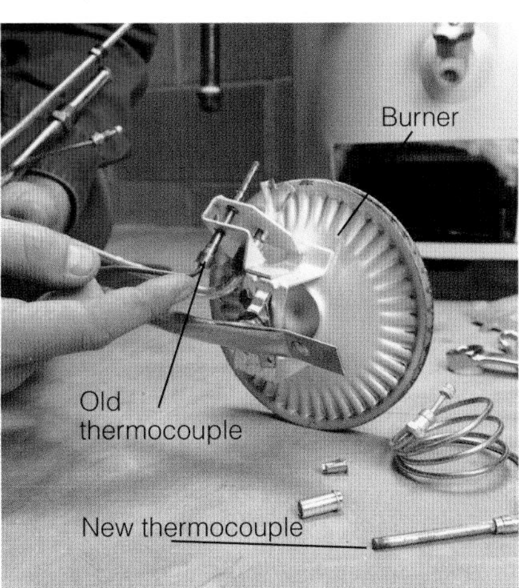

2 Slide the old thermocouple out and push the new one in. Note the position and mounting details of the old thermocouple and install the new one the same way.

3 Reinstall the burner and reconnect the gas lines and thermocouple to the gas valve. Tighten the nuts with moderate pressure and test the gas connections for leaks by coating joints with soapy water and checking for bubbling.

Replacing an Electric Heating Element

If you have an electric water heater that suddenly produces only lukewarm water, it's very likely a heating element has gone bad. Since the lower element in a dual-element unit does 90 percent of the heating, that one usually wears out first.

First, shut off power to the water heater, remove access panels and use a voltage-sensing device to make absolutely certain there's no power running through any of the wires.

1 Shut off power. Disconnect two wires attached to the element and use a water-heater continuity tester to test each one. No light indicates a burned-out element.

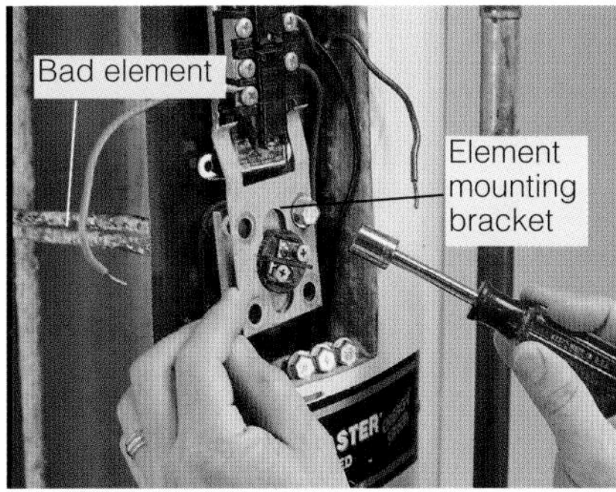

2 Shut off the cold-water supply and drain water from the tank. Remove the bad element by removing the bolts holding its mounting bracket to the tank.

3 Replace the element with one that exactly matches the wattage, voltage, length and mounting style of the old one. Install the new element and gasket, close drain and refill tank.

Tankless Water Heaters

Tankless water heaters, also called instant or on-demand, don't heat and store 40 or 50 gal. (150 or 190 l) of water like conventional heaters. Instead, as water is needed, it's heated with a blast of gas or electric resistance heat.

Tankless heaters have some substantial advantages. They can fit into small spaces. They have great longevity and will provide limitless hot water as long as they're not overtaxed. And they save energy, because they don't have to keep water hot while it's not being used.

The disadvantages of tankless units are that they're expensive and may require larger gas or electric lines and vents for installation. They are also foreign to some repair people, and only the largest units can keep pace while filling a large indoor bathtub or if several showers are being taken at one time.

Tips for Saving Energy

Pipe Insulation 106
Compact Fluorescent Bulbs 152
Attic Insulation 168
Thermostats 184
Cooling with Shade 196
Whole-house Fans 197
Air-conditioner Maintenance 199
Whole-house Humidifier 203
Energy-efficient Windows 369

If history has taught us anything, it's that we can't predict what will happen to energy prices or what will happen with the weather. As homeowners, the best thing we can do is position ourselves and our homes so we don't consume more energy than we absolutely have to. The key is to be prepared.

This book is loaded with energy-saving advice and projects; here are a few more ideas that will help stretch your dollar even further. The happy benefit to all this effort is that not only will you save money and energy, but your home will be a more comfortable place to be.

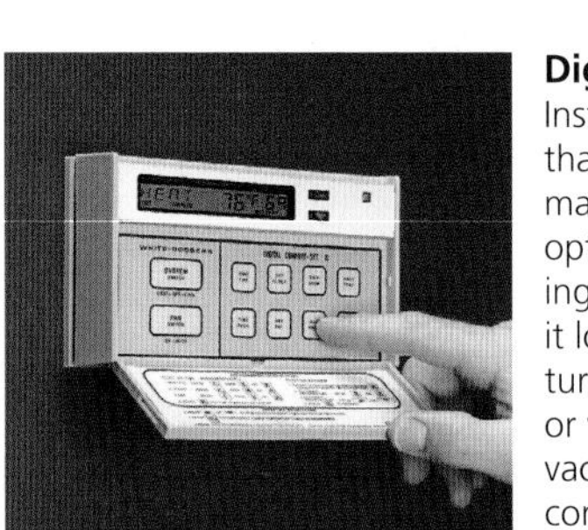

Digital thermostat. Install a digital thermostat that you program to automatically adjust settings for optimum savings. Depending on the season, set it so it lowers or raises temperatures while you're at work or while you sleep. During vacations, set it to hold a constant energy-saving temperature.

Pipe insulation. Tightly insulate pipes with foam pipe insulation, especially those running to dishwashers, clothes washers and other appliances with cycling loads. Hot water in the pipes will retain heat longer when running through cool areas, and the pipes won't radiate heat into areas you don't want heated.

Motion sensors. Install light controls, such as motion sensors, photocell switches and timers, to automatically shut off lights when they're not needed. Motion sensors are even available for interior light switches.

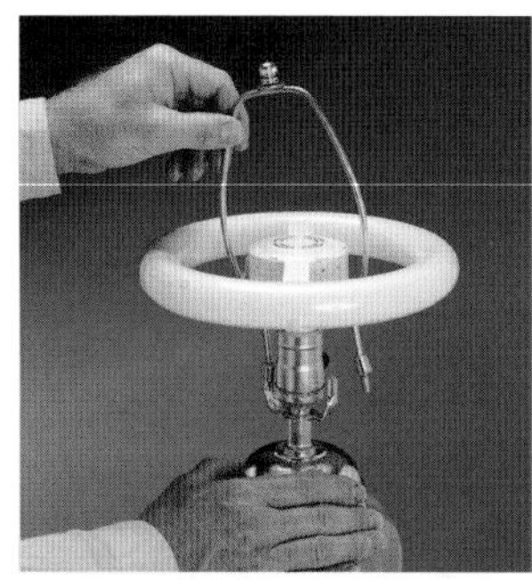

Fluorescent bulbs. Replace lightbulbs used more than two hours per day with compact fluorescent bulbs. Fluorescent bulbs last longer, use only one-third as much energy to produce equivalent light and don't add to the heat load during the cooling season.

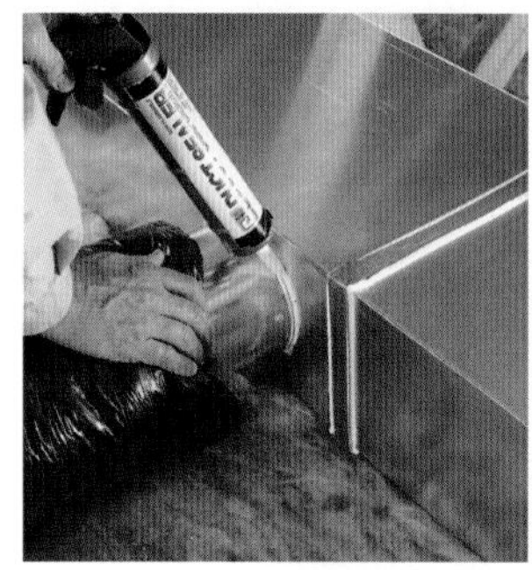

Seal ducts. Seal the joints of heating and cooling ducts near the furnace and those that run through attics and basements with pure silicone or metal ducting tape. Sealing ducts will save energy and help prevent condensation problems.

Water-heater blankets. Wrap the tank of your gas-burning water heater in a special fiberglass blanket to decrease heat loss. Check the owner's manual to make sure a blanket is recommended for your model.

Energy-saving Ideas That Don't Cost a Dime

1. Set the thermostat lower at night during winter.
2. While on vacation, lower the water-heater temperature and raise or lower the heating and air thermostat, depending on the season.
3. Seal unused fireplace dampers with a plastic bag stuffed with insulation.
4. During sunny winter days, open southern shades and blinds for passive solar heat.
5. Close doors, registers and dampers in unused rooms.
6. Clean furnace blower, air-conditioner coils and refrigerator coils with a soft brush and vacuum cleaner.
7. Turn off lights not in use, reduce bulb wattage and use a dimmer switch when possible.
8. Fill clothes and dishwashers to capacity before operating.
9. Skip the dishwasher's drying cycle.
10. Regularly clean all furnace, air-conditioner, dryer lint, humidifier and dehumidifier filters.
11. Cook more efficiently using microwaves, slow-cookers, pressure cookers and toaster ovens.
12. Look into off-peak energy-usage programs that local utility companies may offer.
13. In warm weather, set the thermostat higher and rely more on ceiling and table fans for cooling.
14. Lower water-heater setting to 120 degrees F (50 degrees C) for both energy savings and safety.
15. Ventilate and cool your home with window or whole-house fans during cooler hours.

Interior Repairs & Improvements

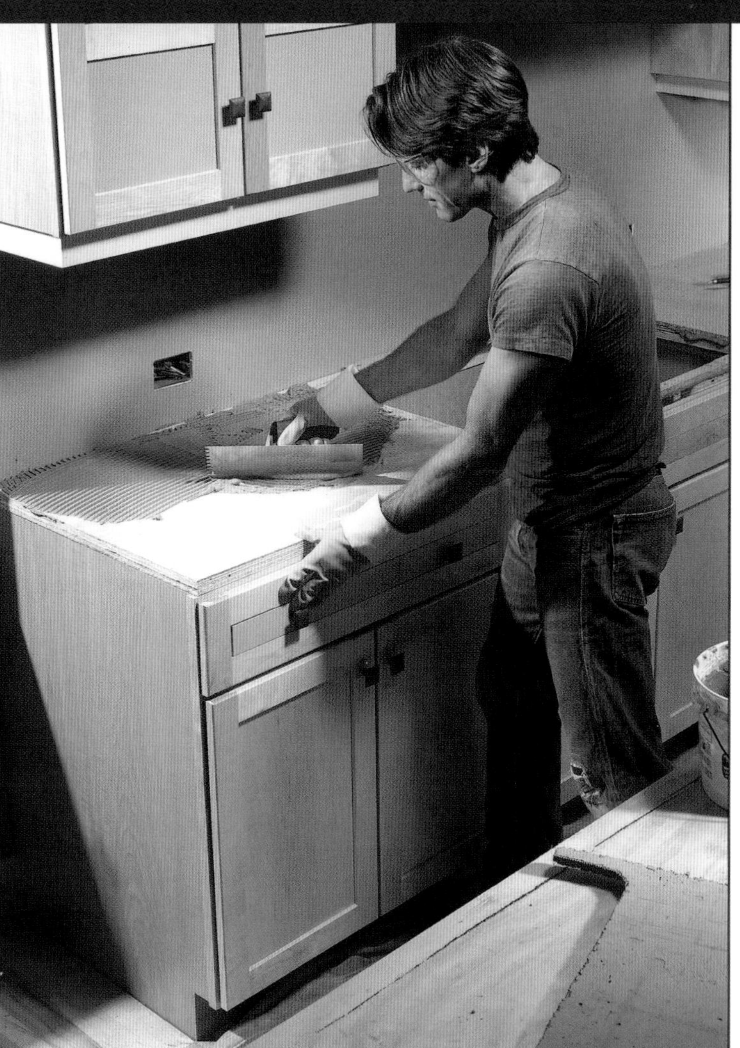

Maintenance Checklist

Septic Systems 91
Heating Systems 172
Cooling Your Home 196
Basement Moisture 272
Exterior Checklist 310
Fire Safety 481

Keeping a house in good working order is a primary concern for all homeowners. It contributes to your comfort and enjoyment, and it's vital to maintaining your property value. The key to peace of mind is preventive maintenance. By checking your home's systems at appropriate times of the year, you can catch and solve small problems before they grow into big expensive problems.

A periodic checkup may take only a few hours a year. You can probably take care of most minor repairs yourself. Having your septic tank inspected and pumped or correcting major structural problems, though, are jobs best left for the pros.

An ideal time to check a system is when it's not in use. In spring a house often shows signs of wear from severe winter weather, so check the exterior. Also check your dehumidifier and cooling system (have its refrigerant level increased, if needed). In late summer or early fall, have your heating system and humidifier checked, cleaned and serviced. If any part of a system seems unduly worn, a replacement may be better than a repair. When in doubt, contact an expert.

When fall comes, clean or change the filter(s) of your heating and air conditioner system(s) and vacuum accessible parts. This is also a good time to inspect for insects and animals that may have taken up residence in unsuspected parts of your house. Your local humane society or your state conservation department will provide information on how to safely remove such invaders as squirrels and raccoons.

Some checklist items are seasonal—to be done in spring or fall. Others can be done any time of year. "As Required" items may need doing only every few years or as often as is necessary.

Handy Hints

Battery Reminder

Pick a memorable day—your birthday, New Year's Day, Memorial Day—and use it as your annual prompter to change batteries in your smoke and carbon-monoxide detectors, flashlights, clocks and other equipment.

Interior Maintenance Checklist

General Interior

- □ Check sealant around tubs, showers and other tiled surfaces. (Annually)
- □ Check egress windows for proper operation. (Annually)
- □ Check weather stripping around windows and doors. (Fall)

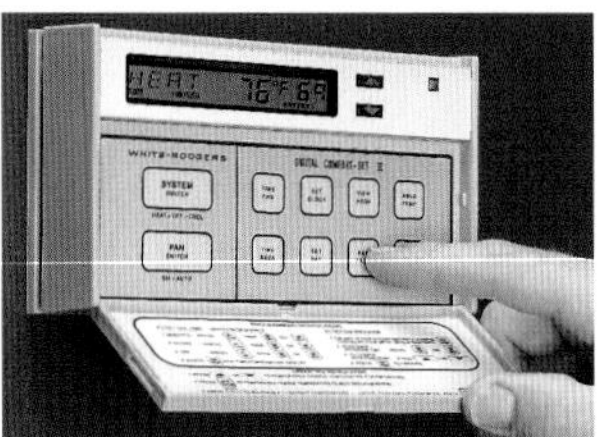

Heating and Cooling Systems

- □ Have furnace or boiler professionally checked and tuned up for proper operation. (Fall)
- □ Check belt tension on furnace blowers. (Fall)
- □ Change filters in forced-air furnace and whole-house ventilation systems. (Monthly)
- □ Clean and service humidifiers and dehumidifiers. (Annually)
- □ Bleed air from hot-water radiators. (Fall)
- □ Have furnace and fireplace flues checked and cleaned, if necessary. (Fall)
- □ Adjust heating-duct dampers based on seasonal changes. (As Required)

Plumbing System

- □ Drain sediment from water heater. (Annually)
- □ Check for dripping faucets and leaky drain traps. (As Required)
- □ Have septic system inspected and pumped. (As Required)

Electrical System

- □ Check ground-fault circuit-interrupter (GFCI) outlets. (As Required)
- □ Inspect cords and plugs for wear. (As Required)
- □ Replace burned-out bulbs, particularly in high-use areas. (As Required)

Foundations and Basements

- □ Check beams and structural members for signs of termites, powder post beetles and carpenter ants. (Annually)
- □ Check for new cracks or movement in old cracks. (Annually)
- □ Check for excess moisture on basement or crawl space walls and floors. (As Required)

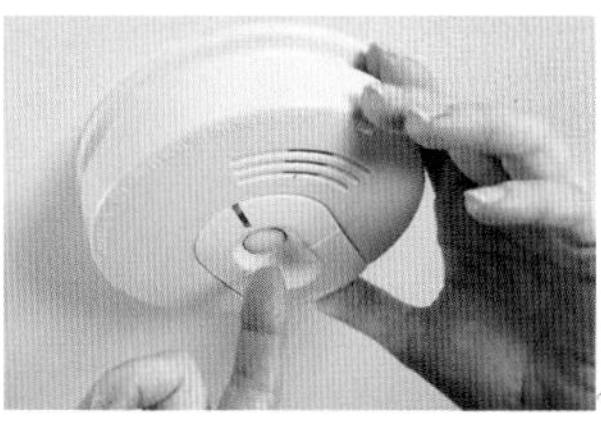

Safety

- □ Check pressure levels of fire extinguishers. (Monthly)
- □ Check smoke detectors and carbon-monoxide detectors for proper operation using the test button. Replace if more than 10 years old. (Monthly)
- □ Conduct family fire drill; discuss evacuation procedures and where to meet. (Annually)

Drywall / Materials

Drywall is commonly used to cover interior ceilings and walls and as a wall underlayment in dry areas for ceramic tiles. Drywall is a simple sandwich of mined gypsum rock wrapped in paper. Alone, neither component has much inherent strength, but together they form a remarkably strong, fire-resistant wall sheathing.

Unlike plaster, drywall doesn't call for expert-level skills. It's affordable, simple to install and finish, and easy to repair and paint. It's also stable and less prone to cracks than plaster.

Working with drywall is hard, awkward, physical work. Panels weigh as much as 100 lbs. (45 kg) each and are as long as 16 ft. Consequently, getting extra help for a big drywall project is a major plus. Common panel thicknesses vary from 1/4 to 1 in.; however, panels more than 5/8 in. thick are generally special-order items. The 4-ft. width and 8-, 12- and 16-ft. lengths are compatible with virtually all standard framed walls and ceilings.

Tools

The following drywall tools are very affordable to buy or rent. Each one saves time and helps pave the way toward a professional-looking installation.

Drywall lift hoists up lower rows of drywall using the floor for leverage.

Screw gun is a dedicated drill used to drive screwheads to a preset depth.

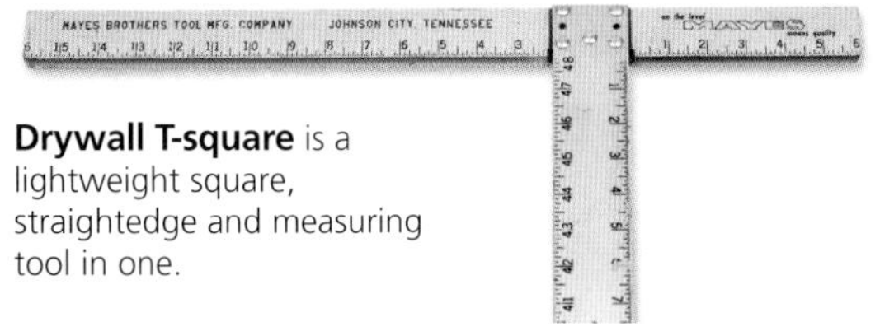

Drywall T-square is a lightweight square, straightedge and measuring tool in one.

Drywall saws cut on the push stroke to avoid tear-out on the finish side.

Types of Drywall

All drywall sheets have a smooth finish face and wrapped, tapered edges along their lengths for easier finishing. They vary in thickness, length, density, core content and backing.

Standard drywall has a medium-density gypsum core for general applications. It is commonly used in 1/2-in. thicknesses but is also available in 1/4-in. and 3/8-in. thicknesses.

Fire-rated 5/8-in. drywall has a dense, fire-resistant core and is normally applied to shared framing between living spaces and attached garages or used on ceilings where framing members are spaced 24 in. apart.

"Green board" has a water-resistant face and core and is used for damp-area (kitchen, laundry, bath) applications.

Specialty drywall includes that which is abuse-resistant, bendable, and an extra-stiff 1/2-in. drywall that can span longer distances than standard drywall. Drywall with a non-paper, non-organic backing that won't feed mold is also available.

Types of Tape

Joint tape covers and strengthens joints between drywall panels. It covers horizontal and vertical joints, and inside corners. Paper tape is cheaper, more versatile and easier, though messier, to work with than mesh tape.

Paper tape is thin, lightly perforated and center creased. It adheres to a bed of wet joint compound (mud).

Mesh tape is a clothlike, self-stick, thick tape best used on flat surfaces and for repairs.

Types of Fasteners

Drywall screws offer the preferred method for drywall installation. They grip tightly and install easily. However, nailing, in combination with adhesives or screws, provides good results.

Drywall screws avoid the common "nail pop" problem since they remain largely unaffected by house movement. Use 1-1/4-in. screws for 1/2-in.-thick drywall, 1-5/8-in. screws for 5/8-in. sheets. Use coarse-thread screws for attaching to wood framing and fine-thread for metal framing.

Drywall nails, usually ring-shanked, are used for nail-on corner bead and for tacking the drywall in place until you can install screws.

Adhesives provide a sturdier bond when securing drywall to framing members or when applying new drywall directly over existing solid surfaces, such as plaster or old drywall.

Drywall / Cutting

Keyhole Saws 27
Utility Knives 28

When you're hanging drywall, the key to saving time and effort is making accurate cuts and knowing the tolerances. The need to fix poor cuts, big gaps and ragged ends will eat time in the finishing stage.

Most long, straight cuts made on any drywall job consist of three basic steps: scoring the face paper, snapping and folding the sheet, and cutting through the paper on the back. When you're scoring with a utility knife, use only enough pressure to cut through the paper. After you score it, the crumbly gypsum breaks cleanly, directly in line with the score.

To make a tough job easier, follow these two rules: First, minimize the number of joints, especially hard-to-finish butt or end joints. Second, don't attempt tight joints. Tight joints often result in cracks and broken corners when you're forcing sheets into place. Instead cut the sheets a hair short.

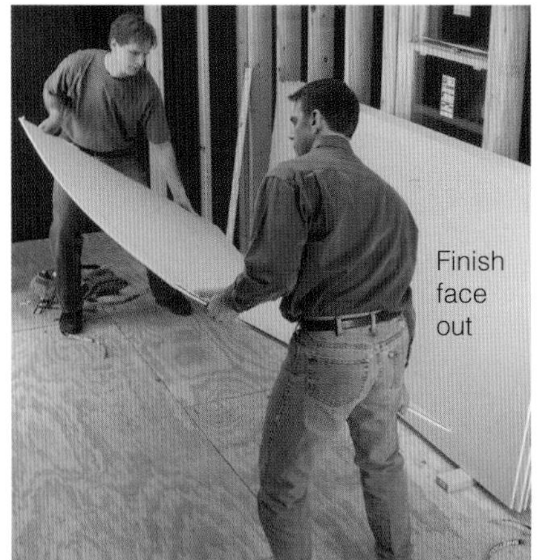

Lean drywall sheets at a slight angle, finish face out, against the last wall to be covered.

Cutting to Length

1 Mark length along the top edge, position and firmly hold the T-square. Score two-thirds of the face on down stroke, one-third on up stroke.

2 Lift one end of the sheet away from the stack. Firmly tap the back side of score line with a knee to break.

3 On the backside, cut two-thirds down along the paper crease. Come up from the bottom to finish the cut.

Cutting to Width

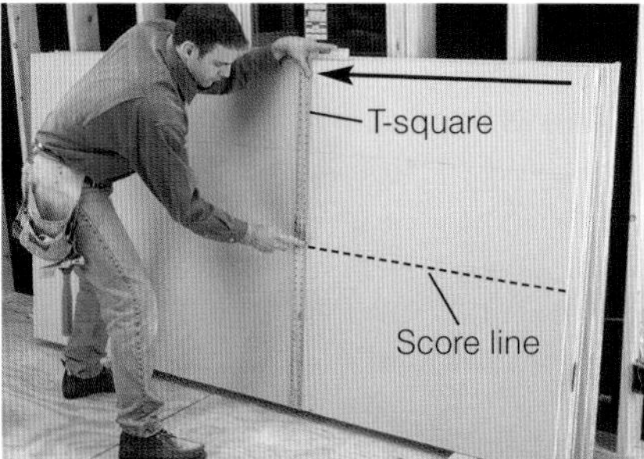

1 Using the sheet edge like a rail for the T-square, rip sheets to width by pulling a utility knife behind the square.

2 Lower a sheet close to a very clean floor and snap the cut open from the back side with a soft punch.

3 Cut through the back side of the paper. For multiple rips, make all scores on the face before lowering the sheet.

Cutting Wall Openings

1 For new construction, install drywall over door openings, then use a drywall saw to cut along sides. For existing doors or windows, cut openings before hanging sheets.

2 Score the back side of an opening's top. Pull out waste piece to snap the sheet. Hold waste piece firmly in center and cut face paper.

Electrical Box Openings

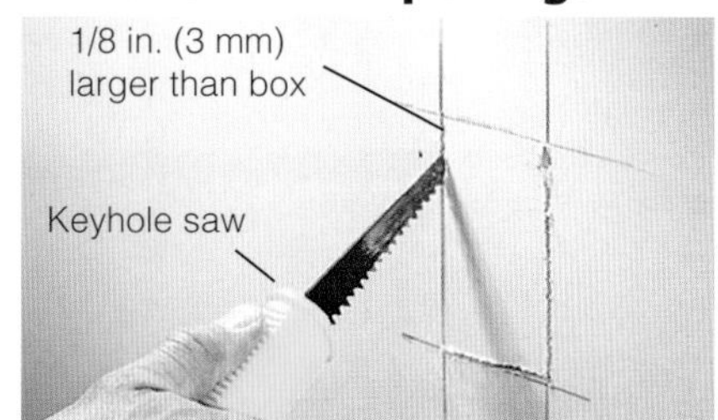

Mark, then cut out electrical box openings slightly larger than the box using a keyhole saw or rotary tool. Don't force drywall over the box.

Drywall / Installing

The best way to hang drywall is to begin with the ceiling and work your way down. It doesn't require a lot of finesse, but it is heavy work, so extra help is almost a necessity. If you do a good job hanging drywall, it paves the way for a smoother finishing stage.

Preparation. Before installation, make sure all lighting, outlets, utility lines (phone, computer, security, TV cable, stereo) and plumbing are in place. Hold a 6-ft.-long straightedge across framing to find problem framing members that will warp the finished drywall surface. If a board varies by more than 1/8 in. (3 mm) from its neighbor, you may need to shim it out or plane it.

Estimating. Estimate materials by adding total surface areas and dividing by square feet (square meters) per sheet. Don't deduct for doors and windows unless they're very large.

Moving drywall. Plan the project so you move the drywall as little as possible. Most suppliers charge an additional fee (money well spent) for drywall delivery.

Fastening. Use the right size and number of screws; codes in many communities spell out the specifics. In standard installations, use 1-1/4-in. screws for 1/2-in. drywall and 1-5/8-in. screws for 5/8-in. drywall.

Final dos and don'ts.

- Always join tapered edges to tapered edges.
- Stagger butt joints with each row of drywall.
- Cut and remove broken corners and loose drywall chunks. Drywall compound won't fix this type of damage.

1 Hoist sheets overhead, position tightly against walls or other sheets, hold in place with T-bar or drywall lift, and tack in place.

2 Install top wall sheet tightly at the ceiling edge. Avoid joints above door and window openings. Stagger butt, or end, joints.

3 Lift the lower row of drywall against the top row using a wall lift. Fine-tune electrical box openings with a knife, if needed.

Worth Renting

Anyone who has tackled a large drywall project will tell you these two specialty tools—a self-feeding screw gun and a drywall lift—available for rent, will pay for themselves in the project's first few hours.

A self-feeding drywall screw gun can cut fastening time up to 70 percent. It holds a strip of screws and offers a depth adjustment for properly setting the screws.

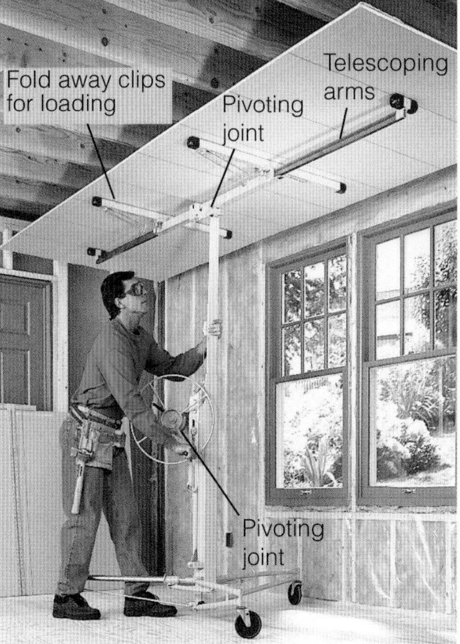

A drywall lift is a "must-have" for ceiling installations, especially for heavier 5/8-in.-thick sheets. The lift makes working alone possible, it disassembles easily and its tilting arms are ideal for angled ceilings or walls.

4 Finish securing sheets with a screw gun. Space screws about 8 in. (20 cm) apart on edges and 12 in. (30 cm) apart in open areas.

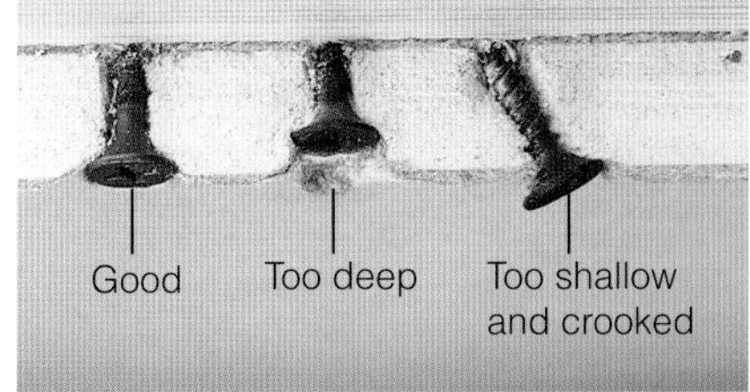

5 Drive screws correctly, straight and just dimpling the paper surface. An overset screw has little holding power.

Drywall / Taping

Corner Beads 216

You can complete any drywall finishing job with only narrow- and intermediate-width broad knives, a wide hand trowel or taping knife, a mud pan and taping banjo. For materials, you'll need joint tape, joint compound (mud), corner bead and sanding materials.

Beginners often mistakenly apply too much joint compound in hopes of sanding it level later. But thick coats take longer to dry and can crack. By building up several thin, gradually wider coats, you reduce the need for sanding until final finishing. Between coats, simply use your broad knife to knock down ridges or bumps.

Tapered joints (below, top) form a gutter that makes obtaining a flat, level surface fairly simple. Butt joints (below, bottom) are tougher because, without the gutter, you must apply and "feather" the joint compound thinly to avoid buildup over the seam.

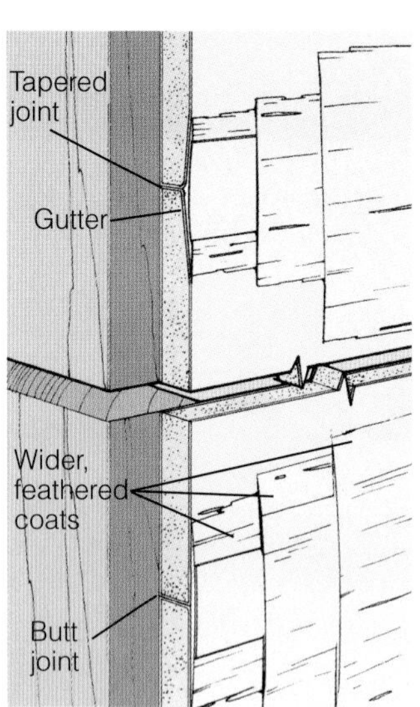

Taping Joints

Begin by applying mud-saturated paper tape first over the butt joints, then the tapered joints, and then the inside corners. Next apply a coat of mud over the corner beads and all screw or nail holes. A banjo evenly saturates the tape with mud as you dispense it. For smaller jobs, you can trowel a thin layer of mud over the joints, then imbed tape in it using a broad knife.

1 Prepare drywall surface by recessing all fasteners and holes. Dent damaged paper with butt of knife handle. Note: We tinted the compound in following steps for better visibility.

2 Apply tape by holding one end and pulling tape out of banjo. Press and center wet tape into the joint with your fingers. Smooth the tape with your broadknife.

3 Lay down a second coat, carefully feathering edges. Let compound on one side of inside corners dry before applying other side.

4 Before the final coat, scrape the ridges. Apply a wide, thin, layer to butt joints, feathering out from the joint's center.

Inside Corners

If you have large gaps, carefully fill these with setting compound before taping. Apply corner tape using the banjo. Use the tape's natural center crease to align it.

1 Smooth tape into a corner with a putty knife, taking care to follow the tape's center crease.

2 Apply second and third coats, alternating sides to avoid digging out wet mud on the opposing side.

Outside Corners

Finishing corners is a fairly simple task because you have hard, defined edges of the metal corner bead to guide application. Use full-length pieces on corners whenever possible. Paper-covered metal corner bead, available in long lengths, is available for special situations.

1 Cut corner beads to length. Trim off sharp corners. Clinch into place with clincher. Secure with nails.

2 "Butter" each face of corner generously with mud, then use a trowel or broadknife to remove excess and feather edges.

Sanding

Final sanding is your last chance to correct problems before painting. Use a light, held against the wall, to shine across the surface to highlight areas that need special attention. Use caution when sanding over butt joints to avoid sanding through to the paper.

1 Use a pole sander with 120-grit sandpaper for large areas. Wear a dust mask and seal off finished areas.

2 Corner sanding sponges are ideal for touching up inside corners. Avoid sanding through to the paper.

Shop Smart: Confounded by Joint Compounds?

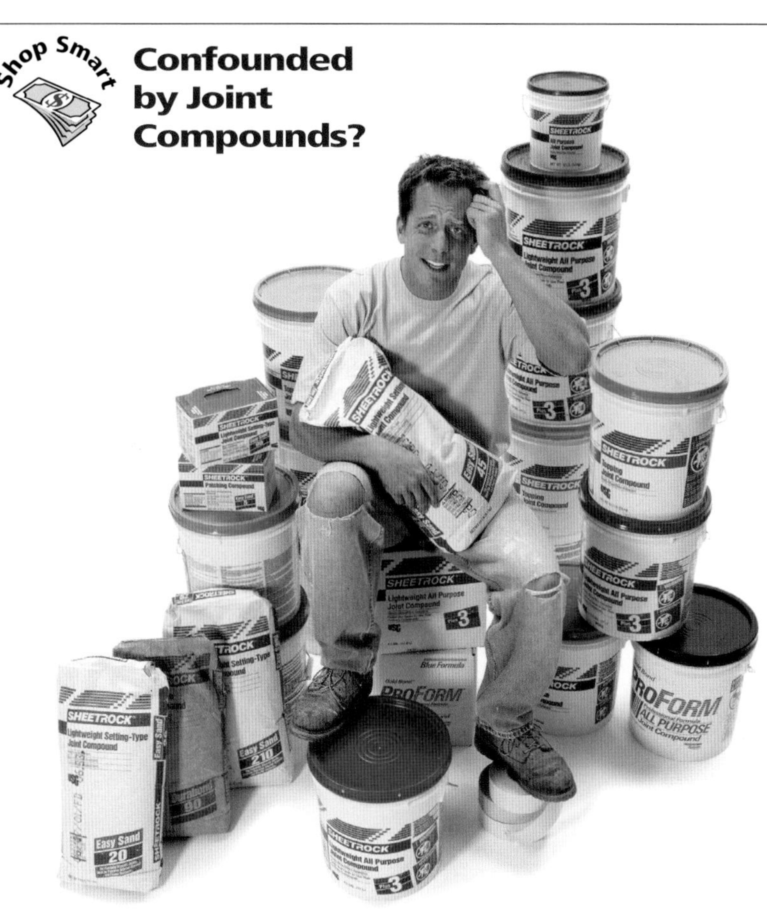

Joint compound falls into two categories: setting compounds, which contain plaster of Paris to make them chemically harden, and drying compounds, which harden through evaporation.

Setting compounds are available with setting times that range from 10 minutes to 3-1/2 hours. The setting time is a rough estimate of how long the compound will remain workable after mixing. For filling large gaps or oversize cutouts around electrical boxes or installing paper-covered metal corner bead, use setting compound. It has great adhesion, shrinks very little and dries hard as rock. Once dry, though, it's difficult to sand, so don't overfill the areas where you use it.

Easier-to-sand setting compounds work much like premixed joint compounds except they speed the finishing process by avoiding the 24-hour downtime between coats—and you can only mix small batches at a time.

Drying compounds are available in powder or premixed form. Most premixed compounds need to be thinned (more for banjo work and spray-on textures, less for knife work) slightly before application. All-purpose compounds work for all coats and even for textured surfaces. Topping compounds are soupy and contain less adhesive than all-purpose compounds. This makes them easy to feather and sand—ideal for the final coat.

Drywall / Other Techniques

Staple Guns 28
Hazardous Materials 480

Specialized Corner Beads

If you're tired of the standard square doorway and corner approach to wall design, look at corner bead options available in most home centers. They add tremendous architectural interest to your room for very little effort. These specialized corner beads don't cost much more than standard corner bead, and they're easy to install.

Rounded, or bull-nose, corners give a soft, adobe-like look to a room and a finished appearance to open doorways. There are two kinds: metal nail-on, and metal or plastic with a paper face. The drywall shouldn't overlap at the corner so the bead fits correctly. Apply the paper-covered, no-nail bead in a bed of setting compound; use the same mud for the first topcoat.

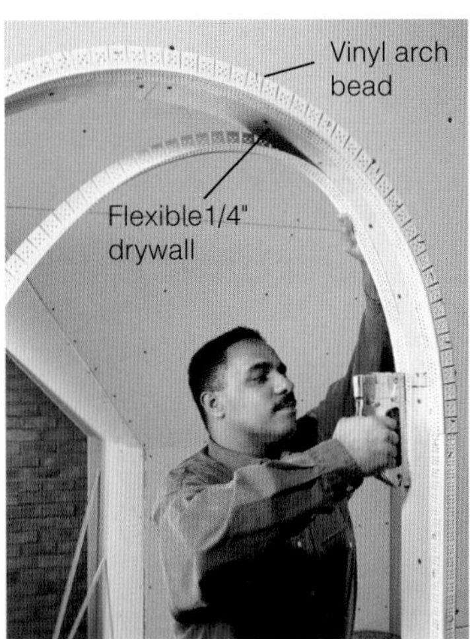

Vinyl arch bead creates a nice, smooth arch with little trouble. Staple the flexible bead to the drywall with long staples. Use vinyl bead for the entire doorway for the smoothest transition. Use a setting-type joint compound to permanently set the bead. This will provide more strength than premixed joint compound.

Knockdown Textures

Knockdown textures give ordinary walls an earthy appearance, similar to stucco. You'll need a spray gun and compressor, knockdown knife, and premixed all-purpose joint compound thinned with 5 pints (2.4 l) of water per 30 lbs. (14 kg) of mud for the initial orange-peel coat and 3 pints (1.4 l) per 30 lbs. (14 kg) for the final topcoat. Mask and cover everything you don't want textured.

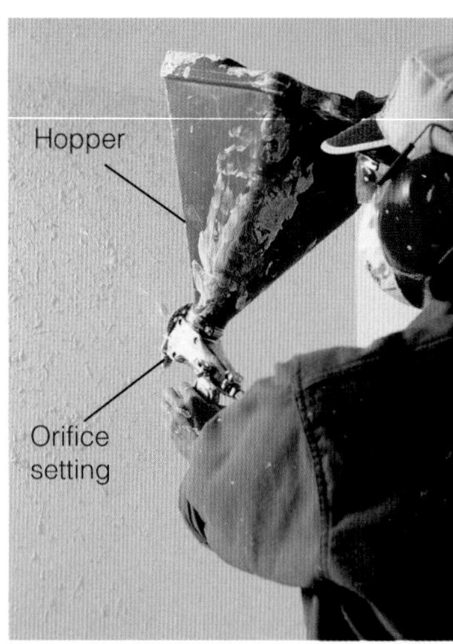

1 Rapidly apply a small-splat, orange-peel base coat with the spray gun set on the second smallest orifice and compressor pressure set at 25 to 30 psi. Let dry for 4 hours. Apply large-splat topping coat with the spray gun set on the second largest orifice and compressor pressure at 10 to 15 psi. Let topping coat set up 10 to 15 minutes before knockdown.

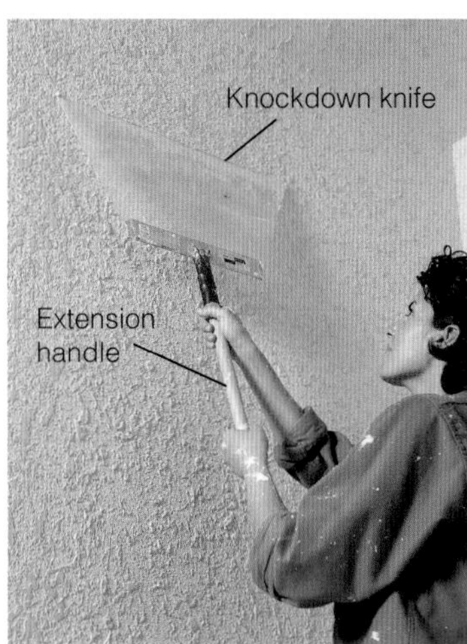

2 Knock down topping coat with a wide Lexan knockdown knife and light pressure. Knock it down in the same order you applied it. On the ceiling, knock down in a direction across the joists or framing to compensate for unevenness. Start each stroke with a clean edge on the knockdown knife.

Ceiling Textures

It's a rare drywall ceiling that's perfectly smooth. There's usually a dip, bump, ridge or crack. Smoothing everything can be a nightmare. Textured ceilings help hide some pesky imperfections. For spray-on textures, like acoustical texture, you'll need to thoroughly mask the walls, floor, light fixtures and yourself.

Stippled ceiling texture can be applied with a crow's foot brush or a plastic looped roller. Thin some all-purpose joint compound, pour a bit onto a scrap piece of drywall, dip the brush, shake off the excess and apply the texture by randomly rotating the brush. For an unusual appearance, any stippled texture can be knocked down while wet.

Spray texture is applied using a spray gun, hopper and compressor. The texture is first mixed with water in a large container; read the spray texture bag for specific instructions. Mask the room and make a poncho from leftover plastic. Practice with the hopper and gun on a scrap piece of drywall. Start in a corner and apply the texture in both directions for even coverage.

Drywall / Repairing

Drywall is easily marred and damaged but, fortunately, almost as easy to repair. Save leftovers from an installation project—joint compound, drywall tape, scrap drywall, screws—for making repairs down the road. If you've run out of drywall supplies altogether, consider buying a drywall patching kit, available at most hardware stores and home centers. Choose one that's suitable for the job and follow the instructions.

Damage. It's easy to accidentally mar drywall panels while moving furniture or tackling other home-improvement projects. Dents, gashes and broken corners can easily occur. Other kinds of damage, like a doorknob banging frequently into a wall, slowly worsen until they need repair. And as your house shifts and resettles, it may even stress the walls to the extent that cracks appear.

If the drywall was not flush to the studs or joists when it was fastened, in time its ringed nails may pop from the wood, breaking the drywall's paper surface. This may also occur if the studs or joists were unseasoned and have shrunk or as a result of moisture changes in the wood.

Tools. You can complete most drywall repairs with basic hand tools: a utility knife for cutting scrap to size and for paring rough edges around holes, 6-in. and 12-in. drywall knives and fine, 150-grit, closed-coat sandpaper to smooth dried compound (or a small-celled polyurethane sponge to wet-sand it). Allow each coat of compound to harden thoroughly (up to 24 hours). Coat with drywall primer and let dry completely (several hours) before painting or wallpapering.

Handy Hints: Spackle in Your Medicine Chest

If you have just a few small nail holes to fill and don't want to break out the tools, fill the holes with regular white toothpaste before painting over them.

Cracks

When houses shift and settle, a drywall crack or two often results, usually above the corner of a door or window. The only lasting fix is to repair these cracks with joint tape and compound.

1 Cut a V-shaped groove into drywall on both sides of the crack. Use a utility knife with a sharp blade (dull blades pull and rip the paper face). Keep the knife blade angled about 45° to form a groove.

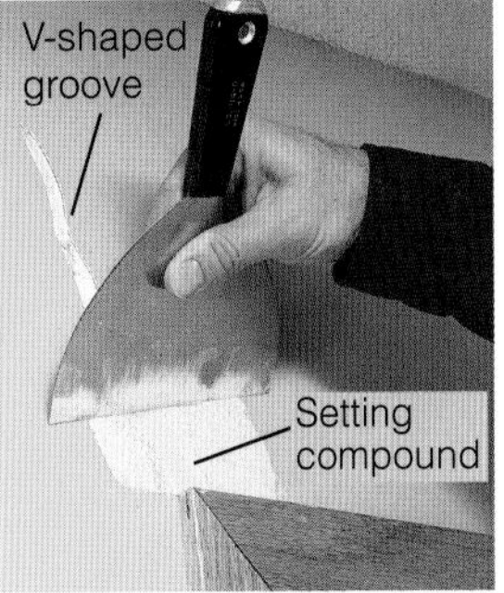

2 Fill the groove with easy-sand setting compound. Powdered setting compound dries faster than premixed joint compound. It's also stronger and shrinks less. Let compound dry and sand smooth.

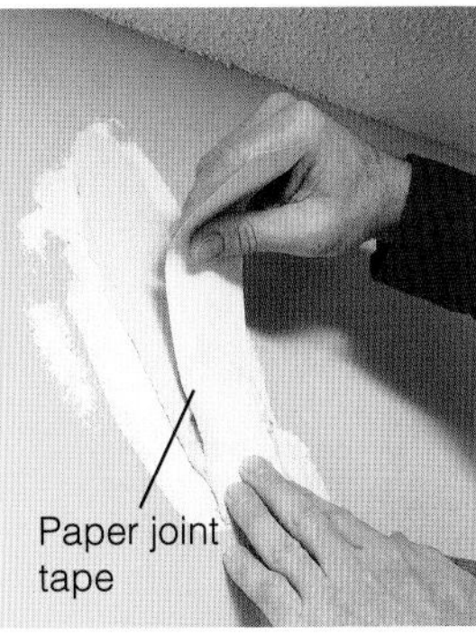

3 Spread a layer of joint compound over filled groove. Lay paper joint tape, centered over the crack, into the wet mud bed. Press the tape into the mud using a flexible knife. Apply topcoat of compound, completely covering tape, and let dry. Continue applying thin layers of compound, feathering away from high ridge, until repair blends with surrounding wall. Then prime and paint.

Popped Nails

As wood studs shrink and swell with changes in moisture content, nails can work loose and pop through the drywall surface. A temporary fix is to reset the nail and cover with spackle. For a permanent fix, do the following:

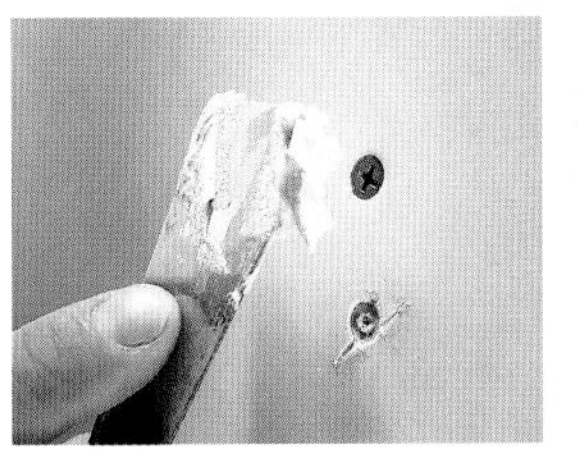

Remove a popped nail with a small flat pry bar. Add a drywall screw just above or below the pop. Fill repair area with two coats of joint compound. Sand smooth, then prime and paint.

Spray-texture Repairs

When water leaks onto a drywall ceiling, ugly coffee-colored stains usually appear. If this happens on an acoustical, or "popcorn," ceiling, texture often flakes off. The challenge is to blend the repair to match the surrounding texture. The solution is an acoustical texture patch in an aerosol spray can.

1 Isolate the repair area with a plastic tarp. Scrape off loose, flaking texture with a flexible putty knife. (**Caution:** Some older ceiling textures contain asbestos.) Catch falling flakes on scrap cardboard or a dustpan. Cover scraped area with stain-blocking primer.

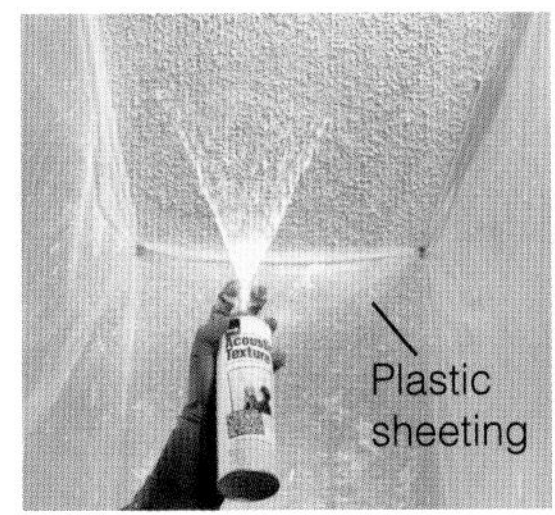

2 Determine whether you have fine, medium or coarse texture and use a matching aerosol acoustical texture patch. Hold can away from ceiling and squeeze the trigger with quick bursts while sweeping over the damaged area.

Drywall / Repairing

Drywall Materials 211
Joint Compounds 215

Holes

Doorknobs, furniture movers and teenagers all have a peculiar knack for creating baseball-size holes in drywall. In fact, such holes are the reason you save that little bit of paint from every painting project.

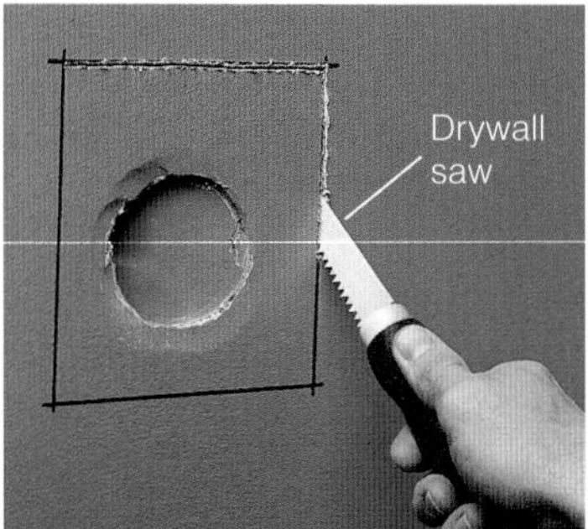

1 Enlarge and square the hole using a drywall saw or rotary tool. If the hole is near a stud, cut damaged drywall back to the stud's center. Square and enlarge the area to make the repair easier.

2 Slip backer boards into hole, then secure them in place with drywall screws. Cut the drywall patch a bit undersized to allow a small gap around all four edges. Attach patch with drywall screws.

3 Finish the repair by covering seams with self-sticking fiberglass mesh tape, then three thin coats of joint compound (fast-setting joint compound lets you finish this repair in a day). Allow compound to dry, then sand smooth, prime and paint.

Corners

Metal corner bead will stand up to everyday wear and tear, but a good whack with a furniture leg can inflict damage. You can restore a damaged corner in an hour or two with quick-setting easy-sand joint compound, as we show here:

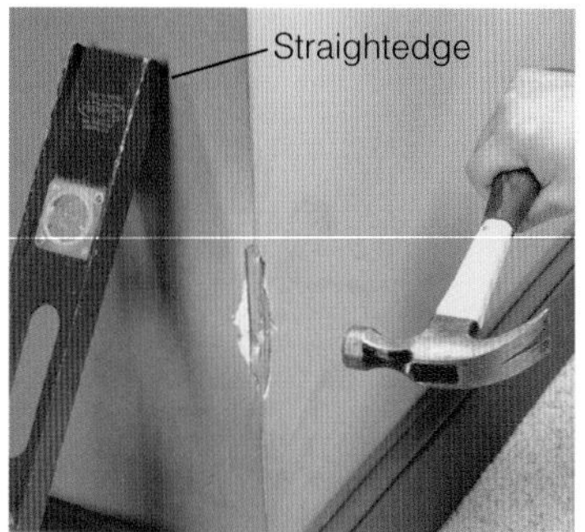

1 Tap corner bead straight with a smooth-faced hammer. Use a straightedge to check the alignment and make sure the bead doesn't protrude past the finished wall. Remove any loose joint compound.

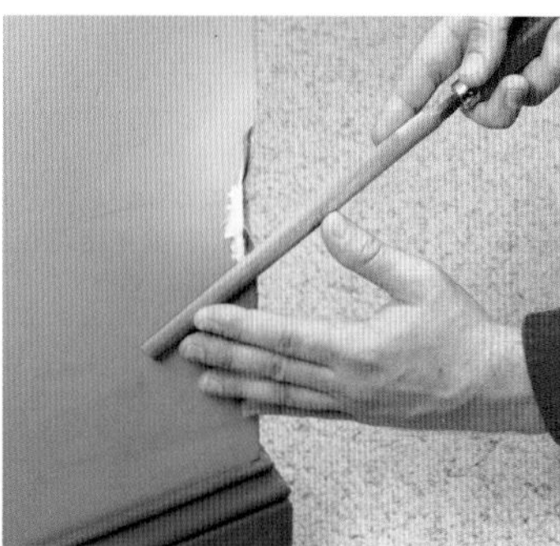

2 File off any remaining sharp edges or burrs using a mill file.

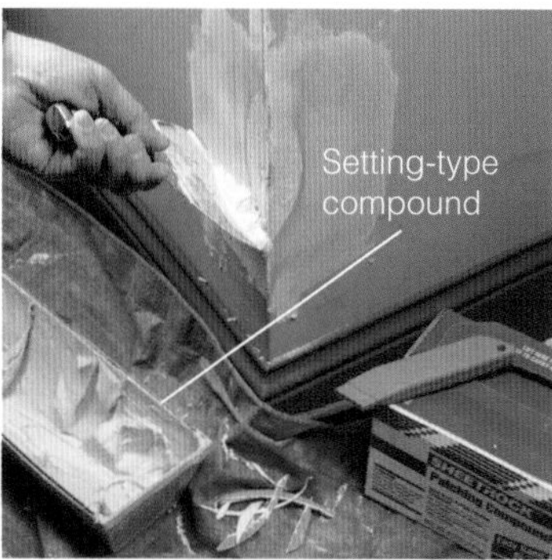

3 Mix setting compound; fill the damaged area. (Remember to protect the floor with a tarp.) Recoat the patch, as necessary, to achieve a straight, even corner. Let dry; then sand, prime and paint.

Removing Drywall

When remodeling or repairing, remove drywall in large chunks to minimize the mess and cleanup. Remove hanging objects from adjoining rooms and tent off the room with plastic to contain the dust. Carefully remove any trim you want to save; then remove the drywall.

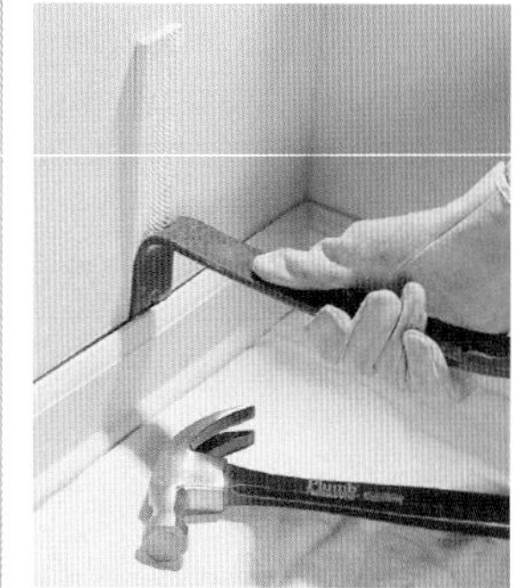

Remove trim carefully for reuse. Slice through paint around the trim using a utility knife. Use a stiff putty knife and flat pry bar to pry off trim. Protect wall surfaces with a wood shim in areas where existing drywall won't be removed. Work trim loose gradually.

Locate nearest studs outside the area to be removed, using a straightedge and level to mark stud centers. Cut drywall over stud centers. Use a utility knife to cleanly separate inside corners and wall-ceiling intersections. Start a hole with a framing hammer; use the hammer and your hands to tear off drywall (remember to wear work gloves and a dust mask).

Protect Your House (and Yourself)

While tearing down drywall, turn off water and electricity in case you accidentally break pipes or cut wiring. Wear safety goggles, a dust mask, work gloves and hard-soled shoes.

Plaster Repairs

Flatten Saggy Ceilings

You can renew a sagging ceiling without messy plaster tear-out by installing strips of wood, called furring, directly over the old ceiling. Then you can cover it with a fresh surface of drywall. The key to this project is starting with accurate level lines on the walls and being patient as you shim the furring strips until they're all level. Be prepared with assorted screw lengths and plan to extend the ceiling electrical box.

Start by finding the lowest spot in the ceiling using a level taped to a long straightedge. Transfer this lowest height to the wall by holding the straightedge level against the low spot and marking where the top of the straightedge meets the wall.

1 Measure 1 in. (2.5 cm) below the low-spot mark. Use a level and straightedge to extend marks around the room. Snap a chalk line to mark the wall.

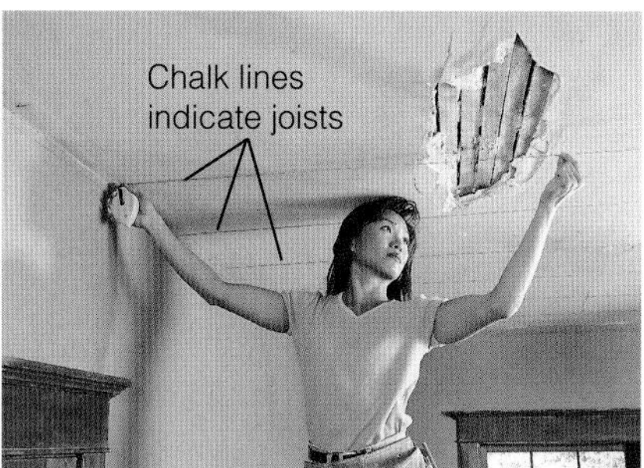

2 Locate the center of each ceiling joist and snap a chalk line to mark it. Probe with hammer and nail to verify joist location.

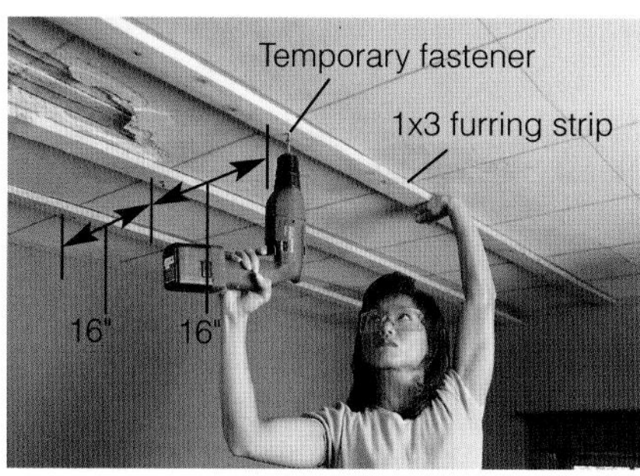

3 Temporarily fasten 1x3-in. furring strips perpendicular to joists, and center them 16 in. apart.

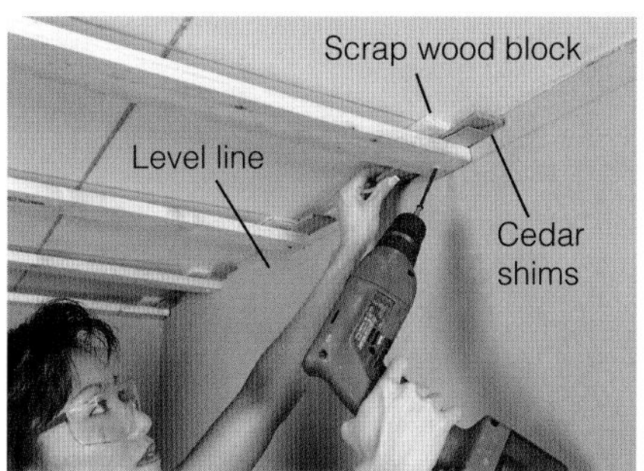

4 Shim furring strip ends to meet the chalk line on wall and secure them. Use scrap wood blocks to reduce shim usage.

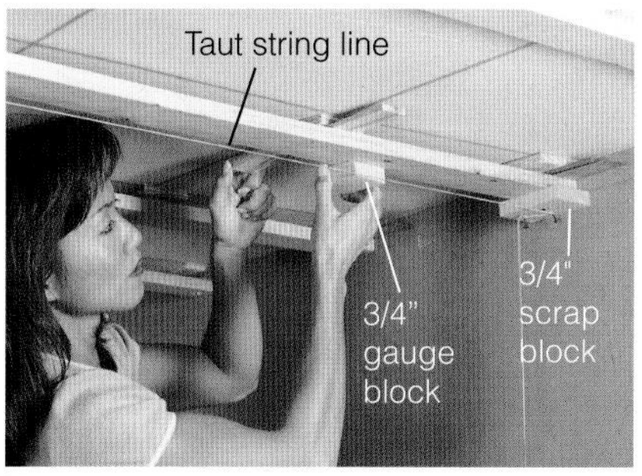

5 Attach scrap block and taut string to each end of furring strip. Use gauge block and string to properly shim furring strip.

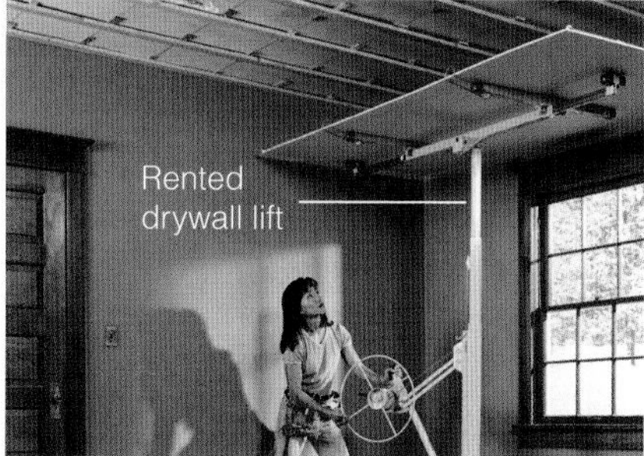

6 Hang drywall perpendicular to furring strips using 1-1/4-in. drywall screws.

Canvas a Wall

Applying wall liner or canvas is a slick way to quickly rescue ratty-looking but structurally sound walls. Canvas will span small gaps and hairline cracks and soften unevenness of heavily painted, textured or patched walls. Some canvas products even function as a vapor barrier and an approved lead paint encapsulation system.

1 Remove flaking paint or wallpaper with a putty knife. Fill gaps or holes with joint compound.

2 Spread special adhesive base coat according to manufacturer's instructions. Work a small area at a time.

3 Apply canvas lining, pressing it into wet base coat. Coat canvas again with base coat. After drying, lining can be painted or papered.

Plaster Repairs

Installing Drywall 213
Lead Paint 288

Plaster is applied to a lath material fastened over studs or joists. The lath may be wooden strips (in pre-1930 houses), metal mesh, or drywall-like gypsum. Repairing old-fashioned plaster walls used to be a real art, requiring a practiced touch, arcane ingredients like horsehair and complex recipes for the plaster. Now the same materials and tools used to repair drywall can be applied to plaster.

Before making a repair, fix any leaks or other causes of excess moisture and give any water-damaged area time to dry thoroughly.

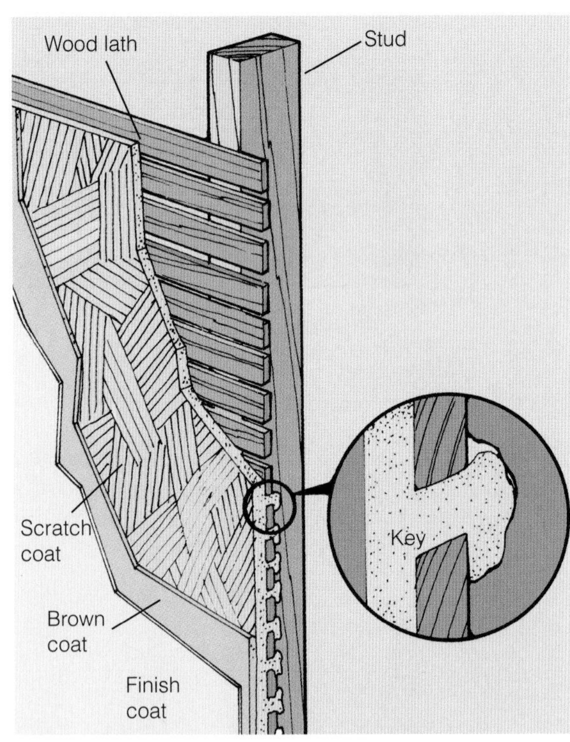

Plaster wall anatomy. When plaster is applied over lath, the first (scratch) coat squeezes through the lath's gaps or holes to create "keys" that bond it to the lath. Sagging plaster is usually an indication that some keys have broken.

Large Area Plaster Repair

1 Secure solid plaster around the damaged area using plaster washers. Concretelike plaster is tough and messy to cut with a circular saw, so carefully use a masonry bit to drill a series of holes around the repair area, then "connect the dots" with a chisel.

2 Hold a cold chisel at a shallow angle to the ceiling to avoid breaking lath or loosening additional plaster. Carefully chip plaster away from wooden lath in damaged area.

3 Patch with drywall of appropriate thickness. Drywall is available in a wide range of thicknesses. Space drywall screws about 6 in. (15 cm) apart along edges and every 8 in. (20 cm) along a joist or stud.

4 Apply joint tape (paper or fiberglass mesh) over joints and skim coat the entire repair area after taping. Work in thin layers to blend the patch with the surrounding surface. Sand smooth, prime and paint.

Securing Loose Plaster

Plaster sags when the keys embedded in the wood lath break loose. You can sometimes stabilize sagging plaster by using plaster washers and screws to pull the plaster back up against the lath. They're perforated to better grip the drywall compound applied over them. Plaster washers are available through specialty drywall supply companies and the Internet.

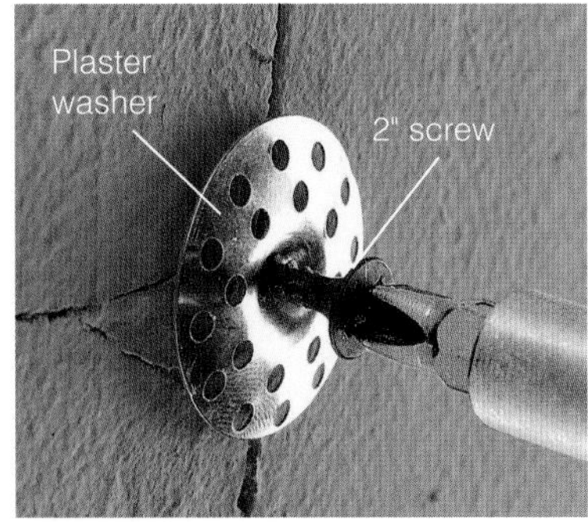

Cracks. Resecure loose or cracked plaster by screwing plaster washers to underlying wood lath or studs. Then skim coat, prime and paint.

Damaged areas. Keep sound plaster secure by installing plaster washers around damaged areas before making more extensive repairs.

Small Holes

1 Undercut the edges of holes with a linoleum or utility knife. Then brush concrete-bonding agent onto lath and edges of old plaster.

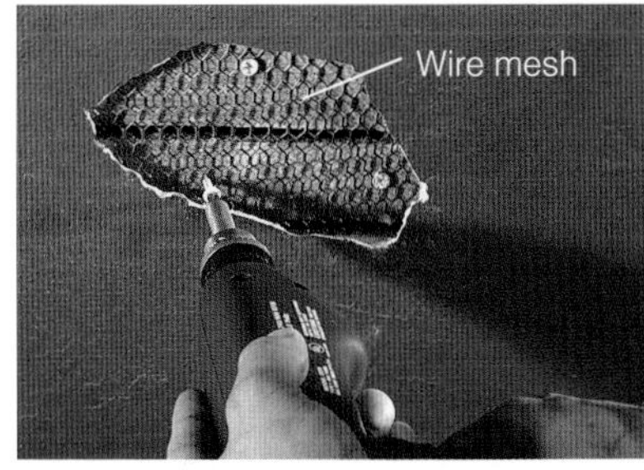

2 Fasten wire mesh to existing wood lath with drywall screws. Wire mesh provides tooth, or a gripping surface, to hold a joint-compound patch.

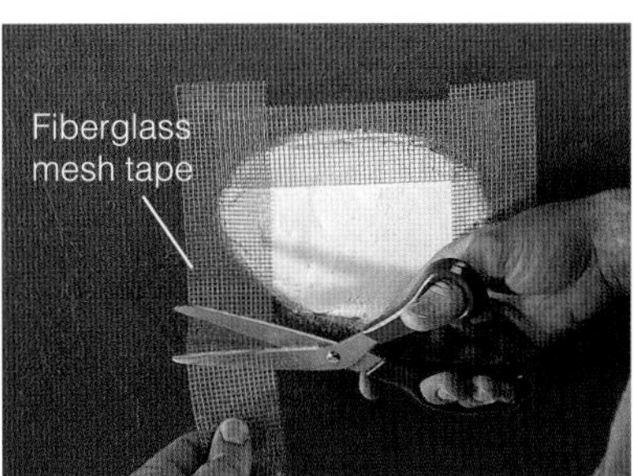

3 Fill the space with setting compound, troweling it level. Cover the seams with self-stick fiberglass tape.

4 Trowel on two or three thin layers of joint compound to cover tape and blend patch with surrounding wall surface. Sand smooth, prime and paint.

Cracks

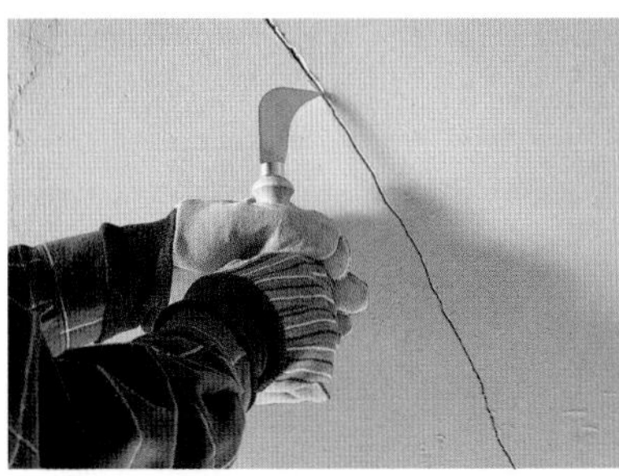

1 Widen and undercut edges of crack with linoleum knife. Vacuum out dust or chips.

2 Fill the crack flush to the surface with setting compound.

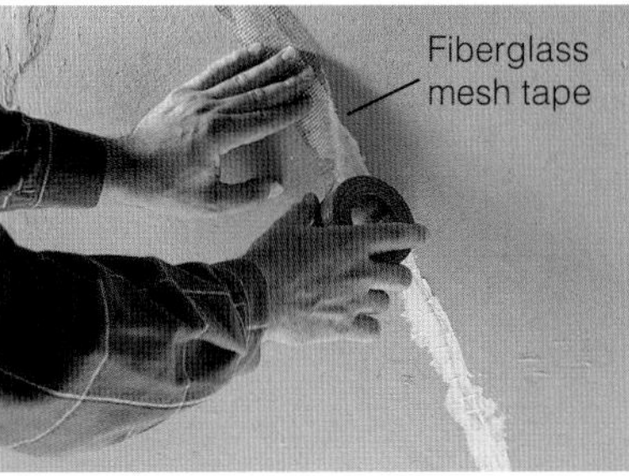

3 Apply fiberglass mesh tape, pressing it firmly over crack. Mesh tape is self-adhesive and remains flexible to inhibit further cracking.

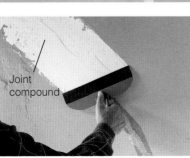

4 Finish repair with two or three thin coats of joint compound. Feather edges with a wide drywall knife. Sand smooth, prime and paint.

Damaged Lath

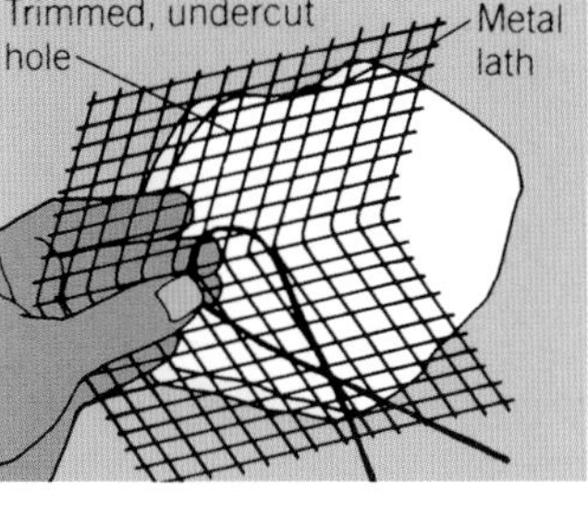

1 Cut away damaged wood lath with a rotary tool or fine-tooth saw. Loop wire through metal lath, fold lath in half and slip it through the hole. Pull lath flush against back side of the plaster.

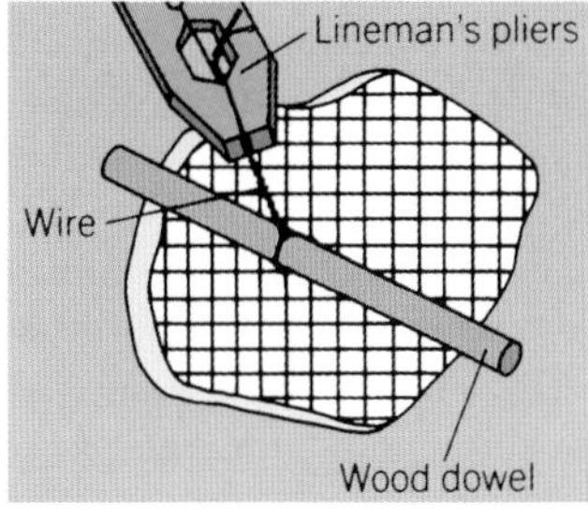

2 Twist wire around dowel to secure metal lath. Coat edges of the hole with concrete bonding agent. Apply a coat of setting compound to lath. Let compound set, snip wire and gently remove dowel. Add finish coats.

Covering Old Plaster with Drywall

Sometimes reskinning an entire wall is faster and easier than patching multiple damaged areas. Find the studs underneath the plaster and mark their locations. Then, install and finish the drywall.

Use drywall adhesive and screws that are long enough to penetrate at least 1 in. (2.5 cm) into the studs or framing material.

Sheet Paneling

Scribing 42
Levels 44

Wall paneling, whether in solid wood planks or sheets, can dramatically change the appearance of any room. Sheet paneling can have a wood surface or a synthetic surface resembling anything—bathroom tiles, living room wallpaper or, of course, wood. It's more durable than paint or wallpaper and, when backed by drywall, has a good solid feel.

Wall paneling falls into three basic categories: solid wood planks, plywood surfaced with top-quality veneer and sheet paneling backed by a substrate of plywood, particleboard, hardboard or even gypsum (predecorated drywall). You can install planks or wood-grained paneling vertically, horizontally or diagonally. Paneling one wall may be enough to dramatically accent a room.

Before installing any paneling, let it acclimate in the room for two days. Grain pattern or color depth may vary slightly or dramatically with real wood paneling, so arrange the panels to make differences less noticeable.

Specialty tools and materials you'll need for the project are a nail set, a rubber mallet, paneling adhesive, color-matched paneling nails, a color-matched putty stick and a felt-tip pen color-matched to the panel grooves.

Caution: Paneling, unless installed directly on drywall or plaster walls, is less fire-resistant than drywall or plaster. Air spaces between studs and furring strips may even encourage airflow, helping flames to spread faster.

How Much Paneling?

Sheets of wall paneling usually measure 4 x 8 ft. Measure the room's perimeter in feet, round up to the next highest foot and divide by 4 to get the number of panels you'll need. If your ceilings are higher than 8 ft., you will have to special-order taller panels. Or to make up a small difference, you can leave a gap between floor and paneling to be covered by baseboard molding.

Preparation for Paneling

Paneling can be fastened to new or existing drywall, plaster, furring strips or to new wall framing (see "Caution," left). Using panel adhesive with paneling nails will provide the most solid installation. Begin by marking the location of all studs on the wall. Remove trim and baseboards, and label their backs with their locations if you intend to reuse them. When replacing baseboard, you'll have to shorten the molding's length by the paneling's thickness on each adjacent wall. Using a carpenter's level as a straightedge, check the wall surfaces you intend to panel. If they are uneven or not plumb, install 1x2 furring strips and insert shimming wedges where necessary to provide a level surface for the paneling. Glue the shims in place.

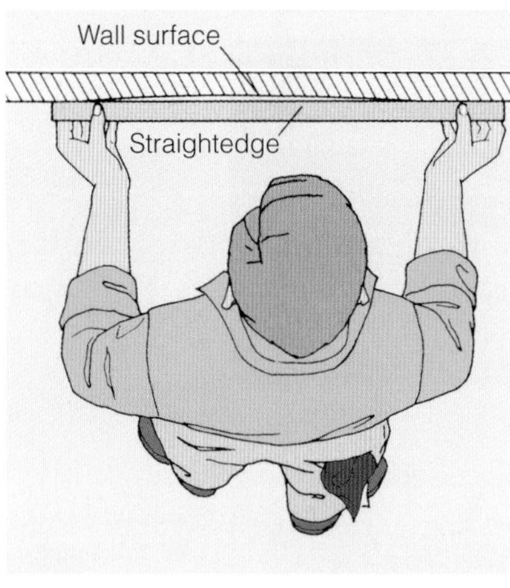

1 Position a straightedge horizontally at several places along the wall. If you observe significant gaps, install furring strips as shown.

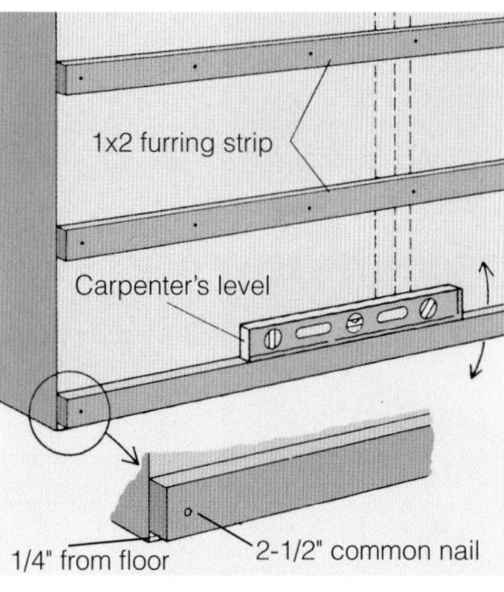

2 Position the bottom furring strip slightly above the floor. Level the furring strip and secure it at high spots only (the points not requiring shimming out). Predrill furring strips' ends to avoid splitting.

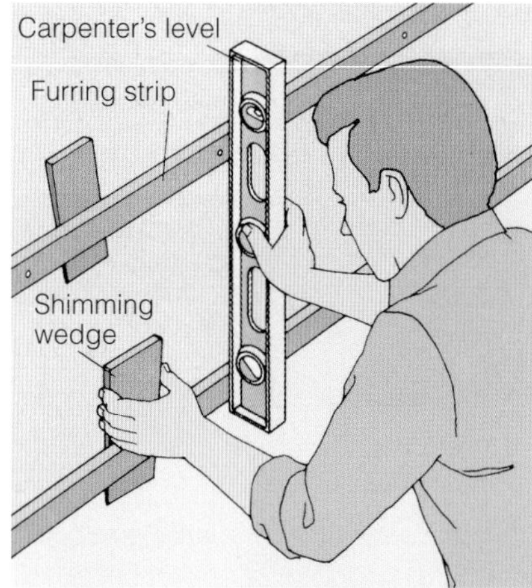

3 Bridge horizontal furring strips with a level to check whether they're plumb. Where out of plumb, insert a shimming wedge under strip to adjust it until plumb. Fasten plumbed spots to studs.

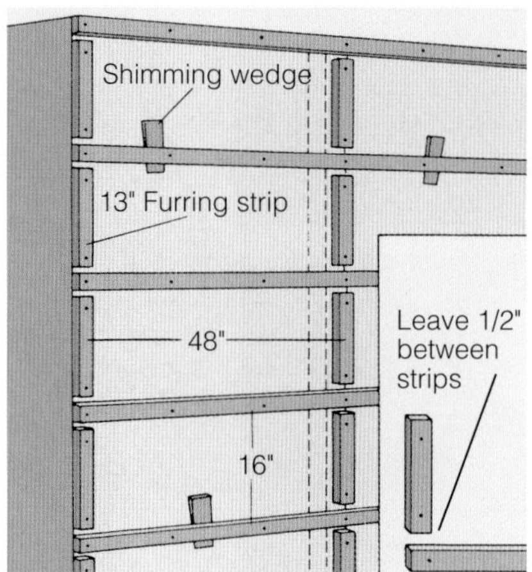

4 Install 1x2s to fit vertically between (but not touching) horizontal strips to support sheet paneling edges. Vertical furring strips should be on 48-in. centers, except at corners.

Installation

Cut panels to length, allowing a small gap at both top and bottom. Gaps will be hidden later with corner, crown and baseboard moldings.

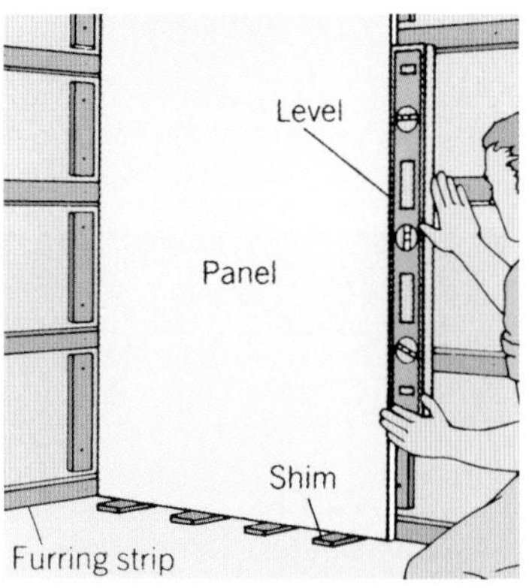

1 Position the first panel with shims under the bottom edge. Level the panel by adjusting shims. Mark the panel's level position on furring strips along the vertical edge. Apply paneling adhesive to furring strips. Tack panel in a level position with four partially driven paneling nails along its top edge.

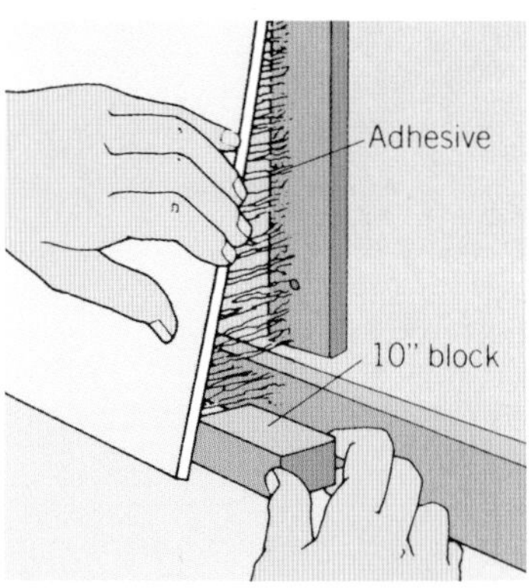

2 Pull panel bottom away from the wall and insert a block to hold the panel out. Let exposed adhesive sit 10 minutes to become tacky. Remove blocks and, with rubber mallet, pound panel over furring strips. Nail panel edges and grooves (if any) to furring strips at 6-in. (15 cm) intervals.

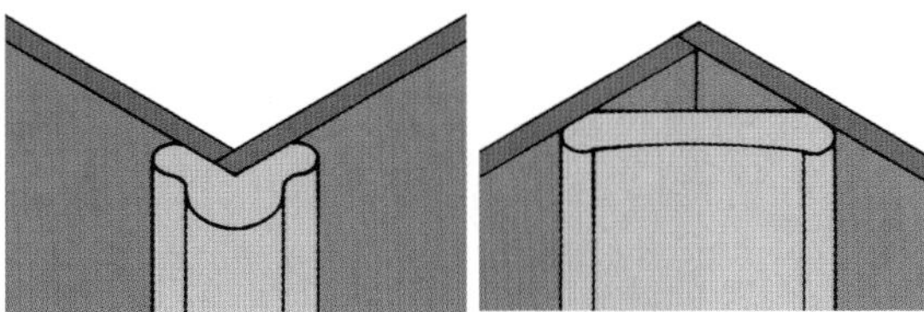

3 Use simple butt joints on inside and outside corners. Finish corners with specialty moldings.

Electrical Considerations

Whether you add new electrical boxes and wiring or simply extend existing boxes' depth, you must do so in a manner that meets electrical codes.

Box extenders. Shield your paneling with a box extender, which is a metal collar that slips over the device and goes inside the box. It's split on one side so you don't need to remove wires to install it. Cut power to outlet before installing extender.

New wiring. If you use furring strips and want to add new electrical boxes, use shallow boxes specifically designed for use under paneling. Use specialty shallow outlets and switches with these boxes. Add protector plates to furring strips to protect wires.

Trade Secrets

Here's a collection of trade secrets that will make the difference between a "pretty good" job and a top-notch professional-looking one:

Install drywall over furring strips before paneling. It makes the wall stiffer, more sound and fire resistant.

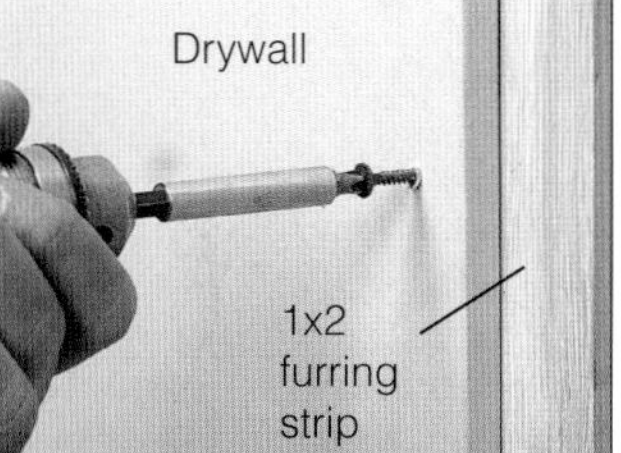

Use a flat pry bar and wood block to help lift and position panels. After lifting a panel, drive in a few nails to hold it in position.

Scribing will give you a good fit against an uneven surface without the use of molding. To mark the scribe line, tack the panel temporarily in place and use a basic compass as shown to mark the contours.

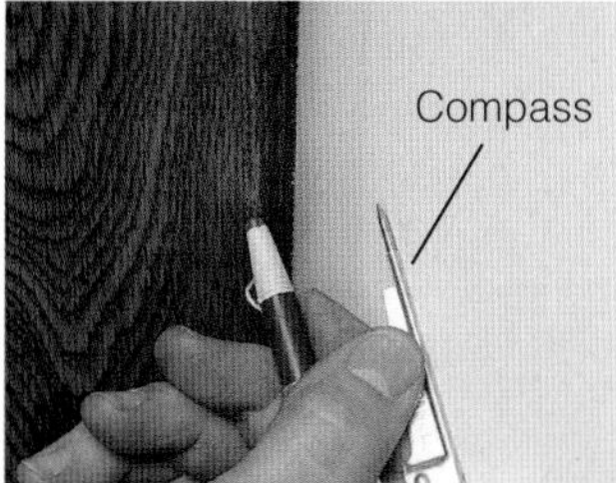

When sheet paneling shrinks, it can leave unsightly light-colored gaps. To hide the problem, apply spray paint that matches the color of the panel's grooves behind each panel joint.

Wainscoting / Styles

Miter Saws **55**
Pneumatic Nailers **74**
Baseboard Moldings **230**
Moldings **430**
Staining Wood **454**

Paneled wainscoting and walls can turn a dull, ordinary room into something spectacular. First, determine where wood walls will seem most at home. Family rooms, dining rooms and studies are all natural fits. In kitchens, paneling can mimic the look of cabinet doors and continue into breakfast nooks and dining rooms to pull the whole scheme together.

Wood walls can be full or partial height. Full wall paneling on every wall can lead to a boxy, closed-in feeling unless the walls are visually broken up by large windows and doors. Combining one wall of taller paneling with three walls of wainscoting is a time-tested approach that strikes a nice balance.

If you plan to paint your paneling, consider using birch plywood or medium-density fiberboard. Birch is affordable and its smooth, close-grain surface makes it easy to paint. For stained paneling, plan to prestain your plywood and moldings before installation.

Casual

This casual style combines wainscoting at one-third wall height and a full wall capped by a display shelf. Its raised-panel look is achieved by applying an additional piece of 1/2-in. plywood over the base plywood and surrounding it with standard door casing. Shoe molding covers the exposed edges of the 3/4-in. plywood rails and stiles.

Traditional

Stained oak offers a traditional warm feel because the wood grain takes center stage. With a base of 1/2-in. oak plywood, solid 1x4 rails and stiles are applied over the top, with cove molding accenting the edges. Another benefit is that unfinished oak outlet and switch covers are readily available.

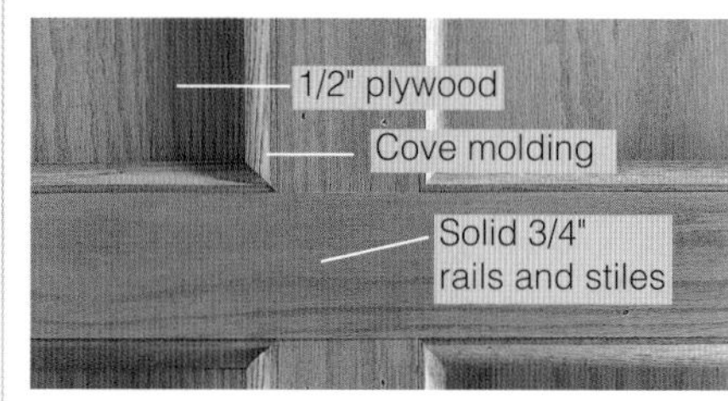

Raised Panel

This raised-panel wainscoting is made primarily with 1/2-in. MDF. The rails and stiles are trimmed with base cap molding and topped with a simple 1x2. The raised center panel is trimmed with panel cap molding.

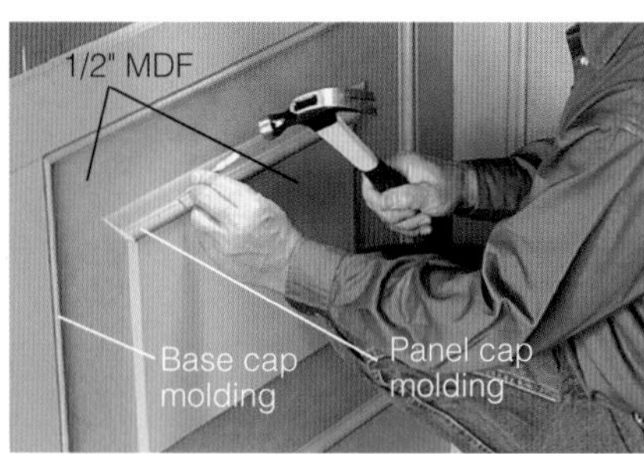

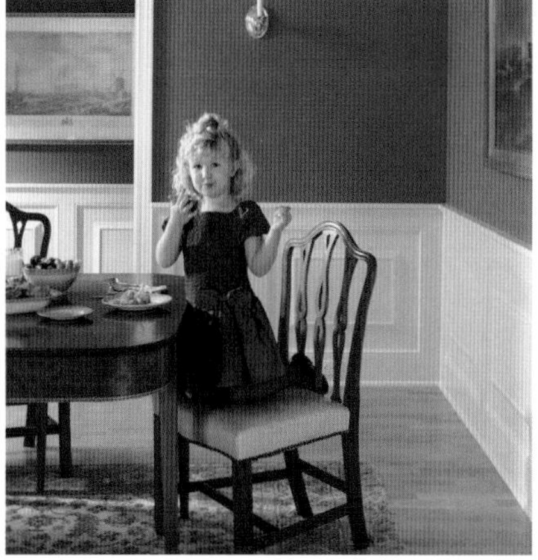

Formal

This painted paneling style has a formal feel achieved through paint, varied-height paneling, lower panels twice as wide as the upper panels and delicate applied molding creating an inner frame. A woodworking store is the best source for a variety of applied moldings.

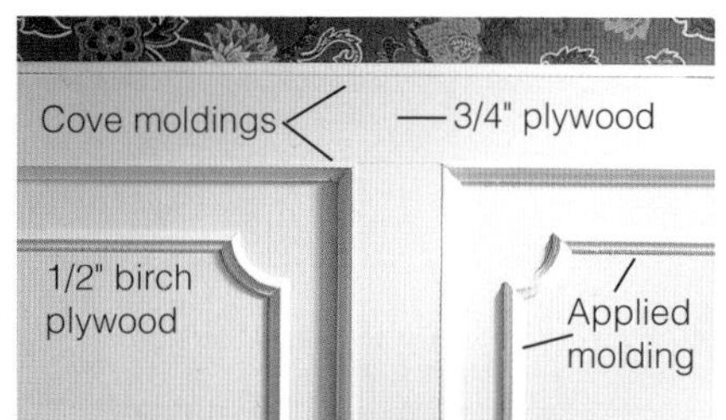

Wainscoting / Installing

A traditional beaded tongue-and-groove wood wainscoting adds warmth and elegance to the simplest room. Add the custom brackets and shelf shown here and it becomes a versatile display wall, too.

Prepare the room by prying off window and door trim and baseboard and installing box extenders. Stack and store the wood wainscoting in the room for several days so it adjusts to your home's humidity level.

Use construction adhesive and a pneumatic finish nailer to install the wainscot. As a rule, start with full-width boards at doors and outside corners. At corners or other tight spots, face-nail the boards and putty the holes after the first coat of finish.

1 Measure up from floor and snap a level chalk line at the desired height. Find studs and mark centers at chalk line and base.

2 Replace old window and door trim with 1x4 moldings. Miter and attach outside corner moldings to trim.

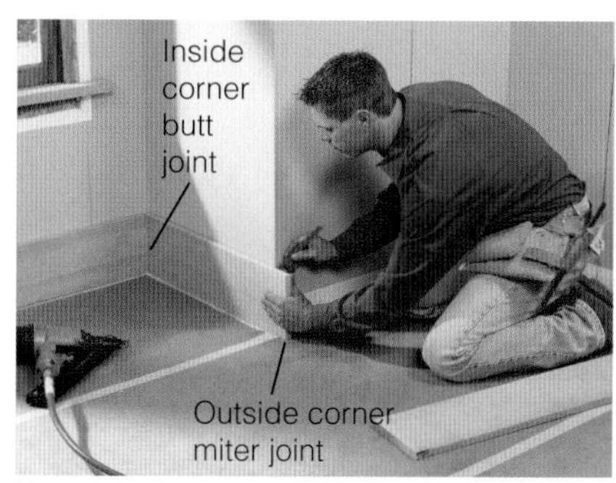

3 Cut and nail 1x8-in. baseboards to studs. Use butt joints on inside corners and mitered joints on outside corners.

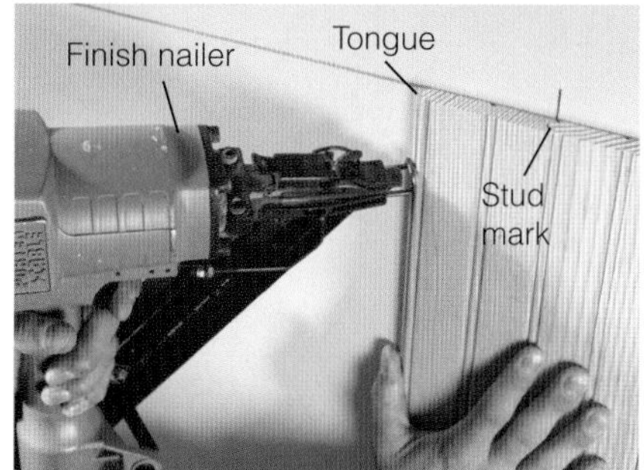

4 Position planks for nailing with tongue exposed. Apply adhesive to back of plank and nail through the tongue at a 45° angle.

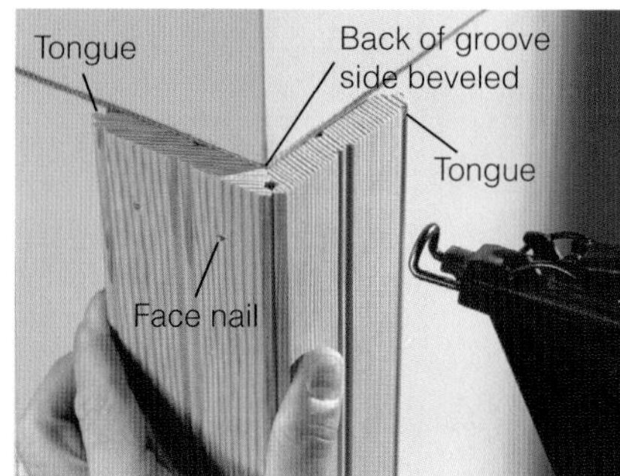

5 Use full planks on outside corners. Bevel the back of the groove side so planks come together snugly. Face-nail corner boards.

6 Using hot-melt glue, temporarily tack brackets in place to determine ideal positioning and spacing.

7 Remove top rail and brackets. Screw brackets to top rail as shown. Install shelf and shelf edging.

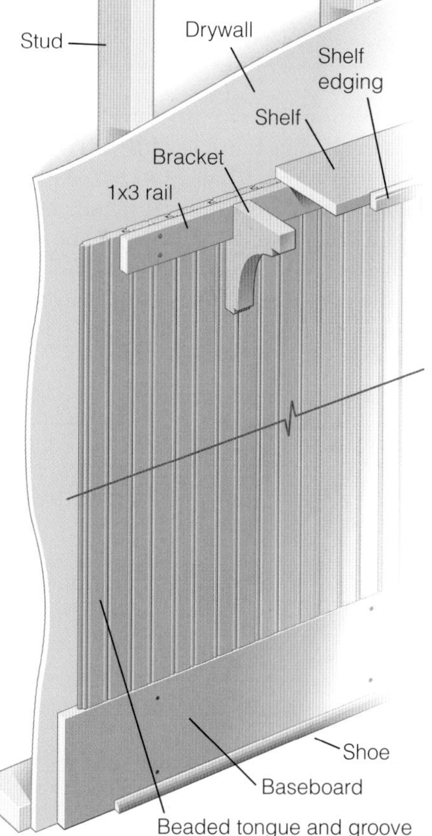

Chair Rails

Miter Saws 27
Pneumatic Nailers 74
Baseboard Moldings 230
Moldings 430

A well-designed chair rail provides a clean dividing line that adds visual interest to a room. Chair rails look best at about one-third wall height and can be painted or stained. For your chair rail, always try to match the look, feel and scale of other moldings in the room.

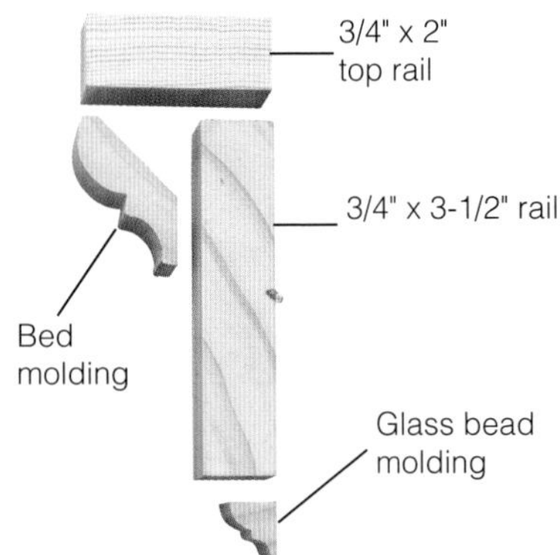

The simple but elegant chair rail shown here consists of four easy-to-find parts. For a painted rail, clear pine is a good choice.

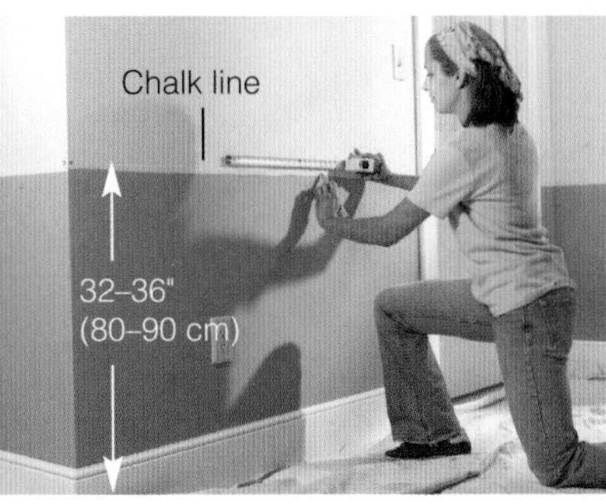

1 Mark and snap chalk lines about one-third up the wall. Locate and mark studs.

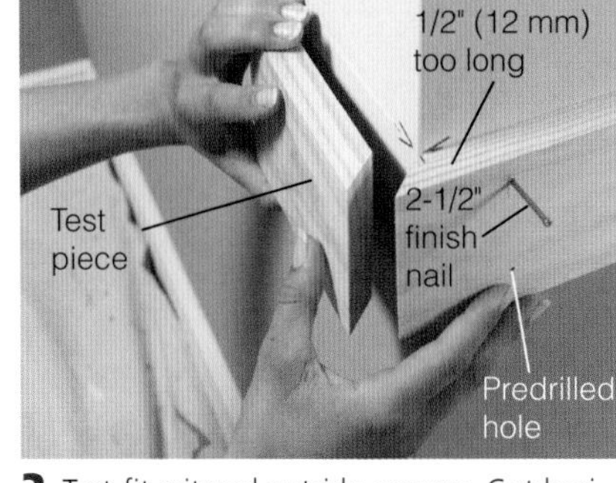

2 Test-fit mitered outside corners. Cut horizontal rails and baseboard to length and nail in place.

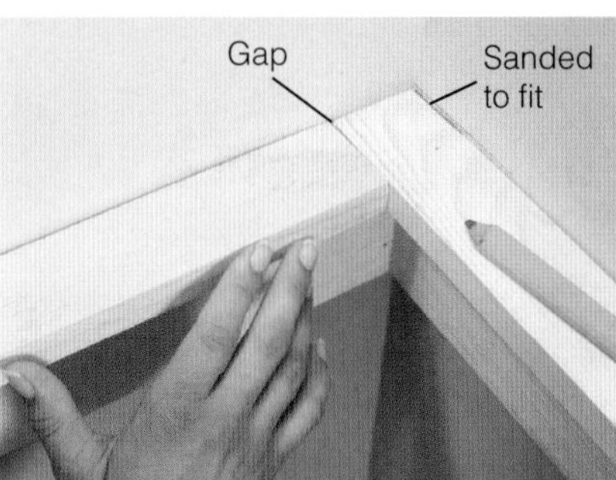

3 Test-fit top rail. Use a belt sander to fine-tune butt joints. Then nail the top rail in place.

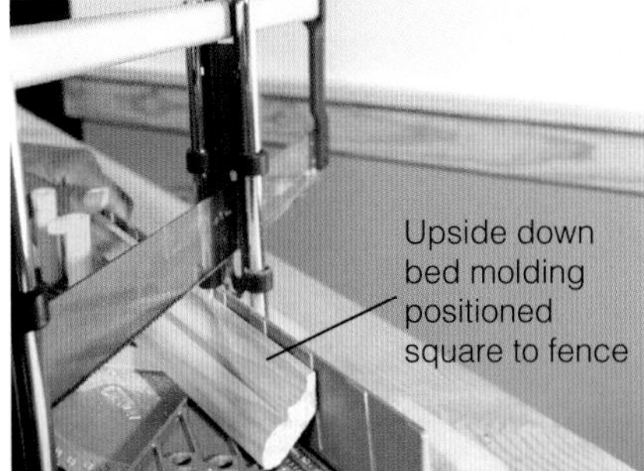

4 Cut bed molding by securing it upside down and tight against a miter saw fence.

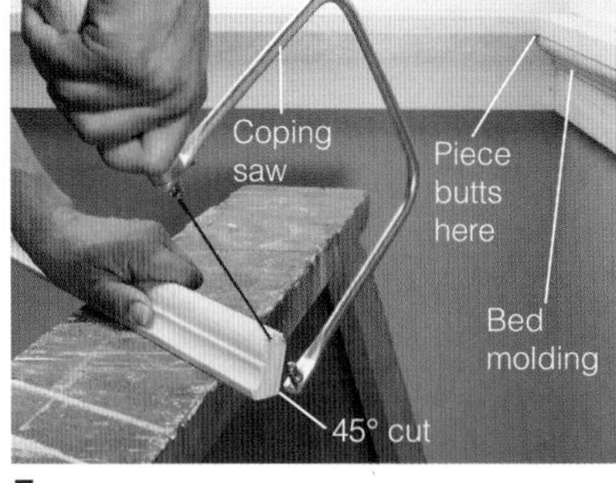

5 On inside corners, cut one overlong piece of bed molding at 45°. Use that profile to cope the joint.

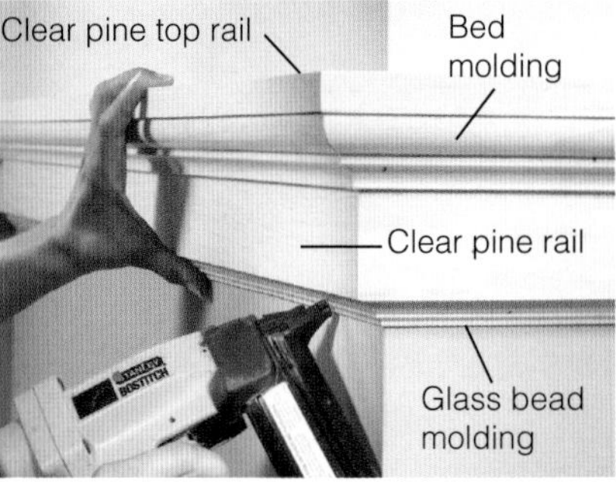

6 Nail glass bead molding to the rail with 1-in. brad nails. Press molding tightly against the wall to close gaps.

7 Putty the nail holes and sand smooth. Ease the top rail edges with sandpaper. Caulk gaps between rail and wall. Prime and paint.

Chair Rail Meets Casing

Pay attention to the transition where your chair rail intersects with door and window casing. For thinner casing, as shown at right, remove a section, add a rosette or corner block, then butt a single piece of decorative chair rail into it. Another option is to add a thicker band of wood around the existing casing to raise its profile. Yet another choice: Bevel the corner of the top rail and bed molding where it butts into the casing.

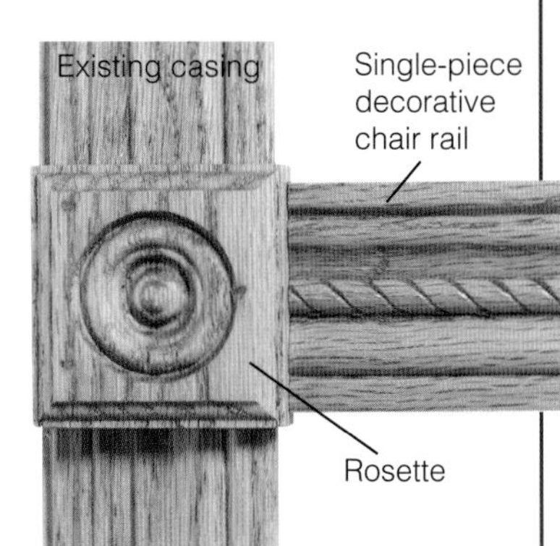

Ceiling Tiles

Acoustical ceiling tiles conceal damage and help reduce noise. If the original ceiling is level and in good condition, the tiles can be glued directly in place. If not, install furring strips, shimming as needed to create a level surface, and staple the tiles to the strips. Let the materials acclimate in the room for at least 24 hours. For installing furring strips, use 1x3s and 2-1/2-in. nails (or 2-1/2-in. drywall screws). For installing the panels, you'll need a hammer (or power screwdriver), a staple gun and 9/16-in. staples, a utility knife, a chalk line, a level or straightedge and a tape measure. The adhesive method requires cutting and measuring tools, a wide putty knife and manufacturer-recommended adhesive. Always wear safety goggles, a dust mask, gloves and long sleeves.

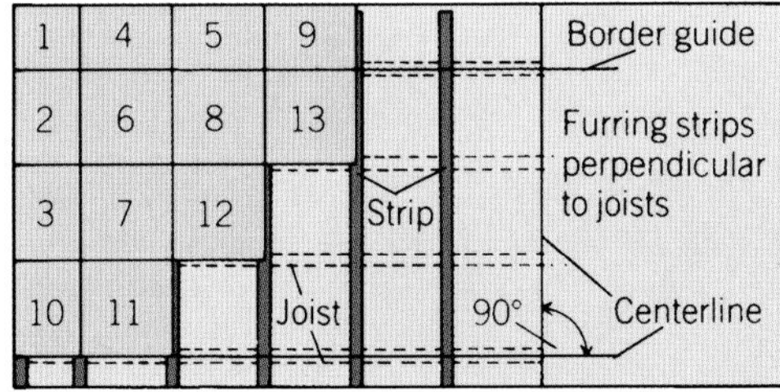

Plan installation on graph paper; then check measurements against the ceiling. Test corners for squareness; the one closest to 90° is the starting corner. Locate joists as you would studs. Measure the ceiling in several places—it may be wider at one end. Plan your layout to minimize small tiles around the perimeter. Mark border guidelines; adjust centerlines so they fall at a seam. If tiles are flanged, shift centerlines an additional 1/2 in. (12 mm) away from starting corner. Snap a chalk line at this position. Install furring strips at 12-in. intervals.

1 Center first furring strip over centerline at right angle to joists. Screw or nail strip to joists. Work from the center out, using a spacer.

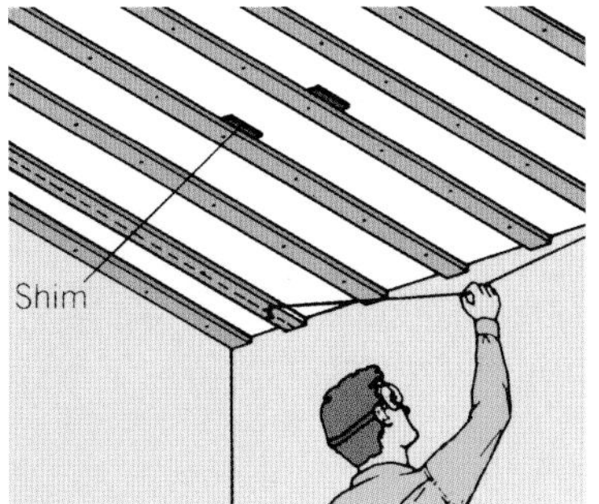

2 At border-tile distance from each wall, snap chalk lines along the ceiling's length and width. These lines must parallel the centerlines.

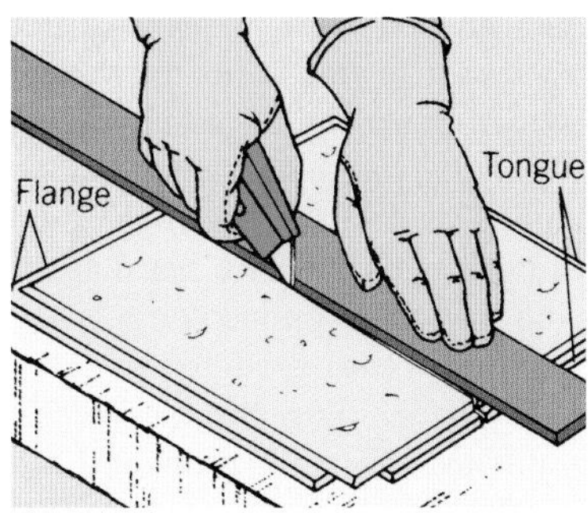

3 Cut border tiles to size, face up, using a utility knife and straightedge. Leave long flanges intact. Cut off the corner tile's tongue.

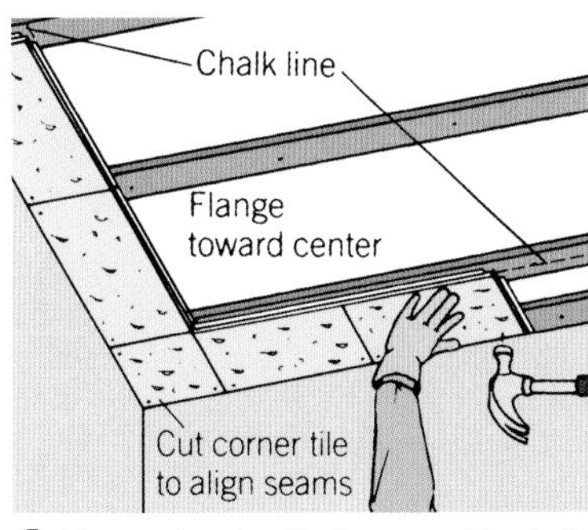

4 Line up border-tile flanges with chalk lines. Use drywall nails to secure the cut edges and staple the flanges. Install tiles in sequence shown at left.

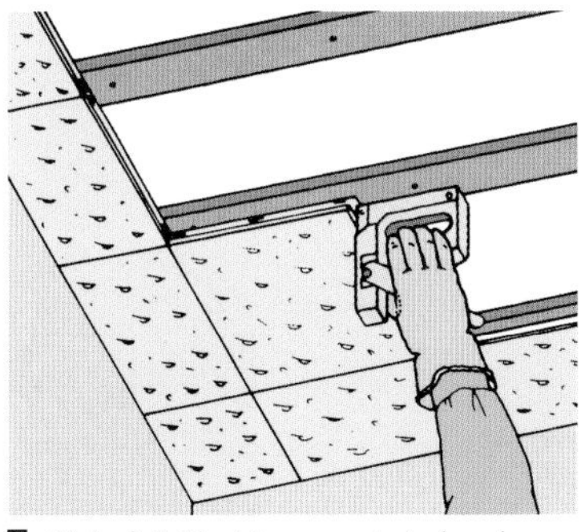

5 Slide full tiles' tongues into border tiles' grooves. They should be snug but not forced. Staple through flange into furring strip.

To glue tile, first prime a tile's back with a light coat of glue. Put golf-ball-size dabs of glue 2 in. (5 cm) from the edges. Press in place.

Replacing a Damaged Tile

1 Cut close to the edges of the damaged tile with a utility knife; pry out tile remains with putty knife. Scrape debris from furring strips or old adhesive from base.

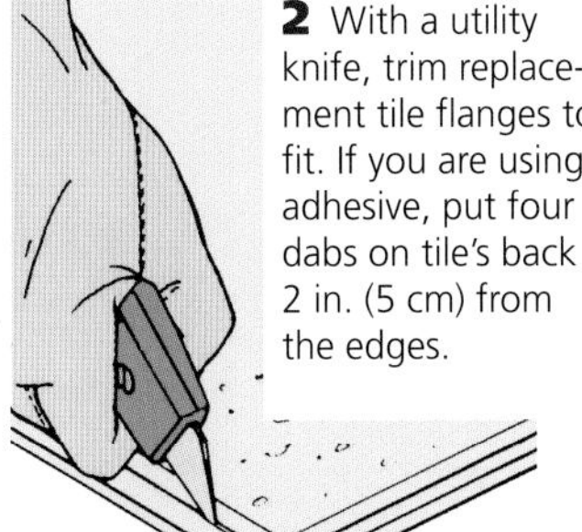

2 With a utility knife, trim replacement tile flanges to fit. If you are using adhesive, put four dabs on tile's back 2 in. (5 cm) from the edges.

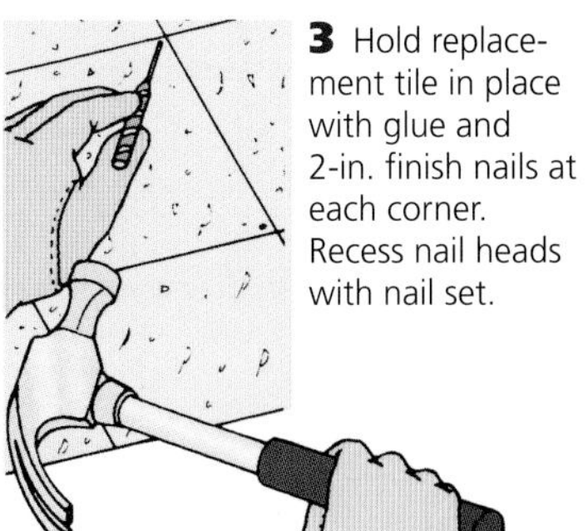

3 Hold replacement tile in place with glue and 2-in. finish nails at each corner. Recess nail heads with nail set.

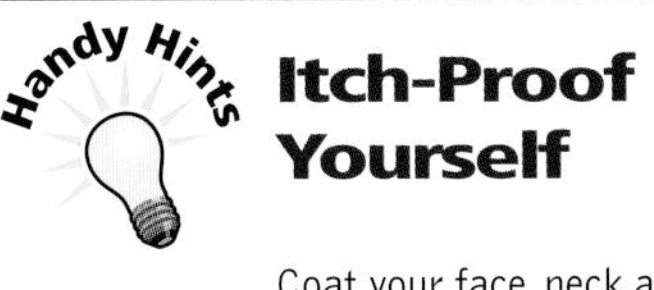

Itch-Proof Yourself

Coat your face, neck and arms with baby powder before working with ceiling tile. It will help keep itchy fibers contained in some ceiling tiles from sticking to you.

Suspended Ceilings

Levels **44**
Fluorescent Lights **152**

Unfinished basements pose unique challenges when you want to transform them into comfortable living spaces. One of the biggest challenges is figuring out how to install a flat ceiling when you have ductwork, pipes and electrical wire crossing underneath the joists. Fortunately, this problem has a fairly simple, affordable solution: a suspended ceiling. Beyond affordability, a suspended ceiling offers access to the mechanical systems you're hiding, provides some insulation, improves acoustics within the room and is easy to repair.

A suspended ceiling system consists of a metal support gridwork that holds the ceiling tile. This metal gridwork has three main components: wall molding, main runners and T-shaped crosspieces.

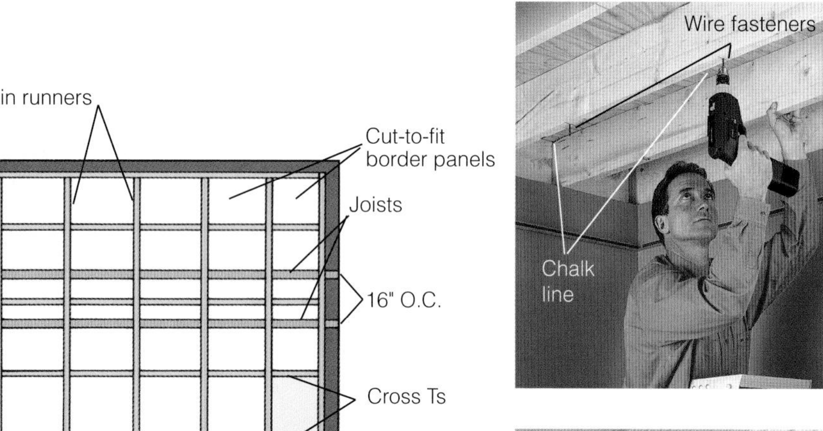

Gridwork layout. L-shaped wall moldings form the perimeter track. Main runners run perpendicular to the joists, divide rows of tile and are supported by 18-gauge wire. Crosspieces divide individual tile panels and are supported by main runners.

Installing a Suspended Ceiling

1 Install L-shaped wall molding at a level line marked on the wall. Use one screw per stud to attach it. Butt, rather than overlap, molding in corners.

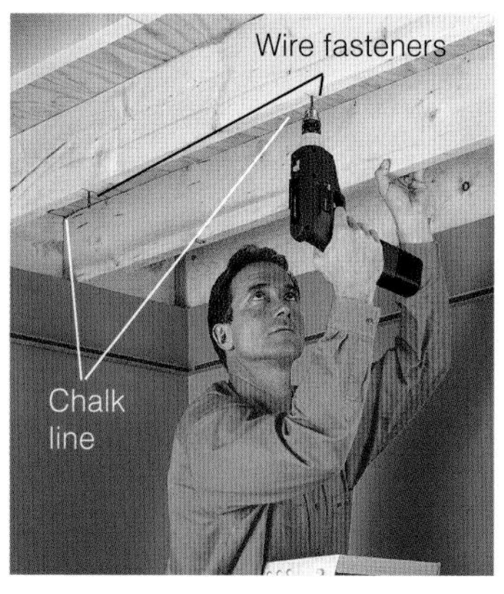

2 Screw wire fasteners into ceiling every 4 ft. (approx. 120 cm) along main-runner chalk lines. Refer to your gridwork layout to determine the position of the first main runner chalk line—its distance should be equal to the width of your border tiles. Chuck fasteners into drill to install them faster.

3 Wrap wire tight to fastener eye to reduce slack and droop in main runner height when tiles are installed. Use wire three times as long as the gap between bottom of joists and the suspended ceiling. Wrap wire around itself three times.

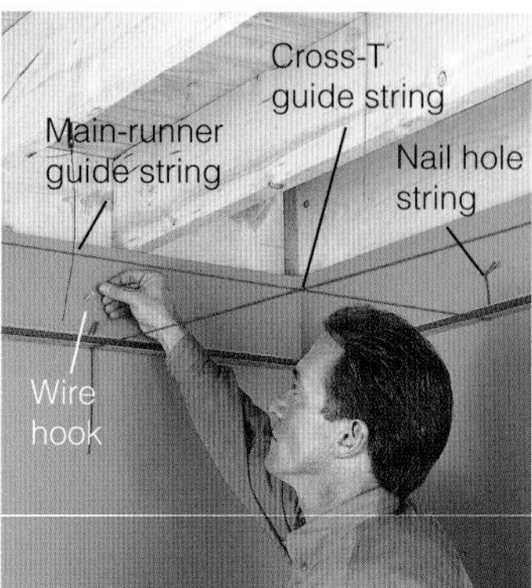

4 Run two guide strings perpendicular to each other. One string guides first main runner; the second string guides the first row of crosspieces. Pull string up behind the wall molding with a wire hook. Wrap string around a nail driven in above the molding to pull string tight.

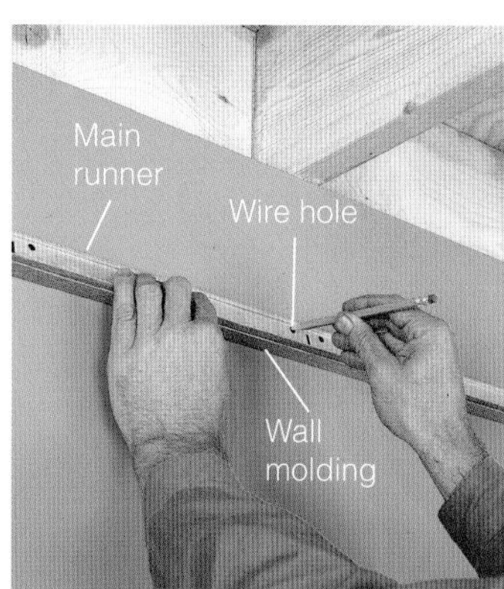

5 On each wall perpendicular to the joists, temporarily lay T-shaped main runner on top of attached wall molding and mark wire support hole locations closest to the joists. Run tight parallel strings between the wall moldings on these marks.

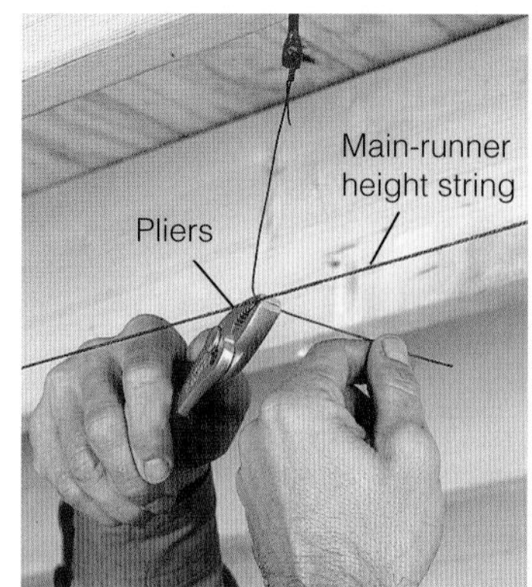

6 Use pliers to bend each wire slightly more than 90° where it touches the guide string. Bending the wires at this string-indicator height helps reduce the amount of leveling and adjusting you'll do later.

7 Install the main runners. Each support wire goes through a predrilled hole most nearly plumb to the fastener. Don't wrap the wire until all leveling adjustments are made after crosspiece installation.

8 Install crosspieces. Crosspieces lock in place to vertical slots in main runners. Start at the crosspiece guide string. Install full-length crosspieces first; then cut border crosspieces to length. Check that entire gridwork is level. Make adjustments to main runners at hanger wire; then tie wire together.

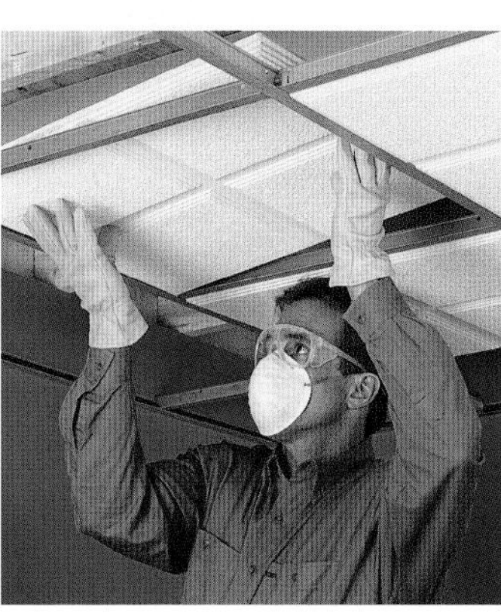

9 Install full tiles first to stabilize the gridwork. Start at room's center and work toward walls. Install border tiles last, since each must be measured and cut.

Installing Lights

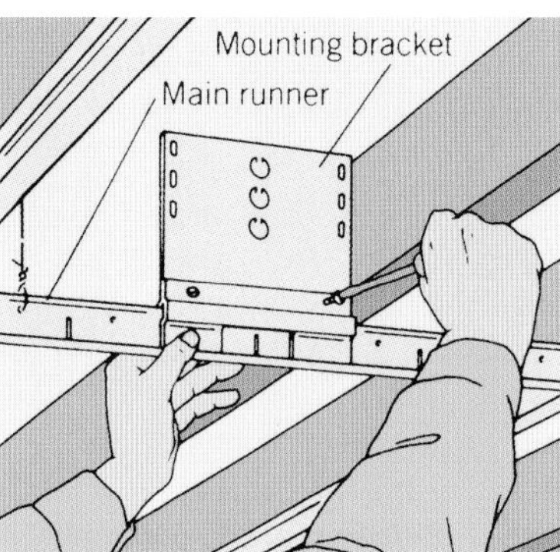

1 To install a fluorescent fixture within a suspended ceiling, position light mounting brackets on the midpoint of a crosspiece's upright leg. Screw bracket sections together.

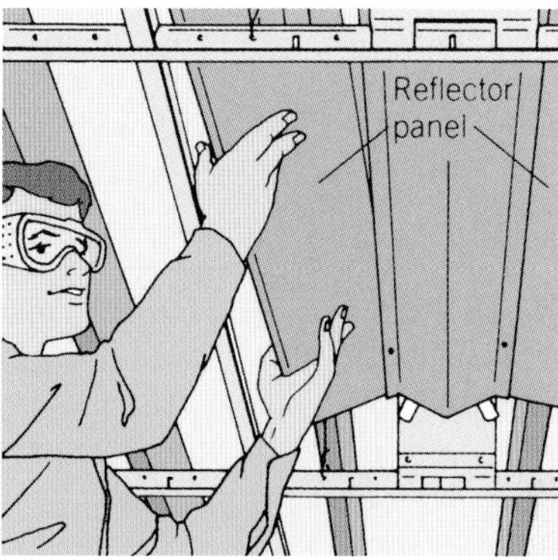

3 Shut off power. Run switch-controlled electrical wire to fixture. Wire fixture and install fluorescent tubes. Install reflector panels over fixture top.

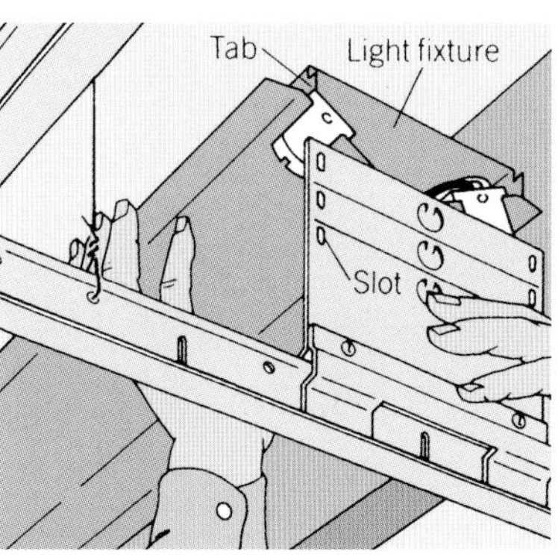

2 Attach fixture to mounting brackets by sliding two tabs at each end of fixture through matching slots of opposing brackets.

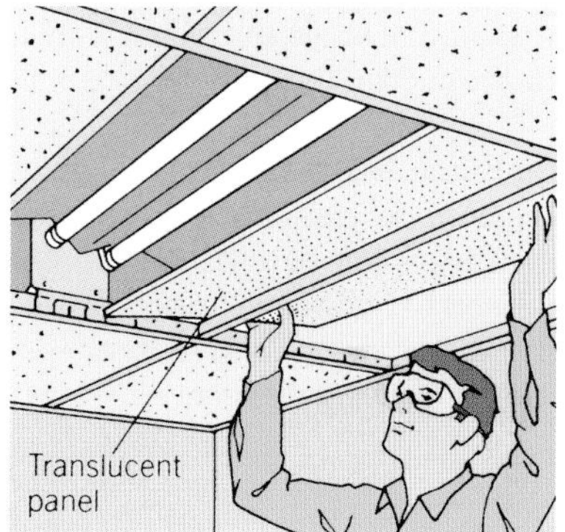

4 Remove panel next to fixture space. Through this space, slide translucent (or diffuser) panel into place below fixture. Replace adjoining panel.

Wood-Frame Suspended Ceilings

An attractive option for suspended ceilings is a luminous ceiling with an entire surface lit up by rows of fluorescent lights. It follows the same basic concepts as metal grids but uses wood and molding to create the grid and plastic diffuser panels instead of ceiling tiles. Install it anywhere you would consider using a conventional suspended ceiling.

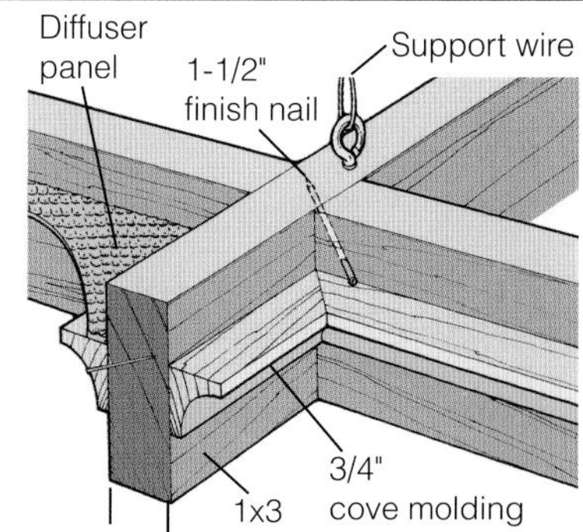

A wood alternative. Placed on edge, 1x3s form a wood frame that's supported by eyebolts and wire. The cove molding creates a shelf for the diffuser panels.

Baseboard Moldings

Coping Saws 26
Miter Saws 55
Inside Corners 233
Interior Trim 388

Interior trim doesn't occupy a lot of space in a home, yet no other element speaks with more clarity about a home's quality of craftsmanship. Because of that quality, installing wood trim ranks high on the list of satisfying do-it-yourself endeavors. In the next few pages, you'll learn the tips and secrets the pros use to get great-looking results time after time. Today, a huge variety of trim choices are available. Make your choice based on what will blend with or complement your home's other trim styles.

Tools. The engine that drives a perfect trim project is a 10- or 12-in. power miter saw with a 40- to 60-tooth thin-kerf carbide blade. With a power miter saw, you can change angles in seconds and nibble off the tiniest amount for a truly accurate fit and cut. A pneumatic finish nailer, while not essential, is certainly a huge plus, especially for smaller trim. You'll also need a coping saw and a nail set.

Preparation. Apply the finish to the trim before you install it. For stained trim, apply the stain and one or two coats of clear finish. For painted trim, apply primer and at least one coat of paint. In both cases, apply final coat after installation. To save footsteps, set up the miter saw in the center of the room where you plan to work.

Handy Hints: Trim Tricks

- Always cut pieces slightly overlong and test-fit before making the final cut.
- To predrill holes, cut the head off a same-size finish nail and use it as a drill bit.
- Where possible, install nails in a dark grain portion of wood to better hide the nail.
- Use a tape measure only when you have to. Instead, set the workpiece in place and mark the cut to improve accuracy.

Molding Types

Molding falls into two basic categories: paint-grade and stain-grade. Paint-grade trim has a smooth, paint-friendly surface. For painted trim, use preprimed solid wood, poplar, polystyrene or finger-jointed pieces.

For trim that will only be stained or finished, use solid pine (no finger joints), hardwood or hardwood veneer (which has an MDF core). Most home centers carry a wide variety of each type; unfortunately, their hardwood selections are often limited to red oak or maple unless you special order.

This vast selection of moldings means you can experiment with many combinations to create your own trim style with two, even three pieces. Single-piece baseboard varies greatly in width. Use a single piece for carpeted rooms and where the style matches the window and door trim. Add quarter-round or base shoe in rooms with hard-surface flooring so it can conform to floor dips and uneven areas. The base cap on three-piece moldings conforms to uneven wall surfaces and helps hide gaps.

Single-piece moldings

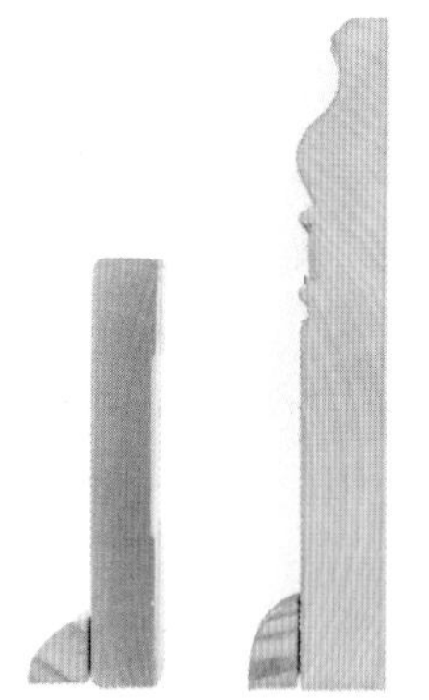

Two-piece moldings

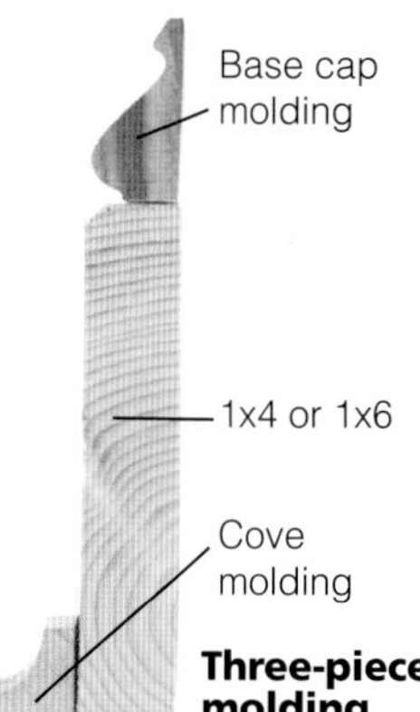

Three-piece molding

Getting Started

Protect the floor with a tarp and set up your workstation in the room's center. Locate the studs and mark their locations with painter's tape. Install door trim before working on baseboard.

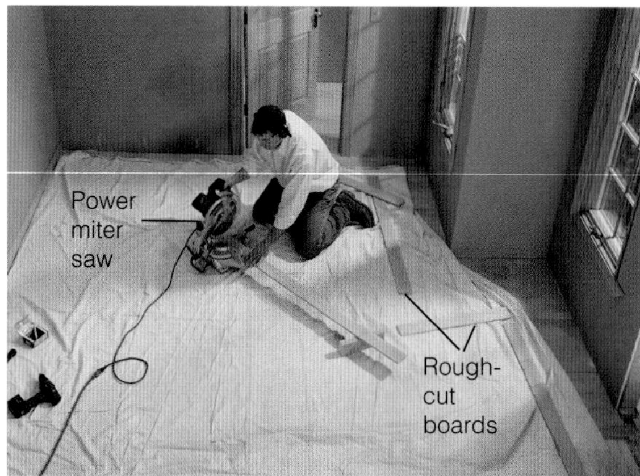

Rough-cut all baseboard pieces about 2 in. (5 cm) overlong and lay them in place. Starting with the longest wall, cut the first piece to length and install it. Continue around the room using butt joints on inside corners.

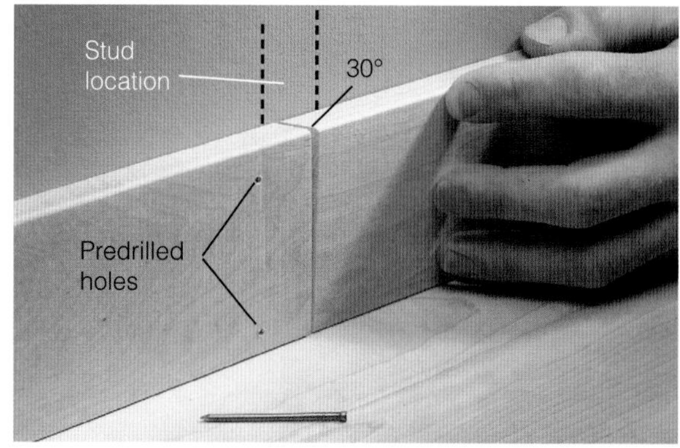

To splice two baseboards, use beveled cuts over a stud location. Select pieces with similar grain color and pattern so the joint is less visible. Cut a 30° angle on each piece.

Inside Corners

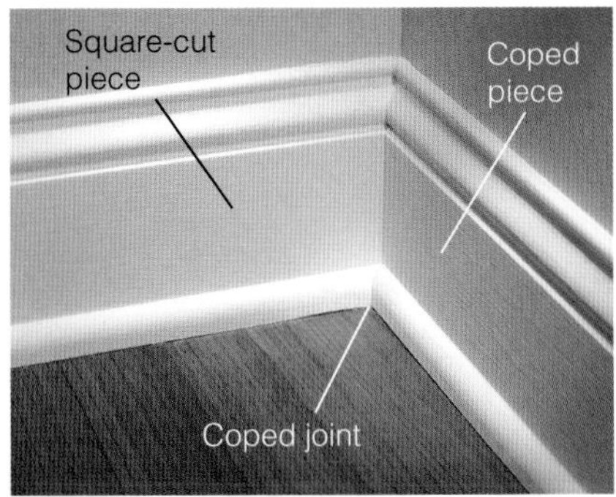

Form the inside corner joints by making a simple square cut on one piece and a coped cut on the other. Floors that are out of level, though, can cause even perfectly coped inside corners to look lousy. Check each joint's fit before you make the final cuts and nail either piece. If a coped joint has a gap at the bottom, shim a square-cut piece using the technique shown at bottom. For a gap at the top, adjust the coped cut on a miter saw.

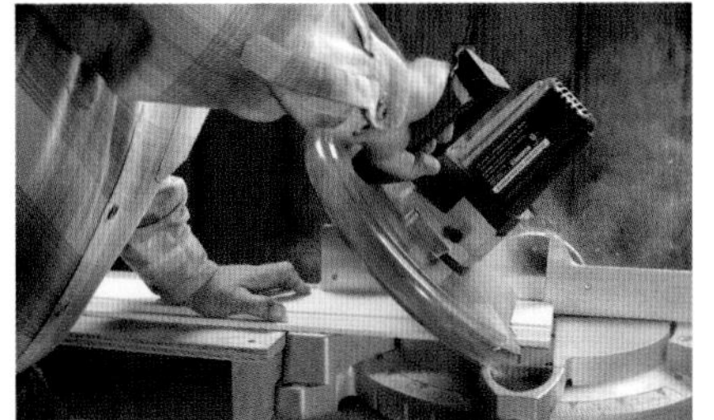

1 Cut a 45° bevel on baseboard pieces to be coped. Then turn each board upside down in a miter saw and carefully back-cut the straight portion until reaching the profiled section.

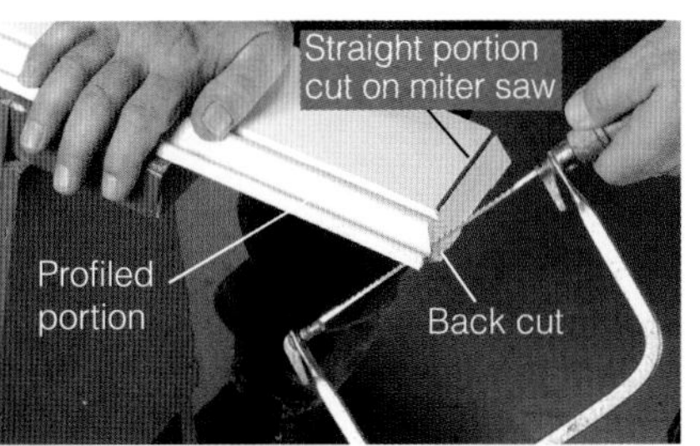

2 Saw out remaining profiled section with coping saw. Tilt saw at least 30° to create a back bevel for a tighter joint on the exposed face.

Outside Corners

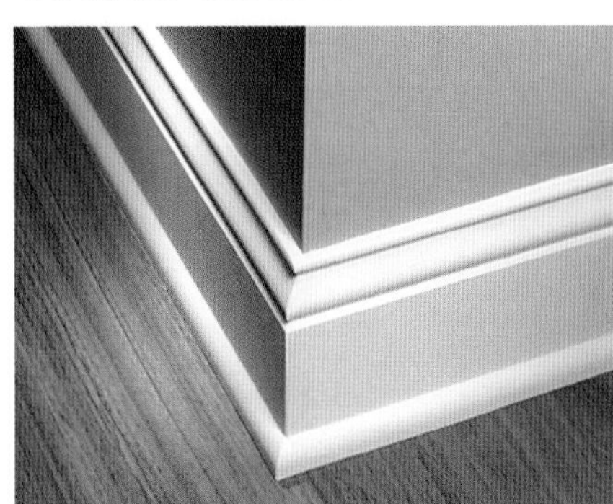

Getting outside corners to fit is trickier than it looks. Start by making accurate marks with the baseboard in place rather than relying on measurements. Use test pieces to gauge the corner's angle. Adjusting for the actual wall angle, cut each piece a little long. Avoid gaps on outside corners by cutting slightly steeper (about 46 degrees) angles on each piece.

1 Mark outside corners with utility knife about 1/8 in. (3 mm) overlong. Repeat marking process on opposite baseboard.

2 Hold boards in place to check fit. If miter is open to front, increase the back-cut angle gradually until a tight joint is achieved.

Better-Looking Trim

Filling nail holes. For painted trim, fill nail holes with latex putty before the final coat of paint. After it dries, remove excess putty with stiff, damp sponge. For stained or clear-finish trim, fill holes with colored putty to match wood color. To get a good color match, mix two putty colors. Oil-based putties should be applied only after the first coat of clear finish has been applied.

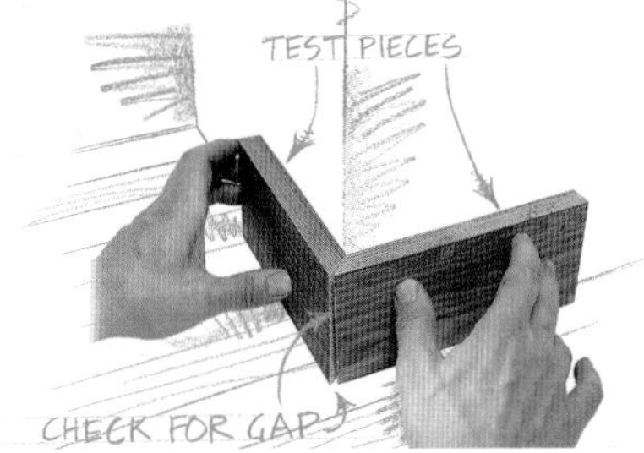

Check outside corners using test pieces. True 90° corners are rare. Adjust your miter saw to compensate.

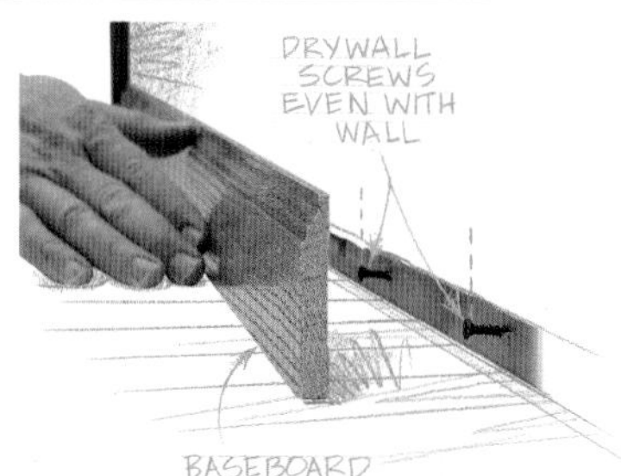

If baseboard "kicks in" because of a gap between drywall and floor, put drywall screws below drywall edge, even with its surface.

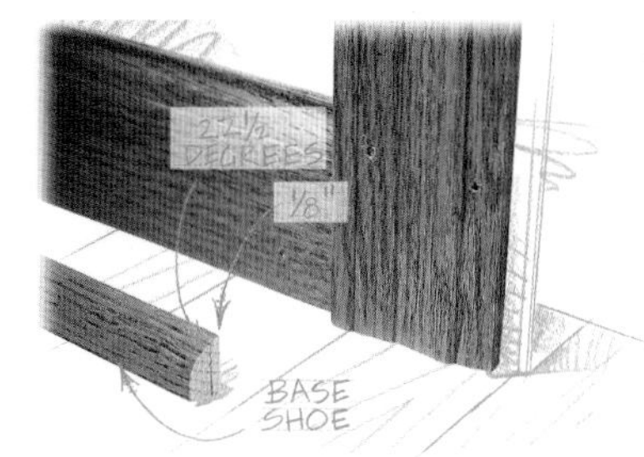

Cut base shoe at 22.5° where it meets door casing. Cope all base shoe inside corner joints and nail it to baseboard, not to the floor.

Crown Moldings

Coping Saws 26
Miter Saws 55
Moldings 430

Crown molding looks so good because it provides the perfect counterpoint to an elegant baseboard and it visually frames the ceiling, creating the illusion that the ceiling is raised. Installing it is not easy, but the result, in the right room, is well worth the effort. It looks best when mounted next to a smooth-surface ceiling. If your ceiling has a heavy texture, especially a spray-on popcorn texture, consider scraping off the texture and skim-coating the ceiling to smooth the surface before you begin.

Most principles and tips that apply to installing baseboard molding also apply to crown molding, but you should be aware of a few twists:

- Always cut crown molding upside down in the miter saw.
- Cut and install outside corners first.
- Enlist another pair of hands—this is not a one-person job.
- Caulk gaps between the molding and the wall and ceiling (whether staining or painting) and paint over the caulk. Don't try to close the gaps with nails.

Marking Stud and Crown Molding Locations

Find the wall studs and ceiling joists using a stud finder and mark the positions with painter's tape or a light pencil mark. Where ceiling joists run parallel to walls, secure a nailer, or cant strip—an angled block of wood, slightly smaller than the hollow behind the installed molding—to the wall-ceiling corner.

Most crown moldings bear on two points out from the wall-ceiling inside corner. Mark these bearing points so you can keep the molding straight when you nail it. To accurately mark the points, make an installation template as shown in the photos below.

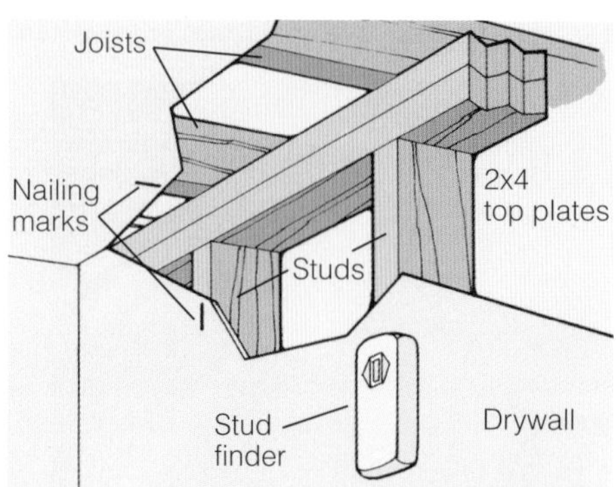

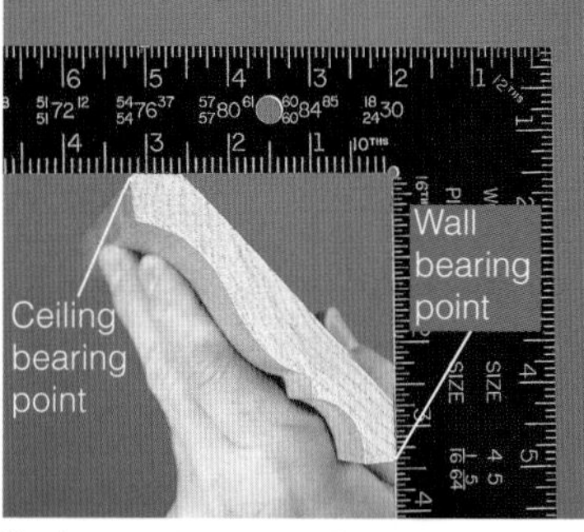

1 Place molding on a framing square as though it were mounted on the wall and measure its bearing points.

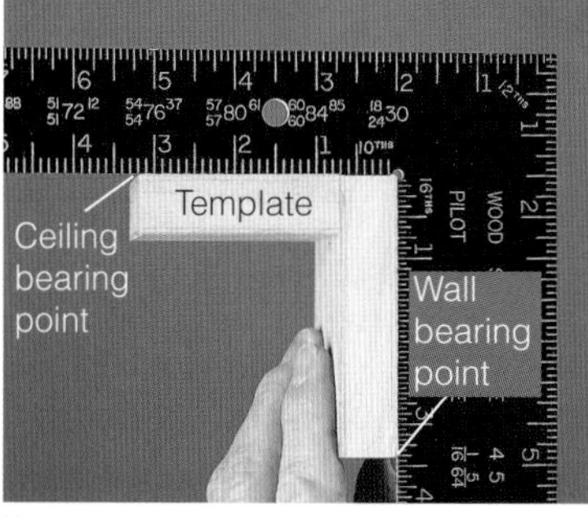

2 Nail together two blocks to make a template that duplicates crown molding bearing points.

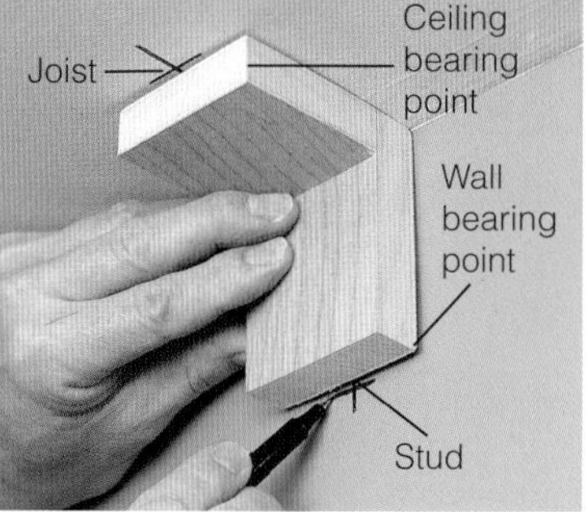

3 Mark correct crown position on walls and ceiling at each nailing point using the template as a guide.

Setting up your Saw

Crown molding must be cut upside down, and most standard miter saw fences aren't high enough for the task. Solve the problem by making a temporary fence secured with C-clamps. Envision the saw fence as the wall and the saw table as the ceiling.

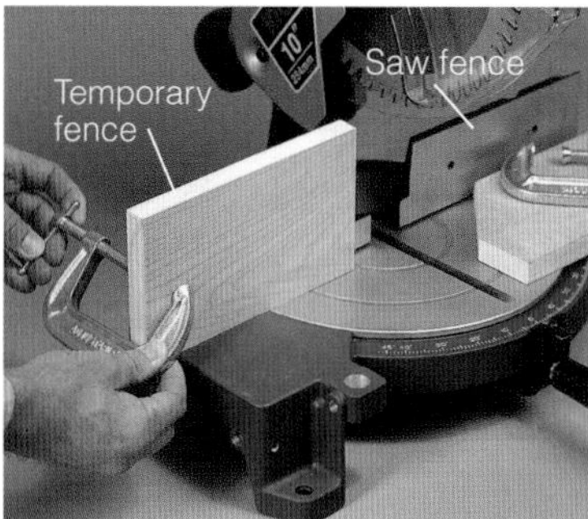

1 Clamp a higher fence to the saw fence so large moldings can be held in position correctly.

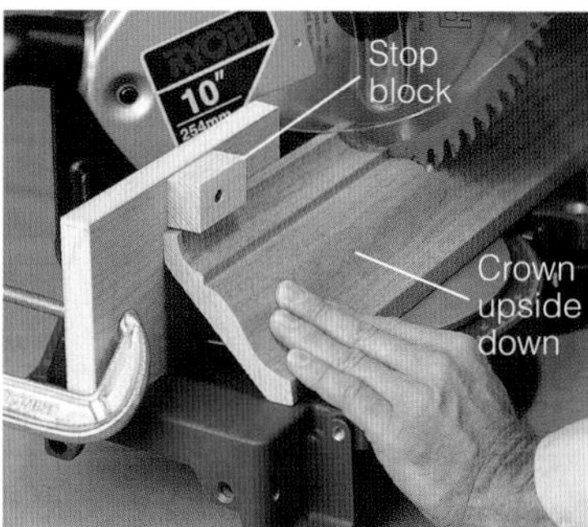

2 Screw a stop block to the fence, at the wall-bearing point distance to hold molding upside down at correct angle.

Outside Corners

The wall corners in your home are rarely, if ever, square. On outside corners, the task falls to your miter saw to compensate for the variance. To get a feel for the outside corner, check it with two short test pieces or a framing square before cutting. The key to a tight outside corner joint is to keep the joint's front edge, or exposed face, tight. To do this, back-cut each miter an extra degree so you have a slight gap along the back edge of the joint.

One way to avoid the difficulties of corner joints is to use premade outside-corner blocks (not shown) that require only a simple butt joint.

1 Before permanently installing outside corner pieces, drill a pilot hole for a 1-1/2-in. nail in the molding's upper edge.

2 Hold mitered corner against test piece to check fit. Then drill pilot holes for 2-in. finish nails on lower edge of molding.

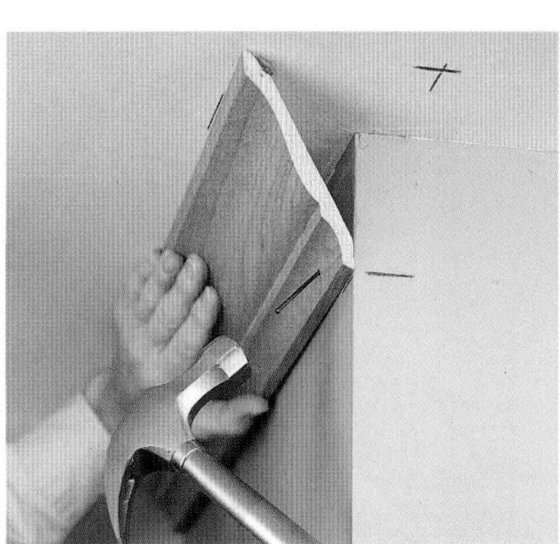

3 Nail up the first piece with a 2-in. finish nail. Coat joint with glue. Then fit, cut and nail second section of molding.

4 Drive a 1-1/2-in. finish nail into a predrilled hole to tighten the miter after second section has been installed.

Inside Corners

Inside corners are likely to be even less square than outside corners. Mitering inside corners accurately is next to impossible because a gap almost always opens when you nail the pieces. Coping a corner solves this problem. A coped piece forces the piece it abuts into alignment. Always let the piece run long until you've cut and fit the coped inside corner, then mark and cut the other end.

Inside-corner blocks (not shown), where the crown moldings can meet at a square angle, are available for some molding profiles. Check your local full-service lumberyard for availability.

1 Cut coped piece several inches overlong and at the same angle for a mitered inside corner.

2 Back-cut the profiled edge 30° with a coping saw. A jigsaw with a thin blade can also be used.

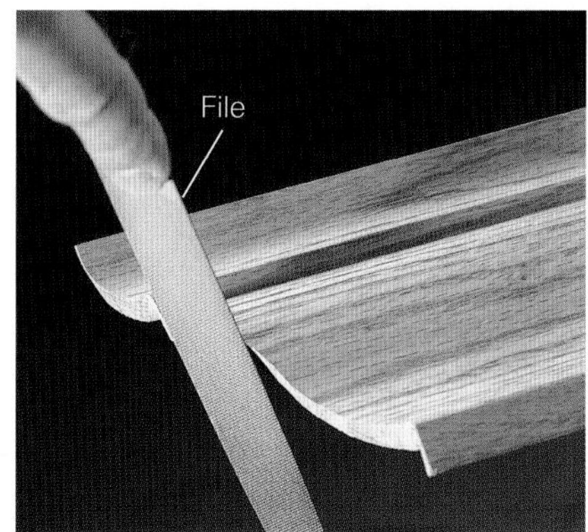

3 File edge clean and test-fit the coped joint. Make final cut to length.

4 Install coped piece, forcing other section into proper position.

Stairs

Stairways can be simple or complex, enclosed or open, a beautiful focal point to your home or just a way of getting from point A to point B.

Whatever type you have, it needs to be soundly constructed and maintained so it remains that way. A safe stairway has four primary elements.

Sound stringers to support the steps. A sound stringer won't have large chunks broken loose or large knots where the board is notched.

Level treads at least 10-1/4 in. (about 25 cm) deep. Walking down steps that are out of level or have shallow treads makes you feel like you're pitching forward.

Evenly matched risers 7-1/4 in. (about 18 cm) or less in height. Even a slight variation can create a tripping hazard.

A firmly mounted handrail and balustrade. The newel post should be rigid and firm and the brackets of a wall-mounted handrail should be screwed directly into studs.

Inside an Enclosed Stairway

Drywall
Nosing
Stair skirt
Tread
Riser
Stringer
2x4

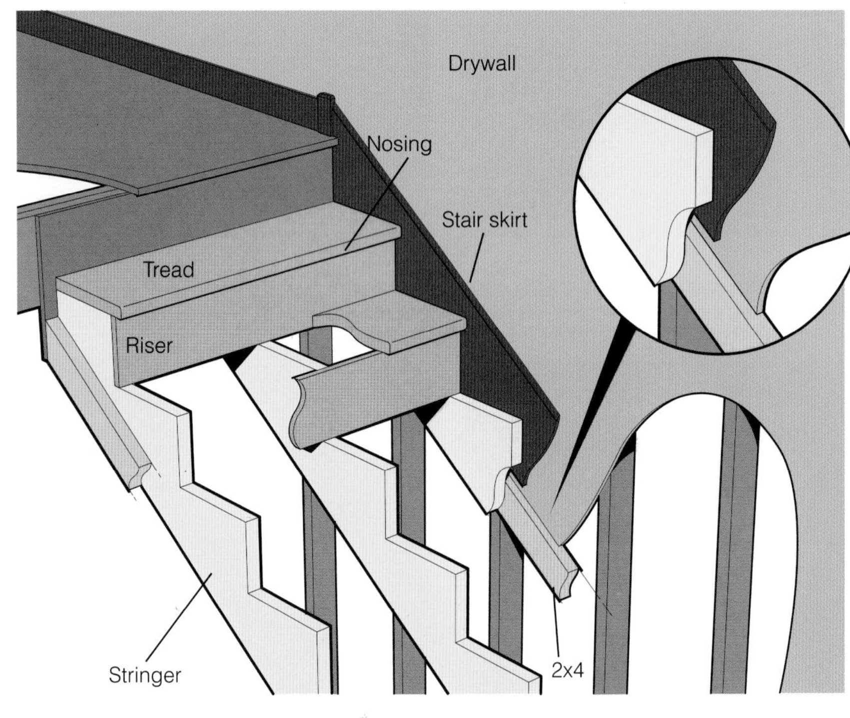

Staircase Language

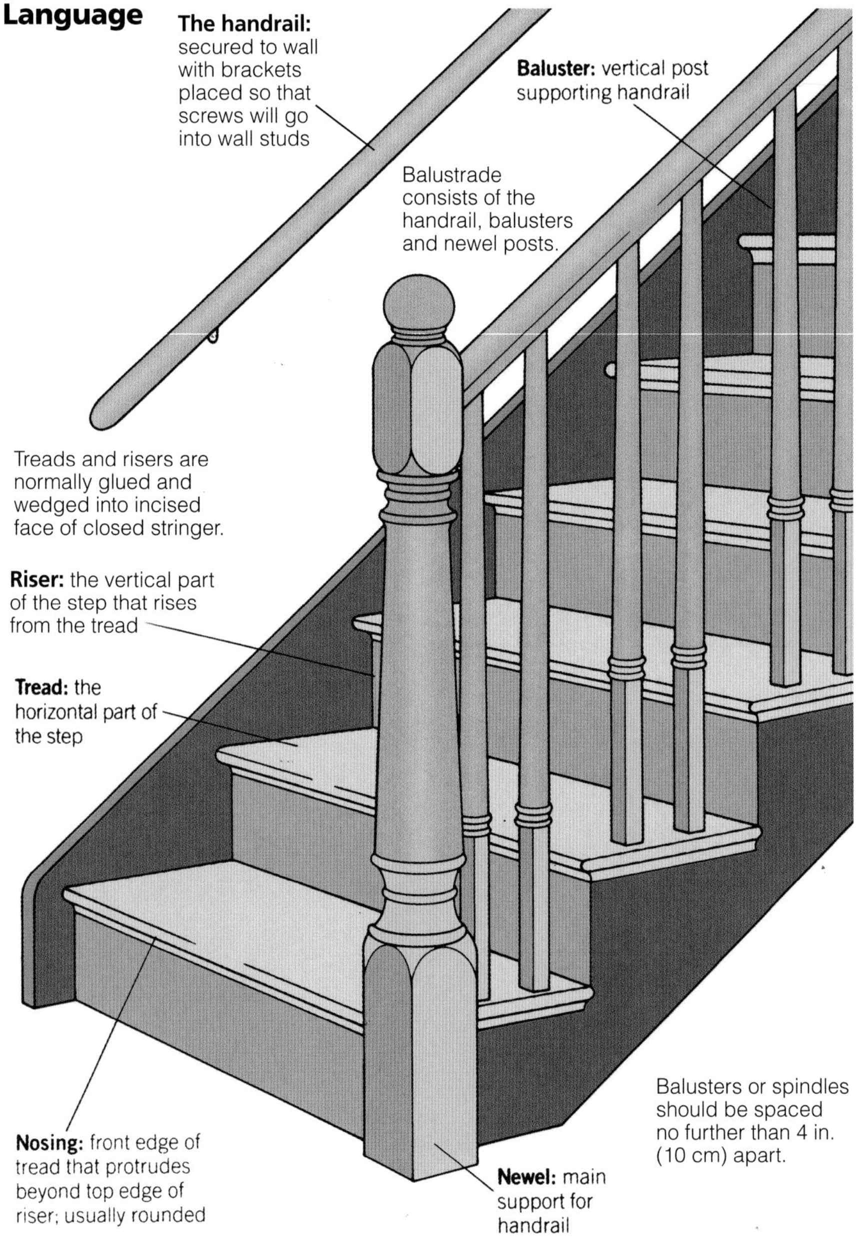

The handrail: secured to wall with brackets placed so that screws will go into wall studs
Baluster: vertical post supporting handrail
Balustrade consists of the handrail, balusters and newel posts.
Treads and risers are normally glued and wedged into incised face of closed stringer.
Riser: the vertical part of the step that rises from the tread
Tread: the horizontal part of the step
Nosing: front edge of tread that protrudes beyond top edge of riser; usually rounded
Newel: main support for handrail
Balusters or spindles should be spaced no further than 4 in. (10 cm) apart.

Stairs / Repair

Most stair squeaks are caused by loosened parts rubbing together. Isolate the source of the noise by walking on the offending step. Even better, if you have access underneath, have someone else walk on the steps so you can mark the squeaky spots from below. First, check and tighten the existing structural elements, including the nails and glue that hold the staircase together and the wedges, if any, that fill the joint between the tread and the riser. A dry lubricant, such as powdered graphite, can silence or considerably muffle some squeaks; however, the effect will likely be temporary.

You can fill gaps with shims or use wood blocks or metal brackets to close gaps. If you use blocks or brackets from below, pay close attention to screw length. Most treads are 1 to 1-1/8 in. thick. Riser material is thinner, usually 3/4 in.

If you can't reach your carpeted stairs from below, you'll have to screw treads and risers to stringers from above with small-headed trim screws. The centers of the two outside stringers should be about 1-1/2 in. (4 cm) from the ends of the tread. The third, if there is one, should be located in the center.

A Last Resort

If all other stair repair techniques fail, try lubricating the joint from above or below with powdered graphite or talcum powder.

Repairs from Above

Trim screws. Drive trim screws through treads and risers into stringers. These can be driven through carpet. In exposed wood treads, they leave a small enough hole to putty.

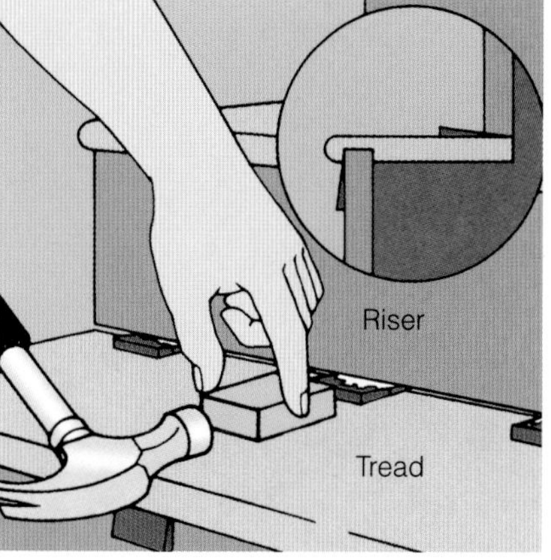

Wedges. Correct squeaks that come from the rear of the tread by inserting thin glue-coated wood wedges between tread and riser.

Trim wedges. With a sharp utility knife, trim wedges so they are flush with the riser. Install quarter-round or cove molding to conceal resulting gaps.

Repairs from Below

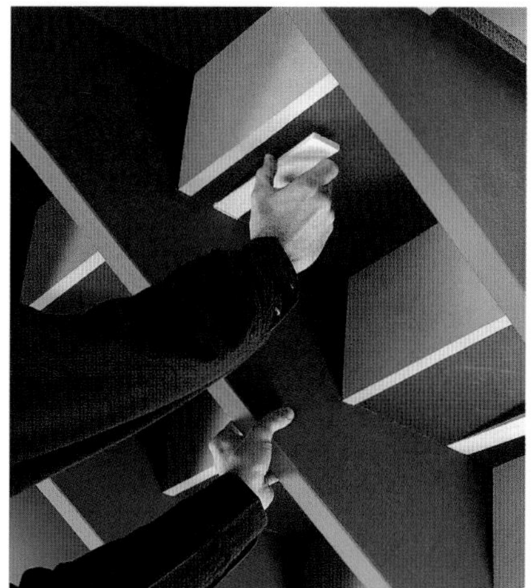

Shims. Coat shims with construction adhesive and force them into gaps between treads, risers and stringers.

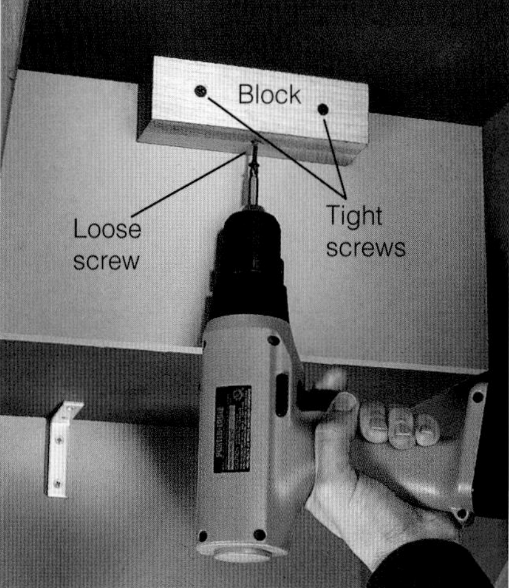

Blocks. Use 2x2 blocks coated with construction adhesive to create a more solid connection between treads and risers.

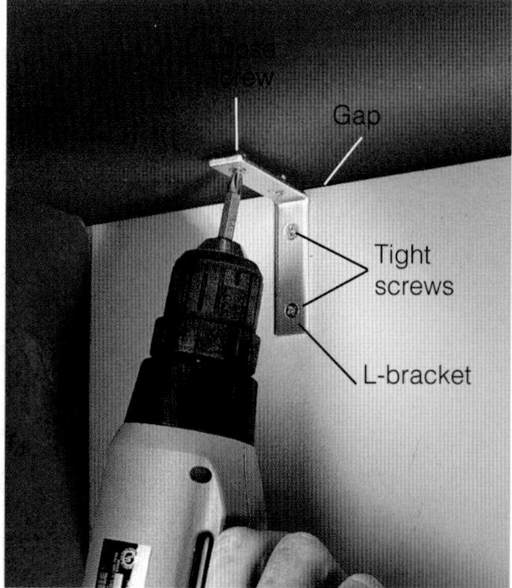

Brackets. Install one leg of an L-bracket to the riser back, leaving a small gap. Draw the tread tightly back down with screws. For extra insurance, coat gap with glue, then tighten.

Stairs / Tightening a Newel Post

A firmly mounted newel post anchors the entire balustrade structure. As the main post, it tends to get abused. Unfortunately, tightening a newel post can be a vexing problem, since anchoring methods vary widely and you may or may not have easy access to key fasteners. The older the house, the more elaborate or obscure the method of steadying the newel post.

One method, not shown here, uses a threaded rod through the length of the post to anchor it. To tighten the post, you tighten the rod from below. Also, look for a possible anchor point inside the hollow area behind the first step.

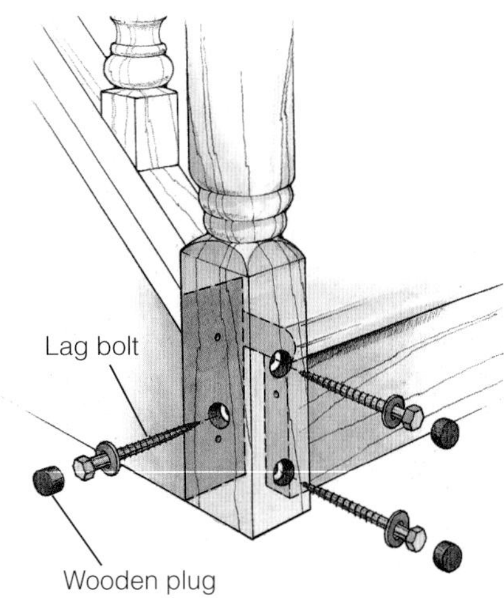

Lag bolts. Look for wooden plugs in the exposed base of the newel post. If possible, remove plugs and tighten bolts. If not, add bolts and plugs to tighten the post.

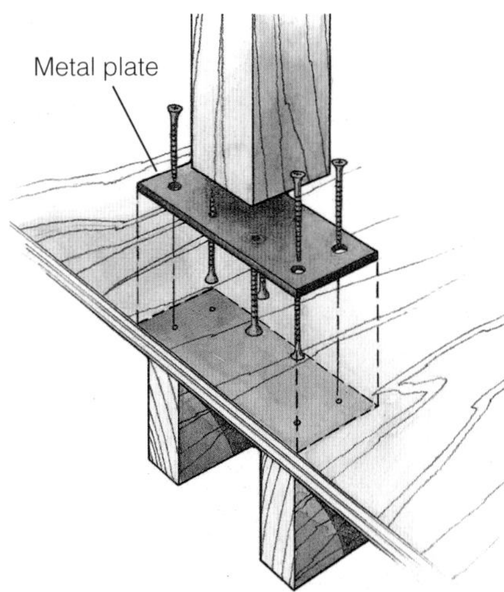

Plates. If a metal plate anchors the post, installing larger screws into the floor may cure the problem. If screws going into the post are loose or stripped, removing the post and the flooring material around it may be required.

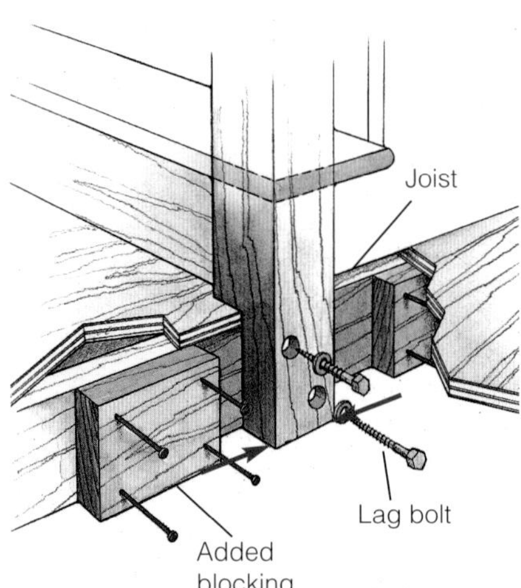

Blocking. When the post extends through the floor, it's usually bolted to the floor joists or other blocking. If necessary, cut out the ceiling of the level below and add blocking, shims and bolts to steady the post from below.

Stairs / Remounting a Handrail

The top of a handrail must be between 34 and 38 in. (about 86 and 96 cm) above the front edge of a stair tread. To accommodate the thickness of the handrail and the bracket, mount the brackets between 31 and 35 in. (about 80 and 90 cm) from that point.

Install one bracket for every three or four treads, making sure to screw each bracket into a wall stud. Attach the top and bottom brackets about 12 to 16 in. (30 to 40 cm) from the handrail ends. When driving the bracket's upper screws, angle them inward to get a good bite in the stud.

Note: Use white chalk when you snap your reference line for mounting brackets. It brushes away easily and is less likely to leave marks.

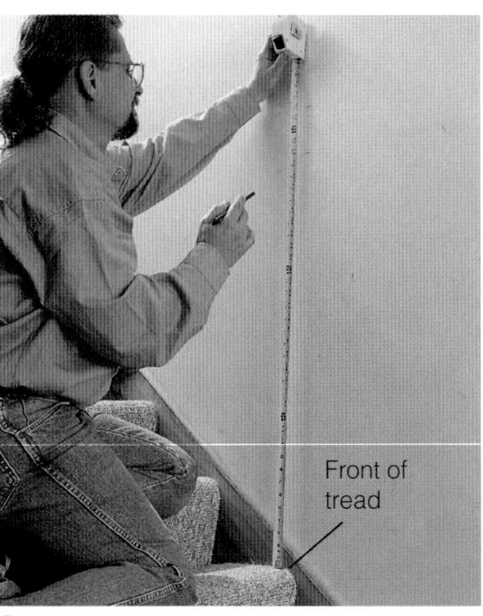

1 Measure up from front of bottom step and mark lowermost point of bracket-mounting plate. Repeat procedure at second from top step. Snap chalk line between two points.

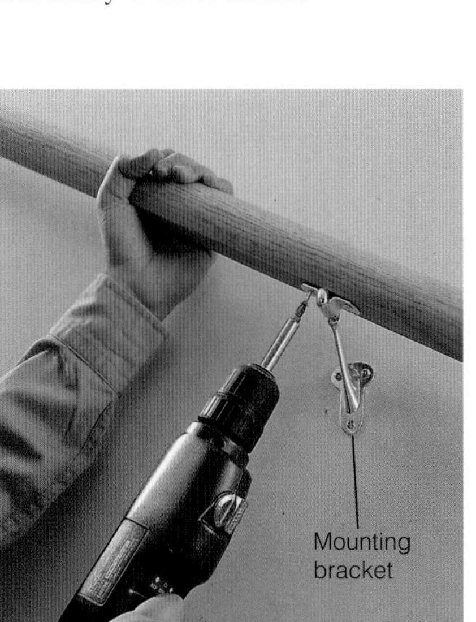

2 Locate stud centers and mark bracket positions along the chalk line. Anchor brackets, in plumb position, to wall studs and attach handrail.

3 Most codes require new handrails to have end returns. With main handrail temporarily installed, measure distance needed for returns. Cut and install returns; then remount.

Wood Floors

Natural wood flooring has a solidness and richness that never goes out of style. It works so well because your floor becomes a canvas for nature's art. It's durable enough to last for decades and easy to keep clean. You'll be amazed at the wide range of wood species, finishes and styles available.

Begin your research by visiting a wood flooring specialty store. As you shop, keep these three characteristics in mind: appearance, durability and stability. The grade of a particular species can greatly affect its appearance: The lower the grade, the greater the color variation and knots. Durability is primarily affected by the hardness, or density, of a particular species and the finish used. Open-grained woods, like hickory or oak, tend to show scratches and dents less than closed-grain woods like maple. Some wood species are more stable than others; however, all wood floors expand and contract with humidity changes. The illustration below shows the approximate changes in wood moisture content in your area.

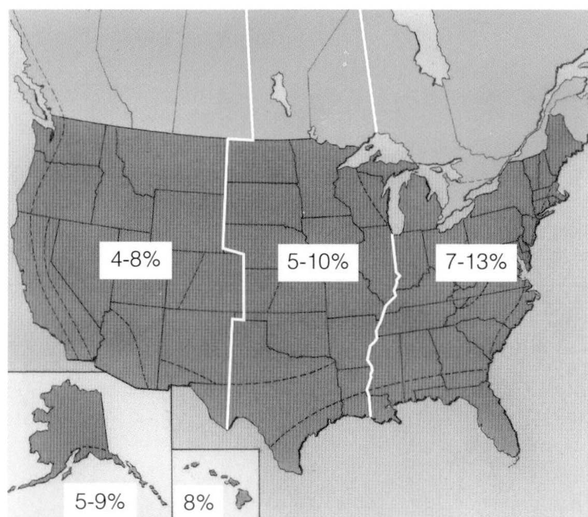

Moisture content. The first number represents approximate wood moisture content during the driest period, usually January. The second number represents the dampest period, usually July. The larger the difference, the higher the potential for seasonal movement.

Solid Wood Flooring

Solid wood flooring has a tongue and groove milled into the edges that interlocks the strips to form a strong, solid floor. Typically milled in random lengths, the finished floor has random butt joints and, depending on the grade, a wide variety of grain patterns and color. The thickness of the material allows repeated sanding and refinishing.

Unfinished strips. These are sanded, finished on site and are available in many species of varying grades (clear, select, #2, #3) and widths. Unfinished strips are labor-intensive initially but can be custom stained and are the easiest to refinish.

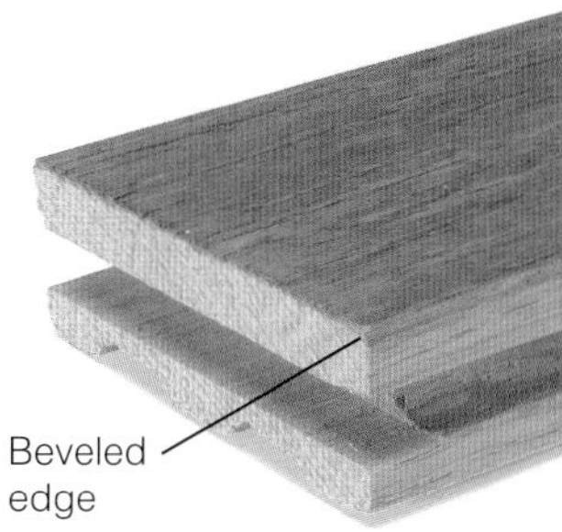

Prefinished strips. These have a tough, factory-applied finish in a limited choice of stains, species and grades. A slight beveled edge creates crisp-looking joints but complicates sanding and refinishing when it becomes necessary.

Planks. Many hardwood species are available in widths up to 6 in. (15 cm); softwoods, like pine, come even wider. They are available with or without tongue and groove. The potential for warping creates bigger installation problems than with thinner strips.

Laminated Wood Flooring

Laminated wood flooring, also called engineered wood consists of layers, as in plywood, with a solid wood layer exposed on top. Laminated boards come in many species, colors, widths and thicknesses. The flooring can be sanded and refinished only a limited number of times, or not at all in some cases, but is less prone to movement than solid wood.

Floating floors. Individual boards are snapped or glued together to create a monolithic floor. Usually installed over a thin foam pad, they can be installed over a concrete or wood subfloor.

Glue-down floors. Most laminated floors can be glued to a wood subfloor or dry concrete. They are more prone to gaps at joints than floating floors and not suitable for damp areas, like kitchens or bathrooms.

Nail-down floors. Thicker types of laminate wood floor can usually be stapled or nailed to wood subfloors.

Wood Floors / Installing

Pneumatic Nailers **74**
Baseboard Moldings **230**
Flooring Over Concrete **243**

It's hard to beat the natural beauty, warmth and durability of a hardwood floor. A well-laid floor can last for a century or more and can be rejuvenated by resanding and finishing to look brand new. If you lay, sand and finish the floor yourself, you'll find it costs about the same as high-quality installed carpet.

A solid hardwood floor must be fastened to a solid base. If your floor has a layer of particleboard, remove it (it doesn't hold nails well). Next, determine whether you'll need an additional layer of plywood over the subfloor. For hardwood flooring that will run perpendicular to the joists, an added layer of 1/4-in. plywood will suffice. For hardwood flooring running parallel to joists or over a subfloor of oriented strand board (OSB), add a layer of plywood at least 1/2 in. thick. To prevent squeaks, use screws to anchor plywood layer(s) to floor joists. Next, sweep or vacuum the floor clean and tack down rosin paper with a stapler. Overlap the paper joints 6 in. (15 cm) and tape the seams.

Before installation, let the hardwood flooring acclimate in your home for several days. Don't install it during high humidity periods unless your home's humidity is well controlled.

To get a straight start, begin the floor on its longest side and work toward the areas with interruptions. If a small jog breaks the long edge, mark a straight line beyond the jog and establish your starting course from there.

Do a trial layout to determine the best arrangement of the floor boards. Scatter end-to-end joints evenly over the floor, avoiding clusters of short boards. Install boards with odd grain patterns or color in closets or other out-of-the-way areas.

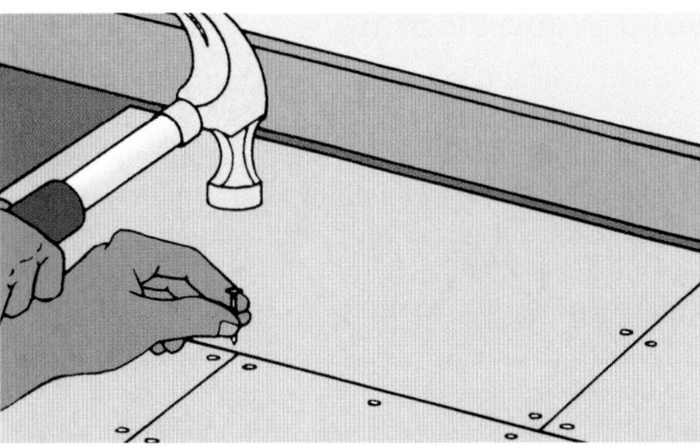

1 Secure existing subfloor or underlayment or install additional plywood, if necessary. Stagger joints and use ring-shank nails or decking screws.

2 Remove baseboard molding carefully with flat pry bar. Avoid wall damage by prying against scrap wood. Preserve molding by pulling nails through backside with wire cutters.

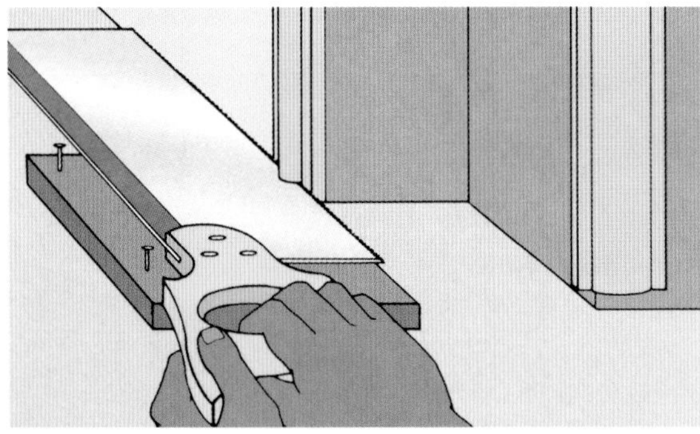

3 Cut door casing to accommodate the new floor height after rosin paper is installed. Rest the backsaw or pull saw blade on scrap flooring and cut through molding.

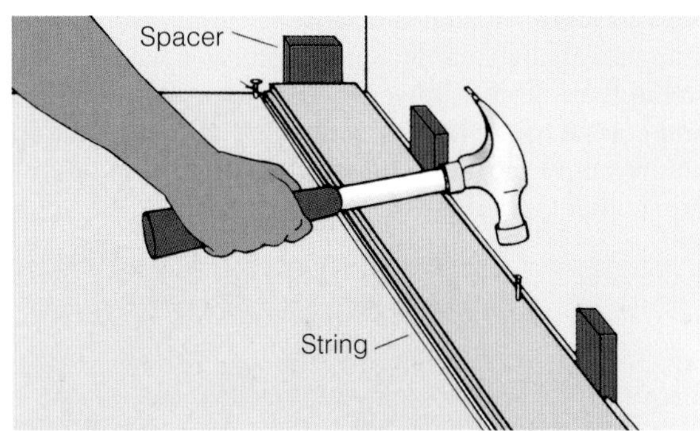

4 Snap chalk line or use string line to align first course of boards, leaving small space between wall and floor for expansion. Use straight, long boards with groove toward wall. Face nail close to wall.

Flooring Nailers

Flooring nailers come in two types—pneumatic and manual. Pneumatic nailers use an air compressor, drive long staples and are less labor intensive than manual nailers. Manual nailers, while physically demanding and somewhat slower, drive a heavy-duty serrated nail with tremendous gripping power.

Besides being much faster, both types offer huge advantages over hand nailing. Flooring nailers automatically tighten the boards as you nail and easily remove minor warps. Flooring nailers set the fasteners and drive them at the correct angle; reduce the chance of marring board edges and splintering; and let you straighten your legs as you nail, reducing fatigue.

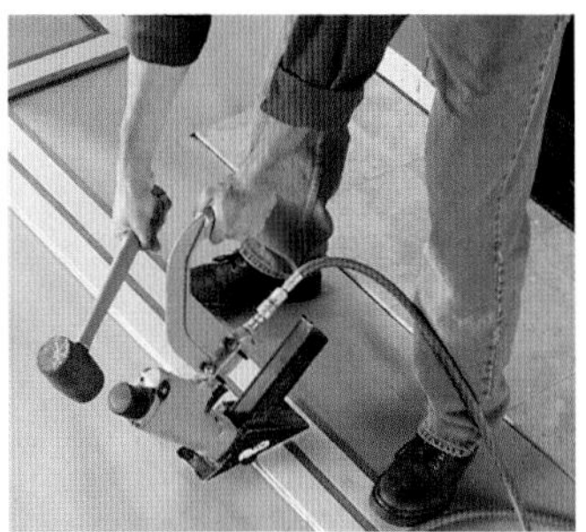

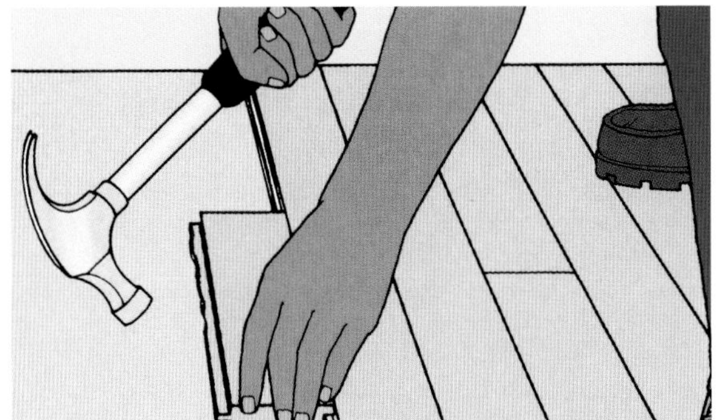

5 Drive each board tight against previous course using a piece of scrap flooring to protect tongue. Stagger joints at least 18 in. (45 cm). Leave spacer blocks in place while tightening.

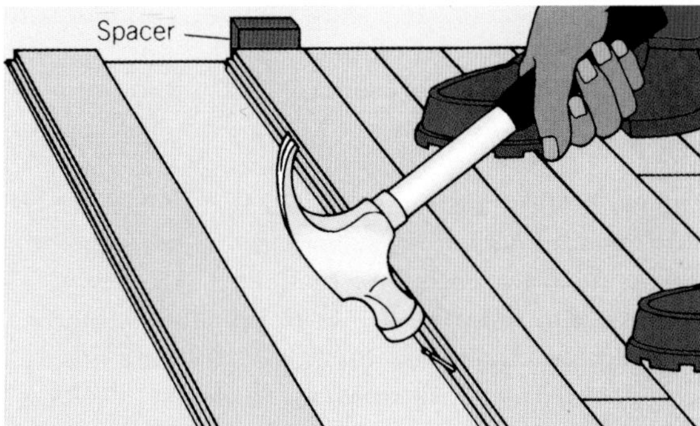

6 Secure boards with flooring nailer or blind-nail boards through tongue at a 45° angle every 10 to 12 in. (25 to 30 cm) or every 6 to 8 in. (15 to 20 cm) for plank flooring. Set nails using a nail-set; predrill holes if splitting becomes a problem.

7 Force warped boards into position by driving a wedge between it and a scrap nailed to floor. Note: It's easier to close a gap in the center of a long board than at its end.

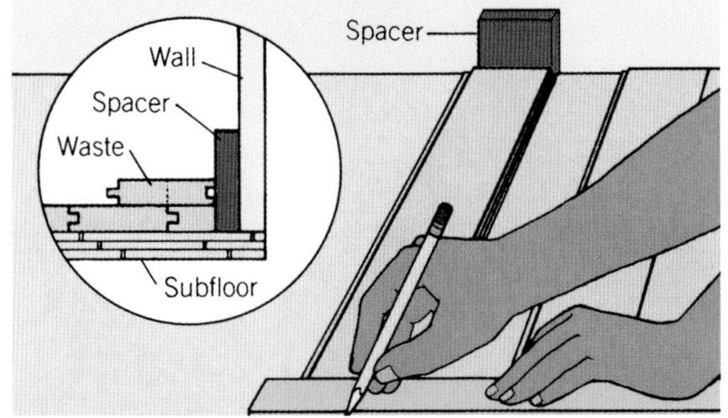

8 Mark length needed for last board in a course by flipping board around (tongue to inside) and butting it against spacer. Tighten joint with flat pry bar between the wall and board.

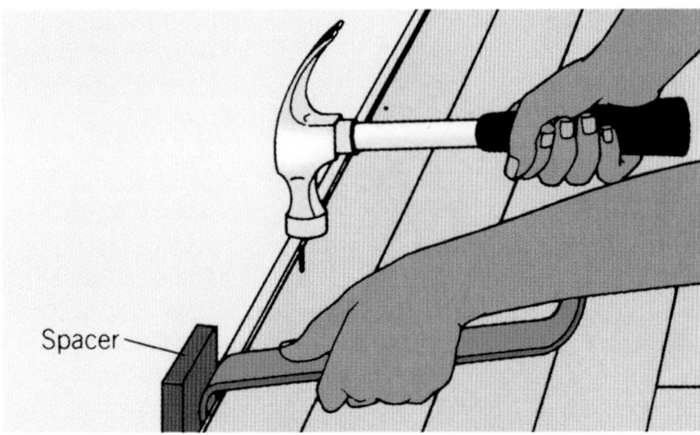

9 Predrill and face-nail final course. Rip course to width so expansion gap remains between wall and floor. Tighten course with flat pry bar and scrap block. Nail as you tighten.

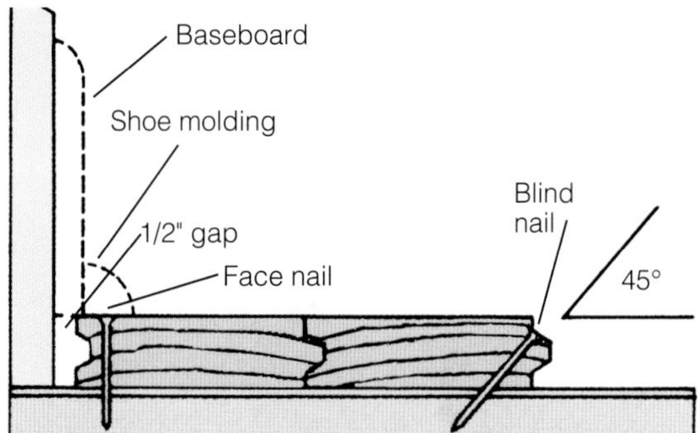

Molding and nailing details. The baseboard covers expansion gap. The base shoe covers first course of face nails and flexes to cover gaps between baseboard and floor. Subsequent courses are blind-nailed.

Transitions

You'll likely have a height difference between your hardwood floor and neighboring floor materials. Use reducer strips to ease this transition. Handle ledges around stairwells and sunken rooms with rounded-over nosing boards. Look for flush-mount or drop-in wood floor registers that match the floor species you're installing.

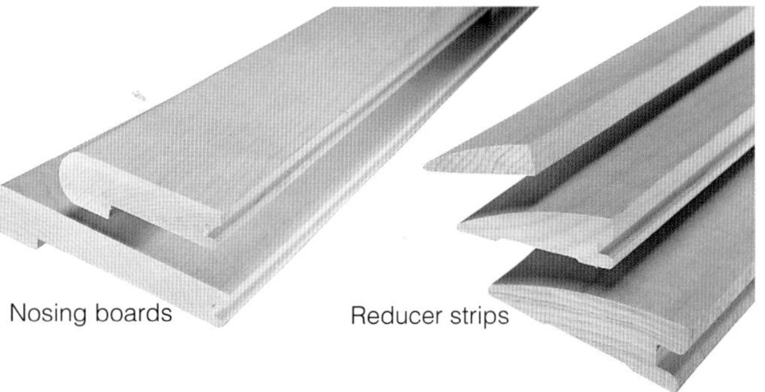

Order Extra

Order 5 to 10 percent extra flooring for waste and mistakes. Also consider ordering a bundle of the next widest size to fill areas where the flooring is just a little too narrow to do the job. This way, you can avoid cutting sliver-thin strips of flooring to fill in areas near walls or against borders.

Wood Floors / Sanding

Sanders 68
Applying Polyurethane 455

To sand or not to sand? The first question to ask is whether the floor is worth sanding and, if it is, does it need to be sanded down to bare wood or will a quick buffing and recoat do the job? Most solid wood floors can be sanded multiple times, but if yours is less than 5/8 in. (16 mm) thick, is laminated wood floor or has deep black stains or other irregularities, consult a pro to see whether it can be safely sanded.

Use the right equipment. You'll need to rent a belt-type floor sander, an edge sander and a floor buffer. You'll need to buy several sanding belts and discs in 24, 36, 80 and 100 grit and sanding screens in 100 and 150 grit. You'll also need to use a shop vacuum, carbide paint scraper, dust masks and hearing protection.

Prepare the space. Remove all furniture from the room. Cover all doorways with 2- or 3-mil plastic sheeting and painter's tape. Tape plastic around all the heating vents and transitions to other floor materials. Set any exposed nails (they can rip very expensive belts) and remove any grills from the floor.

An easier alternative. Square orbital floor sanders, now commonly available, reduce gouging and the amount of edgework needed. These sanders work slower but are worth considering for some jobs.

Smoother Sanding

- Check with local flooring suppliers for rental equipment. Both the equipment and the advice are often better than what's available at a general rental store.
- Before you use the belt sander on your floor, practice on a full sheet of inexpensive plywood to get a feel for the sander and what it takes to control it.
- Overlap your passes—side-to-side and end-to-end—to avoid digging in too much at any point.

The Right Order

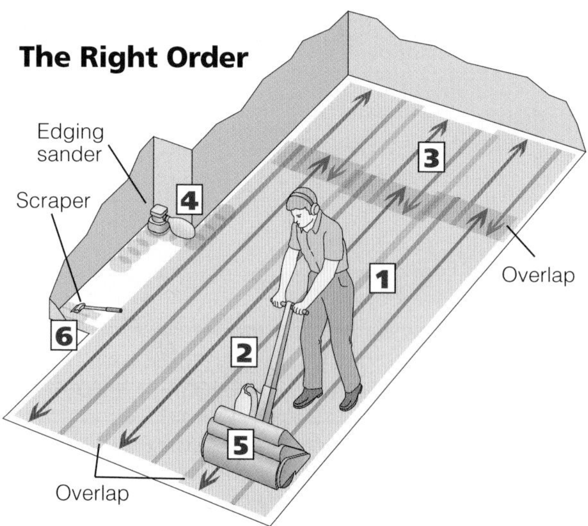

1. Beginning 4 or 5 ft. (120 to 150 cm) from one wall, sand all the way to the opposite wall, and then sand the same path back.
2. Shift and make your next pass, overlapping the previous one by about 2 in. (5 cm).
3. When you've completed that side of the room, go back and sand the swath you couldn't get on your first pass. Overlap your first passes by 1 to 2 ft. (30 to 60 cm).
4. Sand edges with an edging sander before switching to the next grit.
5. Progress from a 24- or 36-grit sanding belt to 80 grit, then 100 grit. Finish using a floor buffer with a 100-grit sanding screen.
6. Use scraper to remove finish from areas the sander can't reach.

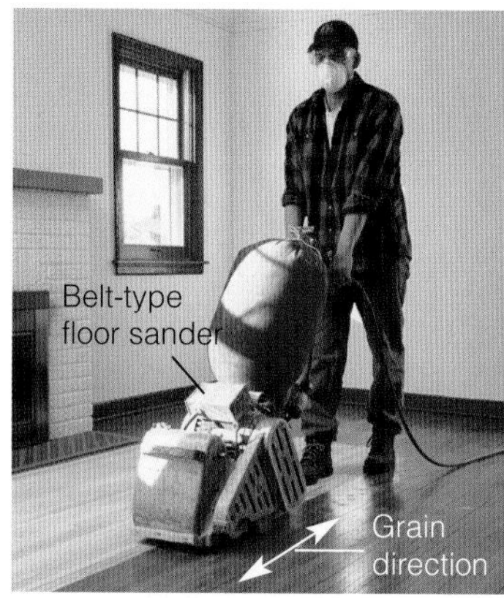

1 Start the machine, move forward with the grain and retrace the same path back. As you approach a wall, lift sander to avoid grooving floor near wall. Keep machine moving. Starting on same side of floor as your first pass, sand another row, overlapping sanded area by one plank.

2 Sand the starting area after finishing the main area. Start about 1 ft. (30 cm) into previously sanded area and work toward the wall. Again, as you approach the wall, lift sander to avoid grooving floor near wall. Overlap each pass by one plank of flooring.

3 Using same grit disc as on the belt, edge-sand areas remaining next to baseboard and other tight areas. Start machine next to baseboard and work out to the sanded area. Gently feather the surface as you meet main sanded area. Work clockwise around the room for better control.

4 Scrape the old finish away in areas the edge sander couldn't reach (inside corners and around radiators). Make these areas even with surrounding floor surface. Use a quality carbide scraper. For later sanding steps, detail sanders with pointed pads work well in these spots.

Wood Floors / Finishing

After the messy business of sanding is done, finishing your floor will feel like a pleasant vacation as the grain starts to "pop" and the floor takes on a shine. Follow these tips to work your way toward a flawless finish:

- Tape edges of vacuum wand to avoid marking raw wood.
- Thoroughly clean floor before each coat. After vacuuming, wipe entire floor with tack cloth if applying oil-based finish; use an alcohol-dampened rag if applying water-based finish.
- Plan your exit—don't finish yourself into a corner.
- After thoroughly stirring finish, pour it into a plastic-lined dishpan wide enough for the wide applicator.
- While finishing, always keep a wet edge and keep the applicator moving.
- Tightly seal applicator in plastic between coats.
- Wait three days to bring furniture back, two weeks for rugs.

1 Vacuum the entire room once the dust settles, including ledges, windows, walls, nooks and crannies.

2 Brush in edge areas. Working in complete rows, spread finish onto main floor area with wide applicator.

3 Buff first coat with 150-grit sanding screen. Buffer should leave white powdery residue as you work.

4 Apply second and third coat the same as the first. If necessary, buff between second and third coats with 220-grit screen.

Which Finish?

Nothing surpasses polyurethane as a do-it-yourself wood floor finish. It provides a tough, long-lasting shell that's resistant to water, alcohol and most cleaners. You'll have to choose between oil-based or water-based and decide on a sheen (gloss satin is the most popular choice for floors). As a rule, the more you spend for the finish, the better its quality.

Oil-based polyurethane adds a warm amber color to wood. Compared with water-based finish, oil-based is a bit less expensive, easier to apply and arguably tougher. However, it's slower drying, gives off irritating fumes and is more difficult to clean off brushes.

Water-based polyurethane adds little color to wood. It dries fast, emits little odor and cleans up with water, but it doesn't self-level as well as oil, making it tougher to apply evenly.

Reviving a Wood Floor

Recoating a floor takes much less time, skill and money than full-scale sanding and refinishing. With a recoat, you'll use a floor buffer and a 150-grit sanding screen to remove blemishes and roughen the old finish, so it will accept a new coat of polyurethane.

1 Test for adhesion. Clean two out-of-the-way areas, mask them with tape, roughen the surface, apply finish and let dry. Orange-peel texture or easy flaking when scraped by a coin indicates poor adhesion.

2 Clean the floor with wood floor cleaner or trisodium phosphate (TSP). Use scouring pad and mineral spirits for tough spots. Buff with 150-grit sanding screen with one or two passes. Roughen the remaining corners and edges.

3 Eliminate all dust from floor and apply finish. To apply, dip applicator in paint tray, unload applicator in dry spot by pressing pad against floor and drag applicator across floor length.

Laminate Floating Floors

Pull Saws 26
Baseboard Moldings 230
Basement Moisture 272

In some ways, installing a "floating" laminate floor is the ideal do-it-yourself project. The project moves along quickly, especially using the locking systems shown here. Frequently, little or no demolition is needed, keeping the mess to a minimum.

Start by testing the floor for flatness. Most manufacturers recommend having a surface with no more than 3/16-in. (5 mm) variation over a 6-ft. (2 m) span. Slight depressions can be built up with roofing felt. Significant humps or ridges pose a more serious challenge and may rule out the project all together.

Engineered floating wood floors have a hardwood top layer and plywood base. Laminate versions have a photographic top layer.

Install floating floors over a manufacturer-recommended underlayment. Some types combine a vapor barrier and padding over concrete or where moisture might be a problem. Others reduce sound transmission. Take extra care to follow directions when installing vapor-barrier underlayment.

Installing Locking Laminate Floors

1 Undercut door jambs, stops and casings using a fine-tooth saw. Guide the saw against a piece of flooring scrap and underlayment. For doors with a transition to different flooring, use a sharp chisel to complete the cut in areas not reached by the saw.

2 Unroll underlayment and, when doubling as a vapor barrier, lap it up baseboards or walls 2 in. (5 cm) and temporarily tape in place. Butt underlayment sheets together and tape seams with manufacturer-recommended tape. Cut starter row to length and width and lock ends together.

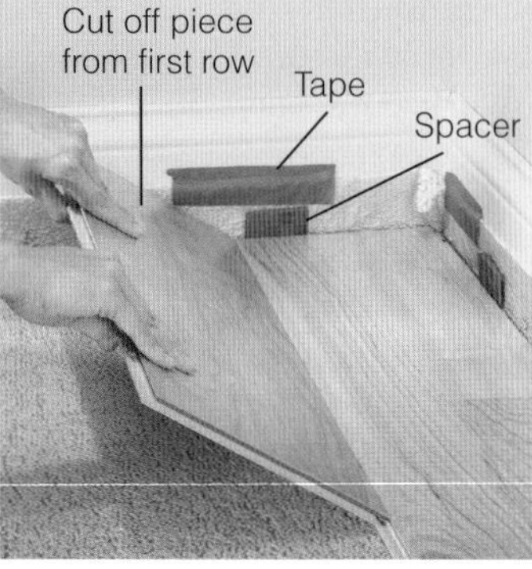

3 Start the second row with a leftover cutoff piece from the first row, making sure end joints are offset by at least 12 in. (30 cm). Add spacers to establish a gap. Install by starting at an angle, pushing in while you push down. Boards should click and draw tightly together.

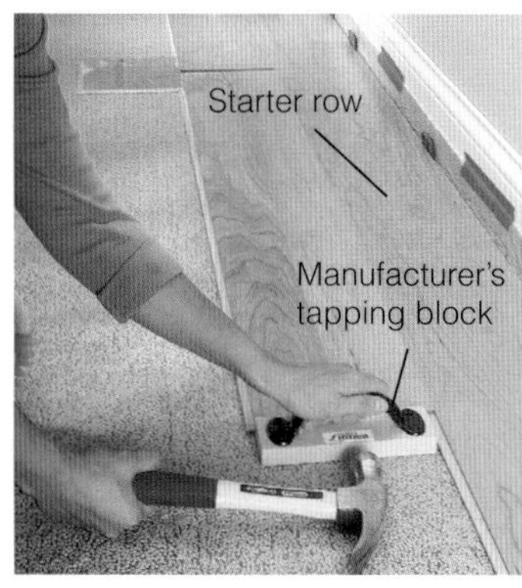

4 Leave a 1/4-in. (6-mm) space between end of the next full piece and previously installed piece. Snap the new piece in place along its length. Use a flooring scrap to temporarily align ends. Then close the gap between ends, using a manufacturer's tapping block.

Selecting Your Flooring

Floating floors, both engineered and laminate, fall into one of three categories:

Glue-together systems have been around the longest and require a clamping system to tighten the joints. This system is the most time-consuming to install.

Snap-together systems, like the one shown above, use a locking tongue-and-groove to tighten and hold the joints. This system installs quickly and is the easiest to repair.

Water-activated systems are the latest generation. On these, the semi-locking tongue and groove has a preapplied glue strip that's activated by applying water. This system needs no clamping, installs quickly and is the most resistant to water penetration.

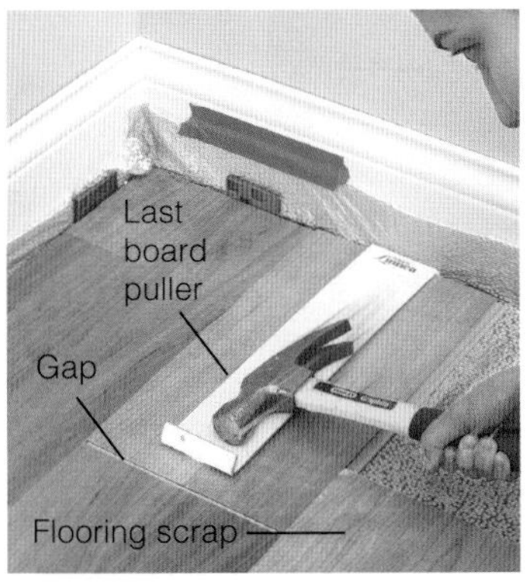

5 Close gap at the end of the row using the "last board puller" hooked over the board end, tapping the puller with a hammer. Use flooring scrap to align joint.

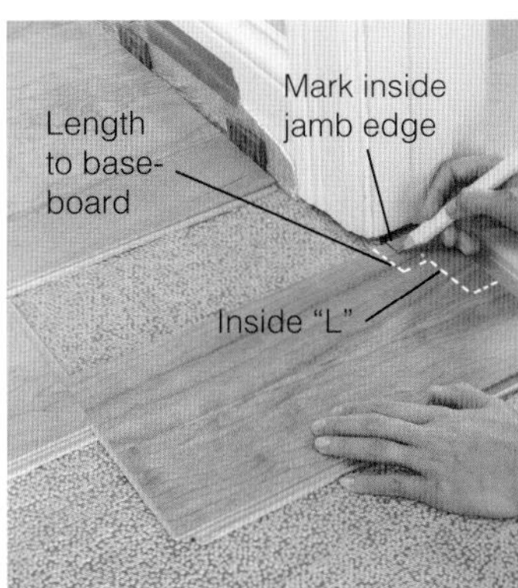

7 Cut the plank to be notched to length. Allow a 1-in. (2.5-cm) gap for a transition strip. Align the board's end with the last plank laid and mark 3/8 in. (1 cm) inside the jamb edge.

9 Install transition strips where necessary and secure them with silicone and temporary weights.

6 Door jambs require planning. On the last board of the row before the one going underneath the jamb, slice off the locking section of the tongue. This technique will help you slide parallel boards together, instead of tilting, as you go underneath the jamb.

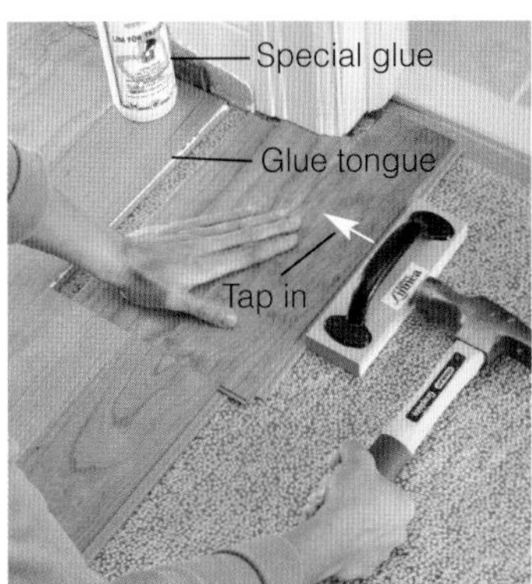

8 Apply a thin bead of manufacturer-recommended glue along the edge where the tongue portion was removed. Slide notched piece into place under jamb and tighten joint with the tapping block.

10 Complete flooring project by trimming off protruding under-layment with utility knife and installing base-shoe molding. Nail base shoe to baseboard, not to floor. For hand nailing, predrill holes and use 1-1/2-in. finish nails.

Flooring Over Concrete

Many laminate and wood floors can be installed over reasonably dry concrete. Floating floors can be installed over special foam or dimpled plastic under-layments. To install a hardwood floor over concrete, you'll need to provide a subfloor under the flooring layer. The thickness of these two layers creates some problems. Unless you do the entire level, you'll have transition issues. If stairs are involved, the rise of the bottom step will change. Finally, doors and jambs will have to be shortened.

Floating subfloors use manufactured tongue-and-groove tiles made with a layer of high-density OSB and a layer of polyethylene cleats that hold the subfloor off the concrete. Because it floats, the floor requires no nails or glue but does require a reasonably flat surface.

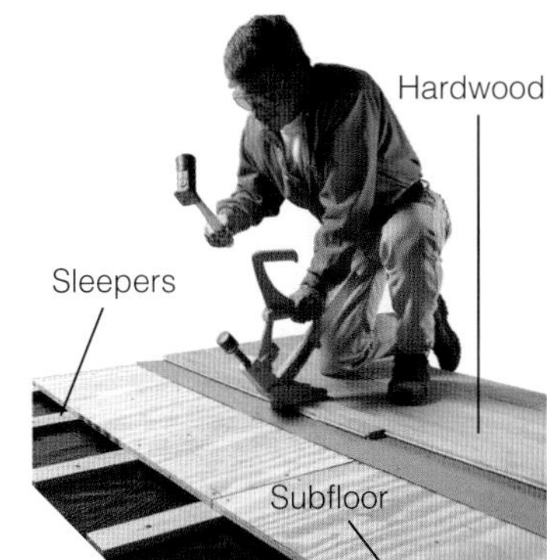

Sleeper subfloors start with a 6- to 8-mil vapor barrier on which you build a frame of treated wood "sleepers." The sleep-ers are screwed to the concrete with concrete screws. A 3/4-in. plywood subfloor is screwed to the sleepers.

Repairing Hardwood Floors

Drills 50
Tablesaws 62
Installing Hardwood Floors 238
Staining 454

Silencing a Floor

The first step in stifling a squeak is to pinpoint its origin. A hardwood floor generally consists of three layers: joists, subfloor and hardwood floor. Squeaks occur where the layers rub together or against nails. A sprinkling of powdered graphite between the boards may silence a squeak temporarily, but for a permanent cure, you'll need to tighten the parts that are rubbing.

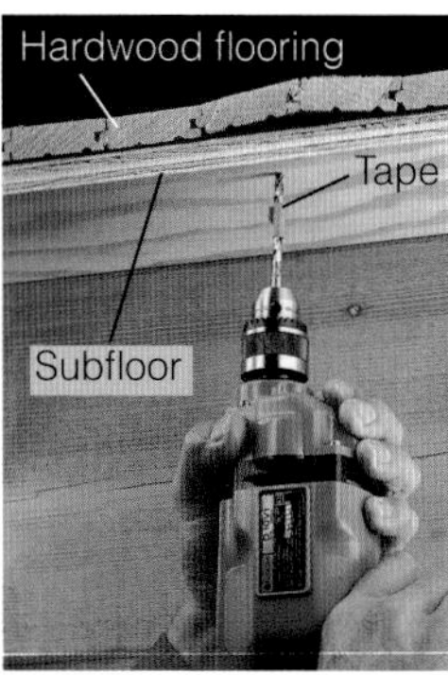

1 Drill a hole slightly larger than your screw through the subfloor and bottom 1/4-in. (6 mm) of hardwood flooring. Wrap tape on the drill bit to act as a depth gauge to prevent drilling through the hardwood floor surface.

2 Squeeze wood glue into the hole. Force in a generous amount of glue so it can surround both sides of any flooring paper between the layers.

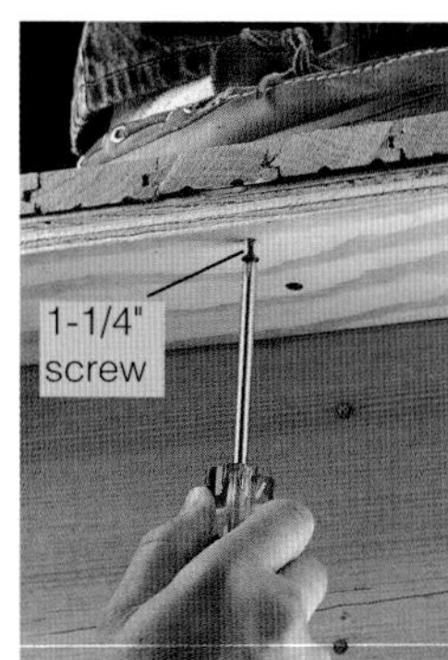

3 Install 1-1/4-in. screws while someone stands on the floor above. Space screws every 6 in. (15 cm). Make sure screws penetrate at least halfway into the hardwood flooring.

Patching a Floor

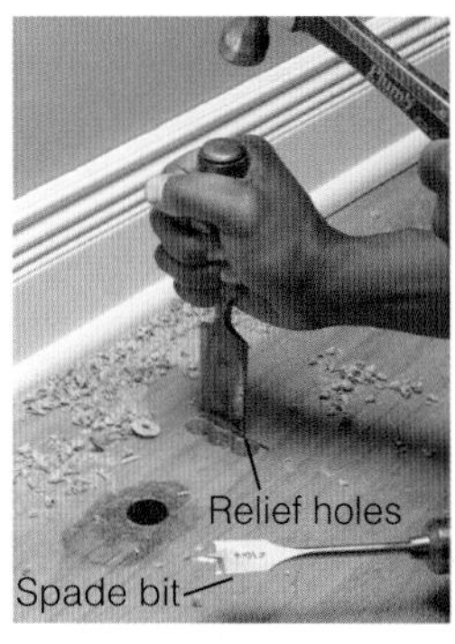

1 Mark across flooring strip(s) beyond the damaged area. Drill three relief holes using a spade bit. Use a sharp chisel to complete a clean cut.

2 Set saw blade depth to floor thickness. Saw two parallel relief cuts through damaged board. Remove pieces with flat pry bar and chisel. Protect the remaining flooring's edges.

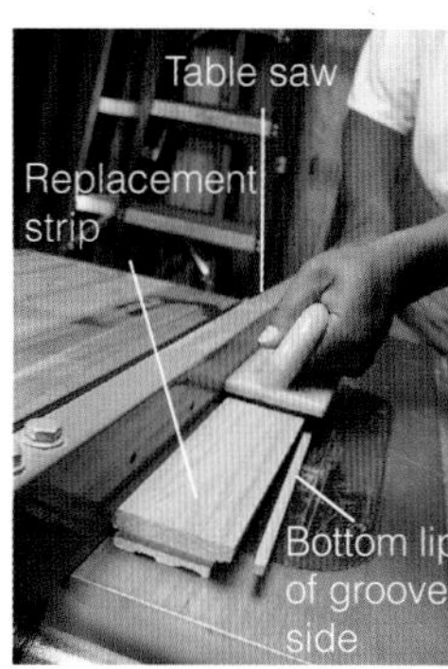

3 Remove the bottom lip on the groove side of the replacement strip using a table saw or sharp chisel and then cut the strip to length.

Caution: Blade guard is removed for photo; if possible, use yours.

4 Install replacement strip and tap into place. Predrill holes over joist locations and fasten board with 2-1/2-in. finish nails. Set nail heads and putty holes.

Removing a Stain from a Floor

1 Sand discolored area with 100-grit sandpaper to start, 150-grit to finish. Vacuum and wipe area with mineral spirits for oil-based stains and finishes, denatured alcohol for water-based stains and finishes.

2 Test-match stain colors on scrap of bare wood that's the same species as the floor. If necessary, mix stains to match color. Check for color match while stains are wet if you're topcoating with oil-based polyurethane, or when semi-dry with a water-based polyurethane.

Fixing a Scratch in a Floor

Repair wood scratches quickly. Left untreated, damaged wood discolors, and repairs won't blend. Use a similar stain color, thinned to half strength. Add more stain until colors match. Most stains contain enough resins to seal a scratch without topcoating.

Fixing Squeaky and Bouncy Floors

Fixing Squeaks from Above

Even without access underneath, you can solve most floor squeaks. Trim-head screws tend to be carpet friendly.

1 Probe for joist location by drilling a small hole and using a bent coat hanger. Joists often line up with wall studs.

2 Push carpet nap away and predrill a hole through the subfloor angled toward the joist. Do not drill into joist.

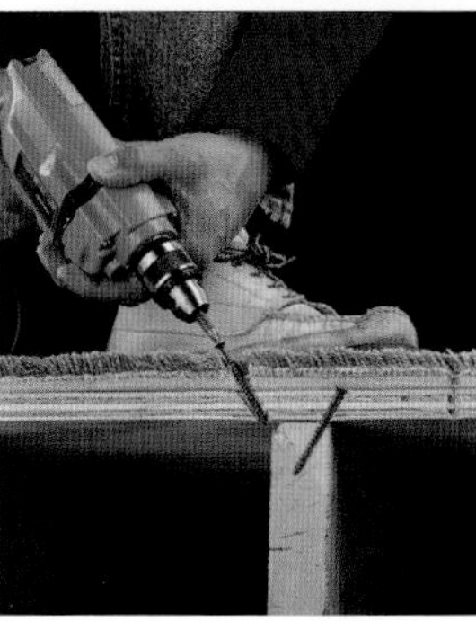

3 Drive trim-head screws into joists while applying weight. Sink screw heads below pad level.

Fixing Squeaks from Below

Many squeak-stopping solutions are available when the floor joists are exposed. Cleats, caulk and bridging all offer potential solutions.

1 Mark squeaks while someone walks and bounces on the floor above. Listen for noises and watch for movement.

2 Nail or screw 2 x 4-in. cleats at least 2 ft. (60 cm) long along joists. Apply construction adhesive on top edge.

Or inject gap-filling polyurethane caulk into gaps between joists and plywood. Push caulk into the gap using a plastic spoon.

Solidifying a Bouncy Floor

Bridging connects joists to one another to limit independent movement and create a more "unibody" floor.

Bridging, made from 1x3s, is installed in an X-shape. Wood bridging is most easily installed during new construction.

Solid-wood blocking is installed between all joists. Snap chalk line and install alternately on each side of the line.

Metal bridging comes in several styles, some better suited to installation from below. Leave a gap between pieces to avoid rubbing.

Replacing a Support Post

Sagging floors, doors that won't close and cracks that appear in interior walls can be symptomatic of a serious structural problem. Floors can sag because the posts supporting a house beam are failing or the footings holding those posts are undersized and sinking. Repairing or replacing footings requires special tools and skills—a job best left to pros.

Caution: As a house beam is raised, rigid plumbing or gas lines can separate or rupture.

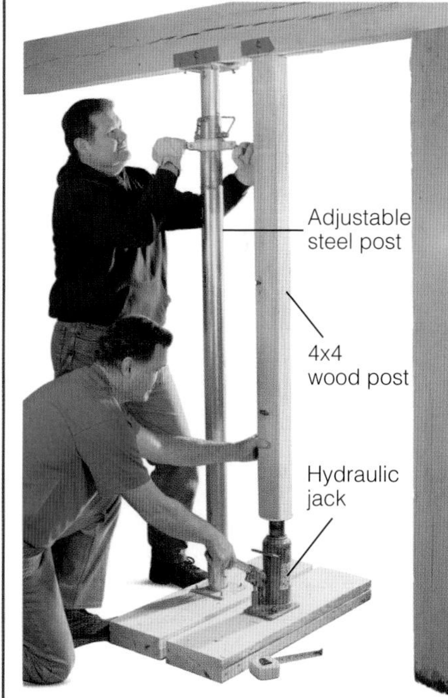

Vinyl Flooring

Scribing 42
Replacing a Toilet 120
Baseboard Moldings 230
Moisture Test 272

For areas exposed to heavy traffic, dirt and moisture, it's hard to beat vinyl flooring. Quality vinyl, also called resilient flooring, is easy to clean and maintain under the toughest conditions. Further, it readily conforms to uneven conditions that might make other types of flooring impractical.

Vinyl flooring can be installed over almost any clean, sound, dry surface, including concrete, old vinyl, ceramic tile and wood floors. If you have an old vinyl floor, it may contain asbestos, and disturbing it may cause more harm than covering it over. Another option, shown here, is to install a quality 1/4-in. plywood underlayment. Check with the manufacturer for specific instructions and products for these types of installations.

As always, careful planning pays big dividends. For flooring styles with distinct patterns, think about how you want the pattern to reveal itself in the space, especially at thresholds and next to tub skirts and walls. Sheet vinyl is commonly available in 6- and 12-ft. widths, depending on style and manufacturer. Keep these widths in mind as you plan and shop to help you minimize seams.

Preparing the Floor

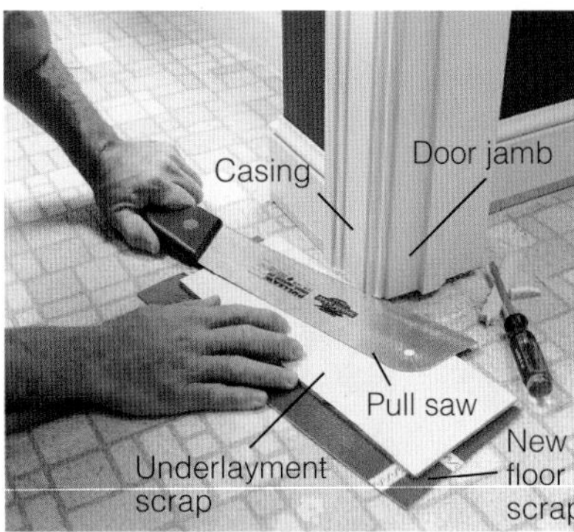

1 Saw off the bottom of door jambs and casing using small pieces of the new flooring as a thickness guide. Remove base-shoe molding. You'll reinstall shoe molding as last step of project.

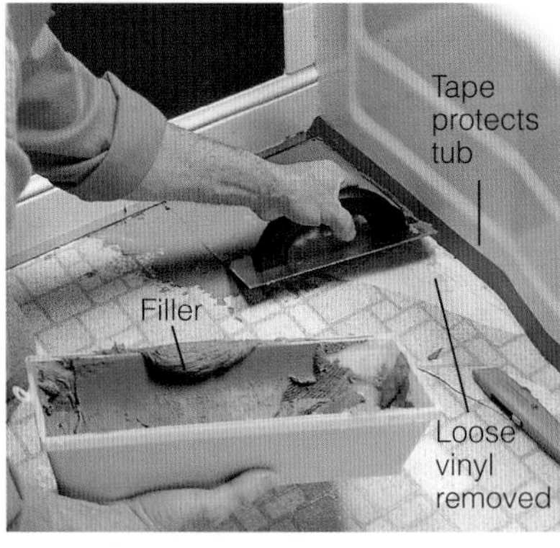

2 Cut out or remove loose flooring; then fill gaps and low spots with manufacturer-recommended filler.

3 Cut underlayment (see next page). Staple it to subfloor with 7/8-in.-long staples. Space staples 4 in. (10 cm) apart in field and 2 in. (5 cm) apart on seams.

4 Mix recommended filler and trowel it onto underlayment to fill gaps in seams, holes and voids. If seams form ridges, sand flat before filling.

Gluing

1 After making a template and cutting flooring (see next page), position vinyl and pull back to expose half of floor. Spread adhesive, re-lay vinyl, pull back the other side and repeat.

2 Press vinyl tightly to the floor and roll out glue ridges with a rolling pin. Work from center out. Roll edges with wallpaper seam roller. Roll vinyl as soon as possible after gluing.

Creating and Using a Template

1 Make a floor template to use as a guide for cutting both underlayment and flooring. Tape pieces of heavy paper together. Cut paper to leave about 1 in. (2.5 cm) of old floor showing around perimeter.

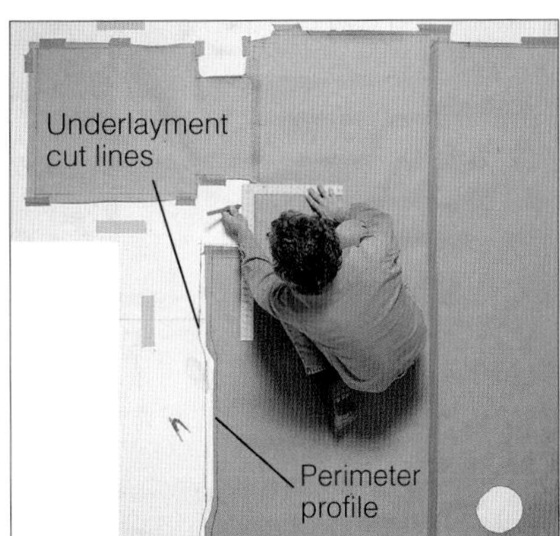

4 Rough-cut underlayment sheets and butt together factory edges. Mark cutlines on underlayment using paper template and adding back 2 in. (5 cm). Install as shown on previous page.

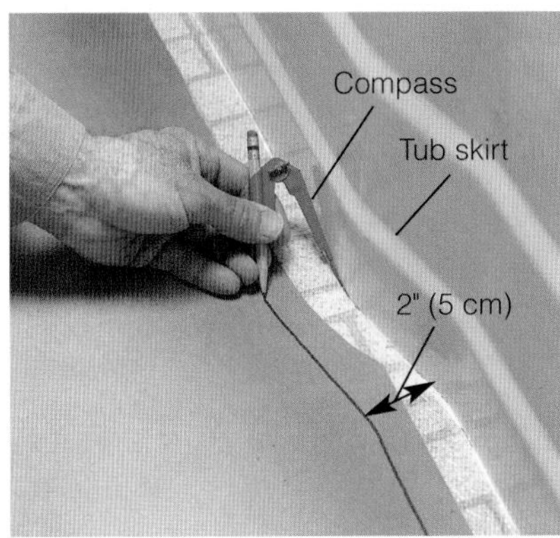

2 Transfer floor shape to template by marking a line on paper 2 in. (5 cm) from walls. Use compass to scribe tub skirt and other odd-shaped profiles.

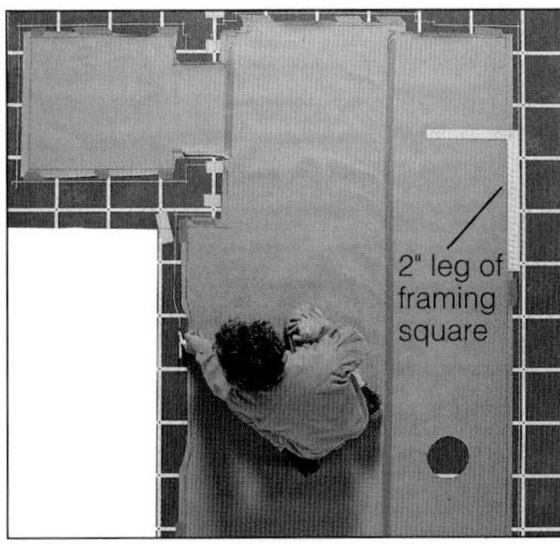

5 Unroll vinyl on clean surface and let it relax. Sheet vinyl relaxes or flattens best at room temperature. Tape template in place on vinyl with pattern in mind. Transfer profile, adding back 2 in. (5 cm).

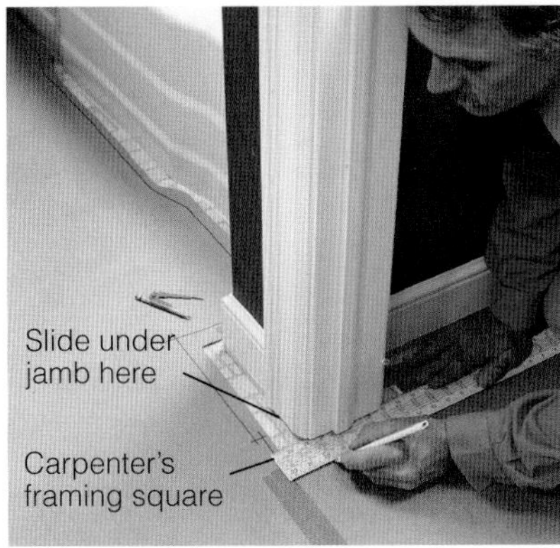

3 Slide 2-in. (5-cm)-wide leg of framing square under moldings and jambs to mark template. New underlayment and flooring will go under casing and jamb and butt to baseboards, tub skirt and toilet flange.

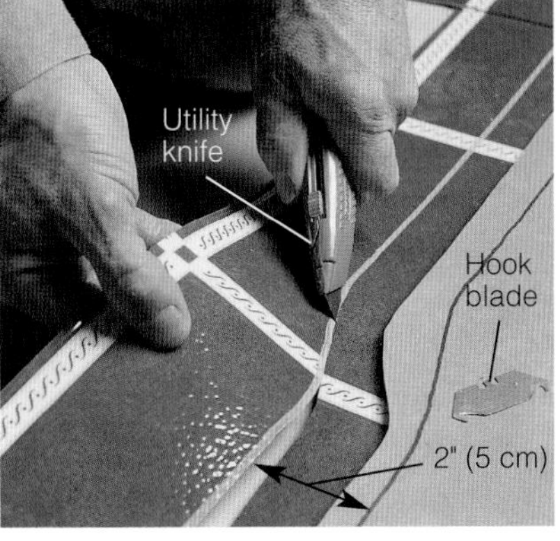

6 Cut vinyl flooring using a utility knife fitted with a sharp hook blade. Fill seams and voids in underlayment. If seams will be present, tape sheets together before using template.

Vinyl Flooring Choices

Vinyl, or resilient flooring, is divided into four basic categories: vinyl tiles, fully adhered sheet flooring, perimeter-fastened sheet flooring and loose-lay sheet flooring. Most home centers stock a wide selection of the first two categories, but you may need to visit a flooring specialty store for more information on perimeter-fastened and loose-lay flooring.

Vinyl tiles (see p. 248) will be either a laminated vinyl with a pattern, a wear layer and a self-stick backing, or a vinyl composition tile (VCT), like the type shown on the following page. VCTs are thick, have no protective wear layer and must be glued. These tiles are more labor intensive to install and higher maintenance because they require waxing, but they have some distinct advantages. They're durable, relatively inexpensive and repairable. They also minimize waste and allow you to create unusual designs.

Fully adhered sheet flooring (see left) requires gluing the entire floor surface. This type of installation makes the floor, slightly more resistant to tearing and water damage and its seams more stable. While working and gluing a large sheet, it's critical to avoid damaging or crimping the sheet.

Perimeter-fastened sheet flooring requires only a thin strip of glue or staples around the edges and glue along each side of a seam. Once installed, this flooring shrinks slightly to pull out bubbles and loose spots. Because there is little or no gluing, it's easier and less messy to cover large areas. However, it's more costly and you must repair cuts and tears immediately to avoid further damage.

Loose-lay sheet flooring has a glass-encapsulated backing that allows the sheet to lay flat once installed. This flooring doesn't shrink and, as the name implies, no gluing is involved. However, it does require a manufacturer-recommended tape under seams, doorways and heavy appliances. Even though it's more costly, it's the easiest to install of the vinyl floor types.

Installing Vinyl Tile

Pull Saws 26
Squaring 41
Asbestos Flooring Materials 480

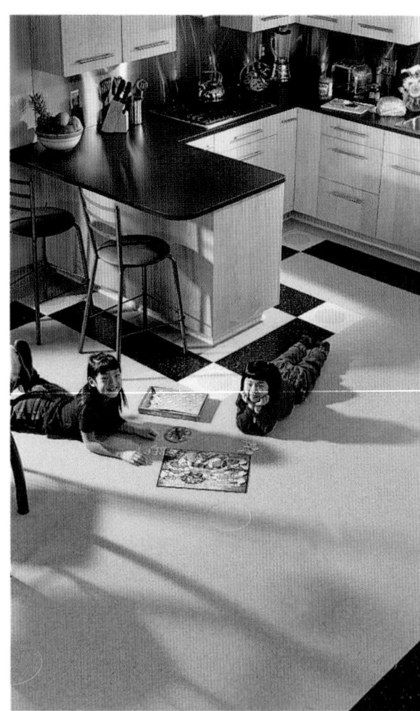

Vinyl composition tile has been around for 60 years and few flooring surfaces can claim a better track record. It's inexpensive, virtually indestructible and easier to install than most flooring materials. Perhaps best of all, these tiles allow you to flex your creative muscles in a way not possible with other materials. Colors can be mixed, matched and contrasted. Individual tiles can be shaped to create unique inlay designs and you can create a border, both of which we show here.

The tiles are relatively easy to cut with a sharp utility knife and straightedge, but a rented cutter will improve your speed and precision, and a heat gun will improve the tile's cutability if you cut and shape by hand.

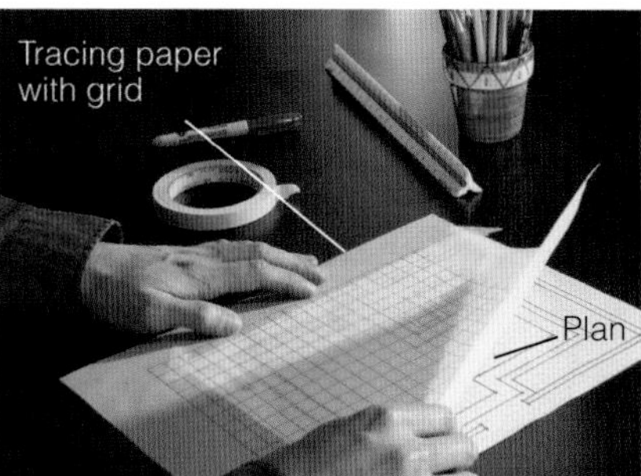

1 Plan your design. Draw a floor plan. Lay tracing paper with a grid proportionate to the tiles' size on top. Move tracing paper grid to determine final layout.

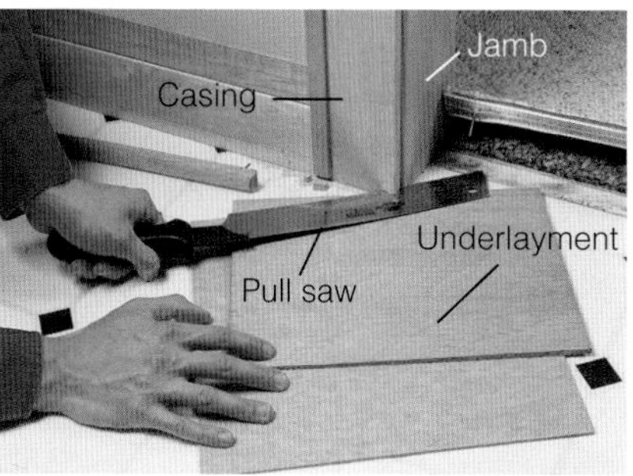

2 Saw off the bottom of casings and door jambs to allow underlayment and tile to slide under them.

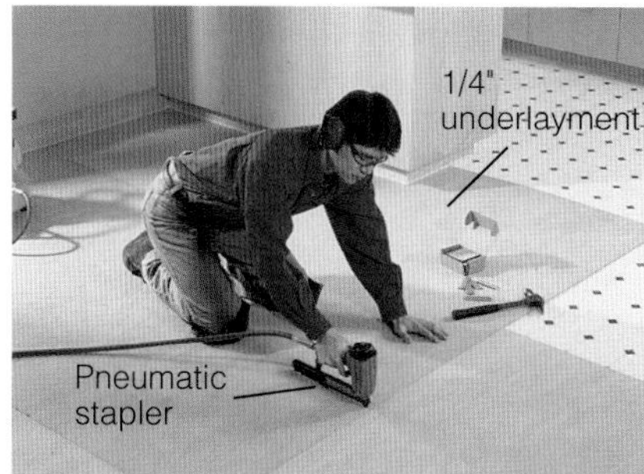

3 Fasten plywood underlayment to the old floor with a pneumatic or underlayment stapler. Ring-shank nails can also be used.

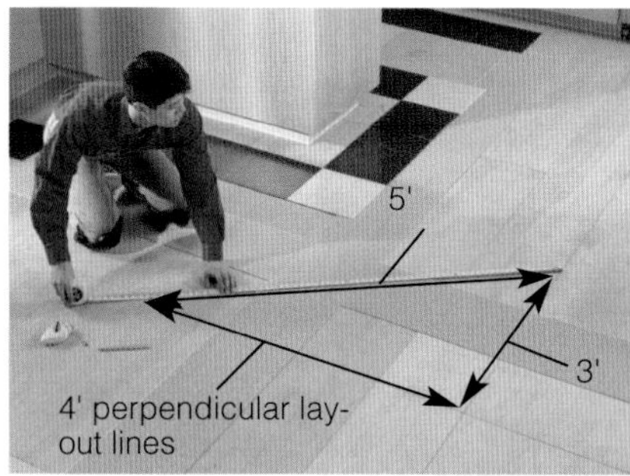

4 Snap perpendicular chalk lines, aligned with edges of full tiles, to establish a layout. Use the 3-4-5 rule (p. 41) to check square.

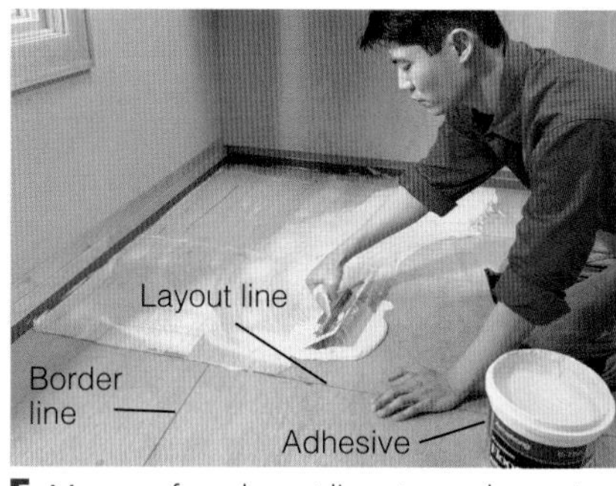

5 Measure from layout lines to mark exact border lines. Spread glue over half the floor. Let dry clear and tacky.

6 Press full tiles in place along layout lines, starting at layout intersection. Stair-step tiles to keep them aligned.

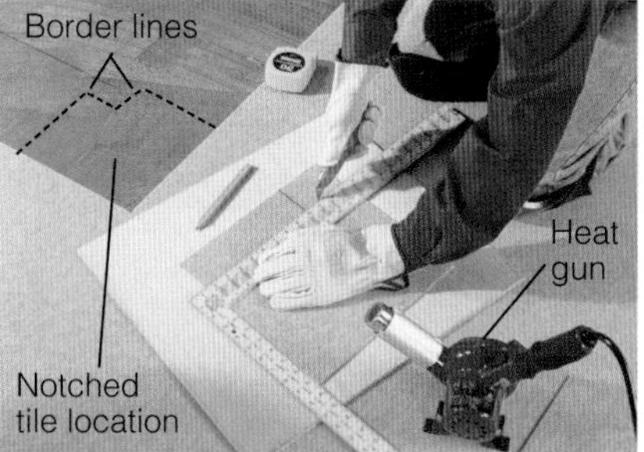

7 Notch tile to fit around border corners. Warm tile with heat gun until it's pliable. Cut using a sharp utility knife.

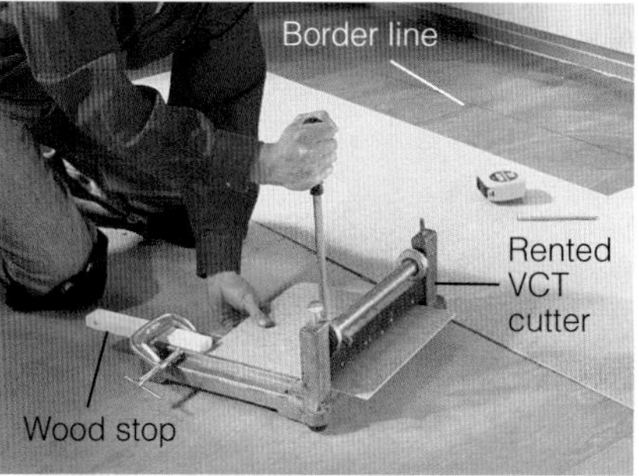

8 Cut to width remaining field tiles that lay next to border. Use special cutter for clean cuts and press tiles in place.

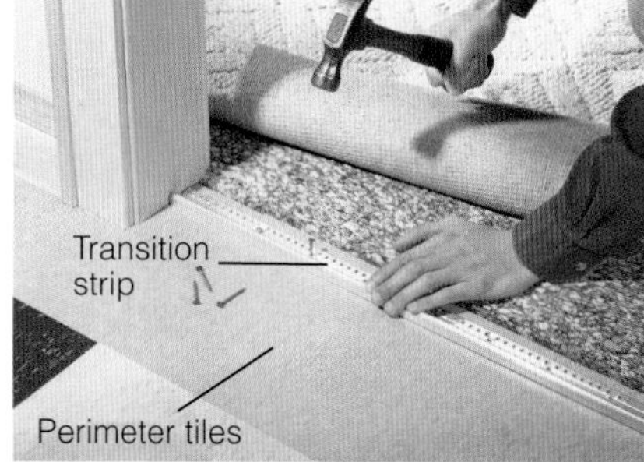

9 Lay decorative border and install perimeter tiles. Install transition strips where the tile floor meets other flooring. Add quarter-round molding.

Repairing Vinyl Flooring

Restoring Small Areas with a Repair Kit

1 Mask off repair area. Cut away loose fragments and clean out dust and dirt using a damp rag. Smooth rough edges with sandpaper. The repair kit shown is available at many hardware and flooring stores.

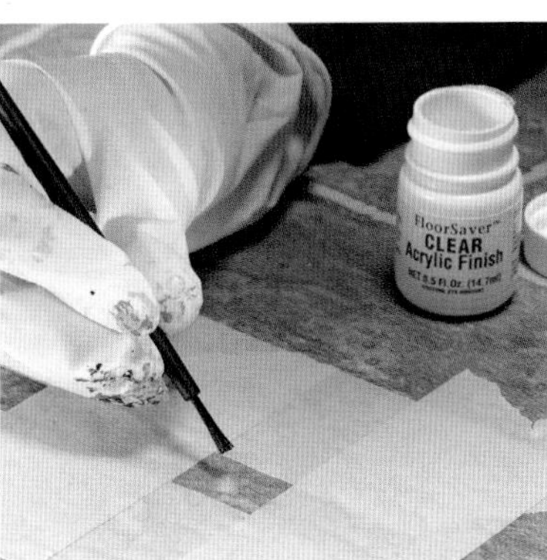

2 Mix paint from the repair kit to match floor color. Paint inside surface and edges of damaged area. Clean off excess paint and dry with a hair dryer on low heat. When wet, the final paint color should be slightly darker than the floor color.

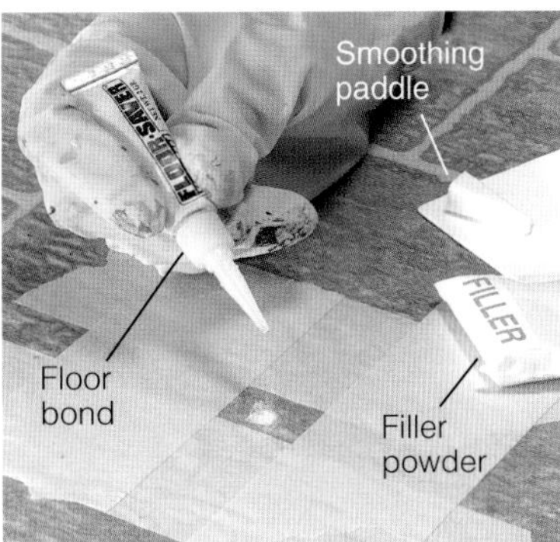

3 Pour filler powder into the hole and level it with a smoothing paddle. Slowly drip floor bond onto the powder until it is saturated. Let compound harden for 15 minutes.

4 Brush the clear acrylic finish over the repair. Allow two hours' drying time before you walk on the area.

Regluing Seams

1 Heat edges of vinyl with hair dryer. Peel edges back and clean out sand and dirt. Protect floor surface with masking tape. Apply multipurpose floor adhesive to backing. Hold edges down with a board and weights.

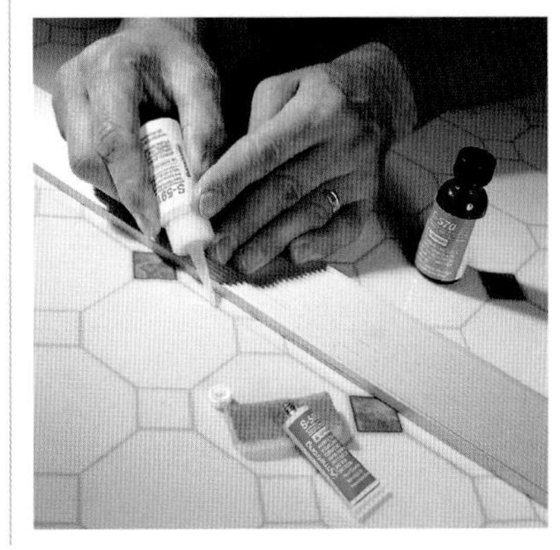

2 Use seam sealer kit (manufacturer-approved, if possible) to fuse the vinyl edges together. A typical kit contains an applicator, cleaner, catalyst and sealer.

Replacing a Section

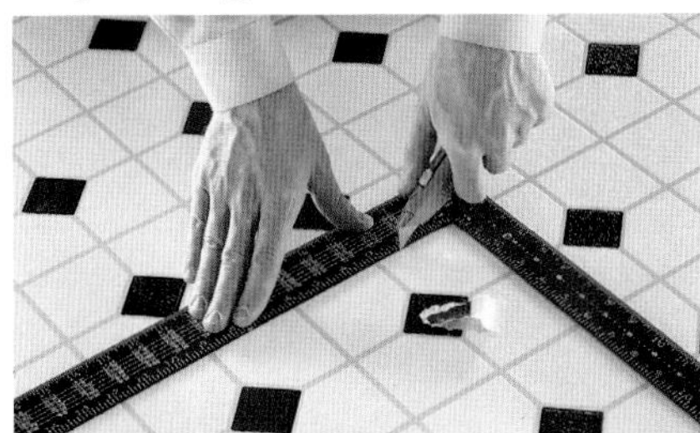

1 Use a straightedge and sharp utility knife to cut out the damaged section. Cut down the center of any simulated grout lines.

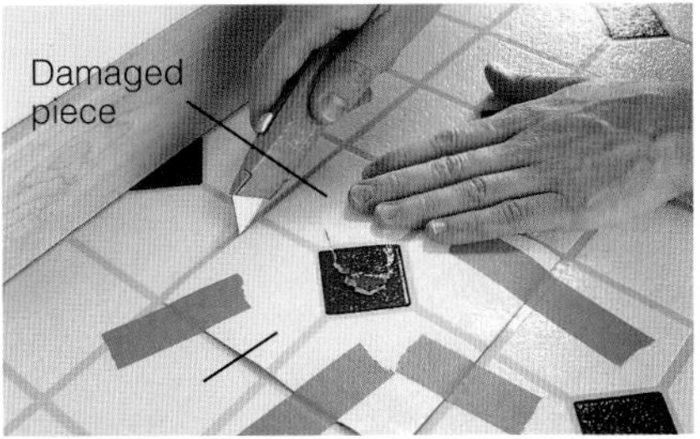

2 Use the damaged section as a pattern to cut a replacement piece from leftover scrap or from behind the refrigerator.

3 Test-fit patch, apply adhesive, set patch and roll flat. Seal seams with manufacturer-approved seam sealer.

Vinyl Tricks

Hair dryer help: Use a hair dryer set on low to make old vinyl flooring pliable and easier to remove for repairs. It also softens adhesive, making it easier to scrape.
Replacement pieces: If you don't have a leftover scrap of flooring material, steal a patch from an inconspicuous area, such as under the fridge or stove or in the back of a closet. Patch it with a damaged or mismatched piece to protect the underlayment.

Ceramic Tile and Stone

The notion that quality begins with planning and preparation is closer to the truth for tiling than for most home-improvement projects. Perhaps that's because tile and stone embody a sense of permanence that's hard to match. The planning involves substrate, grout-line width, layout lines and design. Designing is a challenge because the choices are infinite when considering tile type, size, color and layout.

Carefully plan your project on paper by making a map of the space, including fixtures, cabinets and doors. Make multiple copies of the map and experiment with layouts, tile sizes, borders and colors. Include grout lines in the drawings and color in the tiles.

Planning and Installation Tips

- When you've determined your final design, draw over chalk or pencil layout lines on the floor with a black permanent marker. That way, layout lines will show through if they're covered with adhesive.
- Dry-fit your tile layout, especially on diagonal installations. Use layout lines to place a few full tiles and work toward the pieces to be cut. Once the fit is assured, apply adhesive to the grid and install the tile.
- Except for self-spacing wall tile, most tiles have slight size variations that make cross-shaped spacers difficult to use. For wall installations, however, plastic wedge-shaped spacers are necessary to keep tiles aligned and in place.
- Clear out adhesive that squeezes up between tiles with a small putty knife. For dried adhesive, use a linoleum knife or narrow, flat-bladed screwdriver.
- If you're down to a small area where you can't use the notched trowel, butter the back of each tile (instead of the substrate) before installation.
- Don't use white, or even light, grout in heavy-use areas. Even with a grout sealer, you'll be inviting a maintenance headache.
- After the initial grout cleaning with a sponge, you'll have a heavy grout haze. For the second cleaning, use a damp, smooth cotton cloth (T-shirt material) folded into a square pad. Avoid digging into the grout lines while you work.

Manufactured Tile

Manufactured tile includes any tile, whether machine or handmade, that is baked or dried. The tiles may be glazed or unglazed and vary with respect to wear rating and porosity. Wear rating refers to a tile's durability and porosity may affect its suitability for use in wet areas or outdoors. Ceramic is a general term referring to most manufactured tile; porcelain refers to impervious ceramic tiles, which have the lowest possible absorption rating.

Natural Stone

The most common natural stones available in tile form are granite, marble, limestone and slate. Of these, granite is the hardest and most durable; however, any natural stone in a heavy-use area (like a foyer) will require maintenance. Granite and marble are usually polished; limestone, slate and tumbled marble are sold with a more natural surface. Voids and pits are normally filled in polished marble but left open in limestone. Slate tiles may vary in thickness because the pieces are fractured across the face rather than cut.

Shop Smart

Adhesives, Grouts and Sealers

Adhesives. Thin-set mortar, a cement-based powder, is the adhesive of choice for most tiling jobs. Available, commonly, in gray or in white (for use with lighter grouts and marble), some thin-set adhesives are polymer-modified or latex-fortified for added strength and flexibility; however, a compatible liquid additive is available for most. Pay attention to the set time (some thin-set mortars are very fast setting) and, if installing natural stone, make sure thin-set is suitable. Another option is a premixed latex mastic. Mastics work well for walls in dry areas. They're convenient and offer better slip resistance when installing smaller tiles, but they are much slower drying and don't have the strength of thin-set mortars.

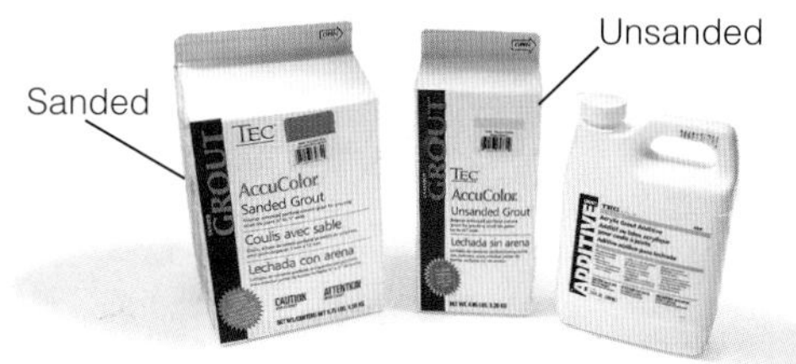

Grouts. Grout is a cement-based powder that's mixed with water or latex additive. Some grouts are already polymer-modified, and others can be mixed with additive in place of water. These additives strengthen grout, making it more resistant to water, shrinkage and cracking. Buy unsanded grout for joints 1/8 in. (3 mm) wide or less and for use with polished marble. Sanded grout works best for wider joints.

Sealers. Unglazed tile, stone and grout all require a sealer. Either water-based or solvent-based, some sealers penetrate, soaking into the material, and some are topical, forming a surface coating. Water-based sealers are expensive but tend to be invisible, retaining the original color of the grout or stone. Solvent-based sealers can sometimes darken the surface.

Cutting Basics

Some cutting is involved with nearly every tiling job. If you have just a few tiles to cut, some specialty tile stores will cut them for you at a reasonable price. For larger projects, it's much more convenient to rent or buy the tools for doing the job yourself.

Straight cuts. Snap cutters are excellent for cutting straight lines in most glazed floor and wall tiles. Depending on the tile, snap cutters make clean diagonal cuts for installations or decorative inlays. They work best for making cuts of 1 in. (2.5 cm) or more. To make very narrow cuts, or for cutting thick tile or stone, you may need a wet saw. An inexpensive wet saw will meet the needs of most do-it-yourselfers. Larger, higher-grade wet saws can also be rented.

Angles and miters. Most wet saws allow you to miter, or bevel cut, up to 45 degrees. Use these on outside corners when installing tile base, wainscoting or decorative trim. Bevel cut a long edge to avoid exposed edges if the tile wraps around an outside corner.

Curves. For the most part, when you need to cut a curve or hole in tile, it doesn't need to be pretty. Decorative faucet and fixture plates usually cover the hole's edges. Cut the curves around valves and toilet flanges by making a series of relief cuts with a wet saw and using a tile nipper to snap off the waste.

Holes. Use a ceramic-tile hole saw (see p. 51) for small holes, keeping the bit wet as you drill. For odd shapes, larger holes and electrical outlets, use a glass/tile bit to drill closely spaced holes around the perimeter.

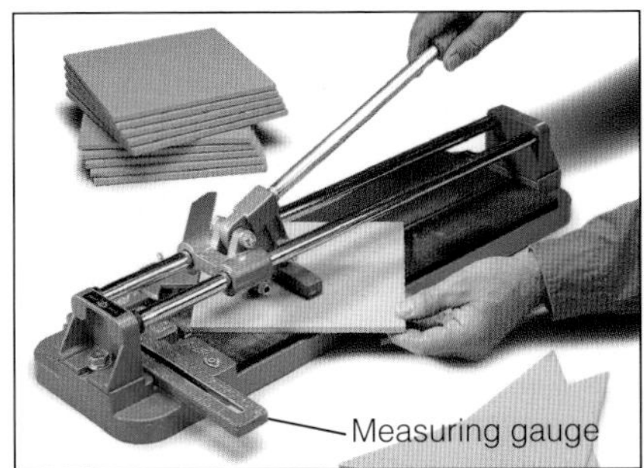

A snap cutter is essentially a guided glass cutter equipped with a measuring gauge, a foam pad and breaker arm for snapping tile.

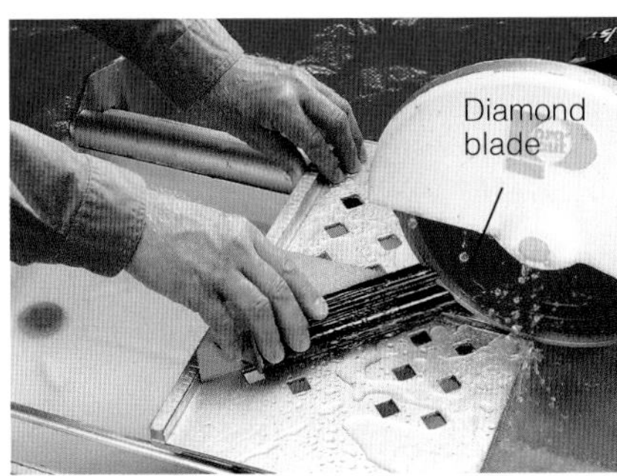

Wet saws cut any tile—ceramic, stone or concrete—using a diamond-coated blade that spins through a tub of water to keep cool.

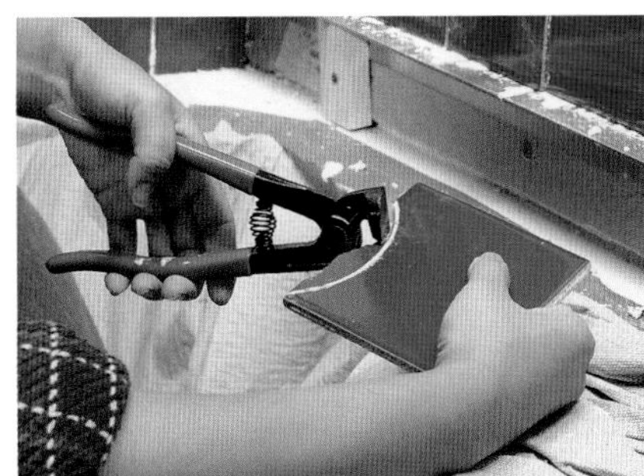

Tile nippers nibble away small bits of tile to create curves, like those around tub or shower valves.

Grouting Basics

Grout fills the spaces between tiles, making the wall watertight and more attractive. Mix grout thoroughly until it has a uniform color and a toothpaste consistency. If necessary, use additive in place of water. Allow grout to sit, or slake, for 10 minutes and then remix before using it.

Don't grout inside corners or where tile meets another material. Instead, use a high-quality latex sealant or silicone, the same color as the grout, to seal these gaps.

If you're installing unglazed tile or unsealed stone, seal the tile before grouting. The sealer acts as a grout release and keeps the grout from staining the tile.

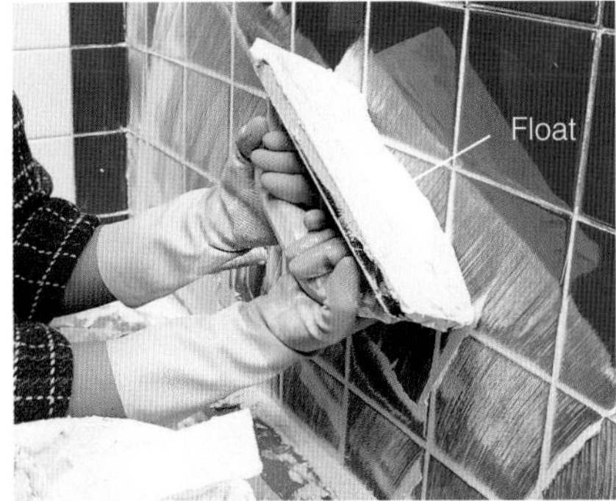

1 Working one area at a time, use a float to distribute the grout and push it into all joints. Holding the float at an angle, scrape away excess grout.

2 Allow grout to firm up, then remove excess grout and shape grout lines with damp sponge. Use circular motion and clean sponge frequently. This may take several passes.

3 After the grout dries, polish off any remaining grout haze with dry cheesecloth. Apply grout sealer after grout has cured for a week.

Grouting Simplified

- Wear rubber gloves while grouting. Cement-based products can cause an alkali burn.
- After initial cleaning with sponge but before polishing, clean heavy haze with a damp, smooth cotton cloth, such as a T-shirt.
- If you have large tiles with wide grout lines, use a grout bag with a spout to squeeze the grout directly into the joints.
- If the grout hardens before you have a chance to remove it, clean it off with one of the specialty grout removers available.

Tiling Walls

Replacing Shower Faucets 103
Tile-cutting Basics 251

Tiling a wall is often part of a larger project—like remodeling a bathroom or installing a new tub or shower. If the wall studs are exposed, take the opportunity to add an antiscald shower valve, install blocking for grab bars and update the bathroom to meet current building codes.

Add blocking around the tub skirt or shower base and extra studs to support joints between tile backer material and drywall. Replace wet or moldy insulation and add a 4-mil vapor barrier.

Install tile backer material, such as cement board, approved for use in wet areas. Cover the tile backer joints with fiberglass tape and a swath of thin-set mortar. With the updated substrate in place, you're ready to do the job right.

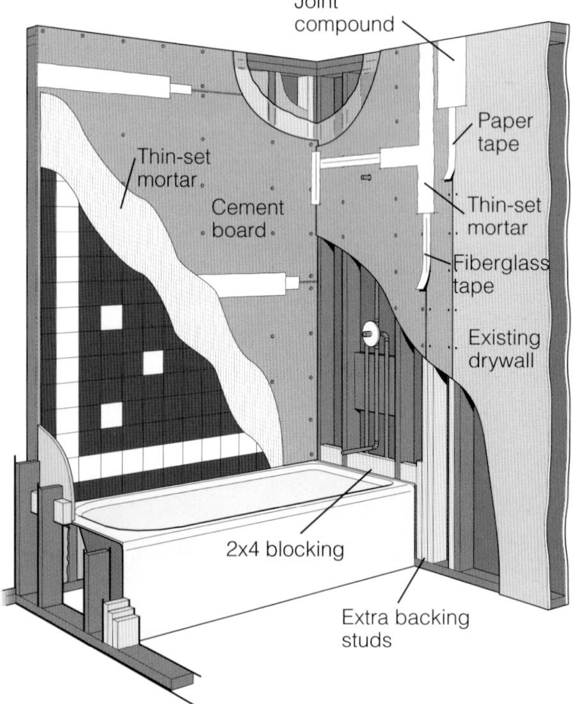

Ceramic Tile Walls

1 Mark horizontal layout line, using a long level, to indicate the first course of full tile. The tile next to the tub, inside corners and floor will be cut to fit. Mark vertical layout line so it centers on a grout line. Layout lines should be level and square. Plan so perimeter tiles will be at least a half-tile wide.

2 Screw a straightedge, aligned with horizontal layout line, to support the first full course. On one side of vertical layout line, spread a layer of adhesive using trowel's flat side; then rake adhesive with trowel's notched side, holding it at a consistent angle. Start setting tiles at a vertical-horizontal layout line intersection. Proceed in stair-step fashion.

3 Make sure grout lines stay straight and tile aligns with vertical line. If tile is not self spacing, use plastic spacers. Continue working in sections until wall is complete.

4 Remove straightedge after adhesive has set. Cut and install perimeter and first-row tiles. Leave 1/16-in. (2-mm) gap in corners for caulk adhesion. Test-fit each tile and grind cut edges smooth. If necessary, butter back of tile instead of wall.

5 Mark tile for holes by resting tile next to and above or below the obstruction. Mark both sides of obstruction and carry marks across tile in a tic-tac-toe pattern. Line intersections form the area to cut. Aim for a 1/8- to 1/4-in. (3- to 6-mm) gap around the obstruction.

6 Cut small holes by drilling a series of holes around the perimeter of your drawn circle with a glass/tile bit. A rotary tool with a tile bit works well for cutting holes and curves in ceramic wall tile, but not in thicker floor tile or stone.

Tiling Floors

Your biggest challenge in a floor tiling project will likely be maintaining the existing floor height. Most tile floors, subfloor and underlayment included, will be 1-1/2 to 1-3/4 in. (3.8 to 4.5 cm) thick. Your goal is a floor sturdy enough to support tile, yet thin enough that it doesn't stand much taller than adjacent floor coverings or change the rise on a stair step. For most tile jobs, subfloor and underlayment must total 1-1/8 in. (2.8 cm).

Use a tile suitable for the floor location. For heavy-use areas, like foyers or kitchens, select a tile with a wear rating of 3 or more and use natural stone only if you're willing to maintain it.

1 After removing interior doors and baseboard moldings, pull up existing underlayment. For easier removal, cut underlayment into smaller pieces using a circular saw. Set the saw's blade depth carefully. Use a cat's paw to remove nails and a flat pry bar to pry up existing underlayment.

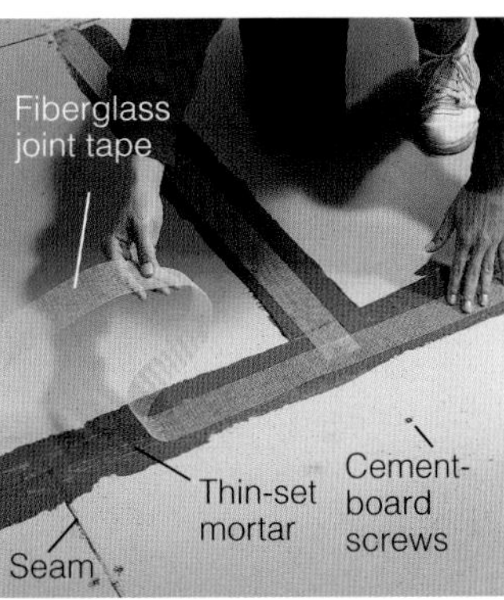

2 Cut and fit a tile backer, like cement board, over entire subfloor. Use thin-set mortar to bond cement board (smooth side up) to subfloor and cement-board screws to fasten. Cover seams between sheets with thin-set mortar, fiberglass joint tape and another coat of the mortar.

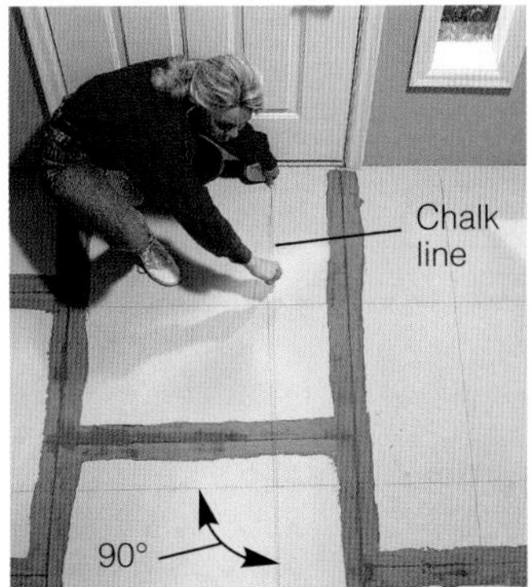

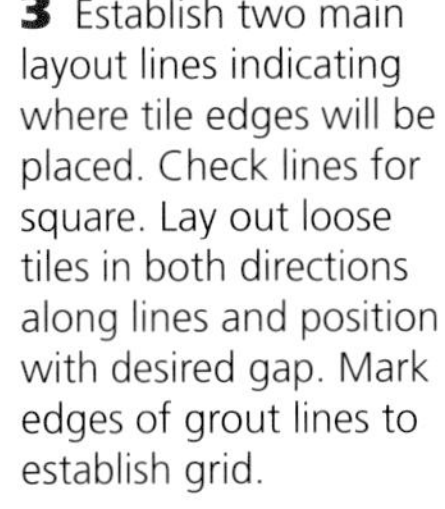

3 Establish two main layout lines indicating where tile edges will be placed. Check lines for square. Lay out loose tiles in both directions along lines and position with desired gap. Mark edges of grout lines to establish grid.

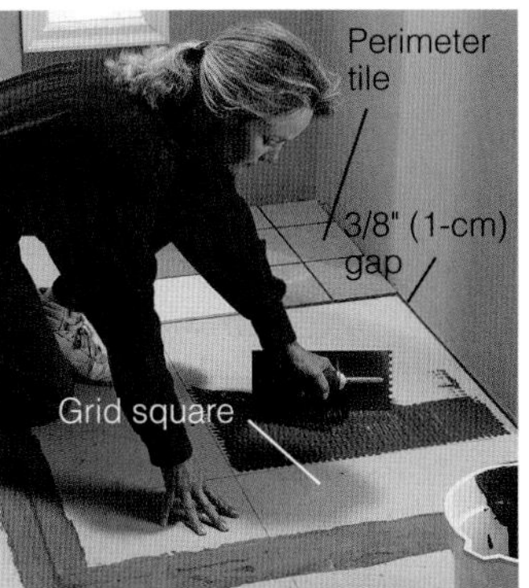

4 Each grid square should be about 3 ft. x 3 ft. (1 m x 1 m). Work in one grid square at a time. Spread thin-set mortar with trowel's flat side, then rake it with notched side. Avoid covering grid lines with adhesive. Measure each perimeter tile and cut to leave 3/8-in. (1-cm) gap at wall.

5 Position tiles using a slight twisting motion. Set each firmly in place with a few medium blows from your fist or rubber mallet. Readjust spacing between tiles, as necessary.

The Right Substrate

Your tile floor will only be as solid as the surface beneath it. Rot-proof tile backer boards (near right) offer do-it-yourselfers an excellent, affordable option to labor-intensive mortar beds (far right). Choose among cement boards, fiber cement or one of the drywall-like products available. Be sure the tile backer you choose is rated for your intended use.

Tile can usually go directly over clean, dry concrete; however, for large areas, you may need a crack isolation membrane to minimize damage from underlying cracks, joints and expansion joints.

For out-of-level and wavy floors, self-leveling compounds offer a solution. When mixed, this liquidlike cement settles into a flat, level surface.

Cement board is made from cement sandwiched between two layers of fiberglass mesh. The sheets come in several sizes and thicknesses. Cement board cuts easily with a carbide scoring tool and utility knife.

Mortar beds are laid over galvanized metal lath and a waterproof membrane or felt-paper. The dry-tamped mortar method is still used by pros and to create sloped custom shower bases. You'll likely encounter a mortar bed when removing older tile.

Carpeting

Even though carpet has some drawbacks when compared to hard surface flooring, there's no denying that nothing else is quite as comfortable, especially for bare feet. Besides being decorative, carpet insulates against cold, helps absorb sound and cushions the floor.

Several types of fibers are used to make carpet. Wool is a soft, natural fiber that's very durable. Unfortunately, it's also expensive. Most likely, you'll be choosing from an assortment of synthetic fibers, such as nylon, olefin and polyester. Nylon is the most common fiber because it's resilient, easy to clean and nearly indestructible. Olefin is also durable and often used in berber carpets. Because it's highly resistant to water, olefin is used in indoor-outdoor carpet and commercial settings. Polyester has traditionally lacked resiliency, but manufacturers have improved it over the years by blending it with other materials.

When shopping, examine the pile's twist. The tighter the twist, the more resilient the carpet. If the yarn is heat set, the twist is built in.

How Much Carpet?

To estimate the amount of carpeting, measure room's longest and widest points in feet (including doorways and alcoves). Add 3 in. to each dimension. Multiply width by length and divide the result by 9 to get the number of square yards needed. Carpet comes 12 and 15 ft. wide. If possible, avoid seams or place them in low-traffic areas (Berbers and textured styles make hiding seams difficult). Lay carpet with pile in same direction and match patterns.

Carpet Installation Tools

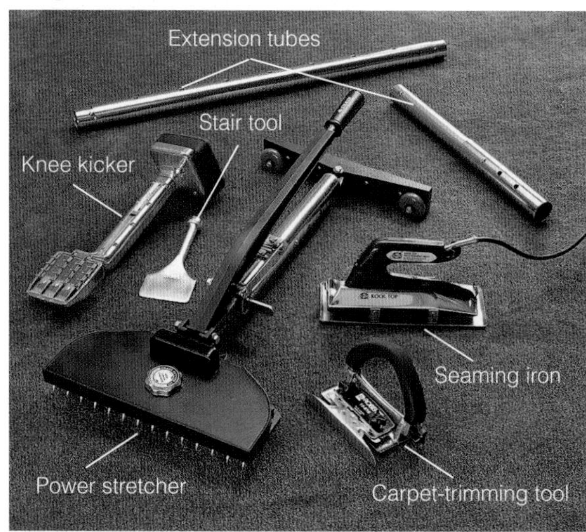

Use professional tools for professional results. A **seaming iron** melts glue on the edges of seaming tape when joining carpet edges. A **trimming tool** is faster and more accurate than a carpet knife for trimming excess carpet. A **power stretcher and extension tubes** pull carpet taut between tackless strips. A **stair tool** sets carpet backing into the inside corners of steps and onto the tackless strips. A **knee kicker** is used for bumping and tightening carpet onto tackless strips and for stretching carpet in closets and other confined spaces.

The Right Products in the Right Places

Carpet. The data on the back of a carpet sample is helpful in comparing carpets of the same style. Pay attention to face weight (the weight of the pile and density or stitches per inch). For a quick test, bend the carpet pile tightly backward—the less backing you see, the better the carpet.

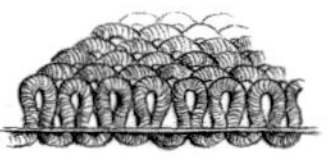

Level loop. Loops are of equal height and size. It's durable, slow to wear and easy to clean.

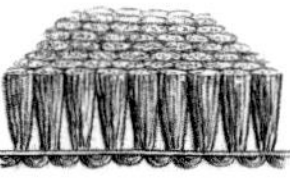

Cut pile. Loops are cut but not twisted. Its flat surface wears more easily than other styles.

Cut and loop. Loops and cut, twisted loops are combined. Its textured look is durable.

Frieze. This cut pile has straight and curled fibers. It's a resilient, trackless carpet that's slow to wear.

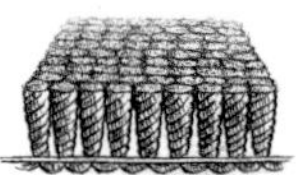

Saxony. All loops are cut, twisted and heat set. Its flat surface is luxurious yet more durable than cut pile.

Berber. Tightly spaced loops of thick yarn form a textured or level surface. It's durable yet can be hard to clean.

Pad. Carpet pad and thickness affect a carpet's longevity and comfort. Attached pad is factory bonded to the back of the carpet and is usually low quality. Unattached pad comes in 6-ft.-wide rolls and is installed independently of the carpet. Different thicknesses and weights (density) are available. For most carpets, a good choice is a 3/8- to 1/2-in.-thick (10- to 13-mm-thick) pad. For more resiliency, opt for a denser, rather than thicker, pad.

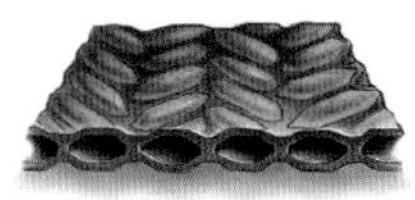

Rubber pads have a waffled appearance with air chambers between two layers. Heavy and dense, they retain resiliency better than most pads but are also the most expensive.

Rebond pads are composed of multicolored foam chunks bonded together. The most commonly used pad in homes, it has a proven track record. For cold concrete floors, look at foil-faced rebond pad.

Urethane pads are single-sheet pads that vary widely in quality. Some are comparable to rebond pads; others tend to compress soon after installation. In this case, price is a good clue to determine quality.

Installing Standard Carpeting

Prepare the floors before laying the carpet. Hammer the nails flush and remove all of the staples. When stretching, begin in center and work toward corners. In most rooms, the basic sequence is:

1. Knee kick or secure carpet along Wall C to tackless strips; **2.** Power stretch toward Wall A; **3.** Knee kick toward Wall D; **4.** Power stretch and/or knee kick toward Wall B.

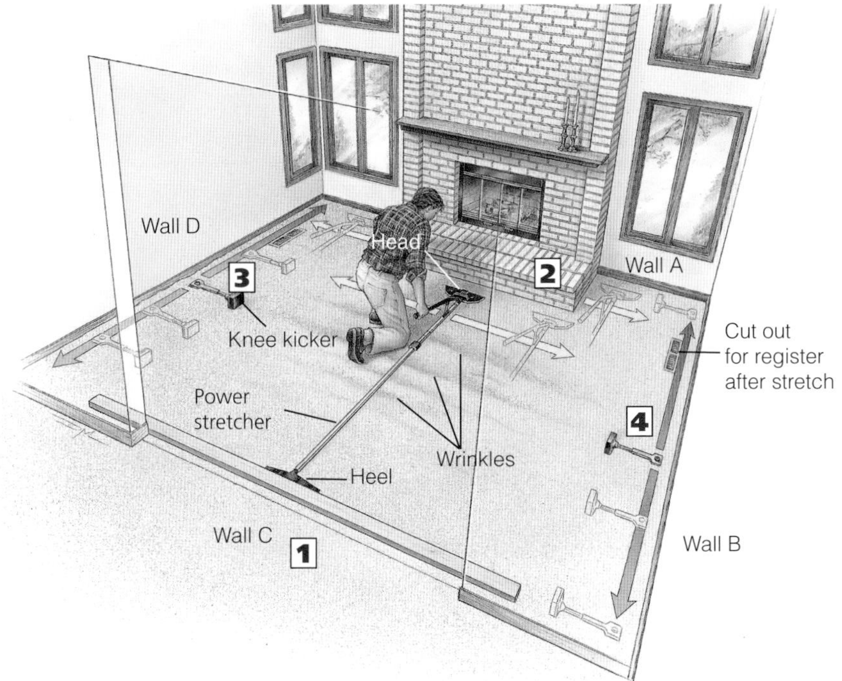

1 Nail tackless strips around room perimeter with pins facing wall. Leave a finger-wide gap between baseboard and strips. Cut strips with aviation snips.

2 Lay pad with smooth side up. Staple every 6 to 12 in. (15 to 30 cm). Use carpet or utility knife to trim even with the inside edge of the tackless strip.

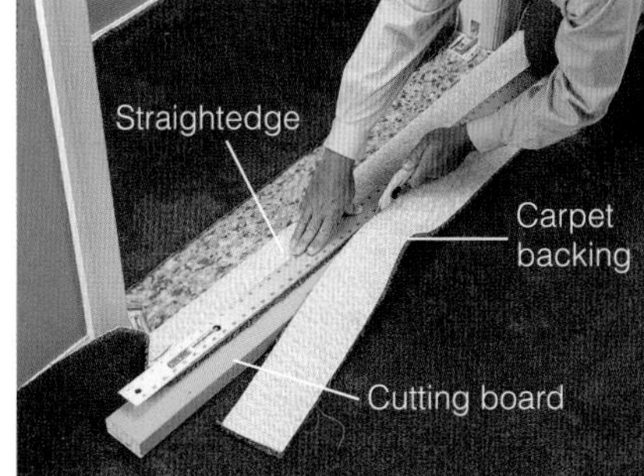

3 Cut and fit carpet so thin strip of excess runs up wall. From the backing side, straight cut edges of carpet to be seamed together.

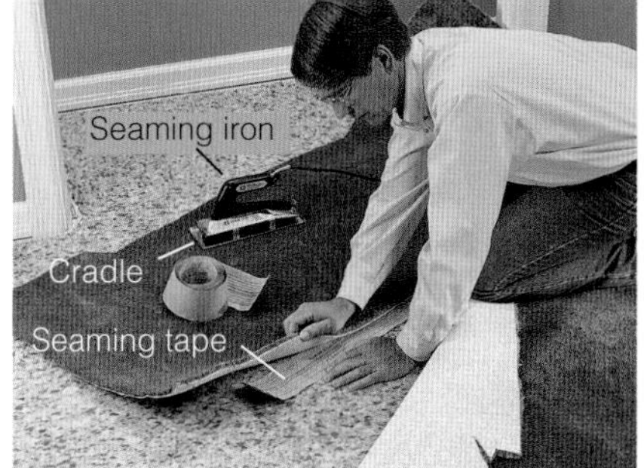

4 Position and center seaming tape under edges to be joined. Pieces are temporarily removed from closet for easier seaming.

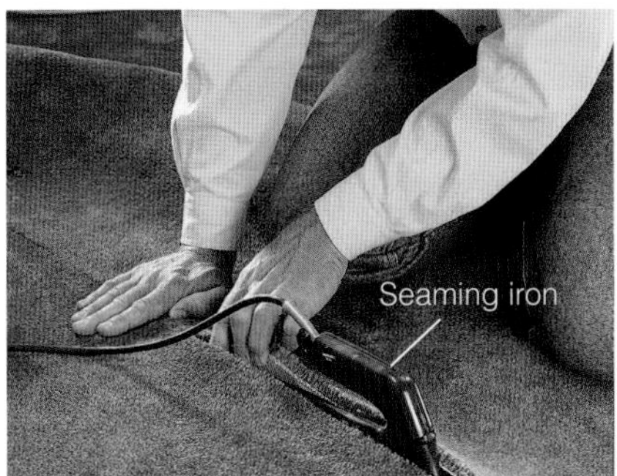

5 Melt edges together with seaming iron. While glue is hot, press down backing. Make edges meet exactly without gaps or overlap.

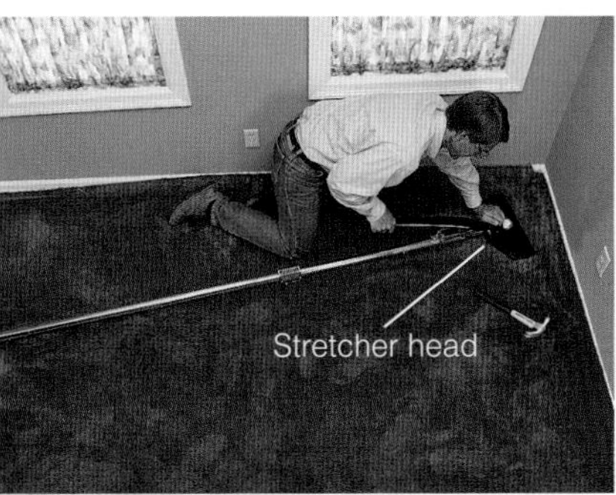

6 Secure carpet to tackless strip on one wall, then power stretch and fasten along opposite wall. Follow same procedure on adjacent walls.

7 Use knee kicker to stretch carpet not stretched by power stretcher head. Use hammer to press carpet onto pins as you stretch.

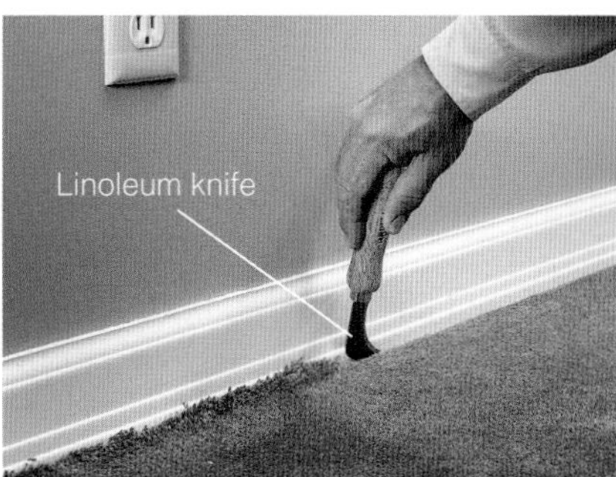

8 Trim excess carpet with trimming tool. Tuck carpet into gap behind tackless strip using dull edge of linoleum knife.

Installing Stair Carpeting

Carpeting Stairs

A staircase can be covered with a runner or fitted with carpet (best laid by a professional if a balustrade is involved). Buy durable carpet and padding. Because a staircase bears heavy traffic, the carpet will wear quickly—especially at the tread's nosing. Before laying the carpet, clear the staircase of old tacks and nails and remove any molding. Paint or refinish exposed wood, if needed. Mark each tread with a pencil for carpet and pad placement. To decrease wear, lay the carpet with the pile facing toward the bottom step. If you use carpet that has unfinished sides, score the backing with an awl 1-1/4 in. (3 cm) from each edge; fold the carpet under. Cut padding for each step 2-1/2 in. (6 cm) narrower than the step width to allow this tuck-under along the edges. Also, cut the pad long enough to cover the tread and wrap around its nosing.

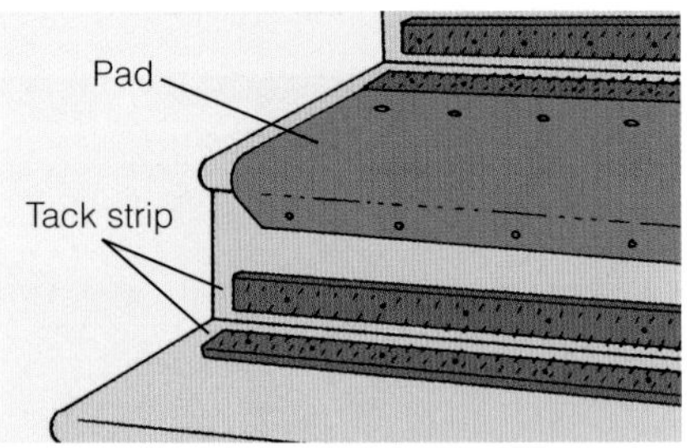

1 Butt padding against tack strip on tread. Staple padding to tread every 4 in. (10 cm) along top and bottom edges. Repeat procedures on all steps, but don't pad the risers.

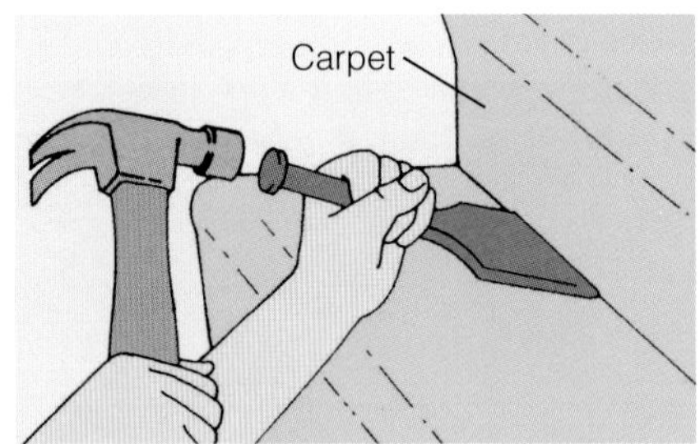

2 Press carpet backing into angle and onto riser strips, using a stair tool and hammer. At top riser, fold end under at the nosing; tack every 4 in. (10 cm). Wear safety goggles while working.

Making Carpeting Repairs

Repairing Seams

1 Pull edges back together and, if possible, hold carpet in place with nails a short distance from each edge.

2 Sew edges together using a curved upholstery needle and fishing line. Needle-nose pliers help punch the needle through.

Repairing Snags

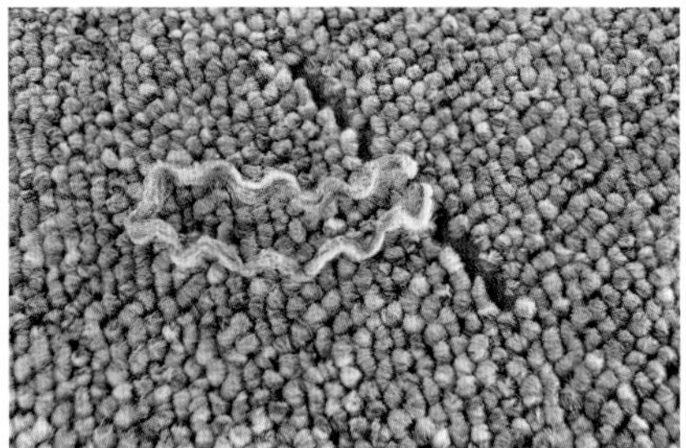

1 Cut away loose yarn and save it. Mask off repair area with tape. Squeeze heavy bead of carpet seam sealer into run.

2 Use a nail set to press each "scab" of the saved yarn's dried glue into the carpet's backing and seam sealer until a loop is reestablished.

Carpet Stain Removal Guide

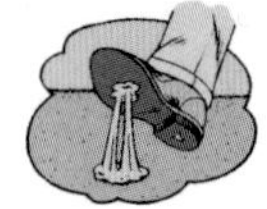

Chewing gum. Freeze with ice cubes. Scrape with butter knife. Let dry. Blot with dry-cleaning fluid.

Grease, oil, lipstick. Blot with paper towel. Sponge with dry-cleaning fluid. Work from edges to center.

Animal urine. Immediately blot up. Soak with carbonated water and blot again. Scrub with carpet shampoo.

Juices and sodas. Mix 1 teaspoon powdered laundry detergent, 1 teaspoon white vinegar and 1 quart (1 l) warm water. Sponge stain.

Shoe polish, ink, dry paint. Dab with paint remover or dry-cleaning fluid.

Coffee, beer, milk. Blot excess. Scrub with diluted carpet shampoo. Cover with paper towels and weigh down.

Repairing Burns

Snip tips of burned carpet threads with sharp scissors. Feather out area around damage.

Installing Glue-Down Carpeting

Laying cushion-backed carpet is simpler than laying standard carpet. The attached backing eliminates the need to install separate padding. The carpeting comes in many styles, such as berber and cut pile, and in a wide range of colors.

The carpet is laid down with an all-purpose white latex adhesive or with double-faced carpet tape. The adhesive is hard to remove, but it holds the carpet in place better, reducing wear. Double-faced carpet tape (below) is easier to remove, but it won't hold the carpet in place as securely.

To lay the carpet, you'll need a linoleum knife, straightedge, hammer and carpet knife. For the adhesive method, add a notched trowel. For seams, buy a seam adhesive recommended by the carpet dealer; spread it along the primary backing (the center layer between the pile and the padding) at the seam edges. To estimate how much carpet is required, see p. 254.

Before laying the carpet, remove any existing base-shoe molding; vacuum and wash the floor. Fill in any holes or cracks; secure loose boards or tiles. If the flooring is concrete, make sure it is dry; damp concrete will decay some carpet backings. Replace the base-shoe molding after you've laid the carpet.

Double-Faced Tape Method

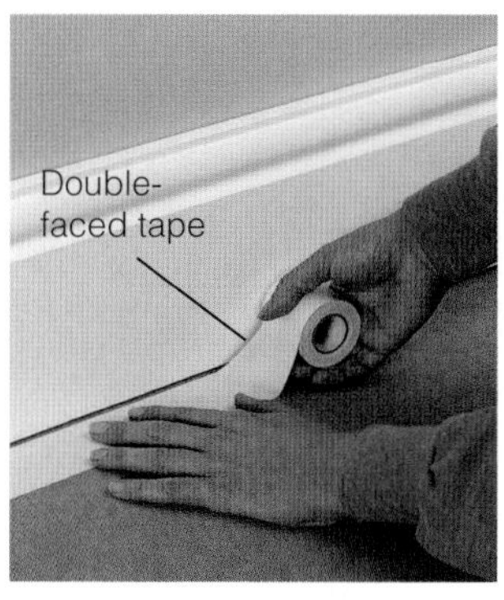

Set 2 in. (5 cm) tape around room's edges; leave top paper in place. In heavy-traffic areas, set tape 1 ft. (30 cm) apart diagonally across room. Rough-fit carpet; fold it back. Remove paper from tape; press carpet down and trim. To make a seam, set double-wide tape halfway under carpet; coat carpet edges with adhesive. Join pieces.

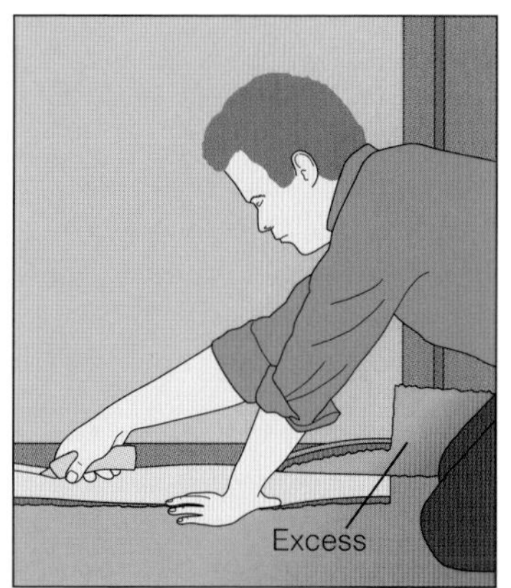

1 Rough-fit carpet, leaving 3 in. (8 cm) excess on all sides. For a seam, snap chalk line on floor. Trim seam edges using straightedge. Spread 3 ft. (1 m) band of adhesive on each side of chalk line. Set one carpet piece in place and spread seam adhesive along its edge. Butt second piece against the first.

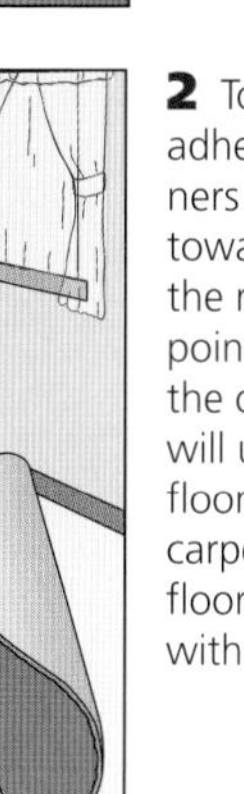

2 To expose floor for adhesive, fold two corners of carpet back toward the middle of the room; then fold point of carpet toward the opposite end. This will uncover half of the floor. After first half of carpet is adhered to floor, you'll repeat step with second half.

3 Spread a layer of all-purpose latex adhesive evenly over exposed half of floor, using a notched trowel. Then let adhesive set until tacky, about 10 to 15 minutes, before continuing with next step.

4 Unfold carpet in reverse order it was folded. Lay each section gradually to avoid bumps. Working from center out, smooth bumps by shuffling your feet along carpet as it is laid. Repeat steps 2, 3 and 4 until all sections are adhered to the floor.

5 To remove air bubbles, push on carpet with a piece of 2x4 held at a 45° angle. Move from one end of room to the other. If carpet has a seam, start on one side of seam and work away from it toward wall. Then work on other side.

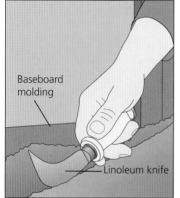

Baseboard molding

Linoleum knife

6 Finish edges at walls, first creasing carpet with back edge of a linoleum knife. Then cut off excess with carpet knife. Carpet should be flush with wall. At a doorway, finish with metal threshold bar. Replace base-shoe molding.

Window Treatments / Mini-blinds

Mini-blinds give you variable amounts of light and privacy, letting you see out the window yet blocking direct sunlight. Mini-blinds' disadvantages are they tend to accumulate dust, won't block all the light and may not fit your room's style.

Stock mini-blinds come in various widths and lengths in a limited choice of colors. Usually limited to vinyl and aluminum, some can be custom cut to width at the store for an inside mount.

Custom mini-blinds are the solution for large or odd-size windows. Generally of higher quality, they come in a wide range of colors and materials.

Micro-blinds have very narrow slats, are often custom ordered and work well for narrow sidelights.

Wood mini-blinds have slats made of stained, clear finish or painted wood. The wood gives these blinds a warmer, more traditional look with all the practical advantages of mini-blinds.

1 Attach side brackets toward the jamb's front edge to avoid interference from window hardware. Predrill frame before driving screws.

2 Snap head rail of mini-blind into brackets. Decorative valance strips, supplied with the blind, attach to the front of the head rail.

Perfect Brackets

To show screw locations without marking your trim, first mark bracket screw holes on a piece of tape and stick the tape to the bracket location. Use an awl to mark the hole's center and guide the drill bit; then predrill for the screws.

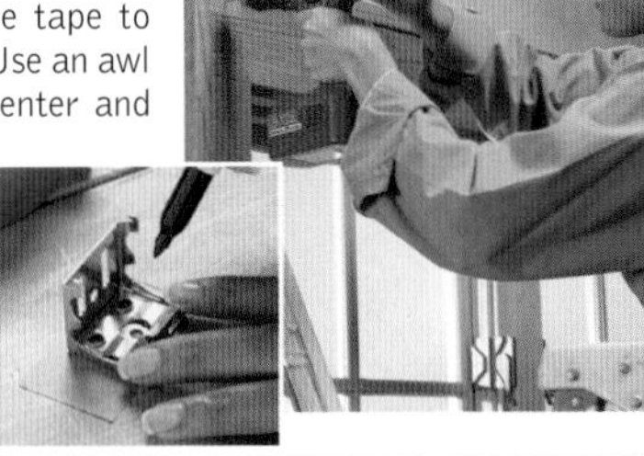

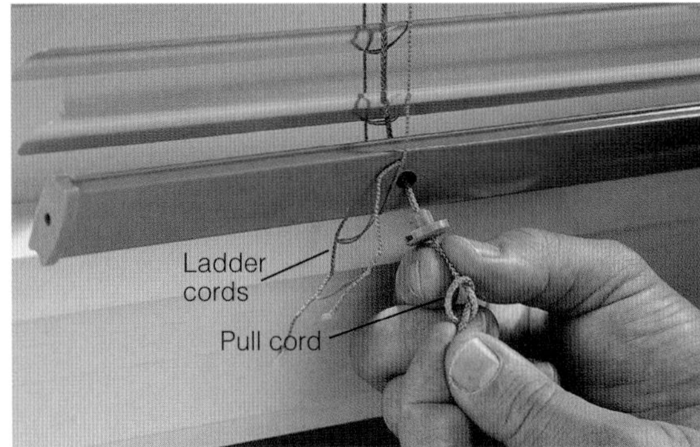

3 Adjust length by cutting ladder cords and pull cord 3 in. (8 cm) below sill. Slide out slats and bottom rail, then reattach bottom rail.

Shortening Blinds

If you buy stock mini blinds, you'll likely have to shorten the blinds to fit your window. To shorten the blinds, you'll have to shorten the ladder cords that hold the slats in position, remove the excess slats and reinstall the bottom rail.

Caution: Install a cleat to wrap dangling cords around so they are out of the reach of small children.

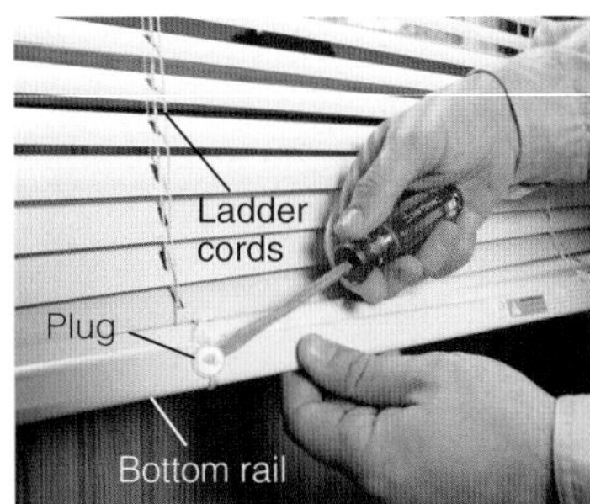

1 Pry plug out of the bottom rail. Cut the ladder cords just above the bottom rail to free it. If pull cord is threaded through the plug, cut close to it.

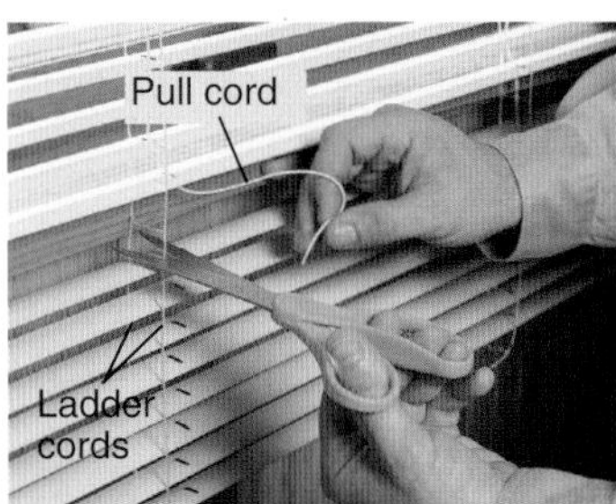

2 Extract the pull cord from the center of ladder cords. Hold the pull cord away and cut both ladder cords about 3 in. (8 cm) longer than final length.

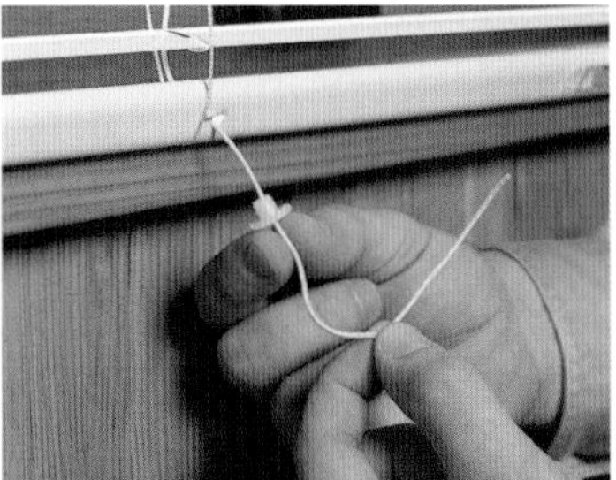

3 Slide the bottom rail back between ladder cords. String pull cord through the bottom rail and knot cord end. Tuck loose cord ends into holes before replacing plugs.

Window Treatments / Roller and Pulley Shades

Building Balloon Shades

Select your own fabric to make a balloon shade. Balloon shades are hung from a mounting board and lifted and lowered by hidden rings and cords. To begin, line the fabric and seam the sides. At the fabric's bottom edge, stitch in a rod casing. Sew rows of rings 12 in. (30 cm) apart along the shade's length and width. Staple the shade to the mounting board and feed cords into the rings. Knot each cord to a bottom ring. Knotting intermediate rings allows the shade to "balloon" out. Slide the rod into its casing and attach screw eyes to the mounting board. Attach the mounting board. Thread the cords through the screw eyes and rings as shown and wrap the pull cord around a cleat for safety.

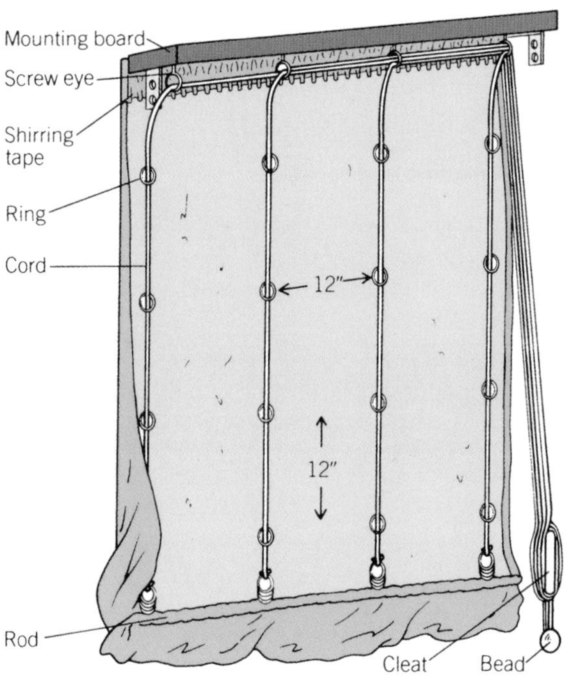

Repairing Pulley Shades

A pulley shade uses a single cord to roll up in a cylinder shape from the bottom. Some feature a headbox and a cord lock. To install a new cord, unroll the shade and remove the old cord. Knot one end of the new cord to a top support. Bring the cord down behind the shade, underneath it and up its front. Feed the cord through the first pulley, then across the shade and over the other pulley. Leave sufficient cord to form a long loop for the pull cord. Bring the cord back over the pulley, down the front and up the back. Tie it to the support. Feed the loop through the equalizing buckle and adjust it so the shade rolls evenly.

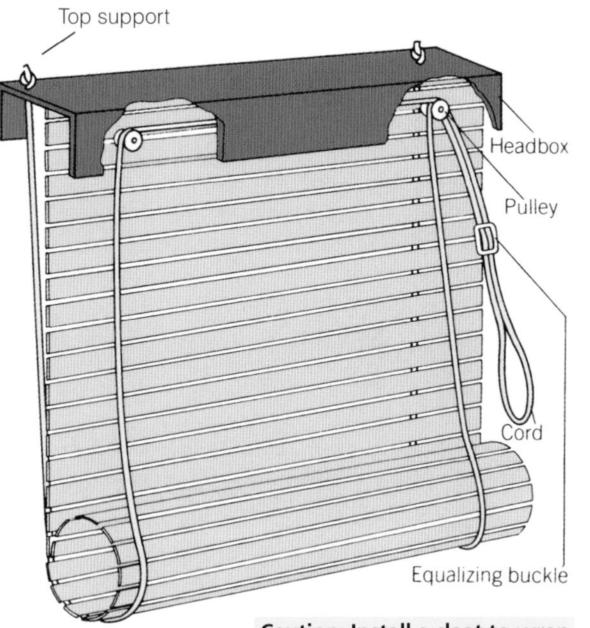

Caution: Install a cleat to wrap dangling cords around so they are out of the reach of small children.

Adjusting Roller Shade Tension

Roller shades are used to insulate, block light and provide privacy. They're sold by the width, measured between the tips of the spear bracket and the pin. The roller is hollowed to house a long spring controlled by a ratchet. The shade is held in position by a pawl that latches into the ratchet tooth. When you lower the shade, the pawl is freed. The more you lower the shade, the more spring tension increases. If the shade doesn't roll up fully, increase spring tension by pulling the shade down halfway. Then take the roller off its brackets and reroll the shade by hand. If the shade winds up too rapidly, release tension by taking down the roller and partially unrolling the shade. If the ratchet fails to hold the shade in place, lightly oil the pawl with machine oil.

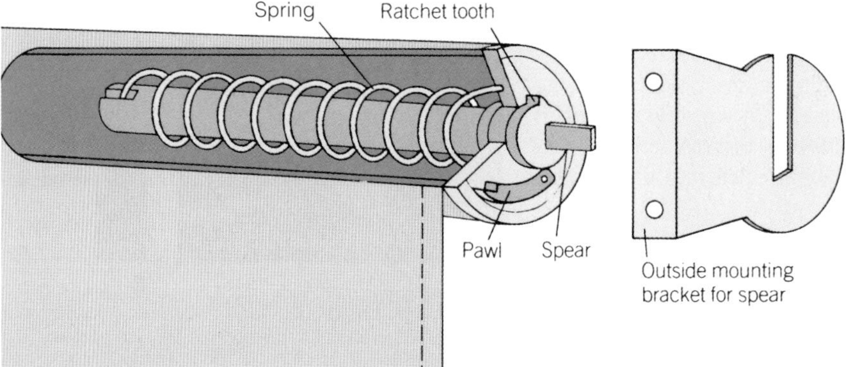

Window Treatments / Traverse Rods

Traverse rods operate draperies and vertical blinds. They may part the window covering at the center, called a two-way draw, or pull it to one side, called a one-way draw. A two-way draw uses two slides: an underlap master and an overlap master. A two-way draw can be converted to a one-way by eliminating the underlap master slide and attaching both cord ends to a single master slide. If a cord breaks or pulls loose, restring it as diagrammed at right. Because a traverse rod telescopes, you can usually adjust its length for a more custom fit. Add intermediate supports for rods that are more than 4 ft. (1.3 m) long.

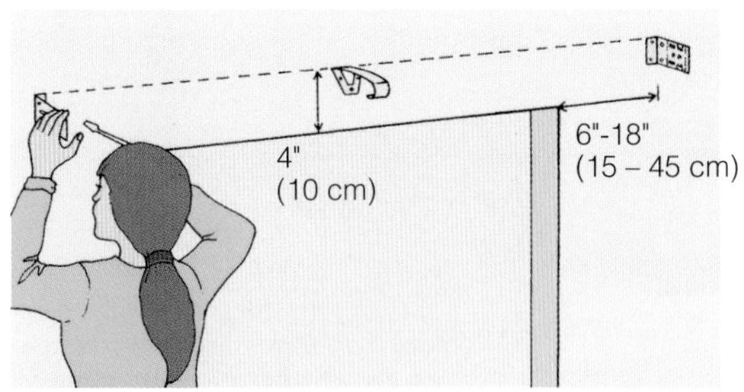

Mount a traverse rod with brackets 4 in. (10 cm) above the window or door and 6 to 18 in. (15 to 45 cm) past each side. If possible, mount brackets into a stud or header.

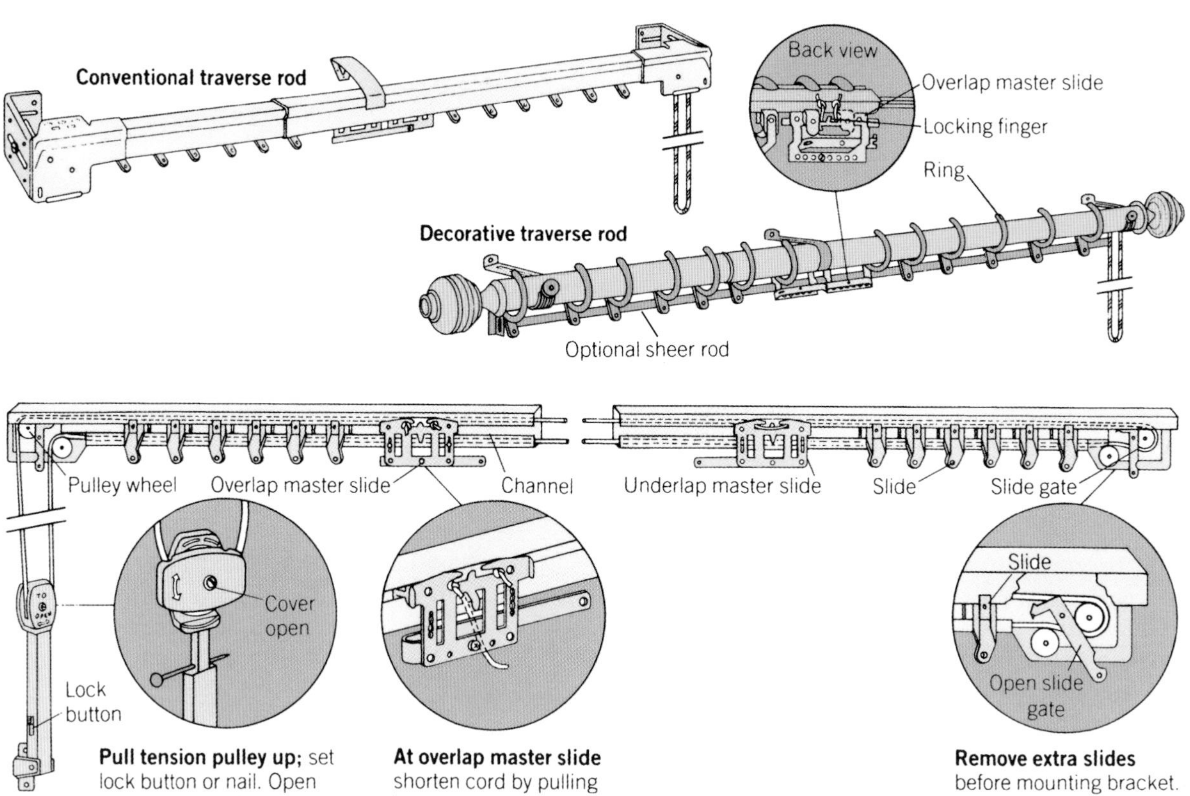

Pull tension pulley up; set lock button or nail. Open cover; slip cord in. Knot cord; reset pulley.

At overlap master slide shorten cord by pulling knot nearest pulley. When cord is taut, reknot it.

Remove extra slides before mounting bracket. Push slide gate open; slip slides out.

Building a Cornice

Using off-the-shelf trim and a miter saw, anyone can create a beautiful window cornice to hide ugly drapery rods and add a touch of custom detailing. If you prefer painted cornices, poplar and aspen work well. For finished hardwood, you may have to special order the moldings.

1 Build a basic three-sided box wide enough to surround the rod brackets. Glue and nail three pieces together.

2 Cut the top board to fit and glue and nail to box frame. Sand box so it's ready for finishing before you install moldings.

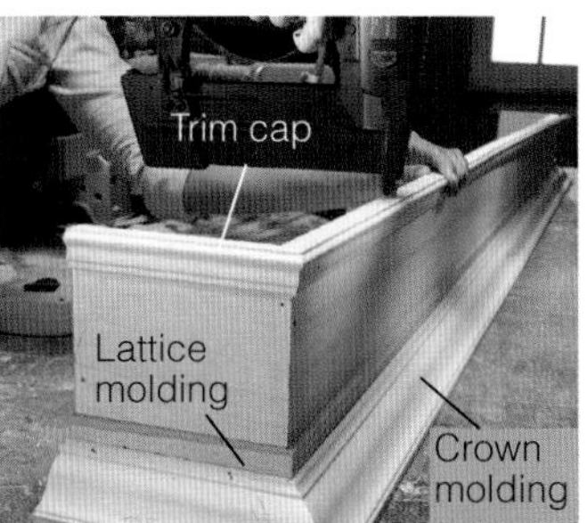

3 Cut, fit, glue and nail on moldings. Install lattice molding first so the crown molding's bottom will butt up to lattice.

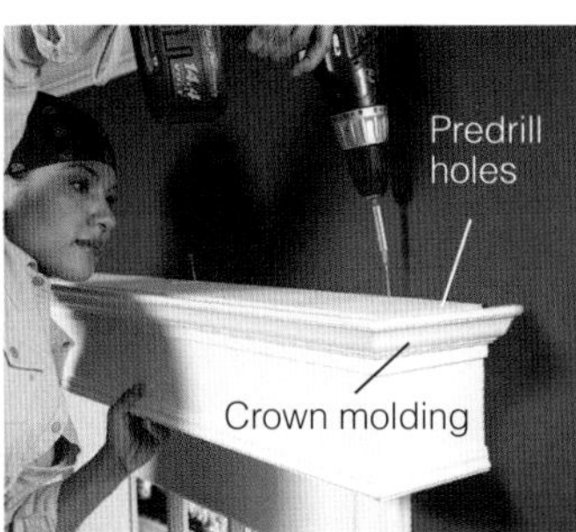

4 Prefinish cornice and install 1x2 ledger boards on wall between rod brackets. Attach cornice to ledger boards.

Window Treatments / Vertical Blinds

Drawn across windows like traverse draperies, vertical blinds look like venetian blinds set on end, but instead of horizontal slats, they have vertical vanes. The vanes rotate 180 degrees to give maximum control of light and privacy. They draw apart at the center, or to the left or right. The vanes, usually about 4 in. (10 cm) wide, may be opaque or translucent and are made of fabric, aluminum or vinyl.

The blinds most often mount outside the frame but can mount inside or even attach to the ceiling. From above, mounting brackets hold the headrail, which houses the track. Carriers, which slide along the track when a cord is pulled, support the vanes with hangers. Some vanes are held straight at the bottom by weights.

To hang vertical blinds with the inside-mount technique, the window recess must be at least 4-1/2 in. (11 cm) deep, as you might find with windows set in a 2x6 wall. Otherwise, the vanes and the headrail will protrude beyond the frame. For an outside-mount approach, mount the brackets on the wall above the trim. Be sure to order vanes long enough to compensate for the higher mounting. You may want to order blinds wide enough that when you pull the vanes to the side, the window or door and its trim remain fully visible.

Vertical Blind Anatomy

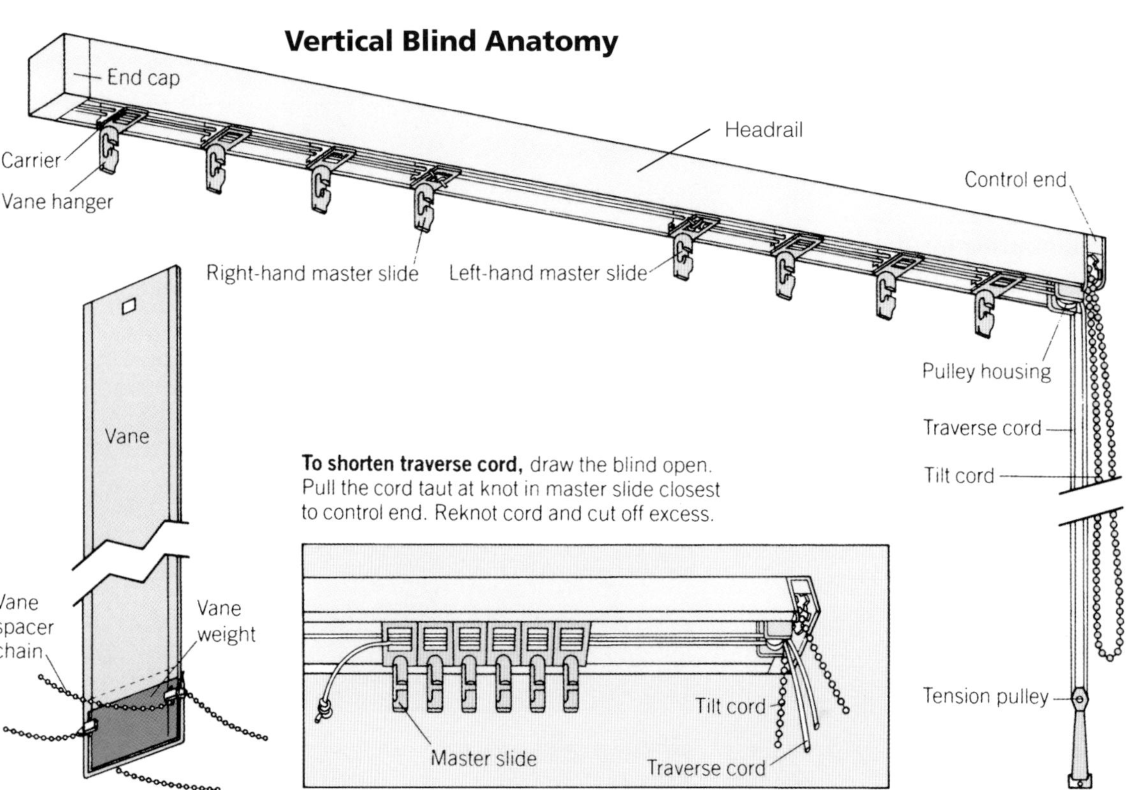

To shorten traverse cord, draw the blind open. Pull the cord taut at knot in master slide closest to control end. Reknot cord and cut off excess.

Installing Fabric Vanes

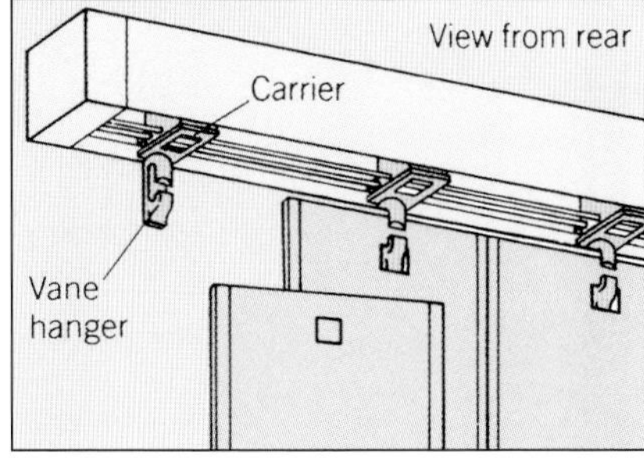

1 With front of vane facing out, slide vane hanger onto carrier and twist hanger and vane until properly positioned.

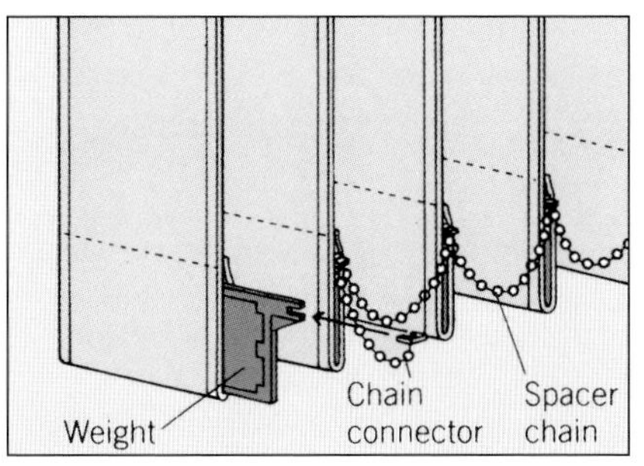

2 Slip a weight into each vane pocket. If present, clip the spacer chain between weights. Operate blinds to test their spacing.

Installing Vinyl or Aluminum Vanes

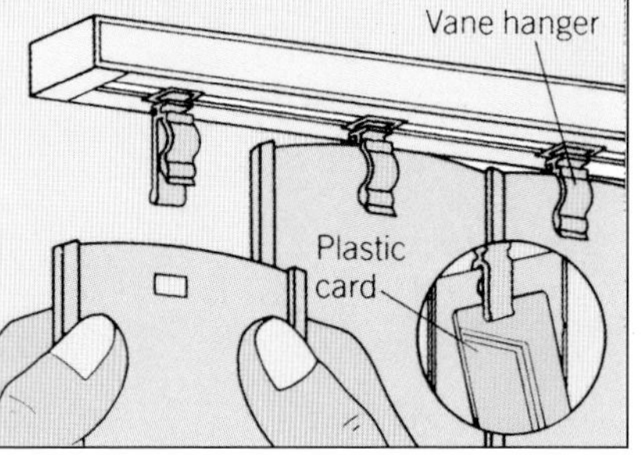

1 Turn vane hangers so short leg faces out. Push vane into hanger until it snaps in place. To free a vane, use plastic card to open hanger.

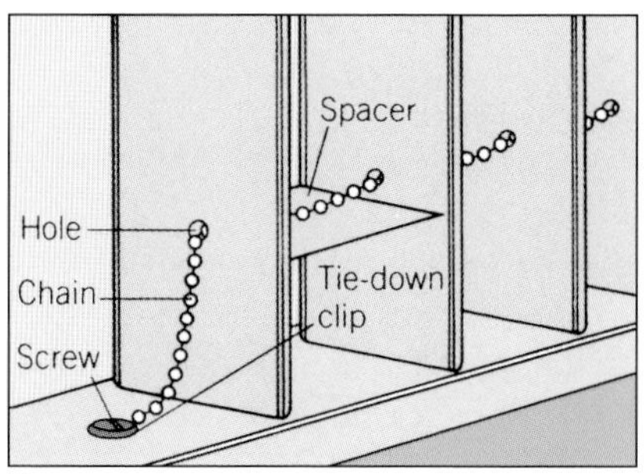

2 If necessary, thread chain through bottom holes on vanes. Use a spacer to determine chain length. Attach chain to tie-down clip.

Warmer Windows

The surest cure for old drafty windows is to replace them with new well-insulated, tightly sealed units; it's also very expensive and labor-intensive.

This page shows three relatively inexpensive options for warming up your existing windows.

The interior insulating window shown at right can be made from Plexiglas, available at hardware stores, and edging materials (magnetic or Velcro) are available online (search "interior storm windows").

Heat-shrink film, available at hardware stores and home centers, can be installed easily and economically using little more than a scissors and hair dryer.

Quilted shades, while requiring more skill to create, will provide privacy as well as warmth.

Interior Insulating Window

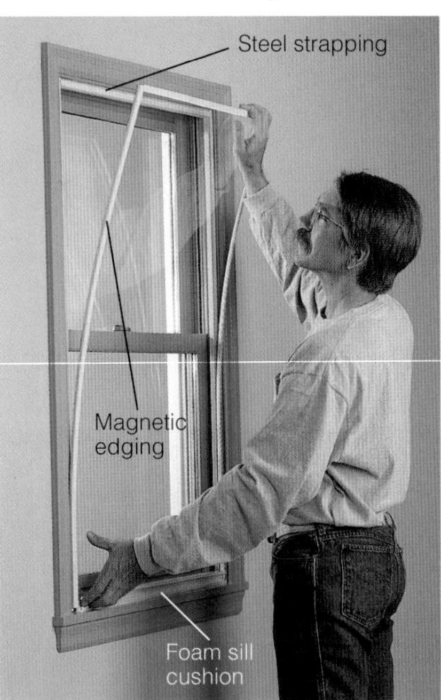

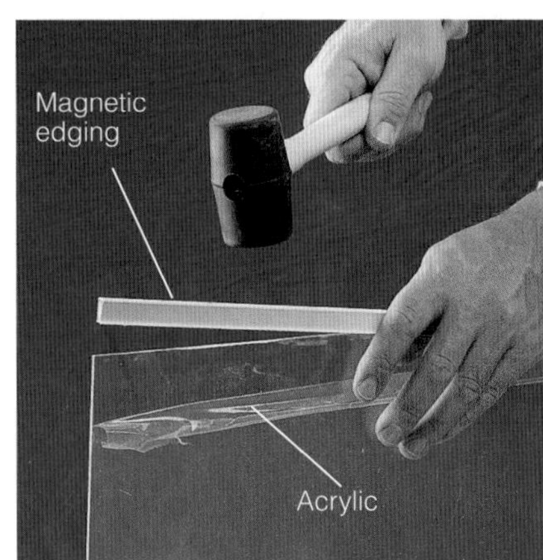

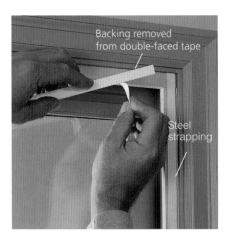

1 Apply steel strapping to the window frame using double-faced tape. For many windows a thin wood parting strip must be installed first.

2 Cut the Plexiglas to size, then install the friction-fit magnetic edging. Install the special foam sill cushion (see top photo), then pop the window in place.

Heat-Shrink Film

1 Clean window trim with denatured alcohol. Leaving paper on one side, apply the double-faced tape to outside edges of trim as shown.

2 Cut film 2 in. (5 cm) larger than taped area. Remove paper from the tape on top trim and position film on top. Uncover remaining tape, stretch film flat and press it into place.

3 Set hair dryer on high, hold it slightly away from film and move it slowly back and forth across window. Film will begin to shrink, removing all wrinkles. Carefully cut off excess film with utility knife or scissors. Avoid marring trim or wall with knife.

Quilted Shades

Quilted shades, basically sandwiches of fabric, curtain lining, fiberfill and other materials, can help hold heat in and keep light out. But they're not without their problems.

First, they block heat but not moisture. This allows ice to build up on windows, which can lead to premature failure.

Second, in extreme cold, if shades are opened quickly, thermal shock can literally shatter a window.

Make certain to weigh the pros and cons and alternatives before installing quilted shades.

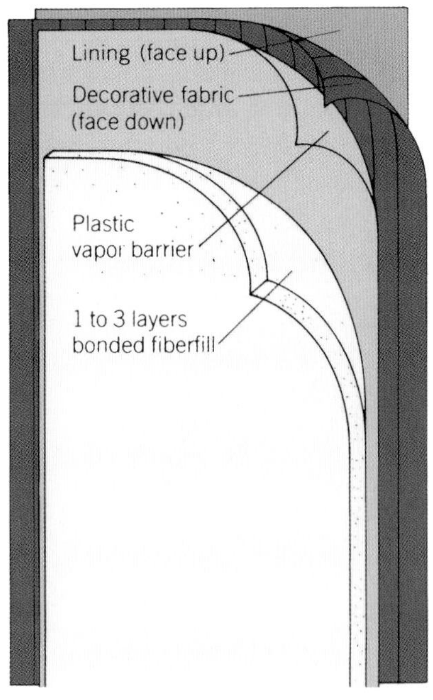

Kitchens / Planning and Layout

The kitchen is the most complex, expensive room in your house, and making major changes to it takes major time and planning. To get through the challenge, you need a strategy. Begin by shooting for everything you really want, assuming from the beginning that you may have to scale down your plans.

Start an idea file. Clip pictures of kitchens you love from magazines and brochures and collect material samples. Look at other kitchens by attending open houses or getting nosy with neighbors who have recently remodeled. Most neighbors love showing off a new kitchen and neighborhood homes will often share many of your home's attributes and problems.

Concentrate on big decisions first, like whether walls should come down or windows and doors should be moved. Look at your kitchen, and even adjacent living areas, as though they were empty spaces. Draw a floor plan that includes only existing walls, windows, doorways and staircases. Make copies of this basic drawing and begin experimenting with ideas, keeping in mind the standard spacing and measurements for kitchen areas.

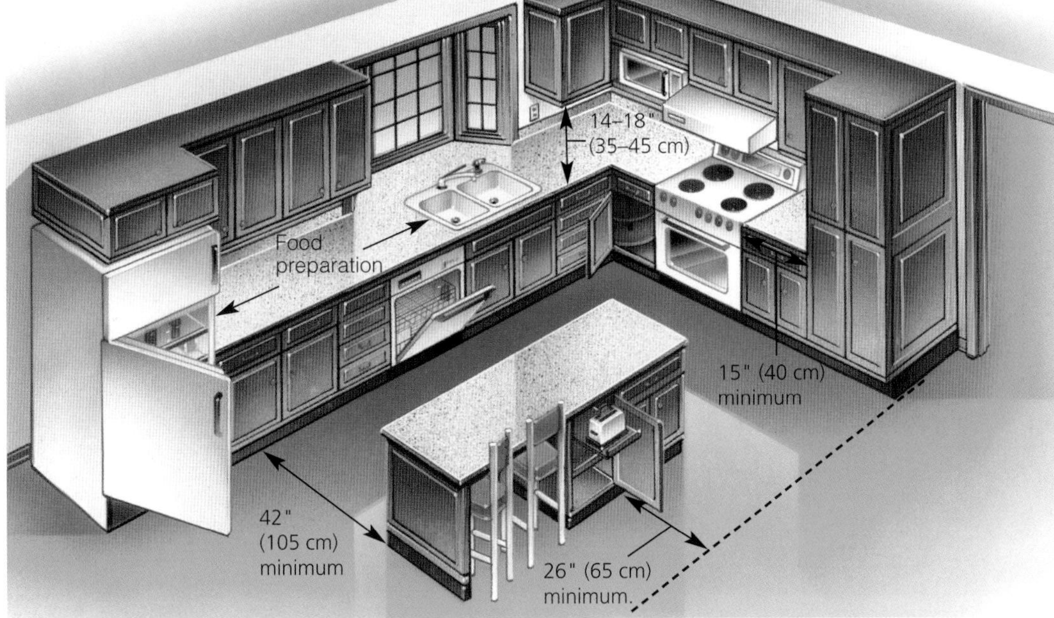

Standard spacing and measurements. The above measurements are suggestions for proper spacing of appliances and adequate counter space, and for allowing comfortable movement. Also, keep these rules in mind as you plan:

- For sit-down counter space, allow at least 2 ft. (60 cm) of counter length per seat.
- Don't place the range any more than three steps away from the kitchen sink.
- Provide at least 6 sq. ft. (.5 sq. m) of counter between sink and stove.
- The work triangle, formed by stove, sink and refrigerator, shouldn't exceed 22 ft. (7 m) in length or be smaller than 12 ft. (3.6 m).
- Place counters on both sides of a range and allow at least 15 in. (38 cm) between a range and a doorway.
- Keep dishwasher near enough to sink to reach without taking any steps.

Kitchen Design Blunders

To avoid experiencing deep regret about your design decisions, here's a list of common blunders and how to avoid them:

Poor corner planning. Base cabinets on inside corners occupy a lot of space while offering little front access. To use the space well, order cabinets with glide-out shelves, L-shaped doors or lazy Susans.

Designing with trendy colors. Kitchen cabinets, countertops, appliances and flooring are meant to last, so avoid the latest trend and choose colors and styles you can live with for a long time. Add pizzazz with paint and accessories.

Colliding doors. Sketch the position of opened appliance and cabinet doors and drawers onto your floor plan. Pay special attention to drawers and doors across from each other, close to inside corners or next to protruding door trim.

Relying on one light fixture. To avoid shadows and badly lit countertops from a single ceiling fixture, plan additional task lighting, spot lighting for islands and sinks and undercabinet lighting for counters.

Designing as you go. Complete a detailed plan before you lift a hammer. Nothing piles up expenses or problems faster than changing plans along the way.

Kitchens / Installing Cabinets

Clamps 34
Jigsaws 54
Countersinking Screws 79
Replacing a Faucet 101
Laminate Countertops 266
Cabinets and Boxes 446

There was a time when getting quality cabinets meant having them custom made. Today, most home centers and specialty stores offer several cabinet lines with quality that rivals that of custom cabinetry. The huge variety of styles, sizes, options and accessories let you achieve a custom-made look for less. Even better, most cabinet retailers provide free computerized layout and design assistance that helps you experiment with and visualize your dream kitchen before you lift a hammer.

As you shop, think carefully about the options. Slide-out shelving and full-extension drawer slides dramatically improve base cabinet and drawer accessibility. Base cabinets can be composed of door-drawer combinations or entirely of drawers. Consider cabinet door swings and how they affect function and hardware location. Full-height pantry cabinets accommodate a variety of swing-out doors that greatly expand storage capacity.

Most cabinet widths change in increments of 3 in., allowing you to fully utilize wall space. Narrow filler strips can be used to fill spaces between two cabinets or between cabinet and wall.

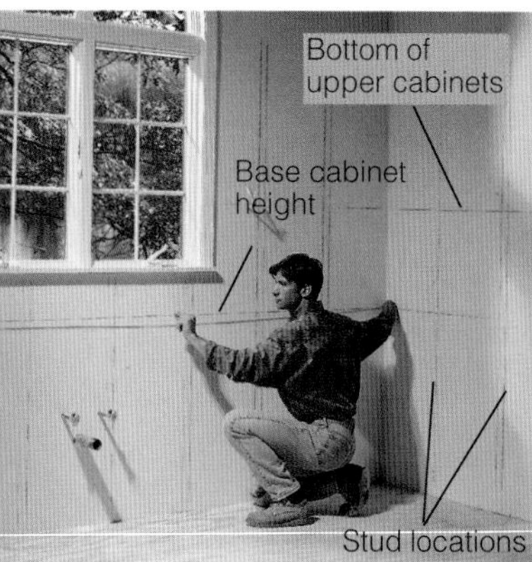

1 Snap two level chalk lines to mark the top of the base cabinets and the bottom of the upper cabinets. Measure up from the high spot in the floor. These measurements allow for standard counter thickness.

2 Clamp together corner base cabinet and adjacent base cabinets. Line up cabinet face frames at top and bottom; then push assembled unit into corner. Realign face frames, if necessary.

3 Level the clamped-together three-unit cabinet using shims. Make sure cabinets are level in all directions and that top edges of cabinet backs are on the chalk line. You may need to shim behind some cabinets to align across face frames.

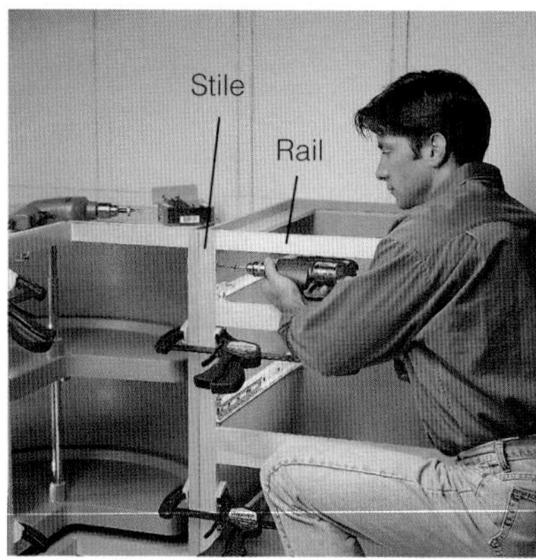

4 Screw leveled cabinets together near top, bottom and midpoint of face frame stiles with 2-1/4-in. screws. Predrill holes with countersink bit. Lubricate screws for easier installation by pulling the threaded part across bar soap.

5 Cut out back of sink base cabinet for sink plumbing with jigsaw or rotary tool. Drill holes in cabinet bottom for supply lines that come up through floor.

6 Secure assembled and level base cabinets to wall studs with 2-1/2-in. screws through the nailing cleat on top of cabinet back. Predrill holes through cleat to avoid splitting.

7 Allow required appliance openings for dishwashers and ovens between face frames. Make sure cabinet tops are level across the span. Screw 1x2 cleats to wall, even with chalk line, to support counters in open areas between base cabinets.

8 Preassemble banks of upper cabinets before installation. Use clamps to pull cabinets tightly together.

Neater Installation

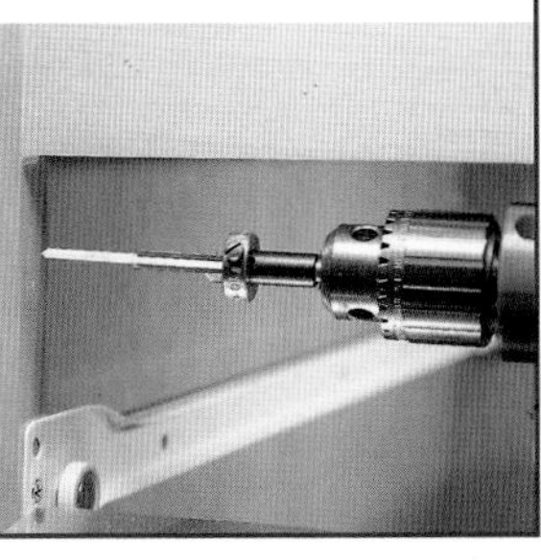

Countersink bits. To join the cabinets' face frames, you can use a three-stage drill bit to predrill holes for screws. The drill cuts the pilot hole, the clearance hole and the countersink. Your cabinet-to-cabinet joints will be tighter and the screwheads will disappear.

9 Where necessary, install temporary support cleats. Position upper cabinets. Predrill top and bottom nailing cleats and screw cabinets to wall studs.

10 After aligning them carefully, glue and clamp decorative end panels in place. Thicker decorative panels need screws (from inside the cabinet) for support.

11 Reattach cabinet doors and adjust hinges. Quality hinges will allow door adjustment in at least two directions; up and down, and left to right. Most can also be adjusted in and out.

Frameless or Face Frame?

The differences between frameless (Euro-style) cabinets and traditional face-frame cabinets go beyond appearance. Here's what you need to know:

Frameless Cabinets

- Essentially are boxes with front edges that are completely covered by doors and drawer faces, making the panels look continuous.
- Have a modern, clean-line appearance.
- Are a bit tougher to install because there is little margin for hiding errors and making adjustments. Plus they can be considerably heavier than face-frame cabinets.
- Are joined to one another through their side panels.
- Generally cost more than a comparable face-frame cabinet.

Face-Frame Cabinets

- Have a hardwood frame attached to the cabinet box that creates a lip on the sides. Door styles are either full overlay (some face frame shows) or partial overlay (more face frame shows).
- Tend to look more traditional.
- Have spaces between doors and drawers that make small deviations less noticeable.
- Are joined through their hardwood face frames.

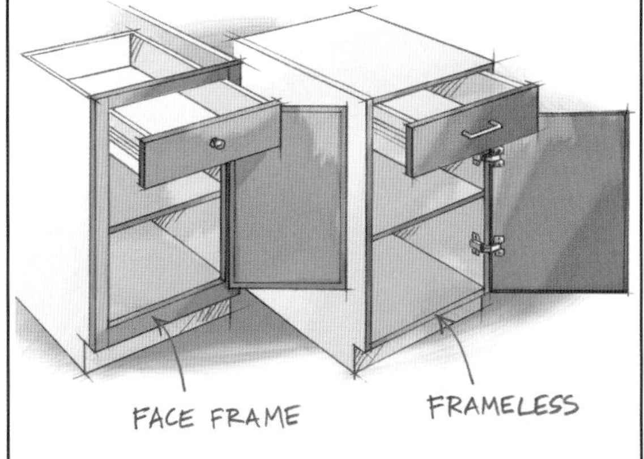

Installing Laminate Countertops

Scribing 42
Jigsaws 54
Belt Sanders 68
Solid-Surface Materials 478

It's no accident that plastic laminate countertops have adorned kitchen cabinets for more than half a century. Plastic laminate is a tough, affordable material that, when applied to particleboard, medium-density fiberboard (MDF) or plywood underlayment, is ideal for kitchens and other wet areas.

You can order custom-made counters from many retailers. You'll be able to choose from various nosing styles, built-in backsplashes and a tremendous selection of colors. Skip the matching backsplash if you're planning a tile backsplash. Use sample chips to test the durability of colors you like. Attack the samples with sandpaper and a knife to see how easily they scratch.

1 Screw build-up strips to your cabinet tops at the ends, over joints and at least every 18 in. (45 cm). You can skip buildup if you have a sufficient amount of face frame exposed above the drawer face's top edge.

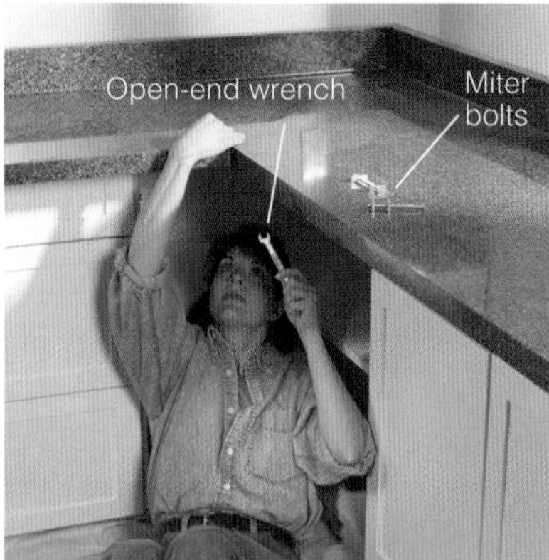

2 Temporarily bolt together mitered corner pieces from below with miter bolts and an open-end wrench. Make sure miter is flush on top as you tighten. With bolts tight, slide counter into corner and check its fit along the wall.

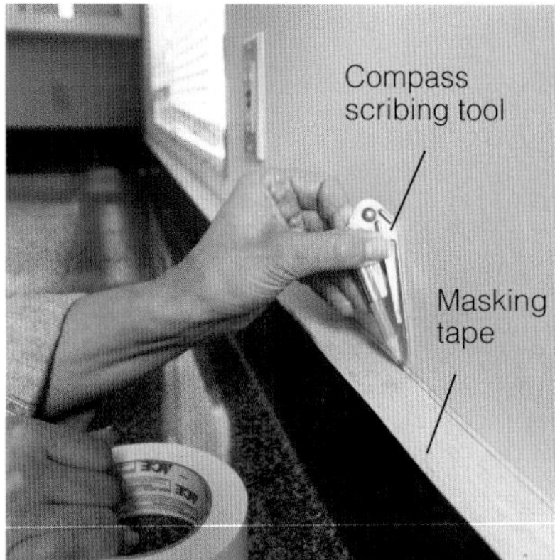

3 Open compass scribing tool to the width of the widest gap between counter and wall. Scribe entire length of each countertop on each wall. Carefully pull out counters and trim to your scribe line using a belt sander with 80-grit paper.

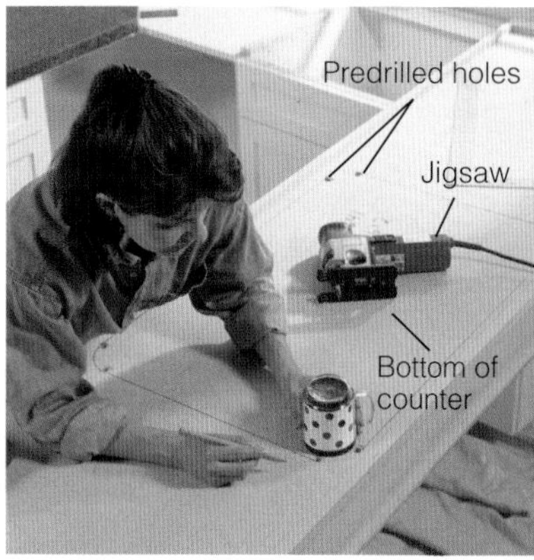

4 Following your new sink's instructions, mark sink cutout on top of counter. From above, drill holes to mark corners. Flip counter, mark cutout and cut hole. To avoid damaging laminate, support cutout until cut is complete.

5 Trim end of countertop, if necessary. First, apply masking tape and mark cutoff line. Cut slightly outside cutoff line and then belt sand to line. Carefully cutting from the back side with a circular saw also works well.

6 Cut and glue end caps for trimmed ends. Use a fine mill file to fine-tune end cap so it conforms to countertop shape. Use half-round file for inside corners.

7 Take apart miter joint. Squeeze a bead of colored silicone onto each mitered edge. Join miters together as before, making sure surfaces are flush as you tighten the bolts.

8 Attach countertop to cabinet sides using L-brackets and short screws. If counters lie flat on the cabinets, you can silicone counters to cabinets.

Selecting Countertops

Maintenance on most countertops is minimal, but fail to do it and costly damage can occur. Preventive daily maintenance includes mopping up spills, using hot pads and working on cutting boards. Long-term maintenance involves caulking, sealing and countertop finish touch up.

Select a countertop you can live with and enjoy for a long time. Texture, cost, glossiness, color, how natural the material looks and feels and how it fits in with your kitchen design and home are all part of the equation. Explore the idea of mixing materials—a laminate top with a tile backsplash, a laminate top with a solid-surface nosing or a granite island top with solid-surface work areas for other countertops.

Material	Repairability	Damaged By	Maintain By	Seams	Cleanability
Laminate	Edge repairs are simple; surface repairs are hard to blend.	Sharp knives, abrasive cleaners, hot pans, water in seams.	Keeping seams sealed.	Seams are visible.	Nonporous surface, very easy to clean and hard to stain.
Granite	Granite is difficult to repair (but rarely needs repairing).	Cutting, severe impact.	Applying quality penetrating sealer annually.	Seams are more or less visible, depending on color and pattern.	Easy to clean, temporarily shows water marks.
Solid-surface	Light damage can be sanded out.	Sharp knives, impact. Hot pans can pop seams and discolor surface.	Resanding and sealing every 5 to 7 years.	Seams are virtually invisible.	Nonporous surface, easy to clean. Subject to some stains.
Wood	Damage can be sanded; wood must be resealed.	Cutting, water seeping into end grain, impact.	Resealing tops with oil-based, or special wood-countertop, finish as needed.	Seams are visible and must be very well sealed.	Can absorb grime and liquids if neglected.
Tile	Individual tiles can be replaced.	Severe impact. Grout is subject to stains.	Keeping grout lines sealed.	Larger tiles mean fewer grout lines.	Grout lines must be sealed frequently to avoid staining.

Repairing Laminate

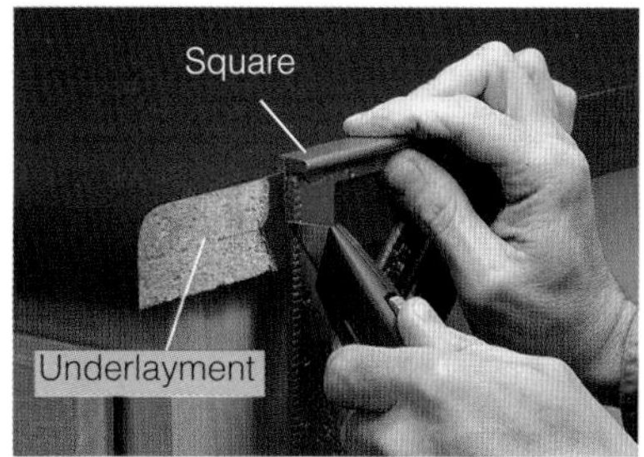

1 Mend a chipped or broken countertop before water increases the damage. First, cut through laminate with a sharp utility knife to create a clean edge.

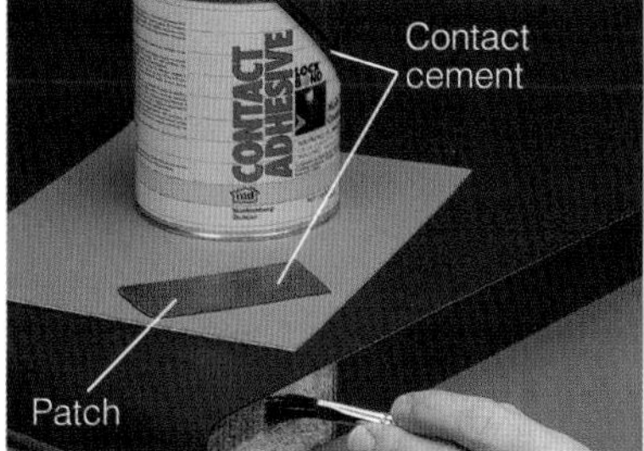

2 Scrape off old adhesive. Apply contact cement to exposed underlayment and patch. With cement dry but slightly tacky, apply the patch.

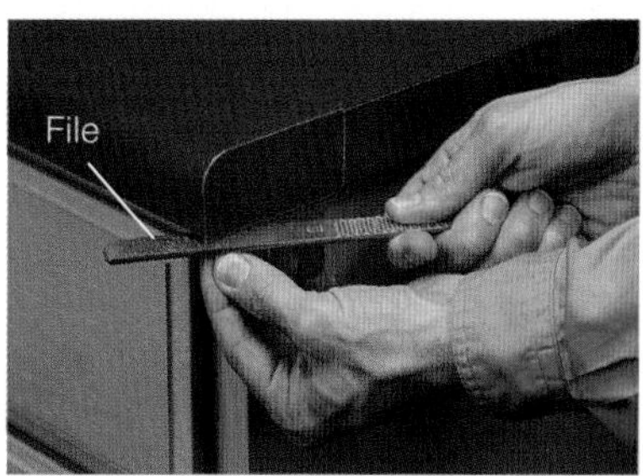

3 File new patch to the contour of the countertop edge. File at a slight angle to avoid scratching the countertop.

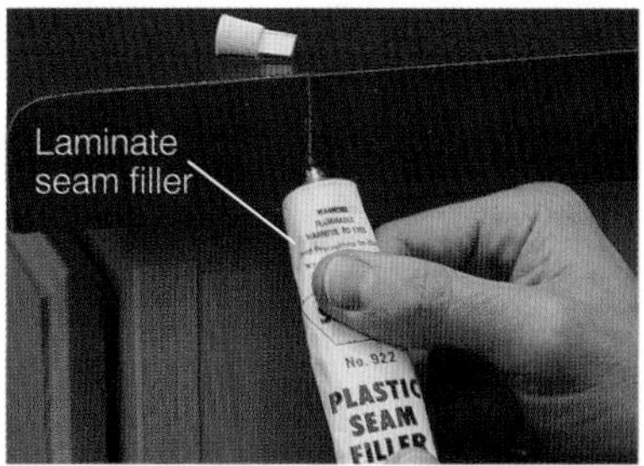

4 Disguise the joint with special laminate seam filler. Seam filler can also be used to fill small dings, dents and seams.

Installing Tile Countertops

Tile Cutting **251**
Grouting **251**
The Right Substrate **253**

Whether you've chosen ceramic, marble or granite tile, the steps for installing a tile countertop remain basically the same. Here we'll focus on granite—one of those natural products that will be as stylish 50 years from now as it is today. Although granite was once only accessible as large slabs affordable to those with equally large budgets, the huge selection of affordable granite tiles now available makes an extraordinary countertop a reachable dream for anyone doing kitchen remodeling.

Although it might seem intimidating to work with stone, it's no more difficult to use than manufactured tiles. You can't score and snap it like ceramic tile, but it cuts easily using any wet saw equipped with a diamond blade. When granite is installed, the biggest problem you're likely to have with it is being able to spot the messes and spills that need cleaning up.

Materials and Tools

To calculate the number of 12 x 12-in. tiles you need, multiply the lineal footage of a standard-width countertop by 2.5 ft. Add as many tiles as you need to cover wider peninsulas or islands and subtract for cooktops, stoves and sinks. Add 10 percent to the total to allow for breakage, miscuts and bad tile. In addition to the tile, you'll need thin-set mortar, grout and color-matching caulk for inside corners, polished-granite sealer, a plywood or MDF base, tile backer underlayment, fiberglass joint tape and tiling tools, including a wet saw.

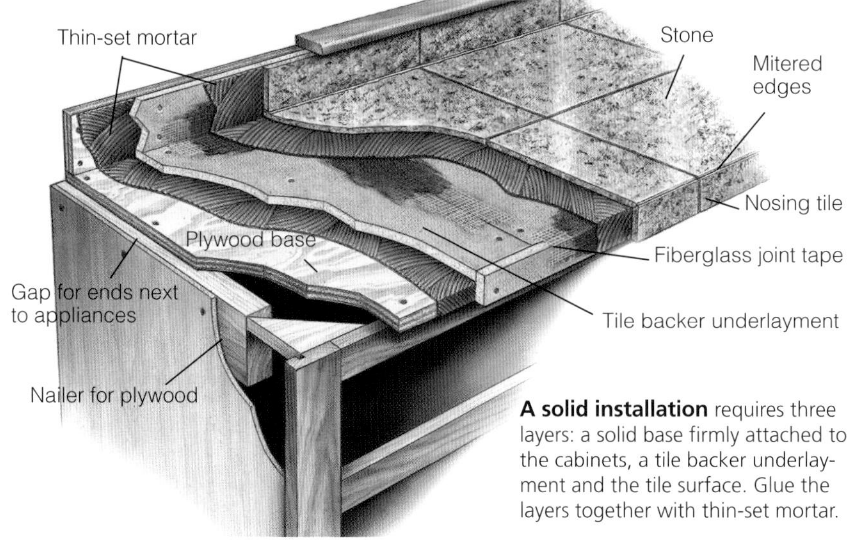

A solid installation requires three layers: a solid base firmly attached to the cabinets, a tile backer underlayment and the tile surface. Glue the layers together with thin-set mortar.

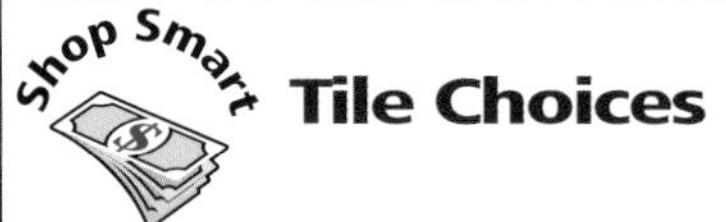

Tile Choices

Tile has many virtues. It's affordable, do-it-yourself friendly, available in an astounding variety of materials and colors and offers design flexibility. Some drawbacks are that its piecemeal nature means some surface unevenness is inevitable and the grout lines are vulnerable to staining.

Not all tiles are created equal. Granite, porcelain and glazed tiles are the least porous and are quite durable. Marble, unglazed clay or limestone tiles are more porous, softer and usually not recommended for kitchens. Here are some other points to consider before you buy:

- High-gloss and solid-color tiles tend to show scratches.
- Create a flatter surface by choosing a flat tile instead of one that has a slight pillow effect.
- Use larger tiles with straight edges (instead of wavy edges) to reduce the number and width of grout lines. Grout lines are prone to staining unless they are well sealed and maintained.
- Backsplash tiles are less subject to abuse and thus open to more options than the surface tile.

Preparing the Substrate

Completely strip the old countertop from your cabinets. Create a new substrate for the tile top with a base of firmly supported plywood and a suitable tile backer underlayment.

1 Install support cleats along unsupported back edges. Cut plywood base and screw it to cabinet tops. Cut out sink based on manufacturer-supplied instructions. Use polyurethane to seal exposed plywood edges on sink cutouts and next to appliances.

2 Set tile backer underlayment on base and mark cut lines from underneath with black marker or carpenter's pencil. Make sink cutouts using a jigsaw and straight cuts using a scoring tool or knife.

3 Adhere tile backer to base with a thin layer of thin-set mortar and with cement-board screws. Cut tile backer for counter nosing and attach with galvanized roofing nails. Seal underlayment seams with fiberglass joint tape and mortar.

Laying the Tile

Installing tile on a countertop is essentially the same as tiling a floor, but with a little less stooping and bending. The following instructions show how to add a decorative border and nosing to complement the surface (or field) tile.

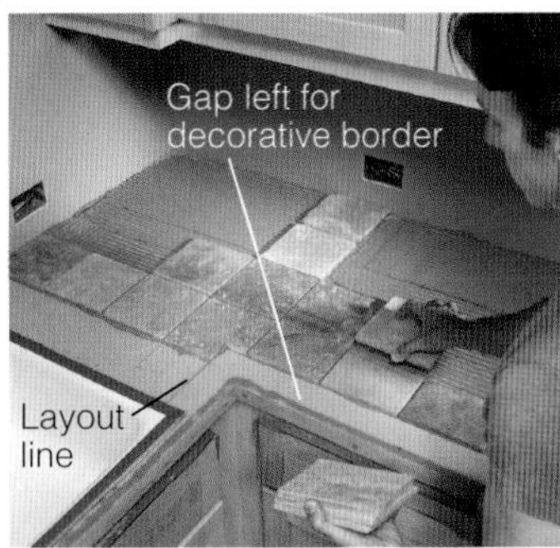

1 Mark layout lines for tiling, planning for the border. Then precut some field tiles to dry-fit a section. Tile the top in workable sections. Spread mortar with a notched trowel, leaving layout lines exposed. Then set the tile.

2 Cut webbed backing to separate strips of decorative trim tiles. Install the trim tiles, making sure they sit flat in the mortar. Leave space for a grout line between the field tile and nosing tile.

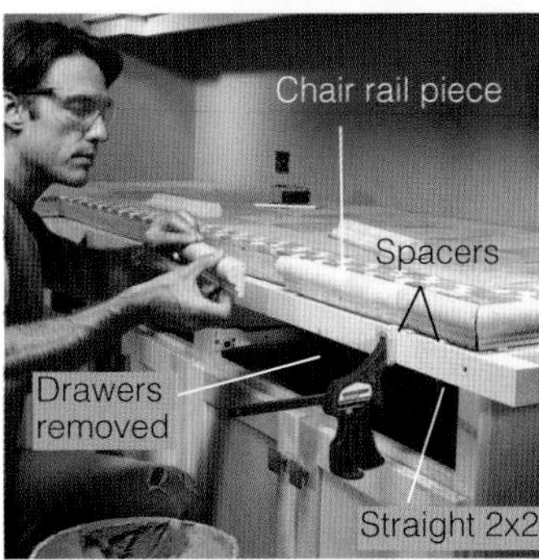

3 Clamp straight 2x2s to the face frame to support nosing tile. Adhere nosing with thin-set mortar. Apply mortar to the back of tile instead of nosing underlayment. Use spacers to bring nosing flush with surface.

Applying Sealers and Grout

Seal the stone before grouting. The sealer penetrates the stone and prevents grout pigments from being absorbed into its surface. Choose a water-based sealer if you want to retain the stone's natural color; oil-based for a deeper color.

1 Coat the stone's face with sealer. Roll out the flat areas and brush any contoured edges. Apply two coats for extra insurance and let dry between coats.

2 Mix grout to toothpastelike consistency with grout additive, unless otherwise instructed. Push grout into joints using a grout float. Work in manageable sections and keep grout out of inside corners.

3 Wipe excess grout from tile with a dense grout sponge. Wash sponge frequently and thoroughly. Wring sponge out dry before wiping tile. Several passes are necessary to clean grout from tile. Seal grout lines and caulk inside corners with color-matched caulk.

Finishing an Attic

Trusses vs. Rafters 18
Egress Windows 277

Before converting an attic, consult a building inspector or architect while developing your plans. He or she can tell you whether your plan is feasible, your budget is reasonable and what permits, inspections and variances you will need. This will help you decide what you can do yourself and what to leave to a professional.

Assessing the space. Building codes specify minimum floor area and ceiling height requirements for different rooms. Generally, 50 percent of the finished floor must have a designated minimum ceiling height. If your attic is crisscrossed with lots of roof supports, you have trusses, and in most cases, trusses cannot be cut or altered. Consult a structural engineer before making any changes.

Have a professional check the foundation and utility systems. If you want to add a bathroom, you must be able to hook new plumbing into the existing system. Check also that your heating system is sufficient for the additional space.

Planning construction. The attic's floor joists must support the increased load. Strengthen them as needed by repairing, doubling or adding joists. You may need to install a new staircase or improve an existing one. Plan a second exit or egress windows for emergencies.

When choosing windows, keep in mind that they may serve as emergency exits and must meet minimum opening size requirements. Provide insulation and ventilation to maintain comfortable temperatures and avoid condensation. Install an auxiliary circuit breaker box, if needed, and new circuits. Be generous with electrical outlets. Install smoke detectors.

Structural considerations. Finishing an attic is a complicated project that affects the house from foundation to roof. In houses built after 1970, the exterior walls' framing, lower floors and foundation may need bolstering to support the increased load. Older houses tend to be overbuilt and may not need any shoring up. A building inspector, contractor or architect can tell you whether reinforcement is needed, what materials to use and where to put them. Adding insulation will impact your roof venting system. Discuss this with a professional as well.

Building sequence. Begin with the floor: Run any pipes, wires, ducts and insulation. If there's no floor in the attic, lay a subfloor. Run the utilities in the walls and ceiling. Install a vapor retarder between the insulation and the drywall in the ceiling and walls. Schedule inspections as you go; for example, the wiring must be inspected before it is enclosed by the floor, walls or ceiling.

Attic Anatomy

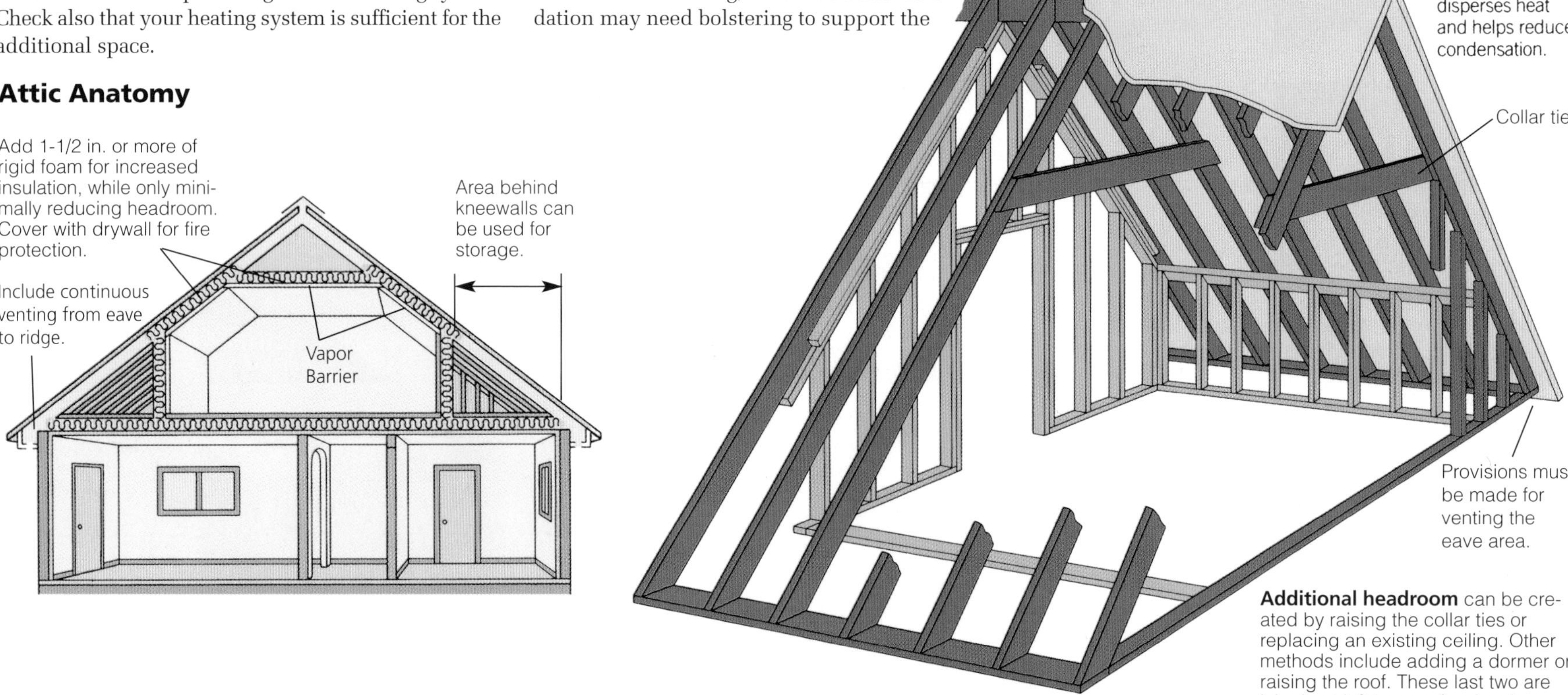
Add 1-1/2 in. or more of rigid foam for increased insulation, while only minimally reducing headroom. Cover with drywall for fire protection.
Include continuous venting from eave to ridge.
Vapor Barrier
Area behind kneewalls can be used for storage.
A ridge vent disperses heat and helps reduce condensation.
Collar ties
Provisions must be made for venting the eave area.
Additional headroom can be created by raising the collar ties or replacing an existing ceiling. Other methods include adding a dormer or raising the roof. These last two are jobs best left to a professional.

An unfinished attic provides ready expansion space since the roof, walls and foundation are already in place. As you plan, talk with your building inspector. Often floor joists must be beefed up to support the added weight, and roof ventilation and insulation must be installed correctly to avoid problems further down the road. The illustrations below provide the basic information for framing attic walls.

Additional information for renovating an attic

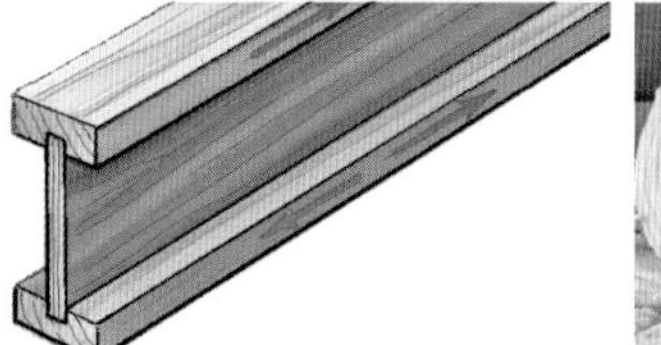

Planning
Guidelines for Home Improvement **10**
Permits, Inspections and Contractors **11**
Utility Shutoffs **12**
Roof Styles **18**
Ladder and Scaffold Safety **311**

Electrical
Circuit Mapping and Planning **129**
Assessing Your Electrical Service **131**
Fishing Cable **141**
Wiring Variations **143**

Structure
Beams and Joists **17**
Trusses vs. Rafters **18**
Attic Venting **169**
Laying Shingles **320**
Dimensional Lumber **427**

Heating
Insulation and Air Leaks **165**
Blowing in Insulation **167**
Ductwork **175**
Heating an Addition **179**

Installing Kneewalls and Partitions

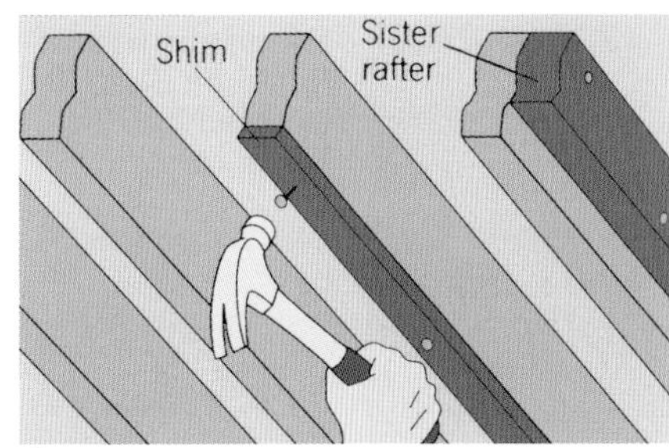

1 Rafter edges must form a level plane for top plate of kneewall. Test by holding a straightedge across edges. Raise low spots with shims. Strengthen or take the bow out of a rafter by nailing a 2x4 or larger member alongside it.

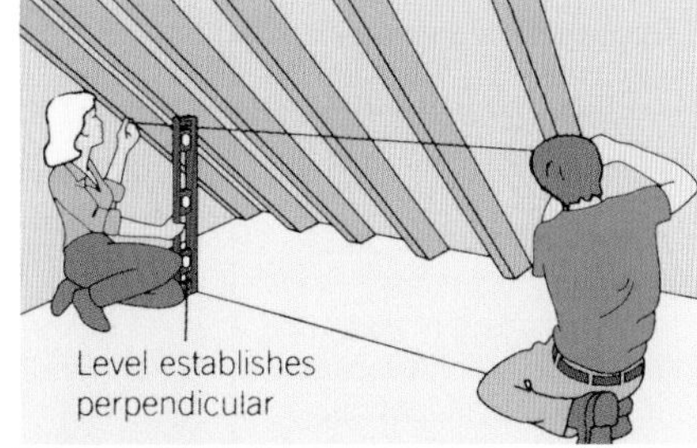

2 Snap a chalk line across floor and rafters to establish position of kneewall. Measure distance between end rafters. Cut two 2x4s to this length (for kneewall's top plate and soleplate).

3 Cut 2x4s for kneewall's studs. Transcribe rafter angle onto one stud; use it as a template to bevel remaining studs. Nail studs to plates, 16 or 24 in. apart.

4 Set kneewall in position. Check plumb with a level; shim as needed. Nail wall to floor and rafters. Add blocking at corners.

5 For top plate of partition, nail 2x4 blocks between rafters inset 3/4 in. from rafter faces, and 48 in. (120 cm) apart. Nail 1x6 to blocks, parallel to rafters. Center 2x4 on 1x6; fasten with nails.

6 Align 2x4 soleplate directly below top plate, and nail it to floor. Mark stud positions at 16-in. intervals along soleplate. Transfer measurements to top plate with level and straightedge.

7 Set tallest 2x4 on its mark. With level, check that it is truly vertical. Mark and cut top bevel. Install stud by toenailing it to both plates. Repeat procedure for remaining studs.

8 Install shortest stud on final mark. Finish walls and ceiling with drywall (1x6 in top plate and doubled studs at end of kneewall provide nailing surfaces in corners for drywall).

Basement Moisture

Sump Pumps 111
Gutters and Downspouts 326-329
Ice Dam Solutions 331
Repairing Concrete 406

Basements are leak prone, but you don't have to live in fear of those leaks and abandon your basement as a living area. Most leakage can be prevented, often with surprisingly little effort and cost. In addition to the solutions on the following pages, here are simple things you can do to avoid the shock of walking downstairs and stepping on soggy carpet.

- Make sure gutters are clean and sloped properly. Install larger 4-in. (10-cm) downspouts to discourage clogging.
- Properly seal around basement windows and doors with caulk or silicone.
- Test sump pump to ensure proper functioning by pouring water in the sump catch basin. Install a battery backup in case of power failure.
- To avoid bursting a water line, remove hoses from outdoor faucets before freezing weather comes.
- Test floor drains for proper functioning.
- Replace low-quality plumbing lines. Instead of flexible pipe, use PVC or ABS pipe for sump pump discharge. Install steel-braided no-burst supply lines on your washer.
- Repair poorly flashed deck ledger boards, windows and doors.

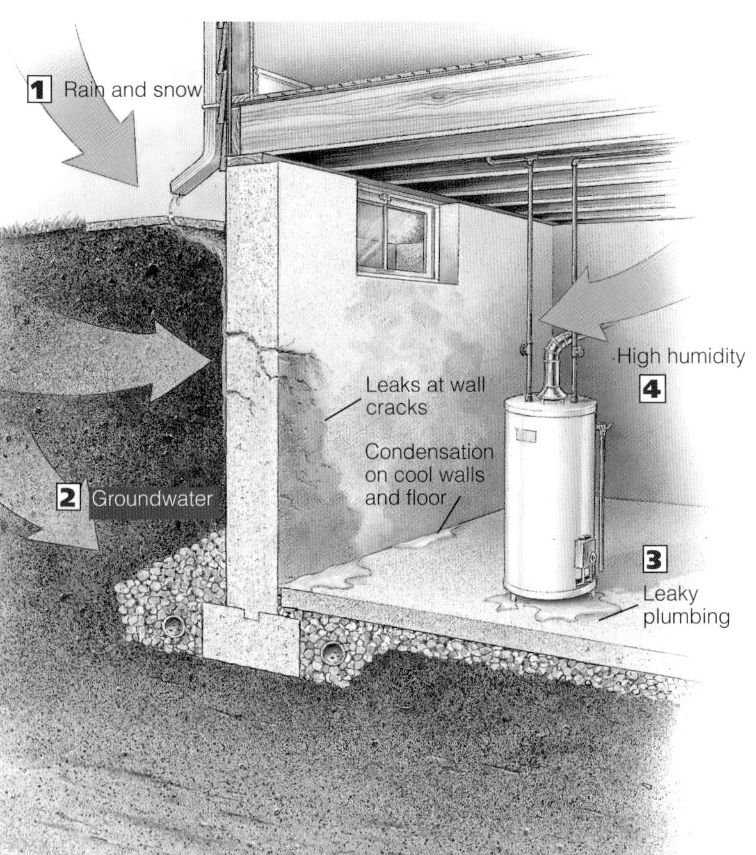

The first step in solving a water problem is to figure out the water source among four possible suspects: rain, groundwater, leaky plumbing or condensation.

1 Rain. Water from rainfall and snow will eventually penetrate your basement if you don't direct it away from the foundation. To do this, keep gutters and other drainage systems functioning properly and make sure landscape and concrete pads slope away from the foundation walls.

2 Groundwater. Leakage from groundwater occurs when the soil around the foundation becomes saturated with water and presses against the basement walls, causing hydrostatic pressure. Rainfall amount, soil type and water table level can all play a role in groundwater problems. To control groundwater leakage, your home may require installation of a drain tile system or repairs to an existing one.

3 Plumbing leaks. Water pooling on the basement floor may come from a leaky water pipe, water heater, outdoor faucet, sump-pump discharge pipe (especially the flexible type) or another plumbing source.

4 Condensation. On warm, humid days, water can condense on the cool basement walls and floors, encouraging the growth of mold and mildew.

Conducting a Moisture Test

Even if you see no visible puddles from leaky cracks, moisture may still be entering through the basement's concrete walls and floor. Many houses are constructed loosely enough to naturally vent this moisture, but tighter homes often trap this moisture inside, resulting in high indoor humidity. This humidity can cause peeling paint, mold and mildew, and condensation on windows leading to wood rot. To distinguish between condensation and seepage, conduct this test: On a warm, humid day, dry a spot on the floor or wall using a hair dryer. Tape a piece of foil or plastic over the dry spot. Thoroughly seal all four sides and wait two days. Then check.

If moisture has collected on the foil's exposed face, but the concrete behind is dry, moisture is due to interior basement humidity condensation.

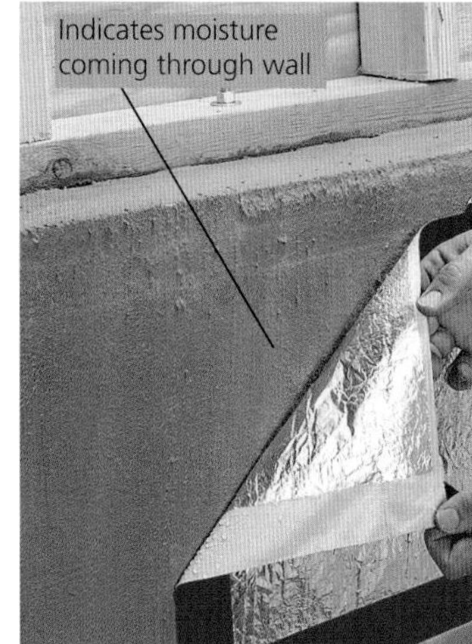

If water has accumulated on the foil's side facing the wall, moisture is coming through wall or floor seepage. If the source is condensation, reduce humidity with a dehumidifier. If your home is equipped with refrigerated air conditioning, it already has a dehumidifier, but the basement area may require additional help. If the source is seepage, see p. 273 for solutions.

Basement Moisture / Interior Solutions

Hydraulic Cement

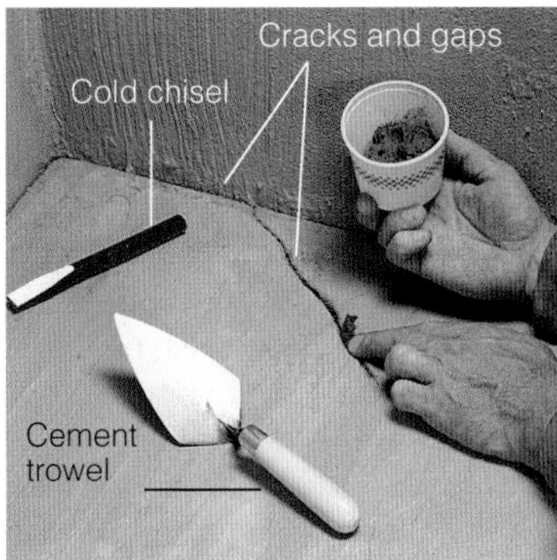

Undercut cracks using a cold chisel. Pack hydraulic cement into gaps and cracks and trowel it smooth. On concrete block walls, chisel a groove only in cracks in mortar joints. Cement hardens in five minutes and can block actively flowing water.

Waterproof Paint

Remove dirt, flaky paint and chalky residue from walls. Apply waterproof paint according to manufacturer's directions. Some products go over raw concrete, others over painted walls. Use only for minor seepage problems.

Water Dam

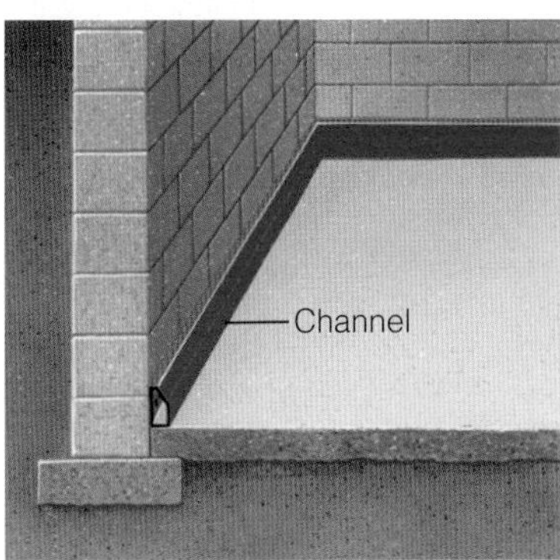

This water dam system catches water at the wall's base above the floor (unlike drain tile, which catches it below the floor). The enclosed channel carries water to a sump where it's pumped outside. The system is less expensive than drain tile, but less effective.

CWM Waterproofing

1 Crystalline waterproofing material (CWM) penetrates deep into concrete to make it waterproof. Chisel or scrape away loose concrete or other coatings, leaving no coating patches larger than a silver dollar.

2 Fill cracks and holes with hydraulic cement. Cement sets quickly, so mix only as much as you can use in three minutes. Both hydraulic cement and CWM generate heat as they cure, so the mixing container may feel warm.

3 Wet the concrete until it's soaked but not dripping. Smear a thick coating of CWM over concrete. Mix only as much CWM as you can spread in 10 minutes. Keep the coating damp for 48 hours after application.

Drain Tile with Sump Pump

If all other measures fail to prevent water penetrating your basement, you may have to install an interior drain tile and sump basin—a massive job. To install this system, first find a location for the sump in an unfinished space and plan for its electrical and discharge requirements. Remove an 18-in. (45-cm) strip of concrete flooring around walls and dig an 8-in. (20-cm)-deep trench along the footing. Fill the trench with 2 in. (5 cm) of gravel and lay the perforated drain tile in a complete loop to and from the sump basin. Cover the tile with gravel, hang 6-mil plastic sheeting on the wall and install corrugated floor edging. Cover the gravel with 6-mil plastic, patch the concrete floor and install the sump pump. Only then should you frame the interior walls.

If you have a concrete block foundation, you'll have to drain the block cores by drilling 1-in. (25-mm) holes through the face of the block. Water will run down the inside of the floor edging and be directed to the drain tile.

Basement Moisture / Exterior Solutions

Beams and Joists 17
Concrete Fasteners 82
Heating an Addition 179
Window Wells 277
Gutters and Downspouts 326-329

The first strategy for drying a damp or wet basement is to channel water from rain or melting snow away from the foundation. Most solutions are low-tech and inexpensive, and you can quickly spot failures and correct them. Approach the problem by beginning at the top—the gutters.

To keep gutters clean, simplify maintenance by installing gutter guards and larger downspouts. Check the pitch of your gutters to ensure they slope toward the downspout (standing water is a giveaway that they don't slope enough). For sagging gutters, replace or reattach any loose fasteners. With the gutters in good repair, look at the surrounding landscape for problems.

When a patio, driveway or sidewalk running along the house settles and tilts toward the house, it directs water toward the basement wall instead of away from it. In these cases, the best solution is to break out the tilted concrete, regrade the compacted soil and pour a new slab.

Sloping Soil Around Foundation

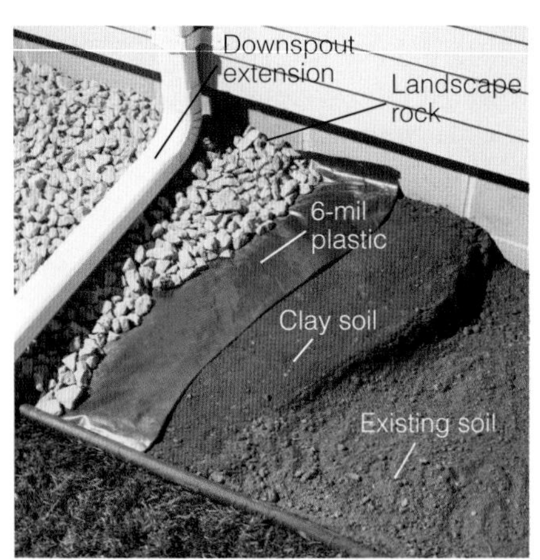

The soil around a house should slope away from the foundation at about 1 in. per foot (2.5 cm per 30 cm) for the first 10 ft. (3 m). Unfortunately, drainage problems are often caused by backfill around the foundation that has sunk over the years. To solve small slope issues, firmly pack clay soil around the foundation at a slope. Cover the clay soil with 6-mil black plastic and cover the plastic with landscape rock. For large problems, you may need to consider regrading and landscaping.

Extending Downspouts

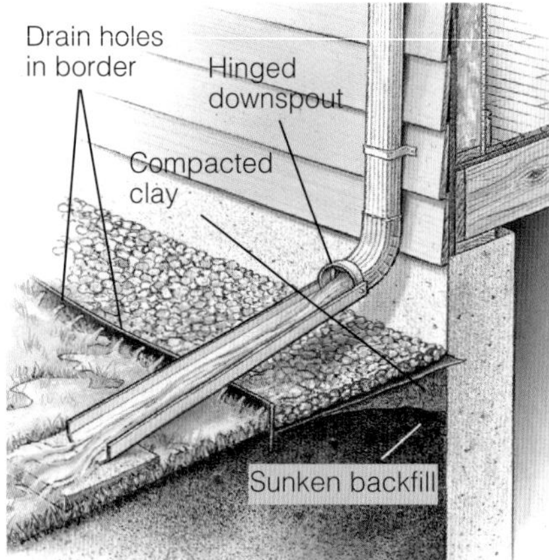

Missing or short downspout extensions, in conjunction with poor landscape drainage, can lead to basement moisture. First, correct slope problems, and then add a longer downspout extension. If you have a plastic border, drill holes in it, or use a perforated border to provide drainage. For convenience, use a hinged extension that can be swung out of the way when you mow the lawn.

Improving Window Wells

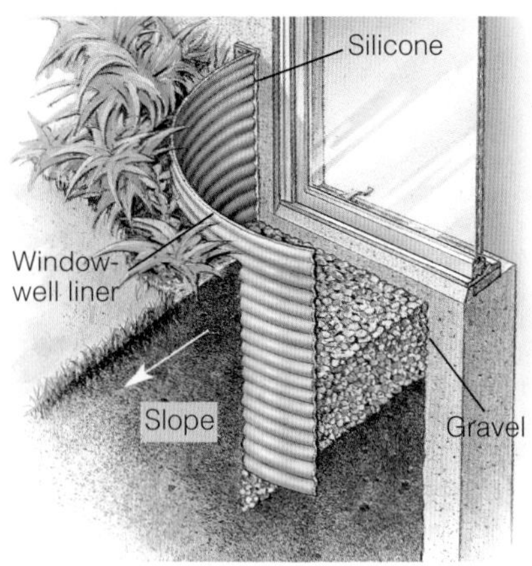

Window wells are a vulnerable spot because they're essentially temporary catch basins for surface runoff and saturated soil. Plastic well covers help somewhat, but a better solution is to keep the well itself in good shape. To do that, extend the window well soil retainer above ground level, seal the edges with silicone and dig the bottom out 12 in. (30 cm) below the sill. Finally, fill the well with stone to make a temporary drainage basin.

Installing Exterior Drainage

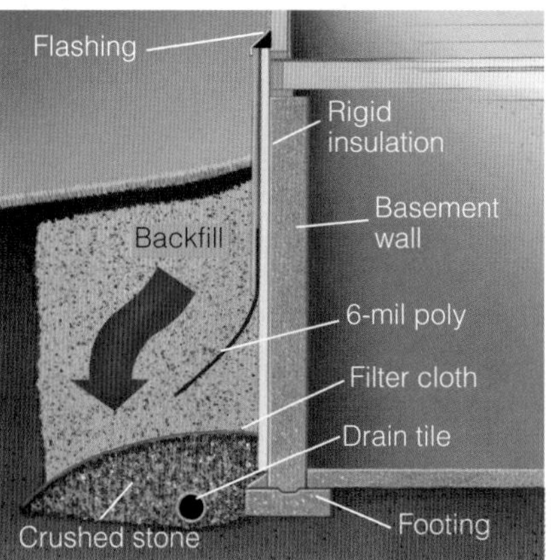

Exterior drainage, while more expensive than interior drainage, usually has the advantage of not requiring electricity (for a sump pump) to work, and you don't have to tear up the basement floor. With this repair, you prevent water from getting to the foundation by using the correct type of fill gravel around the foundation and footings. Filter cloth keeps the gravel clean, and drain tile carries the water away (sometimes to an interior sump pump). Rigid insulation and plastic sheeting help prevent seepage problems.

Finishing a Basement

Compared to building above ground, remodeling a basement is an affordable option to increase your living space. But before finishing your basement, answer these three questions to determine the project's scope:

1. Will the finished headroom meet code requirements? Most codes dictate 7 ft. 6 in. (2.3 m) as a minimum height for a certain percentage of the space. Soffits that cover ventilation and other systems may be as low as 7 ft. (2 m). Consult a local building inspector for a ruling.
2. Will you meet egress requirements? Most basement bedrooms and, in some cases, basements in general must have a legally sized egress window or outer door for occupants to escape through in case of fire.
3. Have all moisture problems been resolved? If not, you'll be throwing money away by finishing your basement.

Basements often have heat ducts, pipes, wiring and exposed concrete walls and floors that need to be dealt with to create a comfortable living space.

Enclosing Ductwork

1 Build soffit sides from 2x2s and oriented strand board or plywood. Where soffits exceed 8 ft. in length, overlap end joints for a more rigid panel.

2 Mount soffit sides to ceiling, using a chalk line snapped along bottom of joists as a guide.

3 Install horizontal blocking to complete the enclosure. Before covering the ductwork, add necessary vents and returns for the basement.

Framing Walls

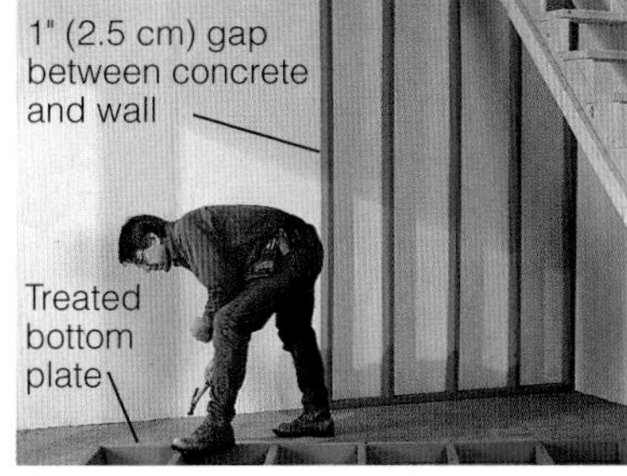

1 Assemble 2x4 walls with a pressure-treated bottom plate. Build them a little short, so they can easily be raised into position.

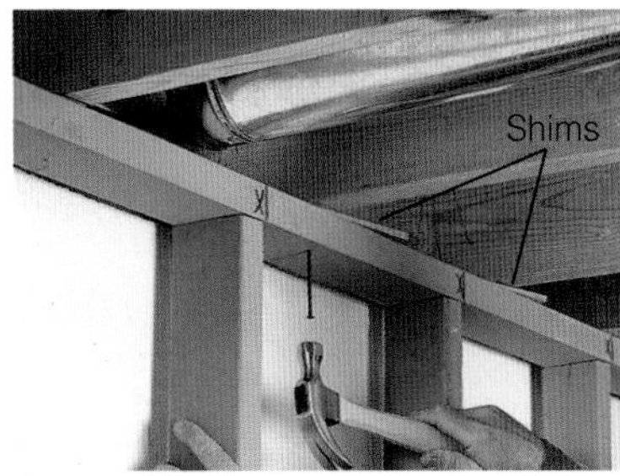

2 Snap chalk line on joists and floor. Attach the top plate using shims and nails. Add the bottom plate using adhesive and cement fasteners.

3 Frame kneewalls. You can install furring strips and rigid foam insulation when space is at a premium (see p. 276).

Dropping Ceilings

1 To encapsulate plumbing and electrical lines, attach furring strips to the ceiling. Install perimeter 2x2s with a 1/2-in. (12-mm) gap below joists.

2 Attach a taut string line between perimeter strips; use it as a guide to attach the framing perpendicular to joists. Use shims to keep 2x2s level.

3 Provide framework for access panels for shutoff valves, duct dampers and drain clean outs. Use duct grills to conveniently disguise access holes.

Finishing a Basement / Insulation and Steel Studs

Surface Wiring 142
Insulation and Air Leaks 165
Timber Retaining Walls 345
Buying Windows 369

Insulating Basement Walls

You can use either method shown to effectively insulate basement walls. Each includes a rigid foam moisture barrier between the framing and the basement wall. The foam eliminates condensation from interior humidity and helps protect walls from minor exterior moisture. Tack the foam to the concrete with construction adhesive while you frame. Don't install a vapor barrier between the insulation and drywall for either method.

Building codes in some colder regions require basements be insulated at least 2 ft. (60 cm) below grade and/or to R-12 or greater.

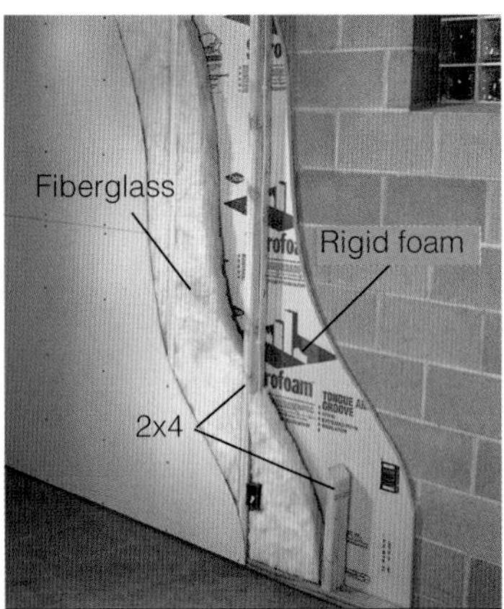

Fiberglass and foam. In a 2x4 framed wall, use a combination of rigid foam and unfaced fiberglass (R-11 or R-13). This method makes plumbing and electrical work easier, but the wall is thicker and consumes more floor space.

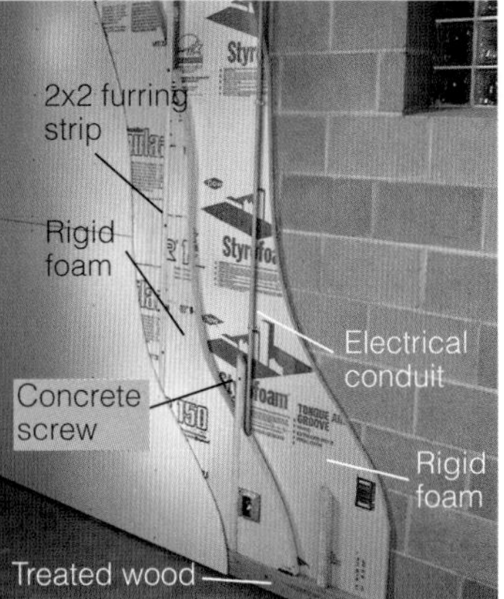

Foam and foam. If you have a plumb, flat foundation wall and want to save floor space, frame with 2x2 furring strips and insulate with rigid foam on the concrete and another layer of rigid foam fitted between the strips.

Using Steel Studs

Steel framing is easy to work with in confined basement spaces, where you assemble it one piece at a time, like a giant Erector set. Even better, it's termite-proof and doesn't soak up water the way wood framing does. The steel framing used here is 25-gauge non-load-bearing track and studs that measure 1-5/8 x 1-1/4 in. The insulation used with steel framing is a semirigid spun-mineral fiber with R-5.4 that fits snugly in the cup of one stud and against the back of another.

1 Fasten track to floor with masonry screws. Snap chalk line on joists and floor to keep wall straight and plumb. Keep framed wall 3/4 in. (19 mm) away from masonry wall at closest point. Overlap track and fasten to floor through overlap.

2 Install studs on 16-in. centers and insert them into the tracks with a twisting motion. Fasten studs to track with sheet-metal pan head screws. Holes in studs are for running electrical conduit, not for plastic-sheathed electrical cable.

3 Attach windowsill level with bottom of window frame. Align window studs with edge of concrete. Use spring clamps to hold sill while fastening. Install wall stiffeners at midpoint of wall. Fabricate stiffeners from short pieces of track.

4 Install plywood window surrounds. Fasten them to framing with drywall screws and to concrete with masonry screws. In some cases you can build surround box first, then slide it into place. Finish plywood with drywall.

5 Run plastic-sheathed electrical cable behind metal framing. Fasten plywood blocks to concrete with masonry screws to support cable and electrical boxes. Use different sizes of plaster rings to compensate for variations in wall depth.

Window Wells and Egress Windows

Installing a basement egress window and building a window well are two projects that go hand in hand. Find the best location and size for the window by considering these three elements:

Light. The best natural light comes from the east and the south.

Exterior look. Centering the window underneath a window in the floor above provides a balanced look, and the header of the upper window, if it's larger, will take most of the load off the egress window.

Obstacles. Buried utilities, shrubbery, indoor wiring and ductwork can all complicate the project.

Terraced Window Well

The bottom of a well can't interfere with window operation. Wells more than 44 in. (110 cm) deep may require ladders unless they are terraced.

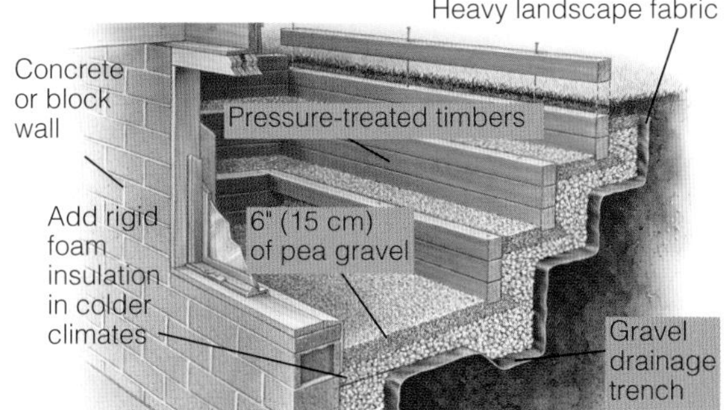

1 Dig out the bottom level 12 in. (30 cm) deeper than the bottom of the window opening. Slope the bottom away from house and dig a drainage trench around the perimeter. Line the well with fabric held in place by spikes. Add a level gravel base.

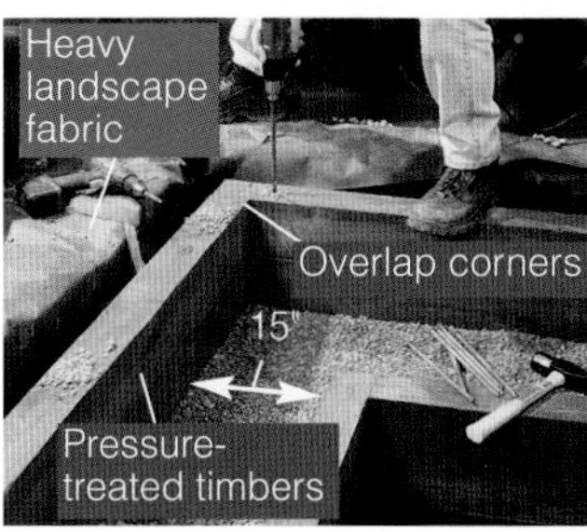

2 Create a level base for each level of the timbers. With the lowest wall in place, use timbers as a guide for the next wall. Alternate overlapping corner joints and screw joints together before predrilling and driving spikes.

Egress Window

An egress window must have a clear opening of at least 5.7 sq. ft. and be at least 20 in. wide and 24 in. high. This size is large enough to allow a firefighter, with equipment, to enter the home through the window. In addition, the bottom of the opening can be no more than 44 in. from the floor. Check with your building code official prior to tackling this project. Note: In Canada, clear openings must not be less than .35 sq. m, with no dimension less than 380 mm.

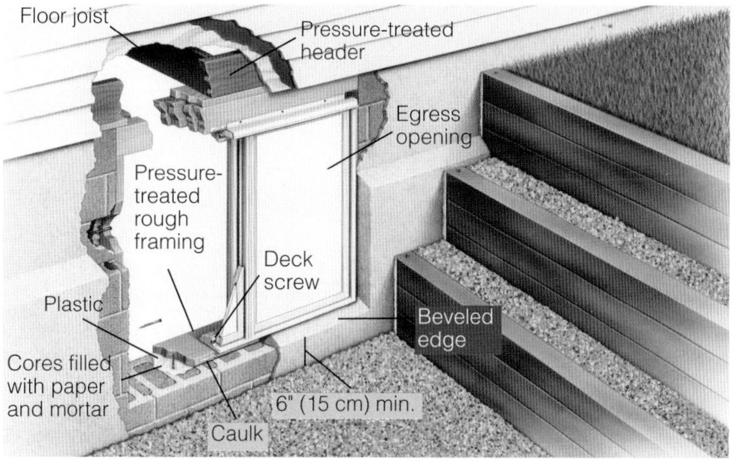

1 Use tape to outline the proposed window size and location. Erect a temporary 2x4 support wall if joists are perpendicular to the wall you're cutting. Fit studs tightly and align each under a floor joist.

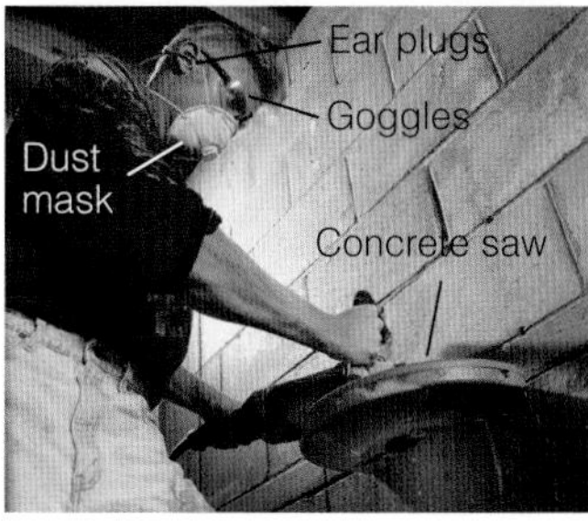

2 Mark cutline for opening using a black marker. Drill level holes through the wall at corners to locate your exterior cutline. Cut concrete wall from both sides using a concrete saw by making a shallow pass first, then cutting through. Use a wet blade to reduce dust and heat.

3 Build the frame from treated wood. In concrete block, fill cores with newspaper and mortar, drive deck screws in the bottom of the frame sill and, while mortar is wet, set sill in place. Make the frame tight fitting and attach it to the concrete.

4 On the outer wall, seal gaps between the rough frame and concrete. Center the frame in the window and level it with shims. Nail shims in place and remove window. Caulk outer frame beneath the window's nailing flange and install window.

Reducing Noise

Ductwork 175
Storm Windows 371
Installing Door Sweeps 374
Hanging Interior Doors 382

Noise is a fact of life, but that doesn't mean it has to disturb your work, play and sleep. There are steps you can take to minimize noise generated both inside and outside the home.

Since noise is simply airborne vibration, the best way to block it is to put something in its path. That something will block noise best if it has mass (like drywall or solid concrete), can isolate noise (like rubber gaskets or acoustic board) and is continuous (noise can sneak through even the smallest gap).

The photos on this page show a few ways you can dampen interior noises. To help block outside noise you can:

- Install high-quality storm windows with thick glass and good weather stripping.
- Add caps to chimneys.
- Add insulation to attics and walls.
- Seal up all holes and gaps around windows and doors and where pipes and wires enter your house.

A Quieter Room

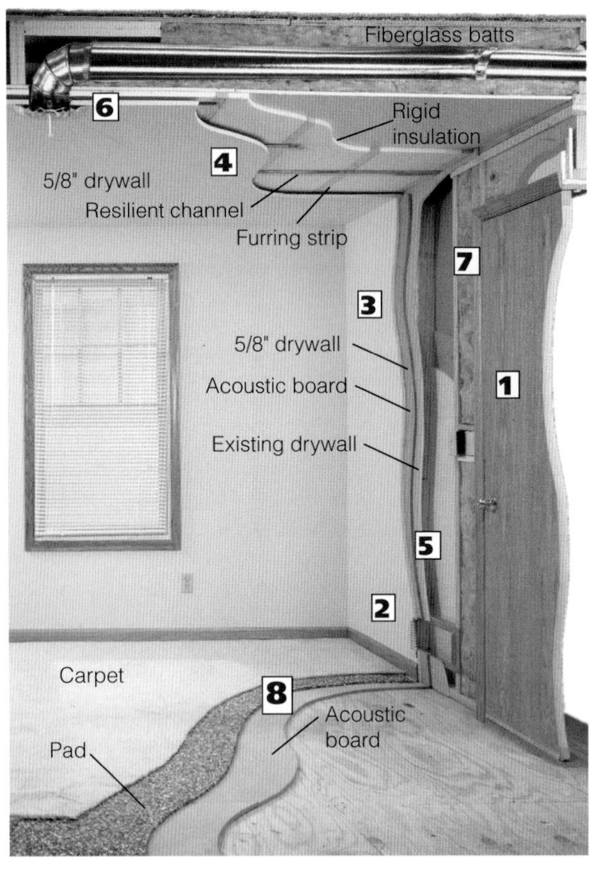

1. Install a solid-core door with weather stripping and bottom sweep.
2. Caulk around ductwork and electrical boxes.
3. Glue a layer of acoustic board, then another layer of drywall to walls.
4. Secure furring strips, resilient channel and rigid insulation to the ceiling.
5. Glue acoustic board and drywall inside wall cavities while remodeling.
6. Surround ductwork with rigid foam and fiberglass insulation.
7. Install fiberglass batts in wall cavities while remodeling.
8. Install acoustic board, carpet pad and carpet on floors.

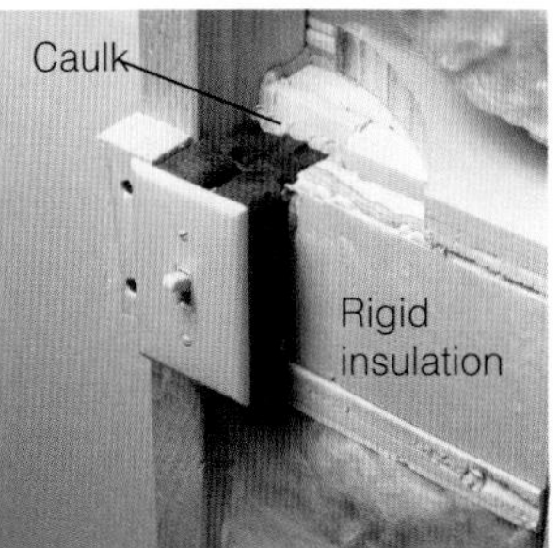

Other Noise-control Measures

Plumbing and heating systems are double trouble since they both create and distribute noise. Here are a few products to help quiet them:

Rubber boots on supply and cold-air return ducts will help isolate furnace vibration and limit noise from traveling along the ductwork.

Vibration pads, available at heating and industrial supply stores, can help isolate noise generated by dishwashers, furnaces and washing machines.

Pipe inserts installed in oversize holes, will help limit bangs, rattles and squeaks.

Pipe hangers, secured to joists with a strip of weather-stripping felt pinched between them, will isolate noise from both copper and PVC pipe.

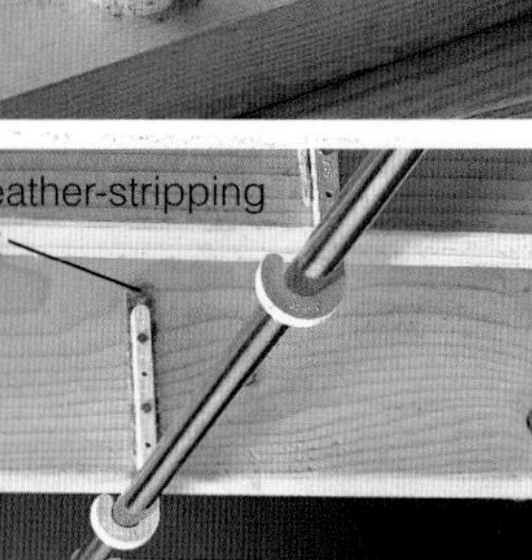

Painting & Wallpapering

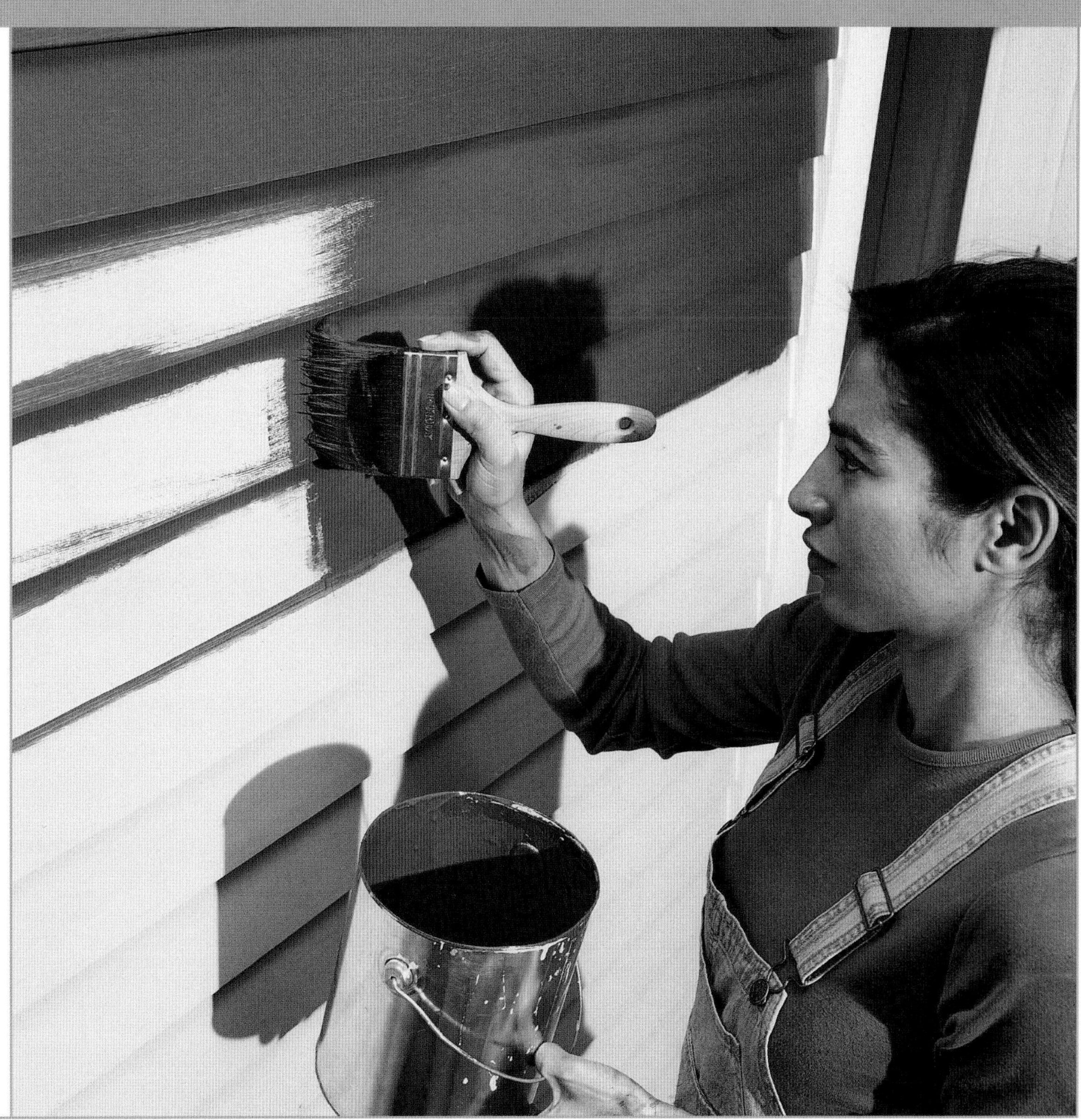

Tools / Brushes

Walk along the paint supplies aisle of any hardware store or home center and you'll be greeted by a selection of dozens—maybe even hundreds—of paintbrushes. Select the right one and you'll be able to apply paint faster and more efficiently and, at the end of the day, your paint job will look better.

Wide wall brush

Angled brush

Trim brush

Brush Size

Paintbrushes come in as many sizes and shapes as there are painting jobs to do. For covering large, flat surfaces like clapboard siding, use a wide, square-edged wall brush. For cutting in along ceilings and baseboards or when painting trim, use a smaller angled brush for better control and line of sight. When painting window muntins and other thin components, use a small trim brush.

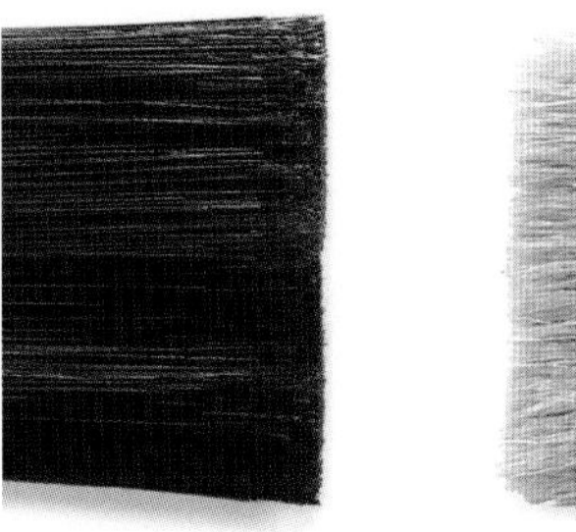

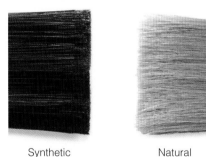

Synthetic Natural

Brush Material

Synthetic bristle brushes, made from nylon, polyester or a blend of both, are economical and work well with all kinds of paints. Natural bristle brushes should be used only when applying oil-based paints and clear finishes. Don't use natural bristle brushes with latex paints or clean them in water; this will eventually make the bristles "fluffy" and more difficult to control.

Low quality

Medium quality

High quality

Brush Quality

High-quality brushes have tapered bristles of several lengths to form a more easily controlled "chiseled" tip. Each bristle is flagged—like human hair with split ends—to hold more paint. They are springy, not stiff, when you press them against your palm, and they should fan out evenly. Medium-quality brushes usually have bristles with split, but not tapered, ends. Low-quality brushes have untapered bristles with blunt ends.

Cleaning

Use these steps to clean brushes used with acrylic paints or with stains. Follow the same steps when using oil-based paints, but use mineral spirits (or a mineral spirit substitute) in place of water.

1 Scrape off excess paint using the rim of the can to be sure the brush is as free of paint as possible. Then work paint onto newspaper.

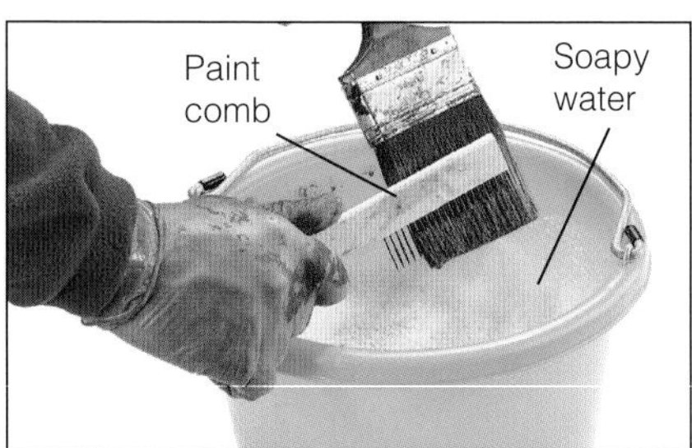

2 Wash the brush in a pail of soapy water using your hands and a paint comb or an old fork.

3 Spin brush in pail to remove any remaining paint and water. Rinse in clean water, then spin again. Finally, rinse in clean water.

4 Wrap the brush with heavy paper and tie it loosely with string so the brush retains its original shape.

Salvaging Petrified Brushes

You can resurrect hardened brushes by soaking them overnight in a specialty brush-cleaning product. Suspend the brushes as shown or they'll look like hockey sticks as they soften and settle.

Tools / Rollers

For large, flat surfaces, no painting tool matches a roller for ease, speed and solid coverage. Originally designed for painting interior walls, rollers with specialized sleeves or attachments simplify other indoor and many outdoor painting jobs as well.

When it comes to roller sleeves, you get what you pay for. The best sleeves have uniform, fluffy, lint-free pile and a tough water-resistant center. Cheap sleeves hold less paint, splatter more, and tend to mat. The smoother the surface you want to paint—and the smoother the desired finish—the shorter the pile you need.

Basics

A roller frame has a spring-type mechanism to hold the pile cover, or sleeve, that applies paint. A well-designed frame will hold the sleeve securely and, at the same time, permit you to slide the sleeve off and on easily. A frame should spin smoothly, and the handle should feel sturdy in your hand. An extension pole (far left) or threaded broom handle lets you tackle ceilings without a ladder and load the roller from a tray on the floor without bending down. Special rollers can solve special problems. The narrow roller is ideal for painting lap siding and wide trim. The skinny foam roller allows you to paint in tight quarters, like behind radiators and toilets, and it leaves a very smooth finish.

Roller frame

3" roller and frame

Thin foam roller

Extension pole

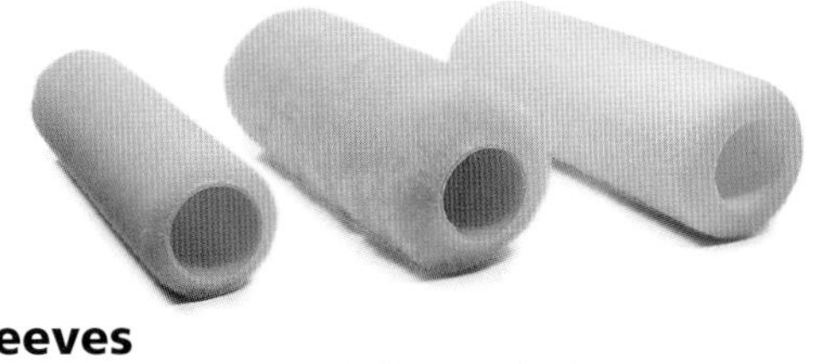

Sleeves

The short nap roller sleeve (left) is standard for most interior wall surfaces. The thicker long nap sleeve (center) is good for painting stucco and other rough surfaces. The foam roller (right) applies an ultra-smooth coat of paint.

Power Rollers

These feed paint from a central source to a specially designed roller sleeve by way of a hose or a paint reservoir in the handle. You don't have to reload the roller from a tray or bucket every few minutes and, when you work from a ladder, you're saved the inconvenience of moving your paint supply.

Cleaning

Clean your sleeves thoroughly after each use, and they'll last for years.

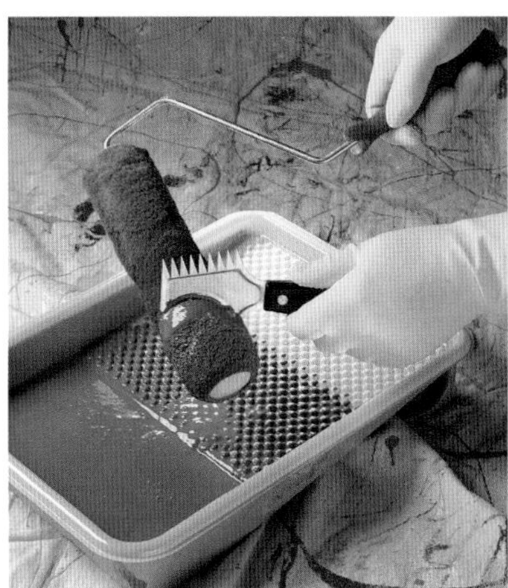

1 To clean a roller, begin by scraping excess paint from the roller using a roller cleaner tool or the notched handle of a stir stick.

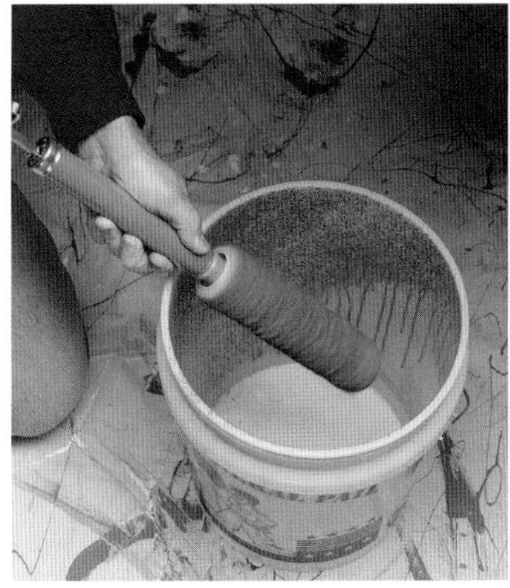

2 Spin rollers into a large bucket or washtub after washing and rinsing. Store rollers on end to keep the nap fluffy and uniform for future use.

Time-Savers

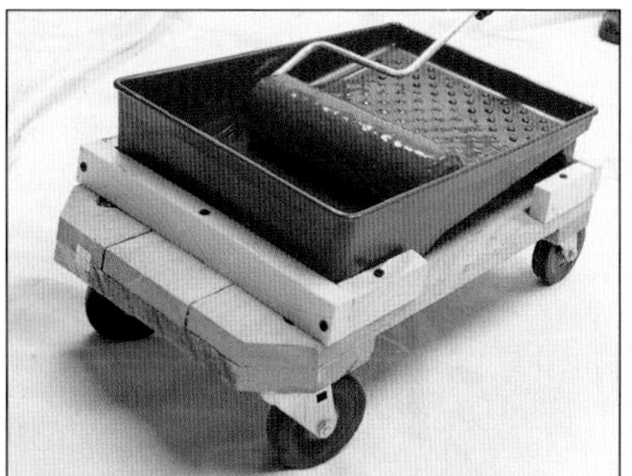

This simple roll-around tray made from casters and scrap lumber minimizes bending and carrying.

Stash roller sleeves in a snack food canister if you're going to paint again in a few hours.

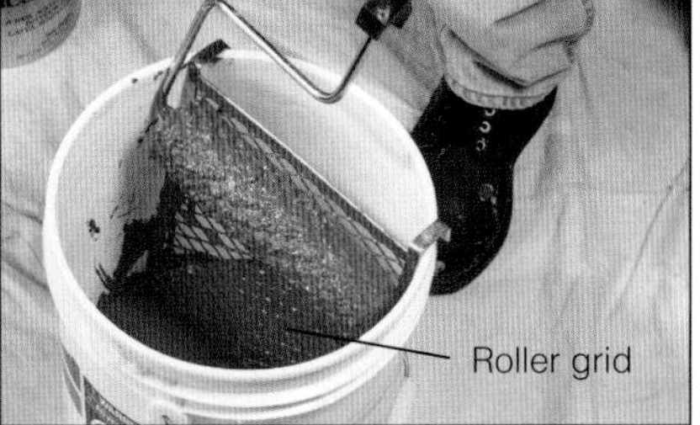

A roller grid in a large bucket helps spread the paint more evenly on the sleeve (and keeps lots of paint at the ready).

Tools / Pads and Others

Pads

There's hardly a painting chore that hasn't had a special paint pad designed to address its needs. Standard pads are normally found in 7- and 9-in. widths. Many have a protruding front edge that allows you to paint the lower edge of one row of lap siding as you paint the face of the row below. Edging pads with adjustable wheels let you cut a straight line as you paint next to the ceiling. Corner pads are L-shaped so they can do both walls that meet at a corner in one pass.

Paint pads come in a wide choice of naps—synthetics for painting flat surfaces, thick mohair for applying smooth stains without brush marks and even deeper piled synthetics for one-coat coverage of rough stucco walls.

Not everyone is comfortable with paint pads. For many painters who use brushes with confidence and satisfaction, paint pads seem to match neither the control brushes offer nor the speed rollers offer. Others, however, find paint pads efficient to use and easy to clean. Many people treat inexpensive foam pads as throwaways.

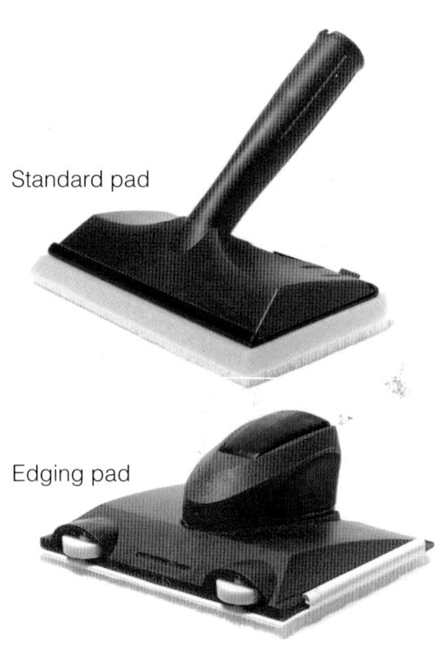

Standard pad

Edging pad

Corner pad

Paint Mitt

A paint glove or mitt has a paint-holding nap for quick coverage of staircase balusters, railings, gutters or pipes. Slide your hand into a plastic bag before sliding it into the mitt to ensure your hand will remain paint-free. Dip the glove into paint, clasp thumb and forefinger together around the object, then move the glove down the length until the surface is coated with paint.

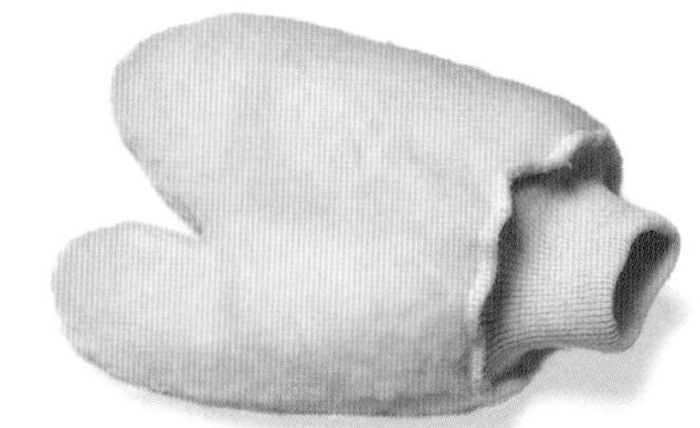

Masking Tape

Masking tape is relatively inexpensive, so always buy the highest quality and the best type for the job.

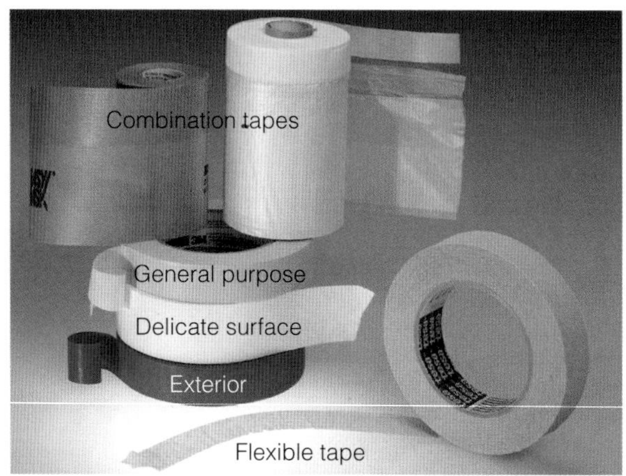

General purpose tape is the standard for interior work. Remove it within 24 hours or it may not come off easily, don't use it outside and, since it has high "tack" or stickiness, don't use it on delicate surfaces.

Long-life exterior tape can be used outdoors and removes easily up to 7 days after it's been applied. This tape has moderate tack and can damage delicate surfaces.

Delicate-surface tape has weak tack, making it ideal for delicate surfaces like fresh paint, wallpaper and drywall. It's perfectly flat and creates very crisp paint lines.

Tape/plastic combination has tape connected to plastic or paper, making it ideal for protecting cabinets, whole walls or fireplace mantels.

Flexible tape is crinkled so it can easily be used to mask off curved or irregular surfaces.

Drop Cloths

Drop cloths take a few minutes to put in place, but protect finished floor surfaces and, in the long run, save hours of clean-up.

Canvas drop cloths are fairly expensive but stay in place, can be reused and are easy to walk on.

Plastic drop cloths are inexpensive and disposable but tend to slip and slide unless they're taped in place. Paint tends to stay wet on a plastic cloth and may track to other rooms. Some pros use plastic with cloth on top for the ultimate protection.

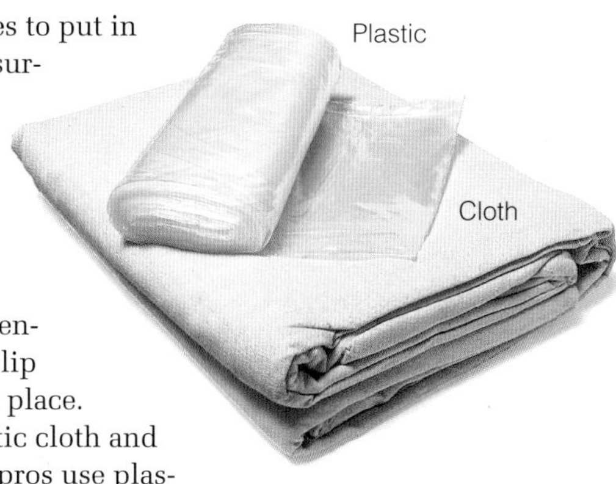

Plastic

Cloth

Tools / Spray Painting

Speed alone could justify the extra masking that spray painting requires. However, spraying has another advantage over brush or roller painting. It covers intricate shapes—louvered shutters, trellises and fencing, for example—far more evenly than hours of handwork with a brush, roller or pad. And spraying does it in minutes.

Several types of sprayers are available, each with its own pros and cons. Select the one that suits your job and budget.

Aerosol cans are ideal for small projects like painting wicker furniture or shutters. Applying several light coats will produce the best results. The first coat, called a tack coat, prepares the surface to accept the final coats. The next light coat can usually be applied before the tack coat is dry, but for subsequent coats wait until the previous coat has dried. Read and follow the instructions on the can; applying coats too early, too late, without proper surface preparation or too thickly can result in a wrinkled surface.

Handheld airless sprayers are portable, lightweight and an excellent choice for intermediate-size tasks, such as fences. These tools basically atomize the paint and direct it through an adjustable spray tip to the surface. They have a limited holding capacity—usually about one quart—and even a slight breeze can disperse much of the paint before it hits its intended surface.

Large airless sprayers work well for large jobs, such as painting entire houses. With these sprayers, paint is drawn into a tube, then pushed through the spray gun's tip at pressures ranging from 1,200 to 3,000 pounds per sq. in. (psi). They allow you to cover large areas in a short time.

HVLP (high-volume, low-pressure) sprayers are excellent for fine finishing tasks. They apply the paint at pressures less than 10 psi and are easy to control. They're portable and can apply most types of finishes.

Whatever type of sprayer you use, clean your equipment thoroughly after each use and wear safety glasses and a dual-cartridge respirator.

Aerosol cans. They work well for small objects and offer a wide range of paint colors. Specialty paints, such as metal primers, textured and high-heat paints, add to their versatility.

Handheld airless sprayers. They're moderately priced, versatile and an excellent tool for do-it-yourselfers. Special flexible tip extensions can be adjusted up and down for painting floors and ceilings.

Large airless sprayers. Ideal for large projects, large airless sprayers can draw from a large container of paint and distribute paint quickly and efficiently. They can inflict serious injury; never point the tip toward yourself or someone else.

HVLP. These tools are small, quiet and deliver paint smoothly and efficiently. They're used for tasks including airbrush artwork, wall painting and applying clear finishes to millwork.

Spray Painting Techniques

Safety and Safety Equipment **20**
Masking Tape **282**
Spray Painting Tools **283**

Any surface you don't want coated must be masked before you begin to spray paint. Although an airless sprayer can be controlled more readily than an air compression sprayer, they both create a mist of paint that can drift onto any nearby surface. Outdoors you need to shield shrubbery and protect your car. Indoors, carry out all the customary preparations, and in addition, mask all windowpanes with newspaper held with masking tape.

Getting started. Set up your spray equipment according to the manufacturer's directions. (If you rent a sprayer, be sure to get instructions with it.) Flush the unit with a solvent—water for latex paint or mineral spirits for oil-based (alkyd). Then start pumping paint either through a suction tube and hose in a paint can or from the paint holder attached to the nozzle. Check that the spray tip you pick is the right one. Thin stains take the smallest spray tip openings, heavy latex paints, the largest.

If you've never used a sprayer before, first load it with water and spray against an outside wall or a piece of scrap plywood. Without making a mess, you can practice using the controls until you are comfortable with them.

Going to work. Hold a spray painter 10 to 12 in. (25 to 30 cm) from the surface and keep it upright. Try a sample spray to check the pattern. The ideal spray pattern is wide, finely atomized and even throughout. Three variables determine that pattern: the viscosity of the paint, the size of the spray tip and the pressure control.

Because it is the easiest variable to adjust, experiment first with turning the pressure control knob. If changing the pressure doesn't help, check the tip and the thickness of the paint. Too small a spray tip for thick paint causes heavy spatters in the middle of the spray and lighter coverage at the edges. Using too large a tip with thin paint produces a coarse spray. The design will be widely spattered and the coverage poor.

Follow the technique shown (right). Arcing the sprayer as you swing your arm creates thin spots at the edges and too much paint in the middle. To overcome the temptation to swing your arm, move your whole body parallel to the surface.

Cleaning up. Pump excess paint out of the hose first. Then use the appropriate solvent to flush out the sprayer. Clean individual components by soaking them in the applicable solvent. When the sprayer is reassembled, lubricate metal parts with an all-purpose oil for rust protection.

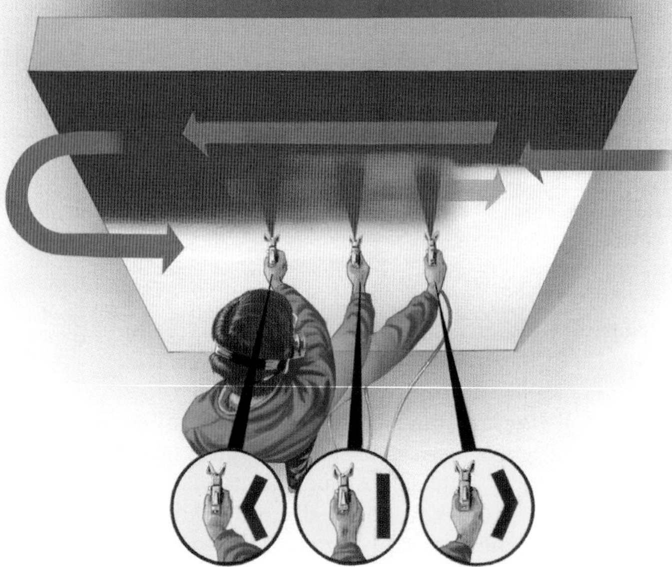

Keep the sprayer parallel to the wall. As you move along, flex your wrist to maintain the same 12-in. (30-cm) distance from the surface. This will result in an even, consistent spray pattern. Make 3-ft. (1-m) horizontal sweeps across the surface you are spraying, slightly overlapping each strip of paint. Go beyond the edges of the area before starting the return pass. The secret to good spraying is multiple thin coats.

Spray it Safe

An airless spray gun must be used with great respect. Paint is forced through the tip at pressures up to 3,000 pounds per sq.-in.

Such powerful propulsion can inject paint through your skin and into your body, causing serious injury that requires immediate attention in a hospital emergency room. When using an airless paint sprayer, at all times follow these safety rules:

- Never point a spray gun at yourself or at any other person.
- Keep children and pets well away when you are spray painting.
- Unplug airless equipment before unclogging a spray tip or before any other disassembly or maintenance procedure.
- Never leave an airless sprayer lying about unattended.
- Always wear safety glasses and a dual cartridge respirator with the proper cartridge.

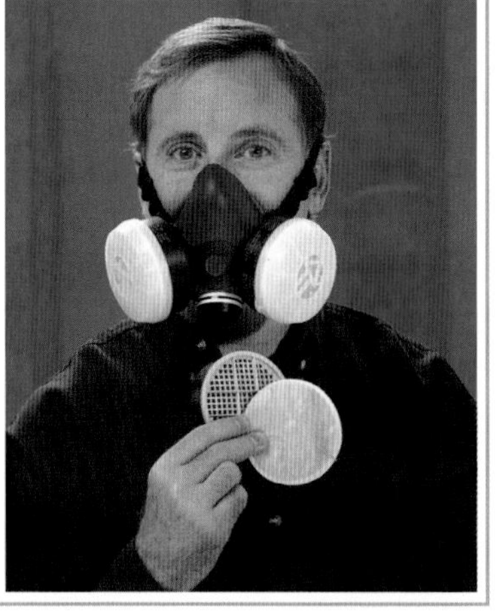

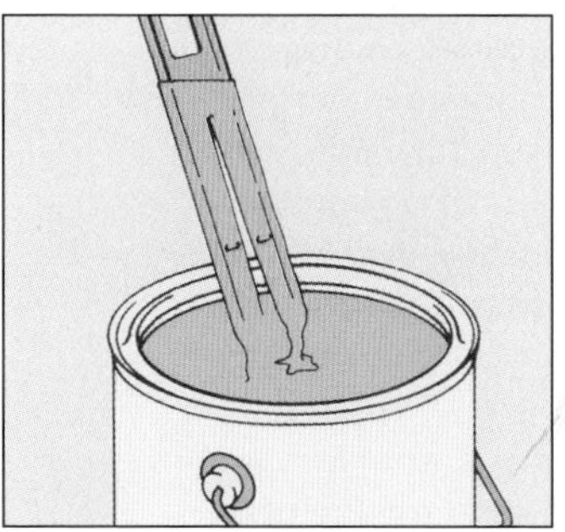

A viscosity test stick helps to gauge whether paint has been thinned enough for a sprayer. To be usable, paint must drain from a notch to a particular point on the stick in a predetermined number of seconds. Most paints need at least 10 percent dilution for spraying.

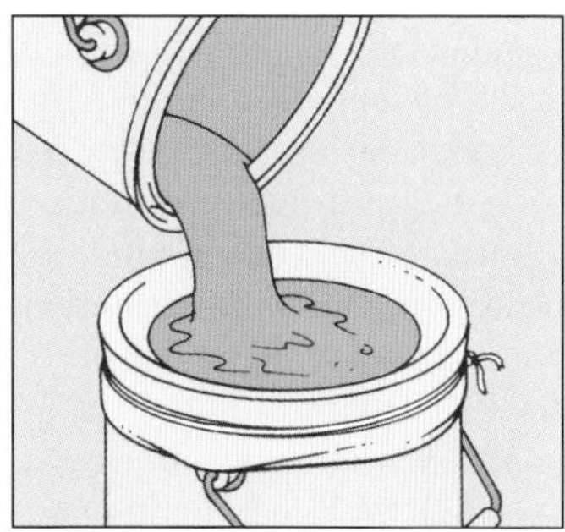

Straining paint through several layers of nylon stocking material or cheesecloth will prevent lumps and debris from clogging the spray tip.

Interiors / Preparing a Room

Begin by removing furniture and rugs. The furniture that stays should be clustered in the middle of the room and covered with drop cloths.

Dismantle hardware. Remove knobs, latches and locks on doors and wood window frames. Take down curtain rods and brackets. Remove picture hooks. Turn off electricity to the room at the fuse or circuit-breaker box, then unscrew plates from electrical switches and outlets. If there's a ceiling lighting fixture, either disconnect it and take it down or loosen its plate and enclose it—plate and all—in a large plastic bag.

Finish masking. Protect wall sconces, radiators and thermostats. Cover the entire floor (or carpeting) with drop cloths and tape them in place. Canvas drop cloths absorb paint and allow it to dry quickly. Paint on a plastic cloth stays wet, and if you step on it, you are likely to track it into other rooms. In a pinch, place several layers of newspaper over plastic.

Make repairs. Fix walls, ceilings and woodwork with the techniques described on the next page. Prime patched areas to ensure uniform paint coverage.

Wash down all surfaces to be painted. Use a heavy-duty detergent, such as trisodium phosphate (TSP) or a nonphosphate equivalent. Even fingerprints can keep paint from bonding properly. Clean any damp or mildewed areas with a 1-to-3 household bleach and water solution. Rinse and let the area dry completely before painting. Glossy surfaces may also need sanding or an application of commercial deglosser for new paint to adhere properly.

1 Cover floor with drop cloths. 2 Move large objects into middle of room and cover with plastic. Remove all pictures, movable objects, hooks and hangers. 3 Remove all switch and outlet cover plates. Remove, mask off or cover light fixtures and thermostats. 4 Patch holes in ceiling and wall, then sand smooth. Spot prime patched areas and all new drywall. 5 Caulk gaps between moldings and walls.

Handy Hints

Masking Tape Tricks

Here are a few hints for applying masking tape fast and neatly:

- Fold over the end after each use. It will be easier to grab and you won't "lose" it.
- Slide the roll over your hand and use your wrist as a tape dispenser as you work.
- Use a putty knife to firmly press the tape down; you'll paint a cleaner line with less overrun.

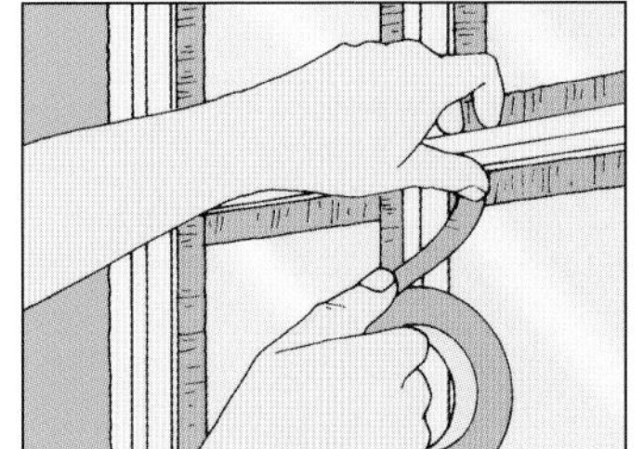

Mask windowpanes leaving a small gap between the panes and the muntins. A small line of unbroken paint film adhering to the panes protects the muntins from harmful condensation.

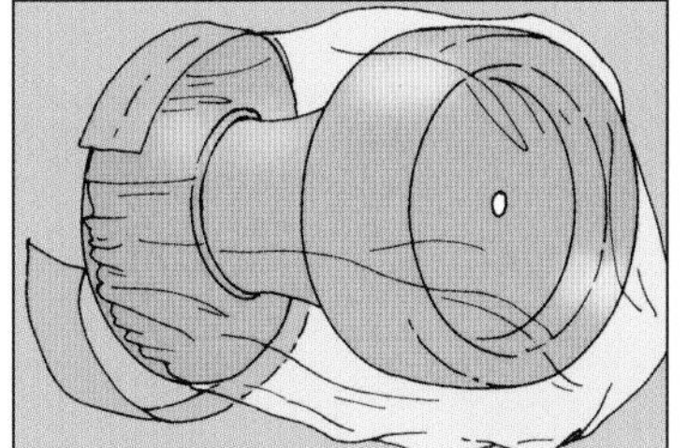

Cover doorknobs with a small plastic bag held by masking tape. Or remove the knob completely to eliminate all the extra detailed cutting in with a brush.

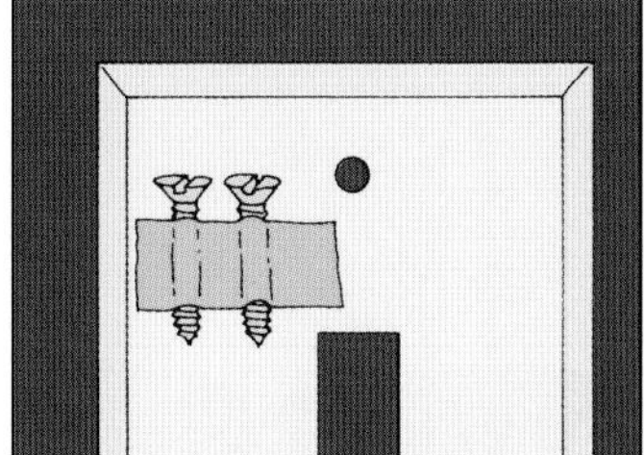

Keep track of screws and small pieces of hardware by taping them to the object with which they're used. Here, the screws are attached to the switchplate they hold in place.

Interiors / Preparing Walls

Drywall Repairs 217
Strippers 451

The key to a good-looking, long-lasting paint job is painstaking preparation. The scraping tools shown below testify to the number of different surfaces that may need stripping before they can be repaired, sanded down, scrubbed and primed for a fresh coat of paint.

The triangular shave hook, or molding scraper, digs accumulated paint and dirt out of the crevices in decorative woodwork. Similar tools with different heads scrape paint off curved wood molding. The razor scraper uses standard blades and takes paint off glass. The flexible wall scraper, or drywall taping knife, removes wallpaper and softened paint from flat surfaces. It is also used to level off applications of plaster compound. The flexible putty knife is equally versatile, but for smaller jobs. The hook scraper, which you draw toward you, takes paint off flat wood surfaces like windowsills and door frames.

Get your room ready in this order:

Check for big problems. A sagging ceiling, for example, may be evidence of a roof leak or a seeping radiator on the floor above. Track down the cause of wall or ceiling damage and clear that up before you repair the drywall or plaster.

Clear the walls. Take down pictures and curtains to look for cracks, holes and peeling paint on walls and ceiling. Check the woodwork for loose paint, nicks, popped nails and separations at corners or at wall junctures. If there is wallpaper, you'll probably want to strip it, whether you are painting or repapering.

Assemble your materials. For masking you'll need drop cloths, newspaper, masking tape and plastic bags. For access, you'll need ladders and boards for scaffolding. For repairs, have on hand spackling compound, wood filler, a heat gun or chemical paint remover, sander and sandpaper, tack cloth, vacuum cleaner and primer. For cleaning you'll want detergent, bleach, bucket and sponge; for safety, goggles and respirators.

Tools

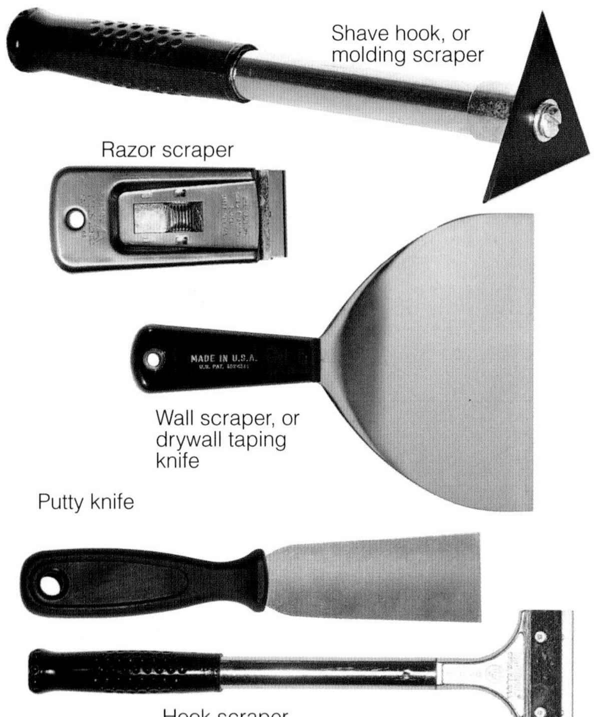

Wall Preparations

1 Wash the ceiling, walls and trim with powdered detergent. Use Soilex or another brand that requires no rinsing. Shut off power and remove outlet covers when done.

2 Fill cracks, holes and dents in walls and trim with latex spackling compound. Sand until smooth, vacuum, then apply primer to seal it.

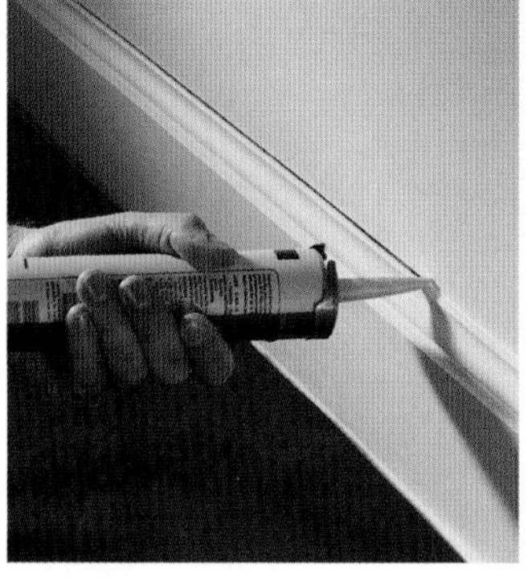

3 Caulk gaps, especially along the top of the baseboards and around window and door trim. Use paintable latex caulk and cut just a small hole in the tip.

4 Seal stains with a latex- or shellac-based stain-killer to keep stains from bleeding through your paint. Prime the sealed areas before painting.

Preparation for wood trim—whether it's painted or natural—can range from a quick cleaning to a complete stripping.

Painted wood trim—if it is in good shape—needs little more than scrubbing with a strong detergent like trisodium phosphate (TSP) or its nonphosphate equivalent before repainting. Very glossy paint may need to be sanded or treated with a deglosser so the new paint will adhere.

Once paint begins to craze (crack) or peel badly, it's better to remove it than to try to repair large patches. You can remove old paint with a heat gun (right) or with a chemical stripper. Nontoxic strippers work slowly—they soften old paint in hours rather than minutes—but they save exposure to caustic substances and fumes.

The finish on natural wood trim can be revived if it's dull, but you must remove it if the finish is in poor shape or the underlying stain has worn through.

Bare wood needs to be sanded smooth, wiped free of dust with a commercial tack cloth (or a cotton rag soaked in paint thinner), and sealed with a primer before it is repainted.

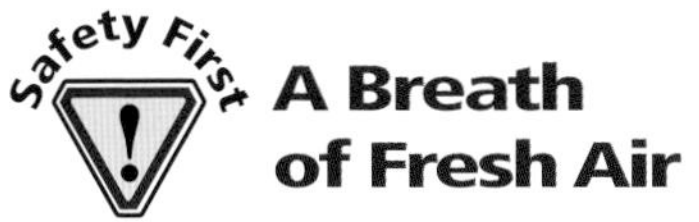

A Breath of Fresh Air

Whether you're removing a finish with a heat gun or chemical strippers, let fumes out and fresh air in by opening windows and using fans.

Stripping Painted Woodwork

Use great caution when heat stripping; guns can reach temperatures as high as 1,200° F (650° C). Protect yourself with heavy work gloves and breathing protection. Protect your home by making certain nothing smolders or inadvertently catches on fire.

1 Hold the gun about 1 in. (2.5 cm) from the paint. To prevent scorching the wood, keep the gun moving constantly. Work it back and forth over one small area at a time.

2 Scrape off softened paint, holding a putty knife in one hand while moving the gun over an adjacent area of paint with the other.

Reviving Natural Woodwork

Reviving natural woodwork is easier, quicker and costs less than stripping. Use the photos below to diagnose whether or not your woodwork is a good candidate for reviving, then test the process on a small inconspicuous area to see if it will work in your situation.

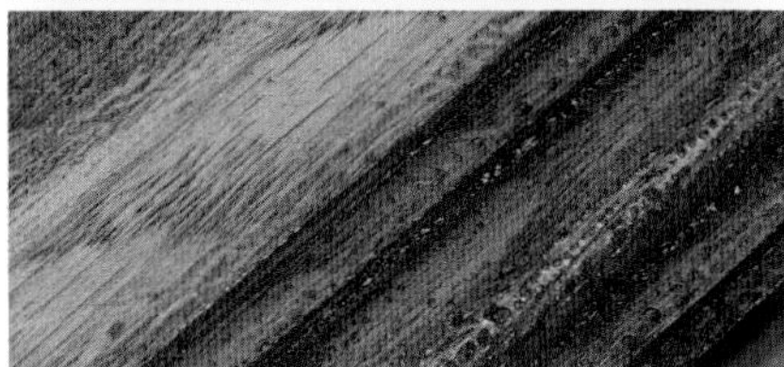

Strip or renew? Even though the woodwork in the top photo is dull and dark, it's generally in good condition with no serious flaws in the finish. It's a likely candidate for reviving. The woodwork in the lower photo is checked, bubbling and peeling. It should be stripped and refinished.

Revive. Scrub the surface with a fine- to medium-grit sanding sponge dipped in mineral spirits. Wipe the surface clean with a rag soaked in mineral spirits. After 30 minutes, spot stain any areas that have worn through, let stain dry, then apply sanding sealer and two coats of varnish.

Stripping Natural Woodwork

Stripping older clear finishes is messy, tedious work. But when you're finished, you'll love the new look. Try using a water-based stripper. It works slowly and, because it tends to raise the wood's grain, you'll sand more, but there are no harmful odors and it's nonflammable.

1 Apply a thick layer of stripper, brushing in only one direction. Protect floors with plastic drop cloths.

2 Lay down newspaper to catch loosened finish. Scrape flat surfaces with a stiff putty knife and contoured surfaces with plastic scrapers. Apply a second coat, scrub with a stiff brush, then clean and sand the surface thoroughly. Apply stain and two coats of varnish.

Interiors / Preparing Other Surfaces

Painting Tools 282
Hazardous Materials 480

No paint job will look good or last long if the surface beneath it is rough, scaly or full of gaps and cracks. Some pros spend just as much time sanding, puttying and priming as they do painting—but the finished result is worth it.

Large gouges and damaged areas in wood surfaces should be slightly overfilled with plastic wood filler, then sanded with 150-grit paper until flush with the surrounding area. Smaller cracks and gaps can be filled with caulk, wood putty or even spackling compound.

Tighten any joints in the trim around windows and doors before painting. You can fill gaps with putty as shown or use corner clamps to pull the joint tight, then predrill holes and drive in finish nails to hold the moldings in place.

Here's how to patch and prepare other damaged surfaces:

Metal doors. Sand dented areas down to bare metal. Mix and spread on two-part epoxy auto body filler. Sand the patch with medium, then fine sandpaper, then prime and paint.

Hollow-core doors. Shoot expanding foam sealant in deep holes. After the foam hardens, trim away the excess with a putty knife so the foam is slightly below the surface. Fill the depression with wood filler; sand, prime and paint.

Spray-textured ceilings. Scrape away loose texture, then prime water stains with a stain-blocking primer. Use a spray texture repair product, available at home centers and hardware stores, to blend the area in with the old, then prime and paint.

Moldings and Trim

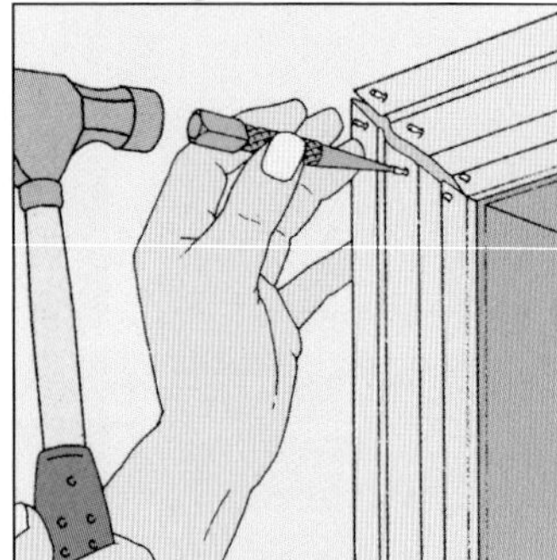

1 Use a hammer and nail set to sink the heads of any popped nails below the surface. Then use your fingertip to force wood putty into the holes. Sand the surface smooth.

2 Fill joint openings in decorative trim using a flexible putty knife and putty. If the opening is deep, apply two layers. Shape and sand the dried material to conform to the shape of the molding.

Paneling

Older plywood paneling can be left in place and painted over. First, fill the grooves with spackle, then lightly sand and prime the surface before rolling on the paint.

Radiators

Metal surfaces should be carefully prepared. First use a stiff wire brush to remove loose paint. Then prime with a primer formulated specifically for metal.

Safety First

Lead Paint Testing

Any house built before 1978 may contain lead paint; older homes almost certainly do. Lead paint isn't a hazard when it's covered and maintained, but renovations and everyday wear and tear can expose lead paint and create dust and chips.

Children are especially likely to ingest lead. And because their neurological systems are still developing, small amounts of lead are dangerous.

If your house is older and has undergone renovation or has chipping or worn paint, you should check for the presence of lead. Buy a test kit (check the Yellow Pages or the Internet for a source), follow the directions, then send the samples to the lab for analysis. The lab report will list micrograms of lead per sq. ft. of area. Currently the U.S. government has proposed recommendations of less than 40 micrograms of lead per sq. ft. of floor and less than 250 micrograms per sq. ft. of windowsill. (Canadians can consult the resources listed on page 516.)

If the lab results show higher levels, contact your local health department for cleanup and control recommendations and have your children tested for dangerous levels of lead.

To test for the presence of lead dust, wipe a 12-in. (30-cm)-square area of flooring with the special wipe included in the test kit, then place it in the special container. Most kits will have you perform a similar "wipe test" on a windowsill. Send the samples to a lab and you should receive your results within two weeks.

Interiors / Choosing Paint

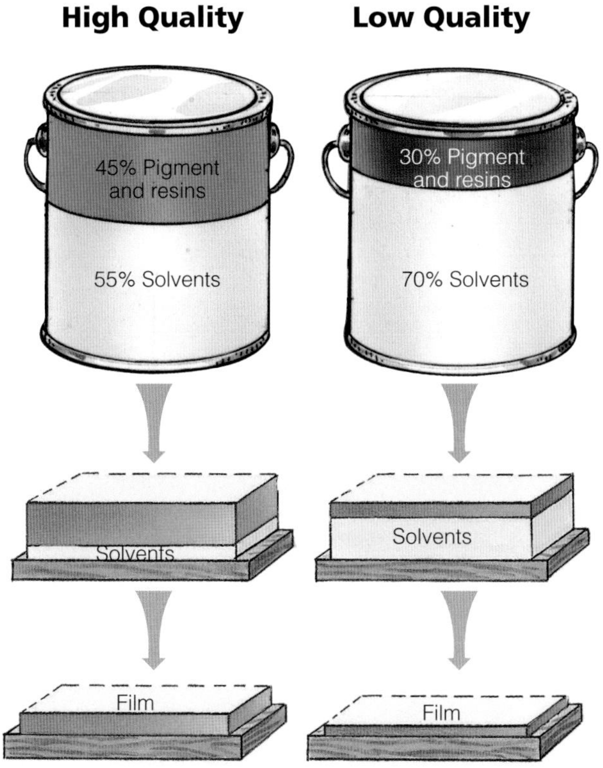

Painting is labor-intensive and material-cheap. So as long as you're spending many hours applying paint, apply the good stuff. It'll cost a little more but it'll last longer, protect better and cover in fewer coats.

All paints contain four basic ingredients. Here's what they are and what separates the good from the bad:

Pigments are the finely ground particles that give paint its opacity. In high-quality paints, these pigments are purer, smaller, more plentiful and do a better job blocking the color of the surface they're applied to.

Resins, sometimes called binders, encapsulate the pigments, penetrate the wood and create the surface film. Paints labeled "100 percent acrylic" are of higher quality than those labeled "vinyl acrylic."

Solvents are the liquids—water in latex paints, mineral spirits in oil-based paints—that transport the pigments and resins from the brush or roller onto the wall, then evaporate as the paint dries. Less solvent means more solid resins and pigments, which translates into better coverage.

Additives include thickeners that help create smoother surfaces, surfactants that help paints adhere better and mildewcides that help limit mildew growth, at least for a few years.

In many ways, the best determinant of good paint is price; you'll get what you pay for. And since high-quality paint can last twice as long as less expensive paint, it's actually cheaper in the long run.

Primers

Primers are designed to help paint stick. There are primers formulated for use on metals, vinyls, bare drywall, wall coverings and other surfaces. Using the right primer will ensure better adhesion and, in most cases, result in fewer coats of paint.

Here are a few tips to remember:
- Both oil-based and latex paints can be applied over an oil-based primer. As a general rule, only latex paint should be applied over a latex primer, but some newer formulas allow for both oil and latex topcoats.
- Tinting a primer will often allow you to get by with one coat of paint.
- When painting over surfaces that have stains that tend to bleed through, prime first with a "stain-blocking" primer.

Drywall primer

Stain-blocking primer

Tinted primer

What Paint to Use Where

Selecting the right primer and paint for the job depends on the composition and condition of the surface it will be applied to, as well as what kind of abuse it will take. Here are some basic guidelines:

PAINT TYPES:

Water-based (latex): Latex paint has the consistency of latex, but doesn't actually contain any of the substance. Withstands moisture, mildew and wood movement. Fast drying and therefore, more likely to show brushstrokes than oils; but new additives are overcoming this tendency. Water clean-up.

Oil-based (alkyd): Most often used for woodwork, trim, cabinets and floors. Slow drying and less likely to show brushstrokes. Mineral spirits clean-up. Use is restricted in some areas.

Enamel: Enamel paint is tougher and more "scrubbable" than other paints. It can be either latex or oil and usually has a fairly high sheen. More likely to yellow and become brittle with age.

Epoxy: Exceptionally durable and moisture resistant. Often used on concrete and wood floors. Some are two-part products. Critical to follow manufacturer's instructions regarding priming and other preparation work.

PAINT SHEEN:

Gloss: Durable and easy to scrub. Best for high-use areas such as bathrooms, kitchens, hallways and children's bedrooms. Often used for woodwork and trim. Most likely to show surface flaws.

Satin/semi-gloss: Often used in bathrooms, kitchens and other areas where a soft yet somewhat glossy look is desired.

Flat/eggshell: The least shiny and least likely to show surface flaws. Often used on ceilings and walls of less likely to be abused rooms like bedrooms and living rooms.

Interiors / Selecting Color

Paint manufacturers have taken much of the guesswork out of selecting paints. Most now have brochures and Web sites that suggest different schemes and combinations based on the style of your house or room.

There are a few rules of thumb in regard to color selections. Pale shades open a room and give it a sense of spaciousness. Because colors with a lot of white in them reflect light, they brighten dark hallways and rooms with a northern exposure, which get the least sunlight. White ceilings seem higher because the color makes them appear to recede.

Dark colors make a room cozy and intimate. They are often used in quiet places like studies and dens. Dark colors can also disguise architectural faults like uneven walls, and they hide signs of wear in heavy-use areas.

Blues, violets, greens and grays give a cool, serene feeling to a room. Intense cool colors are refreshing, while subdued cool hues have a tranquil effect. Reds, oranges and yellows warm a room. Intense warm colors create excitement; subtler hues, sociability.

Pure colors are vibrant, energetic, but, in too great a quantity, a little tiring. Expanses of bright, intense color belong in active spaces like recreation rooms. Bright accents, however, can add excitement to soft color schemes.

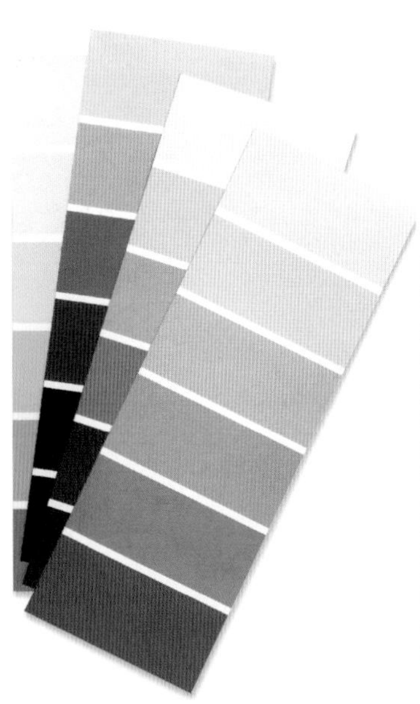

Using swatches. When you choose room colors you can select them all from the families of colors on a single paint swatch; select one for the trim, one for the walls and one for the ceiling. As a rule of thumb, if your ceilings are less than 9 ft. (270 cm) tall, paint them two shades lighter than the walls. If they're taller, paint them two shades darker. For the trim, select a color within the same family.

Light vs. Dark Color

To make a room appear larger and the ceiling taller, paint them both light colors. To make a room feel calm and uncluttered, paint it white.

To make any room feel smaller and more intimate, paint the walls a dark color. Darker ceilings tend to make them feel lower.

Monochromatic vs. Colorful

To unify a room or give an odd-shaped room a sense of wholeness, go with a monochromatic color scheme.

To add liveliness to a room, use bright, contrasting colors. Kids bedrooms are likely candidates for these schemes.

Interiors / Decorative Painting

There are dozens of different decorative painting techniques and tools you can use to liven your walls. You can use sea sponges, rags, newspapers or any number of special tools available in the paint department to help simplify the task. Some companies now offer rollers embossed with random raised patterns so you can roll on a decorative finish. Look around and talk with a paint specialist to get a feel for the full range of tools and materials available.

Whichever method you choose, practice your technique and experiment with your color choices in the back of a closet or on a scrap piece of drywall until you feel comfortable with the look. Decorative painting is very forgiving; if you make a mistake, you can simply paint over it and try again.

Sponging

1 Immerse a sea sponge in water, wring it out thoroughly, then rotate the sponge in the paint until it's lightly and evenly coated.

2 Start applying paint over your base coat by starting at the top and working down. Work in a 2- x 2-ft. area and overlap the pattern slightly so every mark blends with the next.

3 When the first coat has been applied and has dried, add a second color to add richness and texture to the finish. You can use a completely different color or a lighter version of the first.

Stippling

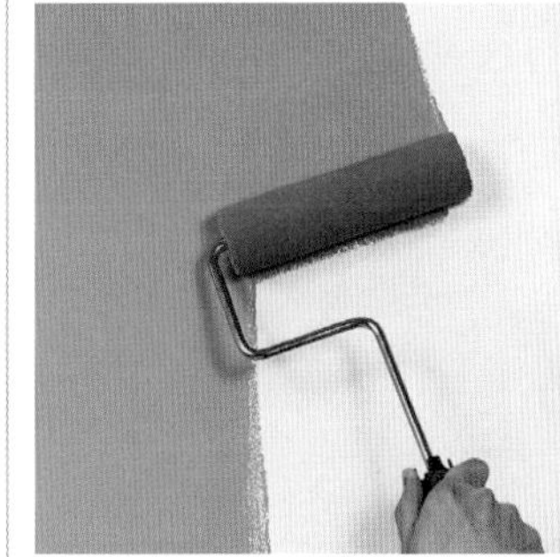

1 In this technique, you get an effect by removing glaze in a pattern. It works best with alkyd paint, which dries more slowly, giving you extra time to work. Apply a coat of alkyd glaze (blue paint in picture) over a thoroughly dried alkyd base coat (cream) with roller or pad.

2 With the glaze still tacky, press a coarse brush against it in quick, firm jabs, which will reveal the base color and give the wall a textured look. Stippling is easiest when two people work: one glazes while the other follows with the stippling tool.

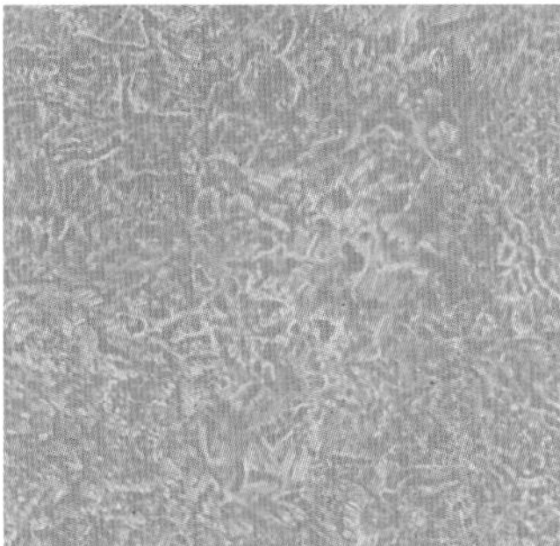
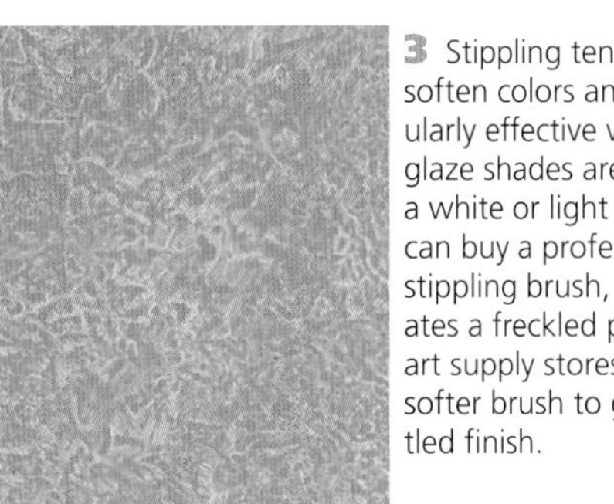

3 Stippling tends to soften colors and is particularly effective when deep glaze shades are used over a white or light base. You can buy a professional stippling brush, which creates a freckled pattern, in art supply stores, or use a softer brush to get a mottled finish.

Rag-Rolling

1 This technique works best with alkyd paint and glaze. Start with a base coat (cream here) and let it dry completely. Have plenty of rags (old cotton sheets or cheesecloth are good) cut up and ready for use before applying the glaze (rose in picture).

2 With folded, rolled, or crumpled strips of cloth, blot off part of the glaze in an irregular pattern that will look consistent over a whole wall. Reroll rags or pick up fresh ones often. Working with a partner will make the rag-rolling go much faster, and the results will be more uniform.

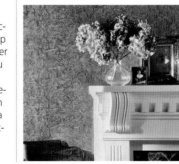

3 Cotton rags were used for this pattern of rag-rolling. Other fabrics will create different textures and patterns. Sharply contrasting colors, like burgundy over tan, will give a more dramatic effect than the rose over cream shown here.

Interiors / Painting Ceilings and Walls

To paint a room efficiently and neatly, work from top to bottom. Start with the ceiling, letting the paint lap onto the walls. Next use a 2-in. angled brush to "cut in" areas along the ceiling and along the baseboard, door and window trim. Hold the brush like a pencil. Dip the bristles one-third of their length into paint; gently press out excess paint against the side of the container. Apply the paint in smooth, overlapping strokes. Finally, roll the walls and paint the trim and moldings.

Mix the paint thoroughly before you use it. Let your paint dealer mix it on a machine if you will be painting right away. If you have had the paint for a while, turn the can upside down and let it sit for 24 hours before you open it. To ensure a uniform color, pour the two or three cans it might take to paint a room into a large bucket and mix them together. Then pour paint back into a smaller container or roller tray for working. Always reclose the can; this keeps your supply from drying out, picking up stray grit or spilling.

Painting order. 1 Paint ceiling. 2 Cut in paint at tops of walls, around doors and windows, in corners, around switches and outlets and along baseboard moldings. 3 Paint walls, starting at ceiling and working down. 4 Paint trim and moldings.

Rolling Paint

Here's a method for rolling paint that's not fancy but gets the job done in record time. It will also eliminate common problems like light areas, roller marks and built-up ridges.

Even the best technique won't work with poor-quality equipment, so invest in high-quality tools. Purchase a good roller frame that won't let the cover slip off, a short- or medium-nap wool-blend roller cover, an extension handle, a large bucket and a bucket screen.

1 Load the roller cover by dipping it halfway into the paint, then rolling it against the screen. Do this two or three times.

2 Start about 1 ft. (30 cm) from the bottom and 6 in. (15 cm) from the corner. Roll upward at a slight angle using light pressure. Then roll up and down quickly toward the corner to spread the paint.

3 Reload the roller and repeat the process in the adjacent space, working back toward the painted area.

4 Roll back over the entire area to smooth and blend the paint. Roll from floor to ceiling, slightly overlapping the previous stroke.

Interiors / Painting Woodwork

Good surface preparation and good brushing technique are the keys to great-looking painted woodwork. Begin by scrubbing with TSP (or TSP substitute) to remove grease and grime; then rinse with clear water. Scrape away any loose paint, and fill any gouges or dents with a wood filler. Sand the filler smooth with 120- and 180-grit sandpaper. Spot prime the filler and any bare wood. Finally, caulk any seams or gaps before painting.

1 Apply putty to any gouges by holding a putty knife at an angle and pressing. Leave the filler slightly higher than the surrounding area, then sand smooth.

2 Start at the top and bottom with a loaded brush and stroke toward the middle. When the brush begins to drag, stop and reload.

3 Holding the brush perpendicular, lightly set the tip of the brush against the wet paint and stroke down the entire length of the board. Move to the next board.

Paint Like a Pro

For pros to make money, they have to work quickly and efficiently. We can all learn something from that! Invest the time it takes to get a room ready for painting; clean out the room, move large items to the middle of the floor and cover them with plastic, put down drop cloths and remove door hardware, light fixtures, picture hooks and switch and outlet covers. Give the walls a quick sanding with 100-grit paper attached to a drywall sanding tool for the smoothest results. Then use the tips shown here.

Remove light fixture globes and covers and mask the bases with plastic bags. Seal old water stains on the ceiling and elsewhere with an aerosol stain blocker.

Paint textured ceilings with a thick nap roller. Roll on the first coat lightly in one direction, then a second thicker coat in the opposite direction.

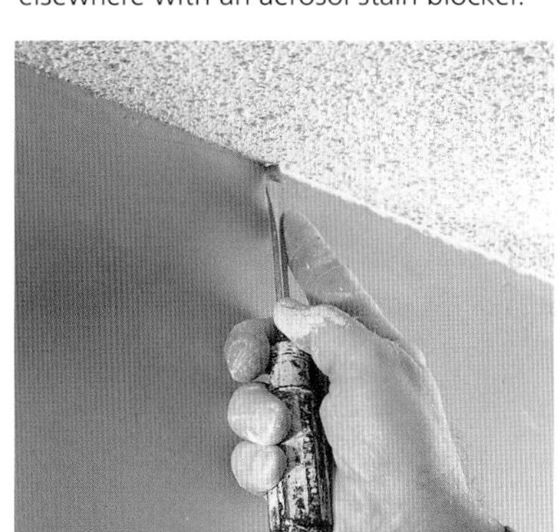

Drag a screwdriver around the perimeter of textured ceilings to remove a thin line of texture to ensure crisp paint lines when you cut in along the ceiling.

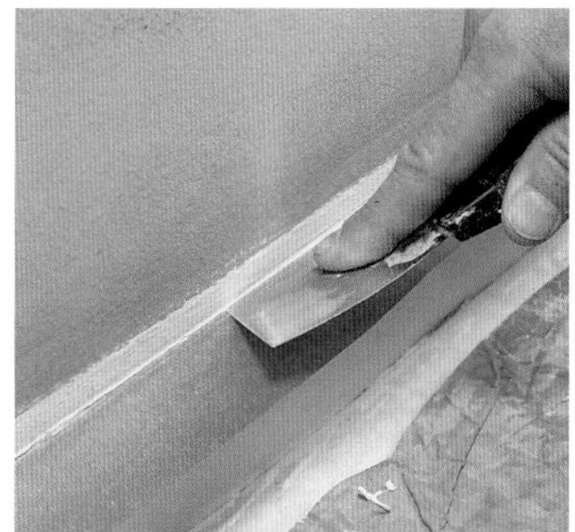

Mask off woodwork using a putty knife to press the tape in place. Let the tape stick out perpendicular to the trim to catch any paint drips.

Interiors / Painting Windows, Doors and Stairs

Painting Windows

If time, weather and window design allow, remove the sashes (the frames that hold the actual glass) from the window frame, as well as operating hardware, so you can paint as many edges and surfaces as possible. Sash removal is fairly easy with most glide-by, casement and newer double-hung windows. Older double-hung windows are usually easier to paint in place.

1 Paint the dividing muntins or grids, then the window sash outer frame. Leave a hairline of paint overlapping onto the glass to seal out moisture and condensation that could cause paint to peel.

2 Alternate the positions of the sashes. Paint the area where the two sashes meet and as many other edges as you can reach. Work the sashes up and down a few times to keep them from sticking.

3 After painting the grids and sash frames, move on to the casing and finally the sill and apron. Don't paint the metal channels in the window tracks. Lubricate channels with silicone spray after the paint has dried.

Painting Doors

Whenever possible, remove a door from its hinges so you can easily access the bottom and top edges for painting. Remove hinges and hardware to help the job go quickly and smoothly. Laying a door horizontally across a pair of sawhorses, or 2x4s laying on the floor, helps minimize drips and runs.

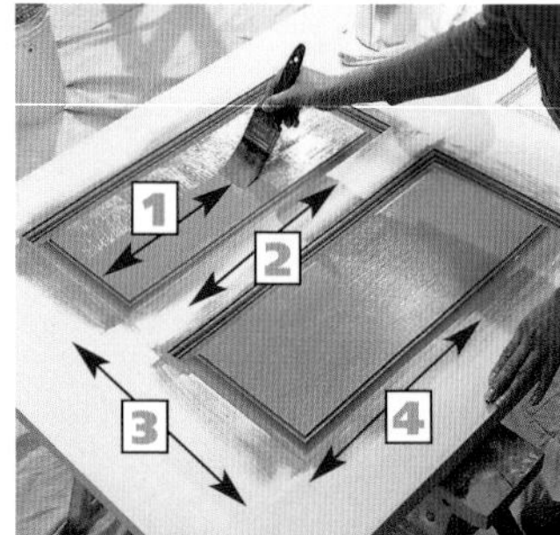

1 Spread paint on the inner panels first; then work outward. Some people prefer to apply the paint quickly with a roller and then work it into corners and around moldings with a brush.

2 Smooth out the paint in long sweeping strokes, mimicking the original direction of the wood grain. Make certain to paint top and bottom edges to seal out moisture that could cause the door to warp.

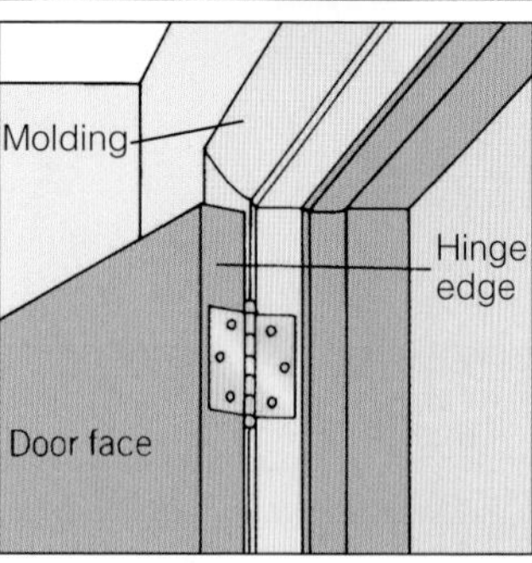

3 Door faces and moldings should match when the door is closed. Paint the hinge edge the same color as the adjacent visible door face; latch edge matches the side of door (not visible) opening into the room.

Painting Stairs

When painting stair treads and risers, purchase a paint formulated for high-use areas. Balusters and handrails are best painted with an easy-to-maintain, high-gloss enamel paint.

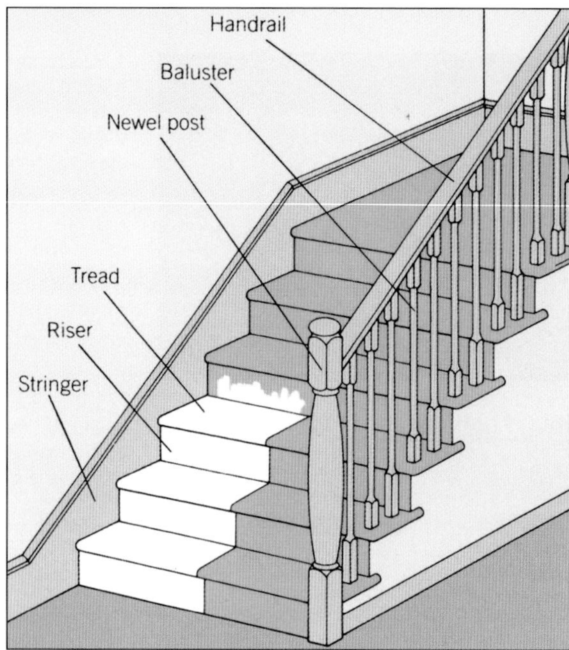

The painting order for stairs starts with the balusters, newel post, and handrail. Then, beginning at the top and working down one step at a time, paint the treads, risers, and stringer on one side of the stairs, leaving the other half open for traffic. When the paint is dry, start again at the top and work on the other half of each step.

Twice as Good

Since the centers of most stairways get twice as much wear and tear as the outer edges, apply twice as much paint to this area. Paint the right two-thirds of each tread, then when the paint is dry, paint the left two-thirds. This way the center area gets a double coat.

Interiors / Painting Concrete Floors

Epoxy paint is a tough, long-lasting coating you can apply to concrete that will resist grease, oil and other substances that would ruin ordinary paint. It comes in a variety of colors and is easy to maintain. Be aware of two things: one, not all concrete will hold a coating and, two, preparing the concrete can be labor-intensive and tedious.

Plan to spend the first day removing oil spots, cleaning and degreasing the floor, etching it with a mild acid and scrubbing. Set aside a second day for filling cracks and applying the first coat and a third day for applying a second coat.

For the best results, rent a walk-behind power floor scrubber with a stiff brush attachment and a wet vacuum if you don't own them.

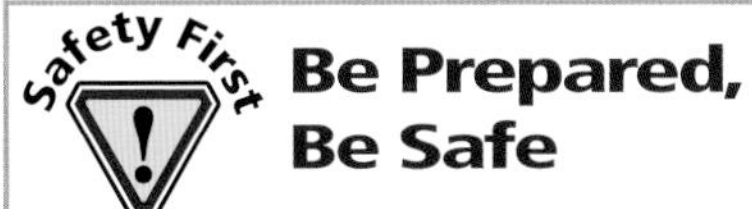

Be Prepared, Be Safe

Wear gloves, eye and lung protection and rubber boots. Turn off gas to the water heater or other appliances in the garage. Keep children and pets at a distance.

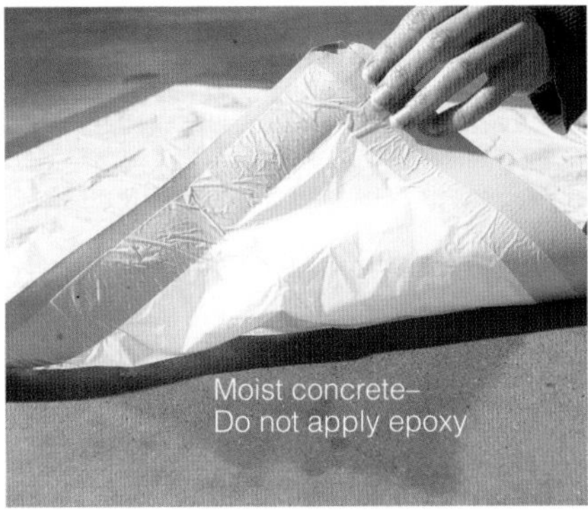

1 Lift the corner of a plastic bag that's been taped to the floor for 24 hours. If it's dry underneath, you can apply an epoxy coating. If you see moisture, don't coat the floor with epoxy; water pressure will break the bond.

2 Use a stiff-bristle brush and cleaner/degreaser to scrub oil stains until the greasy feel is gone. Wet the floor and scrub with the electric scrubber and cleaner/degreaser. Vacuum up solution and dispose of it properly.

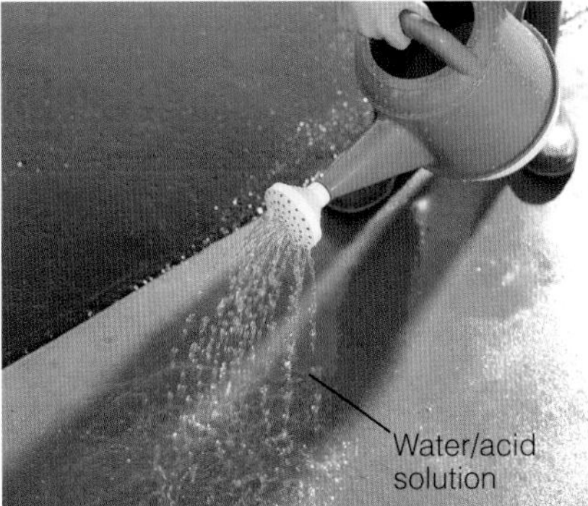

3 Pour 32 percent muriatic acid (a common formulation) into water at a ratio of one part acid to 10 parts water, and then sprinkle evenly over a 10- x 10-ft. (3- x 3-m) area. **Caution: Always add acid to water and wear an organic vapor/acid respirator.**

4 Power scrub each area for 5 to 10 minutes, making sure the entire area stays wet. When completely finished, spray a large volume of water on the floor, power scrub again, then rinse two or three more times. Let floor dry overnight.

5 Mix the two epoxy compounds for 5 minutes using a drill and stirring bit. Pour into a second bucket and mix again to ensure complete blending of the mixture.

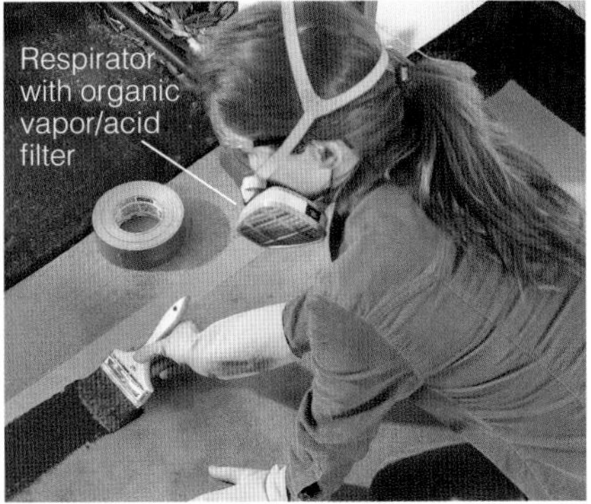

6 Tape the area directly under the garage door with duct or masking tape. Then brush a thin strip of epoxy along the walls and against the tape.

7 Dip a roller half way into the paint. Apply the paint in a "W" pattern the size of the area shown. Then backroll to fill in the pattern—all in about 60 seconds. Go lightly over it to remove roller marks.

8 Let the first coat dry, then apply the second coat. If you don't want a glossy floor, add a nonskid floor coating additive for the second coat. Wait three to seven days before parking your car on the floor.

Exteriors / Choosing Paints and Stains

House siding is usually protected with flat paint, and trim with glossy enamel. Wood shingles and shakes can be painted, stained or protected with a clear finish. The chart (right) suggests types of coatings suitable for various exterior surfaces.

Ask your paint dealer about additives. Houses that are heavily shaded often have mildew problems. You can have a fungus-inhibiting additive mixed into the paint.

Many exterior oil-based paints are designed to be self-cleaning. They gradually "chalk," or give off a powdery white substance that rain washes away along with the dirt and grime that cling to it. This process keeps paint looking fresh but can stain red brick walls or dark siding located below.

Latex paints are easy to apply, dry quickly, and clean up with water. They resist the alkali found in concrete and masonry that disintegrate alkyd paints; they are permeable to moisture, so they blister less and allow dampness to escape.

Oil-based paints and stains take longer to dry and require hazardous solvents for cleanup, but some argue they go on smoother, dry harder and can be applied at lower temperatures.

Paint vs. Stain

Paint is a film-forming finish, which means it lasts longer, offers better protection and has stronger colors than stain. But paint films, especially dark colors, which can blister in the hot sun, are more likely to peel.

Stain is a nonfilm-forming finish. The advantage to this is that it soaks into the wood, won't peel and is easier to renew. However, stain colors are more muted, and they won't protect as well as paint.

How Much Paint?

To estimate paint for a project, add up the length of all walls and multiply by the height of the building. Don't subtract for windo ws and doors unless there are multiple large units.

As a rule of thumb, a gallon (3.78 l) of paint will cover:

- 350 sq. ft. (33 sq. m) of previously painted wood siding.
- 200 sq. ft. (19 sq. m) of rough-sawn wood siding or shakes.
- 100 sq. ft. (9 sq. m) of raw stucco or brick.

In normal situations, you'll need one unit of trim paint for every six units of siding paint.

Exterior Paint Selection Guide

Previously painted wood siding	No need to prime if existing paint is in good condition. Lightly sand to remove gloss and aid adhesion. Spot prime bare areas. Coat with latex- or oil-based paint once surface is clean and dry.
Previously painted wood doors and trim	Prime bare areas. Coat with high-gloss, oil- or latex-based enamel paint.
New redwood or cedar siding and trim	If applying paint, prime beforehand with a stain-blocking primer (or knots will bleed through topcoat). Solid body and transparent stains and clear finishes require no priming.
Hardboard siding	Most new hardboard siding has factory-applied primer. Topcoat with latex paint.
Cement-based siding	Usually comes with factory-applied primer. If not, use alkali-resistant primer. Topcoat with 100-percent acrylic latex paint.
Concrete block	Latex or special concrete primer. Use "block filler"-type primer to fill pores and voids. Topcoat with latex paint.
Aluminum siding	Pressure wash to clean and remove any chalking. Apply 100-percent acrylic exterior paint once siding is clean and dry.
Vinyl siding	Apply latex house paint once siding is clean and dry. Do *not* paint darker than the color of the original siding in order to minimize expansion and contraction problems.
Porch floors	Apply oil-based primer. Topcoat with special "porch and floor" paints. "Nonskid" additives available. (Some treated-wood floor manufacturers suggest *not* priming. Consult literature.)
Stucco and brick	These materials are basically maintenance free; once you start painting them, you'll need to keep painting them (so think twice). Use flat latex paint on clean, dry surfaces.
Metal gutters, downspout, etc.	Wash thoroughly. Apply primer formulated for use over metal. Topcoat with latex paint.

Selecting a Color Scheme

An effective color scheme can draw attention to a building's best architectural features and minimize its defects. When selecting colors, start with the colors you can't change: the roof, brick facing, a stone foundation or chimney. Look for paint shades that match or harmonize with these colors.

Most buildings have three basic color components:

Body color. Pick this first. It should either contrast with the roof color or—to make an integrated whole of a smaller house—be a variation of it. A light color makes a small house appear larger. A dark color can bring a big, rambling house into proportion. Painting an odd-shaped porch or ugly garage door the same as the body of the house will visually integrate the awkward features.

Trim color. This usually is applied to fascias, soffits, cornice moldings, window frames and sashes, door frames and porch railings. To downplay part of a house that is flawed–sagging facia boards, for example–paint it the body paint color. White window frames seem bigger and brighter.

Accent color. A contrasting color that highlights special features is most effective when used sparingly. Often only the front door and shutters are painted with the accent color.

Many paint manufacturers have interactive Web sites that will allow you to test color combinations on your computer screen before applying them to your house.

Bold Color. A bold color scheme draws attention to the various architectural details. Here several accent colors were used to increase eye appeal and make the entry to this house more inviting.

Subtle Color. A monochromatic color scheme helps unify the different elements of the house. A light color helps a small house appear larger.

Problem: Alligatoring and checking.
If paint has many reptilian-looking interconnected cracks, the outer coat has not adhered properly to the paint beneath. It could have been applied to an incompatible paint, a badly prepared surface, a not-yet-dry first coat, or too many layers of paint may have built up over time.

Solution: Strip to raw wood and reapply primer and paint.

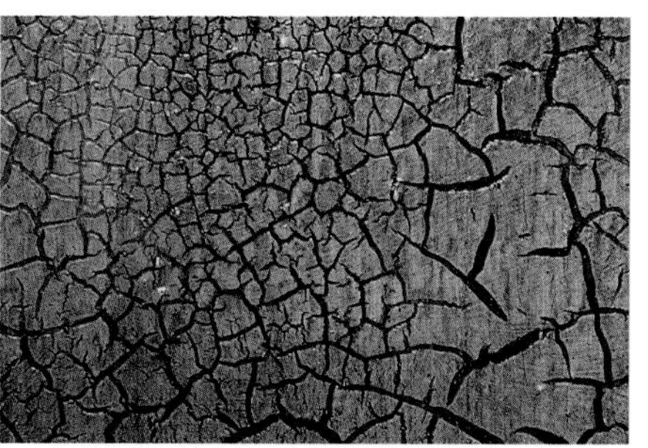

Problem: Blistering and Bubbling.
If bubbles form under paint, open a blister. If it reveals raw wood, moisture has worked its way under the paint and you should check for sources of water, such as leaky gutters, missing caulk, or winter ice dams, and fix before repainting. If the opened blister reveals paint, the temperature was too high when the topcoat was applied.

Solution: Sand and repaint.

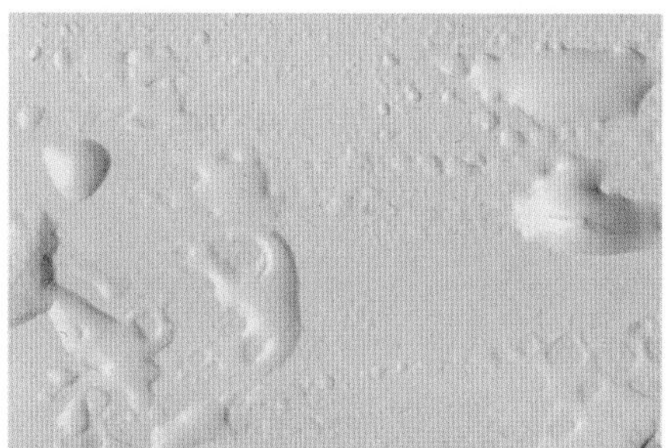

Problem: Chalking.
Most exterior paints are formulated so the surface gradually breaks down into a powdery chalk that takes dirt and grime with it when rain washes it away. This feature keeps the paint looking clean. Chalking surfaces, however, will not hold new paint.

Solution: Scrub a chalking surface with detergent and rinse well before repainting.

Problem: Flaking and Peeling.
If the paint simply didn't stick, the surface might have been dirty, it might have had too many layers of paint already, or the wrong type of paint may have been used. On masonry, flaking can be caused by alkali leaching into paint.

Solution: Strip to the surface, clean carefully, and reapply appropriate primer and paint.

Exteriors / Preparing Surfaces

Sanders 68
Repairing Wood with Epoxy 366

If an exterior paint job is to look good and last a long time, all dirt, grime and loose paint must be removed. Power tools can do some of the work, but a certain amount of handwork—scraping, washing and sanding—is almost always required. Specialized tools designed to shave the paint from lap siding and specialized chemical strippers—some with a paper backing that is applied to the painted siding, and then peeled off—are other, more expensive options to consider. Ridges where well-adhered existing paint meets newly scraped bare wood must be feathered smooth by sanding before you start painting.

Safety First

Lead Paint (again!)

If your home was built before 1978, check the paint for lead. Call your public health department for details. Don't use the methods shown here to remove lead paint because you may create lead dust, the primary cause of lead poisoning.

Removing Old Paint

Pressure washers scour away dirt, grime and chalking, the powder left as paints deteriorate. The high-pressure stream will blast away loose paint. Be careful; it can gouge wood and knock mortar from between bricks.

Remove loose and flaking paint with a sharp steel- or carbide-blade scraper. Pull in the direction of the wood grain and apply enough downward pressure with your other hand to strip paint, but not gouge the wood.

Use a random orbital sander for fast removal of thin paint layers that are difficult to scrape. Start with 60-grit paper for rapid cutting on broad, flat surfaces, then 80- and 100-grit papers to smooth the surface.

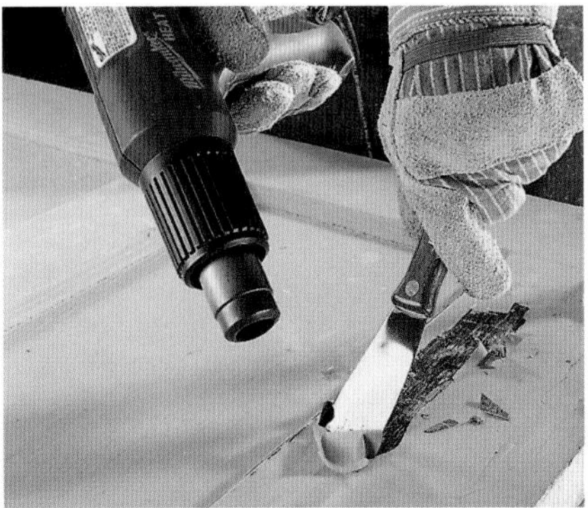

A heat gun softens paint, making it easy to remove with a putty knife. Set it to run no higher than 700° F (370° C) if the paint contains lead. Wear protective gloves, goggles and appropriate breathing respirator.

Preparing and Repairing Damaged Wood

Dig out old loose or cracked caulk with a five-in-one tool or stiff putty knife. Putting new caulk over old hardened caulk is doomed to early failure. Leave old caulk only if it's flexible and tight.

Drive heads of protruding or rusty nails below the wood surface to secure siding, then fill hole with wood filler. Don't sink nails in hardboard siding; moisture can enter the hole and damage the vulnerable siding core.

Seal the end grain of new or replacement boards with primer to keep paint from peeling at seams and butt joints. This may well be the most effective step you can take to prevent paint from peeling.

Fill deep cracks and holes with two-part resin. These resins are expensive, but bond to dry, sound wood, won't shrink, are impervious to moisture and can be sanded and shaped like regular wood.

Exteriors / Priming and Caulking

Priming

Primers are specially formulated to seal the wood, adhere well and form a smooth consistent base for the paint. Don't buy a cheap primer. To make sure it's compatible with the topcoats, buy the same brand as the paint you select. You don't have to apply a primer over old sound paint unless the old paint is chalking or eroding badly.

When painting natural wood siding, use a stain-blocking primer on knots to prevent chemicals in the wood from bleeding through. Consider tinting your primer if you'll be applying a darker color paint.

Spot prime knots with a stain-blocking primer or shellac. Shellac dries fast, but don't use it as an overall primer since it won't let the wood breathe.

Apply an oil or latex primer to all bare wood. Using a roller or sprayer will speed application, but work the primer in with a brush to ensure good coverage and adhesion.

Work primer as far into cracks as possible to waterproof the wood and provide a good adhesive surface for caulk you'll apply.

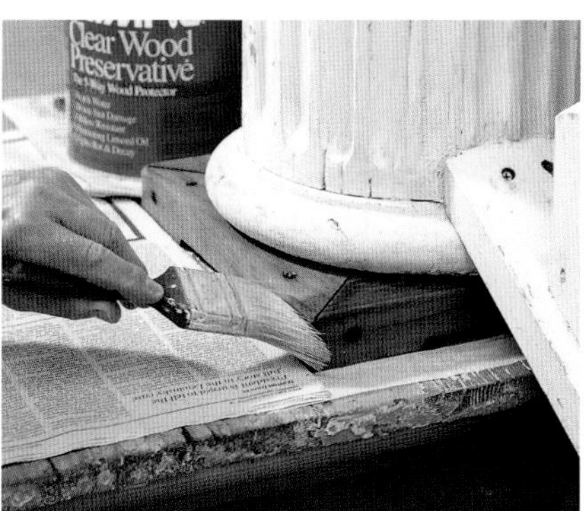

Apply a water-repellent preservative to wood that's likely to get wet often. The wood must be dry for good absorption.

Caulking

A good caulking job ensures that the topcoat will last for years and look good. It plugs the cracks where water can seep in and lift the paint. And it smooths over ugly gaps that make your home look shabby, no matter how well painted. Caulk siding gaps as well as around doors, windows, decks and other places where water or wind-driven rain could penetrate the walls and rot the framing.

Apply caulk after your primer has dried and just before applying the topcoats.

Squeeze a smooth, even ribbon of caulk over the joint, completely covering it. Squeeze steadily, resting the tip of the tube on the wood and dragging it along at an even rate.

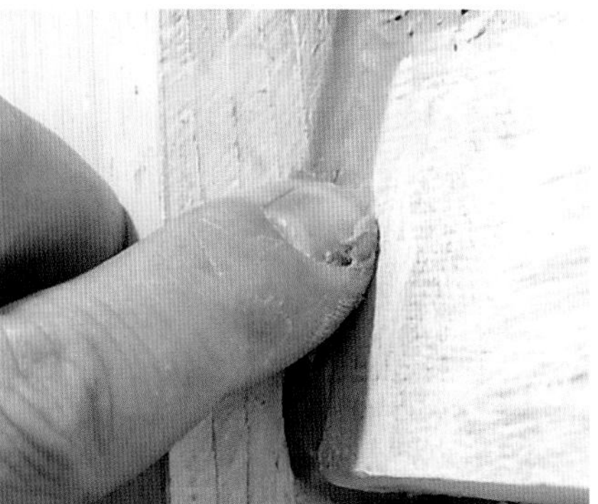

Lightly press caulk against both sides of the joint with a moist finger. Then wipe away excess with a damp cloth. Don't caulk horizontal joints; your walls need cracks to breathe.

Press foam backer rod into gaps larger than a pencil width using a putty knife or other blunt tool. Buy several sizes to accommodate different-size gaps.

Selecting Sealants

Although there are dozens on hardware store shelves, you need only two for your home's exterior.

Acrylic or acrylic latex caulk is a good all-purpose caulk. It's water based, cleans up easily and dries quickly, so you can paint over it almost immediately. Silicone acrylic is more flexible, but be sure the label states it's paintable.

Polyurethane is a good choice when you want extra-strong adhesion. It outperforms acrylic but is stickier and harder to apply. Use it on stucco, masonry and other areas especially vulnerable to water.

Exteriors / Painting Step-by-Step

Rollers **281**
Spray Painting Tools **283**

Exterior painting is a huge job, but when you do it yourself, you'll save thousands of dollars, extend the life of your house, increase the value of your home and make it look like new again. Buy the best paint you can afford. High-quality paint is easier to apply, covers better and lasts longer. Eggshell or satin paint is more fade resistant and easier to clean than flat paint.

For a top-notch job, remember these tips:
Avoid painting in direct sunlight. The paint dries too fast and you're more likely to get lap marks.
Avoid painting on windy days. Again, the paint will dry too fast and blown dirt can stick to wet paint.
Don't apply latex below 50° F (10° C) unless it's formulated for cold-weather application.

House Painting Order

1 Remove shutters, light fixtures, mailboxes and other items. Repaint shutters before reinstalling. 2 Cover foundation plantings and nearby shrubs with breathable canvas or cotton drop cloths (not plastic). 3 Scrape and remove loose sections of paint. 4 Spray or scrub house. 5 Countersink protruding nails; putty holes. 6 Caulk all joints. 7 Patch and prime bare sections of wood. 8 Paint soffits and fascia. 9 Cut in paint along soffits, corners boards, intersecting rooflines, windows and doors. 10 Paint siding, working from top to bottom. 11 Paint door and window trim.

Brush Techniques

For your brushwork, use a straight-bristle brush as wide as each lap for large areas and a smaller angled brush for detailed work. To avoid lap marks, work in sections small enough so the previously painted area stays wet until you can apply paint to the adjacent section. Most drips, runs and sags can be avoided by checking back on your work regularly and brushing out the areas before the paint dries.

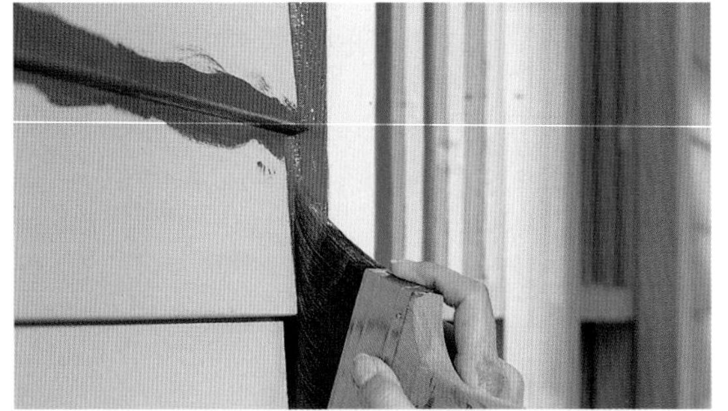

1 Work paint into areas where the siding meets doors, windows and cornerboards. Also paint the lower edge of the siding to seal out moisture.

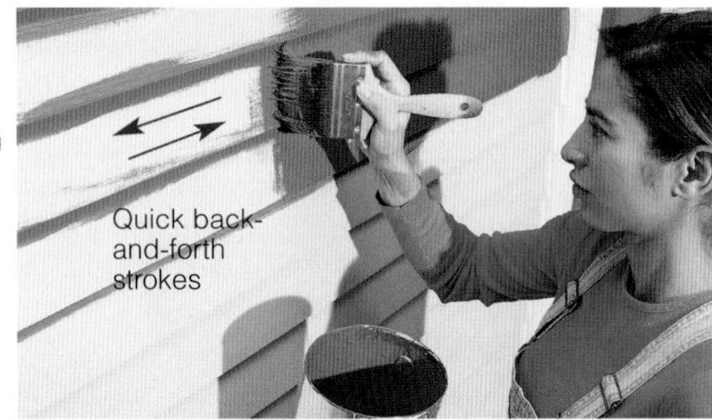

2 Lay on paint thickly with two or three back-and-forth strokes. Reload the brush and repeat until you've covered about 3 or 4 sq. ft. (1/3 sq. m).

3 Smooth the paint without reloading the brush. Use long, sweeping brush strokes, working from the unpainted area toward the painted area. Gently lift the brush while it's still in motion at the end of each stroke.

Rolling

Applying paint with a roller is an excellent way to cover large areas and textured siding quickly and efficiently. Paint pads work equally well. The key is to use a brush to work the paint into crevices and corners for thorough coverage.

1 Place a gallon of paint and a roller screen into a large bucket. Load the roller, rolling it against the screen until the roller is saturated and the excess paint is squeezed out.

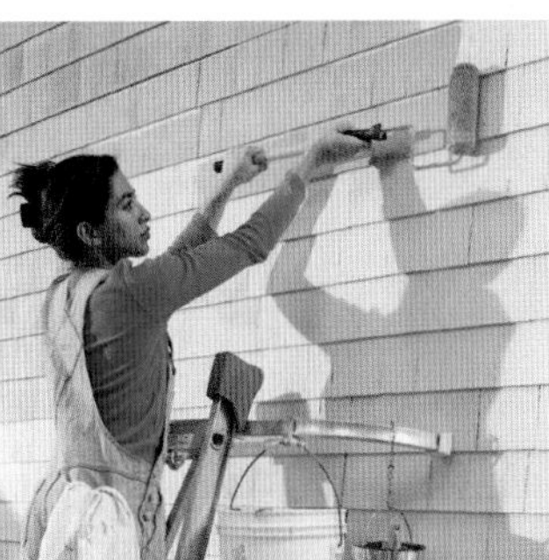

2 Lay the paint on with a roller, using moderate pressure until the paint no longer flows off easily. Cover 3 or 4 sq. ft. (1/3 sq. m) at a time.

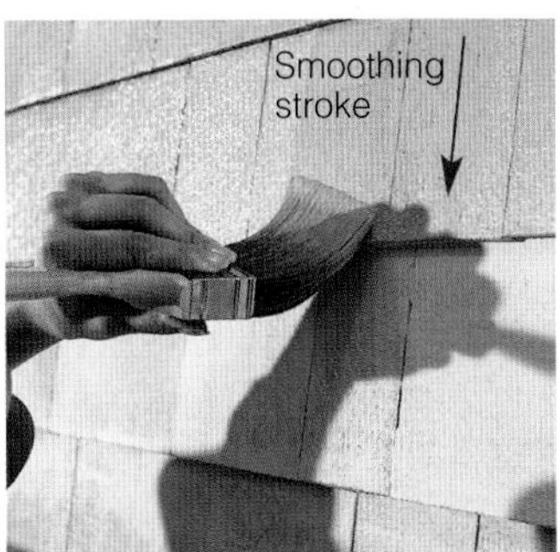

3 Backbrush, working the paint into cracks and onto the bottom edge of shingles and siding with your brush. Then brush with the grain of the wood to smooth the paint.

Spraying

Spraying is a fast, efficient way of applying exterior paint. Masking off windows and areas you don't want painted takes time, but once you're set up, you can work twice as fast as with other methods. Again, backbrushing to smooth the paint and work it into cracks and gaps is essential.

1 Angle the gun upward on the first pass to cover the underside of each lap. The bottom edge of lap and cedar shake siding must be thoroughly coated to prevent moisture damage.

2 Hold the gun at a slightly downward angle and apply the paint to the face of the lap siding. Keep the spray gun perpendicular to the surface as you work.

3 Spray straight onto the surface on the final coat. Use a brush to work paint into any seams, cracks or openings.

Perfect Painting

Lap onto window. When you paint window frames and muntins, let the paint lap slightly onto the glass. This helps keep moisture and condensation from working their way under the paint and damaging the wood.

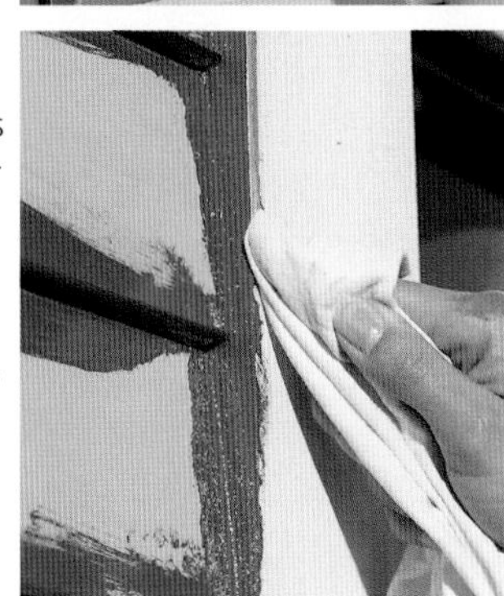

Paint casing edges. Paint the edges of window and door casings the same color as the siding. It looks great from the street and will save you tons of time. And keep a rag in your back pocket to wipe off excess paint from the face of window trim in order to avoid thick edges.

Create crisp edges. Use a putty knife to press masking tape firmly in place to create crisp, sharp edges where two colors meet.

Wallpapering / Tools

Wallpaper Borders 308
Ladder and Scaffold Safety 311

Create a Workstation

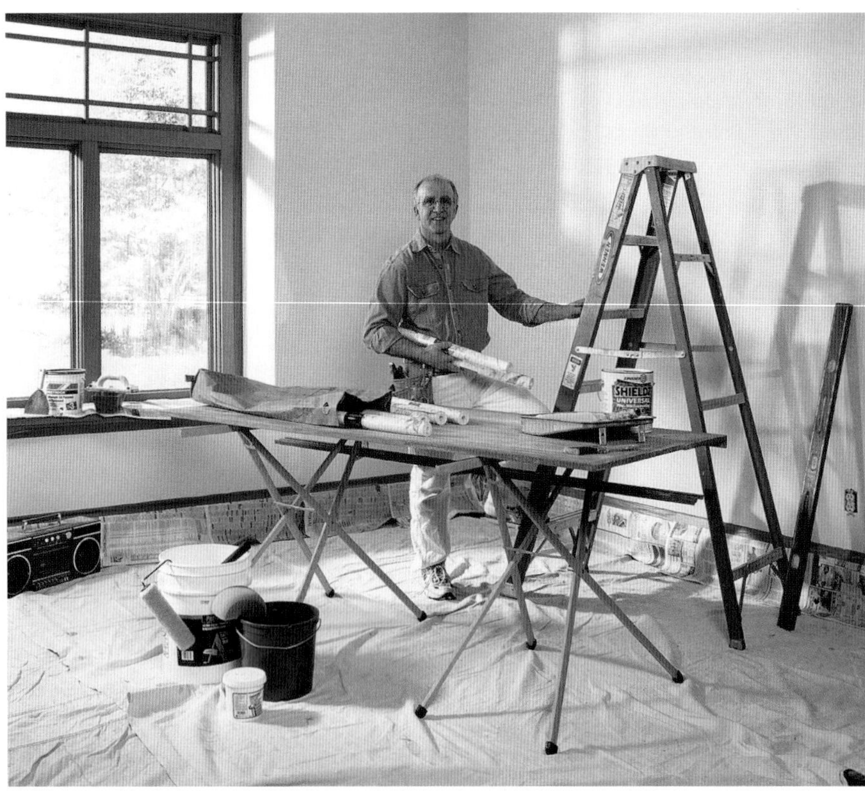

If you want to change the entire character of a room fast, hang wallpaper. You can change a dull room into a dramatic personal statement in less than a weekend, and you don't need a bunch of expensive tools to do the job.

Spend a few minutes getting set up right and, in the long run, you'll be able to work faster with neater results. Clear out movable items and move heavy objects to the center of the room. Turn off all power to the room at the fuse or circuit breaker panel since you'll be working around outlets and switches with metal tools and wet wallpaper.

Pros use a special table made of basswood because it's a good surface to cut on and easy on razor blades. You can rent one from a wallpaper store or substitute a hollow-core door or a piece of thick plywood resting on a pair of sawhorses. Soften the plywood edges with sandpaper so you don't accidentally tear your paper.

Critical Tools

You can buy all the specialty tools you need at a wall covering store or home center. In addition to the tools shown below, you might also need a stepladder, a large bucket, a sharp scissors, a level, a tape measure, a plumb bob and a sponge.

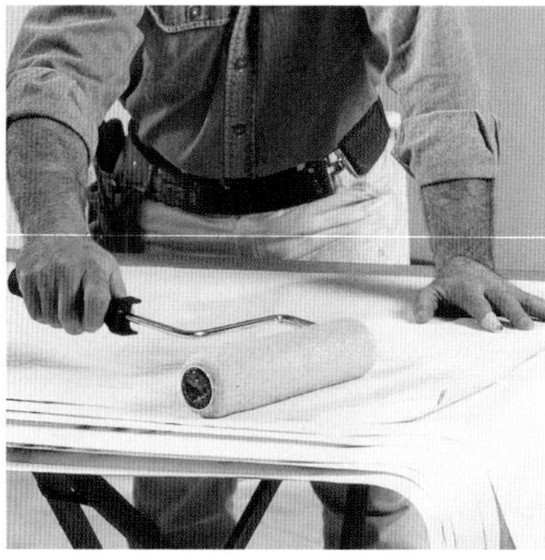

A paint roller with a short nap roller cover is ideal for wetting the back of prepasted papers.

A rigid vinyl smoother with slightly rounded corners is the best tool for working out bubbles and wrinkles.

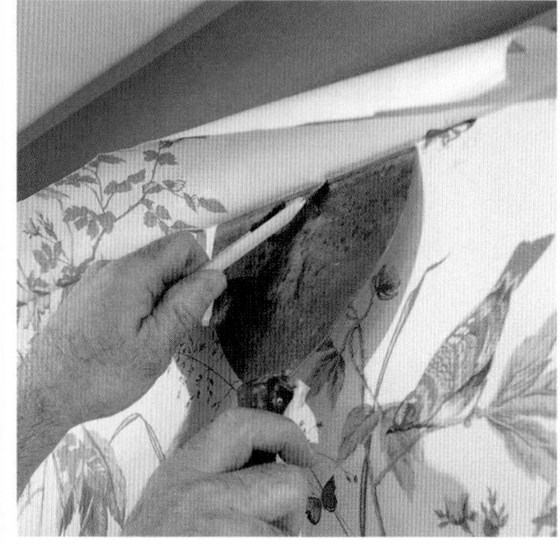

A broadknife serves as a straightedge guide as you trim the paper. Advance a new blade in your snap-off knife every few cuts for best results.

A seam roller helps ensure edges make firm contact with the wall. Don't apply too much pressure; you can squeeze out too much of the adhesive.

The Label and the Match

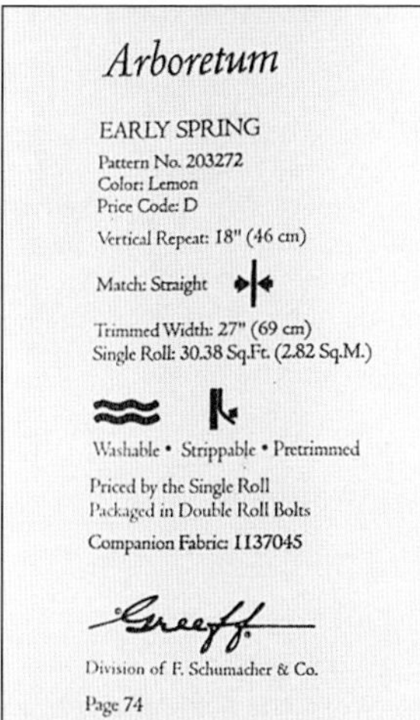

The back of a wallpaper sample can tell you a lot about ordering, durability and the essential hanging details. Before purchasing any wallpaper, you should know about the following:

Vertical repeat. The repeat is the length of the image or pattern before it shows itself again. Repeats can range from none (for a covering without a pattern) to more than 36 in. (91 cm). Order extra paper for repeats more than 24 in. (61 cm); you'll waste a lot when matching the pattern.

Match. The match is how the pattern aligns sheet to sheet. A random match means you don't have to fuss with lining up any pattern from sheet to sheet. A straight match requires shifting the pattern so a main element in a pattern is always the same distance from the ceiling. With a drop match you align the pattern halfway down the repeat.

Single roll/double roll. Look for the sq.-ft. coverage to calculate how many rolls you'll need to cover a room. In double-roll bolts, the paper is twice as long as on a single roll, which usually provides more usable paper.

Drop match. A drop pattern requires extra paper to make a match at the top of two strips.

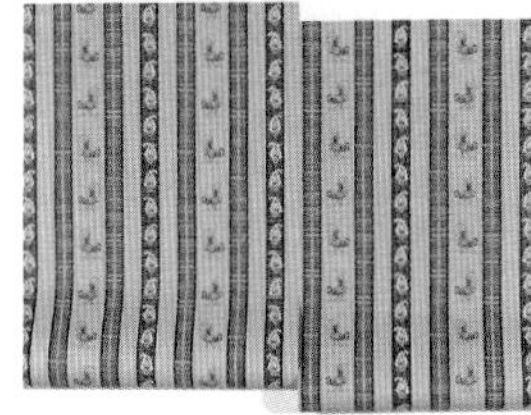

Straight match. A straight match, or set match, pattern aligns easily across strips with minimal waste.

Random pattern. Because these need no matching, waste is minimal.

Papers

In general, small prints and light colors make a room feel larger, while big prints and dark colors make a room feel cozy. If your room has crooked walls, use a paper with a random pattern so crooked corners aren't so noticeable. There are many types of wall coverings:

Standard vinyl papers are reasonably priced, sturdy, scrubbable and hold their colors, making them ideal for use in kitchens, playrooms, bathrooms and children's rooms.

Textured papers can make walls look like they're made of painted plaster or like they've been painted with one of the many decorative painting techniques like rag-rolling or stippling.

Natural-look papers can be made from grass cloth, burlap, cork and other natural materials bonded to a paper backing. Moisture can make the layers separate, so use care when pasting and hanging.

Embossed papers have raised designs, making them ideal for hiding minor imperfections on walls. Use a wallpaper brush instead of rollers and smoothers to avoid flattening the design.

Foils add drama and reflected light to powder rooms, alcoves and other dark spaces. Foils show every fault, so lining paper applied to the wall beforehand is recommended for less-than-perfect surfaces.

Wallpapering / Stripping

In most cases, old wallpaper should be removed before you hang the new. There are a few exceptions. Foil wallpapers and papers that were hung directly over new drywall, without a coat of sizing, can be nearly impossible to remove. Secure loose seams, apply a special paper-to-paper primer and paper over them.

When using a wallpaper remover, be patient and let the chemicals do their job. You may need to spray a wall four or five times to loosen really stubborn papers. For extremely stubborn papers, consider renting or buying an electric steamer.

1 Loosen an upper corner, then pull straight down. If the facing comes off in large strips, you're in luck. Simply remove the rest; then spray the remaining wallpaper backing and scrape it off.

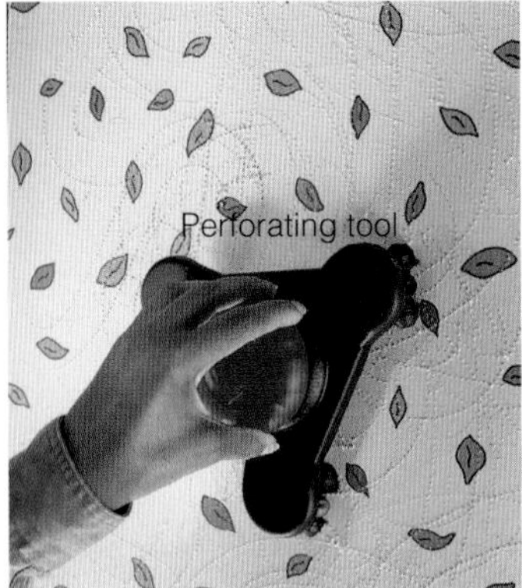

2 Perforate tightly adhered papers. Specialized tools create small holes so wallpaper remover can soak in and break the bond between wall and paper.

3 Soak the paper with remover starting at the top and working down. Wait 15 minutes, apply a second coat then wait again before scraping. Ventilate the room and wear safety gear as shown.

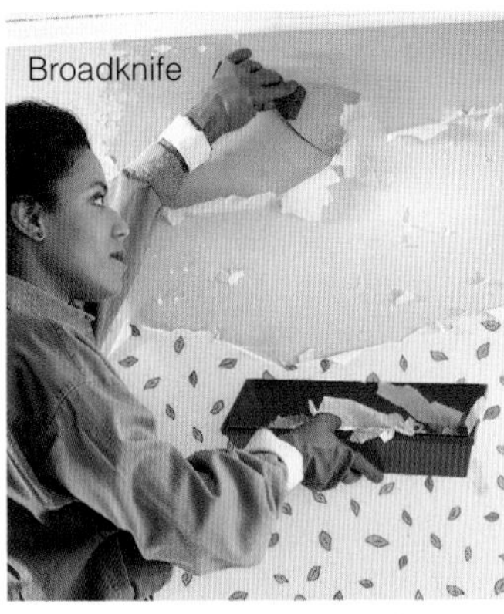

4 Scrape backing from the wall with a broadknife. Spray the wall again if necessary. Use a drywall pan to catch scraps and to wipe your broadknife clean.

5 Scrub the walls with an abrasive pad and TSP (or TSP substitute) to remove remaining backing and adhesive. Rinse with clean water, let dry and apply a new coat of sizing before hanging new paper.

How Much Wallpaper?

Most wall coverings are sold in double or triple rolls. Single rolls contain 36 sq. ft., which average 30 usable sq. ft. after trimming and matching patterns. Papers with large repeats won't have as much usable paper. Order more than you need so all rolls are from the same dye lot (color variations can be significant). Return the extra, or use it as drawer liner or gift wrap; save some for repairs.

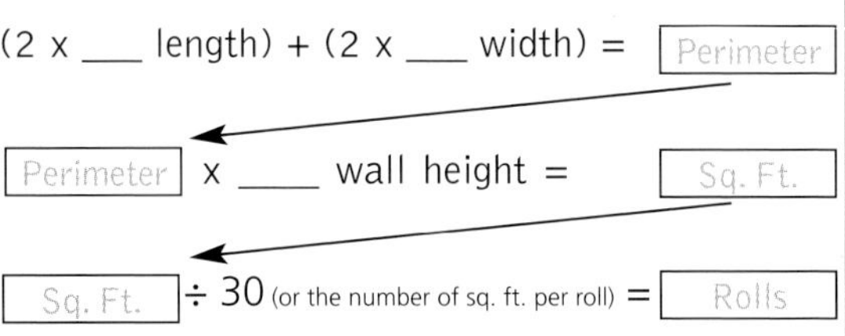

(2 x ___ length) + (2 x ___ width) = Perimeter
Perimeter x ___ wall height = Sq. Ft.
Sq. Ft. ÷ 30 (or the number of sq. ft. per roll) = Rolls

Note: Don't subtract the sq. ft. of windows and doors unless your room is loaded with them.

Wallpaper Smarts

Simple glue remover. Mix equal parts of white vinegar and water to create wallpaper adhesive remover. Spray it on the wall, wait a few minutes, then scrape or scrub. Keep a window open for good ventilation.

First things first. Paint the ceiling and trim before you wallpaper. It's easier to wipe paste off fresh paint than to remove paint splatters from new wallpaper.

Hide those seams. Run a strip of paint, close in color to your wallpaper, in the area where two strips of wallpaper will butt. If the seams separate, the less-noticeable color will show through instead of a white wall.

Recycle the leftovers. After finishing a job, use the leftover pieces to cover wastebaskets, lamp shades, shelves and photo albums.

Wallpapering / Planning

Where to Begin?

For satisfying and lasting results, prepare the surfaces you plan to paper as carefully as those you are about to paint. For less-than-perfect walls and ceilings, put up a lining paper—an economical, unpatterned paper—to cover faults. Lining paper will create a smooth surface. It also absorbs excess paste moisture from water-sensitive coverings, like grass cloth or foil, and keeps their backings from separating.

Always apply a coat of sizing or special primer before hanging paper; this will help your new paper grip tighter and make it easier to remove when the time comes.

For a top-notch job, take these precautions:

Check your paper to be sure all the rolls have the same dye lot or run number. If they don't, they may have color variations. Return them and reorder.

Find the starting point. Mark with a ruler and pencil exactly where each strip will go. This lets you anticipate problems and work out solutions.

Study the paper pattern. Hold it up to the ceiling line. Check where the pattern's repeat looks best. If the ceiling-wall juncture is uneven, for example, don't use a horizontal band as your starting point at the top.

Hide the mismatch. Most rooms have a "point of reckoning"—the area where the first and last pieces of paper meet, often in a mismatch. Try to make this seam as inconspicuous as possible, in this case behind a door that's commonly open.

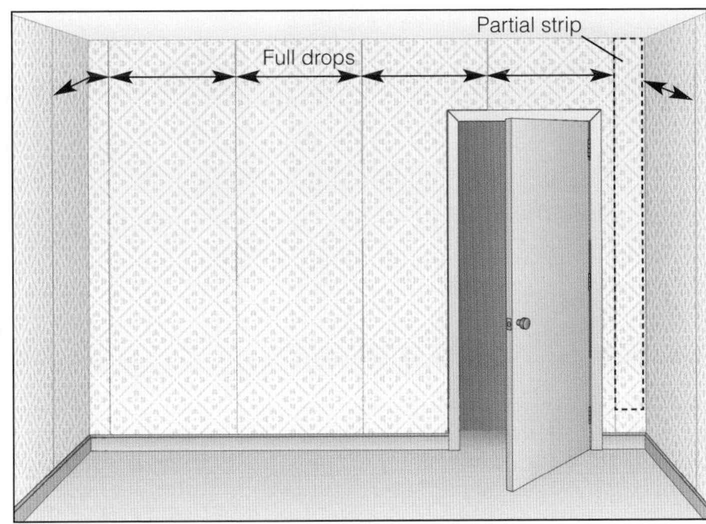

Minimize waste. Planning ahead can minimize waste. In this example, substantial amounts of paper would be wasted by centering the drop on the window (shown over the window) as opposed to centering the seam on the window (below the window).

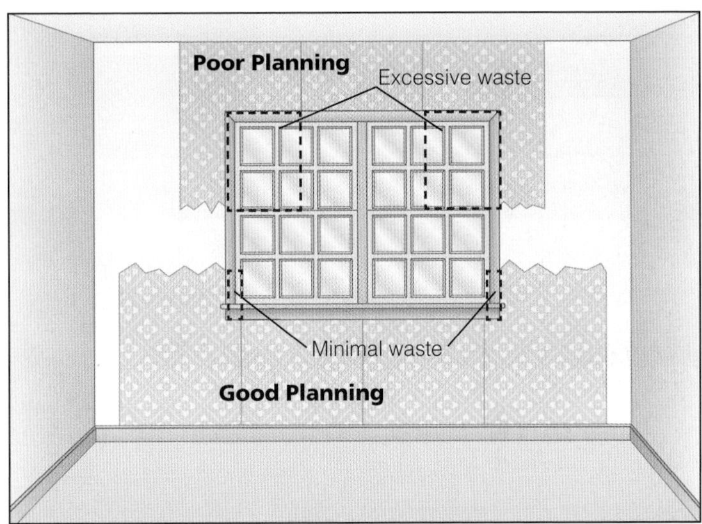

Wall Covering Problem?

Installing even prepasted vinyl wallpapers with easy-to-match patterns can be tricky. Seams can pull apart, edges can curl and air bubbles can appear. The cures range from having to strip off the wallpaper and start over to doing a little touch-up work with a seam sealer.

Here are some preventative measures you can take to avoid the most common problems:

Problem	Cause	Repair	Prevention
Seams pull apart	Wall covering shrinks after it's hung	Strip off the individual strips of wallpaper, called drops, and hang new ones.	Buy high-quality wall coverings; prepare the wall properly; fold or "book" according to manufacturer's instructions; add paste activator when wetting (wallpaper hung when too wet will shrink).
Edges/seams curl when dry	Too much rolling	Apply seam adhesive or vinyl paste to edges.	Don't roll seams immediately but wait until several drops have been hung; roll seams just once; roll a thin layer of clear adhesive on the wall and allow it to dry before hanging paper.
Air bubbles	Overworking the wall covering	Slit the paper over the bubble and glue down with seam adhesive or vinyl wall covering paste.	Smooth the paper without overworking (small air bubbles that you see when the wallcovering is wet should disappear when it's dry).
Dried paste	Not washing paste off before it dries	Use a paste remover or an all-purpose cleaner such as Soilex.	Rinse off excess paste with warm water and clean sponges as you hang each drop. It's very difficult to remove dried adhesive.

Wallpapering / Step-by-Step

No house has perfectly vertical walls. If wallcoverings are to look natural, they must be hung against a plumb line. You can make a plumb line with a weighted plumb bob on a chalked string. Or you can find true vertical with a level and mark it with a pencil against the level or a straightedge.

Your first plumb line will be a guide for aligning the first strip of wall covering you put up. Draw it a strip's width from your starting point. Each time you turn a corner, create a new plumb line to get a fresh alignment. Corners are never perfectly square and usually require a little fudging.

Cut strips of wall covering 4 in. (10 cm) longer than the wall measurement, providing 2-in. (5-cm) allowances at the top and bottom. With a drop match pattern, you'll save time and paper by cutting alternately from two different rolls—one for each part of the drop pattern.

Kill the Power

Shut off power to all lights, outlets and switches in the room at the circuit panel or fuse box before you start. Metal tools, wet wallpaper and open electrical boxes make a dangerous combination!

1 Mark a plumb line for your first drop (precut length of wallpaper) on the wall. Cut each drop the height of the wall plus 2 in. (5 cm) at the top and bottom.

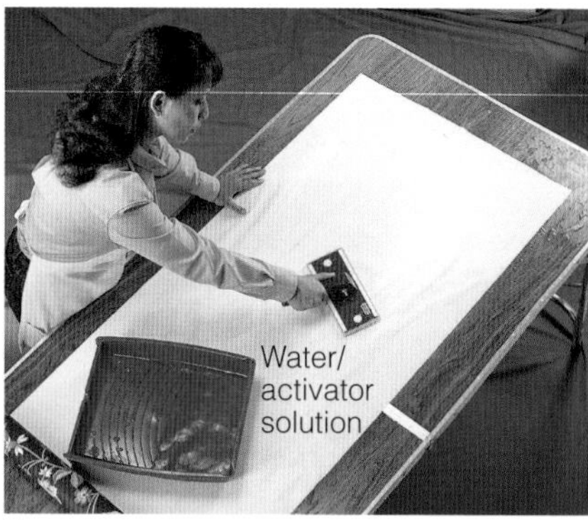

2 Wet the back of the drop thoroughly with adhesive activator mixed with tepid water according to the product instructions.

3 Fold the drop as shown with the pasted side in, without creasing it. Fold edges in again and let the drop rest or "book" according to manufacturer's guidelines.

4 Hang the drop beginning at the top, lining up the right edge with the plumb line. Release the folds gradually, letting the paper overlap onto ceiling and base molding.

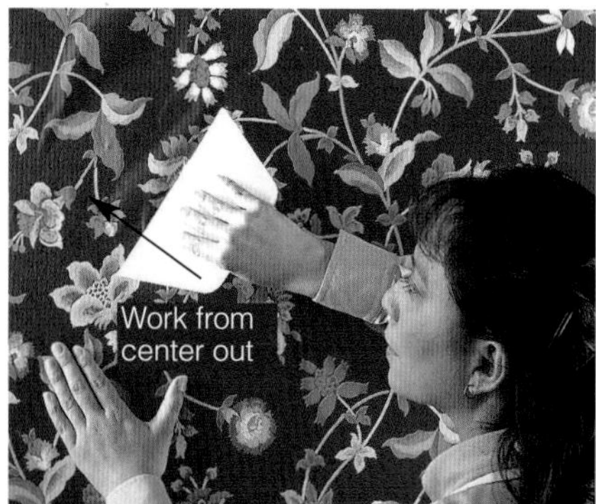

5 Flatten the drop with a plastic smoother. Start at the center and gently push out ripples and large bubbles. Take care not to stretch the paper.

6 Trim off excess paper at the ceiling and baseboard molding using a broadknife and razor knife. Wash paste off wallpaper and molding with a damp cloth.

7 Hang the next drop, which has been cut, wetted and booked beforehand, matching the pattern. Butt the seams, but avoid stretching the paper.

8 After the third drop is hung, go back and lightly roll the first seam as shown. Roll just once, then wash off excess paste.

Windows and Doors

The wider the window, the more difficult it is to make the pattern and seams line up by the time you reach the far side. One trick is to only lightly position the last two or three pieces so you can make adjustments using two or more seams rather than all in one spot.

Make sure to book the individual pieces for equal lengths of time so they expand to equal widths.

1 Hang a full drop over the window or door, then trim the excess, leaving 2 to 3 in. (5 to 7 cm) overlapping onto the trim. Use scissors to cut at an angle toward the corners. Then press the wallcovering into the sides of the moldings with a smoother.

2 Trim the paper around any curved casings by making a series of small cuts. Trim the remaining flaps with a razor knife. Use short pieces to fill in above and below the window.

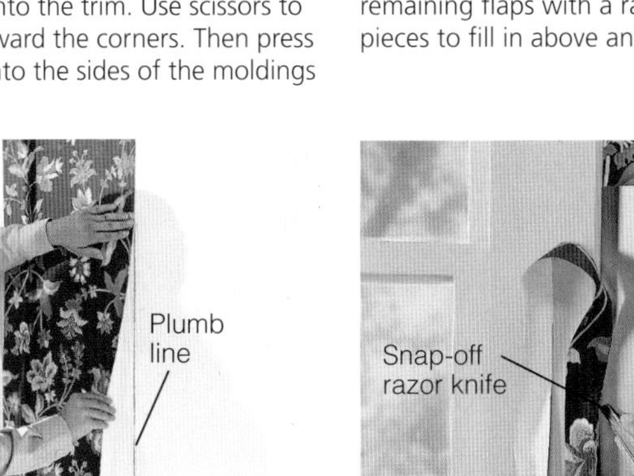

3 Mark a plumb line for the drop on the far side of the window. Hang the drop, trim the excess against the window, then adjust this and previous drops until patterns match and seams are tight.

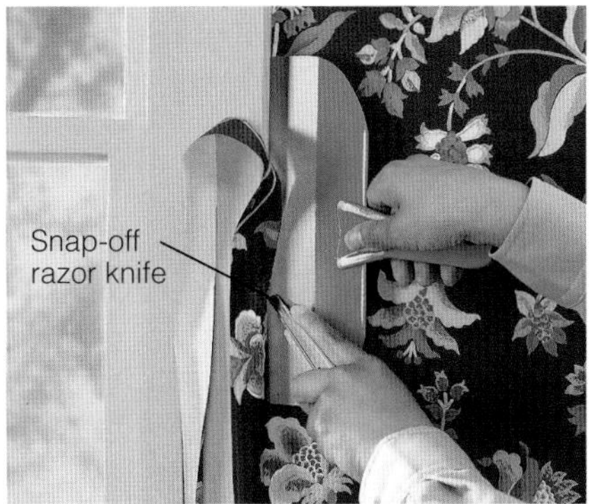

4 Trim the wall covering along the straight edges of the window casing. Wash off excess paste from window, trim and wall covering with a damp sponge.

Outside Corners

Since outside corners are rarely straight or plumb, simply wrapping a full-width drop around a corner usually results in an out-of-plumb edge and bulges at the corner. Install corners in two pieces as shown.

1 Measure from the edge of the last drop hung to the corner, add one inch to that measurement, and cut a drop to that width. Install the drop, wrapping the extra inch around the corner.

2 Hang the leftover piece aligning the edge with a new plumb line drawn on the wall. The wall covering will overlap the previous piece by varying amounts and the pattern may not always match up exactly.

Inside Corners

Like outside corners, inside corners are rarely plumb or straight. Again, installing the corner drop in two pieces will produce crisper results and create a plumb line for installing wallpaper along the rest of the wall.

1 Cut inside corner drop to width so it extends slightly past the inside corner. Trim to 1/16 in. (1.6 mm) the excess that wraps around corner using smoother to guide the razor knife. Mark a new plumb line out from the corner.

2 Hang the leftover piece aligning the edge with a new plumb line. Pull back the edge of the first drop, trim the edge of the piece just installed, smooth it into the corner, and smooth the edge of the first piece back in place.

Wallpapering / Borders and Stencils

Wallpaper borders are a fast, simple, inexpensive way to jazz up nearly any room. Home centers and paint stores stock dozens of selections and can order hundreds more. Some borders look best snug to the ceiling or crown molding, others a few inches down. To get a sense of what looks best, pin up a small section at various heights and take a look.

Whatever style you choose, keep these things in mind:

- Apply sizing to the wall where you'll install the border. The border will stick better and be easier to remove later.
- If you're going to paint, do it beforehand. Wait at least three days for the paint to cure before hanging your border.
- Chances are the pattern won't match by the time you circle the room. Start and end installing your border in an inconspicuous spot, usually an out-of-the-way corner.
- Cut sections of border to the length of each wall plus 1/4 in. (6.5 mm). Overlap the borders this same distance in the corners.

Better Borders

If you're installing your border tightly against a textured ceiling, run a flat-blade screwdriver around the edge to remove loose texture and create a small flat trough so the border fits evenly along the ceiling.

1 Measure down from ceiling the height of border, then snap a white line around the room using a chalk box. Apply sizing above this line.

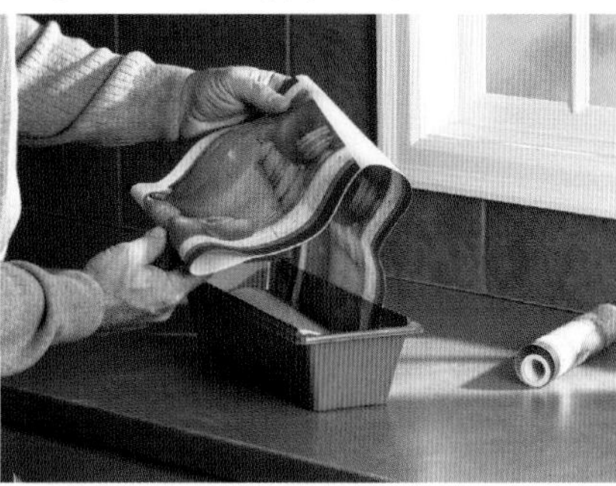

2 Reroll the prepasted border sticky side out, immerse the roll in water and book it sticky side to sticky side. Wait a few minutes while the paste activates.

3 Crease one end sharply into the corner with 1/4-in. (6-mm) lapping onto the adjacent wall. Use a smoother to flatten the border as you install it. Wipe excess glue from the wall and border.

Stenciling is a decorative technique that's easy to learn. If you can handle a paintbrush, you can master the techniques for an attractive border.

The key tools are a stenciling brush, the stencil and paint, all available at craft and art supply stores. You can also find stencil patterns at bookstores and on the Internet. Or buy stencil blanks and cut your own designs.

Match the brush size to the area being filled within the stencil. You can use artists' acrylic wall paints or special stenciling paints.

Position your stencil at the desired height and mark the alignment holes or top edge. Snap a light, horizontal chalk line around the room at that height; white will wipe away easily. Or use faint pencil marks, which can be easily removed or covered later. Avoid awkward pattern breaks at doors, windows and corners. To work out the best spacing, measure the stencil pattern and mark the repetitions on the wall. Vary the spacing slightly as needed to make the pattern fall in a pleasing way. Start your layout at the most prominent part of the room and make compromises in less visible areas. Draw vertical lines at the pattern's center point to make positioning easier.

Don't worry about getting paint on the stencil, but avoid wiping or stabbing too hard around the edges. You can cover the cutout completely or use shading for effect. Cover nearby cutouts with masking tape so you don't accidentally paint in them.

Mistakes are easy to correct. Lift the stencil and wipe any paint that has smeared under the edge with a damp paper towel, or touch it up later with wall paint.

1 Snap lines on the wall to align with the alignment marks on your stencil. Tape the stencil along the top edge with masking tape.

2 Dab the special stenciling brush into the paint; then pat off the bristles on a dry cloth. Leave the brush almost dry.

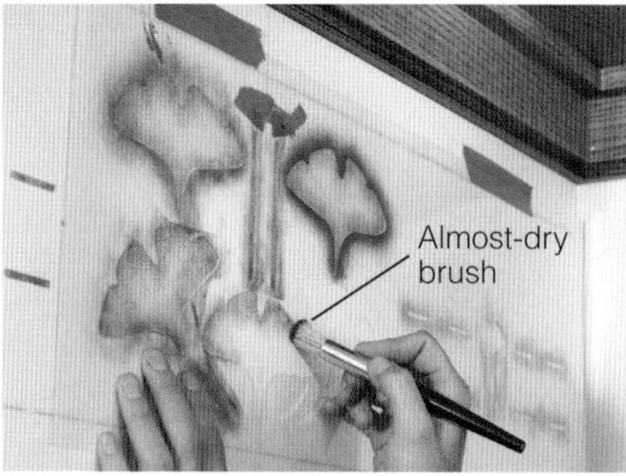

3 Apply the paint to the stencil with light dabbing and swirling motions. Work in from the edges, brushing toward the center. Allow the first color to dry; tape the stencil on the same marks and apply the second color.

Exteriors

Maintenance Checklist

Despite the wide range of building materials—both natural and manufactured—that lay claim to being no-maintenance, there isn't a building exterior in the world that doesn't require some attention periodically. Combined effects of sun, rain, salt air, wind, snow and ice ultimately take their toll. In some regional climates, homes have to endure temperature swings from sub-freezing winter storms to scorching summer afternoons. Even materials we might think of as permanent degrade over time and change in response to temperature and humidity. More vulnerable still are the connections where dissimilar materials meet—glass to metal, wood to stone, vinyl to brick masonry. These areas tend to move the most and create gaps for water to penetrate.

Aside from natural disasters or such catastrophic events as fire, ordinary water damage ranks as the biggest threat to most homes. Making periodic inspections to identify and fix potential trouble spots can prevent many problems, although others won't show up until the damage is already done. Preventive maintenance is much less expensive than repair work, so pay attention to key features on your home before problems grow large.

Start with the roof by viewing the surface with binoculars. If there's apparent damage, follow up with a closer inspection, provided conditions are safe. Look for damaged or missing shingles, bent flashing, loose mortar or bricks in a chimney, and other paths that water might take. Don't assume an exterior roof leak will be directly above interior areas that suffer water damage. Water often migrates along rafters and other surfaces before it sneaks into the house. Also look for water stains and other signs of ice damming at the roof edges, and check to see that gutters are clean and draining properly. On wall surfaces, patch any cracks or holes, tuck-point weak mortar joints and caulk or flash joints between siding and trim to prevent water penetration. For more suggestions, see the checklist at right.

Maintenance Checklist

Think of exterior maintenance as a spring ritual, a routine to follow before summer projects or vacations occupy your time and attention. Taking an inventory of these items will help you catch problems and normal wear while they're still manageable and easy to fix. Remember one basic rule: Water flows downhill. This simple principle can guide you through everything from roof flashing to grading the landscape.

Exterior walls

- ☐ Fill masonry cracks (p. 415).
- ☐ Recaulk joints between siding and other materials (p. 299).
- ☐ Check window wells and cellarways for debris; check window well covers for damage.
- ☐ Check wood surfaces for paint failure and damage.
- ☐ Check for carpenter ants and wasp nests (p. 484).

Roof

- ☐ Check for damaged shingles (p. 319).
- ☐ Inspect flashings at chimney, dormers, valleys and vents (p. 322).
- ☐ Replace loose mortar between chimney bricks; check condition of chimney cap (p. 332).
- ☐ Clean gutters, downspouts and leaf strainers (p. 327).
- ☐ Check for leaks at gutter seams and joints.
- ☐ Checks vents and louvers for broken screens.
- ☐ Check fascia and soffit for paint failure and decay.
- ☐ Check that antenna support wires and satellite dish brackets haven't damaged roof.

Doors and Windows

- ☐ Replace cracked window glass; reputty loose windows (p. 367).
- ☐ Clean and repair screens (p. 371).
- ☐ Replace worn or damaged weather stripping (p. 368).
- ☐ Apply new caulk around windows and doors as needed.
- ☐ Lubricate hinges, locks and closers.
- ☐ Clean and lubricate tracks of gliding doors (p. 381).

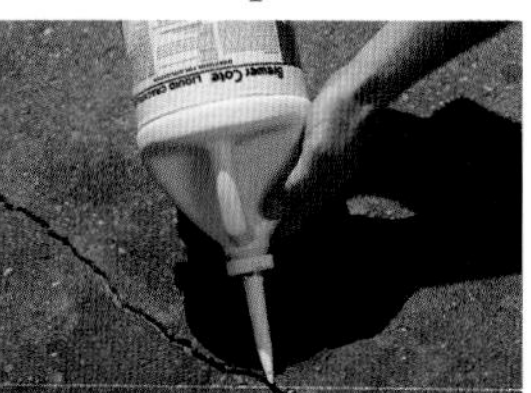

Yard

- ☐ Check storm drains for debris.
- ☐ Fill driveway cracks (p. 422); seal blacktop or concrete, if needed.
- ☐ Check foundation for signs of termites (p. 484).
- ☐ Check ground by house for standing puddles.
- ☐ Trim overgrown trees and shrubs that could damage siding or shingles.
- ☐ Check deck or patio for loose boards, bricks and stones.

How Long Should It Last?

Properly installed or applied, today's exterior materials can weather a lot of abuse. Take shortcuts, however, and you'll often pay dearly. For example, skip the tedious prep work on a paint job and you'll be lucky to see two years free of peeling. Omit the subgrade compaction beneath a new concrete driveway and you'll see cracks develop in short order. That said, here's a guide to what you can expect from some common exterior materials.

Material	Life Span
Exterior paint	5–10 years
Exterior solid-color or semitransparent stain	5–15 years
Asphalt shingles	15–40 years
Tile roofing	50–75 years
Vinyl or aluminum gutters and downspouts	25–30 years
Copper gutters and downspouts	50–75 years
Wood siding*	10–100 years
Vinyl siding	50 years
Stucco	75–100 years
Exterior wood door (with protected overhang)	80–100 years
Exterior wood door (unprotected)	10–25 years
Wood deck (pressure-treated frame)**	25 years
Concrete walkway/driveway	25–50 years
Asphalt driveway	10–15 years
Wood fence	10–20 years

*Depends on species, grade, coatings, and exposure. **Shorter life span likely for decking.

Ladder and Scaffold Safety

Ladders

Falls from ladders constitute one of the leading categories of home injuries, and it's likely that many occur because users don't treat ladders as they do other tools—with respect for their inherent risks. Common sense dictates the basics. Make sure both surfaces that support an extension ladder, at its feet and upper end, are stable. Set up a ladder at an angle that prevents backward tipping or sliding forward, and watch for overhead power lines. Never climb a ladder barefoot, don't stand on the top few rungs, and if you need tools or materials, haul them up in your tool belt or with a rope and bucket.

Wood, aluminum and fiberglass are the common materials for ladders, with quality and price typically increasing in that same order. For general use, fiberglass ladders offer strength and rigidity and don't conduct electricity, a nice safety bonus.

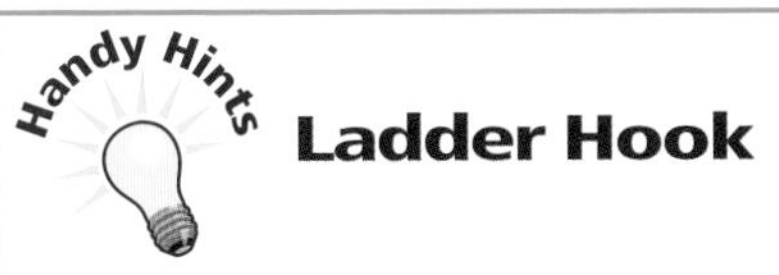

Ladder Hook

Extension ladders don't provide a place to set a paint bucket, but you can improvise. Simply insert a length of 3/4-in. plastic pipe or a wood broom handle through a rung and notch the end to create a hook for the pail or paint-can handle.

Walking a ladder. To walk a ladder upright, set the feet against a solid base and work your way under from the top end. Switch your hands onto alternating rungs as you move forward. Avoid overhead power lines.

The right angle. Check for a correct, stable angle by placing your toes against the feet of the ladder and extending your arms forward and level to grip a rung.

Spiked feet. To prevent unwanted movement on soft surfaces, pivot the ladder feet so the spiked ends are down. Then step on the bottom rung to drive them into the ground.

Cleats. On wood decks or other surfaces that might allow ladder feet to slide, use screws to fasten a wood cleat or stop-block against each foot.

Stabilizers

A ladder stabilizer, also called a standoff, is a bolt-on accessory that provides a wide stance at the top of the ladder, allowing it to straddle windows and other obstacles you can't lean against. It also provides a setback from the surface, so you have access for painting or other work, making it easier to work on roof overhangs with less fear of falling backward.

Scaffolds

Available at most rental centers, scaffolds provide a stable, elevated work platform where you can stack materials and set up tools. They're great for projects that require a lot of detail work or extended completion times.

Assembly. Start by laying the end frames on the ground and installing the adjusting screws and baseplates or casters.

Positioning. After you have the crossbars attached and the baseplates sitting flat on wood blocks, use the adjusting screws to level the frame.

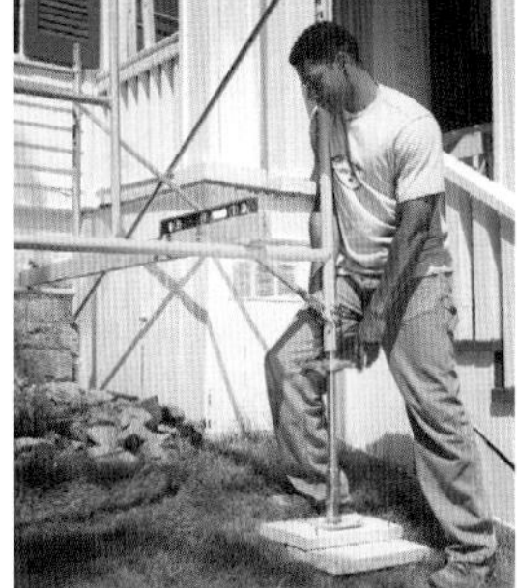

Safety. Use a guardrail system on any open sides to prevent falls. Fit toe boards elsewhere to keep materials and tools from dropping off.

Roof Safety

Flashings and Vents 322
Chimney Flashing 324
Ice Dams 330

Most homeowners don't have to climb on top of their houses very often, so when a damaged shingle or leaky flashing beckons them onto the roof, the inherent danger seems compounded by the unfamiliarity of the task. The height and the sloped surface present a precarious setting that can unnerve most anyone, but simple, effective safety precautions help make rooftop repairs a manageable chore.

As with most home repairs or improvements, working on the roof involves a few specialized tools, but start with some common sense. First and foremost, leave the difficult situations—steep slopes and excessive heights—to professionals. It's just not worth the added risk to tackle those obstacles. Second, wait until conditions are right; wet or icy shingles, gusty winds or high temperatures increase the likelihood of a fall or damage to the roof. Keep away from overhead power lines. Wear soft-soled shoes that offer some grip, and sweep the roof to remove dirt, debris and loose shingle granules that might compromise your footing. Finally, stay off slate or tile roofs to avoid breakage.

Safe rooftop work involves a simple system. Wearing soft-soled shoes and a safety harness is the first step. Beyond that, you need a sturdy extension ladder, a few temporary slide guards and a broom to sweep the surface free of debris.

Installing Roof Brackets

Anyone who has ever slid down a roof knows the panicked feeling of trying to gain traction on a steep, sometimes slippery, surface. By using roof brackets to install temporary slide guards, you can work more safely and with more confidence. And the guards create a convenient place to store tools and materials.

1 Lift a shingle tab, position the tongue of the roof bracket and sink three or more framing nails into a rafter or truss to secure it. Space brackets 48 in. (1.2 m) apart.

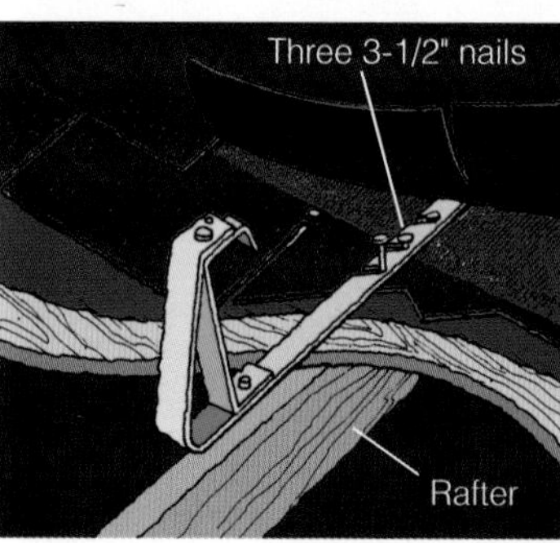

2 This illustrates the correct technique for placing the bracket over a rafter and under a shingle tab. Measure from underneath or use a stud finder to locate the framing members.

3 Use screws to fasten a 2x6 plank onto the brackets. The board's ends should extend 6 to 12 in. (15 to 30 cm) beyond the outer brackets.

Using a Roof Harness

A safety harness offers a reliable means of avoiding injury from a rooftop fall, but without the accompanying system of rope, hardware and roof anchor, it's nothing but an expensive set of suspenders. In trade jargon, the complete system is called a personal fall arrest system; think of it as a lifesaver.

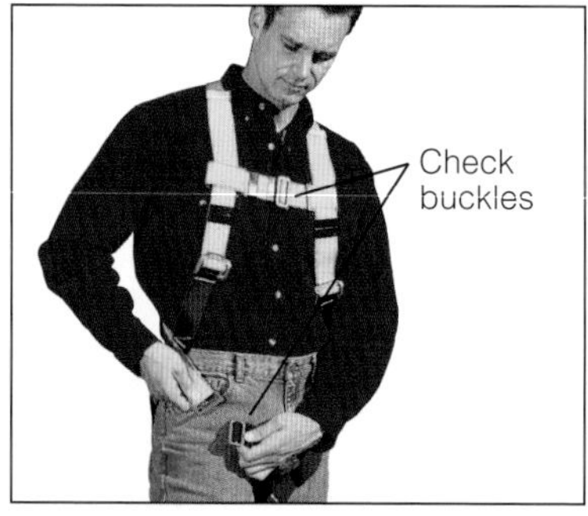

1 Strap on the harness according to the manufacturer's instructions and tighten the straps for a snug fit. Double-check the buckles before you climb onto the roof.

2 Use lag screws or similar heavy hardware to secure the roof anchor to rafters or trusses at the ridge. This placement lets you work on either face of the roof without repositioning the anchor.

3 Clip the safety rope to the ring on the roof anchor. Then clip the lanyard to the D-ring on the back of the harness. Use the rope grab to reposition the lanyard as you work.

Roof Repairs / Locating Leaks

Even minor signs of water damage warrant tracking down a roof leak. Incoming water can migrate in various directions, so you can't assume that what you're seeing inside is all there is.

How Water Can Travel

Water that penetrates a roof often takes a circuitous route before making an appearance below, so check the attic area thoroughly with a flashlight.

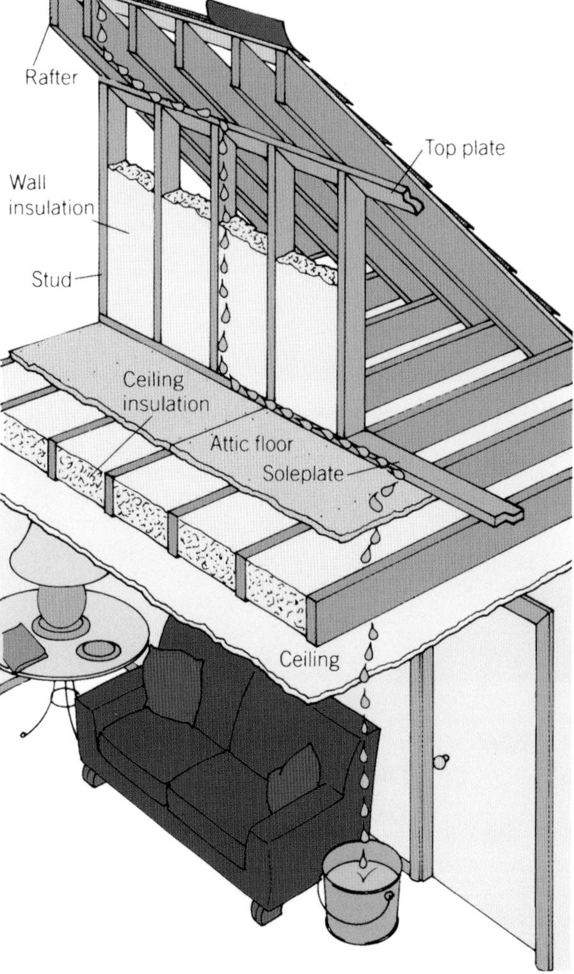

Inside Clues

Water is a determined invader, but it also leaves tracks that can help you identify the source of a leak. Good detective work usually pays off.

Chimney leaks. With the large roof opening, pieced flashing and constant movement between the masonry and surrounding wood, chimneys are a common source of roof leaks. Inspect the area during a rainstorm to see where water is making its way in.

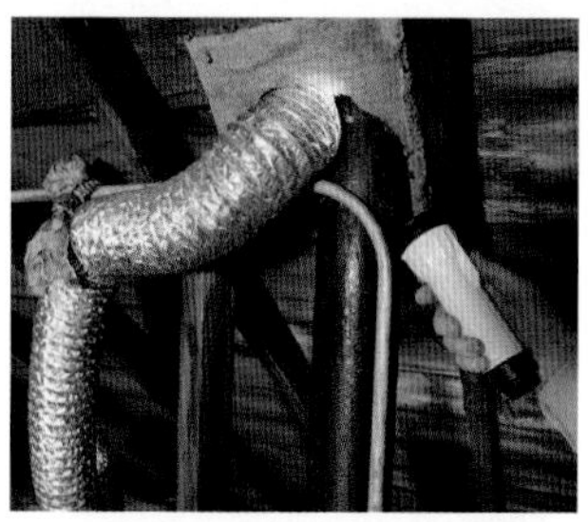

Vent leaks. Vent stacks penetrate the roof and create another opportunity for water to enter where it's not welcome. Makeshift setups, like this combined bathroom fan duct and plumbing stack, increase the odds of a leak.

Valleys. Roof valleys channel rain into a stream that can sometimes get past metal flashing or overlapped shingles. Check roof framing carefully around these areas. Typically, incoming water travels along rafter edges before dripping down.

Nail holes. Any spot where a fastener has penetrated the roof is a candidate for a leak. Old television-antenna hardware is a common culprit, but whatever the source, you'll need to patch or replace the shingle to provide an effective cure.

Outside Clues

Roof penetrations aren't the only sources of water leaks, but they are the most common. Inspect them first; then look for damage elsewhere.

Dormers. Like chimneys, dormers present a risk of leaks just because of their size. Even when step flashing or other preventive measures are used, the connections between side walls and roof are vulnerable. Relying only on caulking or roofing cement, as shown here, almost guarantees a leak.

Soil stacks. With their multiple transitions between dissimilar materials—from cast iron to caulking or gasket, then to the flashing cap and shingles—plumbing vent stacks offer water plenty of opportunity to trespass. Periodic inspection and resealing is your best defense.

Shingle fasteners. A protruding staple or nail head can wear a hole in an asphalt shingle, creating a potential leak. Pry up the shingle tab carefully and drive the fastener flush; then cement a small piece of metal flashing underneath the tab.

Roof Repairs / Asphalt Shingles

Asphalt shingles are the most common residential roofing material used in North America. Color and style choices are plentiful and some of the better, heavier grades are rated to last 40 to 50 years when properly installed. It's not uncommon, however, for these roofs to need spot repairs throughout their life span. Falling tree branches, roof-mounted hardware and uneven weathering can result in damage to individual shingles or small sections. Fortunately, such localized repairs are often easy to make, but before you haul out the ladder and tools, take a few minutes to assess the roof's overall condition.

The Roof Safety section (p. 312) provides basic guidelines for working safely on a rooftop, but the cardinal rule is to leave difficult situations to professionals who have the necessary training and equipment to handle them safely. Anything steeper than a 7:12 pitch—a roof that rises 7 in. for every 12 in. it runs—can be difficult to work on. If your roof pitch is steep, you have a two-story or taller home, or you are unable to set up minimal safety devices beforehand, you're better off having a roofing contractor do the repairs.

Also, make sure the roof warrants the effort to make piecemeal repairs. Shingles that are curled, cracking or discolored from fading or loss of granules are ready to be torn off or covered anyway, so making temporary fixes to individual areas is a losing battle.

Replacing a Shingle

1 Work on a warm, but not hot, day so shingles are flexible. Lift overlapping tab off damaged shingle and pry out nails. Repeat with next row up, since those nails also penetrate the damaged shingle's top edge.

2 Insert the new shingle underneath the row of tabs above. Nail it in place with galvanized roofing nails in approximately the same locations as those you removed.

3 Apply a thin bead of roofing cement under the tabs of the new shingle and any existing tabs you folded back to make the repair. Press them flat to ensure adhesion.

Repairing Damaged Shingles

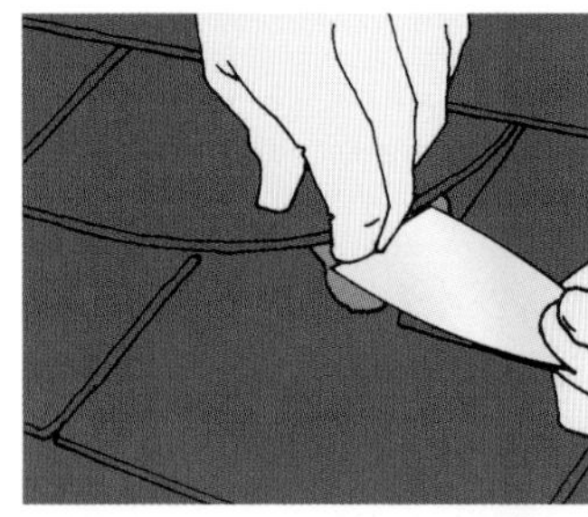

1 A lifted or curled shingle tab can be reglued with a dab of roofing cement under its corner. Do this work in warm weather when the shingles are pliable enough to bend without cracking.

2 Torn shingles can be salvaged by applying roofing cement underneath both sides of the tear and pressing firmly in place. Apply the cement generously if the tear is near a seam.

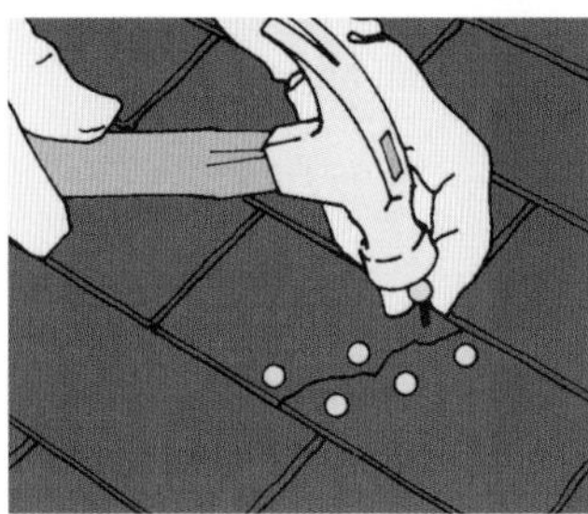

3 Reinforce the repair by driving roofing nails along the torn edges. Cover the nail heads with roofing cement to prevent leaks.

Repairing Blemished Shingles

1 For cosmetic blemishes, such as small gouges that don't require replacing the shingle, start the repair by cleaning the area thoroughly and applying a bead of clear silicone caulk.

2 Rub the top surfaces of two shingle scraps firmly together above the blemished area. Granules will drop and become embedded in the caulk, disguising the scar.

Shingle Cooler

The preapplied adhesive strip on a shingle is tackiest in hot weather. To break the bond before making a repair, set a bag of ice over the shingle, then pry it loose.

Roof Repairs / Slate Shingles

Slate is a natural stone, quarried in blocks and split into thin layers before being trimmed to make shingles. It's not uncommon for slate roofs to last for two centuries or more, and with that extended life span comes the likelihood that individual shingles may become damaged by ice or falling debris.

Because slate is a natural material, you can't expect the uniformity you'd find with a manufactured product. Colors will vary depending on the region of origin, and thicknesses vary because the shingles are split along natural fissures in the slab. Thicker shingles are typically used toward the lower edge of a roof, so take measurements or even a sample with you when you go shopping. Most suppliers stock several varieties; some even have inventories of salvaged roof slate. Slate doesn't tolerate foot traffic well, so if you can't make the repair while working from a ladder, hire a pro to do it.

Shop Smart

Fake Slate

Like most expensive natural materials, slate has a few manufactured imitators that offer a convincing look at a lower cost. Some versions are similar to manufactured stone veneer or fiber-cement siding, which use portland cement, fine aggregate and strands of fiberglass to create a durable surface. They aren't typically as brittle as natural slate, but care must be taken to avoid cracking. Other versions are made from plastic composites but don't have the same life span.

Replacing a Slate Shingle

Knee

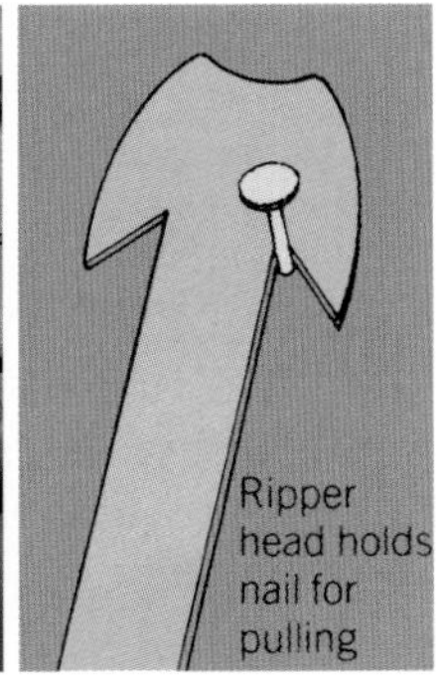
Ripper head holds nail for pulling

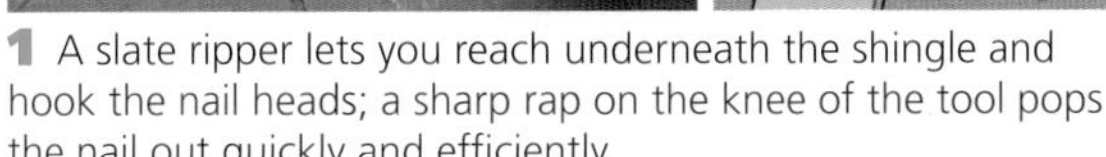

1 A slate ripper lets you reach underneath the shingle and hook the nail heads; a sharp rap on the knee of the tool pops the nail out quickly and efficiently.

Work from back of slate; hole on good side will be beveled

2 Test-fit the new shingle and mark the gap between the two shingles above it. Working from the shingle's back side, use a slate hammer or a nail set to punch two small holes along the gap line.

3 Refit and align the new shingle and drive two galvanized nails through the holes to secure it. Copper nails are traditional but may have heads too large to make these repairs.

4 Gently wedge a pair of screwdrivers underneath the upper shingles to create a slight gap. Insert a copper bib, a slightly curved flashing, to cover the new nail locations. Trim if needed.

Cutting Slate

1 Use a nail set and a hammer to punch a closely spaced series of holes along a marked line where you want to cut. Work from the back side of the slate.

2 A soft slate will separate without much further work. For tougher slate, you may need to tap it against a sharp edge to break it cleanly.

3 Rough edges can be smoothed with hammer taps along the finished cut. Support the shingle on a solid, flat benchtop as you work.

4 A traditional slate hammer has a beveled cutting edge that, if skillfully used, can make clean, accurate cuts, either curved or straight, in the shingle.

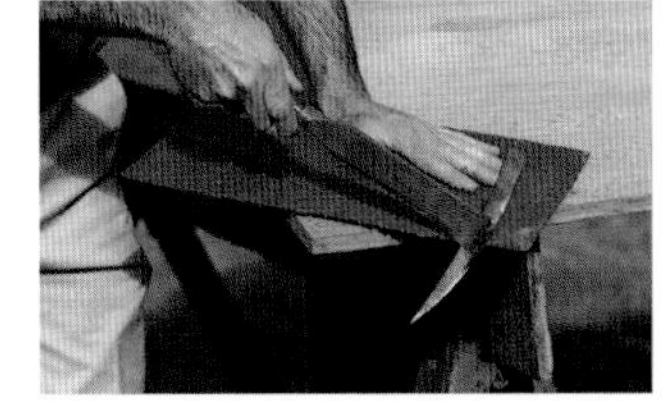

Roof Repairs / Wood Shingles and Shakes

The most common roofing-grade wood shingles and shakes (No. 1 Blue Label) come from the heartwood of western red cedar. Others are made from eastern white cedar or spruce. All must come from high-grade wood. Poor-quality lumber will expand and contract more as it moisture cycles from dry to wet and back again, making splits more likely. Some shingles are chemically treated during manufacturing, but periodic applications of preservative on untreated shingles and good air circulation can help them last 30 years or more. Shakes are thicker and can last a half-century or more.

Wood shingles have two smooth sides because both are sawn; shakes are split and have rough, striated faces. Some varieties feature one sawn face, to be installed down, and one split face. Whatever the style, all are prone to splitting and cracking, either from weather-related stresses or from being walked on. Sometimes repairs can be as simple as fitting a metal patch underneath a cracked shingle, but major splits or deformation will require replacement. Don't replace the entire roof without checking local fire codes first; some communities no longer allow wood shingle roofs.

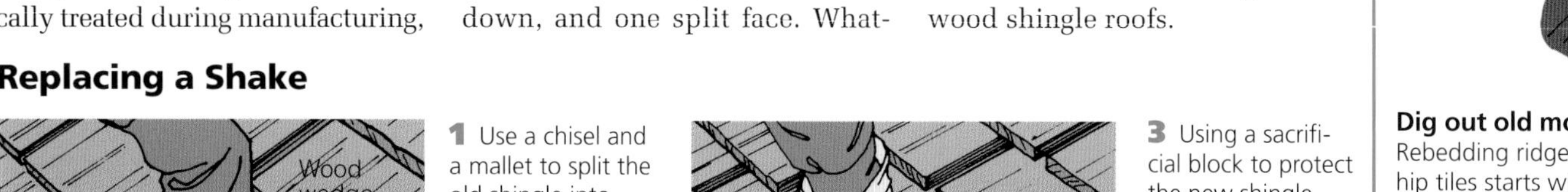

Replacing a Shake

1 Use a chisel and a mallet to split the old shingle into pieces that you can slide out. If clearances are tight, use wood wedges under adjacent shingles to relieve the pressure. Work carefully to avoid damaging good shingles.

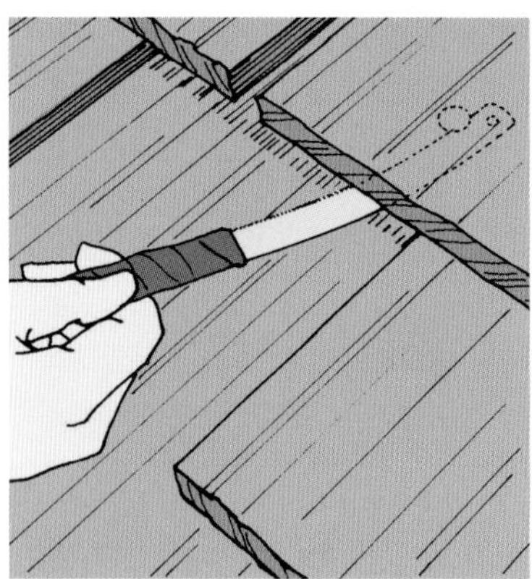

2 Wrap one end of a hacksaw blade with tape and use the other to reach under the upper shingles and cut off the roofing nails that secured the damaged shingle. Cut the new shingle 1/4 in. (6 mm) narrower than the gap it will fill to allow for swelling.

3 Using a sacrificial block to protect the new shingle, tap the shingle in place until its lower edge aligns with the adjacent shingles in the same course. Stiff resistance may indicate you missed a nail, so don't force it or you'll split the shingle.

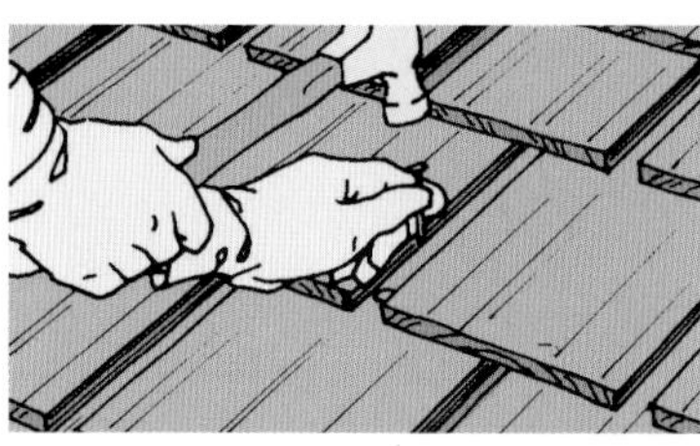

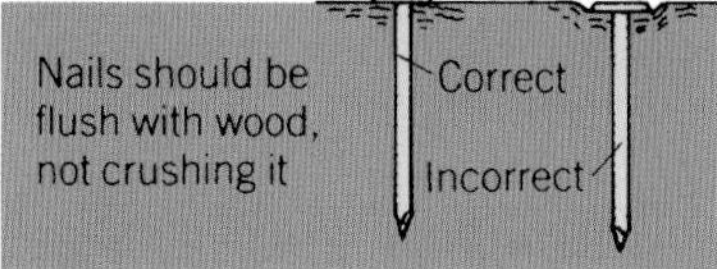

4 Drill small pilot holes, if necessary, and drive two galvanized nails into the gap between the shingles on the upper course. Set the nail heads flush, and insert a small piece of metal flashing under the shingles to cover the nails.

Roof Repairs / Clay Tile

Maintaining a Clay-Tile Roof

Clay tiles don't degrade much from weather, but like slate and other brittle materials, they can break. The tiles come in various shapes, most with a half-round profile, and many have interlocking contours that make them difficult to replace individually. Unless the repair is minor and can be done while you stand on a ladder rather than the roof itself, hire a pro.

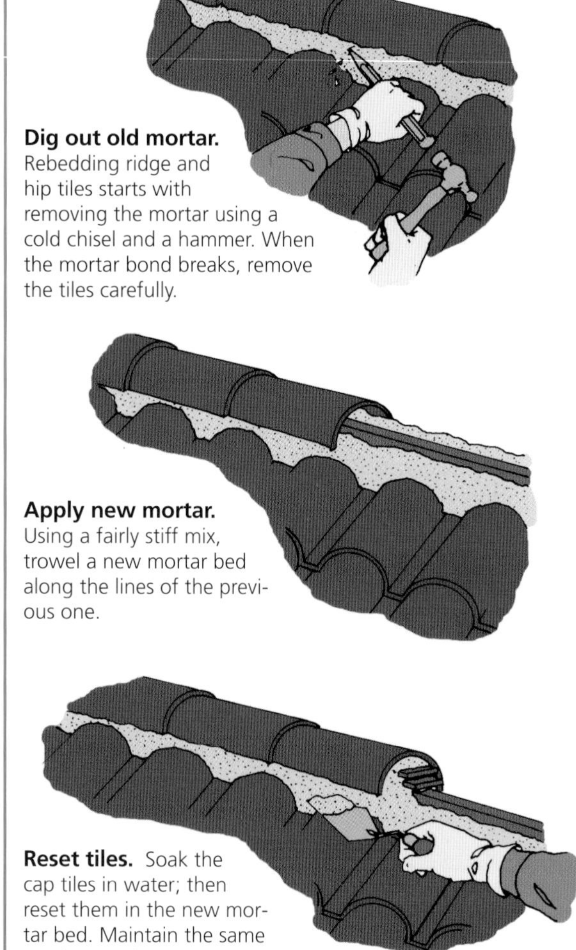

Dig out old mortar. Rebedding ridge and hip tiles starts with removing the mortar using a cold chisel and a hammer. When the mortar bond breaks, remove the tiles carefully.

Apply new mortar. Using a fairly stiff mix, trowel a new mortar bed along the lines of the previous one.

Reset tiles. Soak the cap tiles in water; then reset them in the new mortar bed. Maintain the same overlap used previously.

Roof Repairs / Flat Roof

Because it can't shed rain the way a sloped roof can, a flat roof often requires more care to keep it waterproof, and it can't rely on the shingles or similar loosely overlapped materials used on a conventional roof.

Technically, a flat roof can be dead horizontal or have a very low slope. For a roof, slope is described as a ratio of vertical rise per foot of horizontal run, both expressed in inches. For example, a 7:12 slope indicates 7 in. of vertical rise for every 12 in. of horizontal run. Any roof with a slope of 2:12 or less qualifies as flat and must be covered using one of several techniques.

For years, built-up roofing has been the standard solution for flat or low-sloped roofs. Multiple layers—as many as five—of asphalt-impregnated builder's felt are secured down with alternating layers of hot tar in a hot process or standard roofing cement in a cold process.

To minimize the heat absorption and subsequent damage to the surface, built-up roofing is often covered with a layer of gravel or mineral-surfaced roll roofing. This coating slows the overheating, oxidation and hardening of the tar that eventually creates cracks. More recently, brush-on aluminum-fiber coatings have become popular treatments for built-up or roll roofing; in addition to providing another waterproof layer, these silver-colored coatings keep the roof cooler by reflecting sunlight.

Alternatives to built-up or asphalt roll roofing include soldered metal roofs—an expensive option and one that requires specialized skills and equipment—and a synthetic rubber membrane called EPDM (see below). EPDM membranes can be applied with adhesives or by a system that uses heat to seal the seams.

Patching a Torn Spot on Asphalt Roofing

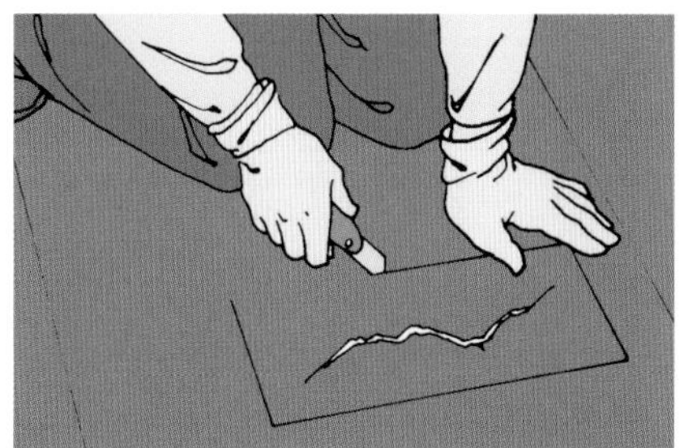

1 Brush the area clean, then cut out the damaged section with a utility knife. Use the cutout as a pattern for cutting a patch.

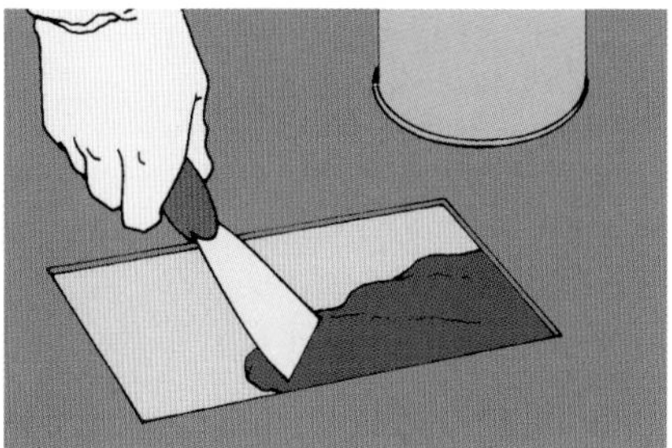

2 Apply roofing cement to the exposed area, using a putty knife to work adhesive under all the cut edges and to cover the center.

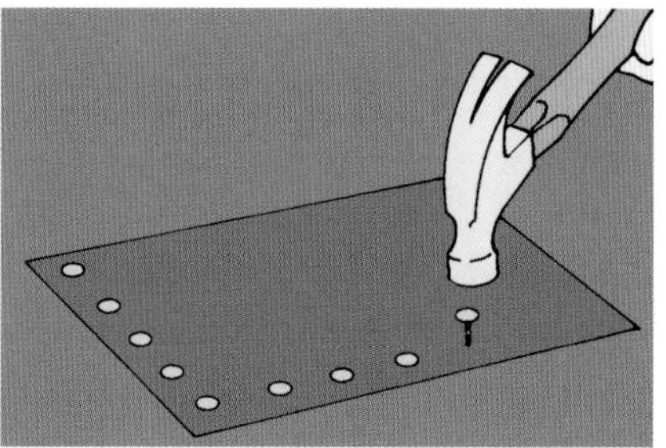

3 Cut one or more patches from new roll roofing and nail them in place so they're flush with the surrounding surface.

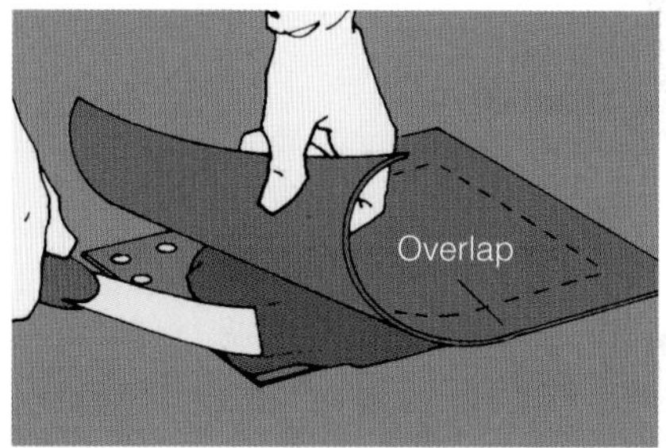

4 Cut a cover patch to overlap the repair by 2 in. (5 cm) along each edge. Apply cement, then press the cover patch down firmly.

Installing Asphalt-Rolled Roofing

Asphalt-rolled roofing typically comes in 3-ft. or 1-m widths and can be used on roofs with a shallow pitch. After removing the old roofing and installing flashing and drip edge, precut lengths of roofing are installed with nails and roofing cement. Consult manufacturer's instructions for exact installation procedures.

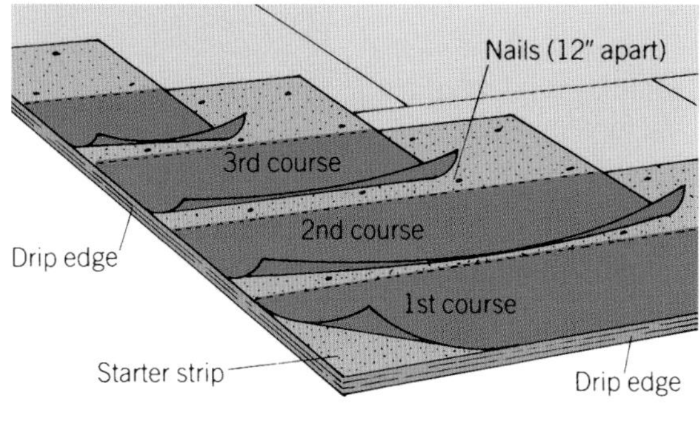

Installing EPDM Roofing

A synthetic rubber membrane called EPDM offers a reliable solution for flat roofs. Available in sheets up to 50 ft. (15.3 m) wide, this material is installed with adhesive and special fasteners, then flashed to cover the edges. Most vendors offer installation advice to do-it-yourselfers. Pros often install this using an open-flame or torch method.

Roof Repairs / Metal Roof

Ladder and Scaffold Safety 311
Soldering 473

Many different metals are used for roofing. Copper, which over time develops a signature green patina, is found in many older cities, especially on prominent ecclesiastical, university or government buildings. Tin roofs common on farm buildings are actually more likely to be corrugated galvanized steel. Other metal roofs are not always recognizable. Terne, which is steel coated with an alloy of tin and lead, is usually painted. Some modern aluminum roofing is die-stamped to look like wood shingles, and some steel roofing panels are preformed to resemble clay tiles. Most metal roofing features some sort of contoured or formed edge that overlaps the edge of an adjacent piece to create a water-shedding joint. Corrugated panels simply overlap a crest and trough. Flat roofing panels have standing seams along their edges that are crimped tightly to connect them to each other.

Copper ranks high in durability; properly installed, it can last a century under the right conditions. Other roofing metals are more subject to corrosion, but even aluminum and galvanized steel can last for decades. Salt air is very corrosive to metals, but a more common factor in metal roof failures is a destructive chemical reaction, called electrolysis, that occurs when dissimilar metals contact one another. For this reason, it's very important to install metal roofing using fasteners made of the same metal.

Painted steel or terne roofs must be repainted and touched up to prevent rust. Pinhole leaks can be fixed with roofing cement or an asphalt-based sealant. Larger holes or tears can be mended by soldering on a patch of the same metal. Steel and terne should be soldered with a noncorrosive resin flux; copper should be soldered with an acid flux. Aluminum roofing does not need to be painted, but it often is for aesthetic reasons. Fasteners are usually screws with sealing washers, as nails tend to loosen over time.

Soldering a Patch

1 Clean damaged area thoroughly. Cut a patch of the same metal at least 2 in. (5 cm) larger in each dimension than the hole. Snip corners and fold edges under 1/2 in. (12 mm). Sand the turned edges and position the patch. Coat edges and the roof surface with flux.

2 Weight the patch with bricks to secure it. Use an electric soldering iron to heat solder at the edges of the patch until solder flows into the joint. Work around the patch until all the edges are sealed.

Patching Aluminum

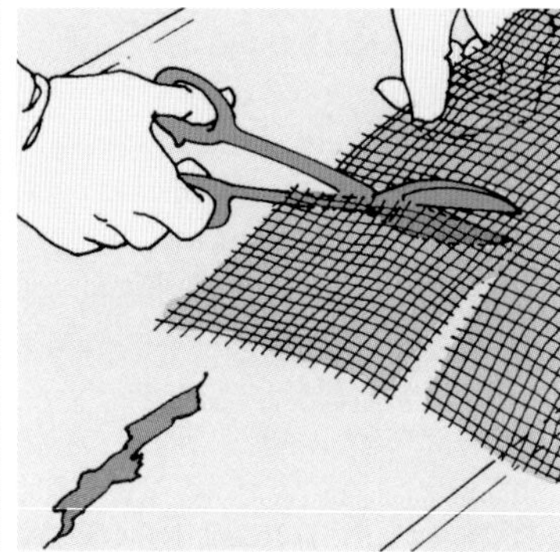

1 Cut two patches from fiberglass screen material, large enough to cover the damaged area. Use a wire brush to scrub the roof surface clean, and then coat the area with roofing cement.

2 Apply one fiberglass patch over the fresh roofing cement. Using a flexible putty knife, cover the patch with more cement. Then embed the second fiberglass patch in that layer. Finish with a third coat of cement.

Coating a Pitted Roof

Over time, the slow corrosion that occurs with metal roofing often results in numerous pinholes or pits that will grow and allow leaks. Modern, factory-applied protective coatings ward off this damage for many years, but once the degradation starts it's almost impossible to stop. You can, however, buy some additional time by applying an asphalt-based liquid sealant. Start at the high end of the roof and work the coating along the flats and seams using a stiff push broom. Work from your ladder to finish the lowest sections. As long as the coating adheres well to the metal surface, periodic recoating will help prevent leaks, but eventually the roofing will have to be replaced.

Asphalt Shingles / Diagnosis and Tear-Off

Although the lifetime rating on a given type of asphalt shingle might be useful for comparing one product to another, it's not always a reliable indicator of how long the roof will actually last. Rain and ice are often considered the worst offenders when it comes to exterior damage on a home, but it's sun and heat that destroy roof shingles. Ultraviolet rays break down the asphalt layer and cause it to become brittle, so a 30-year shingle might last twice as long on the cloudy Northwest coast as it would in the desert Southwest. Even different roof sections on the same house will age differently, depending on their exposure to sun. Also, nonvented roofs suffer heat buildup that accelerates the degradation. To assess a roof's condition, start with the areas that get the most sun, typically the south-facing sections, and use them as a benchmark for deciding on replacement.

Is It Time to Replace?

It's not the only test, but a quick visual inspection from the ground can often indicate whether a roof needs to be replaced. The crisp edges, flat tabs and uniform color of new shingles will be replaced by broken corners, curled tabs and a mottled or spiderweb appearance from the loss of mineral granules and subsequent cracking.

Still good. Consistency of color and shape indicates shingles in good condition. They're flat with edges, corners and granules intact.

Too old. Granule loss, broken corners and curled tabs reveal this roof to be overdue for replacement. Leaks are probably already occurring.

Tearing Off Old Shingles

Roof tear-off and replacement is a messy job that goes much better if you're organized.

1. Rent a roll-off trash bin and position it under a roof edge.
2. Cover plants to protect them from falling debris.
3. Remove the old shingles with tear-off shovels.
4. Cut and install the ice-and-water barrier along the roof edges.
5. Roll out roofing felt over the sheathing and staple in place.
6. Clean up the loose debris and nails around the house.
7. Have the shingles delivered and placed on the roof by a boom truck.

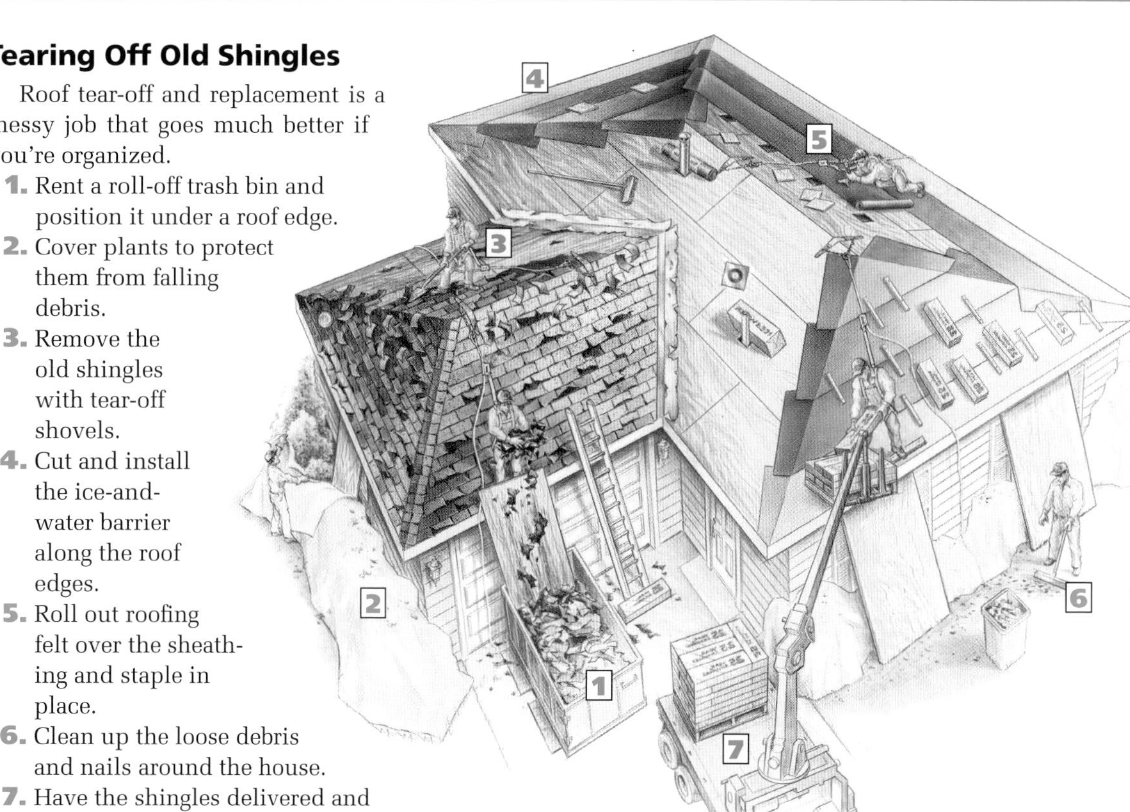

Laying New Shingles over Old

When a roof has a layer of aging but intact shingles and is still sound, you can—if local building codes allow—install new shingles without doing a tear-off first. Install valley flashing as you would for a new roof and use longer nails to penetrate the old shingles and sheathing. Stagger the shingle joints so they don't align with those on the previous layer. This technique works best when new shingles are the same size as the old; switching from the common 3-ft. shingles to those that are metric size and vice versa requires special techniques.

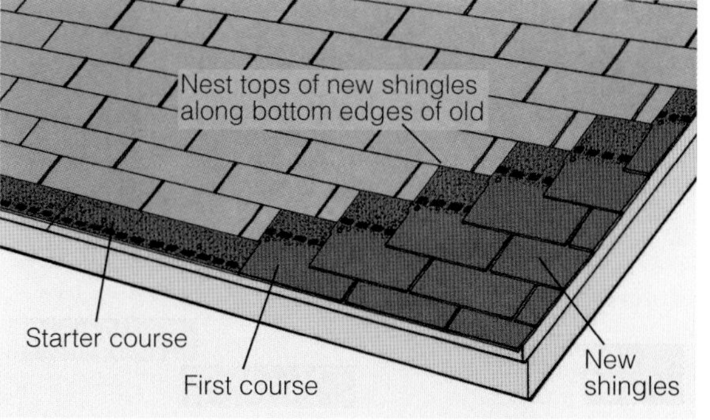

Asphalt Shingles / Installing

Ladder and Scaffold Safety 311
Flashings and Vents 322
Chimney Flashing 324

Roofing a house is not a job for everyone, but if you can handle the mess of tear-off and the planning logistics, the savings can amount to thousands of dollars. It also provides a good opportunity for upgrading or installing soffit and roof vents. Some circumstances warrant turning the job over to professionals. First, complex roof shapes or steep slopes make the work more difficult and dangerous. If that describes your situation, find a safer project to add to your to-do list. If your roof is two stories or higher aboveground, you should use scaffolding, and the cost of renting or buying that equipment may offset any savings you might enjoy. Finally, if the roof has deteriorated to the point that chronic leaks have caused extensive sheathing rot or structural problems, the repairs may require skills and equipment you don't have.

That said, there's good reason to tackle simple reroofing projects yourself, but you should be familiar with the techniques and materials. Shingles are sold by the bundle but estimated in squares that equal either 100 sq. ft. or 10 sq. m. Take rough measurements of your roof area, then add 5 to 10 percent for waste. Single-ply three-tab asphalt shingles are the least expensive type, but you'll get better life and looks from a multi-ply architectural or dimensional shingle.

Handy Hints

Easy Delivery

Find out if your shingle supplier has a boom truck or conveyor belt that can deliver your shingles directly to the rooftop. It may cost more but can save you hundreds of trips up and down the ladder.

Getting Started

After estimating and ordering materials, strip the roof clean of old shingles and felt underlayment. Inspect the sheathing for rot and the flashing for signs of leakage; make repairs as necessary. Then organize your tools, materials and helpers; roofing a house should be a team effort.

1 Install a gutter apron and a self-adhering ice-and-water membrane along the lower edges. Cut the membrane into manageable lengths and overlap the ends 6 in. (15 cm).

2 Finish covering the sheathing with felt underlayment. Nail drip edge flashing along the sloping edges, or rakes, of the roof, overlapping the gutter apron.

Dealing with Valleys

Valleys, where two roof planes intersect at an inside corner, need special attention because they're a main channel for diverting water on its way down the roof. The objective is to ensure that water flowing down one face of the valley doesn't have a chance to make its way under the shingles on the other face. Three common techniques are shown.

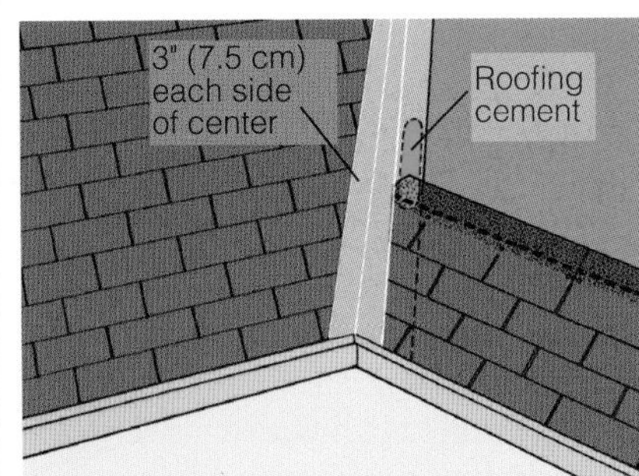

Open valleys, which shed water the quickest, rely on metal flashing nailed along the edges to provide the water channel. The flashing may have a ridge protruding along the center to help direct the flow.

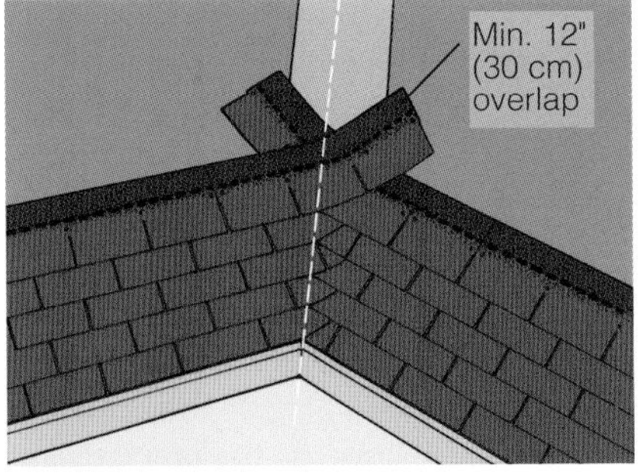

Woven valleys involve laying shingle courses up both sides of the valley simultaneously. Where they meet, the overlap alternates from side to side. These are less obtrusive, but shed water more slowly.

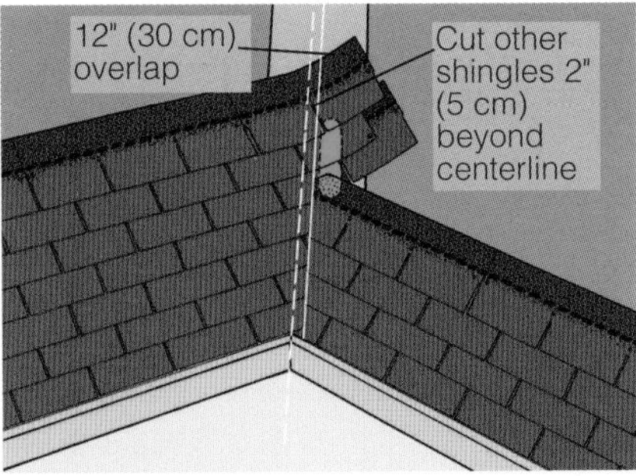

Closed-cut valleys have shingles from one side running at least 1 ft. (30 cm) onto the adjacent roof; shingles from the adjacent roof then lap over these and are cut in line with the valley to present a cleaner look.

Two Methods for Laying Shingles

With a consistent roof that was built straight and square, it's often simplest to begin shingling at a lower corner, cutting the starting shingle in each course down to offset the joints and working from one end to the other. One alternate method starts near the middle, using chalk lines snapped for reference, and works outward toward both ends, trimming the end shingles later.

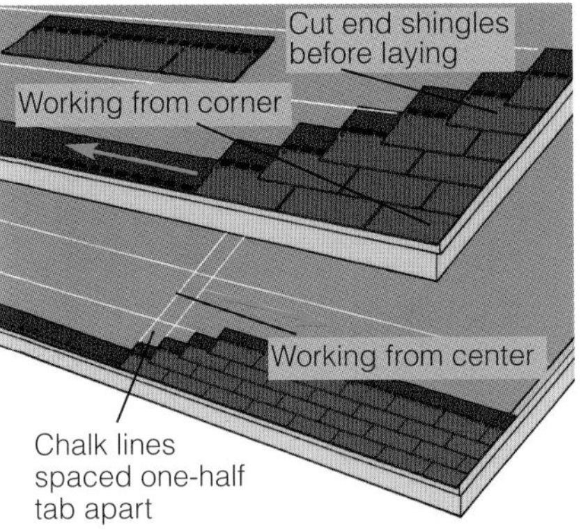

With the prep work done, you can start laying shingles. This is mostly a simple repetitive task, but start by measuring accurately and snapping chalk lines to ensure correct alignment. For the starter course, buy a special starter strip or cut the tabs off the shingles and nail the remaining sections so they overhang the edge about 3/8 in. (1 cm). Follow the nailing instructions on the shingle package. Right-handers usually find it most efficient to work from left to right and left-handers, from right to left. Every few courses, check to make sure shingles are running in a straight line and tab cutouts are lining up.

1 Beginning at a corner or pair of chalk lines, nail the first course of shingles over the starter course. Stagger the subsequent courses with a half-tab offset as you proceed.

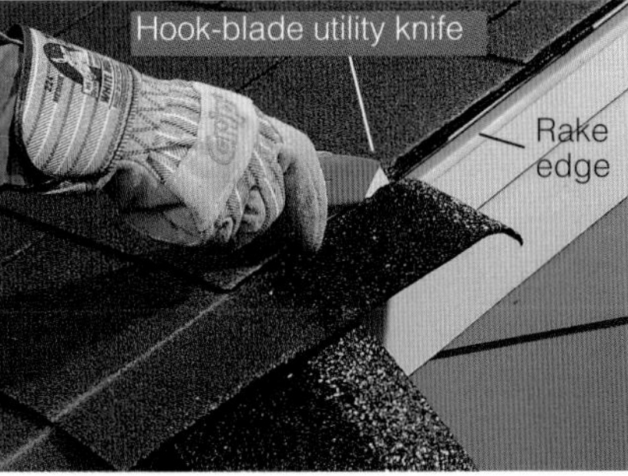

2 Let the end shingles run long until you finish the section. Then snap a chalk line 3/8 in. (1 cm) from the rake edge and cut the excess material off with a hook-blade utility knife.

3 Cut full shingles into thirds at tab cutouts to use for covering the ridge. For a cleaner fit, cut a slight taper so the upper ends are narrower than the tabs.

4 Snap a chalk line along one side of the ridge so tabs line up evenly on both sides. Nail the cut shingles with the same exposure used for the flat sections. Use slightly longer nails.

Installing Vent Flashings

Every structure with plumbing will have at least one or two vent stacks that penetrate the roof. To seal the pipe edge and roof opening, use a preformed vent flashing with a flexible rubber sleeve. These are sized for standard pipe sizes.

1 Shingle up to the vent stack, then fit the flashing sleeve over the pipe and press the metal base down flat. Nail at the lower corners only.

2 Install the next row of shingles, cutting the tabs to accommodate the flashing's raised base and overlap the flat part of the flashing.

Adding a Rain Diverter

Roofs without gutters send water cascading over the edge. When that happens over doorways, it soaks you, your walkways and porch stoop. Fix the problem by installing a D-style metal drip edge as a diverter. Beware: This can create or accentuate ice dam problems in colder climates.

1 Apply a bead of clear silicone caulk along the underside of the drip edge before slipping it under the shingle tabs. Angle it slightly to drain at one end.

2 With the diverter secured, apply a bead of clear silicone caulk in each of the slots between the shingle tabs, so water doesn't seep under the metal edge.

Flashings and Vents / Installing

Installing new shingles is only half the battle in getting a leak-free roof. Wherever roof planes intersect or meet an obstacle, such as a chimney, vent stack or dormer, flashing is required to divert water away from the joint. Because they're pliable enough to bend around corners, asphalt-impregnated felt and asphalt roll roofing—doctored with roofing cement—are sometimes used as flashing. Metal flashing, however, is typically more effective and durable, and more commonly used. Available in rolls of various widths or as smaller preformed pieces of step flashing, aluminum and galvanized steel are the most widely available. Occasionally you can find lead sheets, which are used to flash chimneys because aluminum corrodes in contact with mortar and concrete, or copper flashing. Both are pricier but last much longer. Fasteners should be made of the same metal to avoid an electrolytic chemical reaction.

The strategy for flashing isn't to create a watertight seal but rather to overlap layers of material, diverting rainfall onto the shingles or other pieces of flashing so it can run harmlessly off the roof. Some connections, where flashing is embedded in a mortar joint, for example, do have to be watertight. As long as gravity can keep the water flowing, though, overlapped edges do most of the work.

Can a New Roof Leak?

Certainly, but it's not likely to happen through the shingles themselves. Interruptions in a roof's surface—dormers, vents, skylights—create opportunities for water to get under the shingles and through the sheathing. Every joint is vulnerable, particularly if the surfaces are made of different materials and expand and contract at different rates. To accommodate this movement, sometimes flashing edges are allowed to float rather than be nailed tightly; as long as water is eventually diverted onto intact shingles, it won't find a point of entry into the house.

With age and exposure, thin layers of metal flashing can develop pinhole leaks that allow water to seep through. These minor leaks can be patched temporarily with roofing cement, but they are a sign that the flashing is due for replacement soon. Larger holes in copper or steel flashing can often be repaired with a soldered patch.

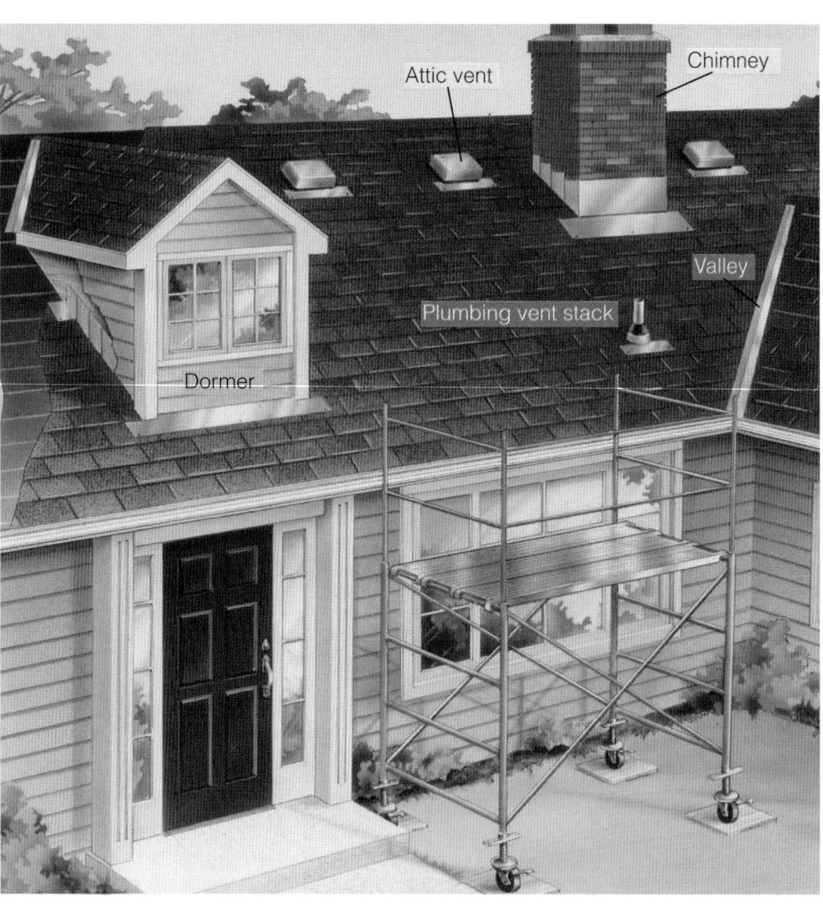

Installing Dormer Step Flashing

1 Start at the lower, or front, face, removing or loosening trim or siding as necessary. Crease a length of metal flashing. Slip one edge underneath the siding and nail the other edge to the shingles. Apply sealant to nail heads. Cut and bend the flashing at the corners.

2 Slip the first step flashing under the siding on the side wall, cutting and bending it to wrap around the corner and cover the front flashing. Seal the joint with silicone caulk and nail the top corner of the step flashing.

3 Lay the next row of shingles to cover the first step flashing. Slide a second step flashing under the siding and nail it at the upper corner, near the top of the shingle. Continue alternating shingles and flashing.

Flashings and Vents / Repairing

Replacing a Vent Flashing

All-metal plumbing vents present two opportunities for leaks—first, where the flashing meets the roof, and second, where the vent pipe meets the flashing. When the latter situation occurs, caulking and similar fixes will prove to be only temporary cures. You'll have to replace the flashing, either with a rubber-sleeve version or the telescoping two-piece type shown at right.

1 Carefully remove any shingles that lap over the top half of the flashing base. Pull the nails that secure the old flashing and remove it.

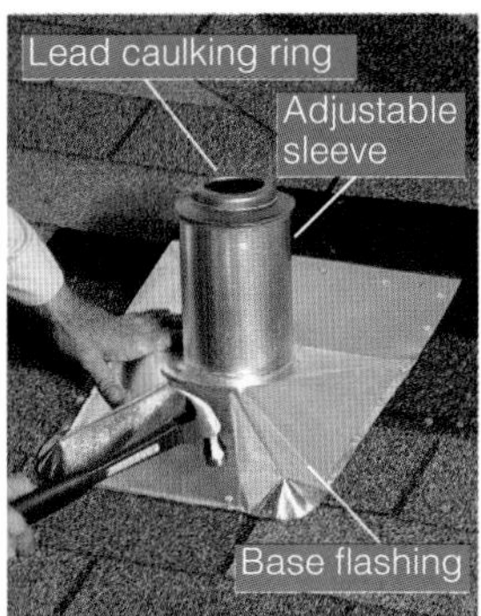

2 Fit the new base flashing over the pipe and nail along the edges. Slide the adjustable sleeve over the base flashing and vent pipe.

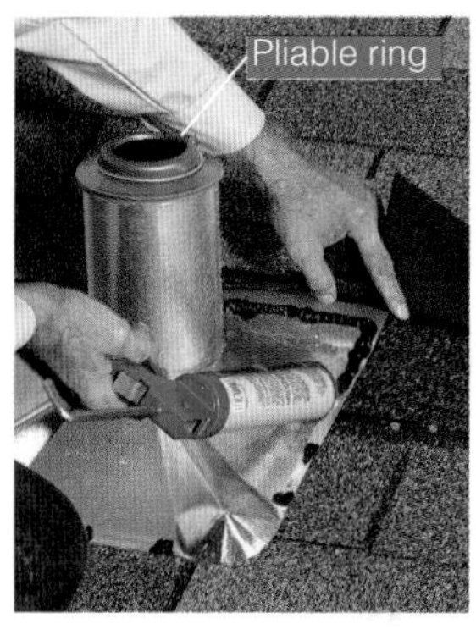

3 Notch and reinstall shingles to cover upper portion of base flashing. Apply roofing cement to overlapping tabs and exposed nail heads. Fold pliable ring over top of vent pipe.

Sealing a Valley Joint

Occasionally, a flashing that's still intact can allow water passage; this is especially true for valley flashing that doesn't have a raised fin or ridge in the center to help prevent fast-moving water from sloshing. If the roofer didn't cement the joint—and many don't—the shingles can curl up at the edge and eventually create a gap that water can easily penetrate.

1 Starting at the bottom edge, lift the shingle and apply a heavy, consistent bead of roofing cement along the flashing.

2 Drop and embed the first shingle into the cement. Lift the next shingle and lay another long bead of cement on flashing and the top edge of the previous shingle.

3 Continue applying cement to both the flashing and the shingles as you work your way up. Press the shingles down to seat them.

Adding a Roof Vent

Roof vents prolong shingle life by letting hot air rise and escape rather than contribute to excessive heat buildup in an attic or rafter space. Ridge vents that extend the entire length of the roof can be effective when installed correctly, but are more easily installed new than retrofitted. Multiple single vents represent a simpler option and can be positioned as needed.

1 With your saw set deep enough to cut through only the shingles and sheathing, cut a square hole the same size as the hole in the vent base.

2 Using a hook-blade utility knife, trim the surrounding shingles to fit around the vent body and overlap the base flange.

3 Pull nails, if necessary, to allow the vent to slide into place. Apply roofing cement and position it with the flange tucked under the upper shingles.

Flashing and Vents / Chimney

Ladder and Scaffold Safety 311
Repairing Brick 414

A chimney, whether it abuts an outside wall or rises from inside the house, is usually built on its own foundation to accommodate the tremendous weight of all that brick and mortar. The whole structure can move and settle independently, causing the joints between chimney and roof to shift, too. Flashing must accommodate this movement and still divert water. Both problems are solved with a two-stage flashing system. First, a base layer of flashing is attached to the roof and bent up the sides of the chimney. This layer consists of two larger apron flashings on the front and rear faces of the chimney and a series of step flashing on each side. The second layer, called cap flashing or counterflashing, is tucked into the mortar joints in the chimney and overlaps the top edges of the base-layer flashing. The layers are not fixed to each other, so they can withstand some movement, and the overlap ensures that water is shed properly. Flashing simply caulked to the side of brick will almost guarantee a future leak.

If a chimney emerges from the roof below the ridge, the joint at the back face creates a V-shaped pocket prone to collecting debris and water, increasing the likelihood of leaks. In these situations, a small A-frame structure called a saddle or cricket is typically installed and flashed to shed water off to the sides.

Whether made of galvanized steel, copper or lead sheeting, the metal flashing for a chimney is often more effective and durable if it can be prefabricated with soldered corners rather than cut and bent on site (see "Ordering Custom Flashings" at far right.) Prefabricated flashing is also easier to install and requires spending less time on the roof. Even so, the process requires grinding and caulking multiple mortar joints and fitting many individual flashings, so—unless you're a savvy or adventurous do-it-yourselfer—hiring a professional may be your best route.

Flashing Details

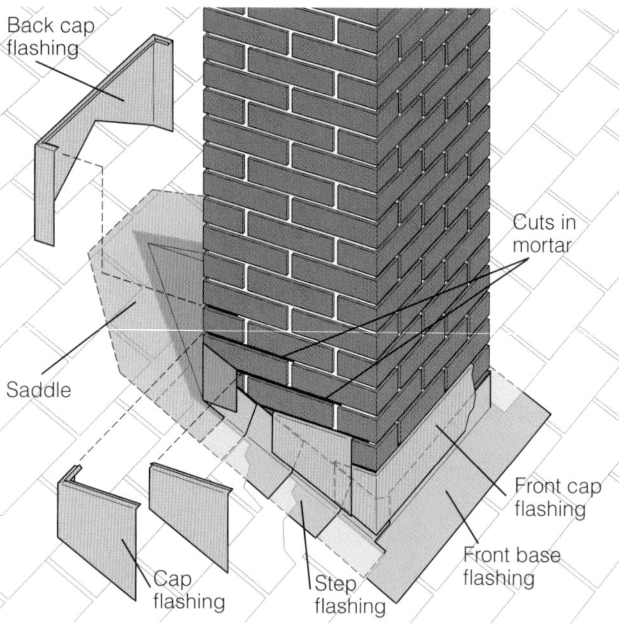

The two-stage system for chimney flashing consists of the base and step flashing fastened to the roof along the front, back and sides of the chimney. The cap flashings are bent with a narrow ledge along their upper edges to be inserted into cuts in the mortar.

Handy Hints: Safer Flashing

Rolled metal flashing can sometimes uncoil abruptly and cut your hand. You can tame that tendency by cutting a slot in the side of a large, lidded plastic bucket and using it as a dispenser. Wearing gloves and eye protection further enhances your safety.

Ordering Custom Flashings

The crisp bends and soldered corners that look and work best on chimney flashings require a bending brake and other equipment no homeowner is likely to have. For best results, consider having a sheet-metal contractor or professional roofer fabricate these pieces for you. All they need from you are the chimney dimensions and the slope of the roof, and they can make the apron base flashing, a metal saddle or cricket, and the step and cap flashings.

Find the slope. Use a scrap piece of plywood with one edge labeled "roof." Set that edge on the roof with the plywood perpendicular to the ridge. Then use a level, as shown, to mark a level line from the lead corner across the face of the plywood.

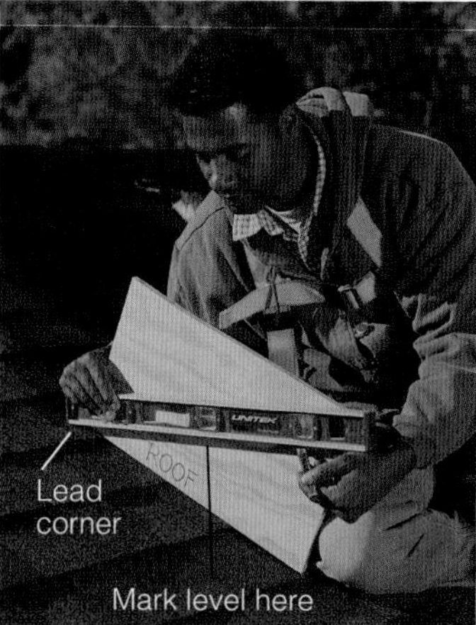

Mark the rise and run. Align a framing square's blade along the level line, with the 12-in. mark at the lead corner. Then mark a line along the tongue of the square and note the dimension. Here, it shows 6 in., or a 6:12 slope.

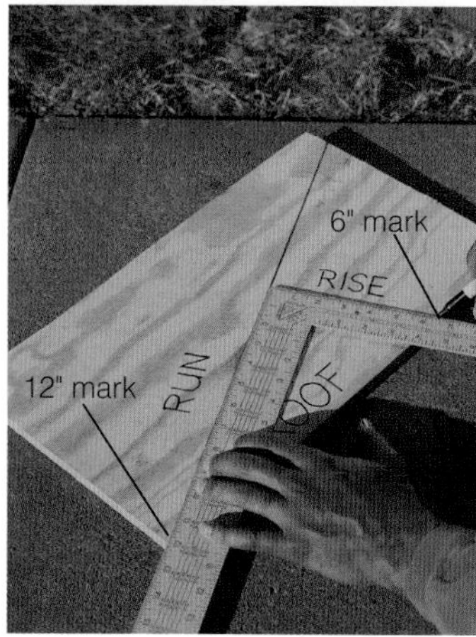

Reflashing a Chimney

1 Use a pry bar and old chisel to remove the old metal flashing and scrape off the old roofing cement. Then cut a piece of pre-bent base flashing equal to the chimney width plus 8 in. (20 cm) to fit across the front of the chimney.

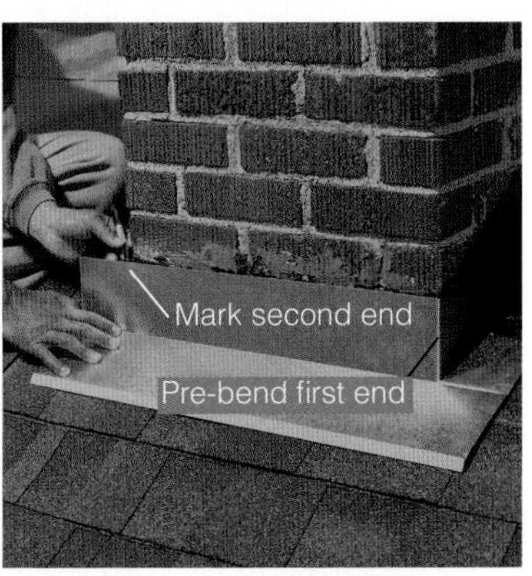

2 Cut a 45° angle on one end of the flashing to bend around the chimney corner and fit the flashing snugly in place. Mark the remaining end and make another angled cut to bend around that corner. Nail the front edge.

3 Snip and bend a piece of square-step flashing to wrap about 2 in. (5 cm) around the front corner. Apply a generous dollop of caulk at the corner, press the step flashing in place and nail the outer edge to the roof.

4 Nail the next shingle over the first step flashing; then nail another step flashing over the top half of this shingle. Work your way up the sides, alternating shingles and step flashing. Cut and bend the last step flashings around the top.

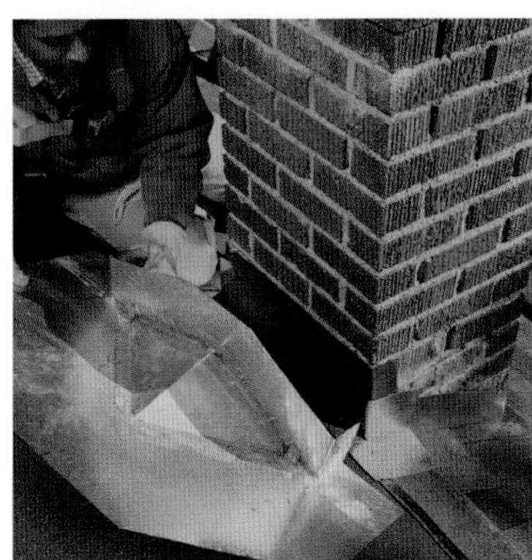

5 Fit the prefabricated chimney saddle into place behind the chimney. Nail it to the roof along its top edge using 1-in. galvanized roofing nails. Nail at intervals close enough to keep the edge flat.

6 Use an angle grinder with a diamond blade to cut 1-in. (2.5-cm)-deep grooves in the mortar joints just above the base flashings. These will accept the L-shaped cap flashing. Wear eye and ear protection, as well as a dust mask.

7 Bend the ends of the front cap flashing around the chimney; then use a hammer and block to drive the flange into the groove in the mortar joint. When it's fully seated, drill and drive an expanding masonry anchor near each corner.

8 Cut the side cap flashings to fit the angle of the roof, so they overlap the base step flashings by at least 2 in. (5 cm). Drive flanges into grooves and secure expansion anchors. Repeat for the back cap and seal all mortar-flange joints with polyurethane caulk.

Prevent Falls

Flashing a chimney means you'll be on the roof a while. Ensure your safety by setting up roof brackets and a sturdy plank as a slide guard to give you a solid footing to step on. Rent a safety harness system as well.

Gutters and Downspouts / Maintaining

Ladder and Scaffold Safety 311
Cutting Metal 469
Riveting 472

Gutters and downspouts channel rainfall and snowmelt off the roof and away from the foundation of a house. To be effective, they must have the proper slope, remain free of debris and obstructions and empty into a downspout or other device that will divert the water. A less common drain alternative is a dry well, basically a large hole in the ground filled with stones. Dry wells have a limited storage capacity and ultimately rely on the water absorption rates of the surrounding soil, so they tend to fill quickly if rainfall is heavy and constant.

Gutters are made from various materials—copper, galvanized steel, aluminum, vinyl, even wood—but with their standard 10-ft. lengths and assorted fittings, galvanized steel and vinyl offer the most do-it-yourself-friendly installation for homeowners. Copper gutters and fittings sometimes require soldered or riveted joints, though they'll last a century or more. Aluminum gutters are often made on site by professionals. These are seamless gutters with each section formed from a single piece, extruded from long rolls of metal and offered in a wide variety of colors. Vinyl gutter systems, typically offered in white and brown, are a low-maintenance option available at most home centers.

Aside from occasional painting of steel or wood gutters, most maintenance requirements involve sealing leaks between fittings or keeping leaves and other debris from building up and clogging the water's path.

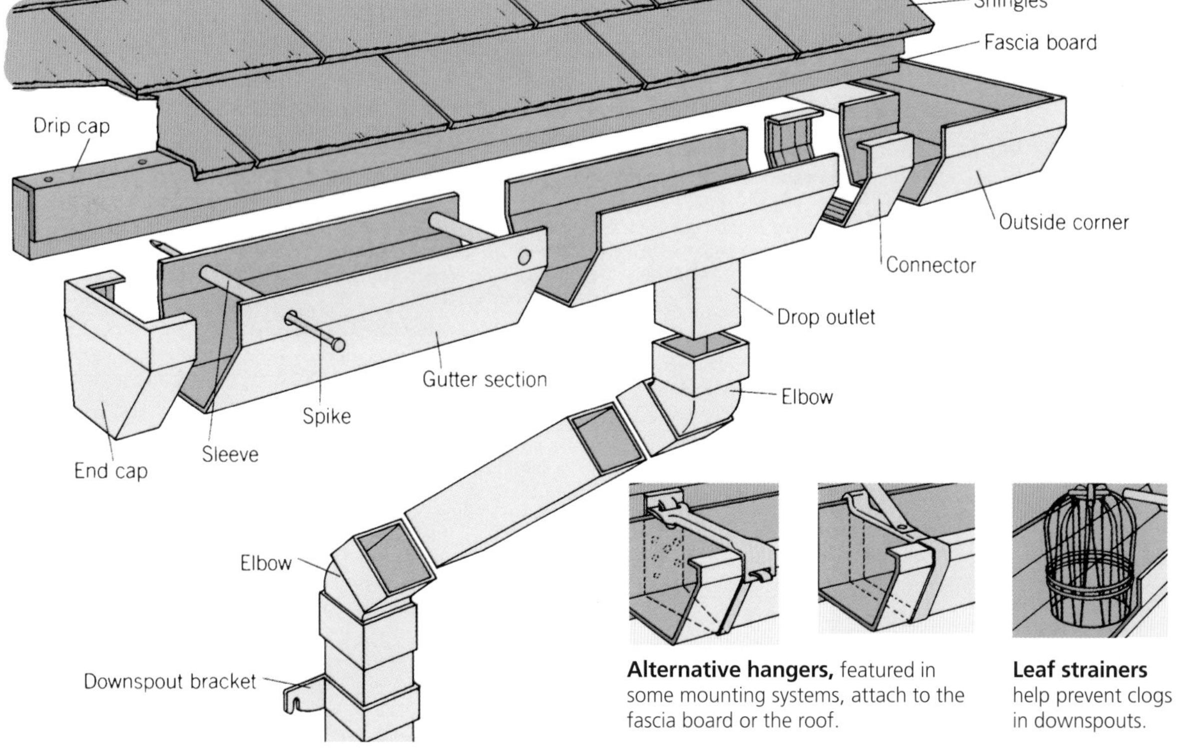

Alternative hangers, featured in some mounting systems, attach to the fascia board or the roof.

Leaf strainers help prevent clogs in downspouts.

Repairing Leaky Metal Gutter Seams

For water to make it to the downspouts and drain properly, it has to stay in the gutter channel. When couplings or other fittings leak, the water drips instead right next to the foundation. A simple repair can stop the leak.

1 Separate the leaking seam by drilling out the pop rivets that hold it together. Use a drill bit slightly larger than the hole in the center of the rivet. Clean off any old sealant using a putty knife and sandpaper.

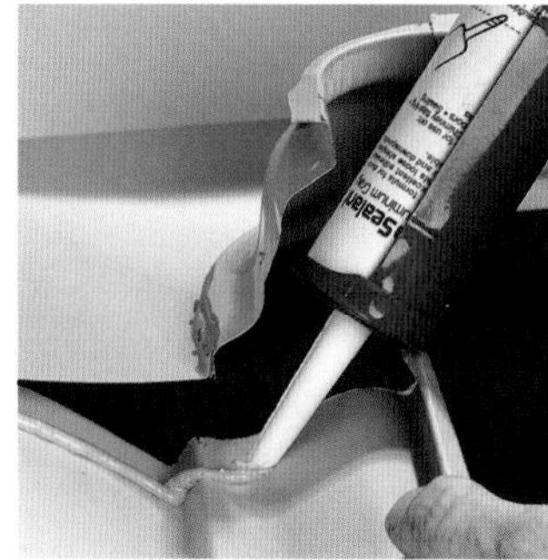

2 Apply a new bead of gutter sealant between the adjoining surfaces. Use a putty knife to work the sealer into corners and along edges. Reconnect the fittings and make sure they're tight.

3 In most cases, you can use new pop rivets that are the same size as the old ones. Check the diameter and depth range to make sure they'll fit the old holes and will cinch the joint tight.

Patching a Leaky Gutter

Left unrepaired, leaks from your gutters can result in water damage to the house siding and eaves, as well as create drainage problems that affect the foundation or basement. Patch small leaks before they grow.

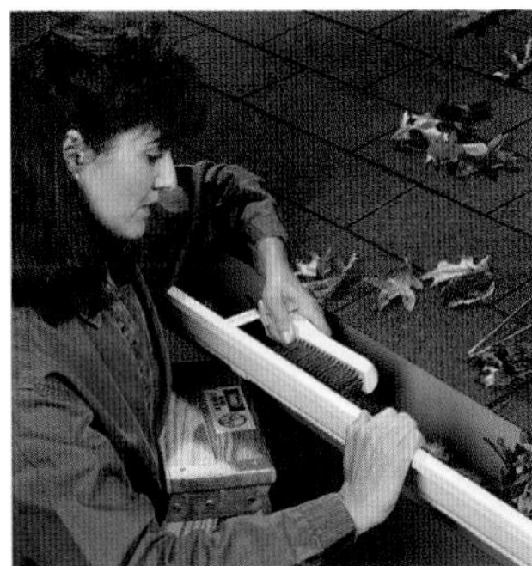

1 Remove any accumulated debris around the leak and spray it clean with water. Use a wire brush to clean off surface rust or corrosion and scuff the surface lightly. Break off loose or fragile edges from the hole.

2 Use an old towel to remove any standing water left from the cleanup. Spread plastic roofing cement directly over the leaky seam or hole and at least 6 in. (15 cm) beyond in both directions.

3 Embed a piece of repair mesh or a piece of prebent metal flashing in the roofing cement and press firmly to seat it. Then recoat with a second layer of cement and apply a coat of aluminum paint.

Resecuring Gutters and End Caps

Over time, ice dams, heavy rains and loose fasteners will undo the secure installation your gutters and fittings had when they were new. Make periodic inspections to locate any loose parts or sagging gutters.

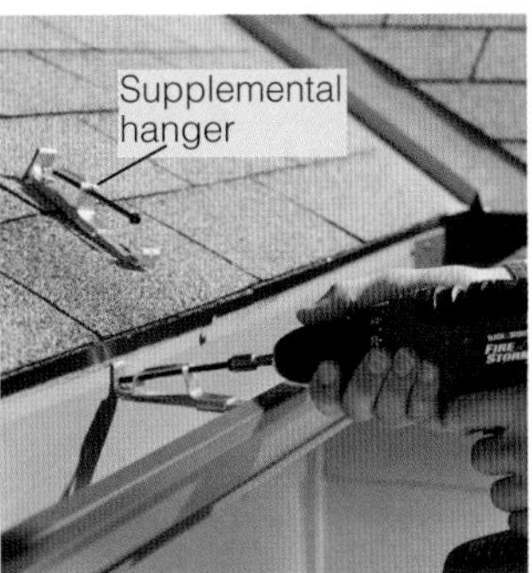

1 Supplement the original spikes or mounting brackets with retrofit hangers. Hook the nose of the hanger under the gutter's front edge and its rear lip over the back edge. Then drive the screw into the wood trim, and preferably the rafter tail or truss tail behind.

2 Loose or leaking end caps can be repaired to make them stay tight for good. Remove the cap and clean it thoroughly. Fill the perimeter groove with a bead of clear silicone caulk and press firmly in place to seal.

3 With the end cap reinstalled, use the existing holes or drill holes to accept 1/8-in.-dia. Pop rivets. Install rivets at the front upper edge and the front lower corner. Small sheet-metal screws will also work. Wipe away any excess caulk.

Gutter Getters

Cleaning gutters can be a tedious chore, so make sure the results you get are worth the time and effort you spend. Here are three simple homemade solutions that will let you work faster and get better results.

Leaf scoop. Retire a worn-out plastic kitchen spatula for use as a gutter scoop. It won't scratch the gutters and, if necessary, you can cut it with snips to fit the contour of the gutter trough.

Leaf catcher. If you pull clumps of leaves from gutters only to toss them on the ground, you end up cleaning them up twice. Instead, cut the wire handle of a bucket and bend it to form two hooks to hang the bucket from the gutter.

Gutter cleaner. To rinse gutters clean without repeatedly climbing and moving a ladder, fashion a gooseneck sprayer with 3/4-in. PVC plumbing pipe and a hose connector. Drill four small holes on one side of the cap, as shown.

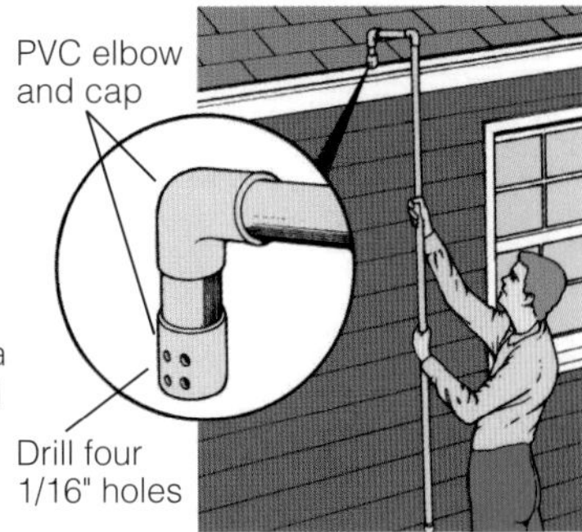

Gutters and Downspouts / Installing Metal Gutters

Rivets 472
Cutting Metal 469

Store-bought metal gutter systems have a lot going for them, especially the relatively low cost. By installing them yourself, you'll enjoy a substantial savings over professionally installed custom gutters. The standard 10-ft. gutter length can't match the clean lines of the extruded seamless type that pros fabricate on site. But if you don't mind a few coupling connectors on long runs, you'll get a solid system that performs just as well—and that you can paint to match your house trim, if desired.

Before you start, sketch a bird's-eye view of your roof outline and mark rough dimensions. You'll need this to determine how many lengths of gutter and how many downspouts you need, plus the various fittings to put it all together. Allow for downspouts at intervals no greater than 35 ft. (10 m), and calculate the number of connectors, drop outlets, corner fittings and hanger straps required. Every downspout needs two elbows to make the return under the eaves, plus a third if you divert the water away from the foundation, and at least two mounting straps.

If you're replacing old gutters, remove them and inspect the fascia boards around the entire roof; patch old spike and screw holes and replace any sections where the wood is rotted or otherwise unsound. Prime and paint any bare wood. Some older homes have narrow or contoured trim nailed to the fascia just under the shingles; this must be removed to create a flat surface for mounting the gutters.

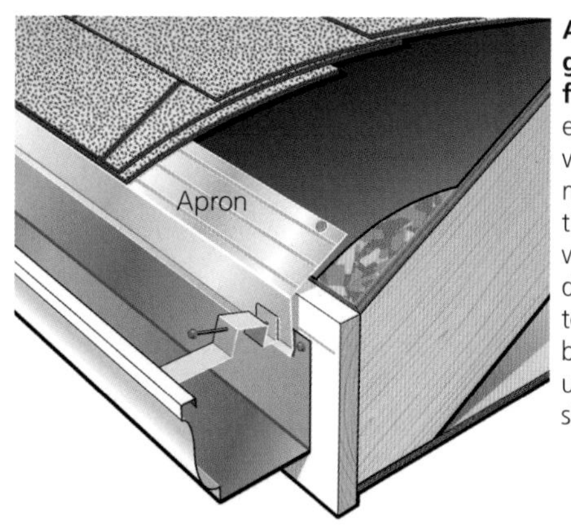

A metal gutter apron flashing will ensure that water runoff makes it into the gutters without meandering behind to the fascia board or under the roof sheathing.

Installing Gutters

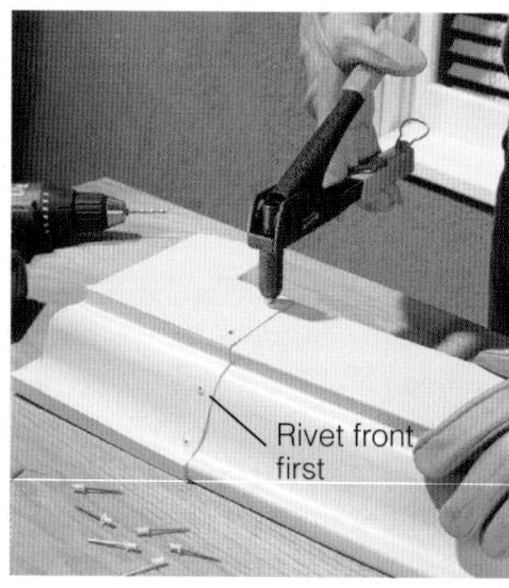

1 Join fittings to the gutter sections by pressing them firmly together and drilling a 1/8-in. (3-mm) hole for a pop rivet in the front face. Cinch this first rivet and recheck the fit. Install more rivets and caulk the inside seam.

2 Mark the outlines for the downspout outlet tubes and use an offset-type metal shears to cut the hole. Test-fit the outlet and drill holes for rivets; then remove it, caulk the rim and fasten with rivets.

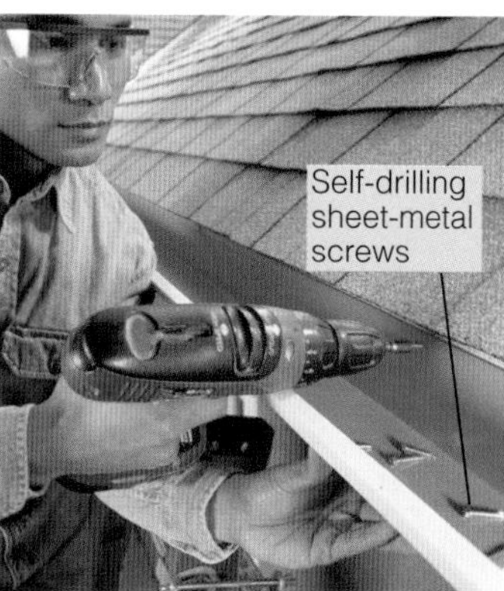

3 Use a chalk line to mark a slightly sloped —1/4 in. per 10 ft. (6 mm per 3 m)— guideline for setting the back edge of the gutters. Use a drill to drive stainless-steel sheet-metal screws every 2 ft. (60 cm) along the gutter's length.

Installing Flashings and Downspouts

1 Slide the gutter apron flashing underneath the edge shingles and make sure it overlaps the back edge of the gutter. Lap the ends at least 2 in. (5 cm) and fasten with roofing nails every 2 ft. (60 cm). Install hanger brackets, too.

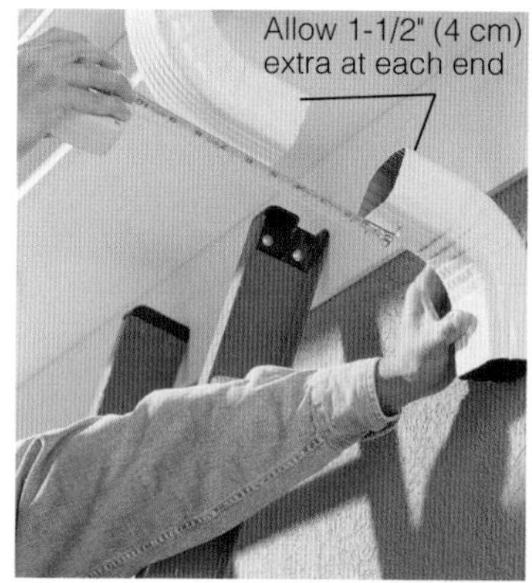

2 Screw an elbow to the downspout outlet and align another elbow against the wall. Measure the gap, add 3 in. (8 cm) and use a hacksaw to cut a connecting section from the uncrimped end of a downspout. Crimp one end and fasten with screws.

3 Use store-bought straps or cut your own from a section of downspout tubing. Fasten at least two to the siding or trim with stainless-steel screws and the appropriate anchors, if necessary. Fit the downspout and fasten with screws.

Gutters and Downspouts / Installing Vinyl Gutters

Plastic replacements for traditional building materials are typically third- or fourth-generation products and, along with their low cost and low-maintenance features, they've improved in appearance and durability. However, color choices are still limited in some categories, and gutter systems is one of them. Most home centers and lumberyards still offer vinyl gutter and fittings in only white and brown, but if you can live with either of those options, these systems are easy to install and maintain. Newer versions even have profile shapes and detailing similar to metal gutters, if you want that traditional look.

Unlike metal gutters, vinyl components snap together with self-sealing gaskets, so no riveting or caulking is necessary. You still have to screw the hanger brackets to the fascia and fasten the downspout straps to the wall, but overall the assembly process is fairly simple. The biggest difference from metal systems lies in the sequence. With vinyl, some fittings, such as coupling connectors and drop outlets, are fastened first to the fascia boards, and the gutter sections are then snapped in place between them. Also, you have to allow for some movement, as the vinyl expands in hot weather and shrinks when it's cold. Clean cuts are easiest with a power miter saw, although a handsaw or hacksaw also will work.

1 After snapping chalk guidelines to indicate the correct slope —about 1/4 in. every 10 ft. (6 mm every 3 m)—fasten the drop outlet and connecting couplers to the fascia board. Align the drop outlets with the corners of the walls below, not at the roof corners.

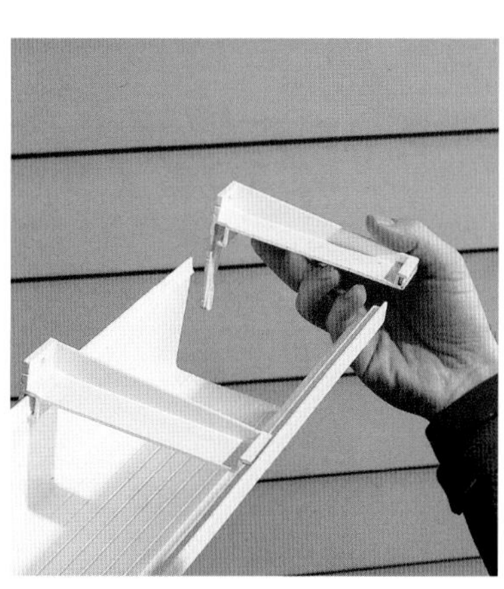

2 Some vinyl systems feature hidden hanger brackets rather than the exposed type that fit around the bottom of the gutter. These slide on from the end of the gutter; space the hangers about every 24 to 30 in. (60 to 75 cm).

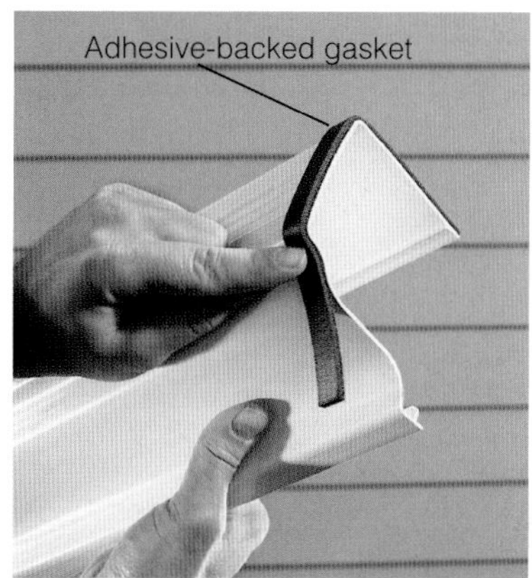

3 Gasket systems on vinyl gutters can vary slightly by manufacturer. This system has adhesive-backed gaskets that you wrap around the end of the gutter. Other types have gaskets built into the fittings.

4 Lift the gutter section into the fittings and snap it firmly in place at each end. Then slide the hanger brackets until they're spaced evenly and fasten them to the fascia board—along your chalk guideline—using galvanized screws.

Shop Smart

Sectional or Seamless Gutters?

In some home-improvement projects, a skilled do-it-yourselfer can use the same materials and produce results equal to most professional efforts, but gutter installation isn't one of them. Most professional gutter contractors install seamless aluminum or steel systems, some complete with a leaf guard—something no homeowner can duplicate.

Seamless systems get their name from the long uninterrupted sections of gutter—up to 45 ft. (14 m)—that are extruded on site using a specialized fabricating machine. Only the corner and downspout connections have joints; the usual splices along the gutter sections are absent. Often this reduces the number of seams by half, reducing the potential for leaks. Most pros also use thicker metal for the gutter and install hanger brackets that are stronger than your typical home-center fare. Another benefit to seamless gutter systems is the much wider range of color choices—often as many as two dozen.

As might be expected, cost is the biggest downside to the seamless strategy. Expect to spend three times as much for an installed seamless system as you would for the materials you'd need to install sectional gutters yourself. However, given the improved quality of materials, the lower maintenance requirements and your being spared at least a weekend's work, seamless gutter systems prove a worthwhile investment for many homeowners.

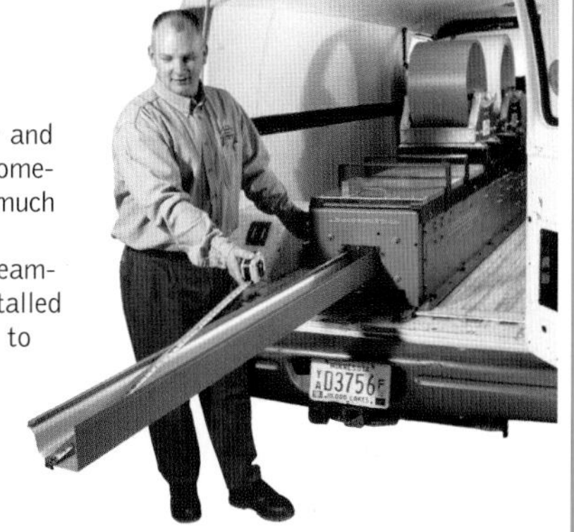

Understanding Ice Dams

Insulation and Air Leaks 165
Attic Insulation and R-values 165
Attic Insulation and Bypasses 168
Locating Roof Leaks 313

A picturesque array of icicles might make a nice image for a holiday card, but there's nothing charming about the damage that built-up roof ice can do to your home, especially the continuous chunks called ice dams. Several conditions are required for their formation (see "How Ice Dams Form," at right), but the factors you can control are heat loss through your roof and proper ventilation to maintain a cold roof.

Spot problem roofs by observing them during the few days following a snowfall. If significant heat loss occurs, the blanket of snow will rapidly develop thin areas or holes from melting. Icicles will soon appear at the eaves; then thicker layers of ice will form above them.

The only effective strategy is to keep the attic cold by preventing heat escaping upward from the living areas of the house and by keeping the roof cold by providing an unobstructed pathway for cold air to move from eave to ridge. Attic insulation between and above the ceiling joists is essential; most modern codes specify as much as 1 ft. (30 cm) of insulation with a heat retention value above R-32. Equally critical is sealing off ceiling penetrations—from a small electrical box to a large access hatch—that allow warm air to leak past the insulation.

How Ice Dams Form

Ice dams can't form from snow and cold weather alone; they need a warm roof, too. This is how they're created:

1. Heat rises through ceiling penetrations and into an attic.
2. The snow on the shingles melts and the water runoff travels down the roof slope until it gets to the edges.
3. Because the heat loss stops at the eaves, they are typically cold enough to refreeze the melted water, forming icicles and ice dams. Gutters magnify the problem by providing a platform for the ice to accumulate and are often damaged by the added weight.
4. As the dams accumulate ice, they form an obstacle to the melted water that's still making its way down the roof.
5. With nowhere else to go, the water backs up under the shingles and eventually finds its way through the sheathing and into the house.

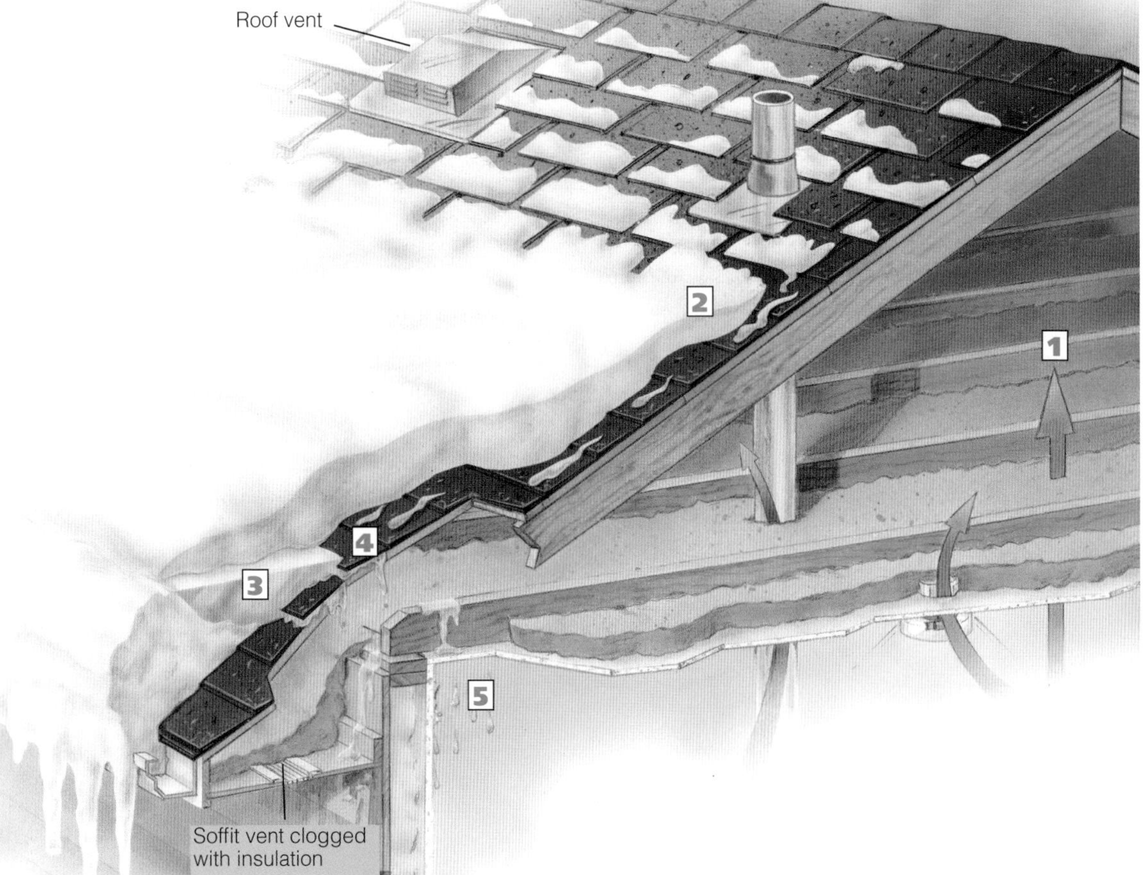

Ice Dam Solutions

When ice dams occur on a roof, it's usually not long before the symptoms move inside. Rust spots from drywall fasteners might show up on the ceilings, paint will peel and water stains will appear around windows and exterior doors. Even under the best conditions, some ice dam formation is often unavoidable; the daytime sun can melt snow on sections of a roof, only to have temperatures drop and the water refreeze as night falls. You can't prevent this melting-refreezing cycle completely, but you can reduce the attic heat loss that aggravates it, and you can also protect your roof sheathing and house from the inevitable ice dams that will form from normal climatic changes.

Above all, stop or at least minimize the heat loss through your attic. Air leaks can occur wherever a ceiling or wall penetration isn't sealed properly. Light fixture boxes, access hatches and open pipe or duct chases can all be routes for warm air to migrate up into your attic, so use caulk, expanding foam insulation or other sealants to close them. This requires a trip to the attic to pull away the insulation and apply a sealant from the top side of the drywall or plaster, so this is a good project to tackle in the fall when the attic will be reasonably cool. Aside from reducing the ice dams' severity, these measures should also lower your energy bills. Upgrading insulation also helps; it's likely the attic already has some—probably fiberglass batting nested between the joists—but additional blown-in cellulose or fiberglass helps seal gaps and improve the R-rating.

Also important is maintaining a cold roof by installing or improving ventilation with soffit vents and roof or ridge vents that keep cold air circulating freely. Even with some attic heat loss, this will reduce the melting rate. Also, the next time you reroof, install a self-sealing membrane along the roof edges.

Keeping a Cold Roof

Insulate and seal every ceiling penetration so heat intended for living areas can't migrate into the attic and warm the roof. Add an extra layer of insulation across the entire attic, if necessary. Make sure there's adequate vent area along the soffits and eaves, so cold air from outside can flow freely under the roof sheathing and out through vents on or near the ridge.

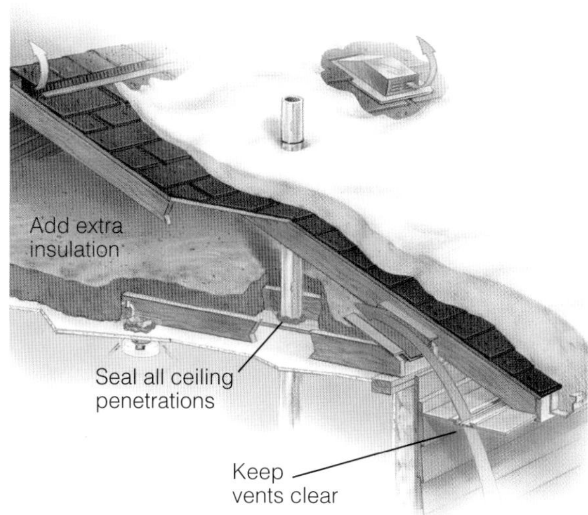

Installing Ice-and-Water Barrier

Even if ice dams do form, you can prevent damage to the roof sheathing and interior by installing an ice-and-water membrane along the roof edges before shingling or reshingling. These 3-ft. (90-cm)-wide adhesive membranes are waterproof and self-seal around nail and staple holes. The membrane should run at least 2 to 3 ft. (60 to 90 cm) up the roof beyond the exterior wall plane.

Using Secondary Measures

If there's no snow on the roof, it can't melt to form ice dams at the edge. You can remove snow manually using a snow rake on an extension handle, although you'll have some cleanup to do on the ground afterward. Beware of overhead power lines. For a surefire preventive measure, place heating cable intended for this purpose along the roof edges and all the way out the downspout to melt the ice and snow. Always follow all manufacturer's instructions.

Repairing Chimneys

More Efficient Fireplaces 192
Wood Stoves 193
Ladders and Scaffolding 311
Repairing Brick 414

Most people think of chimneys only in association with fireplaces or wood-burning stoves, but these tall venting stacks remove smoke or warm gases from any source, including gas- or oil-burning furnaces and water heaters. Natural convection—the rising of warm air and gases—explains most of a chimney's workings. The smoke or fumes rise from the fire or burner and heat the chimney liner, the flue, along the way. As the flue warms, it increases the buoyancy of the airstream and actively pulls, or drafts, the smoke and hot air up through the chimney.

Any obstructions in the flue can create fire hazards or cause the smoke and gases to backdraft into the house, resulting in a dangerous buildup of carbon monoxide gas. Periodic inspection and cleaning will keep a chimney functioning properly, but repairs to the exterior have to be made whenever normal weathering takes its toll.

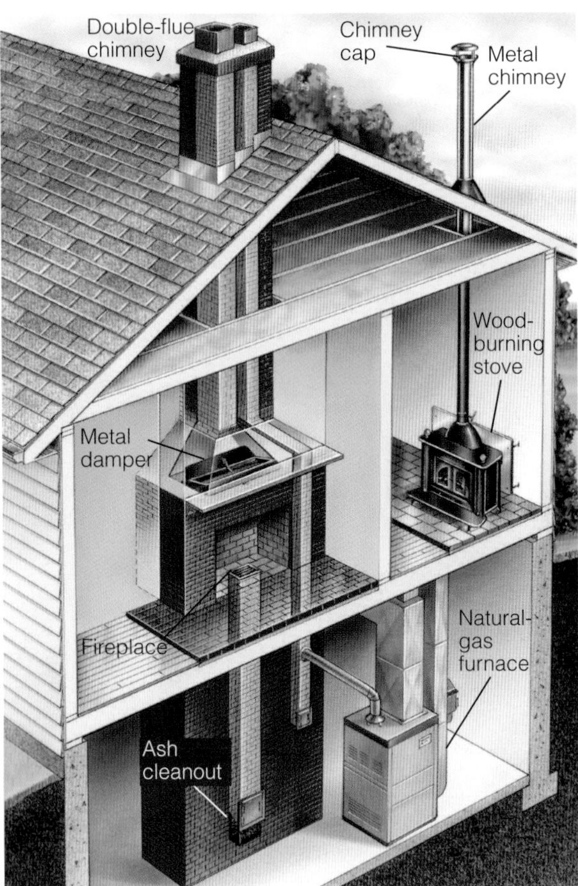

Chimney evolution. In the past, traditional masonry chimneys made of brick or stone functioned largely to vent wood and coal fires used for heating. They have evolved to accommodate furnace and water-heater emissions as well, and lightweight metal chimneys and fireplaces have become more common. The brick chimney here features two flues, one primary flue to vent a wood-burning fireplace and a smaller secondary flue to vent a gas furnace. A metal damper in the primary flue allows closure of the fireplace when not in use, so heat from the house isn't lost. A wood-burning stove features a smaller, independent metal chimney.

Brick Chimney Maintenance

Like any masonry structure, an exposed brick chimney will suffer damage if water penetrates and freezes below its surfaces. The best defense for this is a well-constructed concrete crown, either prefabricated or formed in place atop metal flashing and caulked to seal the connections to the flues. Wire mesh reinforces the concrete and keeps it from breaking apart, should cracks develop.

Periodic inspections and repairs are critical; if water gets past the crown or flashing, it will freeze and expand, breaking mortar joints apart and popping brick faces off, which is called spalling. Metal caps help keep birds, squirrels and other wildlife from nesting in the flues.

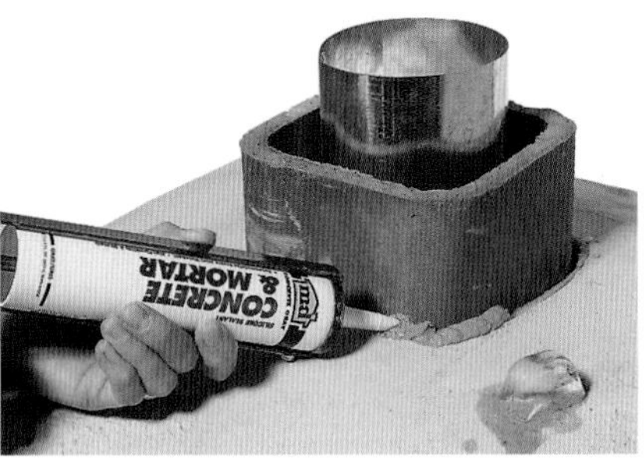

Seal the expansion joint around the flue with concrete caulking. It's sticky, so use an ice cube to smooth it out and spread it into the joint.

Seal the chimney crown and the brick with Siloxane, a water repellent that protects masonry, yet allows it to breathe. Read and follow all warning labels.

Tuck-Pointing

Despite its durability, mortar doesn't last forever. In fact, because of the temperature swings a chimney experiences, its mortar may degrade more quickly than normal. When it loses its strength and adhesion, it's time to tuck-point the joints. This process involves scraping or grinding away the mortar to a depth of at least 1 in. (2.5 cm), and then using a narrow offset pointing trowel to tuck new mortar between the bricks while they're in place. A similar technique is used to replace individual bricks (see p. 415 for more complete how-to information).

Cleaning Chimneys

Over time, unburned gases and resins from wood smoke condense on the inside of a chimney flue. This residue collects soot and forms a tarry substance called creosote, which can accumulate in a thick layer. Certain conditions, such as a weak or smoldering fire or burning undried "green" hardwoods or resinous softwoods like pine, tend to accelerate the accumulation, which can turn dangerous if it catches fire and begins to burn in the flue. Flue tiles or liners aren't designed to withstand that kind of direct, intense heat and the flare-up may cause surrounding framing or other combustible materials to catch fire.

Cleaning a chimney flue regularly—at least once a year if it's used frequently—can help prevent the buildup of flammable residue. Wear a pair of safety glasses and shine a flashlight up the chimney to have a look. If the residue is powdery or crusted, you can often clean it yourself with a chimney brush and a shop vacuum. If the flue is caked with a gummy, hard or glazed surface layer, have a professional chimney sweep do the work.

If you want to tackle the cleaning yourself, prepare for a mess. Wear old clothes, gloves, a respirator and safety goggles. Cover carpeting and furniture with plastic sheeting; if the soot dust billows from the fireplace, it will be extremely difficult to remove from fabrics.

Caution: Before doing any work on a chimney, read pages 311-312 on ladder, scaffold and roof safety. If you have doubts about working on a roof, call a chimney expert.

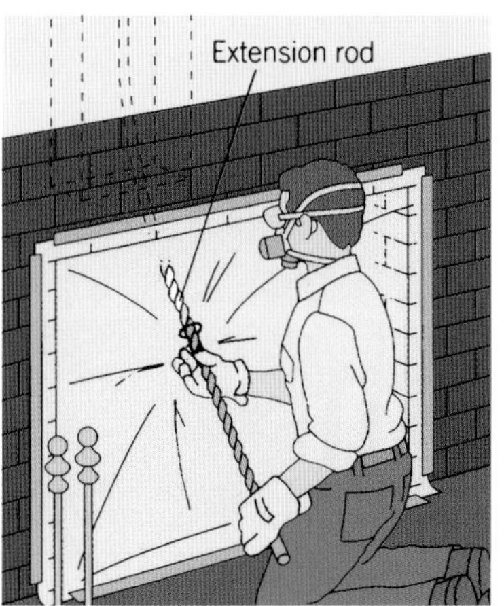

To work up. Tape clear plastic sheeting over the fireplace opening, with a slit in the center for the brush handle. Open the damper and work the brush up and down the flue, adding handle sections as you go higher. Vacuum up the soot after you finish.

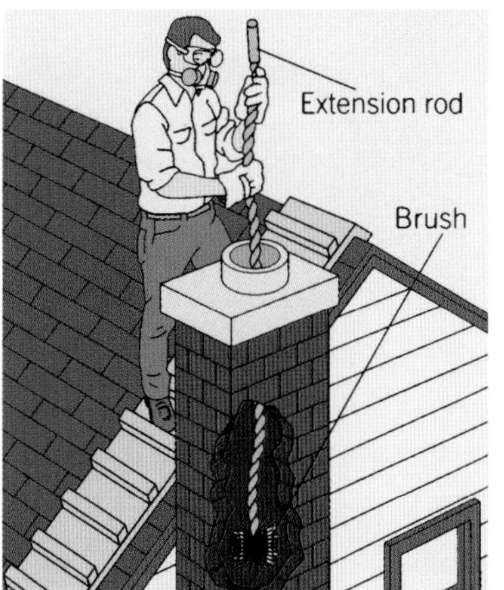

To work down. Seal the fireplace opening(s) inside with plastic sheeting. Build a simple step platform to help you work from the roof. Insert the chimney brush down the flue and scrub vigorously. Add handle sections until you reach the bottom of the flue. **Note**: Always wear a safety harness.

Chimney Accessories

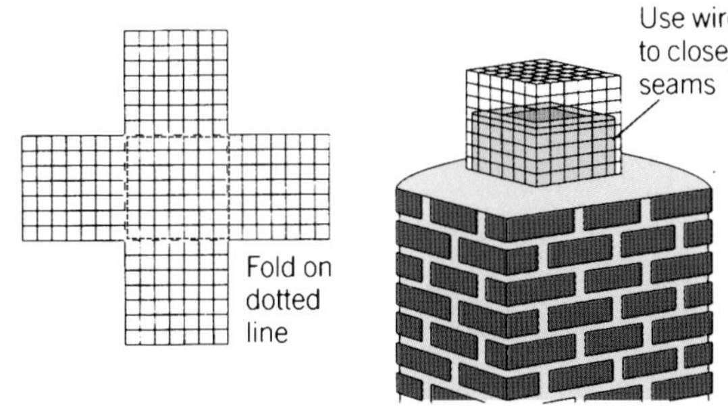

Simple spark arrester. To ensure floating embers don't escape to start a fire on the roof or other surfaces, cut a section of wire-mesh cloth in the shape of a plus sign (+) and fold it to form a cube with one open end. Use wire to tie the corners and to secure it to the flue.

Provide flat surface
Commercial cap
Must be at least 8" above top of flue
Tilt slab
Clamps onto flue

Weather cap. Weather caps keep rain, snow and debris from entering the flue. Build a masonry version by constructing four corner posts of brick and capping them with a stone or concrete slab. For a simpler solution, buy a manufactured metal version that clamps onto the flue edge.

Chimney brushes and handles. Use a brush with stiff wire or synthetic bristles for a wood-burning stove's metal flue. Buy a brush to fit the diameter of the flue. Flexible extension rods are made of fiberglass or braided metal.

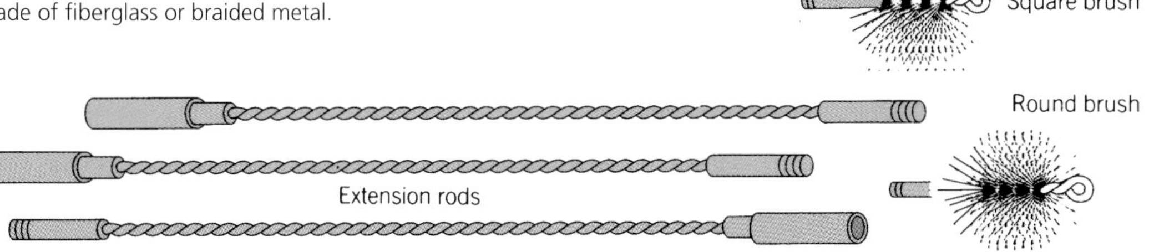

Installing Skylights

Roof Styles 18
Level and Plumb 44
Reciprocating Saws 59
Shingling 320

The search for more natural light can't always end at a picture window. Privacy concerns, lack of exterior wall space and budget limitations can make large windows an impractical solution for some homeowners, but those obstacles don't have to decide the issue. Bringing light in from overhead, through skylights and roof windows, is a method that's often easier and less expensive than retrofitting conventional windows.

The terms are often used interchangeably, but there is a distinction. Typically, a skylight is a fixed unit with tempered glass or translucent plastic glazing; a roof window looks virtually identical but features a hinged sash with tempered glass that can be opened for ventilation or cleaning. Both have similar frames and flashing systems for mounting on the roof. Sizes can vary from narrow units designed to fit between 16-in. on-center framing to wider units that require cutting out rafters to frame a reinforced opening. If your home has roof trusses, they can't be cut to accommodate skylights; use multiple narrow units between the trusses rather than one wide one. Keep daylight patterns in mind. North-facing roofs are often best. Skylight placement should enhance a space, not introduce too much harsh sun and heat or create glare that interferes with the room's uses.

Skylight Styles

Straight shaft. A shaft is the enclosure that makes the transition from skylight to ceiling below. The simplest version is a straight vertical shaft lined with gypsum wallboard or other finish materials.

Flared shaft. A flared shaft can double the amount of light transmitted into the room through a skylight. The tapered well not only allows more direct light transmission, but it increases the reflective surface and sometimes the headroom, too.

Cathedral ceiling. You'll see the largest gains from a skylight when the roofline and ceiling share a common frame, allowing unobstructed light to enter. The shifting position of the sun is more noticeable, however.

Light Pipes

Skylights come in a variety of styles, shapes and sizes. Light pipes, or tubular skylights, have a clear acrylic dome and a self-flashing base that perch on the roof, plus an adjustable, or sectional, tube lined with a highly reflective silver film or metal to magnify the light transmission. With this type, you don't have to frame and finish a conventional skylight shaft to make the transition through attic space.

1 With your layout mark centered between two joists or rafters, use a plumb bob to transfer the mark from the ceiling to the roof.

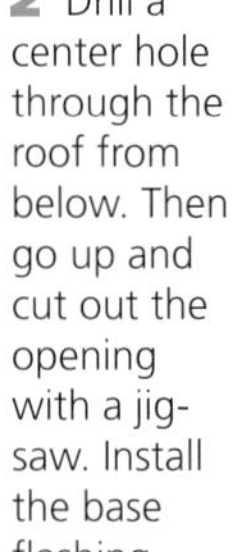

2 Drill a center hole through the roof from below. Then go up and cut out the opening with a jigsaw. Install the base flashing.

3 After fitting the dome to its base, go inside and cut out the ceiling opening. Finally, install the downtube sections and the diffuser.

Skylight Installation

Installing a skylight involves basic construction and roofing skills, plus knowledge of roof framing. Plan ahead and think realistically. This isn't a project you want to begin without knowing how and when you'll finish!

You'll need standard carpentry tools, such as a tape measure, framing square, utility knife, reciprocating saw and power drill, plus safety gear, such as goggles, dust mask and roof safety equipment. When you're scouting the location for a skylight, identify vent stacks, dormers or any other roof elements that might cause interference. For a covered cathedral ceiling, use a stud finder to locate the rafters, mark the opening and use a utility knife or a reciprocating saw to cut and remove the wallboard.

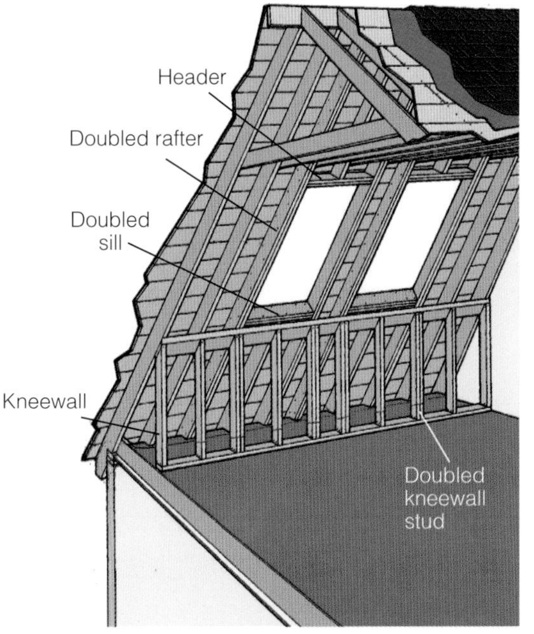

1 With the room's electrical circuit shut off, use a reciprocating saw with a short blade to cut through only the wallboard or plaster and lath, not into the framing or the roof sheathing.

2 After framing a kneewall, if necessary, and double sills and headers to establish the opening, double up the rafters that will flank the skylight. This is necessary to compensate for cutting a rafter for the skylight.

3 Fit a 10-in. or longer blade on the reciprocating saw and cut through the roof sheathing and shingles from inside. Let the blade follow the surfaces around the framed opening.

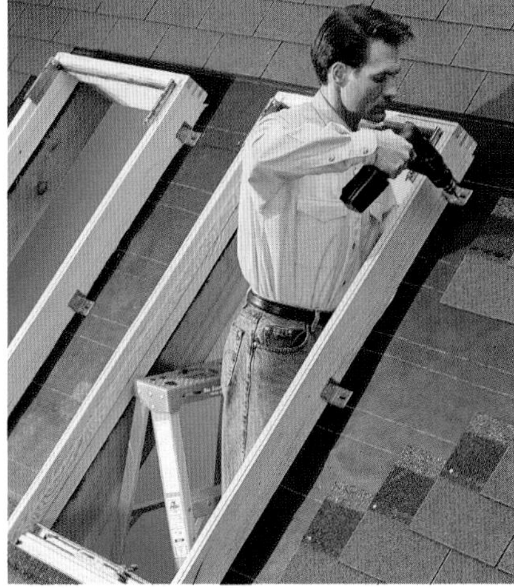

4 Use the hardware provided to secure the skylight frame to the roof sheathing. Center the unit over the opening. Make sure frame corners are square when you fasten them.

5 Fit the lower apron flashing on the bottom end of the skylight frame. Weave step flashing and shingles over each other as you work your way up the frame sides.

6 Slip the head flashing onto the top of the skylight frame, overlapping the step flashing at the corners, and insert its upper flange underneath the row of shingles just above the skylight. Install the glass skylight sash.

Siding / Basics

As the protective cladding that wards off rain, snow, sun and other weather agents, siding is part of the face your house presents to the world. It can help reinforce a home's style, define its personality or give it curb appeal, but beyond these aesthetic qualities, it's there to keep wind and water from making their way inside the walls.

Before industrial manufacturing came along, siding materials were typically simple, individual components—brick, stone, split wood shakes or rough-sawn boards and similar natural materials. Now the options include wood siding, painted steel and aluminum, vinyl, wood-plastic composites, fiber cement and other engineered materials.

Material costs, installation techniques, durability, aesthetics and maintenance requirements have always been key issues for siding. Most homes need a sizable quantity, so installation costs must be weighed carefully. Siding has to remain watertight and withstand repeated cycles of wetting and drying, temperatures that range from frigid to searing and the effects of ultraviolet light from the sun.

Traditional looks remain the overwhelming favorite, but they can be created using traditional natural materials or more recent impersonators. Want the look of wood-shingle or lap siding? Get the real thing if authenticity is an issue, but vinyl, composites and fiber cement convincingly offer a similar look, often with lower maintenance requirements.

Get the appearance of full bricks with thin brick veneers that offer a lower cost and weight; the same goes for stone, which is now mimicked realistically by manufactured stone veneers. The chart below offers upkeep requirements for different kinds of siding.

Note: Many areas now require installation of house wrap or complete water barrier along with an air space behind the siding to promote drying and drainage. Consult local building codes before going to work.

Siding Selections

Types	Cost	Ease of Installation	Life Span	Fire Resistance	Maintenance and Finish
Wood shingles and shakes	Moderately expensive	Moderately difficult	40 yr. or more	Poor	Western red cedar, the most common type, will weather to gray or streaked black-gray. Solid-color or semitransparent stains provide a durable low-maintenance finish; conventional primers and paints are OK, but invite more prep work later. Cracked or damaged shingles must be replaced.
Wood lap boards	Expensive	Moderately difficult	30 yr. or more	Poor	Maintenance issues are similar to those of wood shingles. Lumber quality is a critical factor here; the old-growth trees that sided American homes for decades are mostly gone. Newer juvenile trees produce less stable lumber, which translates into more finish maintenance.
Board and batten	Moderately expensive	Easy	30 yr. or more	Poor	The traditional board and batten look, consisting of wide boards installed vertically with thinner battens covering the seams, is now often replaced by 4x8 sheets of roughsawn plywood with battens applied every 16 in. (40 cm).
Hardboard and plywood panels	Inexpensive to moderately expensive	Easy	20 yr. or more	Poor	Panels install faster and are less costly than lap-board versions; all forms require adequate sealing of cut edges to prevent swelling and delamination. Their fairly stable surface holds paint well, but underneath the surface, water damage can spread quickly once it starts.
Aluminum	Moderately expensive	Easy to moderately difficult	40 yr. or more	Good	With factory-applied coatings, metal needs little care. Dents easily during installation and from later impacts and must be repaired or replaced. Can be repainted.
Vinyl	Inexpensive	Easy to moderately difficult	40 yr. or more	Good (it won't burn, but may melt near intense heat)	Includes complete trim system. Integral pigment means no painting, but also no changing colors later. Darker hues can fade over time. Most types mimic the look of wood lap siding or wood shingles. Allow for thermal expansion when installing. Wash clean.
Cement board	Moderately expensive	Moderately difficult	40 yr. or more	Excellent	Tough material is best cut with diamond blades. Slightly brittle during installation, but durable and stable once installed. Order raw, preprimed or prepainted; holds paints and stains well. Highly resistant to insects. Used mostly as lap siding, but also in shingle panels.

Siding / Shingle and Shake

A traditional and still popular siding material, wood shingles and shakes are typically made of red or white cedar. Both are rot-resistant. Left untreated, red cedar's brown tones weather to a dark streaked gray. White cedar starts as a cream-colored wood and weathers to a light silvery gray. Semitransparent or solid-color stains are a durable, low-maintenance finish for either.

Shingles have a smooth sawn face and measure about 3/8 in. (1 cm) thick at the butt. The best grade is a No. 1 Blue Label with an R/R designation for resquared and rebutted. Shakes are split, resulting in a thicker butt end and a rough, striated texture; they're used less frequently, mostly for roofs. Both types are installed in overlapping courses that leave the lower third to half of each shingle exposed.

Basic Installation

Shingle siding installation follows the same principles used in roofing—the offset joints and overlapped courses shed the water. Shingles are installed side by side, with a small gap to allow for seasonal movement.

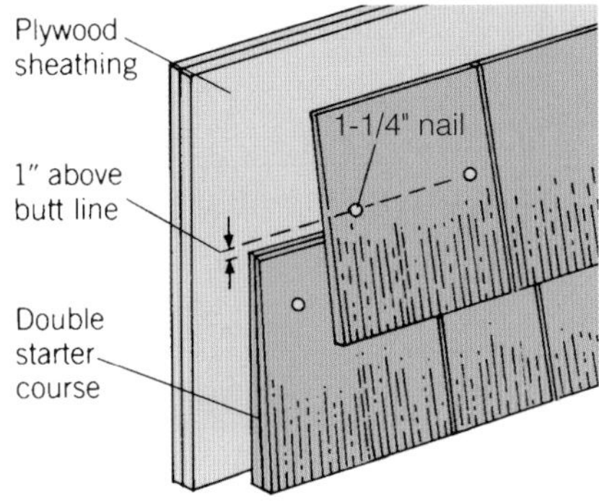

Single course. With this method, you double the starter course and stagger the joints, and then nail subsequent courses just above the exposure line.

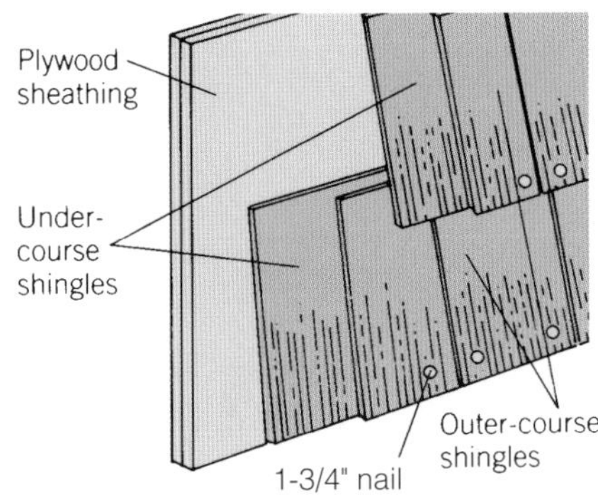

Double course. This method, rarely used now, employs double layers for waterproofing each course. Shingles are nailed at the bottom with nails left exposed.

Repairing Damaged Shingle Siding

1 Remove the damaged shingle by splitting it in several places along the grain with a wood chisel and a mallet. Be careful not to damage the shingle below.

2 Tuck a hacksaw blade underneath the course above to cut away the nails that secured the damaged shingle. Use a hammer to pull any exposed nail heads.

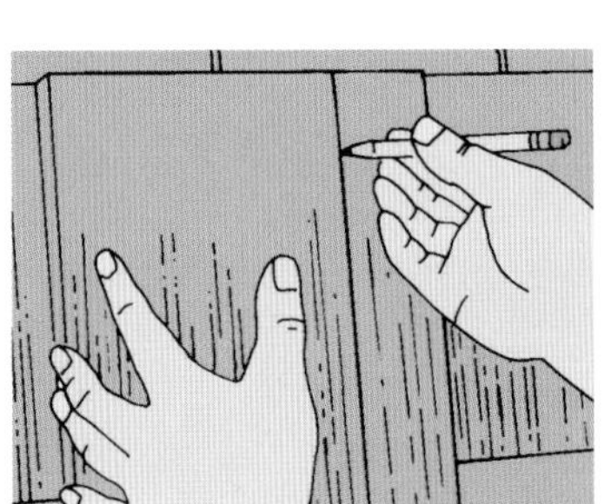

3 Allowing a 1/8-in. (3-mm) gap along each side, measure and cut a replacement shingle. Use a saw or score with a utility knife and break.

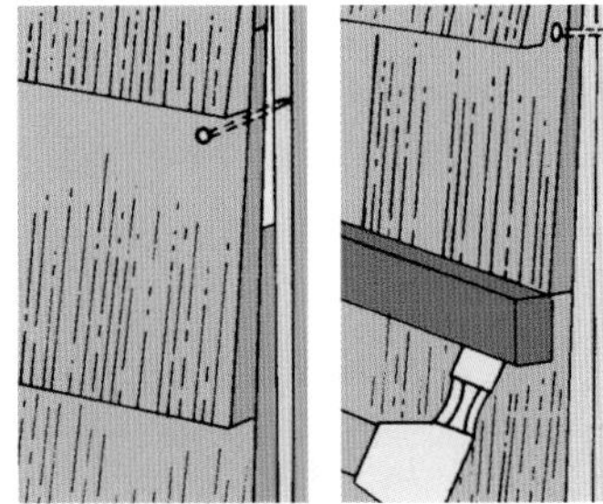

4 Position nails in the new shingle 1/2 in. (12 cm) low, driving them at an angle. They'll straighten as you tap the shingle into place.

Shingle Options

There's more than one way to shingle a wall. One option is to use decorative shapes (see photo, at right). You can mix fancy-cut shingles, such as diamonds, fish-scale, half-round or other profiles, as accent rows or elements amid standard square-cut shingles.

Another option is panelized shingles that are preinstalled on a plywood subbase and fastened in sections. For small wall areas with a lot of windows or other interruptions, they're of limited help, but for large expanses, these panelized shingles let you cover the wall much faster. These panels' cost (per area covered) is higher than that of individual shingles.

Siding / Vinyl and Aluminum

Although they aren't the solution for every house or homeowner, vinyl and aluminum siding do offer relatively maintenance-free protection for your home. Vinyl's integral color means no painting is ever necessary and the material costs can be as little as one-third that of high-quality wood lap siding. Vinyl doesn't rot, is impervious to insect damage and stays free of the cracking and peeling surface that eventually plagues almost any painted wood siding.

That said, vinyl has its detractors. The rolled edges don't have the crisp look that genuine wood siding or some new composite and fiber-cement materials provide. The integral color means you're stuck with the look you've got, although it can be painted. And over time virtually all vinyl siding fades and becomes brittle and prone to cracking. High winds can peel it off a wall that might hold wood siding intact and, although it doesn't share wood's shrink-and-swell response to moisture, vinyl moves noticeably with temperature swings and will buckle if not installed correctly. Better grades feature thicker material, improved colorfastness and sometimes metal edge reinforcements for better shape and wind resistance.

Aluminum siding does offer the crisp edges found on wood and, with durable factory-applied coatings, doesn't need to be painted, although it often can be. Denting is a problem, however, especially during installation. Cost is about 30-percent more than for vinyl. Both materials can—with the addition of foam insulation panels—be installed over old wood siding.

Installing aluminum siding follows most of the same basic steps as the vinyl siding installation shown here.

Vinyl Siding Detail

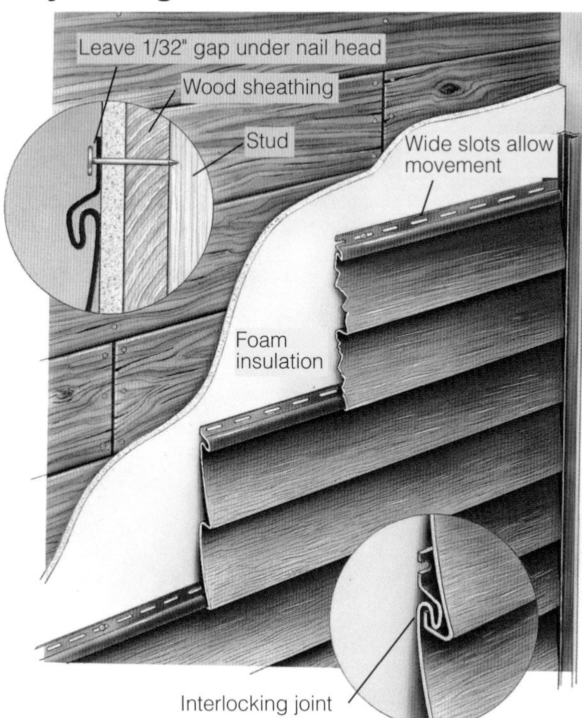

Getting Started

As with many siding materials, vinyl is often installed over an underlayment. For residing over other materials, flat foam panels are typically installed to provide a flat base surface and a small amount of additional insulation. Thicker foams can be used. Matching trim components are installed first, then the siding.

1 Use roofing or washer-head nails to fasten foam insulation panels or matching contoured rigid foam to the sheathing or old siding.

2 Snap a chalk line to establish the baseline height. Install the corner trim. Then fasten the starter strip along the line.

Window Trim

As with any siding system, the transition areas around windows and doors are the most likely to let water leak behind the protective surfaces. Use a combination of conventional metal flashing and vinyl J-channel to create a safe runoff path for water.

1 Trim the J-channel to direct water past the corner and down alongside the window. Be sure to use a metal drip cap along the top casing.

2 With the side trim flange running long and the top trim mitered, nest the J-channels together so the outer flanges overlap, as shown.

Basic Installation

The effectiveness of vinyl siding often depends more on correct installation techniques than it does on the material itself. Vinyl's thermal expansion and contraction rules out rigid connections and watertight seams; the siding needs to "float" without deforming and still channel away water.

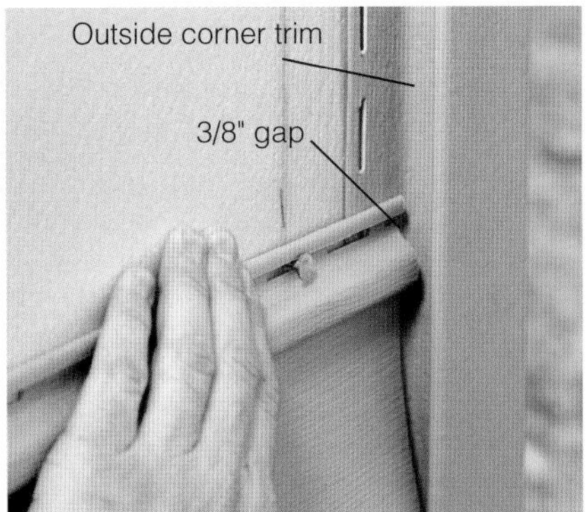

1 Cut the siding to leave a 3/8-in. (1-cm) gap at each end, which will be hidden by the J-channel. Set nails in the slot centers to allow movement.

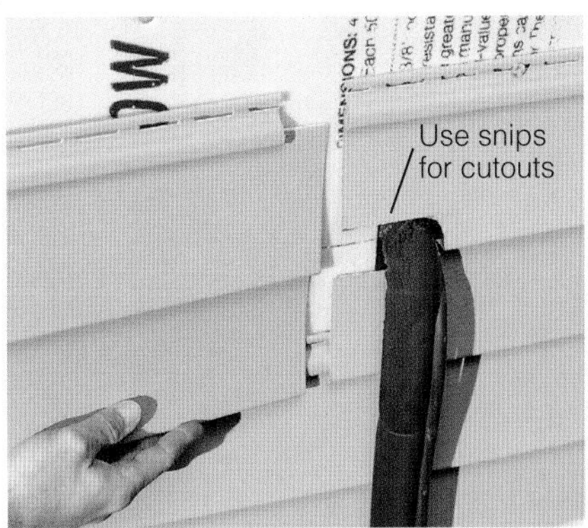

2 Slots or cutouts for obstructions should be slightly oversized to accommodate the siding's movement. Overlap ends 1-1/2 in. (4 cm).

Special Situations

Plumbing and electrical fixtures require penetrations in the wall, and vinyl-siding systems include special components to make these openings weatherproof. Most are two-part fittings: a base to fasten to the sheathing and a cap to fit over the base after the siding has been installed around it.

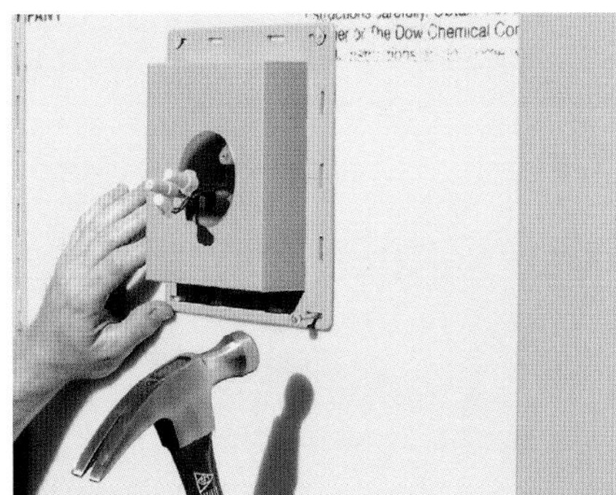

1 Designed for a wall-mount light fixture, this vinyl mounting box fits over a conventional metal or plastic electrical box.

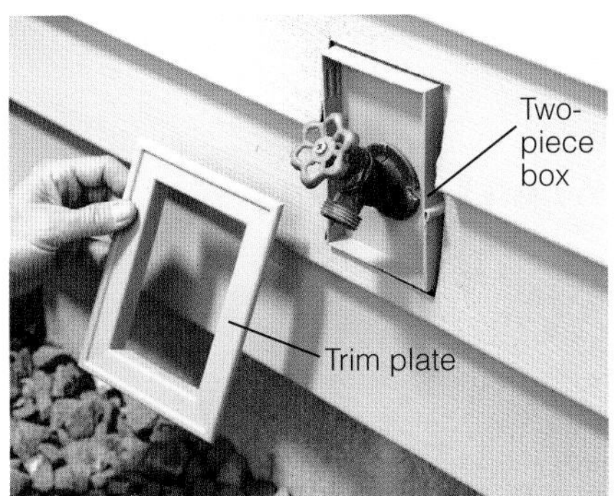

2 An immovable fixture or fitting can be covered with a split, or two-piece, box you assemble around the item. Cover with a trim plate.

Repairing Metal Siding

1 Hook and unlock the damaged piece of siding from the pieces above and below. Work the tool from side to side.

2 Use metal snips to cut out the damaged section of siding. The cut edges will be sharp, so wear gloves.

3 Use blocks to prop the upper piece of siding out of the way. Then pull the nails that hold the damaged section in place.

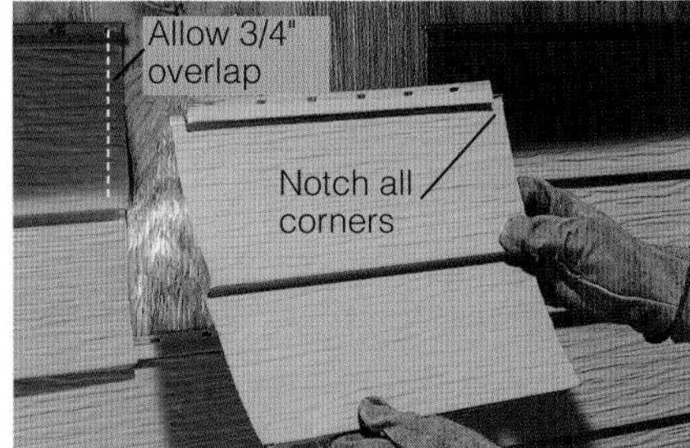

4 Cut a replacement piece to overlap the cutaway area by 3/4 in. (2 cm) on each side. Notch corners on the patch's corners so it seats properly.

Reattaching Loose Vinyl Siding

Sections of vinyl siding interlock along their top and bottom edges. Expansion and contraction cycles, heavy impact or severe weather can sometimes cause the joints to pop open. To reconnect them, use a flat-hooked tool designed for vinyl siding removal to realign the edges, so you can snap them back together again.

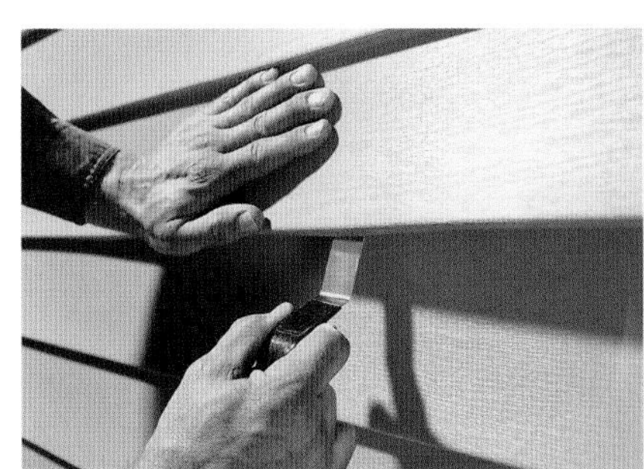

Use the siding tool to hook the edge of the loosened course, and press against the upper course until the two snap together.

Siding / Hardboard and Wood

Installing Hardboard Siding

In its first few decades, hardboard siding earned a reputation for premature failure. The problems were real, but they were due mostly to faulty installation, not defective materials. Today, these engineered composites—a mix of wood fiber and plastic resins—are improved but still require careful handling. The embossed, textured surface is tough, but the cut ends are vulnerable to moisture. Unless they're properly sealed against water penetration, they swell and crack open, creating a vicious cycle that allows even more water inside. Proper fastening techniques, careful sealing and back-priming, and use of splice hardware help ensure the material lives up to its potential.

Drive nails properly. Drive the nail head snug, but don't pound it deep into the surface.

Joint the moldings. Aluminum joint splices help divert water from cut ends.

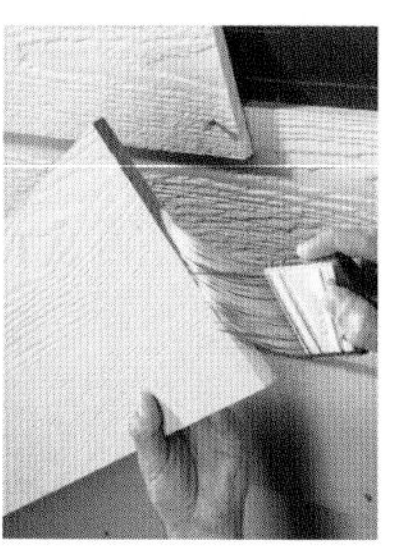

Seal cut ends. Paint and caulk any cut ends to prevent water penetration.

Protect against dampness. Keep lower courses away from damp ground and keep them well primed and painted.

Replacing Rotted Siding

1 Drive wood wedges under the course above the damaged area. Use a hacksaw to cut through the nails.

2 Cut out the damaged sections using a circular saw and a utility knife or keyhole saw to finish the cut.

3 Using a flat shim to protect the good siding, pry off the damaged sections. Remove any protruding nails.

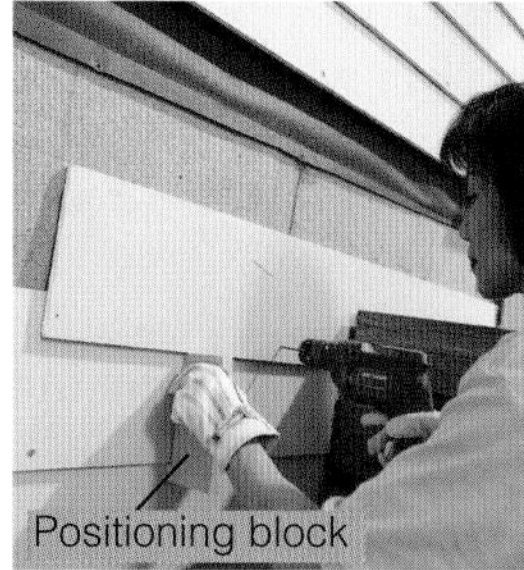

4 Use a positioning block to ensure the correct spacing of the new siding. Then predrill for galvanized nails to secure the siding.

Board and Batten Siding

The system shown uses 1x2 battens applied over sheets of rough-sawn plywood siding—often cedar. Original board-and-batten siding used wide flat boards applied vertically with narrow wood strips, called battens, covering the joints.

Wood Lap Siding

Featuring flat or beveled boards overlapped horizontally, this centuries-old method is still widely used. Cedar, redwood and spruce are favorite species that weather well. Penetrating stains, solid color or semitransparent, tolerate seasonal movement of wood better than most paints. Seal ends and back faces for long-lasting results.

Siding / Fiber-Cement

Made of portland cement, silica and wood fiber, fiber-cement siding is a durable material that pairs the crisp detailing of wood with other properties that include high rot- and insect-resistance, dimensional stability for better paint retention, and reasonable cost. It's so heavy, flat and stable that the top, rather than lower, edge can be nailed during installation, resulting in no exposed nails. It's also virtually fireproof. Early versions were limited to lap siding, but now you can find fiber-cement siding in large faux-stucco panels, faux-brick panels and a wood-shingle look. The abrasive silica and cement quickly dull ordinary saw blades, so you'll need to install a diamond blade on your circular saw or rent special cutting tools.

1 Prepare the wall with a housewrap or felt paper. Mark the stud locations so you know where to nail the siding.

2 Use a diamond blade to cut the siding. Wear safety glasses and a respirator or dust mask to avoid breathing the fine silica dust.

3 Install corner boards and window and door trim (also available in low-maintenance materials) for the siding ends to butt against.

4 Using a story pole, mark layout lines on the trim to indicate the top of each siding course. Snap chalk lines in between.

5 After fastening a treated 3/8-in. (1-cm)-thick starter strip, install the first course. Nail at the studs and leave a caulking gap at end joints.

6 Notch the siding to fit around windowsills, leaving a 1/8-in. (3-mm) gap to be filled with caulk later. Predrill and nail at studs.

Making a Story Pole

A story pole is simply a strip of wood with markings that indicate important height or layout settings. It can be a complex mix denoting positions for the architectural millwork throughout a room's interior or, like this version, a simple scale with regularly spaced increments for siding courses. With a consistent reference height—here it's the trim board under the eaves—the story pole lets you transfer layout marks accurately to trim or wall surfaces so you don't have to measure for each course as you work.

In this case, the height of the story pole's lowest mark accounts for the full width of the first course of siding (6-1/4 in. / 16 cm) and indicates its top edge. Subsequent marks are spaced in increments that match the reveal or exposed dimension (in this case it is 5 in. / 12.7 cm) of the remaining courses.

Siding / Stucco and EIFS

Stucco is a composite of portland cement, sand, lime and water. It has its origins in hand-troweled adobe plaster and other traditional low-tech masonry finishes, but now it's often applied professionally with specialized materials, tools and skills. But patching and repairing smaller areas can easily be managed by a competent do-it-yourselfer. The trick is building it up in layers.

You can buy premixed dry stucco in bags, just like concrete or mortar, and add water until the mix is stiff but pliable. Wait for a dry, mild day so excess heat doesn't shorten the mix's working time. Break or chisel away the damaged area of old stucco and cut away the old metal lath underneath. Remove any loose debris and use a mist sprayer to keep the working area from drying out.

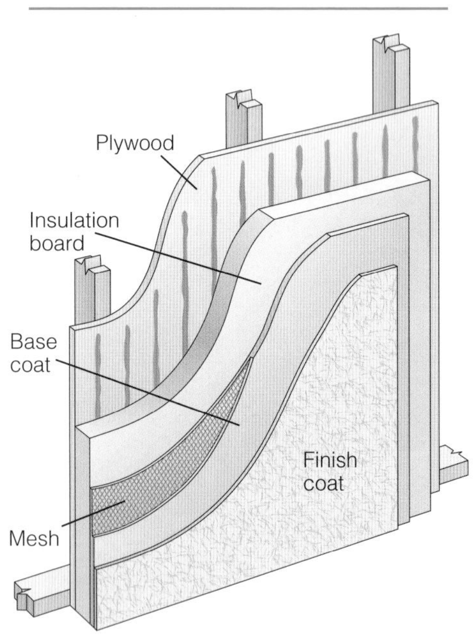

Patching Stucco

1 Cut new metal lath for the repair, sizing it to overlap the old lath by 2 in. (5 cm). Fasten with roofing nails.

2 Trowel the first "scratch" coat on in layers that total 3/8 in. (1 cm) thick, working it vigorously into the metal lath.

3 While it's wet but starting to set, comb the scratch coat with a lath remnant to provide tooth for the next coat.

4 Trowel on the second "brown" coat until it's flush with the surrounding stucco. Use a straightedge to check its flatness.

5 Use a wet sponge float to feather the brown coat so it blends in with the edges of the surrounding area.

6 After using a dash brush to flick bits of stucco onto the surface, knock down the bumps to create a matching texture.

Exterior Insulation and Finish Systems

An Exterior Insulation and Finish System (EIFS), sometimes referred to as synthetic stucco, is an exterior cladding installed in layers. These layers usually consist of high-density insulation board secured to plywood or other substrate, a base coat reinforced with fiberglass or other mesh, and a textured and/or colored finish coat.

Used initially on commercial structures, then later on residential structures, these systems offer many benefits. They can be applied in a wide variety of colors and textures, they're low-maintenance and the foam insulation wrapping the exterior reduces air infiltration and increases the R-value of the wall.

The same weathertight qualities that have made EIFS so popular have also led to moisture-related problems, almost always due to improper installation. If moisture penetrates around windows, doors, flashings and other openings, there is little chance for it to escape or dry out. This sets the stage for severe moisture-related damage ranging from rotting wood to mold growth and insect infestations.

Manufacturers have addressed these problems by creating materials and systems that channel water out and away from walls and by instituting more rigorous installation training programs. EIFS are not do-it-yourself projects; installation should be done only by trained, experienced personnel.

Landscaping

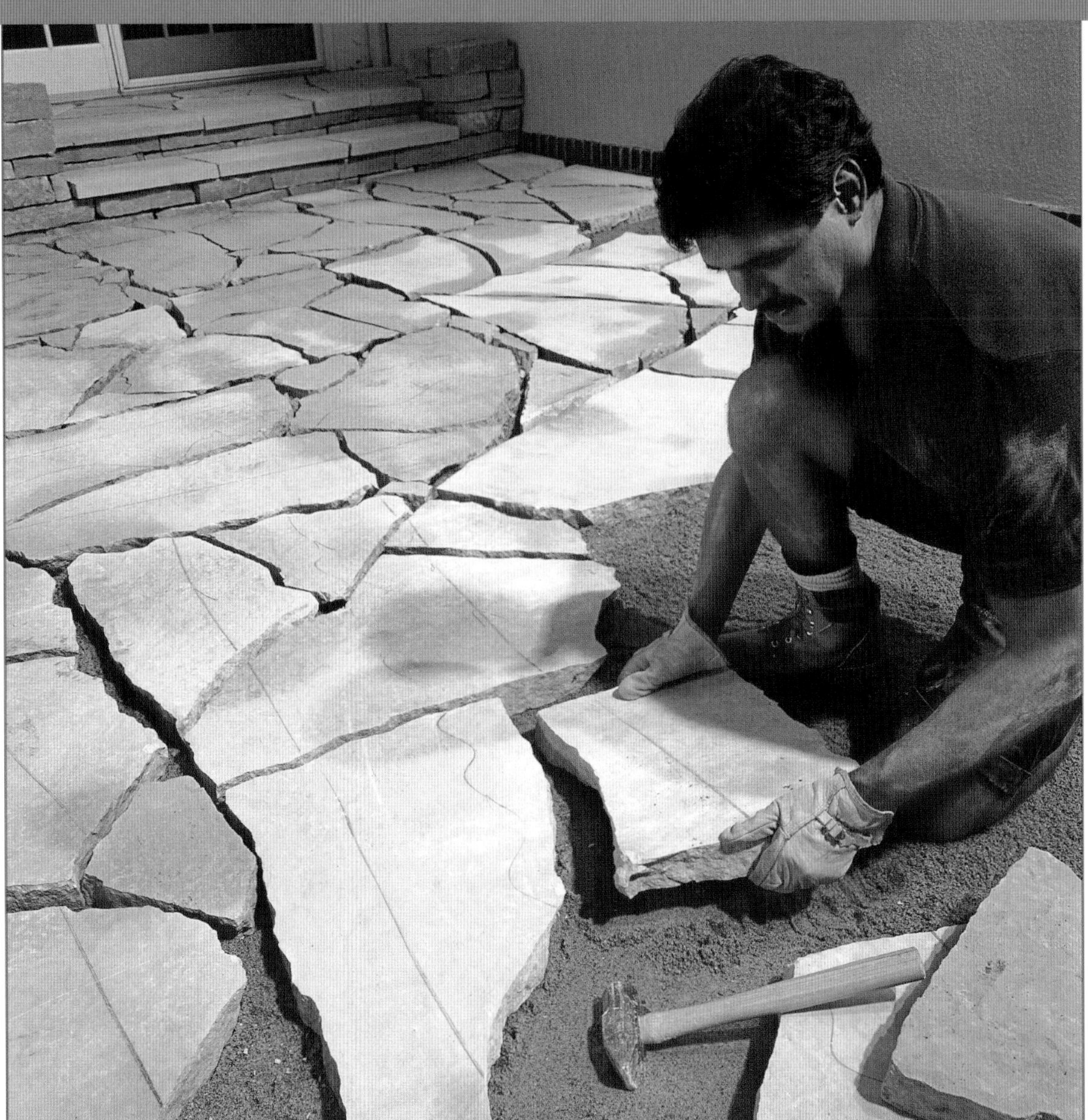

Modular Concrete Retaining Walls

Levels 44
Transits 45

Until a couple decades ago, effective and durable retaining walls were made of natural stone, poured concrete or mortared brick, and they often required professional engineering or building skills. Now modular concrete block offers a solution just right for do-it-yourself installation. These products vary slightly—some have locking pins that secure one course to another, while others feature an integral back lip that aligns the blocks. Virtually all of them are stacking, mortarless systems that create a stepped wall that leans slightly into a hillside or terrace.

The block sides are tapered to allow curved contours, and the faces can be smooth or textured. Gray, tan and terra-cotta are common colors, but some manufacturers offer variegated or tumbled styles that mimic the look of natural stone.

Small-scale projects such as planter bed surrounds can be completed in a weekend or two with little planning. Some systems aren't appropriate for making tall walls, though, so check with the manufacturer or vendor before you proceed. Also, check with local building officials to see whether a permit is required.

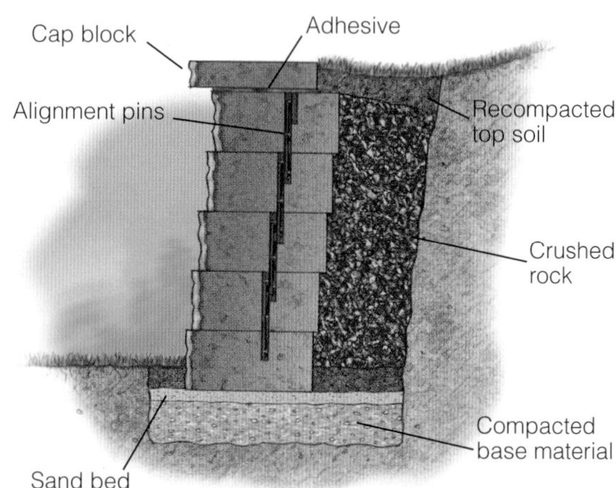

Retaining wall anatomy. A retaining wall requires a strong foundation. Inside a trench of undisturbed soil, start with a 4- to 6-in. (10-to 15-cm)-thick layer of compacted base material, followed by a 1-in. (3 cm) layer of dry sand. Level the first course on the sand, with about half of the block face below grade.

Modular Concrete Blocks

Before your shovel hits dirt, make a call to your local utility providers so they can mark underground lines—it's a free service. Also, purchase your materials in advance and have them delivered. For the base material, specify a mix that has various sizes of crushed rock plus "fines"—the sand and rock dust that help it pack more densely. Spend time building a level, straight first course and the rest of the wall will go up quickly.

Preparing the Base

1 Using a transit or 4-ft. level secured to a long, straight 2x4 to ensure a level line, drive wood stakes along the back of the trench to indicate the finished height of the sand bed. Fill to that height with base material.

2 For smaller projects, use a hand tamper to consolidate and compact the base material until it's 1 in. (3 cm) below the tops of the stakes. For longer walls, rent a gasoline-powered vibrating plate compactor.

3 With the tops of the guide stakes as reference points, use a straight screed board to level the sand bed. Then pull the stakes out and make a pass with a mason's trowel to flatten and lightly compress the sand.

Laying the Block

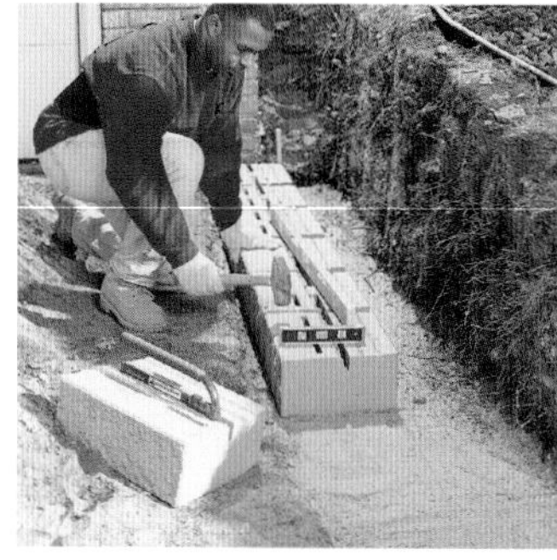

1 Drive end stakes and run a level string line between them. Then set the first course of block. Use a torpedo level and a 4-ft. builder's level to keep the blocks properly aligned as you work. When the row is set, pack soil to grade level along both sides to prevent shifting.

2 As you add courses, backfill the trench with clean, crushed rock (not smooth or round gravel) to keep the blocks from shifting. The rock allows rapid water drainage, reduces the soil pressure against the wall and deters tree roots.

3 Some modular block systems feature separate cap blocks. To install them, apply two beads of concrete/masonry adhesive on the top course block and press the cap into place. You can offset the cap course or align it flush with the course below.

Timber Retaining Walls

Landscape timbers are a user-friendly material ideal for building attractive, moderately priced retaining walls up to 4 ft. (1.25 m) high. The most popular size for landscaping projects is a 6- x 6-in. timber, 8 ft. long.

To withstand direct contact with soil and moisture, landscape timbers are pressure-treated to resist decay. The wood tissue is impregnated with chemical preservatives, giving the lumber a greenish or brown cast. It's safe to handle, but wear gloves and a dust mask.

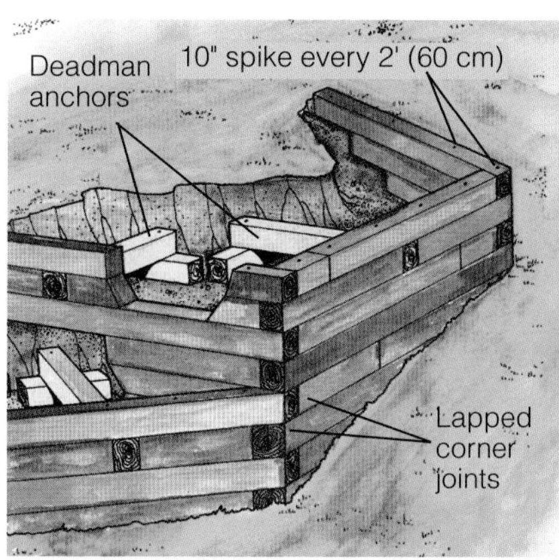

1 Dig a level trench half the depth of the first timber and install it. Tamp with a mallet to seat firmly. This first course determines fit of entire wall, so make each timber level and aligned.

2 Use a long 1/4-in. drill bit to drill through two layers of timber. Secure with 10-in. spikes (galvanized, if possible). Drive spikes at corner lap joints and 2-ft. (.6 m) intervals.

3 Deadman anchors, fitted with cross braces, help resist soil movement. Install them in second or third course up and in second course from top. Secure to front timbers with spikes.

4 Work your way up slopes by excavating a stepped trench and using progressively longer courses of timbers. Make sure soil supports the extended ends of the timbers.

Stone Retaining Walls

Stone retaining walls typically feature the dry laid technique of stacking without mortar. Overlapping the stones helps keep the wall intact, though the structure can still flex if soil movement occurs. Buying and shipping quarried rock is expensive, so find a local source if possible. You'll need about a ton for every 3 linear ft. (1 m) of a 3-ft. (1-m)-high wall, with a mix of sizes. Use angular rock if it's available; it tends to stack and split more easily.

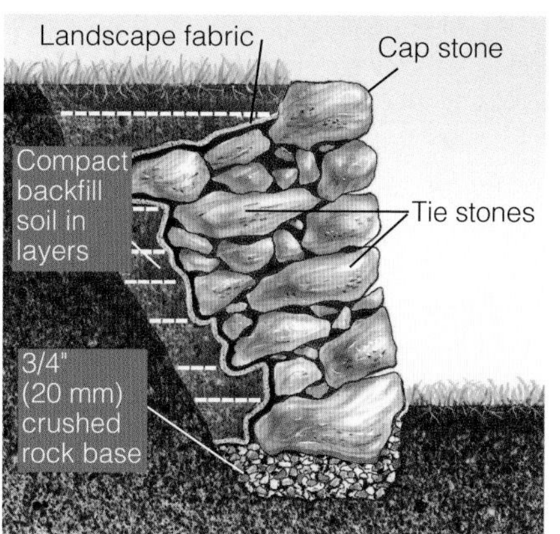

1 Excavate a trench, then fill halfway with 3/4 in. (20 mm) crushed rock. This creates a drainage bed and flexible foundation for the wall. Set aside soil to use as backfill later.

2 Lay landscape fabric against slope and install first courses of stone, with each course progressively wider. Use largest stones at the bottom. Mix sizes for subsequent courses.

3 As you build, fill large gaps in the wall with chinking stones. Small angular stones provide a better locking action to secure the larger stones.

4 Set the final course, or cap stones, level with the embankment. These can be mortared in place if desired. Tuck landscape fabric behind the stone and backfill with topsoil.

Wood Fences

Wood fences rank among the best value-for-cost projects you can build for your home. They define property lines, enhance the landscape, provide privacy and create a safe area for children or pets. Material costs are relatively modest, and installation requires only a few tools and simple techniques most homeowners can manage. Cedar, redwood and pressure-treated pine are the most common woods used. All will weather to a gray color unless stained, painted or sealed with a clear preservative.

Though fences are not complicated structures, their design and installation are often governed by local building codes that specify maximum heights and proximity to property lines. Check with local building officials to see what codes and restrictions, if any, might apply to your project. Also, contact your local utility providers to request marking of underground lines that might be affected when you dig postholes. It's a free service, but the responsibility for making the call is yours.

Fence layouts vary according to the site and design, but as a rule, posts should be no more than 8 ft. (2.4 m) apart, and set at a depth of just less than half the fence height.

Aligning and Digging Holes

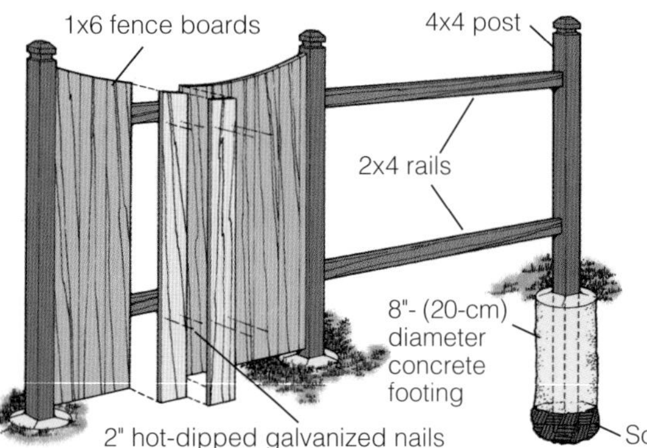

1 Set stakes and guide strings 6 in. (15 cm) inside the property lines (or per local codes), then dig holes for the end and corner posts. For a tall fence, use a posthole digger to create holes a minimum of 8 in. (20 cm) in diameter and 32 in. (80 cm) deep. Tamp the soil firmly at the bottom of the hole.

2 Set the first post, checking to make sure the top end is at the proper height. Then use a pipe to tamp 6 in. (15 cm) of dirt along the sides to steady it. Check for plumb in both directions. Brace with stakes if necessary.

3 Measure and mark the other post locations, taking care to stay clear of buried utility lines. Consider renting a power auger to dig the remaining postholes; it's faster and digs a cleaner hole. Use a wood stake to keep the guide string clear of the auger.

Working with Sloped Terrain

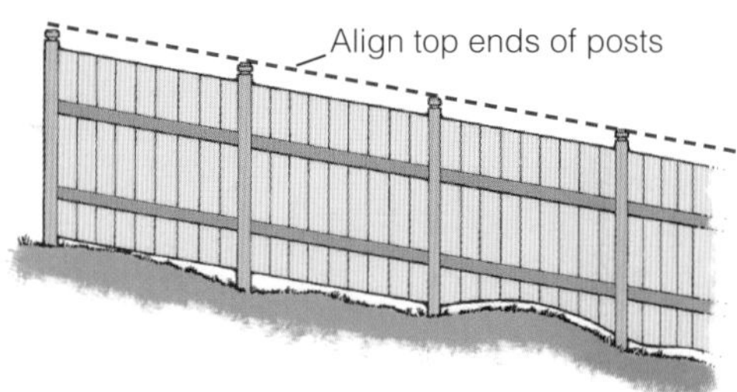

Straight fence. Align post tops using a string stretched between the end posts. Make minor adjustments to soil grade or bottom of fence boards as required.

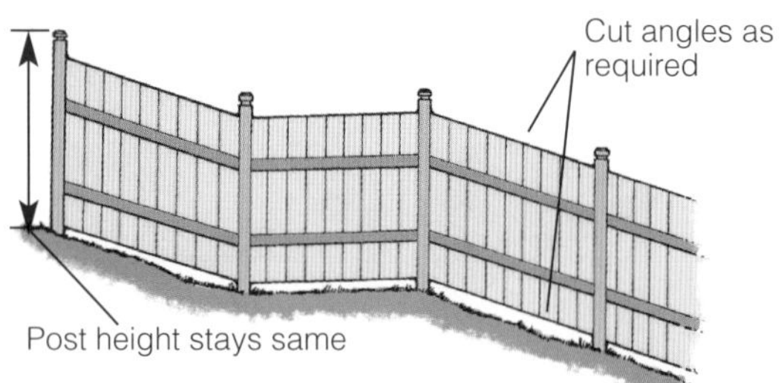

Ground-contour fence. Keep post heights a consistent dimension from ground regardless of terrain changes. Cut rail ends and fence board ends at angles to follow the slope's contours.

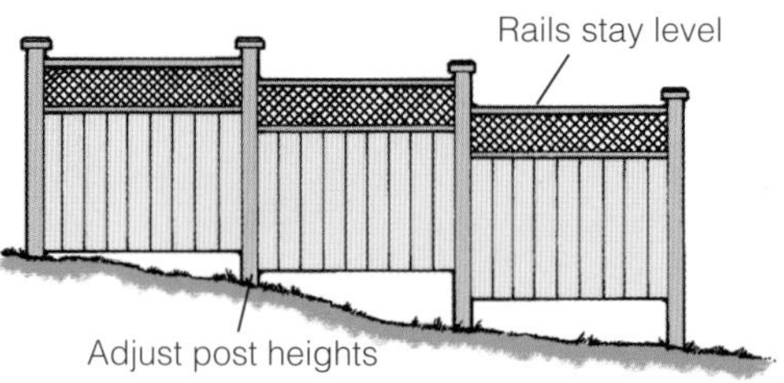

Stepped or terraced fence. To keep the rails of the fence level, adjust their height as the slope descends or ascends. The lower edges of the fence panels can be level to match or angled to fill gaps.

Setting Posts

1 As you make progress along the length of the fence, sight the posts occasionally to check for plumb and to see that the tops are aligned. Make adjustments as required and retamp the soil in the postholes. Brace posts with wood stakes if necessary.

2 Mix concrete (air-entrained where required) and fill the postholes, adding evenly around each post so you don't dislodge or misalign the post. Fill slightly above grade, and check post for plumb. Use a mason's trowel to slope the concrete away for drainage. If a gap appears later, fill it with caulk.

Installing Rails

1 On each post, fasten a temporary support block along the guide string to hold the bottom edge of the lower rail. Draw marks indicating the end cuts, cut the rail to length, and toenail (drive nail at an angle) the rail into the center of the post face. Remove the support blocks afterward.

2 To support the upper rail for marking and nailing, rest identical spacer boards on each end of the lower rail and temporarily fasten them to the posts. This system ensures that upper and lower rails stay parallel. Toenail each rail end to the center of the post face.

Installing Pickets

1 For consistency, build a simple jig to align the tops of the fence pickets above the upper rail. Secure the picket with two 2-in. hot-dipped galvanized nails at each rail. If possible, use a pneumatic nailer or recruit a helper to brace the posts so the hammering doesn't disturb the footings.

2 To get a pleasing, consistent curve, drive nails to mark the ends, called peaks, and the center, called the trough, of each contoured section. Bend a strip of thin hardboard and trace the curve with a pencil. Cut along the line with a jigsaw and sand any rough edges.

Installing a Gate

The gate will require different post spacing than the solid fence sections, so although it comes last in the building process it should be figured into your plans from the beginning. Avoid cutting narrow pickets for the gate. Plan to use full-width boards by multiplying the board width times a whole number to get the gate width. Leave a post-to-post spacing, between inside faces, to allow clearance between the gate and posts.

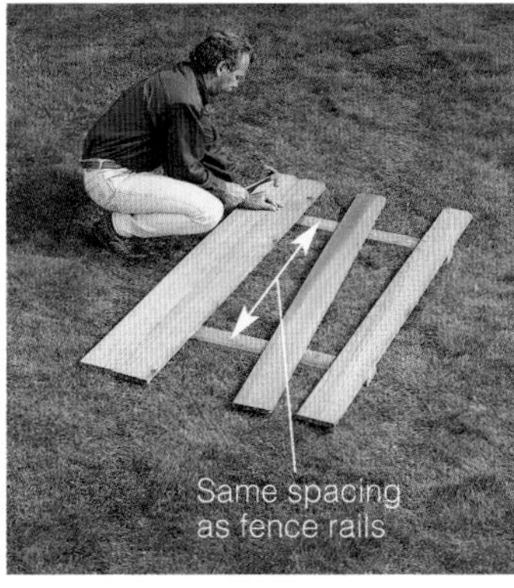

1 Set an upper and lower gate rail on the ground, with the same spacing used for the fence rails. Measure across outside corners and adjust to get equal diagonals. Then fasten the pickets with one nail at each rail. This allows flexibility for the final adjustments.

2 Test-fit the gate until the rails align with the fence rails. Secure temporarily with clamps or wedges and finish nailing the gate pickets. Cut and nail a diagonal 2x4 brace between the gate rails to form a Z-frame for added strength. Install hinges and latch.

Fence Repairs

Mixing Concrete 400
Lumber 427

Fence repair may not be as creative or fun as building a new fence, but it involves a more useful set of skills. The reason is simple: For most homeowners, fence construction is an infrequent project, but fixing the daily wear and tear can be an annual spring ritual. Rain and sun warp the lumber, post ends rot in the ground, the wind beats against the structure, and gravity takes its toll with each passing day.

A fence's structural soundness can deteriorate quietly, then fail suddenly without warning. To prevent mishaps, assess the fence each year by shaking posts, checking rail-to-post connections and inspecting the pickets, gate and hardware. Any problems—post rot, loose pickets and so on—are likely to be found in multiples, so check all sections before you tackle repairs. Numerous problems may warrant replacing the fence rather than fixing it.

If most of the fence is sound, make spot repairs as required. Clear leaf piles and other debris away from the fence; they often contribute to moisture-related problems and termite damage.

Cap the posts. Flat or beveled cap blocks reduce water absorption into the end grain.

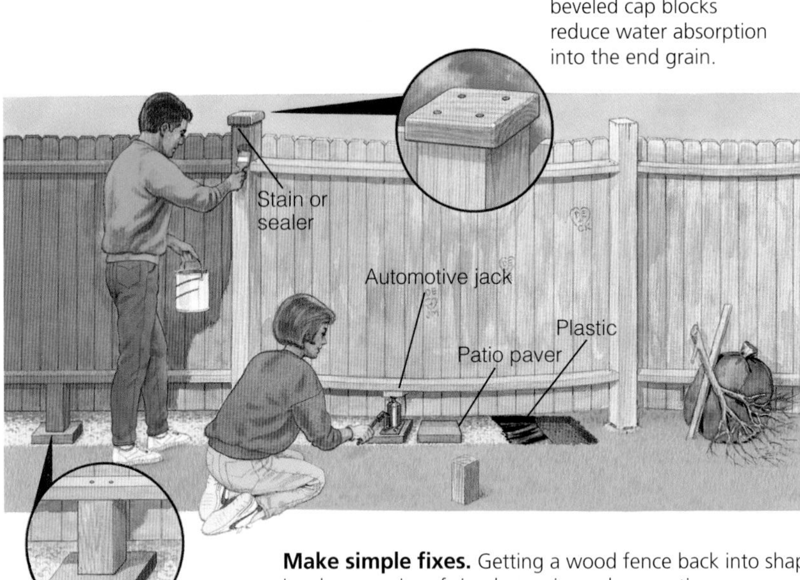

Shore up rails. Use 4x4 blocks, supported on small patio pavers, to realign lower rails and straighten the fence.

Make simple fixes. Getting a wood fence back into shape involves a series of simple repairs and preventive measures. Correct sagging rails by straightening them with an automotive jack and installing support blocks as shown. Install a lined gravel trench to keep grass and plants away and reduce maintenance. Protect against moisture by covering the porous post ends with wood or metal caps and sealing the entire fence with an exterior stain or clear wood preservative.

Replacing a Post

When a post rots at its base, you can often dig the soggy wood debris out of the concrete footing and insert another post. If the damage is higher up, remove both post and footing as shown below.

Use leverage. Fasten a 2x4 block to the post. Use a longer 2x4 as a lever to pry up the post and footing.

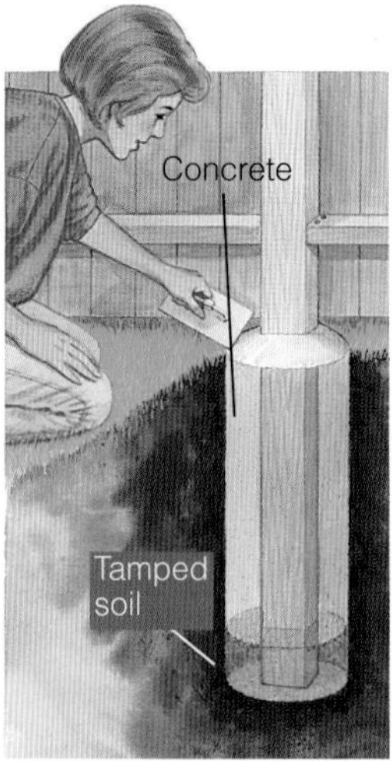

Replace the post and concrete. Tamp a hands-width of soil around the base of the new post. Then pour a new concrete footing. For drainage, shape the top of the footing so it slopes away from the post.

Straightening a Gate

Whether from hardware and fasteners working loose, the seasonal movement of the wood or just plain gravity, virtually all outdoor gates eventually sag or bind. The simplest cure is a turnbuckle and some braided steel cable. Run cable from the turnbuckle's eye bolts to lag screws on the gate corners as shown, then tighten to realign the gate.

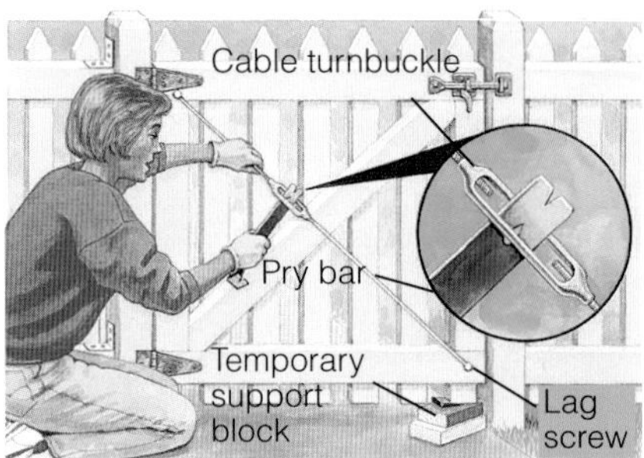

Solidify Loose Posts

Occasionally, posts shrink and become loose after installation, leaving a gap in the footing. Tighten the post by driving cedar shingle wedges along each side of the base. Cut off the excess wedge tops and fill around the post with exterior caulk.

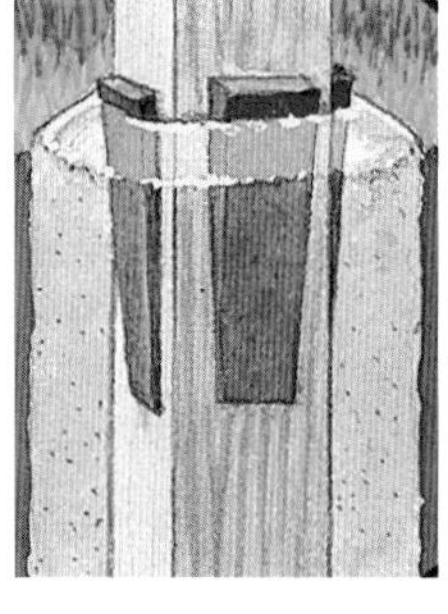

Chain-link Fences

Chain-link fencing is durable, affordable and virtually maintenance-free. Plus it's simple to install. You'll need a helper and at least two days for this project: the first day to dig postholes and set the posts in concrete, and another day (about a week later) to attach the rails, mesh and hardware.

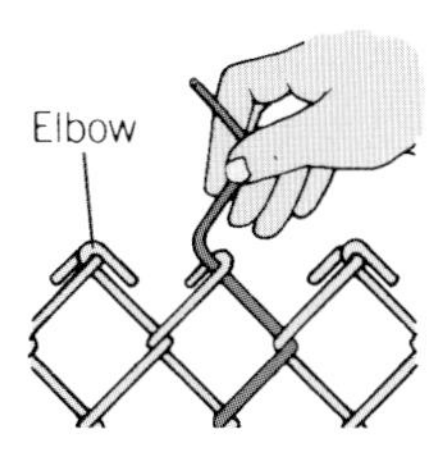

Before beginning, check with local building officials about permit requirements and call your utility company to mark any underground lines. Post spacing is typically 10 ft. (3 m) apart with 12-in. (30-cm)-dia. footings about 3 ft. (1 m) deep for end and corner posts; intermediate or line post footings are slightly smaller. End and corner posts are slightly larger in diameter, and their tops should be 2 in. (5 cm) taller than the wire fence mesh; line posts should be 2 in. lower than the mesh.

The hardware includes metal bands, tension bars, wire ties and other fittings that connect the posts to the wire mesh and the horizontal top rails. Adjust the mesh length by twisting a wire strand out in a corkscrew motion to separate the mesh, as shown above.

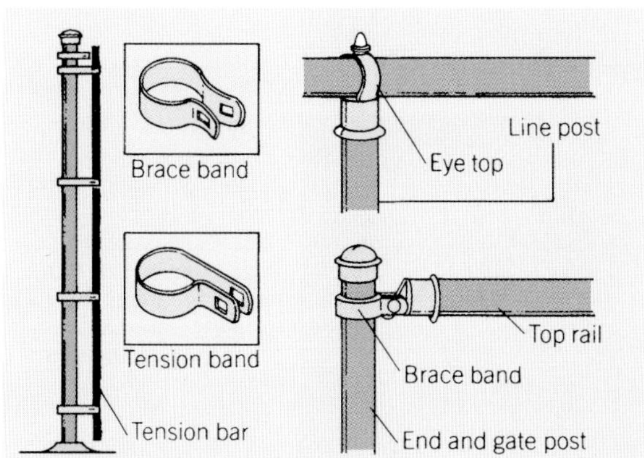

1 Dig a hole and set a post in it. Fill hole with concrete and adjust post height, then check post for plumb. As concrete starts to set, use trowel to slope footing away from post.

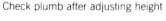

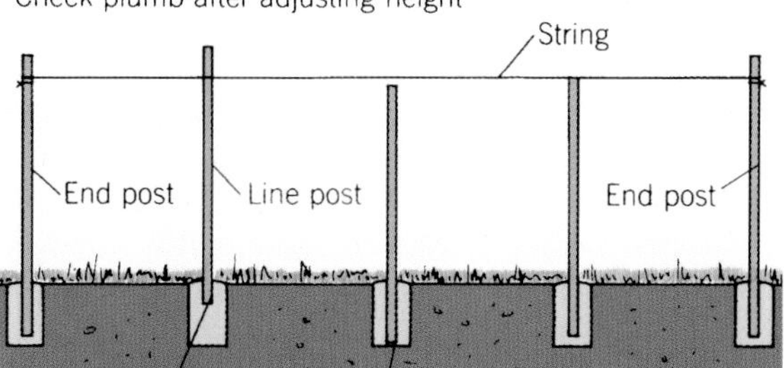

2 Set end posts first, then tie a string 4 in. (10 cm) below the tops to establish the height for the line posts. Let concrete set one week before proceeding.

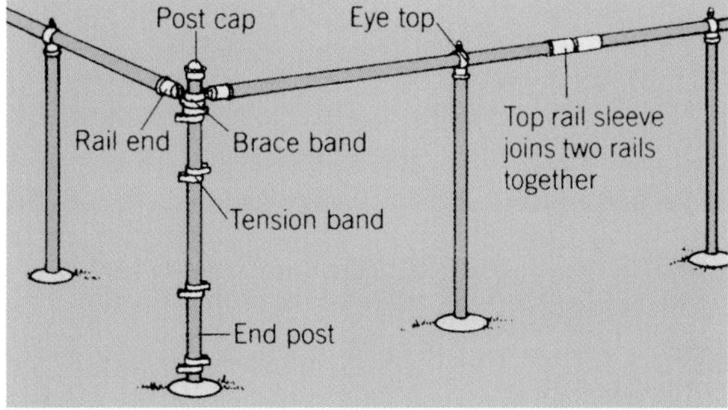

3 Slide tension bands and brace bands onto end posts, and add post caps. Add eye tops to the line posts and slip rails through them. Cut to fit using a hacksaw or reciprocating saw, add rail ends and bolt rails to brace bands.

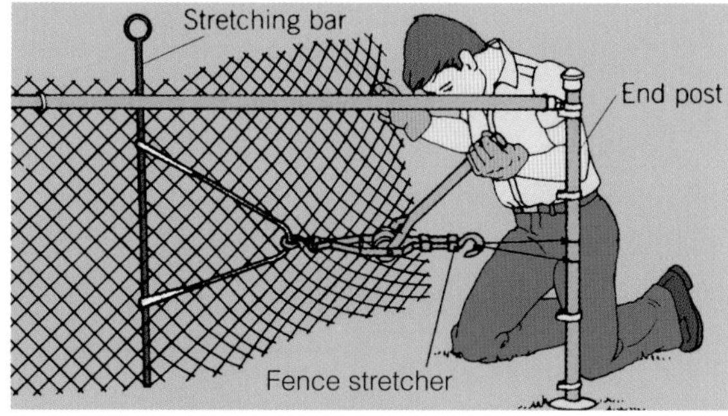

4 Slip a tension bar (illustration bottom, far left) into the first row of wire mesh and bolt the bar to the tension bands. Stretch the mesh at the other end with a stretching bar and fence stretcher (available at rental yards) to tension it.

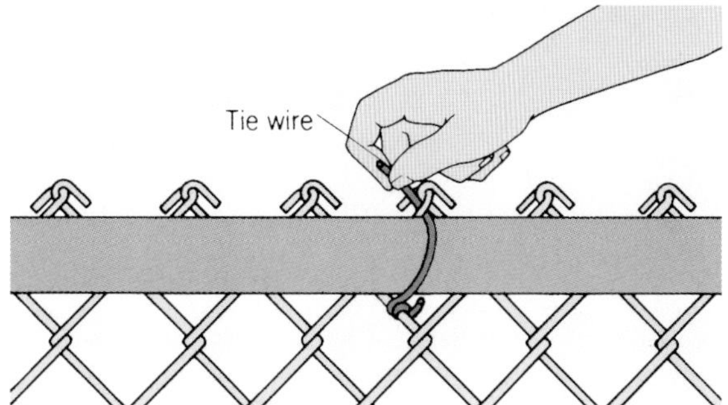

5 When mesh is stretched taut, remove any extra length and insert another tension bar to connect to the other end post as before. Use tie wires to secure the mesh to the top rails (every 24 in./60 cm) and line posts (every 12 in./30 cm).

6 To set gate, install bottom post hinge with pin pointing up and top post hinge with pin pointing down. Align top of gate with fence's top rails; then tighten hinges and install gate latch.

Paths

Outdoor paths that are created naturally from foot traffic often result in mud and dirt being tracked into the house. You can fix that. Gravel, random-edge stone, cut stone or masonry pavers offer a durable surface that won't follow the feet that tread it. Because these materials follow the ground's contour, most paths are simple to build. Looks can include randomly arranged stepping stones, free-form curves, mixed materials or formal geometric designs.

Gravel Paths

Crushed stone makes a simple, low-cost pathway that can be edged with brick or cut stones. The small chips and dust, called fines, allow the stone to pack solidly to create a stable surface. Washed stone or gravel has a cleaner look but shifts more underfoot.

Stone Paths

Large random-edge flagstones create a meandering path of stable platforms to walk on. The irregular shapes are often surrounded by borders of ground cover.

Cut stone, more costly than most random-edge varieties, offers a tighter fit and a less organic look. Unlike bricks or pavers, the sizes, colors and textures are somewhat random, so designs still have a rustic look and flavor.

Paver Paths

Concrete pavers, once limited to a few styles with a manufactured look, now also feature variegated colors and tumbled edges that mimic the appearance of cut stones. The modular sizes make it easy to align them in patterns—even circles and curves.

Clay pavers or bricks lend themselves to a traditional, formal look and allow curved paths despite their rectangular shape. Their uniform size allows for narrow joints that can be filled with sand for a low-maintenance path.

Building a Path

This project takes some muscle, but it's a low-tech process. You'll need a few simple tools, such as a square-nose shovel, a steel rake, a wheelbarrow and a rubber mallet. Excavation is often limited to a shallow trench. If need to dig deeper, ask your local utility provider to come out and mark the locations of any buried utility lines.

Multiply the width and length of the path to estimate the total path area. Then add about 15 percent for stone waste and breakage. Have the sand and stone delivered before you begin, and have it unloaded as close to the path site as possible to minimize hauling by hand. The path shown here features random-edge limestone approximately 2 in. (5 cm) thick. A ton covered about 90 sq. ft. (10 sq. m).

1 If there's lawn where you're building your path, rent a sod cutter to remove it. Check for low-voltage wiring that might have to be removed or relocated. Use marking paint (the can sprays upside down) to outline the path area. Set the sod cutter at full depth to make soil excavation easier.

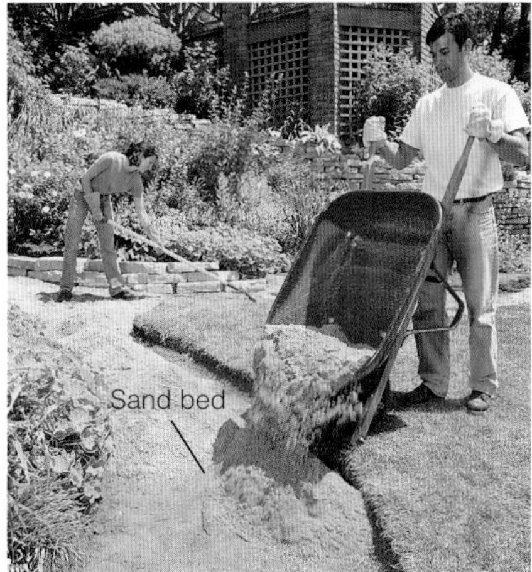

2 Heavy traffic areas might call for a thick base of crushed rock to prevent stones from settling; but for a walkway, a 3-in. (7-cm)-thick sand bed will do fine. Spread the sand evenly with a rake. Then compact it lightly with a hand tamper. Adjust depth so stones will be flush with lawn surface when installed.

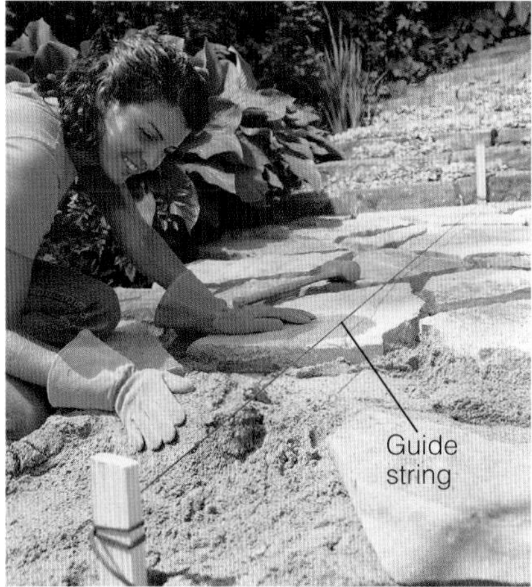

3 Stretch a string between stakes, at a height about 1 in. (3 cm) above the finished path. It should follow the slope of the ground so you have a visual guide to keep the stones even. Place and wiggle the stones until they settle at the desired depth in the sand. Tamp with a rubber mallet to seat them firmly.

4 For a more natural look, leave some irregular spaces and joints between stones. Spread a potting soil mix and sweep it into the joints. This will support low-profile ground cover. If you don't want to plant anything between the stones, fill the joints with mulch, shredded bark or pea gravel.

Building Steps

Stone landscape steps don't require the same precision as a finely crafted wood staircase, but the principles are the same. To begin, measure the total horizontal distance the stair will travel along a level line, called the run. Then measure down from that line to get the total vertical distance, called the rise. Get riser stones of a uniform thickness between 6 and 8 in. (15 and 20 cm). Divide the total rise by the stone thickness to get the number of steps. Steep slopes need taller risers and short treads; gentle slopes get shorter risers and long treads.

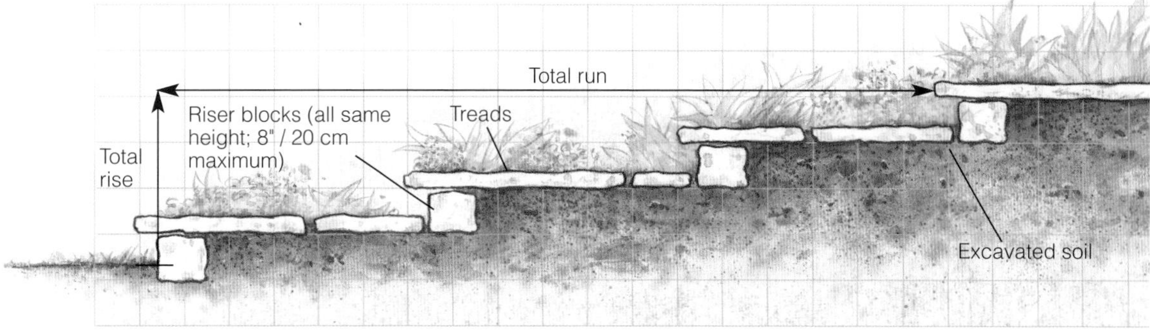

Brick Patios

Levels **44**
Rental Tools **424**

Building a paver patio might seem like a big project, but it's really a series of individual tasks managed one at a time. The critical site requirement is a flat, level area, with a slope of no more than 2 in. (5 cm) in 10 ft. (3 m). Build retaining walls to create a level area, if necessary. Rent a sod cutter, setting it to full depth, to cut the lawn away. Use a square-nose shovel to excavate further until the soil bed is 7 in. (18 cm) below the lawn surface.

Order base materials–crushed limestone and sand–by the ton or cubic yard (meter). Ask your supplier to help estimate the amounts and deliver it. You'll also need wood stakes, plastic edging with steel spikes and two 10-ft. lengths of 3/4-in. steel pipe. For tools, you'll want a wheelbarrow, 4-ft. level, string, handsaw, mallet and push broom. Plan to rent a brick saw and a vibrating plate compactor.

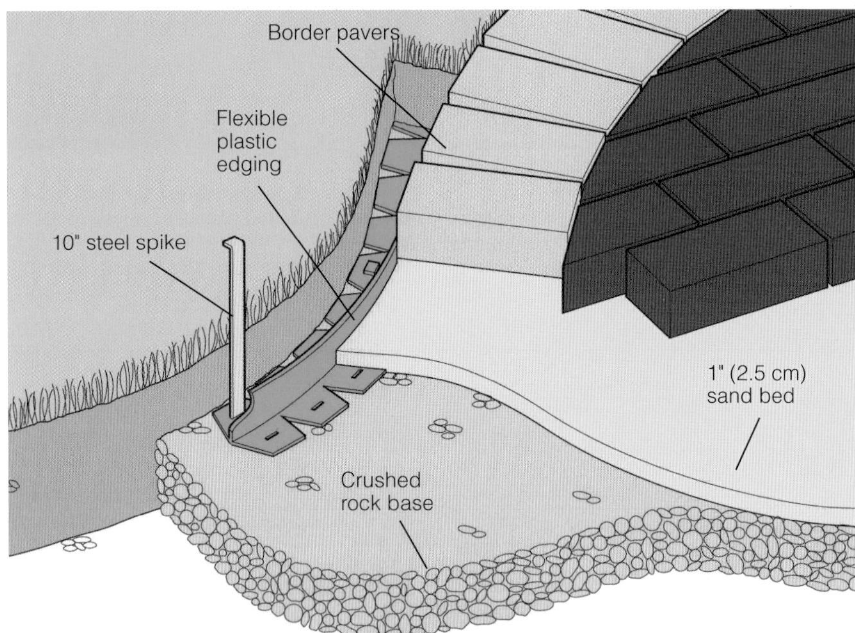

Anatomy of a paver patio. The foundation is provided by a 3- to 4-in. (8- to 10-cm) layer of crushed limestone. The limestone includes fines, which are small chips and stone dust to help it pack tightly. A layer of bedding sand tops that base and supports and helps level the pavers. **Note:** In colder climates, increase depth of rock base to 8 to 10 in. (20 to 25 cm).

Layout

Because manufactured concrete pavers are modular and very consistent dimensionally, it's simple to calculate a layout or pattern for your patio. For rectangular shapes, aim for overall dimensions that use whole pavers and reduce cutting. Curved or angled edges will, of course, require more cut pavers but offer more design freedom.

1 Cut the sod loose using a sod cutter and roll it up for immediate use elsewhere. Finish excavating and leveling the soil using a square-nose shovel.

2 Drive rows of wood stakes at the perimeter and center of your excavated area. Mark the finished height (3 in. or 8 cm minimum) for the crushed rock base material.

Installing Base Materials

Use a screed board to level the base materials. To create a simple guide system, cut off stakes 1 in. (2.5 cm) below the height-measurement marks and secure lengths of black pipe to their tops; screws driven into the tops of the stakes on the sides of the pipe work well. The pipes will act as guide rails for the screed board when you level the base.

1 Use a straight 2x4 as a screed to level the crushed limestone. If you're working in sections, relocate the outside pipe to level the second half of the area.

2 Use a vibrating plate compactor to consolidate the entire base. Fill any low spots and compact the entire area again. (The posts shown are for a future pergola.)

Stone Patios

Installing Sand and Pavers

Take care to level and compact the base material evenly. Like the soil grading, this determines final surface quality. Remove the wood stakes and black pipe and fill those spots. Then lay the pipe on top of the base to act as a depth guide for the sand.

1 Lay the pipe on the compacted base. Then spread and level the sand. To compensate for the taller edging, cut an offset notch on one end of the screed board.

2 Set up a guide string line so rows run straight. Lay pavers in the sand bed. Plywood supports your weight and the stacks of pavers.

Cutting and Tamping

Almost any pattern you choose will require cutting some pavers, but lay all the uncut pavers first. Mark other whole pavers directly from the infill spots and cut them to fit. After all the pavers are placed, compact them so they settle uniformly into the sand.

1 Rent a wet-cutting brick saw to cut the pavers. Wear eye and ear protection and hold each paver firmly. Use the cutting guides for angled or irregular cuts.

2 Make one complete pass with the vibrating compactor, sweep sand into the joints, and run the compactor over the entire patio again.

Building a raised stone patio takes more time, effort and money than a grade-level paver patio, but it will have a more defined character and be a stronger landscape element. In addition to the basic steps shown for building a paver patio, you'll need to build a retaining wall to border the patio, add a much thicker base of crushed rock and spend more time fitting irregularly shaped stones.

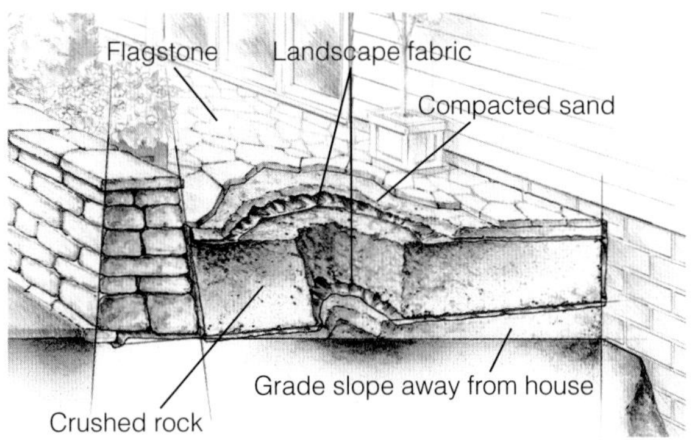

Anatomy of a raised stone patio. A sturdy retaining wall, preferably also of stone or other masonry, must be built before you start the patio. Compact the crushed rock base material in layers no more than 6 in. (15 cm) thick. Plan for the finished height to be 6 in. (15 cm) below the siding.

Natural flagstone will vary in color, texture, size, shape, cost and availability, so scout local supply yards before you design your patio. Allow at least 10 percent extra for waste. Have it delivered as close to your patio site as possible.

Cutting and fitting. Random-edge stone creates a natural look, so don't waste time trying for the precise, tight joints you'd get with pavers. Use a brick hammer or mason's sledge to chip edges to the rough shape you want. Then press stone firmly into the sand.

Filling joints. After all the stone is down, spread coarse sand and sweep it into the joints. Sweep in different directions to ensure consistent levels. Spray the surface with water to help sand settle. Heavy rains will wash some out, so expect to add sand periodically.

Decks

Squaring **41**
Metal Hangers **77**
Concrete Footings **405**
Lumber **427**

A deck consistently ranks as the home-improvement project most likely to recover its entire cost upon resale, but plenty of other reasons exist to build one. Decks create usable living space at a fraction of the cost of an enclosed addition, provide a transition between home and yard and offer a versatile setting. They're great places to entertain summertime guests or have coffee on a quiet weekend morning.

A deck project can be as simple or as complex as you want. Most start with concrete footings, called piers, that support a series of posts (or sometimes the deck frame directly). The posts support beams, which in turn carry a framework of joists—the base for the decking surface and railing. Site factors, such as steep terrain, might require other features or strategies, but almost anyone with basic carpentry skills—measuring, cutting and fastening wood—can manage this project.

Planning and site-preparation requirements include drawing a plan and obtaining a building permit, establishing level and square reference lines, having underground utility lines marked, grading the yard and digging holes for the concrete piers. You may also have to remove siding or otherwise modify the house exterior to attach the deck frame.

Decking options. Although pressure-treated pine is the most common material for a deck's structural frame, the decking surface itself offers many options, including (from top down) hollow-core extruded composite decking, solid composite decking, cedar and pressure-treated pine.

A Safe Deck

Code requirements for decks vary widely among cities and counties, so always consult local building officials during the planning stage. Some decks, if they are small or low to the ground, are exempt from permit requirements or restrictions governing railings, but don't take anything for granted. Because deck building is such a common project for homeowners, many cities publish guides outlining the rules and regulations for their design and construction. Typically they specify acceptable construction techniques, hardware and lumber sizes and types. Regulations may govern such things as footing size and placement, railing height and spacing, stairs and stair handrails, allowable joist and beam spans and methods for attaching the deck to the house. Follow these guidelines accurately, especially for upper-level decks where structural failures can have serious consequences.

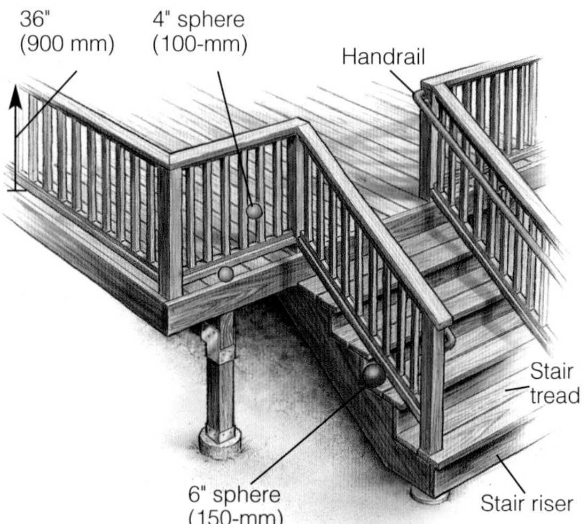

Preventing falls and head entrapment (especially for children) are the two main safety concerns for railings. Typical requirements include a 36-in. (900-mm)-high railing for elevated decks. Higher decks may require 42-in. (107-mm)-high railings in some areas; lower decks may not require any railing. Railings can't have openings large enough to allow a 4-in. (100-mm) sphere to pass through. Similar restrictions govern stair handrail, tread and riser dimensions.

Railings

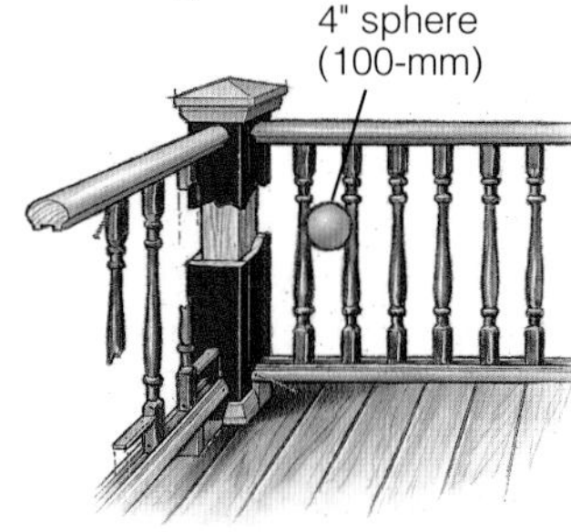

Spindles. Vertical spindles in a railing can be decorative turned spindles, such as those depicted here, or simpler shapes, such as square or flat pickets. To comply with the 4-in. (100-mm) sphere rule for maximum gaps, allow for the smallest-diameter section of the spindles.

Glass. Clear-panel railings are a popular choice for decks that offer great views. Minimum requirements for glass are tempered 1/4-in. (6-mm) panels, though some jurisdictions require thicker glass. Clear acrylic or polycarbonate plastics are sometimes allowed.

Benches. Built-in benches can double as railings if necessary, but keep them limited to sections of the deck rather than the entire perimeter. The 36-in. (900-mm) height requirement still stands, so the bench backs must extend that far above the seat height.

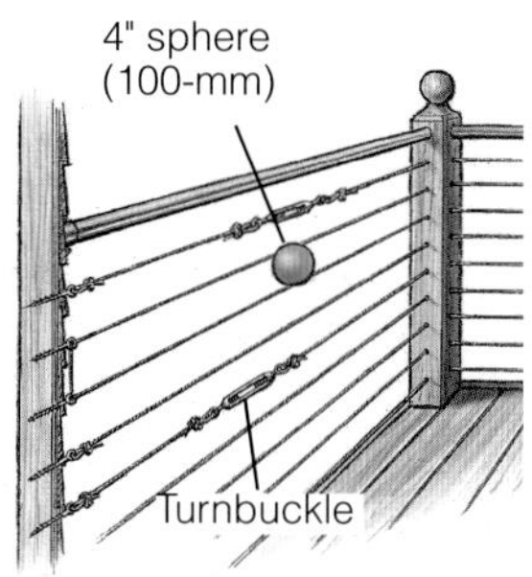

Cable. Braided-steel cable offers a contemporary, industrial look to deck railings, but it requires special tensioning hardware that can stress posts and add to the project cost. The horizontal orientation enables climbing the railing, so some codes don't allow it.

After you draw plans and get necessary permits for your deck, start gathering tools and materials. You'll need a portable circular saw, a sturdy electric drill (corded or 12-volt cordless minimum) with a bit assortment, an angle square, framing square, tape rule, hammer, 4-ft. builder's level, chalk line, shovel or posthole digger and a wheelbarrow for mixing concrete.

For materials, you'll need pressure-treated pine framing lumber for the structural framework, plus the decking of your choice. The deck shown here features 2x6 cedar decking. Because it's built low to the ground, it doesn't use the post-and-beam assembly normally required. Instead, the joist framework rests directly on three concrete piers at the outer end of the deck; the outer rim joist is made from two 2x10s to serve as the support beam. At the connection to the house, a ledger board supports the other ends of the joists.

Fasteners you'll need include bolts or lag screws, decking screws and hot-dipped galvanized or stainless steel nails. Another hardware item typically required is metal framing connectors, such as joist hangers. For footings, you'll need cardboard tube forms, wood stakes and concrete mix.

Typically, decks require two inspections. The first will be for the footing holes before the concrete piers are poured; the second is the final inspection after the deck is completed.

Make certain the land below the deck slopes away from the house so water drains away.

Ledger Board

When placed low on the wall, the ledger board is usually bolted to the house's rim joist. For higher decks, make sure it's secured directly to wall studs, header beams or other solid framing members.

1 Pry off or cut away a portion of siding. Position the ledger board on a level chalk line about 3 in. (7 cm) below the door threshold. Drive a few nails to hold it temporarily.

2 Use 1/2-in. bolts or lag screws to anchor the ledger board to the wall. Mark the joist layout and fasten joist hanger brackets. We spaced ours 12 in. on center. Flashing above the ledger and under the siding will divert water.

Footings

For this project, we temporarily assembled the perimeter frame to mark positions of the footing piers, then dismantled it to dig the footings. The footing depth should be below the frost line.

1 Shore up the joist frame with blocks to level it. Then shift the two outside corners until the diagonals are equal, indicating square corners. Mark the outside corners in the soil.

2 Set 12-in. (30-cm)-diameter tube forms to the required depth and reinstall the perimeter frame to fine-tune the form placement. Then brace the forms with stakes and fill with concrete.

Framework and Decking

Joist layout can vary from 12 to 24 in. on center, depending on their span and the decking material's type and orientation. Check local building codes to determine the required joist size.

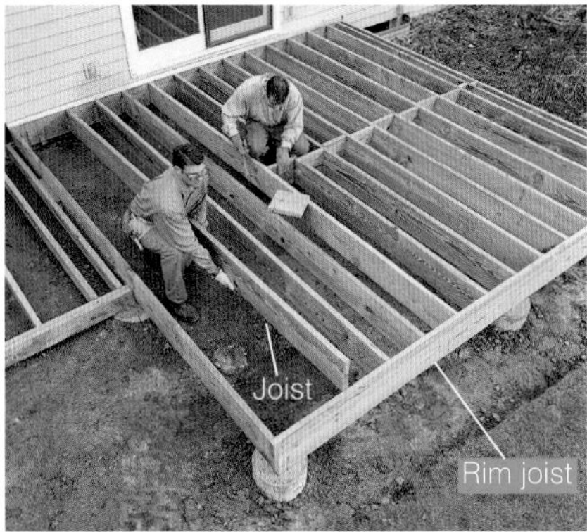

1 To make this deck stiffer, 2x10 joists are fastened at 12 in. on center. Blocking is nailed along the centerline to help them transfer and share loads. This spacing is often required when decking is laid diagonally.

2 Snap a chalk line to start the decking. Wet boards can be butted together so gaps will open as they dry. Otherwise, space the boards about 1/8 in. (3 mm) apart. Use a chisel to pry crooked boards into line.

Deck Maintenance

Refinishing a Wood Deck

The simplicity that makes decks easy to build also makes them easy to restore. All parts are accessible, and most surfaces and hardware are clearly visible, so you can check their condition and make repairs as needed. Inspect everything—decking, railings, stairs and framework. Push or pull firmly to ensure parts are tight, and keep an eye out for discoloration, mold or other indicators of rotting wood. Press a screwdriver into surfaces that appear suspect; if the tip penetrates easily and tears the fibers out, replace the part.

Even if a deck is structurally sound, its appearance will eventually degrade from accumulation of dirt, exposure to sun and rain and ordinary wear and tear. A deck cleaner will renew wood that is raw or has been treated with a penetrating sealer. Film finishes, such as varnishes or paints, will have to be removed with a chemical stripper. When they're off, replace them with penetrating sealers or solid-color stains that are easier to renew. Wear rubber gloves and protective eyewear when working with strippers and cleaners.

1 Most surface finishes—paint, varnish, solid-color stain—will flake off under the pressure of a sharp paint scraper. Remove the bulk of the finish by hand, then sand the remainder or apply a chemical paint stripper.

2 Railings often have the heaviest accumulation of paint or finish. Wearing gloves and safety glasses, apply stripper and watch for finish to blister. Keep the surface moist and work in sections less than 6 ft. (2 m) long.

3 Use a stiff synthetic-bristle brush to scrub loosened finish from the wood. If the finish doesn't come off readily, wait longer or reapply chemical stripper. Clean up crevices and corners with a putty knife or scraper.

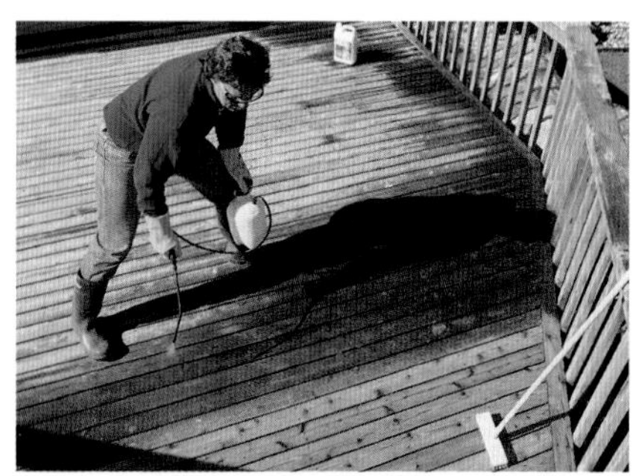

4 After the railing is stripped, renew the decking surface by spraying a deck cleaner. This will work on accumulated dirt, discoloration and minor stains. Cover nearby plants with plastic sheeting to avoid damaging them.

5 Working in sections, allow the cleaner to sit on the wood for about 15 minutes. Then scrub the decking clean with a stiff-bristle brush. Work the brush briskly in the direction of the wood grain. Rinse with water.

6 After the deck has dried for 48 hours, use a paint roller on a pole handle to apply clear or tinted sealer. Weathered wood surfaces are highly absorbent, so apply the sealer generously. Brush between boards, if necessary.

Replacing a Deck Board

Like any natural material, wood varies in appearance and durability. Occasionally you'll find board sections that have aged poorly and need to be replaced. Here's a simple technique:

1 With an angle square as a guide, use a jigsaw to cut the section of deck board from between the joists. Cut alongside each joist.

2 Fasten support cleats to the joists to hold up the ends of the new deck board. Pull them tight against the underside of the adjacent decking.

3 To reduce the chance of splitting the wood, blunt the tip of the nails before driving them. If using deck screws, drill pilot holes.

Water Gardens / Flexible Liner

Stocked with a variety of plants and even fish, water gardens represent an entire aquatic ecosystem but are surprisingly easy to build. There's no precise measuring involved, and nothing has to be square. Still, some planning guidelines apply. As with any project that requires digging or excavating soil, don't start until you've called your local utility company to mark any underground utility lines. Also, check with local building officials about permit requirements or codes for safety fences surrounding the pond. Then you can start construction.

This water garden features a flexible pond liner, the most popular type. Easy to install and relatively inexpensive, flexible liners are typically made of black synthetic rubber and range in thickness from 20 to 60 mils. Buy the thickest you can afford. Garden supply centers and landscape retailers that sell them can help you calculate the size; you'll need to account for pond length, width, depth and a 2-ft. (.6-m) perimeter border. Ideally, the pond should feature multiple ledges so plants can be grown at different depths. If you plan to add fish, at least part of the pond should be between 18 and 36 in. deep (0.5 to 1 m).

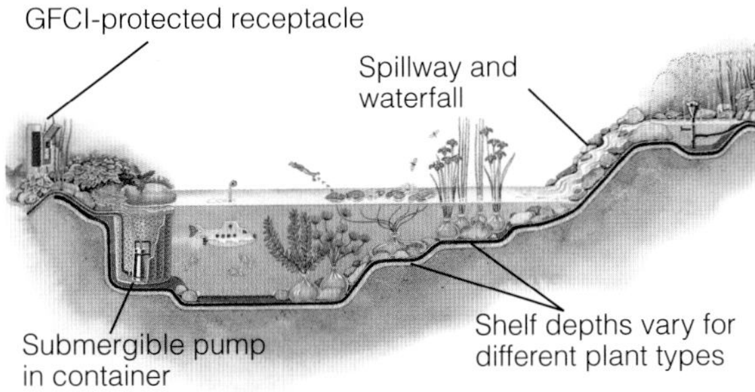

Water garden anatomy. A water garden should mimic the contoured shape of a natural pond, with varying depths for plants. Flexible liners conform to the soil bed. Water is circulated from a pump at one end to an outlet at the other, usually a waterfall feature.

1 Pick an area with a mix of sun and shade. Use a garden hose to outline the pond shape. This outline climbs the slope for a holding pool and spillway into the main pond. Stay clear of trees to avoid large roots.

2 Adjust the surrounding soil grade to make the pond banks level. Use that reference point to measure pond depths. The actual water level will be below the banks, so allow 2 to 3 in. (5 to 8 cm) extra depth.

3 Line the pond bed with a 1/2-in. (12-mm)-thick layer of newspaper. The paper helps prevent punctures to the liner and will eventually form a claylike layer that deters leaks.

4 Insert the liner loosely so it can conform to the contours of the hole. Use rocks to hold the edges. Work your way around to adjust and press the liner more firmly into place. Wear soft-soled shoes to protect the liner.

5 Fill the pond partway to secure the liner. Work in sections around the perimeter to dig niches, shape the bank and place edge rocks where you want them. Finish filling the pond, then trim the excess liner.

Picking a Pump

The amount of water a pump moves, the flow rate, is measured in gallons or liters per hour or minute. This flow rate is affected by the diameter, length and composition of the hose as well as the vertical distance or "lift" the water must travel. You can conduct a simple test by pouring a measured amount of water into your full holding pond and determining which rate of flow looks the best as the water tumbles into the spillway or lower pond. Then do the math and purchase your pump accordingly.

Water Gardens / Preformed Liner

Preformed rigid pond liners offer another option for building a water garden. These durable polyethylene shells simplify the project somewhat by offering a ready-made shape and design for the pond, but they require more careful sculpting of the soil bed to ensure that the liner is supported uniformly. Also, they are limited to more modest sizes (up to about 200 gal./750 l) than ponds with flexible liners. If you want more pond area or a more elaborate design, you can combine multiple shells and join them with a spillway, like the version illustrated below.

Other than the installation procedure, the guidelines for this project stay consistent with other water gardens. Before digging, call your local utility provider to request marking of any underground cables or pipes and check with local building officials for code requirements, such as property-line setbacks and safety fences to prevent drowning hazards. Pick a location that gets a mix of sun and shade, and try to stay away from trees with large root systems. Spillways and waterfalls between ponds create movement necessary to filter and aerate the water so the garden won't become stagnant. For single ponds, install a fountain feature to aerate the water.

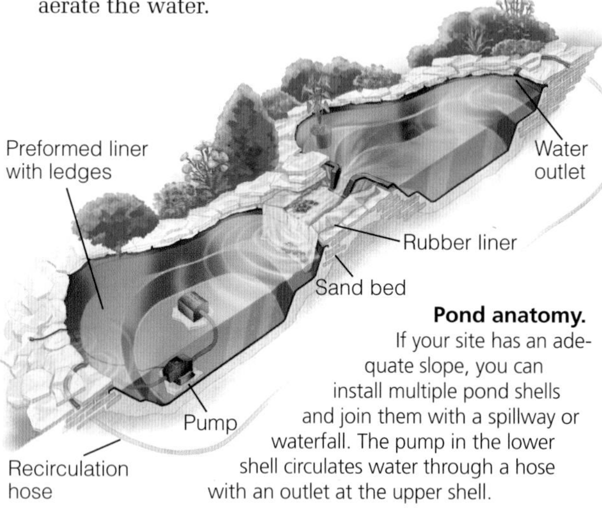

Pond anatomy. If your site has an adequate slope, you can install multiple pond shells and join them with a spillway or waterfall. The pump in the lower shell circulates water through a hose with an outlet at the upper shell.

1 Dig a hole 6 in. (15 cm) wider and 2 in. (5 cm) deeper than the liner shell, with matching contours for ledges and curves. Test the fit repeatedly to ensure every portion of the liner will be supported by dirt, sand or stone when it's full of water.

2 Spread a layer of coarse sand to protect the liner's bottom and ledges. If the soil grading is reasonably accurate, the sand will conform to the contours of the shell, making leveling adjustments easier to make.

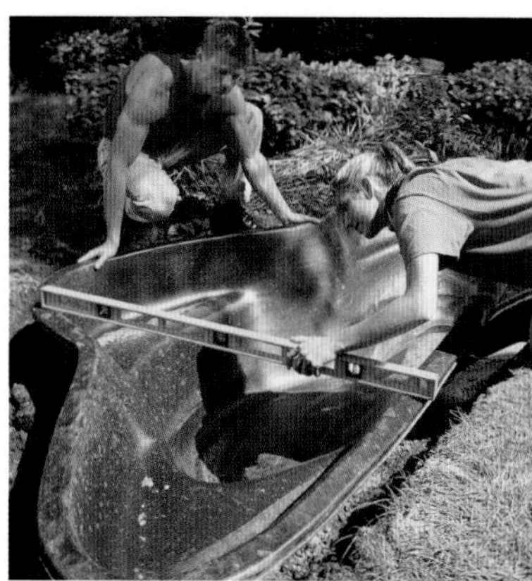

3 Adjust the liner's position until it's level in every direction and the bottom and ledges rest directly on the sand bed. For long spans, support the builder's level with a straight length of 2x4 framing lumber.

4 Backfill around the liner with a half-and-half mix of sand and soil at the same rate water is filling it; this equalizes the pressure on the shell. Compact the sand-soil mix firmly as you place it, especially under ledges.

5 After tucking the corrugated recirculation hose along the lip of the shell, finish backfilling the pond perimeter with the sand-soil mix. Place landscaping stones alongside and level with the rim, then add the cap stones.

6 Connect the filter, pump and hose. Then place them in the pond with the pump and the discharge end of the hose as far apart as possible. This ensures maximum water flow to prevent stagnation. Monitor water level to check for leaks.

Windows & Doors

Windows / Basics

Egress Windows 277
Buying Windows 369

Types of Windows

Casement windows have hinged sashes that swing from the side. They offer a large opening relative to window size, making them a good choice for egress windows, ventilation and viewing. A casement seals better than other window types because of its full-perimeter gasket and locking system. Screens are on the window's interior side.

Double-hung windows have vertically sliding sashes and a traditional look. The two separate sashes offer smaller viewing areas and a style that often complements more traditional homes. Some have a tilt-in feature that makes cleaning easier. An outer screen or storm window offers the glass some protection from the elements.

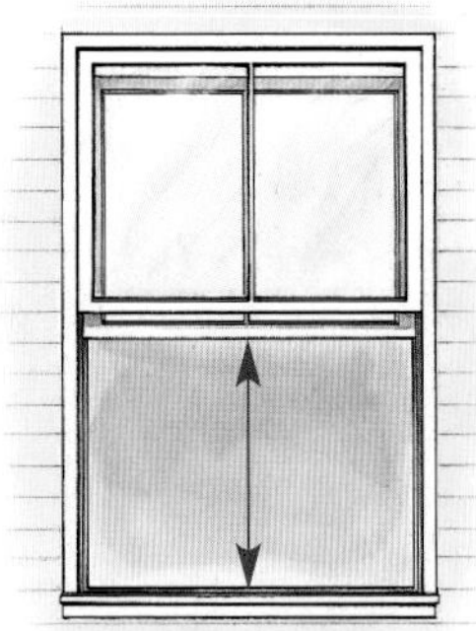

Gliding windows, or gliders, have horizontally sliding sashes. The easiest type to operate, gliders are also the most affordable. But the rolling-sliding action means they don't seal as well as casement or double-hung windows and the bottom track tends to gather dirt.

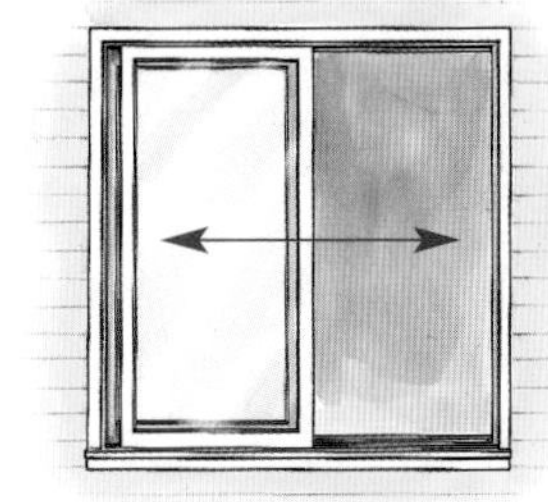

Awning windows have top-hinged sashes. Normally wider than they are high, they are often used for ventilation or light, not for viewing. Usually, they work best above or below other windows, above doors or in basements or bathrooms.

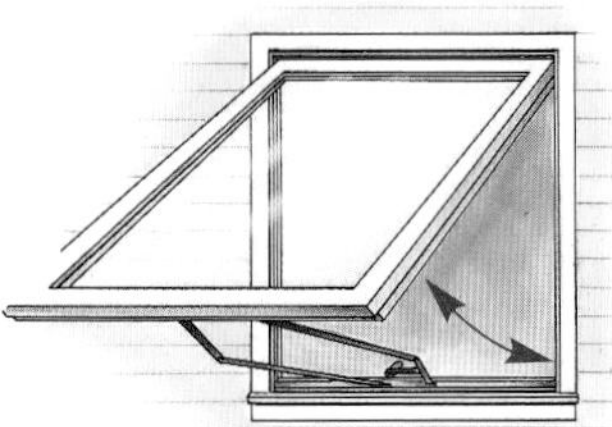

Window Anatomy

The parts related to a double-hung window are common to most other window types. The window's structural support, the frame, consists of jambs, stops, sill and stool (inside sill), and the exterior brick mold. The sash includes the rails, stiles, muntins (if present) and lites (glass panes). The glass layer is called glazing; a window may be single-, double- or triple-glazed.

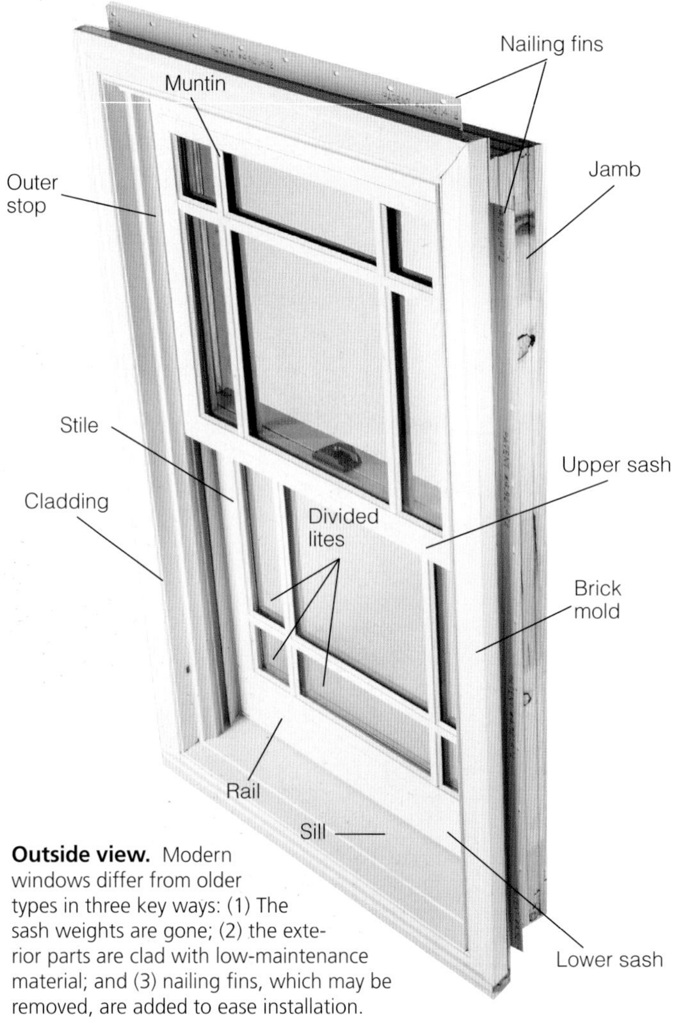

Outside view. Modern windows differ from older types in three key ways: (1) The sash weights are gone; (2) the exterior parts are clad with low-maintenance material; and (3) nailing fins, which may be removed, are added to ease installation.

Older Double-hung Windows

Older double-hung windows have sashes that move up and down in channels. The sash position is controlled by counterweights concealed behind the side jambs.

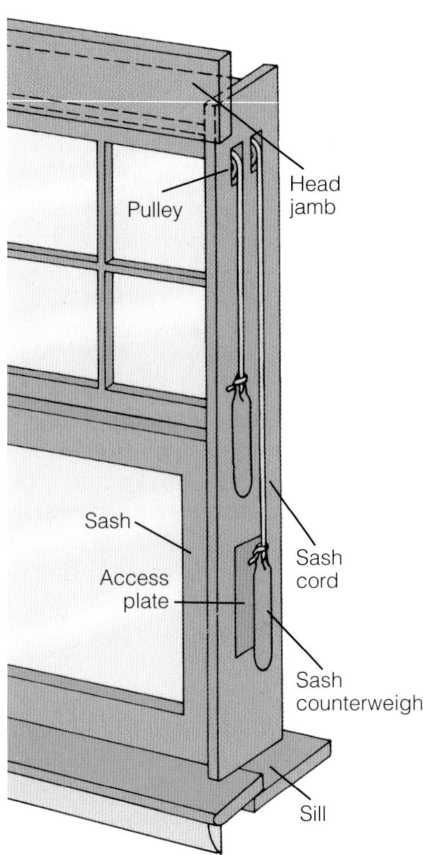

Inner view. The sash weights are held by sash cords that run over a pulley and are attached to each side of each sash.

Windows / Repairing Double-hung

Replacing a Broken Sash Cord

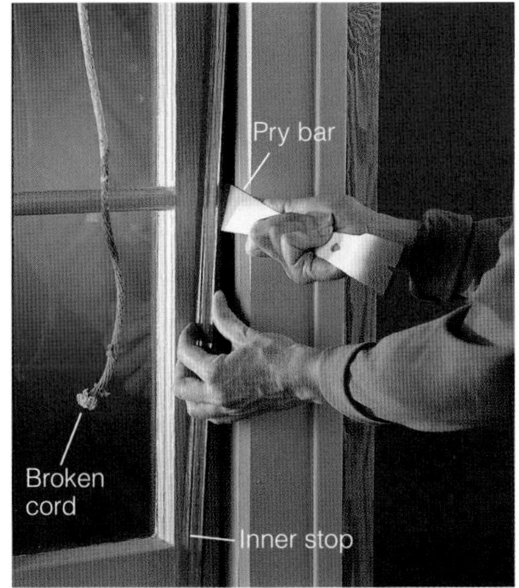

1 Unscrew or pry out inner stop using a putty knife or pry bar. If you have metal weather stripping, carefully remove and save it. Pull bottom sash out from frame. Remove knotted sash cord (or chain) from channel in side of window sash.

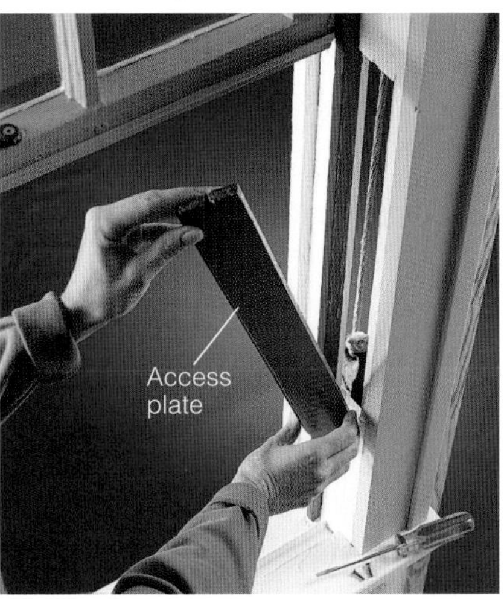

2 Unscrew or pry out access plate in jamb to expose the weights. The plate must come out at an angle, not straight out. If the plate is painted stuck, score around it with a utility knife. If it's still stuck, attach a drywall screw in the center and pull out with pliers.

3 Pull out weight and broken cord. The new cord should be the same thickness as the old. To help feed the cord, use a piece of strong string. Tie a bent nail to one end of string to serve as a weight and direct it over the pulley. Firmly tie other string end to new cord.

4 Feed cord over pulley, pull it down and tie it to the old weight. Rest sash on the sill, pull cord down until weight bumps pulley, and thread cord through channel on the side of the sash. Cut cord 2 in. (5 cm) longer than sash channel. Tie tight knot in cord end and push in hole at bottom of sash channel. Replace sash and inner stop.

Quick Fixes for Falling Sashes

If you don't want to spend time replacing broken sash cords, you can repair the window using a spring-tension device. You have two tension device options: the butterfly and the window spring. To install a butterfly, open the sash fully, push one butterfly wing between the sash and jamb and nail or screw it in place. If the window still doesn't stay open, place another butterfly in the other jamb. To install a window spring, which is the more attractive option, lower the sash, insert the spring between it and the jamb, and screw it in place. Again, use two springs if necessary.

Freeing Stuck Sashes

Do not use force, other than a slight tap with your hand against the sash, to open a stuck window. Look for and repair obstructions in the side jambs, such as loose weather stripping or stops. If the window is painted shut, free it carefully using a paint zipper between the sash and the frame, as shown.

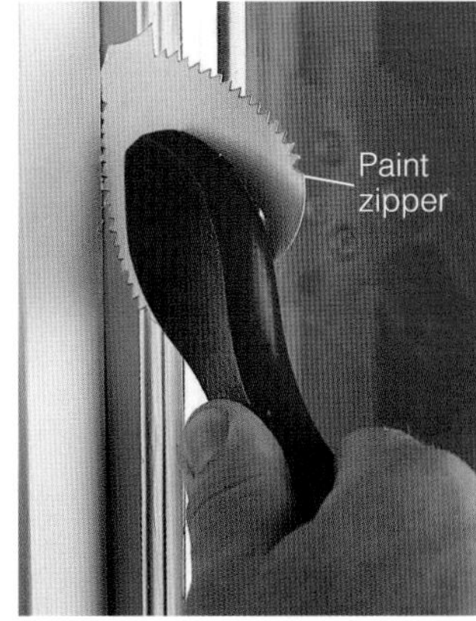

Windows / Upgrading Double-hung

Vinyl Track Inserts

Installing vinyl track inserts in older double-hung windows is an economical option that improves the windows' operation and lets you retain the original sashes' charm. To do this, the inserts replace the function of the sash cords and weights with a counterweight spring held in a vinyl track. The original sashes snap into the new vinyl track, and the springs allow them to lift easily. Plus, you can then snap out the sashes to gain the easy-cleaning feature of modern double-hung windows. This repair's drawback is that it does little to improve the windows' energy efficiency.

You can complete this project with basic tools and little experience in a few hours per window once sashes and tracks are on hand. Begin by using a framing square to check that the window frames are square. Use the tip of a screwdriver to examine the frame and sashes for rot.

If your sashes and frames are in good shape, find a window dealer who will trim and groove the original sashes and sell the vinyl tracks. Also, have the dealer install the counterweight catches on the bottom of the sashes and cut the vinyl tracks to length. If the vinyl tracks are available in more than one color, choose one that blends with the window and trim.

Before installing the new vinyl tracks, remove the counterbalance access plates and fill the cavity with blown-in or minimally expanding foam insulation.

With the sash stiles trimmed and grooved, the original sashes snap into the spring-loaded vinyl track inserts.

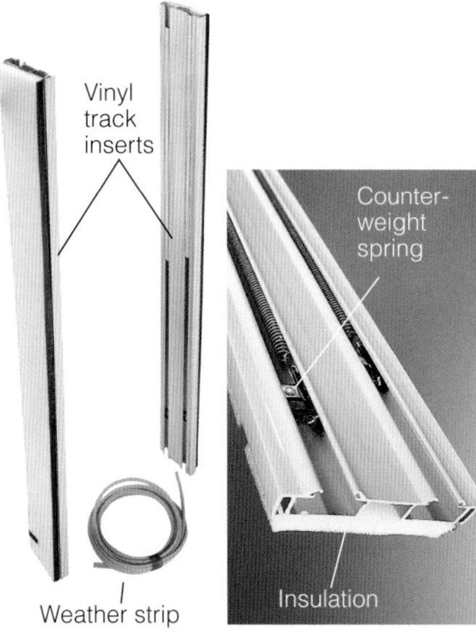

Counterweight springs do the same job as the old sash weights and cords, but more reliably. Improve the seal between the sashes by adding weather stripping to the sash rail.

Vinyl Replacement Windows

Visitors often praise older, double-hung windows for their authenticity, but if you live with their draftiness, sticky sashes and high maintenance, it's more difficult to say nice things about this original equipment. The simplest option to permanently solve these problems is to install vinyl replacement inserts. You won't have to remove any exterior trim or interior casing, and the inserts come as an assembled unit, complete with frame, tracks and sashes. The biggest drawback to these replacements is that, because the window will have two frames, you will lose some viewing area.

First, check your old window frames to make sure they're rot free and within 1/4 in. (6 mm) of level across the sill. Order the inserts 1/2 in. (12 mm) smaller (height and width) than the original frame opening of the sash tracks (not the stops). If the opening is not square, order the largest window that will fit in the non-square opening. To install the inserts, remove the old sashes, sash cord covers, inner stops and parting strips. Save the inner stops and cut the sash cords. Remove the weight-access hole covers and fill the entire area behind the jambs with insulation.

Using shims and a level that will fit inside the frame, establish a level base for the insert across the sill. Set the insert into the frame, pushing it against the outer stop. Insulate the gaps between the insert and the old frame. Caulk the exterior with sealant between the insert and outer stop. In cold climates, caulk the interior as well. Finally, reinstall the inner stops.

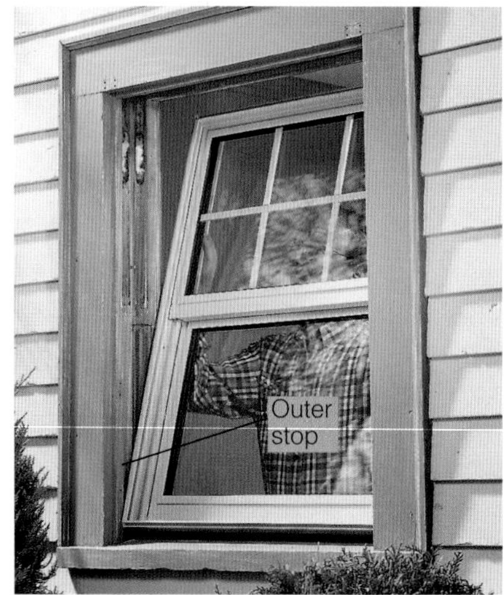

To install a vinyl replacement insert, remove the old sashes, sash cord covers, inner stops and parting strips. Install the insert against the original outer stops, level it, insulate the gaps and reinstall the inner stops.

Vinyl inserts provide an easy-to-install, draft-free window with insulated glass that operates smoothly.

Replacing Sashes and Tracks

Window sash kits let you replace just the sashes without removing the interior trim or tearing out the frame. The new sashes are custom-made to fit your existing frame opening, are airtight, come with insulated glass and allow you to do the entire job from inside. Accurate measurements are essential for a proper fit (see instructions at right).

As with one-piece inserts, sash kits' big advantage is ease of installation. The job can be completed from the inside in a few hours per window without disturbing your trim or wall covering. Unlike one-piece inserts, you don't have an extra frame that reduces your viewing area, and you can order wooden sashes with muntins or grilles to retain your home's traditional look.

Paint or stain the wooden sashes before installation. Also, follow the manufacturer's instructions; each brand has specific steps to follow to ensure that your sashes fit properly.

1 Check the frame for rot, and repair any rotted areas. Remove inner stop carefully with a putty knife or pry bar. Remove parting strip on jamb between sashes.

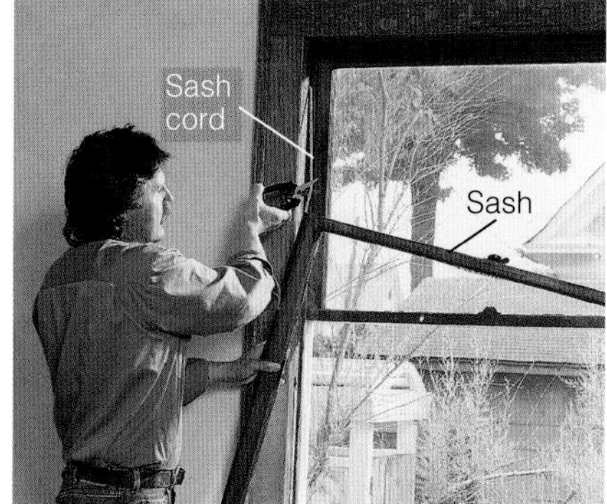

2 Detach the lower sash by angling it out of the opening. Cut sash cords and remove sash. Remove the upper sash and cut sash cords.

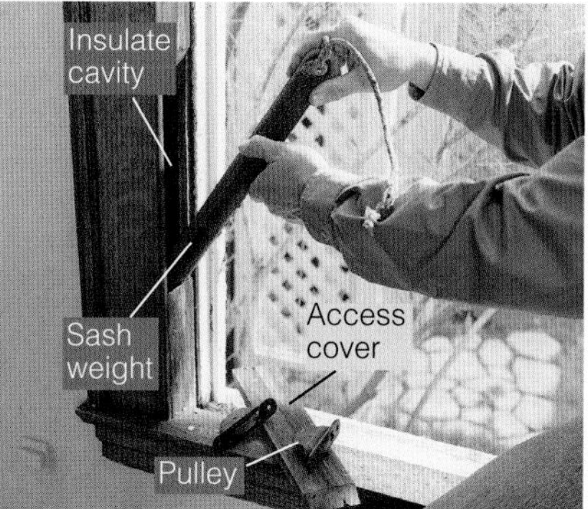

3 Remove access hole covers, weights, cords and the pulleys at the top of the jamb. Fill the entire area behind jamb with minimally expanding sprayed foam or blown-in insulation.

4 Install jamb liner bracket clips, following the manufacturer's instructions for the number of clips needed and required spacing.

5 Snap vinyl jamb liner in place over brackets. Jamb liner provides an airtight track for the new sashes.

6 Install new sashes, starting with the upper sash. Follow instructions for locking the lift mechanisms located in jamb liner. If new sashes tilt out, make sure they tilt properly.

Measuring Accurately for Replacements

Before you order new window sashes, take accurate measurements to ensure a good fit. Measure top to bottom on both sides, and side to side at the top, middle and bottom of the sash opening. Check the opening for square, as well.

You also need to know the angle, or bevel, of the windowsill. The bottom rail of the new lower sash and the bottom edge of the vinyl jamb liners must match the sill's angle. If they don't, the sash won't seal properly and the jamb liners won't fit. To measure this angle, use an angle finder, available at home centers and hardware stores.

Most replacement-window manufacturers can build whatever size sash you need, and some, but not all, can match the original pattern of lites (individual panes) in each sash.

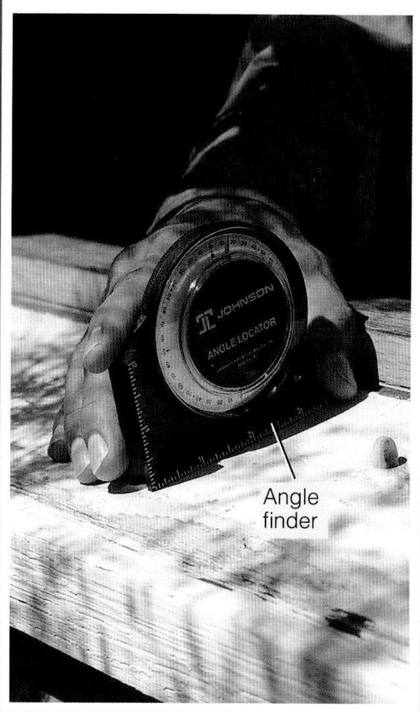

Windows / Repairing Casement

Hand Planes 38
Windows / Basics 360

Replacing an Operator

Casement and awning windows rely on little mechanisms called operators. When a window doesn't operate properly, first make sure it isn't painted shut. Next, remove the crank handle and cover. If the operator is in good shape, clean and lubricate it. If the inside gears are worn or damaged, replace the operator, as shown. See "Resources," p. 516, for information on ordering old, unusual or obsolete window parts.

1 Remove crank handle and gently pull off cover. If your cover is permanently bonded to the operator, go to the next step.

2 Pry up the stop that hides operator arms. Partially open window; then press down on operator arm so roller slips out of the exit notch on the sash track.

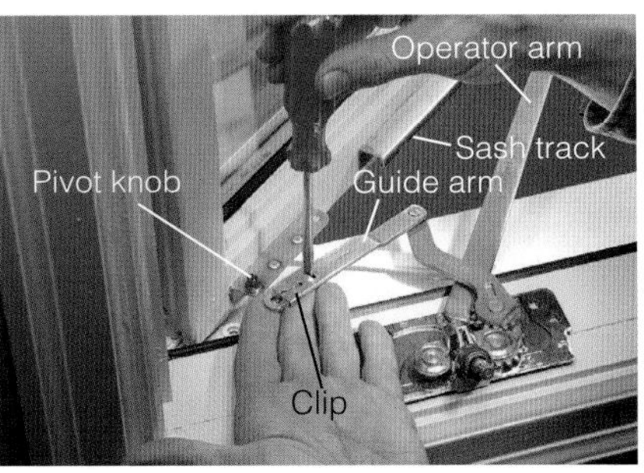

3 Slide guide arm clip off pivot knob. Remove screws, replace operator and reconnect it to window by reversing steps 1 and 2.

Replacing a Crank Handle

When a window crank handle wears out, replace the handle or install a more window-blind-friendly, low-profile T-handle. Before shopping for a replacement, check the window brand. Window manufacturers make unique operator shaft sizes that won't fit other companies' window handles. If you can't find the right handle, generic replacement kits have assorted shaft adapters that fit most window brands.

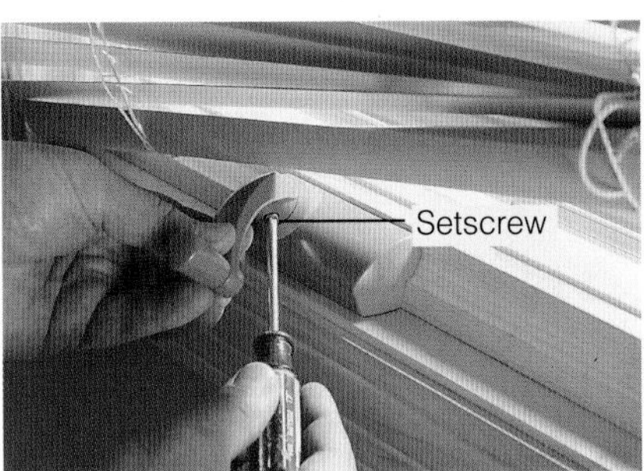

1 Remove the old handle by loosening setscrew with small straight-blade screwdriver.

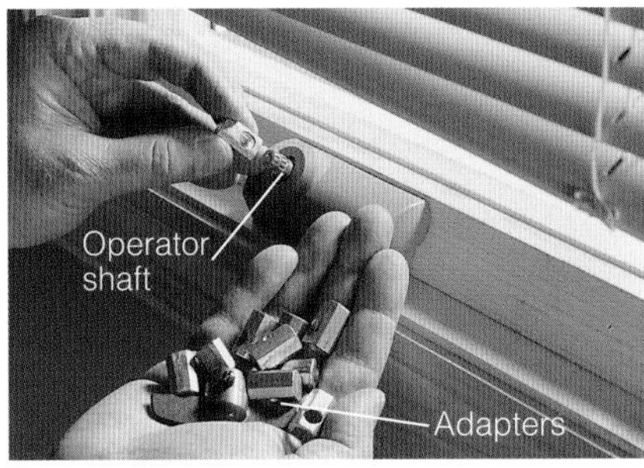

2 Select adapter that fits tightly over your window opener's shaft and slide it in place.

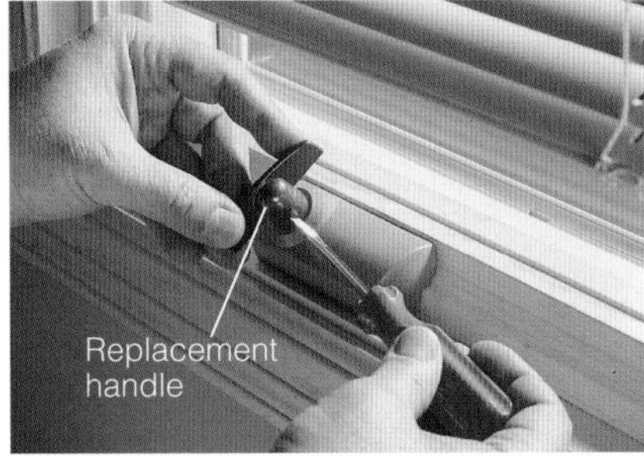

3 Install new handle and tighten setscrew. Note: T-handles are more difficult to operate than crank handles.

Freeing a Binding Sash

Casement window sashes bind or stick because of swelling from humidity, house settling or excessively packed insulation around the window. A little preventive maintenance—sealing or painting bare wood and lubricating moving parts—helps limit swelling and the chances of binding. For a stuck sash, first make sure the window isn't painted shut. To free up painted-shut windows, run a paint zipper (p. 361) between the sash and frame. For other binding problems, follow these steps, as shown.

1 Slip carbon paper between the sash and frame in several places as you open and close the window to determine where binding occurs. Binding points will show up as carbon marks on the sash's side.

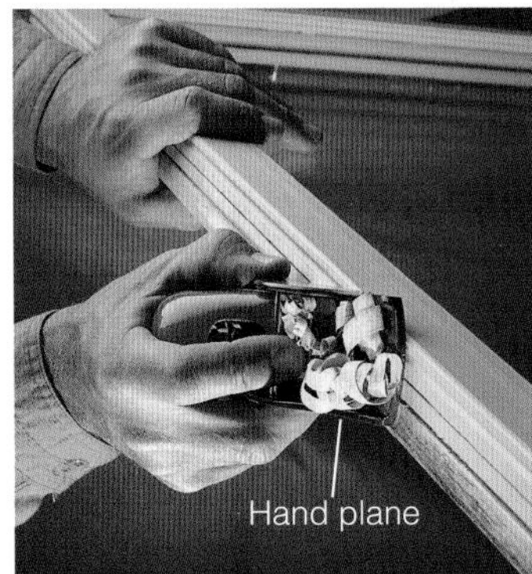

2 Level high spots that bind, using a hand plane or belt sander. Removing just a few shavings is enough to free most windows.

Windows / Repairing Gliding and Jalousie

Tuning-up or Replacing a Gliding Window Sash

A typical gliding window consists of sashes that move horizontally; in some cases one is stationary. The sash is guided by upper and lower tracks. Usually a groove in the sash's bottom rail fits over a ridge in the track. Some sashes may have additional nylon glides or rollers that ride on the ridge.

A glider's bottom track is a dust catcher. Keep it clean with regular vacuuming and an occasional scrubbing. For hardened dirt on metal or wood, use detergent and fine steel wool or an abrasive sponge. Lubricate the track and upper channel with spray silicone. Aluminum sashes can become spotted with oxidation deposits (similar to rust). These are easily removed by washing with a mild abrasive cleaner or with fine steel wool and detergent. A light coat of automobile paste wax will help prevent oxidation in the future.

To remove or replace a sash, unlock it and slide it to the window's center. Grasping the sides, push the sash straight up into the upper channel and swing the bottom out toward the interior. Then pull the sash down out of the upper channel.

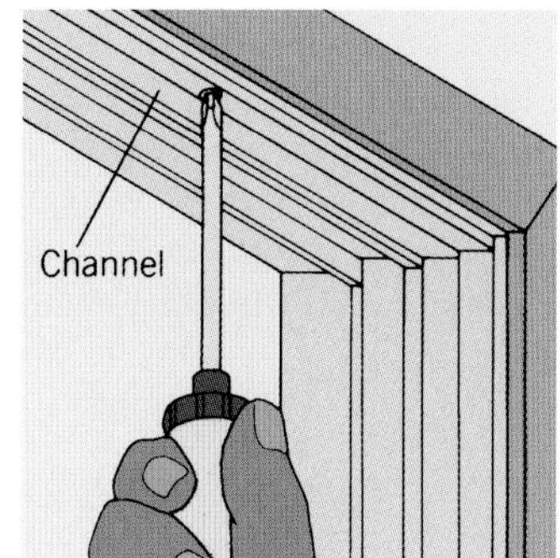

If the sash doesn't come out easily, tighten screws in the upper channel. Pulling up the upper channel should provide enough room to remove sash.

Remove a fixed sash by unscrewing corner brackets at its top and bottom. Unscrew the bumper from the track and slide the fixed sash to the center. Lift the sash up and tilt it toward the outdoors to remove it. To replace sashes, reverse these steps.

Repairing Jalousie Windows

While rarely used as the primary windows in a home, jalousie windows can be a good choice for an enclosed porch because they allow maximum ventilation. The windows are opened and closed by a system of pivots and levers driven by a crank handle. If the window becomes difficult to operate, lubricate the moving parts with a silicone spray. In a jalousie window, the side with the crank handle is the active side; the opposite side is the fixed side. If the pivot mechanism is damaged, you may need to replace the entire active side.

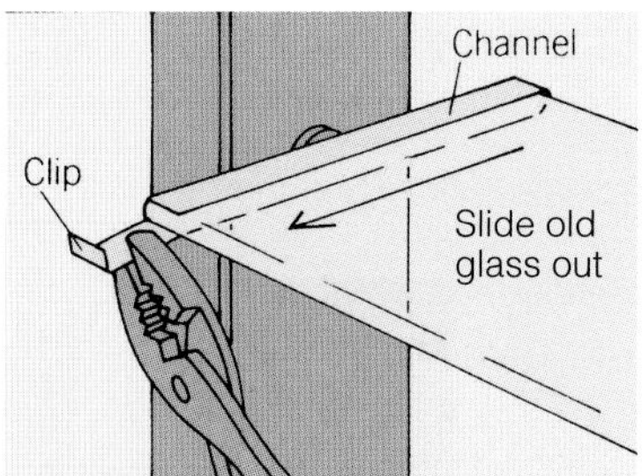

1 To replace a louver, open window until louvers are horizontal. With pliers, gently press back clips just enough to release glass.

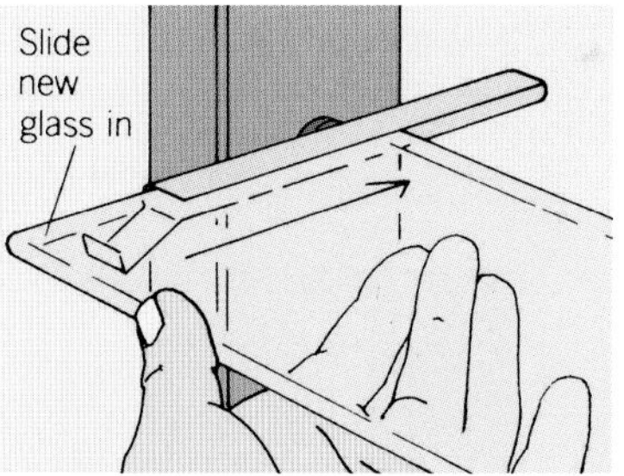

2 Slide new glass into channels. Bend clip ends into their original shape to hold glass firmly in place.

To replace a pivot mechanism, remove all louvers. Unscrew active side unit from jamb and install new unit. Use a level to align channels with those in the fixed side.

Windows / Repairing Wood Frames with Epoxy

Repairing a Rotted Sill

Epoxy is the perfect repair material for windowsills and door jambs that are difficult to remove and for moldings that would be expensive to duplicate. It bonds permanently and is formulated to flex and move with the wood. The repair shown here utilizes a liquid consolidant (usually sold alongside the epoxy) to stabilize the wood and a two-part puttylike epoxy to rebuild the missing sections. Both products are available at well-stocked hardware stores.

1 Probe rot-damaged areas to determine how far decay extends. Gouge or scrape away the large chunks of loose, spongy wood. Scrape paint away from other soft areas.

2 Drill 1/4 in. (6 mm) holes and soak repair area with consolidant. Drive screws to strengthen large repairs in corners. Rebuild one piece of wood at a time using epoxy filler.

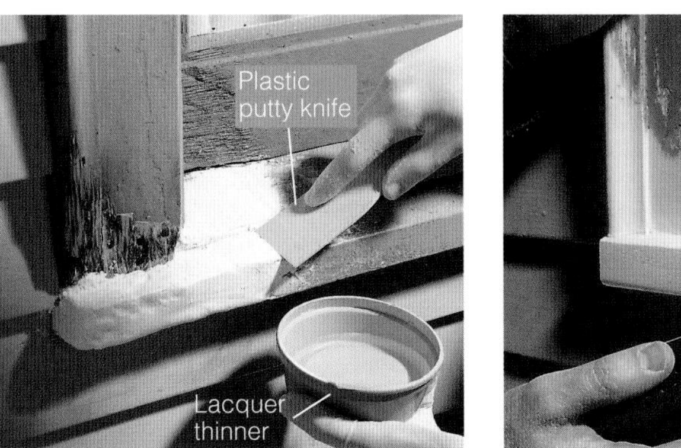

3 Before it hardens, smooth the filler with a putty knife that's soaked in lacquer thinner to prevent sticking. For best bond, apply filler when consolidant is tacky, not fully hardened.

4 Sand epoxy smooth using custom sanding block with 100-grit paper. Filler looks best primed and painted but can also be stained.

Repairing a Sash

Epoxy filler is even strong enough to rebuild the entire corner of a rotted sash. Remove the sash. Support it by attaching a diagonal brace that won't interfere with the repair area, and then build the form.

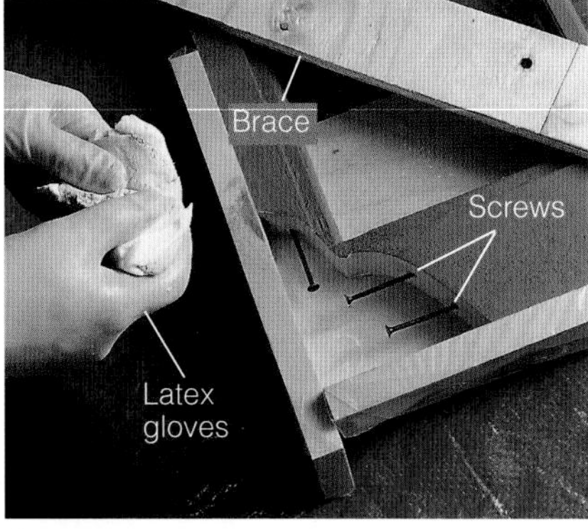

1 Cut away rotted section with a jigsaw and drive screws into rail and stile. Build form, wrap it in 4-mil plastic sheeting and screw form to sash.

2 Soak cut surfaces with consolidant. Pack filler into form, building it up in layers to eliminate voids. Shape repair using a putty knife dipped in lacquer thinner.

Making a Custom Shaping Block

Help rebuilt moldings blend in by smoothing the repair with a shaping block made from auto body filler. Begin by coating a section of undamaged molding with a release agent, such as car wax or cooking spray.

1 Mix auto body filler. With a putty knife, smear it thickly over surface of solid section of molding and edges. Coat all surfaces with release agent beforehand.

2 After 10 minutes, pop off hardened filler with putty knife. Square ends of shaping block. Use solvent to wipe away remaining release agent on molding.

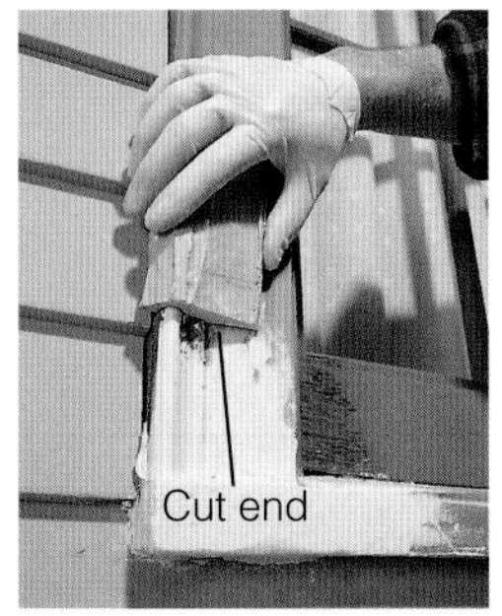

3 Overfill repair area with epoxy. Wet shaping block with lacquer thinner and work it over epoxy until it matches existing profile. After epoxy cures, sand repair smooth.

Windows / Replacing Glass

Single Pane

You can leave a sash in place or remove it to replace a single pane of glass. Order glass 1/8 in. (3 mm) smaller than the opening. Explore the option of installing thicker double-strength instead of single-strength glass.

1 Remove broken glass by scraping away old glazing. Soften difficult compound using a heat gun. Be careful not to cut into the wood while working. Under the old compound, you'll find tiny metal tabs, called glazing points. Remove these with a pliers.

2 Line the sash opening with a thin bead of glazing compound and firmly press new glass into place. Secure glass by placing glazing points every 4 in. (10 cm) around perimeter. Use points with ears and press into place with putty knife.

3 Apply compound around edges of glass and smooth using a flexible putty knife. Wet the knife occasionally so it doesn't stick to the compound. Let putty cure for at least a week before painting.

Double-pane Windows

Insulated glass can get broken or lose the seal between the panes and permanently fog. Start by taking the entire sash to a shop that repairs windows. They'll measure the size and thickness of the insulating unit, help you identify the manufacturer, determine whether a window is still under warranty and discuss energy-efficient replacement options. Manufacturers use one of the three methods for installing the sealed units. Savvy do-it-yourselfers can repair the units themselves. Sometimes it's easier and cheaper to replace the entire sash.

Gasket method. With sash removed, take out screws that hold horizontal rails and vertical stiles together. Tap frame loose from gasket and glass with wooden block and hammer. Remove old gasket from faulty pane and install it on a new glass double-pane unit. Push two frame pieces together around the gasket and fasten the frame back together. Seal any gaps in corners using clear silicone.

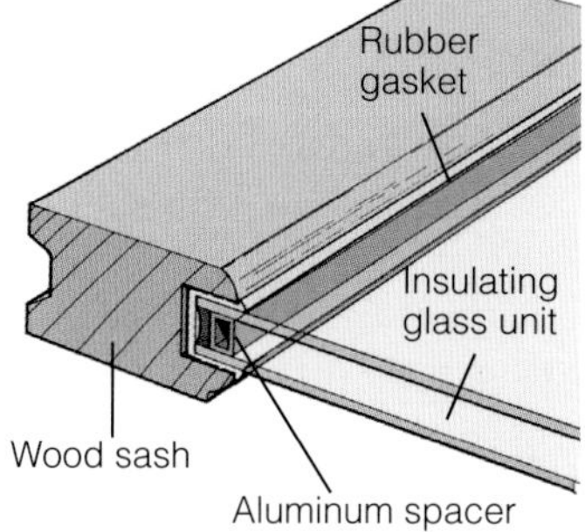

Adhesive tape method. Pry out stops using a putty knife. Flip window over and slice through tape bond with a utility knife blade. Scrape old tape and clean lip with adhesive solvent. Lay new sealing tape in place. Position spacing blocks against one side of frame, position glass against blocks and carefully drop it in place. Replace stops and seal gaps with clear silicone.

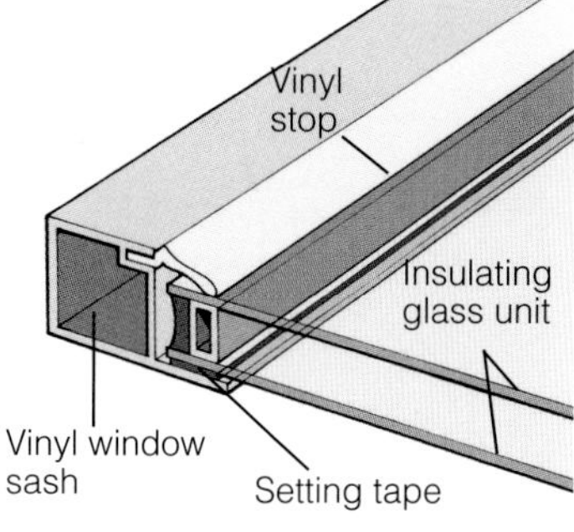

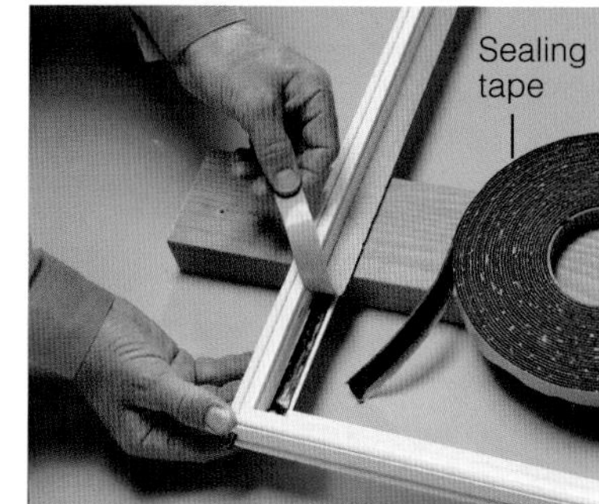

Caulk method. Carefully pry off wood stops. Flip window over and cut caulk with a utility knife. If necessary, break window after covering it with carpet. Soften adhesive using a heat gun, and then scrape and clean edges. Position spacing blocks, apply bead of neutral-cure silicone to frame and drop in new glass unit. Apply silicone to glass's stop side and reinstall stops.

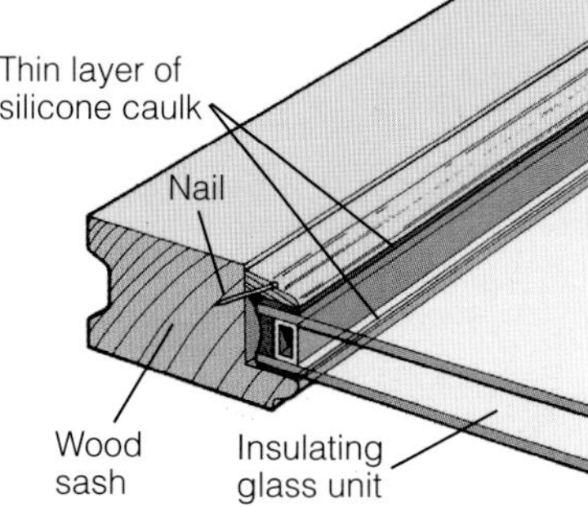

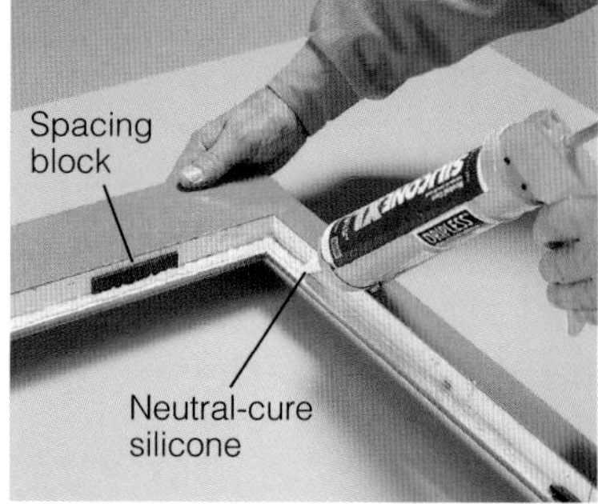

Windows / Increasing Efficiency

Insulation and Air Leaks **165**
Windows / Basics **360**

Tubular Gasket Weather Stripping

Tubular gaskets are made of vinyl or rubber and are durable and effective even when the gaps around windows or doors are uneven. Applied from the outside, gaskets remain pliable in subzero temperatures. When applied to the window's outside sash frames, they can make double-hung and gliding windows more airtight. Although they offer a tighter seal than metal strips, gaskets are very visible.

Spring Metal Weather Stripping

Made of bronze, stainless steel, vinyl or aluminum, these long-lasting strips fit unobtrusively in window or door channels and use pressure to create a seal. However, they may make doors or windows hard to open.

Wood casement windows can be inconspicuously sealed with strips applied to the sash channels with the nailing flange facing outward. In a double-hung window, the metal strips can seal the sash sides while tubular gaskets seal the horizontal joints.

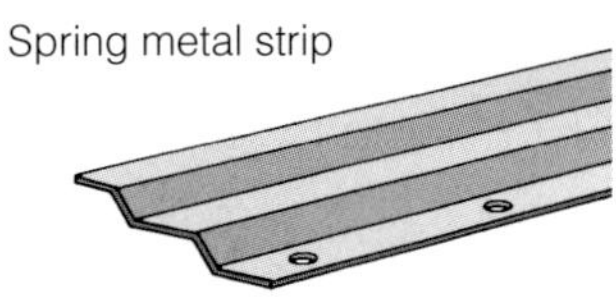

Window Tint Films

If your windows let in too much heat in the summer and too much cold in the winter, a simple, affordable option to improve their efficiency is to apply low-E or tinting film. Low-E films offer these major benefits:

- Like reflective and nonreflective films, low-E films virtually eliminate the ultraviolet ray penetration, helping reduce fading problems, while doing little to affect window visibility.
- They reduce heat gain from the outside in the summer.
- During the winter, they reduce heat loss by 60 percent.
- Glare is reduced by filtering 50 to 60 percent of the incoming light.
- In the case of a broken window, the film helps hold the pieces of glass together.

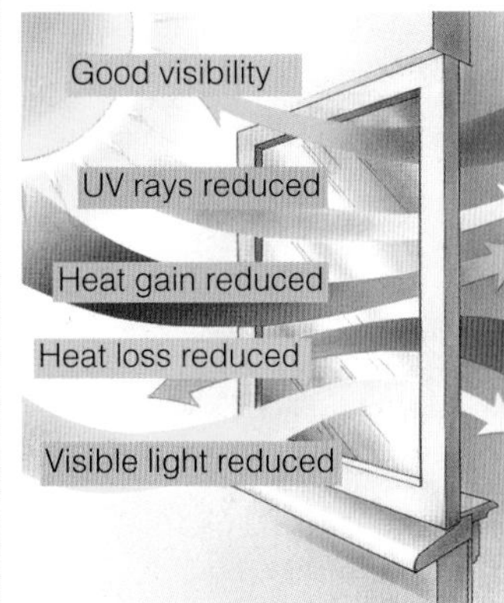

Low-E films reflect both outside summer heat and inside winter heat and offer fade protection.

1 Clean windows thoroughly. Spray window with wetting solution following manufacturer's directions.

2 Position film on dampened window, making sure it overlaps sash on all sides.

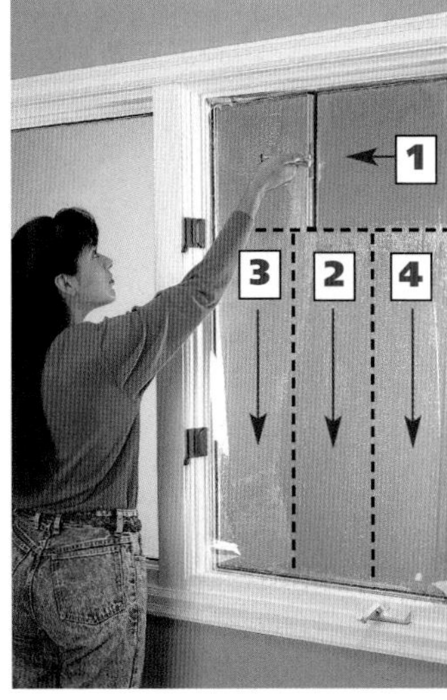

3 Spray film surface with wetting solution. Make a single squeegee pass across the top, then use vertical passes down.

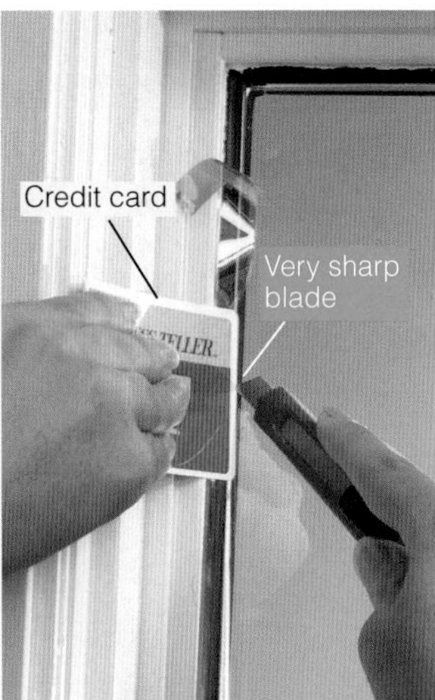

4 Trim excess film using a credit card shield and very sharp utility knife. After trimming, wet and squeegee a second time.

Windows / Buying

Window Choices

Buying windows isn't easy. Dozens of options concerning construction, efficiency, durability, type, size and style make window shopping a sizable research project. The charts at right will help you with some of these decisions.

The basic construction of most premium windows is usually wood, with surfaces exposed to the elements clad in metal, or a foam-insulation core clad in vinyl. The double-pane unit has two layers of glass with a space between the layers filled with an insulating, inert gas. Inside, the glass layers are often coated with a low-E film to reflect heat.

U-value, or ER ratings in Canada, indicates the rate of heat loss of a window assembly. The U-factor ratings generally fall between 0.20 and 1.20; the lower the U-value, the greater a window's resistance to heat flow, and the better the insulating value.

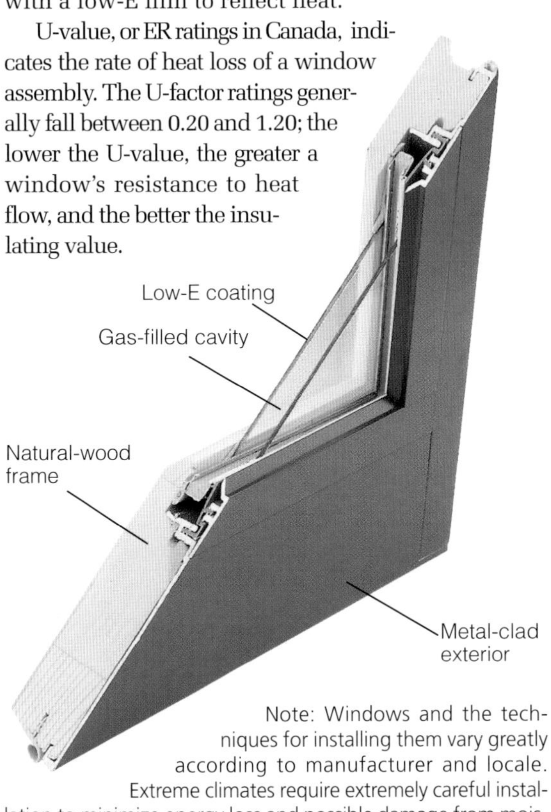

Note: Windows and the techniques for installing them vary greatly according to manufacturer and locale. Extreme climates require extremely careful installation to minimize energy loss and possible damage from moisture. Always install windows based on information from the manufacturer and local building codes.

Frame Options

All window framing materials have their pros and cons. Wood provides a warm look and is very repairable; however, it's prone to rot and insect damage and expands and contracts with humidity changes. Vinyl is low maintenance and a good insulator, but it expands and contracts with temperature changes and becomes brittle in extreme cold and with prolonged sun exposure. The best windows combine materials to utilize the best qualities of each.

Frame Material	Energy Efficiency	Longevity	Maintenance	Cost
All wood	good	good	high	medium
Vinyl or aluminum clad	excellent	excellent	low	high
All aluminum	poor	good	low	low
Thermal break aluminum	good	good	low	low
All vinyl or fiberglass	excellent	good	low	low (vinyl) high (fiberglass)
Insulation-filled vinyl	excellent	good	low	medium

Glazing Options

Single, double and triple glazing refers to the number of layers of glass in a sash. Double- and triple-glazed windows may have low-E film with air or a dense gas (argon or krypton) between the layers to inhibit heat flow. These inert gases slow the exchange of heat or cold between the panes. R-value is a measure of the material's resistance to heat flow; the higher, the better.

Glass Type	R-Value	Pros	Cons
Single layer	0.7	lightweight, easy to repair	poor insulator, poor security
Double layer	2.0	readily available, affordable, medium weight	fair insulator, seals can break
Triple layer	3.0 to 3.5	good insulator, good security	very heavy, expensive, not readily available
Double layer, low-E	2.0 to 4.0	reflects outside heat and inside heat	reduces light, seals can break
Double layer, gas-filled	2.0 to 4.0	excellent insulator, good cost-to-benefit ratio	seals can break, causing fogging
Double layer, low-E gas-filled	2.5 to 4.5	reflects inside and outside heat, excellent insulator	reduces light, seals can break

Windows / Installing

Level and Plumb 44
Reciprocating Saws 59
Ladder Safety 311

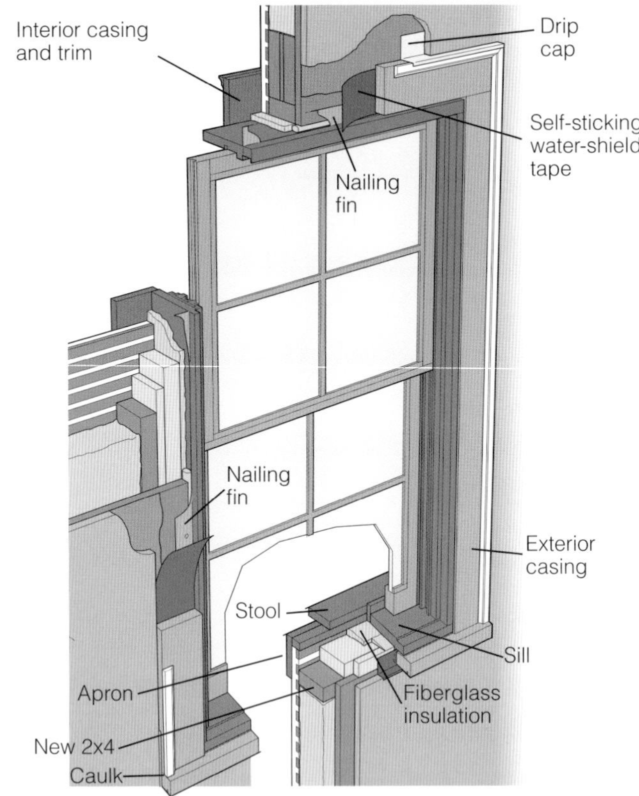

Replacing a window isn't as difficult as you might think. In some ways, the biggest challenge is to order the correct size, and to do that, you need to know the size of your rough opening and the thickness of your exterior walls. The rough opening refers to the width and height of the wall opening after the entire window is removed. As a rule, the rough opening should be 3/4 in. (19 mm) wider and taller than the new window.

Most new windows are held in place by exterior nailing fins, but don't rely on the nailing fins to keep out water. Instead, use a combination of self-sticking water-shield tape, drip caps and polyurethane caulk. Insulate the gaps between window and opening with fiberglass or minimally expanding foam, taking care not to bow the window jamb. Apply primer to all sides and cut ends of exterior trim before you install the trim.

1 Measure the opening's width and height. Measure jamb depth based on wall thickness, plus drywall and sheathing, but not siding material.

2 Tear out old window. Pry off exterior trim. If window frame is nailed to wall frame, cut nails using a reciprocating saw.

3 Nail wood blocking to bottom and sides, if necessary, to adjust rough opening's size. Channels left from sash weights need to be filled.

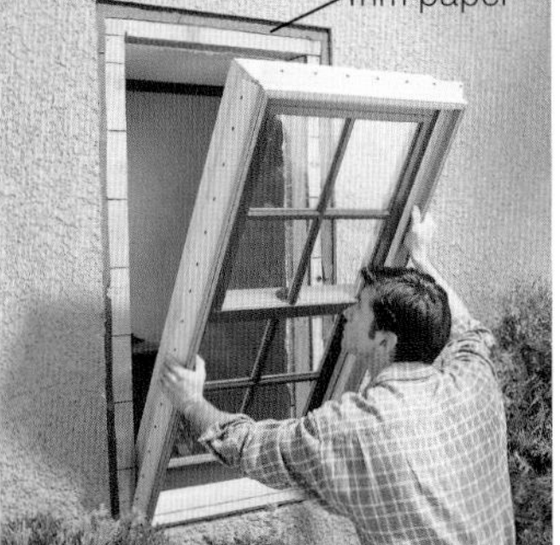

4 Set new window in opening. Caulk behind nailing fins. Trim building paper to improve seal. Center the window in the opening.

5 Level the window with pairs of shims and check with a level. Have a helper hold the window while you complete this step.

6 Secure nailing fins in lower corners, double-check windowsill is level and centered. Measure window diagonally to check square.

7 Use a level to check side jambs are plumb and finish nailing fins. Use a straightedge and pairs of shims to straighten bowed side jambs.

8 Apply self-sticking water shield. Slide drip cap behind siding at top. Attach exterior trim and seal joints between trim, siding and window.

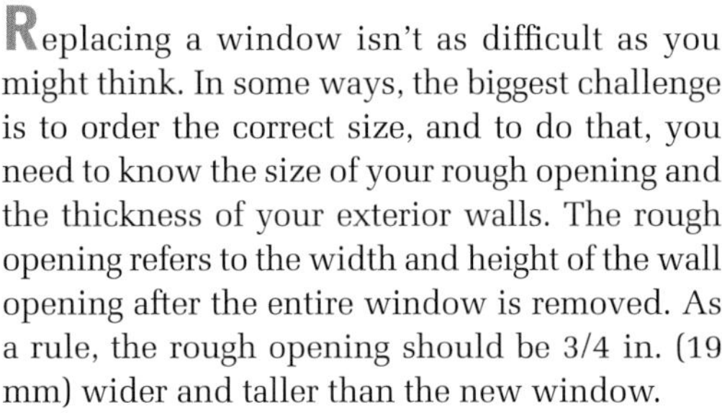

Windows / Screens and Storms

Repairing Screens

Stop pesky insects from invading your home by replacing torn screens. It's a simple and inexpensive project that requires only a few simple, inexpensive tools. For interior spaces that tend to overheat, consider using sun-shading material for the replacement screen. If the old moldings on wood frame screens are rotted, missing or split, replace them. Prime and paint the replacement moldings before installation and, if necessary, paint and patch wood screen frames while the screening is off.

Aluminum Frame

1 Dig out the old spline with a nail set or awl. Remove old screen. Use either fiberglass or metal replacement screening. Metal screening is stronger, but it can dent and is harder to manage.

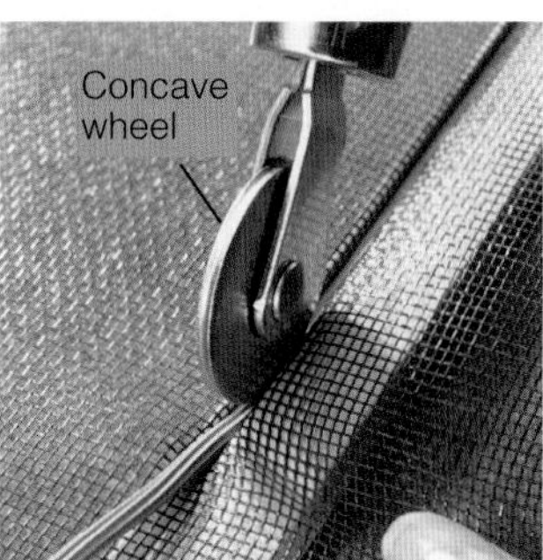

2 Align the new screen grid to the frame's side so it goes in square. Beginning at one corner, seat the new spline in a channel on one side with the concave wheel of a screening tool.

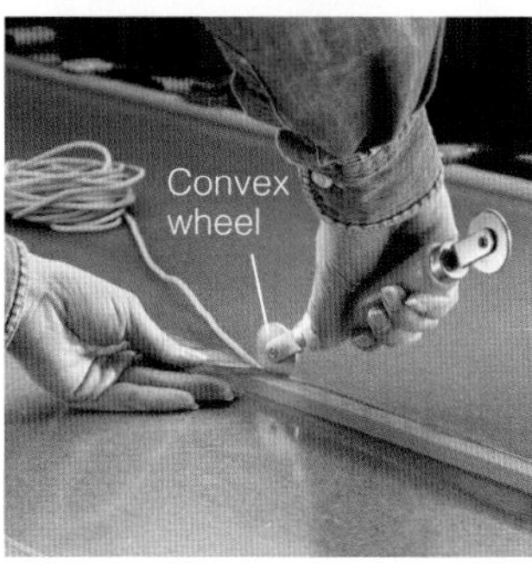

3 Clamp side of finished frame to work surface. Pull screen tight on opposite side and insert spline down that side. Complete two other sides the same way. Re-press entire spline with screening tool's convex wheel.

Wood Frame

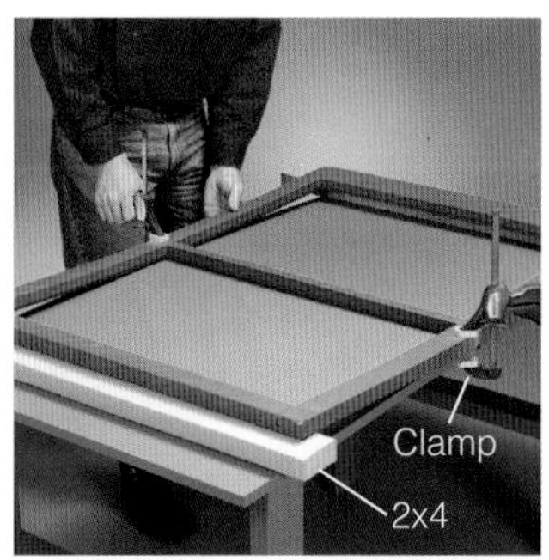

1 Remove screen molding after cutting paint bond between molding and screen frame. Pull staples or nails and remove old screening. Gently bow screen frame by propping up both ends on 2x4 blocks, then gradually apply pressure with clamps in middle of frame.

2 Staple new screen to top and bottom frame rails. Cut screen so it extends 1 in. (2.5 cm) on all sides beyond the molding. Remove clamps so frame straightens and pulls screen taut; staple the two remaining sides.

3 Nail the moldings back in place with small finish nails or brads every 6 in. (15 cm). Cut away excess screening with utility knife using the molding edge as a guide.

Installing Combination Storm Windows

Combination storm windows offer many benefits. They improve a window's thermal efficiency, improve security by adding a layer of protection, help protect primary windows against rain and hail, and act as a screen to allow ventilation. Some standard-size units are available at home centers; others must be special ordered.

1 Measure existing window at inside edges of brick molding and order windows. Predrill holes along outer edges of storm window frame 2 in. (5 cm) from each corner and every 12 in. (30 cm) between.

2 Test-fit the storm window. Use a belt sander to trim its lip, if necessary. Don't twist the window out of square to make it fit or it won't operate properly. Now apply a bead of silicone along the openings' top and sides but not the bottom.

3 Position storm windows in openings. Lift window as high as possible, then lower expansion seal at bottom. Attach window with screws. Make sure moisture can pass freely through weep holes at bottom.

Windows / Increasing Security

Installing Exterior Doors 379
Installing Interior Doors 382

A window is the second choice of entry for a burglar—first choice if it's unlocked. A burglar usually won't risk the noise of breaking glass to release a lock, especially when two or three layers of glass are present. Window style makes a difference as well. A casement window is difficult to open from the outside, but a double-hung window, even one that's latched, can be fairly easy to open. The following techniques will help make your windows more secure against intruders.

Burglar bars. For maximum window security, and if local fire codes permit, mount steel burglar bars to the wall framing on the inside of the window. The bars latch into a mounting bracket but can swing out of the way for an emergency exit.

Locks for Double-hung Windows

To deter or delay intruders, install additional locking devices on your double-hung windows. Don't rely solely on the clamshell, or butterfly, latch often found on double-hung windows. These latches are not really locks, but are meant to draw the sashes together to reduce drafts and rattling.

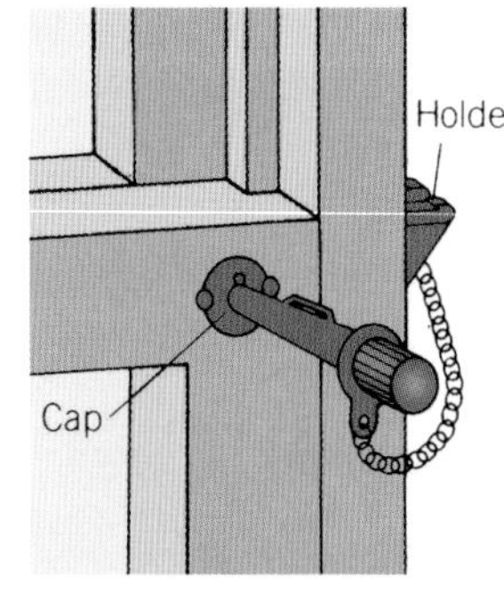

Locking pin. Improvise a lock by drilling a hole through the interior sash and partway into exterior sash. Then insert a bolt, dowel or locking pin. Drill the hole slightly larger than the pinning device for easy removal. Install one pin on each side of sash. Manufactured locking pins have a more finished look and a holder for the pin when it's not in use.

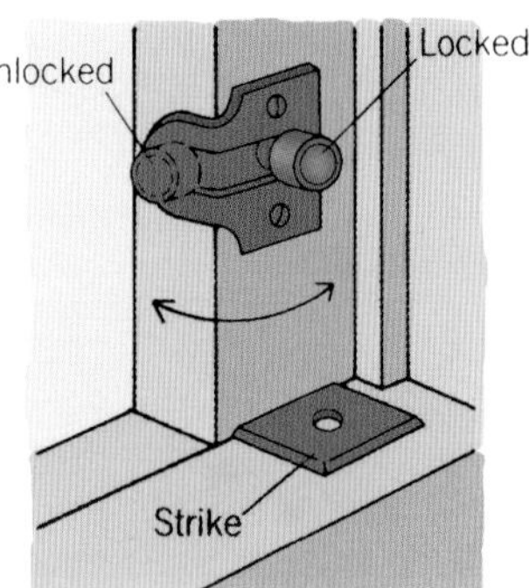

Ventilating lock. These locks remain engaged but also allow the window to be opened slightly for ventilation. Screw lock to stile of upper sash a short distance above the rail. Screw strike plate to top rail of lower sash. Attach one lock to each side of sash. Move lock to inside position for full window operation.

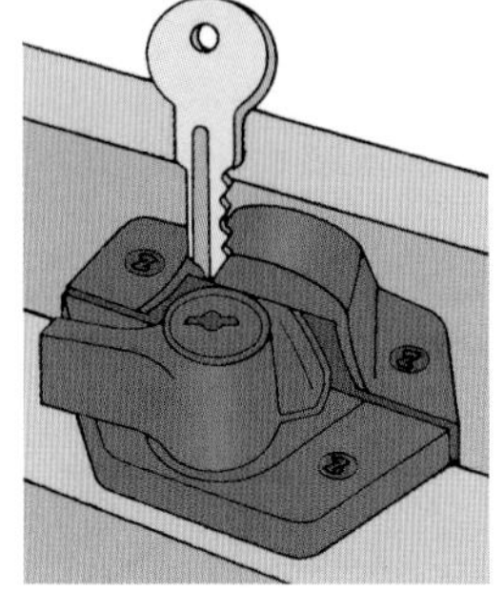

Key turnbuckle. Remove clamshell latch. Mount new lock with one-way screws. If possible, get matched keyed locks from a single manufacturer so one key fits all locks. For emergencies, keep a key near each window, hidden from outside view, and another set for backup.

Locks for Gliding Windows

Gliding windows, like double-hung windows, have sliding sashes, making them easier to jimmy open without breaking the glass. The key to improving sliding windows' security is to prevent the sliding sash from sliding or being lifted out.

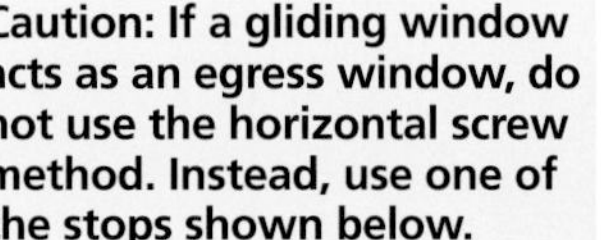

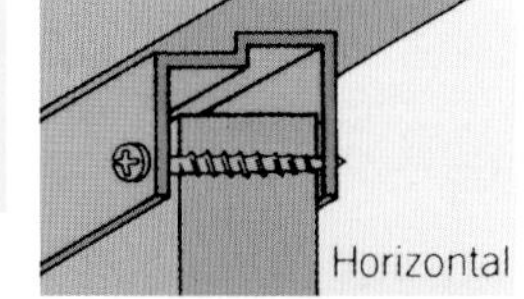

Screw stop. A screw installed vertically in the top channel prevents a sash from being lifted out (top). A horizontal screw (bottom) keeps sash from sliding.

Caution: If a gliding window acts as an egress window, do not use the horizontal screw method. Instead, use one of the stops shown below.

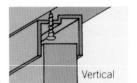

Key track stop. A small slot in this stop fits over the window track. A key anchors the lock in position. If possible, get matched keyed locks from a single manufacturer so one key fits all locks. For emergencies, keep a key near each window, hidden from outside view.

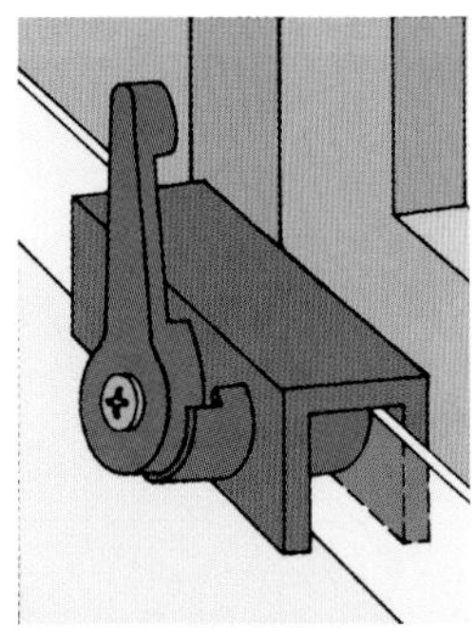

Track stop. Use a track stop to stop a sliding sash from sliding. Slip track stop over window track and turn handle clockwise to tighten bolt.

Doors / Types and Swings

When doors swing freely, latch easily and firmly, have an even gap around the edges of the slab and close with a solid "thunk" instead of a rattle, the impression given is that of a solidly constructed home in good condition.

Doors come in standard widths of 24, 28, 30, 32 and 36 in. and are referred to in a "feet and inches" format (for instance, a 30-in. door is labeled 2' 6"). The measurement refers to the slab or door only, not the frame. Nonstandard sizes can be ordered. For easiest installation, buy a pre-hung door—already hinged in its jamb. Pay particular attention to the door swing (see below) and jamb depth. The pre-hung door's jamb should be as wide as the wall is thick when you add up wall framing, drywall and/or sheathing thicknesses. Also, for exterior use, have the door bored for the lockset and the deadbolt.

Left-hand door

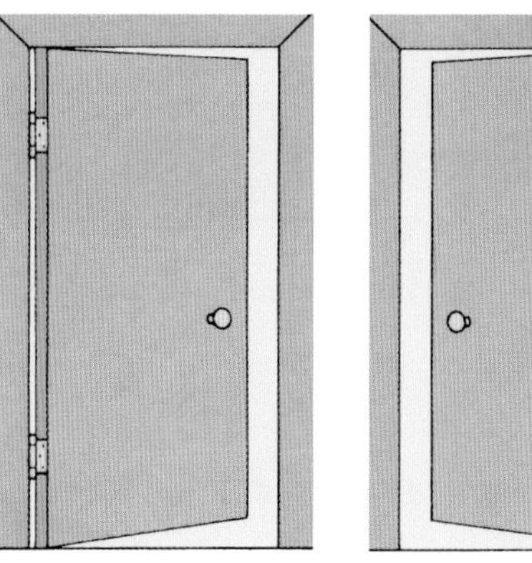

Right-hand door

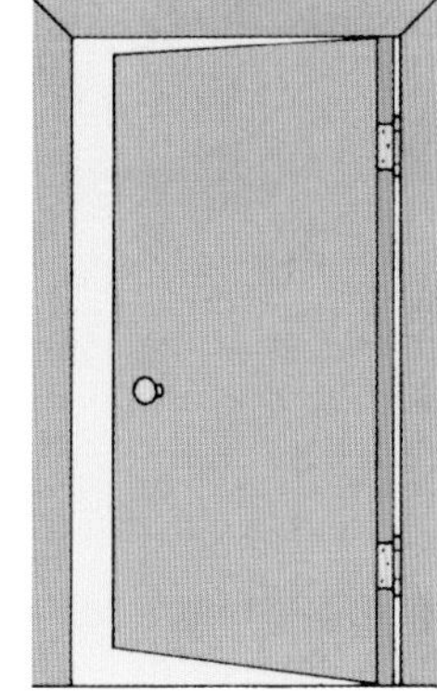

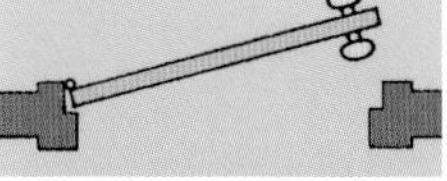

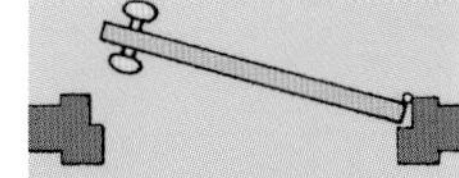

Determining swing. Stand with your back against the door jamb containing the hinges. If the door swings the same way your left arm does as it swings outward, it's considered a left-hand door. If it swings to the right, it's a right-hand door.

Door Composition

Doors come in three basic types—solid wood, solid core or hollow core—all of which may be bought pre-hung. The solid core may be wood, steel or insulating foam. The core of a hollow-core door is usually cardboard. Hollow-core interior doors are lighter and less expensive than solid-core doors but also less durable and less fire resistant.

Exterior doors must be solid wood or solid core. For the most part, wood exterior doors have been replaced by steel and fiberglass to eliminate the main weakness of wood—its vulnerability to the weather. However, steel doors aren't perfect. They can warp from excessive heat, especially if they're painted a dark color and covered by a storm door.

To make them more attractive, manufacturers mold steel or fiberglass skins to mimic traditional wood doors. Some fiberglass skins even have wood-grain patterns that can be stained to look like real wood.

Wood-panel doors consist of rails, stiles and panels assembled in one operation. Gaps between the panels and the stiles and rails allow the panels to expand and contract with humidity changes, reducing the chances of a door binding or cracking due to swelling.

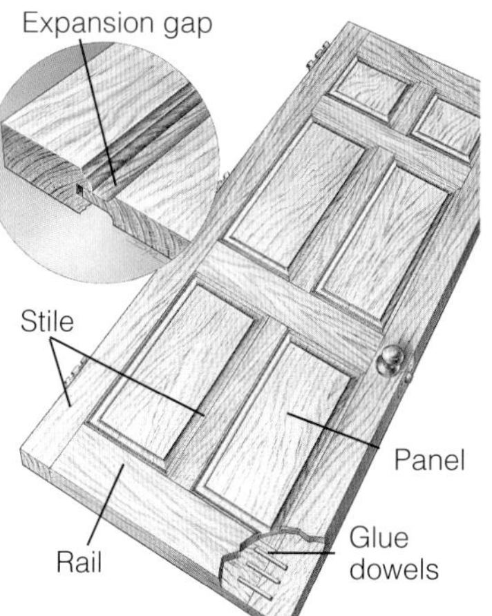

Solid-core flush doors have wood cores sandwiched and glued between two plywood, or sometimes hardboard, skins. The cores may be made from particleboard or short blocks of wood glued together. Solid core doors are easy to shorten, and the door slabs are usually supported by three hinges.

Hollow-core doors are built around a cardboard-lattice core. Wood blocks support the knobs and latch. A hollow-core door is light yet stable, making it easy to install and perfectly suited for interior use. It's not a good choice for an exterior door. The solid framework around the edges is fairly narrow, limiting how far you can cut the door down to fit smaller openings. Hollow-core doors often have two hinges.

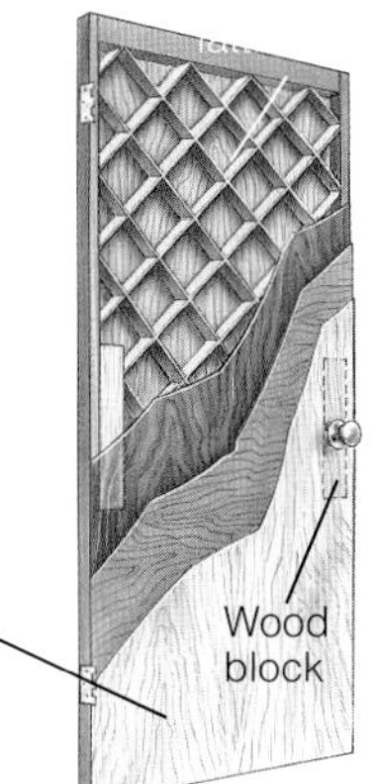

Steel and fiberglass skins make exterior doors more durable and maintenance-free than wood doors. A rigid insulation core provides superior insulation over wood. The thermal break keeps the inside steel skin from developing a film of condensation or frost.

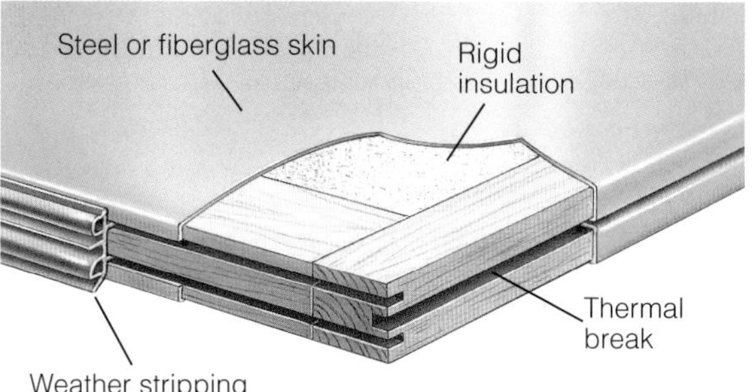

Doors / Warmer

Hacksaws 27
Marking and Scribing 42
Insulation and Air Leaks 165

Installing Flange-type Weather Stripping

For drafty exterior doors, quality weather stripping offers a quick, affordable, long-lasting solution to eliminate drafts and increase comfort. Weather stripping kits are readily available and include two side strips, a top strip and fasteners. The foam type shown below is easy to install, provides an effective seal and retains its flexibility for a long life. The key to positioning the new weather stripping is to shove it against the door so it compresses slightly along the strip's entire length. But if you compress it too much, the door won't latch when you close it.

1 Cut the foam part of the weather stripping with sharp scissors; then cut the wood flange with a fine-tooth saw. Cut side pieces to fit profile of top piece.

2 Position the weather stripping so the entire length seals to door. Tack it in place. Test the door to make sure foam seals but doesn't interfere with the door's operation.

Which Weather Stripping?

Shop Smart

Finding new weather stripping to match the exact profile of the old can be difficult; however, the common types shown here work well for most exterior doors. The wrapped foam type, whether combined with wood (A) or metal (B), is durable, retains its shape, withstands abrasions and conforms to a wide range of gaps. The metal flange (B) with screw slots is more adjustable than the wood flange (A).

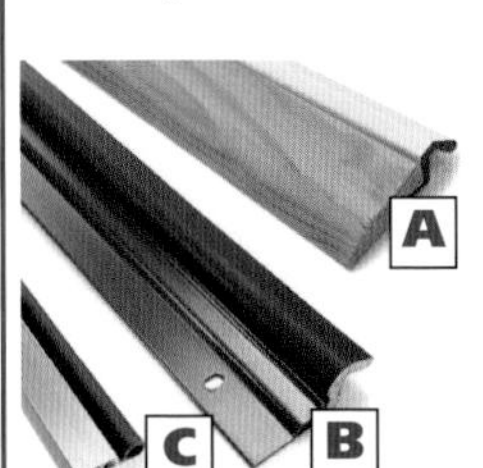

The vinyl or silicone bulb (C) won't cover gaps as well as wrapped foam, but it has a smaller profile with a cleaner look. For steel doors, look for a magnetic-seal replacement kit (see p. 375).

Replacing Threshold Gaskets

To get the right threshold gasket, remove your old gasket and take it to the hardware store with you. The gasket has two splines that fit into the grooves cut into the wood threshold. Cut the new gasket to the right length using a utility knife.

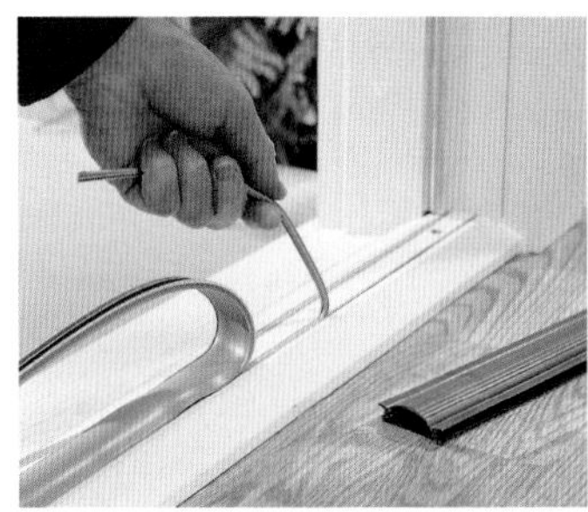

1 Remove old gasket. Splines will likely tear off and stay behind. Pry splines out with a narrow screwdriver or chisel. Clean out grooves.

2 Press new splines into grooves using your finger. Bear down with block of wood to finish the job.

Installing Door Sweeps

You may need a door sweep if you see daylight or feel a draft coming under the shut door. An adjustable face-mount sweep with a flexible flap is easy to install. To cut the sweep to length, cut the flap with a utility knife; then cut the flange with a hacksaw.

1 Position sweep with vinyl flap lightly touching threshold. Mark screw positions and drill pilot holes.

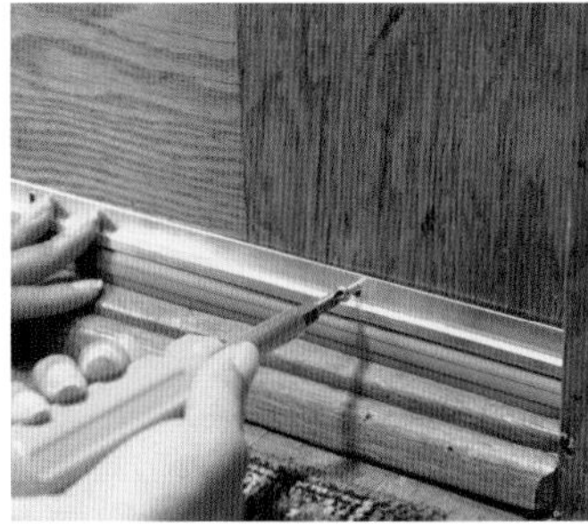

2 Push sweep down against threshold and drive screws. Open and close door to test seal.

Threshold Choices

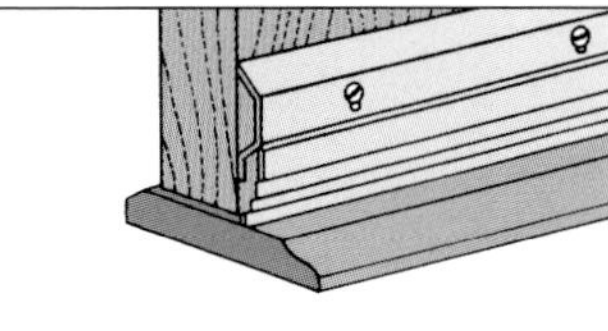

Door sweep has a rigid flange screwed to the door bottom and a flexible flap that seals against the threshold. If floor surface is even with or close in height to the threshold, don't use a sweep.

Door shoe is a U-shaped metal frame with a vinyl gasket under it that slides onto the door bottom. The gasket seals the threshold. Door may need trimming to fit.

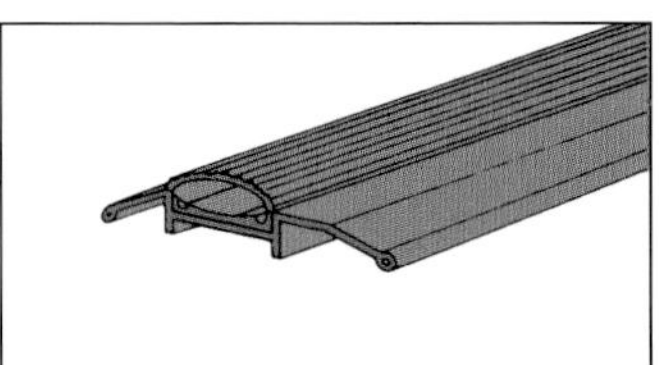

Threshold gasket is a vinyl gasket inserted into channels in a threshold's center. To seal, vinyl presses against the door's bottom when closed.

Doors / Upgrading Exterior

Replacing Compression-type Weather Stripping

Most modern entry doors use a compression weather stripping held in a slot in the stop portion of the doorjamb. This jamb weather stripping can be a simple compression strip or a magnetic strip for the strike side of a steel door. Look at the door and note the style of weather stripping on all three sides before going to the hardware store to pick up replacement seals.

The old weather stripping will usually be tacked into place with small brads so the door doesn't pull the magnetic strip out when it opens. Don't remove the old brads; you'll risk damaging the jamb while trying to remove them or driving them through. Instead, push them back or cut them off, as shown in step 3.

1 Remove the door slab only if replacing the bottom-mount door sweep. To remove door, tap out hinge pins with nail set or 3-1/2-in. nail. Work from bottom to top.

2 Unzip old damaged weather stripping, pulling it through brads that hold it in.

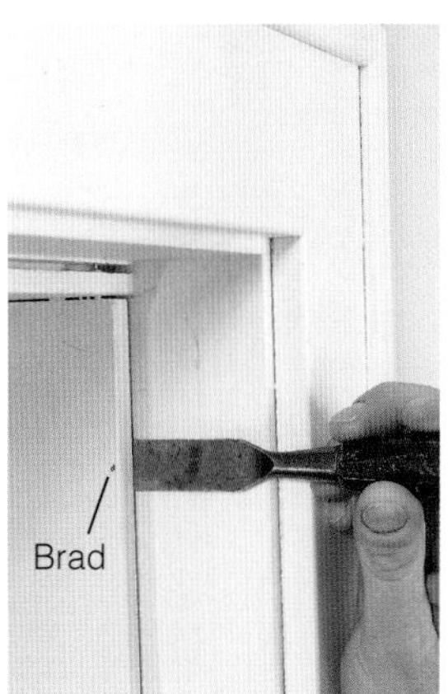

3 Cut off brads with an old chisel or push them all the way back into the groove using a screwdriver.

4 Cut new weather stripping to length. Install weather stripping and pin it with new brads positioned near old ones. Hold brads with needle-nose pliers to make starting them easier.

Self-closing Devices

In most areas, an entry door to an attached garage must be fire-rated and have a self-closing device—either self-closing hinges or a door closer.

Door closers work well for doors that have hard-to-match hinges or trim that will interfere with the larger barrel of a self-closing hinge. Drilling templates and installation instructions come with the closer.

Self-closing hinges look much like ordinary hinges except they have a bigger barrel to house the internal spring that makes them self-closing. Most doors require one or two of these to close properly. To find the right size, take the original middle hinge to the hardware store and find self-closing hinges with screw plates the same size. Switch hinges one at a time so you won't have to remove the door.

Adjust the self-closing device so the door closes and latches on its own from a wide-open position.

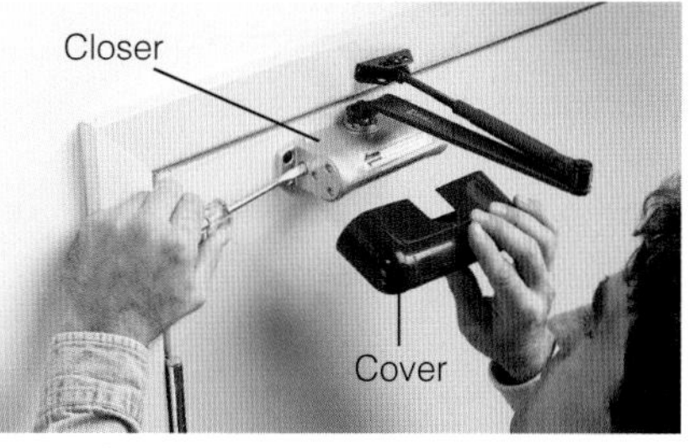

Door closer. Adjust tension on a door closer using the adjusting screw found on the barrel of the closer.

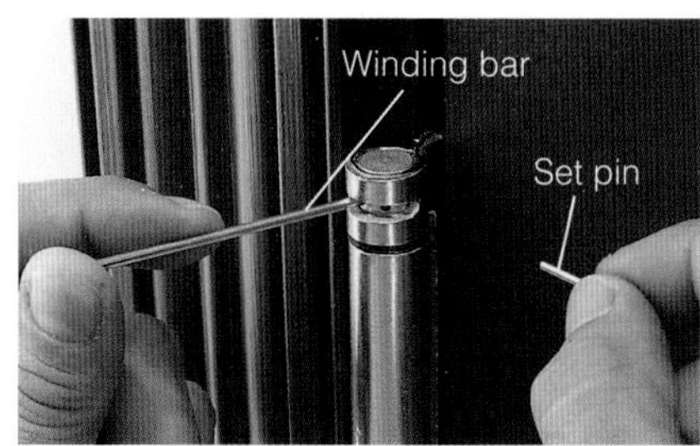

Self-closing hinge. Adjust tension by tightening the spring with the winding bar and inserting the set pin in the hole provided.

Bottom-mount Door Sweep

The hardest part about replacing a bottom-mount sweep is removing the door slab. If you're replacing a sweep on a wood door, apply a bead of caulk along the length of the door bottom and staple on the entire replacement sweep. If the door operates too stiffly, adjust the threshold—usually a wood strip that can be raised or lowered—by turning the four or five large screwheads.

Peel out the old door sweep. Caulk ends of door bottom. Tap in replacement sweep and secure ends with staples.

Doors / Installing a Heavy-duty Deadbolt

Wood Chisels **36**
Files and Rasps **40**
Boring Large Holes **52**

Installing a heavy-duty deadbolt is one of the least expensive and most effective security measures you can take. Single-cylinder deadbolts, keyed on one side, will work fine for most situations. Use double-cylinder deadbolts, which are keyed on two sides, only if everyone in the household knows where the key is stored and leaves it there.

To install the strongest deadbolt, do these three things: (1) buy a Grade 1 security deadbolt; (2) install an all-metal strike box and long screws to spread the impact of an attempted forced entry; (3) use a rectangular faceplate—not a round one that doesn't require chiseling.

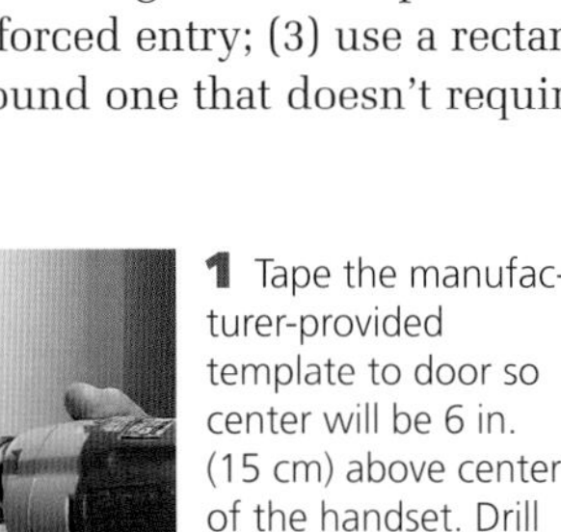

1 Tape the manufacturer-provided template to door so center will be 6 in. (15 cm) above center of the handset. Drill out cylinder hole with 2-1/8-in. hole saw. Buy a deadbolt with same setback (distance from its center to the door edge) as the handset.

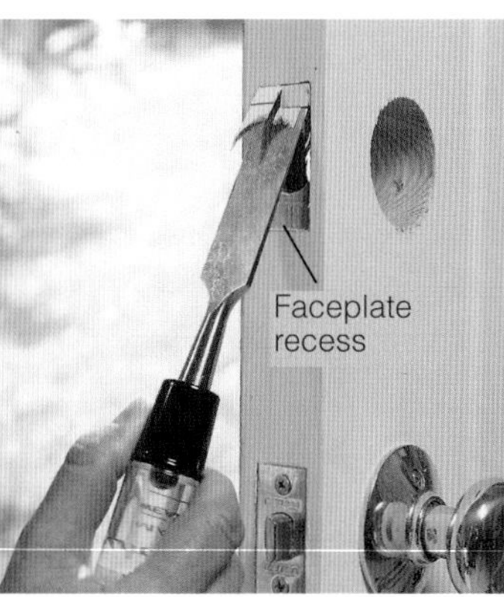

2 Chisel out recess for faceplate with sharp chisel so faceplate will rest flush with door edge. Score vertical edges beforehand with utility knife or chisel to avoid accidentally splitting door with chisel.

3 Install bolt mechanism into door. Unless installed in a steel door, always use a rectangular faceplate for a stronger setup. Assemble cylinder parts following manufacturer's instructions. Coat bolt end with lipstick to mark strike box location on jamb.

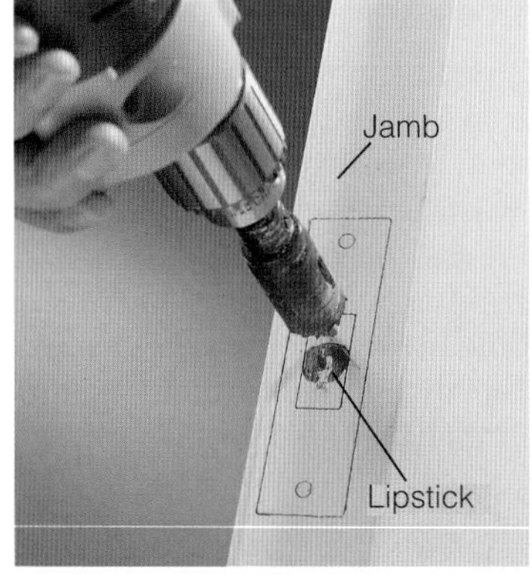

4 Mark profile of strike plate on jamb. Drill out series of holes for strike box recess. Chisel out recess for strike box and plate. To accommodate a heavy-duty strike box, drill all the way through the doorjamb.

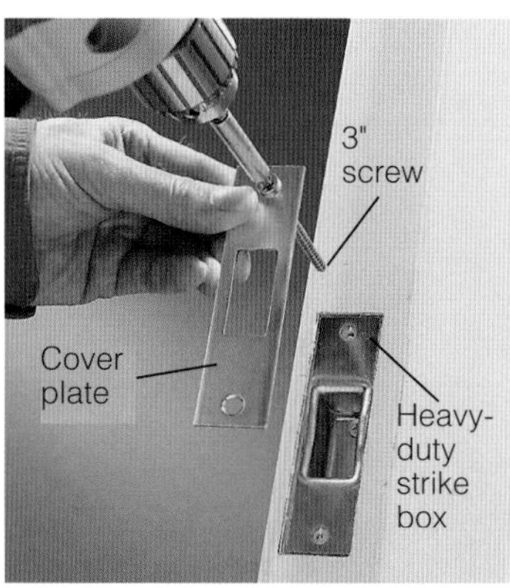

5 Secure strike box and cover plate to jamb and 2x4 frame behind it using heavy-duty screws. Drill pilot holes for screws. Generally, jamb will have hollow space behind it, so go slowly to avoid warping jamb by driving screws in too deep.

How Locks Work

In a cylinder lock, a cylindrical plug is housed in a cylindrical shell. Five or six holes, or pin chambers, are drilled through both the plug and shell. Inside each pin chamber sits a bottom pin, top pin and spring. The top pin sits partway between the plug and cylinder shell, preventing the plug from turning. When the correct key is inserted, the pins align to a point where the plug can rotate.

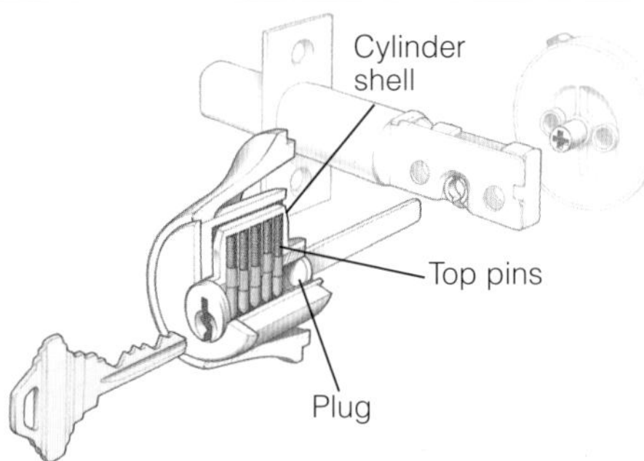

Locked deadbolt. When a cylinder is locked, the top pins protrude partway into the plug to prevent the plug from turning.

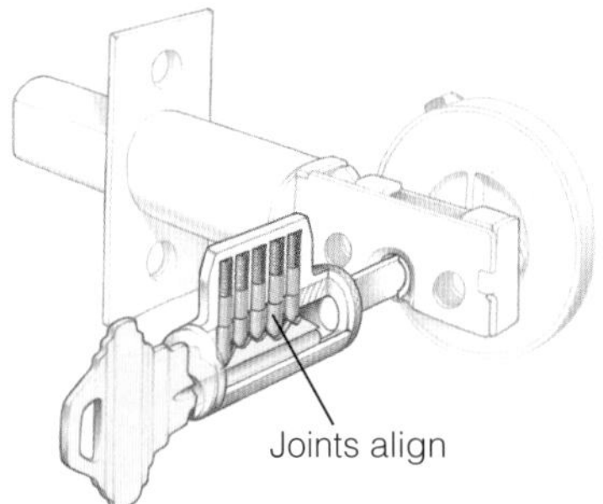

Inserted key. The key lifts each set of pins so the joints between the top and bottom pins align with the plug's outer surface.

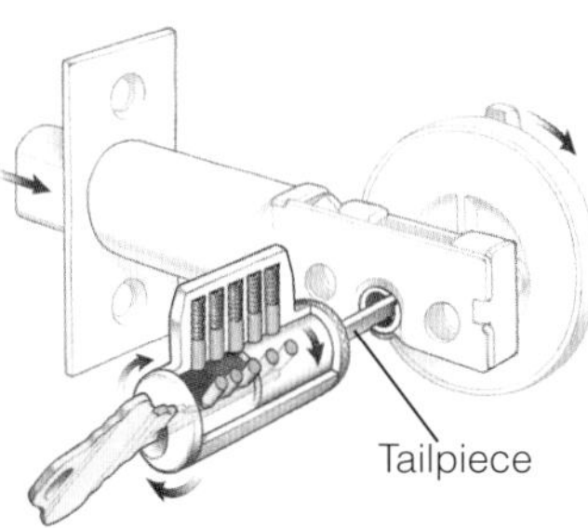

Unlocked deadbolt. With the pins aligned, the plug can rotate, turning the tailpiece, which retracts the bolt so the door can open.

Doors / Adjusting Locks

Rekey a Door Lock

Unless you're the first occupant of a property, you can never be sure how many copies of the keys exist. Fortunately, you can use a rekeying kit to rekey a lock like a pro. These kits are available at hardware stores for most lock brands but are not interchangeable; you'll have to buy a kit for each brand of lock used in your home. The kits will rekey up to six locks for the same key. They work on entrance and deadbolt locks and usually come with two keys and all the tools you'll need, except a screwdriver.

1 Press the wire tool, included in the kit, into knob hole and depress knob clip. Pull knob off door.

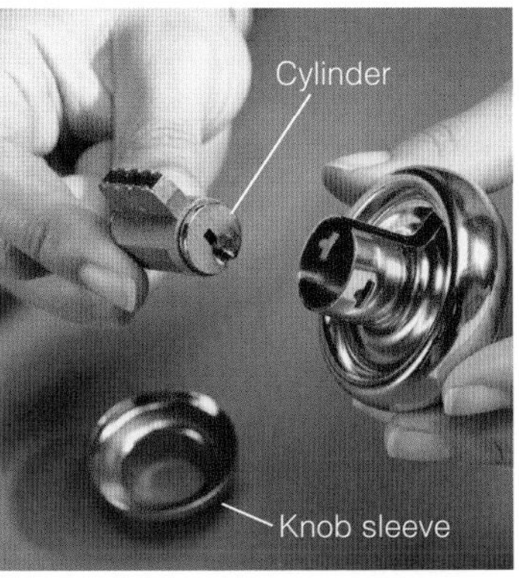

2 Force the cylinder out the back of the knob assembly to pop off the knob sleeve and remove the cylinder.

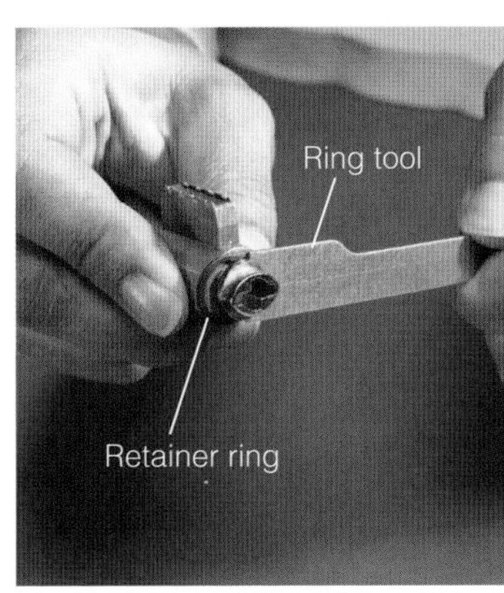

3 Push retainer ring tool against retainer ring to pop it off cylinder. Set ring aside so you can reuse it.

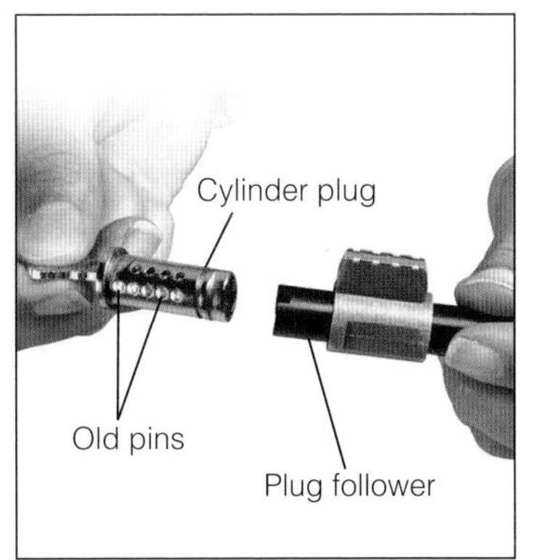

4 Insert old key and turn it either left or right. Remove plug by pushing plug follower, supplied in the kit, through the cylinder. Make sure to keep constant pressure between plug and follower so top pins and springs don't pop out.

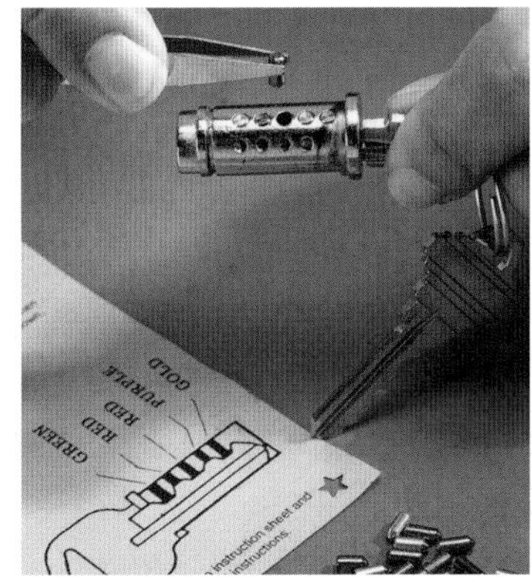

5 Dump out old pins and insert new key. Match new colored pins to color code on the kit's instruction sheet. Install pins using tweezers or needle-nose pliers. When new pins are in, do the previous steps in reverse to reassemble the lock.

Adjust a Latch

When deadbolts, latches and their strike plates are misaligned, doors sometimes won't stay latched or can't be locked without a hard shove. Sometimes the cause is new weather stripping that pushes too hard against the slab. Other times, the door slab may sag, causing the latch or bolt to catch on the bottom of the strike-plate throat. If the simple fixes don't help, you may need to move the strike plate slightly.

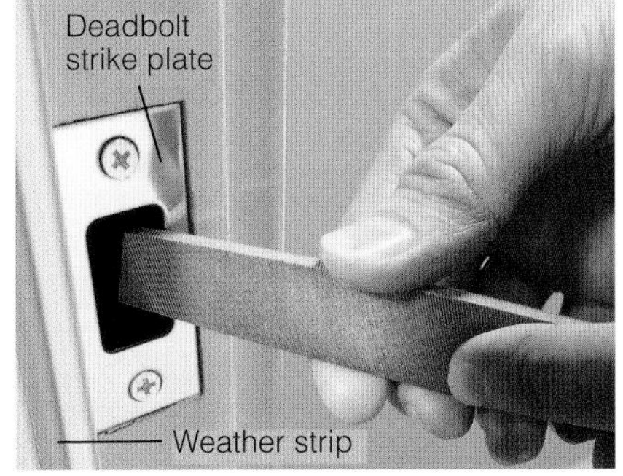

File the inside edge of the strike plate if the door latch won't engage without a hard shove.

Install an adjustable strike plate for cases of severe misalignment.

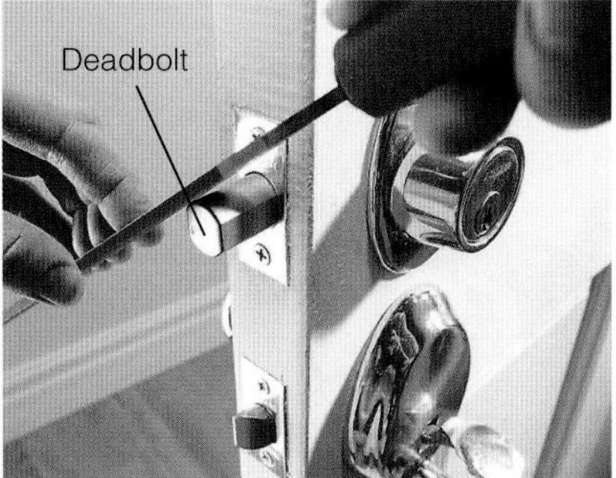

Round off edges of deadbolt using a file for a slight misalignment.

Doors / Reinforcing and Adding Security

Typical Exterior Wall 16
Level and Plumb 44
Boring Large Holes 52

Reinforce an Entry Door

It doesn't matter what kind of entry door you have—wood, fiberglass or solid steel. If the hinges and strike plate are secured with wimpy screws to wimpy wood jambs, they won't offer enough resistance to the efforts of a determined intruder.

Here are two quick steps you can take to help strengthen your door:

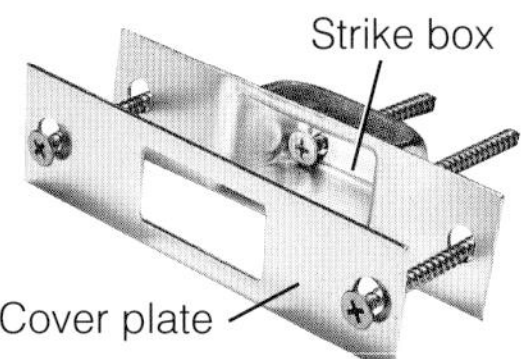

Reinforced strike boxes can be used to replace existing deadbolt strike plates. Enlarge hole as well as the cover plate recess to accommodate the larger strike box. Install two extra-long screws through back of metal strike box into wall framework. Also secure cover plate with long screws.

Reinforce hinges by driving 3-in. screws through hinges and doorjamb into the 2x4 framework. Predrill holes to avoid splitting jamb and ease driving of screws. Take caution not to warp jamb when driving screws.

Reinforce a Door Knob

Install a door reinforcer on your entry or garage service doors to help discourage break-ins. Reinforcers are three-sided metal plates that encase and strengthen a door around the latch—the door's most vulnerable area. You can also buy reinforcers that strengthen deadbolts. A reinforcer extends the door edge about 1/32 in. (1 mm) and may rub the door frame of a tight-fitting door. If so, slightly deepen the hinge mortises with a chisel to widen the gap at the latch.

1 Measure setback (the distance between door edge and center of handset), thickness of door, and handset hole diameter. Buy a reinforcer that fits all those measurements. Unscrew and remove handset. Also take out latch-plate screws, but leave latch in place.

2 Slide reinforcer plate onto door. Secure it to latch with screws provided and remount the handset. Drill pilot holes in both corners of plate on both sides of door slab and install screws. Before drilling, dimple metal with nail set at hole position. This helps prevent drill bit from drifting on slick metal.

Install a Peephole

Tiny peepholes don't always clearly show you who's there, and strangers can hide out of view. Avoid this uncertainty by installing a wide-angled viewer, designed to fit any door up to 2 in. (5 cm) thick.

1 Mark viewer's position on door at the best height for all the home's occupants. Use the correct size hole saw to drill through from inside until pilot bit emerges through outside. Finish boring hole from outside to avoid splintering. Sand edges of hole.

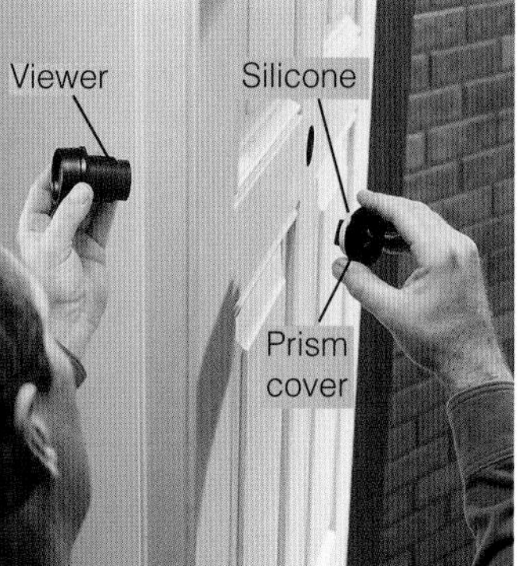

2 Screw viewer body clockwise into prism cover, while holding it level. For metal or fiberglass doors, trim small plastic spikes off the exterior prism cover. Secure cover to door with a bead of silicone. Mount wide-angled viewer so the viewer body faces indoors.

Doors / Installing Exterior

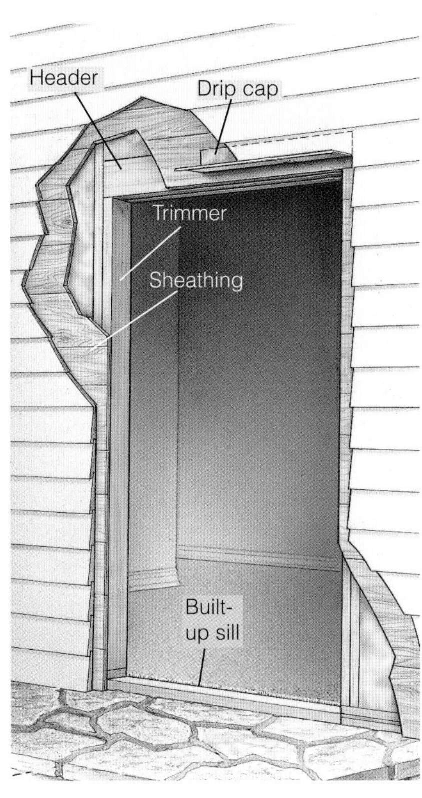

You can install a pre-hung exterior door in a single day. It comes already hinged into its preassembled jamb—complete with threshold and weather stripping—so you get a smooth-swinging, weather-tight fit without all the fuss. Follow local building and energy codes during installation.

Your new door has to be the same nominal size as your existing door. For a larger door or one with added sidelights, you have to rebuild the rough opening.

In some cases, the existing door has a thick threshold that rests directly on the joists. This means you have to build up the sill (the surface the threshold rests on). Unfortunately, there's no way to know how much you'll have to raise the sill until you've removed the old threshold and measured the rough opening top to bottom.

1 Remove old door, brick mold and jamb with pry bar. If you have a drip cap above the door, leave it in place. If not, install one. If exterior trim isn't brick mold, remove it carefully so it can be reused.

2 Hold a level and straightedge against sides, top and bottom of rough opening. Check corners for square. This offers a picture of how plumb and level the opening is and where you may need to make adjustments.

3 Set the pre-hung door into rough opening for trial fit.

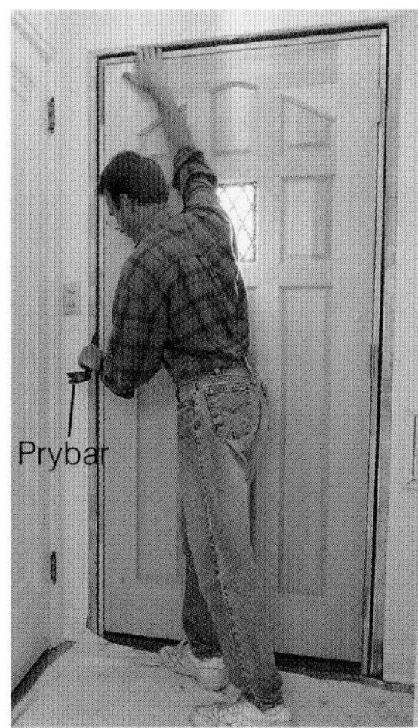

4 Use temporary shims and pry bar to center and level door in opening. Make sure jamb is flush with wall all around and that gaps between the door slab and jambs are consistent along top and sides.

5 Tilt door out and lay three heavy beads of silicone on sill and a bead around rough opening behind brick mold. Set jamb back in place and position correctly. Attach brick mold with 3-in. galvanized finish nails.

6 Secure jamb with 3-1/2-in. screws. First, insert shims behind screw positions to stiffen jamb. Install four screws on strike side hidden behind weather stripping. Use two screws on inside holes of each hinge.

7 Adjust threshold height using adjustment screws so door sweep seals tightly. Insulate gap around jamb with fiberglass or minimally expanding foam. Seal gaps around brick mold with caulk.

Doors / Installing Patio Doors

Bearing Walls 16
Miter Saws 55
Interior Trim 387

Replacing an old sliding patio door with new hinged French doors can improve your home's appearance, energy efficiency and security. It's a big-impact project, but one that is relatively simple to do, provided you select a new, fully assembled door unit that is close in size to your old one.

In choosing a door type, consider the room's size and arrangement. Is there enough room for a door, or doors, to swing into the room without disrupting how you want to use the space? Out-swinging doors are available. Also, find out whether a screen and door hardware are included in the price and what options you have. The hardware may or may not include keyed locks and deadbolts. While most screens are outside-mount, some sliders offer inside-mount screens. Also, look for a low U-rating for optimal energy efficiency.

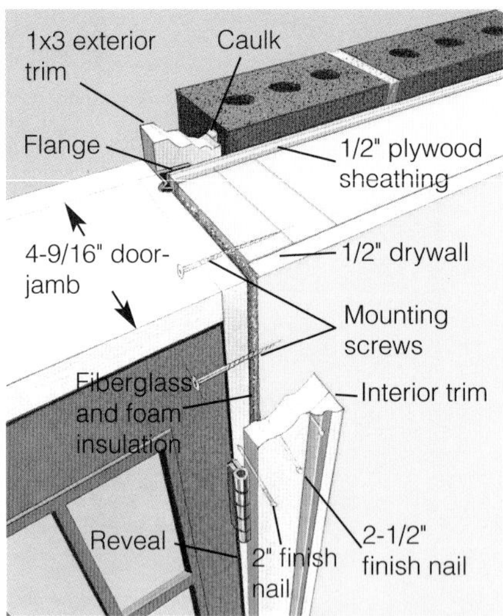

1 Measure width and height of door's rough opening. Remove interior casing to get exact measurement. Purchase or order a new door that will fit rough opening and leave only a 3/8 to 1 in. (1 to 3 cm) gap around frame.

2 Lift and pull sliding panel of door to remove it. Unscrew brackets that hold stationary panel and remove it. Pry off exterior moldings or trim using pry bar. Cut through nails and remove frame.

3 Test-fit new door as you would an exterior door (previous page). Apply two heavy beads of silicone on rough opening sill. Center door in opening and use screws in upper corners to temporarily hold it.

4 Level door and use shims near hinges to hold it in position. If bottom of door needs to be raised or leveled, create a level sill with shims or plywood before permanently installing door.

5 For hinged patio doors, install extra-long screws through the doorjamb and inside hinge holes into wall framing and secure nailing flange. For sliding doors, follow the manufacturer's instructions for securing door.

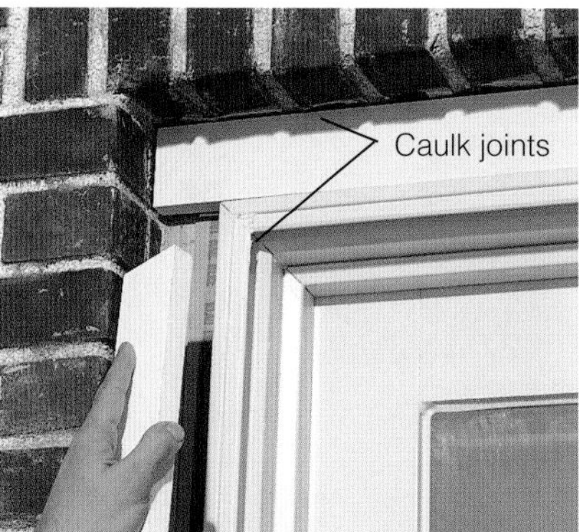

6 Cut exterior trim to fill gap between door frame and siding material. Prime back of trim. Install top trim board first, then side pieces. Caulk joints between trim and siding and door frame.

7 Install door hardware. Many French doors have a three-point locking system to secure door at top, bottom and middle.

Creating or Enlarging a Door Opening

Whether you want to increase the size of an existing door or window or create a new opening, if the wall you're cutting into supports the roof or floor above, you must provide temporary support during the operation. To provide that support, build a shoring wall within 2 ft. (60 cm) of the exterior wall.

The wall should extend beyond the edges of the new opening with temporary studs positioned under each floor joist or roof member above. Protect surface finishes with protective plywood plates tacked to the floor and ceiling by finish nails. Tack the temporary wall's top and bottom plates to the plywood. Note: Make sure there is solid support beneath the new trimmers.

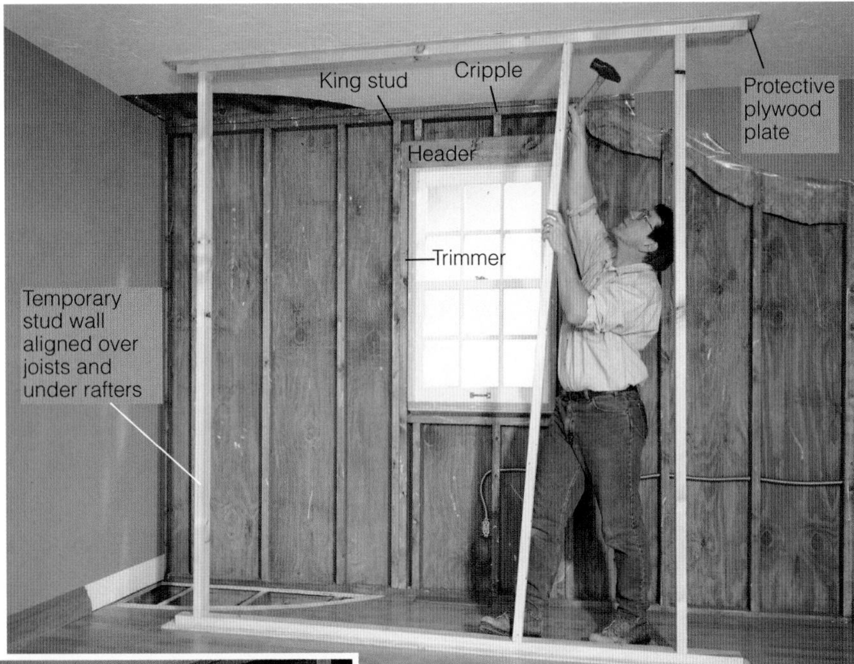

Locate floor joists (below and above, if applicable) and mark locations on plates for temporary wall. Measure for each temporary stud and cut them slightly longer than measurement. Wedge and hammer studs between horizontal plates directly over joists. Remove exterior wall framing to create opening and install king studs and one trimmer. Place one end of new header on installed trimmer and use other trimmer to wedge it up into place. Finish framing opening, remove temporary wall and cut exterior sheathing for new opening.

Tuning-up a Sliding Door

Sliding doors can develop problems due to dirty threshold tracks, misaligned latches and poorly adjusted or worn rollers. In general, these problems are simple and inexpensive to correct. If you need to remove the door, lower the rollers, center the door in the opening, lift, the tilt out the bottom first.

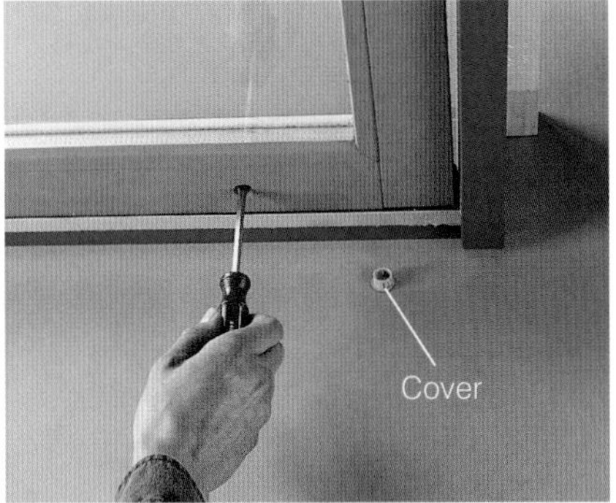

Adjusting rollers. Remove cover over adjustment screw. Adjust roller so door is plumb, just clears threshold, rolls smoothly and latches correctly.

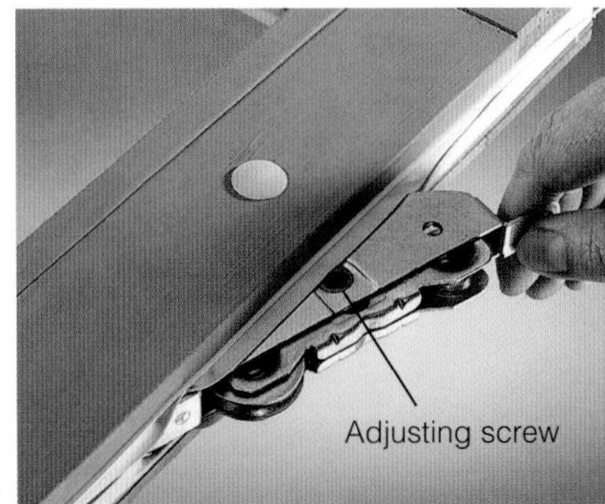

Replacing rollers. Unscrew old roller and work it out of the frame. If possible, use a replacement roller with metal wheels. To install it, follow the removal steps in reverse. Reinstall door and adjust rollers.

Tuning-up a Sliding Screen

Patio screen-door rollers can also stop rolling, break or wear flat. Roller wheels usually mount in the bottom of the door frame. After removing the door, check the upper and lower tracks and straighten them if they are bent. If the screen-door frame is loose, tighten the corner screws.

Adjusting wheels. Set wheel adjustment screws so door aligns top and bottom and side to side with its surrounding frame.

Replacing wheels. Remove adjustment screw to remove wheel and spring assembly. Replace wheel and install door by lifting top into track, then popping wheels over the bottom track.

Doors / Installing Pre-hung Interior

Cutting a Hinge Mortise 36
Circular Saws 56
Door Types and Swings 373

Installing a new interior door is a bit like taking dancing lessons with a partner with two left feet. Fortunately, modern pre-hung doors, with the hinges already mounted on the door and jamb, make this task fairly simple, even if you've never hung a door before.

Begin by determining the swing and measuring the door you're replacing to see if it's a standard size (see p. 373). If it's not standard, you may have to special order a replacement. If you don't like the direction the current door swings, use this opportunity to change it. With the new door(s) in hand, use these tips and the following instructions to help smooth the way:

- Prefinish the door and jamb, including all edges (even the bottom) to minimize warping, before you install it.
- Let the new door follow the wall's plane, even if the wall is slightly out of plumb; otherwise, you'll have problems when you install the trim.
- Unless you're planning to replace all the doors and trim, salvage the original trim to avoid the hassle of matching new trim to the old.
- Remove any fragile objects, such as pictures and mirrors, that hang on nearby walls.

1 Pry off old trim carefully with a stiff scraper and flat bar. To avoid splitting corners, start about two-thirds of the way down one side and work up, around top and down other side.

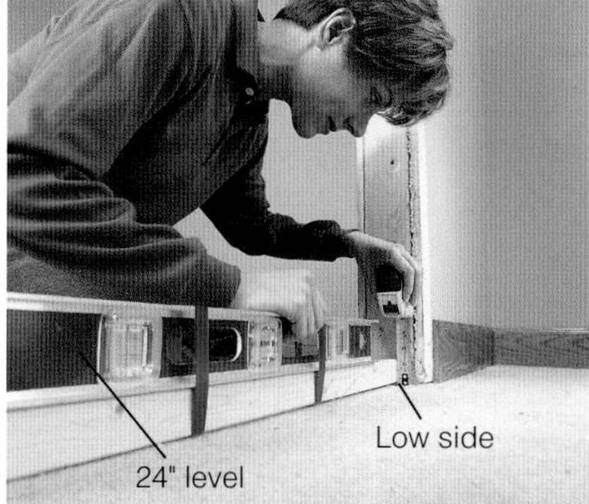

2 Check levelness of floor threshold using a straightedge that's the same width as the rough opening. Measure any variance so you can adjust length of side jambs so top jamb will be level.

3 Cut bottom of side jambs, adjusting for level, so new door will fit in rough opening and door slab will clear flooring by 1/4 to 1/2 in. (6 to 12 mm). Set blade depth, then cut jamb and stop, using square as a guide.

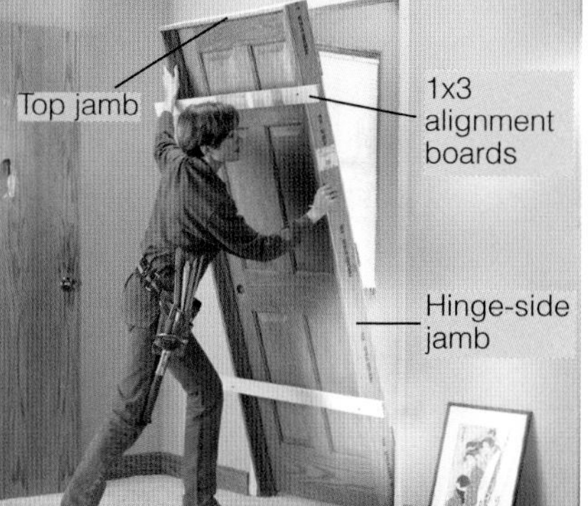

4 Attach alignment boards to jamb edges on non-swinging side to help level and position door. Push door into position. Boards act as stop to align new jamb with drywall surface.

5 Measure and position bottom of hinge-side jamb so trim, when reinstalled, will fit correctly against baseboard. Add pairs of shims on each side of top jamb to plumb hinge-side jamb.

6 Place first nail near top of hinge-side jamb and through shims. Add pairs of shims and nails at bottom and middle of hinge side, checking for plumb and straightness.

7 Add shims along strike side to leave even gap between door slab and jamb. Shim and nail strike side at top, bottom and near the strike. If 2x4 frame is twisted, use shims to adjust jamb.

8 Install handset and adjust strike side stop (which is usually lightly stapled) with softwood block so it lines up with door's face when it's closed. Renail stop to jamb through predrilled holes.

Doors / Hanging a Slab

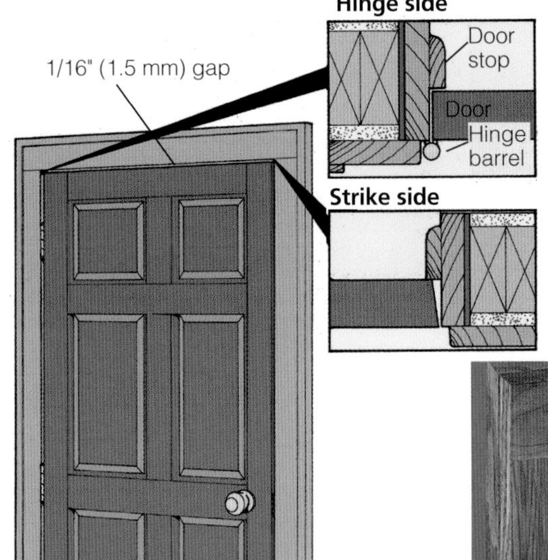

If you have a nonstandard-sized door, want to install a salvaged antique door or don't want to remove the old trim and jamb, hang just the door slab when you replace your door. Some door slabs come with a beveled edge (see "Strike side" illustration at left) on the strike side to ease closing, but most have two square edges and can be hinged on either side.

The first task is to cut the new door to fit into the old, frequently unsquare, jambs. Usually, the side jambs remain parallel but the top jamb (step 1) is out of square with the sides. To adjust a panel door's width by more than 1/2 in. (12 mm), remove equal amounts from both sides.

Be especially careful drilling holes for the handset. The trick is to install the latch so it catches the old strike plate. To complete this step, consider renting a hole-drilling jig for locksets.

There's plenty of room for errors and miscalculations, so "measure twice, cut once" and work carefully.

1 Set framing square against hinge-side jamb and top jamb to measure gap, if any. You can use stiff cardboard as a template to get the angle correct and transfer angle to slab.

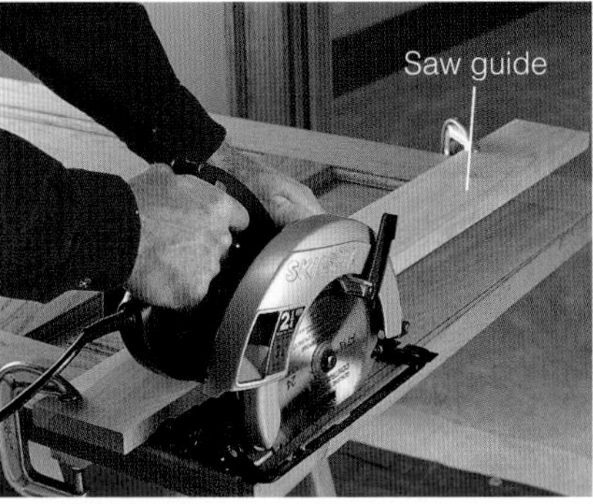

2 Deeply score top of door just inside the cutline using a sharp utility knife to avoid chipping. Using saw guide, cut slightly outside scored line with circular saw. Use sandpaper to slightly round all cut edges.

3 Measure hinged-jamb height, subtract clearances at top and bottom and cut door bottom to that height. Make sure to measure down on the slab's correct side before cutting.

4 Wedge new door against hinged jamb and shim it upward about the thickness of a quarter from top jamb.

5 Mark hinge locations using a sharp pencil or utility knife. Measure width that the hinge leaf is inset into the jamb. Transfer this dimension to the door's edge.

6 Hold hinge leaf in place and score outline with utility knife. Chisel mortise for hinge leaf as deep as leaf is thick. Set leaf in place and use awl to mark the centers of screw holes.

7 Predrill hinge screw holes. Attach leaf, leaving screws slightly loose. Connect leaves with hinge pins and tighten screws. Close door and check gaps.

Doors / Repairing and Adjusting

Hand Planes 38
Specialty Bits 52
Circular Saws 56

Tightening Loose Hinges

Screw holes, especially for the top hinges and for heavy doors, often become stripped, and you can't tighten the screws. To hold the screws firmly, you'll need to plug the hole before resecuring the hinge.

Another option (far right) is to drive a longer screw, angled slightly to bite into the stud, through the hinge hole into the wall framing.

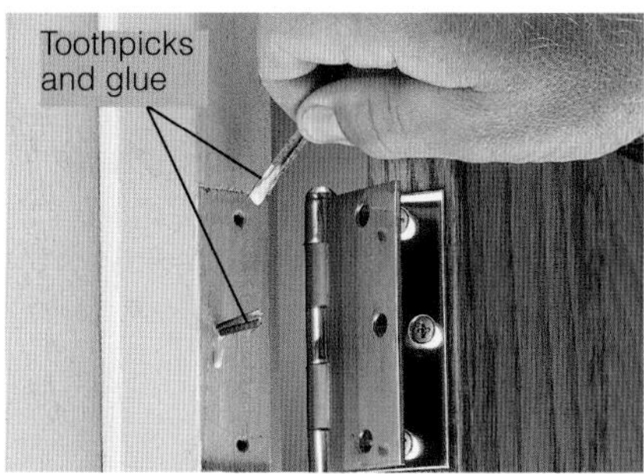

1 Coat toothpicks, matchsticks or a golf tee with glue, then force them into old screw holes. Trim ends flush when glue dries.

2 Drill new pilot holes and drive screws. Use a self-centering drill bit so screws are centered and heads lie flush with surface.

Longer-screw fix. Drive long screws through hinge hole into stud behind jamb. Angle screws through outer holes toward the stop.

Freeing Binding Upper Edge

When a door binds and catches and the hinges are tight, try these simple fixes before cutting: For a slightly sticking door, a light sanding may be adequate. A solid whack with a hammer on a block of wood along the strike side of the frame may widen the opening enough to free the door. If not, try this fix.

1 Mark edge of door where it rubs against frame to allow 1/16 to 1/8 in. (1.5 to 3 mm) gap between slab and frame.

2 Remove hinge pins, place slab across cushioned sawhorses and, if necessary, remove handset.

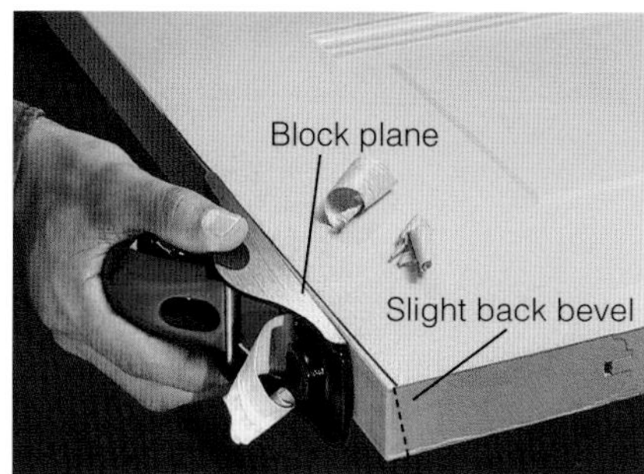

3 Plane or sand door edge, creating a slight back bevel where door meets stop. Seal or paint exposed wood and replace door.

Freeing Binding Lower Edge

When doors bind on the strike side's bottom edge, the lower jamb has probably shifted or pulled loose from its nails, resulting in an out-of-plumb opening. To reset jamb, loosen the casing's bottom section and renail jamb with 3-in. finish nails. As you recess the nail heads, keep closing the door to check for the proper gap so you don't overcorrect.

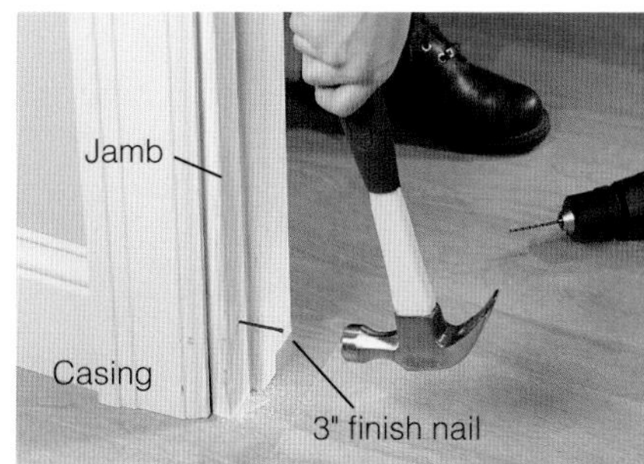

Pry out lower section of casing. Install shims if necessary and nail jamb through shims.

Handy Hints

Dragging-Door Fix

To fix a slightly dragging door without removing it, use a sanding disc, reversing the disc so the sandpaper faces the drill. Protect the floor with cardboard or scrap plastic laminate, and sand the door's bottom. Sanding works only if you need to shave off only a small amount. To reseal the raw wood, put finish or paint on scrap carpet and slide it along the bottom of the door.

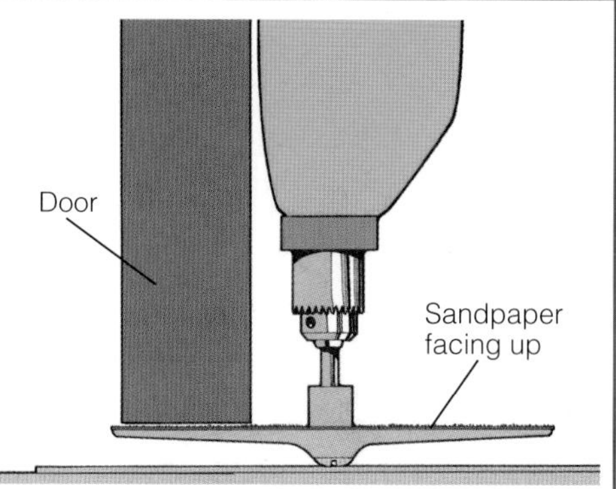

Shortening a Door

When new flooring, such as a carpet with a thicker pad, makes doors drag, shortening the door is required. Cutting down hollow-core doors is often more involved than solid-core doors. In either case, the biggest potential problem you'll face is remembering which end of the door to cut. Cutting the top of the door only creates a bigger problem.

First, remove the door from the jamb by removing the hinge pins. Measure the amount to be removed from the bottom. Use a straightedge and sharp utility knife to deeply score just inside cutline. This will minimize chipping while you cut. Use a circular saw equipped with a sharp blade to make the cut just outside the scored line.

Hollow-core doors have a thin base piece that is often removed or becomes too thin when you cut down the door. Save this piece and reinstall it (see photo far right) by first pushing the cardboard mesh back into the door far enough for the fill piece to fit. After gluing, clamp the door skin to the fill piece.

When the door is correctly sized, seal the bottom edge to prevent warpage before you reinstall the door.

All doors. Using your circular saw's guide, cut slightly outside scored line. Apply tape to the bottom of the saw to protect the door surface. Sand a bevel around all cut edges.

Hollow-core doors. Use a sharp chisel to scrape glue and door skin off base piece, attach drywall screws for temporary handholds, coat it with glue and reinstall. Seal door bottom.

Silencing a Rattling Door

A well-adjusted door should hit the stop and latch at the same time to remain tight and prevent rattling. Use the two fixes shown here to solve most rattling problems. Before adjusting the stop, cut through any paint or varnish on both sides with a utility knife so the stop can break free cleanly.

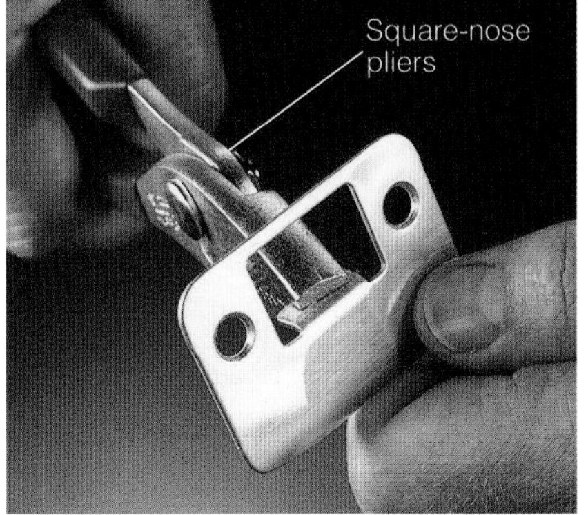

Fix 1. Bend flange in strike plate with square-nose pliers to hold door slab more tightly against the doorstop.

Fix 2. Adjust stop by tapping it with a soft wood block, so it lies flush with door face. Renail stop after adjusting.

Adjusting a Latch Plate

When a door doesn't stay shut, check the wear marks on the strike plate to see how the latch hits it. Adjust the latch hole accordingly.

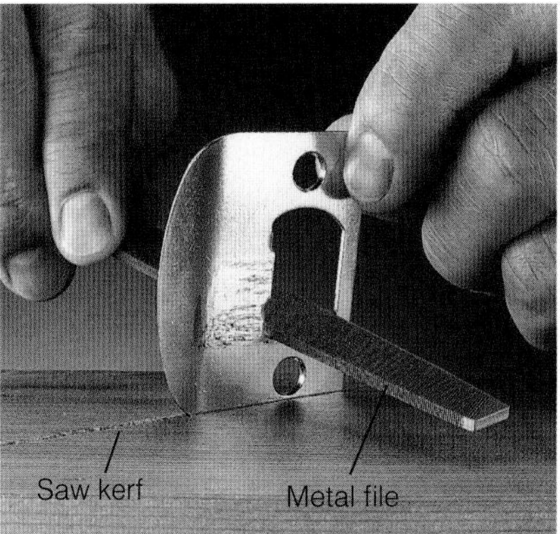

File the latch hole slightly larger until the latch catches. Use a saw kerf in a scrap of wood to hold the strike plate steady.

Lengthening a Door

To "stretch" a solid-wood, rail-and-stile door slab, the add-on piece should be the same thickness and have the same grain direction as the slab.

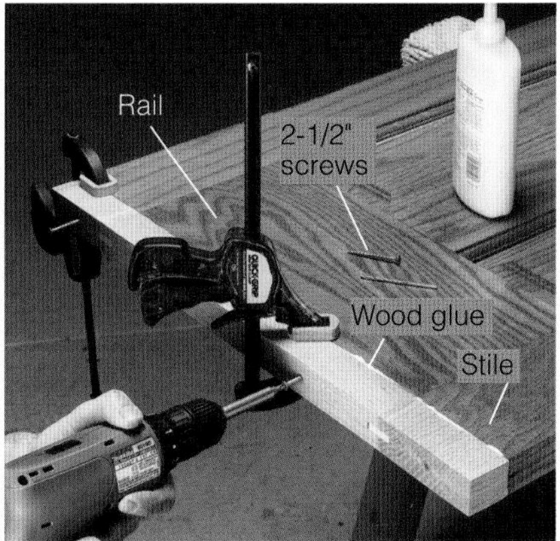

Construct an add-on from three separate pieces, matching the species, width, thickness and grain direction of stiles and rail.

Doors / Bifold

Miter Saws 55
Making Moldings 67
Bull's-eye Corner Blocks 445
Stopped Flutes 445

Adjusting a Bifold Door

Bifold doors start running a little ragged after a few hundred uses. They stick, rub and don't align. Fortunately, adjustable brackets on most doors make tuning them a simple matter. Furthermore, bifold door replacement parts are fairly universal and available at hardware stores and home centers.

Properly adjusted bifold doors have an even vertical gap between doors and an even horizontal space along the top. Also, the door slabs should open and close easily and not scrape on the jambs or floor.

You can't always get the doors perfectly adjusted on all four sides, especially if the opening is out of square. If this is the case, get the highly visible gaps between the doors and the top even and leave uneven spaces along the side jambs or floor.

After the doors are fine-tuned, spray a little silicone lubricant on the track for a smooth glide.

Top adjustment. Loosen the setscrew on top bracket and slide bracket slightly along track to adjust door spacing. Retighten setscrew.

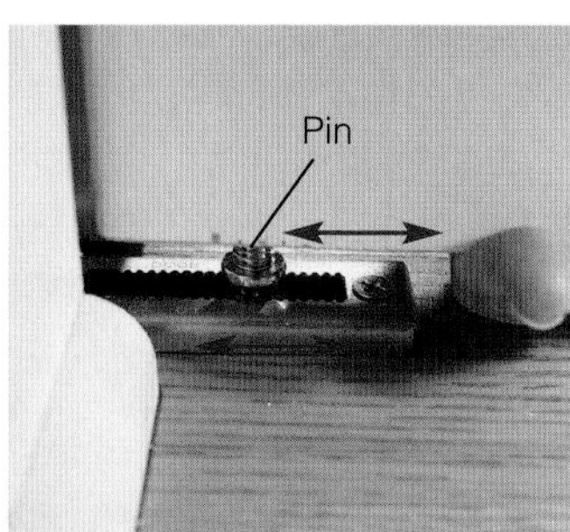

Bottom adjustment. Lift the door and move pin in bottom bracket to adjust gaps between the doors and between the doors and jambs.

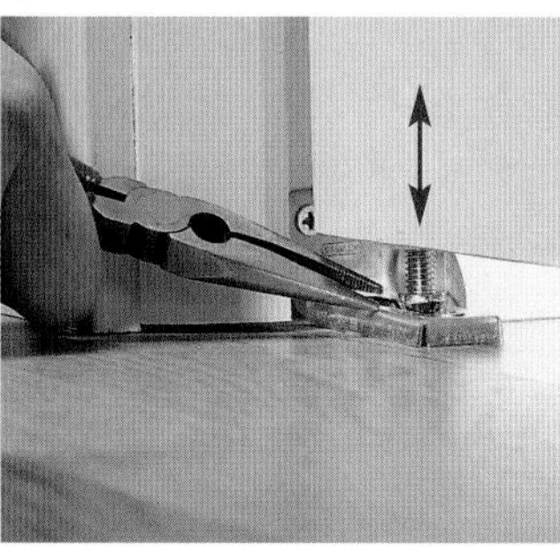

Height adjustment. Screw pin longer or shorter to adjust height. If necessary, remove the door, or take weight off pin using shims or prybar under door.

Re-anchoring Bottom Brackets

A bifold door that wobbles or jerks as you open it might have a loose bottom bracket. When the brackets are installed over concrete or ceramic tile, the floor screw often is not installed, leading to a wiggling bracket especially if the bracket is mounted to a drywall jamb. Heavy solid-wood or mirrored doors are particularly prone to this problem.

For the firmest repair, fasten the bracket to the floor using a masonry anchor.

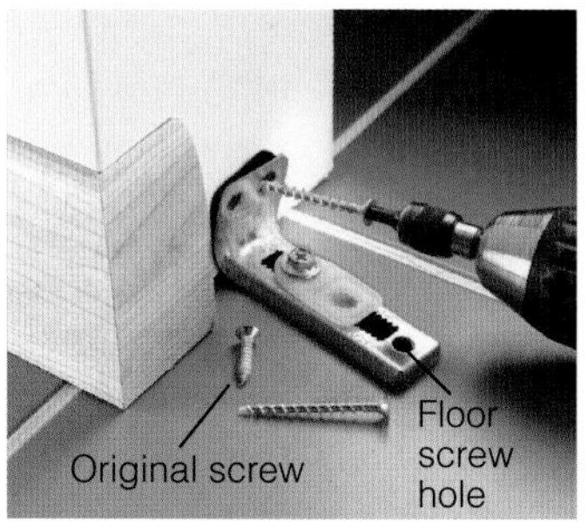

Longer screws. Anchor bracket using longer screws into the jamb. Using a drill and masonry bit, install a concrete screw in the floor.

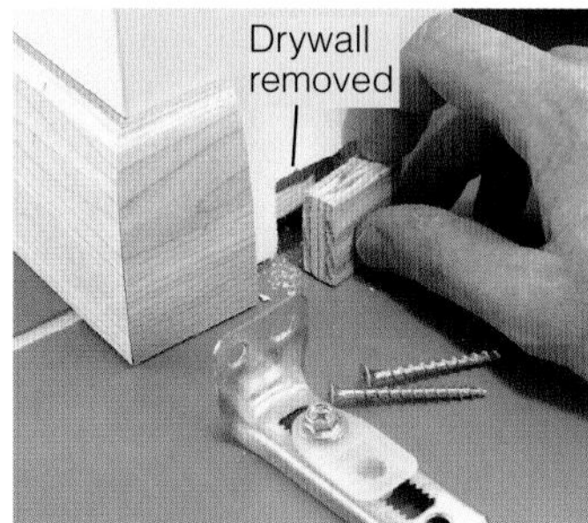

Solid block. Cut out damaged drywall. Fill hole with plywood block and re-anchor bracket.

Installing a Repair Bracket

When a door pivot breaks loose and cracks the edge of the door slab's edge, you can save the door with a repair bracket that provides a firm base for the pivot pin. Remove the door and, if the slab is cracked, glue it. Install the repair bracket following manufacturer's directions and, if necessary, readjust the door height.

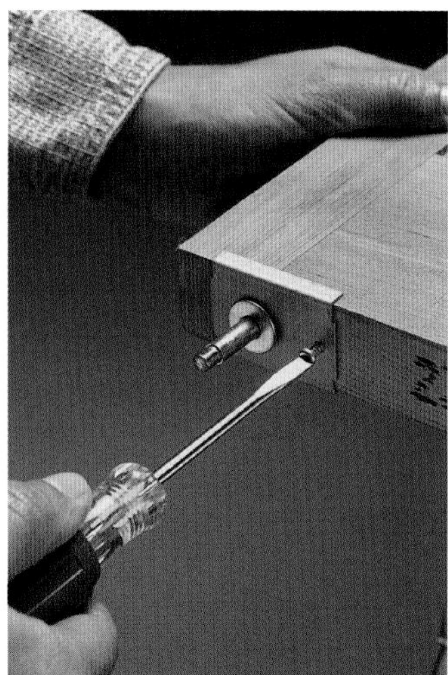

Interior Trim / Styles

What most people notice first in an older or well-crafted home is the woodwork. The rich details give these homes a certain inviting, elegant character. You can add this same special touch to a family room, dining room or your whole house by changing your door and window casing and installing wider baseboards.

A wide variety of hardwood trim is available through your home center or lumberyard. This premilled trim is the way to go if you're still developing your woodworking skills or don't own a tablesaw.

Milling your own trim will save money and expand your options. The back-band and post-and-lintel styles require only basic tablesaw and router skills.

Before you begin, check the distances to any light switch covers to see whether the casing will fit or the electrical boxes need to be shifted. Also, look at adjoining walls, especially at hallway ends, to determine whether tight corners will interfere with the plans.

Mitered

Use mitered corners to achieve a contemporary look. Many wide, thick, elegant trim styles are available that look great with mitered corners. The mitered style offers two big advantages—speed and fewer tools (no tablesaw). Installing mitered trim generally goes faster since it involves fewer parts and cuts and you don't have to mill or sand the trim. The big challenge is creating perfect mitered casing corners in openings that are out-of-square.

Back Band

The simple lines of the back-band method meshes perfectly with Arts and Crafts architecture and furniture. The wide, flat face of the primary casing boards showcase the wood's grain rather than the casing's shape. The side casing boards are often 1x4s, the head casing is a 1x6 and the back band is an L-shaped strip either created with a tablesaw or purchased.

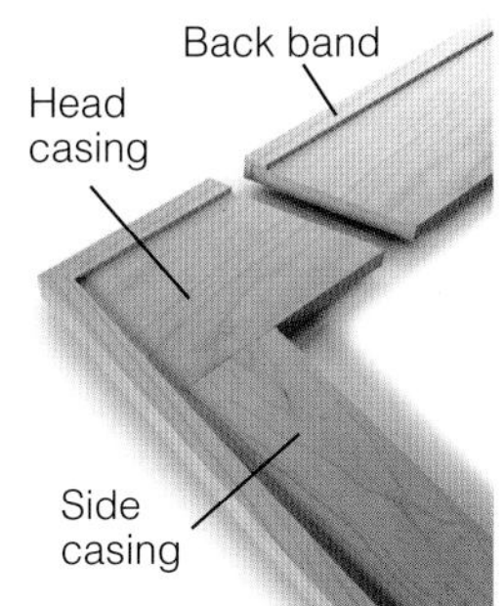

Post and Lintel

This multipiece style echoes the style used in homes around the turn of the 20th century. The 1x4 side casings have eased edges, and the slightly wider head casing has squared edges and ends. The upper part, called the lintel, often has four components: a small round-edged fillet, the head casing, the ogee molding and a cap, with rounded edges and ends extending past the head casing. Side trim terminates with plinth blocks that rest on the floor.

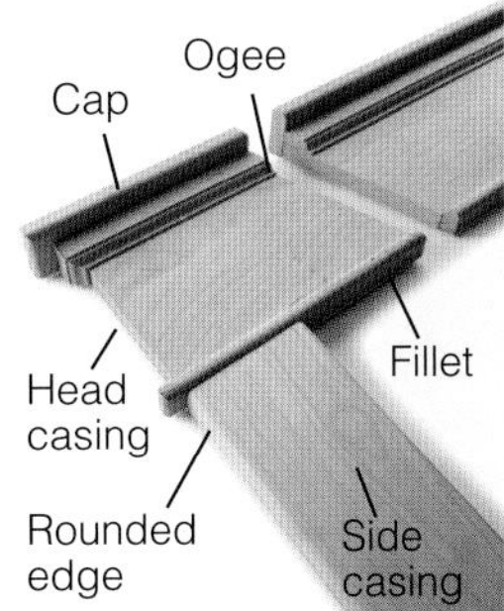

Corner Block Trim

The classical style shown here consists of three parts: square corner blocks, fluted casing and plinth blocks that rest on the floor. Corner blocks of various styles and species can be purchased at larger lumberyards and home centers, special ordered from a millwork store or created with a router and templates. Glue thin backers to the corner and plinth blocks so they stand out slightly from the casing.

Plinth block

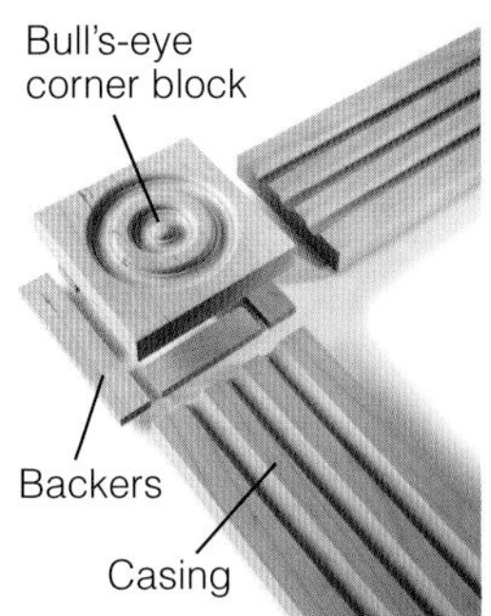

Interior Trim / Door Casing

Miter Saws 55
Air Nailers 74

Installing trim isn't very difficult, especially if you have enough patience to get the details right and a power miter saw with a sharp blade to make clean cuts. It's a deeply rewarding project that adds value to your home and helps put your own lasting imprint on its character. Use these tips and instructions to help you succeed.

- Prefinish all sides of the trim before installation. Finishing the back helps stabilize the wood during humidity changes.
- Use a power miter saw with a 40-tooth or finer carbide blade to make the angled cuts.
- To reduce legwork, set up the miter saw in the room you're trimming and protect the floor with a tarp.
- Make small adjustments when cutting angles to fit. Even 0.25° can make a big difference.
- Match wood so grain pattern is similar at the joints.
- Predrill all nail holes to avoid splitting. Small drill bits break easily. Use the same size nail you're driving, with the head snipped off, as a substitute drill bit. Use a power nailer, if you have one.

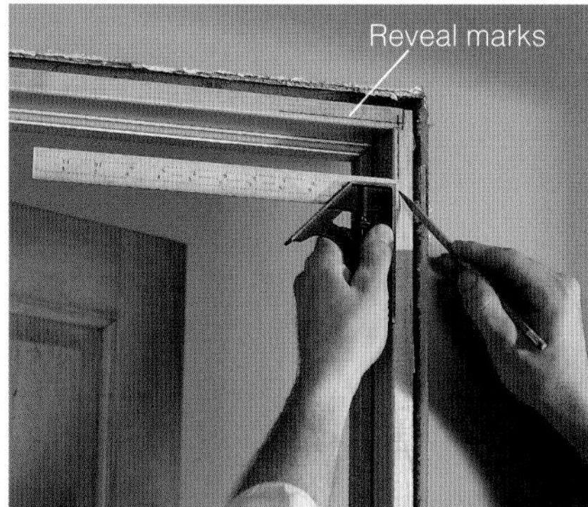

1 Mark reveal line 3/16 in. (5 mm) from jamb edge using a combination square. Use a sharp pencil to position marks in corners and regularly along jamb edge.

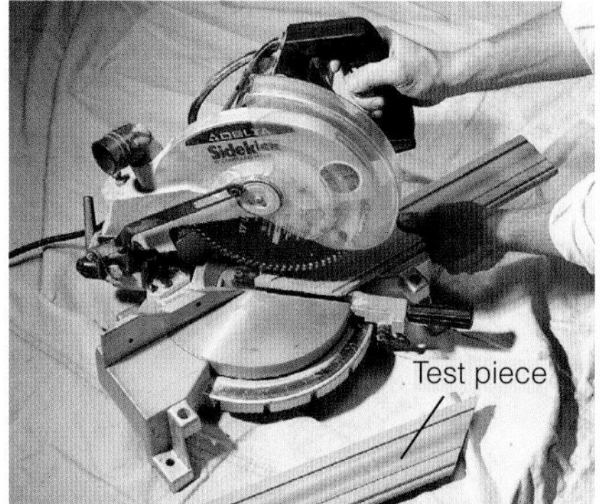

2 Cut two test pieces of casing at opposing 45° angles on a miter saw. Use test pieces to check the casing's fit on each corner of the doorjamb.

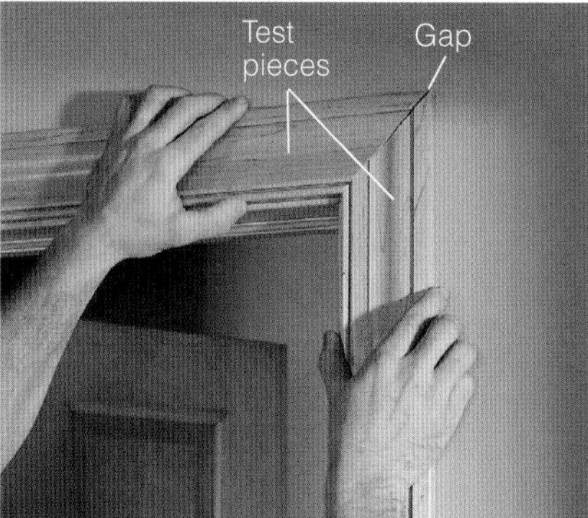

3 Hold test pieces on reveal marks. If the joint is even slightly open at top or bottom of miter, adjust angle on miter saw. Recut test pieces until the joint is tight.

4 Cut side casing about 1/2 in. (13 mm) overlong and hold it in place along reveal marks. Use a sharp pencil to transfer reveal mark from head jamb to side casing. Make final cut.

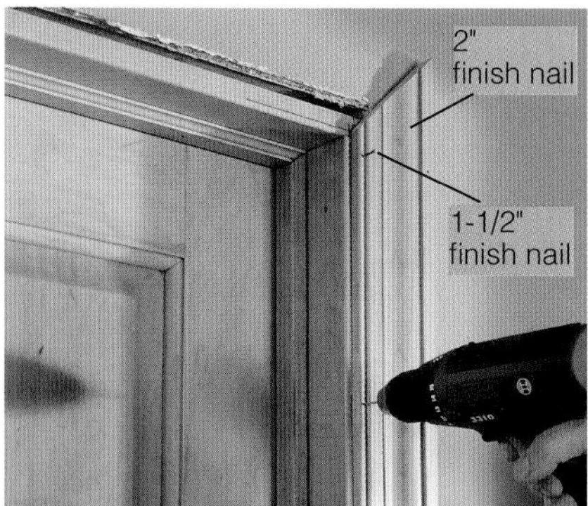

5 Holding the casing in position, predrill and nail inside edge with 1-1/2-in. finish nails every 12 to 16 in. (30 to 40 mm). On outside edge, predrill for 2-in. finish nails. Nail 1 in. (2.5 cm) away from board ends.

6 Cut end of top casing that mates with side casing after determining correct angle with test piece. Position casing, mark length, cut it, glue first mitered end and tack it up.

7 Cut second side casing 1 in. (2 cm) overlong and hold it against top casing backward and parallel to doorjamb. Cut casing slightly long, check fit and trim it to final length.

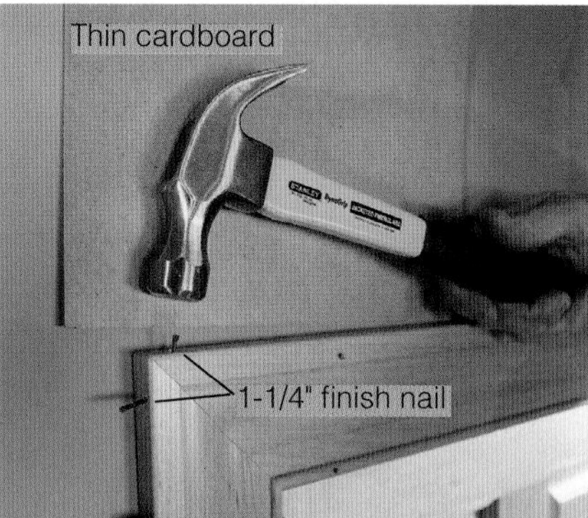

8 Align miters and predrill holes for finish nails—one from the top and one from the side. Protect the wall with cardboard. Apply glue; then drive corner nails slowly, alternating between nails.

Interior Trim / Window Casing

Installing Window Trim

Installing trim around a window requires the same techniques and tips as you use when trimming a door. The primary difference is that if you use the picture-frame method, you have two more mitered corners to sweat over and no simple butt joints at the floor.

1 Trim window by starting with top casing. Mark reveal lines around jamb edges. Use test pieces to gauge angles. Cut and tack top casing, then fit sides and install sides. If possible, place nails in dark portion of wood grain to make holes less noticeable. Glue all miters.

2 Fit one miter on bottom, then overlap opposite miter and mark it. Cut miter 1/8 in. (3 mm) overlong, slide casing into place and trim it gradually, checking the fit frequently.

3 Tap nails just below surface using nail set. After sealing, fill holes with colored putty to match wood color or stain. Mix shades of putty to get a good match.

Making a Window Stool

Classic window trim includes a piece of trim called the window stool that sits on top of the rough opening's sill. Typically, the stool board is a 1x4 notched to fit flush with the drywall and window jambs.

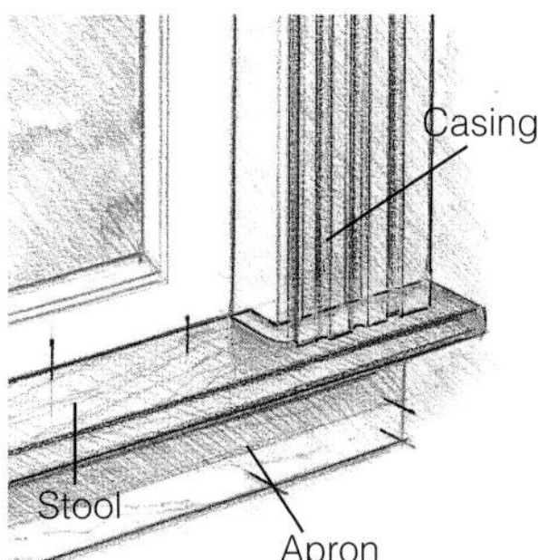

How it all fits. The stool and apron are installed first. Side casing, and sometimes jamb extensions, sit on top of stool. Stool extends about 3/4 in. (20 mm) beyond casing; all exposed edges can be rounded or beveled by a router. Use same routed edge on apron underneath. The apron's ends can be slightly angled.

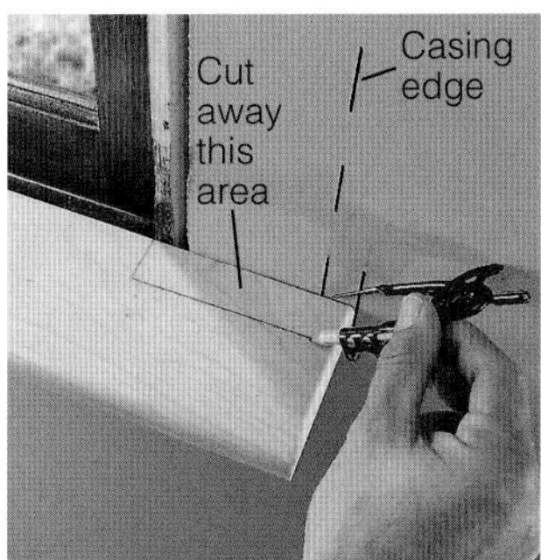

1 Mark stool notches by setting compass 1/8 in. (3 mm) less than the distance from the edge of the stool to the window sash, and by scribing the cutline. Cut out notch using jigsaw and test fit.

2 Cut an apron that extends to casing edge marks. Rout edges same as stool and use 2-1/2-in. finish nails to nail apron to framing behind drywall. Place stool over apron and framing sill. Nail stool to both with 2-in. finish nails.

"Cheating" with a Miter Saw

The secret to tight-fitting miter joints is knowing how to adjust the cuts to make them conform to out-of-square openings, uneven drywall and recessed jambs. Use the first tip below if your saw won't cut angles greater than 45 degrees or is difficult to fine-tune.

For out-of-square corners. For a gap on outside of miter, place shim against fence at point farthest from blade. Hold molding tight against fence and shim and shave miter. Move shim closer to blade for greater angle. For inside gaps, adjust saw to less than 45°. Cut molding pieces overlong until correct fit is achieved.

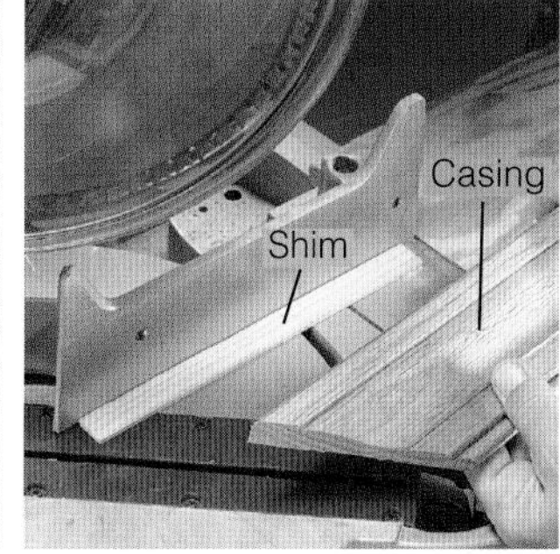

For recessed jambs. Trim back drywall using a utility knife until molding no longer rocks when set against jamb and drywall. Mash and flatten drywall with hammer, if necessary. Set shim(s) under back of casing and shave miter. For proud jambs, place shim under the mitered end of casing and shave the cut.

Air Nailers

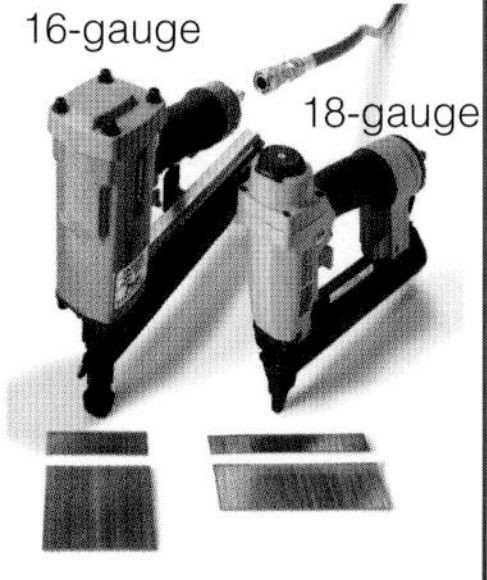

Air, or pneumatic, nailers speed the job, reduce the chance of splitting and eliminate hammer marks. Use a 16-gauge nailer for securing casings to the wall; a smaller 18-gauge brad nailer for securing casings to the edge of the jamb.

Storm Doors / Installing

Hacksaws 27
Repairing Wood with Epoxy 366

Installing a high-quality storm door not only dresses up an entryway but will help keep your house warmer in the winter, breezier and bug free in the summer and a little more secure all year 'round. The basic installation techniques are the same for all storm doors, but read and follow the manufacturer's instructions.

To order the correct door for your entry, determine the width by measuring between the inside edges of the brick mold, top, middle and bottom, and determine the height by measuring between the entry door's threshold and the brick mold on top. An adjustable expander strip accommodates variations in height. A storm door should be hinged on the same side as the entry door. Fortunately, most storm doors are "ambidextrous" and can be mounted as either a left or right swing.

For easiest installation, follow these tips:

- Before installing the door, paint the brick mold.
- Remove any glass inserts before you begin.
- Keep the expander strip pushed up until all other steps are complete.
- Don't warp the frame by overdriving jamb screws.

Caution: A door exposed to direct sunlight shouldn't be tightly weather stripped. Trapped heat can warp vinyl trim and even distort the main door.

1 Check hinge-side brick-mold opening for square to see if it's the low side or high side. Measure hinge-side height from top of threshold to top of brick mold.

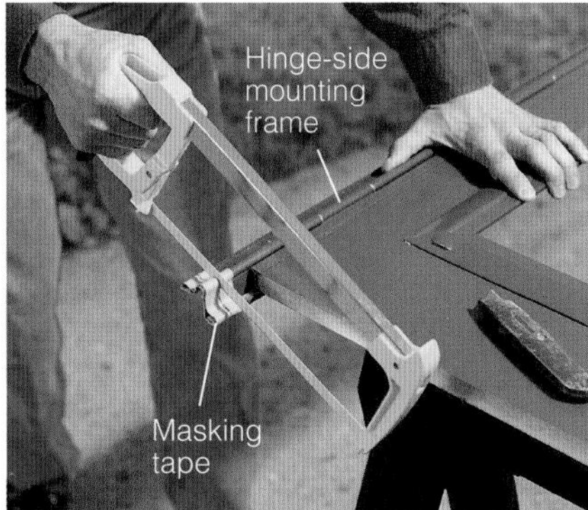

2 Cut the hinge-side mounting frame leg to length using a hacksaw. Angle cut to match threshold angle.

3 Slide vinyl sweep into groove of expander; then slide expander onto door bottom. Pinch ends of sweep groove with pliers to prevent slippage. Center the door in the opening.

4 Plumb the door and secure the hinge-side mounting frame's face to the brick mold. Use shims behind frame to fill gaps; then secure jamb side of mounting frame.

5 Position top mounting frame so the gap between it and door is consistent along entire length. Use a sharp awl to hold one end in place. Attach top mounting frame.

6 Carefully plot position of storm door latch and lock so they won't collide with entry-door hardware. Check by holding storm door hardware in position before drilling holes.

7 Dimple metal with an awl to mark hole locations and to steady drill bit. Remove template and drill hardware holes from both sides to prevent damaging the door's thin metal skin.

8 Level and install door closer. Heavy-duty storm doors have a closer for top and for bottom. Lower the expander so vinyl sweep contacts threshold.

Storm Doors / Repairing

Replacing a Closer

Storm door closers rarely wear out, but if a strong enough gust of wind catches the door and throws it back hard, the closer usually suffers most. The bracket screws can be pulled out of the jamb, or the plunger shaft can be bent. If the shaft is bent, replace the closer.

1 Open the door and lock the plunger open. Pull out pin holding plunger in jamb-mounting bracket. Remove pin on other end holding closer to storm door bracket. If brackets are soundly mounted, leave in place and test-fit new closer before replacing brackets.

2 Remove old bracket from doorjamb. New mounting bracket will cover minor damage from screw pullout. For serious damage, fill voids with wood putty or epoxy wood filler and sand and paint the jamb before installing a new bracket.

3 Secure new closer bracket to doorjamb and wall framing behind jamb with 3-in. screws. Reinstall the plunger unit.

Adjusting a Hold-open Washer

It's nice to have a storm door that stays open on its own when you need to move furniture, groceries or trash. But over time, the hold-open washer can lose its grip. Fortunately, 10 minutes is all you need to solve this annoying problem.

1 Hold the storm door open by clamping locking pliers on plunger shaft against closer tube. Remove pin holding closer to jamb-mounting bracket and pull off washer. Secure washer in vise and bend it over slightly from its previous angle with hammer.

2 Reinstall washer on plunger shaft and test gripping power by pinning closer to mounting bracket. Remove locking pliers and move washer against closer tube and test door. If necessary, remove washer again and bend it until it bites into plunger shaft and holds door open.

Making Seasonal Adjustments

Make adjustments to door closer when you exchange screens for heavier glass storm panels. Move connecting pin into forward hole for winter and rear hole for summer. If necessary, adjust piston pressure with control screw.

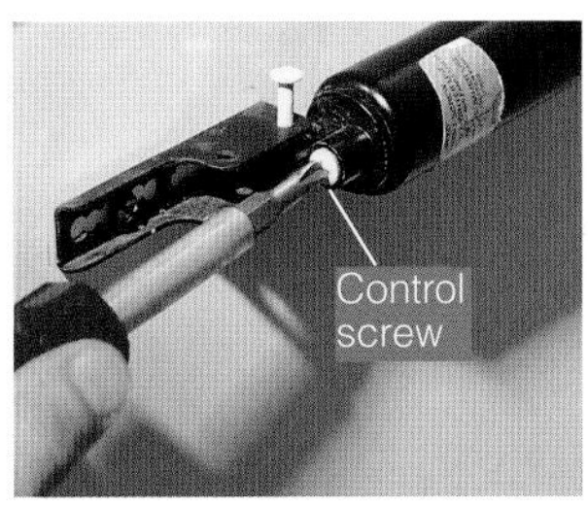

Installing a New Handle

Storm door handles are easy to replace, but upgrading to a quality brass handle usually requires new hole locations. Consequently, look for a handle with cover plates that will cover the old holes, and consider adding a matching deadbolt for extra security.

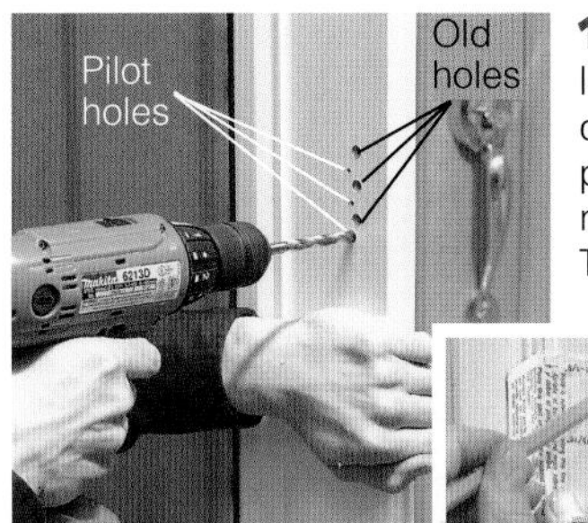

1 Mark door for new hole locations using new handle's template. Drill small pilot holes through door or mark them with an awl. Then drill holes to the recommended size by drilling through both sides.

2 Assemble door handle according to the manufacturer's instructions. Start screws by hand to align with threads. Close door and hold strike plate in position while you mark screw slots. If necessary, use plastic shims provided to shim strike, then attach. Adjust strike until door latches firmly.

Revive a Storm Door

You can successfully repaint a banged-up storm door with epoxy appliance paint. Remove the glass and hardware, sand and prime any scratches, fill any dents with auto body filler and repaint.

Garage Doors / Installing

Wrenches 30
Doors / Maintaining Garage 395

A garage door is the largest moving object in your house. An older door can weigh from 250 to 450 lbs. (110 to 200 kg). This weight, coupled with antiquated designs and hardware, makes older garage doors a frequent scene of home accidents. New steel garage door designs last longer, insulate better and significantly improve safety. The new doors are lighter, have safer spring systems and often have pinch-resistant joints between the panels. Further, some new door systems allow you to complete the project yourself. Be aware, you should always hire a pro to release the tension on existing torsion-type springs and remove the old door.

Garage doors have one of two types of door springs. Torsion springs (step 8, next page) mount on the header above the door. Extension springs (step 1, inset) float above the roller track. Extension springs are noisier and, without a containment cable, become dangerous, heavy whips when they break. Their primary advantage is that you don't need the 12 in. (30 cm) of headroom that a torsion spring requires.

Torsion springs have three advantages over extension springs—they're quieter, safer and easier to fine-tune. Although setting the tension on torsion springs has been very dangerous in the past, several companies now make torsion and extension spring systems with easy, do-it-yourself tensioning.

A standard double door is 7 ft. (213 cm) high by 16 ft. (488 cm) wide. Standard single doors are the same height, but 8 or 9 ft. (244 to 275 cm) wide. Doors are available in wood, fiberglass and steel. Steel doors, like the one shown, are light, maintenance-free, affordable, readily available, and have an insulating value as high as R-19.

Among steel doors, choose from steel only, steel with insulation on the inside and two-sided steel with insulation. Other features that add to the cost are thicker insulation and windows, especially insulated windows. When you replace the door, replace all the hardware and the stop material outside the door with the type that has a rubber weather-strip gasket.

1 Release tension on side-mounted extension springs by lifting door and locking it in place on each side with a pair of locking pliers. Tie extension spring to roller track; then detach cable from bottom bracket with a pair of pliers. Lower a double door by recruiting at least two people to help bear the weight. Before lowering the door, place 2x4 blocks under it to prevent smashing a foot or finger when it's lowered.

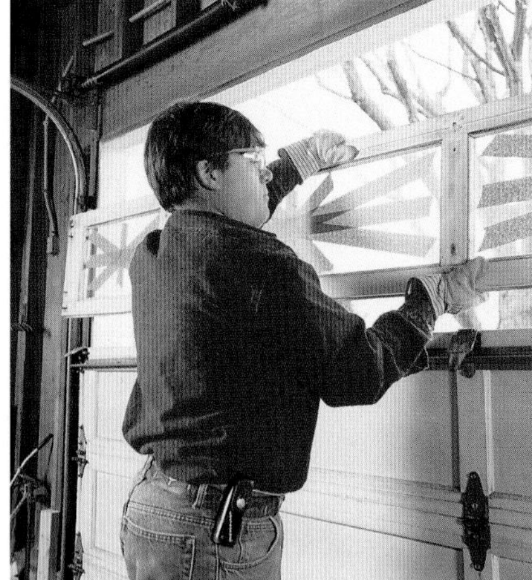

2 Dismantle the door one section at a time by disconnecting rollers and brackets. If you have windows, tape them to control flying shards if they break. With all sections removed, remove old roller tracks and hardware. If your old door has an opener bracket like the one shown in step 4, save it for the new door if it will fit. Your new door kit will not include an opener bracket, and a steel door requires it if you use an opener.

3 Center and level the first section. Door must be level even if floor isn't, so use shims under section to level it. Rubber gasket on bottom section will fill gaps created by unlevel floor. To hold level in place, tape it to the section. To hold section in place, lightly toe-nail 3-1/2-in. nail into frame and bend it over section. Add brackets and rollers before setting sections in place. Stack one section on top of another, toe-nailing as you go up.

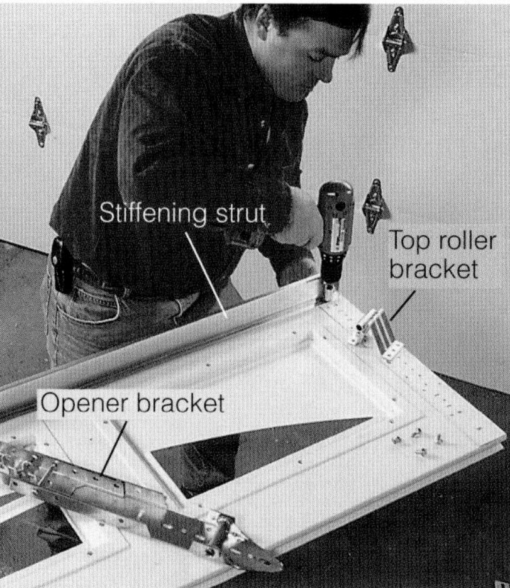

4 Install stiffening strut on top of upper section of steel doors when section is lying flat. To speed assembly, use self-tapping bolts and drill-powered nut driver. Next, install opener bracket (reused or purchased separately) that replaces center bracket between top two sections. Top-section roller brackets mount underneath stiffening strut. Slide the rollers into roller brackets and install top section. Protect door sections from scratches by putting carpet scraps on top of sawhorses.

Safety First

Release Tension Safely

Hire a pro, who will use special tools called winding bars to release the tension on an existing torsion spring system. Doing this on your own is extremely dangerous without the right tools and experience.

Keys to a Safe System

The right door installed with the following qualities in mind can provide decades of safe, reliable service.

Light weight. Newer insulated steel doors, even the heaviest ones, usually weigh less than half that of older doors.

Pinch resistance. The most common injury is a finger that gets smashed, or even amputated, between sections. Look for a door that offers pinch-resistant section designs.

Containment cables. If you have extension springs and don't plan to replace your door, make sure the springs have containment cables, or install them (p. 396), to control the spring if it breaks.

Safe door openers. All openers should have an auto-reverse feature and photoelectric eyes located near the floor on both sides of the door. If the eyes aren't connected or the beam is interrupted, the door won't operate.

Securely mounted hardware and rails. Torsion spring brackets should be firmly mounted to the wooden header above the door. Roller-track support brackets and the opener should be firmly mounted to the ceiling.

Annual maintenance. Make an annual check of all parts of your door system.

Opener switch location. Children like to play with automatic door openers, so opener switches should be mounted at least 5 ft. (1.6 m) above the floor.

5 Install vertical roller tracks first by wrapping track's curved lip around rollers. Top of vertical tracks should be approximately 8 in. (20 cm) below top of upper section. Hold bottom of vertical tracks at least 1/8 in. (3 mm) off concrete floor. Wait to install upper tracks until this step is complete. Check level of top section to make sure tops of vertical tracks are level with each other. After leveling and mounting these tracks, install the horizontal upper roller tracks.

6 Align upper roller tracks by carefully lifting door halfway up. Lock door in place with two locking pliers on tracks. Install supporting brackets on back of rails using perforated angle iron. Install stop bolts, with threads toward the inside of track and at end of each upper track. Stop bolts prevent door from accidentally rolling out the back end of upper tracks.

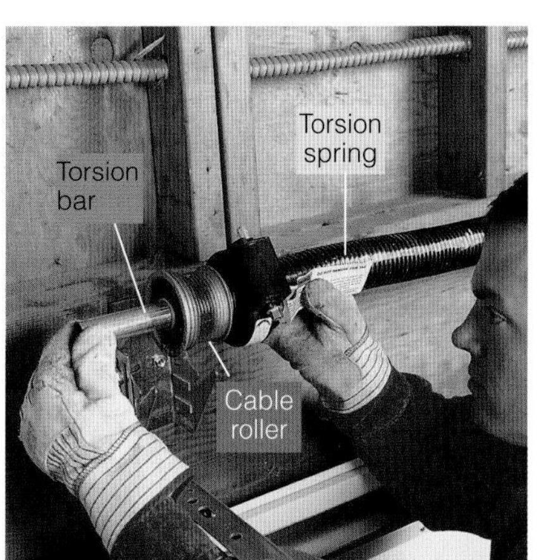

7 Set torsion bar, torsion spring and cable roller in place according to manufacturer's instructions. Some manufacturers use a single torsion spring for a double door, but others use two. The painted line on the spring acts as a gauge for number of turns you put on the spring. Attach lift cables to brackets on door bottom. If installing extension springs, attach lift cables and containment cables according to manufacturer's instructions.

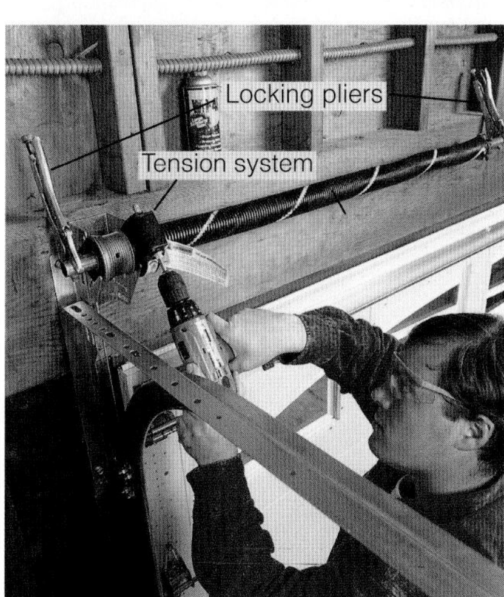

8 Attach locking pliers to torsion bar on both ends of spring to keep bar from turning while adding tension. Apply lubricant to the spring to inhibit rust and reduce metal fatigue. Using your drill, add tension to the spring. Check the tension (door balance) with opener disconnected when lowered halfway. The door should hold its position. If not, adjust tension until door is properly balanced.

Garage Doors / Automatic Openers

Installing an automatic garage door opener, equipped with the modern safety features, not only dramatically improves convenience but makes a garage door system safer than one without an opener because manually opening and closing heavy doors is a common cause of accidents.

Openers are available for most garage door types. The opener shown below works with an overhead door, sometimes called a sectional door. Although overhead doors are the most common type, openers can also be installed on one-piece doors, also called "kick-out" doors, in much the same way.

Before installing the opener, perform these five checks to prepare your door system so it's compatible with an automatic opener:

1. As the door goes up, be sure you have at least 3 in. (7.5 cm) of space above the highest point your door reaches.
2. Verify that you have a grounded electrical outlet within 3 ft. (1 m) of the opener's motor.
3. Inspect the door hardware for damage or wear (see next page) and make the necessary repairs.
4. Make sure the door is properly balanced (see next page).
5. For fiberglass, hardboard, metal or lightweight wood doors, add a stiffening strut (see step 5, below left) to strengthen the top section and prevent damage.

Buy the right opener for your door and follow the manufacturer's installation instructions for your situation. Match the opener's horsepower to the door's size. The 1/4-hp openers should be used only on single doors. Use 1/3- or 1/2-hp openers for double doors.

1 Connect rails and power-drive assembly following manufacturer's instructions. Lubricate chain or screw drive. Fasten header bracket so rail clears torsion spring.

2 After attaching front of rail to header bracket, tie opener in its approximate position with rope.

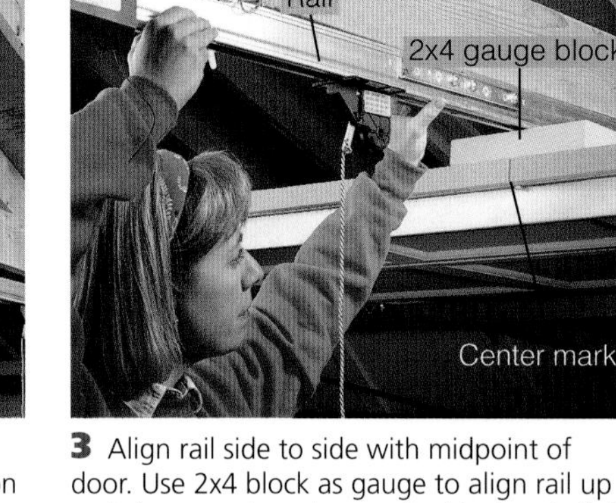

3 Align rail side to side with midpoint of door. Use 2x4 block as gauge to align rail up and down so door clears rail with door in fully open position.

4 Anchor power unit to solid framing using perforated angle iron, lag screws, bolts and nuts.

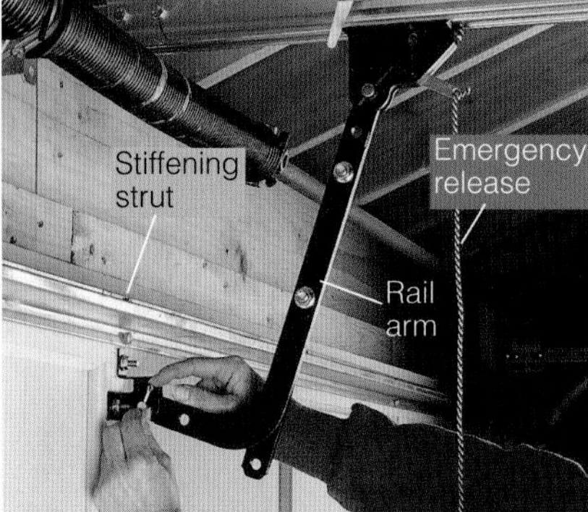

5 Center opener bracket on door. Install stiffening strut on top of upper section to prevent racking door with opener. Attach rail arms to door bracket.

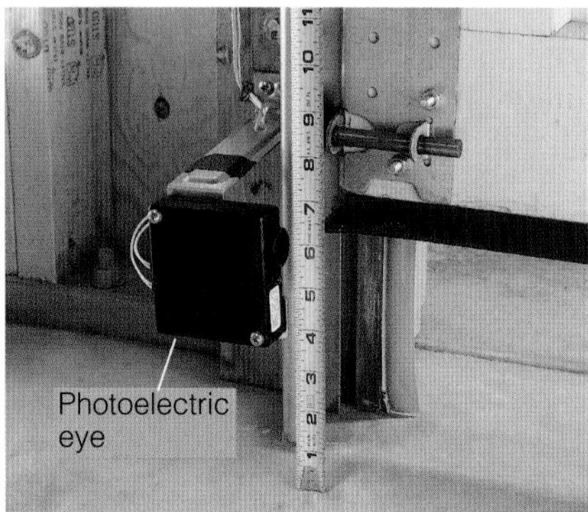

6 Position electric eye 6 in. (15 cm) above floor and clear of roller tracks. Keep wires away from moving parts. The eye stops or reverses opener when an obstruction is detected.

Safety First

Auto Reverse Test

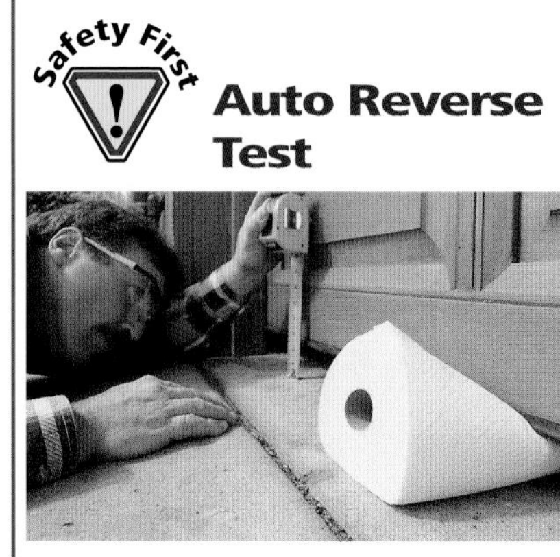

Test your automatic opener's auto-reverse feature by placing a roll of paper towels directly under the point where the opener is attached to the door. The door should get no closer than 1 in. (2.5 cm) to the ground and should reverse direction two seconds after coming to a stop. If your door opener doesn't have an auto-reverse feature, buy a new opener.

Door Maintenance Precautions

Perhaps no other part of your home experiences as much wear and tear as the garage door; it can travel up and down more than 1,000 times a year. A neglected door can become as noisy as a locomotive, and pose a significant safety risk to your family, especially your kids. But when kept in good working order, it provides convenience and security. To be safe while working on the door, take the following precautions:

1. Unplug the automatic door opener so it can't be activated.
2. If the door is open while you're working, clamp locking pliers onto the roller track below a roller to keep door from dropping.
3. Never remove a lift cable while the door is under tension. If released, the cable can cut like a knife.
4. Never attempt to adjust or release the tension on an overhead door torsion spring. This is a job for garage door professionals only.

Test door balance by disengaging the door from the opener. You should be able to lower the door halfway and have it hold its position. If the door rides back up or falls, have tension adjusted by a professional.

Checking Rollers and Brackets

Because the door moves, hardware can loosen. Inspect and tighten all roller brackets and bolts that hold the rails to the support brackets.

1 Inspect rollers for wear and tear. Nylon rollers tend to crack or chip. On steel rollers, bearings wear and wheels begin to tilt like one shown here. Replace worn rollers by removing roller bracket.

Caution: Do not remove bottom roller bracket.

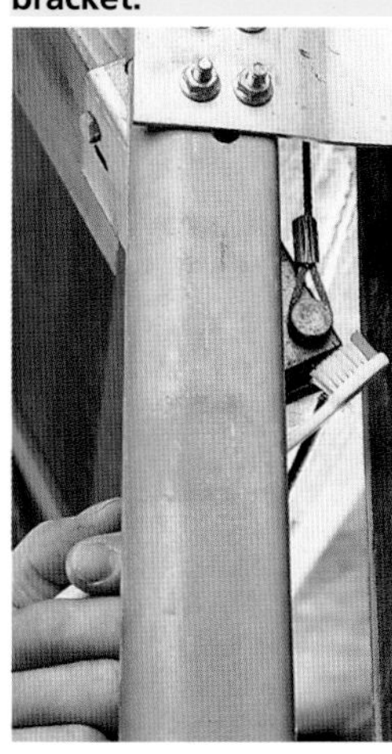

2 Inspect lift cable for wear or corrosion, especially where cable attaches to bottom roller bracket. Clear away the gunk from this area with an old toothbrush to inspect the cable. If necessary, call a professional to replace the cable.

Lubricating Springs and Chains

All springs will eventually break because of metal fatigue or corrosion. Annually lubricating your door lift system will extend the life of springs and opener drives by preventing corrosion. Furthermore, it will make both the door and opener operate more smoothly and quietly and help keep openers working in extremely cold conditions.

1 Lubricate chain- or screw-drive annually with white lithium grease. Spray-on lithium grease is available at most hardware stores.

2 Coat overhead torsion springs or extension springs with lubricant, such as WD-40. Don't wipe off the excess.

Adjusting the Travel Setting

If the door comes back up after it hits the floor or doesn't close or open far enough, you need to adjust the travel on the door opener. Some openers have two setscrews on the back or side of the motor housing, some have knobs on the bottom and others have trip levers on the travel bar that you can reposition.

Adding a Lift Handle

Install a lift handle on both sides of the door to discourage the habit of pulling down on the spaces between the sections—a practice that results in hundreds of crushed fingers every year. Make sure the outside handle will clear the top of the door frame.

Garage Doors / Maintaining

Adding New Weather Seals

Replace the weather seal on the bottom of your garage door if it's brittle, worn or torn. Remove wood door seals with a flat pry bar and attach the new seal with 1-in. roofing nails. The hollow rubber weather seal on metal doors is a U-shaped astragal. An astragal is sized according to its width as it lies flat. To further seal a door, replace wood door stops with vinyl stops that have rubber gaskets.

Wood door seals. Install a new seal with wide angle of flange to the inside of the door. Nail one end of seal, pull it taut, nail other end and then nail from the center out.

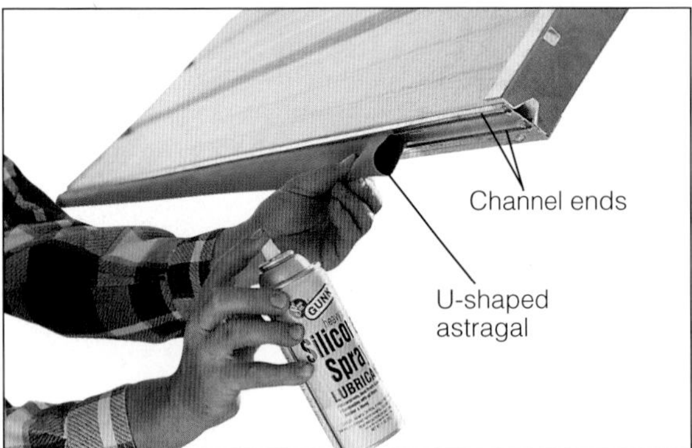

Metal door seals. Use flat-bladed screwdriver to open channel ends and remove rubber astragal. Lubricate channels and install new astragal.

Dealing with Uneven Concrete

When a concrete slab buckles or sinks, it frequently creates a gap between the garage door and the floor. This gap provides easy access for small creatures and sometimes rainwater and snow. It can also knock the door out of level, creating unnecessary wear and tear on the door's hardware and automatic opener. Close the gap with one of these two methods:

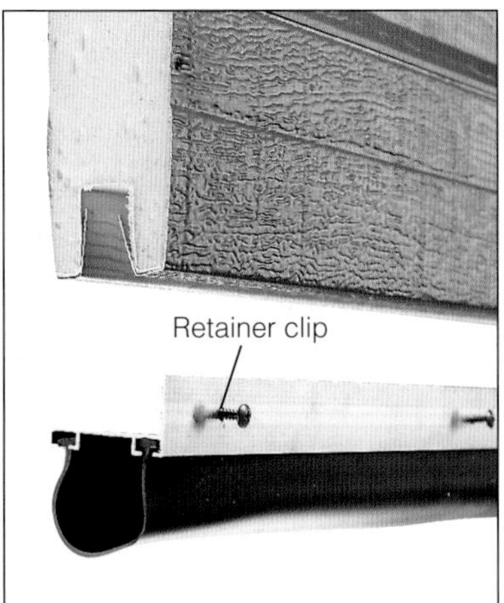

Gap-filling astragals work on metal or wood doors if they are installed in a retainer clip mounted to the door. Astragals are available at garage door supply stores in a variety of widths. These work best if your concrete moves with seasonal changes.

Scribe the bottom of the wood door to fit the concrete. Remove old seal and lower door. Use small wood block that's the same thickness as the widest part of the gap, tape pencil to it and transfer the concrete's profile. Cut the door, seal the raw wood and install a new weather seal.

Adding a Spring Containment Cable

Containment cables should be installed on all extension-spring lift systems. Extension springs are mounted above the roller tracks. Without a containment cable, when an extension spring breaks (and most eventually will), the spring and cable become a heavy, dangerous whip that can smash into cars or unsuspecting victims. These cables contain a broken spring in the space above the track and are inexpensive and readily available at hardware stores.

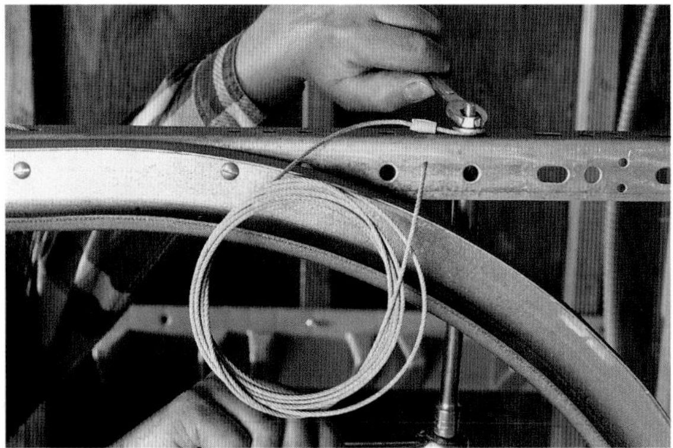

1 Mount an extension spring containment cable by bolting one end to the bracket at the front of the upper rail and feeding the cable through the spring.

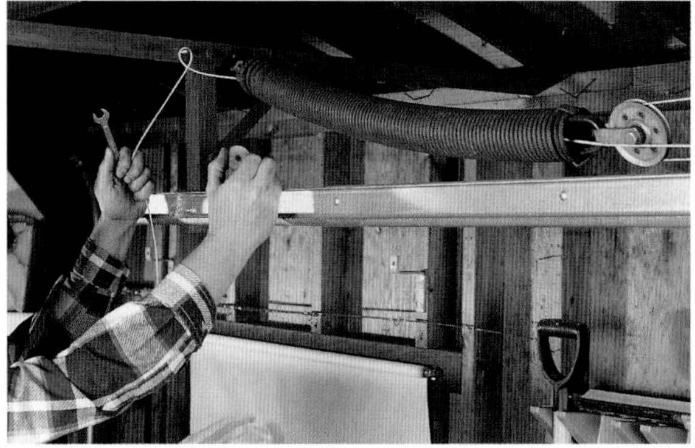

2 Bolt the other end of the cable to the upper support bracket. Make one full loop of cable around the bolt and secure it with a fender washer and locknut.

Concrete, Masonry & Asphalt

Concrete / Basics

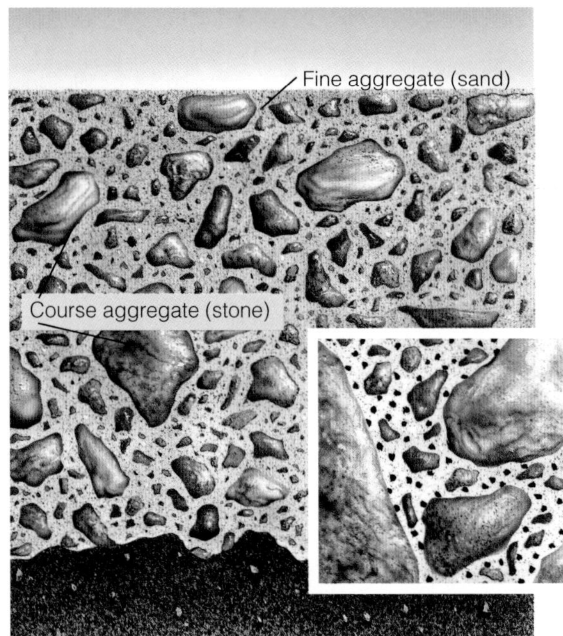

Properly mixed concrete results in the coarse and fine aggregate being suspended uniformly throughout the material. A matrix of cement crystals envelops the aggregate and gives the concrete its high compressive strength.

What is Concrete?

Concrete is the unsung hero among building materials. It is strong and durable enough for use in massive bridges and interstate highways, but economical and versatile enough for a residential patio slab or even a kitchen countertop.

A mixture of fine and coarse aggregate (sand and stone), portland cement and clean water, concrete starts out in a "plastic" or fluid state that conforms to the container, or form, that holds it, then cures to a rigid shape. The portland cement is made by heating limestone and other minerals in a rotating kiln, and then cooling and grinding the clumps, called clinker, into a fine powder. In the presence of water, the cement undergoes a chemical reaction called hydration and begins to form microscopic interlocking crystals. This is what gives concrete its strength. The sand and rock aggregate—suspended throughout the mix—are there mostly to add volume and stiffness and to reduce the cost. Cement crystals will continue to form as long as water is present, but the first week, when the concrete will form about 80 percent of its final strength, is critical. After a month, it will be at 90 percent or greater strength. Fully cured, concrete can be harder than some rocks. A compressive strength of 3,000 pounds per sq. in. (psi) is the benchmark for light-duty residential projects, such as sidewalks and patios, and 5,000 psi is the target for driveways. Cement content and the curing methods are the two biggest factors in the concrete's final strength. Steel reinforcement is also used to control cracks and shifting.

Additives and air entrainment. Aside from the water and cement content, temperature and relative humidity are among the key factors that determine how concrete sets up and cures. Chemicals added to the mixture can accelerate or retard the curing process, but are used mostly by professionals on commercial job sites. Air entrainment is used routinely on projects, however. This process involves a chemical reaction that produces millions of microscopic bubbles. The air bubbles make the concrete easier to finish, but more importantly, the voids later accommodate expanding moisture and help prevent damage from freeze-thaw cycles.

How Water Affects the Concrete Mix

Water is necessary for the chemical process that causes concrete to harden, but too much will undermine the material's final strength. Pros talk about "placing" concrete, not pouring it; the mix should be stiff enough to require moving it with shovels and hoes. Concrete ready-mix suppliers use "slump"—the distance a mix sample settles when unrestrained from a test cone—to gauge the water content; about 4 or 5 in. (10 to 12 cm) of slump is appropriate for a residential mix. The material should flow readily but not pour. If it's too wet, the excess water will result in a looser matrix of cement crystals, with reduced strength.

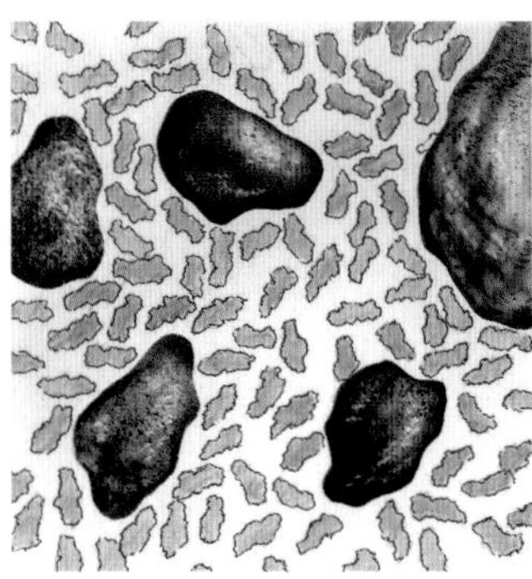
Wet mix. Excess water in a concrete mix not only lets the large, heavy aggregate sink rather than stay suspended in the mix, but it causes greater separation of the cement crystals. Both conditions result in weaker concrete, especially near the surface.

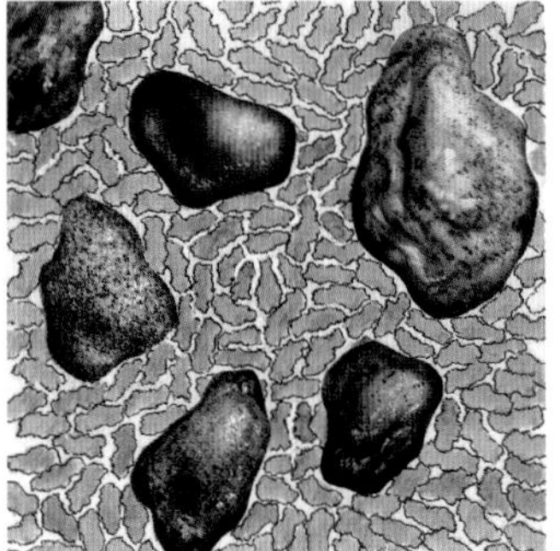
Dry mix. A stiffer mix with less water will cure with fewer, smaller voids between the cement crystals. This makes the concrete stronger and also offers much higher resistance to frost damage, because less water can penetrate and expand within the concrete.

Concrete / Tools

Other than a wheelbarrow, shovel and hoe, most tools you need to mix, place and finish concrete aren't general-purpose items you can use for other projects. Fortunately, they are relatively few, simple and affordable. You'll need general carpentry tools to make and set the wood forms, but after the concrete is inside them, you'll concentrate on bedding the aggregate, shaping the edges and consolidating the surface so it forms a smooth, durable layer. Some tools are worth renting—a vibrating plate compactor (see p. 401) and a bull float, for example. These are too expensive for the average homeowner to purchase for just one or two projects.

One tool you may need besides those shown here is the steel finishing trowel, used when an extremely flat, smooth surface is required.

Concrete work isn't pretty, so wear well-seasoned work clothes. Knee-high rubber work boots let you walk in the concrete while you're placing it—often a necessity for all but the smallest projects. Wear long pants and sleeves, plus safety glasses and gloves to shield yourself from the caustic mix.

Magnesium bull float

About 3 ft. (90 cm) wide, a bull float glides across freshly screeded concrete to push down the rock aggregate and smooth the surface. Whether pushed or pulled, its leading edge is always raised slightly.

Magnesium hand float

This smaller hand float works in areas where a bull float can't fit or isn't required. The magnesium blade works better on air-entrained concrete, where a wood float tends to stick.

Groover

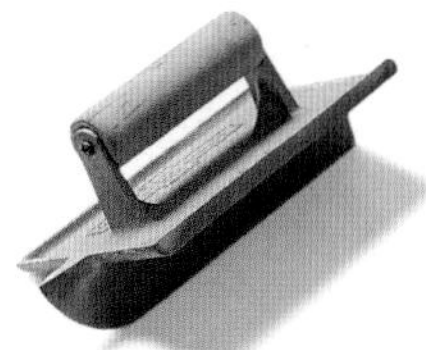

Control joints are grooves formed at intervals in the wet concrete (or sawn in dried slabs) to prevent random cracking at the surface. Sometimes called a deep bronze groover, this is the tool that makes the grooves.

Edger

This tool forms a slightly rounded edge along the perimeter of the concrete, right inside the forms. It makes a nicer-looking edge and reduces the random breakage that would occur if the edges were left sharp.

Broom

There are many ways to add texture to concrete, but this is the simplest. After floating and troweling the surface, allow the concrete to set slightly, and then drag a broom across the surface to create a slip-resistant texture.

How Much Concrete?

Because concrete starts to set up as soon as it's mixed, you have to estimate the quantity accurately beforehand. If it's delivered as ready mix in a concrete truck, you buy it by the cubic yard. You can calculate the amount by this formula (**Note:** You divide by 27 because there are 27 cu. ft. in a cu. yd.):

$$\frac{\text{Width (in feet) x length (in feet) x thickness (in feet or fractions of a foot)}}{27} = \text{cu. yds.}$$

Ready-mix trucks typically hold about 9 cu. yd. Most suppliers add a surcharge if the load is less than half of that. If you're not sure how much or what type concrete to order, explain the project and give the dimensions to the supplier, who can calculate the volume and help you decide on the right slump and added chemicals required, if any. Some suppliers have trucks that carry the ingredients separately and mix the concrete on site, in exactly the quantity needed. The cost is slightly higher, but you won't run short or have excess concrete to dump.

Mix it yourself

In areas so remote that ready-mix concrete isn't available, you can have the ingredients delivered and mix them on site in a gasoline-powered mixer. For a "6-sack mix"—meaning six 94-lb. bags (each holding 1 cu. ft. of cement) per 1 cu. yd.—use a 1 to 2-1/2 to 3 ratio by volume of cement, sand and crushed stone, respectively. Plan on using approximately 30 gal. (115 l) of water per cu. yd.

Amounts of concrete needed for common slabs

Residential walkways and driveways are typically formed with 2x4 framing lumber, making 3- and 4-in.-thick slabs common. These thicknesses are also common for garage, basement and crawl space floors.

One yard of concrete spread 4 in. thick will cover an area about 80 sq. ft.; spread 3 in. thick, it will cover an area about 105 sq. ft. Use this list to estimate the number of cubic yards you need:

Size (sq. ft.)	3-in. slab	4-in. slab
50	1/2 cu. yd.	2/3 cu. yd.
100	1 cu. yd.	1-1/4 cu. yd.
200	2 cu. yd.	2-1/2 cu. yd.
500	4-3/4 cu. yd.	6-1/4 cu. yd.
1,000	9-1/2 cu. yd.	12-1/2 cu. yd.

Note: To convert cubic yards into cubic meters, multiply by .765.

Concrete / Mixing

It's good to know the basics of ordering ready-mix concrete for delivery by a mixer truck, but for many home-improvement projects, you'll end up buying dry, bagged concrete and mixing it yourself. Small walkways, fence or deck-post footings and other modest projects can often be managed in stages that let you mix batches by hand. To do this, you'll need a wheelbarrow, a hoe and a plastic bucket for measuring water.

Using a standard homeowner-duty wheelbarrow like the one shown below, you'll limit your batches to a single 80-lb. (36-kg) bag of concrete mix. Each bag yields only about 2/3 cu. ft., so if you want to mix more—and can handle the extra weight—buy a larger contractor's-type wheelbarrow that can hold two bags' worth. If you want to really reduce the grunt work, rent a portable mixer for the day.

Bagged Concrete Mix

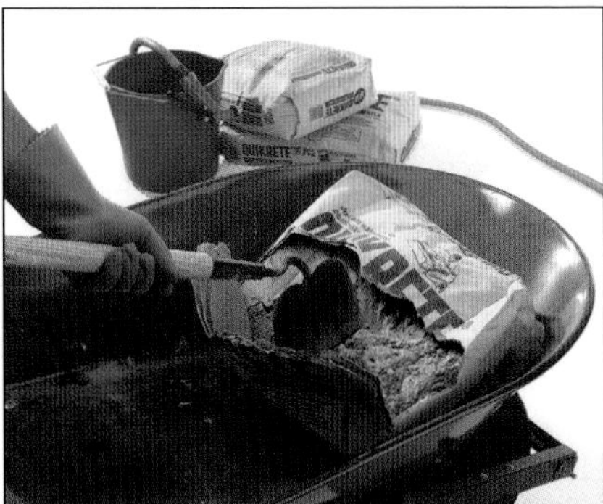

1 Set a bag near the front of a wheelbarrow and cut it open using a hoe. Dump the contents slowly to reduce dust, and remove the bag.

2 Fill a bucket with the water quantity specified on the bag. Pour all but a few cups into the opposite end of the wheelbarrow.

3 Pull a small amount of the dry mix into the water and mix thoroughly. Continue mixing incrementally until the contents are wet.

4 Move to the side of the wheelbarrow, brace it with your knee and mix the concrete from side to side. Pull dry mix up from the bottom.

5 Add the remaining water until the mix is thoroughly wetted but still holds firmly at the sides of the hoe trough. A tamped area should smooth quickly.

Creating Your Own

For areas too large to use concrete mixed bag by bag, but too small for a ready-mix truck, consider buying cement, sand and gravel and mixing them on site by hand or with a portable mixer (see "How Much Concrete?" on p. 399). This is less expensive than bagged mix but requires more work.

Shop Smart: Selecting Bagged Concrete

Standard concrete mix is an economical, all-purpose material. **Fiber-reinforced** concrete has tiny plastic fibers to make it more resistant to shrinkage cracks and chipped edges—a good choice for high-traffic areas. **High early strength** has a higher cement percentage and develops superior strength in about half the time as a standard mix. **Fast-setting** concrete has a higher cement content or additives to accelerate the curing cycle—ideal for projects where you want to work quickly. Use a product labeled as "air entrained" for freezing climates.

Concrete / Pouring: Forming and Preparation

Like any masonry material, concrete's strength lies in its ability to resist compressive forces, such as concentrated weight. Against bending or tension forces, concrete is relatively weak. This means a slab or footing needs firm, stable support underneath it, and providing that is the single most effective thing you can do to ensure your concrete project will last.

Preparation work for a concrete slab starts with determining the surface's finished height and removing any vegetation and loose soil from the slab area. You can't totally prevent movement unless you pour a footing below the frost line, but you can stabilize the subbase to reduce the likelihood of cracking.

1 Outline the slab and rent a sod cutter to remove grass. Clear an area about 3 in. (8 cm) wider on each side than the finished slab will be to allow room for the forms.

2 Excavate to a depth of about 8 in. (20 cm). (Go 2 to 4 in. deeper for clay soil in freezing climates.) Set forms along one side. Use screws to fasten wood stakes to the forms. Space stakes about 2 to 3 ft. (60 to 90 cm) apart.

3 Make a gauge board with cleats on each end to establish a consistent width for the walkway. Place a builder's level on it at regular intervals so you can level the forms on the opposite side as you install them.

4 Rent a vibrating plate compactor to pack the soil firmly between the forms. This won't stop severe frost heaving, but it will prevent settling that might result in a cracked slab.

5 Spread and tamp a 4-in. (10-cm) layer of gravel—crushed 3/4-in. (20-mm) rock is ideal—to provide a stable drainage base for the slab. Vibrating the rock with a compactor helps, but it isn't essential.

Stronger Concrete

Interlocking cement crystals and aggregate provide most of concrete's strength, but you can reinforce a slab with other materials, too. Steel provides tensile strength that keeps cracks from spreading; plastic fibers help prevent early shrinkage cracking.

Rebar. Textured-steel rod called rebar placed around the perimeter of a slab helps reinforce vulnerable areas. Overlap and tie ends with wire.

Mesh. Steel wire reinforcing mesh, typically a 6-in. (15 cm) square grid, helps contain cracks. Place within about 2 in. (5 cm) of the ground for best results.

Fiber. Short plastic fibers dispersed throughout a wet mix helps strengthen concrete. The fibers are most effective at preventing cracks during the initial curing phase.

Concrete / Pouring Sidewalks

Concrete Tools **399**
How Much Concrete? **399**
Forming and Preparation **401**

When the site preparation is done and the forms set, you can get ready for the pour. Calculate the concrete volume and call local suppliers to get price quotes and information about mix types. Watch the weather forecast and try to schedule the work for a dry, cool day. If the hot weather won't let up, plan to start early so you can finish and cover the concrete before peak afternoon heat. Protect against freezing temperatures for at least the first three days. Arrange for at least one helper and get all your tools together the day before the pour. Large projects are often best done in two or three smaller pours.

Skin Alert!

As far as working techniques go, concrete is a fairly user-friendly material, but the high alkalinity of the lime-based cement is caustic to skin and dangerous to your eyes. To avoid sudden splashes, always wear safety glasses when mixing and placing concrete. Wear long pants and sleeves if it's not unbearably hot; otherwise, rinse any concrete from your skin quickly with clean water. Wear tall rubber boots if you have to wade in the mix while you're placing the concrete, and wear lined rubber or leather work gloves to keep concrete from accumulating on your hands. Remove and rinse any concrete-saturated clothing. And keep some pain-relief medicine around for the morning-after aches and pains.

1 Place a few small mounds to support the wire mesh, then start filling. Overworking the concrete segregates the mix, so just place it quickly and keep moving.

2 Level the concrete with the forms by using a straight 2x4 as a screed board. Use a slight sawing motion across the forms as you work the screed along the surface.

3 Before the surface water appears, use a bull float to smooth the concrete and bed the aggregate below the surface. Always keep the leading edge raised slightly.

4 After the bleed water dissipates, use a magnesium hand float to refine the surface. Follow up with a steel trowel, again using broad sweeping motions.

5 Run the edging tool along the forms to round over the edge of the concrete. Lift the leading edge as you work back and forth in sections. Trowel again; then repeat.

6 Set a straightedge across the forms and use a groover to cut control joints. Make each section roughly square. Follow with a trowel to get a clean surface.

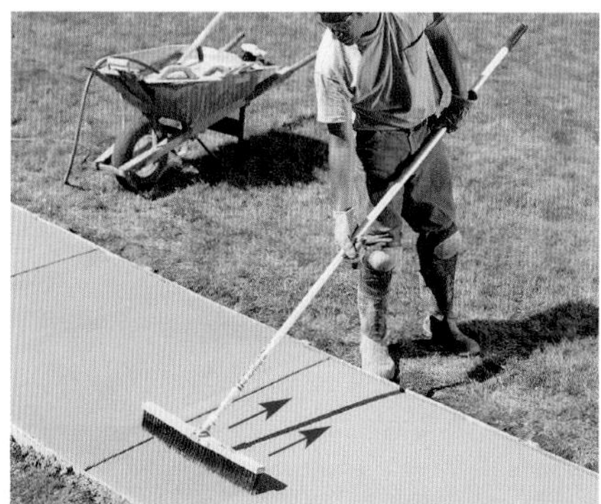

7 After the troweled concrete has a chance to set up somewhat, pull a push broom slowly across the surface to give it a nonslip texture. Overlap passes slightly.

8 If you have to stop progress on a pour, fit a temporary wood bulkhead to hold the concrete. Later, replace it with a felt isolation strip and continue pouring.

Concrete / Pouring Slabs

Although the basic procedure remains the same, pouring a slab presents a few logistical hurdles you won't find with sidewalks and smaller projects. Depending on the access for the mixer truck, getting the larger quantity of concrete inside the forms may or may not be an issue, but screeding, floating and troweling the slab is a little more difficult to do when you're working on a larger scale.

The same fundamental preparations are necessary; in fact, they are even more critical to ensuring the slab doesn't settle unevenly or crack randomly from frost heaving. If the area is too large to remove the sod and topsoil using manual tools, consider renting a rototiller to break it up for removal, or hire a skid loader operator to do the excavating for you. The core elements—compacted sand or gravel base, 2x4 or wider form material and steel reinforcing mesh—remain the same.

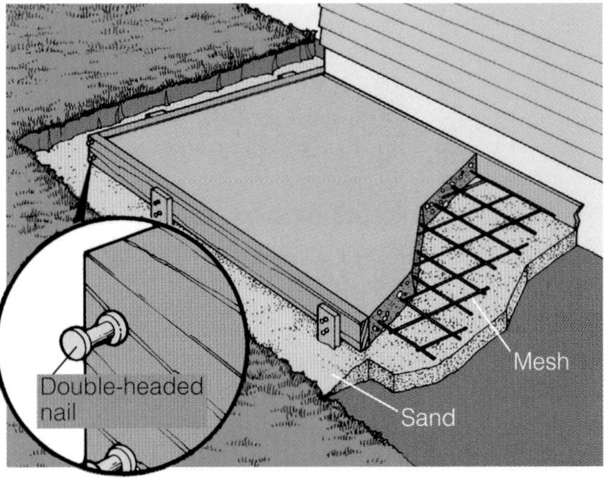

1 When abutting another slab or wall, snap a chalk line and install an isolation strip along the edge. Create a 12-in.-wide (30-cm-wide) concrete curb along this edge to use as a leveling guide for the rest of the pour.

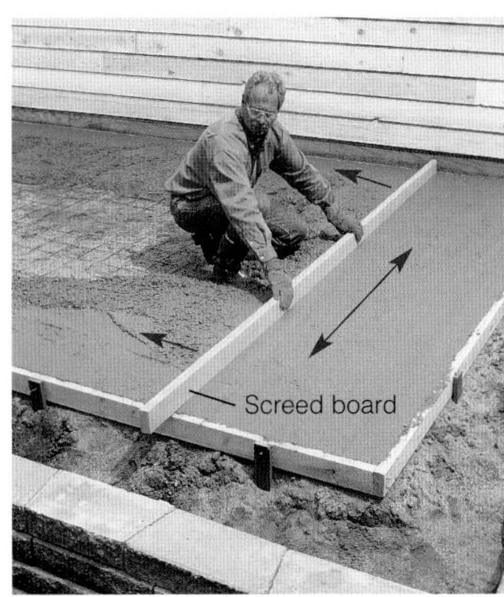

2 Pour the concrete at a manageable pace, pulling the steel mesh up midway as you proceed. Make several passes with the screed to get the section level before you move on. Use a helper on large slabs.

3 Fit an extension handle on the bull float and use it to smooth the surface. Use short, choppy strokes to push the float across the concrete, then pull it back in a long continuous stroke.

4 Use a groover on an extension handle to cut control joints, dividing the slab into squares from 8 to 12 ft. (2.4 to 3.6 m) across. Use a straightedge guide for the first pass and use a series of short strokes.

Ordering the Right Mix

To ensure delivery when you need it, try to place an order several days before the pour; you can cancel if the weather turns sour. Calculate the area of your slab and the amount of concrete required, and ask the ready-mix vendor to confirm your figures. Also, tell the vendor what the project is and ask about options for cement content, air entrainment and slump. A "5-sack" mix (five 94-lb. bags of cement per cubic yard of concrete) is typical for residential concrete rated at 3,000-psi compressive strength, but it doesn't cost much more to bump that to a 6-sack/5,000-psi mix.

Air entrainment (see p. 398) is always recommended, and in most northern regions it's required by code. The flow readiness, measured as slump, is determined at the mixing plant, so don't add much, if any, water to the concrete mix when the truck arrives.

Concrete / Pouring Steps

Demolition Tools **37**
Stronger Concrete **401**
Rental Tools **424**

Like most home features, stairs are subject to specific building codes that govern their design, dimensions and railings. Before you draw a sketch or assume you can rebuild using the same dimensions as an old set of stairs, contact a local building official.

A common width for residential entry steps is 48 in. (122 cm), and the landing should measure at least 3 ft. (90 cm) from the door to the front edge. Each step consists of a vertical face called a riser and a flat horizontal surface called a tread; typically their dimensions add up to 18 in. (46 cm). This allows some discretion for the specific dimensions of each—risers can vary from 6 to 8 in. (15 to 20 cm) high, and treads can vary from 10 to 12 in. (25 to 30 cm) deep—but they must stay consistent for the entire flight of steps.

Concrete steps must rest on a solid concrete footing or other type of support, normally set 2 ft. (60 cm) deep in no-frost areas or below the frost line in regions where soil freezing occurs. Steel tie rods should connect the steps to the home's foundation wall, and you can dig pier footings under the front step. Once the concrete has cured, caulk the joint between the new steps and house. When the time comes, use a sledgehammer or rent a jackhammer to break up old steps.

1 Calculate the overall size—landing plus stairs—and excavate the topsoil in that area, leaving room for the forms. Use a posthole digger to excavate holes for pier footings that extend below the frost line. Tamp the soil firmly. Some areas and projects may require more substantial footings.

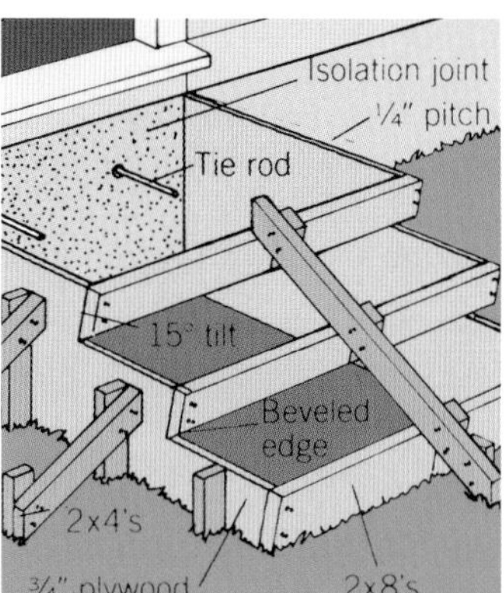
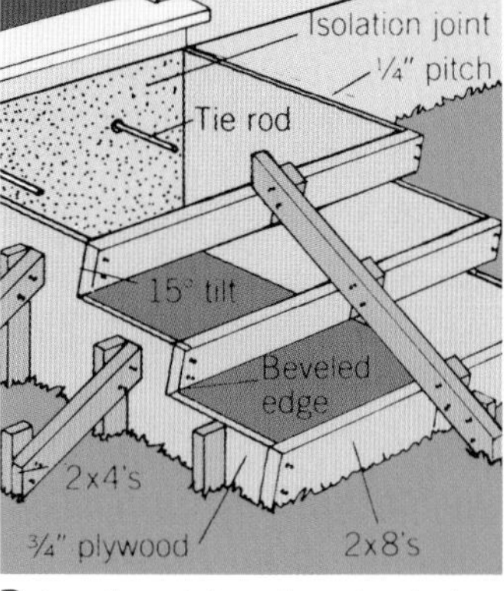

2 Install steel tie rods and an isolation membrane against the house foundation as shown. Cut side forms of 3/4-in. plywood and use dimensional lumber for the riser forms and the bracing. The center brace keeps the risers from deforming under pressure.

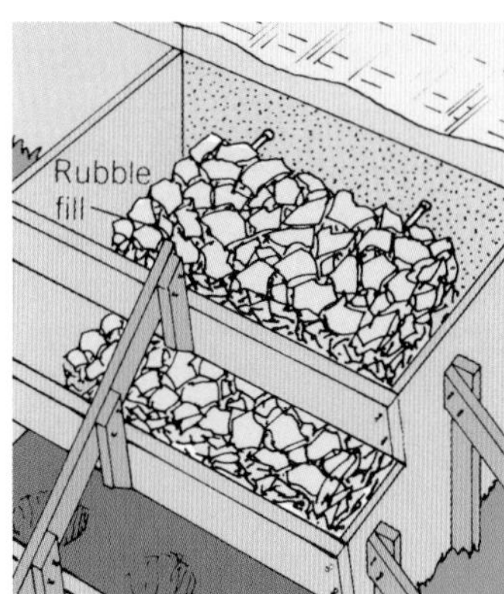

3 After the forms are built and braced, check that the sides are tight against the wall, are level to each other and pitch slightly away from the house for drainage. Fill partially with stone or concrete rubble to reduce the concrete volume required.

4 Place concrete in the footing(s) and the lowest step first. Strike off the excess concrete, and make your way up the remaining steps, working the shovel in the concrete to fill corners and tamping the forms. After screeding, float and edge the landing and treads.

5 When the concrete has set up partially but still responds to hard pressure from a tool edge, remove the riser forms, starting at the top. Float the surfaces and run an inside step tool at the riser-tread joints. Then edge again and finish with a broom.

Precast Alternative

If you don't need to customize your new steps to fit the site, consider purchasing and installing pre-cast concrete steps. They're usually less expensive than site-built stairs and can be set in position in a few hours. In climates subject to freeze/thaw cycles, they still need to be supported on frost footings or brackets that secure the steps to the foundation

Once available only as plain, boring and gray, pre-cast steps now come in a wide variety of styles and finishes. Some manufacturers offer them in a brick (below) or rustic stone look. They're also available in "flights" with side aprons for climbing hillsides and slopes.

Precast concrete steps offer the advantage of quicker installation, and they can also feature built-in railing mounts and brick or faux-stone surfaces for a finished look.

Concrete / Footings

Frost Depth Zones

Footings bear the entire weight of a building and must in turn distribute that load onto soil or another substrate that can sustain the weight without shifting or settling. Frost depth (see zone map at right) is a critical factor for footings, because wet soil expands up to 10 percent as it freezes, generating an immense force known as frost heave. The pressure can crack slabs and foundations.

Typical Frost Depths

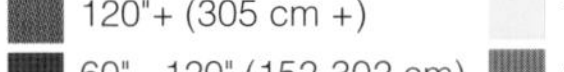

Pier Footings

Pier foundations are typically used under decks, porches, outbuildings and other accessory structures, although it is possible and sometimes desirable to use them to support an entire house. Even homes with a complete perimeter, or stem-wall, foundation sometimes have interior pier footings that support weight in the center of the structure.

The key to a pier foundation is having its footing below the frost line so it won't be pushed up from below. Also, a plastic or other low-friction barrier should surround the concrete pier so the freezing, expanding soil can't grab the sides and lift it up.

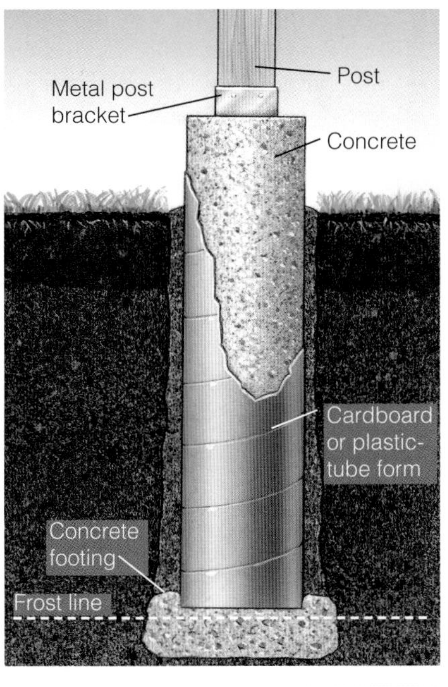

Monolithic Footings

Monolithic foundations—where the floor surface, or slab, and the foundation and footing are one continuous mass—solve the frost-heaving problem by floating atop the soil. Theoretically, the slab will escape damage if the soil freezes uniformly below it and lifts the entire mass gradually and evenly. A thicker edge—reinforced with steel rebar—provides additional strength and will stay intact even if cracks develop.

Monolithic footings are often used for freestanding garages and other small buildings. They are less effective for large slabs because the larger area is more likely to have differences in soil stability or freezing. Whatever the size, a subbase of compacted sand or crushed rock helps drain water and minimize damage from frost.

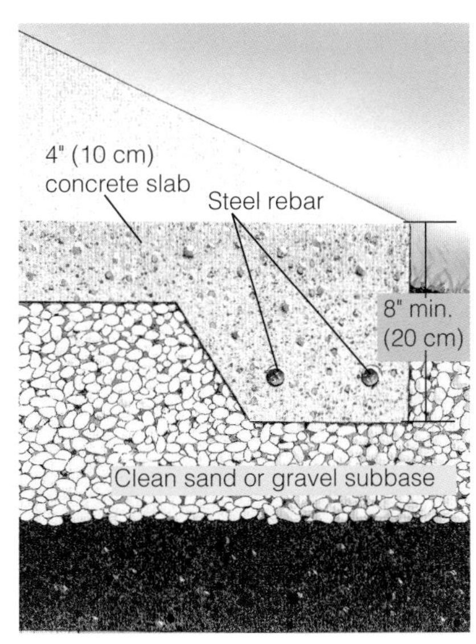

Full Footings

Sometimes called a perimeter or stem-wall foundation, a full foundation features a heavily reinforced footing placed below the frost line. Typically 1 to 2 ft. (30 to 60 cm) wide, the footing supports a foundation wall that is poured separately; the two are fixed to each other by means of a continuous keyway or by protruding rebar embedded in the footing.

In warmer regions, the area inside the perimeter will often remain a crawl space. Farther north, most builders simply excavate well below the frost line—typically to about 6 or 7 ft. (80 to 215 cm) below grade—to create a full basement under the house. A slab is then poured inside the walls to provide a floor.

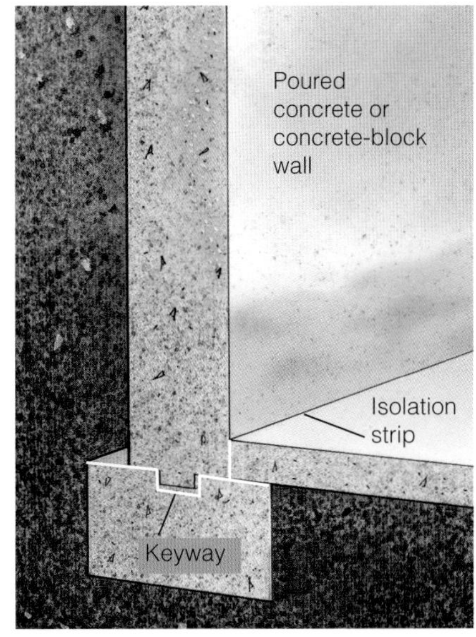

Concrete / Repairing Chips and Craters

Concrete is durable, but it requires the right mix, finishing methods and weather conditions during placement and curing to create a lasting surface. If something goes awry during these early stages, or if a heavy impact creates damage, the surface can spall (separate) to expose the concrete to weather and even more damage. Patching a small problem area is fairly simple, but before you proceed, assess the condition of the entire slab. If the surface degradation is widespread rather than localized, it's likely the concrete wasn't properly finished and cured, so it makes more sense to replace the slab than attempt spot repairs.

To patch concrete, you first have to cut and break away the damaged surface and any loose or flaking material. This normally requires a circular saw fitted with a masonry or diamond blade, a maul, a cold chisel, and safety gear, including goggles, dust mask and hearing protection.

1 With slow but steady pressure on the saw, cut a shoulder around the spalled area. Undercut the edges at a 5° angle to better lock in the patch.

2 Use a maul and a cold chisel to break out all the weak and loose concrete, especially near the edges. This generates flying chips and debris, so wear safety goggles.

3 Clean out all the debris and dust using a hand broom and a shop vacuum. Hose off the patch area with water, letting the excess evaporate.

4 If necessary, remoisten the patch area with a wet sponge, then pack the patch mix into the cutout using a wood float. Build the mix up slightly above the slab.

5 Screed off the excess material by sliding a 2x4 board side to side in a sawing motion. Refill any low spots and repeat until the surface is flat and uniform.

6 To match an existing rough or pitted texture of the surrounding concrete, rub the surface of the patch area with a sponge float, or use a broom to make the patch match.

7 Concrete ends up stronger when it can hold moisture and cure slowly. Keep the patch from drying too quickly by covering it with clear plastic sheeting for three days.

Although repairing a slab using concrete mix is recommended, a shallow area might not accommodate the stone aggregate. For patches less than 2 in. (5 cm) deep, use a topping mix instead. Use acrylic fortifier in either mix.

Concrete / Replacing a Small Section

If an entire section of concrete slab is damaged, it makes more sense to replace rather than repair it. Small sections of sidewalk, especially if separated by control joints, can often be removed and repoured in a single day. The tools and safety gear required are nearly the same as for larger concrete projects, but the small quantities involved mean you can mix bagged concrete in a wheelbarrow rather than order a ready-mix delivery in a truck. If the damage is the result of tree roots or settling, solve the problem first.

Getting Ready

1 Use a sledgehammer to break up the section into smaller pieces for disposal. Start at an open edge, work across and note whether the control joints have cracked all the way through. Wear safety glasses.

2 If the control joints are still intact, use a circular saw with a masonry blade to cut the joints deeper. Cut through at least one-third of the depth. Test by hitting it with a mallet to see if the joint breaks cleanly.

3 Remove the old concrete debris and tamp the soil firmly. Set forms and secure them with wood stakes placed every 2 ft. (60 cm). Drive the stakes until their upper ends are below the forms' top edges.

Pouring

1 Mix the bagged concrete in a wheelbarrow and place the mix inside the forms. Overfill them slightly. Use a board in a side-to-side motion to screed the excess from the surface. Tap the form boards with a hammer to settle the mix.

2 Float the concrete before the surface water appears. Then let the water dissipate as the concrete starts to set up. As it hardens, trowel and edge the section and cut control joints, if necessary, using a groover.

3 After texturing the surface with a nonslip broom finish, cover the new concrete with clear plastic sheeting to prevent rapid drying at the surface. Leave it covered for several days minimum, up to a week, to allow proper curing.

Mudjacking

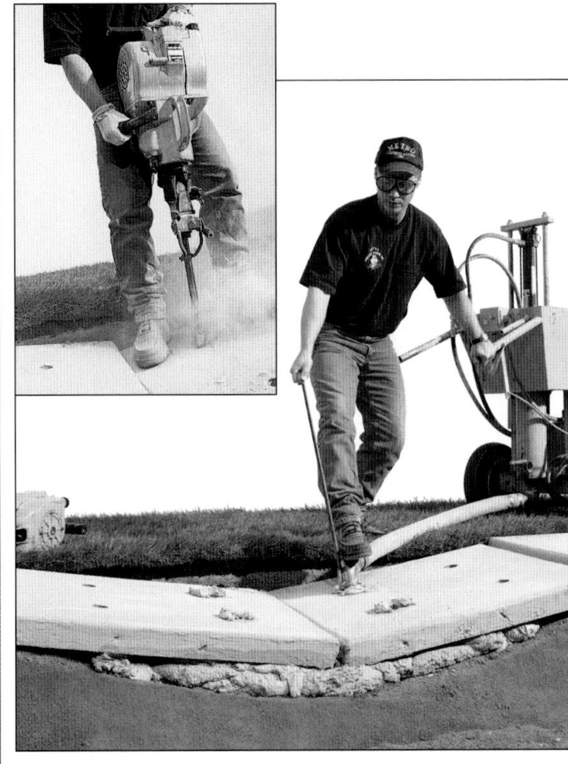

Occasionally, a concrete slab will settle because of shifting soil, subbase erosion or a similar loss of support from underneath. Sometimes the only antidote is to tear out and replace the slab, but if the ground has since stabilized, often the slab can be lifted back into place using a technique called mudjacking (sometimes referred to as slabjacking or pressure grouting).

This method requires specialized equipment and training, so it isn't a do-it-yourself option. The contractor will drill a series of holes through the slab, then use a hydraulic pump to inject a limestone-cement slurry into the holes. The slurry spreads beneath the slab, filling voids in the subbase and raising the slab to its original position.

Concrete / Repairing Steps

Drilling Concrete 51
Circular Saws 56
Concrete Tools 399

Broken Edges

Unfortunately, concrete rarely breaks in places that allow a quick, convenient repair. It breaks where it's most exposed to impact and wear. On steps, that means the edges where a tread meets a riser face. The repair process doesn't differ much from an internal patch, except that on a broken edge, there's nothing to contain the flow of the wet mix, so form boards must be used. As in flat patches in a slab, the newly placed concrete has a much better chance of survival if it is locked in place by deep-faceted sides rather than feathered thin at its edge. Wear gloves, goggles, hearing protection and a dust mask while cutting concrete.

1 Use a circular saw with a masonry blade to make clean cuts just outside the damaged area. Then use a cold chisel to break a flat horizontal ledge at the bottom of the cuts.

2 Place a form board against the step and brace it with brick or heavy blocks. Moisten the patch area with a wet sponge and trowel in concrete or topping mix to fill it.

3 As the concrete starts to set up, use an edging tool to create a slight radius to match the surrounding edge. Remove the form board, and trowel and texture the patch.

Broken Corners

Corner damage requires an approach similar to a broken edge but involves three surfaces rather than two. This means the form will have to wrap around the corner of two adjacent faces to contain the wet patch mix. The increased vulnerability of corners also warrants a little extra reinforcement in the way of embedded metal fasteners. By drilling and driving a few concrete screws into the broken corner and covering them with concrete mix, you create the equivalent of small pieces of rebar to help secure the patch to the step. As with other repairs, cover the corner patch with plastic sheeting to retain moisture.

1 Clean loose concrete from the patch area, then use a masonry bit to drill pilot holes about 1-1/2 in. (3.8 cm) deep for the concrete screws. Drive the screws until about 1 in. (2.5 cm) protrudes.

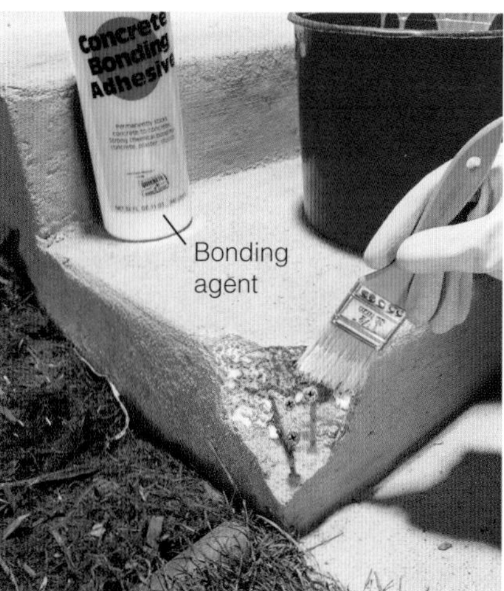

2 Clean the patch area thoroughly using a shop vacuum. Apply a brush-on masonry bonding agent to improve adhesion between the patch material and the old concrete just before making the repair.

3 Use bricks to hold a temporary corner form in place. Fill the patch area with wet concrete mix. Pack firmly and round the edge, then remove the form and finish with a trowel as concrete sets.

Concrete / Repairing Gaps, Cracks, Spalling and Railings

Gaps

Gaps between a concrete slab and other surfaces create problems in any season. Water can leak between and penetrate basement walls or, while liquid or frozen, simply exert pressure that can crack or otherwise damage a foundation.

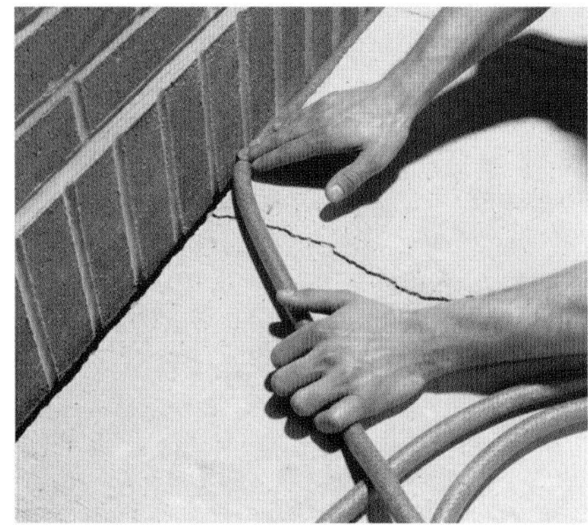

1 If a gap is too large—pencil thickness or greater—to be filled with caulking alone, start with foam backer rod pressed tightly between the surfaces.

2 With the backer rod fitted, follow up with a bead of urethane caulking. Lightly even out the caulking using the back of a spoon lubricated with mineral spirits.

Cracks

Minor cracks can be filled with caulking. It's critical the caulking remain flexible and intact through extremes in temperature, so use a urethane-based caulk or a silicone-modified acrylic caulk rated for exterior use on concrete.

Sealing small cracks with caulking helps prevent water penetration and frost displacement that will worsen the crack if left untreated.

Spalling

Heavy flaking of a concrete surface, called spalling, often occurs as the result of a too-wet mix or other installation mistakes, such as improper curing or sprinkling the fresh concrete with water.

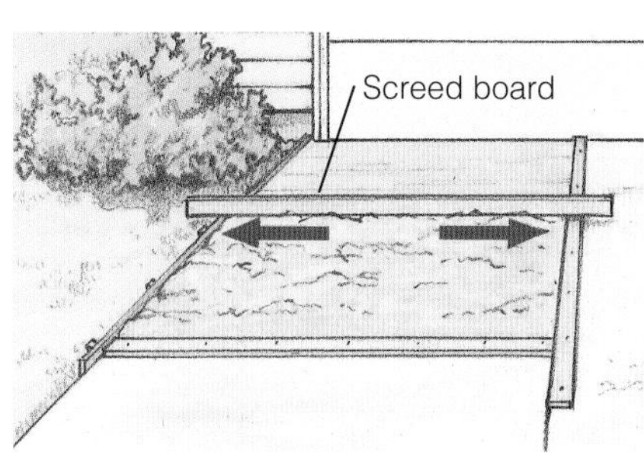

Spalled concrete can be repaired by removing all the weak, flaking material and applying an overlay mix of portland cement, fine sand and water. Screed and finish like regular concrete.

Loose Railings

Loose railing mounts seem to be a chronic problem on concrete steps. Water often corrodes the steel bolts or freezes around them to create "popped" holes in the concrete, weakening the mount to the point where the railing will likely fail just when a person needs it most.

The remedy for this involves new bolts—installed upside down in enlarged holes—and a special anchoring cement that you pour to lock them in place.

1 Detach the railing from the wall by removing the screws or wall brackets. Use a pry bar to lift out the floor-mount bracket and the old bolts.

2 Use progressively larger masonry bits to ream the bolt holes larger, until the new bolt heads will fit inside. Set the new bolts in upside down.

3 Brush the insides of the holes with masonry bonding agent. Mix and pour anchoring cement around the bolts. Let cement set at least one hour.

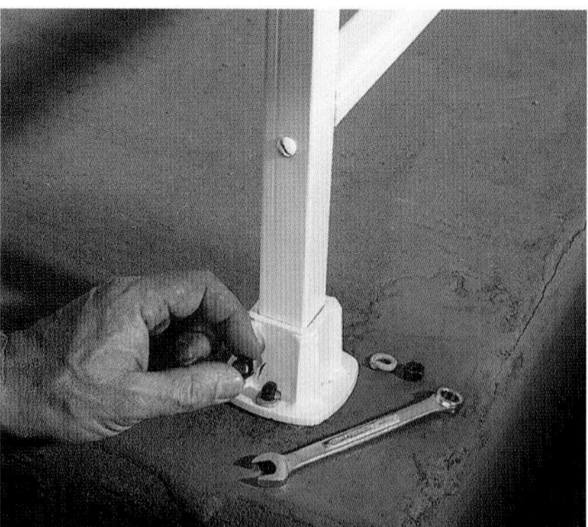

4 After the anchoring cement has cured, apply a waterproof sealer around the bolts. Reinstall the railing and secure it with nuts and lock washers.

Masonry / Basics

Bricks

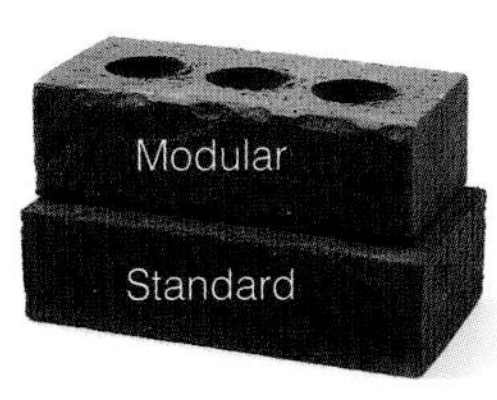

The basic unit of modern masonry—a rectangular clay brick that's fired in a kiln—has an ancient pedigree. Over the centuries, many variations have evolved. You don't have to know all of them, but a working knowledge of brick types and terminology will ensure that you choose the right material for your projects.

Modern manufacturing techniques have remedied the inconsistencies once associated with brick. Traditionally, the best specimens were dubbed face bricks; less-than-perfect bricks, called common, were used where they didn't show. Today, most bricks are face grade, and any variations in color, size or shape are intended. Using a brick's nominal size, which includes the mortar joints when installed, will give you the best idea of the quantity you'll need for a project. Other important ratings involve a brick's resistance to moisture and the effects of freezing and thawing. Bricks are graded as SW (severe weathering), MW (moderate weathering) or NW (no or negligible weathering), depending on their suitability for exterior or interior-only use.

Mortar

A mixture of portland cement, hydrated lime, sand and water, mortar is the bonding material that keeps bricks and other masonry units, such as stone or block, together. The chemical reaction is identical to the cement-crystal formation found in concrete, but no large aggregate is used. Besides anchoring bricks to each other, mortar compensates for irregularities in their surfaces, tethers the assembly to metal ties or reinforcements, and provides a little give should the wall move or settle. Mix according to directions on the bag.

Go Figure: Bricks and Mortar

When using standard-size bricks—those that measure a true 8 x 2-1/4 in.— with 1/2-in. (13-mm) joints, count on using 616 bricks per 100 sq. ft. When using modular bricks—those that measure 7-5/8 x 2-1/4 in.—with 3/8-in. (9.5-mm) joints, count on using 675 bricks per 100 sq. ft. Always increase your total brick order by at least 5 percent to cover breakage and waste. For mortar, plan to use about 8 cu. ft. for every 100 sq. ft. of brick surface.

Tools

As you might expect from such an ancient craft, bricklaying requires mostly simple tools. You'll find laser levels or other high-tech gadgets on commercial sites, but for the basic task of fitting one brick atop another, a batch of inexpensive hand tools works just fine.

Brick trowel. A brick trowel, with an offset triangular blade measuring about 1 ft. (30 cm) long, is used to apply and spread mortar. Skilled masons use an efficient placement technique called throwing.

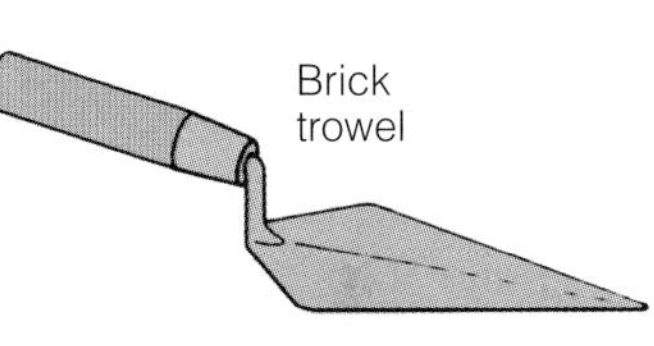

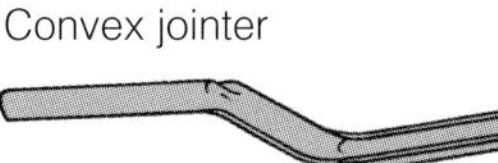

Raking tools. This general category includes rakers and jointers, which shape the mortar joints between bricks. Technically, a raker produces a flat, inset joint, and jointers leave a V-shape or concave profile.

Line blocks. Masonry walls or structures are typically built starting at the ends or corners, then filling in between. Line blocks are fitted to the end bricks, and a string is tensioned between them to provide a straight guideline.

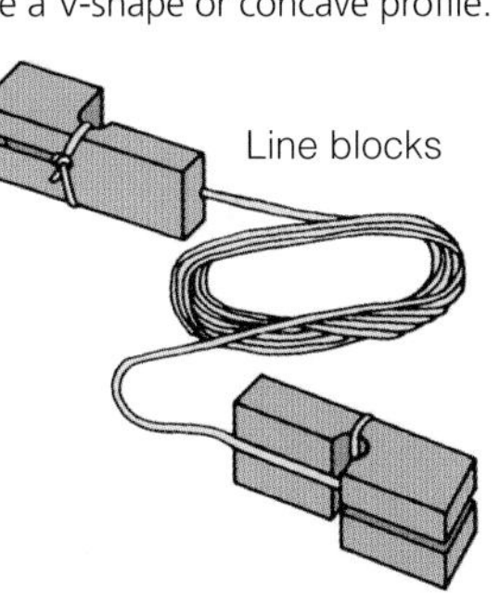

Hammer and brick chisel. A brick chisel features a wide blade that helps create a clean break when you don't have a diamond-blade power saw to cut the brick. A brick hammer has a chisel end designed for the same purpose.

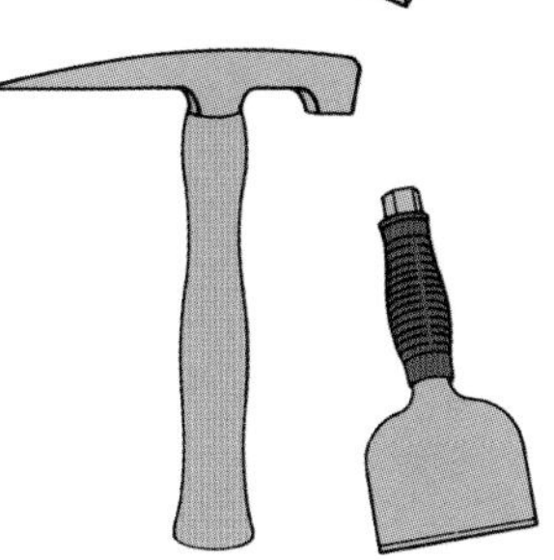

Masonry / Joints and Bonds

All mortar joints perform the basic function of bonding the bricks together, but their exposed edges can take on different shapes and depths, depending on the desired look or the exposure to weather. The wet mortar is very abrasive, so steel tools are best for shaping it.

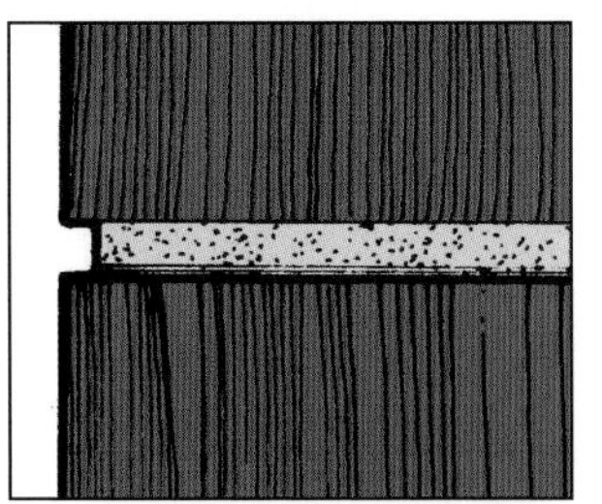

Raked joint. A raked joint has a flat face, inset about 1/4 in. (6 mm) from the brick surface. It has a crisp look but doesn't drain water well and should be limited to interior use.

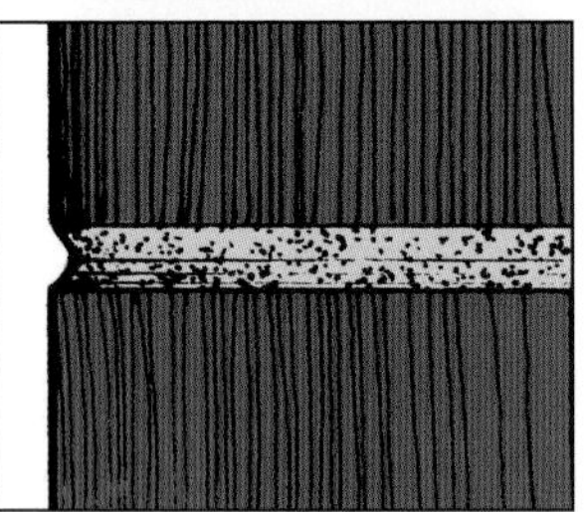

V-joint. As the name implies, this joint features a V-shape profile, yielding a strong geometric or linear look. The tool packs and consolidates the mortar surface.

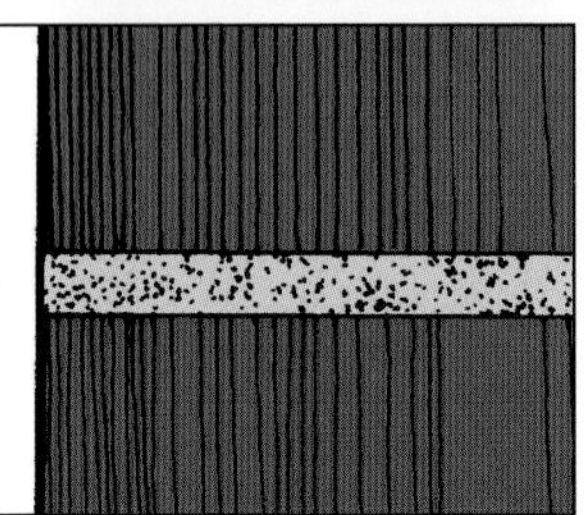

Flush joint. This joint is made by scraping off excess mortar to leave the joint flush with the brick face. It's simple, but it's more porous than a tooled joint.

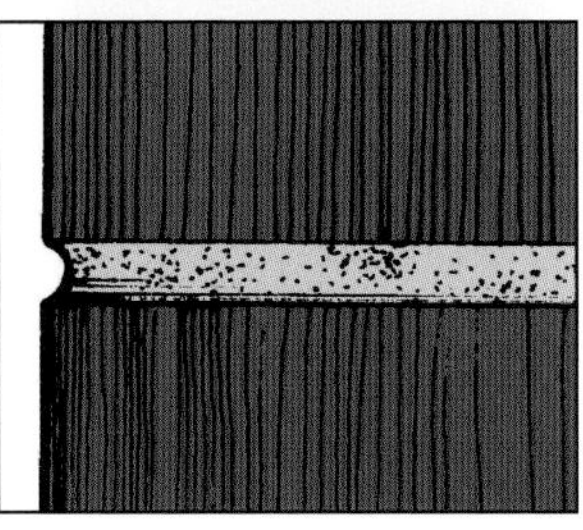

Concave joint. The most common type, the concave joint, does a good job of shedding water, and the tooled surface is dense enough to resist deep moisture penetration.

Bonds

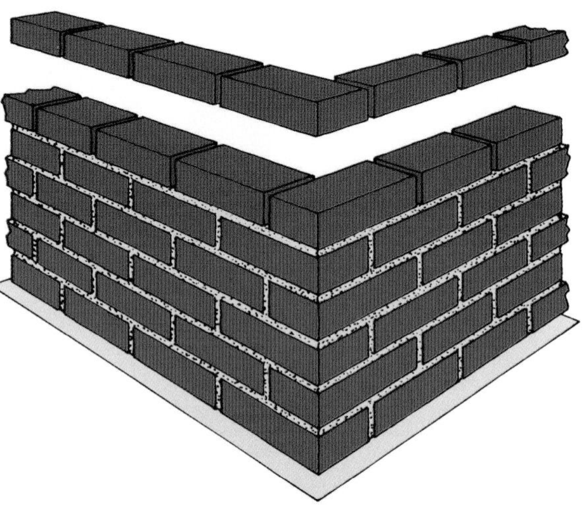

Running bond. This is the simplest and most common pattern. Each brick is a stretcher, overlaid halfway on two bricks below, creating staggered mortar joints. It's typically used for applications only one layer, or wythe, thick.

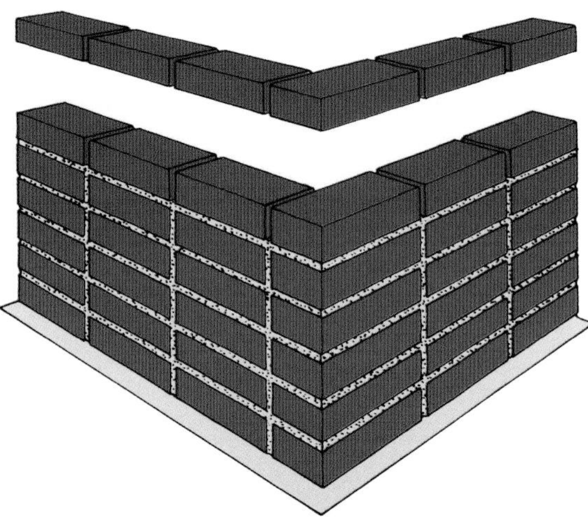

Stack bond. In this all-stretcher pattern, each brick is aligned directly with a brick below. The non-offset mortar joints make this an inherently weak pattern, so it's often used when brick is installed only as a decorative veneer.

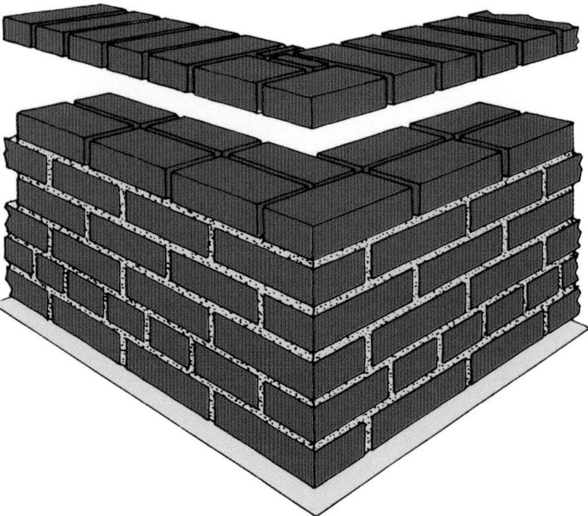

Common bond. This is a double-wythe variation on the running bond. Every fifth course is a header course, exposing the brick ends rather than the sides. On those corners, three-quarter bricks, called bats, are used to stagger the joint pattern.

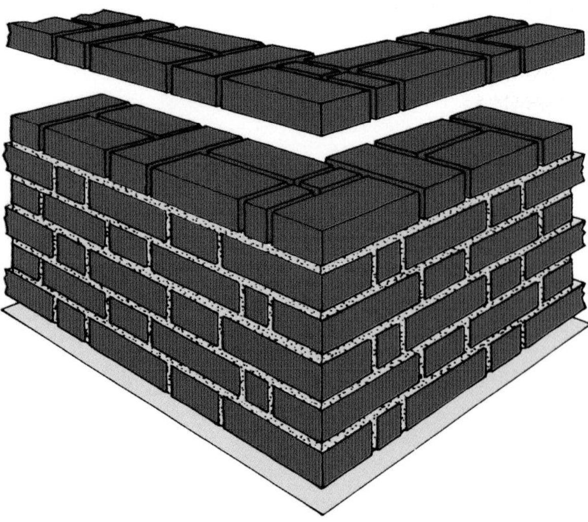

Flemish bond. Another double-wythe pattern, this features courses with bricks laid alternately as stretchers and headers. On alternate courses, quarter-brick closures are used near each corner to stagger the vertical joints.

Masonry / Laying Bricks

Concrete Footings **405**
Masonry Tools **410**

The garden wall shown on this and the next page represents one of the simplest projects you can tackle to learn the craft of bricklaying. With its single-wythe design and running-bond pattern, you can concentrate on your mortaring and leveling techniques without having to worry about making a lot of cuts or repeating a complicated pattern. Before you set a single brick, however, you have to prepare a solid footing for the wall to rest on. Refer to the previous section on concrete to learn about building a footing. For a short wall such as this, the footing can be above the frost line and float with the seasonal soil movement, but reinforce it with steel rebar to help prevent cracking and separation of the concrete in harsh climates.

Try to time the project for moderate temperatures—between 45° F and 75° F (7° C and 23° C)—and allow several days for the footing to cure before you proceed further. Do a dry layout for the first course so you can test-fit the bricks and do any required cutting ahead of time. The bricks should be clean but not bone dry. Hose them off or dunk them quickly in a pail of water, then let the surface moisture dissipate. This will prevent them from wicking too much water out of the mortar as you work.

1 After marking the two ends of the wall at a dimension that will require minimal cutting, snap a chalk line on the concrete footing. Position the line so the bricks will be centered along the footing.

2 Dry-fit the first course of bricks along your chalk line, spacing them with the tip of your little finger to allow for the mortar joints. If there's a gap at the end, cut a brick to fit or widen all the spaces slightly.

Handling Mortar

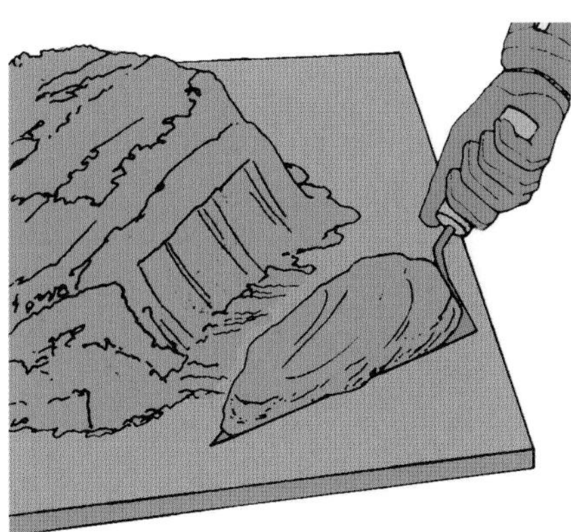

Loading a trowel. Load the trowel by slicing off a section of mortar and sweeping the trowel underneath it quickly. Snap your wrist down slightly to set the mortar securely on the trowel.

Buttering a brick. Hold it upright and use the trowel to swipe a small amount of mortar onto the end. Work the trowel quickly around all four edges to compact the mortar slightly.

3 After making adjustments during the dry run, mark the brick spacing on the footing and remove the bricks. Throw a mortar line about 1-1/2 bricks long next to the line. Don't indent or furrow the mortar on this course.

4 Set the first brick on the mortar bed, pressing it down until the mortar is about 3/8 in. (1 cm) thick. (Check the height alignment mark on your story pole.) Use the trowel handle to tap the brick until it's level in both directions.

5 Repeat the process to lay the first brick at the other end. Then run a string line between the ends. Wrap the string around two loose bricks, stretching it taut and aligning it slightly out from the face of the starter bricks.

6 Working from both ends and using the string as a guide, finish the first course. If necessary, cut the last, or closure, brick to fit. Butter both ends of the closure brick, and the ends of the adjacent bricks, and slide it into place.

7 Make sure the first course is level and straight. Then throw a mortar line at one end to start the second course. Set a half-brick first to stagger the vertical joints, then add two full bricks. Check the height with a story pole.

8 Continue working at the same end to build a lead, making each course a half-brick shorter than the previous course. Alternate full and half bricks at the outside end and check your work frequently with a level and story pole.

9 Build a lead at the other end of the wall. Stretch a line taut along the second course. Use line blocks at the ends, or line pins in the mortar joints, to secure the string. Work in from the ends to complete the second course.

10 Continue filling in each course between the leads, using the string line, level and story pole as guides. In addition, to level and plumb, use the level as a straightedge to keep the bricks aligned. Reset any problem bricks.

11 As you establish a rhythm, you'll be able to throw a mortar line several bricks long and set each course more quickly. Scrape off the excess mortar as you proceed and fill in any holes left by line pins in the mortar joints.

12 As your work progresses, check to see how the mortar joints are setting up. When they yield slightly to firm thumb pressure, use a jointing tool to compress and shape the mortar. Finish vertical, or head, joints first.

Masonry / Repairing Bricks

A brick exterior might look solid, but it faces threats from a variety of unfriendly forces. Foundation settling creates conspicuous diagonal cracks along mortar joints and sometimes through the bricks themselves. Cold walls unconnected to heated interior spaces, chimneys and brick windowsills suffer from freeze-thaw cycles that cause spalling. Gutter or downspout leaks also pose hazards by saturating the surfaces with water.

Why Brick Fails

When a brick structure is new or well-preserved, it seems impervious to damage and wear. But examine some older brick buildings closely and you'll discover they're anything but indestructible. You'll find strange discoloration, cracked or crumbling mortar joints and brick faces entirely missing, leaving a rough, chalky surface exposed. Provided that the right types of brick and mortar were used originally, these failures typically derive from a notorious pair of weather demons—water and below-freezing temperatures. Acting alone, neither does serious harm to a brick home, but teamed up, they'll wreak havoc that can make this enduring material self-destruct before it reaches middle age.

As mentioned earlier, brick is rated according to its resistance to weather-related damage, specifically the freeze-thaw cycles that cause trapped moisture to expand and damage rigid materials. Exterior walls are typically built or covered with bricks carrying an SW (severe weathering) or MW (moderate weathering). Properly installed, the bricks themselves often hold up fine. The weak link is actually the mortar joint, either because the mortar is more porous than the brick or because it has limited elasticity to accommodate thermal expansion and contraction or bigger problems, such as a settling foundation.

When a break occurs, it exposes the mortar and brick to even more stresses and more water penetration, accelerating the deterioration cycle. Any brick surfaces that undergo repeated cycles of heating and freezing are especially vulnerable; chimneys are notorious for premature brick failure.

Resetting a Loose Brick

A brick that works loose isn't just shirking its structural responsibilities—it's clearing a path for water and ice to multiply the damage tenfold. Don't imagine you can take care of the problem with caulking; if the mortar bond is so compromised that the brick can move, you have to extract it, clean out the old mortar, and rebuild the bond with new mortar. Try to reuse the old brick; new brick rarely matches the old brick's color and texture.

1 Extract the loose brick and use a cold chisel and a hammer to chip away the old mortar joint. Working at a low angle often helps pop the mortar loose.

2 Use light, rapid chisel blows at a steeper angle to break the old mortar off the brick. Clean the brick, and the cavity, using water and a wire brush.

3 Trowel a layer of mortar onto the cavity's bottom and sides and onto the top of the brick. Slide the brick into place.

4 As the mortar oozes, use a pointing trowel to pack it firmly into the joint. As the mortar starts to set, tool the joint to match that of the surrounding mortar.

Tuck-Pointing Brick

Restoring the mortar joints in brick, a process called tuck-pointing, isn't much more complicated than actually laying brick, but it involves a lot more dust and sometimes considerable effort to match the color and hardness of the old mortar. This last factor is especially critical when tuck-pointing only small areas in a larger wall; the colors and percentages of the lime, cement and sand in your mortar mix might vary considerably from the original mix. Even if you don't mind a color variation, using a modern, typically harder, mortar with soft older brick can sometimes accelerate damage to the wall. Have an experienced brickmason evaluate the situation to determine whether a close match is necessary.

1 Using a small angle grinder fitted with a diamond blade, cut into the vertical joints first. Push the blade in until the grinder head hits the brick. Make a single pass along the center of all the joints.

2 Position a flat utility chisel at the edge of the brick and drive it toward the cut to fracture and remove the mortar. Repeat along the other edge of the joint. The old mortar should break off at a depth of about 1 in. (2.5 cm).

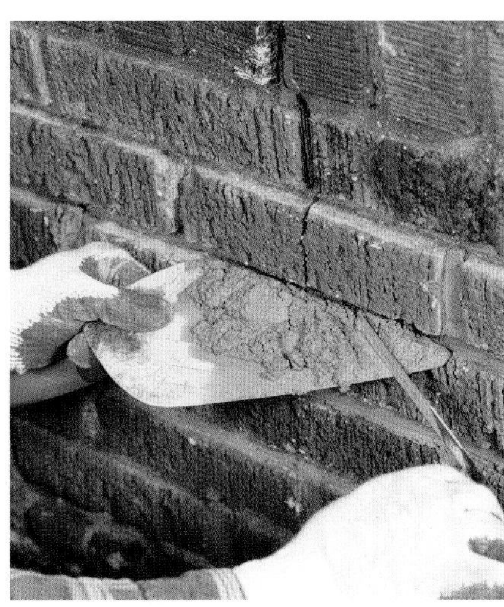

3 Load new mortar onto an overturned brick trowel and hold it against the brick, just under a horizontal joint. Sweep mortar into the joint using a pointing trowel and pack it firmly. Avoid getting mortar on the brick faces.

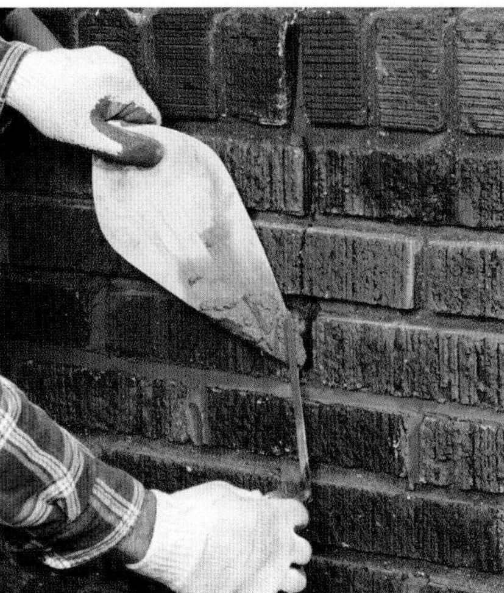

4 For the vertical joints, load smaller amounts of mortar onto the brick trowel and point its tip alongside the joint. Sweep and pack the mortar into the cavity. As it sets up, strike it with a jointing tool.

5 Sweep the loose mortar and residue from the joints and brick faces using a soft-bristle brush. Mist the mortar repeatedly to keep it moist for at least two days. Don't let it dry out between misting; it stresses the mortar.

Firebrick Mortar

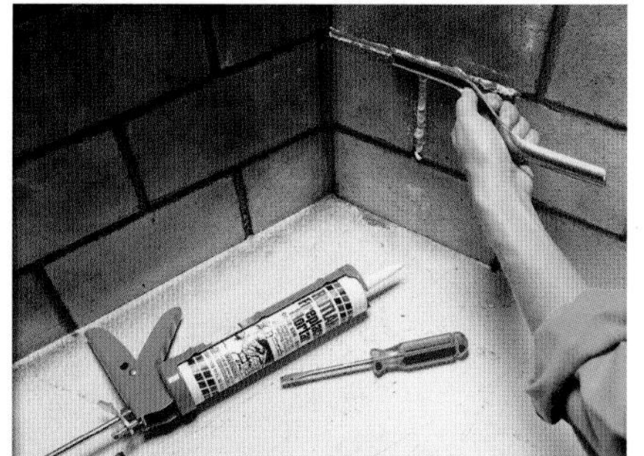

Fireplace masonry introduces a few twists, mostly in materials. Inside the firebox, high-strength firebricks are bonded with refractory mortar that can withstand the blazing temperatures. Repairs can be made using a special premixed fireplace mortar available in a caulking cartridge. Tool it as you would standard mortar.

Efflorescence

Efflorescence, the result of leaching mineral salts such as calcium carbonate, is the powdery white discoloration that can appear on brick, concrete and other masonry. Although it is unsightly it is not harmful to the brick. To remove it, mix a weak solution of muriatic acid and water, brush it on the wall, scrub and rinse with water. Wear goggles and rubber gloves.

Masonry / Stone and Brick Veneer

About a century ago, the common practice of building thick structural stone or brick walls gave way to a hybrid construction of wood-frame walls covered with a masonry skin called a veneer. Lighter and easier to insulate, veneered walls have continued to evolve. Manufactured stone veneers offer even more design options for this type of construction. Here's the basic anatomy:

1. Wood sheathing fastened to a stud frame.
2. Water-resistant, vapor-permeable paper.
3. Galvanized metal lath nailed to sheathing.
4. Scratch coat of mortar applied to lath.
5. Bedding mortar applied to stone veneer.
6. Stone veneer applied to wall. (Apply mortar between joints later.)
7. L-shape stones wrapped around outside corners.

Installation

1 Secure the metal lath to the wall using roofing nails. Mix a batch of mortar and use a concrete trowel to work it into the lath. Cover the lath by at least 1/8 in. (3 mm) of mortar.

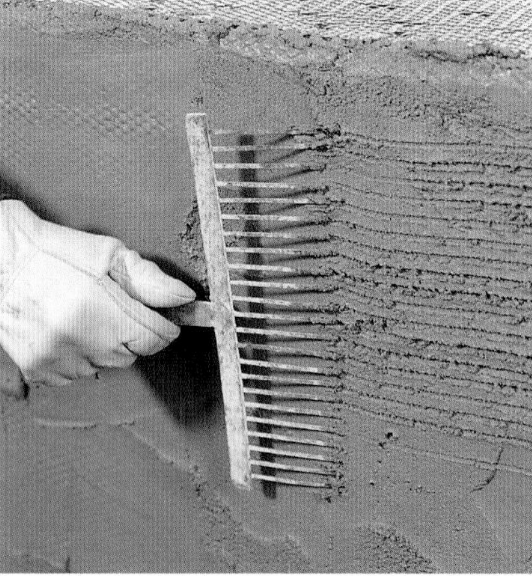

2 While the mortar is pliable, drag a rake or a scarifier tool across the surface horizontally to create rows of lines. This texture, called tooth, improves the veneer bond.

3 Butter the back of each stone with mortar to fill the surface pores. Throw another dollop of mortar on top of that, spreading it into a thick layer.

4 As you would with a conventional brick or stone wall, build the lead ends or corners first. Use string or a chalk line as a level reference to fill in the courses.

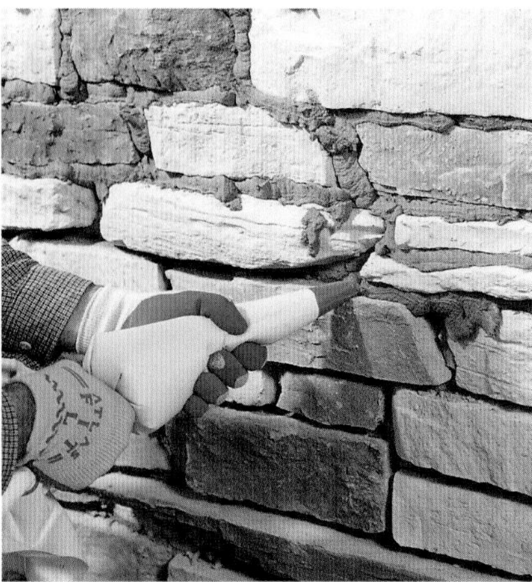

5 Unless you've chosen a mortarless stone veneer design, use a grout bag to squeeze mortar into the joints. Start at the top and work down.

6 As the mortar sets, use a pointing trowel to rake off the excess, leaving an inset joint. Then use a whisk broom to brush away any loose mortar or residue.

Cutting Veneer Stone

Manufactured stone veneer offers advantages other than its low weight, wide range of styles and preformed corner pieces. It's also easier to cut than natural stone. The cement-and-pumice compound is still abrasive, though, and will quickly dull ordinary saw blades. You'll get the best results with a diamond blade, which can be installed in a portable circular saw, an angle grinder or a wet- or dry-cutting masonry saw. Working with synthetic stone presents the same risks as any other masonry material, so wear eye and ear protection, plus a dust mask.

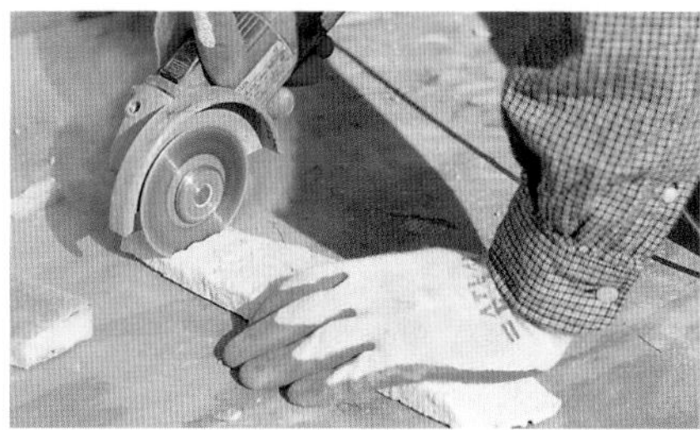

Grinder. Fitted with a diamond blade, a small (4-1/2-in.-dia.) angle grinder is ideal for cutting manufactured stone veneer. Hold the piece firmly on a plywood base.

Tub saw. If you have a lot of cutting to do, rent a wet-cutting masonry saw. Most feature a sliding table that makes cutting safer and more accurate for repetitive cuts or angles.

Brick Veneer over Steps

Concrete porch landings and steps might be practical and durable, but what if you could add charm and good looks to that description? Brick veneer lets you do that. Made of fired clay just like full bricks, brick veneer differs only in thickness and its availability as flat and L-shape corner pieces. Thin brick installs much the way ceramic tile does, so the substrate surface must be flat and rigid. Covering a concrete porch and steps is an ideal application for this material, but make sure the additional height (allow 3/4 in. or 20 mm) won't interfere with the operation of your storm door or send in rainwater over the threshold.

1 Start with the landing edges, bedding the cap bricks in thin-set mortar. Here, flat bricks are added along the riser face so the cap bricks will create a slightly protruding nosing.

2 With the edge bricks firm, spread the mortar with a notched trowel and start placing the field bricks. The pattern shown here is a diagonal herringbone.

3 A sanded grout mix—colored to complement the brick—takes the place of mortar in the joints. Use a grout bag to apply, overfilling the joints slightly.

4 After the grout has become stiff and slightly dry, smooth and pack the joints using a jointing tool. The excess will be crumbly and can be swept away.

Boulder-style Stone Veneer

Not all manufactured or cultured stone comes with angular or flat contours. The type shown here offers the same subtle coloring and texture in the form of round stones, the type you'll often find in a riverbed, worn smooth from the flowing water.

The cutaway corner pieces are especially helpful in a round stone style. Mortar the lower ones in place first and work up from there.

Masonry / Glass Block Wall

Level and Plumb 44
Masonry Joints 411

Installing a Wall

Glass block qualifies as a masonry material largely because of the techniques used to install it, which are similar to those used for brick and concrete block. Fused together from two half pieces, glass blocks aren't intended to be cut like brick or stone; you have to use available sizes, and you'll find it easier to work with dimensions of whole pieces.

Sizes can vary among 6-, 8- and 12-in. square block or 4 x 8- and 6 x 8-in. rectangular blocks. All are about 3 in. thick. The exterior faces are usually flat and smooth; the inside faces may be flat, wavy or textured to create different levels of light transmission and clarity. Lighter weight, more energy-efficient acrylic block is also available. Special hardware and spacers and precise white mortar joints make installation tricky; unless you're already skilled at masonry, this might be a job best left to a professional.

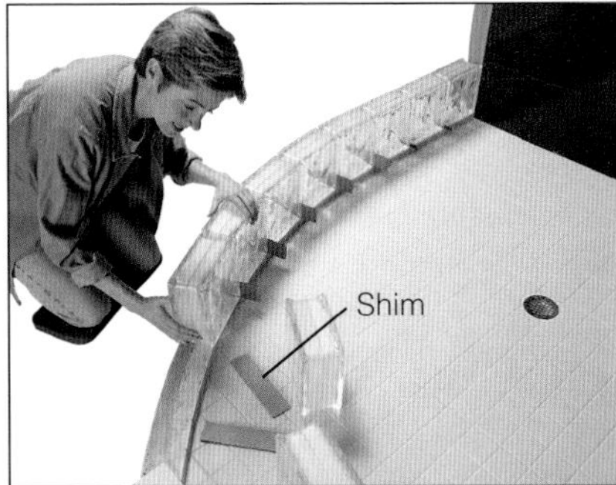

1 Dry-fit the block beforehand to check the layout. Use shims (these are 1/4 in. / 6 mm) to ensure consistent spacing between the blocks.

2 Butter the ends of three starter blocks and set them in a 1/2-in.-thick (13-mm-thick) mortar bed. Check that it's level before proceeding.

3 On every other course, use panel anchors, which are perforated steel strips, and screws to secure the end block to the wall.

4 The indented edges require you to butter each edge heavily, first in the recessed area and then on the outer edges.

5 Use a level to check for plumb and align the block faces as you work. Tap the level with the trowel handle to adjust.

6 Lay reinforcing wire atop every other course. For curved walls, make cuts along one leg of the wire to bend it.

7 Fill joints and spacer holes by dropping a dollop of mortar into the joint and troweling the top smooth.

8 When the mortar has set up firmly but is still pliable, strike the joints with a jointing tool. Follow up with a soft brush.

9 About an hour after setting, use a damp sponge to wipe excess mortar from the joints and block faces. Repeat, then towel dry.

Masonry / Glass Block Window

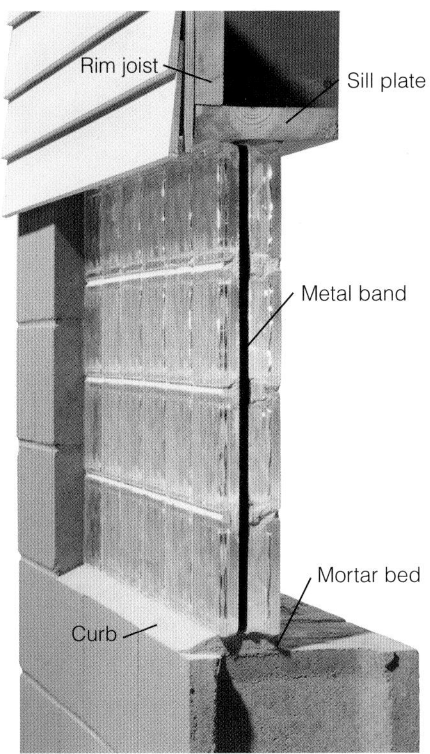

Installing a Window

If you like glass block but are intimidated by the skill requirements, consider a prefabricated block panel instead of individual blocks. Offered through many home centers and local fabricators (check the Yellow Pages under "Glass Block"), these panels come preassembled with mortared joints and a tensioned metal or plastic band around the edges to keep the assembly together. Installation requires only some mortar work around the perimeter. Since glass blocks have to be used in whole sizes, you may have to modify an existing opening if you're replacing an old window.

1 Start by cutting through the center of the old wood sill and prying it out, followed by the side and head jambs. A sloped mortar curb may lie along the sill; remove it also.

2 Fasten a stop block at the opening's inside top edge and cut two wood wedges for temporary sill supports. With a helper inside, fit the panel into the opening.

3 Drive the wedges to adjust the panel position. Then work mortar under the bottom edge and form a sloped sill curb. After it sets up, mortar the side gaps and strike the joints.

4 Wait two hours before pulling the wedges and filling in the holes with mortar. Then caulk the top gap between the panel and the house sill plate and apply a sealer to the mortar.

Glass Block Systems

Although plastic joint spacers have made mortared glass block construction easier, this proven, traditional method is still a tricky, time-consuming part of glass block installation. Mortarless systems offer a simpler option, but they aren't as rigid or secure as a mortared panel. For smaller windows or interior panels, however, they're fine.

Metal grid. These systems feature a perimeter frame and interior partitions that lock together to form a grid. Careful installation is required for a proper fit.

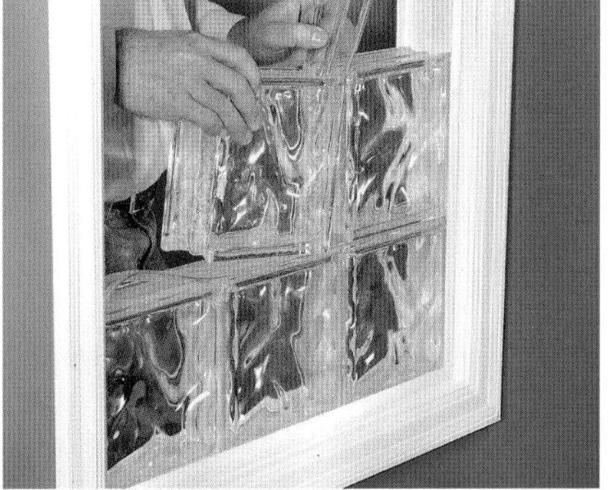

Silicone and spacers. With these systems, use vertical and horizontal spacers to dry-fit the blocks together inside a perimeter channel frame and then caulk the joints.

Masonry / Concrete Block

Measuring Tapes **41**
Masonry Joints and Bonds **411**
Handling Mortar **412**

Considered a utilitarian material since its introduction decades ago, concrete block is still an inexpensive and practical solution for building walls and structures, but today's versions also include decorative blocks. Precision molded from a mixture of portland cement and small aggregate, concrete block is less expensive and faster to build with than brick or stone and can be covered with a decorative veneer of either, if desired. Lightweight versions substitute pumice or other aggregate for the standard gravel, with little loss of strength.

Part of the speed of concrete block construction comes from the unit size. Standard blocks are 8 in. tall and 16 in. long (nominal), typically in either 6-, 8- or 12- in. widths. The basic unit—with two cavities and recessed ends—is called a hollow-core stretcher; corner and end blocks will have one flat end face. Though the blocks can be joined using only mortar, wire reinforcements are usually embedded in the mortar between courses. Additionally, steel rebar and concrete are often added vertically in the cavities to increase the wall's strength. Block walls require a slab base or a concrete footing and are typically laid in a running bond pattern.

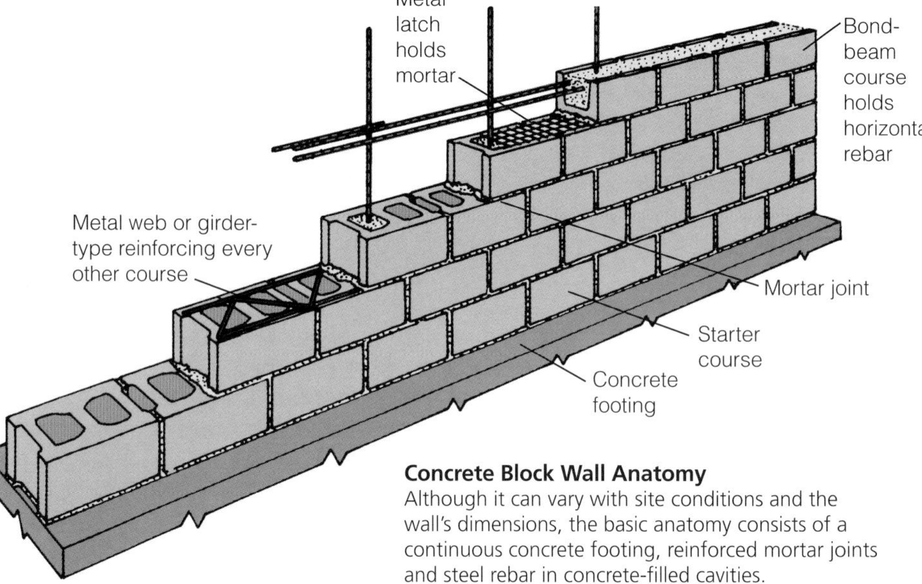

Concrete Block Wall Anatomy
Although it can vary with site conditions and the wall's dimensions, the basic anatomy consists of a continuous concrete footing, reinforced mortar joints and steel rebar in concrete-filled cavities.

Materials

If you want to build economically, standard gray concrete block offers durability in a low-cost package. Aside from the standard modular block, you can add narrower or wider units where required and even upgrade to variations that offer a nicer look. Colored blocks in various shades of tan, gray or terra-cotta don't cost much more. You can also specify a burnished face, which is ground smooth to expose the gravel aggregate, or use split-face block with a texture that mimics the look of handhewn stone. Though not as commonly available, mortarless block systems present yet another option. These blocks feature interlocking edges that let you dry-stack the walls, fill the hollows with rebar and concrete and add stucco to the face.

Decorative Blocks

Concrete block comes in a wide array of colors, sizes and textures. Split-face blocks, or those with vertical ribs or other patterns, are used for above-grade structures and in basement applications, in just the above-grade courses where appearance counts. Check on the availability of specialty corner and cap blocks if your project requires them.

Standard Blocks

These blocks are molded from a mixture of portland cement and aggregate. The most commonly used block is the hollow-core stretcher, measuring 8 in. high, 16 in. long and 4, 6, 8 or 12 in. wide. In general, the taller the wall, the wider the block used. Amount of weight to be supported and depth of backfill (in basement applications) also dictate block width and required reinforcement.

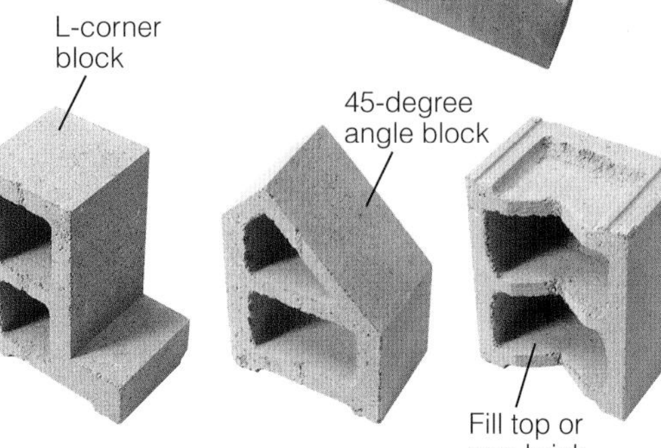

Specialty Blocks

These blocks are used to create finished corners and top surfaces. L-corner blocks are used to create square corners, while 45-degree blocks are used for angled corners. Fill top blocks are used to cap off a wall. Anchor bolts, used to secure top plates and the floor or wall framework to the block wall, are often embedded in mortar joints between blocks.

Installing a Wall

If you're already familiar with brick wall construction, concrete block doesn't pose any new challenges other than heavier lifting, an increased amount of mortar, and adding steel rebar. Standard concrete blocks weigh about 40 lbs. (18 kg) each; figure 25 lbs. (11 kg) each for lightweight concrete block. When you compensate for the unit size difference, however, the weight of a finished concrete-block wall won't differ much from that of a brick wall. Control joints may be required for long or tall walls; consult a professional mason or engineer if you're unsure.

Like any masonry structure, a block wall needs a solid footing of poured concrete, which should cure for at least a week before you start building the wall. Snap chalk lines on the footing and use a full-width bed of mortar for the first course. On subsequent courses, you can apply mortar to just the outer edges of the block. You'll notice that one open face of the block has thicker edges than the other; handle the block by these edges and place them up when you set the block.

Illustrations 1 through 3 (below) show how to build a true corner; illustrations 4 through 8 cover basic block-laying procedures.

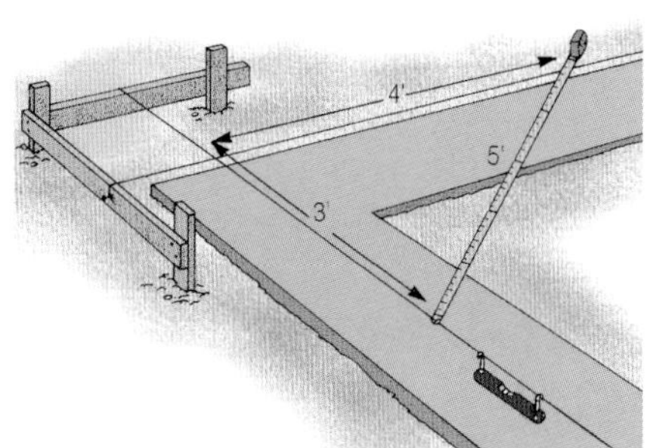

1 Measure out 3-4-5 triangles to establish square corners (see p. 41) and snap chalk lines on the footing to guide the block placement.

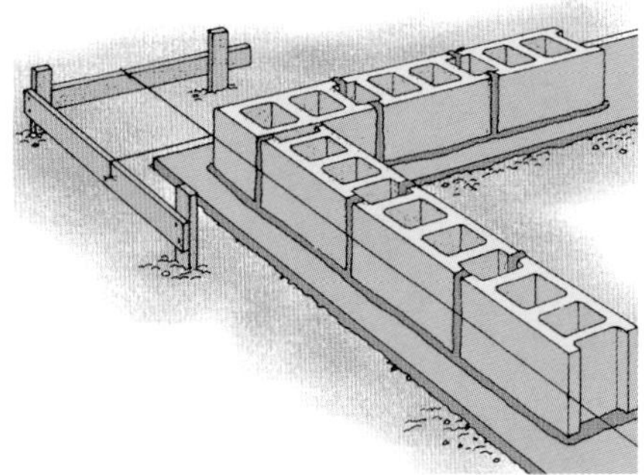

2 Stretch level lines on batter boards, then start each corner with six blocks. Keep the blocks aligned and level as you work.

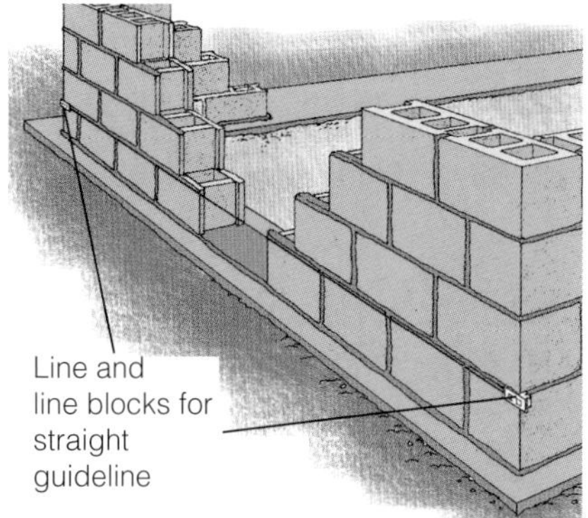

3 Build corners several courses high, checking them with a story pole. Stretch a mason's line between the ends to finish each course.

4 Place the blocks on end and trowel mortar onto the edges with a downward swipe of the trowel. Set in place; check for level.

5 Lift blocks by their thick edges and lower them into place. Bed firmly in the mortar until the block is level and aligned with others.

6 Butter the ends of the closure block and adjacent blocks, then slip the closure block into place. Add mortar to joints, if necessary.

7 Lay the bed joint for the next course by applying mortar only along outer edges of the previous course. Set and level the next course.

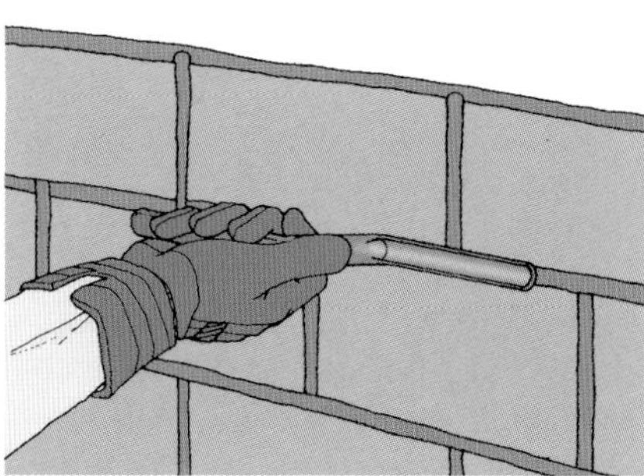

8 As work progresses, check mortar joints periodically. As they firm, use a jointing tool to strike them—vertically first, then horizontally.

Asphalt / Driveways

Contemporary home designs often place the garage at the front of the house, resulting in a short driveway that's typically made of poured concrete. But traditional neighborhoods often feature longer driveways made of asphalt, a lower-cost material that consists of a heavy petroleum tar mixed with small aggregate.

If your home has an asphalt driveway that's more than a few years old, odds are it has a few holes, cracks and stains that need repair. As with most exterior surfaces, asphalt that receives regular maintenance and preventive care is less likely to develop larger, more expensive problems. Left unattended, small holes and cracks become larger ones that can cause widespread surface and structural failures. At that point, minor repairs come too late to avoid replacement.

The elasticity of the petroleum tar gives asphalt some flexibility, especially in warmer temperatures, but as the material ages, it becomes more brittle, and freeze-thaw cycles inflict the same damage they do to concrete and other harder substances. Make a point periodically to clean and fill damaged areas in the surface and then seal it using an ordinary asphalt-emulsion driveway sealer. The tools and materials required are simple, inexpensive and available at any home center.

Patching Holes

1 Use a hammer and cold chisel to break clean square edges around the hole; sweep out loose debris with a whisk broom.

2 Fill the hole with a cold-mix asphalt patch. Work in layers about 1 in. (2.5 cm) thick, tamping firmly before adding more.

3 Build the final layer above the surface, then tamp with a wood post until the patch is flush.

Filling Cracks

Cracks in asphalt present the same opportunity for ice damage that cracks in concrete and brick do, so inspect your driveway annually and repair the cracks before cold weather sets in. Remove weeds and other vegetation from the crack and sweep it clean of any loose dirt and debris. Then apply asphalt crack filler; it will flow and settle, so repeat the application until the crack stays filled. Then seal the driveway as shown on facing page.

Power Washing

If you are ready to patch and reseal your driveway, rent a power washer to clean the surface. A power washer (being used on concrete at right) generates enough pressure to blast loose asphalt and debris from holes and cracks and, with detergent added, will wash oils, solvents and other fluid residue from the surface. Don't power wash without patching and sealing soon afterward, though, or you'll just accelerate weather damage.

Sealers

To be effective, the ritual of applying sealer to an asphalt driveway has to be repeated every two or three years. For some homeowners, this frequency might make the job seem like an exercise in futility. The coating fades relatively quickly from black to gray, so why bother with such regular applications if they don't keep the driveway looking new? You could probably say the same thing about exterior paint, but most people realize that their wood siding and trim would quickly deteriorate without the protection that paint offers. The same is true for an asphalt driveway without sealer.

With time and exposure to the elements, the oils that give asphalt its elasticity eventually leach out or oxidize, making the material brittle and prone to shallow surface cracks known as crazing. In regions with colder climates, these cracks and asphalt's natural pores absorb water that freezes and widens the cracks further. Sealers fill the cracks and pores so water runs off the surface, slowing the cycle of damage.

There are regional differences in sealer availability—western regions tend to have asphalt emulsion sealers, and eastern regions typically have coal-tar emulsion sealers—but whatever type you use should be the highest grade available. Economy-grade asphalt sealers cost less because they are diluted with higher water or solvent content and fewer solids. Those solids are what stay put and protect the driveway, so pay extra for the good stuff.

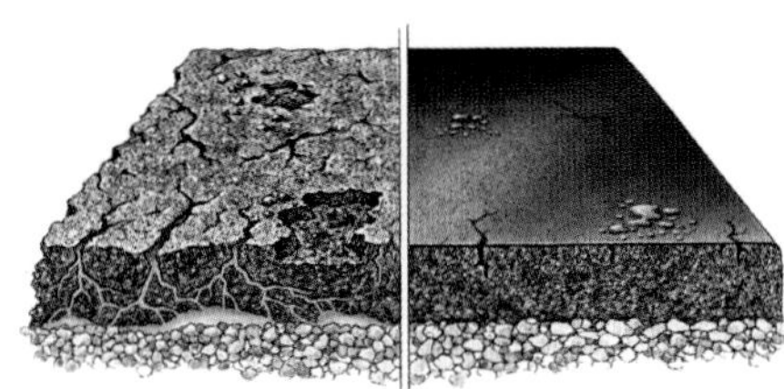

Cracks. A vicious circle can form as an asphalt driveway ages. The surface oxidizes and cracks, and those initially small cracks allow water penetration. Repeated freeze-thaw cycles further widen the cracks, allowing in even more water and accelerating the cycle.

Application. After using a degreaser or detergent to scrub away any oil stains, hose or power wash the surface. When dry, apply sealer with a broom or squeegee.

Keys to a Durable New Driveway

If your brick walkway settled unevenly, you'd correctly blame the substrate and not the bricks, right? The same goes for an asphalt driveway. You need an adequate base—4 to 8 in. (10 to 20 cm) thick, depending on your soil type—of an engineered granular mix, typically crushed rock that still has the small particles and dust, called fines, mixed in. The base thickness should be 6 to 12 in. in cold climates. When properly compacted, these fines help consolidate the base material into a firmer substrate.

1 Your paving contractor should evaluate and upgrade your driveway base by adding and compacting an engineered base material.

2 After the base has settled for a few days and has been recompacted, a 2-in. (5-cm) layer of asphalt is spread over the area.

3 The asphalt should be compacted by heavy rollers right after it's spread. If it cools off, the compaction won't be as effective.

Asphalt / Driveway Aprons

Replacing a Sunken Apron

Minor settling of an asphalt or concrete driveway often goes unnoticed, unless it's in a concentrated area or adjacent to another surface that isn't moving. When it happens along a garage slab, the resulting gap can increase the risk of frost heaving and other damage from water penetration. Short of replacing the entire driveway, the most reliable fix involves installing a small transition area, called an apron. The one shown at right is made of brick pavers.

To begin, snap a chalk line parallel to the front edge of the garage slab, far enough out to where the asphalt or concrete is still sound and its base intact. Better yet, buy your pavers ahead of time and calculate an overall dimension that will let you install only full pavers, without the need for cutting. Rent a pavement or concrete saw and cut a straight line in the driveway. Break up and remove the old material.

Next, excavate about a foot down, tamp the soil, and line the trough with landscape fabric. Then add a base of engineered crushed rock, often called Class V or paver base, in 2-in. (5-cm) layers, using a vibrating plate compactor to consolidate each layer. Stop when you're 3 in. (7.5 cm) below the slab surface. Spread a 1-in. (2.5-cm) layer of coarse sand, lay the pavers and compact them. Finish by sweeping sand between joints.

Shop Smart: Rental Tools You'll Need (and Love)

Jackhammer. An electric jackhammer delivers thousands of percussion blows per minute, enough to reduce the old concrete apron to pieces in short order.

Compactor. Aside from having the right base material, nothing is more critical than having it compacted properly. The best tool for the job is a power compactor.

With a properly compacted base more than 1 ft. (30 cm) thick, this paver apron should stay level with the garage slab and even accommodate slight movement of the driveway.

Woodworking & Furniture Repairs

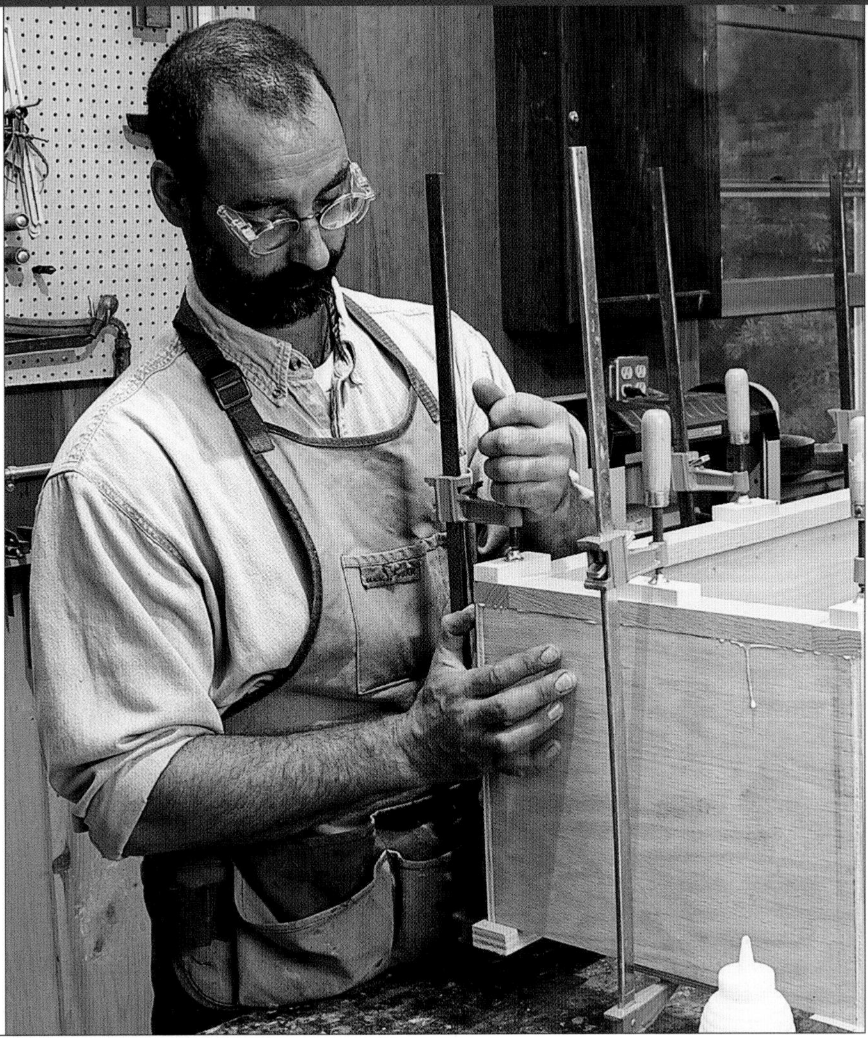

Understanding Wood

Ripping Crooked Boards **63**
Planing Lumber **429**

Wood is the material of choice for most home projects, whether it be small repair or grand addition. Durable, easily shaped and available in an array of sizes, shapes and colors, wood is satisfying to work with. For cutting molding, building boxes, applying a fine finish or restoring old furniture like new—this chapter tells you what you need to know to work with wood with confidence.

Knowing more about wood helps you select the best material for your projects, and the logical place to start is with the tree. You can see its various parts by simply looking at the end of a log. As the drawing on this page shows, every tree is surrounded by a layer of protective outer bark. Beneath this is the living, inner bark, which transports nutrients throughout the tree. Next comes the cambium, a sheath of dividing cells that form more wood and more inner bark. Below this is the stuff we use for our projects: an outer band of sapwood, the growing section that transports sap from the roots to the leaves, and a core of inactive heartwood. In the very center is the pith, an unstable and typically unusable section of wood. Growth rings—one ring per year—mark the yearly growth, with more closely spaced rings generally denoting stronger wood. Crosswise to the rings and radiating from the pith are medullary rays, which are sought after in some wood species for their distinctive markings on finished wood.

Cutting planks from a log involves a series of choices for sawyers as they rotate the log relative to the blade. Outer planks, or slabs, have rounded sides and are usually culled from the pile. The remaining wood is cut into thick or thin stock of varying widths.

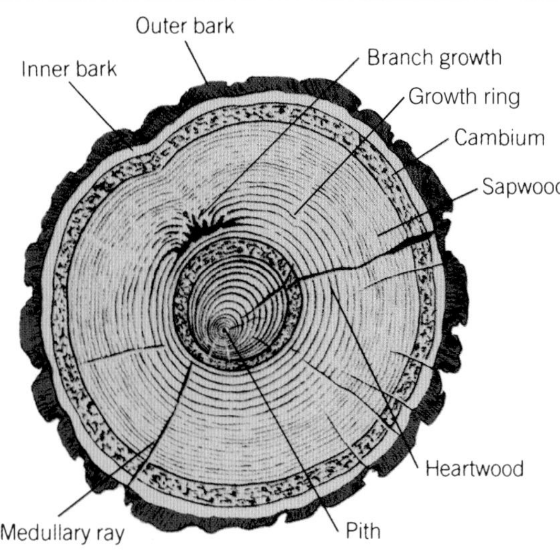

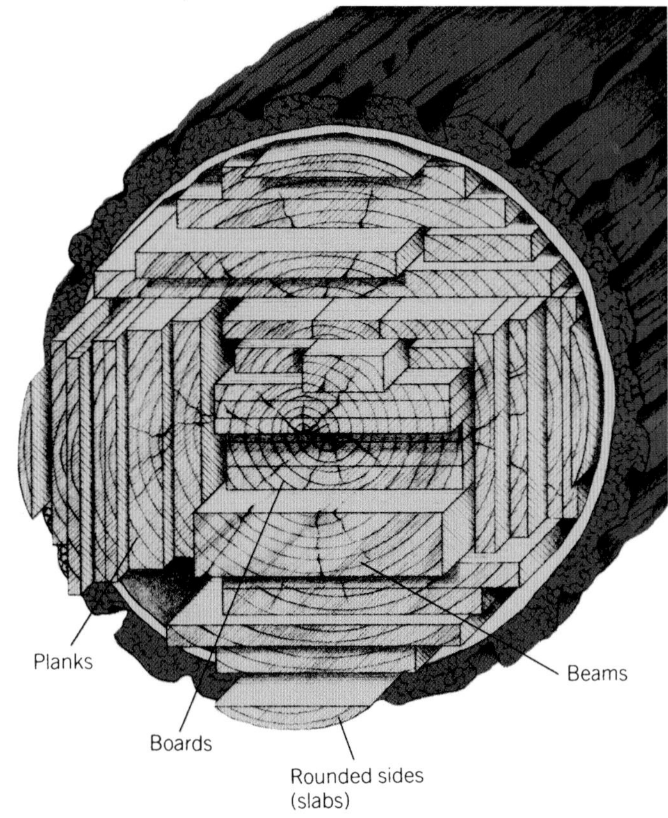

Timber into lumber. Little is wasted when timber turns into lumber. The bark is used as fuel and, with some types, as mulch. The rounded sides, or slash, are ground into flakes or fibers for manufacturing chipboard and fiberboard panels. The remainder is cut into boards of varying widths and thicknesses, depending on the log and the needs of the mill or buyer. Center cuts, which typically contain the pith, are often sawn into large rectangular beams and used for construction or landscaping lumber.

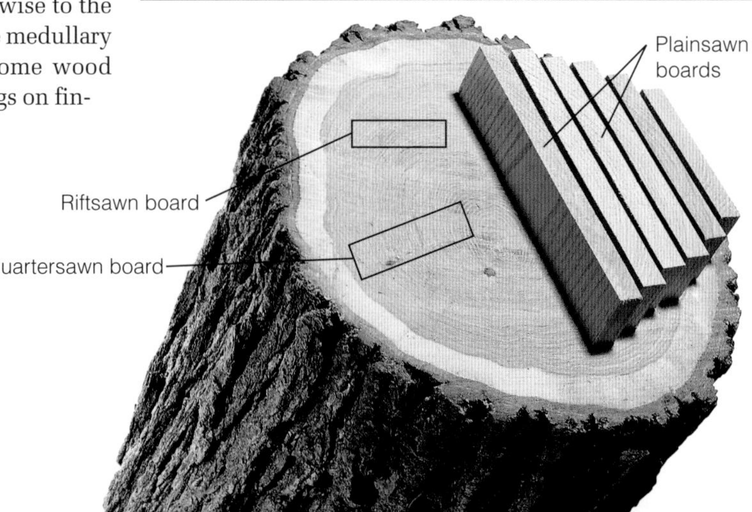

Plainsawn vs. Quartersawn

Most logs are sawn consecutively through their lengths to produce **plainsawn** boards, marked by curved growth rings on their ends. This cutting sequence produces wide boards and makes good use of the log, but the stock is prone to cupping and shrinking. Boards cut like pieces of a pie and with rings that run 90 degrees to their wide faces are quartersawn and have straighter, more even grain that's more stable. The hitch? **Quartersawn** boards are narrower and cost more because of the less-efficient cutting approach. Between these two types of cuts are **riftsawn** boards, with end grain angling roughly 45 degrees to the face.

Lumber

Boards

You'll find wonderfully smooth board lumber at your local lumberyard or home center. Stock planed on both faces, typically to 3/4 in. thick, and ripped straight and parallel on two edges, is called S4S or surfaced on four sides. This material, and dimensional lumber (see far right), are best used for construction-type projects. Boards are sold in nominal sizes, in other words, the thickness and width measured when cut at the mill. Shrinkage and planing make the true size smaller, as illustrated below. The length, however, is the actual measurement. Most boards found at home centers are softwood, such as pine, fir, spruce, cedar and redwood, with occasional hardwood boards of poplar, maple and red oak. Board lumber is perfect for quick projects because cutting it into parts is a snap.

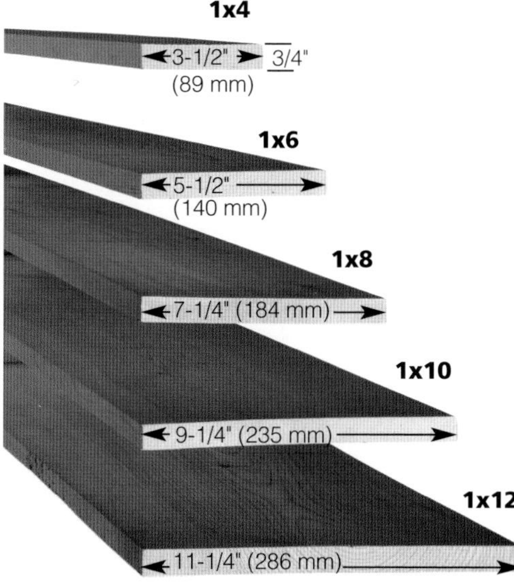

Dealing with Defects

Board lumber usually contains any number of defects, such as knots, splits and other blemishes. Although higher-grade lumber contains fewer flaws (see p. 428), you should always inspect your wood before cutting project parts. Luckily, removing these blemishes is easy when you know where and what to look for. Common defects and how to deal with them are shown below.

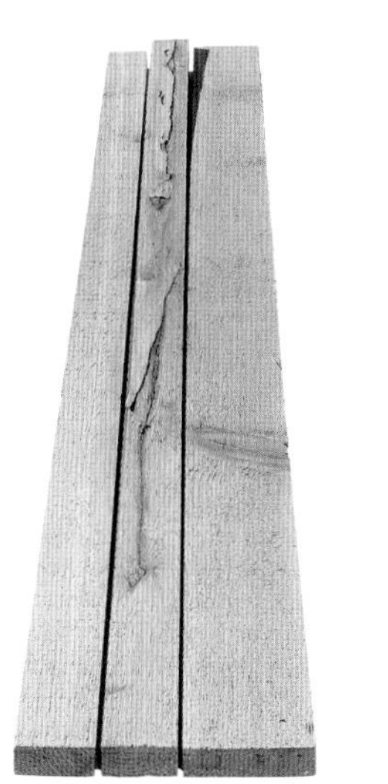

Shake consists of long splits or loose flaps, often deep in the surface. Rip away flawed areas to leave usable material.

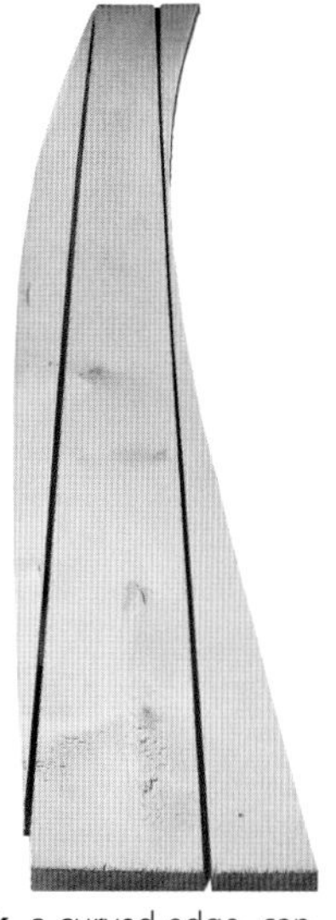

Crook, a curved edge, can be marked with a string and straightened with a circular saw or hand plane. Finish by ripping the opposite edge parallel.

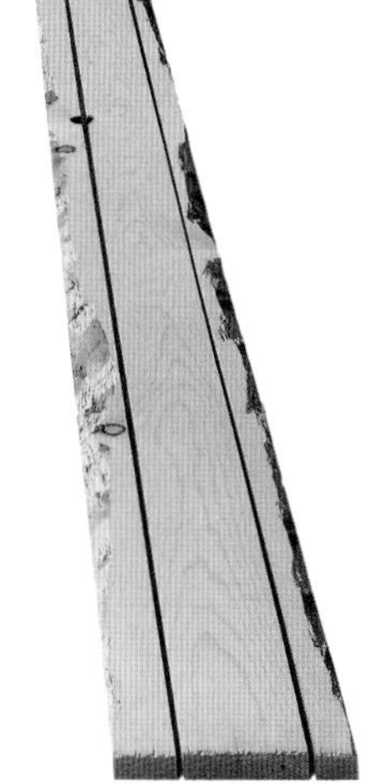

Wane, the rough, barky outer edge of the tree, provides a rustic, natural look. For uniform edges, rip it off on the tablesaw.

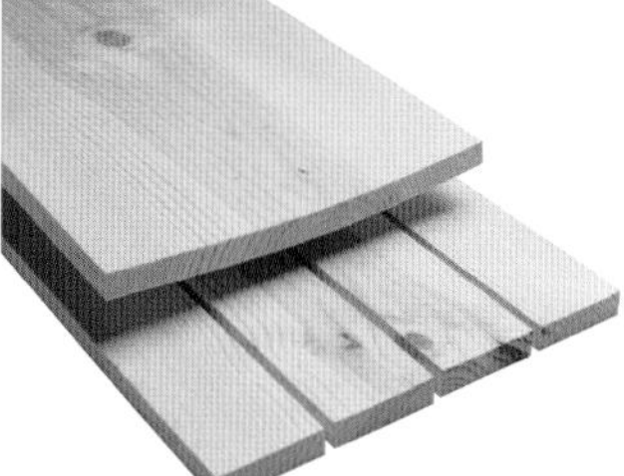

Cup, a concave or convex curve across the face, can be diminished by ripping the board into multiple, narrower strips to reduce the overall cup.

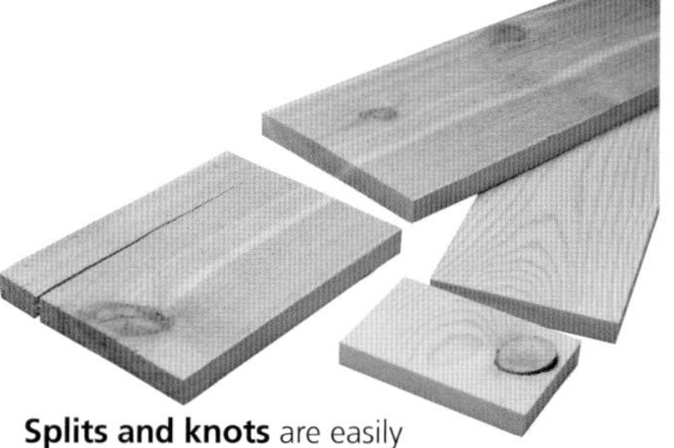

Splits and knots are easily trimmed when they're near ends. Tight knots can add visual interest; trim away loose knots or reinforce with epoxy.

Dimensional Lumber

Lumberyards and home centers carry softwoods in standard dimensions and lengths, called dimensional lumber. Stock is planed to a nominal 2-in. or 4-in. thickness, for instance, a 2x4, 2x10 or 4x4. Actual dimensions are shown below. Cut from fir, spruce, pine, hemlock and larch, dimensional lumber is used for protected structural framing. More weather-resistant species, such as cedar, redwood and cypress, are sold for outdoor use. You'll find such defects as splits and knots but, unless severe, they rarely affect its structural use. Pick the straightest stock you can find, but don't sweat small curves.

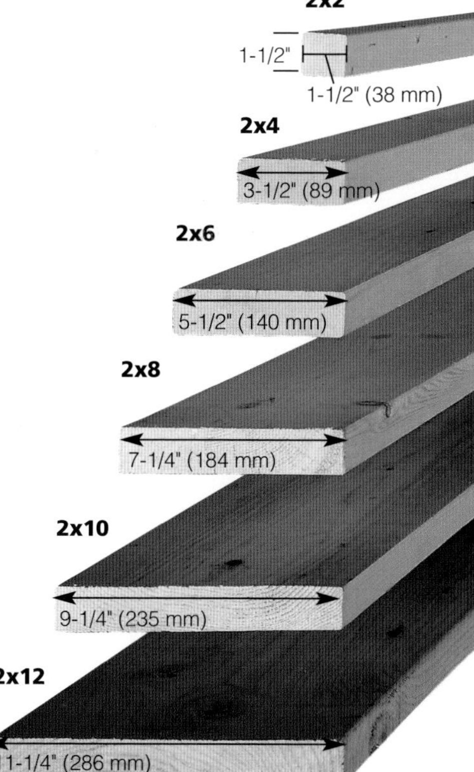

Hardwoods

Jointer 72
Thickness Planer 72

Hardwoods come from deciduous trees, those that seasonally shed their leaves, such as oak, ash and birch. Hardwoods are usually stronger and longer-lasting than softwoods, but they also cost more. They have better surface-finishing properties, and they can be cut, joined and turned as successfully as softwoods, provided your tools are razor sharp. Hardwoods are the best choice for making fine furniture. Not all hardwoods are available at lumberyards. You may have to locate a special dealer (check in the Yellow Pages under "Lumber") or order from a woodworking supply catalog.

Grading

Most lumberyards follow very specific grading guidelines. Grades are based on sound or blemish-free pieces 1 in. wide x 1 ft. long that can be cut from a board. The basic grades, in descending order of quality, are FAS, FAS-1, No. 1 and No. 2.

FAS
Firsts and seconds

Both sides are mostly clear and without knots or splits. Used for fine furniture and solid moldings.

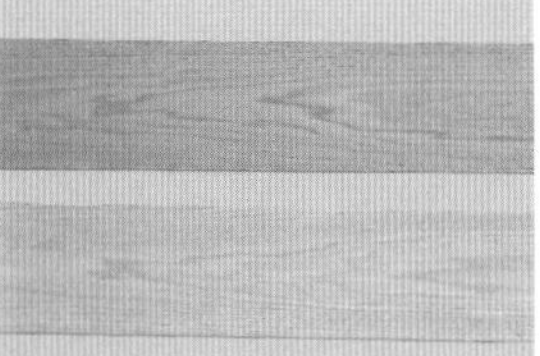

FAS-1
Firsts and seconds on one face

One side is nearly clear; one side has minor defects, such as small knots or worm holes. Used for fine furniture if cut carefully around blemishes.

No. 1
Number one common

Both sides have minor defects, such as small splits or sound knots. Most blemishes can be cut away. Good for furniture and cabinetry.

No. 2
Number two common

Both sides have defects, such as loose or missing knots and splits. Good for lesser-grade cabinets, construction or projects demanding wood with character.

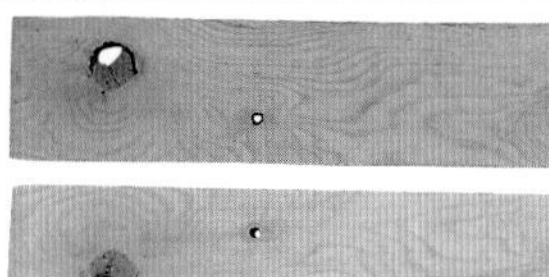

Species

Hundreds of hardwood species are sold throughout the country, some nationally and others only regionally. Domestic hardwoods grow in North America; imported hardwoods grow in the tropics and other regions.

The price of domestic wood varies greatly according to area. If the species you choose is grown locally, it's usually less expensive.

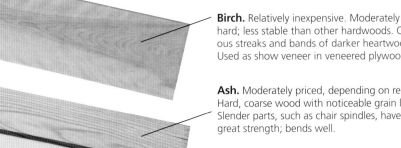

Birch. Relatively inexpensive. Moderately hard; less stable than other hardwoods. Obvious streaks and bands of darker heartwood. Used as show veneer in veneered plywood.

Ash. Moderately priced, depending on region. Hard, coarse wood with noticeable grain lines. Slender parts, such as chair spindles, have great strength; bends well.

Maple. Moderately priced. Fairly hard; fine texture; polishes well. Buy better grades for uniform color. Good for general furniture making.

Hickory. Moderately priced; hard; less stable than most woods. Coarse texture with nonuniform color. Slim parts have great strength; bends exceptionally well.

White oak. Moderately priced. Fairly hard; heavy; coarse texture. Browner tones compared to red oak, with desirable ray flecks when quartersawn. Bends well.

Cherry. Premium price. Moderately hard; fine texture. Pinkish-red color darkens over time. Bends reasonably well. Good for general furniture- and cabinet-making.

Walnut. Premium price, especially for clear stock. Softer than many hardwoods; fairly coarse texture. Striking grain and rich color. Good for general furniture making.

Rough Lumber

Rough lumber is sold with uneven surfaces full of saw marks that require subsequent smoothing. Its nominal sizes differ from those of dimensional lumber. Thickness is in quarters of an inch, beginning at one inch; width and length are always random, or depending on the maximum a log will yield.

The thinnest rough-cut boards are described as 4/4 (pronounced "four-quarter") or stock that's roughly 1 in. thick. Boards are sold in increasingly thicker dimensions by 1/4-in. increments, up to 16/4, which is a 4-in.-thick board. Figure on losing at least 3/16 in. from planing to get flat, smooth surfaces and squared edges.

Go Figure: Board Feet

1" thick
1 bd. ft.
12"
12"

Since roughsawn lumber comes in random widths and lengths, you must buy it by volume or by board feet. You can calculate how much wood you're buying by using the following board-foot formula: width (in inches) x length (in feet) x thickness (in inches) ÷ 12 = total board feet (bd. ft.).

Drying Lumber

Most of us work with kiln-dried lumber. But you can save money and stock up on wood by stacking freshly cut lumber in a pile so air can get around it. Air-drying lumber can take a year or more and you may lose up to 10 percent to drying defects. But given time and a fresh supply of wood, you'll get good results. Buy a moisture meter (at right) to monitor the moisture content (MC) in the stack. Air drying reduces stock's moisture levels to around 20 percent MC. After this, stack it indoors for several weeks to dry to 6 to 8 percent MC.

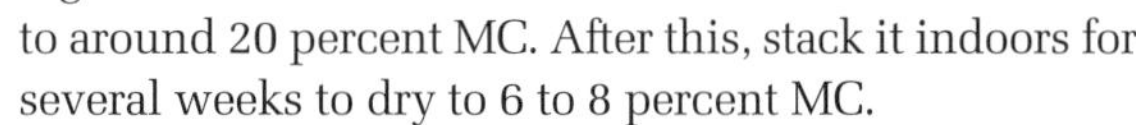

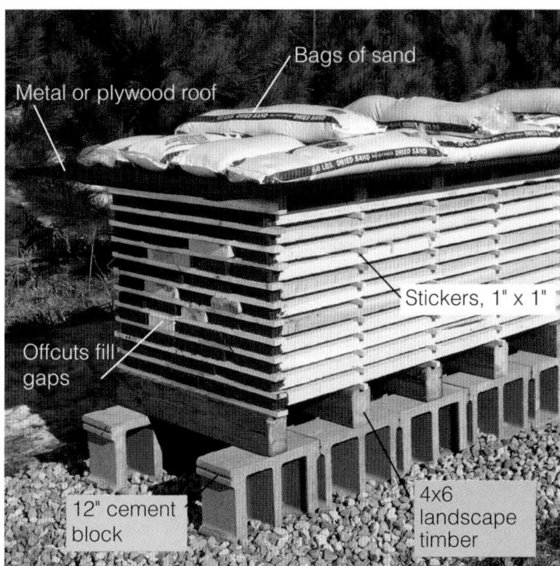

Build the stack on level ground in an open area away from shade. Place gravel over landscaping cloth, then level blocks on gravel, and position timbers every 16 in. (40 cm). Coat ends of lumber with paint or commercial end-sealer. Begin with dry wood stickers, add a course of lumber, add more stickers directly above and so on. Stack to a reasonable height, then cap with a plywood roof and weights.

Planing Lumber

Many lumberyards will plane your roughsawn lumber smooth for a small fee. To save money and gain more control over the process, you can do it yourself with a thickness planer. Floor-model planers are expensive but can take heavy cuts. Benchtop planers (below) cost less and work just as well, although planing occurs more slowly because you can't cut as deeply with each pass. Using your shop vacuum to collect shavings will help keep the mess under control.

A thickness planer is best used alongside a jointer because roughsawn lumber needs to be flat on one side before it's thickness-planed. You can rent time on a jointer at a cabinetmaking shop or ask a woodworking friend to flatten your material. It's possible to skip the jointing process and plane rough stock with good results, especially if you crosscut a long board into shorter lengths after planing, which minimizes overall warp.

For equal-thickness boards, plane all stock at the same time. Place the flattened side down (or cupped, if it isn't jointed) on the bed to plane the top rough side. When the top is smooth, flip the stock over and plane the opposite side. Continue flipping boards after each pass, removing equal amounts from each side until you've planed them to the desired thickness.

Moldings

Miter Saws **55**
Baseboard Moldings **230**
Crown Moldings **232**

Wood moldings are just the ticket to dress up an otherwise plain cabinet or lackluster room and are often used to hide construction seams, for instance, at door openings or where a floor meets a wall.

An assortment of softwood moldings, typically made from clear pine but sometimes from oak and maple, are available at lumberyards and home centers in lengths up to a maximum of 16 ft. Width varies depending on the profile. Moldings made from hardwood, such as cherry or walnut, are more expensive and are usually special-ordered. Picture-frame moldings, with a recess in which the picture rests, can be purchased in a wide range of styles at a frame shop.

Purchase more molding than you need in case you err in cutting. Save money by buying lesser-grade stock if you plan to paint it, which will hide the flaws, such as color variations or knots.

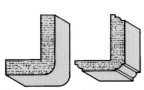

Corner guard protects corners, hides joints.

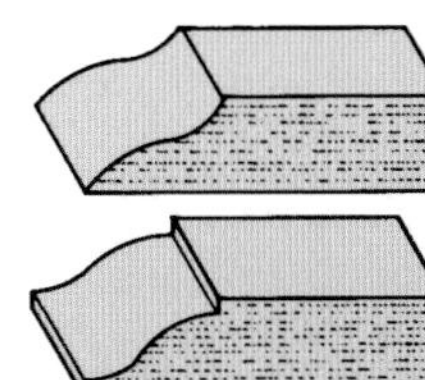
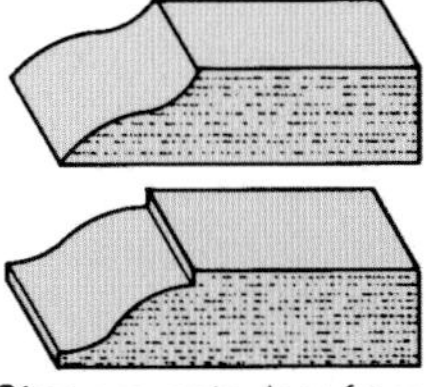

Stop prevents door from swinging through frame.

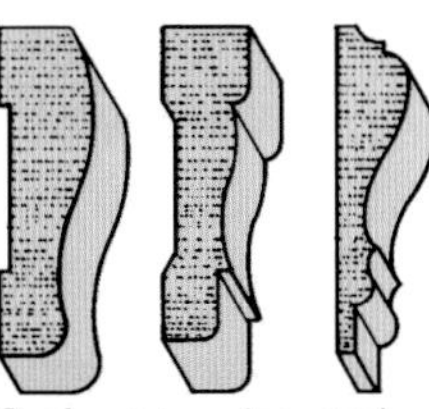

Casing trims door and window openings.

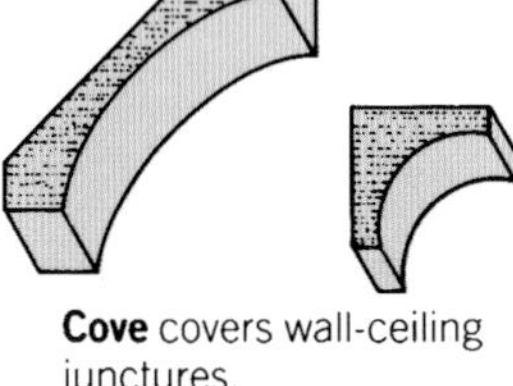

Cove covers wall-ceiling junctures.

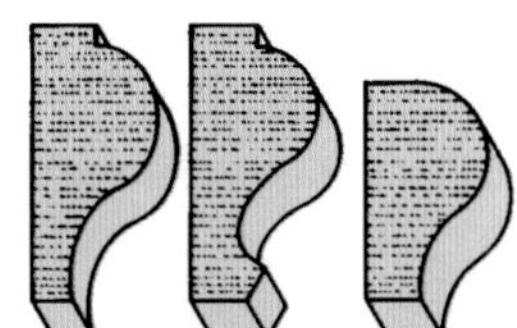

Base cap is applied to the top of a base molding.

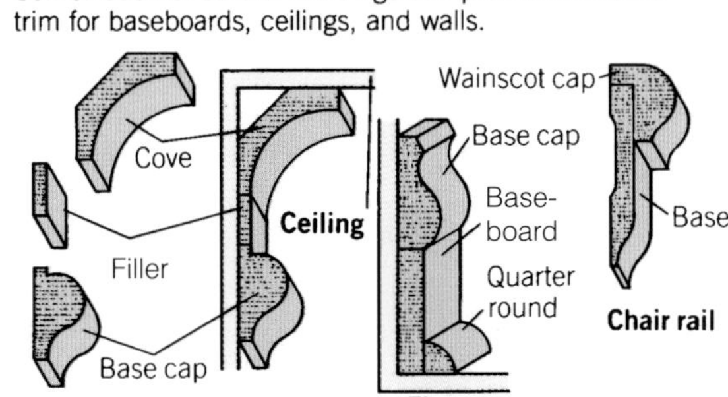

Built-up Molding Profiles

Combination of several moldings can provide attractive trim for baseboards, ceilings, and walls.

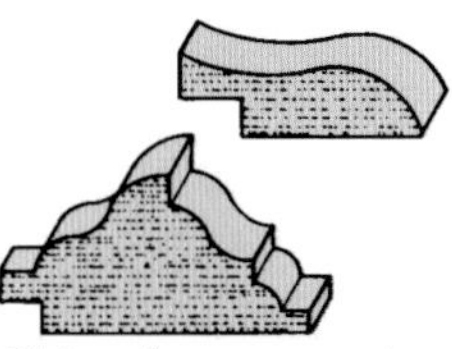

Picture frame presents and protects artwork.

Crown makes ceiling-wall transition.

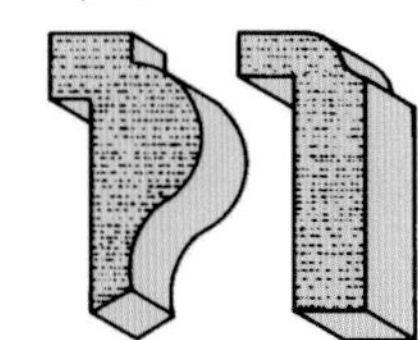

Wainscot cap makes paneling-wall transition.

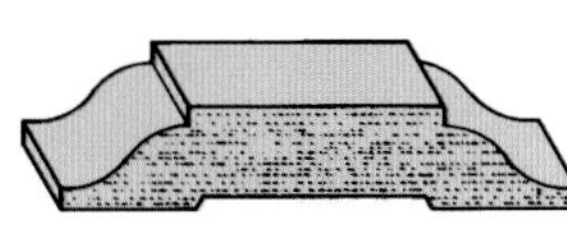

Batten hides the seam where wall panels meet.

Base hides seam where floor meets wall.

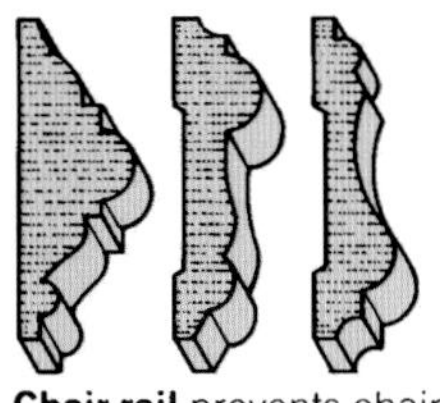

Chair rail prevents chair backs from marring walls.

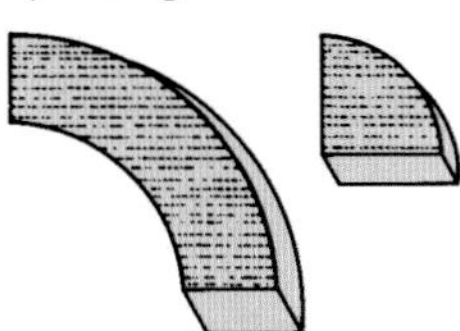

Quarter round is often used in combined profiles.

Measuring and Cutting Moldings

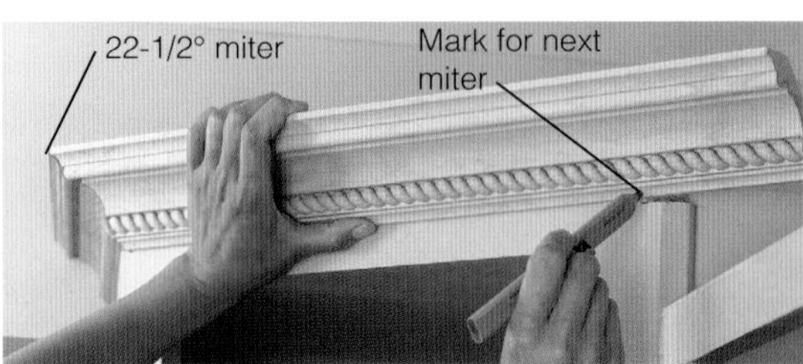

Mark moldings while holding them in place instead of measuring, and then install them in sequence. Position mitered pieces together, then mark the other end for the next miter cut.

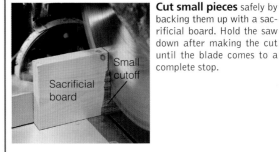

Cut small pieces safely by backing them up with a sacrificial board. Hold the saw down after making the cut until the blade comes to a complete stop.

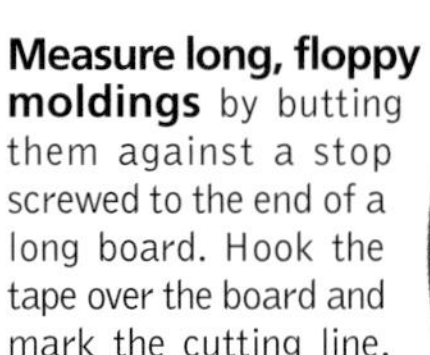

Measure long, floppy moldings by butting them against a stop screwed to the end of a long board. Hook the tape over the board and mark the cutting line.

Plywood

Hardwood Plywood

Made from thin layers of wood, or plies, plywood is cheaper and lighter than most solid wood. Sheets are strong, flexible and don't shrink or expand in the way solid wood does. Best of all, it's readily available at home centers in wide, smooth sheets, making it convenient for cabinet parts and wall paneling. Hardwood plywood has outer plies of super-thin veneer made from hardwood, such as birch, oak or walnut. Veneer-core plywood is common, but other cores such as medium-density fiberboard (MDF), particleboard or strips of solid wood are available. Sheets range in thickness from 1/8 in. to 3/4 in. (3 to 19 mm) and are typically 4 ft. x 8 ft. (1,220 x 2,440 mm), although longer panels can be special-ordered.

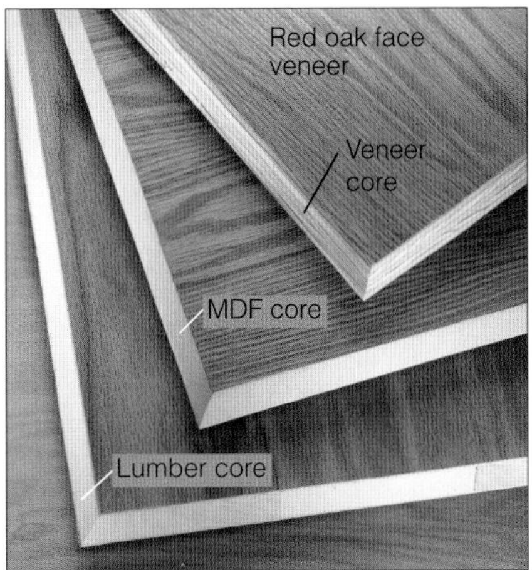

Hardwood plywood has face veneers of thin hardwood. You can choose from a variety of cores, including common and more stable veneer core, cheaper particleboard and MDF cores, or stiffer, screw-holding lumber core.

Softwood Plywood

Commonly called construction plywood, softwood plywood has outer veneers of softwood, such as fir, with inner plies of softwood, hardwood or both. These 4x8 sheets come in thicknesses from 1/4 in. to 3/4 in. and are often used in place of wide construction lumber. You can buy interior plywood for indoor projects, such as subflooring or paneling, or get an exterior grade that withstands the weather, for instance, for outdoor sheathing or sign-making. Sheets are graded alphabetically, with the highest grade having smooth, paintable surfaces free from knotholes and other defects.

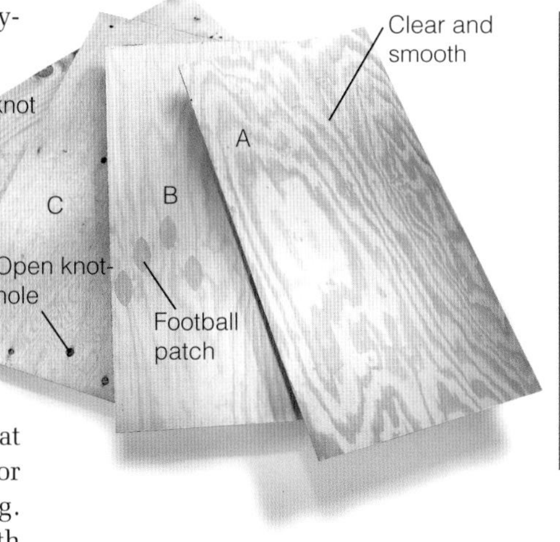

Construction plywood is graded by letter, from A to D. Higher-grade (A) sheets have smoother surface veneers, while lower-quality (D) panels may contain splits and large, open knots. In Canada, the grading runs from A (highest grade) to C (lowest).

Whole log

Fixed knife

Rotary cutting produces a continuous ribbon of veneer.

Squared half-log

Plain-sliced veneer more closely resembles solid boards.

Rotary Cut vs. Plain-Sliced

Hardwood plywood comes with two types of outer veneers. **Rotary-cut** veneers have a wilder, more open and distorted grain pattern and are the most economical choice. **Plain-sliced** veneers have a more natural, boardlike grain pattern and are typically created by gluing layers of veneer side by side to create the standard 48 in. width. Plain-sliced plywood commands a premium price and is popular for higher-quality work. Some sheets are available with plain-sliced veneer on the good-face side and rotary-cut material on the back.

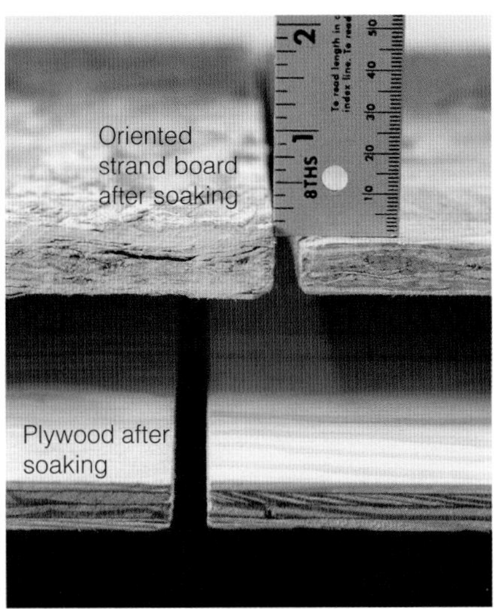

Plywood vs. Oriented Strand Board

Like softwood plywood, oriented strand board (OSB) is made for subflooring, sheathing and other construction. It's less expensive, yet very similar in strength and durability. It weighs about the same, can span equal distances and offers similar nail-holding abilities. Its textured surface is less slippery on roofs and some panels have regularly-spaced lines to help with nailing. One drawback is OSB's tendency to swell when exposed to moisture—then remain swollen when dry. The solution? Store it in a dry place and cover it with tarpaper or siding as soon as possible.

Accurate Marking and Measuring

Measuring Tapes 41
Angles and Curves 43
Miters 441

Angles

Precise marking and measuring is the key to successful projects, and dealing with angles is often the biggest hurdle. Sometimes all it takes is simple math to calculate a desired miter angle; other times the right technique and the appropriate tool make the job go smoothly.

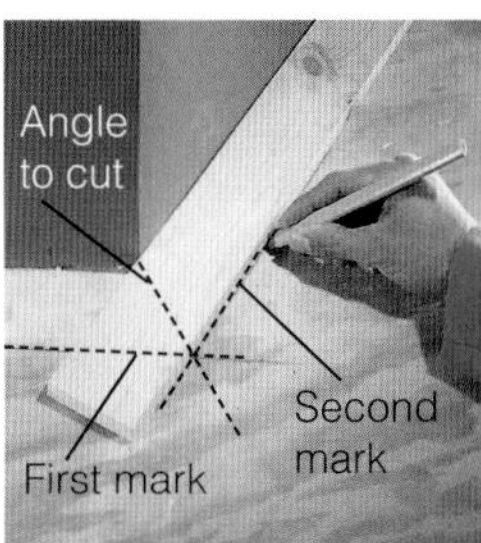

1 To find the exact angle to cut any miter, lay a scrap of wood against the wall and mark the outside edge. Then move the board around the corner and mark again.

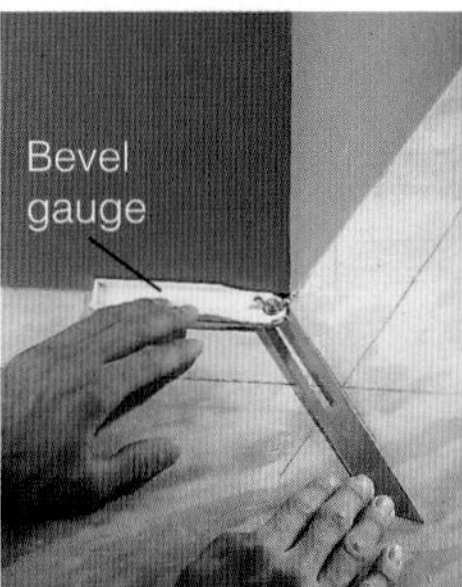

2 Adjust a bevel gauge until it matches the angle. Use the gauge to transfer the angle to a board, protractor, miter saw or other tool.

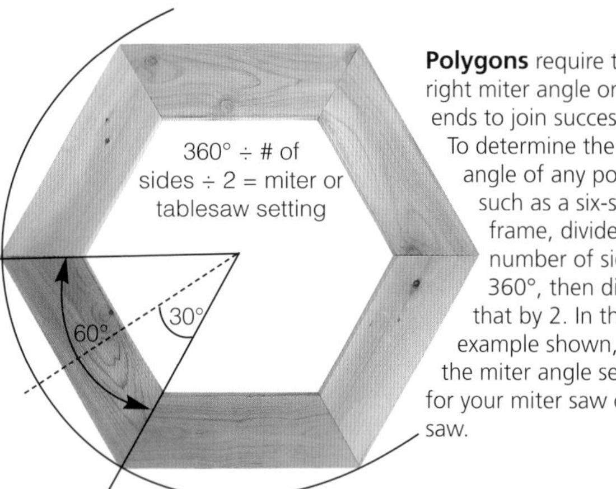

Polygons require the right miter angle on board ends to join successfully. To determine the miter angle of any polygon, such as a six-sided frame, divide the number of sides by 360°, then divide that by 2. In the example shown, 30 is the miter angle setting for your miter saw or other saw.

Curves

Curves add flair to your work but can be challenging to mark. Drawing them freehand usually results in irregular arcs, and the results are usually unsatisfactory. To generate a consistent or fair curve, try tracing around some of the circles that surround you: lids from jars or cans, toy or bicycle wheels or any round item in your house that can easily be traced with a pencil.

After marking the curve, cut out the part as close to your line as possible with a jigsaw or on the bandsaw. Then carefully sand the curve until your eye deems it's fair. For really large circles or arcs of a circle, try one of the techniques below.

Arcs are easy to draw using a piece of thin, straight-grained wood. Drill a small hole in one end and cut a V-notch into the opposite end. Tie string to the hole, then bend the strip to the desired curve and lock it in place by tying a knot in the string and slipping it into the V-notch. Trace the stick to create your arc.

Circles of practically any diameter are possible with a homemade trammel. Drill a hole for a pencil in one end of a stick and tack the other end where you want the center of the circle. The distance between the pencil hole and the tack should equal half the circle's diameter, its radius. Simply spin the trammel to draw the circle.

Assembly

Assembling your work can spell disaster if you forget which part goes where—especially after you've spread glue and can't turn back. To make assembly goof-proof, it pays for you to learn how to mark your work to keep track of its order.

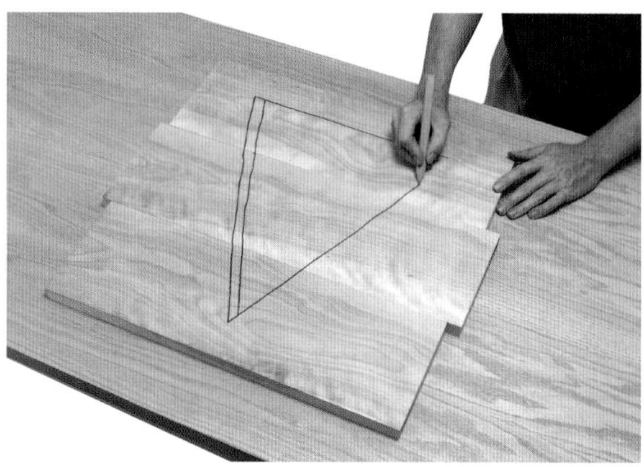

Boards. Use a triangle when laying out boards edge to edge. This way, you can separate the boards for gluing or later assembly and never lose track of their order.

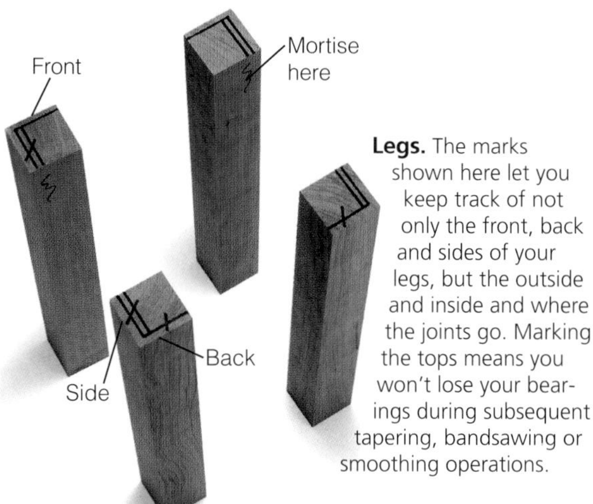

Legs. The marks shown here let you keep track of not only the front, back and sides of your legs, but the outside and inside and where the joints go. Marking the tops means you won't lose your bearings during subsequent tapering, bandsawing or smoothing operations.

Woodworking Joints

You can use many methods to join wood, including simply butting parts together, overlapping them and adding fasteners, such as nails or screws, or cutting precise, interlocking angles. The joints you choose will depend on your own abilities and the tools at hand, as well as the strength and appearance you need for a project. The best rule of thumb when selecting a joint is to keep it simple, but keep it strong. Think twice about using a complex dovetail joint when a simple butt joint will do.

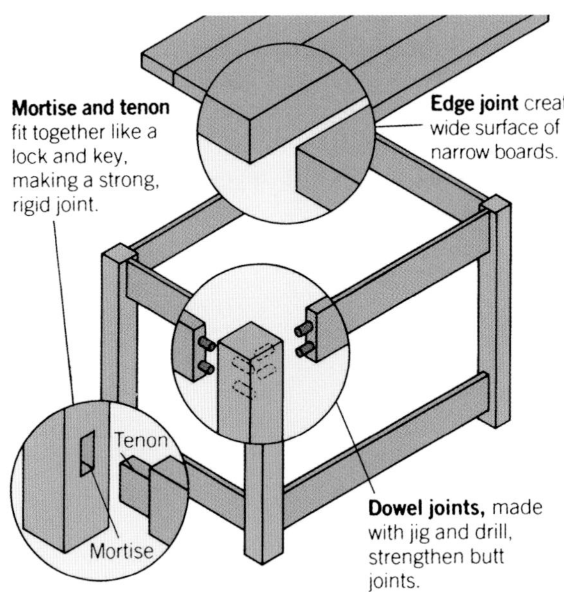
Mortise and tenon fit together like a lock and key, making a strong, rigid joint.
Edge joint creates wide surface of narrow boards.
Tenon
Mortise
Dowel joints, made with jig and drill, strengthen butt joints.

This simple table shows examples of many joinery options. The top, made from multiple narrow boards, is glued together using **edge joints,** which require only straight, flat surfaces that are square to their faces, plus a good coat of glue. The top rails are joined to the legs using **dowels.** Stronger **mortise-and-tenon joints** are shown being used to connect the lower stretcher rails to the legs. When assembled, both types of joints prevent the frame from racking or twisting.

Corner Butt Joints

Joints that butt together at corners are quick to assemble and don't require particularly precise fitting. They do, however, need strengthening with glue and fasteners, such as screws, corner blocks, metal plates or shop-made gussets. That's because all these joints involve joining end grain to either face or side grain, and the open pores of end-grain wood make a poor glue joint.

Use fasteners of the correct size. Oversize screws will split stock; undersize ones won't adequately support the joint. With any type of joint in which you're gluing several parts simultaneously, practice the clamping procedure before you apply the glue.

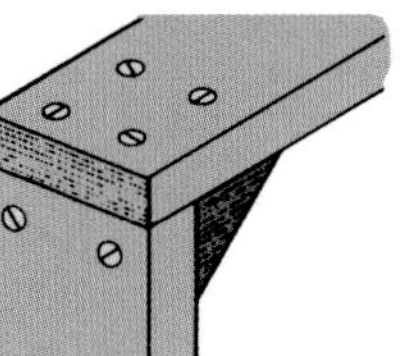

Triangular block, glued and screwed in place, stabilizes inside corner.

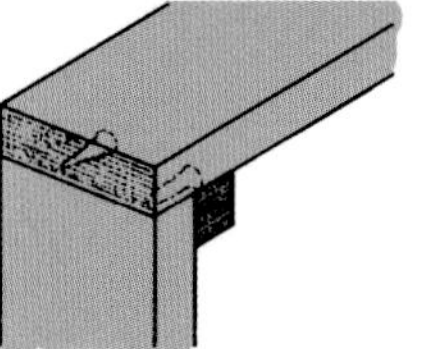

Square block can be attached from inside if you don't want screws to show.

Outside glue block supports joint without obstructing inside corner.

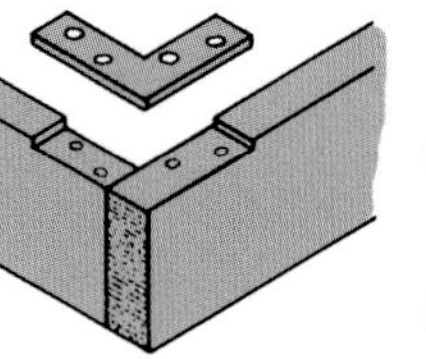

Flat metal corner plate set in recess provides smooth surface across joint.

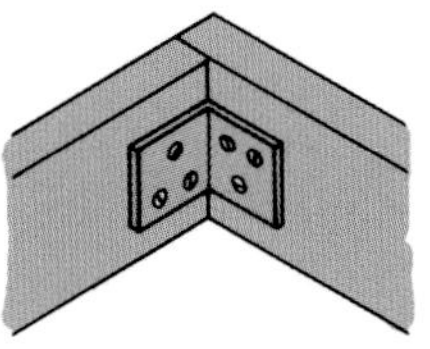

Inside corner brace pulls corner together; supports best if used on all corners.

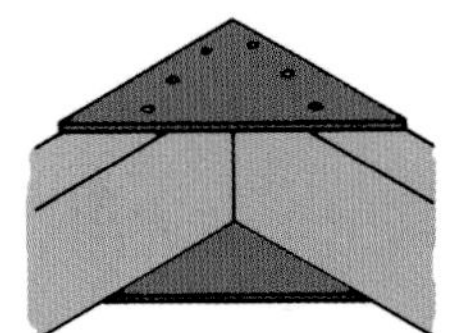

Triangular gussets of 1/4-in. plywood, glued and nailed in place, produce rigid joints.

Overlapping Joints

Overlapping joints are among the easiest to construct and can be strengthened by adding glue and fasteners, typically screws. Notching the piece to form full or half-lap joints that interlock and overlap increases strength by providing shoulders that resist racking. However, it's still a good idea to use both glue and fasteners to reinforce the joint. In addition to its superior strength, a lap joint is a good way to produce flush surfaces for a neater appearance.

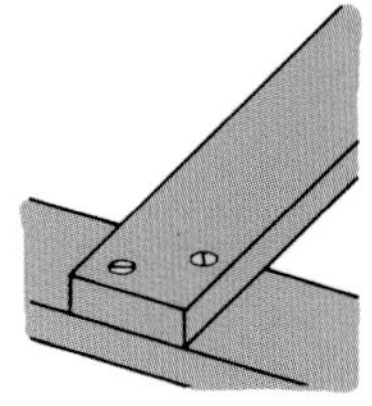

T-joint

Shelf support

T-joints. A T-joint requires no cutting. Place one piece across the other at the desired angle and fasten them with glue and nails or other fasteners. Though strong, the joint is somewhat crude and best used for temporary or hidden construction. Shelf supports, a form of T-joint, are easily assembled. Glue and screw small wooden blocks to the uprights; then simply rest or secure the shelf in position on the blocks.

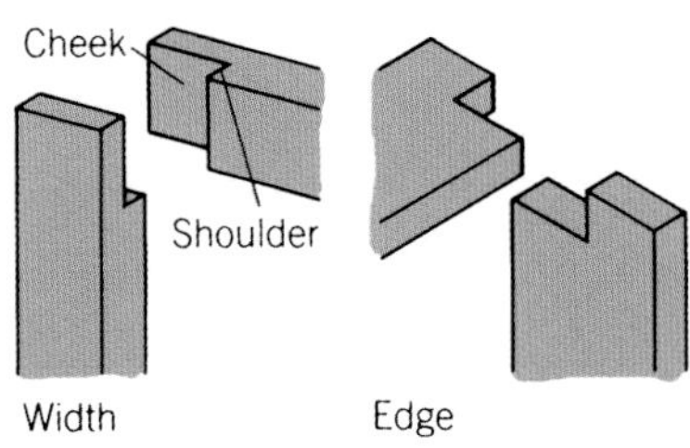
Cheek
Shoulder
Width
Edge

Lap joints. Full and half-lap joints connect width to width, edge to edge or edge to width. In a full lap, a thick piece is notched to receive the entire thickness of a thinner piece. In a half lap, pieces of equal thickness are notched to half their thickness and interlock flush when joined. Cut them in the middle of each board, called a cross lap, at the ends in an end lap, or from one end to one middle in a middle lap.

Dadoes

Tablesaws 62
Push Sticks and Shoes 63
Router Techniques 67

A dado is a channel cut across the grain; when cut with the grain, it's called a groove. The adjoining member can be the full thickness of the board or it can be rabbeted (see p. 435) along its end. A **through dado** goes completely across a board; a **stopped dado** stops short of the edge to conceal the joint. The joint is perfect for case shelves, partitions and drawers, because it resists twisting and warping.

Blade Guard Alert!

Most guards must be removed for non-through cuts, so be careful to keep fingers well clear of the cutting action. Use push sticks and push shoes whenever possible.

Router Method

You can mill dadoes or grooves with this simple T-square jig, a router and a straight bit. Use a framing square to square the jig when you make it, and rout into the right side of the jig's leg to establish the position of the dado. If you're joining 3/4-in. plywood, which is slightly thinner than solid wood, use a special 23/32-in. bit for a snug fit.

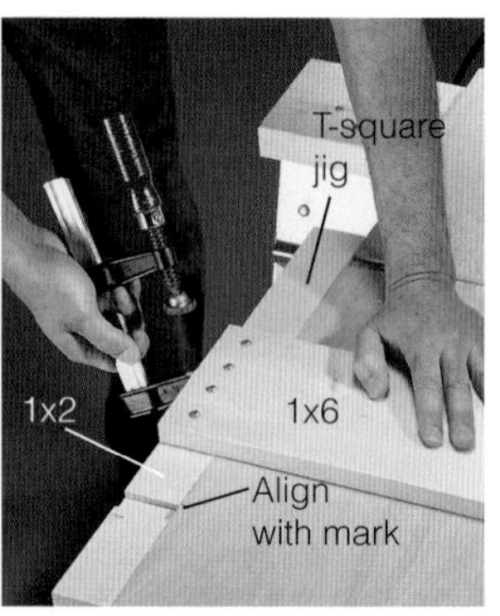

1 Align the dado cut on the jig with the dado marks on your board and clamp both ends of the jig to the workpiece. Make sure the jig is slightly longer than your workpiece is wide.

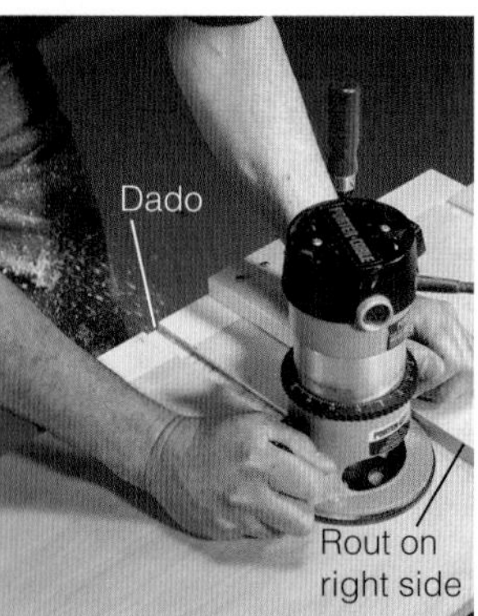

2 Set the desired depth of cut, and guide the router across the jig's leg and workpiece. Keep the router on the right side of the jig and push away from you so the bit pulls the router against the jig, rather than pushing away from it.

Tablesaw Method

The tablesaw cuts dadoes with ease. You can use either a standard blade or a special dado blade, which is a set of thinner blades you stack together to the desired dado width. Set the dado depth by measuring how far the blade projects from the saw's surface. Radial-arm saws can also accommodate dado blades.

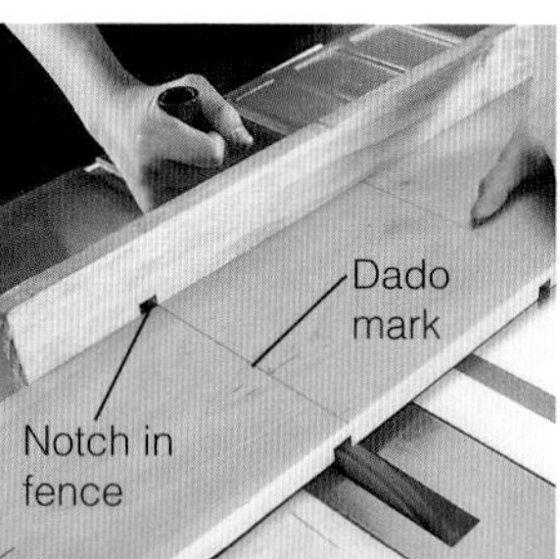

A dado blade is the quickest way to cut dadoes. Screw a 2-in.-high (5-cm-high) wood fence to your miter gauge, cut a deep notch in the fence and then align a mark on the top side of your workpiece with the notch to accurately make the cut.

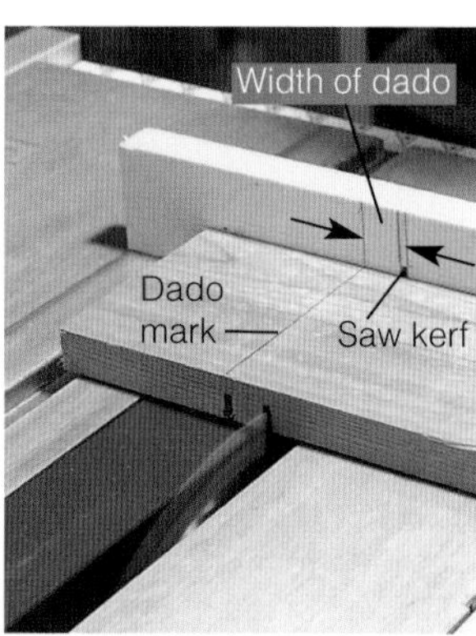

A standard blade can cut great dadoes by way of successive cuts. Saw a kerf in a fence screwed to your miter gauge and mark the dado width. Cut the first dado by aligning the workpiece's dado mark with the kerf. Cut the second shoulder by aligning the mark to the fence mark. Finish by making several passes between the shoulders.

Circular Saw Method

A circular saw cuts serviceable if somewhat rough dadoes. To speed things up, try ganging your parts together side by side to cut the dadoes at one time. Set the dado depth by lowering the saw's base. To guide the saw for the outside shoulder cuts, you can use a jig similar to the router T-square or a carpenter's square.

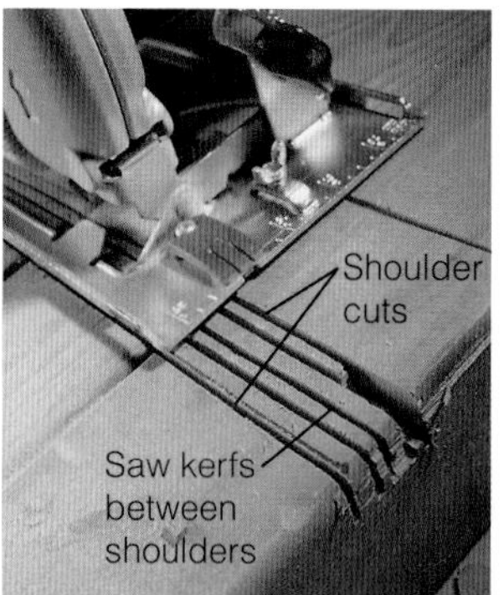

1 Make the left and right outside shoulder cuts first by guiding the edge of the saw with a large square or a T-square. Then cut kerfs between the shoulders by pushing the saw freehand, leaving 1/8-in. (3-mm) strips of wood. Don't fret if the inner kerfs aren't straight.

2 Break out the waste by levering a chisel between the kerfs. Finish up by paring the bottom smooth with a sharp chisel.

Rabbets

Often combined with dadoes or grooves to form interlocking joints, rabbets are L-shaped tongues cut along a board's edges, either across or with the grain. The joint increases the number of gluing surfaces and provides one or more shoulders to help resist racking.

Rabbets are handy for insetting cabinet backs or drawer bottoms into rabbeted case or drawer sides or for making corner joints on boxes, such as cabinets or drawers.

When laying out the joint, be sure to leave enough tongue thickness for strength. It's common to cut the depth of a rabbet about half or two-thirds of the board's thickness. Be sure to set up your cutters so they cut squarely, allowing you to mill square shoulders for a strong, tight fit.

Router Method

Alternate pilot bearings

Rabbeting bit

One of the easiest ways to cut rabbets is to rout them using a special rabbeting bit that automatically cuts the perfect width. The bit comes with different pilot bearings that let you adjust the width of cut by simply installing the correct bearing on the same bit.

Start by selecting a bearing that will cut a groove that's as wide as the thickness of the part you're joining. Adjust the router height for the desired rabbet depth. Clamp the workpiece to the bench. For deep rabbets, adjust the router and make a series of gradually deeper passes.

Make sure the bit's bearing bears against the edge of the work, then move the router from left to right to rout the rabbet.

Dado Blade Method

Rabbets are a snap with a dado blade if you clamp a wood fence to the rip fence to cover a portion of the blade.

1 With a wood fence securely clamped to the saw's rip fence and over part of the blade, slowly raise the spinning blade until it cuts into the fence.

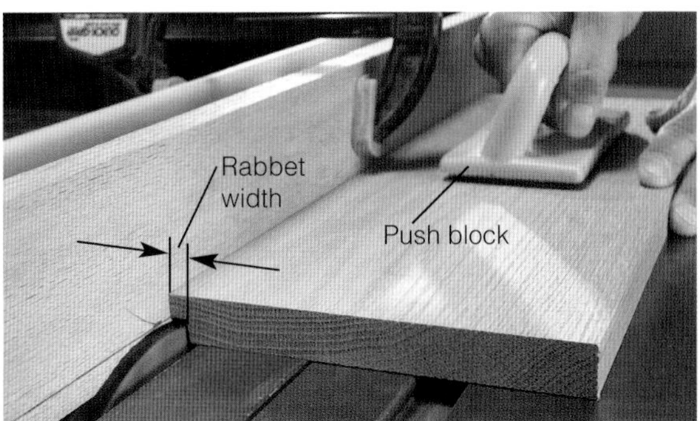

2 Adjust the fence for the desired width of cut and lower the blade for the rabbet depth. Make the cut using a push block, keeping the stock snug against the fence as you push.

Standard Blade Method

A standard tablesaw blade cuts excellent rabbets—especially if you build a jig to guide the work. The jig is a simple box-type arrangement made from plywood, with a tall fence that's square to the saw table. You clamp the workpiece to the jig, and then push the entire assembly past the blade.

First make relief cuts by laying the stock flat on the table and guiding the work against the rip fence. Then stand the work on edge, clamp it to the jig and rip off the waste by pushing the assembly past the blade.

Mortise and Tenon

Mortising Attachment 53
Tablesaws 62
Routers 66

These sturdy interlocking joints are the mainstay of furniture, particularly when joining frame pieces, such as doors, face frames, table bases and chairs. Although a mortise-and-tenon joint usually joins two pieces at right angles, if you plan carefully, they can unite boards at virtually any angle.

The mortise is the hole portion of the joint and is typically cut in the upright leg, or stile, of the work. The tenon is the tongue that's cut in the adjoining member, or rail. A tenon is described by its three dimensions: The shoulder, which defines its length; the cheek, which refers to width; and the edge, which refers to thickness.

A mortise for leg-and-rail construction should be half as deep as the stock is wide. The tenon should be as close to one-third of the stock's thickness as possible and, if blind (see below), about 1/16 in. (1.5 mm) shorter than the mortise is deep, to ensure the shoulders meet tightly. The fit dictates the joint's success: The tenon should be snug enough to require tapping by hand or with a light hammer, but not so loose that it falls into the mortise.

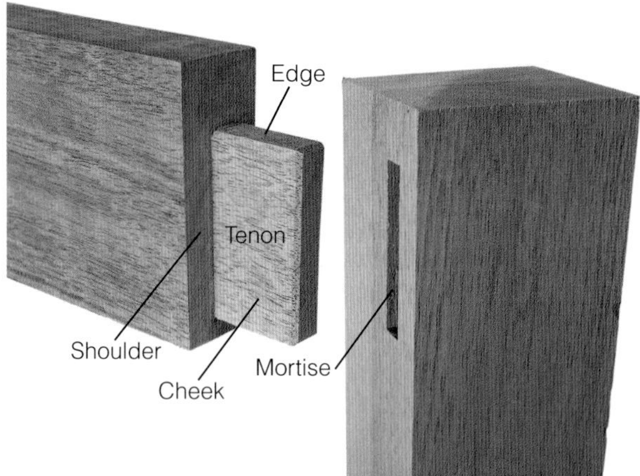

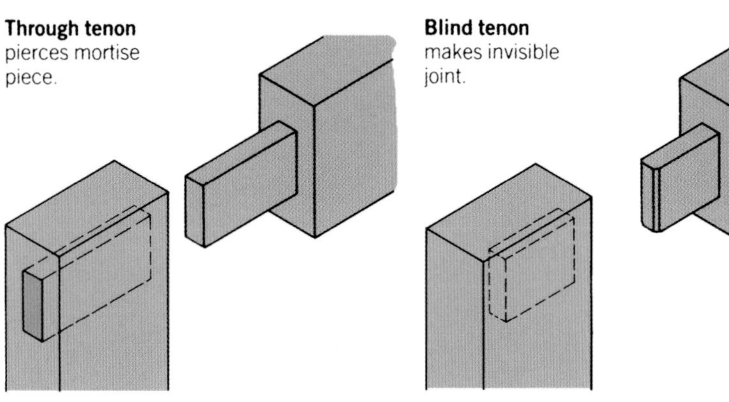

Through tenon pierces mortise piece.

Blind tenon makes invisible joint.

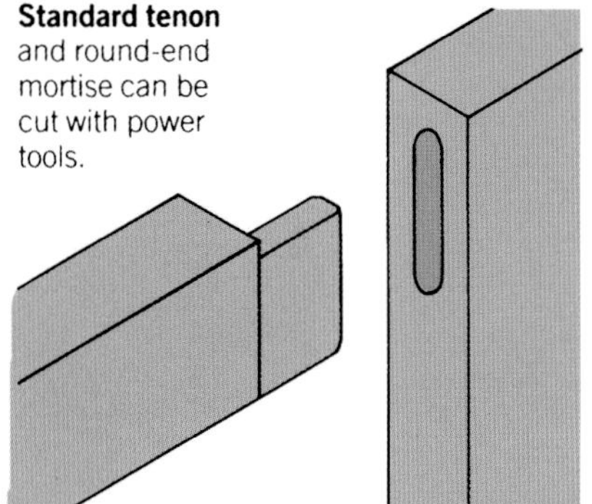

Standard tenon and round-end mortise can be cut with power tools.

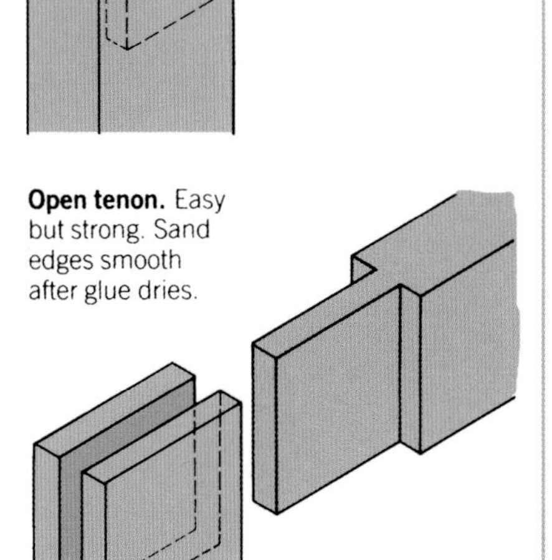

Open tenon. Easy but strong. Sand edges smooth after glue dries.

Cutting Mortises

It's best to cut the mortise first, then fit the tenon. Hollow-chisel bits that work in a drill press or dedicated mortising machine create square-ended mortises that fit square tenons. Use the machine by setting the depth of cut and then drilling a uniform series of holes into the edge of the stock to the desired length of the mortise.

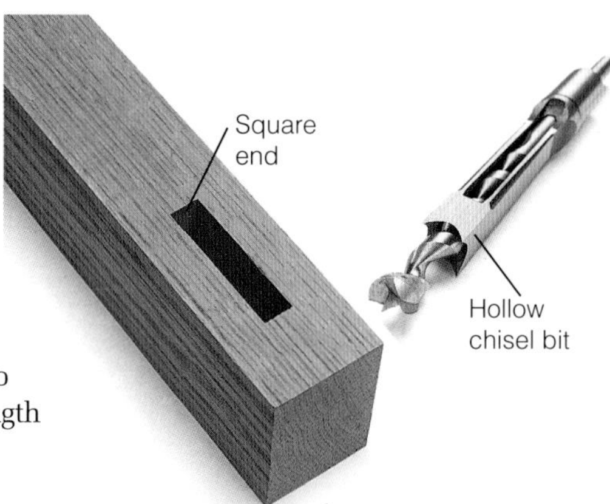

Cutting Tenons

Lay out the cheeks so they fit the exact width of the mortise. Stand the stock vertically on the tablesaw to cut the cheeks, using a similar jig as when rabbeting (see p. 435). Then crosscut the shoulders by guiding the work against a fence attached to your miter gauge. A stop block aligns the work so your shoulders are the perfect length.

Dovetail and Box

Dovetails

Decorative and durable, dovetail joints have flared pins and tails that interlock. Because they resist being pulled apart, dovetails are ideal for furniture parts under stress, such as cabinet boxes and drawers.

Dovetails are commonly made in two styles: through dovetails and half-blind dovetails. Though they can be cut by hand, a router dovetail jig makes cutting the joint foolproof; most come with excellent instructions.

To make a corner joint for a drawer, start by routing the tails in the sides; then cut the pins in the front to complete the joint.

Through dovetail

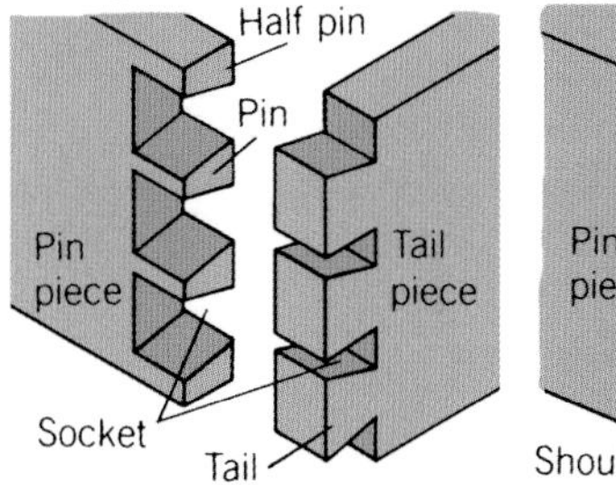

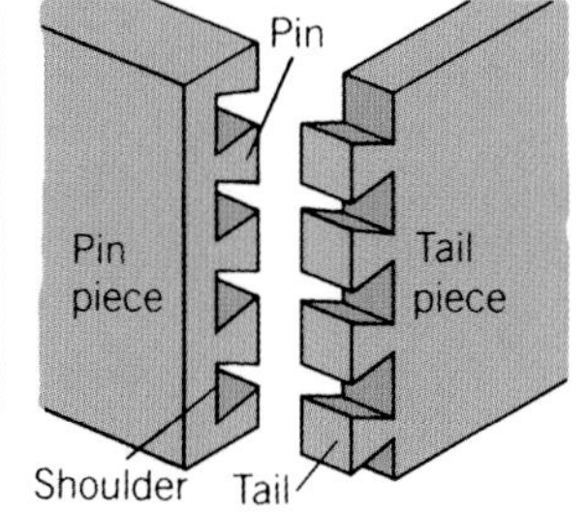

Half-blind dovetail

Through dovetails, the stronger of the two types, are a good choice when you want to expose the joint, such as on a cabinet. Only one-half of the joint is visible with **half-blind dovetails,** making them a good choice for drawers or wherever you want to conceal the joint.

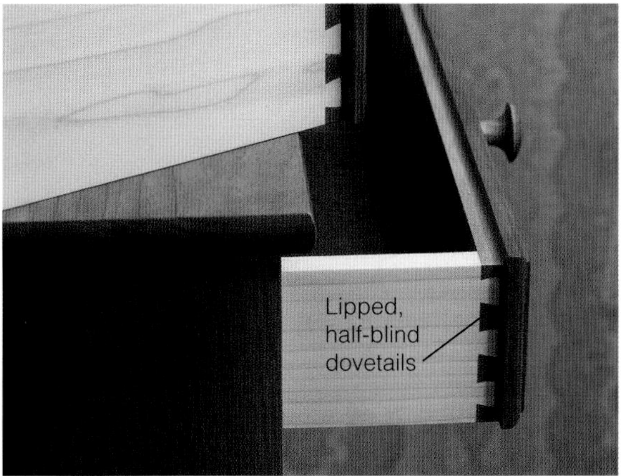

Drawer sides. Clamp the stock vertically in the jig and move the router from left to right to shape the tails.

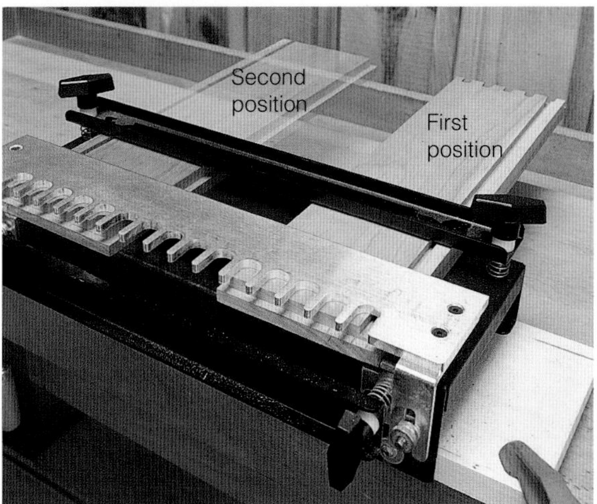

Drawer front. Cut the pins on one end by aligning the stock to the right of the jig. Cut the opposite pins with the stock to the left.

Box Joints

Also called finger joints, the fingers and slots of box joints provide a large gluing area and create a strong joint. Sort of a simplified dovetail, box joints don't have the same flared connection, but they're decorative and a good choice for corner joints, such as box-type constructions.

Make the fingers and slots *exactly* the same width and make them as long as the stock is thick. Simplify the task by using a dado blade adjusted to the width of a finger and attaching a wood fence to your miter gauge. Glue a wood pin into a notch in the fence, equal to the size of a finger and longer by about 1 in. (2.5 cm).

1 With a pin jig screwed to the miter gauge, cut the slots by leapfrogging the most recently cut slot onto the pin, then cutting the next one.

2 Assemble and check for a tight joint. To alter the fit, shift the jig slightly left or right on the miter gauge.

Biscuit Joinery

Clamps 34
Drills 50
Adhesives 84

Fast, strong, invisible and virtually foolproof, biscuit joints can replace box or dovetail joints, mortise-and-tenon, or dowels joints in many situations without sacrificing strength.

The biscuit, made from compressed beech, is shaped like a flat football and comes in three sizes. You cut half-moon slots in adjoining pieces with a biscuit joiner. Squirt white or yellow water-based glue into the slots, slip in the biscuit and clamp. The glue swells the biscuit, locking the joint even if the slots are slightly oversize. The biscuit's elliptical shape allows some lateral movement to help align the joint before the glue sets.

The biscuit joiner is like a small circular saw with a horizontally mounted blade. A good joiner will have a conveniently located on-off switch and a fence that adjusts easily—and locks securely—for right-angled or mitered joints. The fence helps center the slot and holds the blade parallel to the work. After setting up the cut, just plunge the blade into the workpiece to cut a slot. Simple.

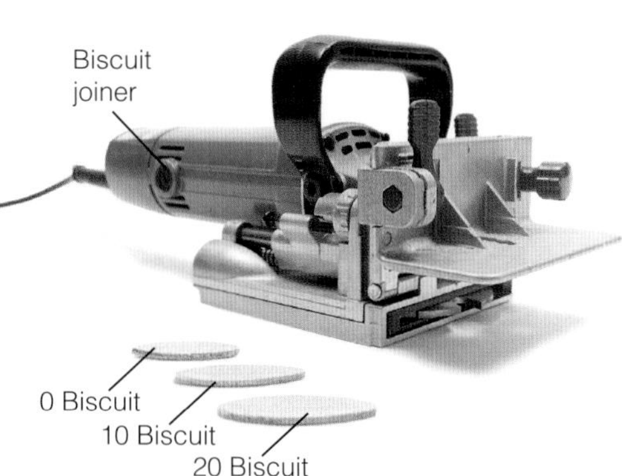

Face-frame Joint

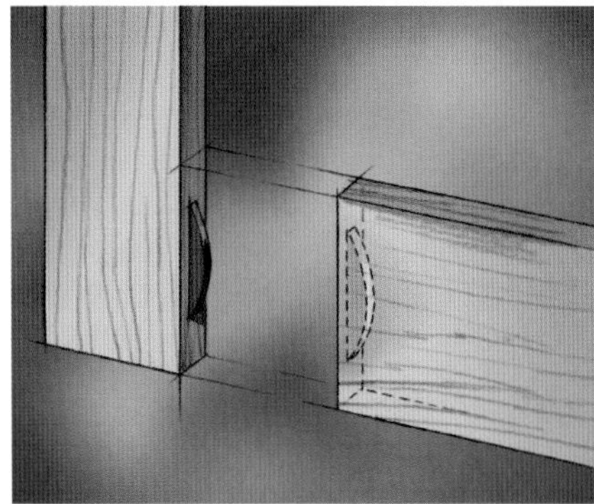

This joint works for door frames, but only for lightweight doors. As with all biscuit joints, position the boards in exactly the position they'll be joined and mark across the joint with a pencil. Adjust the joiner's cutting depth for the biscuit's size and position the fence to cut in the center of the stock.

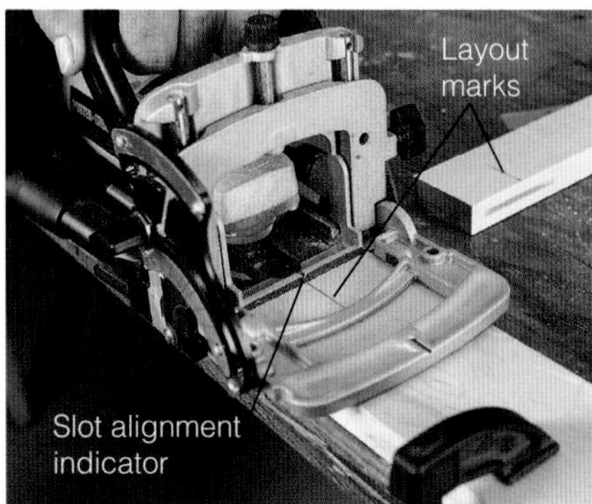

Clamp the stock to the bench, align the mark on the joiner with the mark on the stock and plunge to cut a slot.

Edge-to-edge Joint

When joining long areas, as in an edge-to-edge joint, keep the slots about 2 in. (5 cm) away from the ends of the boards and space them every 6 to 8 in. (15 to 20 cm). While biscuits add strength to this joint, they're particularly helpful in aligning the parts during glue-up.

Apply yellow or white glue inside each slot so the biscuit will be completely coated when inserted. Then run a bead of glue along the edge and clamp.

T-joint

Case joints, such as T-joints or corner joints, are simple to cut. Mark for slots, and draw lines on both sides of the mid-board connection in the T-joint. Cut the end slots with the work vertical in a bench vise. Use a fence clamped to one of your layout lines to create the slot in the middle of the adjoining board.

To slot the middle of a board, clamp a fence to one side of the joint. Adjust the joiner's base, position it against the fence, align guide marks, and plunge.

Pocket Screws

If cabinetmaking intimidates you, pocket screws can be a welcome relief from tedious joint cutting and fancy tools. Armed with a drilling jig and a handful of pocket screws, you can quickly master all sorts of tight-fitting frame and case joinery.

Pocket joinery is best described as a screw version of toe-nailing, where boards are joined by angling a fastener through the edge of one into the other. A drilling jig and special stepped drill bit allow you to drill the precise holes this joinery system requires. You'll need a square-drive bit, special pocket screws, which have narrow shanks and low-profile, square-drive heads.

The downside to pocket joinery is the ugly, oblong holes you'll leave on the backside of your work. But they're easily filled with wood plugs (below) made in several species expressly for this purpose.

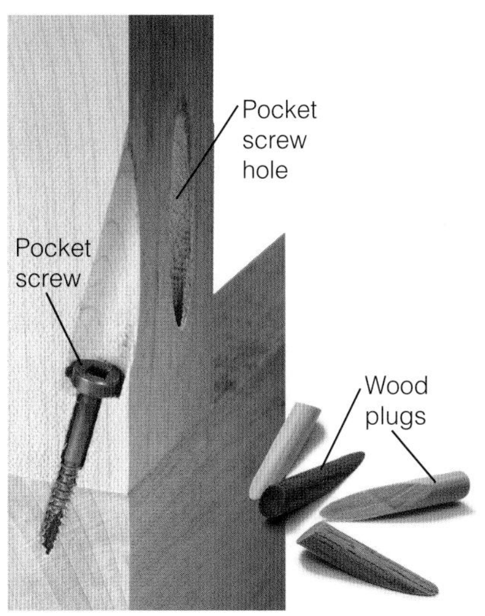

Face-frame Joints

Face frames or door frames are easy to make using pocket screws. Be sure to use at least two screws per joint to prevent twisting. Generally, a 1-1/4-in.-long screw is best when connecting 3/4-in. stock.

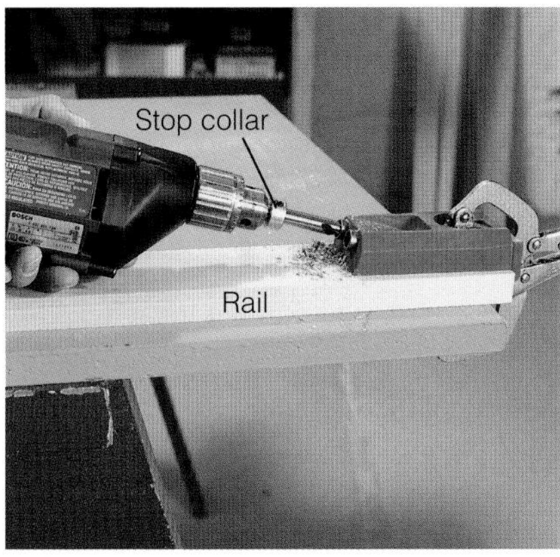

1 Clamp the jig to the end of the rail. Drive the stepped bit through the jig and into the workpiece until it stops against the stop collar.

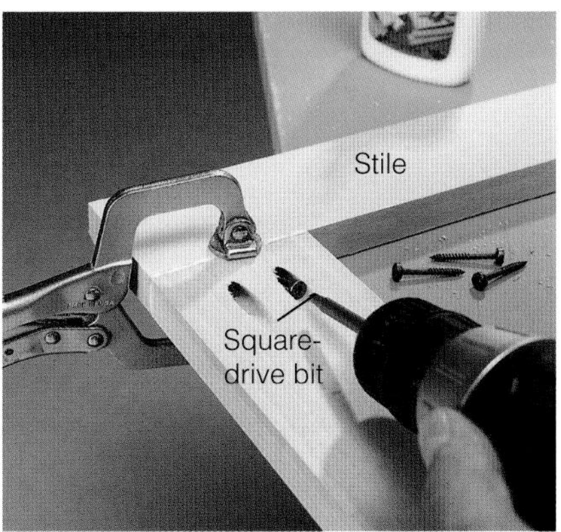

2 Apply glue, align and clamp the joint, and drive the self-tapping screws through the rail and into the stile.

Edge-to-face Joints

You can assemble an entire cabinet with pocket screws in a matter of minutes. As with biscuit joints, you'll need to mark layout lines for midpanel joints and space screws every 6 to 8 in. (15 to 20 cm) for strength.

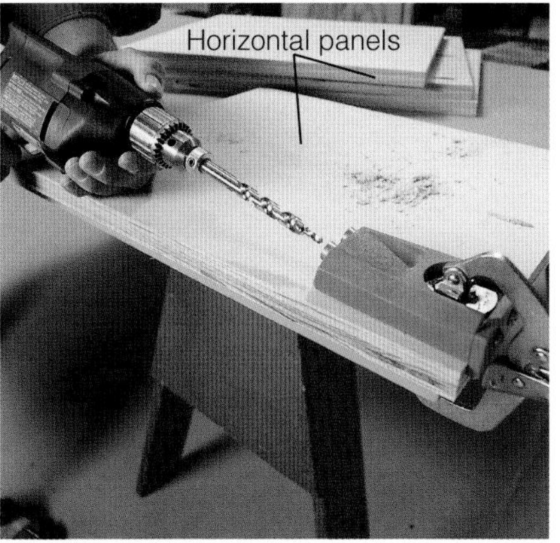

1 Clamp the jig to the end of each horizontal shelf panel and drill the pocket holes.

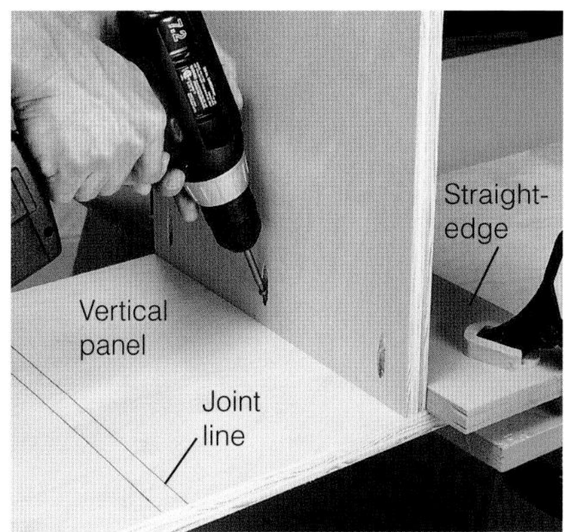

2 Position the horizontal panel on the joint lines of the vertical case-side panel, clamp a straightedge to one side to align the shelf and drive all the screws.

Corner Joints

Pocket screws do wonders holding corner joints for drawers, cabinets or other boxes. Using the drilling jig, bore holes in the drawer ends (or cabinet top and bottom), glue and assemble with screws.

Edge Joints

Hide raw plywood edges by screwing wood banding around its perimeter. Use the drilling jig to bore holes in the plywood, miter the banding to fit, add glue and assemble with screws.

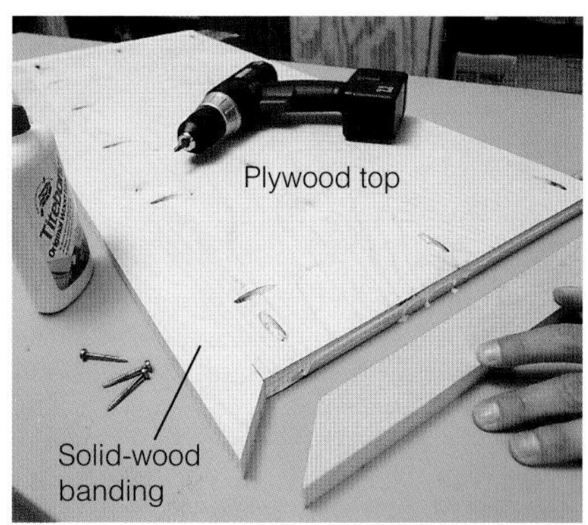

Dowels

Circles and Curves 43
Tablesaws 62
Tablesaw Miter Jigs 444

Correctly made, dowel joints are nearly as strong as mortise-and-tenon joints. Dowel joints connect all sorts of frames, such as doors and face frames, and casework, such as cabinets and other boxes. They require careful workmanship and a few simple tools.

The tricky part is aligning and drilling the holes precisely because you drill complementary holes in each piece. Using a doweling jig solves the problem of drilling the first set of holes, since it guides the drill bit in an exact pattern. To locate the matching holes, you can use dowel centers, which are metal plugs with centered points that fit into the previously drilled holes and prick the adjoining piece to mark its hole locations.

Use at least two dowels per joint to prevent twist. Dowel diameter should be one-third to one-half the thickness of the thinnest piece of wood being joined. Length should be 1-1/4 times the thickness of the thinnest piece. Be sure to drill the holes 1/8 in. (3 mm) deeper than half the dowel's length. And use fluted dowels, which are scored or grooved, so air and excess glue can escape.

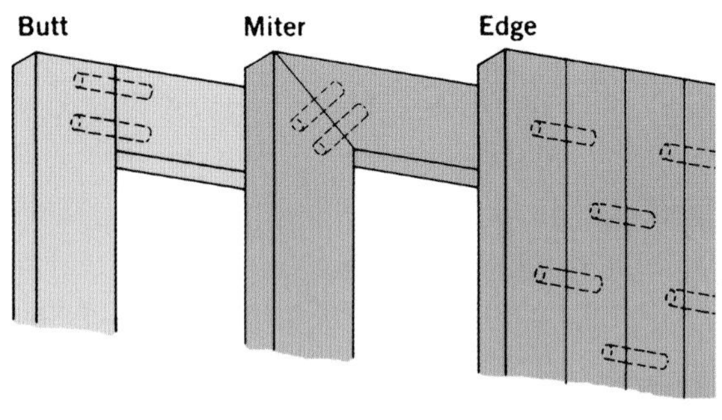

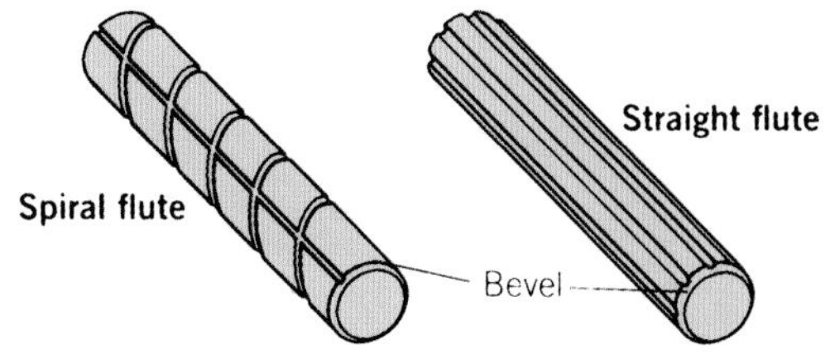

Dowels can connect many types of joints, including square and mitered frame joints, edge-to-edge joints and edge-to-face joints, such as where a case side meets a bottom or top. Fluted dowels make strong connections and are better suited for dowel joints than smooth-sided dowel rods.

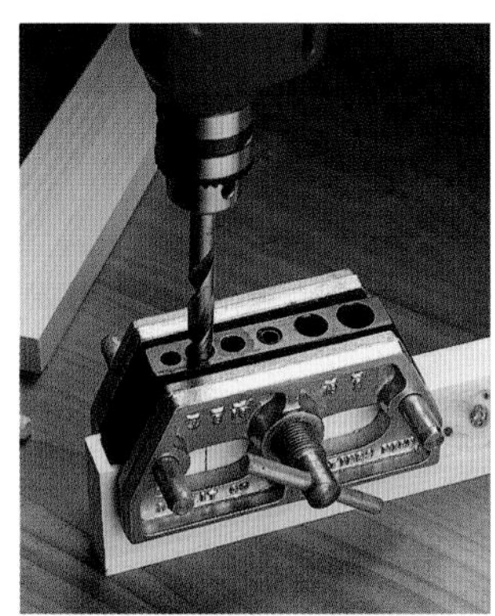

Drill dowel holes using a doweling jig, which guides a drill bit squarely through hardened steel bushings. Most jigs will grasp edges and ends via an integral clamping mechanism.

Transfer dowel hole locations using dowel centers, made from hardened steel with sharp center points. Drop the centers into holes drilled in the stile, align the adjoining piece over the joint and tap it to mark the hole locations in the rail.

Better Doweling

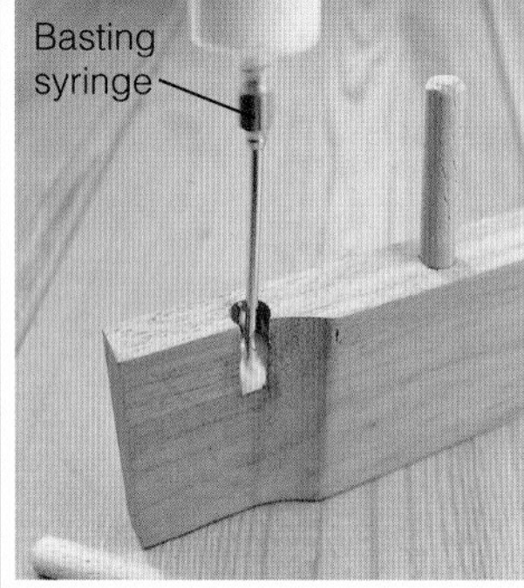

To coat dowel holes quickly and without a mess, use a basting syringe. Pour glue into the syringe, insert the needle into the hole, press the plunger and rotate the syringe to apply an even coat. When finished, pour out remaining glue, fill syringe with water and press plunger to clean needle and needle tip.

Make your own fluted dowels from an ordinary dowel rod. Grasp the end of a rod in a metal vise, clamp locking pliers at the free end and tap them with a hammer so they slide down the rod. Unlock, rotate the pliers, relock and repeat the procedure to cut flutes on other parts of the rod.

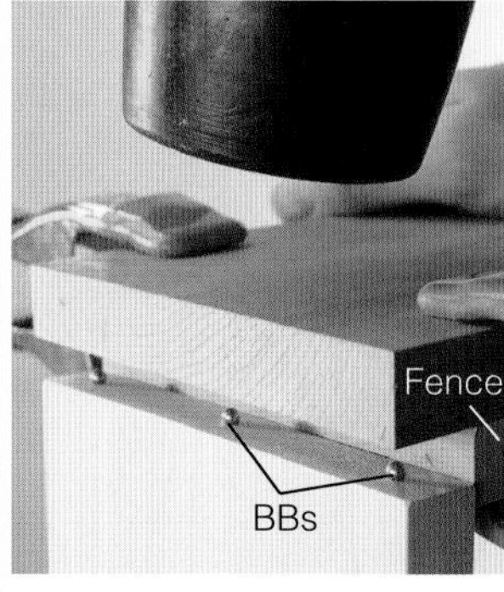

Try BBs for marking complementary dowel holes in both pieces instead of dowel centers. First, use a nail to prick holes in one piece for the BBs to nest in. Then clamp a fence to the adjoining board to align the joint and tap its surface with a rubber mallet. The BBs will make dents in the second board for centering the drill bit.

Miters

Miters are any angled cut on the ends or edges of parts; the most common is 45 degrees so the adjoining pieces connect at a right angle. Cutting a miter is simple if you use a miter saw or a jig for the tablesaw. The real trick, even for seasoned woodworkers, is to glue the joint successfully without gaps.

Miters can be cut either across the face of the stock, called a face miter, or along the edge, for an edge miter. Face mitering is more common, for instance, for picture frames, doors and moldings. Edge miters are useful for cabinet corner joints and other box-type constructions.

Most mitered surfaces are end grain, which does a poor job of holding glue. That's why you need to strengthen the joint with nails, dowels, biscuits or splines. The exception to this is an edge miter whose mating area is either long-grain wood or plywood, which has enough long grain to make a satisfactory glue joint.

Face miter

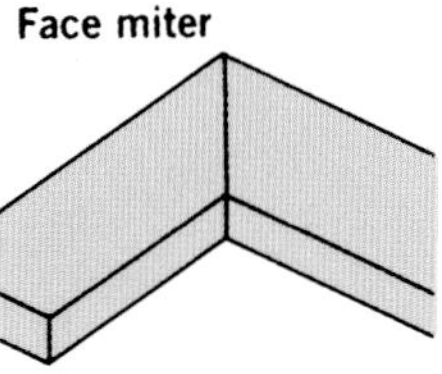

Edge miter

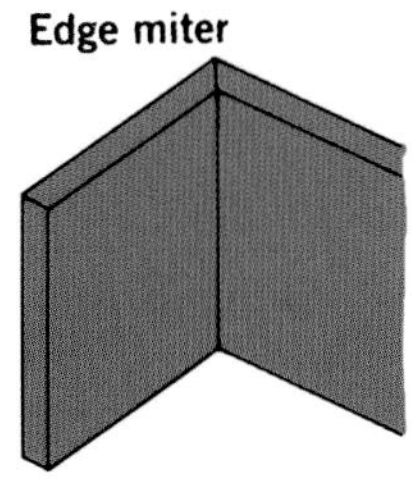

Gluing Miter Joints

Gluing miters is risky, since end-grain pores suck in glue but too much glue makes parts slip. To ensure success, lightly precoat joints with glue, let it get tacky, apply a second wet coat and clamp.

Masking tape makes a great clamp because it stretches to provide tension and removes easily after the glue has dried. Stick one end to one side of the miter, pull the tape to stretch it over the joint and press it to the opposite side.

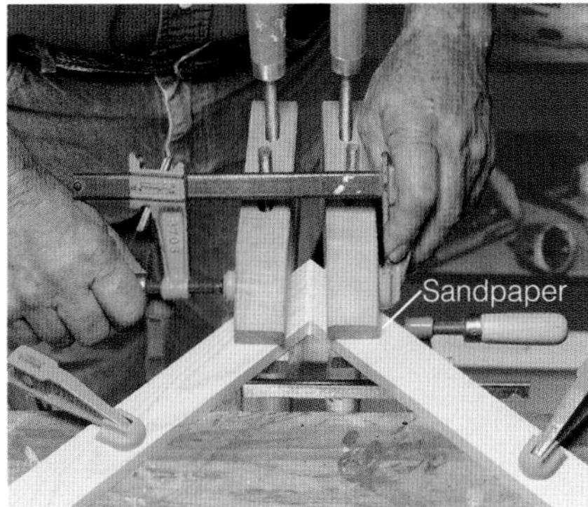

Clamp combinations are often the best solution. Place strips of 60-grit sticky-back sandpaper in the jaws of two handscrews and clamp them parallel and on either side of the joint line. Draw the joint closed by clamping across the handscrews with bar clamps on top and bottom.

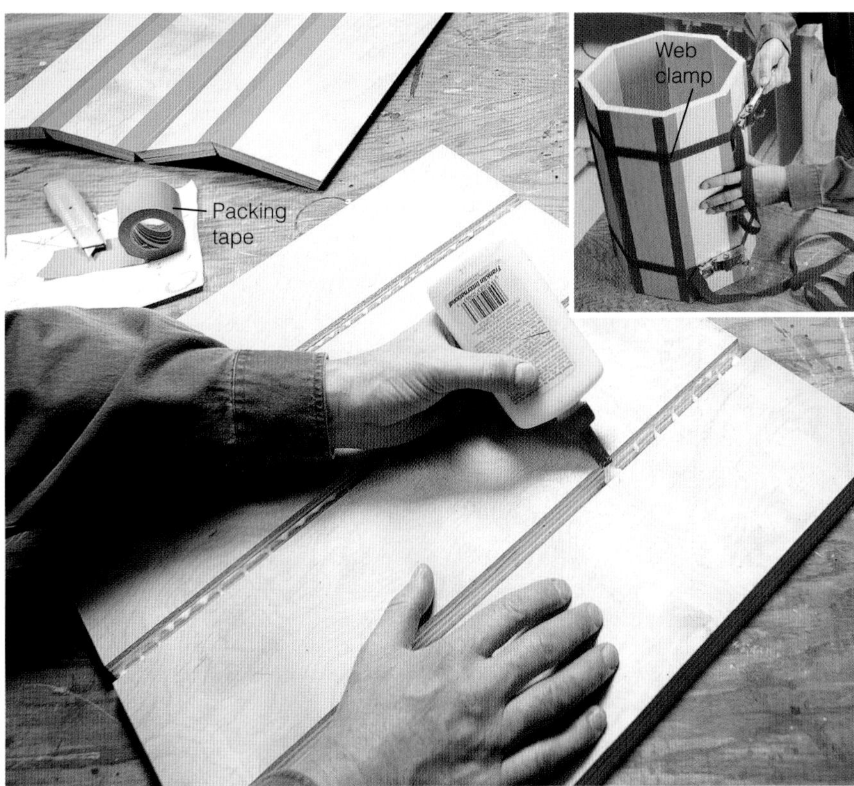

Packing tape and clamps can pull big edge miters together without fuss. Position the parts outside-face up with the joints together and run tape along each joint. Turn the parts over, apply glue into the miters, assemble vertically and secure with web clamps.

Splined Miters

Wood splines make picture-frame miters strong while adding decorative flair. You can make the splines from any wood you like, and glue them into slots cut in the frame. To cut the slots, make a V-shaped jig that rides over your rip fence with a tall fence that holds the frame parallel with the blade and at 45 degrees to the table. Cut the slots in the glued-up frame, glue in oversized splines and trim them flush.

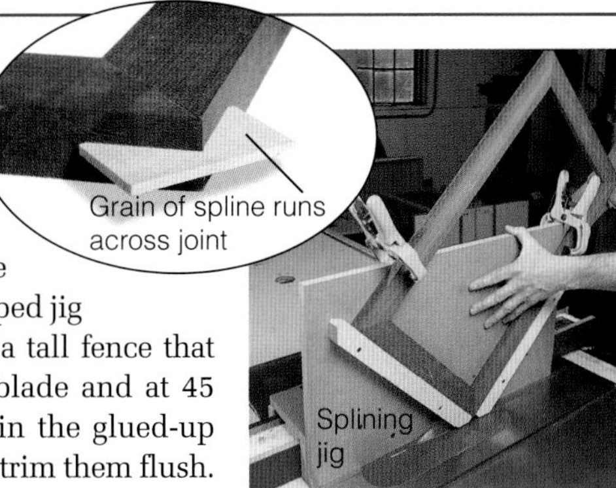

Edge Joints

Pipe Clamps **34**
Bandsaws **61**
Adhesives **84**

To make a wide panel from narrower boards, edge-joining is the answer. Properly cut and glued edge joints form a bond stronger than solid wood. The keys are creating straight, smooth, square edges and then gluing up in a logical manner.

First, cut the boards so the panel will be about 1 in. (2.5 cm) oversize in length and width—you'll trim it to size after glue-up. Arrange the boards as they'll be joined. Decide whether to alternate the end-grain rings (see step 1, below) and check that the grain harmonizes along the joint lines. Then sand the faces of each board and draw a triangle across the joints.

Edges can be jointed with hand or power tools. A jointer requires the least effort, but a tablesaw, router or hand plane will work, too. Don't sand the edges; they'll be smooth but not flat. Stack the boards to inspect the joints.

After jointing, dry-clamp the panel to test your setup. When you're ready, you have two options: Glue-up the entire panel at once or glue one joint at a time. The second method is slower but easier when making really wide panels. Spread glue on each edge, lightly clamp the boards, level the joints by hand and tighten the clamps.

1 Alternate the end grain to minimize any future warp. However, if the panel will be held by a framework, such as a door frame or table base, disregard the end grain and place the best-looking faces up.

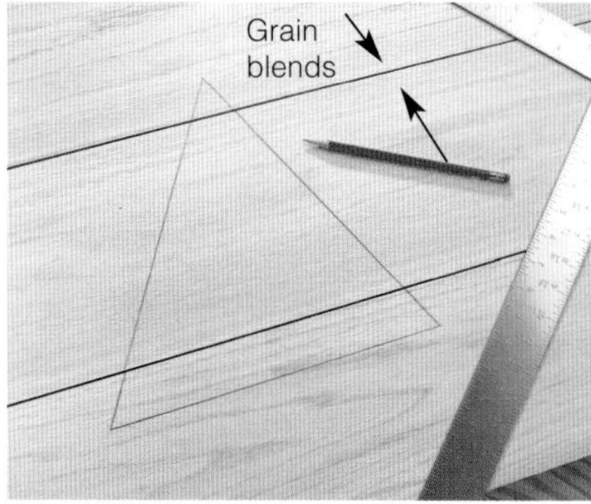

2 Arrange the grain pattern between boards and smooth each face with 100- and 120-grit sandpaper. To keep track of the orientation, draw a triangle across the joints.

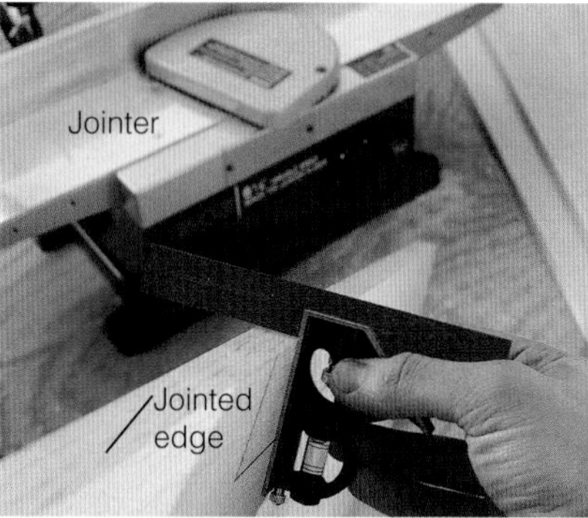

3 Use a jointer, tablesaw, router or hand plane to create a straight, smooth edge that's square to the board's face. Check for 90° using a small square.

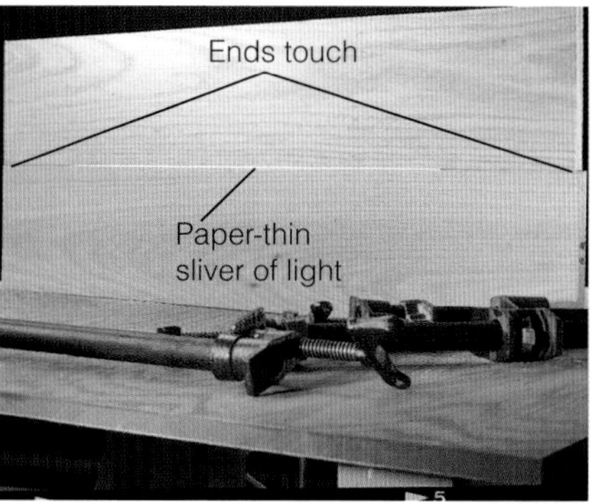

4 Place the joints together and check for straightness by shining a light from behind. The best joints show no light or a thin gap along the middle. Gaps on the ends require rejointing.

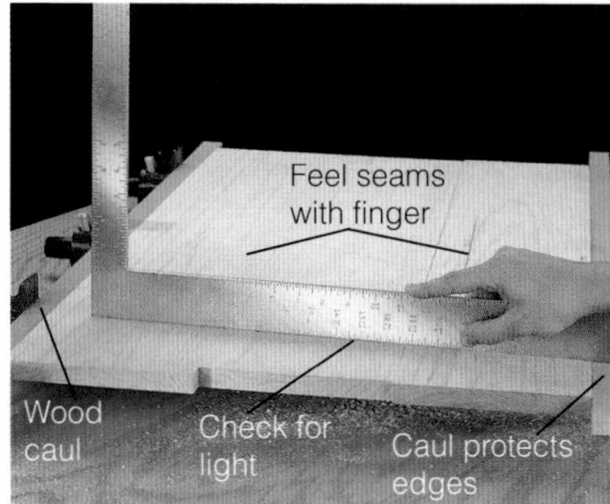

5 Practice clamping without glue, lining up the joints with your finger. Check for flatness with a straightedge and rejoint if necessary. Wood cauls on either side distribute pressure and cushion edges.

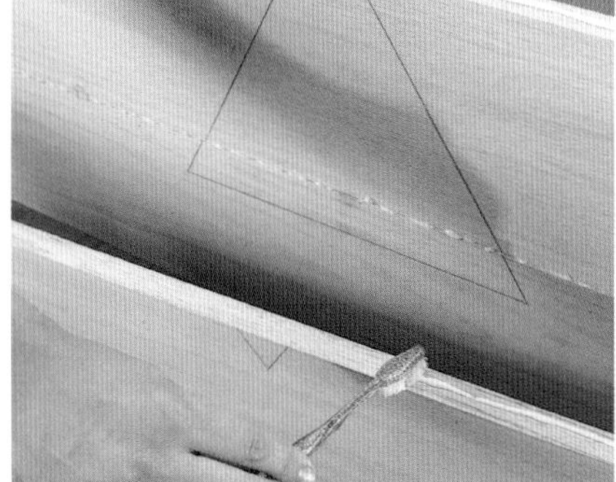

6 Run a bead of glue on both surfaces to be joined and spread it with a water-dampened toothbrush. Both edges should be wet with glue but not thickly coated.

7 Position boards in clamps and gently tighten the middle clamp. Press a finger into the glue line, loosen the clamp and level the joint. Add more clamps, alternating above and below, until the joints are level and closed.

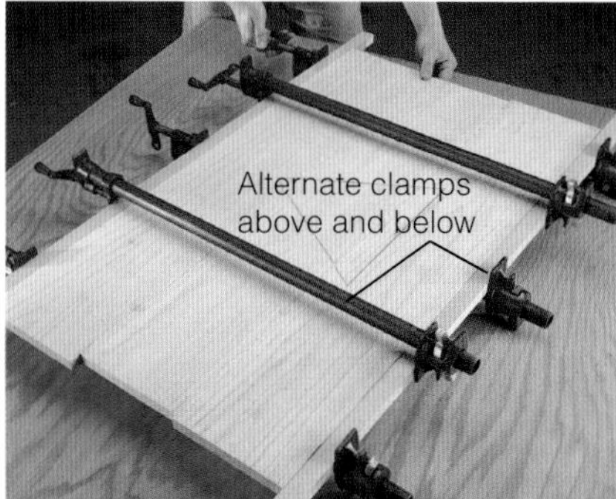

8 After the joints are level and all clamps are tight, reposition them one at a time so each clamp jaw is centered on the thickness of the boards. After 30 minutes, scrape off the dry but pliable glue using a chisel.

Creating Curves

Laminating

Curves add distinction to your work and can be a lot of fun to make. To bend what is normally a very stiff material, you can saw wood into thin, pliable strips and then glue them together using a two-part, curved form. The dried glue holds the curve.

Strips 1/16 to 1/8 in. (1.5 to 3 mm) thick bend best and are easily sawn on the tablesaw and planed using a thickness planer. (A planer produces smooth surfaces that glue-up stronger and more uniformly.)

Make the form from plywood or particleboard. Use a small paint roller to apply glue to all the strips, place them in the form and clamp. Leave the clamps on for at least eight hours.

1 Face-glue sheets of plywood to the thickness of the curved part and draw the desired curve on one face. Cut the form apart on the bandsaw, sawing on each side of the pattern line. Smooth the sawn curves with sandpaper wrapped around a curved block of wood or using a spindle sander.

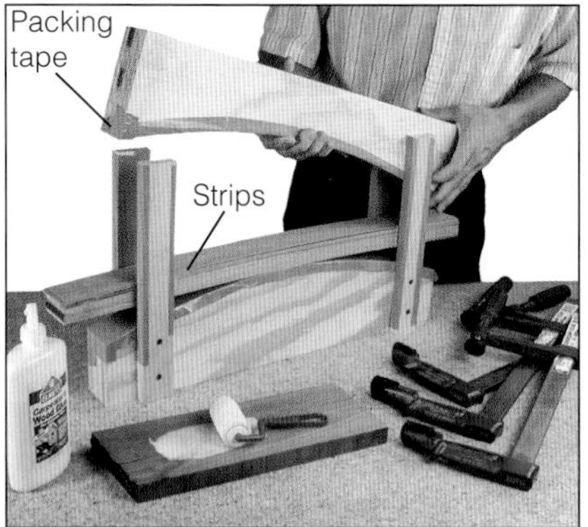

2 Screw wood uprights to the bottom form to keep the strips and top form aligned, and apply packing tape to the inside of the forms and uprights to resist glue. Coat the strips evenly with glue and place them on the bottom form, then position the top form over the strips.

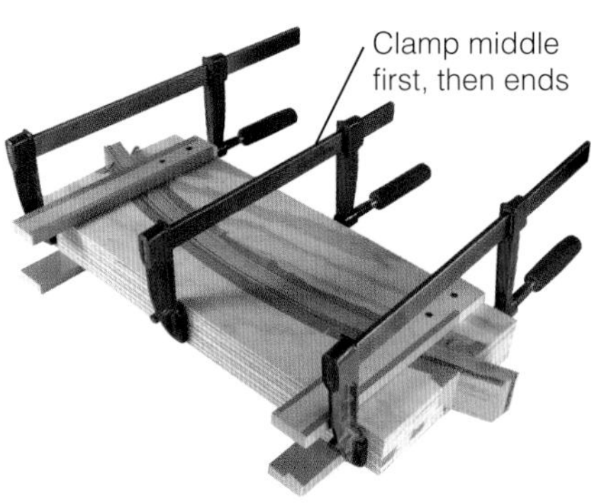

3 Lay the form flat on the bench and lightly clamp across the middle of the assembly. Add clamps to either side, tightening each clamp in sequence until all the joints are closed. Let the glue-up dry for eight hours before you remove the clamps.

Kerfing

Cutting a series of evenly spaced kerfs into one side of a board lets you bend even the thickest woods.

Select a straight-grained piece without knots to avoid breakage and to achieve a consistent bend. Raise the tablesaw blade until it's 1/16 to 1/8 in. (1.5 to 3 mm) below the thickness of the stock. Space the kerfs about 1/2 in. (12 mm) apart and, guided by the miter gauge, make the cuts. Closer spacing allows for a tighter bend. If using plywood, cut just to the final layer of veneer.

After kerfing, glue or nail the part to a curved framework or other structure to maintain the bend. Or fill the kerfs with epoxy and clamp the part temporarily into a curve until the adhesive sets.

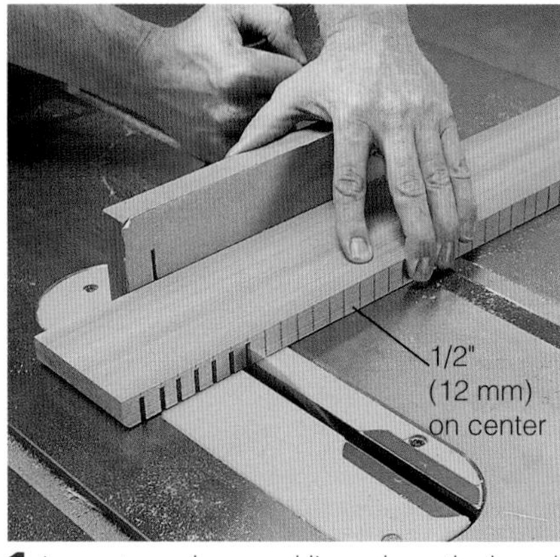

1 Lay out evenly spaced lines along the board and raise the tablesaw blade until it's slightly below the surface of the stock. Using the miter gauge, cut a series of kerfs into the bottom of the board. If the outboard end gets floppy during cutting, support it with a stand placed beside the saw table.

2 To glue the board into a permanent curve, fill the saw kerfs with two-part epoxy wood filler and bend the board to the desired curve. You can hold it in place with clamps or temporarily nail it to a curved structure until the adhesive sets.

3 Installing the curved part to its final structure can help hold the curve while the adhesive sets. If you don't use epoxy, you'll need to brace the part so it remains stiff enough to hold the curve. Cover the sawn side with veneer or paint the board to conceal your kerfed handiwork.

Woodworking Jigs

Drill Presses 53
Miter Saws 55
Tablesaws 62
Router Tables 67

To speed your work and ensure accuracy, it's worth building some hard-working jigs designed for all the major machines, including the miter saw, tablesaw, drill press and router. These clever shop-made devices make your tools more versatile and your woodworking more enjoyable.

When building jigs, use quality materials, such as straight-grained wood, hardwood plywood and MDF, and cut and assemble parts precisely. Time spent now will pay big dividends later in the accuracy of your jigs and projects.

Miter Saw Table Jig

This crosscutting station lets you tackle long boards with ease. Plus, accurate multiple cuts to the same length are possible, thanks to the jig's adjustable stop block.

Screw your saw to the base with its fence aligned with the jig's fences and set up on a flat work surface. If mobility or storage is necessary, simply unscrew the saw and stow the station separately.

Make repetitive cuts by clamping the stop block to the fence at the desired distance from the blade.

1x6
3/4" plywood
8'
Support block
Stop block

Tablesaw Miter Jig

This sled-type jig is simple to construct and turns your tablesaw into a highly accurate mitering machine for cutting picture-frame and other square miter joints.

Cut the runner so it slides in your miter slot without wiggling. Mill the dado so the base overhangs the saw's cutline, attach the runner and trim the overhanging edge by running the assembly past the blade. Add the triangular fence support, making sure its apex is precisely at 90 degrees, and use a combination square to establish its 45-degree orientation on the base. Fasten the fences, handles and stop block, and you're ready for mitering.

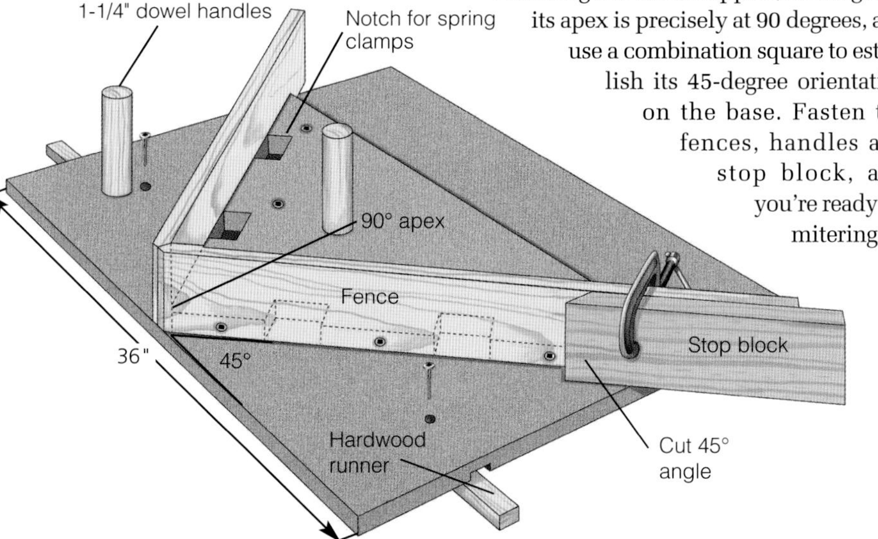

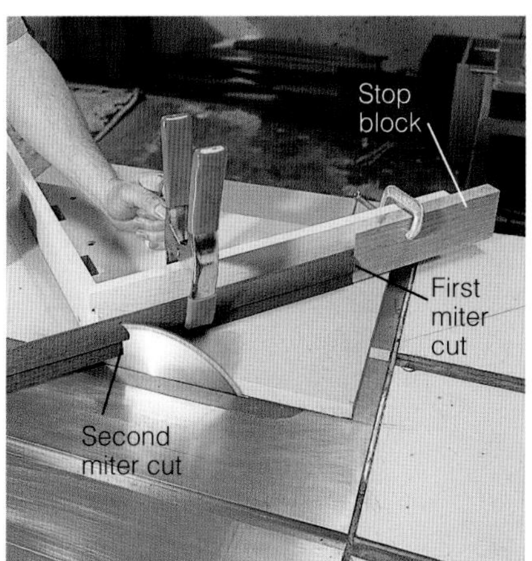

After cutting the first miter using the fence facing you, butt that mitered end against the stop block on the opposite fence, clamp the board in place and make the second miter cut.

Drill Press V-Jig

Drilling holes in round stock, such as dowels and pipes, is dicey without help. This simple V-shaped block, made on the tablesaw, lends a stable hand.

Use the jig by centering the point of the V directly below the drill bit and clamping the jig in place. Then position your work and bore the holes.

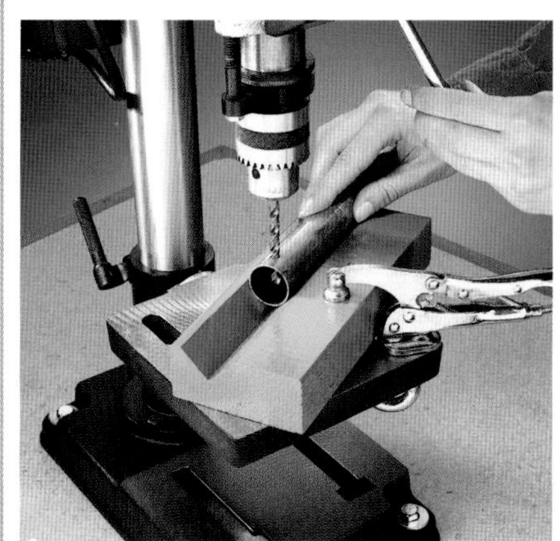

Router Jigs

The jigs and techniques shown at right allow you to shape unique parts using a handheld router. With some of these devices, you can switch bits, using a different profile and the same jig to create an entirely new look. That's part of the versatility of router jigs.

When making a cut, be sure to move the router in the correct direction to avoid having the bit catch and pull the router off course or away from the guide. The important thing is to always move it against the rotation of the bit, not with it. This keeps bits and fences snug against the work for a cleaner, safer cut.

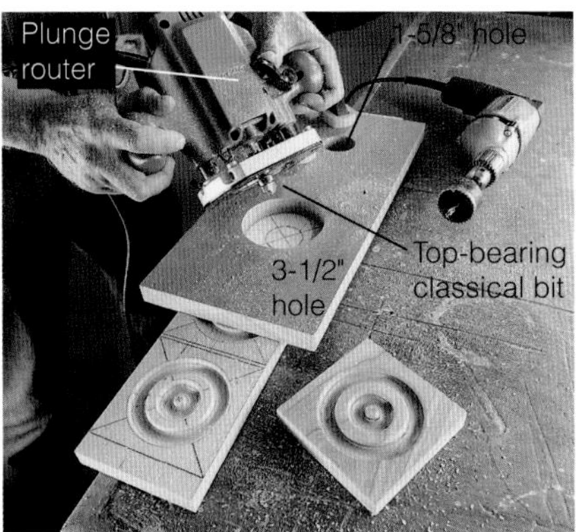

Bull's-eye corner blocks are perfect for decorating door casings and cabinet trim. To make the outer ring, clamp the jig so its larger hole is centered over the work, plunge the bearing-guided bit into the wood and move the router in a clockwise pass. Next, rotate the jig and center the small hole to rout the inner ring, making this second cut using the same bit.

Stopped flutes are a snap to rout with a plunge router, core box bit and edge guide. Draw square start and stop lines across the stock, and adjust the edge guide so the first pass cuts the two outer flutes. Starting at one line, plunge the bit and push the router until you reach the opposite line. Reset the guide to cut the middle flutes and repeat.

Template routing lets you rout multiples from one original, such as a stack of intricately shaped shelves. Make a template shelf and cut the rest 1/8 in. (3 mm) oversize. Clamp template to oversize shelves so edges extend past template. Adjust bearing-guided flush-trimming bit so bearing contacts template and rout the new shelf to the contours of the original.

Router-Table Jigs

The router table is often more convenient than a handheld router for routing small or skinny parts or taking big cuts. When you equip it with the right jigs, the router table becomes even more versatile.

As with handheld routing, be mindful of the bit's rotation and the direction you feed the work. The rotation is reversed with the router mounted upside down. Feed against the bit's rotation, otherwise the bit can grab and the workpiece might scoot away.

Caution: Work carefully around exposed bits and use guards whenever possible. Make jigs and workpieces oversize so you have more room to keep your hands clear of the cutters.

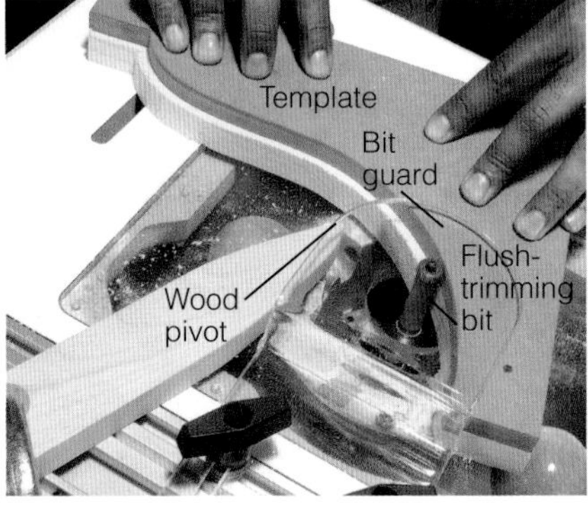

Patterns are easily routed with a template and a flush-trimming bit. The technique is similar to handheld template routing (above) but works better for small parts. Shape the template precisely, then tack it to an oversize workpiece. Clamp a pivot, such as a pointed stick, to the table. Rotate the template around the pivot and onto the bit's bearing. Then safely rout freehand around the template.

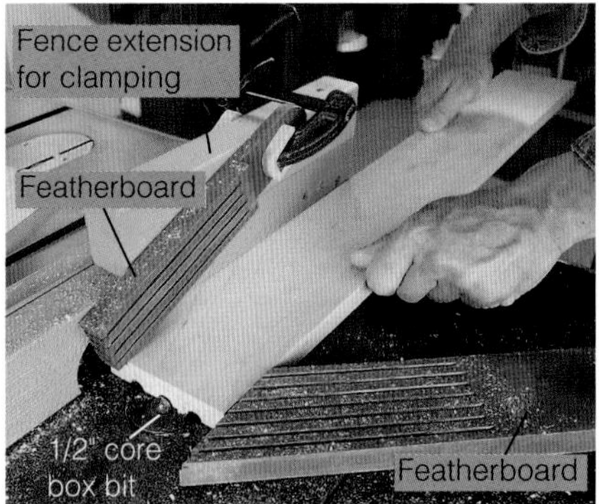

Full flutes for a door casing or cabinet trim are best cut on the router table. Mount a core box bit and set up featherboards (store-bought or homemade boards with flexible "fingers") to press the work down and into the bit. Adjust the fence to cut the first outer flute, then reverse the workpiece end-for-end to rout the opposite outer flute. Move the fence once more to cut a center flute.

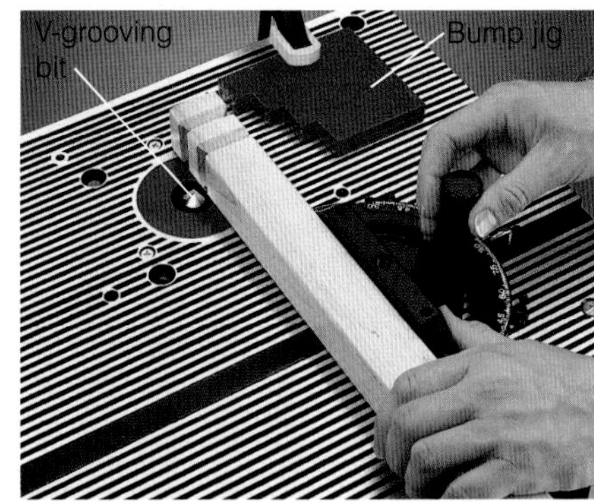

Bump jigs are great for many projects. Clamp this one to the table to rout a series of V-grooves into a leg without measuring or resetting a fence. Cut steps in the jig so they correspond to the distance between grooves. Using a miter gauge, butt the work against the first step to make the first cut. Rotate the work to cut the remaining three faces. Then move to the next step to cut the next groove, and so on.

Cabinets and Boxes

Clamps 34
Checking for Square 41
Dadoes 434
Rabbets 435

The humble box is the building block for all casework. Add shelves, drawers and doors hung on hinges, and you've created handsome and functional cabinets.

There are two kinds of boxes: solid panel, in which the case is made from slabs of solid wood or plywood, and frame-and-panel, a skeleton of frames joined to each other, with panels inside each frame. Either type of box can be frameless or have a face frame attached to the front.

Corner joints can be dovetailed, mitered or rabbeted as shown in the example below. You can use dadoes, grooves and rabbets for interior partitions and backs. The back, which is usually plywood, adds rigidity.

Regardless of the type and style of cabinet you make, do all interior work, such as cutting shelf dadoes, before final assembly. Door and drawer hardware can be fitted after assembly.

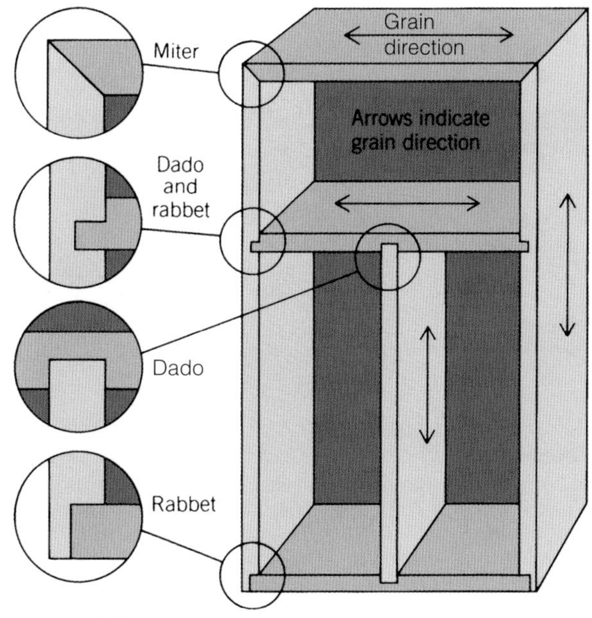

Strong joints can be created numerous ways, as this example shows. Rabbets and dadoes firmly lock the pieces together. Miters provide a wide gluing surface while hiding end grain.

Basic Face-frame Cabinet

Building a simple wall cabinet provides a good foundation for making more complex variations, including kitchen cabinets, vanities and bookcases. This 3/4-in.-thick plywood box is joined with dadoes and rabbets. The face frame adds strength while covering the raw plywood edges.

Start by rough-cutting the plywood parts about 1 in. (2.5 cm) oversize; then trim their coarse factory edges. After ripping each panel to width, crosscut to length using a tablesaw sled, circular saw with straightedge guide or other method.

Mill dadoes and rabbets and use a brad-point bit to drill holes in the sides for an adjustable shelf. Guide the bit with a commercial shelf-hole jig or make a jig from hardwood scrap predrilled with peg-size holes.

Assemble the case, checking for square. Build the face frame using pocket screws (see p. 439), making it 1/8 in. (3 mm) wider than the case. Glue the frame to the case so it overhangs, or is flush with, the sides depending on your design.

1 Use a 60- to 80-tooth alternate-top bevel blade for a high-quality edge right off the saw. Rip parts to width using the rip fence, keeping the good side up. This places any tear-out on the bottom, which is the inside of the cabinet.

2 Assemble the case, keeping the front edges flush. Clamp pads protect the wood surface. Use just enough glue to cover the joint surfaces, similar to applying paint. Old plastic honey bottles make easy-to-use glue bottles.

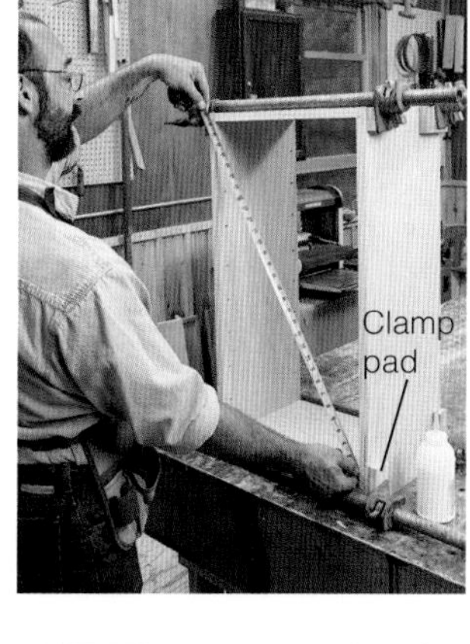

3 Check the cabinet for square by measuring from corner to corner. The two dimensions should be the same. If they're not, squeeze the long diagonal by hand until the two diagonals match.

4 Glue and clamp the face frame to the case. Use clamp pads and be careful not to crush the rabbets on the back. The face frame can slightly overhang the inside, outside or selected edges, depending on how it will be used. Or it can be trimmed flush on all or selected sides using a router or plane after the glue has dried.

Drawers

Legs

A box within a box, well-made drawers are a triumph of planning and layout. Build the cabinet first; then size the drawer to the case opening. For metal drawer slides, subtract 1 in. (25 mm) from the opening's width and about 1/4 in. (6 mm) for height.

You can use rabbets and grooves throughout or use dadoes at the rear and dovetails or box joints at the front for extra strength. A false-front drawer makes it easier to fit the front for even visual gaps, or reveals.

Rabbeted Corners

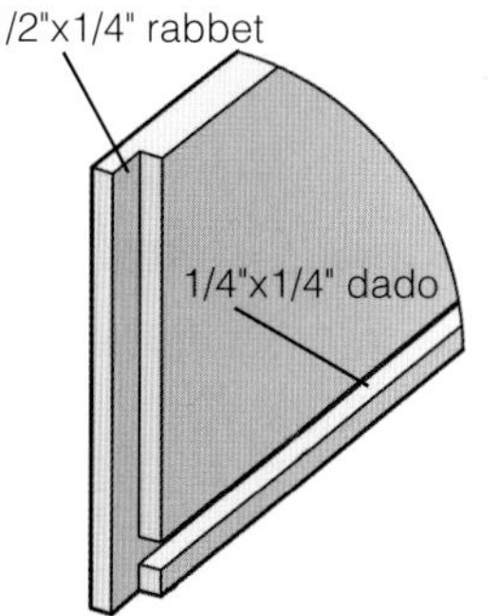

Rabbeted drawers are the simplest to make. Cut grooves around the box sides to house the bottom. Mill rabbets in the sides to secure the front and back. Glue and nail or staple the rabbet joints for strength.

Box-joint Corners

Box-joint corners (see p. 437) are time consuming to make but create a sturdy, attractive joint.

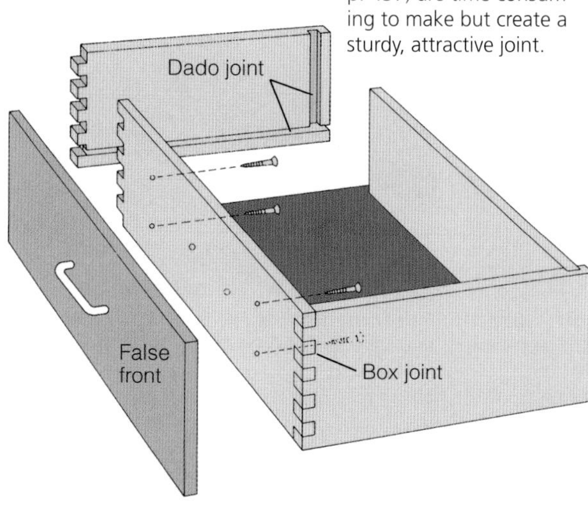

Basic Construction

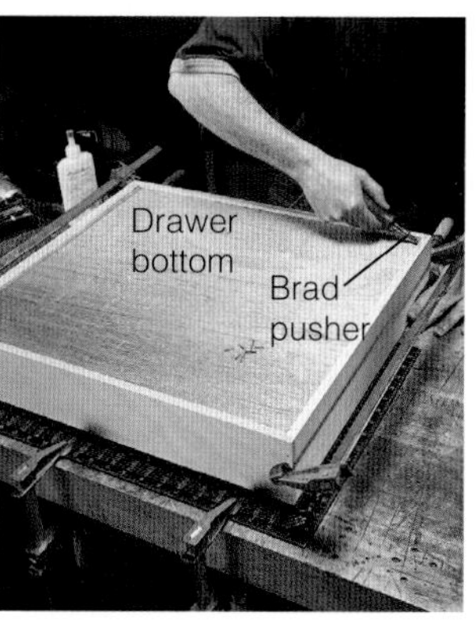

1 Glue, assemble and square the drawer box. With clamps in place, nudge the box against a framing square and push a brad through the bottom near each corner. Let the glue dry before you mount the hardware.

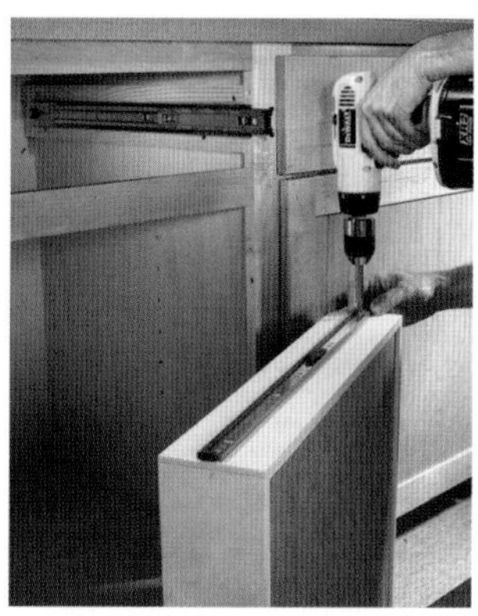

2 Side-mounted slides separate for easy mounting. Screw the cabinet member inside the case, through the horizontal slots in the slide. Screw the drawer member to the drawer side using the vertical slots. Adjust the drawer's fit before adding more screws.

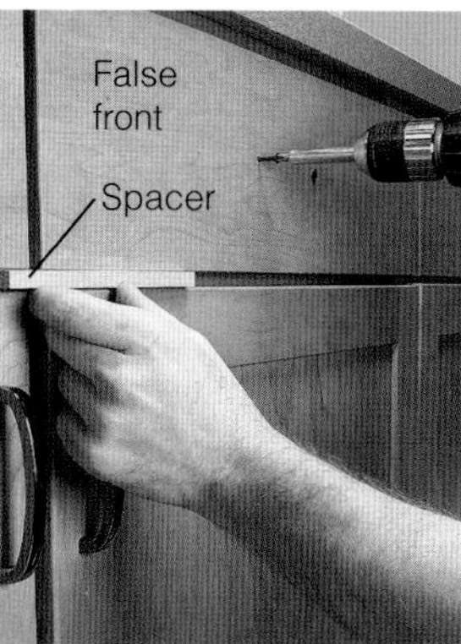

3 Use a spacer to position the drawer front evenly. Drive temporary screws through the existing hardware holes and into the drawer box. Then pull out the drawer and attach the front with permanent screws from inside.

Leg-to-rail Joints

Chairs, tables and other frame-type furniture rely on leg-to-rail joints for strength, as do frame-and-panel cabinets, such as a dresser. Styles of leg-and-rail joints range from utilitarian to elaborate.

Fine furniture calls for hidden mortises and tenons, but dowel joints are very strong, especially if you add corner blocks or braces. If you forgo glue, you can disassemble and reassemble the joint as needed.

Dowels. Install two or more dowels per rail for strength and to resist twist. To keep dowels from colliding, stagger spacing on each side of leg. For knock-down furniture, reinforce each unglued joint with a brace or block.

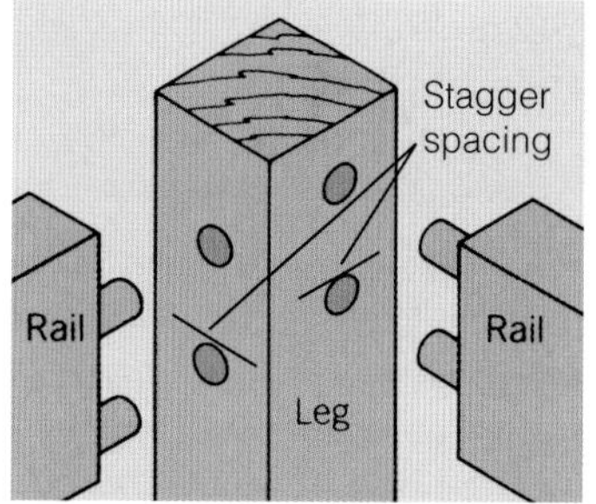

Metal corner brace. These can be used to firm or reinforce a wobbly chair or table leg. To install, saw slots perpendicular to the inside face of rails. Slide brace into slots, drill pilot hole for hanger bolt, install bolt and tighten wing nut.

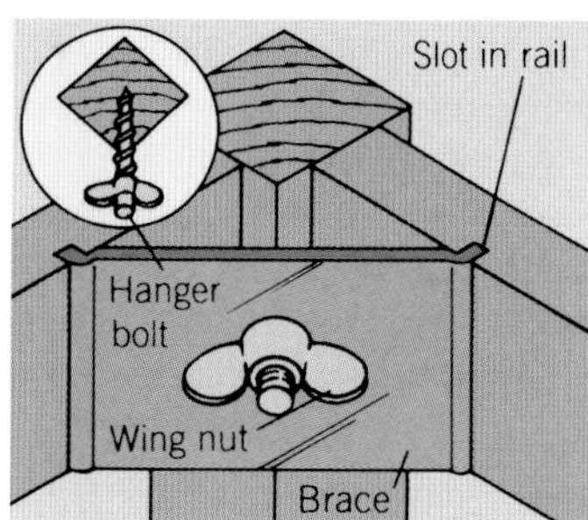

Wood corner block. Miter block to match angle of assembled joints for added stability. Block can replace metal corner brace if hanger bolt is added. Assemble joint first, then position block. Drill pilot holes for screws.

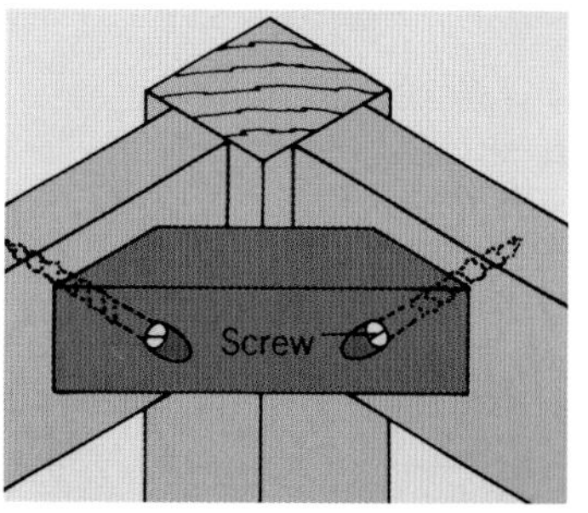

Raised-panel Doors

Drills 50
Router Tables 67

You can use frame-and-panel construction, with its distinctive raised panel, for casework as well as doors. The wide, solid-wood panel can expand and contract freely because it's housed, without glue in its grooves, in the frame, while the frame holds it flat. No cracks, no warp, no problem.

A two-piece matched router bit set, also called rail-and-stile cutters, lets you easily cut the frame joints on a router table. Then you shape the edge of the panel using another specialized bit.

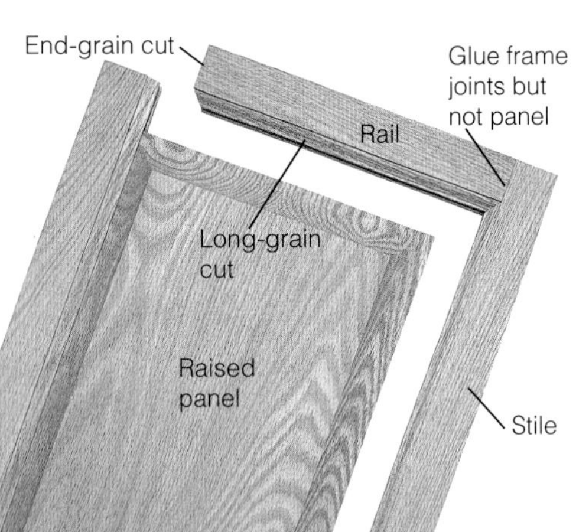

End-grain Cuts

Mill all the end-grain cuts first. A 1-1/2-hp router works fine for the frame joints, and 1/2-in. shank cutters provide the smoothest cuts.

Use 3/4- to 7/8-in. stock and make all the rail cuts with the stock facing down. Build a simple sled with a clamp for making the end-grain cuts. Adjust the bit height by taking test cuts on scrap, fine-tuning the cut until it resembles the profile shown below.

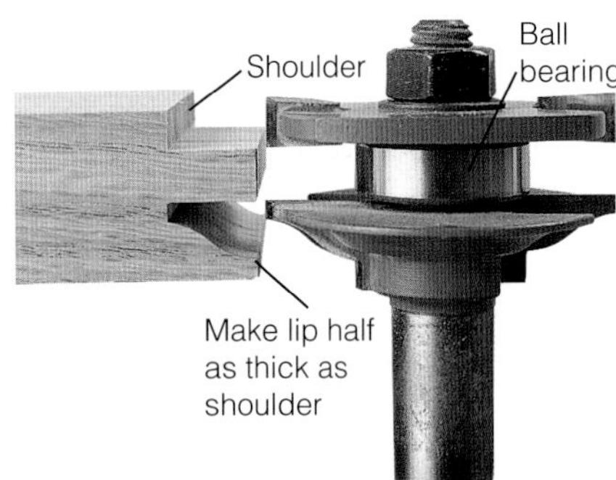

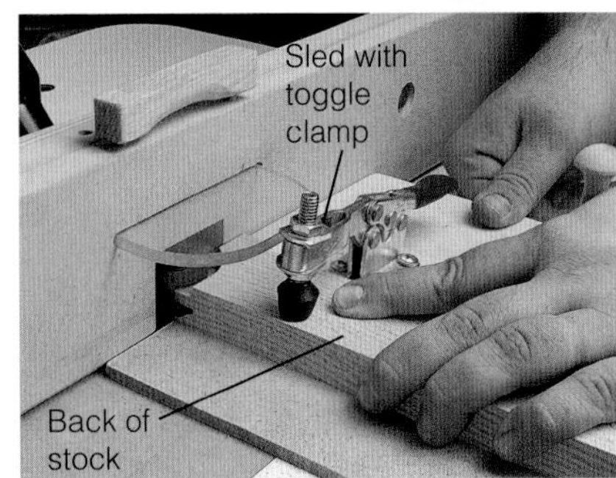

End-grain cuts. With the router table fence even with the bit's bearing, run the sled and workpiece past the bit to shape the end grain. The sled's fence registers the work and prevents blowing out or splintering the long grain at the back.

Long-grain Cuts

With a two-piece matched set, you remove the first cutter and install the long-grain cutter to rout the profile along the inside of both the rails and stiles.

Set the bit height by using one of the previously milled rails to line up the cutter. Use featherboards clamped to the router fence to help hold down your piece and a push stick to move it through. Again, machine the parts with the back side facing up.

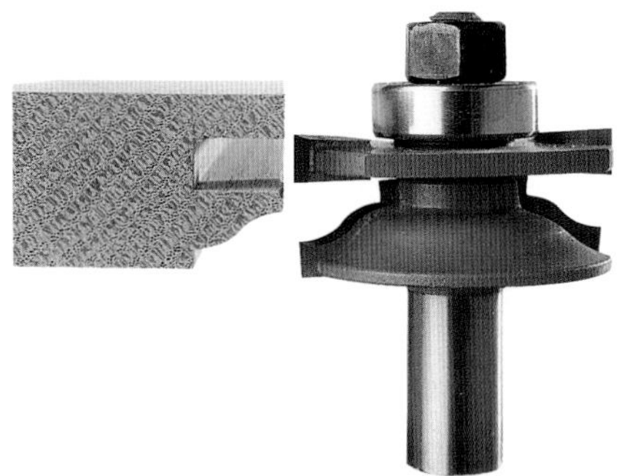

Long-grain cuts. Use a milled rail to adjust the bit height on the long-grained cutter, lining up the top of the groove cutter with the tongue on the rail. When bit height is set, use a push stick and featherboards to rout the profile along the edges of the rails and the stiles.

Raised-panel Cuts

Dry-fit the frame to measure the opening for the panel, adding the combined depth of two grooves, then subtracting 1/8 in. (3 mm) from the width to allow for expansion across the panel.

Use a 2-hp or larger, variable-speed router, slowing its speed to around 10,000 rpm. Align the tongue of a milled rail with the gap in the panel-raising bit. Make at least two successively deeper passes to rout the profile.

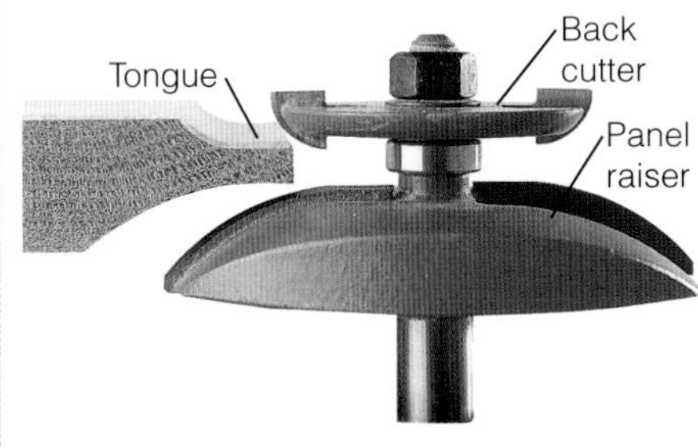

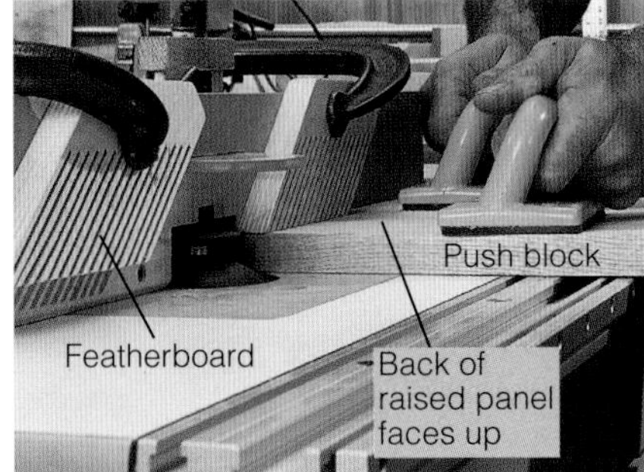

Raised-panel cuts. With the back side up, make the first pass on all four sides with the fence about 1/4 in. (6 mm) out from the bit's bearing, routing the end grain first. Readjust the fence flush with the bearing and make a second, final pass on all four sides.

Hinges

A world of choice exists when it comes to hinging doors. The simplest hinges attach to the outside of cabinets and doors, such as **butt hinges,** which can be surface-mounted or recessed. Choose **overlay hinges** for doors that overlap a face frame. **Partially inset hinges** are for lipped doors.

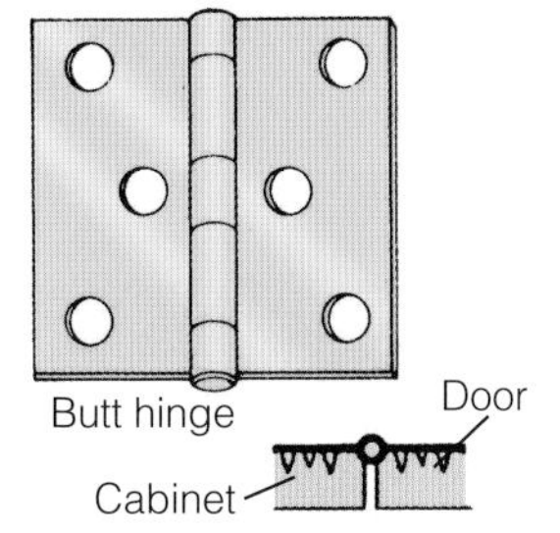

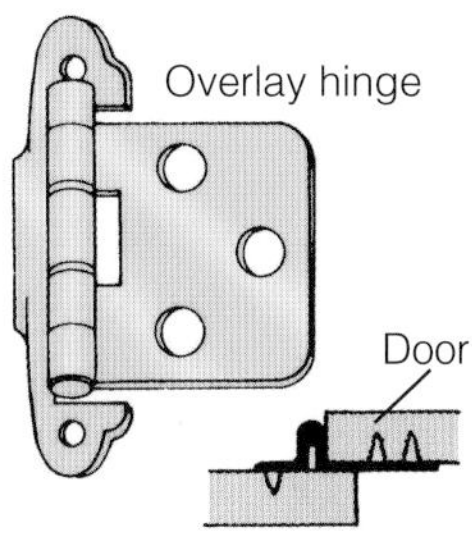

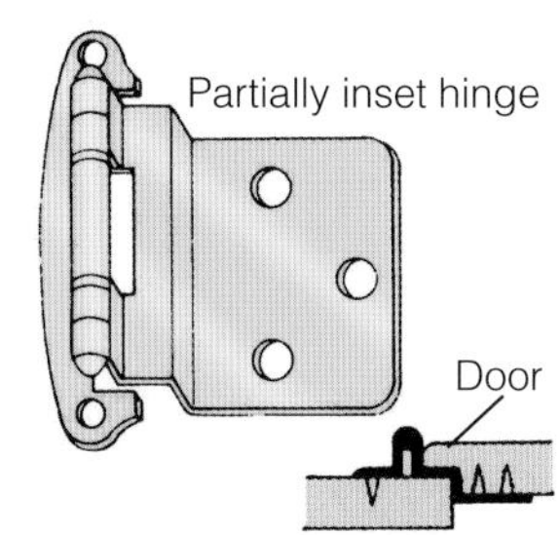

Euro-style Hinges

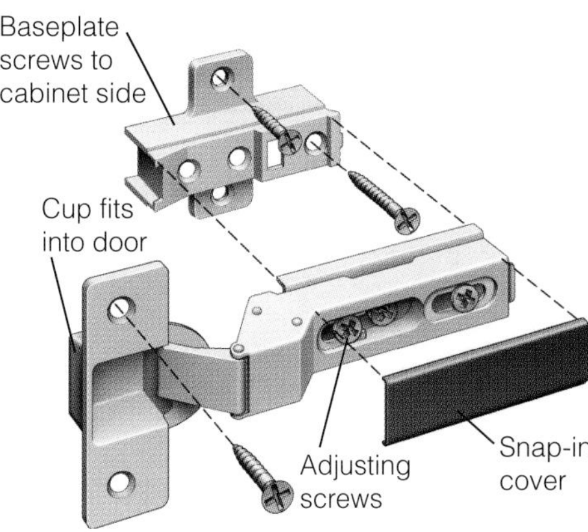

European hinges, also called cup hinges, are easy to install and totally adjustable. They're concealed from view, but beware: When you open a door, their bulky size is immediately apparent inside.

Use the drill press and a 35-mm bit to drill two holes in the back of the door. (You can use a 1-3/8-in. Forstner bit in a pinch.) Screw the cup part of the hinge to the door, screw the baseplate to the cabinet and connect the two. The best part? Simply fine-tune the door's fit with a screwdriver.

1 Drill the cup holes 1/2 in. (13 mm) deep and 1/8 in. (3 mm) from the edge of the door. To position the door, use a jig fitted with a fence and a pin clamped to the drill-press table.

2 Use a square to align the hinge perpendicular to the door. A 7/64-in. self-centering bit drills perfectly centered pilot holes to the correct depth for screws.

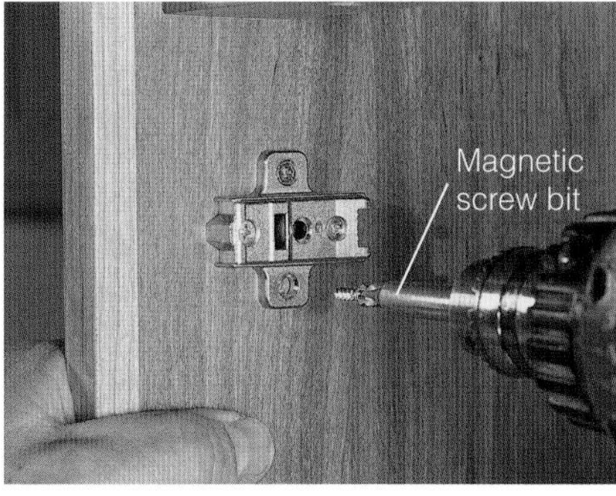

3 Lay out the baseplate location on the inside of the cabinet and fasten it with four screws. A magnetic bit makes it easier to position and drive the small screws.

4 Clip—or screw, depending on the style of hinge—the door to the baseplate. Adjust the screws on the baseplate to fine-tune the door's height, depth and width relative to the cabinet.

Pulls

As with hinges, there's no end to the variety of door and drawer pulls. This simple jig lets you mount machine-screw pulls without fuss by drilling accurate holes for the screws.

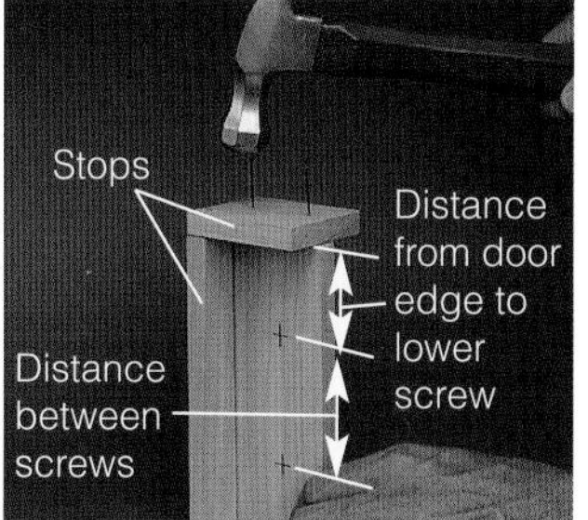

1 Build the jig so the hole spacing is equal to that of the pulls and centered on the vertical stile. Then nail it together.

2 Use the jig to drill holes in cabinet doors. Flip over the jig to drill opposite-hinged doors; turn it upside down to drill lower cabinet doors.

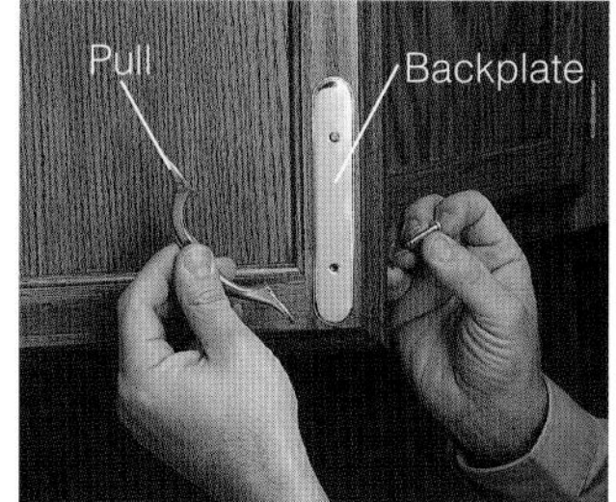

3 Install a backplate if desired. Secure the pull from the back with a pair of machine screws.

Fixing Woodworking Mistakes

Handsaws 26
Scribing 42
Specialty Adhesives 85

We've all done it: a screw hole accidentally drilled too deep, an out-of-level chair or cabinet that wobbles, an ugly knothole right where everyone can see it. Relax. Good woodworkers know how to fix these glitches. Here are some tried-and-true methods for covering your tracks.

Problem: Slipping bits

Router bits can slip in the collet, ruining the cut—or worse.

Solution

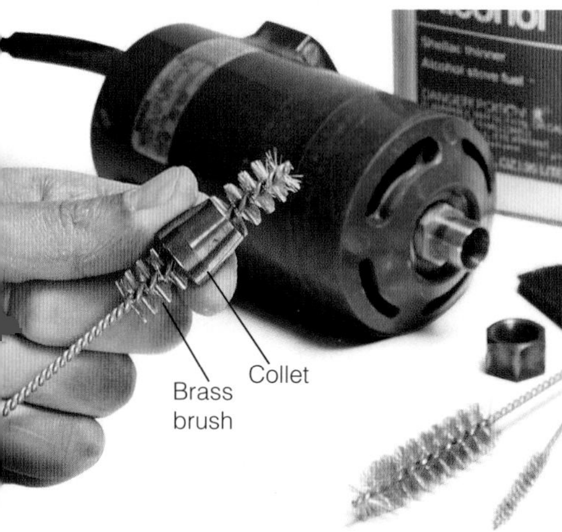

Remove burrs from bit shanks using extra-fine emery sandpaper. Use an abrasive nylon pad and solvent to clean resin or dirt from shanks and the outside of the collet, then scrub the inside with a brass tubing brush. If the collet is scored, buy a new one.

Problem: Rocking furniture

When you build a cabinet or chair slightly out of square (it's OK; we all do it), one of the legs may not touch the floor. The result? Rocking furniture.

Solution #1

Drill a hole in the bottom of the leg and glue in a length of dowel long enough to keep the cabinet from rocking.

Solution #2

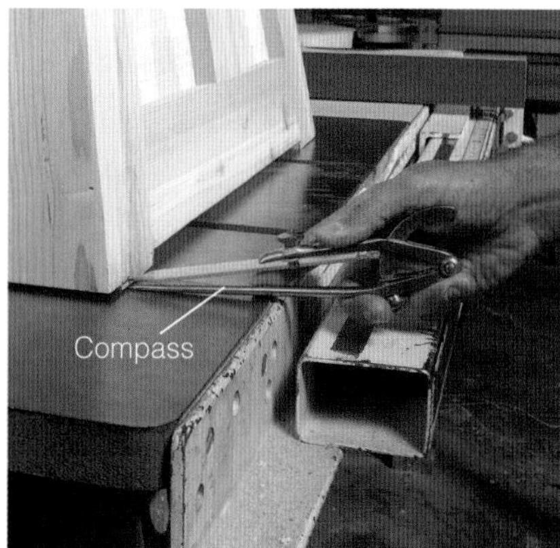

Place the piece on a flat surface, like your tablesaw. Set a compass to the widest gap, run a line around each foot and trim the feet to the line.

Problem: Saw marks

Cutting dowels and other protrusions flush to a surface leaves score marks on the work.

Solution

Cut the rim off of a yogurt lid and drill a hole in the middle, then place this over the work while sawing. Thin cardboard or playing cards work well, too.

Problem: Holes of uneven depth

Wrapping tape around a drill bit indicates the right hole depth, but you might drill too deeply if the tape creeps up the bit or frays during drilling.

Solution

For a reliable drill-bit depth-stop, drill a slightly oversized hole through a block of wood cut to the correct length and slip it over your bit.

Problem: Naughty knots

Loose or missing knots leave unsightly voids in your work surface.

Solution #1

For a loose knot, first remove it, then scrape away any wayward bark from the knot and the hole. Spread some five-minute epoxy on the knot and tap it back into place.

Solution #2

Fill voids with slow-set epoxy, which dries slowly enough to allow air bubbles to escape. Color the epoxy with a few drops of concentrated dye, slightly overfill the hole and sand flush when hardened.

Stripping Furniture

Stripping wood is a great way to resurrect those attic and flea-market finds—and you can do it safely and effectively with the right stripper and the proper setup. Tools and supplies are simple, but suitable precautions are necessary.

Safety is paramount. Wear long clothing under an apron, don splash-proof goggles and put on neoprene gloves with the cuffs turned out. Work in a well-ventilated area—outdoors is good—and wear an activated-carbon respirator with *working* cartridges. Then get ready to reclaim a jewel from the muck!

1 First, remove any hardware. Then apply the stripper in a thick layer, 1/8 to 1/4 in. (3 to 6 mm) thick. Semipaste strippers work best on vertical surfaces because they cling.

2 Seal your piece in a plastic leaf bag and let it sit from an hour to overnight, depending on the brand of stripper. If the work is too big, use polyethylene sheeting to cover it.

3 Scoop off the finish using a putty knife with a dull edge and rounded corners. Spread out the gunk on newspaper to let it dry before you dispose of it. If finish remains, recoat and strip again.

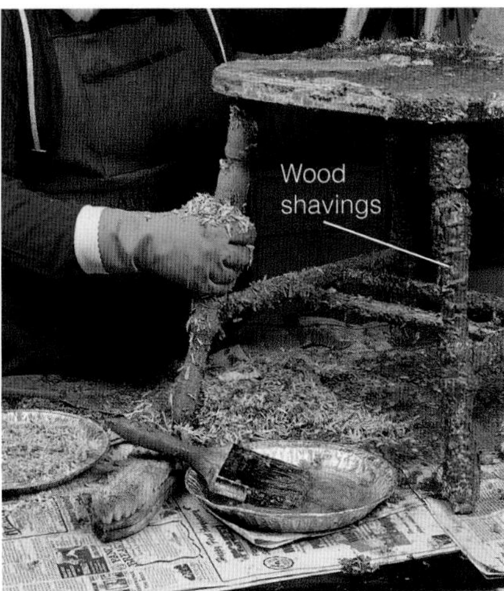

4 Wood shavings help scrub sludge from turnings, carvings and other crevices. Other useful tools for nooks and crannies include string, plastic scrub brushes and pointed dowels.

5 Wash the wood clean with the recommended solvent to remove any bits of paint and any remaining stripper. Then do a final wash with one cup of ammonia in a quart of water.

How Fast? How Safe?

Except for refinishers, which work on only shellac and lacquer, most strippers remove just about any finish. Choose a stripper based on its speed and safety. A good rule of thumb is that the slower it works, the safer it is. Above all, read and follow directions carefully.

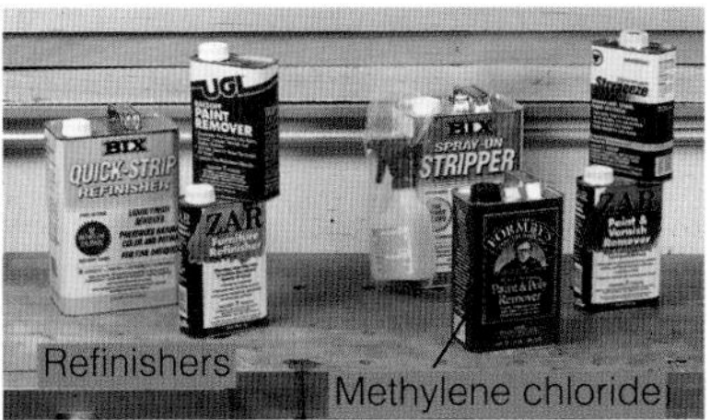

Fast. Refinishers are flammable and work only on lacquer and shellac. Methylene chloride strippers are nonflammable and work fast, but they have harmful vapors.

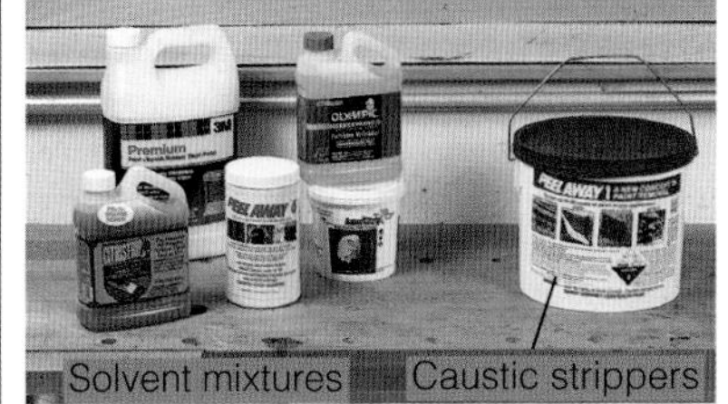

Medium fast. Solvent mixtures require thicker coats and work relatively fast. Don't leave caustic strippers on too long or you'll damage the wood.

Slow. Most effective on oil-based paint and polyurethane, this is the safest-to-use stripper, but it can take as long as 24 hours to soften a finish. Since it's water-based, it can raise wood grain and loosen veneer.

Sanding

Sanding 48
Power Sanders 68

Before Finishing

Sanding might be a chore, but it's critical to a fine finish, because any blemishes in the wood will be magnified when you apply the first coat. With the right approach, you can make the job go more smoothly.

When should you sand? Sometimes it's best to sand before cutting joints or gluing pieces together, as when preparing boards for gluing together into a panel (see "Edge Joints," p. 442). As long as you don't compromise your joinery, sanding before assembly makes sense.

However, some work is easier to smooth after assembly, such as parts joined cross-grain, like the corner joints in a door frame. Here, the joints will need minor leveling, so sanding after glue-up is most effective.

When possible, it's important to sand in the direction of the grain to avoid cross-grain scratch marks. And be sure to sand through a succession of grits. If you skip a grit, you risk leaving deep scratches.

Coarse to fine. Whether you're sanding by hand or with a power tool, start with 80-grit to remove blemishes. Then use 120-grit, 180-grit and finally 220-grit. Exact grits aren't vital (100 to 150 to 220 works, too), but be sure to progress in steps so you remove the deeper scratches and leave finer scratches each time.

Working with the grain. Sand with the grain when hand-sanding or using a belt sander. Scratches are hard to see when they run parallel to the grain. But even the lightest scratches across the grain (as shown) are painfully obvious, especially after staining.

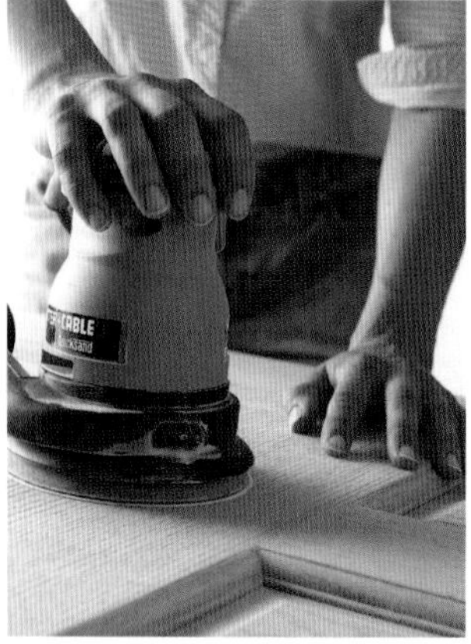

Invisible scratches. A random-orbit sander leaves scratches that are practically invisible, so you can sand across joints where the grain changes direction. Move slowly (about 1 in. / 2.5 cm per second) and apply light pressure. Otherwise, you'll get swirl marks.

Inspection. Before applying a stain or finish, turn out the lights and shine a light at a low angle across the wood to reveal imperfections. Mark problem areas with masking tape or a pencil and sand them out.

Between Finishes

Sanding after each coat of finish (except the last coat) rubs out any imperfections, such as drips or runs, and roughens the surface for better adhesion of subsequent coats.

In general, sanding finishes goes quickly; it's more like wiping the surface than sanding it. It's best to employ a light touch so you don't rub through the previous coat and to use very fine grit—400 or finer.

Wet-dry sandpaper. Sand between coats with 400-grit wet-dry sandpaper, which won't fall apart when it gets wet. A little water provides lubrication and keeps the finish from clogging the paper. Grain direction isn't important, because you're sanding finish, not wood. When you're done, wipe away the residue with a damp rag.

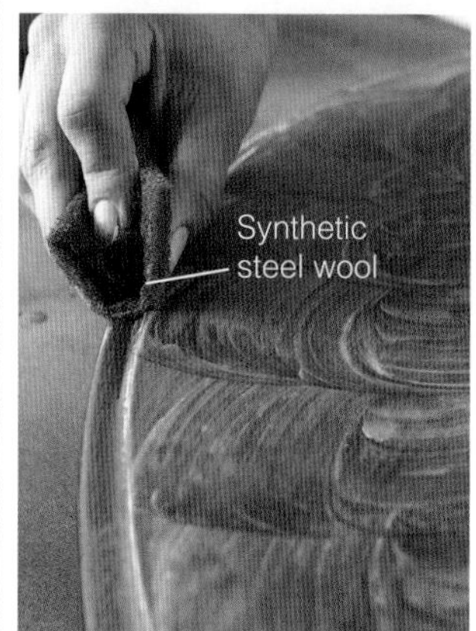

Synthetic steel wool. Use an abrasive nylon pad, also called synthetic steel wool, to sand contoured or otherwise shaped areas, such as routed edges, complex moldings or turnings. The pad conforms easily to the curve and is safer than steel wool, which deposits fibers that can cause stains in the finish.

Wood Preparations

Filling

For a glass-smooth finish, sometimes called a "piano finish" or a filled finish, you can apply multiple finish coats. But open-pored woods, such as mahogany, walnut, teak, ash, oak, rosewood and others have large, open pores that no amount of finish will fill reliably. Instead, you need to use a pore filler first and then apply the finish.

Pore filler, also called semipaste filler, is a thick mixture you apply to bare wood either to fill its pores or to add color contrast. (Don't use wood putty, a thicker concoction meant only for filling gouges or dents.) For most applications, it's best to use a waterborne filler.

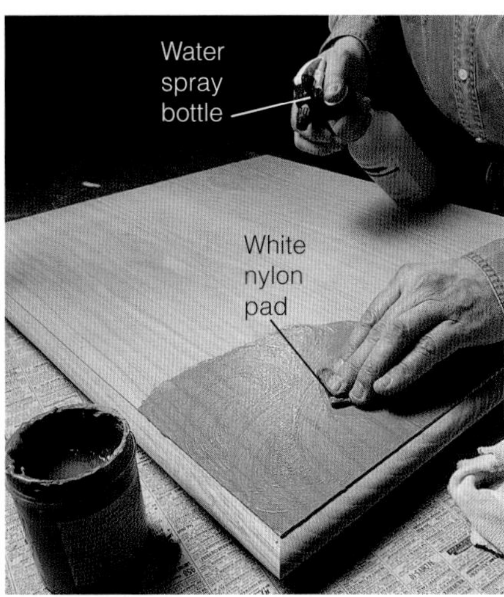

1 Work the filler into the pores by rubbing with a white nylon pad, the finest of the nylon abrasives. If the filler sets up too fast, spray it with water to keep it workable.

2 Scrape excess filler slurry from the surface while it's still wet. A credit card makes a great squeegee. Let the filler dry completely before sanding.

3 Clean a contoured edge using a credit card cut to match the profile. Then sand the dried filler, wipe off dust using a cloth dampened with water, and apply the finish of your choice.

Sealing

An uneven tone in wood, called blotching, is typical when staining many softwoods, such as pine or redwood, and is due to uneven densities in the wood. Even a few hardwoods, such as birch and maple, suffer the same fate. In addition, pine and other softwoods undergo grain reversal, in which the softer earlywood soaks up more stain than harder latewood.

To overcome these visual blemishes, apply a wood conditioner first, which seals the wood's surface so your stain goes on more evenly. Keep in mind that sealing the wood will lighten the finish, so you'll need a darker stain to achieve the same effect.

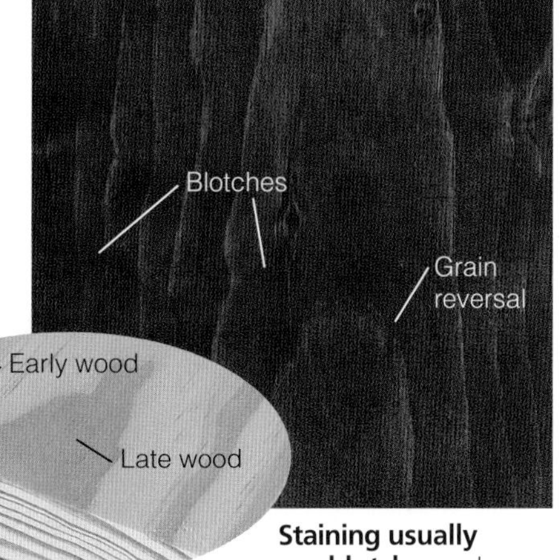

Staining usually causes blotches and always makes pine's porous earlywood darker than its dense latewood, just the opposite of unstained pine (inset). This transformation is called grain reversal.

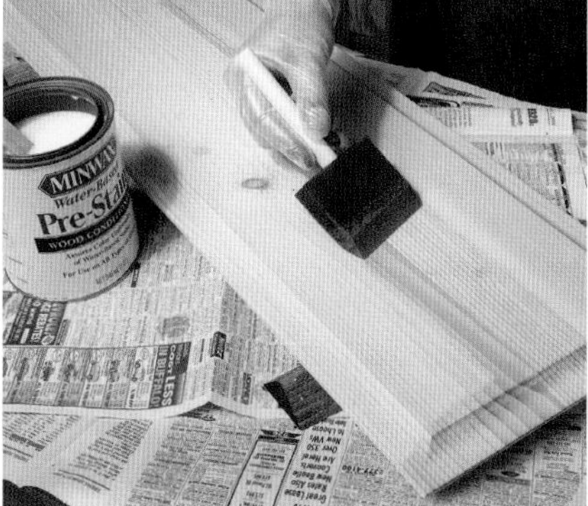

Conditioner. Brush on two coats of waterborne conditioner. With each application, keep the surface wet for three to five minutes, then wipe off excess. Let the conditioner dry, and sand with 400-grit sandpaper.

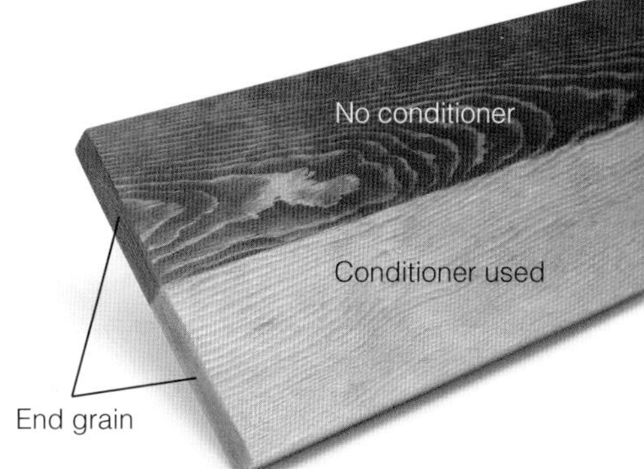

Sealing. Sealing the wood with conditioner gives you a more even finish but lightens its overall tone. To prevent end grain from becoming darker than the face of the wood, give it a double dose of conditioner.

Staining

Brushes 280

Stains add color, providing a richer look to bland woods. Plus, they can unify mismatched colors, such as uneven tones or bands of sapwood.

The final color depends on the wood—even two pieces of the same species can stain differently—and the finish. Experimentation is key.

Penetrating stains, such as aniline dyes, add pure, clear color without obscuring the grain. Work fast, because they absorb quickly into the wood. **Pigmented stains,** such as oil-based wiping stains, are easy to apply, but deposit larger particles that can muddy the grain. **Gel stains** combine the advantages of both: They're almost foolproof, absorb evenly and allow the grain to remain visible.

Tips for a Top-notch Stain Job

- Wear old clothing, a shop apron and gloves, and work on an old bench or cover it with thin plywood. Stains are difficult to remove—from you or from the wood.
- Mix custom colors by combining two or more stains of the same brand and type.
- When making your own colors, mix enough to finish the entire project. You won't be able to get an exact match later if you come up short.
- To test stains on existing work, such as an old table, apply the color first in an inconspicuous area, such as under the top.
- Thoroughly stir oil-based stains to dissolve the pigment that's usually sitting on the bottom of the can.
- When applying oil-based stains, wipe the wood with mineral spirits just before staining to ease and even stain distribution.
- Try spraying penetrating stains, which gets them on the surfaces more quickly. You'll get more even coverage with fewer overlap marks.
- Use alcohol-soluble stains for touch-up. They're easy to pinpoint and they dry almost instantly.
- Place used oil-soaked rags in a flameproof, water-filled container to prevent spontaneous combustion.

Test. Test your stains on scraps of wood from your project that have even been sanded using the same process. Note the type and amount of stain you use and be sure to apply a few finish coats to get a feel for its final color.

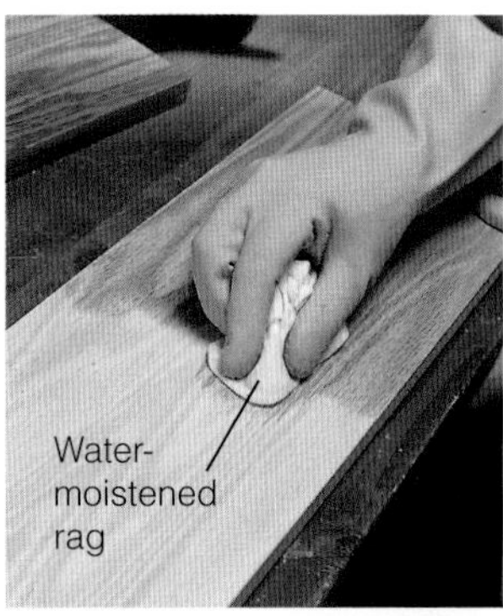

Prewet. When using water-soluble stains, raise the grain first with a damp rag. Sand it smooth when dry, and then stain. Now the water in the stain won't raise the grain.

Rub. With wiping stains, rub the stain into the wood using a soft, clean cotton rag. Stain in any direction you wish, but always make the last pass in the direction of the grain. If you need to remove excess stain, use a rag that has a small amount of stain on it.

What Are Dyes and Glazes?

Dyes and glazes are stains of a different sort. **Dyes** are tiny color particles—much smaller than those in pigmented stains—sold either in powder form or as a liquid. They're great for making custom colors or for staining without obscuring the grain.

Glazes are heavy-bodied pigment-type stains that you apply over a sealed surface to add tone and uniformity. Their thick, workable consistency lets you "age" a piece to make it look old. Glazes come premixed or you can make your own by combining artist's oil with a glazing medium.

Handy Hints: Stain Saver

Recycle your empty pump-type spray bottle for spraying wiping stains. Spray a small section at a time, then wipe. It's a great way to reach intricate areas, such as spindles, and you'll use less stain than you would brushing.

Polyurethane

Polyurethane is a film finish that's built up in layers over the wood and is hard to beat for durability. This makes it excellent for high-wear areas, such as tabletops or floors.

Waterborne and oil-based polyurethanes are applied in a similar manner, although each has its pros and cons. (See "Water-based vs. Oil-based," far right.) Tools for applying oil-based polyurethane are simple: a good quality natural-bristle brush, a well-ventilated space and some patience.

Sand the wood up through 220-grit (see p. 452). Remove dust with a shop vacuum, followed by a wipe-down using a rag dampened with mineral spirits.

Finish the wood in four (possibly five!) steps. First, seal it with a thinned mixture of two parts polyurethane to one part mineral spirits. Next, apply a full-strength coat. After 24 hours, wet-sand the surface. Then apply the final coat. If the last coat is rough, polish it out using rubbing compound.

1 For the first sealer coat, thin oil-based polyurethane with mineral spirits two parts to one part. Brush the sealer on with a natural-bristle brush using long, even strokes.

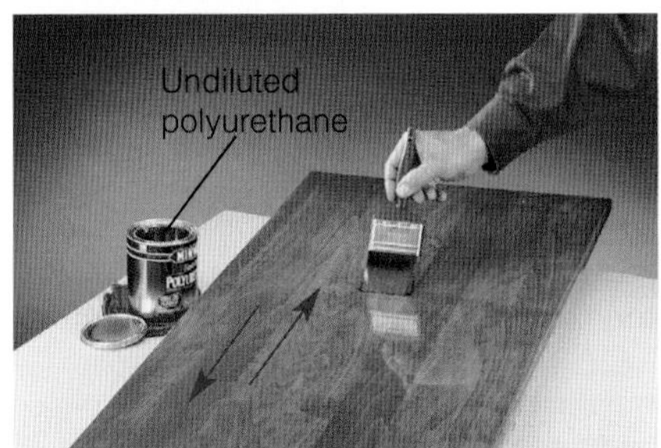

2 Use full-strength polyurethane for the second and third coats. After wetting the entire surface, go back and overlap each stroke following the direction of the grain.

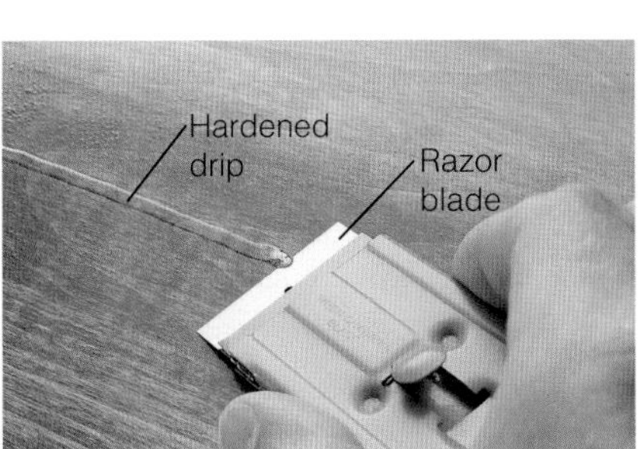

3 Wait at least 12 hours before slicing off any dried drips with a razor blade, being careful not to cut below the surface. Small blemishes will disappear after you wet-sand the finish.

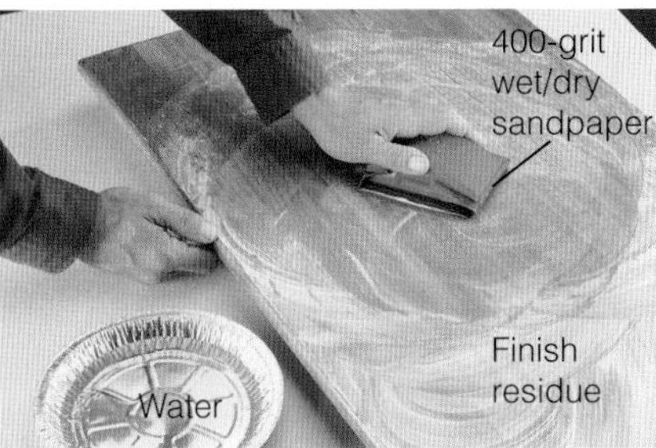

4 After 24 hours, wet-sand with 400-grit sandpaper, using a circular motion to remove bumps and blemishes. Use plenty of water and a light touch to avoid cutting through the finish.

5 If you need to sand the final coat to remove flaws, polish it out with automotive rubbing compound. For greater luster, follow with a polishing compound.

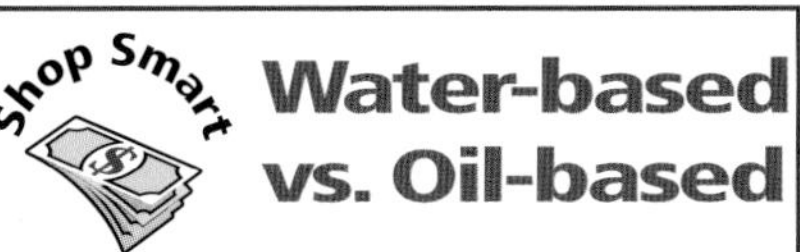

Water-based vs. Oil-based

Both water-based and oil-based polyurethanes offer good protection. The biggest difference is in appearance. Although milky in the can, water-based polyurethanes go on clear. Some people consider them cold looking, especially on darker woods like walnut. Oil-based polyurethanes impart a rich, amber glow, which can highlight certain woods, such as oak or yellow pine.

Working with water-based polyurethanes offers some big advantages. They don't emit strong odors the way oil-based does and they dry fast (two hours vs. 24 hours for oil-based), allowing you to apply several coats in a day and use the room that night. Plus, they clean up with water.

But there are trade-offs. You'll have to apply more finish with water-based: Four coats (vs. two or three coats for oil-based) are recommended for floors. And you may have to recoat more often. Plus, you'll pay more for water-based.

Regardless of which type you choose, you'll prolong the protective life of any finish by eliminating dirt and grime. Dust furniture, sweep or vacuum floors often and put throw rugs in high-traffic areas.

Oil Finishes

Penetrating oil finishes are popular because they're easy to use. They provide a close-to-the-wood effect, soaking into the surface instead of laying on top, as film finishes do.

Oil finishes are actually oil-varnish blends, often called Danish oils. Don't confuse them with natural oils, like boiled linseed oil or pure tung oil, or with nondrying oils, such as mineral or vegetable oil. When oil finishes cure, they seal pores and protect wood from dust, dirt and wear.

Oil finishes, which are technically a blend of oil and varnish thinned with mineral spirits, are extremely easy to apply. They impart a more natural look with a satin sheen, but offer only moderate protection from scratches, water and stains.

Application is simple: Soak the wood with a brush or rag, wipe off any excess and let dry eight hours before you recoat. Sand lightly between coats, applying three to fours coats, and you're done.

Caution: Oil-soaked rags can ignite spontaneously because of heat buildup. Place used rags in a fireproof container or spread them outdoors to dry thoroughly before you dispose of them.

Pros	Cons
• Oil finishes can be wiped on and wiped off without worrying about dust. • You feel—and see—the wood instead of the finish. • You can renew a worn-out finish by simply sanding lightly and recoating.	• The finish can bleed back out of the pores while the surface is wet, requiring vigilant rewiping. • The super-thin mixture builds up less than varnishes and film finishes do, offering minimal protection in hard-wear or high-moisture areas.

Working Tips

Flood surface using a rag or brush, let stand for five minutes and wipe excess before the finish becomes tacky. Continue wiping any oil that bleeds back to the surface.

To smooth the surface while you apply an oil finish, wet-sand after the first sealer coat. Smooth the dried finish by rubbing with paste wax or rubbing compound.

Oil or Oil/Varnish?

Natural oils, like tung and linseed, make wood look rich and beautiful, but because they soak into the wood, instead of sitting on the surface, they don't offer much protection.

Oil/varnish blends are easy to apply, look good and offer more protection than natural oil, but less than straight varnish.

Varnish

Spontaneous Combustion 481

Varnish, a film-type finish, offers excellent protection and adds a warm glow to woods. Two types exist: straight varnishes, which offer superior protection and are made from a blend of resin, oil and solvents, and wiping varnishes, which are simply thinner versions that can be wiped on instead of applied with a brush.

Wiping varnishes (left side) are thinned-down versions that let you wipe instead of brush them on, but you'll need to apply more coats to achieve the same finish thickness. **Regular varnishes** (right side) build quickly with a few coats and protect wood while adding a glossy look.

Wiping varnishes require three to four coats and are similar to oil finishes, except you wipe on thin coats and leave each coat alone without wiping away excess. Regular varnishes are brushed on the same way as polyurethane (see p. 455), which itself is a form of varnish. Their thicker consistency allows you to achieve the same effect in only a couple coats.

Pros	Cons
• Varnishes, including wiping varnish when it's applied in multiple coats, offer good moisture and wear protection. • Spar varnishes can be used outside on doors and patio furniture to protect against the elements.	• Varnish takes six to 24 hours to dry, so keep work areas clean to avoid dust contamination. • Air bubbles can spoil a varnish finish if you don't use a good brush and proper brushing technique.

Working Tips

Use lint-free cloths—washed cotton works great—for applying wiping varnishes. Fold the cloth into a ball, dampen it with finish and wipe on light coats, overlapping each stroke with the grain of the wood. Don't go back over the finish or you'll leave marks.

Thin the first coat of regular varnish 25 percent to 50 percent with mineral spirits. Apply subsequent coats full-strength. Use a natural-bristle brush with flagged ends and a chisel shape.

Allow coats to cure—six to 24 hours, depending on type and brand—before smoothing with fine sandpaper. Rubbing with paste wax or rubbing compound will help smooth the final surface.

Lacquer

Lacquer is the standard film finish in the woodworking industry, because it's fast to apply, offers long-lasting protection and looks great. You can take advantage of these attributes at home by using a can of spray lacquer or investing in spraying equipment and setting up a ventilated place to spray, such as a garage with a fan directing fumes outside.

The nice thing about lacquer is its super-fast drying time. You can spray multiple coats, sanding between each and have an entire piece finished in a day. If spraying is not an option, you can buy brushing lacquers that let you brush on coats almost as effectively as spraying.

Lacquer is a quick-drying finish that looks best when sprayed on, which you can do with a spray can or with an air compressor, spray gun and hoses. Brushing lacquer dries almost as quickly as spray lacquer, allowing you to finish a piece in a day.

Pros	Cons
• Lacquer dries fast, so you can apply multiple coats quickly. • It sands easily and goes on smooth, especially when spraying. • Three to four coats provide adequate protection and sheen.	• Professional results require outlay for spray equipment, such as a midsize air compressor with regulator, fluid and air hoses, and a spray gun. • You need to work in a well-ventilated space to remove overspray fumes. • Good spray technique requires practice.

Working Tips

Dust is not a big problem with lacquer because it dries so fast, but be sure the surface you spray is clean so you don't accidentally trap particles in the finish.

If necessary, thin lacquer with lacquer thinner so it flows easily from the gun without causing drips or "orange peel," a series of pockmarks in the finish that resemble the fruit's rind.

When possible, spray an entire piece at once so the wet finish "melts" together and flows uniformly. Start from the "bad side" and move to the "good," for instance, from the underside of a table to its top, overlapping each spray stroke by about one quarter.

Shellac

Something of a "miracle" finish, shellac has a lot going for it. It's all natural, dries in under an hour, imparts glossy depth and clarity, and is easy to repair, making it a favorite among musical-instrument makers. Shellac will seal stains, grease, soot, odors, silicone, wood sap and knots and is compatible over and under almost all finishes except polyurethanes.

Shellac's biggest downside is its poor resistance to alcohol, so avoid it for bar tops or tabletops. It's best to make shellac yourself using dewaxed shellac flakes dissolved in denatured alcohol. A 1-lb. cut—1 lb. of flakes to 1 gal. of alcohol—works best for brushing or wiping.

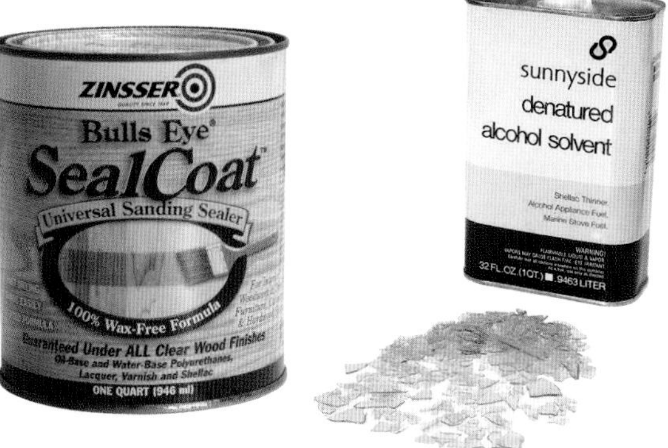

Shellac, a favorite brush-on finish, is easy to work with and adds beautiful clarity and depth to just about any wood. You can buy premixed dewaxed shellac or make your own from flakes dissolved in alcohol.

Pros	Cons
• Nontoxic when dry, shellac is a perfect finish for children's toys or furniture. • It's a good sealer coat for covering blemishes or for applying under problem finishes.	• Shellac offers poor resistance to alcohol; avoid using it for bar tops or anywhere drinks are spilled. • Shellac mixture must be fresh for its dried film to retain moisture resistance.

Working Tips

Keep shellac fresh by mixing it yourself and storing it in an opaque glass or plastic container in a cool, dry place.

The best way to apply shellac is to brush it, although wiping is possible with practice. Use a soft, natural-bristle brush and flow the finish onto the wood slowly and evenly. Don't rebrush or you'll leave marks.

Wait two hours between coats and scuff-sand only if the surface isn't smooth. Three coats provide a nice finish.

Furniture Finishes

Ten to 15 years of everyday use takes its toll on furniture, even if you're careful and your children are angels. The following pages offer some quick-fix techniques that don't require exotic tools or skills for sprucing up finished pieces.

We're not talking about refinishing. Think furniture "triage," or methods for keeping your furniture looking and working great for many years to come. After all, if it's well made, it's worth keeping in the family!

Cleaning

Cleaning dirty furniture can revitalize a piece. But first, make certain you know what type of finish you have.

Most pieces 50 years or younger are finished with lacquer or polyurethane. You'll find shellac on older furniture. Beware of solvents that soften or destroy existing finishes: Alcohol will dissolve shellac and soften lacquer. Lacquer thinner will dissolve lacquer but wrinkle polyurethane. Mineral spirits is harmless to all finishes, especially when used as a cleaning agent.

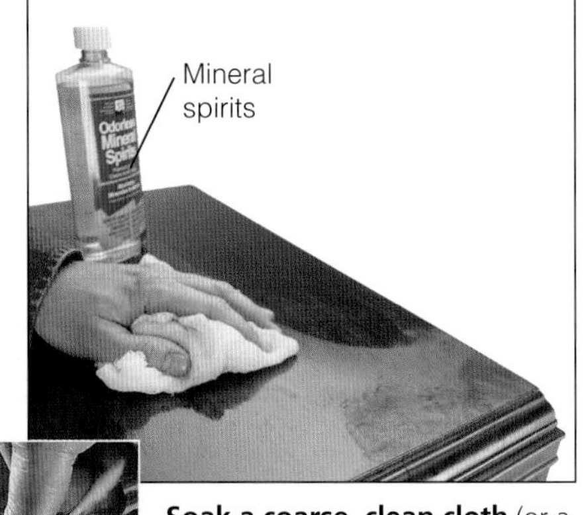

Soak a coarse, clean cloth (or a cotton swab for crevices) with mineral spirits to remove wax build-up and dirt. Keep cleaning until the swab or cloth no longer picks up dirt. Then make a final wash using a fresh rag.

Light Scratches

You can easily remove light scratches in the finish itself, as long as they don't go all the way into the wood.

Rub the scratch with super-fine steel wool saturated with clear Danish oil. Go easy on edges and corners, which wear through quickly, and don't cut into any stain below the clear finish. Clean the entire surface with mineral spirits to remove all excess oil. Allow to dry and spray a top coat of lacquer to blend it all together.

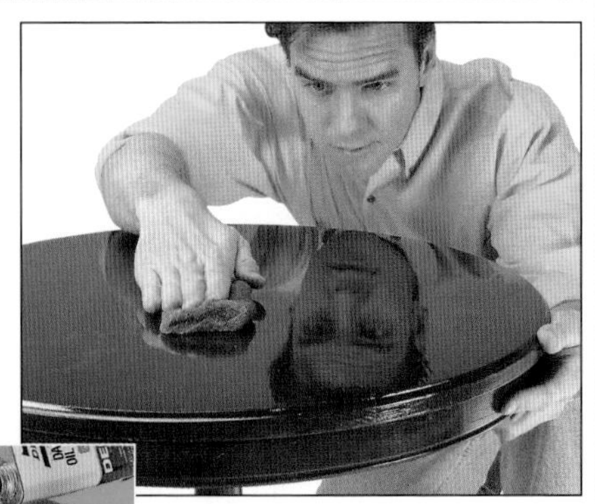

Work the scratch with the grain using oil and steel wool and rub the surrounding area as well to blend it in. Wipe off excess oil, clean with mineral spirits and let it dry. Finish by spraying the entire area with a coat of lacquer.

Deep Scratches

Deep scratches that go through the finish and expose bare wood will disappear when touched up with permanent markers. To get an exact match, pick from a range of colored markers at an art supply store.

Try dotting the ink into the scratch, letting it dry, then evening out the color by stroking lightly with the tip. For hairline cracks, use a fine-tipped marker and keep the ink only on the scratch.

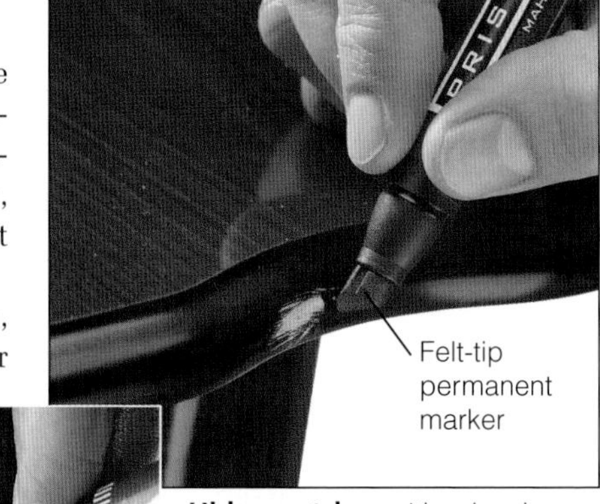

Hide scratches with colored markers. For best coverage, dot the ink onto the scratch and then blend it with the tip. Touch up thin scratches with fine-tipped markers.

Gouges

You can fix a gouge in a light-wear area, such as a table leg, with putty sticks sold at hardware stores. Buy several colors, shave them into flakes and blend them together until you get a good color match.

Apply the putty with a rounded stick; then smooth the surface and wipe the excess with a cloth. Use a permanent marker to color the thin, light-colored line of bare wood. Apply a seal coat of shellac, followed by lacquer.

Pack wax putty into the gouge with a stick, then use a cloth to wipe away excess and smooth the surface. Use a marker to touch up any bare wood. Seal the waxy surface with a few passes of shellac; follow with spray lacquer.

Reviving a Finish

Before you strip your furniture, consider reviving its finish. It may only be hidden by grime, compounded by nicks and water rings—and easily restored.

Examine the piece. Cracked or "alligatored" finishes can't be revived. You can remove white water rings; black rings require stripping. Light and even deep scratches can be disguised.

First, clean the finish with mineral spirits. Then touch up gouges with putty sticks, color any scratches with markers and rub out rings with steel wool and rubbing compound.

Recoat the surface with spray lacquer, let it dry and rub it out using 0000 steel wool and rubbing compound. Finally, protect the finish with paste wax.

1 Clean all surfaces with a cloth soaked in mineral spirits, then touch up gouges and nicks with putty and markers. Use rubbing compound and steel wool to rub out white water rings in the affected areas only.

2 Recoat the surface with spray lacquer, using overlapping strokes and applying three to five coats. Afterward, let the lacquer dry fully, which may take a day or more.

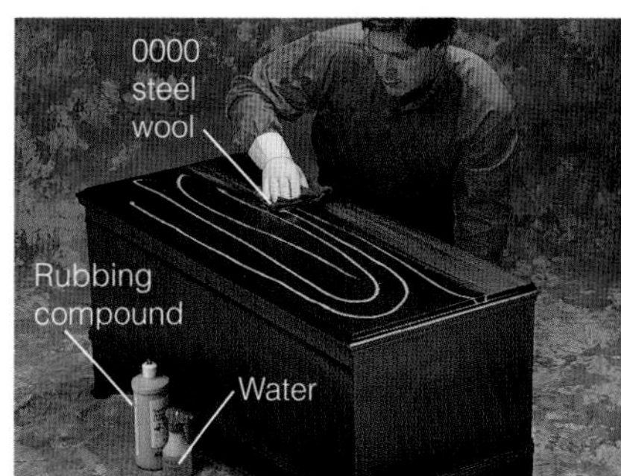

3 Rub the entire surface with rubbing compound and 0000 steel wool. Rub firmly and with the grain, thinning the slurry lightly with water as needed. Wipe clean with a damp rag and repeat if necessary.

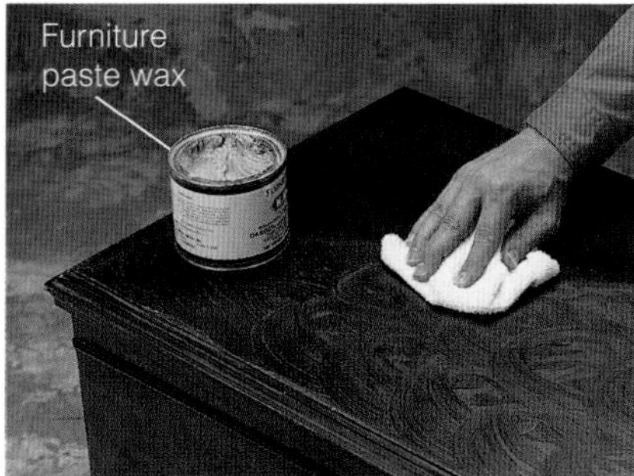

4 Protect the surface and make it more scratch-resistant by waxing the finish with paste wax. Rub a generous amount of wax onto the surface; then use a clean cloth to buff and remove all excess.

Deep Damage

You can fix deep dents using some simple tools and a bit of artistry. First fill the dent with auto body filler, which dries super hard and doesn't shrink. Slightly overfill and, before it fully hardens, use a chisel to shave the filler flush.

Before coloring, and again between each layer, seal the repair with shellac, letting you see the true color. To match the surrounding area, mix some powdered pigment with shellac and dab it on the filler with a brush.

Use a darker color and a fine brush to add grain lines to the repair, "erasing" them with steel wool and starting over if necessary. Seal with a few more coats of shellac, and then topcoat with the appropriate finish.

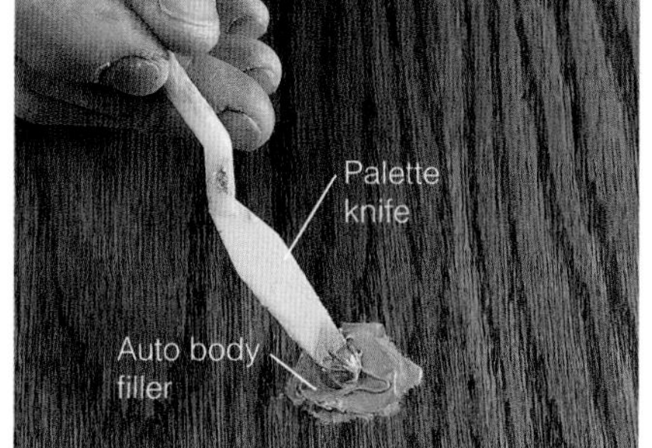

1 Fill the center of the hole with auto body filler, working it firmly to the edges. Try to mound the filler as much as possible, and let it begin to harden.

2 Before it fully cures, shave the filler flush with the surface using a razor-sharp chisel. Then dab a sealer coat of shellac onto the patched area.

3 Color the patch a shade lighter than the surrounding area's background color, using an opaque mix of powdered pigments mixed with shellac.

4 Add grain lines with a fine artist's brush. Use a darker color and try to connect the wood's grain across the patch. You might see the repair, but your friends won't!

Solid Wood Repairs

Clamps 34
Straight-cut Jig 58
Adhesives 84

Cracked Tabletop

Split tabletops are all too common. Fortunately, they're a snap to repair.

Sometimes you can pry the crack open, inject or force in glue and clamp it closed. But distorted fibers and grime often prevent the crack from closing.

The surest fix is to clamp a straightedge to guide a circular saw down the center of the crack, to separate the top in two. Then glue the halves back together with clamps or wedges.

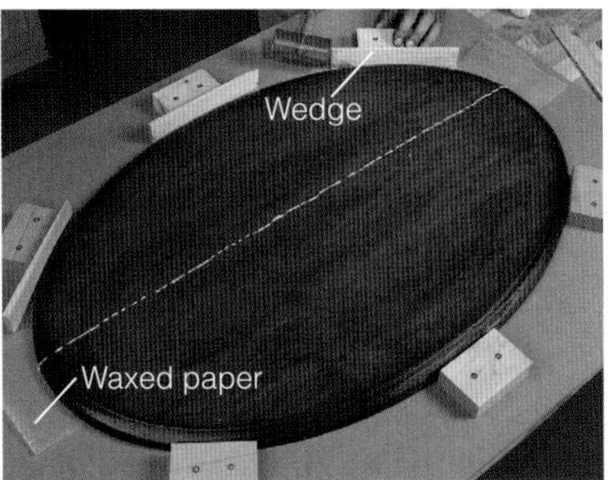

Round tops. Squeeze together curved tops with blocks and wedges. Screw blocks to plywood and drive in shims to apply pressure.

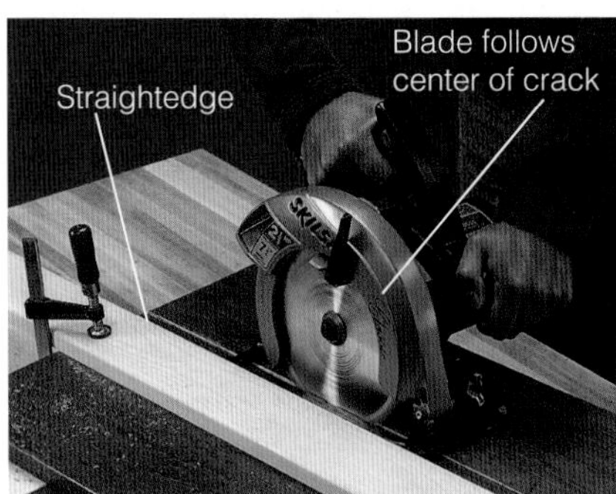

1 Saw the top in two, using a straightedge for cutting along the center of the crack. It may take two or three passes to remove the blemish.

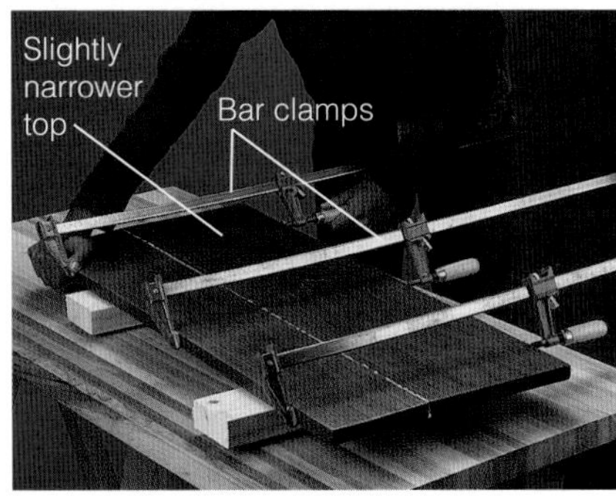

2 Spread glue on each half, and clamp them together until the glue dries. Drill new mounting holes and reinstall the top to its base.

Shop Smart: Glues for Repairs

Yellow or white glue is plenty strong for most repairs, but others are better for special situations.

Slow-set glues, such as liquid hide glue or Titebond's Extend, are handy when you need more time for complex assemblies.

Fast glues like cyanoacrylate (Super Glue) are perfect for small repairs because they set in seconds, letting you hold awkward shapes in place instead of using clamps.

Gap-filling two-part epoxies will fill and support a loose joint. Don't use polyurethanes: they fill, but without much strength.

Table Leg Support Block

Wood corner blocks have a nasty tendency of letting go after years of hard use. To make a new one, dismount the leg, pull out the old block and use it as a template to trace its shape onto a fresh piece of hardwood, such as oak or maple.

Test-fit the new block, then glue it in place and reinstall the leg and hardware.

Nicked Corner

To restore a nicked corner or table edge, make a straight or L-shaped mold (depending on the repair) and clamp the mold to the table with plastic wrap in between to prevent the clamp from sticking.

Fill the missing area with wood putty or auto body filler. When the filler has hardened slightly, remove the mold and shave the repair flush to the surface with a chisel. Paint on a wood grain pattern and refinish.

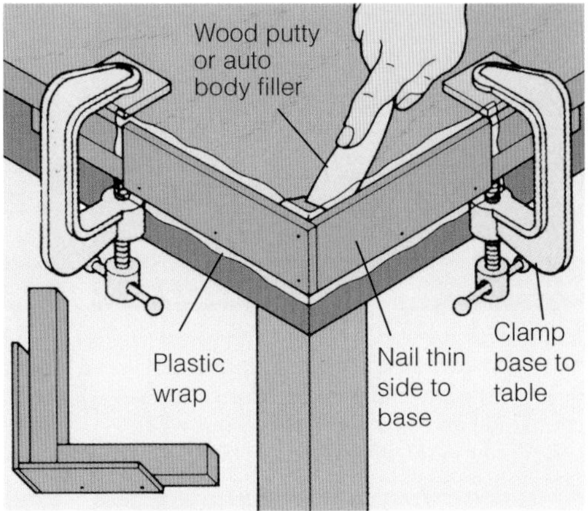

Broken Corner

Rebuild a broken corner by patching it with a precisely cut piece of similar wood, carefully choosing color and orienting grain lines.

Use a router and straight bit or a sharp chisel to create a smooth bed for the patch, making sure to leave square edges so the patch butts up tightly. Glue and clamp the patch in place. Sand the edges flush after the glue dries.

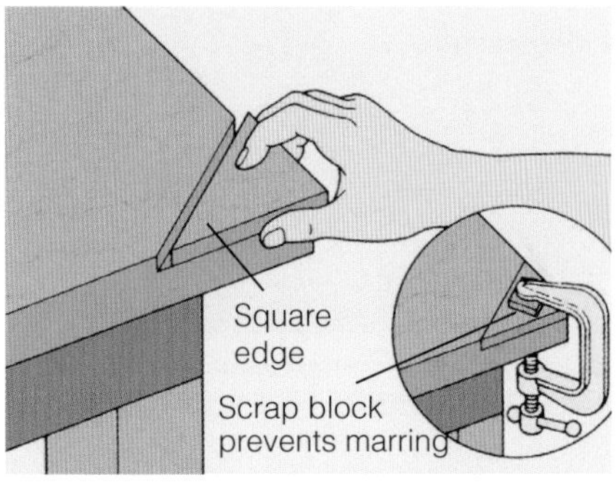

Veneer Repairs

Missing Pieces

Replacing small sections of chipped or damaged veneer is easy to do. Pieces of veneer are readily available in a variety of species from mail-order or retail woodworking suppliers.

For replacing large sheets, such as the top of an entire chest, it's best to use regular white or yellow glue and to place a sheet of plywood topped with weights; books or concrete blocks work great for pressing the veneer. For large sheets, cut the veneer oversize so all the edges overhang, then trim flush after gluing.

For small repairs, you can use contact cement, which sticks without clamping. After you've cut a small patch, spread contact cement on both surfaces being joined. Let the glue become dry to the touch before pressing the patch down.

Regardless of the size of the patch, finish by staining to match and applying your favorite topcoat.

1 Straighten the edges of the damaged area with a ruler and utility knife, cutting parallel to the grain as much as possible to hide the seam.

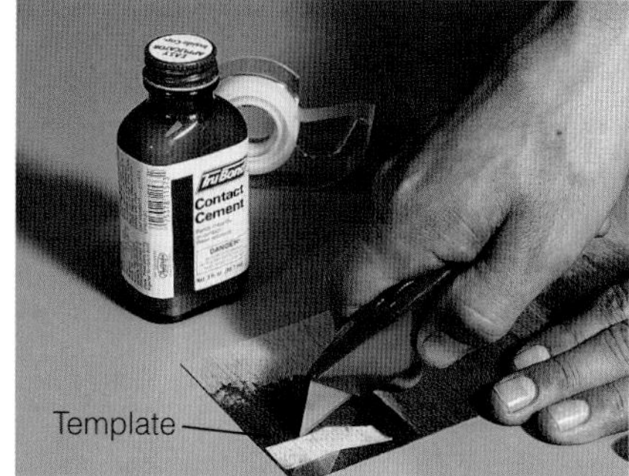

2 Cut an exact replica of the chipped area from a template. Make the template from a paper rubbing of the damaged spot, using the side of a pencil point.

3 Test-fit the patch and trim if necessary. Apply contact cement to both surfaces, let the glue dry and press the veneer in place.

4 Stain veneer to match. Then apply a coat of oil, varnish, lacquer or shellac. After the finish dries, touch up seams with a wax putty stick.

Blisters

It's common to find blistered or bubbled veneer in the middle of a veneered piece. In fact, you can detect unsound veneer by lightly tapping the surface with your finger, listening for a change in sound. A hollow note reveals loose veneer.

If heat and steam won't restick the veneer (see "Lifted Veneer," below), slit the area with a craft or utility knife along the wood's grain. Use a glue syringe, available from woodworking catalogs, to inject glue into the slit.

Press the bubble down by hand to distribute the glue and remove any excess with a damp rag. Then place some waxed paper and scrap wood over the area and lay weights on top.

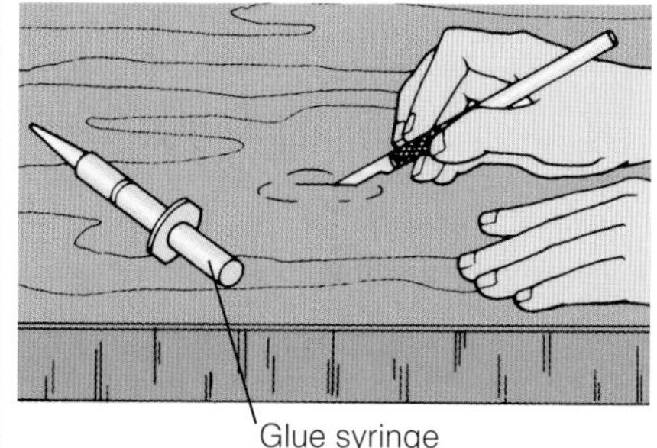

Lifted Veneer

Lifted veneer can be readily glued back in place. If the veneer is old, it's probably glued with hide glue, which you can restick using heat and moisture. Place a damp cloth on the damaged area, turn a household iron on low and press the veneer flat.

If the iron doesn't work, carefully lift the veneer and scrape off as much old glue as possible. Use a small brush to apply liquid hide glue. Then clamp the veneer flat with a scrap of wood.

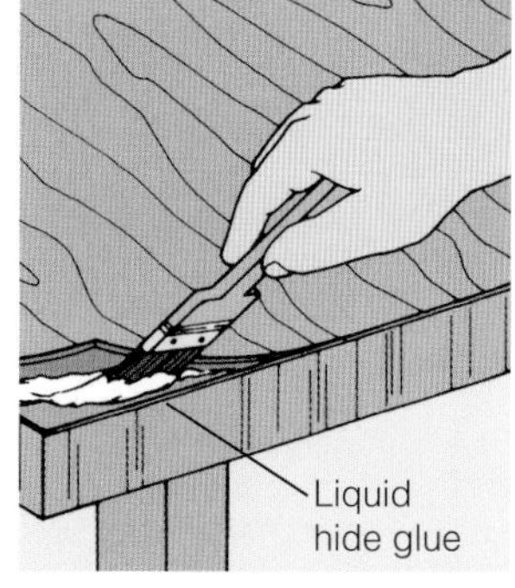

1 Pry up the loose veneer and scrape off old glue with a razor blade. If the glue isn't hide glue, scrape vigilantly. With hide glue, simply remove any big clumps. Apply a thin coat of fresh hide glue to the core and the underside of the veneer.

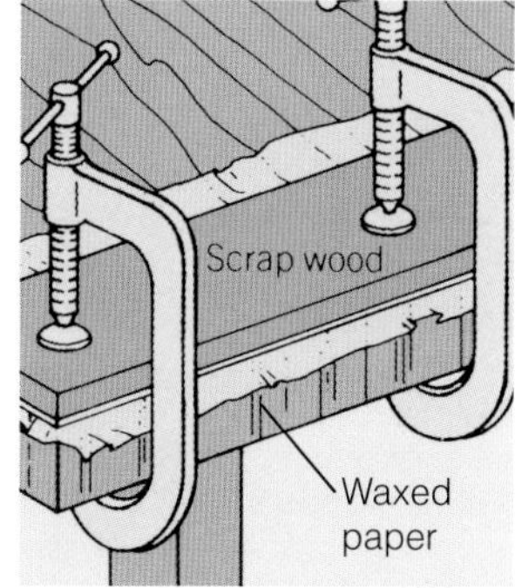

2 Press the veneer back in place and use a damp rag to remove any excess glue. Then position a sheet of waxed paper over the repair, extending it past the damaged area. Clamp a piece of scrap wood over the top and allow the glue to dry for 12 hours.

Regluing Furniture

Clamps 34
Drills 50
Adhesives 84

Chairs

Chairs probably need fixing more than any other type of furniture—particularly when they start to wobble. Here's how to tighten up things.

Start by labeling all the parts and then disassemble any loose joints. If necessary, take the whole chair apart.

Carefully scrape all the old glue from tenons and holes. Be persistent, because new glue won't stick to old yellow or white glue. If the original adhesive was hide glue, you're in luck: Simply soften it first with hot water and then scrape.

Make or replace any missing or broken parts, such as turned spindles. If a tenon fits loosely, "fatten" it by gluing a wood shaving or two around it.

Once all the parts fit, reglue the chair using liquid hide glue. Then fill any chips or nail holes and touch-up the finish.

1 Make reassembly a breeze by labeling all the joints beforehand with bits of masking tape. Use arrows to indicate alignment of mating parts. Then remove any nails or other connecting hardware.

2 Loosen stubborn joints by laying the chair on a padded workbench and giving the joint a sound rap with a rubber mallet. If necessary, take apart intact joints to gain access to loose ones for regluing.

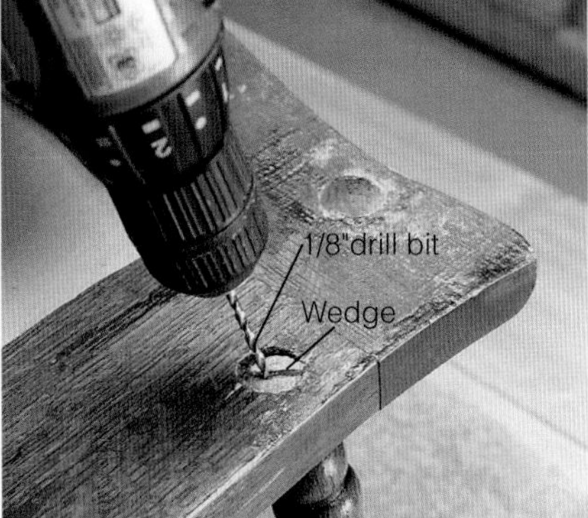

3 Remove wedges from wedged joints by drilling a series of 1/8-in. (3-mm) holes along the wedge. Pick out the remaining pieces of the wedge using an awl, a narrow chisel or a screwdriver.

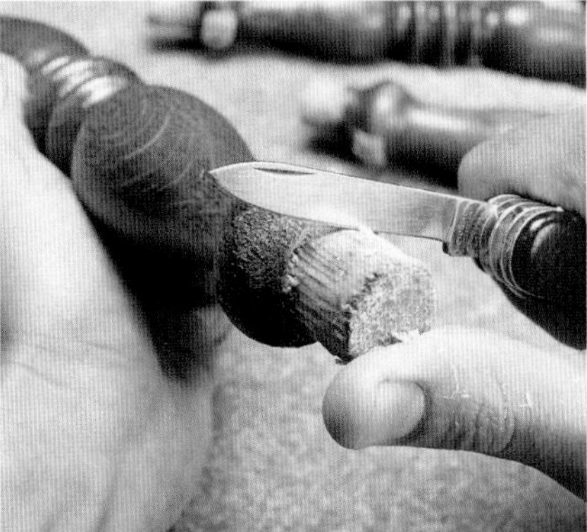

4 Scrape all the old glue from tenons with a pocketknife or utility knife. Don't remove wood fibers or you'll reduce the tenon's diameter and loosen the joint.

5 Remove old glue from the sides and bottom of the holes. File down the point of a spade bit or use a small chisel to clean out holes. Clean remaining bits with a plumber's fitting brush.

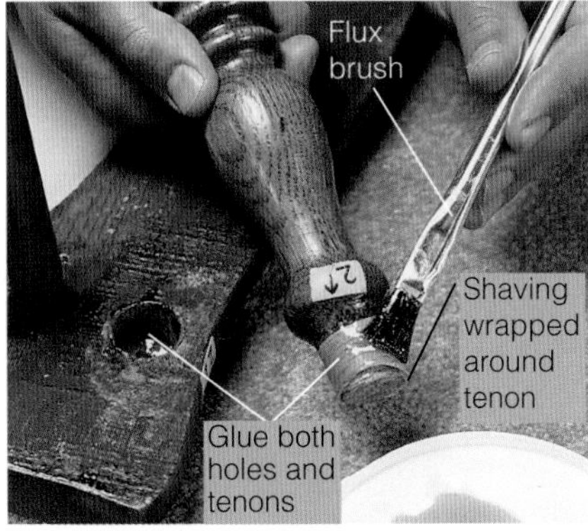

6 Repair bad-fitting joints by applying liquid hide glue to the tenon and wrapping a thin wood shaving or a piece of veneer around it. Let the glue dry. During reassembly, spread hide glue on both parts of every joint.

7 Fit glued parts together by tapping with a mallet, beginning with the legs. To secure wedged tenons, cut a small wedge from scrap wood and apply glue to the wedge and its slot. Then tap the wedge into the slot.

8 Pull glued joints together with clamps. Cut wedges to direct the clamping pressure in line with the joints, holding them with C-clamps. Use web clamps or tightly-stretched bicycle inner tubes to draw parts together.

Loose Joints

There are shortcuts that might prevent you from having to disassemble an entire piece just to fix a few loose joints.

You can repair loose joints from the outside, by adding dowels through both parts of a joint or by injecting gap-filling epoxy into the joint. If a single leg or stretcher is loose, try removing that part only. Then enlarge the tenon by wrapping it with a shaving.

1 Drill a pair of holes through the joint. First, drill holes in a block and then clamp the block to the joint to guide the bit and prevent tear-out. Use another clamp to keep the joint from spreading as you drill.

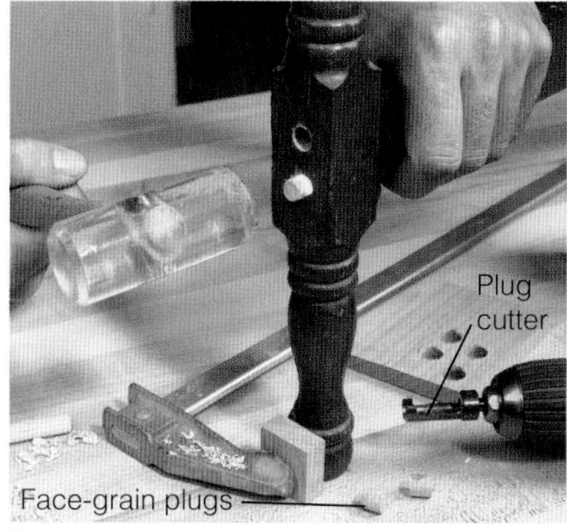

2 Glue and drive dowels through the joint. Set the dowels deep enough so you can conceal the holes with glued-in plugs.

Epoxy. Drill a 1/8-in. (3-mm) hole diagonally into the hole, then pump slow-setting epoxy into the joint with a glue syringe. Wiggle the joint as you inject the epoxy to distribute the adhesive around the tenon.

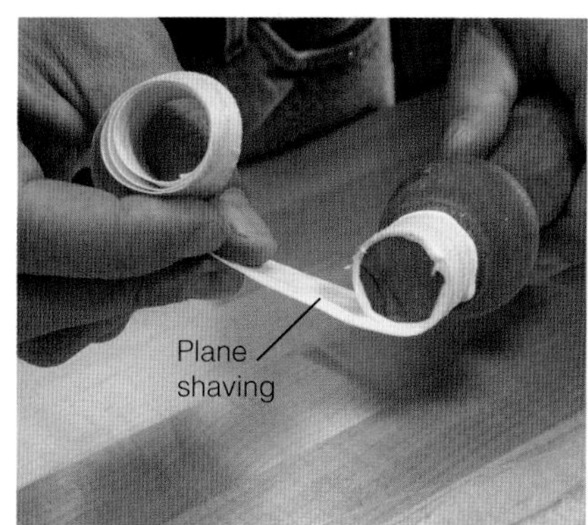

Shaving. Enlarge a loose tenon to get a good fit by wrapping it with a shaving from your plane. Keep in mind that wear and shrinkage turn round holes into ovals, so be sure to sand and shape the new tenon to fit.

Table Legs

Tables may not get as much abuse as chairs, but it's not unusual for one to break when kicked or moved. To repair the joint, save any fractured pieces, and remove old dowels by drilling them out.

Glue fractured parts back together, positioning them in their original order and wrapping them with masking tape until the glue dries. Then install fresh dowels with glue and clamp the joint.

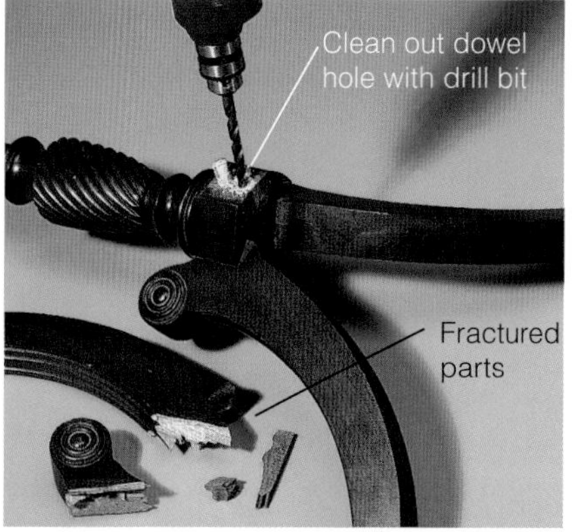

1 Be sure to save even small shattered pieces so you can glue them back together. Drill out broken dowels using a bit the same diameter as the dowel.

2 Scrape all old glue from the surfaces of the joint. Then apply fresh glue to one half of each dowel's length and tap or push them into the holes.

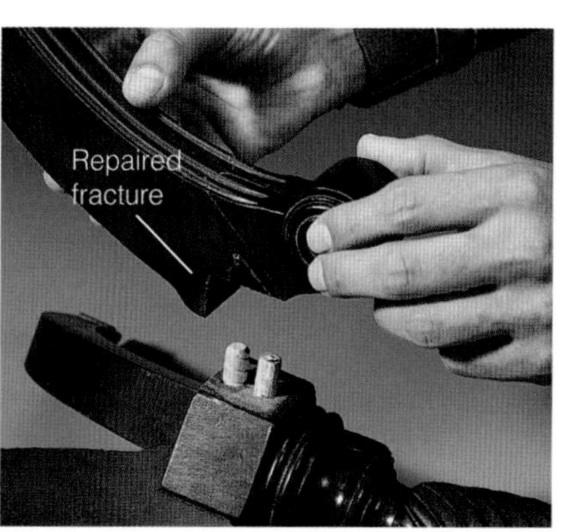

3 Be sure the fractured repair is sound and the glue has dried before you reassemble. Apply glue to all the joint surfaces, including the dowels, and carefully fit the part back together.

4 If regular clamps won't work or fit, use a bungee cord or band clamp to pull the parts together. Let the glue dry overnight. Then fill any visual blemishes with putty and touch up the finish.

Outdoor Furniture Repairs

Lawn Chairs

Resurrect your comfy lawn chair by replacing its broken or frayed nylon webbing. Rolls large enough to reweb one chair are available at hardware stores and home centers.

Remove the fasteners that hold the webbing straps. Measure from hole to hole and add 3-1/2 in. (9 cm). Cut each strap to length, folding its ends into triangles. Attach using the original hardware, and your favorite chair is as good as new—maybe even better!

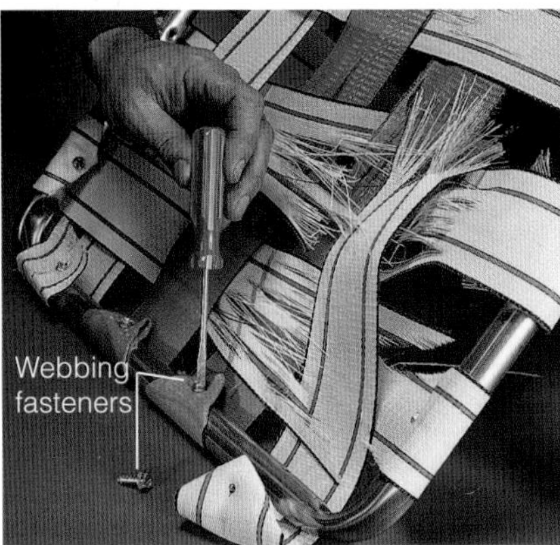

1 Remove the fasteners and old webbing straps from the chair frame. Save the screws for reattaching the new straps.

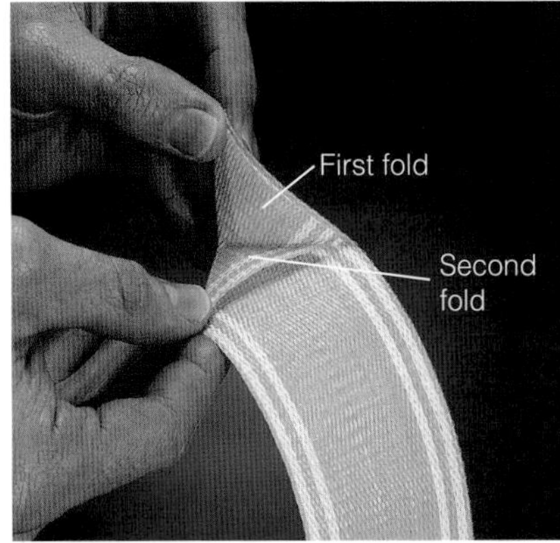

2 Double-fold each end of the strap to create a strong, four-layer-thick triangle, through which you insert the fastener.

3 Poke a hole through the strap with an awl. Install screws through the strap and into holes in frame. A washer strengthens the connection.

4 Secure all the straps in one direction first. Then weave the second set over and under the first and secure it to the chair frame.

Wicker

Repairing wicker furniture is easier than you might think. You can buy the material, whether it's cane, fiber rush, Oriental seagrass, rattan, reed or willow, by looking under wicker or rattan in the Yellow Pages or on the Internet. Be sure to soak the material in warm water for 30 minutes to make it more pliable before you work with it.

To fix a damaged, unraveled area, remove the loose strip and tack its free end to the furniture's frame. Tack a new piece near the old strip, and wrap it tightly around the frame. Tack the trailing end and add glue.

To plug the gaps where woven strips are missing in seats, seat backs and cabinet panels, first cut away damaged material from the underside, back or inside. Cut a new piece 1 in. (2.5 cm) longer than the original and weave it following the existing pattern.

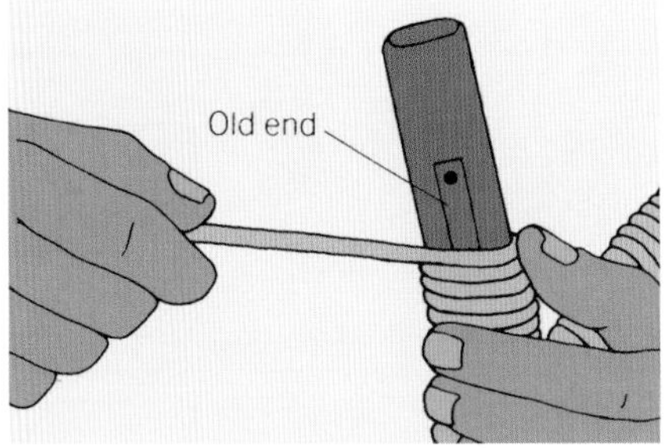

1 Fix a broken strip by cutting off the old piece and tacking down its end. Near the old end, tuck and tack down new end. Wind new piece tightly and evenly around frame.

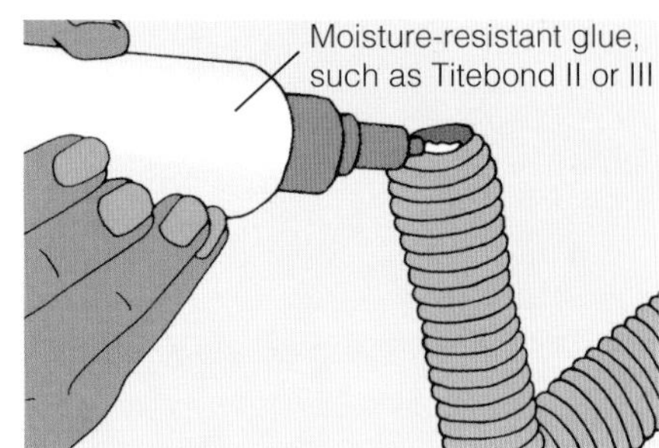

2 To finish, tuck the end under the final turn and tack it in place. Snip off the end flush and apply glue around the end of the wrap.

3 Weave a new strand by first cutting away the old one with wire cutters, working from the underside. Let the spokes support the cut ends. Cut a new piece 1 in. (2.5 cm) longer than the old piece.

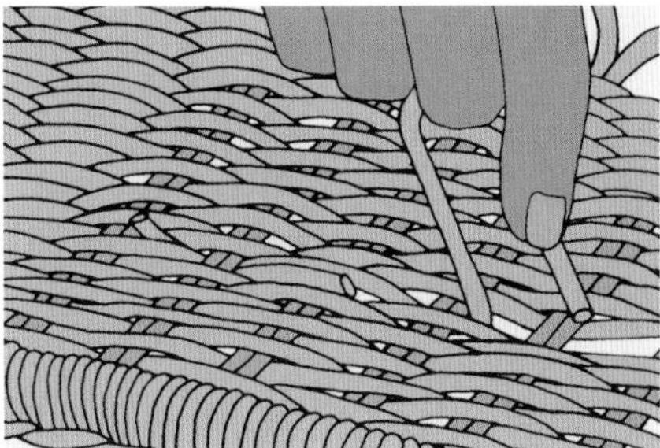

4 Starting on the underside, weave the new strip over and under spokes, following the pattern and pulling tightly as you weave. Snip ends and tuck them against the spokes.

Recaning

Most caned chairs less than 60 years old can be recaned using machine-woven sheet cane, which is far easier than hand-weaving individual cane. In fact, you can use the material to reseat any cane chair that has a groove in which to secure a spline.

All you need is sheet cane, a length of spline sized to the width of the groove and about 10 caning wedges. (Look in the Yellow Pages or search the Internet under "Wicker" or "Rattan" for materials.)

The photos on this page show the caning process. After you've installed the new cane, give it a light coat of lacquer and let it sit for two days before putting it to use.

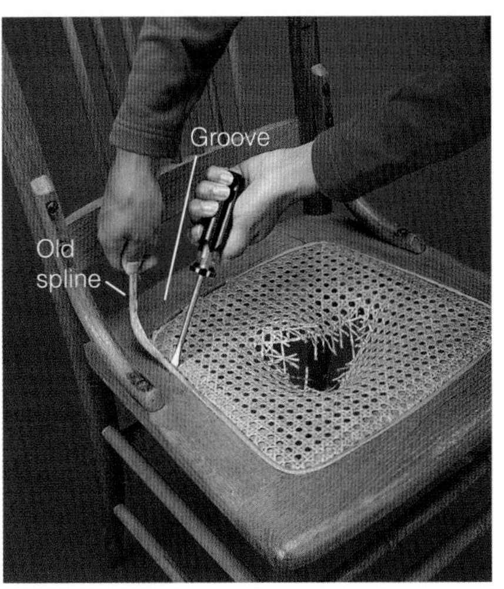

1 Pry up the old spline with a screwdriver, after you have sliced alongside it on both sides with a utility knife to break the glue joint. Then remove the old cane.

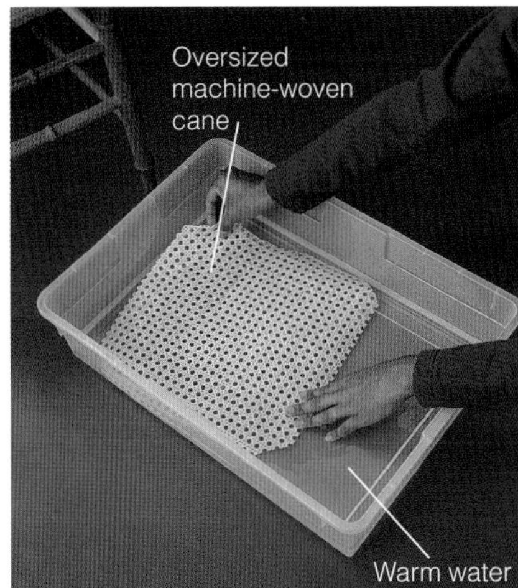

2 Cut the new cane so it extends 1 in. (2.5 cm) past the chair groove on all sides. Soak the sheet in warm water for an hour. Then place the smooth or shiny side up on the chair frame.

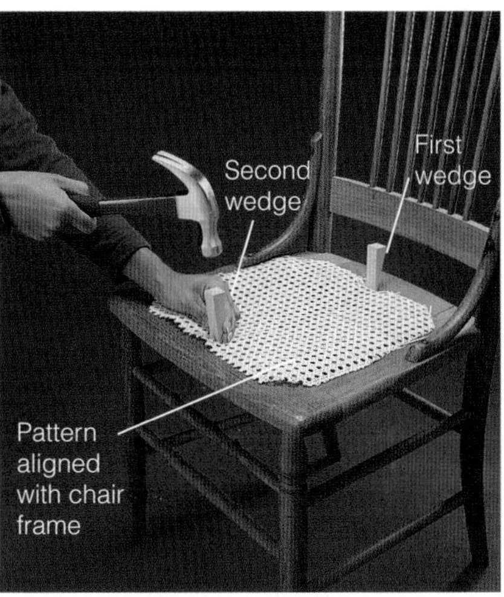

3 Starting at the back, drive in a caning wedge. Drive a second wedge in front, stretching the sheet slightly and checking that the pattern runs straight and square across the seat.

4 Install wedges around the entire seat. If the cane starts to dry out, give it a mist of water from a spray bottle. Use the tip of a spare wedge to press the remaining cane into the groove, then remove the wedges.

5 Soak the rough-cut spline in water for 15 minutes. Run a bead of yellow glue into the groove, and press the new spline into place. If the groove has square corners, miter-cut the spline and install it in four separate sections.

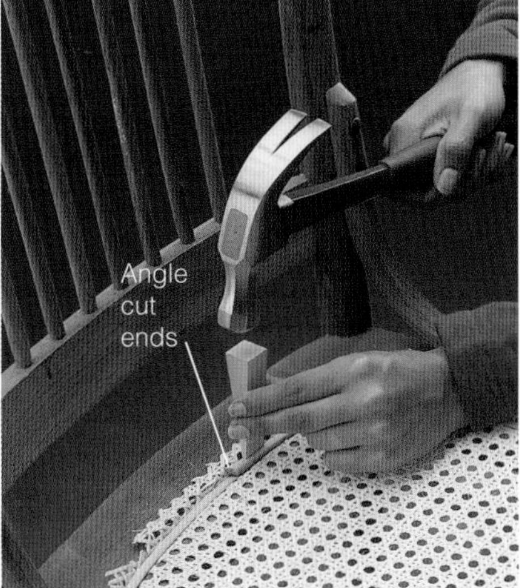

6 Trim the end of the spline and tap it into the groove using a wedge. Cut an angle on the ends of the spline with a utility knife so they meet at a tight joint. Go back around the entire spline and retap it until it's flush with the seat.

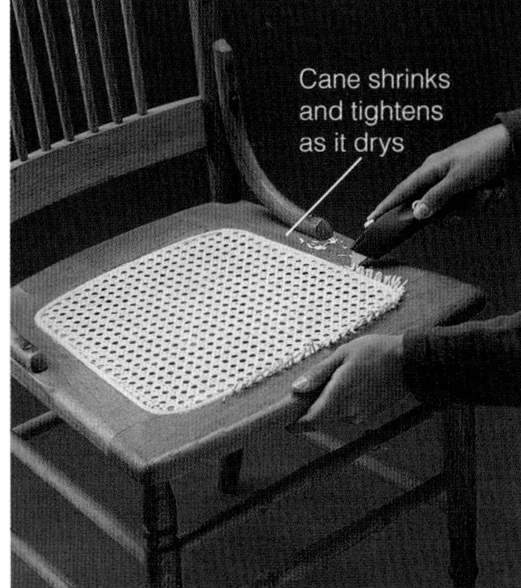

7 Trim excess cane with a utility knife. Let sit for two days to allow cane to dry fully; it will shrink and pull tight to the frame. Sand with 220-grit sandpaper; then spray with lacquer.

Re-covering a Chair

Staple Guns 28

Worn or dated chairs with removable "wraparound" seats are a snap to renew. If the seat is in good shape, you can add new fabric and batting right over the old, as shown.

If the old padding is lumpy, remove it, cut a piece of foam the exact shape of the seat and apply it along with the new batting and fabric.

Most fabric stores carry batting and foam, and you can select cotton or synthetic fabrics in a variety of colors or patterns. Polished cotton, with the pattern printed on the surface, is less durable than other fabric options.

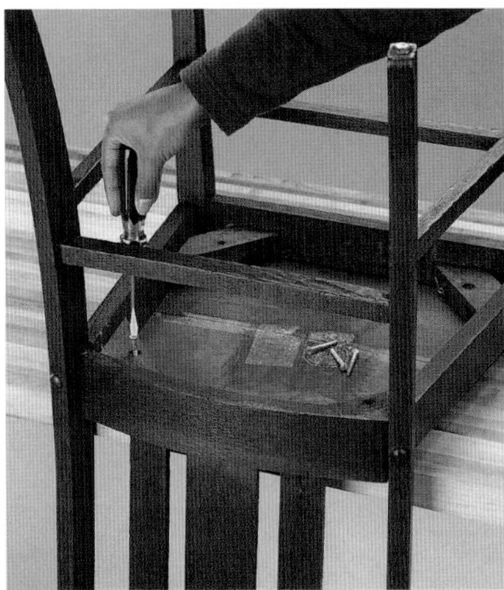

1 Remove the chair bottom by taking out the screws that secure it to the frame. Save the screws for reassembly later.

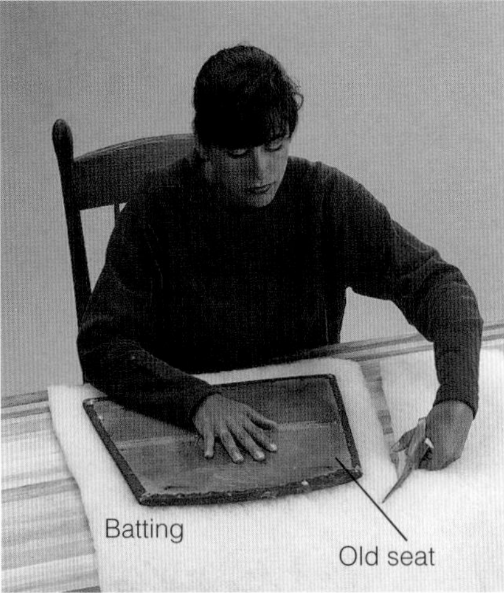

2 Cut new batting about 2 in. (5 cm) oversize on all sides, using the seat bottom as a pattern.

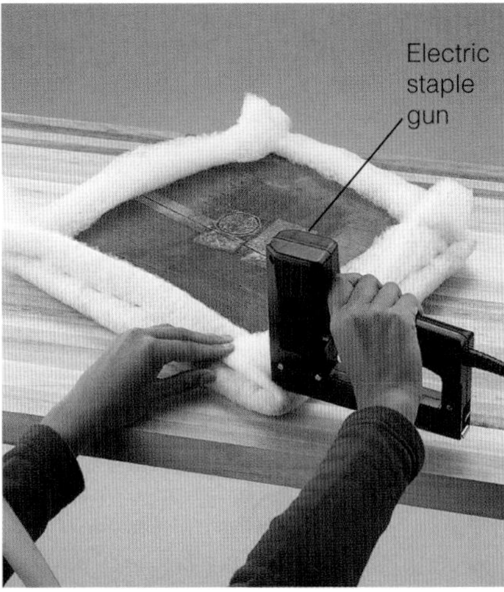

3 Secure the batting by pulling it tightly around the seat and fastening with 1/4-in. staples. Trim any excess.

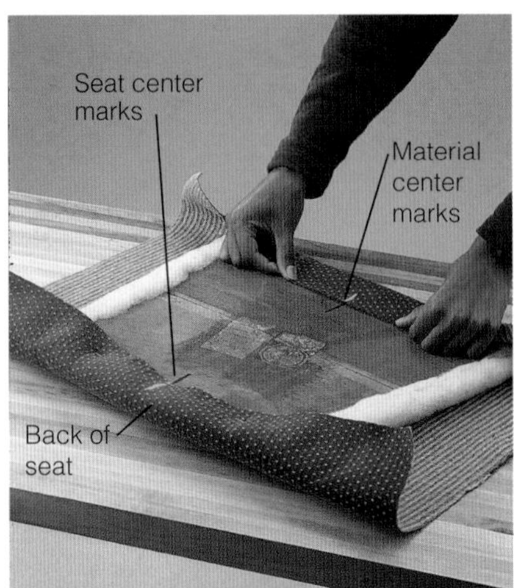

4 Mark centerlines on the chair bottom and the fabric. Align them so the fabric runs straight from front to back.

5 Staple fabric in place, completing the front edge first, back edge next and the two sides last. Start stapling at the center and work toward the corners. Flip the seat often to make sure the pattern is running straight.

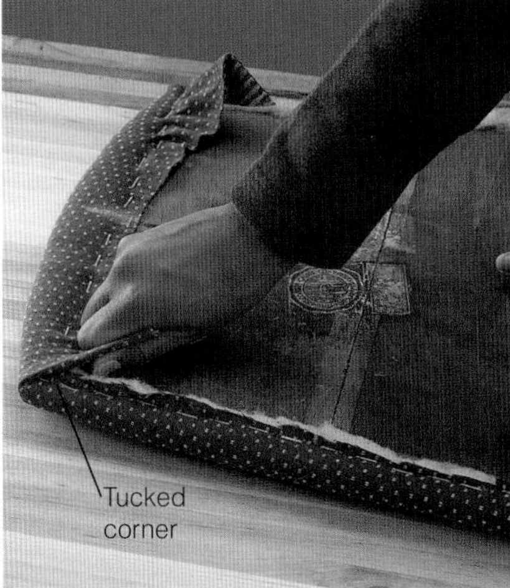

6 Fold fabric at the corners; then secure with staples. Trim excess using sharp scissors after all the corners are complete.

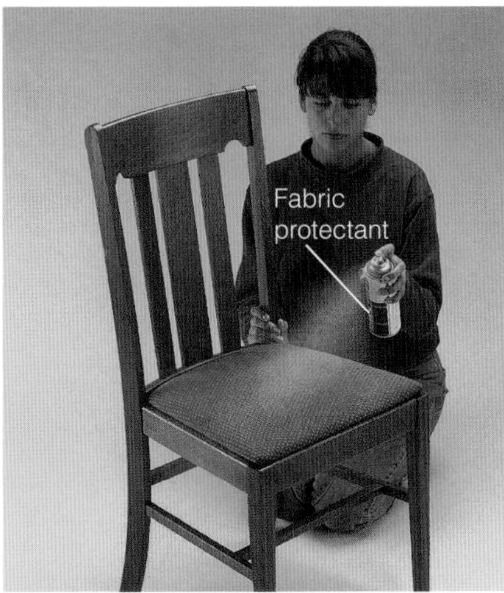

7 Protect the new upholstery from stains, spills and sunlight by spraying it with one of the many fabric protectants available.

Metals & Plastics

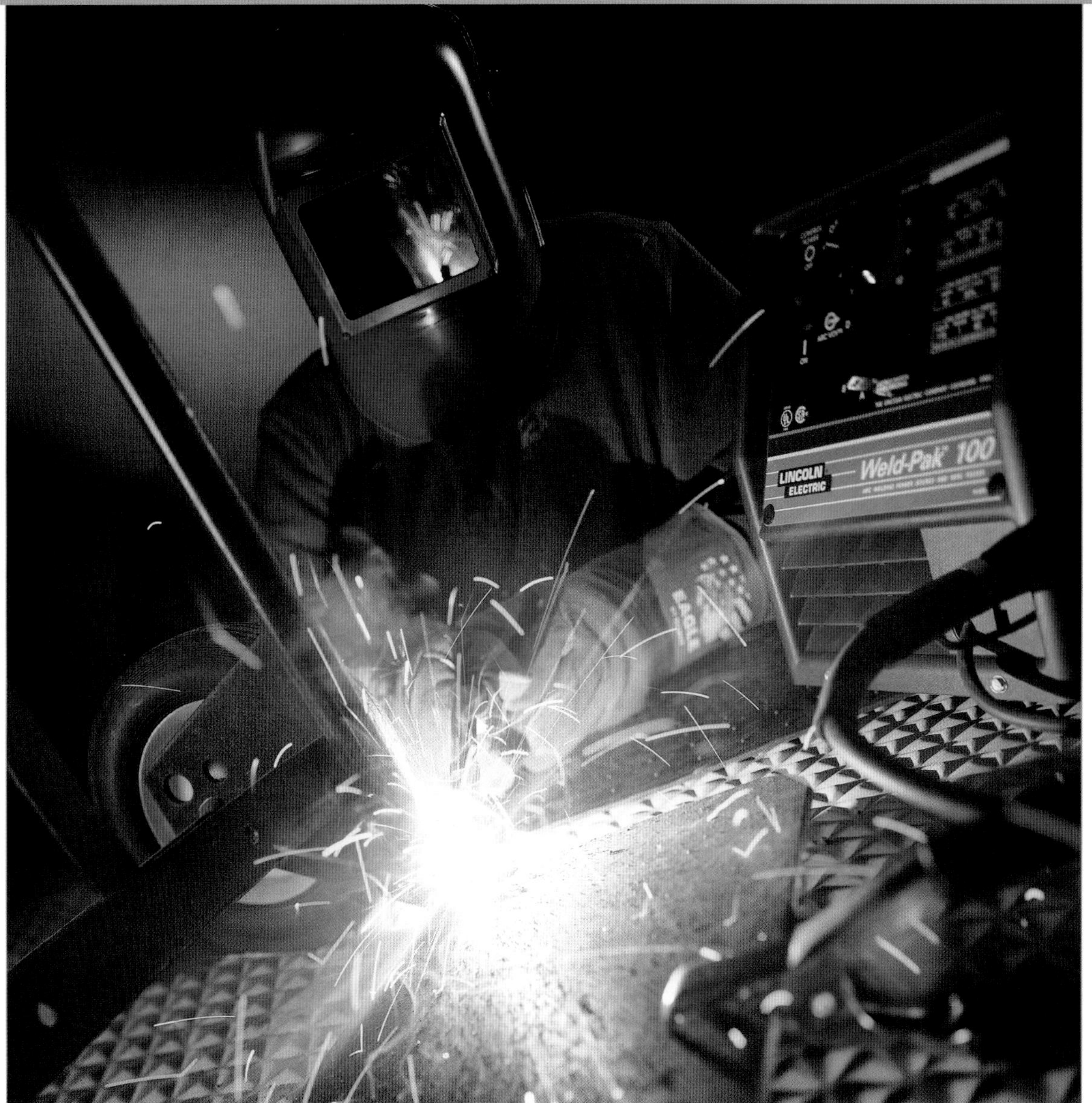

Metal / Bending

Vises 33
Circular Saws 56
Ductwork 175

Whether you're making flashing for your chimney or creating a drip cap for over your patio door, sometimes you need to put on your metal fabricator's hat. You can buy most simple flashings, and complex ones may be best left to pros; it's for those in-between projects that some basic metal-bending know-how comes in handy.

Four methods are shown below. Whichever one you choose, think "safety." Firmly clamp or hold the metal you're working on. Wear thick leather gloves when cutting, bending or installing sheet metal and discard scraps immediately to prevent accidents. Unfurl rolls of flashing carefully; some tend to uncoil like a rattlesnake. Round or bend over any exposed edges where people could cut themselves.

A vise, with protective wood blocks on each jaw, is ideal for bending small pieces of metal, like this step flashing. Draw a layout line to mark the location of the fold. Lightly scoring the line with an awl can help create an even crisper bend.

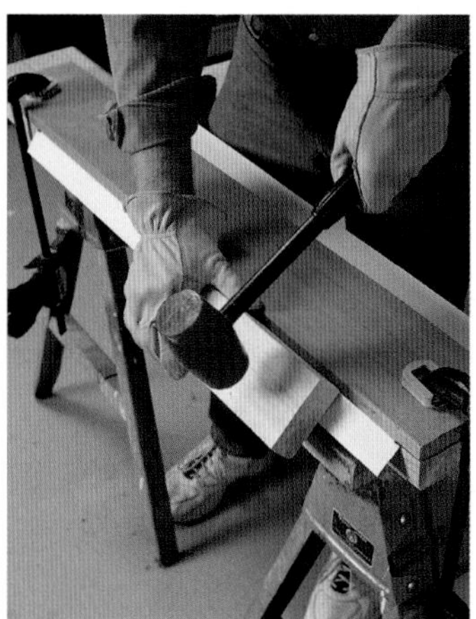

A simple metal bender can be created in 15 minutes using two wide boards and a pair of clamps. Draw layout marks on the metal and clamp it between the two boards. Gradually bend the metal by sliding a 2x4 block back and forth, striking it with a mallet until the proper angle is created.

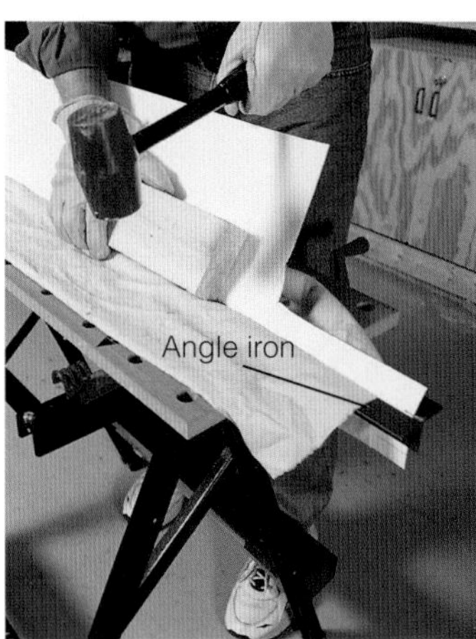

A portable workstand equipped with a pair of angle irons can deliver long, sharp creases with minimal setup time. Use a striking block and mallet to gradually make the bend. Fabricate longer flashings by using longer, wider angle irons in conjunction with a second workstand.

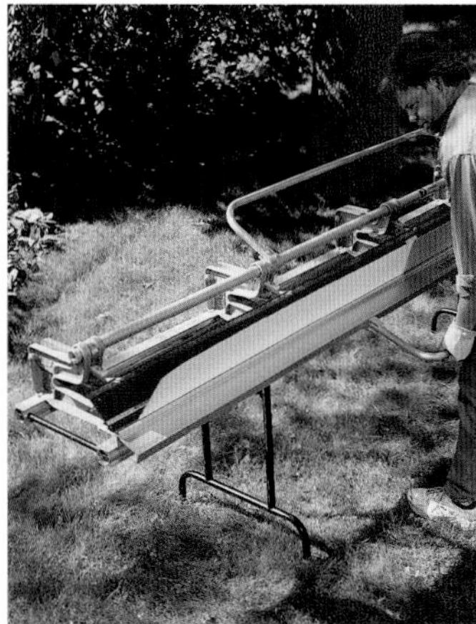

A sliding brake is worth renting if you have dozens of long flashings to fabricate. Position the workpiece in the clamping jaws and secure it with the locking handle. Lift the bending handle to fold the metal to any desired angle between 0° and 180°.

Making a Safe Edge

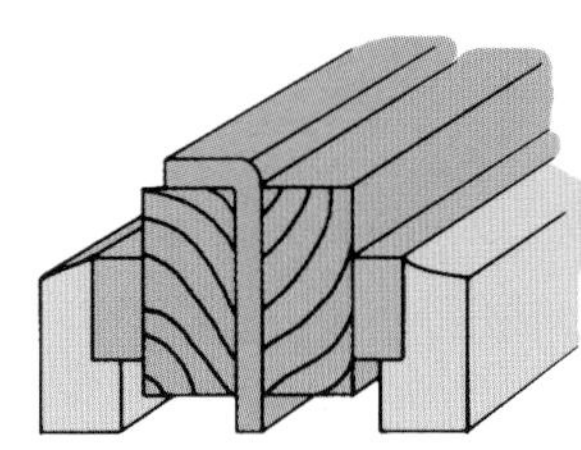

Scribe a line about 3/8 in. (10 mm) from the metal's edge. Clamp the metal at the line between squared blocks of wood. Tap with a mallet to make a 90° bend.

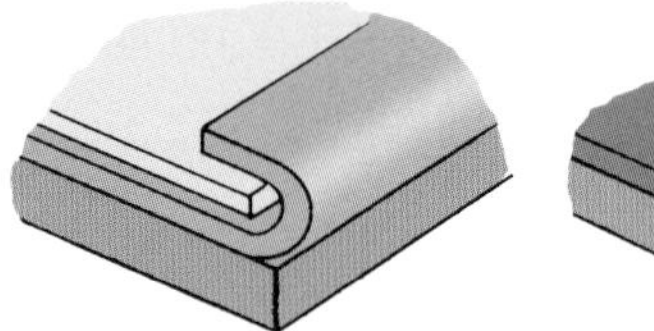

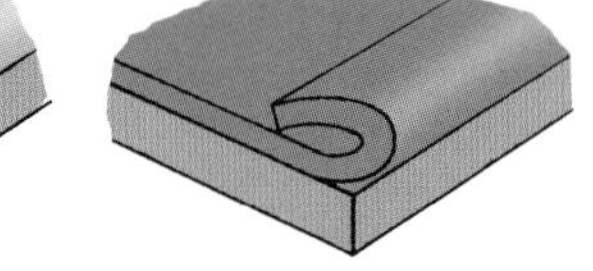

Bend edge to 180° over a piece of scrap sheet metal to keep a slight opening. Then remove the scrap and tap the edge down until it meets the sheet's surface.

Folding a Seam

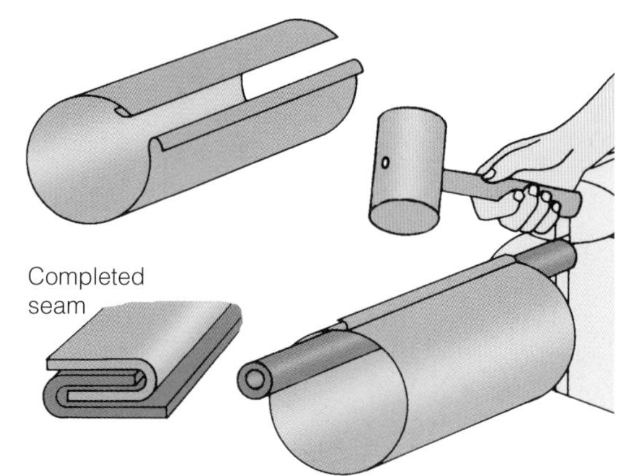

To join two edges, make a hem in each, just as you would for a safe edge, but hook the edges together just before you tap them down. Curved pieces can be supported on a pipe held in a vise while you tap.

Metal / Cutting

Snips

Snips are the tool of choice for cutting ductwork, flashing and other thin metals. The basic scissorlike tin snips will handle most straight cuts, but for angles, curves and tight spaces, consider buying a set of aviation snips. They cut using a more powerful compound-lever action and are easy to control. The handles are color-coded: Straight-cutting are yellow, left-cutting are red and right-cutting are green. Wear gloves and protective eyewear when working with snips.

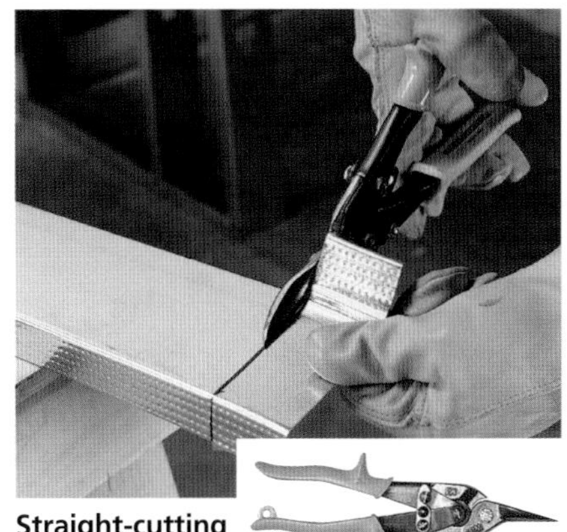

Straight-cutting snips have a compound-lever cutting action that makes them easier to operate and control. When cutting metal studs, snip both flanges, and then bend one flange up and cut across.

Left-cutting snips are designed to cut efficiently in a counterclockwise direction. Create a starting slit for the snips by using a hammer to rap the tip of a screwdriver into the metal.

Right-cutting snips cut most efficiently in a clockwise direction. Here one is used in a confined space to finish a cut started by the left-cutting snips.

Abrasive Blades

Abrasive metal cutting blades (shown at left) basically wear the metal away. Toothed carbide blades cut more like their wood counterparts.

The toothed blades usually have 40 or more small teeth and are most often used on softer, nonferrous metals like aluminum, brass or copper.

The abrasive blades sacrifice themselves as they work; the more you cut, the smaller they become.

Whichever type you use, set the cutting depth only slightly deeper than the thickness of the metal you're cutting. Ease slowly into the cut and don't force the blade. Wear protective long sleeves, gloves, hearing protection and eyewear.

Cutting Thin Metal

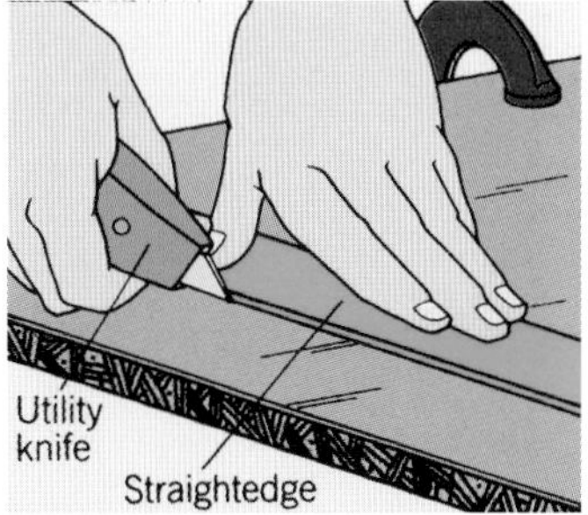

Utility knife. Use a utility knife to cut very thin metal sheets. Clamp metal over scrap wood and scribe a line. Position straightedge along cutline and score line with utility knife. Break the sheet apart with gloved hands. File the edge to remove sharp burrs.

Keyhole saw. To cut very thin sheet metal, clamp it between pieces of thin scrap wood and saw through both wood and metal. Use a coping saw with a metal-cutting blade for deep curves, and a keyhole saw for interior cuts.

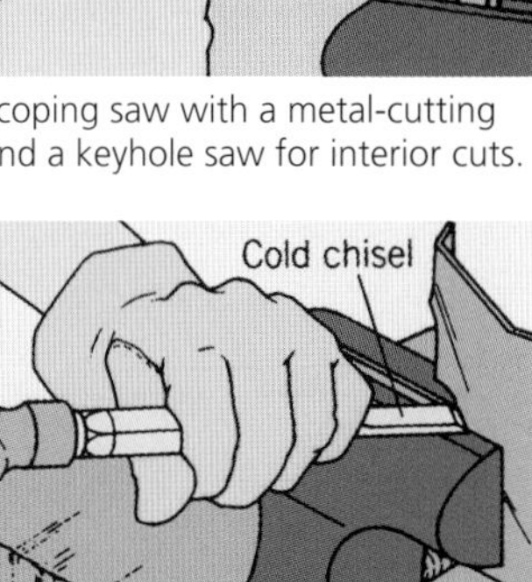

Cold chisel. Clamp the work in a vise with the cutline just above its jaws. Rest the chisel blade on the vise's jaw and tilt it to about a 30° angle so its cutting edge is against the cutline. Strike chisel with a ball peen hammer to make the cut.

Metal / Drilling

Safety Equipment 20
Drill Presses 53

Any handheld drill can be used to bore a hole in metal, but a drill press offers the greatest accuracy and safety. Use regular twist bits (preferably with carbide tips) or high-speed steel bits.

Clamp the work securely so it doesn't become a dangerous whirling helicopter blade. If you're drilling all the way through the metal, back it up with scrap wood. Before drilling, make an indentation in the metal to keep the bit from wandering off center.

When drilling thick metal, lubricate the hole, back the bit out from time to time and brush away waste fragments. Otherwise the fragments may overheat and partially weld themselves to the bit.

Clamp the workpiece in a wood "sandwich." The top and bottom wood layers will help keep the bit in line and ensure a clean-edged hole.

Lubricate the bit and hole with metal-cutting oil to prevent overheating. A washer taped around the area where the hole will be drilled helps confine the pool of oil.

Special Situations

Flashings and ductwork may be the metal items do-it-yourselfers most frequently encounter, but in the course of hanging a garage door or building a woodworking jig you may work with thicker or tubular stock. Use the same precautions and safety equipment you'd use for thinner metals.

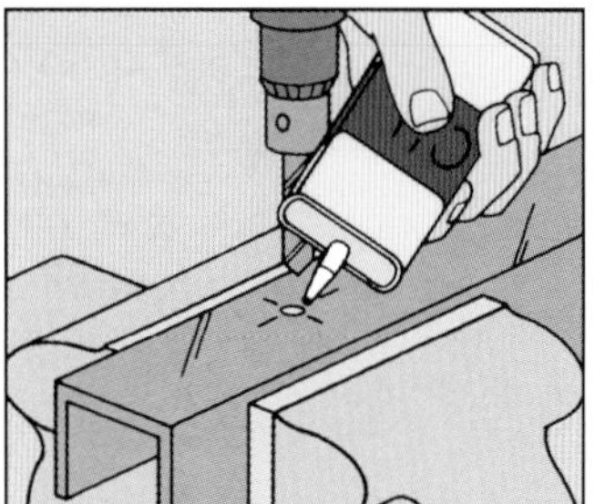

Drill large holes in stages. First drill a 1/4-in. (6-mm) hole, and then increase its size with progressively larger bits. Lubricate the bit and hole as you work.

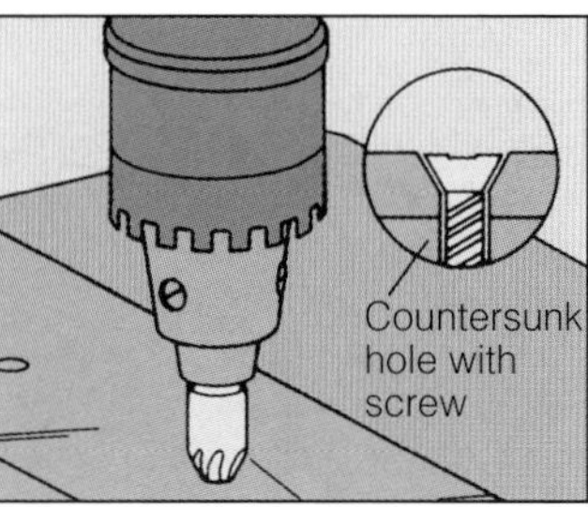

Countersink screwheads so they're flush with the surface of the surrounding metal. Enlarge and taper the top of pilot hole just enough to contain the screwhead. Set the drill at lowest speed, and lubricate the hole liberally.

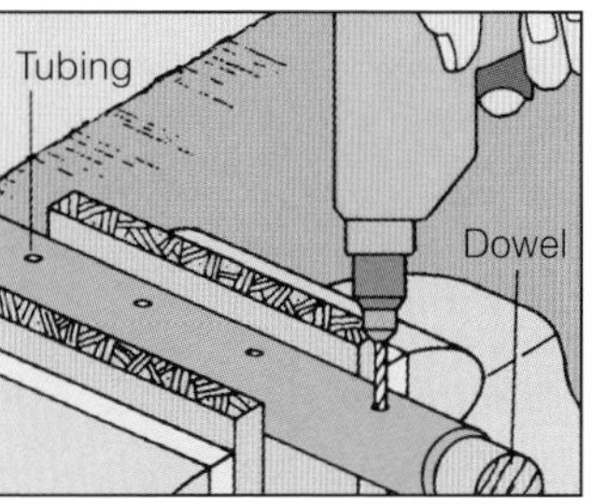

Tubing and pipe can be drilled without distortion by inserting a snug-fitting wood dowel to reinforce them.

Clamps, Goggles and Gloves

Metal is relatively safe to work with, providing you take a little care:

- Clamp work securely. Never hold work with your hands.
- Wear safety goggles; tiny particles of metal or sparks may fly into your eyes if they're not protected.
- Wear thick work gloves when working; edges can be sharp enough to cause serious cuts, and tiny burrs can do painful damage to unprotected fingers.
- Keep drill bits sharp and clean; never force a tool.
- File or grind cut edges of newly drilled holes as soon as possible to prevent cuts.
- Make use of all available safety shields and devices on your power tools.

Perfectly Centered Holes

If you want perfectly aligned holes when drilling pipe (or wood dowels, for that matter) try this trick: Saw a V-shaped channel along the center of a 2x6 block. Place the V-block on the drill press, align the bit with the bottom of the V-channel and clamp it to the table in that position. Clamp your pipe, tubing or dowel to this jig, and then drill your perfectly centered and aligned holes.

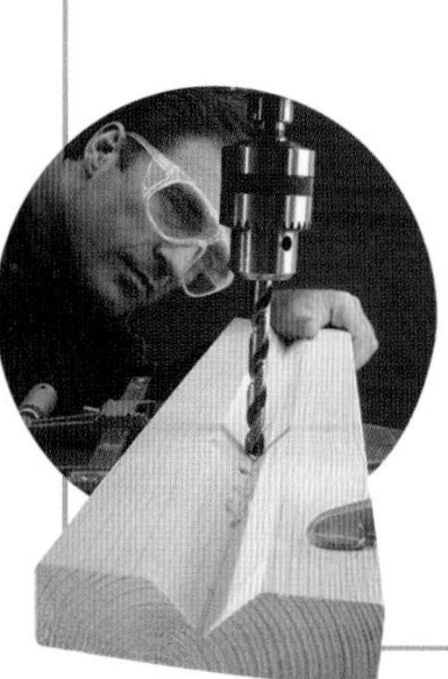

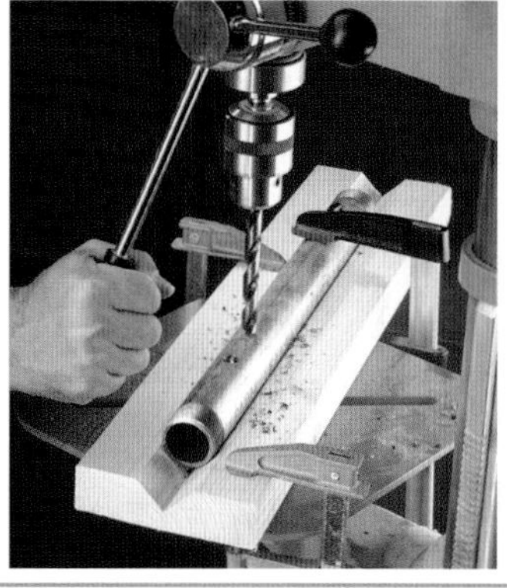

Taps and Dies

Taps

Threaded holes can be created by inserting a tap into a predrilled hole and turning it with a special wrench. The tap's slightly tapered end helps ease it into the hole and start the cutting process.

Tapered taps and plug taps have the first three or more threads tapered, which makes starting easier but prevents threading close to the bottom of a blind hole. A bottoming tap cuts threads to the bottom of a blind hole, but threads must be started with a plug or tapered tap. Taps and dies (for cutting exterior threads) are available in kits along with the special wrenches. The size of a tap is stamped on its shank and is given in three parts: its diameter, the number of threads per inch and the type of threads. The tap should match the bolt for which it is cutting threads.

Tapered tap
This section cuts full-size threads.

This section cuts full-sized threads

Plug tap
This section cuts full-size threads.

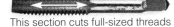

This section cuts full-sized threads

Bottoming tap
This section cuts full-size threads.

This section cuts full-sized threads

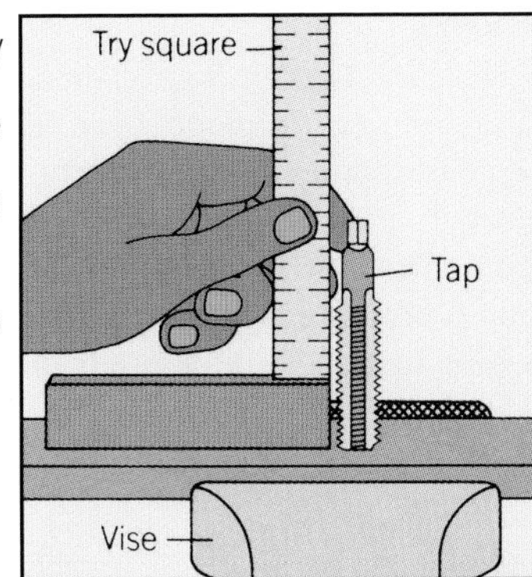

1 Drill hole slightly smaller than tap's diameter. Lubricate threads with cutting fluid. Insert lubricated tap in hole. Check tap against a square to make sure it is straight.

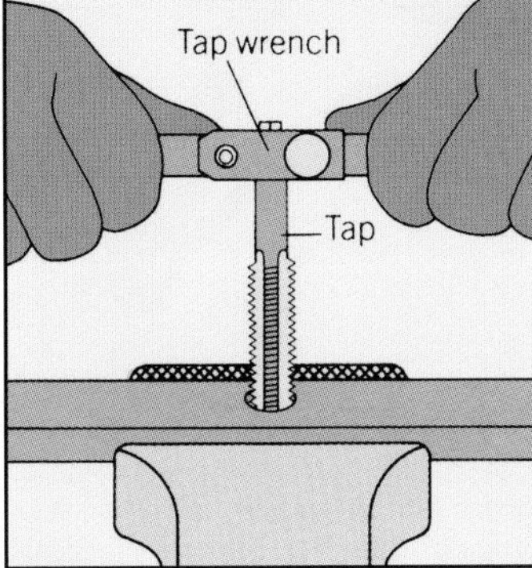

2 Turn tap clockwise, exerting moderate downward pressure. After each turn, back tap out, file burrs from edge, brush away filings and add more lubricant.

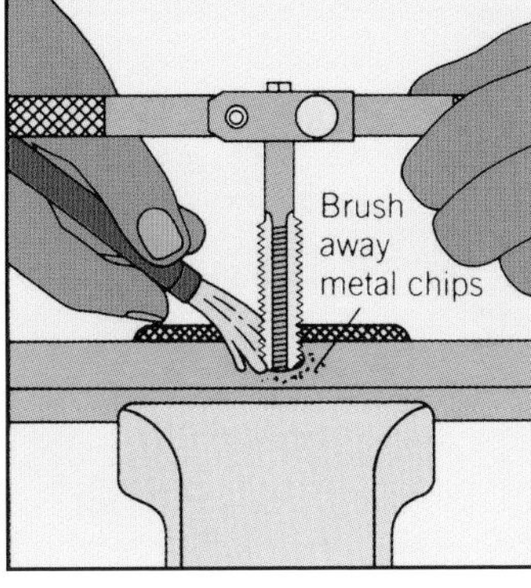

3 Continue turning tap, backing it out and adding lubricant. When threading a blind hole, as you near the bottom, remove tap after each turn or two, and clean out chips.

Bar-type tap wrench

Dies

Bolts and pipes can be threaded, or rethreaded, using a die. The procedure is similar to cutting an internal thread with a tap. A threading die, with sharp internal threads, is fitted over the metal rod or bolt and cuts threads as it's turned. The threads in the die are ground away slightly on one side to make starting easier. Like taps, dies are sized the same as bolts and the size is marked on the die.

In most cases you'll turn the die with a diestock. On some diestocks, the die is simply dropped in and secured by tightening a screw. Other diestocks have guide plates and guide fingers to ensure accuracy.

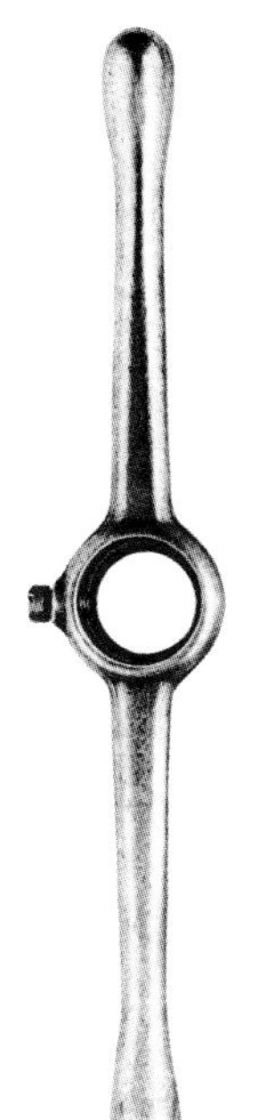

Diestock

An adjustable die has a recessed bolt that can be loosened or tightened to let you cut bolts slightly undersize or oversize.

A solid die, or button die, is the most common type. It can be used on rod or pipe up to 1/2 in. (13 mm) in diameter.

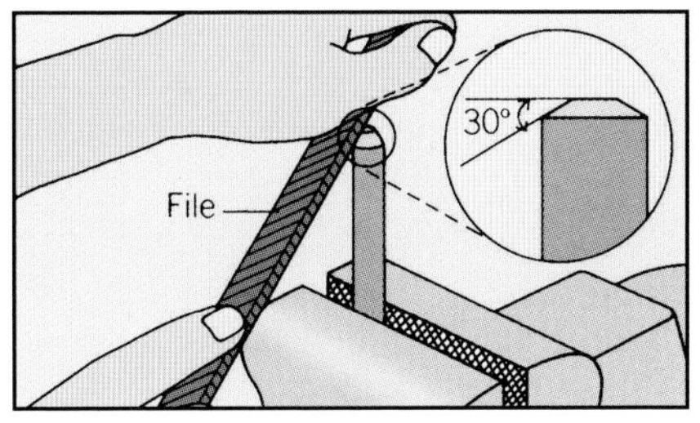

1 Clamp the rod, tubing or old bolt into a vise and mark the place you want the threads to stop. With a file, cut a 30° angle around the top of the stock. This will help get the die started cutting the threads.

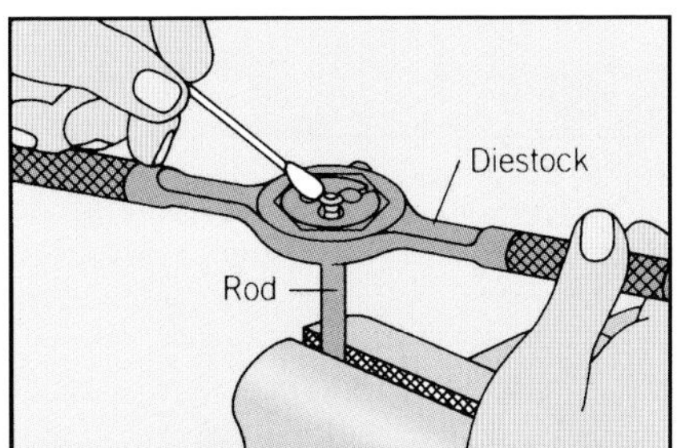

2 Fit the die into the diestock. Position the die over the rod, holding the diestock at a right angle to the rod. Lubricate the die by swabbing on semisolid vegetable shortening or adding cutting fluid.

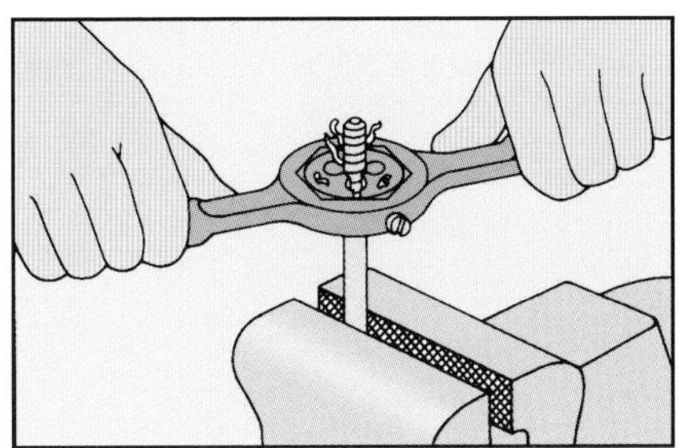

3 Applying downward pressure, turn diestock clockwise one or two turns. Back off, check threads, brush away chips and add more lubricant. Repeat process as needed, but don't apply pressure after first threads are formed.

Fastening Metal

Clamps 34
Drills 50
Drill Presses 53

Bolts

Bolts are generally used by inserting them into slightly oversize holes in the metals being joined, and then securing them with washers and nuts. Taps and dies can be used to join thick metals; even epoxy glues and liquid solder can be used in certain situations.

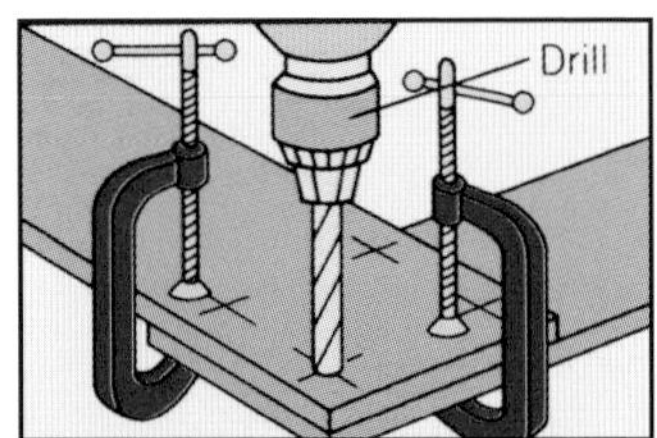

1 Clamp work together firmly and mark positions of all bolts. Drill first hole just large enough to let bolt slip through.

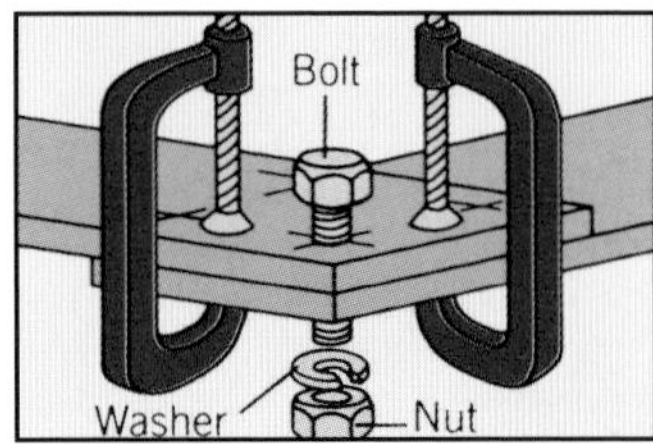

2 Slip bolt into hole, slide on a washer, thread on a nut and tighten. Check alignment of work and reclamp.

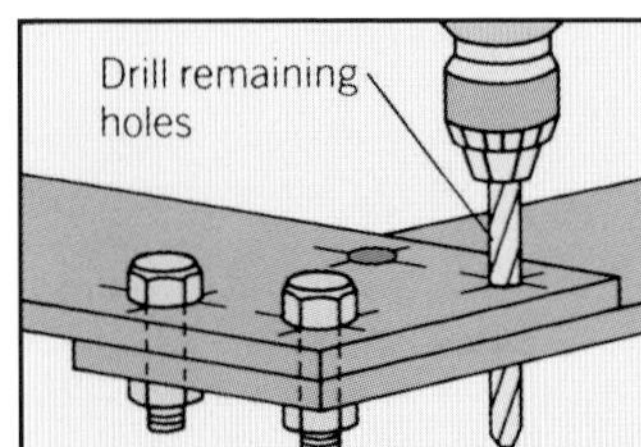

3 Drill second hole. Insert bolt. Add washer and nut to keep work from shifting. Drill remaining holes; add bolts, washers and nuts.

Screws

Self-tapping screws and sheet-metal screws are used to fasten sheets of metal together or attach metal to another material. They cut their own threads as they're driven in. Generally, they pass through slightly oversize holes in the top piece of metal and into smaller pilot holes in the back material.

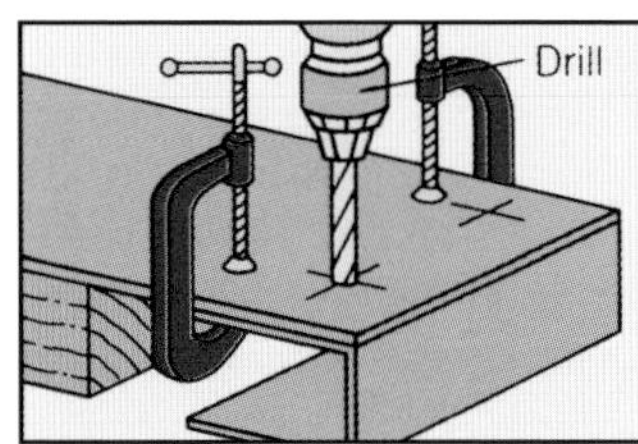

1 Clamp work securely and mark positions of screws. Drill pilot holes slightly smaller than screw shanks through both pieces of metal or through metal and into back material.

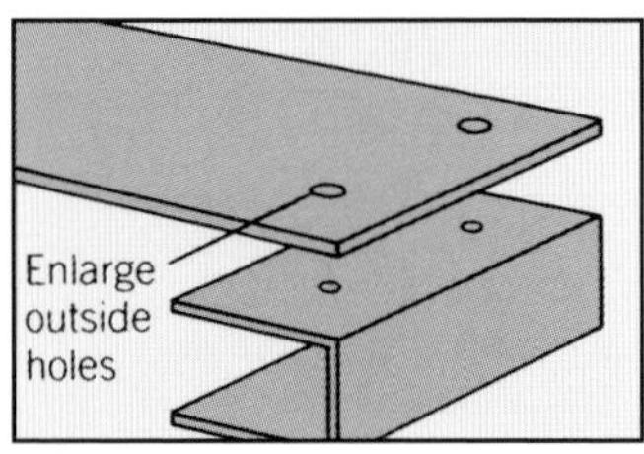

2 Unclamp work and enlarge holes in top piece of metal so screw shank will pass through it easily. Then reclamp work, making sure all holes align.

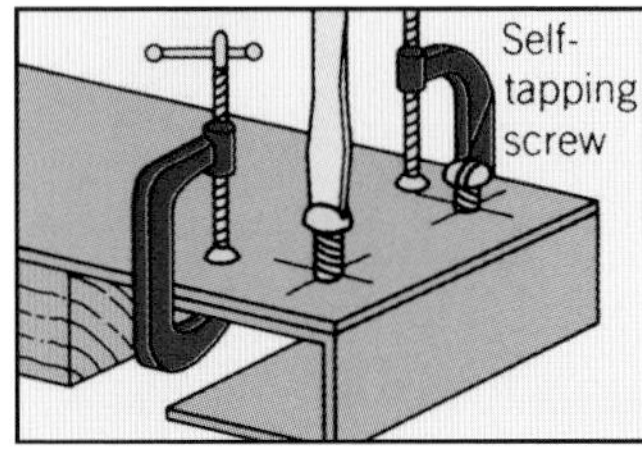

3 Drive in all screws most of the way, then go back and tighten one at a time. Screws will bite into walls of smaller holes in back piece.

Rivets

Rivets are great for repairing everything from gutters to tool belts. There are two basic types: A **solid rivet** is placed through a predrilled hole, then mushroomed over with a hammer or other tool. A **pop, blind or snap rivet** (shown) is also inserted into a predrilled hole, but a special riveting tool mushrooms the end when the handle is squeezed. Select a rivet the right length and diameter, made of the same materials you're joining to avoid a corrosive reaction. Wear eye protection while riveting.

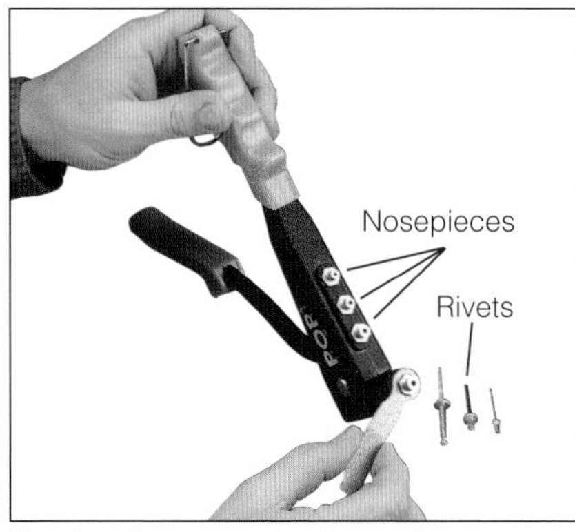

1 Select the correct size rivet and nosepiece for the job. Nosepieces are often stored on the riveter's handle and are easily switched with the supplied wrench.

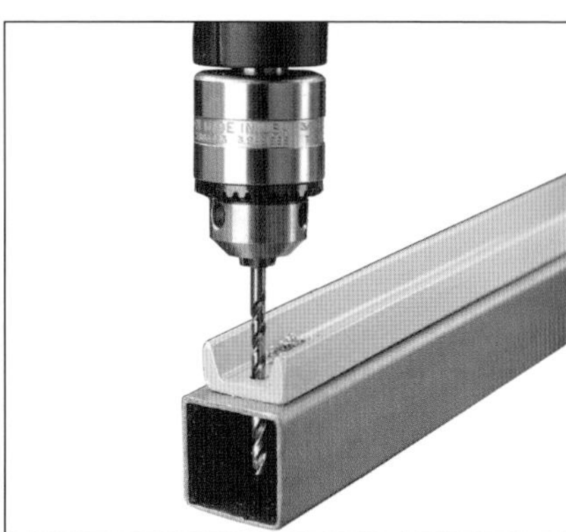

2 Drill a hole the same diameter as the rivet shank. Keep pieces aligned and tight to one another, using clamps or tape, if necessary.

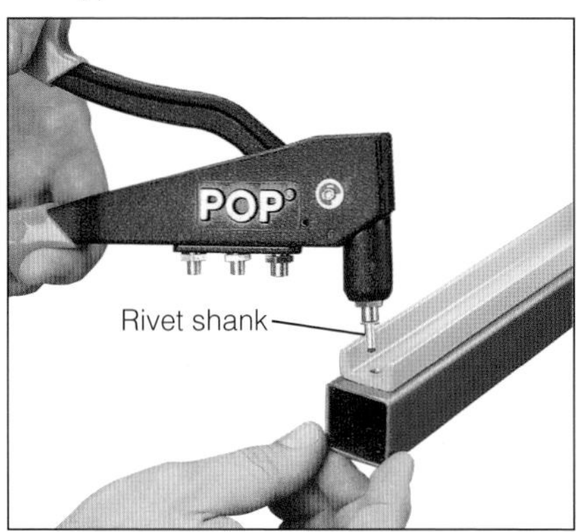

3 Insert rivet's stem into the nosepiece and its shank into the hole. Squeeze handle so the tip is drawn up into the shank, expanding it. The stem will pop off.

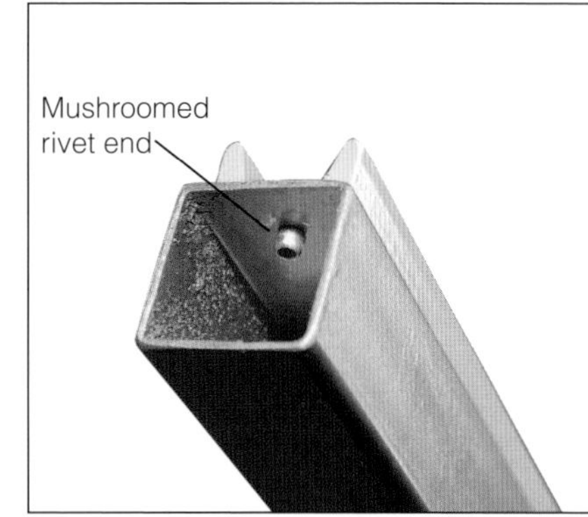

4 A secure connection is made as the two metal pieces are pinched between the rivet head and the expanded or mushroomed end.

Soldering

When repairing electric appliances and electronic components, you'll create stronger, longer-lasting connections when you solder the wires. The slip-on tabs many components use do a good job, but a well-soldered joint is a sure thing.

Making a solid connection involves four basic steps:

1. Clean the two surfaces that will be connected. The best way is to apply paste flux.
2. Make sure the tip of the iron is clean and coated with solder.
3. Heat the connector or tab, not the solder.
4. Touch the solder to the tab and wires and let it flow.

Choosing solder. Soft solder is used for the connections shown. It has a relatively low melting point, making it easy to use. Solder with a rosin core is best. It has flux in it to further help clean and bond the connections. *Never* use acid-core solder for electrical connections. It's designed for plumbing and will corrode small wires.

Safety First

Soldering Dos and Don'ts

Besides keeping an eye out for fire dangers, remember these tips:

- Allow the soldering iron sufficient time to heat up; 3 to 5 minutes is usually sufficient.
- Always heat with the tapered surface of the tip. Trying to heat with the point of the tip is useless.
- Securely wrap the wires through the hole in the connector.
- Place protective material, such as cardboard, under the working area to avoid damaging other components.
- Use a metal stand for the iron when it's heating or not being used. Most tools come with some sort of stand.

Tinning a New Soldering Iron

For best results, you should tin new or pitted soldering irons or those with a dark coating. This allows even heat transfer and prevents oxides from forming on the heated connectors or wires.

1 With the iron unplugged, use a bastard file to dress the copper tip. Remove any old solder or coatings from the tapered surface. You need to get down to the bare copper.

2 Heat the soldering iron and touch the solder to the tip to tin it. A hot iron will cause the solder to flow immediately. Coat the entire cleaned area of the tip. Wipe off any excess with a damp sponge.

Tinning Stranded Wires

Tinned stranded wires make a more solid connection because all of the individual wires will be bunched together under a connecting screw. Bend the wires into the shape needed beforehand; after wires are tinned, you can't bend them without breaking the solder.

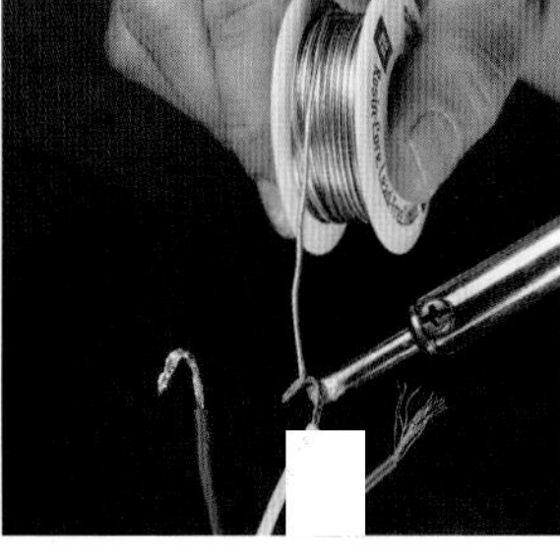

Tightly twist the stranded wires, heat them with the iron and touch the solder to the wires, not the tip. Sufficiently heated wires will melt the solder.

Soldering a Connection

When soldering, remember to always heat the wires and connectors, not the solder. If the solder flows, the connection is hot enough. If not, keep heating. Note: Tabs without holes are designed for slip-on connectors.

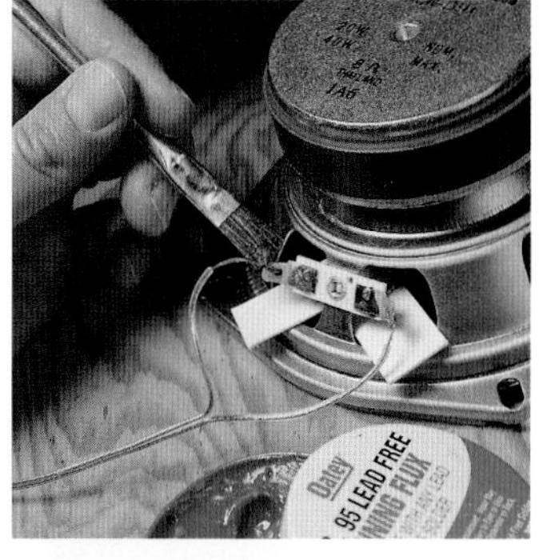

1 After slipping the wires through the hole and bending them around the tab, apply paste flux to the tab and wires.

2 Touch the heated tip of the soldering iron against the tab and wires. Keep the flat surface of the tip against the tab, and then touch the connection with the solder.

3 Solid connections should be shiny, smooth and even. If there are any gaps in the joint, reheat it and apply a bit more solder.

Welding

Drills 50
Lead Paint 288

A wire-feed welder is a portable tool suited for light-duty tasks, such as repairing metal fences, railings, tools and shop equipment. It uses an electric arc to melt both a special wire it feeds and the metals to be joined. The 115-volt units work off standard household electrical current.

For those doing only occasional repairs, rent rather than buy a unit. Note: If you have structural repairs, like the framework on a car or trailer, take the job to an experienced welder.

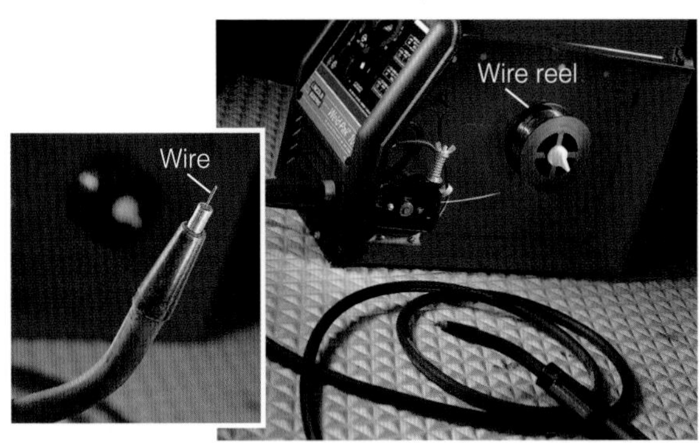

A roll of wire is housed inside the main unit and is fed through the rubber tube to the welding gun tip. Depressing the trigger feeds the wire and sends electrical current to the tip.

Welding Dos and Don'ts

Be sure to read the manufacturer's instructions before going to work, and remember these tips:

- Weld outdoors or in a well-ventilated area; the fumes can be dangerous.
- Keep flammable material away from the work area; never weld on a container that may have contained flammable material.
- Always use a face shield to protect your face from sparks and your eyes from the intense light. Wear heavy leather gloves and a long-sleeved shirt.
- Don't touch the workpiece until it has cooled for 15 to 20 minutes.

Preparing the Surface

Attach a magnet to the metal; if it sticks to the metal, and the metal isn't cast iron, it can probably be welded. Aluminum can be welded but requires special materials. The area to be welded must be free of oil, dirt, paint and rust.

1 If the metal passes the magnet test and nicks easily with a metal file, it should be easy to weld.

2 Clean all paint, dirt, oil or other contaminants from the metal surface using a wire brush or other tool.

Making Repairs

Most wire-feed welders have two setting knobs: one controls the wire-feed rate, the other, the voltage. The thicker the metal you're welding, the faster the feed and higher the heat required. Heat is created when direct current completes a cycle from the main welding unit through the wire that exits the tip of the gun to the object being welded, then back to the unit via a wire that has been clamped to the workpiece.

1 Secure the work clamp to the metal surface as close to the weld area as possible. Move the tip across the area to be welded while pressing the trigger. The tip should be raised slightly above the surface. There should be a snapping and crackling sound as you work. Don't touch the electrode or the metal that you're welding.

2 When the weld is complete, chip any excess metal, called slag, from the workpiece, using a welder's hammer and wire brush.

Painting Metal

Painting metal involves many of the same skills, tools and paints used with wood. The keys are properly preparing the surface and using the right primers and paints. Here are a few tips on painting outdoor metals:

Steel siding. Thoroughly power-wash it using a TSP additive (or TSP substitute). Rinse and let dry for two or three days. There's no need to prime if original paint is firmly adhered. Paint using 100-percent acrylic latex.

Downspouts and gutters. Apply metal primer. Then paint the same way as you would siding.

New galvanized metals. Roof flashings or vents should weather for six months. Apply special galvanized metal primer, then two coats of latex paint.

1 Remove flaking paint using a wire brush or wire brush accessory in a drill. Wear eye and breathing protection.

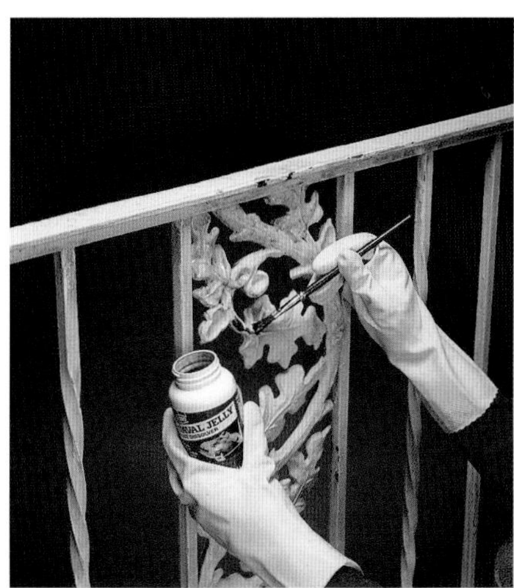

2 Apply a rust dissolver to intricate areas. Let the areas sit for 30 minutes, then spray off with a garden hose.

3 Coat entire railing with a primer. A direct-to-rust primer bonds with any remaining rust, solidifies it and prevents it from spreading. Spray or brush on the final topcoat.

Repairing Dents

Metal is strong, but not indestructible. If you have a dent in thin metal and can reach the opposite side, try pushing it out using the heel of your hand. If the back side is inaccessible, drill a small hole in the dented area, insert a screw, grasp the head with locking pliers and pull straight out. If the dent doesn't come out, tap around the raised border of the dent with a hammer to release the pressure, and then pull again. For repairing large dents, follow these illustrations:

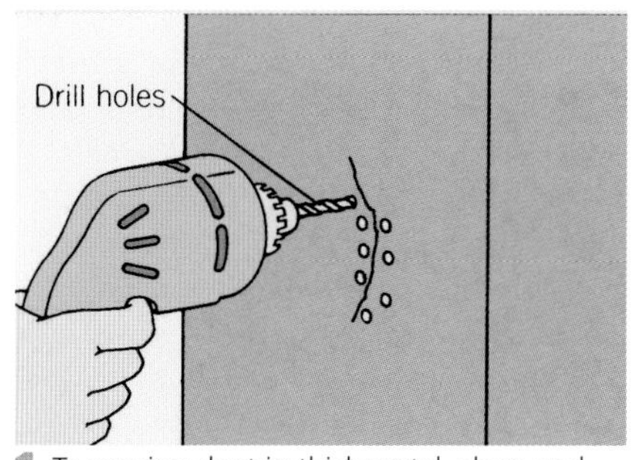

1 To repair a dent in thick metal, clean and sand the metal, and then drill a series of small holes to help anchor some filler.

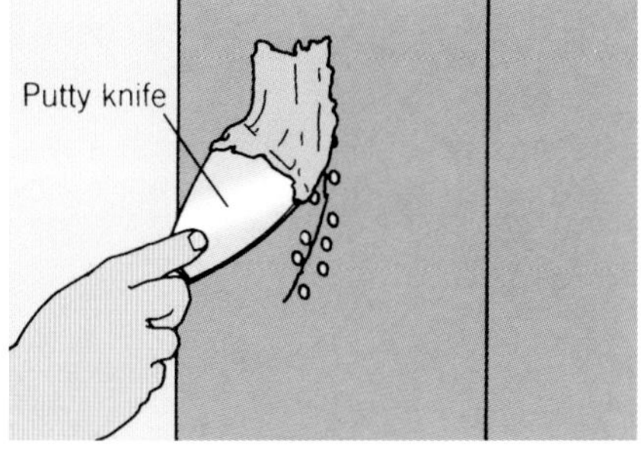

2 Prepare epoxy filler from a fiberglass repair kit. Use a putty knife to fill dent with epoxy, pressing it into holes, mounding it slightly above surface and overlapping the edges of the undented area.

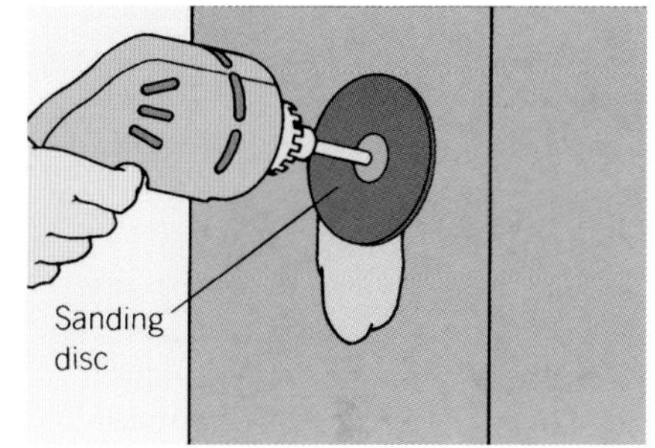

3 Let filler cure completely. Sand even with surrounding surface. Clean and paint the area.

Hammer Away Dents

To remove a small dent, push it out by hand from the opposite side. If that fails, hold dented area against a bag filled with sand, and tap it gently with a mallet until the area smooths out.

Laminate Tops

Circular Saws 56
Tablesaws 62
Routers 66
Belt Sanders 68
Adhesives 85
Installing Laminate Tops 266

Plastic laminate has dozens of uses in the kitchen, in the bathroom, even in the workshop. You can use it to create countertops, tabletops, doors, assembly benches and other areas where a durable, easy-to-clean surface is needed. No sanding, staining or painting is required and you only need a few specialty tools.

Plastic laminate is made with layers of paper and resins pressed together under high temperature and pressure. The top layer of paper gives laminate its color. Since laminate is only about 1/16 in. (1.5 mm) thick, the surface it's mounted to, called the substrate, must be solid. Both particleboard and the more expensive medium-density fiberboard (MDF) work well. Laminate adds significant strength to its substrate. For example, a particleboard shelf with a laminate top, bottom and edge can hold three times the weight of a raw particleboard shelf.

Tools and Materials

You may already own some of the basic tools and supplies required, but you may need to purchase a few specialty items.

Contact cement is the best adhesive. It creates an instant bond and eliminates the need for clamps. A disposable brush and a 9-in. roller cover specially designed for spreading adhesives are all you need for applicators.

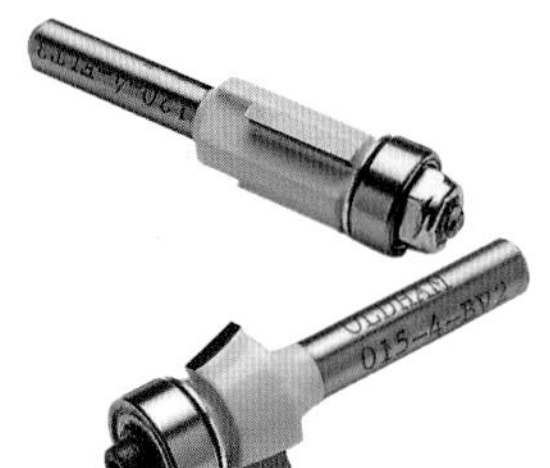

Router bits with roller bearings are the best tools for trimming, both where laminate meets particleboard and where laminate meets laminate along an edge.

Rollers are used to roll the surface of the laminate to ensure a complete adhesive bond with the substrate.

Shop Smart

The Toughest Laminates

One of the simplest ways to check the durability of a laminate is to conduct your own torture test on a sample chip. In general you'll find laminates with solid colors, especially dark colors, are the quickest to show wear and tear. Glossy finishes are also quick to show scratches. Those with mixed colors, matte finishes or slightly textured surfaces tend to show scratches less easily.

Three Ways to Cut Laminate

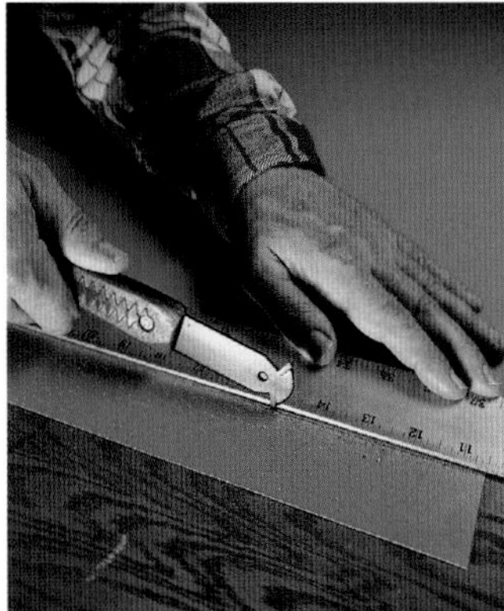

Scoring tool. Make at least four firm passes on the face of the laminate with this carbide-tipped tool to score a deep line. Gradually fold the laminate, pulling up from one end of the score, to make the break.

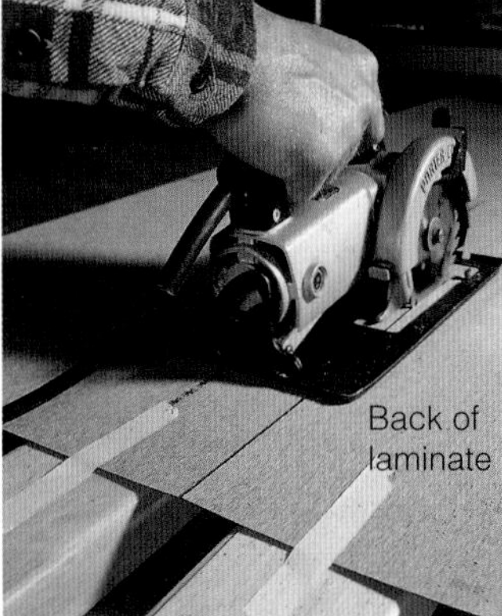

Circular saw. Cut the laminate, face down, with a high-tooth-count carbide blade set at 1/4 in. (6 mm) depth. Support the laminate well with 2x4s and tape it in place. Use a straightedge guide for best results.

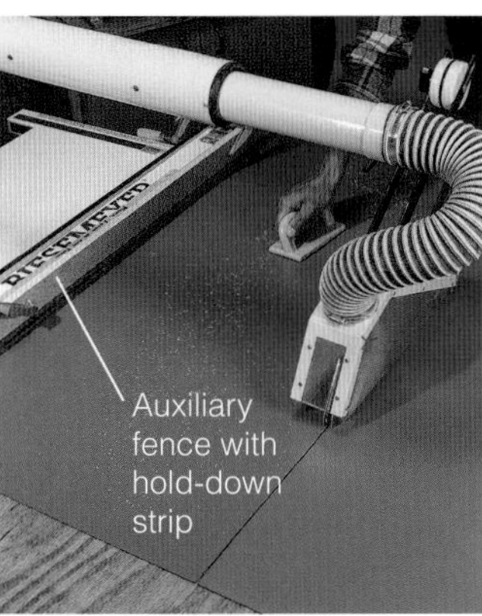

Tablesaw. Cut laminate, good side up, with a high-tooth-count carbide blade. For best results, build a subfence that fits tightly to the top of your tablesaw so the laminate can't slide under the fence. The narrow acrylic strip holds the laminate down while allowing you to still see the fence.

You can order factory-made laminate tops in almost any size, shape and pattern; a few large home centers even stock ready-to-go tops. But if you're the hands-on type, you can create your own custom top in less than a day. The huge variety of laminates available, including metallics, bright colors and faux-stone, opens up a world of possibilities for woodworkers and experienced do-it-yourselfers. Sheets of laminate, up to 5 x 12 ft. in size, can be special ordered through home centers and many lumberyards.

If you tackle this project, remember these tips:

- Make certain your substrate is clean, flat and free of blemishes.
- Contact adhesive, as its name implies, sticks (and sticks instantly) upon contact. Work carefully and use the slip sticks, as shown at right.
- For countertops, always install the vertical surfaces first. That way the horizontal top overlaps and protects the vertical edge from chipping.

Build the Substrate

Glue and clamp buildup strips to substrate's bottom edge. Apply glue, position the strips, tack them in place and clamp.

Applying Edges

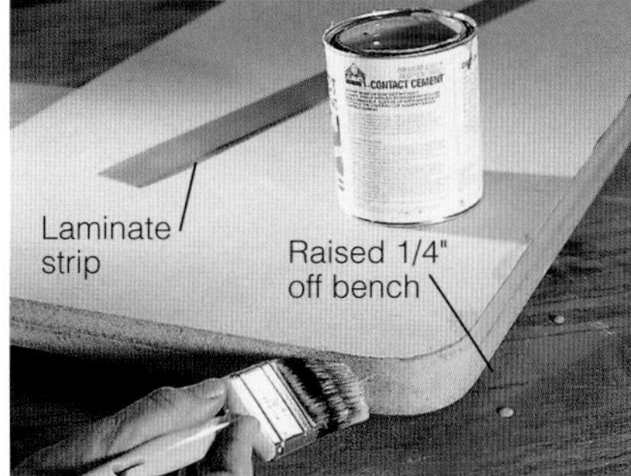

1 Brush on contact cement; porous particleboard edges may require a second coat after the first dries. Apply cement to laminate strips.

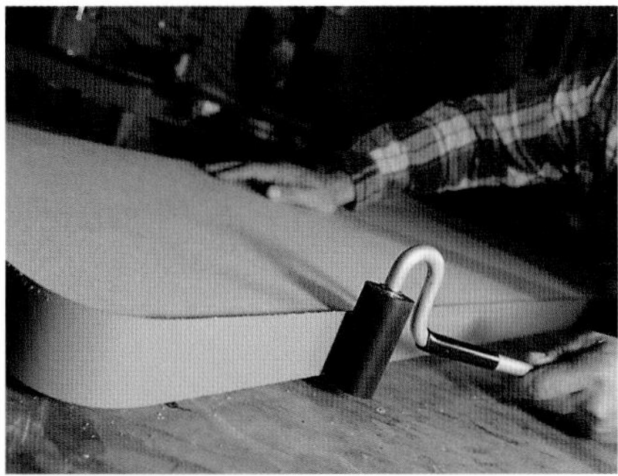

2 Roll the surface of the laminate to ensure a good bond. On curves, use a heat gun to soften the laminate as you press it into place.

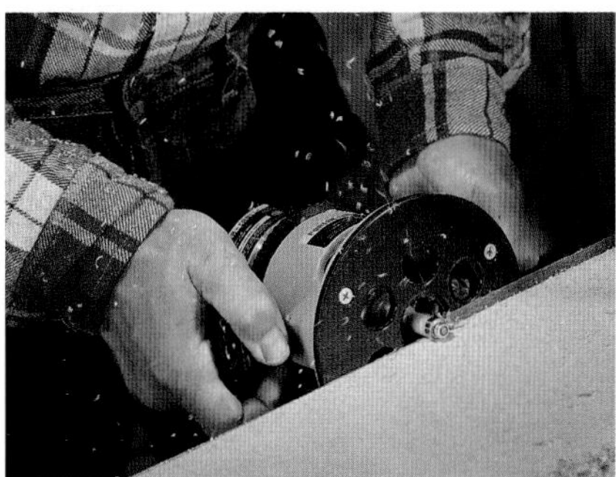

3 Trim the top and bottom edges flush using a laminate flush-trim bit. Keep the router perfectly perpendicular to avoid uneven edges.

Installing the Top

1 Roll contact cement onto the substrate and the back of the plastic laminate. Let it dry on both surfaces before assembly.

2 Use slip sticks to separate laminate from substrate. Start in middle and remove sticks, pushing down as you work toward edges.

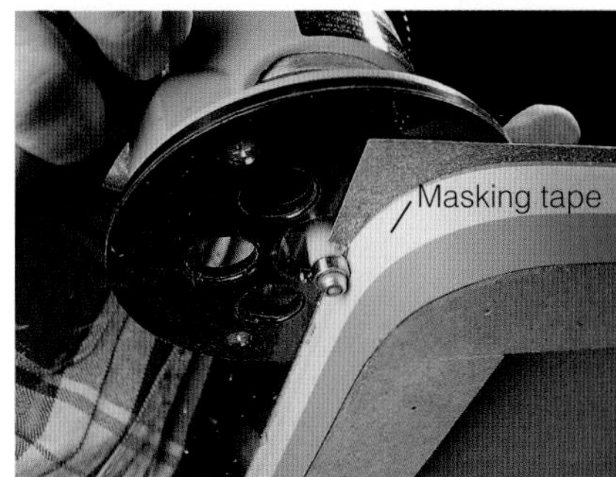

3 Trim laminate flush with substrate. Masking tape protects laminate from possible damage. Ease the edge using a bevel-trim bit.

Wood-edge Tops

A wood-edge top not only looks great but is easier to make and holds up better than laminate edges. Prepare the substrate, then cut and glue 3/4-in. x 1-1/2-in.-hardwood strips along the edges. Miter the corners and slightly round them if they are sharp.

1 Sand the wood edge flush with the substrate. Clean the top and apply contact cement to top and laminate.

2 Apply laminate top, then use a chamfer bit to shape the top edge of the countertop. A 25° to 30° bevel looks best.

Solid-Surface Materials

Circular Saws 56
Adhesives 84
Selecting Countertops 267

Solid-surface materials are a blend of acrylics, polyesters and fillers that have been tinted and textured to resemble everything from earthy granites to elegant marbles. Dozens of manufacturers offer materials in hundreds of colors and designs.

Since shaping the material and creating invisible, durable seams requires special tools and skills, most solid-surface materials are installed only by trained professionals. However, there are a growing number of exceptions. Some 1/4-in.-thick solid-surface shower surrounds, as shown at right, and bathroom vanity tops are available for do-it-yourself installation. Some companies (check the Internet) will sell homeowners the raw materials, but be aware that most manufacturers will not warranty tops that aren't installed by a certified installer.

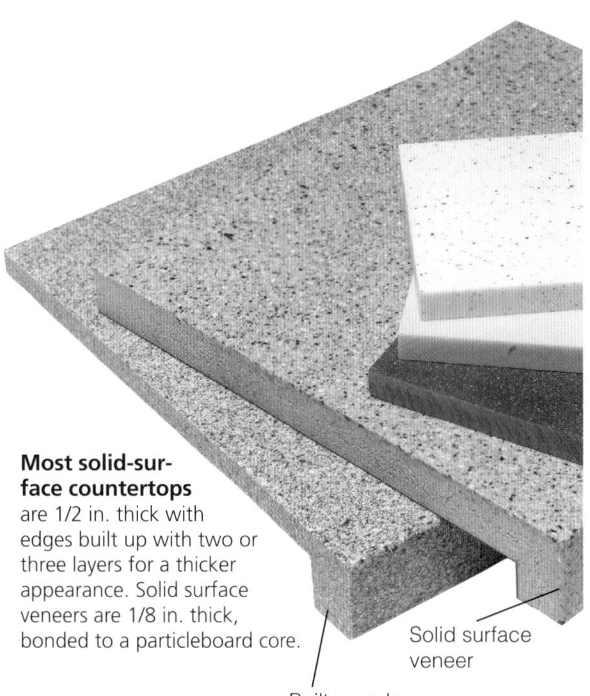

Most solid-surface countertops are 1/2 in. thick with edges built up with two or three layers for a thicker appearance. Solid surface veneers are 1/8 in. thick, bonded to a particleboard core.

Working Tips

The 1/4-in.-thick shower surround material shown below should be handled carefully, as you would a sheet of glass. Fully support it while moving it. Cut and drill it only on a flat, well-supported surface. When cutting, wear a dust mask. Cut outdoors if possible.

Always dry fit each piece before gluing it into place. Use moldings at the corners to cover gaps from uneven walls and cuts. Less-expensive cultured-marble surrounds can be installed the same basic way.

Cutting and shaping can be done using a circular saw with masonry blade and a belt sander. Cut good side up. Prevent scratches by covering the bases of your saws with duct tape.

Making templates of cardboard for walls containing valves or spouts is cheap insurance when handling an expensive product. Use the template to transfer hole locations onto the solid-surface material.

Attaching panels is best done with a combination of pure silicone and hot-melt glue, which holds the panel in place until the silicone sets. Apply thin beads of silicone around the perimeter and small blobs every 12 in. (30 cm).

Sealing the inside corners and corner moldings with 100-percent silicone sealant ensures a long-lasting installation. Seal around faucets, spouts and their trim pieces, too.

Renewing Cultured Marble Tops

Cultured marble countertops can be renewed using the same tools and techniques used to spiff up fiberglass. First wet sand with 1,000-grit paper to remove shallow scratches and surface stains. Don't sand too deep; you don't want to go through the top gel coat. Buff using a very light abrasive cleaning powder, available at auto parts stores. Protect the restored finish with a specialty cultured-marble polish.

Healthy Home & Emergency Repairs

Hazardous Materials

Cordless Tools 60
Lead Paint 288
Chimney Cleaning 333
Indoor Pollutants 482

Lurking Dangers?

Your home may be your sanctuary, but you may be sharing it with a host of hazardous building materials. Keep an eye out for the products listed below. (Note: All dates are approximate.) When in doubt about a particular building material, call a pro. Check your Yellow Pages under "Home and Building Inspection" and "Inspection Services."

Aluminum wiring is dull gray in color with "Aluminum" or "AL" stamped on the wire's plastic jacket. Installed in homes between 1965 and 1973. Wire shrinks and swells, loosening splices, outlet and switch connections, which can lead to increased risk of fire. Repairs can be made using special products and techniques but should be performed only by a licensed electrician.

Asbestos ceiling and wall covering products. Asbestos was used in sprayed and troweled coatings (1935 to 1978), surface and joint compounds (1930 to 1978) and in some vinyl wallpapers (exact dates unknown). Fibers can be released through cutting, sanding, water damage, impact and deterioration causing lung damage.

Asbestos flooring materials. Asbestos was used in vinyl-type tiles (1950 to 1980), asphalt-based tile (1920 to 1980), resilient sheet flooring (1950 to 1980) and mastic adhesives (1945 to 1980). Fibers can be released through sanding, scraping or cutting. Often it's best to leave material undisturbed and install new floor covering over it.

Asbestos pipe wrap was used extensively from about 1925 to 1975 and can be either corrugated or preformed. It contains a high percentage of asbestos. Fibers can be released through damage, cutting or deterioration.

Asbestos roofing and siding. Asbestos was used in roofing felts (1910 to recently), roofing and siding shingles (to present) and clapboards (1944 to 1945).

Formaldehyde, used in particleboard, plywood, some foam insulations and other products, can be an irritant to eyes, nose and throat. Some people are allergic to it and have strong reactions. It eventually dissipates, but the best solution in newer homes and projects is to use alternative products or ventilate well with outside air.

Lead paint is in most homes built before 1950; those built between 1950 and 1978 may or may not. Primary danger is posed by ingesting or inhaling dust or chips. The paint affects nerves and internal organs particularly in children, pregnant women and the unborn. Flawless paint can be encapsulated (painted over). For information on removal, check Resources, p. 516.

Vermiculite insulation, usually small, shiny and light brown in appearance, was installed in nearly one million homes. Much, but not all, of this type of insulation contains asbestos. If it's sealed tightly in walls or isolated in an unfinished attic, it may be best simply to leave it alone. If renovations involve disturbing it, contact a certified professional.

Dispose of It Safely

A typical home contains 100 to 200 products and chemicals for cleaning, painting, lubricating, fertilizing and home improving. Listed below are recommended procedures for safely disposing of some of those products containing hazardous substances.

There are a few steps you can take to keep the disposal problem to a minimum in the first place: Look for less hazardous products, buy just enough of a product to do the job and keep leftover products in their original containers so you can refer to the directions for proper disposal.

Many communities have hazardous waste disposal centers or designated days when hazardous waste is collected curbside. Check with local officials for more details.

Car, boat and other wet-cell batteries contain sulfuric acid and lead. Most outlets that sell new batteries will recycle old ones.

Rechargeable batteries, including those found in cordless tools, laptops, digital cameras and cellular phones, can contain nickel cadmium, nickel metal hydride and other hazardous constituents. Many retailers including The Home Depot, Target, RadioShack, WalMart, Best Buy, Batteries Plus, Rona and Home Hardware have drop-off centers.

Fluorescent bulbs can contain mercury. Dispose of spent bulbs using your community's hazardous-waste disposal facility.

Motor oil contains heavy metals which can cause nerve and kidney damage and hydrocarbons that may be carcinogenic. Never throw it in the trash or burn it. Take it to the used-motor-oil collection center found at most full-service oil change centers or service stations.

Paints, particularly those that are oil based, contain solvents that can be an irritant to you and the environment. When possible, use up the paint or give it away. If it's totally dried in the can, place it in the household trash; if not, bring it to a hazardous-waste collection center.

Treated lumber should never be burned. Bury it, reuse it or dispose of it in a sanitary landfill.

Weed killers, paint strippers and other hazardous household chemicals should be disposed of using your community's hazardous-waste disposal facility.

Fire Safety

Most fires are unexpected because they're caused by ordinary, everyday items and situations normally considered safe. What makes them dangerous are mental lapses, poor judgment, hurried actions and simple carelessness. Here's a rundown of the seven most common causes of preventable fires and steps you can take to keep them from starting.

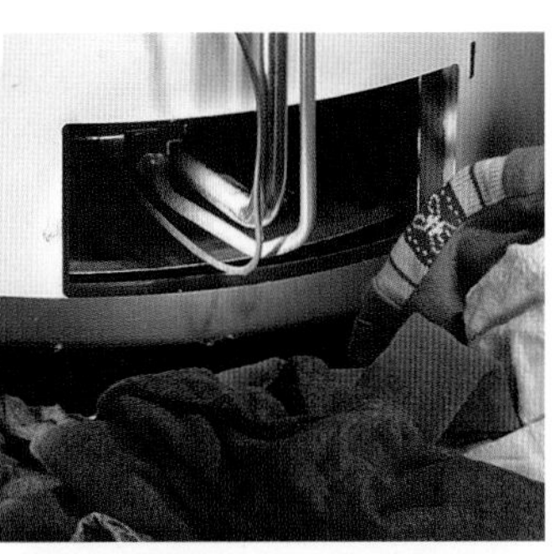

Appliances, more specifically lint in dryers and combustibles near gas water heaters, can spark a fire. Keep dryer and duct free of lint and keep combustibles at least 3 ft. (1 m) from water heaters.

Cooking fires occur most commonly on the cooktop in the first 15 minutes of cooking. Keep curtains, packaging and other combustibles 3 ft. (1 m) away. If a pan catches fire, slip a lid over the top; carrying it outside can leave a trail of dripping, flaming grease.

Smoking kills more people than any other cause because the fires usually start when occupants are asleep. Never smoke in bed and use large ashtrays on tables.

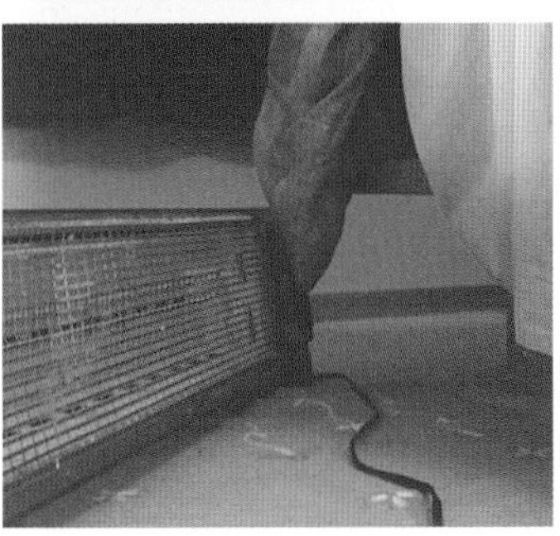

Heating equipment, particularly wood stoves and space heaters, can ignite nearby combustibles. Keep drapes, bedding and other flammables 3 ft. (1 m) away. Plug heaters directly into outlets, not extension cords.

Candles, particularly unattended ones, can easily ignite nearby combustibles. Use tip-proof containers and keep combustibles 3 ft. (1 m) away.

Electrical fires can be caused by overloaded extension cords, hidden electrical shorts, bad connections, and oversize bulbs in fixtures. Replace frayed and undersized cords and call an electrician to track down recurring problems.

Kids playing with fire start 5 percent of residential fires; children are also the most likely to die from those fires. Store matches and lighters up high, well out of reach.

A Word on Fire Extinguishers

Use a fire extinguisher *only* on a fire confined to a small area, after you've evacuated the house and called the fire department. Keep extinguishers away from possible fire sources and near exits so you can easily escape. Locate fire extinguishers in kitchens, garages and other rooms that present fire hazards.

Spontaneous Combustion

A pile of oil-soaked rags can generate enough heat as they dry to spontaneously catch on fire. For safety, spread out rags containing linseed, tung and other oils one layer thick so air can circulate around them and heat can dissipate.

Fireplaces and Chimneys

Ashes can smolder for up to two weeks. Empty them into a covered steel container and store it outside away from combustibles for several weeks. Have your chimney inspected and cleaned annually.

Indoor Pollutants

Lead Paint **288**
Radon Mitigation **483**

Most indoor pollutants are microscopic, which makes them hard to detect, but easily able to infiltrate our bodies. They can cause symptoms such as sore throats, headaches, infectious diseases and worse. Detailed information on controlling these pollutants can be obtained through your local public health department, Health Canada or regional EPA office.

Biologicals include the pollen, spores and dust mites shown below. Control the latter two by eliminating standing water and maintaining relative humidity between 40 and 60 percent.

Insecticide dust can easily drift, or be tracked, into a house. Minimize insecticide use and don't store it in the house.

Lead in dust and fumes can enter lungs first, then the entire body. Test paint before removing it to see if it's lead based. See p. 288 for more detailed information.

Asbestos fibers can lodge in lungs and cause scarring and cancer. Leave asbestos insulation alone. Have testing or removal done by professionals.

Tobacco smoke can contain any of 4,700 different compounds, gases and particles. Stop smoking and stay away from second-hand smoke.

Combustion particles from wood and refined fuels can cause irritations, diseases and cancers. Vent all combustion devices outside.

Organic compounds in household products, including paints and solvents, can be absorbed into your body. Limit your contact, work in a well-ventilated area and keep containers tightly closed.

Radon is a naturally-occurring radioactive gas that creates dangerous particles as it breaks down. Test your house for radon and take steps to reduce it, if necessary.

Formaldehyde is used in manufacturing particleboard, plywood and other building products, and is an irritant to some people. Ventilate well or use alternative products.

Carbon monoxide and nitrogen dioxide, which are odorless, colorless gases, can rob the body of oxygen leading to dizziness, headaches, even death. Make sure fumes from all appliances go up a chimney or out a vent.

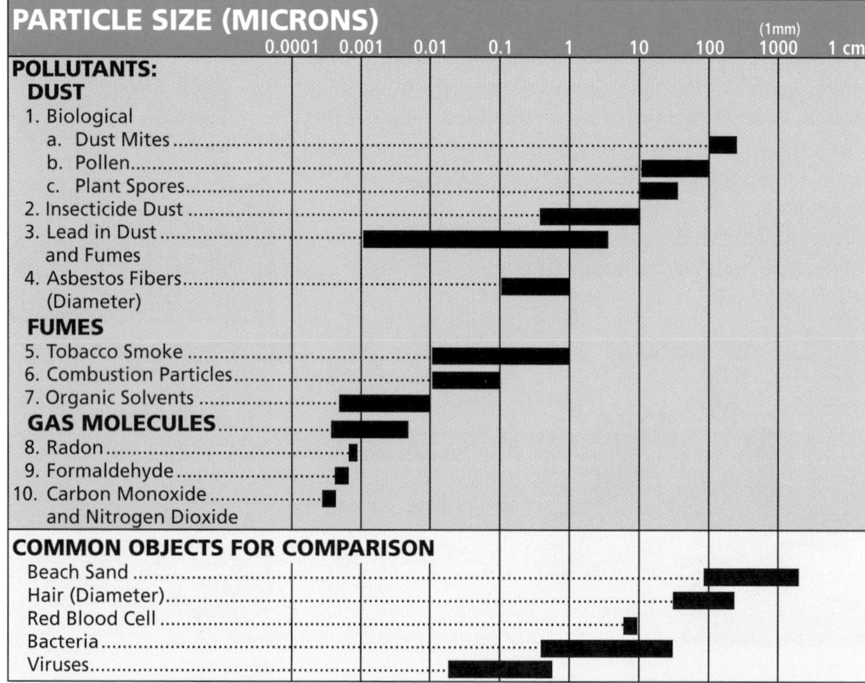

Note: The top scale of the chart indicates "microns," one-thousandth of a millimeter. The letter "o" on this page is about one millimeter wide, so you'd need about 1,000 particles of insecticide dust to span its width. Each vertical line represents a particle size 10 times greater (or less) than the adjacent one. Pollens, for example, are 5 lines away from gas molecules, so pollen is about 100,000 times larger. This smallness makes gases hard to detect and they infiltrate our bodies easily.

Spores are tiny seeds released by the thousands by fungi and mold.

Pollen is released by flowering plants. This chickweed pollen is a common nose and throat irritant.

Asbestos fibers, about the width of a human hair, can fragment into even smaller fibers that can lodge in lungs.

Dust mites scrounge through bedding and carpets, consuming tiny flakes of dead skin. They're the size of a fine grain of sand and live by the thousands in our homes.

Radon

Radon is a naturally occurring radioactive gas that, upon reaching high enough levels, can increase your risk of getting lung cancer. This colorless, odorless gas can seep into your home through cracks and gaps in the foundation or crawl space or in gaps around a sump pump.

Radon levels can be tested using either a home test kit or a professional testing service. If you discover very high levels of radon (4 picoCuries per liter or higher), it may be best to hire a certified professional radon mitigator. They'll take steps including sealing holes and cracks in basements, placing gas-tight seals over sump-pump basins and pouring concrete over dirt floors and crawl spaces. These are tasks many homeowners can do, but bear in mind that some practices, if applied incorrectly, can actually increase radon levels. Conduct a second test after work is complete to check for sufficient reduction.

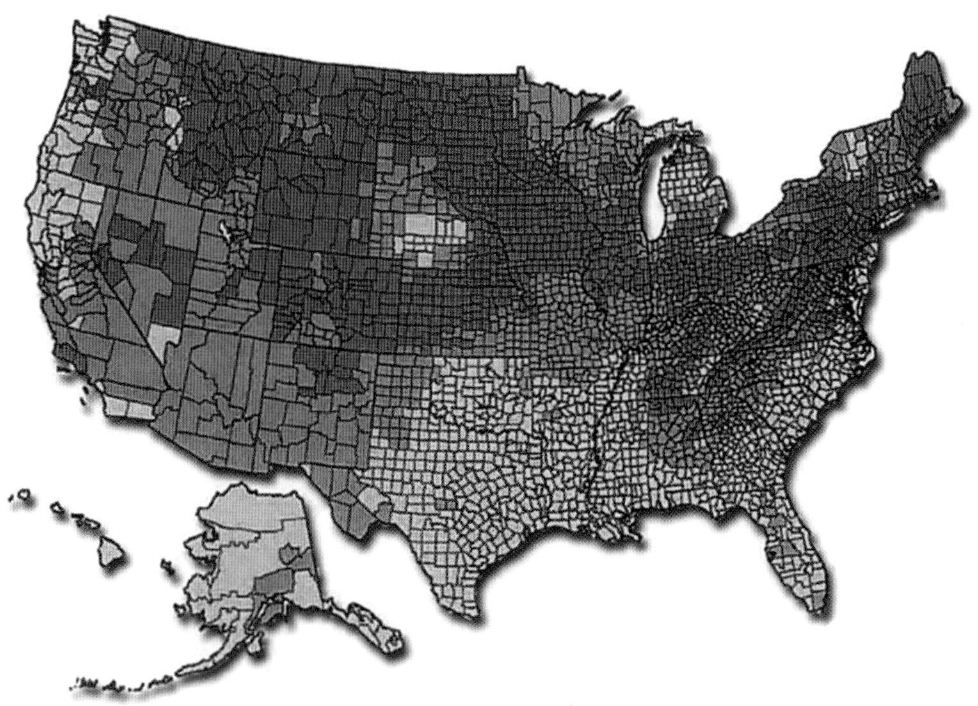

Legend

- **Zone 1** Potential exists for dangerous levels of radon
- **Zone 2** Potential for moderate levels of radon
- **Zone 3** Predicted low levels of radon

See Resources on p. 516 for information on radon levels in Canada.

Testing for Harmful Substances

There is a wide array of in-home test kits homeowners can purchase for checking for the presence of harmful substances in and around the home. In some cases, swabs or samples are taken and sent to a laboratory for further analysis. In other cases the presence of the substance is revealed by a change, usually in color, of some indicator.

There are kits available that will test for the presence of mold, asbestos, lead paint, pesticides in water, lead in water, radon and more.

Bear in mind that test kits can produce false negatives (the hazard is present but the test doesn't indicate so) and false positives (the test indicates the hazard is present, but, in reality, it isn't).

The best approach is to use the results of these test kits as a preliminary step to more thorough investigation and testing.

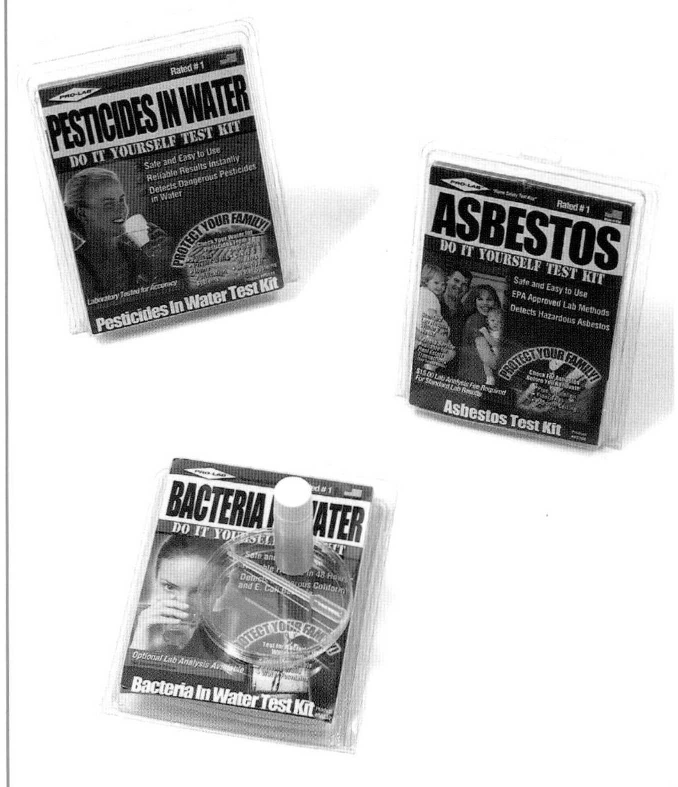

Insect Control

Chimney Repairs 332
Adding Garage Door Weather Seals 396

When insects invade a house, they also invade your peace of mind. Some physically damage a house and its contents, while others are simply unwanted pests.

Some solutions involve the use of insecticides. Be sure you use them carefully and in the right doses—what's toxic for bugs can also be toxic for humans. Always follow the guidelines on the container and avoid using insecticides near children and pregnant women. Try to avoid using products with the warning "Danger." And if you use an insecticide indoors, make sure it's labeled for indoor use.

Carpenter Ants

Carpenter ants are attracted by wet wood, so correcting moisture problems in the home is part of the long-term solution. Cut back tree branches contacting the house and remove wet piles of wood near the foundation. If you locate the working ants—they're large and black with a pronounced waist—find the nest and apply insecticide directly. Severe infestations may require professional help.

Wasps

Watch the wasps to see where they go—it will be to either a nest or a hole in the ground. Spray the nest or hole with an aerosol wasp and hornet killer. Most shoot a stream of quick-acting insecticide up to 30 ft. (10 m).

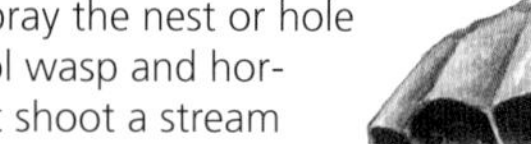

Ants

The best way to control ants is to kill them in their nest. Look for a trail or pattern in their appearance. If you locate the nest outdoors, apply an ant insecticide directly to it. If it's inside a wall, you can drill small holes and squirt an insecticide or boric acid dust into the cavities. If you can't find the nest, use one of the ant baits on the market.

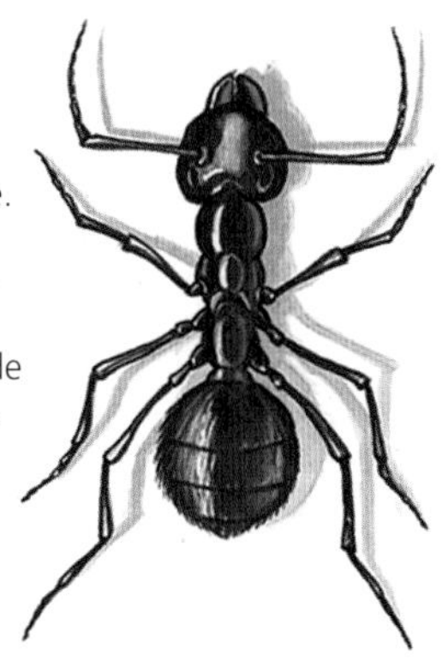

Roaches

Begin by cleaning up every speck of food from shelves, drawers, under appliances and under the sink. Store any accessible food in plastic containers. Fix leaky sinks and drains to remove the roaches' water supply. Then place sealed bait containers or boric acid pesticide powder (read the instructions carefully) around active areas. Avoid using spray insecticides, especially in kitchen areas.

Meal Moths

Meal moths get into dry food like flour, cornmeal, beans, birdseed and dog food. You can toss out the affected stuff, freeze it for four days or heat it in a 130° F (55° C) oven for 30 minutes. In the future, store food in glass or sturdy plastic containers with lids.

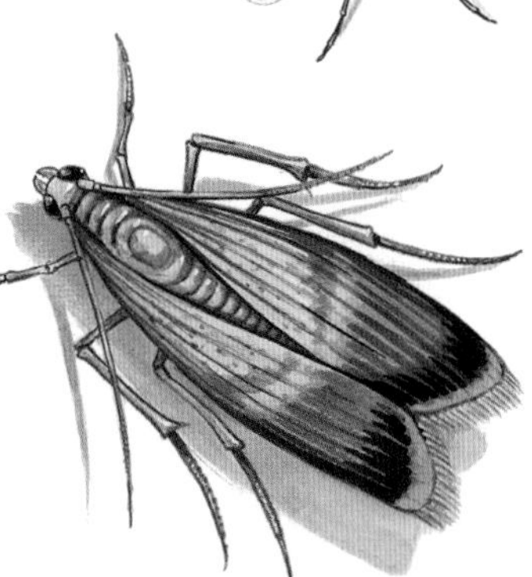

Termites

It's estimated that termites cause more than one billion dollars a year in structural damage. If you suspect you have termites, don't fool around—call a state-certified pest management professional to inspect your home.

Signs of termite activity include mud tubes (far right) leading from the soil to wood parts of the house closest to the ground, swarms of flying termites and hollowed wood near the ground in which you can poke a screwdriver.

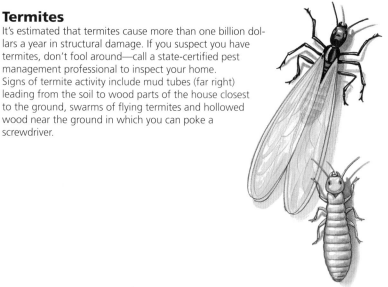

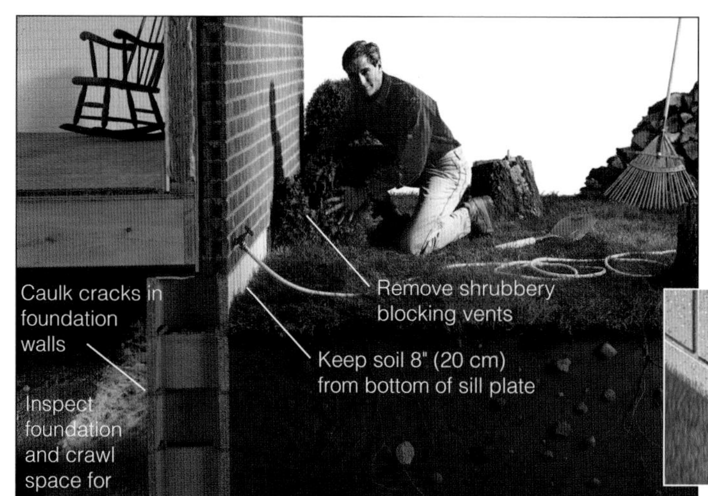

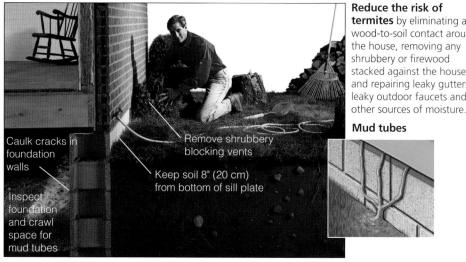

Caulk cracks in foundation walls
Inspect foundation and crawl space for mud tubes
Remove shrubbery blocking vents
Keep soil 8" (20 cm) from bottom of sill plate

Reduce the risk of termites by eliminating all wood-to-soil contact around the house, removing any shrubbery or firewood stacked against the house and repairing leaky gutters, leaky outdoor faucets and other sources of moisture.

Mud tubes

Critter Control

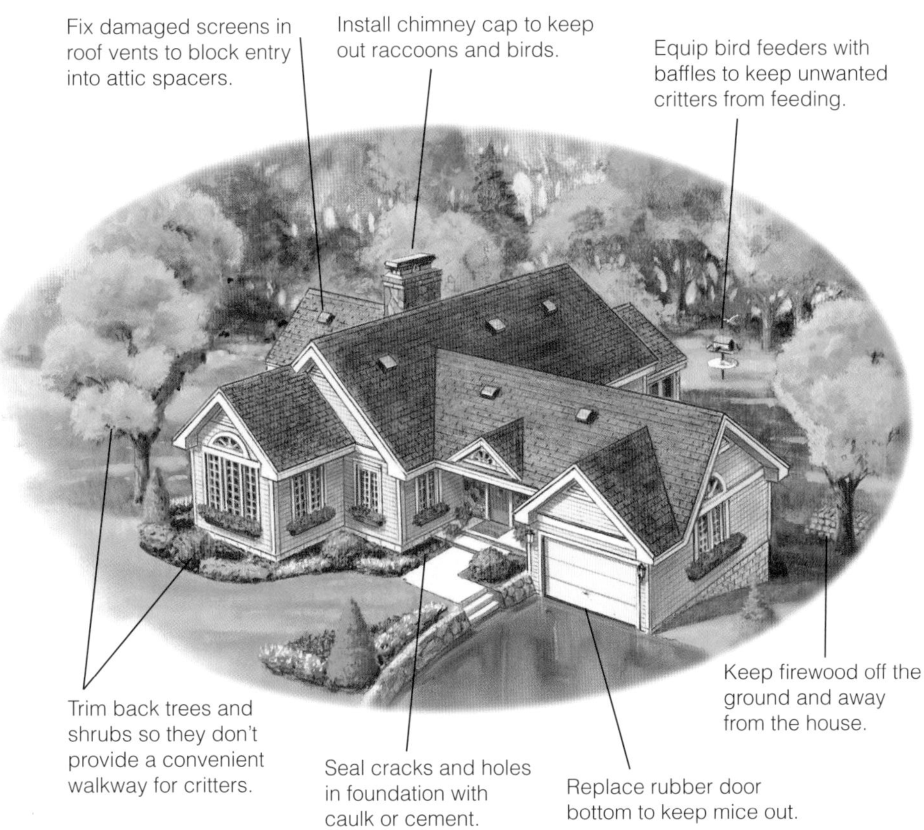
Fix damaged screens in roof vents to block entry into attic spacers.
Install chimney cap to keep out raccoons and birds.
Equip bird feeders with baffles to keep unwanted critters from feeding.
Trim back trees and shrubs so they don't provide a convenient walkway for critters.
Seal cracks and holes in foundation with caulk or cement.
Replace rubber door bottom to keep mice out.
Keep firewood off the ground and away from the house.

Furry Critters

Mice, squirrels, raccoons and bats are the most common fur-covered pests that invade our homes. They really don't mean any harm; they're just looking for food, water and shelter. Some evictions, such as removing a raccoon from a chimney or dealing with skunks, are best handled by the pros. Other tasks, like getting a bat out of your house, can be as simple as opening a window until it finds its way out. (It wants out as badly as you want it out!)

The illustration above gives more specific ideas for keeping critters out.

Mousetraps work best when set in pairs—side-to-side or back-to-back. Use chocolate or nut meat as bait. If you catch a mouse, dispose of it and reuse the trap; the scent of the first mouse will attract others.

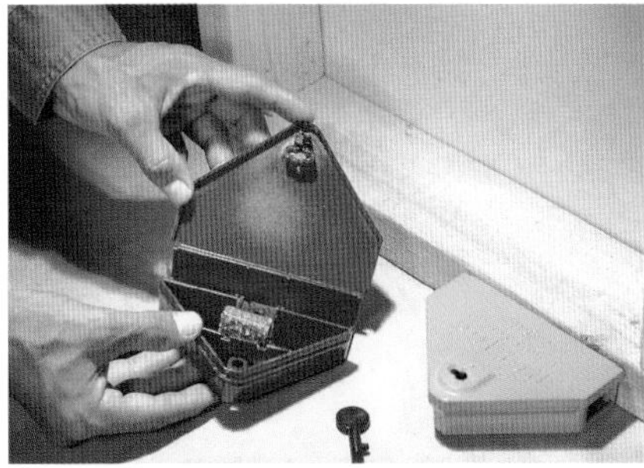

Bait stations are effective, but the poisoned animals crawl off and die somewhere, usually in your house. Use bait stations that lock and keep them away from kids and pets.

Live traps are ideal for capturing squirrels in the attic. Release any captives outside immediately and wear heavy gloves to avoid being scratched or bitten.

Moles

Moles thrive on the grubs, worms and insects that lie just below the surface of your lawn. Methods of eradication range from placing poisonous bait and smoke bombs in their tunnels to eliminating them with choke-type or spear-type traps (below). Other techniques include compacting the soil, installing vibration devices or applying chemicals to drive moles away.

Deer

Deer can be incredibly persistent. You can try using sprays and other repellents or planting plants, like spirea and potentilla, which deer don't like. The surest solution is to build a fence 8 ft. (2.5 m) tall (yes, they can jump that high) or to put a screen over a lower fence. Home remedies range from hanging bars of scented soap around the yard to sprinkling dog hair around the garden.

Dealing with Mold

Insulating Crawl Spaces 167
Replace a Bathroom Fan 170
Energy Recovery Ventilator 171
Basement Moisture 272
Flashing and Vents 322
Installing Gutters 328

Mold Infestations

Mold and mildew need only a damp, moist environment and organic material to establish themselves and thrive. Roof and foundation leaks, high interior humidity, leaky plumbing and flooding are common sources of moisture. Fix the moisture problem before attacking the mold. The organic materials mold and mildew commonly attack are drywall backing, wallpaper, carpet backing, household dust and wood products. A few types of mold are highly toxic. If you have an allergic reaction or a heavy infestation, call your local health department and ask for mold-testing advice. Wear proper safety equipment as you work.

1 Seal room and duct openings with tape and plastic sheeting. Remove carpet by first wetting it with a pump sprayer to control the spread of spores. Cut carpet and pad into small sections, roll them, wrap them in 6-mil plastic and dispose of them.

2 Increase ventilation by using a fan in a window. Remove baseboard and trim from contaminated areas. Remove heavily stained drywall, plaster and insulation. Mist drywall and insulation with pump sprayer. Double bag moldy material.

3 Vacuum up moldy debris with wet/dry vacuum. Keep vacuum outside to avoid spore spread. If necessary, buy an extra length of hose for the vacuum. When done, clean the vacuum with a mildew-cleaning mixture.

4 Scrub surface mold stains from wall cavities and floor with mildew-cleaning mixture. Use a soft brush and work until signs of mold disappear. Wipe, but do not rinse these surfaces. Replace any rotted wood.

5 Allow surfaces to dry completely. Then seal all previously infested areas with pigmented shellac, oil-based primer or latex primer containing mildewcide. Install new insulation, vapor barrier and drywall.

Surface Mold

Surface mold grows in any damp location, such as bathroom walls and corners of a tiled shower. Scrub away surface mold with mildew cleaner. Standard detergent, like dish soap, is also effective. Even for simple cleaning, protect yourself from contact with mold and cleaning products by wearing a long-sleeved shirt, long pants, rubber gloves and goggles.

Scrub surface mold with mildew cleaner or standard detergent. If mold is still visible, reapply mixture and let sit; then lightly scrub again. Seal clean, dry surfaces with grout sealer or paint containing mildewcide.

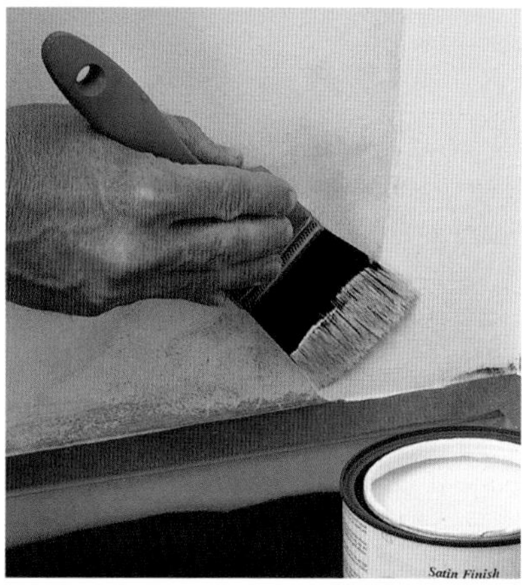

Paint cleaned areas with paint containing mildewcide to help control surface mold.

Mold Problems and Their Solutions

Problem Area 1

Leaky duct joints, especially noninsulated ones running through attics, create a moist environment for mildew.

Solution

Seal these joints with flexible mastic or metal tape and insulate the ductwork.

Problem Area 2

In warm environments, impermeable vinyl wall coverings can trap moist air in walls as the air moves from the warm exterior to the cool interior, degrading the drywall and the adhesive behind the wall covering.

Solution

Remove the vinyl wall covering and apply paint or wall coverings that have permeable paper backings.

Problem Area 3

When a washing machine overflows, a water heater leaks or hoses burst and no functioning floor drain is nearby, water soaks into carpet, drywall and insulation.

Solution

Always provide a functioning floor drain near washing machines and water heaters. Install an overflow pan underneath the washing machine and make sure the washer has no-burst supply lines instead of rubber hoses.

Problem Area 4

Drywall used as a tile backer quickly degrades when subjected to moisture.

Solution

For tile backer in moist areas or floors, use cement board or a similar product.

Problem Area 5

Poorly ventilated bathrooms allow surface mold to grow.

Solution

Remove the surface mildew and seal the surfaces (see previous page). Then install and use a bathroom fan.

Problem Area 6

Crawl spaces with bare earth floors transmit huge amounts of moisture (and occasionally radon gas).

Solution

Cover bare earth with 6-mil plastic sheeting and, if necessary, heat, cool and humidify the crawl space as you do the house.

Problem Area 7

Humidifiers, especially reservoir units, provide both a growth medium and a distribution system for mold and mildew.

Solution

Clean and treat the reservoir often with an antimicrobial solution.

Problem Area 8

The condensation pan under the coil of your refrigerated air conditioner can harbor mold, and the drain system can plug up, causing leaks.

Solution

Before each cooling season, clean the pan with a 1/2 percent bleach solution and make sure the pump and drain are clear.

Problem Area 9

Finished concrete basements that aren't thoroughly waterproofed from the outside can let moisture through; it's then trapped behind vapor barriers, carpet, layers of insulation and drywall.

Solution

Before finishing a basement, conduct moisture tests and perform any waterproofing measures necessary to ensure the basement remains dry after finishing.

Problem Area 10

Yards that slope toward foundations invite water to enter basements and crawl spaces.

Solution

Regrade the yard surrounding the house so it slopes away from the foundation.

Problem Area 11

Improperly flashed or caulked windows (and those with large amounts of surface condensation), doors and deck ledger boards let moisture seep into the surrounding wood, drywall and insulation.

Solution

Properly flash and seal these critical areas during installation or when installing new siding. Minimize window condensation with good ventilation and airflow.

Problem Area 12

Leaky roofs, especially poorly flashed areas, allow rain to infiltrate attics, insulation, eaves and other difficult-to-inspect areas.

Solution

Keep your roof in good repair by performing yearly inspections, using binoculars from the ground, and solving problems quickly.

Preventing Rot

Curing a Wet Basement 274
Gutter Repairs 326
Chimney Repairs 332
Mold 486

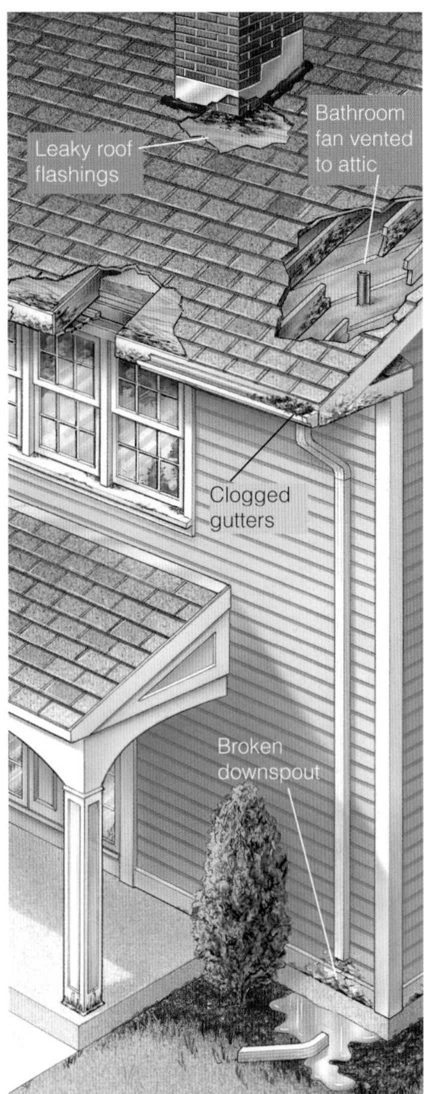

Rot on your home is likely to begin wherever water frequently dampens the wood and is slow to dry out again. Leaky roof flashings, worn shingles, wet areas around the foundation and clogged gutters are all weak points that can lead to decay. Peeling paint usually indicates damp wood.

From the day the carpenters drive the last nail, your home is under continuous threat from decay. Rot, essentially the breakdown of wood fiber, is almost always caused by fungi that invade wood and live off the fiber. Spores—fungi's microscopic offspring—float in the air and spread everywhere; you really can't keep them out of your house. However, to become established, these spores need three things: temperatures between 40° and 105° F (5° to 40° C), oxygen and moisture. You can't control the temperature or oxygen level, but you can control the moisture conditions.

The best way to keep your house decay-free is to maintain its "armor." Inspect the siding, shingles, paint and gutters seasonally and keep them in good repair.

Bathrooms/Laundry Areas

The floor under a toilet can rot when the wax seal between the toilet and toilet flange breaks and water leaks when you flush. If your toilet rocks, the seal is most likely broken and should be replaced. The walls around showers—especially ones that contain windows—can also rot when water and condensation penetrate around sills and uncaulked joints.

To minimize rot in laundry rooms located on wood floors, install a watertight pan under the washer to catch overflows.

Foundations and Exteriors

Poor drainage around the house leads to damp foundations, crawl spaces and rotting wood members and deck posts. Make certain the soil around the house slopes away from the foundation. Clogged or leaky gutters and worn-out shingles allow water to soak into the roof edge and rafter tails. Keep an eye out for peeling paint in soffit and fascia areas and maintain good attic ventilation to minimize the chance of harmful ice dams.

Windows and Doors

Decay around windowsills and doors can be especially bad on the south side where warmth from the sun can drive moisture deeper into the wood. Once decay begins, problems compound because decaying wood soaks up water faster than solid wood. Scrape off flaking paint, apply a wood preservative, then repaint and caulk.

Condensation on the inside of windows and doors can soak through sills, saturate wallboard and also cause wall framing to rot. Running a dehumidifier is a short-term solution; installing an air-to-air heat exchanger or more efficient windows are two long-term, though expensive, solutions.

An Inside Safe Room

Force 5 tornadoes and C5 hurricanes—the two most serious storms—can pack winds of more than 200 mph (320 kmh) and drive even a well-built house right off its foundation. An inside storm shelter or "safe room" can buy both safety and peace of mind. Safe rooms are completely independent of the house structure and secured to a concrete slab. They can be created using wood and steel, like the example shown, or poured reinforced concrete, welded steel and other materials.

The Federal Emergency Management Agency offers free booklets and complete information on constructing a variety of safe rooms. See Resources on p. 516 for more information.

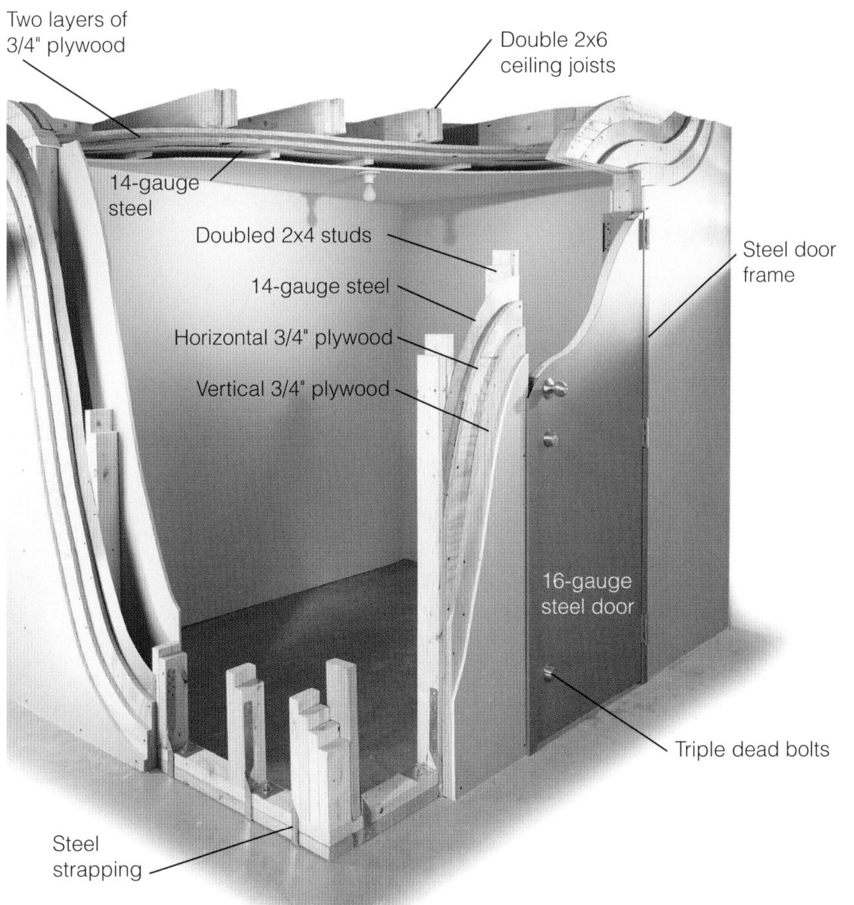

Emergency Power

A back-up generator linked directly to your electrical service panel can provide enough power to keep your furnace, well pump, refrigerator and basic lights operating during a power failure. The system, which should be installed by a licensed electrician, includes:

A transfer switch, mounted next to your service panel, which allows you to selectively operate essential equipment. It also serves as an automatic disconnect switch to protect electrical utility line workers from electrocution by preventing the generator from supplying power back into the utility supply system.

A generator. Purchase a model that will provide enough power to run essential items on an intermittent basis. Never operate it inside any type of enclosure.

Weatherproof outdoor inlet. This allows you to connect the generator to your electrical system without having to run a cord through an open window.

Generator. A 5,000- to 6,000-watt unit is usually large enough to provide power for essential items during a long power outage.

Transfer switch. The transfer switch allows you to run essential equipment as needed and serves as an automatic disconnect switch to protect utility line workers.

Natural Disasters

Protecting Pipes 106
Mold 486

Be Prepared

Natural disasters can affect anyone, any place, any day of the year. Severe weather, floods, tornados, hurricanes, earthquakes, national emergencies, and the utility outages that can accompany them, are conditions worth being prepared for. And it takes surprisingly little time and resources to be ready.

Here are six ways you can be prepared:

Water. Fresh water supplies can be cut off or become contaminated. Store a minimum of one gallon (4.5 liters) of water per person per day—and store enough for three days. Use clean plastic containers and replace the water every six months to ensure it's safe.

Food. Again try to store a minimum three-day supply of food. Canned foods such as meats, fruits and soups, and dried foods such as crackers or cereals keep well. Rotate your food supply every six months to maintain freshness.

Basic tools and supplies. Keep a battery-operated radio, flashlight and fresh batteries in a convenient location. "Crank-operated" radios and flashlights are also readily available, inexpensive and require no outside power source beyond your arm. A can opener, candles, matches and basic personal hygiene items should also be stored. A folding all-purpose tool containing knife, screwdriver, pliers and other implements can also prove invaluable. And don't forget the duct tape, a cell phone and charger.

Emergency medical supplies. In addition to a prepackaged first aid kit containing bandages and other basics, keep non-prescription medicines (aspirin, antacids, etc.), antiseptic, towelettes and latex gloves on hand. Consult your pharmacist about storing prescription drugs.

Clothing. Keep an extra set of clothes on hand as well as sturdy shoes, rainwear, hats, gloves and rescue blankets.

Documents. Keep passports, birth certificates, insurance policies, medical records and emergency numbers in a waterproof, fireproof container. If you keep these items in a bank safe deposit box, keep copies of them at home in your safe box. Consider keeping some cash on hand, too.

Note: For information on shutting off your electricity, water and gas in emergency situations, see p. 12.

Protecting Your Home

Tornado

Before tornado season find a low, windowless, structurally strong place where you can take shelter—in the basement, under stairs, in a safe room or in an inside hall or closet on the lowest floor. Conduct drills with family members.
After a tornado, enter a building only after authorities or an inspector have checked the foundation for shifting or cracking and the walls and ceilings for structural soundness.
If you smell gas, shut off the main gas valve immediately.
Shut off the electricity. Have an electrician check for short circuits.

Hurricane

Take in outdoor equipment, furniture and any other loose items. Tie down objects too large to move. Take in awnings.
Shutter windows or cover them with plywood or boards.
Store candles and flashlights in case of power failure.
Cut dead branches from trees on your property and any branches that are dangerously close to the house.
Lock all doors and windows to reduce vibration. Close draperies and blinds to contain flying glass.

Flood

Move valued belongings to the highest spot in the house if time permits, or to a neighbor's house if it is on higher land.
Raise heavy appliances and furniture by putting concrete blocks, bricks, or layers of boards under the corners.
Open basement windows in severe cases to allow water in and avoid a cave-in due to unequal pressure between the inside and the outside.
If you're told to evacuate, turn off the gas, electricity, and water, lock the house, and leave immediately.

Winter Storm

Protect water pipes with heat tape and insulating jackets, or let water trickle from faucets to prevent freeze up.
Clean out gutters and downspouts ahead of time to prevent ice blockage and aid runoff.
Tightly shut windows and storm windows. Plug window drafts.
Be prepared for a power failure and loss of heat.
Store food and water to last several days. Buy extra fuel for fireplace. Keep flashlights, candles and a battery-powered radio at hand.

Earthquake

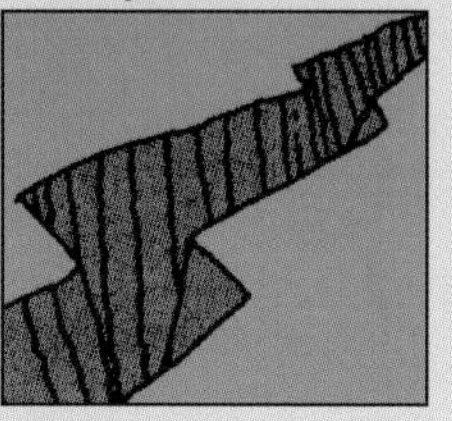

Add extra bracing and foundation bolts and have the chimney and hot-water tank strapped in place in earthquake zones.
Position yourself under a strong doorway, against an inside wall, in a safe room or under stable, heavy furniture, such as a desk or bed.
After an earthquake be wary of flooding and tidal waves. If you're in a low-lying area near a large body of water, head for high ground. Enter a damaged building carefully, as described for tornado, above, and shut off the utilities.

Storage Projects

Garage Storage

Drills 50
Jigsaws 54

Metric Conversions—inside back cover

Rotating Corner Shelves

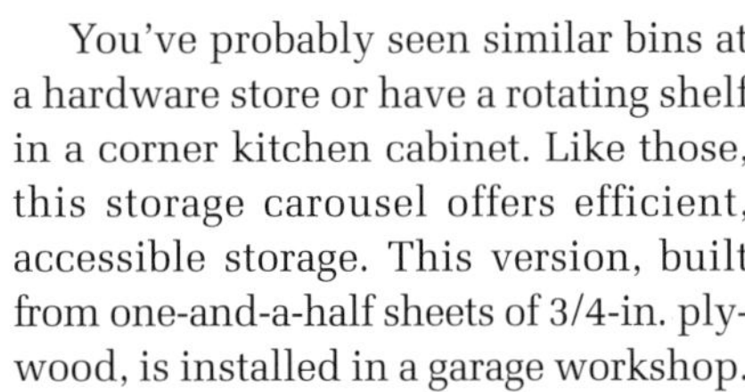

You've probably seen similar bins at a hardware store or have a rotating shelf in a corner kitchen cabinet. Like those, this storage carousel offers efficient, accessible storage. This version, built from one-and-a-half sheets of 3/4-in. plywood, is installed in a garage workshop.

Most of the work of supporting and spinning the shelf assembly is done by a 12-in. (30-cm) round lazy Susan bearing. Fastened to a wall-mounted corner shelf, a smaller 3-in. (7.6-cm) square lazy Susan helps stabilize the top.

In addition to the plywood and the bearing hardware, you'll need wood glue, a box of 2-in. drywall screws, vinyl base edging, a box of 1-in. tacks, and masonry anchors or concrete screws if you want to fasten the floorboard to the slab.

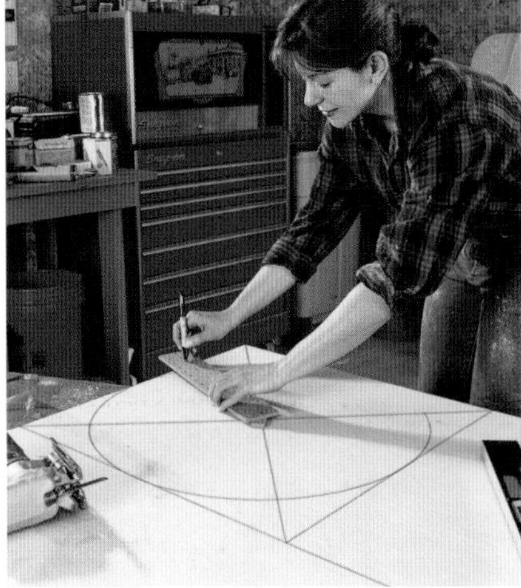

1 Make a compass from scrap pegboard and use it to mark the layout for the bin base. Cut out the base with a jigsaw; use the base to mark the shelf arcs.

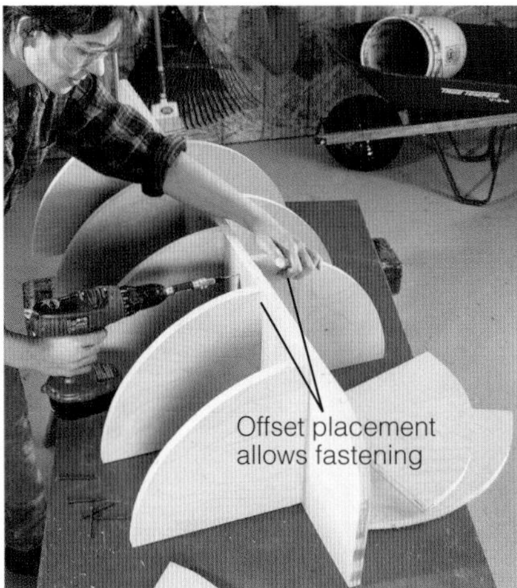

2 Attach the shelves to the narrow dividers, staggering the placement and fastening with 2-in. drywall screws. Countersink the screw heads.

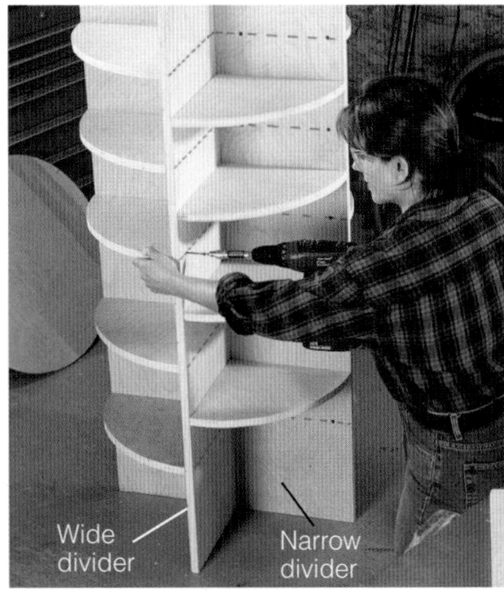

3 Connect the two shelf half-assemblies to the wide divider with drywall screws. Then center them atop the bin base and fasten with screws from underneath.

4 Install lazy Susan hardware following the manufacturer's instructions and mount the top shelf to the corner walls. Tack vinyl base along the shelf edges.

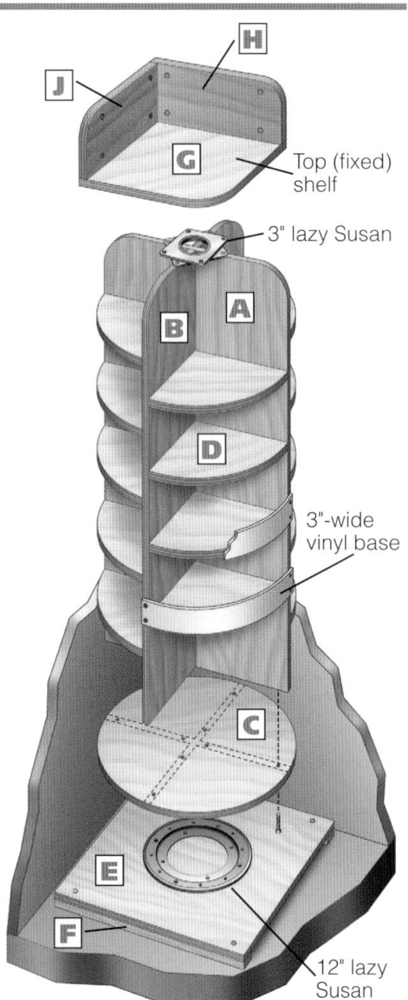

Cutting List

Key	Pcs.	Size & Description (in.)	
A	1	Wide divider	3/4 x 24 x 54
B	2	Narrow dividers	3/4 x 11-5/8 x 54
C	1	Bin base	3/4 x 24 dia.
D	16	Shelves	3/4 x 11-5/8 x 11-5/8
E	1	Floorboard	3/4 x 24 x 24
F	2	Floor cleats	3/4 x 1-1/2 x 24
G	1	Top shelf	3/4 x 18 x 18
H	1	Shelf side (right)	3/4 x 7-1/2 x 18
J	1	Shelf side (left)	3/4 x 7-1/2 x 17-1/4

Folding Pegboard Cabinet

Pegboard panels have always offered a simple, low-cost solution for organized tool storage, but not everyone can spare enough wall space for a full 4x8 sheet. By wrapping smaller pegboard panels in a set of hinged frames, this project provides nearly the same storage area in a far more compact package. Start by cutting the pegboard lengthwise into two pieces, one 24 in. wide and one 23 in. wide. Cut these pieces into 31-1/2-in. lengths. The panels, separated by 1x2 spacers, nest inside frames made from solid lumber in 1x6, 1x8 and 1x2 sizes.

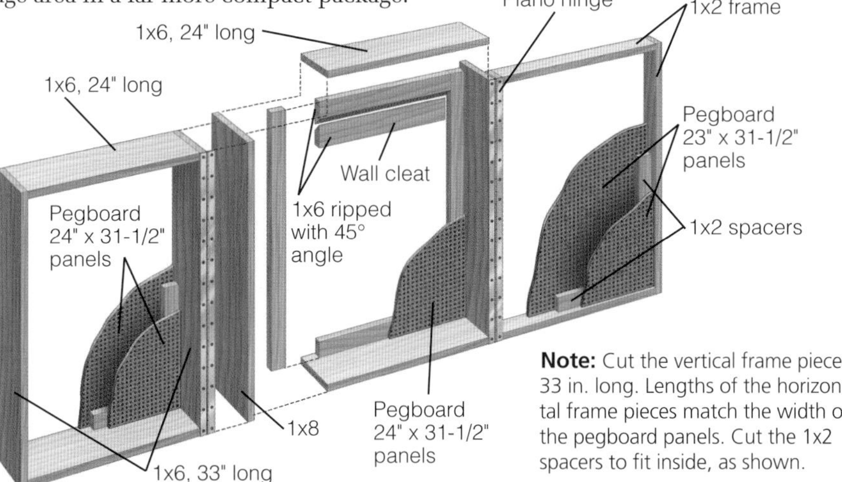

Note: Cut the vertical frame pieces 33 in. long. Lengths of the horizontal frame pieces match the width of the pegboard panels. Cut the 1x2 spacers to fit inside, as shown.

1 It's simpler to build this project from the inside out, assembling the pegboard panels first. Fasten a pegboard panel to the 1x2 spacers using screws, with the outside edges flush. Then flip it over and fasten a panel to the other side. For the center cabinet, fasten pegboard on only the front of the spacer frame and modify the frame by incorporating the beveled mounting cleat along the top, as shown. Note that the center and left-hand cabinets feature the wider (24-in.) pegboard panels; the right-hand cabinet's pegboard is 23 in. wide so it can nest in place when the cabinet is closed.

2 After assembling the pegboard panels, build each cabinet around its panel. Glue and nail the top and bottom frame pieces first, with their ends flush to the panel edges. For the center cabinet (shown here resting on its right side), use a 1x8 for the left vertical frame piece. The extra width creates the offset necessary for the right-hand cabinet to nest inside so you can swing the left-hand cabinet closed. Orient the parts as shown, so the beveled mounting cleat is at the top and the 1x8 side frame piece is on the left as you face the cabinet front.

3 When you have all three cabinet sections assembled, you can hinge them together. To join the center and left-hand sections as shown, prop the left-hand cabinet on two scrap 2x4 support blocks so the front edge is flush with the 1x8 frame piece in the center cabinet. Clamp the sections together. Use a hacksaw to cut a piano hinge to just under 33 in. long and fasten with screws, as shown. Use the same technique to install a piano hinge joining the right-hand section with the center cabinet. Fasten the beveled wall cleat and hang the cabinet.

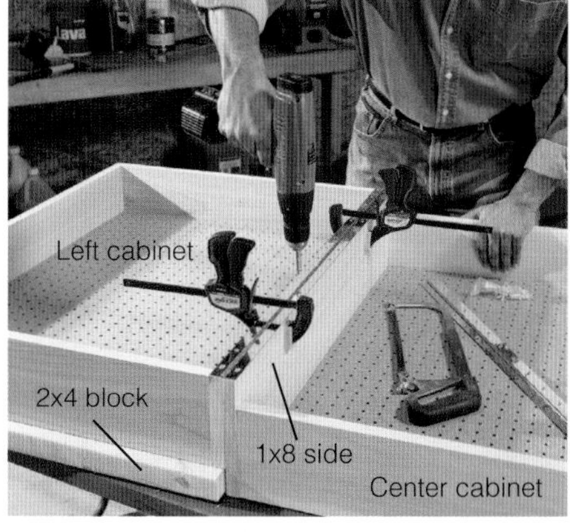

Garage Storage

Circular Saws 56
Screws 78
Plywood 431

Metric Conversions—inside back cover

Swing-out Plywood Storage Rack

Want to store plywood and sheet goods efficiently? This hinged storage rack pivots away from the wall for easier access to contents and even has vertical bays for storing solid lumber. Flanked by 2x6s along its lower edge, a 4x8 sheet of 3/4-in. plywood is the backbone of the assembly. Cut one end at a 45-degree angle, leaving a square 6-in. nose as shown, and make a similar cut on the 7-ft.-long front panel. A triangular plywood remnant provides support on the back side.

1 Cut five 2x6 dividers 46-1/2 in. long and use 2-in. drywall screws to fasten them, along with one 8-ft. bottom plate, to the plywood center divider.

2 Fasten the plywood front panel to the 2x6 dividers and bottom plate, then add the other 2x6 parts and plywood back panel to the main assembly.

3 To reinforce the rack assembly, use 2-in. screws to fasten four plywood cleats—three at the hinged end or base and one under the front end.

4 After mounting casters to the bottom plywood cleats, install hinges to anchor the tall end of the rack to the wall studs. Fasten with lag screws.

Materials

Pcs.	Description
2	4x8 sheets 3/4-in. plywood
5	8-ft. 2x6s
4	3-in. plate casters (one with a lock)
2	6-in. T-hinges
2- and 3-in. drywall screws	
1/4 x 1-1/2-in. lag screws	

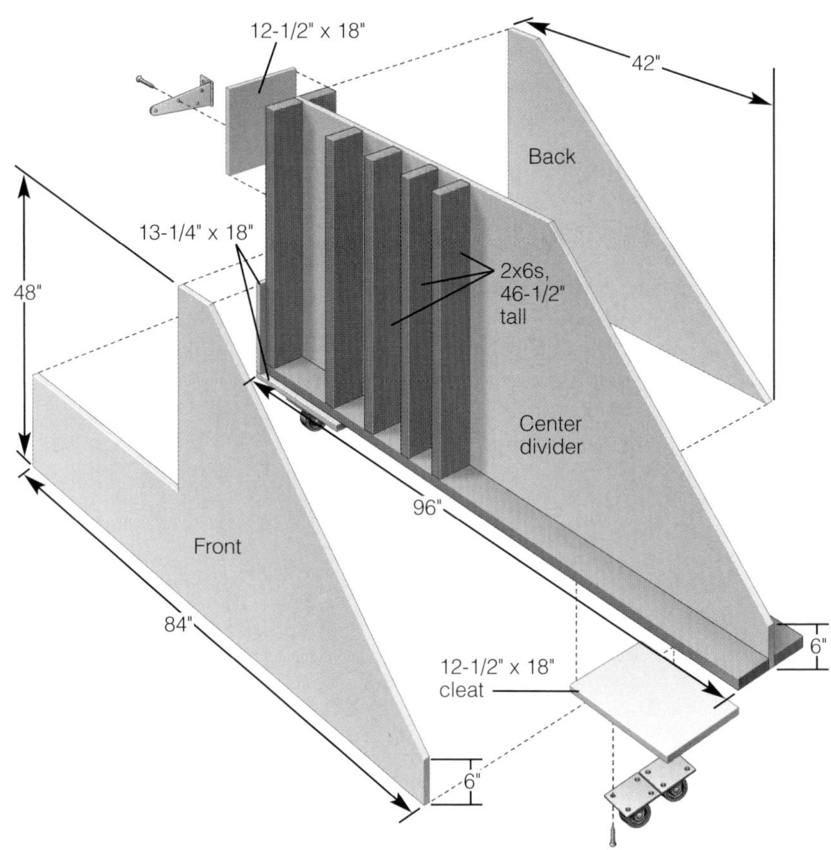

Compact Shovel Rack

Shovels and other long-handled yard tools are ideal candidates for wall-mounted storage, but perched on a nail or hook they aren't very stable and can't be doubled up to save space. This inexpensive rack fixes that and takes only a couple of hours to build.

Start with the 3/4-in. plywood deck. Mark the placement for four 12-in. (30-cm)-long slots about 2 in. (5 cm) wide and cut them with a jigsaw. Next, use 2-in. screws to fasten the plywood to the top edge of the 2x6 ledger, as shown. Then cut five 2x6 braces, each 12 in. (30 cm) long and use screws to attach them to the deck and the ledger. Be sure to offset braces from the wall-stud locations so you don't block access for the mounting screws. Mark a level line on three adjacent studs and mount the rack with lag screws.

4" hook and eye for added safety

Materials

Pcs.	Description
1	16 x 48-in. piece of 3/4-in. plywood
1	10-ft. 2x6 for ledger and braces
6	3/8 x 4-1/2-in. lag screws with washers
4	4-in. hook-and-eye sets
2- and 3-in. drywall screws	

2" drywall screw

3/4" plywood deck

Lag screws

Studs

2x6 ledger, 48" long

3" drywall screw

2x6 braces, 12" long

Closet Rod Bike Holder

You can find fancy bicycle storage racks at a bike shop, but this system does the same job and requires just two inexpensive closet rod shelf brackets. Use large screws to fasten the brackets securely to two adjacent wall studs. Line the rod hooks with a soft material to protect the bike frame. You can even install a shelf for storing helmets and other equipment.

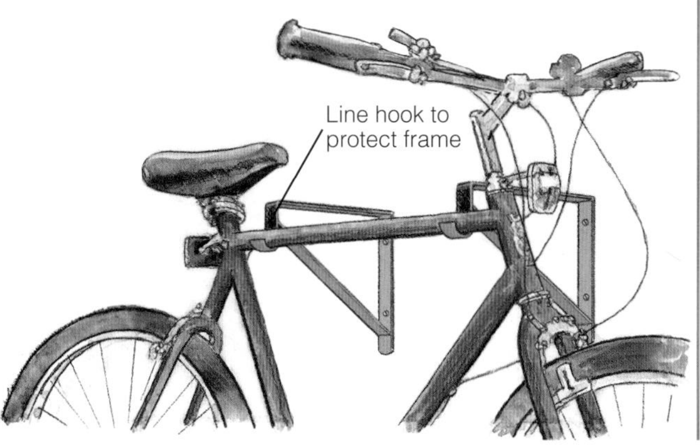

Megastorage Hooks

If the truss chords or ceiling joists in your garage are sitting idle, put them to work supporting these oversize storage hooks. Cut and glue 2-in. PVC pipe together with four 90-degree elbows, as shown, to create customized hooks for ladders, bicycles and other large items. Glue the joints securely.

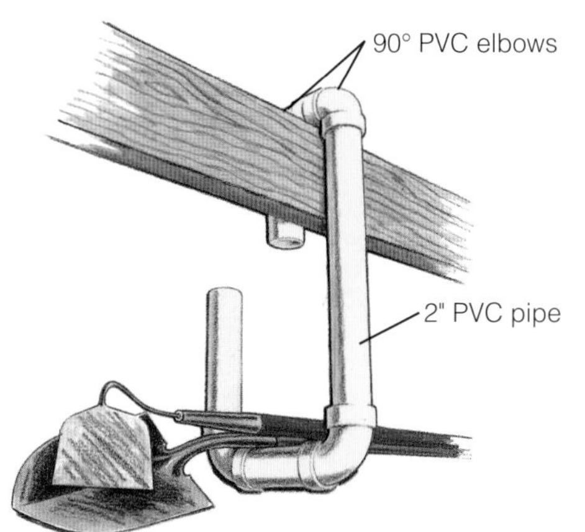

High Hanging Helper

Nobody wants to give up prime, easily accessible storage space for seasonal or infrequently used items, so a lot of this stuff ends up perched overhead among garage rafters. Here's a simple trick to get it down: Attach a spring clamp to the end of a length of plastic pipe. The clamp grips tightly to the pipe and the open end of the handle functions as a hook to retrieve the item you need.

Spring clamp

Plastic drain pipe

Kitchen Storage

Routers **66**
Moldings **430**
Cabinet Drawers **447**

Roll-out Pantry Cabinet

If you've seen the cabinetry selections at a home center or kitchen showroom lately, you know that cabinet manufacturers now offer features that used to be available only in high-priced custom goods. Improvements in hardware and design make the storage much more user-friendly. Slide-out shelves in base cabinets are among the most popular features; the back-saving convenience they offer makes most homeowners want to retire their old cabinetry quickly and permanently.

But what if your existing cabinets are well constructed and still attractive? Rather than tear them out, you can retrofit them with a roll-out pantry like the one shown. All you need is a sheet of 1/2-in. plywood, some 1x3 and 1x4 lumber and readily available drawer-slide hardware. This project uses a pair of bottom-mounted slides and one center-mounted top slide, with a combined weight rating of 130 lbs. (60 kg); check your local home center, hardware store or woodworking supply retailer for the specific types and sizes they carry.

Prepare your cabinet by removing the door and clearing the interior of shelves. You can discard the door hinges, but save the door so you can reuse it on the front of the new pantry shelf assembly. To determine the assembly's overall size, measure the cabinet face-frame opening; for the vertical dimension, subtract the combined height allowances for the upper and lower glide hardware, and deduct 1/2 in. (13 mm) from the width for clearance.

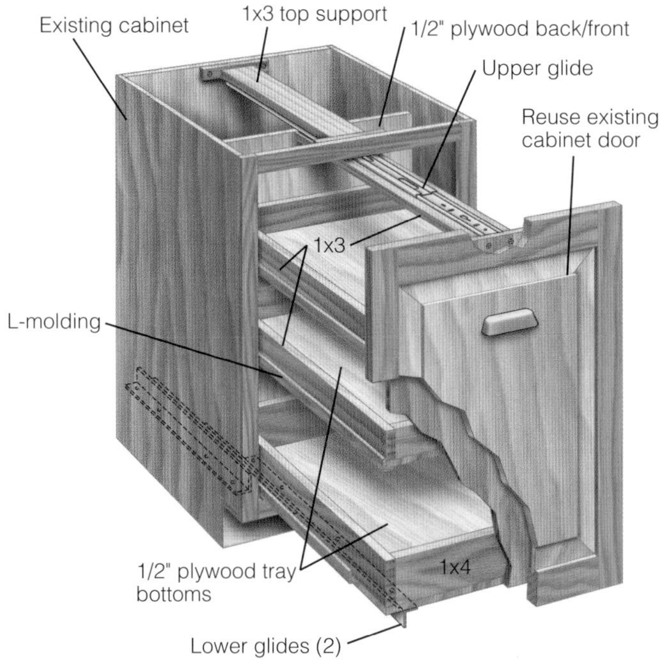

1 Install lower glides even with lower face frame. Fasten plywood end flanges to the 1x3 upper glide support and install it level, with its lower face flush with the top of the face-frame opening. Screw flanges to the cabinet.

2 Assemble pantry trays using 1x4s, 1x3s, 2-in. finish nails and glue. Fit plywood bottom to square up tray sides; then glue and fasten. Add molding to hide plywood edges.

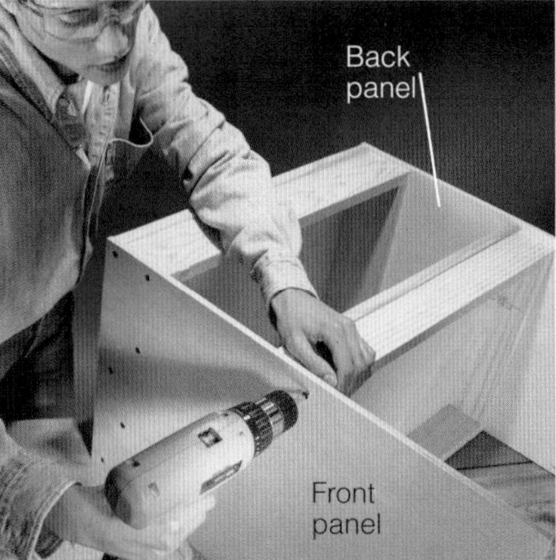

3 Use glue and drywall screws to secure the front and back plywood panels to the trays. Space the trays according to the items you want to store, allowing a minimum 4-in. (10-cm) height.

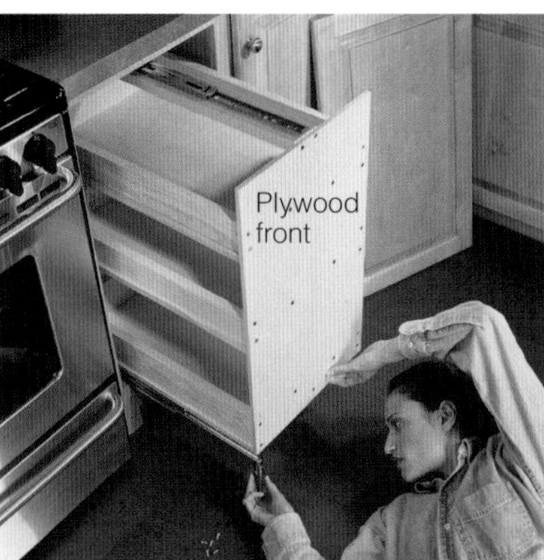

4 Slide the extension arms of the lower glides forward and fasten them to the tray assembly. Adjust the upper glide, if necessary. Fasten cabinet door to plywood front using screws driven in from the back side.

Slide-out Tray

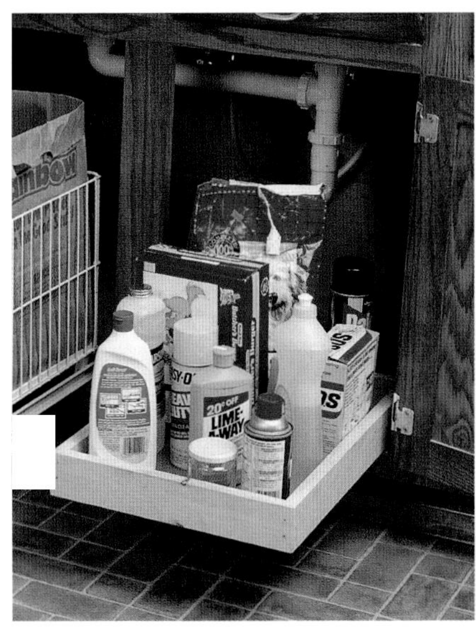

The roll-out pantry cabinet project on the previous page demonstrates that good storage solutions are as much about access as they are about volume. This slide-out tray is a simpler version designed for smaller spaces or cabinets with interior obstructions—such as the plumbing inside a sink base—that prevent the use of a full-height shelf unit. To determine the tray width, simply deduct 1 in. (25 mm) from the width of the face-frame opening; size the length according to the bottom-mounted drawer slide used. Use two glides for heavy loads.

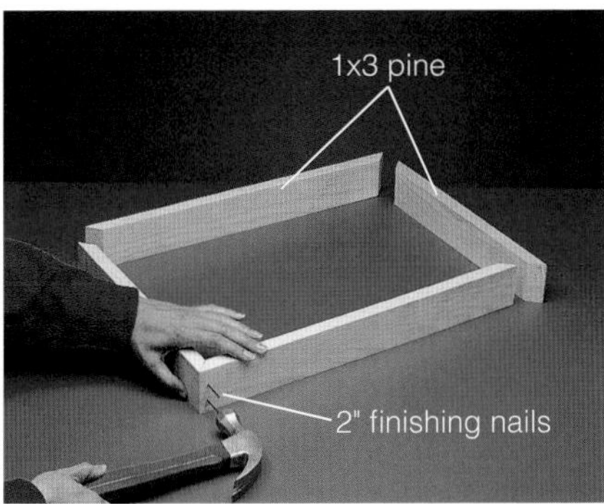

1 Assemble frame using butted or mitered corner joints secured with glue and nails. Predrill holes and keep nails away from edges.

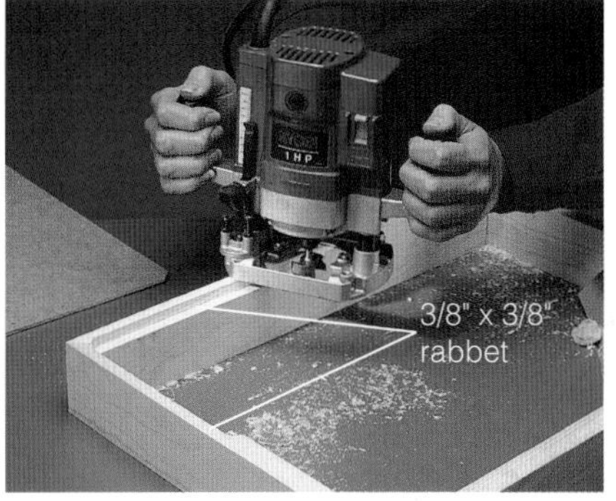

2 Rout a rabbet along the inside lower edge of the frame to accept a bottom drawer panel of 1/4-in. plywood or pegboard.

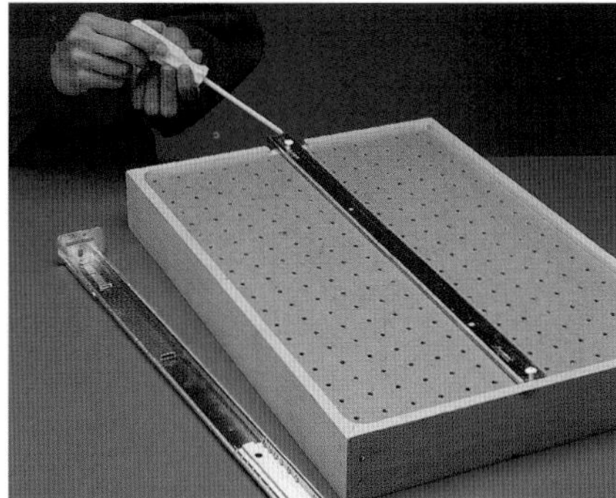

3 Fasten the top component of the drawer slide to the underside of the tray. Install the lower part on the floorboard of the cabinet.

Tilt-down Sink Front

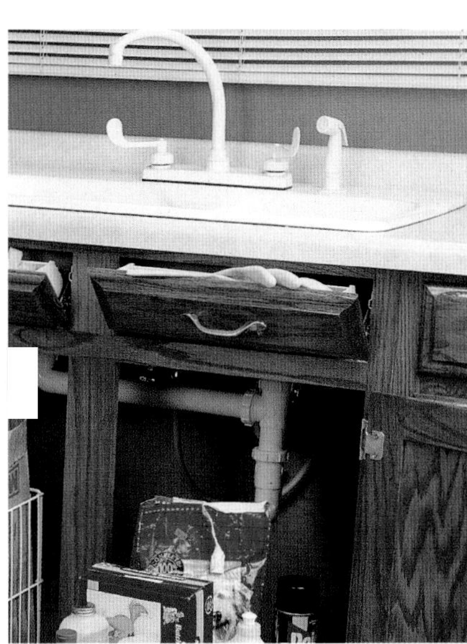

Here's another modern convenience that might not have made it into your kitchen's original cabinetry. Though they yield only a small pocket of storage space, tilt-down sink fronts earn their keep by stowing sponges, scrubbers and dishwashing gloves out of sight but well within reach. Installed with concealed hinges and plastic cut-to-fit tray inserts, they upgrade the cabinet's storage without altering its appearance.To get started, remove the false front panel(s) by twisting the mounting brackets or loosening the screws on the back side of the face frame.

1 Remove the false front and measure the width of the opening. Minus clearance for hinges, this will be the length of the tray insert.

2 Install hinges on the edges of the cabinet opening. Reposition the front panel to mark and drill for screw holes.

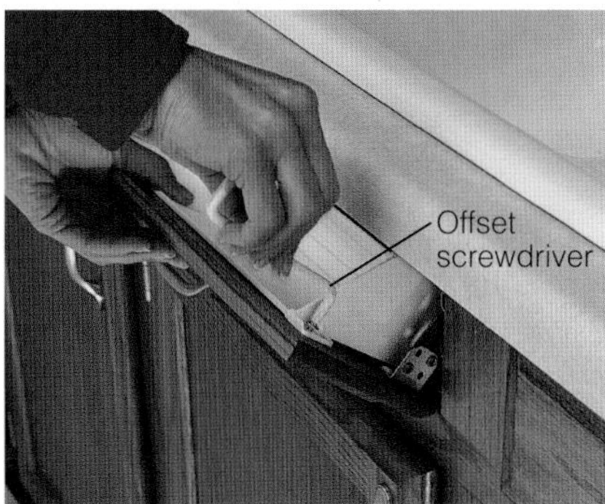

3 Install a handle on the false front. Fit the panel and drive hinge screws in the pilot holes drilled earlier. Install the tray insert.

Kitchen Storage

Saws **26**
Drills **50**
Jigsaws **54**

Door-mounted Spice and Lid Racks

Ornate or simple, traditional or contemporary, a kitchen cabinet is still basically a box built for storage. But volume isn't the only goal. Good storage keeps items organized and accessible, and sometimes that means dividing up that space into separate sections. Shelves are the most common example of such a strategy. This door-mounted rack system takes the divide-and-conquer approach a step further. Because it occupies part of the cabinet interior, there's no net gain in storage space—in fact, it requires cutting the cabinet shelves narrower to create a shallower depth—but it makes the stored items easier to locate and retrieve.

Whether built for use as a spice rack (main photo, left) or to hold lids for pots and pans (inset left), the basic anatomy remains the same: a pair of 1x3 side uprights joined by wood dowels and/or shelves. Typically, you'll want to choose a wood species that matches your kitchen cabinets. Most home centers offer premilled oak, maple and poplar lumber, so odds are good you can get a close match. Or you can paint the rack to suit your tastes. Keep in mind that most hardwoods require predrilling for nails.

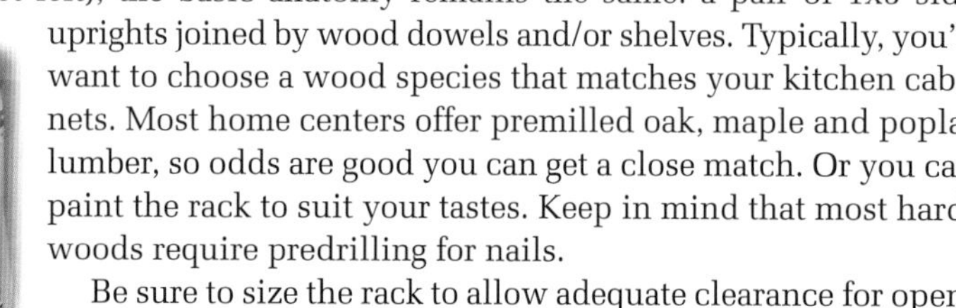

Be sure to size the rack to allow adequate clearance for opening and closing the cabinet door. For this version, that meant fitting the rack into the inside perimeter of the door frame so it nests on the back of the center panel.

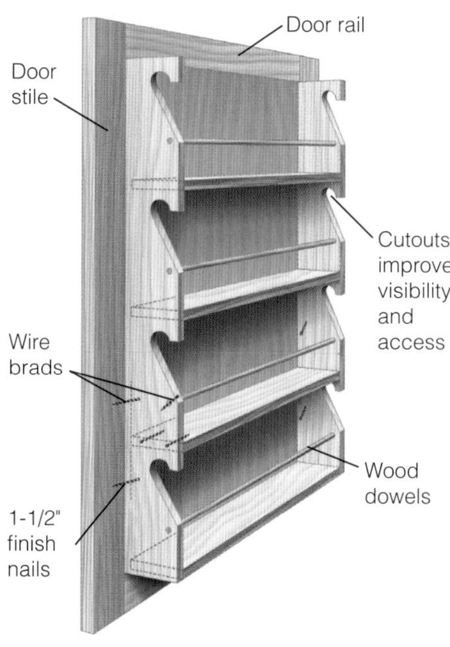

1 Measure inside the vertical stiles and the horizontal rails to determine the outside dimensions for your rack. If necessary, cut the existing cabinet shelves narrower to make room for the rack's depth.

2 Mark the shelf and dowel layout on the inside faces of the side boards. Use a 1-in. drill bit to create the circular end of each cutout and finish the shape with a jigsaw. Sand the edges smooth.

3 Glue and nail the shelves in place one at a time. Then drill holes, fit the dowels and pin their ends with wire brads. Countersink and fill the nail holes, and apply stain or finish to match the cabinet.

4 Clamp the finished rack to the back of the door; then drill angled pilot holes through the side boards into the door frame. Space the holes about every 8 in. and drive brads to secure. (Glue is optional.)

Space-saving Cabinet

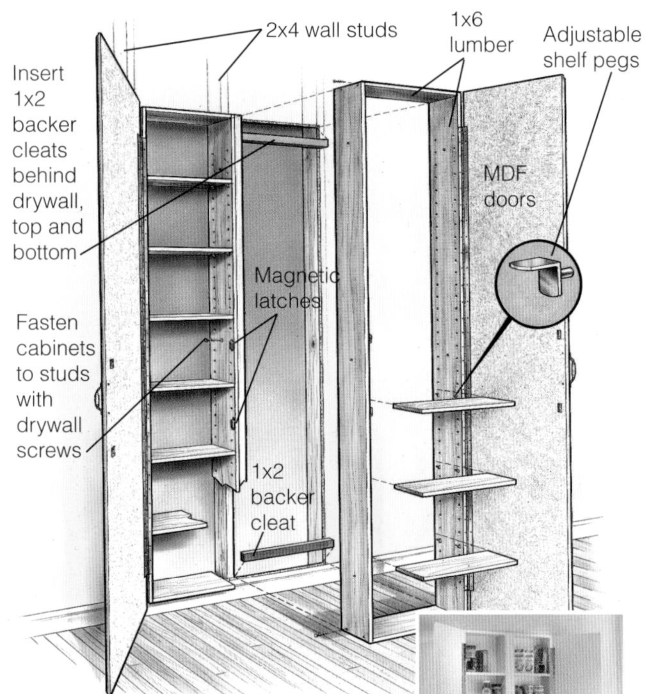

To discover hidden storage, look behind the surface. Most homes have interior walls harboring empty but unseen cavities, bays between the studs, many of which have no plumbing, wiring or ductwork running through them. This tall twin cabinet—recessed among three studs—can turn that idle space into a big storage gain.

Target an interior wall area free of electrical outlets, vent registers and other obstructions. Locate three adjacent studs and cut peek holes in the drywall to scout for wiring and pipes between them. Finding the bays completely clear is ideal, but often you can work around obstructions simply by reducing the cabinet height.

1 Cut nominal 1x6 lumber to lengths for the cabinet box parts. To allow adjustable shelves, use a pegboard jig to drill two rows of 1/4-in. holes for shelf pegs. Then use simple butt joints—reinforced with glue and drywall screws—to secure the cabinets at the corners.

2 After gluing in backer cleats behind the drywall (top and bottom), fit the two cabinet cases between the studs and shim to align them level and plumb. Insert a 1x2 strip between the cases, flush with their front edges, and clamp. Fasten the cases together and to the studs using screws.

3 The doors are medium-density fiberboard (MDF). This material stays flat and stable, but it's heavy, so use piano hinges to hang the doors. Fasten hinges to the cases first. Then prop up the doors with books and drive a few screws to check and adjust the fit. Drive the remaining screws. You can also have custom doors made to match your existing cabinets.

Open Baskets

A solid bank of cabinets might make storage efficient, but the look can be monotonous. Basket drawers, designed to replace shelves or standard drawers, add flair and easy access. To retrofit an existing cabinet, remove the door or drawer fronts and install a basket-drawer kit, available through woodworking supply catalogs and even some home centers.

1 To create better access and a more open look, use a flush-cutting pull saw to cut out any intermediate face-frame rails separating drawer and door openings.

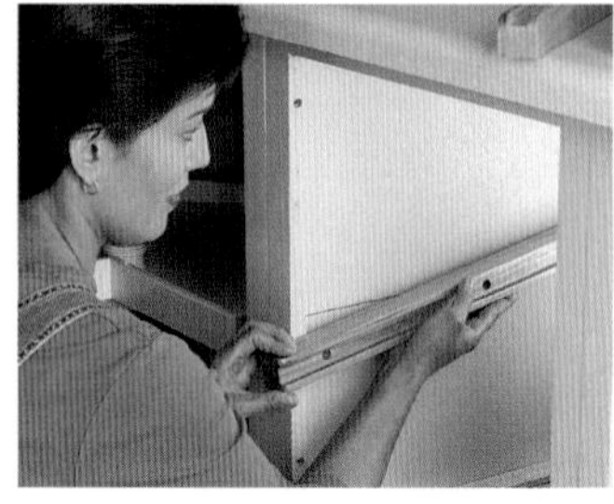

2 Cut the wood glide tracks to the cabinet depth, level them and fasten them with screws to the sides of the cabinet. Trim basket side flanges to the required width and slide into the glide tracks.

Laundry Room Storage

Circular Saws 56
Straight-cut Jig 58
Hollow-wall Fasteners 81

Under-the-Sink Shelf

In an active do-it-yourself household, a laundry-room sink probably handles paint cleanup chores more frequently than it does clothes washing, so providing some handy storage for painting supplies makes perfect sense. The floor space underneath offers a ready-made space, but mounting a shelf midway up the sink legs improves the utility and makes items easier to reach.

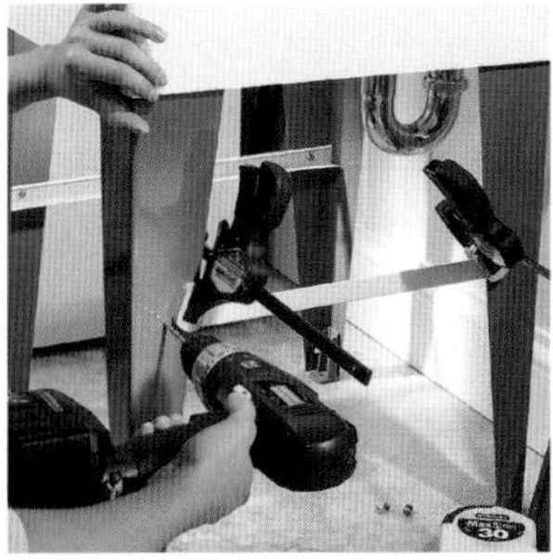

1 Cut two lengths of 3/4-in. suspended ceiling wall angle and clamp them opposite each other about halfway up the sink legs. Check for level and drill a 1/4-in. (6-mm) hole at each end for a machine screw or bolt. Fasten with nuts and washers.

2 Cut a shelf from 3/4-in. plywood, melamine-coated particleboard or another suitable material, preferably with a water-resistant surface. Allow about 1/4 in. (6 mm) of clearance in each dimension for an easier fit, and cut small notches, if necessary, to fit over the bolt hardware.

Towel Bar

Why drape wet towels or shop rags over the sink edge when there's often room along the sides for a towel bar or two? The towels will dry faster and be out of your way while you use the sink. Pick a unit with simple mounting brackets (exposed screw heads are fine) and a bar you can cut to length. For tools, you'll need a hacksaw, a file and a portable drill.

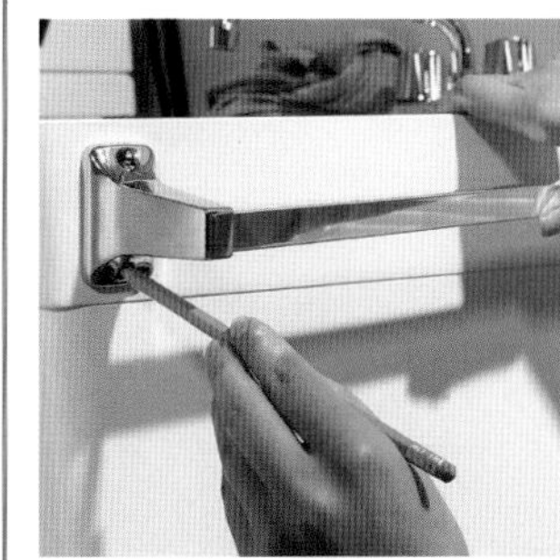

1 Use a hacksaw and a file to trim the bar length, if necessary. Fit the brackets and position them against the sink rim to mark the holes. Keep in mind that this technique is for a plastic laundry sink; if you have an older cast-iron sink, mount the bar on the wall.

2 Make sure your layout marks are all on the thick part of the rim. Drill four 3/16-in. (5-mm) holes to accept stainless-steel machine screws. Use a screw length that protrudes about 1/4 in. (6 mm) past the inside sink face and thread an acorn nut onto the end.

Soap Dispenser

Want to add even more convenience to your laundry sink? Replace the grungy bar soap or disappearing liquid hand soap with a built-in soap dispenser. You can buy refillable dispenser units at a home center or plumbing supplies retailer. For installation, drill a hole in the faucet deck of the sink, insert the threaded base and install the retaining nut.

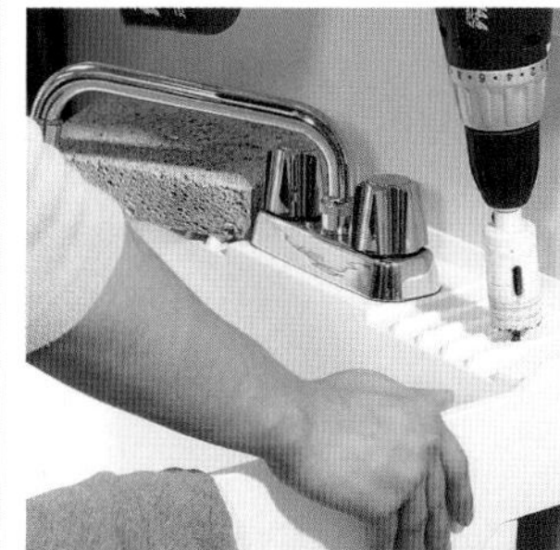

1 Use a hole saw to drill through the sink deck on one side of the faucet. The standard size for the threaded dispenser base is 1-1/4 in. (32 mm), but confirm this beforehand by measuring. Be sure the hole position allows enough clearance for the soap reservoir below.

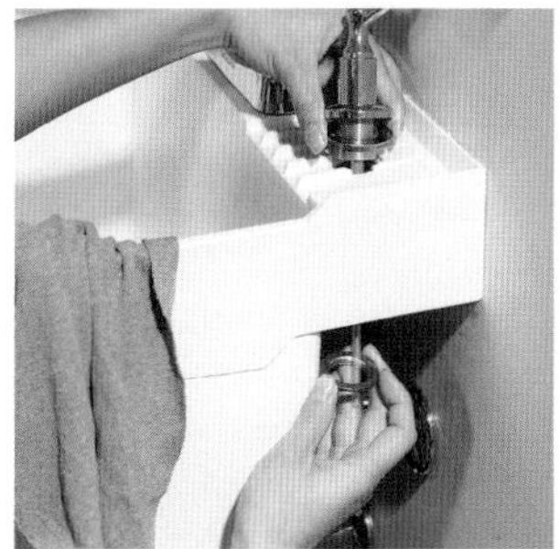

2 Insert the threaded base through the hole and thread the retaining nut up from underneath to cinch the base tightly onto the sink deck. Fill the soap bottle and thread it onto the base of the pump.

Fold-away Countertop

The mixed feeling most of us have about our laundry rooms—wanting a generous work area but making use of it only intermittently—often results in compromises that make nobody happy. If your home has the square footage to spare, you allocate a sizable space that sits idle a lot; if you don't have the luxury of that much extra space, you make do with a cramped area and try to fold clothes on top of the dryer. Here's a simple project—a fold-away work table—that helps out when you need it but takes very little space when you don't.

Aside from the basic tools required, you'll need a few ordinary items: some pine boards and a section of prefabricated laminate countertop with end cap from your local home center. And you'll need one specialty item: a set of folding brackets available through woodworking supply catalogs or a cabinetmakers' supply outlet. One pair is plenty if you keep the countertop length to less than 5 ft. Space brackets no farther than 32 in. (81 cm) apart.

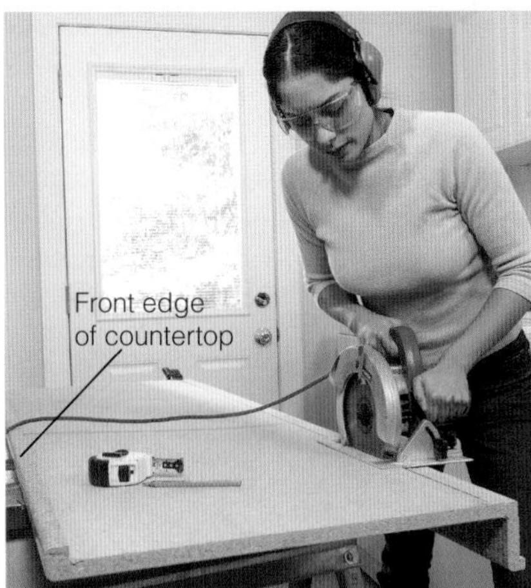

1 With the countertop turned upside down, use a circular saw to cut about 2 in. (5 cm) off the back edge. This removes the backsplash portion, which you won't need. Then trim the counter to length. Use an edge guide for perfectly straight cuts.

2 Glue and screw the pine boards to the underside of the counter for reinforcement. Use 1x4 stock along the back edge and perpendicular 1x2 cleats located where the brackets will mount. This will stiffen the countertop and provide a better fastening base for screws.

3 Mount vertical 1x3 cleats to two wall studs, fasten the brackets to them and attach the countertop. If a wall runs along one end, leave about 1/8 in. (3 mm) of clearance there. Add a filler strip at the exposed end and iron on the laminate end cap.

Closet Rod and Shelf

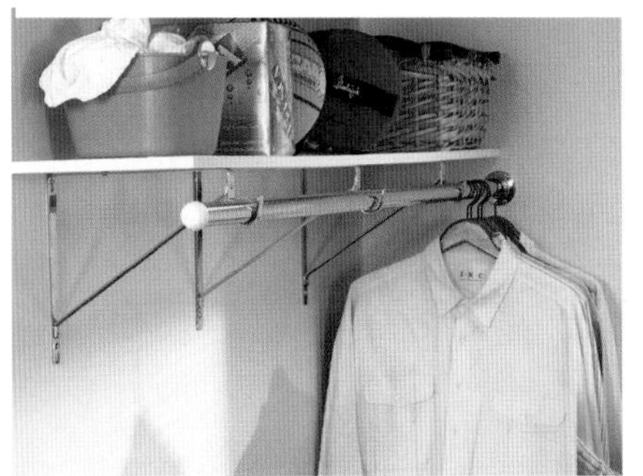

While you're scouting for unused space in your laundry room, try looking overhead. Odds are there's room for at least one wall-mount shelf, and if you mount it with closet shelf brackets, you can add a closet rod for hanging laundry. Use one bracket for every 2 ft. (60 cm) of shelf length.

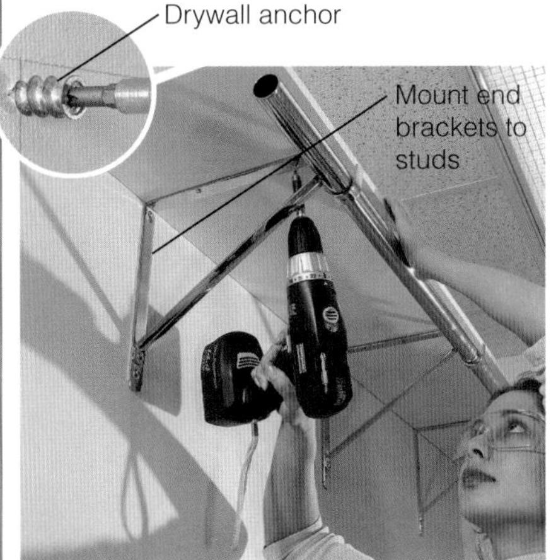

Mount the two end brackets securely to wall studs, positioning them for a shelf height of about 6-1/2 ft. (2 m). Center bracket may be mounted to the wall surface using drywall anchors if shelf and rod will be supporting only light items. After they're secured, fasten the shelf and closet rod in place with screws.

Laundry Room Storage

Hollow-wall Fasteners **81**
Fishing Cable **141**
Ductwork **175**

Ironing Center

An ironing board is another part-time-use laundry item that occupies too much space to be left standing full-time. Fortunately, its narrow, flat shape lends itself to being tucked into the cavity between wall studs. A few savvy manufacturers have realized this and designed wall-mount models that nest inside a decorative cabinet; you can install the simplest versions in an afternoon. The model shown here takes a little longer to install because it has an integral electrical outlet; wiring it directly is easier if the stud bay has an existing receptacle on a circuit with extra capacity.

1 Mark stud locations and use a drywall saw to cut along the inside faces. Position the opening for a comfortable working height.

2 Shut off power. As you install the unit, feed electrical cable into raceway. Fasten the cabinet sides to the studs using drywall screws.

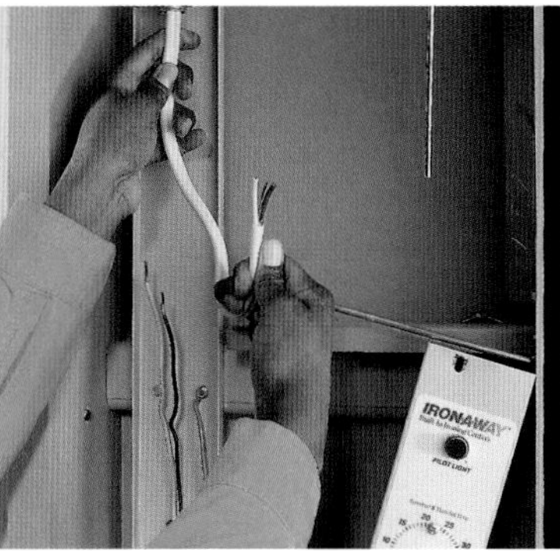

3 Remove the raceway cover and make the wiring connections, including the ground wire, following the manufacturer's instructions.

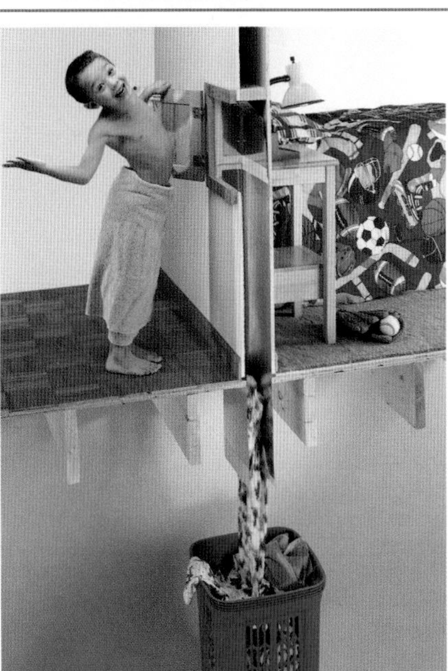

Clothes Chute

Laundry chutes, common in older homes, rarely make their way into newer homes. If your laundry center is below your living areas—and if local fire or building codes don't prohibit installation—you can retrofit a chute inside an existing wall. Hallways between bedrooms are a good central location.

Installation is easier if the wall runs parallel with the floor joists (but not directly over one) or if studs are "stacked" directly atop joists. Before opening the stud cavity, cut a small hole and check for wires and other obstructions. Tape the seams in the clothes-chute ductwork to avoid snagging delicate clothes.

1 Cut drywall along stud centers; then cut away exposed section of bottom plate. Reinstall that block at the top of the cutout.

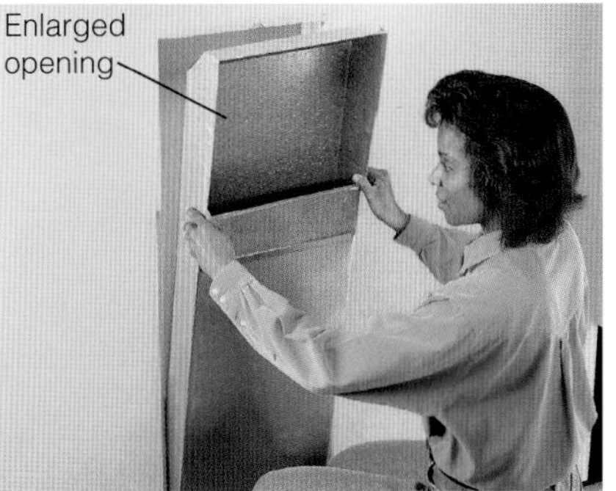

2 Fit a heating duct inside the stud bay. You'll need a 90-degree corner bend with a register opening. Use metal snips to enlarge opening.

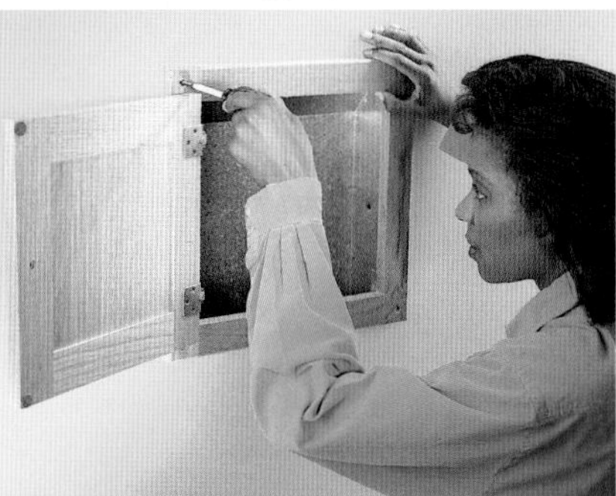

3 Patch and paint the drywall, fit a prefabricated laundry door unit over the opening, and then fasten the door to 2x4 studs and block.

Bathroom Storage

Glass Shelves

Wall space above the toilet offers one of the most common storage opportunities in a bathroom, inspiring many cabinet and accessories manufacturers to market special "over-the-john" cabinets to put that space to use. Too much closed cabinetry can make a small room feel cramped, however, especially if the unit is at eye level. Glass shelves can provide decorative, functional storage that doesn't impose so much on the room. The systems vary slightly, but the installation shown here is typical.

1 Using painter's tape to protect the walls, mark the heights and centerlines of the shelf brackets—on studs where possible.

2 Dry-fit the bracket to mark the screw-hole locations. Use a screwdriver to dimple the wallboard at those points. Remove the tape.

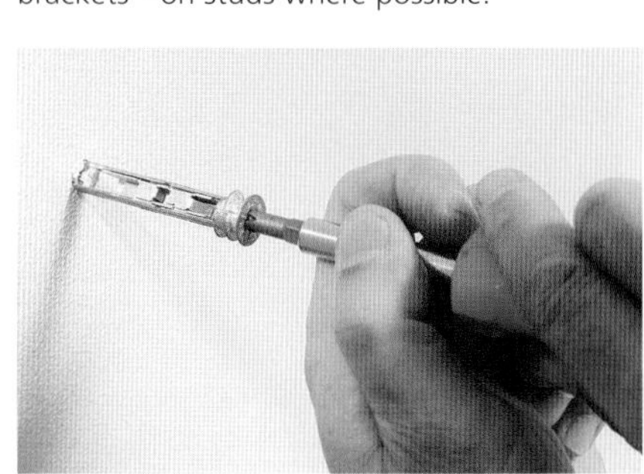

3 For bracket locations not backed by a wall stud, drive a self-threading hollow-wall anchor into the drywall.

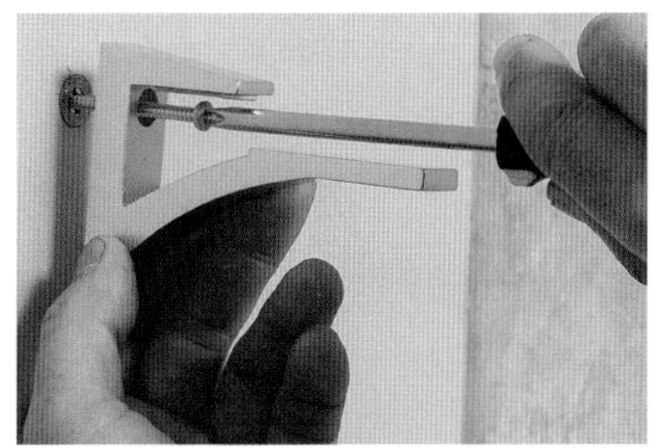

4 Screw the shelf brackets to the wall. You may need two different screw lengths if some are going into studs and others into anchors.

Swing-out Wastebasket

Here's a 15-minute project that conceals that less-than-gorgeous bathroom wastebasket, yet makes it easily accessible. Hang the waste bin on the inside of a vanity door so it's out of sight but swings out when you need it. Rather than the typical wire-cage bracket, a pair of ordinary mirror clips supports a standard plastic wastebasket.

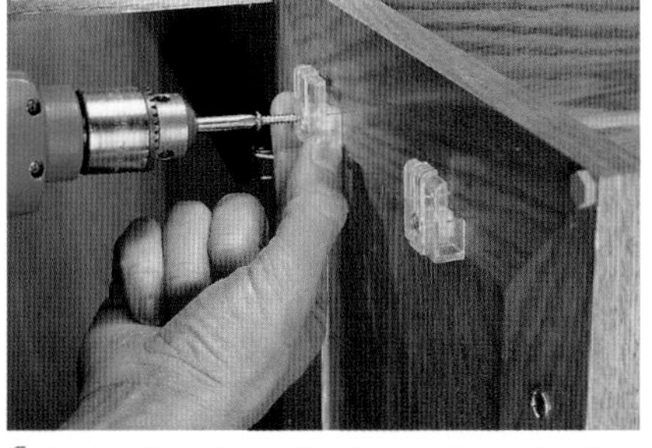

1 Fasten the mirror clips level with each other and low enough to allow clearance for the lip of the waste bin.

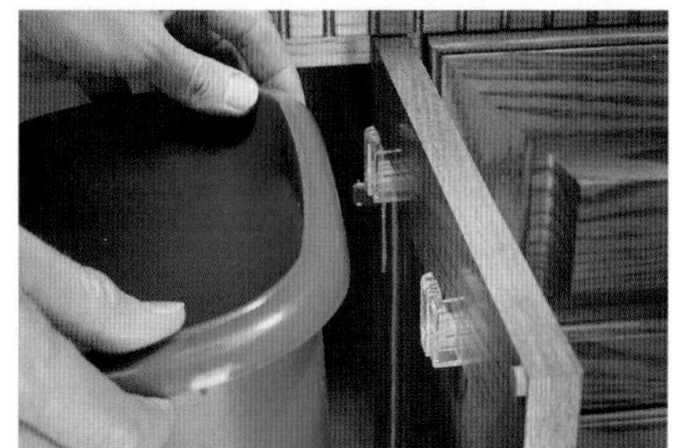

2 Fit the lip of the waste bin over the mirror clips and press down slightly. Opt for metal clips if you would prefer that look.

Bigger Medicine Cabinet

If you want more storage space (and a larger mirror) than a standard recessed medicine cabinet can provide, consider installing a surface-mounted unit. There's no interference with plumbing pipes or electrical wires inside the wall, and the larger mirror surface will make the room itself appear bigger. Temporarily support and level the cabinet on wood blocks while fastening the back to wall studs.

Bookcases and Shelves

Straigh-cut Jig 58
Air Nailers 74
Router Jigs 445

Metric Conversions—inside back cover

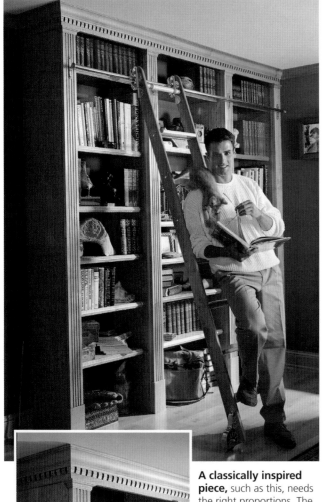

A **classically inspired piece,** such as this, needs the right proportions. The center shelf section shown here is about 8 ft. (244 cm) tall and 36 in. (1 m) wide, which happens to be the span limit for the ladder rail hardware. The two flanking sections are slightly narrower, about 30 in. (76 cm).

Floor-to-Ceiling Bookcase

Despite its elegant appearance, this bookcase is within the range of homeowners with basic woodworking skills. The plan and design shown can easily be adapted to fit a variety of situations.

This bookcase is easier to manage when approached as a series of individual components. These components include the upright panels, called standards, the top panel or cap, the shelves and the various trim pieces. The ladder system is optional and typically comes in a ready-to-assemble kit. If you're going to finish the bookcase with a stain or clear finish, opt for a cabinet-grade hardwood plywood with plain-sawn face veneers; be sure you can buy or make the required moldings out of the same wood species.

Any built-in feature has to accommodate such irregularities as out-of-plumb walls and floors that aren't flat. To get an accurate baseline, mark a level line on the wall, about 1 in. (2.5 cm) below the ceiling. The dentil and crown moldings will compensate for any irregularities there; each standard can be sized according to the floor height and angle where it fits.

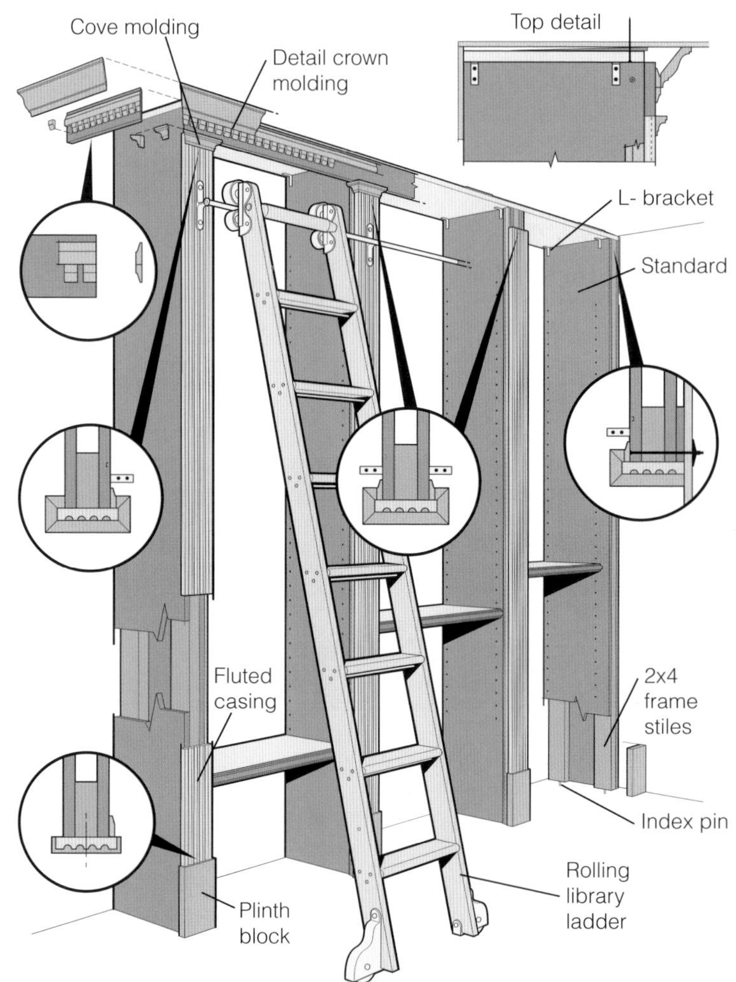

Materials

Pcs.	Description
5	4x8 sheets of 3/4-in. plywood
8	8-ft.-long pine/fir 2x4s
Assorted solid stock (1x2, 1x4, 5/4x6) for shims, cleats, dentil molding and plinth blocks	
Assorted trim and moldings, including fluted casing, shelf edging and crown and cove molding	
Hardware requirements include 1/4-in. shelf pins, screws, finish nails, a steel strip for making a shelf-pin drill guide and ladder and ladder-rail hardware.	

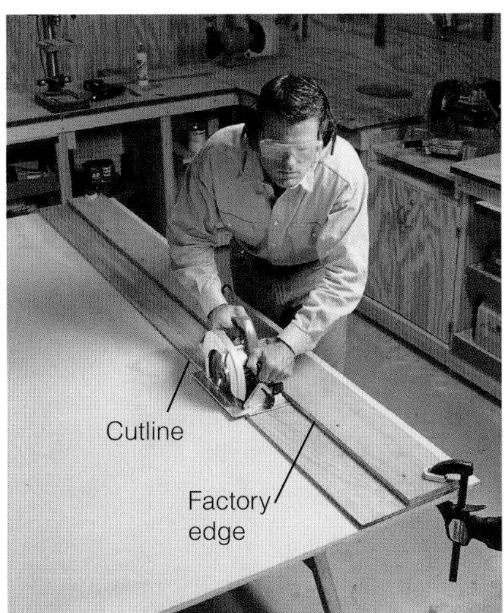

1 Use a cutting guide or tablesaw to rip plywood into eight panels for standards, plus the top panel and shelves. See p. 58 for building a jig like the one shown here.

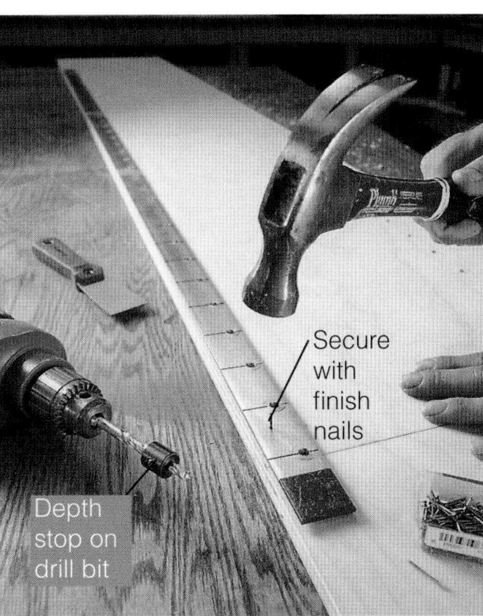

2 Use a jig to drill accurately spaced holes for the shelf pins. This flat-steel bar features 1/4-in. holes spaced every 2 in. (5 cm) on center and 3/4 in. (19 mm) from the edge.

3 Sandwich a pair of 2x4 uprights between two plywood panels to form each standard. Align them evenly at the front edge, but leave an inset along the back edge for scribing.

4 Make your own dentil molding by gluing a filler strip along one edge of a 1x4 and adding 7/8-in. (22-mm) segments cut from a colonial-style stop molding.

5 Two index pins nest in holes in the floor to position each standard. Secure the end, or corner, standard first, then use temporary cleats called stringers to align the others.

6 Slide the top panels over upper ends of standards, align the front edges flush, and connect them with metal angle brackets. Next, screw through the top panel into the ceiling joists. Use shims to prevent bowing.

7 Nail plinth blocks at the base of each standard. Cut and fit the fluted casings to the front edges of the standards. Secure the casings with finish nails.

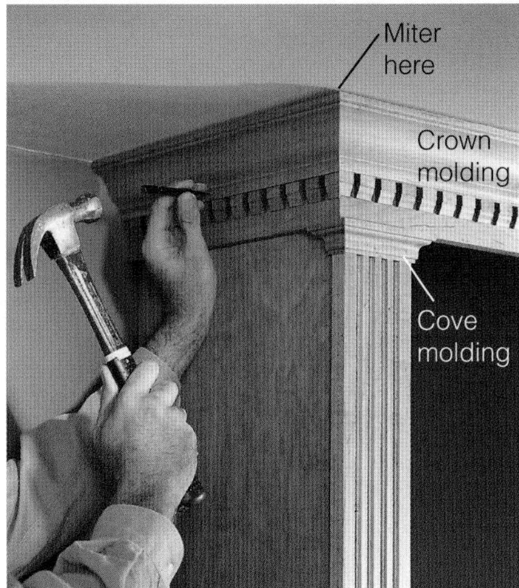

8 Cut and install the cove, dentil molding and crown molding to the top of the bookcase. Miter the front corner joints and butt the back ends to the wall. Set the nails and putty the holes, then apply clear finish.

Bookcases and Shelves

Jigsaws 54
Template Routing 445

PVC Pipe Shelving Unit

For this project, posts made of 3-in. PVC pipe are used to support four shelves made of 3/4-in. birch or melamine-laminated plywood. The size can vary, but you can get four 12 x 48-in. (30 x 122-cm) shelves from a half-sheet of plywood. A shelving unit like this is appropriate for a child's bedroom, but be sure to secure it to the wall with L-brackets and be careful not to load it with heavy objects, such as books.

With a power miter saw or a handsaw, cut the four posts; align the posts side by side with ends flush and mark the shelf locations. Use a handsaw to cut four 3/4-in. (19-mm) slots halfway through each post, taking care to align the notches precisely. Finish the cuts with a keyhole saw or jigsaw. Paint the plywood and the 1x2 lumber used for the shelf aprons and apron blocks; cut a 9-degree bevel on the ends that abut the pipe. Attach the aprons with glue and finishing nails. Top the posts with round painted-plywood caps or 3-in. PVC pipe caps.

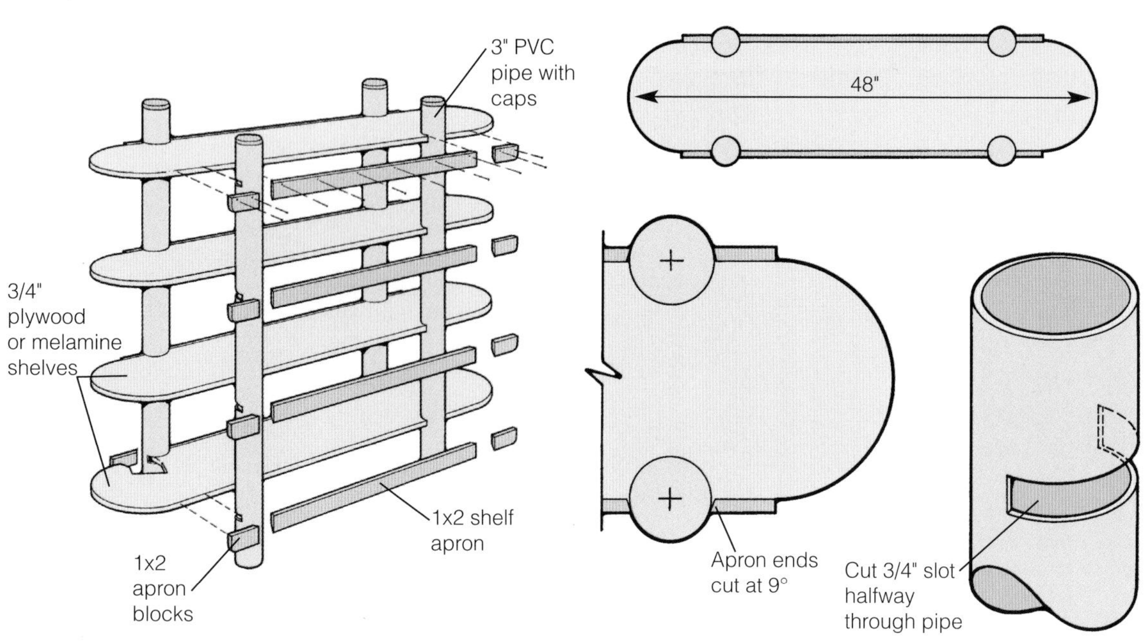

Glass Wall Shelves

Thanks to the simplicity of its two upright supports, this glass-shelf display unit almost appears to float on the wall. The uprights are fashioned from 1/2-in. birch plywood, glued and finish-nailed into a U-shaped channel. The slots for the shelves are cut after assembly; this can be done with a tablesaw, a radial-arm saw or a handsaw and miter box. For shelves, use 1/4-in. (6-mm) tempered plate glass with polished edges and rounded front corners.

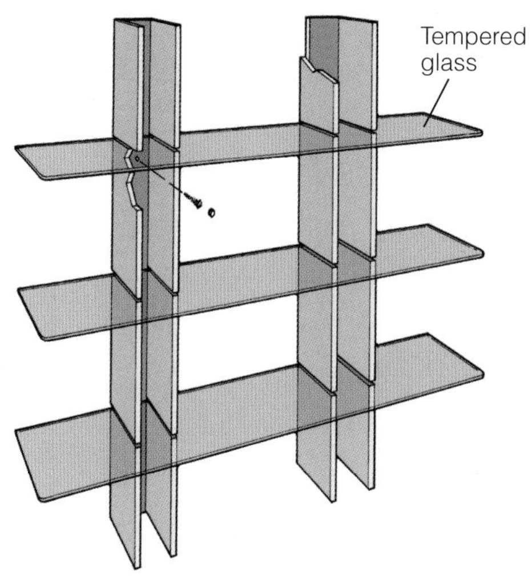

1-1/2" finish nails
1-1/4" x 5" slot
14"
15"
14-1/8"
13"
14-1/8"

Stacking Totes

Modular storage solutions are practical and efficient, whether you're building or using them. This project yields four stacking storage totes from a single 4x8 sheet of 1/2-in. plywood, and the stack takes up less floor space than most single-story toy chests. With swivel casters mounted on the underside of the bottom tote, you can roll the entire set into a closet or corner.

For tools, you'll need a circular saw, straightedge guide, jigsaw, hammer, nail set and screwdriver. For faster, more accurate results, a tablesaw and a router (with a pattern or flush-trim bit; see p. 445) will make quick work of cutting and shaping the parts, and you'll have exact replicas that ensure a good fit when the totes are stacked.

To create four cubes, start by cutting the eight smaller square-cornered side panels and the four bottom panels for each tote. Then cut the contoured side panels to size. You'll need eight of these, but make one finished piece first and use it to mark the others for cutting. Use a jigsaw to cut the radius corners and the handle slots. Then lay this pattern atop each of the other blanks and trace the outline. You can cut the other panels freehand with the jigsaw or clamp the template and the blank together and use a router with a flush-trimming bit to clean up the edges and create an identical shape. Glue and nail the parts together, and paint the boxes and add casters, if you like.

Stacking Shelves

This stacking shelf set relies on the same modular principle as the storage totes, but it is built for heavier loads. The five-module version shown is made from one-and-a-half sheets of 3/4-in. oak plywood. Birch or fir plywood are fine also, especially for a painted version.

Because these shelf units stack directly atop one another and need a precise fit, use a tablesaw for greater consistency when cutting the parts. If that's not possible, use a cutting guide with your portable circular saw to ensure accurate dimensions. Note that the end panels for the bottom unit are taller than those for the other modules. Mark the outlines of the half-round tongue and half-round cutout on one of the end panels. Make sure the two contours are identical in size and position, because they must nest together precisely as you stack the shelves. Cut the outlines with a jigsaw and sand the edges smooth; use this piece as a template to mark the others. Cut with a jigsaw or use a router with a pattern and a flush-trimming bit to cut them to shape. Assemble the shelves with glue and finishing nails.

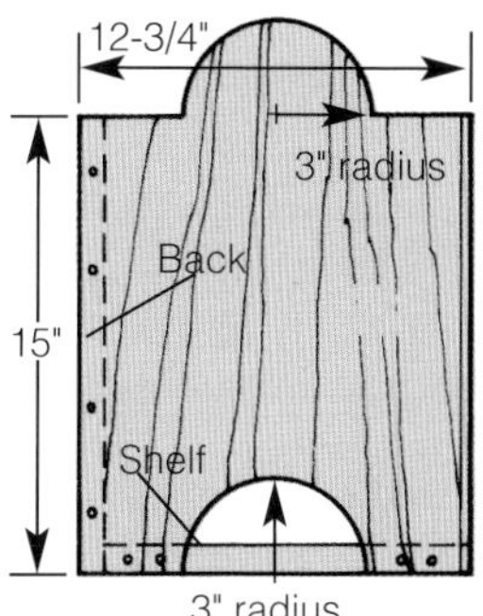

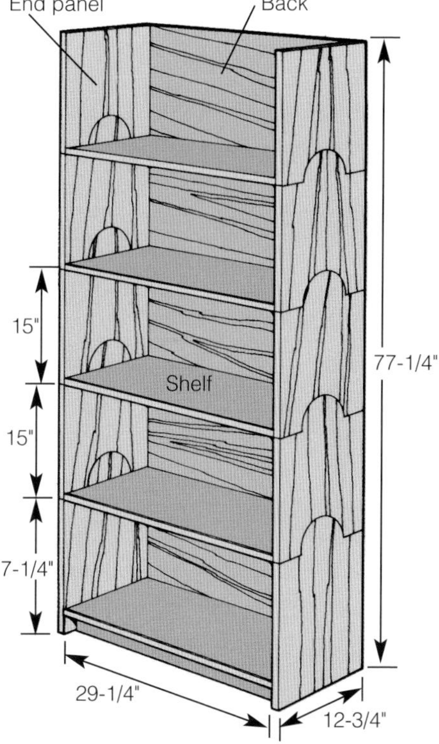

Bookcases and Shelves

Clamps 34
Miter Saws 55
Air Nailers 74

Metric Conversions—inside back cover

Leaning Shelves

Simple projects don't have to be boring or ordinary. With nothing more than a few angled cuts to create its lean look, this shelf unit brings a creative touch to the world of traditional bookshelves. Its anatomy is basic: A pair of uprights and a series of cleats have their ends cut at a 10-degree angle, supporting a set of progressively wider shelves.

The shelves (parts A through E) are cut from plywood and have veneer tape applied to their front edges; 1x3 rails are glued and nailed to their back and side edges. The two side rails also get the 10-degree cut on their front ends. When assembled, the unit leans at a 10-degree angle against the wall, with the shelves level. Use nonskid pads on the bottom ends or secure the tops of the uprights to the wall.

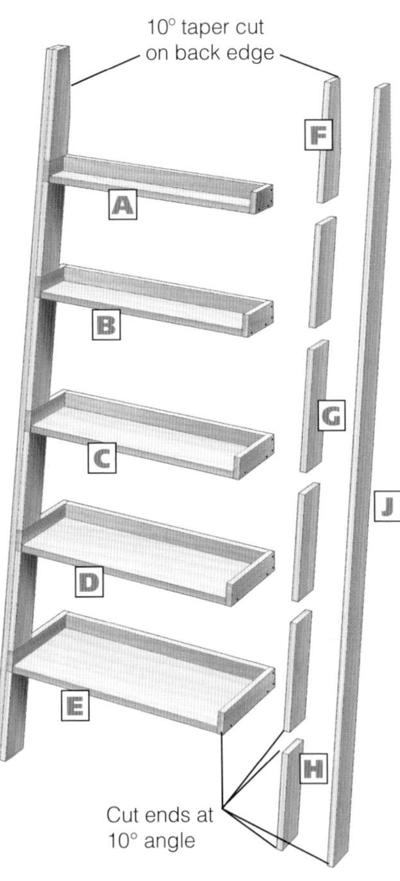

Cutting List

Key	Pcs.	Size & Description (in.)	
A–E	5	Shelves	3/4 x 30-1/2 long;
		(Widths = 3-3/8, 5-3/4, 8-3/16, 10-5/8, 13)	
F	2	Top cleats	3/4 x 3-1/2 x 14-1/2
G	8	Step cleats	3/4 x 3-1/2 x 11-3/4
H	2	Base cleats	3/4 x 3-1/2 x 10
J	2	Uprights	3/4 x 3-1/2 x 84

Cut five back shelf rails (3/4 x 2-1/2 x 30-1/2) and 10 end rails; end rails should be 1 in. longer than the width of the shelf they fit and have front ends cut at 10° angle.

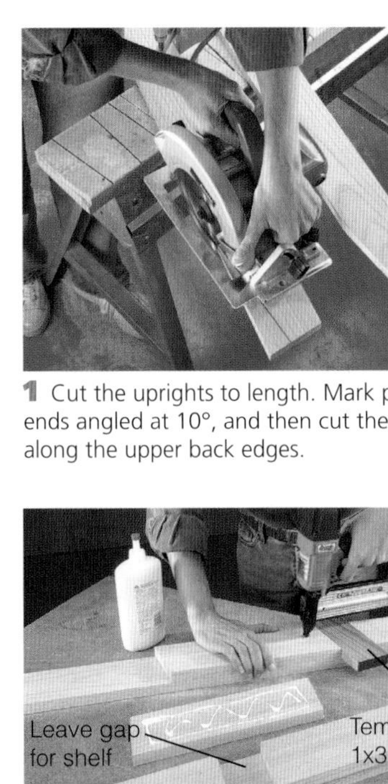

1 Cut the uprights to length. Mark parallel ends angled at 10°, and then cut the taper along the upper back edges.

2 Apply iron-on adhesive veneer tape to the front edges of the plywood shelves. If you plan to paint the unit, simply sand the edges smooth.

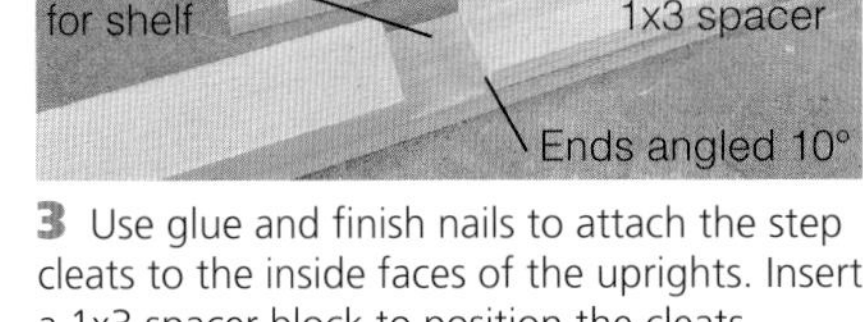

3 Use glue and finish nails to attach the step cleats to the inside faces of the uprights. Insert a 1x3 spacer block to position the cleats.

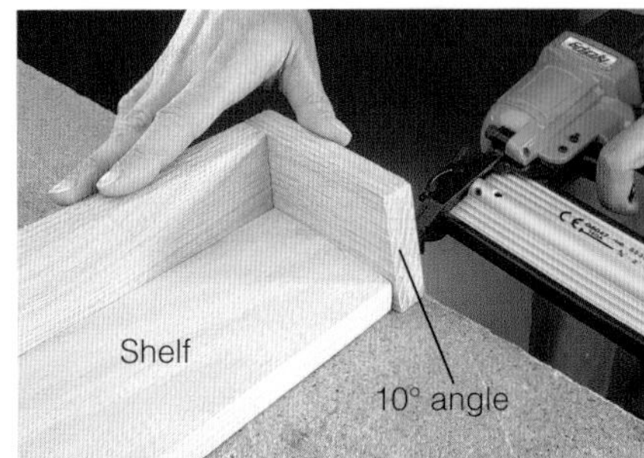

4 Fasten the back and side rails to the shelves with glue and finish nails. Cut the front ends at a 10° angle to match the lean of the uprights.

5 Clamp the shelves into one upright and set the assembly on its side. Spread glue in the notches of the other upright and nail it to the shelves. Flip and repeat.

6 Immediately after glue-up, position the shelf unit against the wall and check that the assembly is square. Clamp until the glue sets.

Floating Shelves

This wall shelf project is a perfect example of how to use inexpensive building materials creatively. Appearing to float on the wall with no visible means of support, the shelves are actually two halves cut from an 18-in.-wide hollow-core closet door. They nest over wood cleats attached to the wall studs. Wider doors will work also, but the practical depth limit for a shelf system like this is probably about 12 in. (30 cm).

Cut the door lengthwise to expose the cavity and the cardboard filler between the door skins. You'll have to cut some of the cardboard away with a utility knife, but aside from scribing the back edge to fit an uneven wall and ripping the wall cleats to the right size, that's all the woodworking required. Glue and finish nails do the holding.

1 Use a circular saw with a straightedge guide or use a tablesaw to cut the door lengthwise. Measure the inside gap to determine cleat thickness.

2 With tape to mark the stud locations, use lag screws to mount straight wood cleats that run the length of the door's inside cavity.

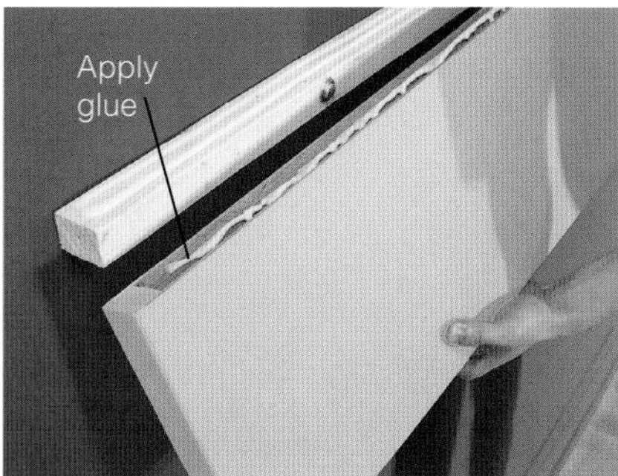

3 Test-fit each shelf and scribe its back edge if necessary. Spread glue on cleat and the lower shelf skin. Press the shelf onto the cleat.

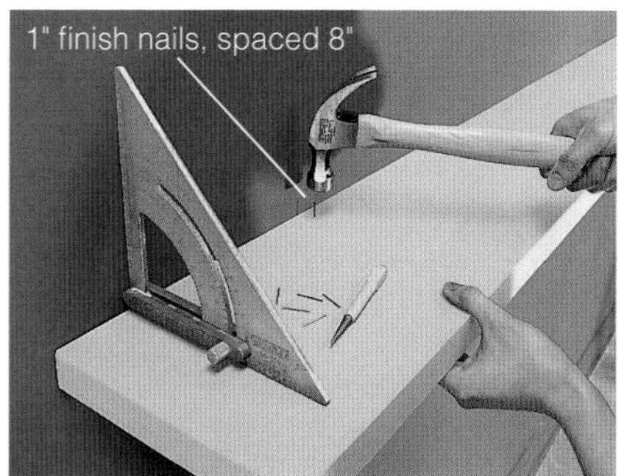

4 Rest a square on the shelf to ensure proper angle. Then drive 1-in. finish nails into the cleat every 8 in. (20 cm).

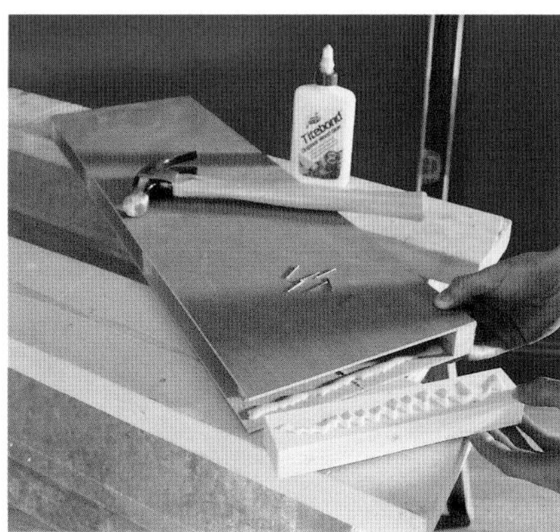

Shorter shelves. If the full length of the door makes a shelf longer than you need, cut the pieces shorter and fit a filler block between the skins at each cut end. Secure the blocks with glue and nail them in from both sides of the shelf.

Supporting Shelves

If you have only the wall to provide support for a shelf, you have to rely on store-bought standards and shelf brackets or site-built fixtures that do the same job. If the installation involves solid sides at each end of the shelf, you can choose from the options below:

Shelf pins. These supports come in steel and plastic in a variety of styles, including offset. Most fit in holes either 1/4 in. or 5 mm in diameter.

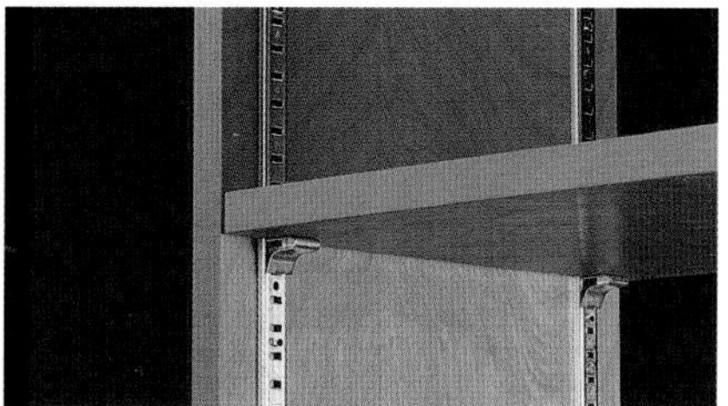

Metal standards. Recessed in grooves or surface-mounted, these slender tracks accept pressure-fit metal clips and allow adjustment in small increments.

Cleats. Though not easily adjustable, wood cleats, secured with nails, glue or screws, provide solid support. Cove, quarter-round and other moldings work well. The shelves can be left loose for easy repositioning.

Closet-Organizing Systems

The storage volume inside a closet is often a given that you can do little about. What really counts is using the space efficiently and keeping items organized and accessible. You can borrow principles from storage professionals to create your own customized unit.

How Much Space Do You Need?

Think about closet space in terms of both quantity and type. For example, a very narrow storage space might make a great niche for hanging bathrobes if it's oriented vertically; arrange the same space horizontally near the floor, and shoe storage makes more sense.

Take a look at the typical contents of your closet to see how you might best divide the space. Drawers for small items should be at least 16 in. (41 cm) deep. You can use these rules of thumb for general planning:

- Slacks and shirts need about 40 in. (100 cm) of vertical hanging space.
- Dresses need about 72 in. (180 cm) of vertical hanging space.
- A pair of shoes requires approximately 8 in. (20 cm) of shelf width, slightly less for women's shoes, slightly more for men's.
- Allot 1-1/2 in. (35 mm) of closet rod length for each item on a hanger.

Ready-to-Assemble Organizer

This store-bought closet organizer system belongs to a product category called knock-down or ready-to-assemble (RTA) furnishings. Note how the overall space is subdivided into smaller bays that organize clothing by size or type. Wood cleats secured to the wall studs suspend the entire system off the floor, leaving that area free for additional storage. The system is installed in modular fashion, starting with the shelf and drawer tower, then adding other sections as required. Made from plastic-coated wood-composite panels, these systems require few tools for installation and assembly.

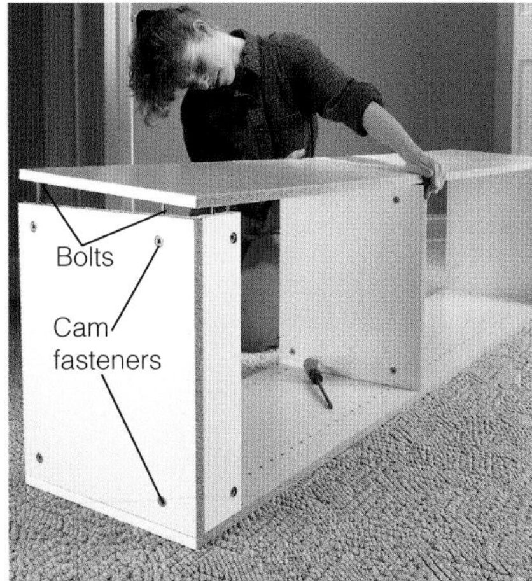

The tower. The corner and shelf joints of the tower assembly feature fixed steel pins that fit into predrilled holes. With the pins seated, you simply use a screwdriver to turn the cam-lock fasteners that cinch them tight.

Shelves and drawers. All the vertical panels feature rows of predrilled holes that accept shelf pins or fasteners for drawer guides. This modular approach lets you decide on the number and placement of shelves and drawers.

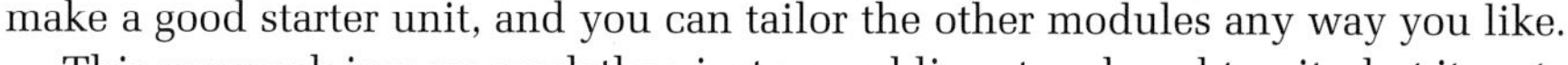

Melamine Closet Organizer

If the options available in ready-to-assemble (RTA) closet organizers don't suit you and you have some basic woodworking tools and skills, you can buy the materials and build your own custom version. Most lumberyards and home centers sell 4x8 sheets of melamine-coated particleboard or MDF. Its white plastic surface provides the same clean look you'd get in a store-bought unit.

This version sits on the floor and, although it doesn't use knock-down hardware, it does follow a simple modular approach. The central drawer and shelf tower section make a good starter unit, and you can tailor the other modules any way you like.

This approach is more work than just assembling store-bought units, but it costs less and offers you more flexibility in how to divide the storage space.

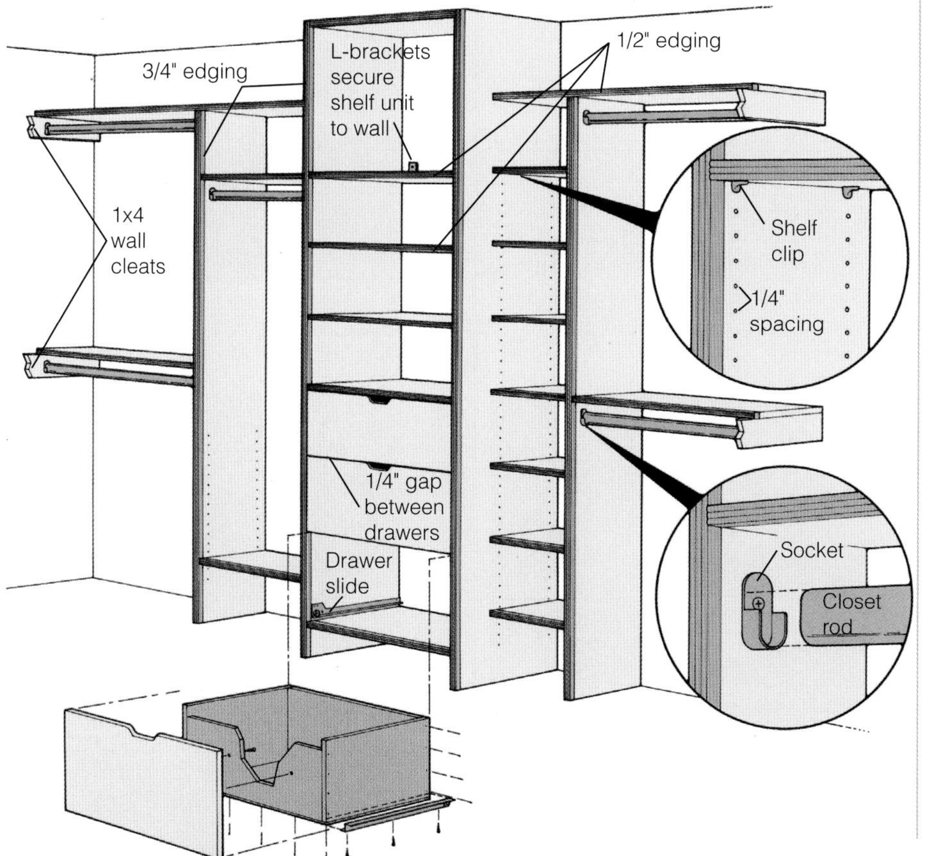

Wood Closet Organizer

If you have a master suite fitted with stained hardwood trim and doors, odds are a white melamine closet organizer will look out of place among those richer-looking elements. For something more appropriate, use cabinet-grade plywood for your system and finish it to match the existing woodwork.

Like the melamine organizer, this closet system consists of simple box modules and vertical panels, but you'll have to add a few twists to give it a furniture-grade look.

Cut the components carefully to minimize splintering the face veneers, and fill nail holes with a stainable wood filler. Select pieces carefully for the drawer fronts and other conspicuous elements, and apply an iron-on wood-veneer tape to cover the plywood edges. The shelf and closet rod hardware are similar to those in other systems.

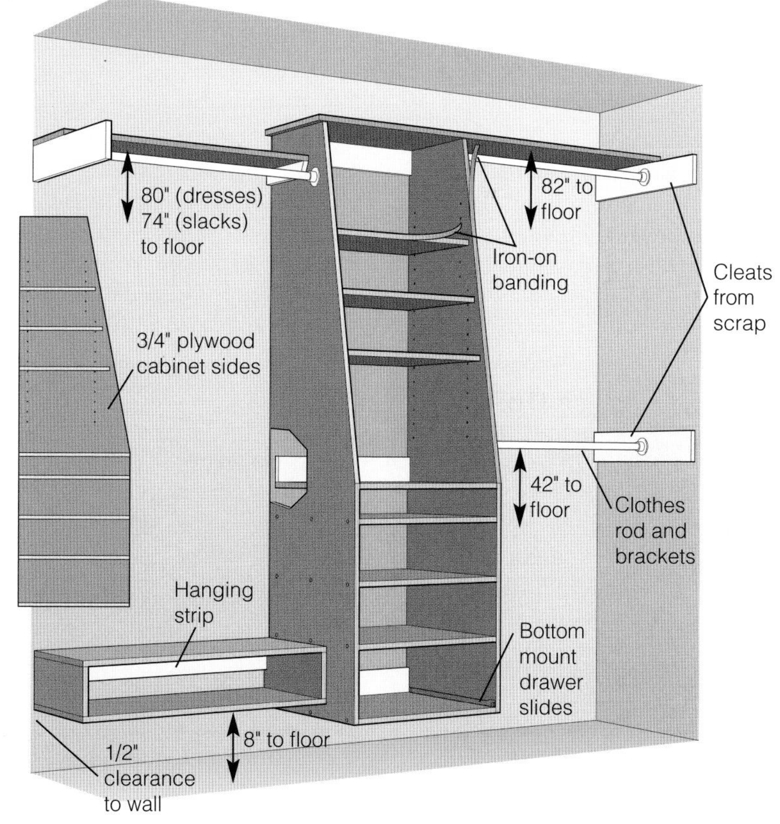

Workshop Storage

Sharpening 46
Router Tables 67

Benchtop Tool Hanger

As affordable substitutes for large stationary equipment, benchtop tools have transformed the possibilities of the home workshop. But where and how do you store them all? Here's a system that keeps them within easy reach but frees up your workbench.

Mount your smaller benchtop tools—portable tablesaws and thickness planers might be a little unwieldy—to a 3/4-in. plywood base and attach a pair of 40° beveled cleats on the underside of each base. Use lag screws to secure a pair of wood rails to the wall studs; the upper edge of the top rail is back-beveled. The tools hang securely in place and are easy to retrieve.

Stored. The interlocking bevels of the wall rail and the base cleat provide a secure perch for the tool. The lower rail doesn't support any weight directly; it simply acts as a stop to keep the tool base from swinging under.

In use. Easily retrieved from the wall, the tool will sit firmly on the workbench top, thanks to the large plywood base. Always clamp the base to the benchtop so it doesn't shift or slide while you're working.

Pull-out Router Table

This convenient router-table system features hardware commonly used for keeping kitchen mixers and other heavy countertop appliances concealed—but at the ready—inside a base cabinet.

Here, the four steel arms mount to sturdy wood blocks and hang underneath the benchtop. When you're ready to work, pull the table up and toward you until it's level with the bench's sur-

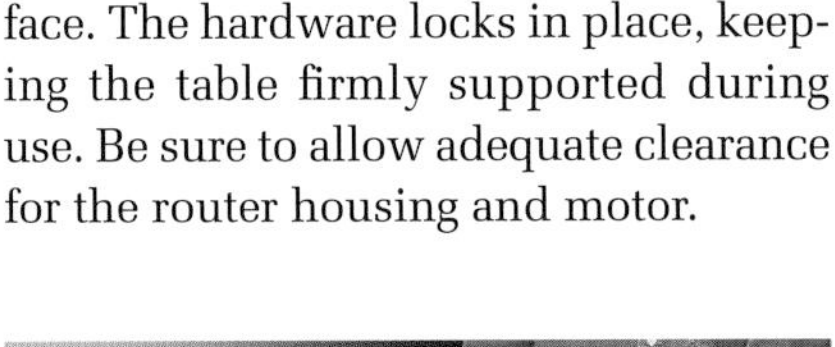

face. The hardware locks in place, keeping the table firmly supported during use. Be sure to allow adequate clearance for the router housing and motor.

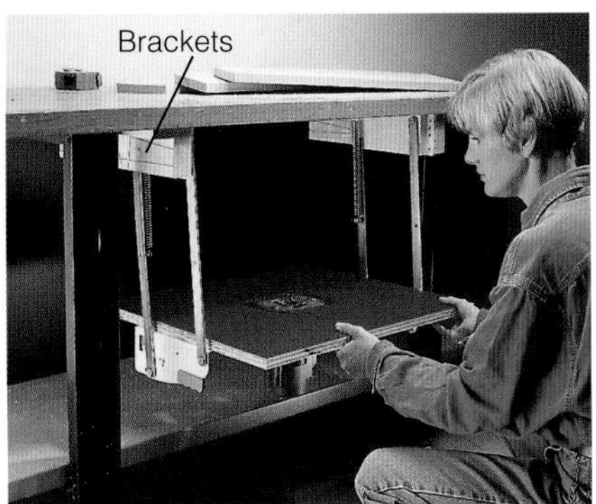

Stored. When not in use, the table swivels down below the benchtop. The shelf area must be kept clear for the router.

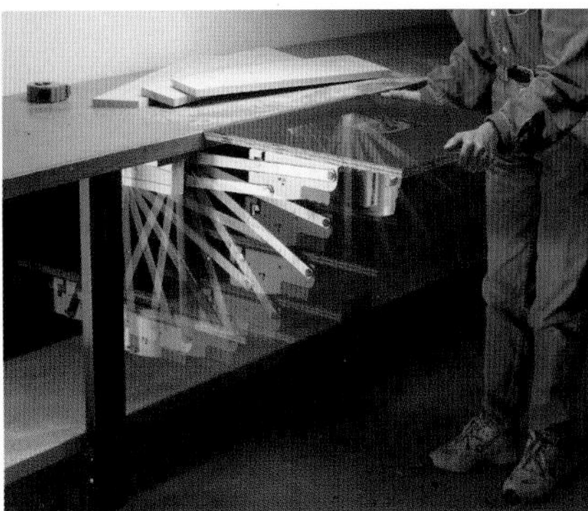

In motion. A firm tug on the front of the table and the brackets pivot up, to bring the router to working height, where it locks in place.

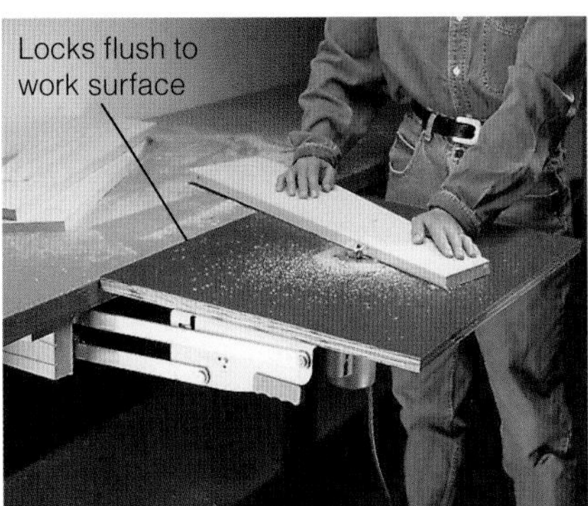

In use. Mount the hardware so the router table ends up flush with the benchtop when it's in the locked position.

Swing-up Grinder

If you don't want to dedicate prime workbench space permanently for a bench grinder, try the swing-mount installation shown. The system requires a 3/4-in. plywood base, a pair of strap hinges and a hook-and-eye set. Bending one leaf of each hinge lets you suspend the grinder on the underside of the benchtop and swing it into place quickly when you need it.

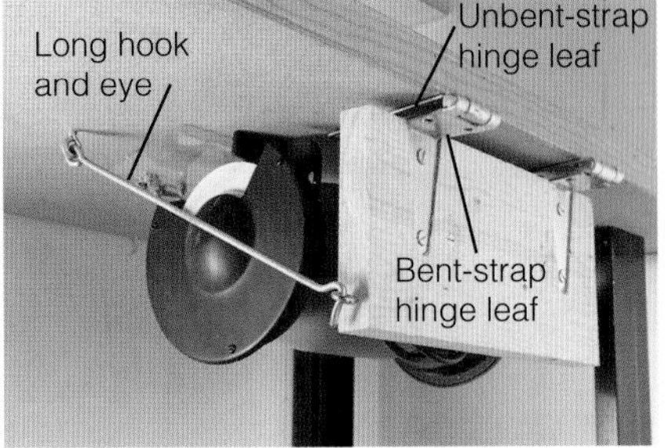

Stored. With the unbent hinge leaf screwed to the underside of the bench, the grinder pivots up so the hook can latch the base.

In use. As the grinder pivots up, the bent leaf hinges nest against the workbench edge, allowing the tool to rest on the benchtop.

11 Quick Tips and Projects

Nest of Crickets

Assembling projects often means clearing the workbench of tools or working on the floor. Crickets, also called lowboys, are simple supports that offer a convenient alternative. Made from a single sheet of 3/4-in. plywood and assembled with glue and drywall screws, the four progressively larger sizes nest in a compact stack. The uniform height allows use in multiples.

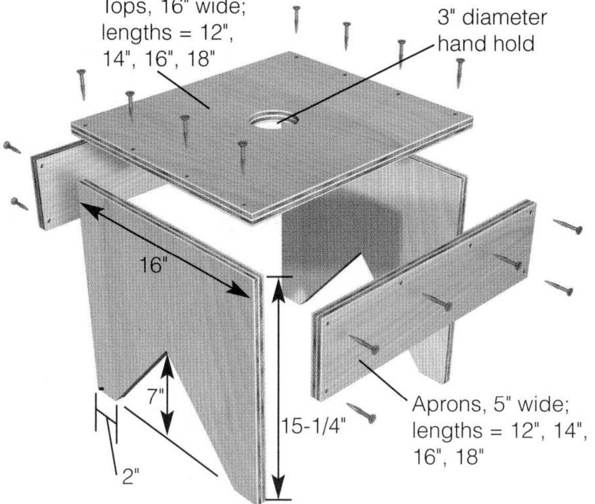

Workbench with Storage

Lumber and sheet-goods storage always present a challenge in a home workshop. After a few projects, you've accumulated plenty of spare usable material, and this workbench provides a tidy way to store those materials so you can put them to good use later.

The heart of the bench is a simple frame (left) built of 2x4 stock secured with 3-in. drywall screws; the tall rear bay holds sheet goods, while the three cubby holes up front store lumber. Build multiple frames—one for every 2 ft. (60 cm) of bench length. Then install a benchtop of your choice, plus a shelf and pegboard backsplash for tool storage. For a neater look, cover the front of the bench with paneling or plywood. Or if you prefer, you can leave the front open for easier access.

12"
53"
32"
Approx. 36" tall

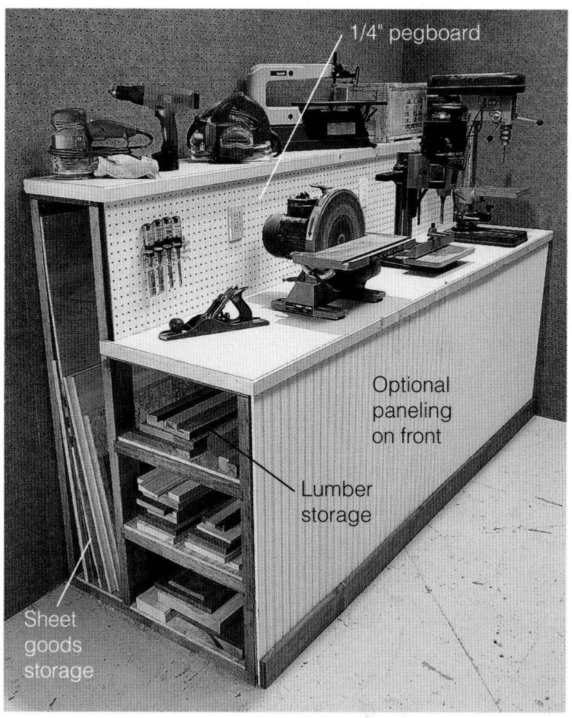

Folding Assembly Table

Sometimes the phrase "fast and cheap" is the perfect description for a good workshop aid. If the occasional need for more work surface or a large assembly table has you frustrated but reluctant to spend time and money building another workbench, consider this alternative. Made from an inexpensive entry door—lightweight hollow-core or heavy-duty solid-core, depending on your preference—fastened to a pair of folding metal sawhorses, this assembly table could hardly be quicker to make or use. And the simple materials requirements keep it affordable. Drive several large sheet-metal screws through each of the sawhorse tops into the door face near the edges. Collapse the sawhorse legs and stow the table when it's not in use.

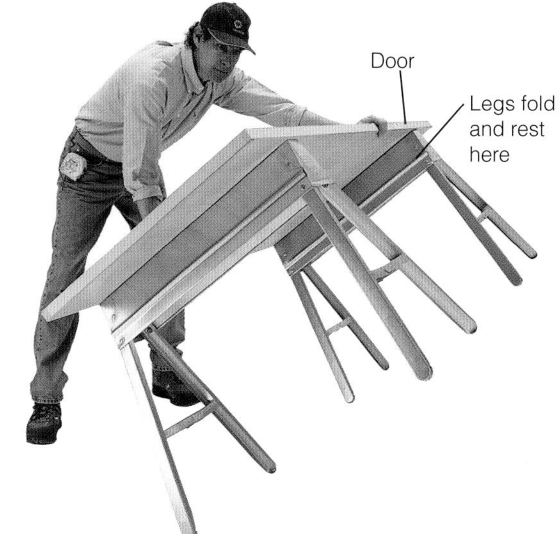

11 Quick Tips and Projects

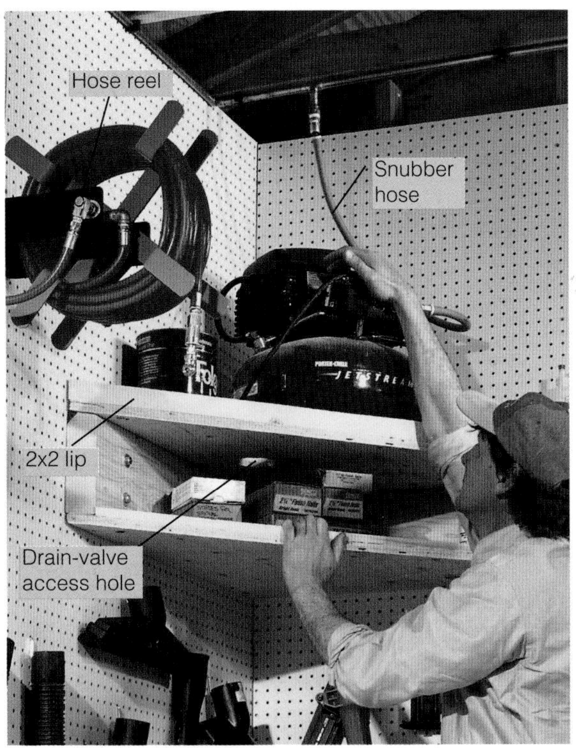

Air-Compressor Loft

Small air compressors offer the portability that professionals need for on-site work, but in a home workshop, the compact size translates into easier storage, not mobility. This project spares valuable floor space by tucking the compressor onto an elevated corner shelf.

Although a single shelf would do, this twin-shelf unit offers a secondary platform for storing collated fasteners or other accessories. Use 3/4-in. plywood for the shelves and fasten the 2x6 rails firmly to wall studs with lag screws. On the upper shelf, add a 2x2 lip along the front edge so the normal vibration doesn't send the compressor shimmying off the shelf. Also, cut or drill an access hole in the top shelf so you can access the tank drain valve regularly. You can even route air lines through the shop to provide outlets.

Ceiling Drawers

Basement shops may not be overflowing with natural light, but they offer some benefits—climate control, convenience, and plenty of opportunity for savvy storage. For example, the joist bays overhead are idle space that can house all kinds of lightweight tools and materials, if there's a convenient way to store them.

These simple wood boxes, built from 3/4-in. plywood, provide one solution. Size each drawer about 1/4 in. (6 mm) narrower than the joist bay it will occupy, and make the depth slightly less than the joist's width. A pair of pivot bolts holds each unit in place, and retractable plywood cleats on the lower edges of the joists hold the drawer in the up position. Keep the loads light and include safety rails where required to keep objects from falling out when the drawer is lowered.

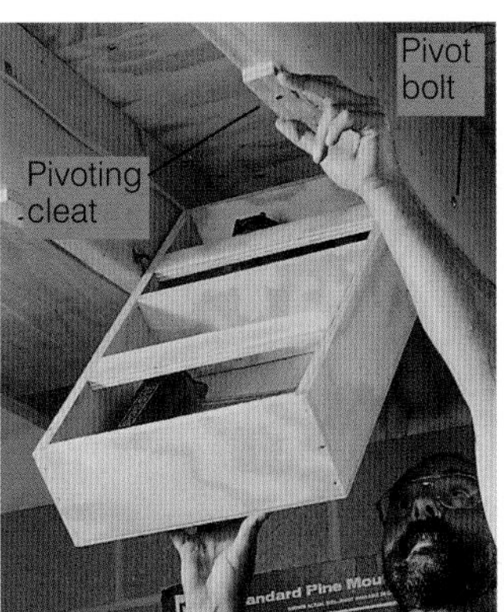

Overhead Cradle

Suspended from ceiling joists, this storage cradle can be installed to hold moldings, pipe and other long materials. Use 5/16-in. bolts or lag screws to secure a pair of vertical 2x6 hangers to two joists. For the cradles, glue and screw two layers of 3/4-in. plywood together and bolt them to the hanger. The angled edge on each side creates a large inclined hook perfect for storing lightweight moldings and other items.

Jar Storage

Plastic food jars are more durable and often larger than glass jars, making them ideal for storing fasteners and other small hardware items. To mount jars to the underside of a cabinet or shelf, simply fasten the lid with a few screws and thread the jar on securely. If you have room to side-mount the jar lids on vertical surfaces, cut part of the jar body (not the threaded rim) away with a utility knife to create open storage bins.

PVC Pipe Storage

Unless you're a plumber, the leftover pipe from a project will likely sit idle for years or get tossed in the trash during a spring garage cleaning. Put those remnants to good use with these shop storage aids. For the fastener trough, make two lengthwise cuts with a circular saw or jigsaw just above the halfway line in a section of PVC pipe. Use one end of the cut pipe to trace divider outlines onto a scrap piece of 1/2-in. plywood; then cut the dividers and glue (or screw) them into the trough. To stabilize the trough, cut contoured base blocks from scrap 2x4 stock and fasten them to the bottom of the pipe.

Build the dowel quiver by cutting out sections of pipe as shown, capping one end and then screwing the unit vertically to the wall.

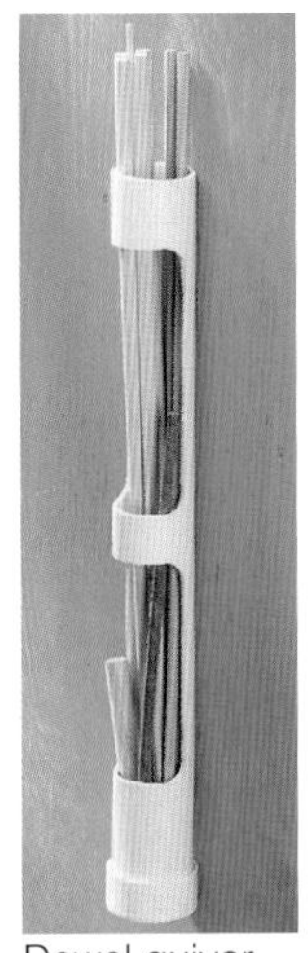

Dowel quiver

Tool Belt on a Shelf

Old leather belts often wear out at the ends while the center portion is still strong and intact. Rather than toss the belt, cut the ends off and nail the good section onto the front of a shelf. Leave bulges between the nails to create small tool-storage pockets.

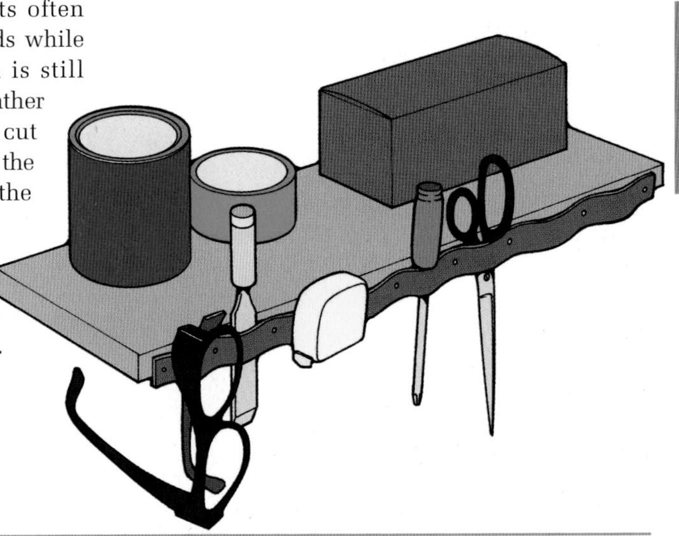

Fastener Bins

Purchasing commonly used screws and nails in large quantities makes sense. Keeping them organized and ready to go makes sense, too. To create sturdy storage bins for these items, use a fine-tipped marker to trace around the top of a plastic laundry detergent bottle. Leave the handle area intact, and cut away the section with a utility knife. The generous container size offers room for hundreds of fasteners, and you've got a built-in carrying handle. Stick a label under the handle to identify the contents. Plastic milk bottles and bleach bottles work well, too.

Nuts and Washers Storage

You can waste a lot of time sorting through boxes and bins for that one little item you need. Here's a simple solution to keep your inventory of nuts and washers—even small wrenches—organized and clearly visible. Buy a package of metal shower curtain rings and load the washers and nuts on them, dedicating each ring for a certain size item. Tape a label on the top of the ring and hang them on pegboard, and you can tell at a glance what you've got on hand. This technique also makes it easy to toss the hardware into your nail apron and take it where you need it.

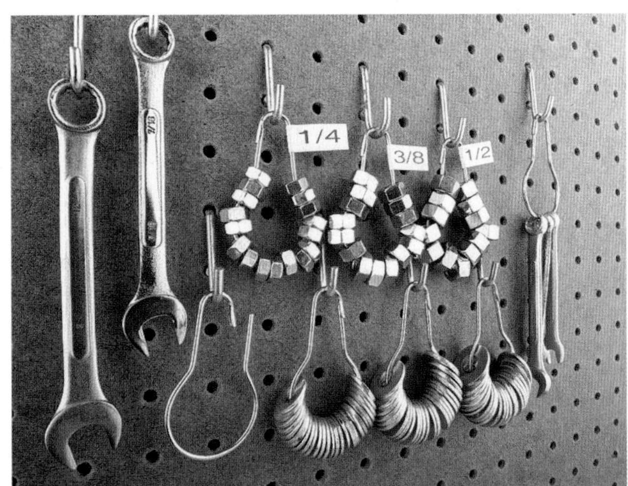

Resources

Accessible housing and universal design (p. 15)

For more information and guidelines on accessible housing, contact these organizations:

Center for Universal Design
NC State University/ College of Design
50 Pullen Road
Brooks Hall, Room 104
Campus Box 8613
Raleigh, NC 27695-8613
(800) 647-6777
www.design.ncsu.edu/cud
Information and technical assistance in the areas of residential and public universal design.

Adaptive Environments Center, Inc.
374 Congress St, Suite 301
Boston, MA 02210
(617) 695-1225
www.adaptiveenvironments.org
Information and education on accessibility.

National Council on Independent Living
1916 Wilson Blvd, Suite 209
Arlington, VA 22201
(703) 525-3406
TTY: (703) 525-4153
www.ncil.org
Information and technical assistance for helping those with disabilities.

Septic systems (p. 91)

The National Small Flows Clearinghouse is a non-profit organization that provides information about septic systems and wastewater treatment for small communities. Contact them at (800) 624-8301 or visit www.nesc.wvu.edu/nsfc.

Canadian electrical code (p. 129)

The Canadian Standards Association (CSA) offers information and publications on a wide range of topics. For information on the Canadian Electrical Code, visit http://www.csa.ca/standards/electrical.

Indoor air quality (p. 205, 482, 486)

For information, links and publications on mold, asbestos, radon and other indoor air quality issues visit the Indoor Air-Quality Association at www.iaqa.com or the Environmental Protection Agency at www.epa.gov.

Lead paint (p. 288)

More information on lead paint can be found on Health Canada's website at www.hc-sc.gc.ca or the Canada Mortgage and Housing Corporation (CMHC) website at www.cmhc-schl.gc.ca.

Window replacement parts (p. 364)

A tremendous source for ordering old, unusual or obsolete window hardware is Blaine Window Hardware, (800) 678-1919
www.blainewindow.com.

Radon (p. 483)

For more information on radon levels in Canada you can view a "Radioactivity Map of Canada" at www.gamma.nrcan.gc.ca/images/canrad.gif. There is overall a good correlation between general radiation mapping and household radon problems.

Safe rooms (p. 489)

The Federal Emergency Management Agency provides booklets and information on safe rooms. Call (888) 565-3896 or visit www.fema.gov.

Natural disasters and emergency preparedness (p. 490)

For information on reducing your risks from natural disasters, including earthquakes, flooding, tornadoes, fire and hazardous materials in the home, visit the Federal Emergency Management Agency website at www.fema.gov.

Index

Index

D

E

Index

Index

R

Index

T

Index

Nails

Nail lengths are identified by numbers from 4 to 60 followed by the letter "d" which stands for "penny." The imperial and metric equivalents are listed here.

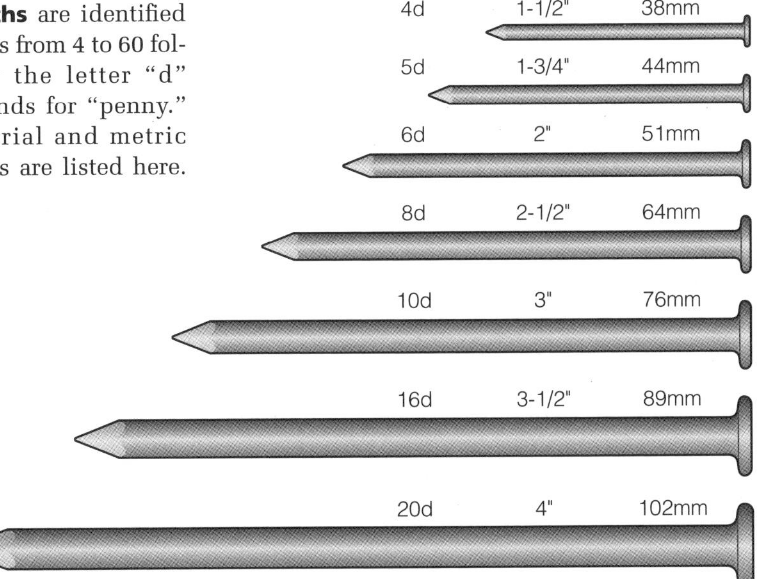

Temperature

Fahrenheit and Celsius. The two systems for measuring temperature are Fahrenheit and Celsius (or centigrade).

To change from degrees Fahrenheit, used in the United States, to degrees Celsius, subtract 32, then multiply by 5/9.

For example:

68°F - 32 = 36; 36 x 5/9 = 20°C.

To convert degrees Celsius to degrees Fahrenheit, multiply the degrees by 9/5, then add 32 to that figure.

For example:

20°C x 9/5 = 36; 36 + 32 = 68°F.

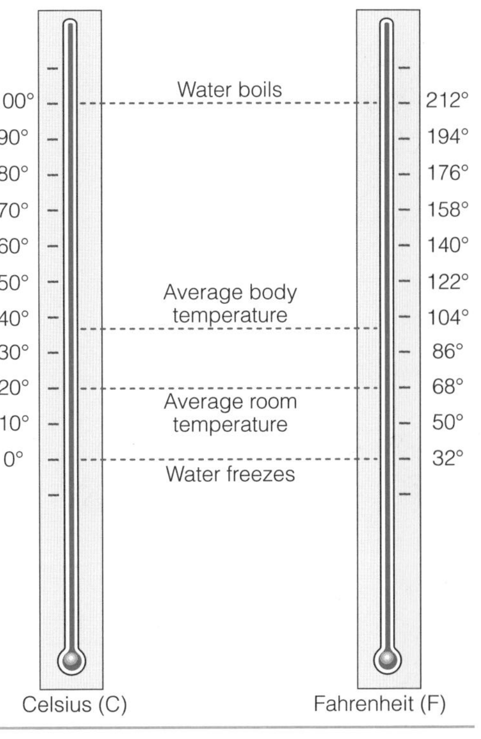

Fractions and Metric Equivalents

Inches (in.)	1/64	1/32	1/25	1/16	1/8	1/4	3/8	2/5	1/2	5/8	3/4	7/8	1	2	3	4	5	6	7	8	9	10	11	12	36	39.4
Feet (ft.)																								1	3	3-1/4†
Yards (yd.)																									1	1-1/12†
Millimeters (mm)*	0.40	0.79	1.0	1.59	3.18	6.35	9.53	10	12.7	15.9	19.1	22.2	25.4	50.8	76.2	101.6	127	152	178	203	229	254	279	305	914	1,000
Centimeters (cm)*							0.95	1	1.27	1.59	1.91	2.22	2.54	5.08	7.62	10.16	12.7	15.2	17.8	20.3	22.9	25.4	27.9	30.5	91.4	100
Meters (m)*																								0.30	0.91	1.00

*Metric values are rounded off. † Approximate fractions.

(actual size)

Credits

Manufacturer-supplied photos

PEX plumbing (p. 111)
Tools and materials supplied by Plumb-Pex, www.rtisystems.com

Doorbell chime (p. 157)
Broan-Nutone, www.nutone.com

Home automation photos and illustration (p. 159)
Smarthome, www.smarthome.com

High-efficiency furnace (p. 173)
Lennox, www.lennox.com

Wall-mount and towel warming radiators (p. 178)
Runtal Radiators, www.runtalnorthamerica.com

Solar battery charger (p. 189)
Real Goods/Gaiam, Inc., www.realgoods.com

Ground-source heat pump (p. 195)
Econar, www.econar.com

Power roller (p. 281)
Airless sprayer (p. 283)
Wagner, www.wagnerspraytech.com

Library cabinetry (p. 290)
Omega Cabinets, www.omegacabinets.com

Faux-slate shingles (p. 315)
Tamko, www.tamko.com

Fancy cut shingles (p. 337)
Shakertown, www.shakertown.com

Pre-cast stairs (p. 404)
Shea Concrete, www.sheaconcrete.com

For *The Family Handyman* and *American Woodworker*

Editors:
Spike Carlsen, Tom Caspar, Ken Collier, Jeff Gorton, Duane Johnson, Randy Johnson, Tim Johnson, Travis Larson, Dave Munkittrick, Dave Radtke, Gary Wentz

Copy Editors:
Donna Bierbach, Jean Cook, Mary Flanagan

Contributing Editors:
Carl Hines, Jeff Larson, Kurt Lawton, Eric Smith, George Vondriska

Art Directors:
Patrick Hunter, Vern Johnson, Sara Koehler, Becky Pfluger, Bob Ungar, Marcia Wright Roepke

Contributing Art Directors:
Hope Fay, Barbara Pederson

Administrative Team:
Lori Callister, Roxie Filipkowski, Alice Garrett, Shelly Jacobsen,

Production and Technical Team:
Shannon Hooge, Lisa Pahl Knecht, Judy Rodriguez

Additional Photography:
Jill Greer, Gene and Katie Hamilton, Morris Karol

Additional illustrations:
Ron Bertuzzi, Sylvia Bokor, Gordon Chapman, Chris Duerk, Mario Ferro, John Gist, Karin Kretschmann, Victor Lazzaro, Lieu & Silks, Ed Lipinski, Mari Maléter, Max Menikoff, Ken Rice, Gerhard Richter, Ray Skibinski, Allyson Smith, Robert Steimle, Victoria Vebell, Robert Villani

Nails

Nail lengths are identified by numbers from 4 to 60 followed by the letter "d" which stands for "penny." The imperial and metric equivalents are listed here.

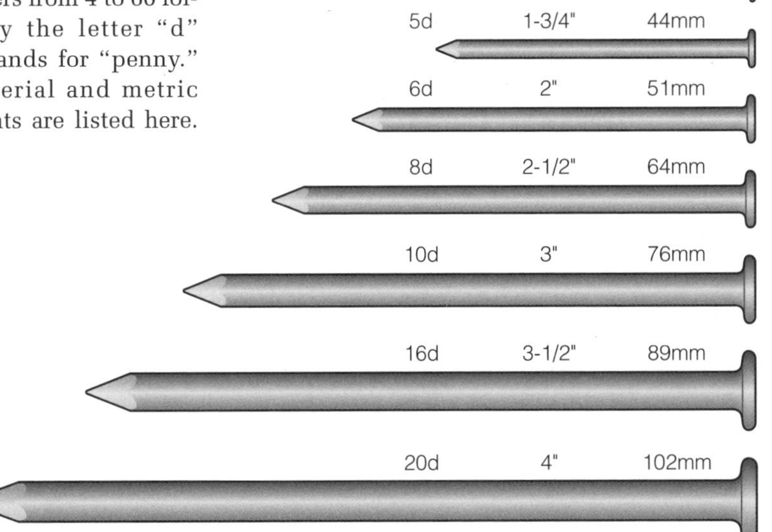

Temperature

Fahrenheit and Celsius. The two systems for measuring temperature are Fahrenheit and Celsius (or centigrade).

To change from degrees Fahrenheit, used in the United States, to degrees Celsius, subtract 32, then multiply by 5/9.

For example:

68°F - 32 = 36; 36 x 5/9 = 20°C.

To convert degrees Celsius to degrees Fahrenheit, multiply the degrees by 9/5, then add 32 to that figure.

For example:

20°C x 9/5 = 36; 36 + 32 = 68°F.

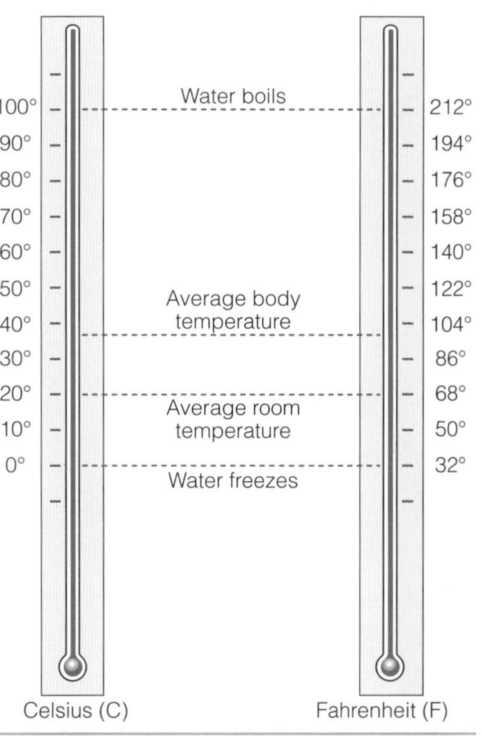

Fractions and Metric Equivalents

Inches (in.)	1/64	1/32	1/25	1/16	1/8	1/4	3/8	2/5	1/2	5/8	3/4	7/8	1	2	3	4	5	6	7	8	9	10	11	12	36	39.4
Feet (ft.)																								1	3	3-1/4†
Yards (yd.)																									1	1-1/12†
Millimeters (mm)*	0.40	0.79	1.0	1.59	3.18	6.35	9.53	10	12.7	15.9	19.1	22.2	25.4	50.8	76.2	101.6	127	152	178	203	229	254	279	305	914	1,000
Centimeters (cm)*							0.95	1	1.27	1.59	1.91	2.22	2.54	5.08	7.62	10.16	12.7	15.2	17.8	20.3	22.9	25.4	27.9	30.5	91.4	100
Meters (m)*																								0.30	0.91	1.00

*Metric values are rounded off. † Approximate fractions.

(actual size)